The Legal and Social Environment of Business

The Legal and Social Environment of Business

FOURTH EDITION

DOUGLAS WHITMAN
University of Kansas

JOHN WILLIAM GERGACZ
University of Kansas

McGraw-Hill, Inc.
New York St. Louis San Francisco Auckland Bogotá Caracas
Lisbon London Madrid Mexico City Milan Montreal New Delhi
San Juan Singapore Sydney Tokyo Toronto

This book is printed on acid-free paper.

4 5 6 7 8 9 0 DOC   DOC 9 0 9 8 7

ISBN 0-07-070005-2

This book was set in Times Roman by Better Graphics, Inc.
The editor was Kenneth A. MacLeod;
the designer was Leon Bolognese;
the production supervisor was Paula Keller.
Project supervision was done by The Total Book.
R. R. Donnelley & Sons Company was printer and binder.

Library of Congress Cataloging-in-Publication Data

Whitman, Douglas.
    The legal and social environment of business / Douglas Whitman,
John William Gergacz. — 4th ed.
        p.   cm.
    Rev. ed. of: The legal environment of business. 3rd ed. 1991.
    Includes index.
    ISBN 0-07-070005-2
    1. Industrial laws and legislation—United States.   2. Trade
regulation—United States.   3. Commercial law—United States.
I. Gergacz, John William.   II. Whitman, Douglas. Legal environment
of business.   III. Title.
KF1600.W47   1994
346.73'07—dc20
[347.3067]   93-31671

ABOUT THE AUTHORS

Douglas Whitman is a Professor at the School of Business Administration of the University of Kansas and a member of the Kansas and Missouri bars. He received his B.A. from Knox College, his M.B.A. from the University of Kansas, J.D. from the University of Missouri, and LL.M. from the University of Missouri at Kansas City. He has served twice as a staff editor for the *American Business Law Journal*. He is a past president of the Midwest Business Law Association. He has written articles on advertising law and products liability and has published in such journals as the *Indiana Law Review; St. John's Law Review; Southwestern Law Journal* (at Southern Methodist Law School); *The University of California Davis Law Review; The University of Pittsburgh Law Review; The Journal of Products Liability; Brigham Young University Law Review; New Mexico Law Review*; and *American Business Law Journal*. His articles have also been reprinted in *The Advertising Law Anthology, The Personal Injury Desk Book, The Corporate Counsel's Annual*, and by The American Trial Lawyer's Association. He has also written a number of articles for the Advertising Compliance Service. He is a coauthor of *Modern Business Law*, McGraw-Hill, 1989; *The Legal Environment of Business: Regulatory Law and Contracts*, McGraw-Hill, 1992, Random House, 1987; *Law and Business* and *Commercial Law*, John Wiley & Sons. He edited a book of readings, *Reading in Business Law and the Legal Environment of Business*, McGraw Hill, 1994. Professor Whitman is a consultant on business law matters.

John William Gergacz is a Professor at the School of Business Administration of the University of Kansas and a member of the Illinois and Indiana bars. He was appointed as School of Business Alumni Faculty Scholar at the University of Kansas from 1984–1986. Since joining the KU faculty in 1978, he has received eight awards for excellence in teaching. Gergacz received his B.S. from the School of Business, Indiana University, Bloomington, Indiana, and his J.D. from the School of Law, Indiana University, Bloomington, Indiana, where he was an editor of the law review. He is currently editor-in-chief for the *American Business Law Journal*, for which he previously served in other editorial positions. He has also served as editor-in-chief of the *Corporate Information and Privacy Reporter*. He has written numerous scholarly articles in such journals as *The Business Lawyer, Boston College Environmental Affairs Law Review, New Mexico Law Review, Wake Forest Law Review, Real Estate Law Journal*, and the *American Business Law Journal*. Professor Gergacz is an authority on attorney-client privilege and has published a treatise on the topic, *Attorney-Corporate Client Privilege*, now in its second edition. He is coauthor of *The Legal Environment of Business* (McGraw-Hill).

To
Doyle Collins Whitman and Anna Mary Whitman;
John W. Gergacz and Ann K. Gergacz,
our parents,
and to Joan M. Gergacz

CONTENTS IN BRIEF

CONTENTS

**PART 7
Regulation of Business Activity:
Property and the Market**

LIST OF LEGAL CASES

PREFACE

The Legal and Social Environment of Business, Fourth Edition, integrates the teaching of law into the business school curriculum. For too long business law and legal environment courses have been limited to summarizing an enormous number of legal rules without providing the connection between the principles underlying those rules and *business*. The structure of those courses and texts has been more suited to review for a bar exam than for preparing the student for a professional career in business. Yet the law plays a very important role in providing an understanding of the business system and decision making.

Thus, when a student successfully completes the legal environment of business course, the law should be viewed as far more than an unconnected series of rules. The law should, in fact, be seen as providing the foundation for the operation of the economy and an executive's activities as a part of this economy. *The Legal and Social Environment of Business* provides the student with this perspective and understanding. It also provides the background for further courses in business law, either elective or required, that can focus more precisely on other substantive areas (for example, business organizations, contracts, or commercial law). However, without "the big picture" that is provided by this text, such courses can be no more than an unconnected rehash of law school and not appropriate for future business executives, who will be hiring lawyers and who have very special legal educational needs.

Legal studies should be an exciting and dynamic experience, and we believe that this book preserves the excitement and tension that accompany great legal issues. Because tomorrow's business executives undoubtedly will be affected by such issues, today's business students should understand the scope and complexity of legal issues. To that end we have written the fourth edition of *The Legal Environment of Business*.

THE AMERICAN ASSEMBLY OF COLLEGIATE SCHOOLS OF BUSINESS STANDARDS

The American Assembly of Collegiate Schools of Business (AACSB), the organization which accredits business schools in the United States, feels that organizations and managers face the following challenges in the years ahead:

- Strong and growing global economic forces
- Conflicting values

- Changing technology in products and processes
- Demographic diversity among employees and customers

Management education needs to assist managers in meeting these challenges. With respect to curriculum content, AACSB Standard C.1.1. states: "Both undergraduate and MBA curricula should provide an understanding of perspectives that form the context for business. Coverage should include:

- Ethical and global issues
- The influence of political, social, legal and regulatory, environmental, and technological issues
- The impact of democratic diversity on organizations"

This text addresses all of the AACSB's curriculum requirements.

We have divided the text into eight parts. Part 1 serves as an introduction to the law and the legal system. Part 2 then examines the American legal system. The future business manager needs to understand not only the rules that govern business, but how our system creates, modifies, and implements these rules. These chapters present the American legal system's structure and its actors—judges, lawyers, legislators and administrators—all of whom have as much to do with the law affecting business as do the legal rules.

Part 3 deals with a topic of great importance in business decision making: ethics. This section gives students an analytical structure for evaluating decisions that have an ethical component. We placed ethics early in the text to give students some familiarity with ethics because many legal topics lend themselves to ethical, as well as legal, analysis.

Part 4 focuses on the legal foundations of American business and is designed to illustrate the fundamental nature of law to all other areas of study in the business school. Those areas presume a system of property where rights are established, protected, and owned; they presume a system of contract law under which private transfers of those rights occur; they presume a system of tort law whereby costs imposed (injuries in tort) on innocent parties by business will be borne by that business. The chapters in this part do not dwell on every legal rule associated with those topics, although basic principles are discussed. Instead, the primary emphasis in Chapters 9–12 is on the development and purposes of the topics and the changes or trends that are occurring in them.

In light of the great importance of contract law to business relationships, this text devotes two chapters to contract law. Chapter 9 discusses the historical development of contract law, followed by a brief discussion of the role of negotiation in contracts. It concludes with a discussion of the essential elements of an enforceable contract. Chapter 10 deals with the balance of the law of contracts.

Part 5 focuses on the legal aspects of the firm and its regulation. This section has two purposes. First, it provides students with an understanding of the various ways the law permits businesses to be organized and the legal implications of being part of a certain legal organizational structure. Chapter 13 deals with legal aspects of the business organizational form. Chapter 14 addresses the legal rules relating to members of the business organization. The second purpose of this section is to provide the student with some information on how the laws regulate the power of the business organization.

Part 6 concerns the regulation of business activities that relate to customers or employees. Chapter 16 discusses the liability of businesses for the products they sell and Chapter 17 concerns the liability of businesses to consumers. The final three chapters (Chapters 18–20) in this section deal with employer/employee law. Chapter 18 covers all important aspects of employment discrimination. Chapters 19 and 20 outline American labor relations laws.

Part 7 focuses on several important regulatory topics of interest to business. Chapter 21 deals with environmental law. Chapter 22 provides students with a study of how law acts to regulate organizational power in the capital markets through the federal securities laws. Chapters 23 and 24 discuss the U.S. antitrust laws.

Part 8 addresses some international law problems of interest to the business community. When business managers deal with companies located in other nations, they need to realize how dealing with foreign firms differs from dealing with domestic companies.

FEATURES OF THE FOURTH EDITION

New Organization

The fourth edition has a *revised organization*. As indicated above, we have divided the text into eight parts. The first seven chapters in this text explain the influence of the political and social environment on business. Chapter 8, ethics, gives students an analytical structure for analyzing decisions that have an ethical component. The next four chapters discuss the common law. The material in Part 5 concerns the business organizations and their regulation. Chapters 16–20 concern the relationship of business to customers and employees. We address the question of demographic diversity, conflicting values, and the influence of technological issues in these chapters. Part 6 concerns the influence of regulatory and environmental law on the operation of a business. The text concludes with a discussion of international law.

Prologue

In response to requests from reviewers, we added some additional introductory material at the beginning of this text. Following a brief discussion of the distinction between civil and criminal law, we present some material on how to analyze the cases in this text.

New Additions and Revisions

Many portions of this text have been extensively revised.

- Chapter 3—Civil Litigation. The alternative dispute resolution material from the third edition has been expanded and clarified

- Chapter 8—Ethics. This material has been rewritten, emphasizing the link between ethics and law and providing a means for managers to make ethical evaluations.

- Chapters 9 and 10—Contracts. We have a new chapter on contracts that includes the historical development of contract law, the role of negotiation theory in contracts, and a discussion of the elements necessary for a valid contract. The second chapter on contracts covers additional contract rules.

- Chapter 11—Torts. We have added a great deal of material on intentional torts.

- Chapter 12—Property Rights. This chapter was revised. The material dealing with land use regulation was moved later in this text to Chapter 21.

- Chapters 13 and 14—Business Organizations and Agency. We added a new chapter and a discussion on limited liability companies.

- Chapter 17—Consumer Law. We added an expanded section on bankruptcy law.

- Chapter 18—Employment Discrimination. We increased the coverage of material and added coverage on such topics as the Americans with Disabilities Act, the Age Discrimination Act, and the reasonable woman standard.

- Chapter 21—Environmental Law. We blended a discussion of land use regulation with environmental law. We discussed the market-oriented approach to controlling pollution.

In every chapter we updated our textual material and added many recently decided cases.

Case Selection and Presentation
A great deal of time was spent selecting case material for this text. It has been a goal of the authors ever since writing the first edition to locate cases that have the greatest interest to the students but at the same time illustrate points of law of interest to businesspeople. We have chosen what we consider to be the most interesting, readable, and pertinent cases—both classic and recent—to illustrate the various points of law.

OTHER SPECIAL PEDAGOGICAL FEATURES

Starting with the very first edition of this text, we tried to include other material in addition to the cases and the text.

Boxes   In virtually every chapter you will find boxes that discuss such matters as ethics, international issues, current events, and historical matters. For example:

Managerial boxes	Abortion pills
Historical boxes	The film rights to *Gone with the Wind*
Ethical boxes	The sale of a baseball card
Global boxes	Military weapons sales
Economics boxes	Cost/benefit analysis and contracts law

We all know that it is often easier to understand material by looking at a picture than by reading text. To help students understand the material in this text, we have expanded the number of charts, figures, forms, and illustrations in the text. Chapters conclude with a summary of important concepts and review questions.

Supplements   In order to assist professors in preparing to teach a legal environment course, we have provided all of the supplements necessary for a person with little familiarity with the law to teach a course in the legal environment of business. Many adopters have commented on the outstanding quality of the supplementary materials available with this text.

Instructor's Manual Prepared by the Text Authors

A computerized version of the *Instructor's Manual* is also available.

Study Guide to Accompany the Text

A Study Guide to accompany this text was prepared by Professor Susan Grady at the University of Massachusetts, Amherst.

Test Bank Prepared by the Text Authors

Computerized Test Bank

It is possible to have questions randomly selected and a test generated for you by McGraw-Hill.

Person who wish to generate their own tests can receive the test bank on 5.25″ or 3.5″ floppy disks. You can create tests from these disks, add your own questions to the tests on disk, and store your tests.

Contact your local McGraw-Hill sales representative for a detailed discussion of all supplements available with this text.

Readings Supplement

A new edition of *Readings in Business Law and the Legal Environment of Business*, edited by Douglas Whitman, has been prepared with this revision.

Leading business law professors throughout America contributed chapters that were written expressly for this book. Professor Whitman selected each contributor on the basis of his or her extensive writings on the law.

Professor Whitman keyed the chapters in the *Readings* book around the most commonly covered material in the typical legal environment text. The large number of excellent chapters enables adopters to pick and choose the topics they with to emphasize in class.

Each chapter in *Readings* gives the reader some background information about the area of law discussed in that chapter. This material is followed by a discussion of an important case. Thereafter, each article deals with the managerial implications of the law, reinforcing the importance of the relationship between the law and a student's future business career. Helpful case questions and answers as well as relevant references have also been provided by each author.

Readings in Business Law and the Legal Environment of Business can be used in the introductory business law course as a supplement to this or any other business law text.

PRIMIS— Customized Publishing

The computer age has definitely reached the publishing industry. This text, as well as the *Readings* book and many other McGraw Hill texts, can be adopted in customized form. Contact PRIMIS for more details at 1–800–962–9342, or call your local McGraw-Hill representative.

ACKNOWLEDGMENTS

We are grateful to the following reviewers who suggested numerous excellent revisions and additions which we incorporated in the fourth edition of this text. This text could not have been produced without the efforts of these people: Andy Abrams, College of Charleston; Debora Ballan, Ohio State University; Robert Bennett, Butler University; Suzanne Dreifus, University of Detroit–Mercy; Jerald Engelman, University of North Dakota; Paul Fiorelli, Xavier University; Gale Heiman, Aims Community College; Janine Hiller, Virginia Polytechnic Institute and State University; John Houlihan, University of Southern Maine; Nancy Klintworth, University of Central Florida; Gene Marsh, University of Alabama; Susan Martin, Hofstra University; John Murry, Henderson State University; Jill Olson, Northern Illinois University; Ramona Paetzold, Texas A & M University; Mark Phelps, University of Oregon; Laura Pincus, De Paul University; Gary Sibeck, Loyola Marymount University; Mark Usry, James Madison University; Wayne Wells, St. Cloud State University; and Larry Zacharias, University of Massachusetts–Amherst.

Finally, we would like to thank our colleagues at McGraw-Hill for assisting us in the preparation of the fourth edition of *The Legal and Social Environment of Business*.

Douglas Whitman
John William Gergacz

PROLOGUE

THE IMPORTANCE OF KNOWING THE LAW

During the Industrial Revolution in the nineteenth century most of the rules governing business arose from private agreements. Federal, state, and local governments tended to regulate businesses only to a minimal extent. This worked to the advantage of the nation, as it permitted the rapid industrialization of America. At the conclusion of the nineteenth century many American businesses such as Standard Oil spanned the globe.

As we no longer needed to concern ourselves with developing our industrial base, the concerns of people in America by the end of the nineteenth century began to turn to the distribution of wealth brought about by such multinational enterprises as the Standard Oil Trust and the Carnegie Steel Corporation. The perception of many people during that era was that private agreements could not bring about the social changes that many people desired in American society. For this reason, people turned to government in an attempt to change the relationship between business and society.

As the decades unfolded in the twentieth century, we began to see more and more laws created at all levels of American government. We entered a new era of supervision of business by government. Today's business manager not only needs to know the fundamentals of business—finance, marketing, and accounting—but he or she must also keep abreast of the law. In many ways the law controls what can and cannot be done in business, and how various managerial functions must be performed. Something that may seem to make sense in terms of finance or marketing may nonetheless not be possible because of the law. For this reason, before embarking upon a given course of action, a wise manager needs to consider the legal environment of business.

The law is dynamic and ever changing. It responds to social forces such as public opinion. What may have been permissible in one year may no longer be legal behavior. A manager needs to consult with lawyers. This book will greatly assist you in your dealings with the legal profession, and with your own attempts to stay current in the areas of law that affect your particular business position. The chapters in this book will first of all give you a broad overview of the legal system itself. This will assist you in understanding how laws are created, how they are enforced, and how they are interpreted. At the same time, one needs to bear in mind that even if a given course of action is lawful, it may nonetheless be unethical. To give you some insights with respect to appraising business behavior, we devote a specific chapter to business ethics.

The balance of the text is broken down into chapters that discuss various bodies of law that govern certain types of behavior or transactions. Once you have completed this material, it will be much easier to communicate meaningfully with your attorneys, and to understand articles that appear in such publications as *The Wall Street Journal*, *Business Week*, or *Money Magazine*. When you take other courses in the business school such as marketing or accounting, this material will give you a better understanding of any references to the law.

CIVIL AND CRIMINAL LAW

One concept that students sometimes find confusing is the difference between civil law and criminal law. Civil law concerns the body of laws that governs the legal duties one private party owes to another private party. Civil law also deals with the duties that exist between a private party and the government. Suppose that XYZ Corporation enters into an agreement to employ Bill. We call such an agreement a contract. An entire body of civil law, the law of contracts, governs the relationship between Bill and XYZ Corporation. In most civil suits, a party is accused of having somehow injured another private person or entity. People who bring civil suits generally want monetary damages.

Criminal law, on the other hand, concerns behavior which the government has deemed contrary to the public good. A person who violates the criminal law is thought to have committed a wrong against society. In a criminal suit, the government files suit against a person or an entity that is alleged to have committed a crime. In such a suit, the government creates some penalty for breaking the law—such as imprisonment or a fine. Suppose that ABC, Inc. violated a provision of the antitrust laws. The federal government may bring a criminal suit against the firm, and perhaps may even seek a prison sentence and fines for its executives.

You will note as you read this text, some actions violate both the criminal law and the civil law. Suppose that John strikes Bill, causing serious bodily injury to Bill. Bill could bring a civil action against John—called a tort. Civil law governs situations like this where one private party owes a duty to another private party—in this case, the duty not to strike another person. The government could also bring a criminal action against John. The government makes such conduct a criminal offense because such behavior is contrary to the public good.

THE COMMON LAW

A great deal of the law in America today appears in statutes—laws passed by a legislative branch of government such as Congress or a state legislature. Some areas of law, however, are not governed by statute. This law can be found in the decisions of judges in the course of resolving disputes between people—referred to in this text as the common law. When we speak of the common law, we are referring to the entire body of law created by judges when they decide cases. In Part 4 we discuss three very important areas of common law: contracts, torts, and property law.

Some areas, such as the law of contracts, for the most part come entirely from the decisions of judges. Judges also create law, however, by interpreting statutes and other sources of law discussed in this book. For this reason, cases are very important and a considerable portion of this text is devoted to the presentation of decisions of judges.

Read

ANALYZING CASES

Because cases are a very important source of the law, you should have some systematic method of analyzing them.

It may be useful to you to "brief" the cases in this text. Briefing the cases will assist you in understanding the material dealt with in each case. You should ask yourself the following questions about a case:

1. Who is the party bringing the suit and who is the party being sued?

2. What are the facts of the case?

3. What issue of law was involved in the case?

4. Which party won the case?

5. Why did the judge rule in the manner he or she did?

Most of the cases in this text include an initial statement concerning the facts of the case. The authors of this text wrote this material. This initial statement generally indicates who brought the suit and which party won the case. The material after the judge's name is the actual language of the judge's report in the real case. This generally deals with the legal issue involved in the case and it explains the basis of the judge's ruling. You should carefully consider this material in order to develop an understanding of the judge's rationale for his or her decision.

Many cases involve technical issues beyond the scope of this text; therefore, we have edited the cases in this book. We present only the portions of the case that are relevant to the point we are trying to illustrate with the case. The following case is a typical example:

(1) State Farm Mutual Automobile Insurance Company v. Davis
(2) United States Court of Appeals, Ninth Circuit
(3) *937 F.2d 1415 (1991)*

(4) Walter Davis, a United States Marine, purchased a 1984 GMC van. State Farm issued Davis (the insured) a policy of automobile insurance covering the vehicle. On November 23, Davis and two other Marines, Brian Painter and David Roberts, were in the GMC van. Painter was driving the van. Davis was riding in the front passenger seat. Roberts occupied the rear seat. While driving on Interstate Highway 5 a Corvette passed them. Davis told Painter to overtake and pass the Corvette. As the van approached the rear of the Corvette, Davis fired his .44 caliber revolver at the Corvette. A bullet struck the driver, Charles Keukelaar, in the back of the head.

In this case, Shellie, a passenger in the Corvette, and Charles Keukelaar sued Davis. Davis's insurer, State Farm, asked the Court for a ruling that it was not obligated to provide coverage for this incident because the shooting did not result from Davis's use of the vehicle. The trial court ruled for State Farm. The Court of Appeals ruled that this shooting did result from the use of the vehicle. It remanded (sent the case back) to the trial court for further consideration of the question of State Farm's obligation to provide insurance coverage to Davis.*

(5) Singleton, Judge

(6) State Farm argued that it should not have to provide coverage to Davis because the injuries were not caused by an accident resulting from the ownership, maintenance or use of Davis's car.

The policy which State Farm issued to Davis contains the following relevant language: "We will: 1. pay damages which an insured becomes legally liable to pay because of: bodily injury to others caused by accident *resulting from* the ownership, maintenance or *use of* your car."

In *State Farm Mutual Automobile Insurance Company v. Partridge*, the Supreme Court of California addressed similar language in an automobile insurance policy. The court found coverage where a gun discharged injuring a passenger while the vehicle was being driven off-road in pursuit of rabbits. The court noted that a "use" of a vehicle need not be the proximate cause of an injury in order to require coverage. It was sufficient if some minimal causal connection existed between the vehicle and an injury.

Davis's shooting of Keukelaar was not merely incidental to his use as a passenger of the GMC van. At the time of the shooting, Keukelaar was proceeding rapidly down the highway in his Corvette. Had Painter not heeded Davis's request to overtake and pass the Corvette, Davis would not have been in a position to shoot at Keukelaar. Further, it is not unreasonable to assume that Davis counted on the speed of the van to escape after the shooting. Under the facts of this case, the van was more than minimally connected with the injuries Keukelaar suffered.

Painter had to chase Keukelaar so that Davis could shoot at him. Davis did not leave the vehicle, but shot Keukelaar while both were traveling down the highway. Finally, Painter had to drive the van into position next to the Corvette, giving Davis the opportunity to fire his gun. The presence of these factors supports our conclusion that the vehicle was more than incidental to this shooting.

In conclusion, we are satisfied that Painter's and Davis's use of the GMC van insured by State Farm had more than a minimal causal connection with the incident leading to Keukelaar's injuries.

(7) We therefore reverse the decision of the District Court and remand this case in order for that court to consider State Farm's other defenses.

---

* The parties asked the appeals court *not* to consider the question of whether Davis's shooting of Keukelaar was or was not an accident. California law prohibits insurance coverage for losses caused by the willful act of the insured. The question of whether the shooting was or was not intentional had not been resolved at the time of this appeal.

Note the following information about the *Davis* case.

Section 1 is the name of the case: *State Farm Mutual Automobile Insurance Company v. Davis*. In this particular case State Farm instituted the suit to obtain a determination from the court whether it was obligated to provide insurance coverage in the suit between Keukelaar and Davis. Generally, at the trial court level the plaintiff's name (the party that institutes a suit) is listed first and the defendant's name (the party who is being sued) is listed second. On appeal, the name of the party who filed the appeal is generally listed first. Virtually all of the cases in this text are appellate court decisions.

Section 2 states the name of the court which decided the case. In this case, the United States Court of Appeals for the Ninth Circuit decided the case.

Section 3 contains what lawyers refer to as the case citation. We give a case a citation to enable persons to locate the case. The citation system creates an orderly system for categorizing cases. The citation in this case is "937 F.2d 1415 (1991)." The first number refers to the volume of the Federal Reporter in which this case appears. The *Davis* case can be found in volume 937 of the Federal Reporter. "F.2d" refers to the second set of the Federal Reporter. "1415" refers to the first page on which this case appears in volume 937. "1991" refers to the date this case was decided by the court of appeals.

Section 4 of this case generally includes the names of the parties, the facts of the case, frequently the issue dealt with in the case and a statement as to who won the case. We see this case involved State Farm, the plaintiff, which filed suit against Walter Davis, the defendant. This case arose out of a shooting incident. Davis shot a bullet into Keukelaar's vehicle. The issue on appeal is whether Keukelaar's injuries *resulted from* Davis's use of the car.

Section 5 states the name of the judge who wrote the opinion—in this case, Judge Singleton. Several judges hear each appellate case; the number of judges who participate in any given case varies from court to court. Judge Singleton wrote this particular opinion. Other judges agreed with his reasoning and joined in this opinion; however, we use only the name of the judge who wrote the opinion in this section.

It should be noted that all the judges on a court may not agree with the thinking of the majority of the judges on the court. In such a case, the judges who disagree with the decision in a case will render a dissenting opinion. In this text, we have included a number of dissenting opinions. Judges also may agree with the decision in the case, but disagree with the reasoning of the majority opinion. Such a judge may write a concurring opinion.

Section 6 states the rationale for the judge's decision. This section, for the most part, is in the judge's own words. This decision represents the thinking of the majority of the judges hearing this case. In this case Judge Singleton states that the accident could not have happened had Davis not been using his vehicle; therefore the incident arose out of the use of Davis's vehicle.

One might also note that Judge Singleton referred to another, similar case in his opinion—the *Partridge* case. Judges quite frequently examine other, similar cases in order to determine what should be the proper outcome in a particular case. Judges find it useful to consider the reasoning of other judges. In other cases, judges will look at a variety of other factors in arriving at a decision.

Section 7 indicates that the appeals court overturned the decision of the trial court and sent the case back to the trial court for consideration of other issues that were not considered by the appellate court in this appeal.

An appeals court has a number of options in any case. The appeals court may affirm, that is, uphold, the decision of the trial court. It might instead reverse, that is, overturn, the decision of the trial court. It could also reverse part of the trial court's decision and affirm part of the trial court's decision. Finally, it might do what the appeals court did in this case—reverse and remand. This means that the appeals court is overturning the decision of the trial court and is sending the case back to the trial court for further proceedings not inconsistent with the appeals court's decision.*

CASE BRIEF

The clarity of judges' opinions varies. When you begin studying law for the first time, the points judges want to make in their written opinions do not always "jump right out at you." It takes some time to become comfortable reading judicial opinions. For this reason, case briefs may assist you in developing a clearer understanding of the cases.

Briefing a case involves several steps. The first portion of a brief discusses the important facts in the case. Step two requires the student to identify the issue dealt with in the case. The next portion of the brief generally indicates who won the case. Finally, the brief notes the reasons for the judge's decision.

A sample case brief of the *Davis* case follows:

Figure 1   Sample case brief

State Farm Mutual Automobile Insurance Company v. Davis
United States Court of Appeals, Ninth Circuit
937 F.2d 1415 (1991)

FACTS: State Farm issued an automobile insurance policy covering Walter Davis's 1984 GMC van. While Brian Painter was driving this van, Davis was riding as a passenger. When a Corvette passed them, Davis told Painter to overtake and pass the Corvette. When Painter reached the Corvette, Davis fired a shot into the Corvette, injuring the driver, Charles Keukelaar. The trial court found that State Farm was not obligated to provide insurance coverage for this incident.

ISSUE: Did Charles Keukelaar's injuries in this case result from Davis's use of Davis's GMC van?

DECISION: Yes.

RATIONALE: The court found that it would not have been possible for Davis to have shot Keukelaar had Davis not been using the van. Therefore, Davis's use of the GMC van had more than minimal causal connection with

* In this case there are still some issues that need to be resolved by the trial court before a decision can be made that State Farm must provide Davis coverage under this automobile insurance policy.

the incident that led to Keukelaar's injuries. Keukelaar's injuries consequently resulted from Davis's use of Davis's GMC van. As the trial court decided this question incor- rectly, the appellate court reversed the decision of the trial court and returned the case to the trial court for further consideration of other issues involved in this case.

Your instructor may require you to brief cases. Even if he or she does not make this a requirement in your class, you will find it useful to brief the cases in this text.

When lawyers prepare a brief for an appellate court, the brief quite often follows a very similar form: a statement of the facts of the case, a statement of the questions presented by the case, followed by an argument in support of a particular position. Not surprisingly, judges tend to follow a similar approach in writing their opinions in cases.

WHERE TO FIND THE LAW

If you want to locate the original source of some of the material in this text or to find material in addition to that in this text, consult Appendix A, ''Where to Find the Law.''

We hope this information will be useful to you in your study of the law.

Douglas Whitman
John William Gergacz

The Legal and Social Environment of Business

Part 1

Introduction to Law and Business

CHAPTER 1
Introduction to the Law and the Legal Environment of Business

CHAPTER 1

Introduction to the Law and the Legal Environment of Business

- Law in Business and Society
- How Law Affects Business
- Recurring Themes in the Study of the American Legal Environment of Business
- Historical and Social Movements and the Development of Law: From Slavery to Employment Discrimination
- The Law and Its Efforts to Control Concentrations of Power: Drug Testing in the Workplace
- The Law as a Means of Adjusting Competing Values

The study of law is the study of a people, a civilization, as it has existed and as it currently exists. As a discipline, the law embodies the history, values, and culture of a society. It is a series of concepts and rules that shifts to meet social changes. The productive activity of a society—its business practice—is one of the major facets of this study. The legal environment of business, therefore, involves the legal system, its principal actors, and the major substantive rules of law that influence economic activity.

Legal rules and institutions exist and have evolved throughout American history. Thus, the reader of this text will find numerous references to historical developments that led to today's legal rules. Trends in the legal environment will also be explored—that is, how today's social issues and culture interact to reshape the configuration of current legal doctrine. Tomorrow's business executive must be aware of the changeable nature of the legal environment and the forces that lead to that change.

But law is neither magical nor mysterious. It is merely rules of conduct and relationships that are formally recognized by a government. These rules, however, are not necessarily just, nor are they necessarily designed for the good of the people. Law existed in ancient Greece, in Elizabethan England, and in Nazi Germany. In each of those societies there was a body of rules called law that regulated conduct and relationships among people. The existence of law does not ensure that a just society will also exist. As Grant Gilmore, the prominent legal scholar, wrote, "The better the society, the less law there will be. In Heaven there will be no law, and the lion will lie down with the lamb. The values of an unjust society will reflect themselves in an unjust law. The worse the society, the more law there will be. In Hell there will be nothing but law, and due process will be meticulously observed.''[1]

LAW IN BUSINESS AND SOCIETY

Law and business are inextricably intertwined. Business is the organization of capital and labor to produce a product or service with every aspect of that organization regulated by law. Buying and selling, employment practices, and even the nature of the business organization itself are examples of business activity controlled by law. Therefore, any business decision has a legal component, and the prudent business manager should take care to consider it.

However, it is folly to presume that the business manager will be an authority on law, able to evaluate the legal rules and determine their influence on the problem at hand. Such a task is best left to lawyers. Business managers instead must understand law in the general sense. They must appreciate the nature of the legal environment in which their businesses operate. The law, as distinguished from legal rules, needs to be understood as managers understand other people— what motivates them, angers them, pleases them—without becoming authorities in anthropology, sociology, or psychology.

Limits of Law

A law cannot make a person just, sober, or ethical. It cannot make people love their neighbors, nor can it make a business prosper. Many desirable goals cannot be achieved through law. Other social institutions—the family, church, and community—have major roles to play in the makeup of society.

Law provides minimum rules of conduct that society will sanction. Those rules must possess several general characteristics to be effective: predictability, flexibility, and reasonable application and coverage. If any of the characteristics is missing, then often the rule will have an inconsequential effect without excessive law-enforcement efforts. In a free society, such an occurrence is intolerable.

#1

Predictability

One must be able to predict with some accuracy the legal effect of future conduct. Otherwise no activity would ever be legally safe. However, predictability does not necessarily mean certainty. That snow will fall in Vermont during December and that the Chicago Cubs will not win the pennant are predictions of future events that are reasonably assured to occur. However, warm New England Decembers have happened.

Similarly, when a corporation sells its redesigned personal computer, hires new employees, or raises additional capital, legal issues arise. These common business activities would be impossible to complete if executives could not rely on a body of law for predictable resolutions, even though absolute certainty is impossible. Imagine an economic system in which the law provided no means to

German Reunification and Property Ownership

The fall of the Berlin Wall and the freeing of the East German people from the grip of a totalitarian regime was one of the most breathtaking events of the last decade. The two Germanies, severed at the end of World War II, reunited. No longer were there East or West Germans; all were simply Germans. However, major economic problems loomed, particularly in the east. One of the difficulties was to encourage investment in that area of the country.

Investors were plagued with uncertainty. Private property had been expropriated in eastern Germany, first by the Nazis and then by the Communist government. After reunification, the original, long-dispossessed owners were laying claims to it. Should they be considered the current owners? How can one be sure about any such claims made after fifty years of use by others? Should the West German government, successor to the Communist regime in the east, instead be deemed the owner? With the uncertainty over ownership, an investor's risk in buying property was enormous.

Consequently, the German government created an administrative agency, Treuhandanstalt, that was charged with privatizing properties that were formerly controlled by the Communist government. Treuhandanstalt's mission was to settle conflicting ownership claims, return the property to its rightful owners, and pay compensation when appropriate. Furthermore, the agency was authorized to exempt buyers from certain environmental clean-up laws. This was a major concern, given the uncertainty of the pollution problems that the former East German government had ignored. During its first six months of operation, Treuhandanstalt disposed of over twenty-five percent of the property it was charged with privatizing.

reasonably assure the enforceability of bargains between buyers and sellers. Such a system would have no effective contract law, since any predictability about an agreement's enforcement would have to be based on extra-legal means such as threats, violence, or social condemnation. Thus, it is clear that an effective law must be such that those governed by it are able to anticipate its application.

#2

Flexibility

Most law was developed by people who are no longer alive. Those lawmakers had few of the experiences common in modern society. Many never saw an automobile or an airplane. Many never watched television or used computers. Yet the rules of law are applicable and relevant to new situations that have occurred in modern life. They can grow and develop to reflect changes in society around them.

One issue involving this characteristic is the application of copyright law to computer-created works. A copyright provides protection for original works of authorship. (Note the copyright statement on the page following the title page of this book.) The holder of the copyright owns the work. In order to be copyrightable, the work must show some intellectual creativity and must not have been plagiarized. Books and musical compositions are common subjects of copyright protection.

Today, some computer programs are testing the flexibility of the copyright law. One type of program can create a work of fiction or a poem by applying grammatical rules to words chosen at random. In order to produce a poem the "poet" would simply need to run the program. Who, then, should have the right to seek copyright protection for that poem? The work was "created" by the computer. All the user did was select the time to run the program. The programmer created the system that would write the poem, but the poem that was written was not envisioned by the programmer.

At present, the answer is unclear and the issue remains unresolved. However, the key with this example is to note how the law is pliable enough to be applied to new problems. So, while an effective law in our system must have a predictable outcome in its application, it must also be flexible enough to meet changing conditions.

#3   #4

Reasonable Application and Coverage

Law must be reasonable both in its application and in its subject. In order for the law to have reasonable application, those affected by it must have the opportunity to know its requirements. This concept is contained in the **due process** guarantee in the Constitution and is meant to prevent secret laws from being applied. However, it does not mean that a person who does not know what the law is at a given time need not be concerned with its application. The old maxim "Ignorance of the law is no excuse" does have applicability. No one, lawyer or nonlawyer, knows all the law. What the requirement means is that all people will have access to the laws and to legal advisors to assist them in conforming their conduct to existing standards.

An example of a legal system without the protection of reasonable application was described in *The Trial* by Franz Kafka. In the novel, K awoke one morning to find that he was placed under arrest for a crime that he did not know he had committed. In fact, he never knew what law he had allegedly violated. He was to be tried in a court that had no known procedures, and he had no known way of defending himself. The novel offers a frightening example of a system of laws that is not reasonable in its application.

The subject of the law's regulations must also be reasonable. Our system presumes that people will voluntarily obey the laws because laws that reflect the norms of society will be considered reasonable. However, laws that a large number of people find to be unreasonable will soon become unenforceable. The best example of this phenomenon in the United States was Prohibition in the 1920s. The temperance movement was not strong enough to convince Americans to stop drinking. So its leaders, through lobbying and political pressure, had the law forbid people to drink liquor. The result was over a decade of growth of organized crime as criminals eagerly supplied illegal liquor. People's respect for the rule of law was seriously harmed, and corruption was common. Ironically, people did not drink less. Unless we are willing to change our form of government, unreasonable or unpopular laws will not be effective in our society.

HOW LAW AFFECTS BUSINESS

Not every rule of law will have the same effect on business. Some may be seen as creating new opportunities for business. Entrepreneurs may develop new services, demand for which can be traced to changes in the legal environment. New markets can be opened for creative corporate managers who are attuned to developments in the law. For example, deregulation of the television industry in Europe has created a need for thousands of hours of new programming. American professional sports leagues have sought aggressively to take advantage of this new income source. Executives anticipate increased television revenue and a new market for sports logo trinkets such as T-shirts and caps.

Law also may be seen as restricting or prohibiting certain business conduct. Note the materials in Chapter 22 on federal securities regulation. In general, it is illegal under federal securities law to buy securities based on important information that is not publicly available. However, the same behavior in the purchase of an antique clock would not be illegal. The scope of permissible conduct in the antiques market is different than that in the securities market. Thus, business executives need to rely on the advice of counsel in defining the acceptable range of their activities.

A third effect of law on business is that it acts to facilitate the obtaining of certain benefits. For example, assume that a group of investors decides to market snacks in buses and subways. These investors fear that this unique idea might fail and are concerned that creditors may thereafter seek to attach their personal assets. The law contains an organizational form, the corporation, that provides a means by which those investors can limit their losses to the investment in the business. Procedures in their state's incorporation statute will provide a way to form a corporate organization. These legal procedures facilitate the investors' realizing their aim to operate a business in which their personal assets are protected from creditor claims.

Finally, the law acts to formalize and recognize certain private decisions made by business. The primary example of this function is the law of contracts. As will be noted in Chapters 9 and 10, a contract is an agreement that the law recognizes and enforces. Not all agreements meet the standard of a legal contract. But all are the manifestations, at least theoretically, of some bargaining intent of the parties. For example, assume that ABC, Inc. agrees to buy six trucks from XYZ, Inc., with delivery in two weeks. There is no statute or regulation that requires trucks to be delivered within a certain time. However, in the ABC–XYZ example, if the trucks are not delivered as promised, the courts will be available to enforce the bargain, just as if a statute or regulation was in place. Thus, the law acts to provide a formal power to private agreements.

RECURRING THEMES IN THE STUDY OF THE AMERICAN LEGAL ENVIRONMENT OF BUSINESS

Rules of law, the workings of institutions, current legal issues, and past conflicts raise and restate over and over what might be characterized as *themes*. Beethoven used the four-note theme that opened his Fifth Symphony as a pattern around which the masterpiece was woven. Similarly, the rules and current disputes in today's legal environment of business are woven around three themes to be discussed in the balance of the chapter and illustrated by materials in this text.

First, the development of legal rules and institutions is closely associated with historical and social movements. For example, an understanding of such complex regulatory areas as antitrust and labor relations is enhanced by an appreciation of the historical movements that led to their creation. As an introduction to this theme, a brief summary of the civil rights movement will be made in this chapter. In Chapter 18, current manifestations of this movement will be explored under the topic of employment discrimination.

A second recurring theme is that the law seeks to control concentrations of power. The risk the law tries to avoid is that those who have power will abuse it to the detriment of others. Lord Acton, in his letter to Bishop Creighton, aptly characterized this theme: "Power tends to corrupt, and absolute power corrupts absolutely."[2] At first, the concern was concentration of power in government. A study of the constitutional structure of this country is a study of the decision to diffuse the massive power any government will have (see Chapter 6). Recently, concern has developed about concentrations of power in private hands in corporations, which are beyond the diffusion of power commands of the Constitution. Therefore, the law will also be seen throughout this text as a means of limiting concentrations and abuses of corporate power.

The final theme in the legal environment of American business involves the concept of legal rights. The law recognizes and adjusts claims of individual values within a society. At times, important values conflict and the law must act to balance them. Yet the suggestion that individual values may be controlled raises the problem of that control's discounting them in practice. The tension in the law between protecting individual rights and allowing some control over their exercise is one of the recurring American legal problems.

HISTORICAL AND SOCIAL MOVEMENTS AND THE DEVELOPMENT OF LAW: FROM SLAVERY TO EMPLOYMENT DISCRIMINATION

The study of black Americans' struggle for equality under the law illustrates the effect of historical and cultural attitudes on the law. The Constitution was, in part, a product of compromise between the interests of Northerners and Southerners. As originally drafted, it permitted slavery and the importation of slaves. Slaves were considered to be capital assets of their owners, and many pre–Civil War cases concern various aspects of buying, selling, and transferring the legal rights to a slave. An 1829 case from North Carolina will serve as an example. A female slave was leased by John Mann for one year. While Mann was chastising the slave, she began to run away. Mann then shot and wounded her. The court held that it was not an indictable crime in North Carolina to shoot a slave: "The slave, to remain a slave, must be made sensible that there is no appeal from his master;

that his power is in no instance usurped; but is conferred by the laws of man at least, if not by the law of God. The Court, therefore, disclaims the power of changing the relation in which these parts of our people stand to each other.''[3]

Although a bloody civil war was necessary to resolve the question of slavery, it did not provide equality for black Americans. People may have abhorred slavery in the mid-nineteenth century, but they did not seek integration of the races. The Northern states were not a mecca of racial harmony, and the law reflected this. The case of *Roberts* v. *City of Boston* (1849) is an example of Northern attitudes toward blacks before the Civil War. In that case, a suit was filed on behalf of a five-year-old black girl who was required to attend a public school devoted to the exclusive instruction of black children. This school was at a greater distance from her home than another public school limited to white children. The case was based upon a Massachusetts statute that provided that damages might be recovered by any child who was unlawfully excluded from public school instruction. The court held that the school laws of Massachusetts provided that the local school committee had the power to make operating decisions regarding public schools, and there was nothing inherently illegal in creating a dual public school system, one for black students and one for white students.

After the Civil War, the Thirteenth, Fourteenth, and Fifteenth Amendments, called the **Civil War Amendments,** were added to the Constitution. They were designed to forever abolish slavery and to treat the races equally in the eyes of the law. However, the legal interpretations of those amendments were consistent with the mores of the day rather than with an abstract notion of equal or civil rights.

In 1896, the United States Supreme Court decided *Plessy* v. *Ferguson.* That case involved a claim that a Louisiana statute, which required railway companies to carry white and black passengers in separate coaches, violated the Fourteenth Amendment. Justice Brown, writing for the Court, denied that claim by translating late 19th-century values into the rule of law.

> The object of the amendment was undoubtedly to enforce the absolute equality of the two races before the law, but in the nature of things it could not have been intended to abolish distinctions based upon color, or to enforce social, as distinguished from political, equality, or a commingling of the two races upon terms unsatisfactory to either. Laws permitting, and even requiring, their separation in places where they are liable to be brought into contact do not necessarily imply the inferiority of either race to the other.
>
> We consider the underlying fallacy of the plaintiff's argument to consist in the assumption that the enforced separation of the two races stamps the colored race with a badge of inferiority.
>
> The argument assumes that social prejudices may be overcome by legislation, and that equal rights cannot be secured to the negro except by an enforced commingling of the two races. We cannot accept this proposition. If the two races are to meet upon terms of social equality, it must be the result of natural affinities, a mutual appreciation of each other's merits and a voluntary consent of individuals. Legislation is powerless to eradicate racial instincts or to abolish distinctions based upon physical differences, and the attempt to do so can only result in accentuating the difficulties of the present situation. If the civil and political rights of both races be equal, one cannot be inferior to the other civilly or politically. If

one race be inferior to the other socially, the Constitution of the United States cannot put them upon the same plane.

"Separate but equal" as a constitutional doctrine survived for nearly sixty years after the *Plessy* v. *Ferguson* case. Separate schools, segregated eating facilities, segregated rest rooms, separate drinking fountains, and black- or white-only businesses were common. The post–World War II civil rights movement's demand for an end to racial segregation was given a legal boost in 1954 by *Brown* v. *Board of Education*. In that case, the plaintiffs were black children who challenged a Kansas statute that permitted cities to maintain separate school facilities for blacks and whites. The district court found that segregation in public education had a detrimental effect upon black children, but it denied relief on the ground that the school facilities were substantially equal. The United States Supreme Court, in an opinion by Chief Justice Warren, reversed, holding that "separate but equal" had no place in public education. Note how the Court used social norms to reach its conclusion in much the same way as the Court in *Plessy*. In both cases, the Court was construing the same language in the Fourteenth Amendment.

In approaching this problem, we cannot turn the clock back to 1868 when the Amendment was adopted, or even to 1896 when *Plessy* v. *Ferguson* was written. We must consider public education in the light of its full development and its present place in American life throughout the Nation. Only in this way can it be determined if segregation in public schools deprives these plaintiffs of the equal protection of the laws.

Today, education is perhaps the most important function of state and local governments. Today it is a principal instrument in awakening the child to cultural values, in preparing him for later professional training, and in helping him to adjust normally to his environment. In these days, it is doubtful that any child may reasonably be expected to succeed in life if he is denied the opportunity of an education. Such an opportunity, where the state has undertaken to provide it, is a right which must be made available to all on equal terms.

We come then to the question presented: Does segregation of children in public schools solely on the basis of race, even though the physical facilities and other "tangible" factors may be equal, deprive the children of the minority group of equal educational opportunities? We believe that it does.

To separate black children from others of similar age and qualifications solely because of their race generates a feeling of inferiority as to their status in the community that may affect their hearts and minds in a way unlikely ever to be undone. Whatever may have been the extent of psychological knowledge at the time of *Plessy* v. *Ferguson,* this finding is amply supported by modern authority. Any language in *Plessy* v. *Ferguson* contrary to this finding is rejected.

Brown v. *Board of Education* was the first major legal development implementing the goals of the civil rights movement. Thereafter, legally imposed racial segregation fell. In 1964, the Congress enacted a historical bill with profound and wide-ranging implications. The Civil Rights Act of 1964 set in motion newly created federal rules designed to ensure fair and equal treatment for all persons in public accommodations, housing, and employment, regardless of race, sex, religion, color, or national origin. Today the struggle continues. Issues of preferential treatment for minorities, racial quotas, and the economic plight of the black family carry forward the debate over integrating black people into the mainstream of American life.

THE LAW AND ITS EFFORTS TO CONTROL CONCENTRATIONS OF POWER: DRUG TESTING IN THE WORKPLACE

POLITICAL $\xrightarrow{TEND}$ *ECONOMIC*

The study of law is the study of attempts to limit exploitation by the powerful. Chronicles of this exploitation can be found in innumerable novels. Charles Dickens and Anatole France are examples of writers whose works illuminated the perils of unregulated power. Philosophers as diverse as John Locke and Karl Marx were concerned about the abuse of power caused by the concentration of property in the king (government) or in the capitalist (business). American legal history is replete with examples of laws being enacted to curb activities of the powerful. A prime example is the United States Constitution.

Having freed themselves from a British government they regarded as tyrannical, the early leaders of this country established a government with limited powers and divided the important functions of government among three distinct branches. Furthermore, numerous centers of authority were created (the states and the federal government systems) to further diffuse government power. Such a division of responsibility may be described as planned organizational inefficiency. The drawback to such a system is that it does not yield prompt action to combat national problems. The advantage is that in times of national hysteria (the McCarthy era in the 1950s, for example) a demagogue will be unable to gain control. The Constitution thus has fostered individual liberty by creating numerous and competing governmental authorities that inhibit the concentration of power.

However, concentrations of power are not limited to the government. New concentrations of power arose in the late nineteenth century as very large corporations developed. Before the Industrial Revolution, most businesses produced products sold by the maker directly to the purchaser. With the growth of mass production techniques tied to improved systems of delivering goods, the advantages of economies of scale became apparent. Large pools of capital met this need through the development of major corporate organizations. By the late nineteenth century the concentration of economic power in such industries as the railroads, oil, steel, and sugar triggered movements in the law to control that power. The platforms of both the Democratic and Republican parties in the 1888 presidential election contained planks that promised solutions to the abuses of these large moneyed interests.

In 1890 the Sherman Antitrust Act was passed. It was the first nationwide attempt to control economic monopoly. Chapters 23 and 24 of this text contain a discussion of the antitrust laws. Additionally, the labor union movement, discussed in Chapter 20, rose out of conflicts between workers and big business. The consumer movement grew from consumer complaints over the relationship between business and the public (see Chapter 17).

Today, drug testing in the workplace is a volatile issue that the law is seeking to control. Drug abuse has become a major concern for both government and private employers. Loss of productivity and increased employee absenteeism have been cited as problems that justify drug screening programs. One study estimated that this loss may be as high as one hundred billion dollars annually. Furthermore, as noted in Chapter 14, expanded employer liability for worker-caused injuries imposes financial risk on corporations having drug-impaired workers. In 1987 an Amtrack train crashed, killing fifteen people, and injuring seventy-five more. The crash was found to have been caused by an engineer who had been smoking marijuana. Lawsuits were filed against Amtrack, which settled for seventy-five million dollars.

A survey of human resources managers in 1991 found that sixty-three percent of their companies tested for drugs—triple the number that did so five years before. Some of this increase can be attributed to strong federal government advocacy of drug testing programs, particularly for public employees and companies that do business with the government. However, the power of major corporate employers and the federal government to implement drug testing in the workplace has been a concern.

Numerous cases have been filed that questioned the constitutionality of public employee drug testing programs. Since the employer in those situations was the government, the Fourth Amendment, which protects public employees from unreasonable searches, would be applicable. The United States Supreme Court has upheld some drug testing programs, although it has not ruled on random testing. During the Reagan administration, the Customs Service, the agency charged with interdicting the importation of illegal drugs, adopted a policy requiring a drug test of any employee applying for promotion to certain sensitive positions. This urine testing policy was upheld in *National Treasury Employees* v. *Von Raab* as the Supreme Court focused on the compelling government interest in the work of the Customs Service as a justification.

But the effect of the use of this power on innocent individuals should be considered. One customs employee who was compelled to take a drug test stated: "I would say everybody who has taken one either finds it humiliating or asinine. I've been with the Customs Service for eleven years. If they don't know me by now, they're never going to know me. When I arrest somebody I have to respect their rights. I don't see why I should be subject to an indiscriminate test when I haven't done anything."[4] Furthermore, note that the Customs Service had tested 5,300 of its employees as of June 30, 1988. A mere one-tenth of one percent tested positive.

Private employer drug testing also raises concerns. Although constitutional issues generally do not arise, litigation has been filed over the effects of the testing programs. In 1988 an oilfield worker was fired after testing positive for drug use. However, the drug test was inaccurate. The worker sued the laboratory that processed the test. He was awarded $4.1 million in damages, most of which was punitive.

Generally, a finding of reasonable private employer conduct (that is, self-restraint in the exercise of power) precludes decisions that favor the employee. The following is one court's analysis of a drug screening policy. How might an employer design the policy in order to satisfy the decision?

Borse v. Piece Goods Shop, Inc.
United States Court of Appeals, Third Circuit
963 F.2d 611 (1992)

Sarah Borse was employed as a sales clerk by the Piece Goods Shop for almost fifteen years. In January 1990, the shop adopted a drug and alcohol policy which required its employees to sign a form giving their consent to urinalysis screening for drug use.

Borse refused to sign the consent form. On more than one occasion, she asserted that the drug and alcohol policy violated her right to privacy. The shop continued to insist that she sign the form and threatened to discharge her unless she did. On February 9, 1990, the shop terminated Borse's employment.

This appeal requires us to decide whether an at-will employee who is discharged for refusing to consent to urinalysis screening for drug use states a claim for wrongful discharge under Pennsylvania law.

Becker, Circuit Judge

Ordinarily, Pennsylvania law does not provide a common-law cause of action for the wrongful discharge of an at-will employee. Rather, an employer may discharge an employee with or without cause, at pleasure, unless restrained by some contract. However, the Pennsylvania Supreme Court recognized the possibility that an action for wrongful discharge might lie when the firing of an at-will employee violates public policy. In order to evaluate Borse's claim, we must attempt to discern whether any public policy is threatened by her discharge.

Our review of Pennsylvania law reveals evidence of a public policy that may, under certain circumstances, give rise to a wrongful discharge action related to urinalysis drug screening. Specifically, we refer to the Pennsylvania common law regarding tortious invasion of privacy. Pennsylvania recognizes a cause of action for tortious intrusion upon seclusion. The Restatement defines the tort as follows: "One who intentionally intrudes, physically or otherwise, upon the solitude or seclusion of another or his private affairs or concerns, is subject to liability to the other for invasion of his privacy, if the intrusion would be highly offensive to a reasonable person."

We can envision at least two ways in which an employer's urinalysis program might intrude upon an employee's seclusion. First, the particular manner in which the program is conducted might constitute an intrusion upon seclusion as defined by Pennsylvania law. The process of collecting the urine sample to be tested clearly implicates expectations of privacy that society has long recognized as reasonable. In addition, many urinalysis programs monitor the collection of the urine specimen to ensure that the employee does not adulterate it or substitute a sample from another person. Monitoring collection of the urine sample appears to fall within the definition of an intrusion upon seclusion because it involves the use of one's senses to oversee the private activities of another.

There are few activities in our society more personal or private than the passing of urine. Most people describe it by euphemisms if they talk about it at all. It is a function traditionally performed without public observation; indeed, its performance in public is generally prohibited by law as well as social custom. If the method used to collect the urine sample fails to give due regard to the employee's privacy, it could constitute a substantial and highly offensive intrusion upon seclusion.

Second, urinalysis can reveal a host of private medical facts about an employee, including whether she is epileptic, pregnant, or diabetic. A reasonable person might well conclude that submitting urine samples to tests designed to ascertain these types of information constitutes a substantial and highly offensive intrusion upon seclusion. Indeed, it may be granted that there are areas of an employee's life in which his employer has no

legitimate interest. An intrusion into one of these areas by virtue of the employer's power of discharge might plausibly give rise to a cause of action, particularly where some recognized facet of public policy is threatened.

We hold that dismissing an employee who refused to consent to urinalysis drug testing would violate public policy if the testing tortiously invaded the employee's privacy. The sketchy nature of Borse's complaint makes it difficult to ascertain whether the Shop's drug and alcohol program would constitute a substantial and highly offensive intrusion upon Borse's privacy, however. Although she alleges that the program violates her right of privacy, she fails to allege how it does so. Because we can envision at least two ways in which an employer's drug and alcohol program might violate the public policy protecting individuals from tortious invasions of privacy by private actors, we will vacate the order of the district court dismissing the complaint.

Additionally, a few states have enacted drug testing legislation that is designed to regulate unbridled exercise of this corporate power over its employees. A 1991 survey indicated that fourteen states had such laws. The Rhode Island statute is an example.

Thus, note that the ''simple solution'' of employee drug testing imposed by powerful corporate or government bodies fundamentally involves the law as a means of controlling the exercise of that power. Further developments are certain to occur. As Justice Scalia noted in his dissent to the *Von Raab* case mentioned previously:

Those who lose because of the lack of understanding that begot the present exercise in symbolism are not just the Customs Service employees, whose dignity is thus offended, but all of us—who suffer a coarsening of our national manners that ultimately give the Fourth Amendment its content, and who become subject to the administration of federal officials whose respect for our privacy can hardly be greater than the small respect they have been taught to have for their own.[5]

THE LAW AS A MEANS OF ADJUSTING COMPETING VALUES

Sources of Rights ''You cannot do that to me. I have my rights.'' People who make this assertion usually mean that some injustice, sometimes perceived only by them, has been done, and they believe that it should not be allowed. However, in order to know

---

General Laws of Rhode Island
Chap. 6.5 Urine and Blood Tests As a Condition of Employment

28-6.5-1. Urine and blood testing generally prohibited.—No employer or agent of any employer shall, either orally or in writing, request, require or subject any employee to submit a sample of his urine, blood or other bodily fluid or tissue for testing as a condition of continued employment. Nothing herein shall prohibit an employer from requiring a specific employee to submit to such testing if:

(A) the employer has reasonable grounds to believe, based on specific objective facts, that the employee's use of controlled substances is impairing his ability to perform his job; and

(B) the employee provides the test sample in private, outside the presence of any person; and

(C) the testing is conducted in conjunction with a bona fide rehabilitation program; and

(D) positive tests are confirmed by means of gas chromatography/mass spectrometry or technology recognized as being at least as scientifically accurate; and

(E) the employer provides the employee, at the employer's expense, the opportunity to have the sample tested or evaluated by an independent testing facility and so advises the employee; and

(F) the employer provides the employee with a reasonable opportunity to rebut or explain the results.

---

what is meant by **rights,** the nature and source of the injustice must be understood. Sometimes, the injustice arises through the activities of the government. The Bill of Rights in the United States Constitution protects an individual from the power and activities of the government. Its provisions were deemed necessary because of experiences under British rule before independence.

However, injustice may also arise from the acts of other individuals or private business. These injustices, too, lead to the creation of rights through the balancing of conflicting values. These rights involve the regulation of individual, private conduct, either through legislation or through judicial decision. One example of such regulation is the Equal Pay Act, which makes it illegal for an employer to pay women and men differently for the same job. The conflicting values were the discretion of employers to set wage rates for any employee and the interests of workers not to have sex discrimination affect that decision.

Courts, too, may be seen as a source of legal rights. For example, the Supreme Court created the constitutional right of privacy through judicial decision. Furthermore, legal philosophers argue that rights exist independent of any formal government recognition, since all persons have certain natural rights by virtue of being human. The concept of natural rights is very old. It was advanced by Aristotle, by the drafters of the Declaration of Independence, and more recently by the Carter administration's human rights foreign policy. Calls for natural rights or human rights occur when individual freedom is lacking. Totalitarian regimes that jail or kill dissenters, prohibit or discourage religious worship, or arrest people without charge and punish them without trial give rise to the assertion that there are natural or human rights of which no government may deprive its people.

But constitutions, statutes, court decisions, and philosophical ideas are not the sources of our rights. At most, they are their outward manifestations. Constitutions, statutes, and judicial decisions are only words. The concept of natural rights is a philosophical idea. Yet these mere words and ideas represent the real source of our rights—us. Quite simply, we have certain rights in this country because we as a nation want to have them. When we no longer believe in those rights, the law that recognizes them can easily be ignored. Clarence Darrow, the noted trial lawyer, once stated, ''It is all right to preserve freedom in constitutions, but when the spirit of freedom has fled from the hearts of the people, then its matter is easily sacrificed under law.''[6]

In order to understand this idea, it is helpful to look into early American history. We can review the nineteenth-century cases, such as *Bradwell* v. *State* (Chapter 18), with twentieth-century eyes and see a couple of important things. Today, no state could prohibit a woman from becoming a lawyer solely because she was a woman. We can say that she would have the right to pursue her chosen profession. However, as noted in *Bradwell*, this was not the case in 1872. Second, as we change as a society our rights will change to reflect our new values. The status of women in America has changed vastly since 1872. The law and our rights reflect that change.

Limitations on Rights: Which Value to Choose?

In a complex and crowded nation, an individual's rights may well involve impositions on other people. For instance, if you distribute handbills outlining your disagreement with the current administration, then others are subjected to your standing on the street corner waving the handbills as they pass by. If a newspaper has the right of freedom of the press, then a politician arrested for drunk driving will be embarrassed if named on the front page. Even rights that are most zealously protected, like freedom of speech, are not without restriction. You may have the right to give a speech for your favorite political candidate. But you do not have the right to give that speech at 2:00 A.M. outside your professor's bedroom window. Both you and your professor have certain rights: you, to give a political speech; your professor, to be able to sleep undisturbed by loud speeches. If a dispute between you and your professor arises, a court may be called upon to determine the conflict of rights. The court will weigh and balance various factors, including the importance of both your rights to society, and render a decision.

Rights are not absolute, because the values that they represent often clash in a complex society. For example, should a person be able to read any book that is published? Little dispute arises if one is considering the Bible, the works of Shakespeare, or the poetry of Carl Sandburg. However, controversial books such as J. D. Salinger's *Catcher in the Rye* and Mark Twain's *Huckleberry Finn* have been the subject of censorship efforts by those who claim the books offend their values. Which values to choose?

The fact that the law makes the choice raises a danger that any limits placed on rights will lead to their loss in practice. This is the central difficulty courts face in deciding disputes that raise such issues as employee privacy, advertising restrictions, and land use regulation.

Totalitarian governments frequently have constitutions that provide many of the same freedoms that exist in the United States. Yet it is clear that their citizens have no such rights in practice. The Constitution of the People's Republic of China, for example, grants its citizens the freedom of assembly and the freedom to demonstrate. The regime, uninfluenced by considerations of law, conveniently ignores these mere words—most notably when its army massacred student demonstrators in Tiananmen Square on June 4, 1989.

The following cases illustrate the complexity that sometimes arises when important interests or values clash. The first case, *Schley* v. *Couch*, concerns property and the task of assigning its ownership. The second case, *Regina* v. *Dudley and Stephens*, involves a clash of the most basic values in any civilized society—the value of survival and the duty of a society to prohibit the killing of its members. For each case, carefully consider the values in dispute. Make sure you note the implications of any decision that you reach.

Schley v. Couch
Supreme Court of Texas
284 S.W. 2d 333 (1955)

Griffin, Justice

The petitioner was the owner of a tract of land upon which was situated a house with an attached garage and storeroom. The petitioner had acquired these premises from a Mr. Adams about June 15, 1952. At the time petitioner moved upon the premises, there was a concrete floor covering only the front half of the garage, and the remaining half was a dirt floor. A few days prior to July 7, 1952, petitioner employed a Mr. Tomlinson and his crew of workmen to put a concrete floor in the rear half of the garage. While working on the project, respondent's employer directed respondent to take a pick and loosen up this hardpacked soil. While digging in this soil, respondent's pick struck a hard object and respondent found $1,000 buried in the ground. The money was in currency. Included in this currency were two Hawaiian bills issued during World War II. All bills were fresh, and well preserved and of the size of present currency. A glass jar top and some glass from a jar were found nearby, evidencing that the money had been buried in a glass jar. The erection of the garage had been begun by a Mr. Allen, a predecessor in title, who had sold the property in April or May of 1948, at which time the garage was in the process of being built but had not been completed. The owner of the money is unknown.

No proof having been made in the present case as to who is the true owner of money found, we will indulge the presumption that he has forgotten where he secreted it, or has died since he secreted the property.

[Who should be considered the "owner" of this money? The finder? His employer? The current owner of the land? Previous owners? Decide.]

Regina v. Dudley and Stephens
Queen's Bench Division (England)
14 Q.B.D. 273 (1884)

Indictment for the murder of Richard Parker on the high seas within the jurisdiction of the Admiralty.

On July 5, 1884, the prisoners, Thomas Dudley and Edward Stephens, and Brooks, all able-bodied English seamen, and the deceased, an English boy, between seventeen and eighteen years of age, were cast away in a storm on the high seas sixteen hundred miles from the Cape of Good Hope, and were compelled to put into an open boat. In this boat they had no supply of water and no supply of food, except two one-pound tins of turnips. For three days they had nothing else to subsist upon. On the fourth day they caught a small turtle, upon which they subsisted for a few days. This was the only food they had up to the twentieth day, when the act now in question was committed. On the twelfth day, the remains of the turtle were entirely consumed, and for the next eight days they had nothing to eat. They had no fresh water, except such rain as they from time to time caught in their oil-skin capes. The boat was drifting on the ocean, and was probably more than one thousand miles away from land. On the eighteenth day, when they had been seven days without food and five without water, the prisoners spoke to Brooks as to what should be done if no succour came. They suggested that someone should be sacrificed to save the rest. Brooks dissented, and the boy, to whom they were understood to refer, was not consulted.

On July 24, the day before the act now in question, the prisoner Dudley proposed to Stephens and Brooks that lots should now be cast who should be put to death to save the rest. Brooks refused to consent, and it was not put to the boy, and in point of fact there was no drawing of lots. On that day, the prisoners spoke of their having families, and suggested it would be better to kill the boy that their lives should be saved, and Dudley proposed that if there was no vessel in sight by the morrow morning the boy should be killed.

The next day, July 25, no vessel appearing, Dudley told Brooks that he had better go and have a sleep, and made signs to Stephens and Brooks that the boy had better be killed. The prisoner Stephens agreed to the act, but Brooks dissented from it. The boy was then lying at the bottom of the boat quite helpless, and extremely weakened by famine and by drinking sea water, and unable to make any resistance, nor did he ever assent to his being killed. The prisoner Dudley offered a prayer asking forgiveness for them and that their souls might be saved. Dudley, with the assent of Stephens, went to the boy, and telling him that his time was come, put a knife into his throat and killed him then and there. The three men fed upon the body and blood of the boy for four days. On the fourth day after the act had been committed the boat was picked up by a passing vessel, and the prisoners were rescued, still alive, but in the lowest state of prostration. They were carried to the port of Falmouth, and committed for trial at Exeter. If the men had not fed upon the body of the boy they would probably not have survived to be picked up and rescued, but would within the four days have died of famine. The boy, being in a much weaker condition, was likely to have died before them.

At the time of the act in question there was no sail in sight, nor any reasonable prospect of relief. Under these circumstances there appeared to the prisoners every probability that unless they then fed or very soon fed upon the boy or one of themselves they would die of starvation. There was no appreciable chance of saving life except by killing someone for the others to eat. Assuming any necessity to kill anybody, there was no greater necessity for killing the boy than any of the other three men.

[You write the opinion. How should these rights be balanced?]

SUMMARY

Law is not separate from the culture, history, and times in which it exists. The study of law is not limited to learning legal rules. Understanding the legal environment of business, therefore, requires a broad understanding of the people and basic trends that influence the relationship between law and business.

Three such trends or themes may be identified: first, that historical and social movements affect the development of law. A brief history of the attitude of the law toward equal rights for black Americans chronicled the historical movements that led to today's civil rights laws. A second recurring theme is the efforts of the law to control concentrations and abuses of power, whether it be in the hands of government or private business. Finally, the law may be seen as a mechanism for adjusting claims of conflicting rights. These themes will surface time and again throughout the remaining chapters of this book. More importantly, they influence the legal environment in which the business manager operates.

REVIEW QUESTIONS

1. Define the following terms:
   a. Civil War Amendments
   b. Rights
   c. Separate but equal

2. Why does the law act to control or limit the concentration of power and its exercise? Is there a paradox inherent in this control?

3. Why are there no absolute rights?

4. Is there a danger in limitations that the law places on the exercise of rights?

5. Discuss the themes that recur in the law.

   Give examples other than those mentioned in the text.

6. What characteristics must law possess in order for it to be effective in our system?

7. Discuss the historical and social trends which led to the development of civil rights laws.

8. What are the four effects law might have on business activity? Give an example of each, other than what was noted in this chapter.

9. You are an executive of the ABC Corpora-

tion, a very large multinational firm. One afternoon you are reviewing the terms of a deal that one of your subordinates has negotiated with XYZ, Inc., a small distribution company. The agreement provides that if XYZ does not sell a certain quota of ABC products, it will pay ABC a penalty of ten times the cost of those products. Without discussing applicable legal rules, would you expect a potential problem to arise with such a clause? If so, give reasons.

10. Smith is a highly trained engineer who is in charge of computer design changes at High Tech, Inc. He has been instrumental in developing numerous features of the corporation's line of computers and is currently involved in its secret work involving artificial intelligence. AI, Inc., a competitor of High Tech, lures Smith from High Tech in order to organize its newly formed artificial intelligence division. Smith eagerly accepts the new position, and High Tech is upset that he has left. Without discussing applicable legal rules, what are the concerns of Smith and High Tech that could be central to a suit filed by High Tech against Smith?

11. You have been assigned to Hong Kong by your company to head its Far East division. You are in charge of operations in Taiwan, Korea, and Malaysia. Discuss the sources of differences in law between those areas and the United States, without focusing on legal rules. How might you begin to understand, or at least appreciate, those differences?

12. Jones is marketing manager for Sellit, Inc. She supervises fifteen sales representatives. Jones is an avid professional football fan and each year plans an outing with the representatives as a way to build "team spirit." Carson, one of the sales representatives, dislikes professional football. He believes it is overcommercialized and panders to primitive violent instincts. One year he mentioned casually to Jones that he would prefer a different type of group outing, since he had no interest in football. Jones listened but thereafter began to criticize Carson's work regularly. Finally, she fired him. Previously, Carson had been one of the top sales representatives. Without reference to applicable legal rules, discuss any legal problems that might arise.

NOTES

[1] G. Gilmore, *The Ages of American Law* (New Haven: Yale University Press, 1977), pp. 110–111.

[2] John Bartlett, *Familiar Quotations,* 15th ed., E. Black, ed. (Boston: Little, Brown & Co., 1980).

[3] *State* v. *Mann,* 13 N.C. 229 (N. Car. 1829).

[4] *American Bar Association Journal,* 63 (October 1, 1988).

[5] *National Treasury Employees Union* v. *Von Raab,* 109 S.Ct. 184, 1402 (1989).

[6] A. Weinberg (ed.), *Attorney for the Damned* (New York: Simon & Schuster, 1977), p. 57.

Part 2

The American Legal System

CHAPTER 2

Introduction to the Courts

- The Power to Hear a Case
- Structure of the Court System
- Personnel in the Judicial System

Courts are institutions designed for settling disputes. They are the units of government concerned with the administration of justice. At times individuals, businesses, and the government disagree over the application of various laws in society or seek to use the law as a means of controlling the behavior of others. A function of the court is to settle those disputes. However, courts do much more than decide who was at fault for an accident, whether an accused person actually stole the goods, or whether a marriage should be dissolved. In the course of deciding these and other questions, courts make law. Judicial lawmaking is not the same as lawmaking by a legislature, yet it has the same effect.

Judicial lawmaking may be divided into three categories. First, there is the creation of a body of law, called **common law,** arising solely from judicial decisions. These decisions give an indication of probable future court rulings to other parties with similar problems. The parties rely on the courts following their past decisions or giving them precedential effect. Such areas of law as contracts and torts emphasize this type of judicial lawmaking.

A second type of judicial lawmaking occurs when a court interprets a statute. For example, the Uniform Commercial Code, a statute regulating personal property transactions, provides that buyers and sellers are to act in a commercially reasonable manner. But what precisely does the term *commercially reasonable* mean? A particular buyer and seller may have differing opinions, resulting in a dispute that finds its way into court. In the process of settling that dispute, the court must interpret the term *commercially reasonable*. By interpreting the term, the court makes law through its decision in the case. Thereafter, other buyers and sellers will have the advice of that particular case to assist them in understanding the statute requiring commercially reasonable conduct.

The third type of judicial lawmaking occurs through the interpretation of the Constitution. This is a special type of lawmaking simply because of the profound effect constitutional rulings may have. This type of judicial lawmaking is frequently controversial. The argument that judges should not make law or impose their views of policy in cases usually arises in situations of constitutional lawmaking. This criticism is not peculiarly modern, but has been made throughout American history.

Although courts do their work within the limited context of settling particular disputes between parties, at the same time they have a much greater effect on the law. This chapter and the next two chapters discuss important facets of the judicial branch. This chapter provides an introduction to the courts, focusing on important actors in the judicial process and some issues that affect their roles, while Chapter 3 is a very practical discussion of civil litigation. Chapter 4 provides the theoretical background for understanding various aspects of the judicial process and judicial dispute settling.

THE POWER TO HEAR A CASE

Jurisdiction   A person with a legal claim may not simply bring a case to any court in the nation. The court in which the plaintiff files the case must have **jurisdiction**—the power to hear and decide the case. To begin with, the court must have jurisdiction over the *subject matter* of the case. A court has jurisdiction over subject matter if the case is one which the court is authorized to hear. Some state courts are courts of general jurisdiction—they can hear any case arising in the state. Other courts are courts of limited jurisdiction—they can hear only certain types of cases. For example, suppose that a judge presides over a probate court in a given state. A **probate** court handles the estates of deceased persons and guardianships. If a plaintiff filed suit in the probate court for damages arising out of an automobile accident, the probate judge would be required to dismiss the suit for lack of jurisdiction. An automobile accident case has nothing to do with the power of the court to hear probate and guardianship matters.

It is not sufficient for a court merely to have jurisdiction over the subject matter of the case. The court must also have power over the person involved in the case. *In personam* jurisdiction over the plaintiff is obtained by the plaintiff's filing the suit. In personam jurisdiction over the defendant normally is obtained by the service of a summons and petition on the defendant. A court has jurisdiction over anyone who can be served with a summons and petition while physically present within the state.

In *Burnham* v. *Superior Court of California,* the United States Supreme Court reaffirmed the longstanding rule that a court may obtain in personam jurisdiction over a defendant if the plaintiff serves a summons and petition on the defendant while the latter is physically present within the state. While the justices of the United States Supreme Court agreed upon this rule, they disagreed on a rationale for the rule. We have included two of the opinions supporting the decision against Dennis Burnham to illustrate the differing thinking of the rationale for this rule of jurisdiction.

Burnham v. Superior Court of California
United States Supreme Court
110 S.Ct. 2105 (1990)

Francie Burnham separated from her husband, Dennis, and moved from New Jersey to California with their children. Mrs. Burnham brought a divorce suit in California in June 1988. In late January, Dennis Burnham, who lived in New Jersey, was visiting California on business, after which he went north to San Francisco, where his wife resided, to see his children. Upon returning one of his children to Mrs. Burnham's home on January 24, 1988, he was served with a California court summons and a copy of Mrs. Burnham's divorce petition. He then returned to New Jersey.

Dennis Burnham made a special appearance in California. He alleged that the court lacked personal jurisdiction over him because his only contacts with California were a few short visits to the state for the purposes of conducting business and visiting the children. Burnham argued that the due process clause prohibited California from asserting jurisdiction over him because he lacked "minimum contacts" with the state of California. The California superior court held that since he was personally served with the summons and petition in California, there was a valid basis for in personam jurisdiction over him. The United States Supreme Court agreed with the ruling of the superior court.

IF SERVED, MUST SHOW IN ANY STATE

Justice Scalia (announced the judgment of the Court and delivered an opinion)

The proposition that the judgment of a court lacking jurisdiction is void traces back to the English Year Books (1482), and was made settled law by Lord Coke in *Case of the Marshalsea* (1612). Traditionally that proposition was embodied in the phrase *coram non judice*, "before a person not a judge"—meaning, in effect, that the proceeding in question was not a *judicial* proceeding because lawful judicial authority was not present, and could therefore not yield a *judgment*. American courts invalidated, or denied recognition to, judgments that violated the common-law principle long before the Fourteenth Amendment was adopted. In *Pennoyer v. Neff* (1878), we announced that the judgment of a court lacking personal jurisdiction violated the Due Process Clause of the Fourteenth Amendment as well.

Among the most firmly established principles of personal jurisdiction in American tradition is that the courts of a State have jurisdiction over nonresidents who are physically present in the State. The view developed early that each State had the power to hale before its courts any individual who could be found within its borders, and that once having acquired jurisdiction over such a person by properly serving him with process, the State could retain jurisdiction to enter judgment against him, no matter how fleeting his visit. That view had antecedents in English common-law practice, which sometimes allowed transitory actions, arising out of events outside the country, to be maintained against seemingly nonresident defendants who were physically present in England.

Despite this formidable body of precedent, petitioner contends, in reliance on our decisions applying the *International Shoe* standard, that in the absence of "continuous and systematic" contacts with the forum, a nonresident defendant can be subjected to judgment only as to matters that arise out of or relate to his contacts with the forum. This argument rests on a thorough misunderstanding of our cases.

Nothing in *International Shoe* or the cases that have followed it offers support for the proposition that a defendant's presence in the forum is no longer sufficient to establish jurisdiction. The short of the matter is that jurisdiction based on physical presence alone constitutes due process because it is one of the continuing traditions of our legal system that define the due process standard of "traditional notions of fair play and substantial justice." Where, as in the present case, a jurisdictional principle is both firmly approved by tradition and still favored, it is impossible to imagine what standard we could appeal to for the judgment that it is no longer justified.

Because the Due Process Clause does not prohibit the California courts from exercising jurisdiction over petitioner based on the fact of in-State service of process, the judgment is affirmed.

Justice Brennan (concurring in the judgment)

I agree with Justice Scalia that the Due Process Clause of the Fourteenth Amendment generally permits a State court to exercise jurisdiction over a defendant if he is served with process while voluntarily present in the forum State. Unlike Justice Scalia, I would undertake an independent inquiry into the fairness of the prevailing in-State service rule. I therefore concur only in the judgment.

I believe that the minimum contacts analysis developed in *International Shoe* represents a far more sensible construct for the exercise of State-court jurisdiction than the patchwork of legal and factual fictions that has been generated from the decision in *Pennoyer v. Neff.*

The potential burdens on a transient defendant are slight. Modern transportation and communications have made it much less burdensome for a party sued to defend himself in a State outside his place of residence. Finally, any burdens that do arise can be ameliorated by a variety of procedural devices. For these reasons, as a rule the exercise of personal jurisdiction over a defendant based on his voluntary presence in the forum will satisfy the requirements of due process.

In this case, it is undisputed that petitioner was served with process while voluntarily and knowingly in the State of California. I therefore concur in the judgment.

A difficult problem arises for the plaintiff when the defendant is not physically present within the state. For many years, the courts adhered to the position that service could be accomplished only by personally serving the defendant while that person was physically within the borders of the state.

The following case recognizes the power of the state, in civil suits, to serve a summons and petition beyond the physical borders of the state. It should be noted that the discussion here applies only to *civil*, as opposed to criminal, suits. This case is of great importance because it permitted the state of Washington to obtain in personam jurisdiction over the International Shoe Company even though the company asserted that it never was physically present in the state. Note that the Supreme Court declares that in personam jurisdiction may, under certain circumstances, be obtained over a person or company not physically present within the borders of the state.

International Shoe Co. v. State of Washington
United States Supreme Court
326 U.S. 310 (1945)

This case deals with a dispute between International Shoe and the state of Washington. Though International Shoe's principal place of business was in St. Louis, it conducted business in other states. It was engaged in the manufacture and sale of shoes. International Shoe, the appellant in this case, had no office in Washington, made no contracts there, and maintained no merchandise there. From 1937 to 1940, it employed eleven to thirteen salesmen whose principal activities were confined to the state of Washington. The salesmen exhibited samples and solicited orders in Washington and transmitted the orders to St. Louis for acceptance or rejection.

The state of Washington brought suit against International Shoe for payments it felt International owed the Washington unemployment compensation fund. In this case, notice of the assessment for the years 1937 to 1940 was personally served upon a salesman in Washington, and a copy of the notice was mailed by registered mail to International Shoe's home office in St. Louis. International Shoe challenged the power of the courts in Washington to force it to go to Washington to defend this suit. International Shoe claimed that forcing it to defend the suit in Washington would violate the due process clause of the Fourteenth Amendment.

Chief Justice Stone

Appellant insists that its activities within the state were not sufficient to manifest its "presence" there and that in its absence the state courts were without jurisdiction, that consequently it was a denial of due process for the state to subject appellant to suit.

Historically the jurisdiction of courts to render judgment in personam is grounded on their de facto power over the defendant's person. Hence his presence within the territorial jurisdiction of a court was prerequisite to its rendition of a judgment personally binding him. But now due process requires only that in order to subject a defendant to a judgment in personam, if he be not present within the territory of the forum, he have certain minimum contacts with it such that the maintenance of the suit does not offend "traditional notions of fair play and substantial justice."

Since the corporate personality is a fiction it is clear that unlike an individual its "presence" without, as well as within, the state of its origin can be manifested only by activities carried on in its behalf by those who are authorized to act for it.

"Presence" in the state in this sense has never been doubted when the activities of the corporation there have not only been continuous and systematic, but also give rise to the liabilities sued on, even though no consent to be sued or authorization to an agent to accept service of process has been given. Conversely it has been generally recognized that the casual presence of the corporate agent or even his conduct of single or isolated items of activities in a state in the corporation's behalf are not enough to subject it to suit on causes of action unconnected with the activities there. To require the corporation in such circumstances to defend the suit away from its home or other jurisdiction where it carries on more substantial activities has been thought to lay too great and unreasonable a burden on the corporation to comport with due process.

Whether due process is satisfied must depend upon the quality and nature of the activity in relation to the fair and orderly administration of the laws which it was the purpose of the due process clause to insure. That clause does not contemplate that a state may make binding a judgment in personam against an individual or corporate defendant with which the state has no contacts, ties, or relations.

The activities carried on in behalf of appellant in the State of Washington were neither irregular nor casual. They were systematic and continuous throughout the years in question. They resulted in a large volume of interstate business, in the course of which appellant received the benefits and protection of the laws of the state, including the right to resort to the courts for the enforcement of its rights. The obligation which is here sued upon arose out of those very activities. It is evident that these operations establish sufficient contacts or ties with the state of the forum to make it reasonable and just according to our traditional conception of fair play and substantial justice to permit the state to enforce the obligations which appellant has incurred there. Hence we cannot say that the maintenance of the present suit in the State of Washington involves an unreasonable or undue procedure.

We are likewise unable to conclude that the service of the process within the state upon an agent whose activities establish appellant's "presence" there was not suffi-cient notice of the suit, or that the suit was so unrelated to those activities as to make the agent an inappropriate vehicle for communicating the notice. It is enough that appellant has established such contacts with the state that the particular form of substituted service adopted there gives reasonable assurance that the notice will be actual. Nor can we say that the mailing of the notice of suit to appellant by registered mail at its home office was not reasonably calculated to apprise appellant of the suit.

Appellant having rendered itself amenable to suit upon obligations arising out of the activities of its sales-men in Washington, the state may maintain the present suit in personam to collect the tax laid upon the exercise of the privilege of employing appellant's salesmen within the state. For Washington has made one of those activities, which taken together establish appellant's "presence" there for purposes of suit, the taxable event by which the state brings appellant within the reach of its taxing power. The state thus has constitutional power to lay the tax and to subject appellant to a suit to recover it. The activities which establish its "presence" subject it alike to taxation by the state and to suit to recover the tax.

As a result of the *International Shoe* case, states have adopted what are commonly called long-arm statutes. These statutes permit a plaintiff to obtain service of the summons and petition beyond the physical borders of the state. However, as noted in the *International Shoe* case, a defendant may not be required to appear in court in another state if such an appearance would violate the due process clause of the United States Constitution. The due process clause requires that individuals have fair warning that a particular activity may subject them to the jurisdiction of a foreign sovereign.

All states have provisions that permit the courts to obtain jurisdiction over nonresident individuals and corporations. A typical statute authorizes service of process outside the state on individuals or corporations for in personam actions arising out of (1) the transaction of any business in a state, (2) the commission of a tortious act within a state, or (3) the ownership, use, or possession of real estate in the state.

The typical procedure is to file a lawsuit in the appropriate state court, sending a copy of the petition and a summons to the secretary of state. The secretary of state then sends this information to the defendant by registered mail. Although the defendant is beyond the physical borders of state X, he or she must return to state X to defend the suit.

In some situations, a court need only have jurisdiction over the property involved in the case—this is called *in rem* jurisdiction. A court that has jurisdiction over property involved in a case, but not over a person, may render a judgment that is binding on the property that is the subject matter of a case. If a court is unable to obtain in personam jurisdiction, but property that is the subject matter of the suit is located in the state, the court may permit the trial of a case. Any judgment may be enforced with respect to the property involved in the case. The judgment may not, however, be enforced beyond the borders of the state, because the court lacks in personam jurisdiction over the defendant. Assets owned by the defendant that are located beyond the borders of the state court exercising in rem jurisdiction may not be used to pay the judgment.

Venue

Venue deals with the issue of which court is the proper court in which to bring the suit in a given state. Once a determination has been made that a suit may be brought within a given state, the plaintiff examines the venue statute to determine where in the state suit may be filed. The typical state statute specifies which courts in the state may hear a case.

For example, a state statute might permit suit to be brought in any county in which the defendant resides, or in which the plaintiff resides if the defendant is served therein, or in which the cause of action arose. Suppose that Smith was involved in an automobile accident in Johnson County. The defendant was a resident of Shawnee County—which is located in the same state as Johnson County. The plaintiff is a resident of Wyandotte County, which is also located in the same state as Johnson County. Such a statute would permit the plaintiff to bring suit in either Johnson or Shawnee County. The plaintiff could also file in Wyandotte County if the defendant is served with the summons and petition while in Wyandotte County. Suit could not, however, be brought in Saline County.

Venue statutes generally provide special rules for corporations, partnerships, and nonresidents of the state.

The Distinction Between Law and Equity

Centuries ago in the United Kingdom people who had a disagreement went to the common law courts to obtain relief. For the most part, the common law courts awarded monetary damages. Over time it became apparent that it was not always possible to obtain adequate relief in the common law courts. In response to the complaints of dissatisfied people, the king established separate **equity** courts. These courts provided relief to litigants when there was no adequate remedy available in the common law courts. Thus, two separate court systems developed with their own set of rules—the common law courts and the equity courts.

CASE AT LAW = MONEY

One important new form of relief available from the equity courts was the decree of specific performance. Such a decree obligates a person to perform his or her obligations under a contract. Suppose that Mr. Rich contracts to sell his Picasso painting to Ms. Anderson. Thereafter, Mr. Rich refuses to deliver the painting to her. Ms. Anderson may then go to court and ask for a decree of specific performance—or an order compelling Mr. Rich to deliver the painting.

In its early years, the United States followed England's lead by creating separate law and equity courts. Today most states no longer have separate courts to hear law and equity suits. In the federal and state court systems, the trial courts hear both legal and equitable claims. The principles developed in the equity courts have been blended into the legal rules followed by the courts. Even so, some vestiges of the distinction between law and equity persist today. For example, if a person is seeking equitable relief, that person is not entitled to a jury trial.

EQUITY ONLY IF, MONEY WONT WORK

STRUCTURE OF THE COURT SYSTEM

A very general description of the court systems in the United States will provide a foundation for understanding how courts operate. This discussion will describe courts from two different perspectives: first by their jurisdiction (federal or state courts), and second by their function (trial or appellate courts).

The Federal and State Systems

There are two jurisdictional groups of courts in this country: federal courts and state courts. There is one federal court system in the United States, while each state (and the District of Columbia) has its own court system. Discussion of judges, courts, or judicial lawmaking in fact requires generalization about many different and separate court systems.

Federal District Courts

The federal court system has three major levels of courts (see Figure 2.1). The first level is the federal district courts. These are the trial courts of the federal system. In these courts, juries are impaneled, witnesses are heard, and verdicts are rendered. Federal district courts are generally confined to all or part of one state, the number of districts within that state depending upon the population. For example, there are two federal districts in the state of Indiana: the northern federal district and the southern federal district. Delaware has one federal district,

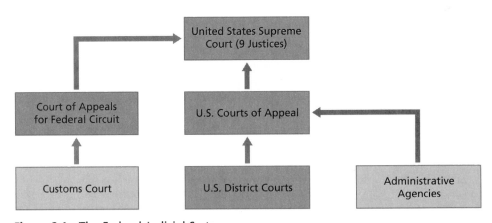

Figure 2.1   The Federal Judicial System

while California has four. In addition to the district courts at the first level of the federal system, there are also some specialized federal courts that are designed to hear cases arising under one major area of law. For example, federal bankruptcy courts hear cases arising under bankruptcy law. The federal tax court is empowered to hear cases concerning federal taxation. If a taxpayer disputes the amount of tax the IRS claims is due, the taxpayer may appeal through the IRS and then seek relief in the tax court. Alternatively, the taxpayer may pay the amount in dispute and pursue relief through the federal district court.

Figures 2.2*a* and *b* give us some idea of the number of suits handled by the U.S. district courts. The types of cases and the number of suits handled by each district judge are presented in Table 2.1.

Federal courts are limited in the types of disputes that they can decide. Article III, Section 2 of the United States Constitution states: "The Judicial Power shall extend to all cases . . . arising under this Constitution, the laws of the United States, and Treaties made . . . under their authority." The Constitution thus gives the federal courts the power to hear cases involving a **federal question**— that is, cases arising at least in part under the United States Constitution, a treaty, or a federal law. If a case deals with a right created by a law adopted by Congress, the federal courts possess the power to hear the dispute. Likewise, a person who alleges that his or her constitutional rights have been violated can sue in federal court as well.

In Article III, Section 2, the Constitution also grants the federal courts jurisdiction over cases involving **diversity of citizenship**. If a case involves citizens of different states and the amount in dispute is fifty thousand dollars or more, then

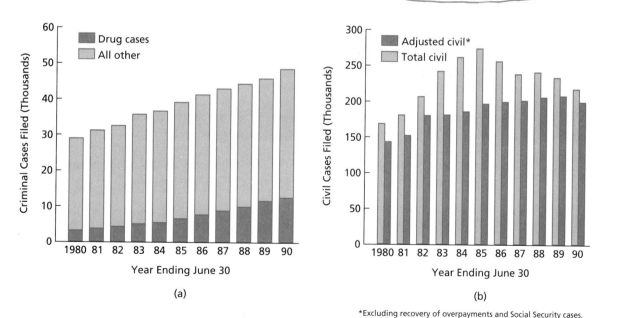

Figure 2.2   Suits Handled by U.S. District Courts
Source: Annual Report of the Director of the Administrative Office of the United States Courts, 1990.

TABLE 2.1		U.S. District Courts: Civil Cases Filed, Terminated, and Pending, 1980 Through 1990						
				Commenced				
Year	Author-ized Judge-ships	Total	Cases per Judge-ship	Recovery and Enforce-ment Cases	Social Security Cases	All Other Cases	Termi-nated	Pend-ing
1980	516	168,789	327	15,588	9,043	144,158	160,481	186,113
1981	516	180,576	350	18,161	9,780	152,635	177,975	188,714
1982	515	206,193	400	30,048	12,312	163,333	189,473	205,434
1983	515	241,842	470	41,213	20,315	180,314	215,356	231,920
1984	515	261,485	508	46,190	29,985	185,310	243,113	250,292
1985	575	273,670	476	58,160	19,771	195,739	269,848	254,114
1986	575	254,828	443	40,824	14,407	199,597	266,765	242,177
1987	575	239,185	416	24,233	13,338	201,614	238,001	243,361
1988	575	239,634	417	18,676	15,152	205,806	238,753	244,123
1989	575	233,529	406	16,467	10,206	206,856	235,219	238,389*
1990	575	217,879	379	10,878	7,439	199,562	213,922	242,346
Percent Change 1990 over 1989		−6.7	−6.7	−33.9	−27.1	−3.5	−9.1	1.7

* Revised.

Source: Annual Report of the Director of the Administrative Office of the United States Courts, 1990.

the case may also be heard in federal court. For example, suppose that Mr. Peters, a resident of Illinois, drives his family down to Disney World in Florida for a vacation. While in Orlando, Peters hits a car driven by a resident of Florida. If the plaintiff's damages are fifty thousand dollars or more, the personal injury suit may be filed in federal district court based on diversity of citizenship, even though no federal question is involved in the case. It should be noted that the plaintiff could also choose to file suit in state court rather than federal court.

Federal Courts of Appeals

Within the federal court system there is a hierarchy of courts; that is, certain courts have control over other courts. The federal district courts are grouped geographically in circuits. For example, the seventh circuit contains the federal district courts in Indiana, Illinois, and Wisconsin. The second circuit contains the federal district courts in New York, Vermont, and Connecticut. There are thirteen federal judicial circuits in the United States; eleven contain the district courts from various states. A separate circuit exists for Washington, D.C. There is also a court of appeals for the Federal Circuit. Each circuit has one court of appeals (see

Figure 2.3). The Seventh Circuit Court of Appeals is located in Chicago. The Second Circuit Court of Appeals is located in New York City. The court of appeals is an appellate court. It does not hear witnesses or preside over trials. Its function is to decide questions that are appealed to it by parties who are dissatisfied with the decision of a district court.

The ruling of a court of appeals is binding **precedent** for all the federal district courts within that circuit. If another similar case arises in one of the district courts, a prior decision of the court of appeals on the relevant point of law is binding. However, a decision of a court of appeals is not binding outside its circuit. For example, recently some state legislatures have enacted statutes providing state tax benefits for residents who send their children to private schools. This type of statute has been challenged in federal district court by others who contend that the statute violates the First Amendment of the United States Constitution in that it impermissibly entangles the government with religion. These people contend that most of the private schools are church-operated. One federal court of appeals struck down such a statute as unconstitutional. Thereafter, any state enacting such a statute within the geographical boundaries of that circuit would virtually be assured that it would be declared unconstitutional. However, in another circuit, the federal court of appeals found a similar statute to be constitutional. Thereafter, other states within the circuit that enacted this

Figure 2.3   The Thirteen Federal Judicial Circuit Courts

TABLE 2.2	Appeals Commenced, Terminated, and Pending, 1980 Through 1990				
	Authorized	Commenced			
Year	Judgeships	Number	Cases per Panel	Terminated	Pending
1980	132	23,200	527	20,887	20,252
1981	132	26,362	599	25,066	21,548
1982	132	27,946	635	27,984	21,510
1983	132	29,630	673	28,660	22,480
1984	132	31,490	716	31,185	22,785
1985	156	33,360	642	31,387	24,758
1986	156	34,292	659	33,774	25,276
1987	156	35,176	676	34,444	26,008
1988	156	37,524	722	35,888	27,644
1989	156	39,734	764	37,372	30,018
1990	156	40,898	787	38,520	32,396
Percent Change 1990 over 1989	—	2.9	3.0	3.1	8.0

Note: Excludes the U.S. Court of Appeals for the Federal Circuit.

Source: Annual Report of the Director of the Administrative Office of the United States Courts, 1990.

statute could be virtually assured that it would be upheld as constitutional. Thus, although there is one federal court system, its organization into separate jurisdictions may well lead to results that are not consistent from circuit to circuit.

Table 2.2 shows the number of appeals filed in the U.S. Court of Appeals.

The Supreme Court

Of course, there is one more level of the federal court hierarchy—the United States Supreme Court. It, too, is an appellate court, although on rare occasions it may exercise original jurisdiction—that is, hear a dispute without the requirement that it first be decided by a lower level court. The United States Supreme Court is the highest court to which an appeal may be taken. It is located in Washington, D.C., and has nine judges, called justices, who together, decide its cases.

Appeals may be taken to the United States Supreme Court from a number of sources. A party displeased with the decision of a federal circuit court of appeals may seek to have that case reviewed by the Supreme Court. Even if the case did not go through the federal court system, it may be appealed to the Supreme Court in some circumstances. For example, after a case has gone through the state court system and the state supreme court has ruled on the matter, a final appeal may be made to the United States Supreme Court, provided that there is a federal question in the case. Even though the Supreme Court is the highest court in the land, it too is limited in the cases it may hear by the concept of jurisdiction.

At one time the law obligated the Supreme Court to hear certain types of cases. Today, all persons wishing for the Court to hear their appeal must apply for a *writ of certiorari*—a request in effect that the Court agree to hear their appeal. Whether the Court grants a writ of certiorari is entirely up to the discretion of the nine justices on the Court.

State Courts

The federal court system is complemented by the judicial systems of each of the states. These state court systems may differ, making a single, complete description of their structure impractical. Some states do not have an intermediate court of appeals. Those who object to a decision reached at trial appeal directly to the state supreme court. Some states, especially those with large cities, have different divisions of trial level courts. There may be a criminal division that handles the trial of criminal cases, or a probate division that handles matters dealing with wills and estates, or a family law division that handles divorce and related matters. Furthermore, many states have special courts at a level lower than that of the trial court. These courts are generally limited to very minor disputes, such as minor traffic offenses or disputes involving only a few hundred dollars. Often these courts act more like informal arbitrators, with more relaxed rules of evidence and no jury trials. In fact, in some of these courts the appearance of lawyers for the parties is prohibited. A party who wants to appeal from such a lower level court usually may obtain a trial de novo (a total retrial) in the regular trial courts of that state. Figure 2.4 illustrates a typical state court system. Some states have more courts, but this figure is similar to that of most states.

The organization of the courts within a state is very similar to the federal court organization, with trial level and appellate level courts. The trial level courts may hear the cases that arise in their particular area of the state. For example, assume the state of X has two counties, Jefferson County and Jackson County. Each county has its own trial court. A case arising in Jackson County will be heard by the court in Jackson County. The Jefferson County court would not be the proper one to hear the dispute. Figure 2.5 shows that a state trial court typically has jurisdiction over legal disputes that arise in one or more counties. The Fifth Kansas district court, for example, hears disputes arising in Lyon and Chase counties. In states that have more than one intermediate appellate court (like the courts of appeals in the federal court system) the same organizational concepts and issues arise. However, there is one important difference between the state court system and the federal court system. As already stated, a federal court must have jurisdiction to hear a case; that is, there must be a federal law issue involved in the dispute (statutory or constitutional) or the parties to the dispute must be from different states. However, state courts may hear disputes concerning federal law as well as disputes concerning the law of that particular state. But there is still one jurisdictional limitation on the state courts. Just as the the federal courts of the United States do not hear disputes arising in Canada (those are for the courts of Canada), the courts of one state do not hear disputes arising in another. Geographical boundaries are important in the structure and organization of court systems.

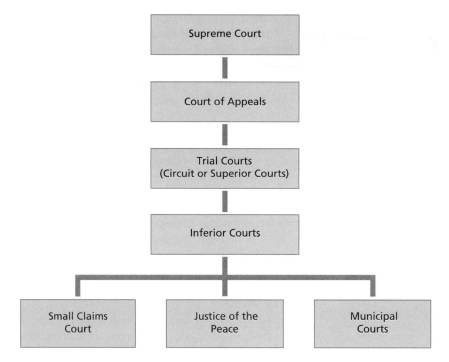

Figure 2.4 Typical State Court System

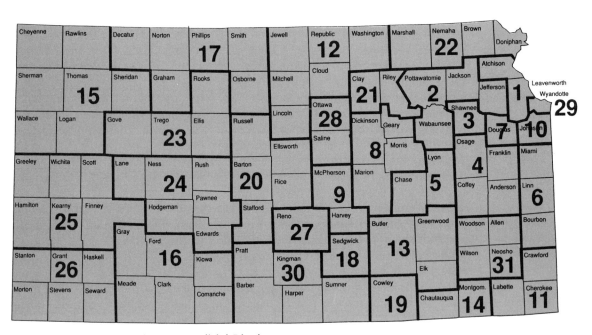

Figure 2.5 The State of Kansas Judicial Districts
Source: Kansas Secretary of State, *Kansas Directory,* 1991.

Trial and Appellate Courts

In the previous section, we described courts by their jurisdiction, as state or federal courts. Courts may also be described by function, as trial or appellate courts. Although procedures in one jurisdiction's trial court or appellate court may differ from those in another, the basic function of the courts would be similar.

Trial Courts

The **trial court** is the first place the judicial system considers the disputes of parties. The trial court listens to the evidence and renders a verdict or judgment based upon that evidence. Trials may be heard by a jury or only by a judge. A trial heard only by a judge is called a **bench trial.** Contrary to popular belief, most trials are bench trials.

The following example illustrates the basic features of the trial function of courts. Mary Smith took her automobile to XYZ, Inc. auto repair shop for a tune-up. When she returned for the car, she noticed that the paint on the trunk and sides of the car was badly scratched. Smith claimed that the car was in perfect condition when she brought it in. XYZ claimed that the scratches were already there. Since the parties were not able to agree concerning the damaged vehicle, Smith hired an attorney, who filed a suit against XYZ for $1,000 in damage to her car. XYZ also retained an attorney to represent its interests in the lawsuit.

At the trial, witnesses were called and examined under oath. Smith and a couple of acquaintances testified that the car was in perfect condition prior to the day of the tune-up. XYZ employees testified that the car was scratched when they first saw it. Exhibits were shown at the trial. One was a drawing showing the relationship between the location of the scratches and sharp objects in the tune-up area. (In major cases, films and scale models may be developed to help the attorney present the case.)

At the trial level, the facts of the matter are determined and the relevant law is applied, resulting in a verdict. In the process of reaching a verdict, what actually happened in the events under dispute will have to be decided. This is frequently a difficult task, because witnesses will often offer conflicting versions of the same event. The trier (either a jury or a judge) must decide which of the witnesses is to be believed and which of the witnesses' testimony can be discounted. However, the verdict itself does not include a summary of the facts of the case. Most often a simple decision in the matter will be reached (e.g., the jury finds for the plaintiff, Mary Smith, or the jury finds for the defendant, XYZ). Occasionally, a jury will be required to render a special verdict. A special verdict requires the jury to answer a number of questions concerning the major issues in the case. The jury, therefore, must make a special finding on each material issue in the case. However, the jury does not draft a summary of the facts of the case.

Most disputes go no further than the trial court stage. In fact, very few of the cases that are filed actually result in a trial. Trials are expensive and time-consuming. Usually, the parties must pay their own attorneys' fees. Therefore, there are substantial incentives for the parties to settle the matter out of court. These incentives also inhibit people from pursuing valid legal claims. The Smith-XYZ example is illustrative of this point. The costs to each party to litigate the matter would probably exceed the amount of money (one thousand dollars) in dispute. It is unlikely that they would pursue their dispute through trial.

Appellate Courts

Sometimes a litigant wants to have another judicial review after the trial stage, usually because that party was dissatisfied with the verdict. The party may then file an appeal with the **appellate court** designated to hear such an appeal. An appellate court does not conduct a new trial. It hears no direct evidence in the case. Instead the appellate court reviews the entire record of the case in order to determine whether any errors were made during the trial. The record includes copies of all the pleadings and documents filed in the case, all the exhibits entered as evidence in the case, and a transcript of all the testimony during the trial itself. Both parties in the case also file **briefs.** The briefs are written arguments to the court concerning the points the parties want the court to consider. The party seeking the appellate review (called the **appellant**) will point out the errors in the application of law made by the trial judge and argue that the verdict should be overturned because of those errors. The opposing party (called the **appellee**) will usually argue that no errors were made at trial or that they were minor errors that would have no effect on the outcome of the case. The appellee will argue that the appellate court should simply affirm the decision reached at trial.

In addition to the briefs, sometimes the parties present an oral argument to the court. Appellate oral argument does not involve the questioning of witnesses or the presentation of evidence. Instead, the attorneys are given a certain period of time to argue their position before the court. Frequently the appellate court justices will interrupt the attorney to ask questions concerning the case, the applicable law, and the attorney's basic argument. Later, the appellate court will render a decision with an opinion discussing the reasons for its decision. These opinions are usually published and are available in all law libraries. Sometimes a justice may agree with the appellate court's decision but disagree with the reasoning of the court. That justice may then file a separate opinion in the case, called a **concurring opinion.** However, appellate court justices do not always agree concerning the outcome of a particular case. In that event, a separate opinion, called a **dissenting opinion,** may be filed outlining the reasons for the disagreement.

An appellate court's role is considered to be the correction of errors of law made by the trial court judge, not the making of factual determinations. These errors of law may involve various rulings made by the judge concerning evidence during the course of the case, or they may involve the judge's instructions on the law to the jury.

Although appellate courts are said to consider questions of law rather than questions of fact, it is sometimes rather difficult to determine exactly when questions are legal and when instead they are factual. Some people suggest that if a question is (or should be) decided by a judge, then that question is one of law; if not, then it is a question of fact. Clearly, this argument begs the question. Yet it shows that often appellate courts, in making decisions, base them on a reading of the facts that may not be at all consistent with the interpretation of the facts that led to the verdict in the trial court.

■■■■■ PERSONNEL IN THE JUDICIAL SYSTEM

The judicial system is made up of a variety of different people, each of whom has a role to play in the administration of justice. Two of the most important members of the judicial system, the judge and the lawyer, are the focus of this section.

The Judge   There are several different types of judges: state court and federal court judges, judges who handle trials, and judges who handle appeals. Some judges hear only one type of legal matter. For example, there are tax court judges who decide only questions dealing with federal taxation, and in some states there are criminal court judges who hear only criminal cases. Although there are differences among the types of work judges do, there are enough similarities to observe some major characteristics of the judiciary.

Function of a Judge in General

Judges decide cases and make law—at the same time. Of course, some cases are relatively routine, involving issues and kinds of facts that have been ruled upon numerous times in the past. In such cases, the case-deciding function of the judge is paramount. For example, assume a judge is hearing a simple traffic violation case. The defendant is accused of driving through a stop sign. However, the defendant contends that a full stop was made. The only witness for the state is the arresting police officer. The only witness for the defense is the defendant. In the hundreds of similar cases preceding this one, the judge has found the stop-sign runner guilty even though the testimony at trial conflicted, the fine being thirty-five dollars. If the same result occurs in the present case, the most evident thing done by the judge is the finding of guilt—the settling of a dispute between the state and a driver. Yet, in a sense, law was being made at the same time. First, it continues to be the legal rule in that judge's court that defendants in a stop-sign-running case will have to produce more evidence than their own testimony in order to prevail, in light of conflicting testimony by a police officer. This is the law as to the particular judge's consideration of the evidence. Second, the thirty-five-dollar fine has been imposed so often as to become almost administrative in nature. You ran a stop sign, you pay thirty-five dollars in this judge's court.

However, take the same basic facts with a different result and the judicial lawmaking function becomes dominant. Assume, in the same case, that the judge refused to find the defendant guilty of running the stop sign because the state had not proved its case "beyond a reasonable doubt," the standard necessary for a conviction. The only evidence was the word of the police officer against the word of the defendant, and there was no indication that the defendant was a habitual liar or somehow untrustworthy in giving testimony (except for an interest in not being convicted and having to pay a thirty-five-dollar fine). In this case, too, a dispute was settled between the state and an allegedly errant driver. However, a potentially important new law was made. In the future, the state will have to do much more than produce a police officer in order to convict stop-sign runners. More evidence will be necessary. The state may have to change its law-enforcement procedures: perhaps assign two police officers to each traffic detail, perhaps film certain intersections (assuming there are no constitutional problems), perhaps seek a witness who may have been strolling by during the incident in question. Clearly, the new evidence rule in this minor traffic matter would make a change in law-enforcement procedures. If the alternatives were too expensive, fewer stop-sign-running cases would be brought before the courts.

The lawmaking done by courts is confined to the particular disputes that come before them. Courts do not have the ability to seek out problems in the law that need correction or clarification and simply draft a new rule. In fact, federal courts and the courts of most states are prohibited from giving advice on the law or on the constitutionality of a proposed law to other branches of government. Such advice is called an **advisory opinion.** A few states do permit this practice, but it is not often used.

As the preceding examples illustrate, judicial decision making can have a broader effect than simply rendering a judgment directly relating to the parties in a case. The decision often indicates to others how they should act in order to prevail in the courtroom. In one example, the investigative practices of the state may have to change.

Judicial Activism

Judicial decision making often involves reviewing the activities of other branches of government. Historically, courts would either find the activity inconsistent with the Constitution (unconstitutional) or uphold the action. In effect, the decision would be a yes-or-no type of judgment. The court would use its reviewing power to set limits concerning what other branches of government could do. Today, however, judges frequently find themselves going well beyond merely setting limits on the activities of other units of government. Judges today may require that certain specific action be taken by the government in order to cure a constitutionally defective practice. For example, a lawsuit may be brought by inmates of a prison contending that the conditions of the prison are so poor as to violate their constitutional rights. A court, in finding that the prison indeed violates prisoner rights, may fashion a remedy that involves the court in day-to-day prison decisions.

The following case involves a decision by a judge to increase the taxes of people in Kansas City—powers normally thought to be reserved to the legislative branch of government.

Missouri v. Jenkins
United States Supreme Court
110 S.Ct. 1651 (1990)

Up until 1954, the state of Missouri mandated segregated schools for black and white children. Vestiges of the dual school system still exist in the Kansas City Missouri School District (KCMSD). KCMSD and the state have not met their obligations to disestablish that system. The school buildings in the KCMSD have literally rotted. In order to correct these vestiges of unconstitutional segregation, Judge Clark, United States District Judge for the Western District of Missouri, ordered a number of improvements in the school system. To enable the district to fund its share of the cost of the desegregation plan, Judge Clark, among other things, imposed an increase in the property tax levied by the Kansas City Missouri School District. The State of Missouri challenged this decision. It argued that the district court lacked the power to raise local property taxes. The United States Supreme Court agreed that the district court abused its discretion by imposing the tax increase.

Justice White

We turn to the tax increase imposed by the District Court. It is accepted by all the parties that the imposition of a tax increase by a federal court was an extraordinary event. In assuming for itself the fundamental and delicate power of taxation the District Court not only intruded on local authority but circumvented it altogether. Before taking such a drastic step the District Court was obliged to assure itself that no permissible alternative would have accomplished the required task. We have emphasized that although the remedial powers of an equity court must be adequate to the task, they are not unlimited, and one of the most important considerations governing the exercise of equitable power is a proper respect for the integrity and function of local government institutions. Especially is this true where, as here, those institutions are ready, willing, and—but for the operation of state law curtailing their powers—able to remedy the deprivation of constitutional rights themselves.

The District Court believed that it had no alternative to imposing a tax increase. But there was an alternative: it could have authorized or required KCMSD to levy property taxes at a rate adequate to fund the desegregation remedy and could have enjoined the operation of state laws that would have prevented KCMSD from exercising this power. Authorizing and directing local government institutions to devise and implement remedies not only protects the function of those institutions but, to the extent possible, also places the responsibility for solutions to the problems of segregation upon those who have themselves created the problem.

The District Court therefore abused its discretion in imposing the tax itself. The Court of Appeals should not have allowed the tax increase to stand and should have reversed the District Court in this respect.

It is difficult to see how relief can be afforded in cases such as this without an expanded role for the courts. In a sense, this type of extraordinary relief has always been available to the courts. In contract disputes, the traditional damage award to the party injured by a breach of contract is money damages. If X agrees to sell Y a textbook for twenty dollars, a contract will be said to exist between X and Y. If, however, on the agreed day of sale, X instead sells the book to Z for twenty-two dollars, X has breached the contract. Y rushes to the bookstore and purchases the needed book for twenty-five dollars. Y has been injured by the contract breach in the sum of five dollars. That would be the usual money damage relief granted by the court. However, if the book were a one-of-a-kind masterpiece and X refused to sell it to Y as agreed, money damages would probably not be sufficient. In that event, a court might require that X perform the contract as agreed—that is, impose on X a duty to act in a certain way to provide full relief to the other party. This is called the **doctrine of specific performance in contract.**

Expansive judicial decisions—decisions in whose implementation the court has a part—are the source of the current criticism of judges and courts as being too activist. The use of such decisions in constitutional disputes is a major extension of judicial decisions into areas that had usually called for political decisions: decisions based on trade-offs made by the other branches of government. Many people contend that a judge has no expertise in making specific decisions concerning the operation of a prison system or the structure and operation of a school system. Another frequent complaint is that such decisions are most often made by federal court judges who are appointed for life with no direct accountability to the general public who would be affected by their decisions. Traditional court action, such as ordering remedies like specific performance, merely affected parties to the lawsuit. Many of the activist decisions today, however, affect the general public, since often tax money must either be raised or shifted to pay for the court-imposed remedy. Yet the taxpayers have no way to influence that spending decision, since it was mandated by a court in response to a lawsuit.

Other people claim that such judicial activity is necessary in today's complex legal world. Government does many more things for (and to) people today than in the past. Furthermore, today more individual rights are recognized in the law, and people are demanding that those rights be protected. Equal rights under law for people irrespective of race, sex, national origin, or a number of other factors is a very recent development in the law. Segregated public schools were declared unconstitutional barely forty years ago. In addition, certain groups, such as prisoners, welfare recipients, and mental patients, have been found to have basic rights in relation to government activity aimed at them. For a court to say no to government action today may not be enough, especially when the problem is government inaction. When a prison system is so underfunded as to cause unreasonable overcrowding or when school boards do not act to dismantle the vestiges of a once racially segregated school system, a more intrusive remedy may be needed to correct the wrong. Judges may require government to act to fulfill the minimum requirements set out by a statute or by the Constitution. Lack of certain government activity may be just as harmful to individual rights as too intrusive activity. However, each type of problem may require a different type of judicial solution.

One effect of such judicial activism is, in a sense, to shift some very difficult political decisions from the legislature, where the voters have an influence, to the judiciary (especially the federal courts), where the judges are not accountable to the electorate. For example, politicians may call for harsher penalties and longer jail terms for a wide variety of criminal offenders. However, the same politicians may refrain from making the extremely tough budgetary decision to go along with their anticrime position—namely, funding for more prison facilities to house the additional inmates. This would require either additional taxes or a switch of funds from an already existing program. Neither of these alternatives would be popular. So the politicians may simply enact popular, strict criminal laws that soon begin to increase the prison population. After a time, conditions become so crowded that a lawsuit is brought by a prisoner and a judge is asked to solve an essentially political question. The only way to solve the problem is to require certain government action, either building additional facilities or releasing prisoners before they have finished serving their time. The judge then catches the political heat. One may not agree with certain activist judicial decisions, but one should realize that such decisions are a product of the increasing role of government in our lives coupled with the greater recognition of individual rights. The legal and political systems have become very complex, often leading to litigation involving not only disputes between parties but also grievances against entire institutions.

Selection of Judges

Given the importance of the judge and the potential broad effect of judicial decision making, it is important that judges be carefully selected. This section will briefly review the two general methods of putting individuals on the bench: the election of candidates and the appointment of candidates. Federal judges are appointed by the president with the advice and consent of the Senate, as provided in the Constitution. They serve for life, with impeachment as the means for removal. Impeachment is very rarely used. Since federal judges are appointed rather than elected, the focus of this section will be on state court judges. However, a few of the issues concerning appointment of the state court judiciary may also be applicable to federal judges.

Some states elect their judges in the same manner as any other official. The political parties nominate candidates to fill the judicial positions. The judge is then chosen by the voters in the general election. The elected judge serves a term like other elected officials and is then subject to renomination and election at the next general election. Some people contend that election of judges is consistent with our form of government in that it ensures that the judicial branch will be held accountable to and be a reflection of the demands of the citizens. Popular control of judges may be seen as highly desirable. Since judges, like all public officials, exercise a great deal of power and control, the people should have a part in selecting the individuals who hold judgeships.

However, others argue that the election of judges risks placing individuals on the bench who are not especially qualified. Candidates for judgeships may be selected in part on the basis of their politics and party loyalty rather than on their judicial qualifications. This political litmus test may be more important than objective criteria in selecting the candidates for the job.

Furthermore, how are voters to determine the most suitable candidates for the judgeships? Much of a judge's work involves only a few members of a community and is not especially newsworthy. Studies have suggested that voters often have little knowledge about candidates for judgeships. If this is so, the argument that the election process makes judges accountable to the public is weakened. Instead it makes judges accountable to the political party that nominates them. Voters may be expected to show an interest in a judicial election if the candidate for election were involved in a highly controversial matter. The result may be that a judge exercises less independent decision making. The very nature of politics, with campaign contributions, campaign slogans, and advertising, raises problems about the independence of the various judicial candidates.

Yet these elected judges do have a limited term in office and can be removed by the voters. Political parties may use politics as a selection factor, yet the political leaders should be interested in competent candidates, since each candidate reflects and has an effect on the party ticket as a whole. Mistakes made in the election of judges are more easily corrected than mistakes made in the appointment process.

However, the problems inherent in the election of judges, as well as the appearance of political influence on judicial candidates, have led a number of states to move away from the election of judges toward an appointive system, often called the **Missouri plan.** The Missouri plan involves a governor-appointed panel, including a judge, lawyers, and lay members, that recommends suitable candidates for judicial appointment by the governor. Periodically, the appointed judges' names appear on a ballot where voters may vote on whether or not to retain the judges for an additional term. This is not a contest between candidates, but a yes-or-no decision by the voters. The plan removes political parties from the process yet retains periodic voter approval. However, given the general lack of voter knowledge about judges, the removal of poor judges from the bench by this process is unlikely.

Although proponents of this plan contend that it removes the selection of judges from the harmful and partisan effects of the political arena, others argue that it merely changes the type of politics involved. Instead of traditional political party influence, those who seek judgeships are subject to private political infighting between the organized bar and the governor. The governor could be expected to appoint members of the nominating panel and to select judges with compatible political views. Therefore, a judicial candidate may seek political favor from powerful persons in the state in order to be nominated by the panel or selected by the governor. It is as if political activity by candidates for a judicial post somehow becomes untainted when it occurs outside of the traditional political system. Another major criticism of the Missouri plan is that the judges who are selected are not necessarily representative of the community at large. Some people contend that the makeup of the selection committees does not reflect the varied interests of the public in general. A political party must develop sensitivity to the community in order to have its members elected to office, but no such pressures exist on the selection committee. The selected judges may be better in terms of objective judicial criteria; however, they may not reflect the makeup of the community.

The selection of individuals to judgeships is a very important task. Methods of selection are designed to find the best candidates as well as make them accountable without sacrificing their independent judgment on the cases that come before them. The plans just discussed have elevated fine people to the bench. Yet these plans are not without problems.

Independence and Accountability of Judges

The discussion of judges so far raises two conflicting points. A judge should be independent of influence but at the same time should be somehow accountable to the public. Judges should not be beholden to certain individuals for their positions. In virtually all court cases, there will be a winner and a loser, and one of the parties will leave the courthouse with an adverse decision. This fact of judicial decision making does not make the judge popular with fifty percent of the litigants. It is in the interest of the community and the law, however, that judicial decisions be based upon the law and facts relevant to the dispute, not on the identity of the parties before the court. A judge who is independent of extraneous pressure is an important factor in achieving justice in the courtroom.

Independence of the judiciary is important in ensuring that the judge makes decisions based upon the law and the facts in dispute. However, this independence cannot be absolute. To have no control on the work of judges would be as dangerous to justice as it would be to have judges who were controlled by others.

Two major factors act as controls on the judiciary. These factors temper the independence given to the judiciary and help prevent that independence from being abused. One factor is that of peer and community pressure. The other factor is the possibility of removal from the bench for misconduct.

Although, ideally, judges are insulated from various influences on their decision making in particular cases, they also want to do a competent job as measured by others. A competent job for a judge is not tied to "who wins" in a given suit. Instead, it is a combination of things that make up the notion of a good judge. Briefly, these things include skill in understanding and applying the law to a given set of facts, fairness and evenhandedness in decision making, and judicial temperament. Judges err, sometimes by making a simple mistake in applying the law. More often, as will be shown in later chapters, the law in question is subject to varied interpretations in a particular case. In these instances, courts of appeal will act to reverse the decision of a judge, showing in their opinion exactly where the judge erred. These opinions are published and form a record of mistakes made by judges in their work. Judges who regularly err feel the pressure of lawyers on their reputation as a judge. Law reviews, publications that comment on legal issues and judicial decisions, are another source of peer pressure. It is one thing to have an article published that criticizes a judge's work on a philosophical or political level; it is quite another to have the article point out a judge's misapplication of the law in reaching a certain decision. A judge's reputation and constant scrutiny by other courts, by attorneys, by the law reviews, and by newspapers work to control the behavior of a judge.

The same peer pressure affects the competence of the judge on the bench. Since judicial decisions are not secret, judges who are inconsistent in their decision making or who are not evenhanded in their treatment of litigants before them are also subject to criticism. A good judge not only works hard in conscientiously applying the legal rules to a given case but also is fair in that certain people are not favored (or disfavored).

Another factor in the makeup of a competent judge is an intangible called judicial temperament. Judicial temperament includes such things as tolerance, patience, and understanding of the parties in litigation. It means looking at the case at hand and not being influenced by the lifestyle of the litigants, as well as showing respect to those people who appear in court. Often, people involved in a lawsuit are very tense and behave in a manner unlike their normal conduct. Judges must have a feeling for the pressures on the litigants in the course of a trial.

Improper Remarks by a Judge

In open court during a hearing on a settlement agreement, before trial or any evidentiary hearing, Federal District Court Judge Miles W. Lord made the following remarks to the firm's president, vice president, and general counsel, who were present in court that day. In the agreement, the A. H. Robins Company, the manufacturer of the Dalkon Shield intrauterine contraceptive device, agreed to pay $4.6 million in a products liability suit. Excerpts of his remarks follow:

Today as you sit here attempting once more to extricate yourselves from the legal consequences of your acts, none of you has faced up to the fact that more than nine thousand women claim they gave up part of their womanhood so that your company might prosper. . . .

If one poor young man were, without authority or consent, to inflict such damage upon one woman, he would be jailed for a good portion of the rest of his life. Yet your company, without warning to women, invaded their bodies by the millions and caused them injuries by the thousands. And when the time came for these women to make their claims against your company, you attacked their characters. You inquired into

their sexual practices and into the identity of their sex partners. You ruined families and reputations and careers in order to intimidate those who would raise their voices against you. You introduced issues that had no relationship to the fact that you had planted in the bodies of these women instruments of death, of mutilation, of disease.

Mr. Robins, Mr. Forest, Dr. Lunsford: You have not been rehabilitated. Under your direction, your company has continued to allow women, tens of thousands of them, to wear this device—a deadly depth charge in their wombs, ready to explode at any time. . . . You have taken the bottom line as your guiding beacon and the low road as your route. That is corporate irresponsibility at its meanest. . . .

What corporate officials could learn a lesson from this? The only lesson they might learn is that it pays to delay compensating victims and to intimidate, harass, and shame the injured parties.

The United States Court of Appeals for the Eighth Circuit criticized Judge Lord for his verbal reprimand of the Robins executives. It ruled he had deprived the officials of notice and an opportunity for a hearing.

However, sometimes peer and public pressures are not enough to discourage abuse of judicial independence by a judge. It would be unwise to provide the necessary independence for the judiciary and then rely solely on the conscience of the individual judge and the peer pressure of colleagues to ensure that no abuse of that independence occurs. Using voters as a check, either through elective judgeships or by having appointed judges subject to voter removal, will not really act as a control mechanism. This will be a check on unpopular decisions rather than a check on the abuse of judicial independence. Judges who exclude evidence from a trial on the basis of the current state of Fourth Amendment law may face harsh public condemnation and potential loss of their judicial positions, especially if a case involves a noteworthy criminal. Yet the legal decision may be correct. The result may be to discourage judges from making legally correct but unpopular decisions, or to encourage judicial gamesmanship—delaying the release of such decisions until after election day. In any event, independence is sacrificed, but control is not really enhanced. A more powerful form of control is the existence of a judicial code of conduct coupled with procedures for removal of misbehaving judges from the bench.

It is impossible to remove all abuses of judicial independence. Some judges may be intoxicated with their power in the courtroom, and attorneys, witnesses, and the parties in litigation may be uncomfortable appearing before such judges. But it must be remembered that there is a trade-off. More weight being placed on judicial independence will necessarily mean less weight being placed on judicial control. A judicial system that values independent decision making requires this trade-off.

The following is an example of a case in which the judge clearly abused his power.

Aetna Life Insurance Co. v. Lavoie et al.
United States Supreme Court
106 S.Ct. 1580 (1986)

Aetna Life Insurance refused to pay the full amount of a hospital bill. The insured brought suit in an Alabama state court for Aetna's alleged bad-faith refusal to pay a valid claim. The jury ruled for the insured. On appeal, the Alabama Supreme Court affirmed the jury verdict in an opinion written by Justice Embry. It was later learned that Justice Embry had two cases pending against insurance companies at the time he wrote the opinion in question, which alleged bad-faith failure to pay claims. Aetna filed a motion challenging Justice Embry's participation in the case. The Alabama Supreme Court denied this motion. Aetna appealed to the United States Supreme Court which, ruled that Justice Embry should not have participated in the case.

Chief Justice Burger

It certainly violates the Fourteenth Amendment to subject a person's liberty to the judgment of a court the judge of which has a direct, personal, substantial, pecuniary interest in reaching a conclusion against him in his case.

More than 30 years ago Justice Black, speaking for the Court, reached a similar conclusion and recognized that under the Due Process Clause no judge "can be a judge in his own case or be permitted to try cases where he has an interest in the outcome."

Justice Embry's opinion for the Alabama Supreme Court had the clear and immediate effect of enhancing both the legal status and the settlement value of his own case. When Justice Embry made the judgment, he acted as a judge in his own case. His interest was direct, personal, substantial and pecuniary.

We conclude that Justice Embry's participation in this case violated Aetna's due process rights. We make clear that we are not required to decide whether in fact Justice Embry was influenced, but only whether sitting on the case then before the Supreme Court of Alabama would offer a possible temptation to the average judge to lead him to not to hold the balance nice, clear and true. The Due Process Clause may sometimes bar trial by judges who have no actual bias and who would do their very best to weight the scales of justice equally between contending parties. But to perform its high function in the best way, justice must satisfy the appearance of justice.

Because of Justice Embry's leading role in the decision under review, we conclude that the appearance of justice will best be served by vacating the decision and remanding for further proceedings.

Lawyers

The following section will examine another important actor in the legal system—the attorney. Three topics will be examined under this section. First, the function of an attorney in representing a client; second, the attorney's relationship with a client, focusing on the concept of the attorney-client privilege; and finally, the age-old question, "How can an attorney represent a guilty client?"

Function of Lawyers

Contrary to popular belief, most lawyers never appear in court. Their work in representing clients involves a variety of tasks often called **preventive law.** Preventive law involves advising clients on a variety of matters so that the clients minimize the chance of having legal problems. Just as plenty of exercise and a proper diet are techniques of preventive medicine, properly drafted legal documents and legal analysis of proposed business activities are elements of preventive law. In advising their clients, these lawyers seek to predict the outcome of legal matters before the issue arises. In order to make this determination, each lawyer studies past judicial decisions. The work of the court, therefore, is very important to these noncourtroom lawyers.

Trial lawyers, on the other hand, play a larger role as actors in the judicial process. The court system in the United States is operated as an adversary process. The adversary process is based upon the idea that the truth will emerge and justice will ultimately be done if each side in a dispute presents its case to an impartial hearing officer (the judge or the jury, depending on the case). The adversarial nature of the process involves being able to attack and test the arguments, evidence, and proof of the opposing party throughout the proceedings. Attorneys play a key role in this process because they represent the competing sides in a conflict and, through their courtroom skills, attack and test the case of the opposing party.

Although attorney courtroom strategy, tactics, and flair may make impressive reading, the most successful advocates win on the basis of thorough and exhaustive preparation of the case. Trial skills are important during actual courtroom confrontation, but the key to success is hard work and preparation of the

Hiring the Right Lawyer

Margaret Mitchell, the author of *Gone With the Wind,* sold her book to Macmillan. Prior to the time of publication, the company clearly realized her book would be a best seller. Macmillan retained an agent to convince a movie studio to make a film based on Mitchell's book. After a period of time, the agent succeeded in eliciting an offer of fifty thousand dollars for the book. Macmillan forwarded the contract to Mitchell for her signature.

Mitchell's father and brother were attorneys in Atlanta, primarily engaged in patent law. They reviewed the contract for her and suggested changes in it. Among other things, Mitchell was concerned about a clause in the contract related to libel suits. She also wanted final script approval of the film. Mitchell, her brother, attorneys for Macmillan, and attorneys for the film studio met to iron out the differences in the contract, which Mitchell eventually signed.

Mitchell became very unhappy soon after signing because she learned from a friend that movie studios make a great deal of money from such matters as licensing. Nothing about this was ever discussed at the meeting with the attorneys, mainly because her brother was not familiar with negotiating movie rights.

While a person should review a contract before signing it, preferably with an attorney, this example suggests that a person should hire an attorney familiar with the specific issues dealt with in the contract. Although Mitchell received fifty thousand dollars for the movie rights and did get the changes in the contract with respect to liability that she desired, one could argue that she might have gotten a better deal had her attorney had some experience in negotiating this type of contract.

case. Pretrial work includes studying the applicable law and gathering evidence and data needed to bolster the client's argument.

Attorney-Client Relationship

The attorney's first and utmost duty is to the client. An attorney owes the client a fiduciary duty of highest care, trust, loyalty, and good faith in the exercise of the representation of that client. Clients do not often understand the law and the procedures necessary for the protection of their interests. By necessity, the client places trust in the attorney. Although the lawyer is ethically bound to zealously represent the client, there are limits to that representation, for the attorney also owes a duty to the courts and to the legal system. The lawyer is considered an officer of the court, and may not lie or misrepresent to the courts, fabricate evidence, or encourage the client to lie.

The following case discusses the ethical dilemma that confronts an attorney who must zealously represent his client but at the same time prevent frauds upon the court.

Nix v. Whiteside
United States Supreme Court
106 S.Ct. 988 (1986)

Whiteside was accused of murder. While consulting with his attorney, Gary Robinson, prior to trial, he indicated that he thought he saw a gun in the hands of the deceased. Shortly before trial, while conferring with his attorney, he changed his story. He stated that "in Howard Cook's case there was a gun. If I don't say I saw a gun I'm dead." His attorney believed this to be perjury and told Whiteside he would not allow him to perjure himself in court. As a result of this, Whiteside did not testify to this effect at trial. Whiteside was thereafter convicted. He brought this appeal on the theory that he had been denied effective assistance of counsel and of his right to present a defense by his attorney's refusal to allow him to testify as he had proposed. The Supreme Court found that Whiteside's constitutional rights had not been violated.

Chief Justice Burger

We granted certiorari to decide whether the Sixth Amendment right of a criminal defendant to assistance of counsel is violated when an attorney refuses to cooperate with the defendant in presenting perjured testimony at his trial.

In *Strickland v. Washington,* we held that to obtain relief by way of federal habeas corpus on a claim of a deprivation of effective assistance of counsel under the Sixth Amendment, the movant must establish both serious attorney error and prejudice. To show such error, it must be established that the assistance rendered by counsel was constitutionally deficient in that "counsel made errors so serious that counsel was not functioning as 'counsel' guaranteed the defendant by the Sixth Amendment." To show prejudice, it must be established that the claimed lapses in counsel's performance rendered the trial unfair so as to "undermine confidence in the outcome" of the trial.

Whether Robinson's conduct is seen as a successful attempt to dissuade his client from committing the crime of perjury, or whether seen as a "threat" to withdraw from representation and disclose the illegal scheme, Robinson's representation of Whiteside falls well within accepted standards of professional conduct and the range of reasonable professional conduct acceptable under *Strickland.*

Robinson's admonitions to his client can in no sense be said to have forced respondent into an *impermissible* choice between his right to counsel and his right to testify as he proposed for there was no *permissible* choice to testify falsely. For defense counsel to take steps to persuade a criminal defendant to testify truthfully, or to withdraw, deprives the defendant of neither his right to counsel nor the right to testify truthfully.

We hold that, as a matter of law, counsel's conduct complained of here cannot establish the prejudice required for relief under the second strand of the *Strickland* inquiry. Although a defendant need not establish that the attorney's deficient performance more likely than not altered the outcome in order to establish prejudice under *Strickland,* a defendant must show "that there is a reasonable probability that, but for counsel's unprofessional errors, the result of the proceeding would have been different." According to *Strickland,* "[a] reasonable probability is a probability sufficient to undermine confidence in the outcome." The *Strickland* Court noted that the "benchmark" of an ineffective assistance claim is the fairness of the adversary proceeding, and that in judging prejudice and the likelihood of a different outcome, "[a] defendant has no entitlement to the luck of a lawless decisionmaker."

Whether he was persuaded or compelled to desist from perjury, Whiteside has no valid claim that confi- dence in the result of his trial has been diminished by his desisting from the contemplated perjury. Even if we were to assume that the jury might have believed his perjury, it does not follow that Whiteside was prejudiced.

Another matter related to the attorney-client relationship is the **attorney-client privilege.** Attorney-client privilege provides that a client's confidential discussions with an attorney remain confidential. The purpose of the privilege is to encourage client disclosure of all the facts to the lawyer, even those harmful to the client. An attorney cannot adequately represent a client unless all the facts (both favorable and unfavorable) about the matter are known. The information is needed so the attorney can prepare the client's case.

Attorney-client privilege has existed for a long time in the law. Some writers date it to Roman time, when advocates were barred from testifying against their clients. Other writers date it to the reign of Elizabeth I of England. At that time, the privilege was based not upon the rationale of protection of client's interests but instead upon the honor of the lawyer. Trial lawyers were considered gentle- men and it was a point of honor with gentlemen to keep their confidences. Today, as already shown, the privilege belongs to the client and exists as a matter of law to further the goals of the adversary system rather than for the protection of the attorney's honor.

Of course, at times the existence of the privilege may cause an injustice to occur. A wrongdoer may be set free. A person who breaches a contract may not be held liable. The end result of the privilege is that evidence which may be central to the case, if it is privileged information may not be used in court. A case therefore may proceed with incomplete information. For example, assume George confides in an attorney, after being arrested for auto theft, that he did indeed steal the car. George refuses to say anything to the police. At trial he is acquitted. George did not testify, and because of the attorney-client privilege, the attorney could not reveal the client's confession. Was justice served in that particular case? The truth was withheld from the adversary system by the attorney-client privilege doctrine. Yet the possibility of this type of result (which is rare) must be balanced against the overall good the attorney-client privilege is seeking.

Clients, even with the existence of the privilege and of an ethical bar to attorneys discussing client confidences with others, are reluctant to confide in their attorneys. Often an important task of the attorney is to gain the trust of the client in order to obtain full information. Few people are eager to confess an error, whether it is a crime they committed or the fact that they were not attentive as they were driving down the street prior to an accident.

Clients, when discussing very personal and sometimes emotional facts, may try to rationalize their conduct. The privilege is a tool to reassure clients that no court will use their attorneys to bring evidence against them. The privilege therefore serves a crucial function in the administration of justice in our legal system. Without it, attorneys would have little hope of gaining the confidence or a truthful statement of the facts from their clients. Consequently, the adversary system would not work properly. The case would be argued and prepared on the basis of false or incomplete facts. (In the law, small factual differences often will cause a change in the way a case is handled by an attorney and perhaps even affect which legal rules are applicable.) The expected result is that clients will most likely not receive a fair trial. Injustice to clients and to the system that relies on the clash in the courtroom in the search for truth would result. The concept of attorney-client privilege is an ideal strongly protected by the courts, since it furthers the search for truth and justice through the operation of our adversary system.

How Can an Attorney Represent a Guilty Person?

One of the most persistent questions asked of attorneys, and one that troubles a great number of people, is: How can an attorney represent a guilty person? A related question is: How can an attorney, in good conscience, seek to have evidence thrown out of court, resulting in a criminal's being set free to prey on other victims? These difficult questions have been responded to in a variety of ways. Some have argued that an attorney cannot let personal considerations overcome professional obligations to the legal system, which provides that accused parties shall have the right to counsel to represent their interests in court. Others have contended that the attorney's role in the adversary system is to zealously represent clients. The decision-making role rests with the judge or the jury and is not a part of the role given to the lawyer in the judicial system. Samuel Johnson once said: "An argument which does not convince yourself, may convince the Judge to whom you urge it; and if it does convince him, why, then, Sir, you are wrong, and he is right. It is his business to judge, and you are not to be confident in your own opinion that a cause is bad, but to say all you can for your client, and then hear the judge's opinion."[1]

Such arguments focus on the lawyer's responsibility to the legal system and the lawyer's role in the legal system. The question is still not answered, and the inquirer is left to ask, "What kind of system is this, which encourages attorneys to use all the devices of the law to set free a guilty person?"

It is impossible to respond adequately to that question, since it is much like asking, "Do you still kick your dog?" The inquirer presupposes an unsatisfactory response owing to a lack of insight into the nature of the adversary system. Therefore, a response to the question of how an attorney can represent a guilty person must be rather involved. First, the term *guilty person* has two meanings. One of them is the everyday usage of that term, covering actual and, in a sense, moral guilt. Did the accused commit the act? Did the defendant steal the car? Did the corporation dump waste in the river? This concept of guilt or innocence focuses solely on the actions of the wrongdoer. It is the way the term *guilt* is used by the questioner.

However, the legal system's concept of guilt is much broader. In the legal system, guilt means that the state has proved its case beyond a reasonable doubt and may punish the wrongdoer. Legal guilt is a prerequisite for an individual's loss of liberty under our system of government. *Guilt* is a shorthand term for this occurrence and includes many more considerations than simply whether the accused did or did not commit the act, although that is a major factor.

Guilt describes the amount of proof (beyond a reasonable doubt) which must be provided by the state before a person can be punished by the state. Thus, the person who committed a crime might be set free simply because the state could not gather enough evidence. Additionally, guilt in the legal system presumes that the state used proper procedures throughout the case. The necessity for such procedures is twofold. First, uniform procedures are necessary for evenhanded administration of justice. That is, all accused parties must be afforded the same rights and the same process before they may be punished by the state. This is important in that it prevents favoritism being built into the legal process.

A second important function of the procedures for determining legal guilt is that they operate as a safeguard for individual freedoms. The procedures are important in order to protect us, in the long run, from the power of the government. When people are forced to speak against their will in a police station, when a person's home may be invaded at any time by the police, a feeling of terror and a loss of liberty will result. Under such a system, wrongdoers would be punished, but at a very great cost to society. People would not know when the knock on the door would come for them, and when it did occur, how they would defend themselves.

Our adversary system of justice is based on the theory that justice—the goal of the system—can best be served through vigorous argument and testing in a courtroom of all aspects of the case. In the adversarial context, guilt is made up of a number of factors (such as the accused's mental state, the way evidence was obtained, whether the accused understood the consequences of cooperation with the authorities, whether the prosecutor presented enough evidence, and whether the accused did the act). Sometimes those factors clash. In order for legal guilt to be established, all factors involved in that concept must be established.

Contrary to popular notions, people who commit crime (do the act) and face trial are usually found legally guilty. The system *does* work. The lawyer who appears to "get the criminal off" really does not do so. Instead, what has happened is that in the testing of the state's evidence and procedures, flaws have been found.

The idea of an attorney representing a guilty client is more complex than the question as originally posed implies. That question usually results from a desire to see the wrongdoer brought to justice. But the process of bringing the wrongdoer to justice by establishing legal guilt calls for a broader inquiry than one that focuses merely on whether that person actually did the criminal act. At times these other factors are central to the finding of a court that an individual was guilty. The testing of these other factors is the lawyer's task, and legal guilt cannot be established until those factors are tested.

SUMMARY

Courts are major institutions in the legal environment. Courts render decisions that can have a profound effect on the operation of a firm. A general study of courts or the judicial system is therefore important. The judicial system may be reviewed by structure—state or federal courts—or it may be reviewed by function—trial or appellate courts.

Understanding the judicial system involves more than gaining an appreciation of its form. It also requires understanding the roles of the major participants in the system: the judge and the attorney. One of the important features of the judicial role is the balance between an independent judiciary and controls on the power that independence brings. Fair decision making is hampered by a judge who is unable to assess a matter free of influence. However, given the powers of a judge, a lack of controls could also cause harm to the administration of justice.

The role of the attorney is another important element of the judicial system. An attorney's task involves zealously guarding a client's interests within the policies and goals of the adversary system. Often, questions concerning the secrecy of client communications with counsel or the representation of a "guilty" client ignore the important functions of the legal system.

REVIEW QUESTIONS

1. Define the following terms:
   a. Appellate court
   b. Attorney client privilege
   c. Common law court
   d. Equity court
   e. Missouri plan
   f. Trial court

2. What are the major characteristics of the federal judicial system? Can federal courts hear any case that arises? What are the differences and similarities between the federal court system and a state court system?

3. What is the difference between a trial court and an appellate court?

4. Briefly describe the general functions of a judge. Is it accurate to say that a judge should not make the law? What is meant by judicial lawmaking?

5. Devise a system for the selection of judges. The criteria for you to use include: highly qualified candidates, sensitivity to the community, independence of outside influence, a public voice in selecting and retaining the judge, and accountability to the general public.

6. Why does the judicial system value the independence of its judges? What would be the effect on a judicial system of greatly restricting the independence of the judiciary?

7. What is meant by the term *attorney-client privilege?* What is it designed to accomplish in the legal system?

8. Should an attorney represent a "guilty" person? What would be the effect on our legal system if attorneys did not represent people who actually committed criminal acts?

9. A woman was brought to court on a disorderly conduct charge. Judge Yengo made certain judgments about the woman on the basis of his perception of people like her. He told her to shut up. He arbitrarily raised the time she had to serve in jail from ninety to

one hundred and twenty days solely because of a remark she made to her mother during the court proceeding. Should Judge Yengo be disciplined for misconduct in office?

10. What is the purpose of the concepts of jurisdiction and venue in the operation of the civil litigation system? Describe problems that might arise if those concepts were removed from the process.

11. Javor's attorney dozed off during a substantial portion of his trial. Should Javor be given a new trial?

12. Johns was accused of a crime. At trial, Johns did not testify, and his attorney did not present the court with jury instructions that could have included a less serious crime than Johns was accused of in this case. Johns was subsequently convicted. The reason Johns's attorney did this, he later testified, was that he felt he could not in conscience argue to the jury that Johns should be acquitted because of what Johns had previously told him. In light of the attorney's actions, should Johns be entitled to a new trial?

13. The inmates at Cummins Prison Farm and the Tucker Intermediate Reformatory assert that there is a lack of housing, a lack of medical care, infliction of physical and mental brutality, and numerous other abuses of the prisoners. The Eighth Circuit Court of Appeals agreed with the prisoners and took over operation of the prison system. Is the decision in this case an example of activism or judicial restraint?

14. While trimming her lawn, Steffey was injured by the electric mower. She purchased it from a retail dealer near her home in Chicago, Illinois. The manufacturer of the mower had its principal place of business in Cincinnati, Ohio. The manufacturer attended trade shows around the country, and it solicited business in all the states through its advertisements in various trade journals. It sold the mower that injured Steffey to the dealer in Chicago. Steffey wishes to bring suit against the manufacturer in Illinois. The manufacturer argues that in light of the fact that it could not be personally served in Illinois, the Illinois courts could not have jurisdiction over it. Who is correct?

15. Shack was a resident of Arizona. Morris was a resident of Oregon. A dispute arose between the two of them and Morris wanted to file suit against Shack. Shack went to Oregon on a vacation. While in Oregon, he was served with a summons and petition. Shack thereafter returned to Arizona. Shack contends that the Oregon courts have no jurisdiction over him because his contacts with the state of Oregon were not continuous and systematic. Is Shack correct?

16. Miller revealed to her attorney, Padgett, in the course of Padgett's representation of her, that she had in fact violated the antitrust laws. The government now wishes to call Padgett and force her to reveal what Miller told her. Can Padgett be forced to reveal what Miller said?

NOTE

[1] James Boswell, *The Life of Samuel Johnson* (1791), p. 333.

CHAPTER 3

Civil Litigation and Alternative Dispute Resolution

- Civil Litigation
- Trial Procedure
- The Appeal
- Alternative Dispute Resolution Procedures

Judges perform their duties of making law and settling disputes through litigation. To understand those duties we must focus on the process of litigation—more particularly, civil litigation. Civil litigation may be distinguished from criminal litigation. **Civil litigation** is all the trial work of our system that does *not* involve the violation of a **criminal law.** Most areas of the law therefore are affected by the civil litigation process: tort law, contract law, property law, and labor law are examples.

Often factors other than the rules of law are crucial to the outcome of a dispute. Yet these factors are frequently considered to be ''mere technicalities.'' A portion of this chapter will discuss a very important factor in any trial—the jury. Much of the discussion of the jury in the context of civil litigation will also be relevant to criminal trials. The jury is one of the most important institutions in our legal system. It is the one direct day-to-day method in which persons without legal training can have an effect on our legal system.

CIVIL LITIGATION

In General

A trial is a search for truth. It is not a perfect mechanism for obtaining the truth, however. There is no process or procedure that will guarantee that the just and correct result will be obtained in all cases. As we have already discussed, in our system a trial is conducted through an adversary process—one in which each side in a dispute presents its case in the best possible light. The decision maker at the trial, either the judge or the jury, listens to the arguments presented by the parties and essentially chooses which one to accept. A trial is a competition. The parties compete by presenting their different versions of the facts and making analyses of the applicable law. For if the parties agreed upon the facts and application of the law, then there would be no dispute and no need for a trial.

This does not mean that in every trial there is one truth teller and one liar and that the function of the decision maker is to select the truth teller. ''Facts'' are difficult to pinpoint. Both parties may be telling the truth, yet the evidence presented at the trial may conflict. Witnesses may see the very same event differently.

The views of parties directly involved in the dispute will most likely differ, and their views may in turn differ from the views of a casual witness. The decision maker must decide which of the factual versions is closer to the events that actually took place. However, as will be discussed in Chapter 4 on judicial reasoning and in the material on the jury that follows, the decision makers too have personality factors that influence their work in deciding the case.

This section examines the various stages of a case as it works its way through the judicial system.

Petition

The statements of the respective contentions of the parties to a lawsuit are called **pleadings.** They are written documents filed with the court prior to trial that state the position of each party to the suit. In order to start a civil lawsuit, the plaintiff must file the first pleading, a document commonly referred to as a petition (sometimes called a complaint or a declaration), which generally the defendant responds to with a document called an answer.

The **petition** is a document filed with the court asking that the plaintiff be granted some type of relief. The petition states paragraph by paragraph the nature of the claims the plaintiff has against the defendant and the relief requested of the court. The petition thus tells the defendant what the plaintiff believes the defendant did or failed to do and what the plaintiff wants the defendant to do or cease doing.

Steps in a Typical Civil Lawsuit

1. Plaintiff serves the defendant with a summons and petition.
2. Defendant files an answer to plaintiff's suit.
3. Discovery stage of the lawsuit begins.
4. Pretrial conference is held.
5. Jury is selected for trial.
6. Opening statements are made at the trial.
7. Evidence is presented at the trial.
8. Closing arguments are made at the trial.
9. Instructions are given to the jury.
10. Jury deliberates.
11. Jury renders verdict.
12. Judge enters judgment.
13. Post-trial motions are made.
14. Appeal is entered.

Summons

To institute a suit, the plaintiff requests that the court serve the defendant with a **summons.** It is not a part of the pleadings, but rather is a command of the clerk of the court that the defendant answer the allegations in the petition within a designated period of time. The summons thus notifies the defendant that suit has been brought against him or her and the time period in which the defendant must reply to the petition. The summons and a copy of the petition are commonly served by the sheriff or other law-enforcement personnel on the defendant. However, in some circumstances, private service may be authorized by a court. Generally, someone, such as the sheriff, actually hands a copy of the summons and petition to the defendant. In certain circumstances, the law permits service on the defendant by a simple delivery of the summons and petition to the defendant's home, or by mail, or by publication.

Answer

In response to the plaintiff's petition, the defendant files with the court an **answer** or reply within the time designated in the summons. A copy of the answer is also sent to the plaintiff's attorney. In the answer the defendant states his or her response to the plaintiff's allegations. Quite frequently the defendant denies all or most of the matters stated in the plaintiff's petition. Any matter denied must be established by the plaintiff if the case goes to trial.

A **counterclaim** is a claim presented by a defendant against the plaintiff. Answers often contain counterclaims against the plaintiff. Some types of claims, called compulsory counterclaims, must be asserted by the defendant in his or her answer. If a counterclaim is compulsory, it must be asserted in the action or is forever barred. Other types of counterclaims are not compulsory but may be stated in the answer. These are called permissive counterclaims.

Suppose the plaintiff alleged in its petition that the defendant failed to pay for goods delivered by the plaintiff. The defendant could allege in its answer that the plaintiff failed to deliver some goods pursuant to another contract. This claim that the defendant has against the plaintiff arising out of another contract is a counterclaim.

A sample petition appears in Figure 3.1. In this petition, the plaintiff claims that his landlord has wrongfully retained certain items of property owned by the defendant. The plaintiff wishes to recover the value of this property from the landlord. Figure 3.2 illustrates a typical response to such a petition. In this case, the landlord admitted renting the home for the time in question and to terminating the tenancy and reentering the home. However, the landlord denied taking possession of the tenant's property and therefore denied any liability to the tenant.

Motion to Dismiss

Attorneys seldom file suits unless they believe a recovery in the case is possible. On occasion an attorney may file suit based on a theory of recovery not recognized at that time in the jurisdiction. In response to this, the defendant quite likely will file a **motion to dismiss.** In essence, what the defendant is saying is that even if everything the plaintiff says is true, the plaintiff still is not entitled to a remedy.

Following the filing of such a motion, the parties argue the motion before the judge. The judge, after listening to the arguments of the attorneys, decides

IN THE DISTRICT COURT OF DOUGLAS COUNTY, KANSAS

JOHN DOE,   Plaintiff,

vs.   Case No. 10011

MARY SMITH,   Defendant.

Proceeding Under K.S.A. Chapter 60

PETITION

COMES NOW the petitioner and states as his cause of action the defendant.

1. From November 1, 1992 to January 7,1993 plaintiff occupied, as defendant's tenant, defendant's house located at 140 Main, City of Lawrence, State of Kansas.

2. On January 3,1993, defendant terminated such tenancy by sending a written notice to the plaintiffs demanding the trailer be vacated by January 8,1993.

3. On January 7,1993, the defendant re-entered the home, and took possession of it and all personalty therein.

4. On that date, the following items of personalty in the home were owned solely by plaintiff: a 1992 RCA color TV and a Pioneer stereo. The reasonable value of such property on that date was $900.00.

5. At the time defendant took possession of the home, she took possession of the plaintiff's property. Plaintiff demanded that the defendant return possession of such personalty to plaintiff, but defendant with willful disregard of plaintiff's legal right to possession of such personalty has refused and failed to surrender possession thereof to plaintiff and still refuses to do so.

6. By reason of defendant's willful conversion of such property with knowledge of plaintiff's legal right to its possession, plaintiff is entitled to compensatory damages in the amount of $900.00.

7. WHEREFORE, plaintiff prays judgment against the defendant for $900.00 compensatory damages for the loss of his personal property, for court costs, and for such other and further relief as to the court may seem just and proper.

DEMAND FOR JURY TRIAL

Plaintiff herein demands trial by jury on all issues of fact contained in plaintiff's petition.

_____

John Doe
Attorney for plaintiff
100 Tennessee Street
Lawrence, Kansas 66044
1-913-845-0000

Figure 3.1   Sample Petition

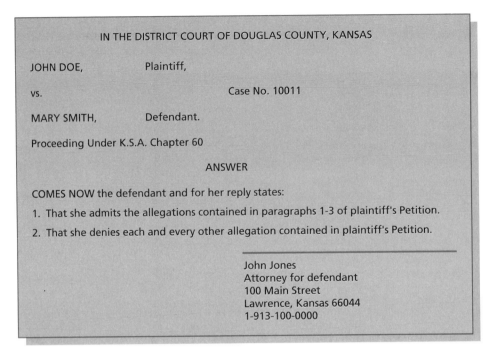

IN THE DISTRICT COURT OF DOUGLAS COUNTY, KANSAS

JOHN DOE,   Plaintiff,

vs.   Case No. 10011

MARY SMITH,   Defendant.

Proceeding Under K.S.A. Chapter 60

ANSWER

COMES NOW the defendant and for her reply states:

1. That she admits the allegations contained in paragraphs 1-3 of plaintiff's Petition.

2. That she denies each and every other allegation contained in plaintiff's Petition.

John Jones
Attorney for defendant
100 Main Street
Lawrence, Kansas 66044
1-913-100-0000

Figure 3.2   Sample Answer to a Petition

whether to permit the suit to proceed. If the judge grants the motion to dismiss, the case ends (subject to the right in many cases to refile a new petition stating new factual allegations, or subject to the right to amend the petition by inserting these new allegations in the petition).

If the judge declines to grant the motion to dismiss, this does not mean the plaintiff wins the case. It merely means the defendant must answer the petition and proceed with the case.

Normally the defendant's counsel makes a motion to dismiss in response to the plaintiff's petition. However, a motion to dismiss may be raised at any stage of the lawsuit—including on appeal.

As the prior material indicates, motions are simply applications to the court for some type of order. The motion to dismiss is merely one type of motion that may be made during the course of a legal proceeding. Motions may be filed prior to trial and argued before a judge, made orally during a trial and decided at that time, or lodged following a trial and argued before a judge. Other motions might be made in response to a petition: for example, a motion to strike a paragraph or paragraphs from the plaintiff's petition, or a motion requesting the plaintiff make its petition more definite.

Judgment on the Pleadings

At the close of the pleadings, the plaintiff or defendant may make a motion for a **judgment on the pleadings.** Essentially, this serves the same function as a motion to dismiss, but the attorney files it after the pleadings are closed rather than in response to the petition.

Suppose the judge finds no basis for a verdict on behalf of the plaintiff, even if the allegations in the plaintiff's petition are assumed to be true. In that case, the suit may be dismissed. However, if the petition is deficient, the judge may allow the plaintiff to amend its petition if the defect can be corrected.

Motion for Summary Judgment

After the plaintiff files a petition, the defendant answers, and the parties have learned something about the facts of the case, one of the parties may believe he or she is entitled to a judgment as a matter of law. Generally, the parties have at least taken the affidavits (sworn statements) of some of the important parties to the case. In some cases, other devices, such as depositions, which are discussed later in this chapter, may have been obtained.

Thus, unlike the judgment on the pleadings, in a **motion for summary judgment** the judge considers matters outside the pleadings—such as affidavits and depositions.

Essentially, the party making a motion for summary judgment is saying that no genuine issue of material fact remains to be decided in the case, and therefore the judge should grant the motion. If any issue of material fact remains, the judge should deny the motion.

Even assuming the judge grants the motion for a summary judgment, she or he still must rule on how the law applies to the facts in question. If the judge feels the law favors the plaintiff, the judge rules for the plaintiff. If the judge decides that the law requires a verdict on behalf of the defendant, he or she enters a judgment for the defendant. The critical concept here is that no trial is required because all issues of fact have been resolved. That being the case, the judge merely needs to apply the law to the facts.

Statute of Limitations

One important aspect of the filings in a civil suit is a time limit imposed on the party who files. This time limit is called a **statute of limitations.** A statute of limitations sets a time period. These periods vary, depending upon the type of document that is to be filed in a given lawsuit, the type of lawsuit that is originally filed, and the jurisdiction in which the case is brought. For example, if an accident occurs today, the statute of limitations may require that any lawsuit concerning such an accident be filed within two years of its occurrence. A party who waits longer than two years may find that its otherwise justifiable legal claim is denied.

In certain instances, the statute of limitations is tolled; that is, certain acts or events cause the statute of limitations to not begin running or to stop running. For example, statutes of limitations often provide that if a person goes into hiding, the statute will not run while the person is concealed; or if after the **cause of action** accrues the defendant absconds from the state, the time of absence will not be counted as any part of the period within which the action must be brought.

We have seen thus far that a plaintiff must institute a suit by filing a petition, to which the defendant responds by filing an answer or a motion such as the motion to dismiss. Suit also must be filed within a certain period of time, specified in the statute of limitations. Once suit is under way, the discovery phase begins.

Discovery   **Discovery,** in a civil case, is a process through which opposing counsel can learn, before a trial begins, the case to be presented by the other side. In general, each side must disclose the identity of its witnesses to the other. In addition, opposing sides have the opportunity to interrogate those witnesses. Documents relevant to the case are generally disclosed. Briefly, then, the discovery rules permit each side in a civil case to fully learn about the other.

The purpose of discovery is to do away with the element of surprise in a trial and encourage settlement out of court. Once both sides are fully aware of the facts they can usually reach a negotiated resolution of the dispute.

There are a number of mechanisms for obtaining discovery in civil litigation. Although the discovery rules are designed to operate without court order, the courts do exercise a supervisory role in the process. Courts may limit discovery if they believe it too burdensome. They may impose sanctions upon a party that refuses to permit discovery. Sanctions may include ordering a party to pay the attorneys' fees of the opposing party or may even include entering a default judgment against that party.

Discovery may be obtained through the interrogation under oath of witnesses and parties to the lawsuit. This discovery technique is called **deposition.** It may be used to preserve the testimony of witnesses who will not be available at trial because of death or illness, or for some other reason. A deposition may also be used to raise questions concerning the truthfulness of a witness at the trial. Consider, for example, that a witness's deposition and trial testimony may conflict. A deposition may also be used as a general tool for having facts revealed about the incident in question and the case of the opposition.

Other discovery tools include the submission of written questions to be answered under oath. The written questions are called **interrogatories.** Documents may also be obtained through the discovery process. Additionally, parties are encouraged to admit to certain portions of the litigation in order to reduce the number of issues to be decided at the trial. This may be accomplished through a request for admissions.

The discovery rules contain a number of techniques litigants may use to gather facts relevant to the litigation. As a result, such techniques help foster fair, fast, and inexpensive resolution of cases through settlement rather than waiting for a disposition through trial.

However, liberal discovery rules sometimes create problems. Many attorneys argue, especially in very large cases, that the discovery stage of a proceeding is the portion of the case where the most decisive "battles" are waged. These battles often involve abuse of the discovery tools, either by the party seeking information or by the party providing it. For example, the party responding to discovery requests may attempt to relinquish the minimum amount of information required to avoid court sanction. As a result, the discovering party must work extremely hard to gather the needed information. Techniques used include providing evasive or incomplete answers to requests for discovery made by the opposing party. This technique will require the discovering party to try to have the requested material supplied through further discovery or through judicial proceedings. Additionally, a responding party may delay in responding to the discovery requests or provide a very large amount of material (usually in the form of

The Ethics of Delaying a Case

One technique often used by well-financed litigants is the practice of delaying the resolution of the case by prolonging the discovery phase of the case. This is called **dilatory** tactics. Suppose that Wilson broke her arm in an automobile accident. She filed suit against the driver of the other car, Sullivan. Sullivan's attorney might attempt to drag the case out. Attorneys use such tactics in order to wear the other side down. As the years pass, Wilson may become more amenable to settling the case on Sullivan's terms. The defendant also profits from such a strategy because he earns interest on the money he eventually must pay to the plaintiff up to the moment Sullivan actually makes a payment to Wilson.

If the goal of the justice system is to obtain a speedy and fair resolution to every suit, does it further the interests of justice to engage in such tactics?

requested documents) in an unorganized manner. The discovering party will be required to spend a great deal of time and money sorting through the information.

However, not all discovery abuses may be claimed by the party to whom the discovery is aimed. The discovering party, too, can abuse the system—for example, by bombarding the other side with a huge number of discovery requests. Again a great deal of time and expense will be involved in responding to discovery requests. The litigation costs increase as a result. The better-financed party may be able to coerce a settlement from the other party through abuse of the discovery system. It should be noted that states have adopted rules to try to limit abusive practices in the discovery phase of a trial.

Though discovery can be abused, such abuses do not, of course, occur in all cases; they occur most frequently in very large, complex cases. Discovery is a portion of the system of civil litigation in which many business managers and other nonlawyers are involved.

We are now ready to examine the actual steps of a civil trial. Trials begin at the conclusion of the discovery period. Great attention is devoted in this material to the function of the jury system in civil litigation—one of the great institutions of the American legal system.

TRIAL PROCEDURE

Pretrial Conference   After suit has been filed and the parties have finished with discovery, if it appears the parties intend to litigate or try a case rather than settle it, the judge sets the case for a **pretrial conference.**

Formal or Informal

At the pretrial conference, the attorneys representing all parties to the dispute meet with a judge. Quite frequently, in many parts of the country, this person is the judge who will actually preside at the trial. In the more metropolitan areas, however, one or two judges may conduct all pretrial hearings for that district.

The degree of formality of this hearing depends upon the judge. Some pretrial hearings are quite formal. Other judges may elect to keep the proceeding more casual—they may meet with opposing counsel in their chambers.

Narrowing the Issues

The primary function of the pretrial conference is to narrow and simplify the factual issues. The judge usually tries to get the parties to stipulate (agree to) as many facts as possible at this stage. By agreeing to certain facts, the parties reduce the amount of time necessary to try a case.

Once the case is set for trial and the parties have completed the pretrial conference, they may settle the case. Quite often, a case is settled on the very day it is scheduled for trial. If this does not happen, the parties appear on the scheduled date.

United States Constitution

The Seventh Amendment to the Constitution deals with civil trials. It provides: "In suits at common law, where the value in controversy shall exceed twenty dollars, the right of trial by jury shall be preserved, and no fact tried by a jury, shall be otherwise re-examined in any court of the United States, than according to the rules of the common law."

Take note of the fact that the Seventh Amendment merely *preserves* the right to trial in suits at common law. It does not *create* a right to trial by jury. Without going into the details of what the common law is, suffice it to say that if a matter was regarded as part of the common law at the time of the drafting of the Constitution, litigants may request a trial by jury for such issues today. If the case was not a common law matter, no right to a trial by jury exists under the United States Constitution. A right to a jury trial may exist, however, under the applicable *state* constitution.

Selection of a Jury

The courts chiefly use one of two types of juries, grand juries and petit juries. (There are other so-called juries, as well. Coroner's juries, which are used in many cities, determine whether a deceased person died of natural causes. A hearing is held by the coroner with the assistance of a jury.) Grand juries, which do not function as part of an actual trial, are discussed in Chapter 15.

Petit Juries

It is the function of the **petit jury** to hear evidence presented by witnesses at the trial and, following instructions given to them by the judge, to render a decision in a case. Petit juries are used in both civil and criminal cases.

Keep in mind the function of a jury—a jury decides the *facts* of a case. It applies the law that controls in the case to whatever set of facts it finds. The judge instructs the jury on the law. Thus, when using a jury, the *judge determines the law* applicable to the case, but the *jury determines the facts.*

If the parties try the case without the assistance of a jury, the judge decides both the facts and the law.

If the parties schedule a trial before a jury, the court instructs the clerk of the court to call in on the day set for the trial a specified number of persons, called veniremen, for possible service. Typically, the court asks for two or three times the number of people needed for the trial because some will be unable, for one reason or another, to serve on the jury.

Statutory Exemptions

Some states are very liberal in excusing people from jury service. Some state statutes excuse a large number of categories of persons, such as employees of the state, physicians, and ministers, while other states permit very few excuses. The theory in those states which exempt certain categories of persons from jury service is that some of these people will better serve society by working on their jobs. Others (state employees, for example) are excused because of their possible prejudice.

The problem for the parties to a trial, however, is to get enough people in the pool of available jurors to constitute a fair cross section of the community. When the state automatically exempts certain categories of persons, these people never even appear at the trial. They simply sign a form and return it to the clerk listing the reason for their exemption from jury service. Permitting too many people an excuse from jury duty lessens the pool of available jurors.

Exemptions by the Judge

Not only do some state statutes permit certain categories of persons to avoid even appearing as potential jurors, but judges also have considerable discretion in excusing people from serving at a trial. For example, if someone were to state that jury duty would pose a hardship, a judge would normally allow that person to be excused.

Voir Dire

After dealing with the basic matters, the judge then permits the attorneys to question the jurors about the case. This stage of the trial is called the **voir dire,** the purpose of which is to determine the qualifications of the prospective jurors to sit as triers of fact in the case and to determine whether they are subject to challenge. In some places, the judge conducts the voir dire based on questions submitted to him or her by the attorneys. The length of the voir dire is substantially up to the discretion of the judge. However, in very serious cases, judges typically allow extensive questioning of the jurors to avoid challenges of the jury on appeal.

The courts allow two types of challenges to a juror. The first is a **challenge for**

cause. There is no limit to the number of challenges for cause. These are made to the court, and the court determines whether sufficient cause exists to remove the challenged venireman. The for-cause challenge allows an attorney to challenge any venireman on the grounds of bias or prejudice. That is, if the attorney can show that a person is not able to make a fair and impartial decision, the attorney can request the judge to dismiss that person. If he or she can show that the venireman is either unwilling or unable to follow or decide questions, the attorney can request that person be dismissed for these reasons as well.

The other type of challenge, the **peremptory challenge,** is designed to serve the other purposes mentioned: to give an attorney's client the best chance possible. This type of challenge is determined solely by the party exercising the challenge. The court may not refuse to excuse a challenged venireman, nor is the party required to give any reason for a peremptory challenge. Unlike challenges for cause, of which there can be an unlimited number, the peremptory challenge may be exercised only a limited number of times, a number usually specified by statute.

Exercising any challenges or deciding which prospective jurors to challenge is largely a matter of strategy. Some attorneys may argue that it makes no difference who serves on a jury. However, seasoned trial attorneys are quite attuned to the fact that the makeup of the jury may be critical to the outcome of a trial. Psychological studies of small-group decision making tend to support this thinking. For this reason, the voir dire is a very important stage in the trial.

In most cases, the attorneys question prospective members of the jury in great depth. They want to know as much as possible about each juror. Here is what Clarence Darrow had to say about the process of picking a jury:

> Choosing jurors is always a delicate task. The more a lawyer knows of life, human nature, psychology, and the reactions of the human emotions, the better he is equipped for the subtle selection of his so-called "twelve men, good and true." In this undertaking, everything pertaining to the prospective juror needs to be questioned and weighed: his nationality, his business, religion, politics, social standing, family ties, friends, habits of life, and thought; the books and newspapers he likes and reads, and many more matters that combine to make a man; all of these qualities and experiences have left their effect on ideas, beliefs and fancies that inhabit his mind. Understanding of all this cannot be obtained too bluntly. It usually requires finesse, subtlety and guesswork. Involved in it all is the juror's method of speech, the kind of clothes he wears, the style of haircut, and, above all, his business associates, residence and origin.

Why do seasoned trial attorneys like Darrow want to know so much about the jurors? The reason is that not everyone thinks the same. Some people are quite bigoted. Others are very tight with the dollar. Still others invariably favor the plaintiff or the defendant.

What the trial attorney is trying to do, to put it crudely, is to stereotype people—to put each person into a category on the basis of the attorney's life experiences and trial experiences. The attorney hopes to eliminate people adverse to his or her cause and to assemble a group of people favorably disposed to the trial strategy he or she plans to adopt.

This brings up an important point: In theory, parties to a trial are entitled to a jury composed of fair and impartial jurors. In practice, however, a trial attorney does not necessarily want fair and impartial jurors. Attorneys want people predisposed toward certain positions and ideas. The law as it operates in practice is very different from what one would gather simply by reading a few cases.

Fortunately, the Supreme Court intervenes from time to time to help assure participants in a trial that those who serve on a jury do not come to court with certain preformed opinions. For example, a person might be so biased as to base a decision of guilt or innocence on the defendant's race. The Court permits questions on the issue of bias.

Lawyers ask, or try to ask, a variety of questions concerning the jurors. Why would an attorney be concerned that members of the jury might harbor some prejudice against his or her client? The juror might vote against a minority person's position because of her or his prejudices, not because of the evidence presented at the case. Naturally, persons who refuse to decide a case on the basis of the evidence ought to be excluded from the jury.

Racial prejudice is one of the more obvious prejudices. Every individual is a composite of attitudes, any of which might play a critical part in the juror's hearing or recollection of the evidence or in his or her attitude toward various witnesses, the judge, and the other jury members. A person's personality also influences the manner in which he or she interacts in small-group decision making—such as occurs on a jury! An attorney, usually operating on gut instinct,

Selecting a Jury

MCI Communications Corporation brought an antitrust suit against AT&T. At that trial, MCI was awarded $1.8 billion. MCI's attorneys spent a considerable amount of time preparing for every facet of this trial.

One of the factors the attorneys were interested in was the type of juror who would be of greatest use to MCI. In order to determine this information, attorneys representing MCI hired a public opinion pollster to learn about the attitudes of persons in Chicago, the place where the trial was scheduled to take place, toward big business. MCI wanted to determine the type of juror who would keep an open mind about MCI's case.

As a result of the work done by the public opinion pollster, MCI's attorneys developed a profile of the type of person they needed to get on the jury. The poll told them to select self-made people who understood competition, who were first- or second-generation Americans, and who were intelligent enough to understand this rather complex case. Six of the twelve jurors who eventually heard the case had college backgrounds.

Obtaining information of this nature is obviously useful to attorneys in selecting the proper group of persons to look for during the voir dire. The size of this verdict suggests that MCI's attorneys selected the jury very astutely.

IN THE SEVENTH JUDICIAL DISTRICT COURT OF THE STATE OF KANSAS
IN AND FOR THE COUNTY OF DOUGLAS

JUROR QUESTIONNAIRE

You have been selected for the privilege to serve as a juror in the District Court of Douglas County. Please carefully read and answer the questions on this form and return it immediately in the enclosed self-addressed, stamped envelope: Questionnaires *must be returned within five days*, whether or not you may expect to be excused from reporting. This questionnaire is for the purpose of determining your qualification for jury duty. Your answers to these questions are for Court use only and will not be made public. Your cooperation and willingness to serve as a juror are appreciated. *PLEASE PRINT OR TYPE YOUR ANSWERS.*

1. Name _____ Age _____
2. Residence Address _____ City _____ Zip _____
   Residence Phone Number _____ Work Phone Number _____
3. Years in residence in Kansas _____ In Douglas County _____
4. Former Residence _____
5. Marital Status _____ Married _____ Separated _____ Widower
   (Please check) _____ Single _____ Divorced _____ Widow
6. Number of children _____ Ages _____ Can care be provided? _____
7. Have you any ill dependents who require your personal and constant care? _____
   If so, give details: _____
8. Occupation _____ Employer _____
   Do you own your business? _____ Number of employees _____
9. Full name of spouse _____ Occupation _____
   Employer _____ Work Address _____ Phone _____
10. If you are not now employed; give your last occupation and employer: _____
    _____
11. Have you ever served as a juror? _____
    Civil case? _____ When and where _____
    Criminal case? _____ When and where _____

Figure 3.3   Juror Questionnaire

tries to evaluate each person as a prospective juror. The more information he or she possesses about each person, the easier this decision becomes.

Before conducting the voir dire, however, the attorney must do some initial investigation and preparation. The attorney must first learn about the backgrounds of all prospective jurors to determine whether she or he wishes to challenge any of them. This will also help to establish the necessary jury rapport. Some of this information can be obtained through various public sources, including the city directory, telephone directory, and other such public listings. Perhaps the best method is simply talking to people who know the juror, such as neighbors and co-workers.

12. Have you or any members of your immediate family been a party to any lawsuit? _____

    Criminal?_____ Civil? _____ When and where _____
    Who in your family was involved? _____
13. Have you ever been convicted of a felony? _____ For what _____
    Where and when _____
14. If you believe you have a physical disability which would prevent you from
    serving as a juror, please state what: _____
15. Has any Court ever found you to be incompetent or incapacitated? _____
    Where and when _____ If restored, give date _____
16. Are you a close friend of, or are you related to any law-enforcement officer?
    If so, please check: _____ Federal _____ State _____ Sheriff's Office _____ City Police
17. Do you drive an automobile? _____ Is transportation available?_____
    If you live outside city limits, state mileage one way to city limits _____
18. Can you read, write, and understand English?_____
19. Please show the extent of your formal education. (Circle highest level completed.)
    Elementary or secondary school: 1 2 3 4 5 6 7 8 9 10 11 12 College: 1 2 3 4 5 6 7 +
20. Have you had any vocational or professional training?_____
    If so, please state what kind and to what extent: _____
    _____

21. If enrolled in a college or university, please state year and course of study:
    _____

22. If you feel there is any reason you cannot serve as a juror, please state:
    _____
    _____
    _____
    _____
    _____
    _____
    _____
    _____
    _____

    I affirm that the answers I have given to the above questions are true and correct.

                              Signed: _____
                              Dated: _____

Some states provide information of this type to attorneys prior to trial. In other states, attorneys must search out information about jurors prior to trial or at trial. The juror questionnaire in Figure 3.3 is a typical example of a form prospective jurors might be asked to fill out.

Having accumulated as much information as he or she desires, both prior to trial and during the voir dire, the attorney must now apply some practical psychology. What strategy does the attorney hope to follow in the conduct of the case? That strategy should be a factor in selecting the jurors.

As far as possible, an attorney tries to eliminate persons perceived to be unfavorable through for-cause objections. Basically, the attorney objects to a particular juror on the ground that the person is ''incapable of sitting as a fair and impartial juror.'' For example, a person who flatly states she or he could not fairly decide the case because the defendant is a minority member clearly would be excused for cause. Convincing the judge to excuse prospective jurors for cause is an art and is not easily accomplished. Furthermore, such objections must be made tactfully, or an attorney will destroy any rapport with the jury. An important factor with respect to for-cause objections is they are unlimited in number.

At the close of the questioning of the veniremen, a few people will always have managed to stay on the panel in spite of the best effort of the attorneys to exclude them for cause. Either attorney will then ask the judge to strike these people from the jury by exercising a peremptory challenge. Each attorney possesses the right to exercise only a few peremptory challenges.

Opening Statement

Following the voir dire, the attorneys present their **opening statements.** In a civil case, the plaintiff's attorney makes her or his statement first. The defendant then has the option of making an opening statement at that time or waiting until the plaintiff has finished presenting evidence. (In a criminal case, the state presents its statement, then the defendant may elect to make a statement at that time or after the state finishes presenting evidence.)

EACH STEP

The purpose of the opening statement is to give the jurors a broad overview of the case. The attorney probably will introduce his or her witnesses, describe their anticipated testimony, stress certain rules of law, tell the jurors what the attorney hopes to prove, and comment upon what the other side intends to do. The attorney ought to present plausible reasons why, after hearing the evidence, the jury should find in his or her client's favor. Thus, the opening statement amounts to a broad overview of the trial to come. The jurors are fresh at this point. They listen avidly. Such information may help clarify points in the trial they might misunderstand or fail to hear. The attention span of the jurors surely is best at this point, and for that reason alone the opening statement is of critical importance.

Nothing said during the opening statements is part of the evidence. They are merely statements of what the attorneys expect the proof to be, merely outlines of the case. The decision in a case must be rendered on the basis of the testimony of witnesses who appear at trial. Nonetheless, a good lawyer starts the jury thinking about his or her position in the case during the opening statement, and possibly even influences the jurors' thinking at this point.

Burden of Proof

One matter often discussed in the opening statement is **burden of proof.** The burden of proof is the duty of a party to substantiate an allegation or issue to avoid dismissal of that issue early in the trial or to convince the trier of facts of the truth of the claim and therefore win at trial.

In a civil case, the plaintiff must establish its case by a **preponderance of the evidence**—that is, the evidence presented by the plaintiff must be more convincing than the opposing evidence in order for the plaintiff to prevail at trial. This does not mean that the trier of fact is absolutely convinced of the plaintiff's position, but simply that the plaintiff's evidence, on the whole, looks more convincing than the evidence presented by the defendant.

In a civil case, the plaintiff has the initial burden of proof. If the plaintiff fails to establish its burden of proof, the judge dismisses the case—even if the defendant never presented any evidence at trial!

Because the plaintiff has the initial burden of proof, it must present evidence first. It must convince the judge that there is sufficient evidence to meet its burden of proof. Once this is accomplished, the burden shifts to the defense to dispute the points brought up by the plaintiff. In other words, the defense automatically loses the case if it fails to meet its burden of proof.

Motions

At the close of the plaintiff's case, the defense may make a **motion.** A motion is a request to the court for an order or rule in favor of the party making the request. Motions may be made prior to or during the trial.

Quite frequently, when counsel for one of the parties makes a motion during a trial, the judge either asks the jury to retire to the jury room or moves the proceedings to her or his chambers. All the remarks made during such a break, like those made during the rest of the trial, are recorded by the court reporter. The judge often considers whether to admit certain testimony during these breaks. If the judge decides not to admit the testimony, jurors will never hear the evidence in question. In certain cases, however, the parties record the evidence or at least some indication of the nature of the proffered evidence in case of an appeal.

When the defendant makes a motion to dismiss the case at the close of the prosecution's or plaintiff's case, many states refer to it as a **motion for a directed verdict.** The moving party really is saying that the other side has failed to prove all the facts necessary to establish a case. If the court grants such a motion at this point, the judge dismisses the case and discharges the jury. Such motions are routinely made at trial.

At the close of the defendant's presentation of evidence, both sides may ask the judge for a directed verdict. Again, if the judge grants such a motion, he or she enters a verdict for one party or the other.

Rules of Evidence

Certain evidence may be admitted at trial, other evidence may not. Certain rules of evidence result in evidence being suppressed (not admitted). A good example is the rule against the admission of hearsay evidence.

Hearsay is evidence that a witness offers not from personal knowledge, but based upon a statement made by another person. The hearsay rule applies to both oral and written statements. It is subject to a number of exceptions.

An example of the hearsay rule follows. Mr. Smith is on the stand. He has just testified that the president of his company said at a meeting of the board of directors that Ms. Jones fired an employee because he was a Native American.

GOV'T REPORTS NOT ADMISSIBLE

This is hearsay—Smith's testimony is based, not on his own personal knowledge, but on a statement he heard from someone else. If this statement is offered to prove that Jones improperly discriminated against the employee, the judge will not admit it in evidence. The judge, following an objection to the statement, will order the jury to disregard it.

The contemporaneous-objection rule requires an *immediate* objection following the introduction of evidence. Also, the attorney cannot just stand up and say "I object to the introduction of this evidence," but must give a reason for objecting—for example, stating that the evidence violates the hearsay rule.

Many other objections exist. Some of them relate to the form of a question—such as the objection that a question is "leading and suggestive." Suppose an attorney asks the witness, "Were you wearing a beard on June 12, 1991?" Such a question suggests the possible answer an attorney wants the witness to give. A question of this nature should be stated in this manner: "Tell us about your physical condition on June 12, 1991," or some similar wording that does not suggest the desired answer.

Cross-Examination

If a party calls a witness to the stand and asks questions, the courts refer to such questioning as the **direct examination.** When the attorney for the opposing party questions this same witness, the courts call such questioning the **cross-examination.**

The purpose of the cross-examination is to permit the opposite party to test what has just been stated by the witness. The attorney tries to demonstrate that the witness's memory is faulty, or that he or she was not in a position to perceive the events in question, or that the witness has not explained the facts clearly.

Closing Arguments

Following the close of the defendant's case and after the judge considers any motions made by the parties, each side presents a **closing argument.** In a civil case, the plaintiff has the option of opening. The defendant may then make concluding statements, followed by the plaintiff's response. (Criminal cases operate in the same fashion, with the state making the first comments.)

A closing argument really is a review of all the evidence heard during the trial. The attorneys refresh the jurors' memory of important points made during the trial. Generally, there is some theme to the closing remarks that the attorney wishes to convey to the jury. Through this theme she or he tries to analyze and review the testimony. The attorneys also review the instructions of law that the judge will present. They try to explain these instructions so the jurors apply the law correctly. The attorneys must attempt to explain the law because the judge generally just reads the instructions to the jurors.

Making a good closing argument is an art. It involves a combination of strategy and logic. An attorney must make the jurors think about his or her position. Sometimes overly zealous and unethical lawyers misstate the evidence to try to confuse the jurors. If the opposing counsel catches the error, she or he objects and asks the judge to admonish the attorney for misstating the evidence. Of course, poor preparation for the closing or excessive emotion may also result in an unintentional erroneous presentation of the testimony.

Quite often, the closing argument is based on pure emotion—in other words, rule for my client because he or she is a very sympathetic person. Such appeals work well in certain tragic or pitiful cases, as when a child is injured by a truck owned by a large company. The attorney representing the child often tries to convince the jury to rule for the child because the child has been injured—as opposed to deciding the case based on the law and facts presented in court.

The following quotation is a classic example of an appeal to emotion, rather than the law, in the closing argument. It was delivered in the case *Burden* v. *Hornsby* in the Court of Common Pleas at Warrensburg, Missouri, September 23, 1870. This case involved a matter of principle—the death of a man's dog, Old Drum, for which he claimed fifty dollars damages. The speech was delivered by Senator George Graham Vest. During it, counsel for the defendant sensed the cause was lost. He is rumored to have whispered facetiously to his partner, "We had better get out of the courtroom with our client, else all might be hanged."

EULOGY, TO THE DOG

Gentlemen of the Jury: The best friend a man has in this world may turn against him and become his enemy. His son or daughter that he has reared with loving care may prove ungrateful. Those who are nearest and dearest to us, those whom we trust with our happiness and our good name, may become traitors to their faith. The money that a man has he may lose. It flies away from him perhaps when he needs it most. A man's reputation may be sacrificed in a moment of ill-considered action. The people who are prone to fall on their knees to do us honor when success is with us, may be the first to throw the stones of malice when failure settles its cloud upon our heads. The one absolutely unselfish friend that a man can have in this selfish world, the one that never deserts him, the one that never proves ungrateful or treacherous, is his dog.

Gentlemen of the jury, a man's dog stands by him in prosperity and in poverty, in health and in sickness. He will sleep on the cold ground where the wintry winds blow and the snow drives fierce, if only he may be near his master's side. He will kiss the hand that has no food to offer; he will lick the wounds and sores that come from encounter with the roughness of the world. He guards the sleep of his pauper master as if he were a prince. When all other friends desert, he remains. When riches take wing and reputation falls to pieces, he is as constant in his love as the sun in its journey through the heavens.

If fortune drives the master forth an outcast in the world, friendless and homeless, the faithful dog asks no higher privilege than that of his company to guard against danger, to fight against his enemies. And when the last scene of all comes, and death takes the master in its embrace and his body is laid away in the cold ground, no matter if all other friends pursue their way, there by his graveside will the noble dog be found, his head between his paws, his eyes sad but open in alert watchfulness, faithful and true even in death.

Appeals to emotion can and do work on closing—with the right jury. They may lead jurors to react emotionally as opposed to thinking about the evidence.

Instructions to the Jury   Following the closing statements of counsel, the judge instructs the members of the jury on the law. Generally, a judge merely reads the instructions to the jury. They may be long, complex, and confusing. Some states permit the jurors to have a copy of them during their deliberations. It is critical for an attorney to explain the meaning of the instructions to the jury in the closing argument. Merely hearing or reading the instructions often does little to clarify the law for the jurors.

Basically, the instructions state the facts a jury must find to arrive at a decision in the case. The instructions are arrived at as a result of suggestions by the attorneys to the judge. Sometimes a judge gives an instruction that an attorney thinks misstates the law, or the judge refuses to give a requested instruction. When this happens, the losing party generally challenges on appeal the instructions given at trial. Erroneous instructions may result in a retrial.

Today, most states have suggested instructions that must be used at trial. This eliminates the need for the attorneys to write their own instructions. The attorney merely selects the instructions he or she wishes the judge to deliver at trial. If the judge consents, they are read to the jury. The parties and the judge discuss which instructions to give out of the hearing of the jury, normally in the judge's chambers.

Jury Deliberations

The jury retires to the jury room at the close of the judge's instructions. The judge tells them to elect a foreman. As indicated earlier, attorneys often try to determine who the foreman will be because of the influential position the foreman occupies.

Jurors deliberate in secret. The deliberations may not be recorded or witnessed by nonjurors. However, jurors usually may discuss the case following the announcement of the verdict if they wish.

Formerly, all the jurors were required to agree upon a verdict. Today, the United States Supreme Court has ruled that the Constitution permits less-than-unanimous verdicts in civil or criminal cases. For example, a vote of nine jurors for the plaintiff could be sufficient for the plaintiff to win, even if three jurors think the plaintiff should lose. Whether juries must come to a unanimous verdict in civil or criminal cases is controlled by the law of the state in which the trial takes place. (In the federal courts, federal rules control this issue.) Thus, states may require a unanimous verdict, or they may permit less-than-unanimous verdicts.

If the jurors are unable to arrive at a verdict, the judge declares the jury a **hung jury**; that is, the jurors are said to be deadlocked or unable to reach a decision. The judge then dismisses the case. Such cases, *criminal or civil, may be retried.* However, it costs money and takes time to retry cases. If a case ends in a hung jury, the parties may just drop the case.

Judges may try to encourage the jurors to resolve a case. The judge frequently calls the jurors back to the courtroom to urge them to come to a decision. The forcefulness of this message depends upon the personality of the judge—as does the time the judge gives the jury to resolve a case. Many jurors do not realize they need not resolve a case. Some think they must stay until they arrive at a decision. For this reason, as a strategic matter, an attorney who hopes for a hung jury may find it advantageous to try to get a person on the jury who has participated before in a jury that hung. This person knows the jury need not arrive at a decision and doubtless will tell the other jurors so. This *may* result in less pressure to resolve a case and a higher likelihood it will hang.

The judge, although she or he possesses considerable discretion, may not hold the jurors forever. If the judge keeps the jury too long, the losing party may challenge the verdict on appeal.

The Verdict   When the jury reaches a decision, the jury foreman fills out the appropriate form provided by the judge. The jurors return to the courtroom, and the judge or bailiff announces the jury verdict in open court.

At this point, the attorney for the losing party may ask to *poll* the jury. Each juror is then asked individually if he or she agreed with the verdict. What the attorney polling the jury hopes for is that a juror will state he or she disagreed with the verdict, but was pressured into agreeing with it. In such a case, the judge probably will declare a mistrial and refuse to accept the verdict.

Jurors may render two types of verdicts: a general verdict and a special verdict. In a **general verdict,** the jury decides for one of the parties without any special findings of fact. A **special verdict** requires the jury to answer a number of questions concerning the major issues in the case. The jury must make a special finding on each material issue in the case. The court then applies the law to these facts.

In certain cases, the jury may arrive at a compromise verdict. The jurors may, in a case involving damages, merely add up the amount each juror feels the plaintiff deserves and divide by the number of jurors. This is called a *quotient verdict,* and it is improper. If the jury arrives at a verdict in this manner, the decision of the jury will be set aside. A decision of the jury is supposed to be a verdict of all the jurors. All jurors should agree on the same amount as damages.

Post-Trial   Following the announcement of the jurors' verdict, the judge enters a judgment
Motions   consistent with that verdict. However, if the judge thinks the jury arrived at a decision inconsistent with the evidence presented at trial, the judge may decline to enter the jury's verdict.

Counsel for the losing party, when the jury announces its decision, makes a **motion for a judgment notwithstanding the verdict**. If the court grants this motion, it enters a verdict that the court feels is consistent with the evidence, as opposed to the jury verdict, because the judge feels the jury verdict was not supported by the evidence or the law.

Following the entry of the verdict, usually within thirty days after the end of the trial, counsel for the losing party may make a motion for a new trial. The attorney points out any reversible errors that he or she thinks took place during the trial. If the trial judge agrees, the judge may set the verdict aside and order a new trial.

If the judge denies this motion, the attorneys and clients must either live with the verdict or appeal.

THE APPEAL

A decision to appeal generally must be made fairly quickly after the termination of the trial—for example, within thirty days. The costs associated with an appeal quite often discourage the losing party from appealing the case from the trial court to an appeals court.

Unlike the trial court, an appeals court does not actually hear witnesses and admit evidence.

At the appellate level, the appeals court merely examines the record of the trial court to determine if the trial court made any reversible errors. The appeals court often hears oral arguments of the attorneys in the case. It also receives a written discussion of the case—called a brief—from each side, and in certain cases, from other interested parties. The court examines only that part of the transcript provided to it by the parties. It does not review the entire trial transcript. It does not hear witnesses. The appeals court generally considers only issues of law.

If it agrees with the trial court decision, the appeals court affirms the decision. If it finds an error, it may merely reverse the decision, or it may reverse and remand (send the case back to the trial court) for a new trial.

As a practical matter, it costs a fairly substantial sum of money to appeal. The losing party must evaluate its interests in the case and the expense of the appeal in deciding whether to continue with the case. Sometimes a party may feel the decision was in error but lack the money or the interest to pursue the case to a higher court.

ALTERNATIVE DISPUTE RESOLUTION PROCEDURES

Quite often, rather than going through the process discussed earlier in this chapter, the parties resort to some means to bypass or complement the formal legal system. The following material discusses these techniques.

Settlement   Relatively few legal disputes actually result in a trial; most are settled out of court. There are incentives for litigants to do so. The time and expense of proceeding to trial must be weighed against the advantages of immediate settlement. An injured party may want to collect money damages as soon as possible, thereby hastening an out-of-court settlement. Additionally, settlements can be structured so that payments can be made in ways other than in one lump sum (that is, they may be spread over a number of years). This option also makes settlement attractive to the party who must pay damages.

There is often great delay in getting a case into court, another reason litigants are willing to settle rather than wait for a trial. Then, of course, there is always the risk of loss at trial.

A useful book that a manager might wish to consult on negotiation is *Getting to Yes: Negotiating Agreements Without Giving In*, by Fisher & Ury (Houghton Mifflin, 1992).

Arbitration   Arbitration is sometimes used as a substitute for a trial and is quicker and less costly than litigation in a court. The arbitrator, the person who hears and decides the dispute, is selected by the parties. Frequently, the arbitrator is an authority in the area in which the dispute arises. Arbitration is often used in labor disputes and in construction contract disputes. The parties, informally and at convenient times, submit their cases to an arbitrator. The arbitrator, like a judge, weighs the evidence, applies the law, and renders a decision. Arbitration is another practical alternative to the delay and expense of the court system. In addition to being quicker and cheaper than trying a case in court, arbitration has the advantage of being more informal. Furthermore, if the parties desire to keep the matter out of the public eye, arbitration can be used to keep a matter private. This is a major factor in many cases for resorting to arbitration.

Various means may be used to select an arbitrator. Sometimes as many as three arbitrators hear a case. These arbitrators are often provided by an organization such as the American Arbitration Association.

The arbitration is dependent on the parties' agreement to arbitrate rather than litigate the dispute through a court. If they decide to submit the dispute to binding arbitration, a court will refuse to rehear the entire matter. At most, the court will review the work of the arbitrator for egregious errors. When the parties have signed an agreement that contains a broad arbitration clause, the courts will order the parties to arbitrate any dispute arising under or related to the agreement in the absence of clear evidence the parties did not intend to arbitrate the matter.

LAWSUIT SETTLEMENT

Steve Jobs was one of the founders of Apple Computer, Inc. In June 1985, Jobs was removed from any management responsibility with the firm and later resigned in a dispute with Apple management concerning his role in his new computer business, Next, Inc. Next is an effort to bring sophisticated computer technology to the university, to create a "scholar's workstation."

In September 1985, Apple sued Jobs, contending that he was using Apple research for his other company and that he was enticing key Apple personnel to join Next. Prior to this suit, five of Apple Computer's top young engineers had resigned to join Jobs's new venture. The suit was settled in early 1986. Some key provisions of the settlement barred Jobs from marketing his new scholar's computer for eighteen months and from using certain undisclosed technology in it. Additionally, Apple Computer was given the right to inspect any newly developed computer for thirty days prior to marketing to determine if any Apple proprietary information was used. However, authorities on trade secrets noted that in other technology-use disputes the inspections have lasted for months. Jobs agreed not to hire additional Apple Computer employees for six months. Finally, the parties agreed that any further disputes over the use of technology were to be submitted to arbitration.

Both parties were pleased with the settlement. Apple Computer's general counsel noted that the corporation's goals were met, and rights were protected by the settlement. Jobs, although convinced he would win at trial, was pleased to have the emotional stress of major litigation behind him.

An example of a broad arbitration clause is as follows: "Any controversy or claim arising out of or relating to this contract, or the breach thereof, shall be settled by arbitration in accordance with the Commercial Arbitration Rules of the American Arbitration Association, and judgment upon the award rendered by the Arbitrator(s) may be entered in any Court having jurisdiction thereof." It is not necessary to include such a broad arbitration clause in a contract. The parties may limit the scope of the clause by specifying that only certain matters be arbitrated or by excluding certain kinds of disputes. However, if a contract is ambiguous, the terms of the contract will be construed in favor of arbitrability where such construction is not obviously contrary to the intent of the parties. This point is illustrated by the following case.

Kansas City Royals Baseball Corp. v. Major League Baseball Players Assn.

United States Court of Appeals, Eighth Circuit

532 F.2d 615 (1976)

Dave McNally and Andy Messersmith, two major league baseball players, "played out their options" during the 1975 baseball season in an attempt to gain free-agent status. (McNally retired during the 1975 season, however.) The baseball owners denied Messersmith the right of free agency at the end of the 1975 baseball season because of the practice and contractual term that allowed a team to renew a player's contract on a year-to-year basis for a reasonable number of years. In practice, this tied the player to one team throughout his career unless the team decided to trade him to another team. Messersmith claimed that after he had fulfilled his contract for the 1975 season, he was able to join any other team he chose. Messersmith sought arbitration of his grievance through the arbitration panel set up by the 1973–1975 collective bargaining agreement of the Players Association and the team owners. The arbitrators, by a two-to-one vote, declared Messersmith a free agent. The baseball owners attempted, in federal court, to have the decision overturned.

Heaney, Circuit Judge

Article X of the agreement between the Major League Players Association and the team owners set forth a comprehensive procedure for the resolution of certain grievances. "Grievance" was defined as "a complaint which involves the interpretation of, or compliance with, the provision of any agreement between the Association and the Clubs or any of them, or any agreement between a Player and a Club. . . ." Certain disputes not pertinent here were excepted.

The Club Owners responded to both Messersmith-McNally grievances on October 24, 1975. Their primary contention was that the claims raised fell outside the scope of the agreed upon grievance procedures and were, therefore, not subject to the jurisdiction of the arbitration panel. They argued that Article XV of the 1973 agreement excluded disputes concerning the "core" or "heart" of the reserve system (the system which bound a player to one team) from the grievance procedures set forth in Article X.

A party may be compelled to arbitrate a grievance only if it has agreed to do so. In resolving questions of arbitrability, the courts are guided by Congress's declaration of policy that arbitration is the desirable method for settling labor disputes. Accordingly, a grievance arising under a collective bargaining agreement providing for arbitration must be deemed arbitrable "unless it may be said with positive assurance that the arbitration clause is not susceptible of an interpretation that covers the asserted dispute. Doubts should be resolved in favor of coverage."

If it is determined that the arbitrator had jurisdiction, judicial review of his award is limited to the question of whether it "draws its essence from the collective bargaining agreement." We do not sit as an appellate tribunal to review the merits of the arbitrator's decision.

We begin with the proposition that the language of Article X of the 1973 agreement is sufficiently broad to require arbitration of the Messersmith-McNally grievances. We think this clear because the disputes involve the interpretation of the provisions of agreements between a player or the Players Association and a club or the Club Owners. The grievances require the construction of agreements manifested in paragraphs 9(a) and 10(a) of the Uniform Player's Contract.

Although we find that the grievances are arbitrable under Article X standing alone, we cannot ignore the existence of Article XV, which provides inter alia, that the agreement "does not deal with the reserve system."

We cannot say that Article XV, on its face, constitutes a clear exclusionary provision. First, the precise thrust of the phrase "this Agreement does not deal with the reserve system" is unclear. The agreement incorporates the provisions which comprise the reserve system. Also, the phrase is qualified by the words "except as adjusted or modified hereby." Second, the impact of the language "This Agreement shall in no way prejudice the position . . . of the Parties" is uncertain. Third, the "concerted action" which the parties agree to forego does not clearly include bringing grievances. Fourth, Article XV affords no basis for the Club Owners' distinction between the "core" and the periphery of the reserve system. Finally, Article X(A)(1), which declares certain disputes non-grievable, is silent as to the reserve system. We find, however, that Article XV creates an ambiguity as to whether the grievances here involved are arbitrable. Accordingly, we must look beyond the face of the agreement and determine whether the record as a whole evinces the most forceful evidence of a purpose to exclude these grievances from arbitration.

The weight of the evidence, when viewed as a whole, does not support the conclusion that Article XV was intended to preclude arbitration of any grievances otherwise arbitrable.

We hold that the arbitration panel had jurisdiction to hear and decide the Messersmith-McNally grievances, that the panel's award drew its essence from the collective bargaining agreement, and that the relief fashioned by the District Court was appropriate. Accordingly, the award of the arbitration panel must be sustained, and the District Court's judgment affirmed. In so holding, we intimate no views on the merits of the reserve system. We note, however, that Club Owners and the Players Association's representatives agree that some form of a reserve system is needed if the integrity of the game is to be preserved and if public confidence in baseball is to be maintained.

Parties may elect to arbitrate virtually any dispute. In general, federal law favors the arbitration of all disputes.

In 1925, Congress adopted the Federal Arbitration Act. It made agreements to arbitrate disputes enforceable. The history of the act indicates a desire by Congress to reject the tendency of courts to refuse to defer cases to nonjudicial personnel. A court must stay its proceedings if the parties agreed in advance to arbitrate disputes and if the matter in question is arbitrable.

In the following case, the United States Supreme Court decided that even statutory claims may be arbitrated. This decision sends an important signal to the courts that the Supreme Court wants to encourage the policy set forth in the Federal Arbitration Act that disputes should be arbitrated, if at all possible.

Shearson/American Express, Inc. v. McMahon
United States Supreme Court
107 S.Ct. 2332 (1987)

Customers of Shearson/American Express filed suit against Shearson and its representative who handled their accounts. They alleged violations of the 1934 Securities and Exchange Act (Exchange Act) and of the Racketeer Influenced and Corrupt Organizations Act (RICO). Shearson moved to compel arbitration of the claims pursuant to Section 3 of the Federal Arbitration Act. The Court held both claims were subject to arbitration.

Justice O'Connor

This case presents two questions regarding the enforceability of predispute arbitration agreements between brokerage firms and their customers. The first is whether a claim brought under § 10(b) of the Securities Exchange Act of 1934 (Exchange Act), 48 Stat. 891, 15 U.S.C. § 78j(b), must be sent to arbitration in accordance with the terms of an arbitration agreement. The second is whether a claim brought under the Racketeer Influenced and Corrupt Organizations Act (RICO), 18 U.S.C. § 1961 *et seq.*, must be arbitrated in accordance with the terms of such an agreement.

The Federal Arbitration Act, 9 U.S.C. § 1 *et seq.*, provides the starting point for answering the questions raised in this case. The Act was intended to "revers[e] centuries of judicial hostility to arbitration agreements," *Scherk v. Alberto-Culver Co.*, by "plac[ing] arbitration agreements 'upon the same footing as other contracts.'" The Arbitration Act accomplishes this purpose by providing that arbitration agreements "shall be valid, irrevocable, and enforceable, save upon such grounds as exist at law or in equity for the revocation of any contract." The Act also provides that a court must stay its proceedings if it is satisfied that an issue before it is arbitrable under the agreement, § 3; and it authorizes a

federal district court to issue an order compelling arbitration if there has been a "failure, neglect, or refusal" to comply with the arbitration agreement, § 4.

The Arbitration Act thus establishes a "federal policy favoring arbitration." This duty to enforce arbitration agreements is not diminished when a party bound by an agreement raises a claim founded on statutory rights.

Absent a well-founded claim that an arbitration agreement resulted from the sort of fraud or excessive economic power that "would provide grounds 'for the revocation of any contract,'" the Arbitration Act "provides no basis for disfavoring agreements to arbitrate statutory claims by skewing the otherwise hospitable inquiry into arbitrability."

To defeat application of the Arbitration Act in this case, the McMahons must demonstrate that Congress intended to make an exception to the Arbitration Act for claims arising under RICO and the Exchange Act, an intention discernible from the text, history, or purposes of the statute. We examine the McMahon's arguments regarding the Exchange Act and RICO in turn.

The suitability of arbitration as a means of enforcing Exchange Act rights is evident from our decision in *Scherk*. Although the holding in that case was limited to international agreements, the competence of arbitral tribunals to resolve § 10(b) claims is the same in both settings.

We conclude that Congress did not intend for § 29(a) to bar enforcement of all predispute arbitration agreements. In this case, where the SEC has sufficient statutory authority to ensure that arbitration is adequate to vindicate Exchange Act rights, enforcement does not effect a waiver of "compliance with any provision" of the Exchange Act under § 29(a). Accordingly, we hold the McMahon's agreements to arbitrate Exchange Act claims "enforce[able] . . . in accord with the explicit provisions of the Arbitration Act." *Scherk v. Alberto-Culver Co.*

Unlike the Exchange Act, there is nothing in the text of the RICO statute that even arguably evinces congressional intent to exclude civil RICO claims from the dictates of the Arbitration Act. This silence in the text is matched by silence in the statute's legislative history.

Because RICO's text and legislative history fail to reveal any intent to override the provisions of the Arbitration Act, the McMahons must argue that there is an irreconcilable conflict between arbitration and RICO's underlying purposes.

[W]e find no basis for concluding that Congress intended to prevent enforcement of agreements to arbitrate RICO claims. The McMahons may effectively vindicate their RICO claim in an arbitral forum, and therefore there is no inherent conflict between arbitration and the purposes underlying § 1964(c). Moreover, nothing in RICO's text or legislative history otherwise demonstrates congressional intent to make an exception to the Arbitration Act for RICO claims. Accordingly, the McMahons, "having made the bargain to arbitrate," will be held to their bargain. Their RICO claim is arbitrable under the terms of the Arbitration Act.

Not only does the Federal Arbitration Act encourage the use of alternative dispute resolution, the laws of many states also lend support to a party who wants to resort to other means of resolving his or her dispute short of a full-blown trial. Most states have adopted the Uniform Arbitration Act.

There is little question that an agreement to arbitrate will be enforced in light of the Federal Arbitration Act, the *Shearson/American Express* case, and the state arbitration acts. Courts will compel arbitration if persons refuse to arbitrate a matter.

It probably will come as a surprise to many people that an arbitration award generally is final even if the award has an error of law on its face and a substantial injustice results from the arbitrator's decision. In the following case, the California Supreme Court formally adopted this position.

Moncharsh v. Heily & Blase
Supreme Court of California
832 P.2d 899 (1992)

Philip Moncharsh, an attorney, was hired by a law firm, Heily & Blase. As a condition of employment he signed an agreement that, among other provisions, contained a provision relating to any clients he might take with him in the event he left the firm. The contract provided that Heily & Blase would receive eighty percent of any fee generated from such clients and Moncharsh would receive twenty percent of any fee generated. The contract provided that any dispute arising out of the contract would be subject to final and binding arbitration.

After leaving the firm, Moncharsh continued to represent six clients for whom he had worked while at Heily & Blase. When Blase learned that Moncharsh had obtained fees in these six cases, he demanded eighty percent of the fees generated by Moncharsh. Thereafter, the parties invoked the arbitration clause and submitted the matter to an arbitrator. The arbitrator ruled in Heily & Blase's favor.

Moncharsh petitioned the superior court to vacate and modify the arbitration award. He contended that the arbitrator failed to apply the law correctly. Nonetheless, the California Supreme Court held that the arbitrator's decision was not subject to review.

Lucas, Judge

We granted review and directed the parties to address the limited issue of whether, and under what conditions, a trial court may review an arbitrator's decision.

Title 9 of the Code of Civil Procedure, as enacted and periodically amended by the Legislature, represents a comprehensive statutory scheme regulating private arbitration in this state. Through this detailed statutory scheme, the Legislature has expressed a strong public policy in favor of arbitration as a speedy and relatively inexpensive means of dispute resolution.

The arbitration clause included in the employment agreement in this case specifically states that the arbitrator's decision would be both binding and final. The parties to this action thus clearly intended the arbitrator's decision would be final. Even had there been no such expression of intent, however, it is the general rule that parties to a private arbitration impliedly agree that the arbitrator's decision will be both binding and final. Indeed, the very essence of the term "arbitration" [in this context] connotes a binding award.

Because the decision to arbitrate grievances evinces the parties' intent to bypass the judicial system and thus avoid potential delays at the trial and appellate levels, arbitral finality is a core component of the parties' agreement to submit to arbitration. Thus, an arbitration decision is final and conclusive because the parties have agreed that it be so. By ensuring that an arbitrator's decision is final and binding, courts simply assure that the parties receive the benefit of their bargain.

Because it vindicates the intentions of the parties that the award be final, and because an arbitrator is not ordinarily constrained to decide according to the rule of law, it is the general rule that the merits of the controversy between the parties are not subject to judicial review. More specifically, courts will not review the validity of the arbitrator's reasoning.

Thus, it is the general rule that, with narrow exceptions, an arbitrator's decision cannot be reviewed for errors of fact or law. In reaffirming this general rule, we recognize there is a risk that the arbitrator will make a mistake. That risk, however, is acceptable for two reasons. First, by voluntarily submitting to arbitration, the parties have agreed to bear that risk in return for a quick, inexpensive, and conclusive resolution to their dispute.

A second reason why we tolerate the risk of an erroneous decision is because the Legislature has reduced the risk to the parties of such a decision by providing for judicial review in circumstances involving serious problems with the award itself, or with the fairness of the arbitration process. Private arbitration proceedings are governed by title 9 of the Code of Civil Procedure, sections 1280–1294.2. Section 1286.2 sets forth the grounds for vacation of an arbitrator's award. It states in pertinent part: "The court shall vacate the award if the court determines that:

(a) The award was procured by corruption, fraud or other undue means;

(b) There was corruption in any of the arbitrators;

(c) The rights of such party were substantially prejudiced by misconduct of a neutral arbitrator;

(d) The arbitrators exceeded their powers and the award cannot be corrected without affecting the merits of the decision upon the controversy submitted; or

(e) The rights of such party were substantially prejudiced by the refusal of the arbitrators to postpone the hearing upon sufficient cause being shown therefor or by the refusal of the arbitrators to hear evidence material to the controversy or by other conduct of the arbitrators contrary to the provisions of this title."

In addition, section 1286.6 provides grounds for correction of an arbitration award. That section states in pertinent part: "The court, unless it vacates the award pursuant to Section 1286.2, shall correct the award and confirm it as corrected if the court determines that:

(a) There was an evident miscalculation of figures or an evident mistake in the description of any person, thing or property referred to in the award;

(b) The arbitrators exceeded their powers but the award may be corrected without affecting the merits of the decision upon the controversy submitted; or

(c) The award is imperfect in a matter of form, not affecting the merits of the controversy."

The Legislature has thus substantially reduced the possibility of certain forms of error infecting the arbitration process itself. . . . In light of these statutory provisions, the residual risk to the parties of an arbitrator's erroneous decision represents an acceptable cost—obtaining the expedience and financial savings that the arbitration process provides—as compared to the judicial process.

Although it is thus the general rule that an arbitrator's decision is not ordinarily reviewable for error by either the trial or appellate court, Moncharsh contends that a court may review an arbitrator's decision if an error of law is apparent on the face of the award and that error causes substantial injustice.

In *Pacific Vegetable Oil Corp. v. C.S.T. Ltd.*, it was bluntly held that "the merits of the controversy between the parties are not subject to judicial review." After surveying cases that note an arbitrator need not rule in conformity with the law, the court made a dramatic conclusion: "Under these cases it must be held that in the absence of some limiting clause in the arbitration agreement, the merits of the award, either on questions of fact or of law, may not be reviewed except as provided in the statute."

This view is consistent with a large majority of decisions in other states. Although California has not adopted the Uniform Arbitration Act, more than half the states have done so. The statutory grounds to vacate a private arbitration award set forth in the uniform law largely mirror those codified in section 1286.2, and most states have concluded that these grounds are exclusive.

We conclude that an award reached by an arbitrator pursuant to a contractual agreement to arbitrate is not subject to judicial review except on the grounds set forth in sections 1286.2 (to vacate) and 1286.6 (for correction). Further, the existence of an error of law apparent on the face of the award that causes substantial injustice does not provide grounds for judicial review.

We conclude that Moncharsh has demonstrated no reason why the strong presumption in favor of the finality of the arbitral award should not apply here.

The decision in the *Moncharsh* case certainly suggests that a person ought to be exceedingly cautious about signing contracts that require all disputes to be settled by final and binding arbitration. Many courts, like California, take the position that the decision of an arbitrator will not be set aside even if the arbitrator failed to follow the law in arriving at his or her decision.

Among the numerous problems associated with the U.S. legal system is the fact that many attorneys make money by billing on an hourly basis. If an attorney bills on an hourly basis, in the absence of a surfeit of business, the system tends to reward the attorney who prolongs cases as much as possible. Once the parties resolve their dispute, the meter stops running. Furthermore, many attorneys are combative by nature. They want to take a case to trial and slug it out with the other side. People with such a macho outlook on life may view any move to settle the case as a sign of weakness.

Sandra Day O'Connor

In a speech to students at Wake Forest University, U.S. Supreme Court Justice Sandra Day O'Connor stated that lawyers should not resort to the confrontational, ''Rambo-style tactics'' to win a case. (Sylvester Stallone created the fictional war hero, John Rambo, which he depicted in several Holly-wood films.) Justice O'Connor stated that the U.S. system of discovery that allows for an exchange of information prior to trial leads to a confrontational style of litigation. ''It is better to use our energy working on a case rather than working over an opponent,'' she observed.

'' 'Rambo-style' Courtroom Tactics Hurt Law Profession, Justice O'Connor Says,'' *K. C. Star*, April 4, 1993, A.10.

In an atmosphere like this, clients must act aggressively to take control of their own cases. In the final analysis, the client, not the client's attorney, must live with the outcome to a dispute. Alternative dispute resolution procedures give a client the chance to hear, from the other side, the shortcomings in his or her position and the strengths of the other side's case, and can help a client reach a mutually satisfactory settlement with another party in an expeditious fashion.

Court-Annexed Arbitration

Unlike a contractual agreement that requires arbitration of disputes, or unlike voluntary agreements to arbitrate after a dispute arises, sometimes courts order a court-annexed arbitration. The courts that utilize this form of alternative dispute resolution compel the parties to certain disputes selected by the courts to engage in nonbinding arbitration of their cases. The judges hope to encourage the parties, after hearing a miniversion of the facts and issues of the case, to resolve the case short of a full-blown jury trial. In this way, the judges attempt to reduce their caseloads by shifting cases to a court-annexed arbitration proceeding.

Many federal courts use court-annexed arbitration. If a party disagrees with the decision of the arbitrator, the case proceeds to a full-blown trial in front of a judge.

A lot of aggressive lawyers like court-annexed procedures such as court annexed arbitration because there is less fear of showing weaknesses. The court *orders* the parties to engage in revealing any limitations in the case to one's client and to some extent to the other side.

Mediation

One procedure used to try to expedite the resolution of disputes is *mediation*. All federal courts are now using mediation and many large corporations routinely utilize it. Both arbitration and mediation are commonly used in the labor-relations field. The federal government operates the Federal Mediation and Conciliation Service to help parties to a labor dispute mediate their differences. A number of private companies now provide mediators: The American Arbitration Associa-

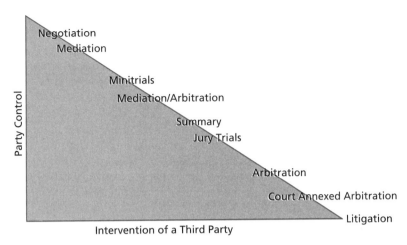

Figure 3.4   Degree of Control That a Party May Exercise over a Dispute

tion, Judicial Arbitration & Mediation Services, Inc. (JAMS), United States Arbitration, Endispute and Judicate among others. Private industry is thus beginning to challenge the state-owned monopoly in dispute resolution.

Most of the time, no one forces the parties to mediate—although a court may forcefully urge the parties to mediate their case. (In some types of cases, for example, domestic relations, courts around the country now require the parties to participate in mandatory mediation.) The parties generally voluntarily agree to mediate their disagreement which keeps them in control.

NO POWER TO BIND

Look at Figure 3.4. This illustration graphically depicts the loss in control that *all* the parties to litigation experience depending on the type of dispute resolution mechanism they utilize to resolve a disagreement. When parties rely upon a formal judicial trial, they in essence transfer the power to settle their dispute from themselves to someone else. A party involved in a dispute ought to ask himself or herself: If I can end this disagreement myself, why should I transfer the power to resolve it to someone else?

If a person fails to understand the strengths and weaknesses of both his or her case and the other side's case, that person may opt for a judicial trial because the litigant incorrectly appraises the likelihood of prevailing at trial. Many clients regrettably overestimate the prospects of winning and possess unrealistic expectations with respect to what they will recover. If the attorneys on both sides of a case attempt to keep each other from learning about weaknesses in the case, it becomes very difficult for anyone to objectively access the prospects of winning or losing at trial. A client needs to attempt to view a conflict *objectively*.

In the American legal system, built as it is on a confrontational, adversarial, macho mode of resolving disagreements, litigants cannot necessarily count upon their attorneys to help them see the case *objectively*. Additionally, an attorney may fear that a client will misinterpret any comments with respect to flaws in the case. The client might think the attorney is "in cahoots" with the other side, is not aggressive enough or is incompetent. Consequently, many attorneys would rather not point out such shortcomings in a case to their clients. Mediation, as well as the other alternative dispute resolution procedures, gives a client the chance to hear, from the other side, the shortcomings in his or her position and the strengths of the other side's case.

Unlike an arbitration proceeding in which the arbitrator actually decides the case for the parties, in mediation, the mediator tries to help the parties work out their differences. A mediator searches for ways to satisfy and promote the mutual interests of the parties. Mediation evolved to assist parties who wanted to maintain a relationship but who were having trouble negotiating. The mediator helps the parties negotiate and at the same time maintain their relationship.

Mediation is thus *consensual.* Mediation is voluntary, as opposed to the coercive, authoritarian approach followed in the judicial system. Mediators have *no power*—other than the mediator's ability to facilitate negotiation. The mediator works with the parties to attempt to facilitate negotiation. The mediator focuses on the parties' *needs*—not on their *rights*. This gets the parties into a problem-solving mode. A judge, on the other hand, must in effect force a decision on the parties based on the parties' rights.

Different mediators employ different styles of mediation. A commonly followed approach is a form of shuttle diplomacy. Following an opening statement by both sides, the mediator speaks in private with each side and goes back and forth between the parties attempting to arrive at a settlement of the case. In contrast to the deal maker style of mediation, some mediators view themselves merely as orchestrators. Rather than trying to strike a deal, they merely want to facilitate discussion. Orchestrators take a less active role in the process than deal makers.

Not every case is suitable for mediation. Timing is critical. At the outset of discovery, for example, a case might not be ready for mediation. The parties must have a desire to settle the dispute. They must trust one another. If one of the parties wants to create a new precedent in the law, that party probably will insist upon a trial and appeal in order to get a change in the case law.

Unlike in the case of an arbitration proceeding, a decision of a mediator generally may be appealed. If the parties fail to arrive at a settlement of the disagreement, they can proceed on to trial. The parties have much to gain and relatively little to lose by mediating their dispute.

Minitrial   Another method of resolving a dispute is the **minitrial.** Corporations sometimes utilize the minitrial to resolve their differences. Each party to a dispute sends a person with decision-making authority to represent it on a panel. These people, along with a neutral third party, serve as a panel whose function is to listen to evidence presented by the parties according to expedited and streamlined procedures. The hope is that after hearing the evidence, the parties will be able to come to some sort of settlement of their dispute. If they do not settle the dispute in this manner, they can always try the case at a later date. Minitrials are currently being extensively used in business litigation.

Summary Jury Trial   The **summary jury trial** is the jury equivalent of a minitrial. Many federal judges impanel a regular jury for use in a summary jury trial. The judge may or may not tell the members of the jury that their decision will not be final. In other cases, the parties themselves assemble a group of persons to act as jurors. The lawyers representing each side present their cases in a capsulized form. The attorneys then instruct the jury to reach an advisory verdict. The jury members provide the parties with their advisory evaluation of the case. In some jurisdictions, the rules permit the attorneys to question the jurors to divine their reasoning. This helps the parties evaluate the case. To the extent that a summary jury trial simulates the prospective jury trial, the litigants get a pretrial advance view as to the reaction of jurors to the case. One also hears both attorneys expound on the major issues likely to arise at trial. If the summary jury indicates that it views the position of one side as weak, that party ought to seriously consider compromising its position and settling the case.

Settlement Conferences

As noted earlier in this chapter, prior to trial, judges call the parties together for a pretrial conference. This conference, at which the judge is present, can be used to encourage the parties to settle the case. In effect, a judge can act as a mediator at the conference.

Expert Fact Finding

With expert fact finding, the parties employ a neutral third party to make a decision, based either on a limited set of facts or, in some cases, on a set of facts concerning the entire case. Thus, a decision of the expert fact finder may resolve only a few issues rather than the entire case. As the decision of the expert fact finder is similar to an agreement to arbitrate, it probably will be enforced.

Private Judging

More and more parties throughout the country now contract with a referee to hear their dispute. The referee acts just like a judge in a case—and quite often former judges serve as referees. The referee determines the facts of the case and applies the law to these facts in order to arrive at a resolution of the disagreement. These decisions are treated like court decisions and are therefore appealable. A California state statute permits persons engaged in civil trials to request that the case be heard by a private referee.

Many people dislike the lottery system by which the government assigns judges to hear a case. With the ''Rent a Judge'' system, the parties can set their own rules to govern the procedure, meet in any place they desire and may select anyone they want to act as the judge in their case.

Critics argue that the ''Rent a Judge'' system of resolving disputes encourages the best judges to leave the bench because they earn more money working for private dispute resolution companies. Important cases are handled in secret and thus the public is kept in the dark about the proceedings. The secrecy of the proceedings troubles many people. Litigants can bypass the long wait for trial in the public court system and receive an immediate airing of their dispute should they so desire it. Furthermore, some states allow the parties to bypass the trial court system entirely and appeal the decision of a private judge to an appellate court. This accelerated access to justice creates a two-tier system of justice in America—one for the affluent and the public system for everyone else.

Organizations such as Judicial Arbitration and Mediation Services, Inc. of California provide such services. JAMS employs only former judges for their cases.

Private Panels

Because certain companies find themselves embroiled in disputes with consumers, it behooves them to set up procedures for handling disagreements. For example, your local Better Business Bureau probably operates a mediation and arbitration procedure in which it attempts to resolve disputes between disgruntled automobile buyers and automobile manufacturers. A consumer with a complaint fills out a complaint form and turns it in to the Better Business Bureau. The Better Business Bureau then attempts to mediate the dispute. If that fails, the consumer may then resort to arbitration. Alternatively, some trade associations operate their own arbitration panels—for example, new car dealers operate a panel called AUTOCAP.

Mediation/ Arbitration

This form of dispute resolution combines both mediation and arbitration. The case starts as a conventional mediation proceeding. If the parties are unable to resolve their disagreement through mediation, the case proceeds to *binding* arbitration.

Small Claims Courts

For the average person, the cost of hiring an attorney for representation in a minor matter often exceeds the amount sought. Courts generally refuse to award litigants attorney's fees. This means that if a person sues to recover a small amount, the attorney collects a fee but the client fails to recover anything. The American Bar Association has long recognized the fact that legal services often are out of the reach of the middle class. For this reason, the ABA worked to encourage the states to create small claims courts. Today, all the states permit persons to file suits in these alternative forums. Most states permit suits for between one thousand and five thousand dollars in their small claims courts.

Suppose that Mary purchases a refrigerator from Acme. A month later, the refrigerator stops working. Acme refuses to repair the machine. Mary cannot afford to pay an attorney fifty to one hundred dollars per hour to litigate this matter. She instead turns to her state's small claims court. Her claim is for five hundred dollars. She fills out a petition at the court and subpoenas Acme. The firm must then appear or risk a default judgment, which means that Mary automatically wins her case if Acme does not appear. The proceedings in small claims court tend to be more informal than at a trial. In this case, Mary presents her position, Acme presents its position, and then the judge rules.

Advantages to Using Alternative Dispute Resolution Procedures

As indicated in this chapter, in the 1980s the courts became much more receptive to the use of alternative dispute resolution (ADR) procedures. No doubt the large number of suits flooding some courts contributed to this change in attitude. Courts also have come to realize the substantial advantages associated with settling cases in some manner other than the traditional courtroom battle. These advantages are described in the following paragraphs.

The classic trial takes a great deal of time and money. Delays in cases are legendary. Trials sometimes result in adverse publicity which a firm would like to avoid. Worse yet, many participants in trials often find the entire process to be alienating and frustrating. A judge or jury ends up *imposing* a decision on the parties—a decision that often leaves one side the winner and the other side the loser.

Alternative dispute resolution procedures are designed to try to *facilitate* a settlement—rather than force a decision upon persons unwilling to come to a voluntary agreement. By involving all the parties in a dispute, the process facilitates a settlement. The fact that the parties become more involved in the resolution of their dispute, and have a direct role in settling it, encourages them to reach an agreement.

Quite often the participants in an ADR procedure listen to a short presentation of the facts and theories of the case. The parties try to reduce even a major case to just a brief presentation of the crux of the dispute. By getting people to appear at this presentation, even if they are somewhat hostile, the parties hear a succinct version of the case. However, it should be kept in mind that ADR clauses in contracts do not *compel* a party to come to an agreement. The goal of this process is to bring the parties together to try to facilitate a settlement. If a party cannot be persuaded to settle, he or she is always free to insist upon a trial. The information presented may persuade the party to settle the matter. In such a case, it may be possible to preserve any business relationship the parties had in the past—as opposed to a trial that ends in a bitter resolution, in which case the parties may even refuse to talk to one another in the future.

Other positive features associated with handling a case in this manner are the fact that such procedures generally are nonbinding and confidential. People have little to lose by listening to this process. If they disagree with the proposed resolution of the dispute, they may generally take the case to trial anyway. Additionally, a settlement at this point prevents most other people from hearing of the dispute. Suppose that the transmission in Acme Automobiles' Victory automobiles tends to fail at twenty thousand miles. If a number of persons take their cases to trial, these trials might attract attention in the newspapers and on television. This adverse publicity may encourage other persons to file suit. On the other hand, quietly settling these disputes short of trial tends to squelch publicity. This, in turn, may result in very few persons learning about experiences of other consumers.

The Pinto automobile serves as an illustration of the dangers of publicity. In the 1970s, some people filed suit over injuries arising from the flange-mounted gasoline tank in the Pinto. Rather than quickly settling the suits, Ford chose to take the cases to trial and then on to the appeals courts. This strategy merely generated more publicity about the defect in the Pinto. In addition to making the corporation look bad, this publicity put ideas in the heads of plaintiffs' lawyers. Numerous suits followed.

United States Federal Rule of Civil Procedure 68 also favors the use of ADR. Rule 68 can be used against a person who refuses to accept a reasonable offer of settlement. This rule permits a judge to assess costs against a person who turned down an offer of settlement and then won less at trial than the amount proposed as a settlement prior to trial.

Disadvantages to Using Alternative Dispute Resolution Procedures

• MAY LOOSE RIGHT TO APPEAL
• MAY BE BAD DECISION w/ NO RECOURSE

Some people feel it is useless to engage in alternatives to a trial in certain instances. For example, if the other side obstinately refuses to cooperate in any fashion, and if she or he agrees to go to an ADR proceeding only as a result of a court order, one might question whether such a person would keep an open mind with respect to any proposed settlement that might be suggested. As noted earlier, however, these procedures are designed to *facilitate* settlements. It is possible that even a totally hostile person might profit from participating in such procedures, since she or he hears the entire case.

A very serious criticism of such proceedings is they are often conducted in secret. This keeps information about the cases out of the hands of the general public. Furthermore, handling a case in this fashion may deprive the courts of an opportunity to handle a matter of great public importance and thus create a precedent that will govern other similar cases. It could also be argued that the whole process of alternative dispute resolution proceedings is creating a two-tier system of justice—one for the affluent and the public system for everyone else.

Enforcement

Although a contract may contain a provision for alternative dispute resolution, one of the parties to the agreement may refuse to cooperate in the process. In such a case, the question comes up: Can a party be *forced* to engage in some form of pretrial alternative dispute resolution procedure? It seems somewhat questionable at first to force a person to participate in a process that he or she refuses to cooperate in. On the other hand, if a court forces a person to listen to an abbreviated presentation of the facts and issues, and to both sides of the case, he or she, no matter how obstinate, may decide upon hearing the facts that a trial will be a useless waste of time and money. Furthermore, such a person may see some merit to the other side's position. This may soften his or her resolve. That person may not feel as bad about settling the matter voluntarily as the loser in a trial might feel.

There is some question about the enforceability of ADR clauses in contracts because some courts still question the value of forcing a person to participate in a voluntary proceeding. The following case is an example of a court decision that forced the parties to participate.

AMF Inc. v. Brunswick Corp.
United States District Court, Eastern District New York
621 F. Supp. 456 (1985)

AMF alleged that Brunswick had advertised certain automatic scoring devices in a false and deceptive manner. In 1983, the parties resolved a suit over this matter by agreeing to submit any future dispute involving an advertised claim of data-based comparative superiority of any bowling product to an advisory third party, the National Advertising Division (NAD) of the Council of Better Business Bureaus. In

March of 1985, Brunswick advertised a synthetic laminated material called Armor Plate 3000 in the *Bowler's Journal.* The advertisement strongly suggested that research supported the durability of the Brunswick lanes as compared to the wood lanes produced by AMF. AMF asked for the supporting research. Brunswick refused to turn it over. AMF then invoked the dispute clause and requested that Brunswick provide substantiation to an independent third party. Brunswick refused. AMF brought this action to compel Brunswick to submit its data to the NAD for nonbinding arbitration. The court ruled that Brunswick must submit the data to the NAD.

Weinstein, Chief Judge

Whether or not the agreement be deemed one to arbitrate, it is an enforceable contract to utilize a confidential advisory process in a matter of serious concern to the parties. The agreement may be enforced in equity. Through the equitable relief of specific performance Brunswick may be compelled to surrender its "comparative data based" information to the NAD for inquiry as to deceptiveness.

The Second Circuit has recently made clear the strong public policy requiring agreements between parties in settlement of litigation to be construed as enforceable contracts. *See Berger v. Heckler.* In the words of the Court of Appeals:

> A defendant who has obtained the benefits of a . . . termination of the litigation . . . cannot then be permitted to ignore such affirmative obligations as were imposed by the decree.

The alternative dispute resolution (ADR) procedure agreed upon in the settlement is designed to reduce the acrimony associated with protracted litigation and to improve the chances of resolving future advertising disputes. This form of ADR is designed to keep disputes of this kind out of court.

General public policy favors support of alternatives to litigation when these alternatives serve the interests of the parties and of judicial administration. Here AMF and Brunswick agreed in June 1983 that a special ADR mechanism would serve them better than litigation. Such decisions are encouraged by no less an observer than the Chief Justice of the United States. In his words, ADR devices are often superior to litigation "in terms of cost, time, and human wear and tear."

Brunswick shall submit its substantiation for the following claim: "Continuing independent research projects that Armor Plate 3000 will now last over 20 years before the possible need arises to replace a small lane area much like replacing a broken board in a wood lane" to the National Advertising Division of the Council of Better Business Bureaus, Inc., for an advisory opinion as provided for in Paragraph 9 of the Agreement of June 30, 1983.

So Ordered.

A business may choose to voluntarily appear at an ADR hearing. Even if a representative of a business is voluntarily present, the company may be making only a token appearance. In such an event, one of the parties may allege a breach of the covenant of good faith and fair dealing inherent in any contract. Good faith requires that the parties not do anything to deprive the other party to the contract of the benefits of the agreement. One could argue that the refusal to participate in an ADR proceeding or the refusal to cooperate in the proceedings constitutes bad faith. The nonbreaching party may be able to obtain some damages for a bad-faith breach of contract, as the *Gilling* v. *Eastern Airlines* case illustrates.

Gilling v. Eastern Airlines, Inc.
United States District Court, District of New Jersey
680 F. Supp. 169 (1988)

Passengers aboard an Eastern Airlines flight to Martinique allege they were wrongfully ejected from their flight during a stopover in St. Croix. They allege numerous claims against Eastern, among them breach of contract and negligence. The court referred the matter to compulsory arbitration. The defendants did not attend the arbitration. They appeared through their attorneys. The Eastern attorney presented summaries of Eastern's position and read a few passages from depositions and interrogatories. The arbitrator found for the passengers. Eastern thereafter moved for a trial de novo. The passengers argued that Eastern should be denied a trial de novo in light of its failure to participate meaningfully in the arbitration. The court referred the matter back to the arbitrator for a factual finding on this question. The arbitrator found that Eastern did not participate in the arbitration proceeding in a meaningful manner. The court permitted the trial de novo but assessed certain costs to Eastern.

Sarokin, District Judge

General Rule 47(E)(3) provides that the arbitration hearing may proceed in the absence of any party who, after notice, fails to be present. In the event that a party fails to participate in the arbitration process in a meaningful manner, as determined by the arbitrator, the Court may impose appropriate sanctions, including, but not limited to, the striking of any demand for a trial de novo filed by that party.

Defendants ask the court to vacate the arbitrator's finding that they did not participate in the arbitration in a meaningful manner. After examining General Rule 47, the court is unable to discover any standard of review of an arbitrator's findings. The rule simply authorizes the court to devise a sanction "in the event that a party fails to participate in the arbitration process in a meaningful manner, *as determined by the arbitrator.*"

The arbitrator, examining the totality of the defendants' participation at the arbitration, concluded that the reading of brief position summaries and deposition and interrogatory excerpts did not amount to meaningful participation in the context of this case. The court concludes that this finding was supported by substantial evidence and was not clearly erroneous.

Defendants argue that the enforcement of General Rule 47(E)(3) against them would deprive them of their constitutional right to a jury trial and conflict with the Federal Rules of Civil Procedure. The court notes that compulsory pre-trial arbitration procedures like the one at issue in this case have withstood constitutional attack.

The court, however, need not reach the defendants' constitutional claim, for the rule does not require the court to deny the application for trial de novo. Rather, it allows the court to choose an "appropriate sanction," only one of which is the rather draconian striking of a demand for trial de novo.

In this case, where the defendants demonstrated such contempt for the arbitration proceeding, it is only fair that they should have to pay for it. The court therefore orders that defendants reimburse plaintiffs for all costs and fees which they incurred in preparing for and participating in the arbitration, as well as costs and fees incurred in opposing defendants' demand for a trial de novo.

Many contracts contain negotiate-in-good-faith clauses in which the parties to the contract agree to discuss certain contractual matters in the future. Most courts will enforce an obligation to bargain in good faith.

As an alternative to a *good-faith clause* in a contract, a party might insert a clause in the contract that prohibits a party from filing suit for a certain predetermined period of time, such as a month. These clauses generally require a party to give notice to the other party to a contract if it intends to litigate. This starts the time limit running. Courts tend to enforce such an agreement.

Other contracts include a *liquidated damages clause*—a clause that specifies how much the aggrieved party will receive in the event of a breach of contract. If the other party fails to cooperate in good faith, one could obtain damages under the **liquidated damages** clause.

Litigants quite often rely upon negotiation to settle their disputes. Most cases arrive at some form of negotiated settlement of the dispute. The parties need only cooperate in the process. Parties can strike any sort of bargain they desire through negotiations. In the process, they may save themselves time and money.

SUMMARY

The American system of civil litigation is adversarial in form; that is, each party to a case is permitted the opportunity to present his or her version of the dispute. It is widely believed that this process is the best possible system to achieve a just and fair resolution of disputes.

In order to institute a suit, the plaintiff must file a petition with the appropriate court. In response to the petition, the defendant files an answer with the court. Suits may not be instituted willy-nilly. A court must have the power to hear the type of dispute described in the petition. This is referred to as a court having jurisdiction over a particular type of dispute and over the parties to the suit. Only recently has the United States Supreme Court permitted state courts to obtain personal jurisdiction over persons who are not physically present within the state.

If a given case is not settled prior to trial, which is the outcome of some disputes, a party may elect to have a jury trial under certain circumstances. Attorneys to a case are permitted some control over the composition of the jury. They may ask questions of prospective jury members during the voir dire, and depending on the answers received, the attorneys may disqualify certain persons from serving on the jury panel. The process of selecting a jury involves a good deal of psychological thinking on the part of attorneys.

A trial gets under way after the opening statements by the attorneys trying the case. The rules of evidence govern which and in what form statements can or cannot be admitted. Witnesses may be cross-examined by the opposing side. At the conclusion of the presentation of the evidence, the attorneys present their closing arguments, the judge instructs the jury as to the applicable law, and the jury retires to deliberate the case. Once the jury verdict is announced, the losing party usually makes a motion for a new trial. If that fails, the losing party must either live with the judgment or attempt to get it reversed on appeal.

In 1925, Congress adopted the Federal Arbitration Act. This act made agreements to arbitrate disputes enforceable. Even so, for years the courts permitted people to try cases rather than submit them to arbitration. The courts regarded arbitration agreements as an infringement on their power to resolve disputes.

The flood of litigation in recent years has altered the attitude of the courts with respect to alternative methods of resolving disputes. Recent United States Supreme Court cases support the enforcement of alternative dispute resolution procedures and, in particular, arbitration agreements. The Court permits compulsory arbitration of even statutory matters, such as those involving the trading of securities.

But contractual agreements today contain many other alternatives to a trial besides arbitration agreements: mediation, court-annexed arbitration, minitrials, summary jury trials, settlement conferences, expert fact finding, private judging, private panels, and small claims courts. Parties use these alternatives to litigation to facilitate a settlement rather than forcing one on a party. These dispute resolution proceedings involve the parties in the resolution of their disagreements. Additionally, these agreements are generally nonbinding and confidential.

The courts today must enforce arbitration agreements, even those dealing with statutory matters. The law is evolving with respect to the enforceability of other types of alternative dispute resolution proceedings; however, many courts will force parties to participate in them. Furthermore, parties often may be penalized if they fail to participate in such proceedings in good faith.

Thus, we clearly are entering a new era in which people will be expected to explore means of resolving their disputes other than the traditional trial in front of a judge or jury.

REVIEW QUESTIONS

1. Define the following terms:
   a. Adversary system
   b. Burden of proof
   c. Deposition
   d. Discovery
   e. Expert fact finding
   f. Mediation
   g. Minitrial
   h. Peremptory challenge
   i. Petit jury
   j. Preponderance of the evidence
   k. Private judging
   l. Private panels
   m. Settlement conferences
   n. Small claims court
   o. Statute of limitations
   p. Summary jury trial
   q. Voir dire

2. Mary was injured in an automobile accident on August 30, 1992. The accident was caused by Tom, who negligently drove his car through a red light and struck the vehicle being driven by Mary. The statute of limitations for filing an automobile negligence lawsuit is two years. When must Mary file her lawsuit? Why does such a rule exist? If Mary files her suit after the date you gave above, are there any additional facts that could be added to this problem to allow Mary to argue that her claim should be allowed to proceed?

3. Discuss the advantages and abuses that exist in our system of discovery. What would you suggest as possible remedies for the abuses?

4. Sally bought a bag of apples, which was to have contained one dozen. After she re-

turned home from the store, she discovered that the bag contained only eleven apples. Sally wants to sue the store for breach of contract. Would you advise her to file that suit? If so, why? If not, why not? Are there alternatives other than filing a lawsuit that Sally might pursue?

5. Duren was indicted for murder and robbery in Missouri. The state's jury selection procedure allowed women an automatic exemption from jury duty. As a result, approximately fifteen percent of the jurors on the jury panels at trial were women. Duren's jury of twelve was chosen from a panel of forty-eight men and five women. He challenged the fairness of his trial in light of the automatic exemption of women from the jury. Is Duren entitled to a jury panel with more women?

6. Do attorneys select people for a jury solely on the basis of whether a person appears to be fair and impartial?

7. Linda Anaya challenged the jury selection in her case. She alleged that blue-collar workers were underrepresented in the jury pool. Does a jury pool of this nature violate the fair-cross-section requirement?

8. International Securities requires that any dispute arising between its customers and its brokers be submitted to arbitration. What is an arbitration proceeding?

9. Rodriguez de Quijas signed a standard customer agreement with Shearson/American Express brokerage house when he set up his stock account. The contract obligates the parties to settle any controversies through binding arbitration. De Quijas sued Shearson and his broker. He alleged that his money was lost in unauthorized and fraudulent transactions. One of the allegations involved a violation of the 1933 Securities Act. Must de Quijas arbitrate his claim under this act?

10. What are some of the advantages associated with using an alternative dispute resolution proceeding?

11. Are there any disadvantages to employing alternative dispute resolution procedures to resolve a dispute?

12. Acme Brick Corporation enters into a contract with Smith's Pool Company. The contract provides that any dispute between the parties will be resolved in a summary jury trial. What is a summary jury trial? Can Smith be forced to participate in this proceeding even if he feels it is a waste of his time?

13. Stevens Construction Company entered into a contract with Acme Electrical Supply. The contract requires the parties to submit any dispute to a private judge. A dispute arises between the parties. Acme appears at the proceeding, but presents no evidence. What is a private judge? Can Acme be penalized for its failure to participate?

14. Rockford Corporation entered into a contract with Acme Corporation. The contract provided that any dispute arising out of the contract would be subject to final and binding arbitration. A dispute arose between the parties. Rockford asked for the dispute to be submitted to an arbitrator. After reading the decision of the arbitrator, the president of Acme felt that the arbitrator misunderstood the law. He vowed to take the case to court. Will he be able to get the decision of the arbitrator reversed by a court?

CHAPTER 4

Judicial Reasoning and Decision Making

- The Judge As a Person: The Personality Factor
- Factors in Judicial Decision Making

The study of the methods by which judges reach decisions provides an understanding of the functioning of courts in our system, as well as an understanding of the law in general. This chapter will examine a number of important components that make up a judicial decision. One factor, the personality of the judge, is not to be found in any written judicial opinion. Yet it has an important effect on the outcome of any case. The other factors that influence how a judge makes a decision are history and custom, a balancing of the various interests involved in a particular case, deferring to other branches of government, reaching a decision that is ''right'' under the circumstances, applying social science studies, and the doctrine of stare decisis, or the application of legal precedent. These factors are used by the judge to justify whatever decision is finally reached. As will be shown, judicial opinions may well be based on one or more of these factors' being applied to a given case.

However, no set mixture of ingredients combines to make a judicial decision. The weight of each factor may differ with each judge and with each case before a judge. Therefore, a study of the components of judicial decision making should provide a needed supplement to the legal rules that are presented throughout this text. Determining what the law is in a given situation is far more complex than simply looking up the relevant legal rules. Gaining an understanding of the nature of judicial decision making will provide the manager with a more sophisticated view of the legal environment.

THE JUDGE AS A PERSON: THE PERSONALITY FACTOR

A frequently heard saying about our legal system is that it is a system of laws, not of people. As with most folk wisdom—''wind from the west, fish bite the best''— there is an element of truth in it. Our system of government and the decisions of our courts are based upon established rules and procedures that apply to all parties affected by the system. For instance, the general rule that contracts for the sale of land must be in writing before they will be enforceable in a court of law applies to all land contracts, whether the parties are rich or poor, black or white, politically powerful or politically weak. In that sense, our system is one of laws. But it is also a system of men and women. Judges are people, not computers or mechanical devices programmed to decide cases on the basis of existing laws or procedures. Judges do not become any less human upon donning their black robes. As a result, the personality of the judge—who the judge is, the background of the judge, the likes and dislikes of the judge—all must be considered in determining how a particular judge will decide a particular case.

When a judge's personality is studied, a major distinction between the law and legal rules becomes apparent. Legal rules, like theorems in geometry, exist in a vacuum; that is, in discussions of their applicability, no mention is made of the effect of a certain person applying them to a situation. For example, the rules for applying the tort of negligence are stated as if a ''correct'' outcome is readily apparent to all who understand them. However, in fact, numerous ''correct'' outcomes can exist when different people accurately apply those rules.

Throughout this text, cases appear with both a majority opinion (the ruling in the case) and a dissenting opinion. These cases most readily illustrate the application of the personality factor in judicial decision making. In both opinions, the same legal rules are being applied. However, the personal characteristics of the individual judges caused their differing resolutions. It is this aspect of legal decision making, called here ''the personality factor,'' that distinguishes the study of legal rules from the study of law.

Without doubt, President Reagan appreciated the importance of this factor. In fact, Reagan and Franklin D. Roosevelt have been accused (or praised, depending upon the analyst) of packing the federal judiciary with judges sharing their philosophies. The effect of President Reagan's efforts can be seen by the decisions of the Supreme Court during the 1988–89 term, which one commentator noted provided the most profound change in legal interpretations in fifty years. A five-justice conservative majority prevailed in decisions ranging from employment discrimination to drug testing in the workplace. Notably, that conservative group determined the Court's holding in over sixty percent of 5–4 decisions that year.

President Bush continued to appoint conservative judges to the federal courts. By the end of the 1991–1992 term, seven of the nine Supreme Court Justices, including Clarence Thomas, could be considered ''conservative.'' However, during that term a ''swing group'' took form with Justice Kennedy often joining moderates Souter and O'Connor. Their votes have kept the Court from overturning certain precedent from the 1960s and 1970s, including the school prayer decision and abortion rights cases. Furthermore, compare President Clinton's first appointee Ruth Bader Ginsberg with the Bush-appointed Clarence Thomas. Their political and personal philosophies are in stark contrast. Thus, one can expect a further movement by the Court away from the conservative holdings that characterized the Reagan era.

However, the personality factor does not suggest that a judge is deliberately biased concerning various litigants who appear in court, or that a judge decides a case beforehand or cannot divorce personal feelings from professional efforts. A good judge attempts to keep any bias, prejudice, or personal feelings from affecting the decision in a case. As Samuel Johnson said: ''If he [the judge] was such a rogue as to make up his mind upon a case without hearing it, he should not have been such a fool as to tell it.''[1] Judges who let bias or prejudice influence their decisions are scofflaws: Such judges are beyond the scope of this discussion of judicial decision making and unfit for their jobs.

Judges are not unique in having their individual characteristics affect their decision making. Such characteristics as personal values, social and family background, likes and dislikes, and basic philosophy of life undoubtedly affect a person's decision to, say, become an accountant instead of a teacher. These and other characteristics are involved in legal decision making as well.

A humorous example appeared on a Public Broadcasting System program, imported from England, titled *Rumpole of the Bailey*. Rumpole was a crafty old barrister (trial lawyer) who had tried many cases before various judges in London for a number of years. As a result, Rumpole knew those judges and their personality quirks. In one episode, a young attorney was trying her first case before a certain elderly judge. Rumpole was representing the opposing party. Rumpole, ever the crafty advocate, told the young attorney that the judge was particularly fond of lengthy argument consisting of a great deal of citation of legal precedent. In fact, the judge became annoyed if attorneys cited cases as authority in his courtroom. He liked short arguments based upon the principle of the case at hand. As expected, the young attorney made a strong, legitimate argument on behalf of her client, citing numerous cases and quoting from the opinions of other judges, while the elderly judge seethed with annoyance. When the young attorney finished, Rumpole made a few comments, and the judge in short order found for Rumpole's client.

The viewer of that television program had no way of knowing whether justice was done in that case or whether a different argument by the young attorney would actually have changed its outcome. However, it was clear that one style of argument carried very little persuasive weight before that judge. Quite possibly, however, a different judge would have been more impressed with lengthy citation. Thus, understanding the personality quirks of the decision maker is an important component of the legal environment.

Another example further illustrates the personality factor as it influences the application of legal rules. Apply this statute to the facts that follow: ''It shall be a criminal offense to willfully damage public property (including trees and vegetation) in public parks.'' As judge you may assess, on those who violate this statute, any combination of the following penalties:

1. *Jail*—zero to thirty days in the county jail. The judge has the option of deciding which days (for example, weekends only).

2. *Fine*—zero to five hundred dollars.

3. *Probation*—no jail or fine. However, conviction goes on criminal record and defendant must report to a probation officer for six months.

4. *Diversion*—no jail or fine. If the defendant stays out of trouble for one year, then there will be no criminal record.

The following are two cases that come before you one day while you are performing your duties as a judge. For each case decide: (1) Did the person violate the statute? (2) What penalty should be assessed against the violator?

PROBLEM 1

Mary, age twenty-one, is a senior at college. Her father and mother are doctors. Mary plans to go to medical school. Her premed grades are 3.95/4.00. Mary belongs to the top sorority on campus. She is active in campus events. She is engaged to be married in June.

On the weekend before final exams, Mary's sorority threw its annual Christmas party. This was a traditional event. In the afternoon, the sorority hosted a Christmas party for underprivileged children. Mary was in charge of that event. In the evening, the party would become a wild celebration of the end of another semester and an outlet before final exam studies began.

When the last child left (about 5:30 P.M.) Mary and her sorority friends began to drink some wine. After the first glass, Mary was a bit giddy and ran from the house laughing and saying, "We need another Christmas tree." She went to a local park and cut down an evergreen. However, a passing police officer stopped her and arrested her. She spent the night in jail.

The next day the local newspapers carried stories concerning Mary's arrest. She was released from jail (pending trial) but was humiliated. She could not face returning to school for finals and took incompletes in all her classes.

Mary pled guilty to the offense. The tree was worth fifty dollars. She had never even had a parking ticket before.

PROBLEM 2

Leroy, age twenty-one, dropped out of high school during his junior year. His parents are divorced and he lives on a farm with his uncle. He is currently unemployed—by choice. Leroy has had a number of jobs: grocery store clerk, farm laborer, gas station attendant. He was fired from each because of his "don't give a damn" attitude. He refuses to help work on his uncle's farm and refuses to look for another job.

Leroy is a 1950s-style hood, although he has never been in trouble with the law. He is clean shaven and has long hair, which he greases back. Leroy dresses in black, keeping his shirt front open. His pleasures consist of driving his souped-up pickup truck around town and playing pool at the local tavern.

Leroy does not attend any church nor does he participate in the community. In short, Leroy does not care about anything.

On the Saturday before Christmas, Leroy was on his way home. He was thrown out of a local tavern for insulting the owner. He was not intoxicated—he had not even finished his first beer. While driving, Leroy decided to stop by a local park. He got out of his pickup truck and chopped down an evergreen—for the heck of it. A passing police officer stopped him and arrested him. He spent the night in jail.

The next day the event was reported in the local newspapers. Leroy was released from jail (pending trial) but did not care. The evergreen was worth fifty dollars.

Make a decision in each case and compare your decisions and the reasons behind them with those given by your fellow students.

Of course, judges realize the effect of personality on their perception of legal issues, legal arguments, and the facts of a case. Therefore, the competent judge will make every attempt to separate personal feelings from a final decision. As just suggested, however, removing personal feelings from the decision-making process does not entirely erase a personality factor, just the most obvious outward manifestations of it.

Attorneys recognize the profound effect the personality factor may have upon the outcome of a particular case. At times, an attorney may seek to have a particular judge removed from hearing a case. The attorney may also seek to ''judge shop''—that is, to file the initial complaint in the court of a judge whose personality is such as to increase the likelihood of success in the case. This does not necessarily mean that attorneys believe that the judge assigned to hear a case is biased, prejudiced, or predisposed to rule in a certain way (although this too is a reason for an attorney to seek to have a judge removed from a case). It may well mean that the personality of a particular judge may be more (or less) compatible with the client, arguments, or facts to be presented in court.

Sometimes a judge may be concerned that the personality factor may bias the outcome of a pending case. In such a circumstance, the judge may decline to hear the case. This process is called **recusal.** It usually occurs when the case concerns a factual matter or a party with which the judge is so personally involved as to risk a possible conflict of interest—for example, a case upon which the judge has worked on behalf of one of the parties prior to becoming a judge, or a lawsuit against a corporation in which the judge is a shareholder. Recusal reflects two things: first, the judge's realization of the importance of the personality factor and of the possible influence of that factor on the decision; second, the importance of a recusal to the appearance of justice where a judge's personal interest may raise questions about the fairness or impartiality of a decision. When a judge's quirks or background unfairly interferes with the professional judgment needed to resolve the dispute, recusal is appropriate.

The following case, although not from a court within the United States, is an example of the personality factor becoming an issue in the litigation. The judge is responding to an attempt to have members of the judicial panel removed from hearing a case because of their personal feelings about the crimes the defendant committed.

State of Israel v. Adolph Eichmann
District Court of Jerusalem
April 17, 1961

Adolph Eichmann was given the responsibility for the extermination of the Jews by the Nazis during World War II. He established death camps, such as Auschwitz, as the "final solution" to the Jewish "problem." After the war, Eichmann escaped from Germany and was given refuge in Argentina. In 1960, Israeli agents captured Eichmann and brought him to Israel for trial.

Landau, Presiding Judge

After reading out the indictment, Dr. Servatius—the Defense Counsel for the accused—voiced arguments regarding the invalidity of the judges sitting in this court, and regarding the lack of competence of the court to judge upon the counts in the indictment. We shall deal with the two matters in their order, and we shall reason our decision.

Regarding the invalidity of the judges: Dr. Servatius said that the accused fears that the judges will not be able in this case to be unprejudiced. The fear is not against one judge in particular, but against the three judges, being members of the Jewish nation and citizens of Israel. The counsel for the Defence says that it is to be feared that the memory of the catastrophe and the holocaust which exterminated their people—this which is the background for the counts and offences in the indictment—may influence the judges and may impair their ability to do justice. He also requested that every one of the judges examine himself, if his personal suffering or the suffering of his relatives during the years of the catastrophe invalidates him from sitting in judgment.

And this is our reply to these arguments:

The subject of the indictment is the responsibility of the accused for the acts described in the indictment. And when these acts are being clarified, it will not be difficult to safeguard the interests of the accused according to the procedure of our Criminal Code Ordinance, that everyone appearing before the court is innocent and his judgment will be declared only in accordance with the evidence brought before this court. Those who sit in judgment are professional judges, used and accustomed to weighing evidence brought before them and do their work in the public eye and the criticism of the public. Learned lawyers and counsels defend the accused. And as far as the fears of the accused regarding the background which is the background for this case, we must only repeat what has been said and what holds good in all courts: That when a court of judgment sits to judge, the judge is still a human being, flesh and blood, with feelings and senses, but he is ordered by the law to restrain those feelings and senses, because otherwise there will never be a judge fit to sit in a criminal case where the abhorrence of the judge is aroused, like treason, murder, or any other serious crime. It is true that the memory of the catastrophe and the holocaust stirs every Jew, but when this case has been brought before us, it is our duty to restrain those feelings when we sit in judgment in this case. And this duty we shall keep.

After weighing all arguments brought by the counsel for the Defence, the learned counsel for the Defence, the Court finds and each judge finds himself fit to sit in judgment.

FACTORS IN JUDICIAL DECISION MAKING

The remainder of this chapter will discuss a number of factors that judges acknowledge in making decisions. The factors to be examined are (1) history and custom (how the norms of society become a part of the law and influence the law); (2) balancing of interests (how a court will weigh the varied interests involved in the particular lawsuit in reaching its decision); (3) doing "what is right" (this factor involves the concept of natural law and notions of what may be called fundamental rights); (4) deferring to other branches of the government (a court may suggest that any change in the way it has decided a particular case is not within its province as a court); (5) use of nonlegal materials to justify the legal decision (often this involves the court's reviewing current sociological, psychological, or behavioral studies and making the conclusions of those studies a part of its justification); (6) the doctrine of stare decisis or precedent (focusing on the conflict between stability and flexibility in the law).

These factors are not used by a judge in the same manner that a recipe is used by a chef. A judicial decision does not contain one part history, two parts precedent, and a dash of doing "what is right." In fact, some judicial decisions may be justified entirely by one of the factors, while others may use two or more factors in arriving at the result. No set rule exists for using or weighing them. The use of factors in justifying a decision is up to the judge.

Notice too what we are saying about the factors to be discussed in the balance of this chapter. They are used by the judge to *justify* the decision reached in a case. This once again suggests the importance of the personality factor. A judge cannot be compared to an empty slate as a case is being presented. Upon hearing the case, the judge makes an initial decision based upon the law. Then, with a decision firmly in hand, the judge uses the applicable factors to legally justify it. If the decision cannot be justified by the usual factors, then the judge will usually alter the initial decision. This is the essence of judicial decision making, which is also judicial lawmaking.

History and Custom

History (a nation's past) and custom (a nation's present habits—formed, of course, by its history) are important factors that may influence a judge's legal opinion. The law does not exist apart from the world around it. Law evolves as a result of a nation's (or within the United States, even a state's) history. Law is based on and is derived from the values of the people. It is a function of all that has affected a nation in its history. The judge may look to the history and norms of the community in formulating the decision in a case. Furthermore, the judge, as a person, is a part of that community and is a part of the history of the people.

Custom is like the historical factor, but with a much shorter time span. Frequently it concerns a type of business practice adopted by a firm or industry that has become standard. The following case is an example of a court's using custom to justify its decision.

Ghen v. Rich
Federal District Court, Massachusetts
8 Fed. 159 (1881)

In the early spring months, the easterly part of Massachusetts Bay is frequented by the species of whale known as the finback. Fishermen from Provincetown pursue the whales in open boats from the shore and shoot them with bomb lances fired from guns made expressly for the purpose. When killed, the whales sink at once to the bottom, but in the course of from one to three days they rise and float on the surface. Some of them are picked up by vessels and towed into Provincetown. Some float ashore at high water and are left stranded on the beach as the tide recedes. Others float out to sea and are never recovered. The person who happens to find them on the beach usually sends word to Provincetown, and the whaler comes to the spot and removes the blubber. The finder usually receives a small salvage for his or her services. A whale swims with great swiftness, and for that reason cannot be taken by the harpoon and line. Each boat's crew engaged in the business has its peculiar mark or device on its lances, and in this way it is known by whom a whale is killed.

The libelant has been engaged in whaling for ten years past. On the morning of April 9, 1880, in Massachusetts Bay, near the end of Cape Cod, he shot and instantly killed with a bomb lance the whale in question. It sunk immediately, and on the morning of April 12, was found stranded on the beach in Brewster, within the ebb and flow of the tide, by one Ellis, seventeen miles from the spot where it was killed. Instead of sending word to Provincetown, as is customary, Ellis advertised the whale for sale at auction and sold it to the respondent, who shipped off the blubber and tried out the oil. The libelant heard of the finding of the whale on the morning of April 15, and immediately sent one of the boat's crew to the place and claimed it. Neither the respondent nor Ellis knew the whale had been killed by the libelant, but they know or might have known, if they had wished, that it had been shot and killed with a bomb lance by some person engaged in this species of business.

Nelson, District Judge

The usage on Cape Cod, for many years, has been that the person who kills a whale in the manner and under the circumstances described, owns it, and this right has never been disputed until this case. The libelant claims title to the whale under this usage. The respondent insists that this usage is invalid. In a previous case, it was decided by Judge Sprague, that when a whale has been killed, and is anchored and left with marks of appropriation, it is the property of the captors; and if it is afterwards found, still anchored, by another ship, there is no usage or principle of law by which the property of the original captors is diverted, even though the whale may have dragged from its anchorage.

Judge Lowell, in another case, decided that a custom among whalemen in the Arctic seas, that the iron holds the whale, was reasonable and valid. In that case a boat's crew from the respondent's ship pursued and struck a whale in the Arctic ocean, and the harpoon and the line attached to it remained in the whale, but did not remain fast to the boat. A boat's crew from the libelant's ship continued the pursuit and captured the whale, and the master of the respondent's ship claimed it on the spot. It was held by the learned judge that the whale belonged to the respondents. The usage for the first iron, whether attached to the boat or not, to hold the whale was fully established; and he added that, although local usages of a particular port ought not to be allowed to set aside the general maritime law, this objection did not apply to a custom which embraced an entire business, and had been concurred in for a long time by every one engaged in the trade.

I see no reason why the usage proved in this case is not as reasonable as that sustained in the cases cited. It has been recognized and acquiesced in for many years. It required in the first taker the only act of appropriation that is possible in the nature of the case. Unless it is sustained, this branch of industry must necessarily cease, for no person would engage in it if the fruits of his labor could be appropriated by any chance finder. It gives reasonable salvage for securing or reporting the property. That the rule works well in practice is shown by the extent of the industry which has grown up under it, and the general acquiescence of a whole community interested to dispute it. It is by no means clear that without regard to usage the common law would not reach the same result. I hold the usage to be valid, and that the property in the whale was in the libelant.

Balance of Interests

The statue of justice, a robed, blindfolded woman holding an evenly balanced scale, is a familiar symbol of a court. This statue is a good representation of the next factor to be considered: the balancing of the various interests in the case. When a judge decides that X or Y should win a particular case, that decision may have an effect on persons other than the parties in the case. Courts, of course, are aware of this effect. So are other interested parties. Often, those other interests will file their own written arguments with the courts, called **amicus curiae briefs.**

Thus, judges may note the competing interests at stake in a case as a means of justifying their decisions. Frequently, these balanced interests will be offered as illustrations that the decisions are consistent with some applicable legal principle. In *United Steelworkers* v. *Weber* (1979), the United States Supreme Court used this approach to justify upholding an affirmative action plan. Numerous interests were involved: that of Brian Weber, the white employee who contended he was denied a place in a training program because of his race; that of black workers who, as a class, had been denied job opportunities prior to the enactment of Title VII of the Civil Rights Act of 1964; that of the company and union, both of which risked discrimination lawsuits from black workers if no affirmative action plan was created; and that of other white workers who would be denied certain training program class slots reserved for black workers, but for only a time.

These interests were not legal issues before the Court. The case involved only the applicability of Title VII to an affirmative action plan negotiated between an employer and a union being challenged by a white employee. However, in justifying its decision to uphold that plan, the Court suggested that it considered those other interests that would be affected. The decision, therefore, gained practical legitimacy as those groups observed that the Court took care to consider their interests.

Doing "What Is Right"

A third factor that a court may use in justifying a decision is that the decision is right, just, or fair. This factor is called many different things. Legal philosophers call it **natural law**—that is, an overriding sense of justice or fairness that is fundamental to the law. This concept may be said to arise from God or from the rational sense of the people. Natural law is based on the assumption that there is some natural or fundamental order in the universe. Its ideals serve as a means for a judge to test rules made by people.

Courts use a number of legal doctrines in making a judicial decision based upon "what is right." For example, the law of equity is based on principles of fairness. The Constitution contains the due process clause, which has been interpreted to mean fundamental fairness in our system of justice. Some statutes, like the Uniform Commercial Code (UCC), contain provisions concerning reasonableness or fairness. One provision in the UCC gives the courts the power to refuse to enforce a term of a contract if it is found to be unconscionable. Courts have defined **unconscionability** as meaning something that is grossly unfair or that shocks the conscience of the court. In addition, courts in the common law would refuse to enforce certain contracts because they conflicted with public policy. For instance, a clause in a contract that provides for the removal of a finger of the breaching party will not be enforced in the courts. Note that no statute or legal doctrine explicitly tells a judge that "contract clauses involving the removal of fingers from those who breach a contract will not be enforced in courts.'' In fact, the general policy in the law is to favor and enforce various contractual terms that parties to a contract have provided. Yet courts will refuse, upon grounds of public policy or unconscionability, to enforce such a contractual clause. Both those grounds are based upon a judgment of the court that such a provision in a contract is simply not right.

Determining whether a contract clause (or any other dispute before the court) involves a question of what is right is not an objective exercise. No complete list of "right" exists, nor is there a test that will produce the answer. The judge reaches such a decision on the basis of collective personal experiences, general societal norms, and ethical reasoning. (Once again the personality factor can influence a decision. Who a judge is and what the judge's experiences have been may well be crucial in determining whether something is "right.")

Certain behavior or the results of certain behavior may be so unsavory as to clearly yield a conclusion that the behavior is wrong. If society cannot agree on basic principles of right and wrong, then there is no society, no civilization, and no law. This does not mean that on all issues there is agreement concerning "what is right." Murder is wrong—it involves the killing of another human being. But is killing someone, as a soldier does, in the performance of duty, also wrong? Is the production of nuclear weapons wrong? People strongly disagree concerning such issues, but underlying that disagreement is a fundamental ideal of right and wrong conduct. This norm is what judges apply, filtered through their own personalities, when they use the "what is right" factor.

Note how this factor incorporates the ethics and corporate responsibility material in Chapter 8. The applicability of a rule of law or the remedy that it provides can well be affected by the ethical behavior (or its lack) of the parties before the court. Corporate managers, thus, can limit the effect of this factor by implementing an ethically based decision-making process.

Riggs v. Palmer
New York Court of Appeals
22 N.E. 188 (1889)

On August 13, 1880, Francis B. Palmer made his last will and testament, in which he gave small legacies to his two daughters, Mrs. Riggs and Mrs. Preston, the plaintiffs in this action, and the remainder of his estate to his grandson, the defendant Elmer E. Palmer. Elmer lived with Francis Palmer as a member of his family, and at Francis Palmer's death was sixteen years old. He knew of the provisions made in his favor in the will, and that he might prevent his grandfather from revoking such provisions, which he had manifested some intention to do. To obtain the speedy enjoyment and immediate possession of his property, Elmer willfully murdered his grandfather by poisoning him. The defendant now claims the property, and the sole question for determination is, can he have it?

Earl, Justice

The defendant says that Francis Palmer, the testator, is dead; that his will was made in due form, and has been admitted to probate; and that therefore it must have effect according to the letter of the law. It is quite true that statutes regulating the making, proof, and effect of wills and the devolution of property, if literally construed, and if their force and effect can in no way and under no circumstances be controlled or modified, give this property to the murderer. The purpose of those statutes was to enable testators to dispose of their estates to the objects of their bounty at death, and to carry into effect their final wishes legally expressed; and in considering and giving effect to them this purpose must be kept in view.

But all laws, as well as all contracts, may be controlled in their operation and effect by general, fundamental maxims of the common law. No one shall be permitted to profit by his own fraud, or to take advantage of his own wrong, or to found any claim upon his own iniquity, or to acquire property by his own crime. These maxims are dictated by public policy, have their foundation in universal law administered in all civilized countries, and have nowhere been superseded by statutes. These maxims, without any statute giving them force or operation, frequently control the effect and nullify the language of wills.

Here there was no certainty that this murderer would survive the testator, or that the testator would not change his will, and there was no certainty that he would get his property if nature was allowed to take its course. He therefore murdered the testator expressly to vest himself with an estate. Under such circumstances, what law, human or divine, will allow him to take the estate and enjoy the fruits of his crime? The will spoke and became operative at the death of the testator. The defendant caused that death, and thus by his crime made it speak and have operation. Shall it speak and operate in his favor? If he had met the testator, and taken his property by force, he would have had no title to it. Shall he acquire title by murdering him? The defendant cannot take any of this property as heir. He made himself an heir by the murder, and he seeks to take property as the fruit of his crime. He cannot vest himself with title by crime.

Deferring to Other Branches of Government

Judges are limited in what they can do by the issues brought before them and the facts and information involved in a particular case. A court cannot conduct its own investigation, call its own witnesses, or hire its own experts to study a matter before rendering a decision. Legislatures and administrative agencies, which also make law, are not as limited as a court. They can initiate investigations of issues. They may call witnesses and consult experts to assist in gathering the information that is necessary to make a legal rule. Legislatures are made up of a large number of officials who are directly accountable to the people. An administrative agency is created to provide expertise about a particular problem. The Environmental Protection Agency, for example, was created by Congress to regulate pollution and other environmental problems.

Because of the practical differences just mentioned between judges and other branches of government, courts may refuse to change the law in a case and instead defer the possibility of change to the legislature. Also, a court may decide to uphold a rule of an administrative agency in recognition of the superior expertise of that agency. A court thus recognizes its institutional limitations. Often deference to another lawmaking branch is used when the issue involved is highly controversial and perhaps may be more readily settled through the political process and its inevitable compromises rather than by judicial decision.

TVA v. Hill
United States Supreme Court
437 U.S. 153 (1978)

The Little Tennessee River originates in the mountains of northern Georgia and flows through the national forest lands of North Carolina into Tennessee, where it converges with the Big Tennessee River near Knoxville.

In this area of the Little Tennessee River, the Tennessee Valley Authority, a wholly owned public corporation of the United States, began constructing the Tellico Dam and Reservoir Project. Of particular relevance to this case is one aspect of the project, a dam that the TVA determined to place on the Little Tennessee a short distance from where the river's waters meet those of the Big Tennessee. When fully operational, the dam would impound water covering some 16,500 acres —much of which represents valuable and productive farmland—thereby converting the river's shallow, fast-flowing waters into a deep reservoir over thirty miles in length.

A discovery was made in the waters of the Little Tennessee that would profoundly affect the Tellico Project. Exploring the area around Coytee Springs, which is about seven miles from the mouth of the river, a University of Tennessee ichthyologist, Dr. David A. Etnier, found a previously unknown species of perch, the snail darter.

Until recently the finding of a new species of animal life would hardly generate a cause célèbre. This is particularly so in the case of darters, of which there are approximately one hundred thirty known species, eight to ten of these having been identified only in the last five years. The moving force behind the snail darter's sudden fame came some four months after its discovery, when the Congress passed the Endangered Species Act of 1973.

Chief Justice Burger

The Tellico Dam will either eradicate the known population of snail darters or destroy their critical habitat. Petitioner does not now seriously dispute this fact. In any event, under §4(a)(1) of the Act, the Secretary of the Interior is vested with exclusive authority to determine whether a species such as the snail darter is "endangered" or "threatened" and to ascertain the factors which have led to such a precarious existence. By §4(d) Congress has authorized—indeed commanded—the Secretary to "issue such regulations as he deems necessary and advisable to provide for the conservation of such species." The Secretary promulgated regulations which declared the snail darter an endangered specie whose critical habitat would be destroyed by creation of the Tellico Reservoir. There is no suggestion that the Secretary exceeded his authority or abused his discretion in issuing the regulations.

It may seem curious to some that the survival of a relatively small number of three-inch fish among all the countless millions of species extant would require the permanent halting of a virtually completed dam for which Congress has expended more than $100 million. The paradox is not minimized by the fact that Congress continued to appropriate large sums of public money for the project, even after congressional Appropriations Committees were apprised of its apparent impact upon the survival of the snail darter. We conclude, however, that the explicit provisions of the Endangered Species Act require precisely that result.

Here we are urged to view the Endangered Species Act "reasonably," and hence shape a remedy "that accords with some modicum of common sense and the public weal." But is that our function? We have no expert knowledge on the subject of endangered species, much less do we have a mandate from the people to strike a balance of equities on the side of the Tellico Dam. Congress has spoken in the plainest of words, making it abundantly clear that the balance has been struck in favor of affording endangered species the high-est of priorities, thereby adopting a policy which it de-scribed as "institutionalized caution."

Our individual appraisal of the wisdom or unwisdom of a particular course consciously selected by the Con-gress is to be put aside in the process of interpreting a statute. Once the meaning of an enactment is discerned and its constitutionality determined, the judicial process comes to an end. We do not sit as a committee of review, nor are we vested with the power of veto.

In our constitutional system the commitment to the separation of powers is too fundamental for us to pre-empt congressional action by judicially decreeing what accords with "common sense and the public weal." Our Constitution vests such responsibilities in the political branches.

Use of Social Science Data

A fifth factor that courts use to justify their decisions is different from the others. The other factors include arguments and rules created by the legal system that a court uses to bolster its conclusion in a given case. This factor involves studies performed by various social scientists—sociologists, psychologists, and the like. Studies by such people are made outside the confines of the particular case and not at the behest of the courts or a litigant. Therefore, this factor is different from the use of expert testimony given during a trial. Expert testimony by a sociologist or other social scientist presented at trial is used as an advocate's tool and focuses specifically on the facts of the case at hand. The social science factor discussed in this section does *not* arise from testimony at trial, although the existence of the data most likely was brought to the attention of the court by one of the attorneys or witnesses in the case. The social science data that make up this factor were gathered independently of the trial, perhaps as part of a general study, perhaps long before the case at hand arose. The conclusion of the study, however, could support a decision in favor of one of the parties.

The earliest use of this factor was in a 1908 United States Supreme Court case concerning whether a state could constitutionally make it a crime for an employer to require female employees to work more than ten hours in a day. Louis D. Brandeis (who later served as a justice of the United States Supreme Court) filed a brief on behalf of the state of Oregon arguing that the law should be upheld as constitutional. His brief contained extracts from more than ninety social science studies and reports that showed that long hours of work are physically dangerous for women. The Court used this information in deciding that the state of Oregon could constitutionally limit the working hours of women. This technique for writing briefs came to be called a **Brandeis brief.**

Use of sociological studies as a factor in justifying legal decisions has been subjected to criticism. Such studies are not designed for use in an adversary proceeding. Furthermore, some people contend that courts do not use such studies properly, nor are judges familiar enough with social science studies in general to use them as support for certain legal propositions. Of course, what is generally accepted by social scientists at one time is not necessarily still accepted at a later time, but the rule established by the case is not generally changed to reflect modifications in the social science studies relied upon by the court in its original decision. Note, for example, the social science information supplied by Brandeis in the case concerning restrictive legislation for working women. Today the law generally rejects work classifications and requirements based solely on the sex of the worker.

Precedent: The Doctrine of Stare Decisis

One of the most important factors used by judges in justifying their decisions is the concept of precedent, or the doctrine of **stare decisis.** This factor embodies two competing notions. The first notion is that the law is stable; that is, because it has a firm foundation in legal history, and is built on the legal rules and decisions of the past, it must therefore be certain and predictable. The second notion is that the law is flexible, that it is not so rigid as to become antiquated. The law is able to change, to move, to be modified as circumstances and society change. Recall the materials in Chapter 1 concerning predictability and flexibility as factors that are necessary for a law to be effective. The doctrine of stare decisis embodies both of those factors.

The doctrine of stare decisis means that the court applies rulings made in similar cases in the past to justify a decision in a current dispute. The past cases are said to be precedents. Decisions of a higher court become what is called binding precedent for the lower courts. For example, assume that the supreme court of the state of X held that walking barefoot across a city park precluded a person from collecting damages from the city if a piece of glass injured the walker. Assume that later a very similar injury occurred and a case was brought to a trial level court in the state. That trial court is considered to be bound by the ruling of the supreme court. Under the doctrine of stare decisis, the supreme court's decision would be applied against the injured walker. If that case was then appealed to the state supreme court, the supreme court could simply cite its previous case as authority (or precedent) for the decision that the walker cannot collect damages from the city.

However, if a similar case occurred in the state adjacent to state X, the decision mentioned would not be considered precedent in that neighboring state. Of course, the courts of the other state are free to refer to that decision, but they have no obligation to consider or follow that case. In fact, they could reach an opposite decision without even considering or discussing the ruling of the neighboring state's supreme court. The doctrine of stare decisis thus is limited in its application to the geographical boundaries of a certain judicial system.

Purpose, Function, and Use of Precedent

Precedent is an important feature of our legal system. It lends stability, certainty, and predictability. Of course, in law, as in life, nothing is ever absolutely certain. In an athletic competition between a very strong team and a very weak team, it is predictable, virtually certain, that the strong team will win. However, an upset victory by the very weak team is not unheard of. The situation is similar with the use of legal precedent as a provider of certainty to the legal system. Legal rules (that is what precedent becomes) are not applied to facts as if they were a mathematical formula. The other factors discussed in this chapter influence and are part of the decision and its justification as offered by the deciding judge.

Judges, however, are careful to follow precedent. They understand the importance to those who are affected by the law's being predictable and based on past decisions. Attorneys predict what a future decision will be in order to advise clients concerning how to conform their conduct to the law and stay out of legal trouble. In fact, precedent and the importance to the legal system of certainty and predictability are so highly valued that good lawyers are usually accurate predictors of future outcomes of legal disputes. Judges usually stay with tradition and follow precedent in deciding cases. A judge who regularly ignores past legal decisions will be considered arbitrary and somewhat dangerous by attorneys, who, with this judge, would have no way of advising their clients concerning the status of the law or how to conform their conduct to the requirements of the law.

The following case is an example of a court that justified its decision by the doctrine of stare decisis. Note how important the values of certainty, predictability, and stability in the law are to the court in this case. The court applied past judicial decisions to the dispute at hand to justify its decision that professional baseball was exempt from the antitrust laws.

Flood v. Kuhn
United States Supreme Court
407 U.S. 258 (1971)

The petitioner, Curtis Charles Flood, born in 1938, began his major league career in 1956 when he signed a contract with the Cincinnati Reds for a salary of four thousand dollars for the season. He had no attorney or agent to advise him on that occasion. He was traded to the St. Louis Cardinals before the 1958 season. Flood rose to fame as a centerfielder with the Cardinals during the years from 1958 to 1969. In those twelve seasons, he compiled a batting average of .293. He ranks among the ten major league outfielders possessing the highest lifetime fielding averages. Flood's St. Louis compensation ranged from $13,500 in 1961 to $90,000 in 1969.

At the age of thirty-one, in October 1969, Flood was traded to the Philadelphia Phillies of the National League in a multiplayer transaction. He was not consulted about the trade. He was informed by telephone and received formal notice only after the deal had been consummated. In December, he complained to the commissioner of baseball and asked that he be made a free agent and be placed at liberty to strike his own bargain with any other major league team. His request was denied.

Flood then instituted this antitrust suit in January 1970, in federal court for the Southern District of New York. The defendants (although not all were named in each cause of action) were the commissioner of baseball, the presidents of the two major leagues, and the twenty-four major league clubs. In general, the complaint charged violations of the federal antitrust laws.

Flood declined to play for Philadelphia in 1970, despite a $100,000 salary offer, and he sat out the year. After the season was concluded, Philadelphia sold its rights to Flood to the Washington Senators. Washington and the petitioner were able to come to terms for the 1971 season at a salary of $110,000. Flood started the season but, apparently because he was dissatisfied with his performance, he left the Washington club on April 27, early in the campaign. He has not played baseball since then.

Judge Cooper, in a detailed opinion, held that *Federal Baseball Club* v. *National League* and *Toolson* v. *New York Yankees, Inc.* were controlling. On appeal, the Second Circuit felt "compelled to affirm." The Supreme Court granted certiorari in order to look once again at this troublesome and unusual situation.

Justice Blackmun

For the third time in 50 years the Court is asked specifically to rule that professional baseball's reserve system is within the reach of the federal antitrust laws.

Federal Baseball Club v. National League (1922) was a suit for treble damages instituted by a member of the Federal League (Baltimore) against the National and American Leagues and others. Mr. Justice Holmes, in speaking succinctly for a unanimous Court, said:

> The business is giving exhibitions of baseball, which are purely state affairs. The restrictions by contract that prevented the plaintiff from getting players to break their bargains and the other conduct charged against the defendants were not an interference with commerce among the States.

Federal Baseball was cited a year later, and without disfavor, in another opinion by Mr. Justice Holmes for a unanimous Court. In the years that followed, baseball continued to be subject to intermittent antitrust attack. The courts, however, rejected these challenges on the authority of *Federal Baseball.*

In *Toolson v. New York Yankees, Inc.* (1953), *Federal Baseball* was cited as holding "that the business of providing public baseball games for profit between clubs of professional baseball players was not within the scope of the federal antitrust laws." . . . The emphasis in *Toolson*

was on the determination, attributed even to *Federal Baseball,* that Congress had no intention to include baseball within the reach of the federal antitrust laws.

In view of all this, it seems appropriate now to say that with its reserve system enjoying exemption from the federal antitrust laws, baseball is, in a very distinct sense, an exception and an anomaly. *Federal Baseball* and *Toolson* have become an aberration confined to baseball. It is an aberration that has been with us now for half a century, one heretofore deemed fully entitled to the benefit of stare decisis, and one that has survived the Court's expanding concept of interstate commerce. It rests on a recognition and an acceptance of baseball's unique characteristics and needs.

Accordingly, we adhere once again to *Federal Baseball* and *Toolson* and to their application to professional baseball. If there is any inconsistency or illogic in all this, it is an inconsistency and illogic of long standing that is to be remedied by the Congress and not by this Court. Under these circumstances, there is merit in consistency even though some might claim that beneath that consistency is a layer of inconsistency.

And what the Court said in *Federal Baseball* in 1922 and what it said in *Toolson* in 1953, we say again here in 1972: the remedy, if any is indicated, is for congressional, and not judicial, action.

When Precedent Is Not Followed

The doctrine of stare decisis also embodies the notion that law is flexible, is subject to change, and has the capacity for growth. Keeping the law stable yet flexible is one of the great functions of the doctrine of stare decisis.

Good lawyers can find precedent or cases from the past to support almost any position taken in court. One of the skills of a good lawyer is the ability to demonstrate that a precedent case supports a certain line of reasoning, yielding a result under the doctrine of stare decisis. This does not involve any trickery or misrepresentations to the court, for no two cases are exactly alike. Even though a past case may have arisen from similar facts, there are usually enough factual differences between the past case and the present case to render the precedential case distinguishable. Legal argument before the court often involves distinguishing away cases cited as having precedential effect by one's adversary while arguing that other cases deserve precedence.

Often, since different cases from the past will be offered to a court as precedent, judges will also engage in distinguishing cases. Case reports are not always clear concerning the rule made by the court. Sometimes cases are read very narrowly as applying only to very similar facts. Other cases are read rather broadly; that is, they stand for a very general proposition of law, which is thereafter considered precedent in a variety of different matters. Attorneys urge such different interpretations of the same case on a court, and judges often use the reading that best suits their decisions. Precedent, therefore, is not as clear or so easy to establish as one might first think.

In some judicial opinions, the court makes remarks about the law that are not precisely at issue. In *Parker* v. *Foote,* a leading easements case from the early nineteenth century, adjoining landowners were in dispute over a building addition one had constructed. This addition blocked the light and air which had been flowing without obstruction into the other's home for a number of years. That party contended that he had a right to the uninterrupted flow of light and air. The legal issue in the case was whether the jury or the judge should decide. The court, in addition to resolving this issue, went on to discuss whether American law would permit a landowner to acquire the right to light and air merely by its long-term enjoyment. It was this "extra" judicial discussion that today is considered the precedential effect of that case.

However, that discussion was not the ruling of the case, from which precedent is usually obtained. A discussion of this kind is called **dicta.** Dicta are not considered to have precedential effect. However, it is not always easy to clearly predict what a court will consider dicta from a past opinion or what legal ruling will deserve precedential value. Sometimes, as with *Parker* v. *Foote,* a case is read in such a way as to give precedential effect to what are usually considered dicta.

A court may also comment on an issue beyond that which is necessary for its decision. This may be the judge's opinion of the ramifications of the ruling on a closely related issue. It too is considered dicta and is not the rule of the case that has precedential value. However, a court may use it as precedent supporting a decision in a future case. One of the best-known instances of such dicta was Justice Stone's footnote number 4 in *United States* v. *Carolene Products Co.* (1938). The Supreme Court at that time was, after enormous pressure, beginning to uphold various controls of economic activity enacted by Congress as part of Roosevelt's New Deal. The footnote in *Carolene Products* suggested that the Court might continue very strict constitutional review of legislative attempts to regulate liberty rights even though it was loosening its review standard for legislation that regulated property rights. That footnote, which was merely an opinion about the Court's standard of constitutional review for certain legislative restrictions, was the starting point for the development today of the distinction between property rights and liberty rights treatment by the courts. (See the materials in Chapter 12.)

Sometimes, although rarely, courts will choose not to follow clear legal precedent. In such situations the existing legal rule is usually outdated, and a need for change in the law is quite evident. Perhaps following the long-established legal precedent will yield an injustice or retain a legal rule when the purposes and reasons for the rule no longer exist. Remember that the ultimate goal of the law is justice. However, the temptation to ignore precedent in order to achieve that end must be balanced with the importance of stability and certainty in the law. This struggle in the law between stability and flexibility is most clearly embodied in the doctrine of stare decisis. The following case is an example of a court's disregarding long-standing precedent and changing a legal rule that it believes is no longer fair or just.

Flagiello v. Pennsylvania Hospital
Supreme Court of Pennsylvania
208 A.2d 193 (1965)

Mary C. Flagiello was injured during her stay at the Pennsylvania Hospital in Philadelphia. It is enough to say that she avers that, through the negligence of two employees of the hospital, she fell, sustaining in the fall a fracture to her right ankle. She and her husband, Thomas Flagiello, brought an action in trespass against the hospital and the two employees alleged to have been immediately responsible for the accident. The defendant hospital answered that it was an eleemosynary institution engaged in charitable enterprise and, therefore, not responsible in damage to the plaintiffs.

Musmanno, Justice

In the early days of public accommodation for the ill and the maimed, charity was exercised in its pure and pristine sense. Many good men and women, liberal in purse and generous in soul, set up houses to heal the poor and homeless victims of disease and injury. They made no charge for this care. The benefactors felt themselves richly rewarded in the knowledge that they were befriending humanity. Charity in the biblical sense prevailed.

Whatever the law may have been regarding charitable institutions in the past, it does not meet the conditions of today. Charitable enterprises are no longer housed in ramshackly wooden structures. They are not mere storm shelters to succor the traveler and temporarily refuge those stricken in a common disaster. Hospitals today are growing into mighty edifices in brick, stone, glass, and marble. Many of them maintain large staffs, they use the best equipment that science can devise, they utilize the most modern methods in devoting themselves to the noblest purpose of man, that of helping one's stricken brother. But they do all this on a business basis, submitting invoices for services rendered—and properly so.

And if a hospital functions as a business institution, by charging and receiving money for what it offers, it must be a business establishment also in meeting obligations it incurs in running that establishment. One of those inescapable obligations is that it must exercise a proper degree of care for its patients, and, to the extent that it fails in that care, it should be liable in damages as any other commercial firm would be liable. If a hospital employee negligently leaves a sponge in the abdominal cavity of a paying patient, why should the hospital be freed from liability, any more than a restaurant owner should escape responsibility for the damage inflicted by a waitress who negligently overturns a tray of hot dishes on a guest?

A person may recover damages if he is injured, as the result of negligence, in a hotel, theater, street car, store, skating rink, natatorium, bowling alley, train or ship, yet he cannot recover if he is hurt in the place where accidents are considered most unlikely to occur—in a hospital, where one goes to be cured of an already existing infirmity and not to be saddled with additional woe and torment. This is indeed the paradox of paradoxes. It has no logic, reason, and, least of all, justice, to support it. And still more paradoxical is the argument that, by refusing recovery to the victim of a hospital's own negligence, one somehow is serving charity!

If there was any justification for the charitable immunity doctrine when it was first announced, it has lost that justification today. Each court which has upheld the immunity rule has relied for its authority on a previous decision or decisions, scarcely ever placing the subject for study on the table of self-asserting justice. No attempt is ever made by the advocates of the immunity doctrine to justify in moral law and fair dealing a doctrine which deprives an injured person of a forum guaranteed to all others.

Nor is it to be feared that with the imposition of liability for torts, accidents in the hospitals will disproportionately increase. It would be a voodoo prediction that with the lifting of the immunity doctrine, hospital patients would leap out of beds to break legs, scar themselves with X-ray machines, rip off bandages, smash plaster of Paris casts, and ingest wrong medicines, in order to further disable themselves and thus collect money damages. No sane person would prefer money to a sane and healthy body, free of pain, agony and torment.

Stare decisis channels the law. It erects lighthouses and flys the signals of safety. The ships of jurisprudence must follow that well-defined channel which, over the years, has been proved to be secure and trustworthy. But it would not comport with wisdom to insist that, should shoals rise in a heretofore safe course and rocks emerge to encumber the passage, the ship should nonetheless pursue the original course, merely because it presented no hazard in the past. The principle of stare decisis does not demand that we follow precedents which shipwreck justice.

Stare decisis is not an iron mold into which every utterance by a Court—regardless of circumstances, parties, economic barometer and sociological climate—must be poured, and, where, like wet concrete, it must acquire an unyielding rigidity which nothing later can change.

The history of law through the ages records numerous inequities pronounced by courts because the society of the day sanctioned them. Reason revolts, humanity shudders, and justice recoils before much of what was done in the past under the name of law. Yet, we are urged to retain a forbidding incongruity in the law simply because it is old. That kind of reasoning would have retained prosecution for witchcraft, imprisonment for debt and hanging for minor offenses which today are hardly regarded misdemeanors.

A rule that has become insolvent has no place in the active market of current enterprise. When a rule offends against reason, when it is at odds with every precept of natural justice, and when it cannot be defended on its own merits, but has to depend alone on a discredited genealogy, courts not only possess the inherent power to repudiate, but, indeed, it is required by the very nature of judicial function, to abolish such a rule.

Of course, the precedents here recalled do not justify a light and casual treatment of the doctrine of stare decisis but they proclaim unequivocally that where justice demands, reason dictates, equality enjoins and fair play decrees a change in judge-made law, courts will not lack in determination to establish that change.

SUMMARY

It is important to understand the nature of the decision-making process in order to appreciate the complexity and difficulty of predicting what a legal result will be in any case. The factors that compose the judicial decision-making process may clash, thereby yielding the sometimes logically conflicting rulings in certain cases. Law is not a logically based, mathematically precise instrument. It is a means of civilizing a society whose goal is justice.

Seven factors involved in the judicial reasoning and decision-making process may be identified. One is unacknowledged in judicial opinions but, nevertheless, is central to understanding law. It is the personality factor. The decisions made by any particular judge are a function of that judge's personality. Six other factors appear as acknowledged justifications for the judicial decision reached in a case. These factors reflect important policies in the law. At times, one or more of these factors may conflict if applied to a given case. The first of these factors is history and custom (how the practices and norms of a society are reflected in its laws and in the judicial decisions rendered in its courts). A balancing of the interests involved in the case is the second factor. This involves the recognition that at times not only do each of the parties in a court dispute have interests to be considered, but so also do others who are not directly affected by the case. Their interest focuses on the possible precedential effect given to that case by other courts. A third factor is doing "what is right." This involves an ideal of the law—to render fair and just results in decisions made in the courts. It may be used by a court to modify an existing legal rule in order that an unjust result not occur. A fourth factor is deferring to other branches of government. A fifth factor is the use by courts of social science data to lend support to their decisions and conclusions in a case. That final factor is one of the most important: the concept of stare decisis, or legal precedent. This notion embodies the conflicting values of stability and flexibility in the law.

REVIEW QUESTIONS

1. Define the following terms:
   a. Brandeis brief
   b. Custom
   c. History
   d. Natural law
   e. Precedent
   f. Recusal
   g. Stare decisis

2. What are the six factors (leaving the personality factor out of consideration) identified in this chapter as components of a judicial decision?

3. For each of the six factors discuss the following: (a) What the factor attempts to ac-

complish in the law. (b) Advantages involved in each factor: What in each factor is good for the legal system and its goal of justice?

4. The case *TVA* v. *Hill* was used to illustrate the "deferring to other branches" factor. Render a decision in that case using the "balance of interests" factor.

5. Justices of the United States Supreme Court place their assets in a **blind trust.** A blind trust is a legal device by which a person is appointed to invest the property of the justice. However, the nature of those investments is kept secret. Why is this done?

Assuming that there are no dishonest justices, why is this necessary?

6. In 1967, State University had restricted hours for its women students. All women students were required to live in campus housing and could not be out later than midnight. Based upon some or all of the factors raised in this chapter, what justifications could be made by a decision maker either for refusing to abolish such a rule or for abolishing the rule?

7. Discuss the doctrine of stare decisis and the effect of precedent on the legal system. Give an example of a case in which precedent should be followed and a case in which precedent should not be followed.

8. Brewing, Inc., is a beer manufacturing corporation. It agreed to supply the Dew Drop Inn with five barrels of beer per month. A barrel is defined by statute as containing 31 gallons. After a few months, managers of the inn noticed that they seemed to be receiving barrels containing fewer than 31 gallons. Upon checking, they learned that the barrels ranged from 31 gallons to 29.7 gallons. In the beer industry, as a barrel ages, it holds less and less liquid because the hoops that hold the barrel together must be driven closer to the center in order to keep them tight. Over time, this reduces the size of the barrel. The Dew Drop Inn sues Brewing. What might the corporation argue in defense?

9. You are an executive with the XYZ Corporation. The corporation has been sued by a disgruntled supplier. Counsel has informed you that five cases that discuss the issue in the lawsuit have been found in your jurisdiction. All five cases support the position of the supplier. How might you expect the issue to be resolved?

10. Given the facts in question 9, under what circumstances would you expect the opposite outcome?

11. Jenkins is very liberal politically. She supports increased government regulation of large corporations and has participated in numerous causes, such as the pro-choice movement, gay rights, and nuclear freeze activities. She is a top-flight attorney and legal scholar and is considered one of the best-qualified judicial candidates in the country. Would you anticipate her being nominated for a federal judgeship by a very conservative president? Give reasons.

12. Grace and Sam Stamos are an elderly couple who recently moved to the United States from Greece. They understand only a little English. Richards visited them at home in order to sell them a freezer. At first, they were not interested, since they did not have a great deal of money. However, Richards discussed the matter with them for ten hours that day. Finally they agreed to purchase a freezer and signed a fifteen-page contract. The contract was written in English, with complex legal terminology, and was in very small print. No one explained the terms of the contract to the Stamoses. One provision provided that if they were late making a payment on the freezer, all their other property could be taken by the seller and sold to pay their debt. The freezer was worth three hundred dollars. The contract required a thirty-dollars-per-month payment for five years.

Without discussing applicable legal rules, if the seller attempts to enforce the contract against the Stamoses and a court rules in their favor, how might the court justify its decision?

13. Foreign policy activities are generally considered to be within the province of the President and, to some extent, Congress. Assume that your company had a contract to build two government-ordered cement factories in a certain foreign country (Overseasia). Although your company had finished the work, it has not been paid by Overseasia. In fact, the United States and Overseasia have become bitter enemies, and various hostile (and retaliatory) actions have

occurred between the two nations. Last month, after a lengthy secret negotiation, the presidents of the two countries announced a "friendship" treaty in which all disputes between the countries or their citizens would be submitted to a special arbitration panel that will meet in Geneva. Thus, under the terms of the treaty your cement factory payment dispute will be heard by the panel in Geneva.

After studying the terms of the arbitration, you realize that your company could obtain a more favorable ruling by filing a breach-of-contract action in an American court. Without discussing applicable legal rules, if you file such a lawsuit, what might the court decide?

14. Grades seem to be an almost indispensable part of college life. However, at Veritas College, a proposal has been made to abolish the school's grading system. Based on some or all of the factors raised in this chapter, what justifications could be made by a decision maker either for refusing to abolish the grading system or for retaining it?

15. Late one winter afternoon two people, Jack and Sally, slip on some unshoveled snow in a retail store's parking lot. Jack is a transient, unemployed by choice. He makes ends meet by occasional thefts. He had planned to go into the retail store to warm himself. Sally is a CPA who was hurrying into the store to make a major purchase. She has been a valued customer there for a number of years. Sally is married with three children, and is active in charitable organizations. Both Jack and Sally have the same type of injury. For each choose among the following (or a combination):

a. The store is not liable to pay damages for their injuries.

b. Each injured party will receive the same amount in damages for his or her injuries.

c. There is no requirement that Jack and Sally be treated alike in whether the store is liable or the amount of damages.

Justify your decision and base your reasons on the materials in this chapter.

NOTE

[1]James Boswell, *The Life of Samuel Johnson* (1791), p. 958.

CHAPTER 5

The Legislature, Legislation, and the Executive Branch

- A Comparison of Lawmaking by the Courts and the Legislature
- The Legislature and Lawmakers
- Statutory Construction
- The Executive Branch

This chapter will first focus on an overview of various issues surrounding the legislature and the legislative process. Thereafter, an analysis of judicial construction and interpretation of statutes will be presented. The concluding section of the chapter will outline the activities of the executive branch that can influence the makeup of the legal environment.

A COMPARISON OF LAWMAKING BY THE COURTS AND THE LEGISLATURE

Context in Which the Lawmaking Occurs

Judicial Case-by-Case Approach

Courts make laws on a case-by-case basis. Judge-made law is the decision in a particular case. However, a judge is not a roving ''do-gooder'' sitting on the bench and resolving all society's problems. For example, if no cases arise involving tort law, then there can be no judge-made tort law. Even if a particular judge is convinced that a doctrine of tort law should be modified because it causes gross injustice, that judge may not simply declare such a legal rule to be henceforth changed. The legal rule can be changed only within the context of a dispute brought before the court. Furthermore, in making law on a case-by-case basis, courts have no power to investigate independently the facts and gather information that may be helpful in rendering a decision. Courts generally are limited to the facts presented to them by the parties at trial. However, simply because judicial lawmaking must occur within a case, its effect is not therefore narrow. Courts have announced very broad principles while deciding particular cases.

Legislative Approach

A legislature's lawmaking ability is not as confined as that of a court. At the outset, note that statutes do not arise to settle private cases. In fact, a legislature is not the proper forum for the settlement of individual disputes. Thus, the scope of legislation is institutionally restricted only by the Constitution. For example, a problem or general issue may exist that interests only certain legislators. The legislature has mechanisms—committees, subcommittees, and special investigatory panels—to study that issue. In studying the issue, legislators may call witnesses representing a broad spectrum of opinion. Witnesses may be required to appear and answer questions posed by the legislators. In addition, legislative staff and investigators may seek data and prepare reports. The purpose of the investigation is to provide the legislature with information—facts from which to draw in its decision whether to enact a statute. Additionally, the information gathered assists the legislature in drafting the statute so as to take into account its full range of effects.

Since information and facts are needed by the legislature to properly draft a statute, legislators have broad authority to order pertinent studies, to hold hearings, to call witnesses, and even to require certain witnesses to testify. Some legislative investigations have been highly publicized and very noteworthy. In the early 1950s, Senator Joseph McCarthy of Wisconsin conducted investigations of contrived communist infiltration of and influence on various segments of American life. In the early 1960s, Senator John L. McClellan led a committee that investigated organized crime in the United States. These hearings enabled the American people to witness the spectacle of alleged mobsters refusing to answer questions posed by the legislators on the grounds that those questions violated their constitutional rights. In the 1970s, the Watergate investigation by a Senate committee led by Senator Sam Ervin uncovered corruption in the Nixon White House that led to the only resignation of a president in American history.

These examples are legislative investigations that have become almost a part of American folklore. The stated purpose of these investigations was to provide background information to the legislature concerning a particular problem. The investigating committee would then ideally be in a position to recommend legislation regulating the area from which the problem or issue arose.

Although the power of the legislature to investigate is very broad, it is not without limit. Individuals are protected from government activity by various provisions of the Constitution. For example, the Fifth Amendment provides the right to refuse to answer incriminating questions.

Relationship to the Past of Any Newly Made Law

The doctrine of stare decisis is a very important factor in judicial lawmaking. Courts seek to apply past decisions to current disputes in order to promote stability and certainty in the law. Judges are therefore reluctant to ignore the precedential effect of past cases. Consider, however, the legislature's right to make new law to meet present needs, without being doctrinally bound to the law as it had previously existed. Broad investigative powers give the legislature the ability to study thoroughly the effect of a new approach to a problem before enacting any legislation.

When courts defer to the legislature it is often because a new approach is needed, and the legislature is institutionally designed to provide that new approach without being confined by past work in the area. The New Mexico Solar Rights Act is an example of a bold enactment by a legislature seeking to resolve a troubling problem—protecting the access to sunlight that is necessary to power a solar energy collector. Before the enactment of this statute, the only law in New Mexico that provided for such access was the common law. In general, the common law provided that solar access could be protected only if the solar energy user purchased the needed access rights from adjoining landowners. The New Mexico statute provided that solar rights could be obtained by the first person to use a path of sunlight to power a solar energy collector. In short, the first solar use established a legal right for continued use of the sunlight. The New Mexico legislature did not limit its lawmaking to a step-by-step progression, as courts usually do under the doctrine of stare decisis. Instead, the Solar Rights Act outlined a radical change in the relevant law.

Although the legislature does not operate under a doctrine similar to stare decisis, it too seeks to avoid being labeled arbitrary in its work. Therefore, the legislature is considerate and ever mindful of the policies behind the doctrine of stare decisis when devising a new statute. In a sense, legislators are like architects who rehabilitate an old office building. The interior is transformed, its function and use completely different than originally intended. Yet the outside appearance of the building remains the same. A legislature often performs much the same feat when enacting a statute.

The legislator is more confident of the success of a particular statute if it is similar to one that already exists. For example, although the New Mexico solar rights statute was a new approach for protecting solar access, it was built on an existing body of law: rules of civil procedure that provide mechanisms for the enforcement of legal rights; rules that govern eminent domain or the power of the government to take private property for public use; and rules that govern the transfer and use of property rights, including those created by the statute in favor of the solar energy user.

Additionally, the solar rights statute was patterned after New Mexico's water allocation law, which had years of use and numerous judicial constructions of its terms. In fact, many of the terms used in the solar rights statute were identical to the terms in the water law—"prior appropriation" and "beneficial use," for example. These terms have a special meaning in water law. The New Mexico legislature expected a similar meaning to exist in their new use as a part of the solar energy access scheme. Furthermore, the entire procedure for acquiring a legal right to solar access was modeled after the procedure for acquiring a legal right to use water in New Mexico.

Legislatures may also look to the experiences of other states in determining the type of statute to enact regulating a certain area. A legislature often uses another state's statute as a model for the one it is enacting. Perhaps upon study, the legislature will make a refinement in the statutory language to repair weaknesses that have surfaced. Perhaps the refinements will reflect some differences between the states. In any event, the legislature uses existing statutes as guides for what is to be newly enacted. In this way, legislation is built on the past while a new and unique identity is maintained.

THE LEGISLATURE AND LAWMAKERS

Historical Development of Legislation

Legislation as a general means of regulating conduct in this country is only about one hundred and twenty years old. Before the end of the nineteenth century, most of the law in the United States was common law. Such bodies of law as torts, commercial contracts, and negotiable paper were a function of long-time judicial lawmaking, first in England and then in the United States. For the most part, statutes enacted before the late nineteenth century were used to fill in ''gaps'' in various areas of common law or to change a judicially created common law doctrine.

The nature of common law is that it is a body of cases that acts as precedent for deciding disputes. Its rules were created on an ad hoc basis, determined by the type of disputes before the courts. The common law as a whole, therefore, could not be modified or changed. Near the end of the nineteenth century, a movement in American law for codification of the common law was begun. This would enable a legislature to clear away confusion existing because of conflicting precedents and to pass one act governing a given area. The first area to receive attention was civil procedure—the mechanical rules of bringing a case and proceeding with it through a court of law.

Later, committees worked to draft uniform laws to be proposed in the state legislatures. These uniform statutes were drafted on the basis of the common law. For example, one such law, the Uniform Sales Act, was derived from the judicial decisions in sales of goods transactions. This common law was in part based on the law merchant, a body of informal law developed in Europe in the Middle Ages by merchants settling their disputes at fairs. The Uniform Sales Act was an attempt to give some form and structure to this area of law. It and other uniform acts were enacted by various state legislatures. The Uniform Sales Act has been replaced by another uniform law—the Uniform Commercial Code.

Today, much of the law has been codified. Such major areas as commercial law, partnership, corporations, limited partnership, wills, and trusts have been put in statutory form. Additionally, state legislatures and Congress have drafted statutes for new areas of legal coverage, such as civil rights, the environment, health and safety in the workplace, and consumer problems.

Functions of Legislators

Although Congress as an institution seems to have image problems, political scientists have found, curiously, that the same attitude does not necessarily attach itself to one's own representative. It is as though the problems with Congress are caused by someone else's. This impression is more than just a curiosity. It tends to reflect the wide range of tasks performed by a representative as well as the nature of a legislature as an institution.

Lawmaking Function

A representative (and a state legislator, although this discussion will be limited to Congress) serves a number of functions. One of them is that of lawmaker. The statutes just mentioned and discussed elsewhere in this text are examples of the end product of this legislative function. This function is, of course, also the most visible. If Congress enacts a statute we may praise it or condemn it, depending upon how that statute affects us. However, more criticism comes from the seeming inability of the Congress to pass *any* statute that concerns a problem affecting the voters. For example, when the economy is faltering, the most that usually occurs in Congress is debate, delay, and perhaps a watered-down compromise bill—never "decisive action." People complain when Congress takes a recess while national problems are not yet solved. When it returns, the problems are still there, but no action ever seems forthcoming. Much of the hostile reaction toward Congress comes from this perceived flaw—inactivity and indecision in the face of problems. Yet the very source of the criticism of Congress is also the nature of its strength.

The power of Congress is dispersed rather than centralized, as it is in the case of the president (or governor) in the executive branch and the judge in the judicial branch. As an institution, Congress represents the factions and interests that surround any issue in this country. Therefore, Congress is unable to decisively act upon an issue until a consensus has been reached.

One may yearn for a decisive, powerful, and efficient legislative branch to spew forth statutes to meet the problems of the day. Yet strong, decisive leadership may well not be responsive to legitimate interests involved in an issue. Ultimately, in a system of government based on a philosophy of limited power and voluntary compliance with the law, the present concept of Congress is the best mechanism for producing effective legislation.

Overseer Function

A second function of the legislator is that of overseer of other areas of government, primarily the bureaucracy and the executive branch. The investigative function of the legislature permits review of activities of various other government units. Legislation may be enacted as a result of abuses found in the course of that investigation. Congressional limitations on the power of the CIA and on the president's war-making power were an outgrowth of the Watergate and Vietnam era investigations.

Ombudsman Function

A final general function of the legislator is constituent service, to, in a sense, serve as an ombudsman for voters who become frustrated in dealing with the bureaucracy. This service function is an important element in keeping the voter at home satisfied and enhancing the image of the individual legislator.

The Legislative Process

A statute is merely a group of words that expresses the legislature's ideas concerning a certain policy. Much of the materials in this text—for example, antitrust and environmental law—are based on statutes. However, the legislature does not act alone. The executive branch often wields great influence in the legislative policy debate. Courts and administrative agencies must implement the statute by applying it to specific situations.

Nonetheless, legislation may be described as the cornerstone of the government process. It is a fundamental element of the legal environment of business, since the outcome of legislative policy ideas (statutes) can materially affect business activity. For example, in 1964 Congress enacted the Civil Rights Act which, in part, prohibited certain types of employment discrimination. Thereafter, business personnel practices changed, since applicants and employees could not be treated differently on the basis of race or sex. Subsequently, through administrative agency activity (Equal Employment Opportunity Commission) and court decisions, the statute was applied to related issues, including affirmative action and sexual harassment. None of those issues was directly addressed in the statute, but each relates to the general nondiscriminatory policy that it represents.

The process of enacting a law generally operates the same at the federal or state level. However, the steps in the legislative process illustrate only the procedure for enacting a statute. The substance of the statute itself is what is of concern to business. How (or whether) Congress decides to regulate acid rain is of greater concern than the path the bill will follow through the House and Senate. That statute will reflect numerous compromises, deals, bargains, and political pressures that arise throughout the process and may bear only slight resemblance to the bill that was initially proposed. The process is not very tidy. Since the legislature is a political body, its actions are influenced by practical political considerations.

Statutes, in a sense, may be viewed as political documents. The campaigns and candidates that are chosen on election day will be those enacting legislation that can greatly affect personal or business behavior. That point, of course, is obvious, but statutes are sometimes treated as if they were handed down by some Higher Authority instead of being the creations of politicians. In practice, the final bill may be passed as much because of political influence (campaign contributions, endorsements, or logrolling) as because of its merits.

Therefore, business maintains a presence during the legislative process. Primarily this is done through lobbyists or with campaign contributions to certain legislators. Business requires access to the legislature so that its interests can be considered during the bargaining that occurs in order for a bill to be passed.

The legislator's role in the statutory process is primarily political: to translate certain policy ideas into a bill that can garner enough votes. Frequently, the legislator never reads the bill before voting, although the committee report may be consulted. That legislator's vote may be based on directions from party leadership, public opinion, advice of an aide who has studied the bill, or the arguments made by a lobbyist. In fact, the bill itself is most often drafted by aides or lobbyists and not by any individual legislator.

Thus, the most effective efforts to influence law occur during the political stages of the legislative process. One of the most common means is through campaign contributions. These contributions are designed to influence the legislator or to reinforce a legislator's voting record that has been beneficial to the donor. Common types of contributions are those made to members of a certain key committee that oversees bills that directly affect the business of the donor. These donations are made usually without regard to the political leanings of the legislator or to whether the legislator needs the funds to wage an electoral campaign against a tough opponent. Frequently, newly elected legislators will receive contributions from donors who did not support them during the election. These funds are not necessarily from businesses and individuals in the legislator's district. Instead, they are from those who are interested in the outcome of certain legislative policy debates.

Donors hope that the contributions will at least provide access to the legislator. Given the legislator's limited time, such access would permit the donor to make arguments and provide information that might be persuasive in the legislator's ultimate actions on the issue.

The political arena is a vital component of the legal environment of business. Once a statute is enacted, the role of the legislature ceases (except to possibly modify the statute at some point in the future). The courts are then charged with interpreting the statutory language. As will be noted in the next section, the courts use various methods in applying a statute, none of which includes the private interests of the parties.

STATUTORY CONSTRUCTION

As soon as a statute is enacted, business begins conforming to its terms and conditions. One of the important functions of preventive law is assisting business managers in planning to stay within the confines of newly enacted legislation. However, disputes may arise concerning the meaning of a particular statute or statutory provision. Legislatures do not give indications concerning meaning other than what was originally conveyed by the statute in question. They do not later clarify portions of their statutes that have caused interpretation problems. This job falls to the courts.

The process of understanding the meaning of statutes not only involves reading the words drafted by the legislature, but also involves reading judges' opinions. Courts play a major role in interpreting the work of the legislature. A court and the legislature work together in the area of legislative lawmaking in order to produce an understandable standard of conduct.

Not all statutes, of course, become subject to judicial scrutiny. For instance, a statute that prohibits driving on an expressway faster than sixty-five miles per hour is clear: No difficulty arises in interpreting the amount of speed that will create a violation. A person arrested for driving seventy miles per hour cannot argue that the statute should be construed to allow seventy miles per hour within its terms. Judges, in interpreting statutes, simply do not have the right to do whatever they like in a case. Even if the judge believes that a sixty-five-miles-per-hour limitation is foolish or unwise, that judge may not simply ignore the statutory command. In fact, in cases brought before courts under such a statute this notion is accepted; no one will argue that the court should substitute its own miles-per-hour standard for that imposed by the legislature.

Not all statutes are as straightforward as the speed limit example. Perhaps the terms of a statute, when confronted by the facts in a case, seem ambiguous or outdated. Perhaps applying the statute to such facts creates a great injustice or actually defeats the purpose of the statute. Perhaps technology has changed in such a way that the wrong the statute sought to correct is being done in a way not contemplated by its exact words. If so, then a court will be called upon to interpret those words—make law along with the legislature—by applying the statute to particular facts.

The need for judicial construction of legislation may be shown by a hypothetical statute enacted in 1876. The statute says that "it is unlawful to walk across or drive a vehicle across a public flower garden." Apply those words to the following facts. Does the conduct violate the statute?

1. A person runs across a public flower garden.

2. In 1881, a person drives a horse and buggy across a public flower garden.

3. A doctor, while strolling in the park, sees a child fall from a tree and become seriously injured in the middle of a public flower garden. The doctor walks across the garden to administer aid to the child.

4. In 1994, a person drives a car across a public flower garden.

As shown by the example, proper application of the words of the legislature is not always clear. This portion of the chapter will discuss the construction and interpretation of statutes by a court. After an introduction to statutory construction, three general interpretative techniques will be discussed: first, the use of legislative history; second, interpreting the words of the statute themselves; and finally, the construction of a statute based upon its purpose.

Statutory Construction in General

The study of English literature often involves interpreting poems and novels on a variety of levels. The investigation into the "true" meaning (or meanings) of those literary works is very similar to what a court must do in order to interpret a statute. The writer and legislator put their ideas into words. The English professor and the judge will then be called upon to interpret or construe those words. The same word may have multiple meanings and may have to be interpreted differently depending upon the way it is being used. In a standard dictionary you will notice that such commonly used words as *front*, *fence*, and *frog* have very different meanings depending upon the context in which they are being used. Language itself is vague. Interpretation is needed.

Consequently, a single literary work may have a number of meanings depending upon which style of interpretation is being applied to the work. Some scholars consider Herman Melville's *Moby Dick* to be the greatest of all American novels; however, they disagree about its meaning. In one interpretation, only the words of the book will be considered, and it is read as an adventure story about the sea and whaling. Another method of interpretation requires a study of the life of the author, the influences on his life, and the historical events taking place during the writing of the novel. These factors will be used to gain an understanding of what Melville was attempting to say in *Moby Dick*—other than simply relating a story about the sea. A third method of interpretation will review the work apart from its author and attempt to extract from the book some basic principles or theories, which may not have even formally existed at the time it was written, but which scholars contend are contained within the novel itself.

Note that the very same novel, the same group of words, can have vastly different meanings to scholars of literature, depending upon the technique used to interpret the work. The question is not what Herman Melville intended when he wrote the novel. First of all, Melville is dead and cannot be of assistance in interpreting his work. All that we have is the novel that he left us, and the question instead is, ''What does the book mean?'' Perhaps Melville had nothing specific in mind when he wrote the book, except to earn a few dollars. Perhaps he actually intended the novel to be able to be read in a number of ways—in a sense, purposely made its meaning vague and ambiguous.

Literary interpretation is similar to statutory interpretation. Understanding what the ''texts'' mean is at the heart of the work of the judge and the literature scholar. Note, that often no one *true* meaning can be agreed upon.

Sources of Statutory Ambiguity

Technical Statutes

Sources of statutory ambiguity that call for judicial interpretation may be divided into three categories. First, the nature of the area of statutory regulation may be so technical and difficult as to raise questions concerning the meaning and applicability of the statutory language to particular facts. Examples of such ambiguity may be found in the federal securities laws and the tax laws. Courts have been asked to determine if a complex business arrangement would be a security within the provisions of the securities act. Orange groves in Florida and beauty products have been found by courts to be securities, because the promoters were actually selling investment interests rather than those products.

Nature of Language

A second source of ambiguity in statutes may be the language of the statute itself. In the example of the flower garden statute earlier in this section, the nature of the term *vehicle* had changed between the time when the statute was enacted (1876) and the time when an individual drove an automobile across the flower garden. In 1876, use of the term *vehicle* could not have been meant to include technology that did not even exist. Yet the mischief which the statute sought to control—damaged flowers—would occur to an even greater extent with an automobile. The job of a court would be to interpret the 1876 statute to determine if it should encompass the automobile violation.

Deliberate Vagueness

A third source of ambiguity in statutes is the deliberate creation of vagueness by the legislature when drafting the statute. A statute may purposely be worded imprecisely to garner enough votes to pass. Or several legislators may interpret a provision in a statute differently. The vague provision may enable enough legislators to vote in favor of the bill, yet determining what the terms of the statute actually meant would fall to the courts.

A statute may also be kept deliberately ambiguous to discourage those subject to its regulation from loophole finding—staying within the terms of the statute, but violating its spirit. The Uniform Commercial Code contains numerous examples of this type of vagueness. Many of its provisions require reasonable or commercially reasonable conduct. Nowhere does the legislator or drafter of that statute precisely outline the type of conduct that will meet the reasonableness test. Undoubtedly, if a series of clear guidelines were presented, someone could conform to those guidelines but under the particular facts of a case exercise unreasonable conduct. Courts are given the leeway to interpret *reasonableness* in the statute, and people are notified to exercise caution, at least in sharp business practices.

A final reason for deliberate ambiguity is that the circumstances which the statute is created to regulate are so varied that more particularized language may be impossible to insert. For example, Section 2-205 of the Uniform Commercial Code provides that a "firm offer," unless otherwise stated, will remain open for acceptance for a commercially reasonable time not to exceed three months. A "firm offer" to sell a crate of just-picked strawberries and a "firm offer" to sell a crate of books may be the same thing legally, but the facts of each situation make the length of time such an offer could remain open very different. That is, since strawberries will rot, a commercially reasonable time will be much shorter for them than for a crate of books.

Thus, courts often must work with legislatures in statutory lawmaking. The task of the court is to give meaning to a statute as it applies to specific facts. Although courts frequently claim that they are searching for the legislative intent, no such inquiry is possible. Courts do not have at their disposal the means to read the minds and determine the mental state of the legislature when it enacted a particular statute. Instead, the courts apply judicially created doctrines to try to determine what the words of the statute mean. Interpreting a statute is, in the end, an act of human judgment by the court, much like the human judgments that make up any judicial decision.

The following three sections will outline the most basic techniques used by judges in interpreting legislation. These techniques are an inquiry into the legislative history, use of the words of the statute, and inquiry into the purpose of the statute—what it was meant to accomplish. Although the interpretive techniques do give the judge some leeway in deciding how to construe a particular statute, the judge may not simply rewrite it.

In construing a statute, a court may consult a body of documentation called the **legislative history.** Legislative history consists of reports, studies, speeches, statements, committee findings, and similar materials that were created at the time the statute was drafted. These documents are consulted to determine the legislature's purpose in enacting a statute. The English language is not so precise an instrument as to always convey ideas clearly. Sometimes in order to understand a statement, a reader must consult additional source material. The judge, in consulting legislative history, acts in much the same way. By doing research into the deliberations of the legislature, the judge may be able to better understand the statute.

Use of legislative history, although a solid research technique, has been criticized. It assumes that there is only one meaning for the statute and that if the judge searches hard enough in the background documents, that one meaning will appear. Statutory construction involves judicial interpretation, and a statute, like a piece of literature, may be interpreted in different ways by different readers.

More practically, actually finding the legislative purpose through a review of the statutory history may be very difficult. How can the study of the statements of a few legislators and the reports of a committee or two enable a judge to determine that the legislature as a whole passed the statute with a certain purpose in mind? Maybe the deciding vote was cast because of political pressure or as part of an agreement that delivered legislative support on a wholly different issue. Some writers argue that use of legislative history by a court may encourage a legislator to create a historical record of a particular interpretation of an act, which in fact is not the one most fellow legislators would have agreed upon.

Use of legislative history involves judgment, as does use of historical materials by a scholar writing about, say, the presidency of Thomas Jefferson. Which ''historical'' material should be considered reliable and which unreliable? If the documents clash, how are the inconsistencies to be resolved? How much documentation is enough to allow one to safely make a conclusion concerning the historical background? Use of legislative history might not produce a clear answer.

The following case is an example of the use of legislative history. *United Steelworkers* v. *Weber* (1979) upheld a voluntary affirmative action plan that was challenged as a violation of Title VII of the Civil Rights Act of 1964. Such a claim was commonly called ''reverse discrimination.'' In *Weber,* Kaiser Aluminum Co. and the Steelworkers Union instituted race-based admissions to Kaiser's craft training program. Completion of this program would lead to a better paying job. The excerpt that follows, from the dissenting opinion of Justice Rehnquist, uses legislative history to bolster the argument that the Civil Rights Act does not allow race-conscious employment practices that favor black workers. Note his use of materials from the debates in Congress in the mid-1960s, when the Civil Rights Act was passed. The majority of the Court did not agree with this historical analysis.

United Steelworkers of America v. Weber
United States Supreme Court
443 U.S. 193 (1979)

Justice Rehnquist (dissenting)

By a tour de force reminiscent not of jurists such as Hale, Holmes, and Hughes, but of escape artists such as Houdini, the Court eludes "uncontradicted" legislative history in concluding that employers are, after all, permitted to consider race in making employment decisions. It may be that one or more of the principal sponsors of Title VII would have preferred to see a provision allowing preferential treatment of minorities written into the bill. But a reading of the legislative debates concerning Title VII, in which proponents and opponents alike uniformly denounced discrimination in favor of, as well as discrimination against, Negroes, demonstrates clearly that any legislator harboring an unspoken desire for such a provision could not possibly have succeeded in enacting it into law.

When H.R. 7152, the bill that ultimately became the Civil Rights Act of 1964, reached the House floor, the opening speech in support of its passage was delivered by Representative Celler, Chairman of the House Judiciary Committee and the Congressman responsible for introducing the legislation. A portion of that speech responded to criticism "seriously misrepresent[ing] what the bill would do and grossly distort[ing] its effects:

> [T]he charge has been made that the Equal Employment Opportunity Commission to be established by Title VII of the bill would have the power to prevent a business from employing and promoting the people it wished, and that a "Federal inspector" could then order the hiring and promotion only of employees of certain races or religious groups. This description of the bill is entirely wrong. . . .
>
> Even [a] court could not order that any preference be given to any particular race, religion or other group, but would be limited to ordering an end of discrimination. The statement that a Federal inspector could order the employment and promotion only of members of a specific racial or religious group is therefore patently erroneous.
>
> It is likewise not true that the Equal Employment Opportunity Commission would have power to rectify existing "racial or religious imbalance" in employ-

ment by requiring the hiring of certain people without regard to their qualifications simply because they are of a given race or religion. Only actual discrimination could be stopped. 110 Cong. Rec 1518 (1964).

In the opening speech of the formal Senate debate on the bill, Senator Humphrey addressed the main concern of Title VII's opponents, advising that not only does Title VII not require use of racial quotas, it does not permit their use. "The truth," stated the floor leader of the bill, "is that this title forbids discriminating against anyone on account of race. This is the simple and complete truth about Title VII." 110 Cong. Rec. 6549 (1964).

At the close of his speech, Senator Humphrey returned briefly to the subject of employment quotas: "It is claimed that the bill would require racial quotas for all hiring, when in fact it provides that race shall not be a basis for making personnel decisions."

A few days later the Senate's attention focused exclusively on Title VII, as Senators Clark and Case rose to discuss H.R. 7152. Of particular relevance to the instant litigation were their observations regarding seniority rights. As if directing their comments at Brian Weber [the plaintiff in this case], the Senators said:

> Title VII would have no effect on established seniority rights. Its effect is prospective and not retrospective. Thus, for example, if a business has been discriminating in the past and as a result has an all-white working force, when the title comes into effect the employer's obligation would be simply to fill future vacancies on a nondiscriminatory basis. He would not be obliged—or indeed permitted—to fire whites in order to hire Negroes, or to prefer Negroes for future vacancies, or, once Negroes are hired, to give them special seniority rights at the expense of the white workers hired earlier.

Thus, with virtual clairvoyance the Senate's leading supporters of Title VII anticipated precisely the circumstances of this case and advised their colleagues that the type of minority preference employed by Kaiser would violate Title VII's ban on racial discrimination.

Kaiser instituted an admissions quota preferring blacks over whites, thus confirming that the fears of Title VII's opponents were well founded. Today Title VII, adopted to allay those fears, is invoked by the Court to uphold imposition of a racial quota under the very circumstances that the section was intended to prevent.

Construing the Meaning of the Words Themselves

In addition to the review of the proceedings surrounding the enactment of a particular statute (its legislative history), courts have adopted doctrines that assist them in interpreting the words of the statute themselves. Three will be discussed: plain meaning, ejusdem generis, and reference to other parts of the same statute.

Plain Meaning Doctrine

The **plain meaning doctrine** is the most straightforward of statutory interpretation techniques. The court will look solely to the ordinary and usual meaning of the words of the statute in order to determine what the statute says. In a sense, this technique is akin to reading *Moby Dick* as a whale-hunting adventure story. Frequently, judicial opinions that use this technique refer to normally accepted usage or simply cite a dictionary definition of the terms. The following case is an example of the Court's using the plain meaning doctrine in applying and construing a particular statute.

Diamond v. Chakrabarty
United States Supreme Court
447 U.S. 303 (1980)

In 1972, Chakrabarty, a microbiologist, filed a patent application, assigned to the General Electric Co. The application asserted thirty-six claims related to Chakrabarty's invention of a bacterium. This human-made, genetically engineered bacterium is capable of breaking down multiple components of crude oil. Because of this property, which is possessed by no naturally occurring bacteria, Chakrabarty's invention is believed to have significant value for the treatment of oil spills.

Chakrabarty's patent claims were of three types: first, process claims for the method of producing the bacteria; second, claims for an inoculum comprised of a carrier material floating on water, such as straw, and the new bacteria; and third, claims to the bacteria themselves. The patent examiner allowed the claims falling into the first two categories, but rejected claims for the bacteria. His decision rested on two grounds: (1) microorganisms are "products of nature" and (2) as living things, they are not patentable subject matter under 35 U.S.C. § 101.

Chakrabarty appealed the rejection of these claims to the Patent Office Board of Appeals, and the board affirmed the examiner. The board concluded that § 101 was not intended to cover living things such as these laboratory created micro-organisms.

Chief Justice Burger

The Constitution grants Congress broad power to legislate to "promote the Progress of Science and useful Arts, by securing for limited Times to Authors and Inventors the exclusive Right to their respective Writings and Discoveries." The authority of Congress is exercised in the hope that the productive effort thereby fostered will have a positive effect on society through the introduction of new products and processes of manufacture into the economy, and the emanations by way of increased employment and better lives for our citizens.

The question before us in this case is a narrow one of statutory interpretation requiring us to construe 35 U.S.C. § 101, which provides:

> Whoever invents or discovers any new and useful process, machine, manufacture, or composition of matter, or any new and useful improvement thereof, may obtain a patent therefore, subject to the conditions and requirements of this title.

Specifically we must determine whether respondent's micro-organism constitutes a "manufacture" or "composition of matter" within the meaning of the statute.

In cases of statutory construction we begin, of course, with the language of the statute. And "unless otherwise defined, words will be interpreted as taking their ordinary, contemporary, common meaning." We have also cautioned that courts should not read into the patent laws limitations and conditions which the legislature has not expressed.

Guided by these canons of construction, this court has read the term "manufacture" in § 101 in accordance with its dictionary definition to mean the production of articles for use from raw or prepared materials by giving to these materials new forms, qualities, properties, or combinations, whether by hand-labor or by machinery.

Similarly, "composition of matter" has been construed consistent with its common usage to include all compositions of two or more substances and all composite articles, whether they be the results of chemical union, or of mechanical mixture, or whether they be gases, fluids, powders or solids. In choosing such expansive terms as "manufacture" and "composition of matter," modified by the comprehensive "any," Congress plainly contemplated that the patent laws would be given wide scope. This is not to suggest that § 101 has no limits or that it embraces every discovery. The laws of nature, physical phenomena, and abstract ideas have been held not patentable.

Judged in this light, respondent's microorganism plainly qualifies as patentable subject matter. His claim is not to a hitherto unknown natural phenomenon, but to a nonnaturally occurring manufacture of composition of matter—a product of human ingenuity "having a distinctive name, character [and] use."

It is, of course, correct that Congress, not the courts, must define the limits of patentability; but it is equally true that once Congress has spoken it is "the province and duty of the judicial department to say what the law is." Congress has performed its constitutional role in defining patentable subject matter in § 101; we perform ours in construing the language Congress has employed. In so doing, our obligation is to take statutes as we find them, guided, if ambiguity appears, by the legislative history and statutory purpose. Here, we perceive no ambiguity. The subject-matter provisions of the patent law have been cast in broad terms to fulfill the constitutional and statutory goal of promoting "the Progress of Science and the useful Arts." Broad general language is not necessarily ambiguous when congressional objectives require broad terms.

Ejusdem Generis Doctrine

The **ejusdem generis doctrine** refers to a technique of interpreting a catchall phrase that had been inserted in a statute after a series of specific words. The doctrine provides that the general phrase shall be interpreted to include words of the same kind as those used in the series of words before it. For example, suppose a legislature has redrafted the flower garden trespass statute discussed earlier in this section. The statute now prohibits going across the flower garden by "car, bicycle, motorcycle, van, truck, bus, or other vehicle." If someone drives a moped across the flower garden, the court would have to determine whether the statute would include moped within its terms even though the word *moped* appears nowhere within it. Under the doctrine of ejusdem generis, the court could read the general term *other vehicle* to include a moped, since it is of the same type as the vehicles specifically listed in the statute.

Referring to Other Parts of the Statute

Often we may be unsure of the precise meaning of a word in a book we are reading. Frequently, the meaning of a word can be gleaned by reference to the accompanying subject matter. Courts may use the same style of interpretation when construing language in a statute. Sometimes statutes are quite lengthy and contain a number of separate provisions all aimed at regulating a certain area. If a word or phrase in a particular section is not clear, there may be some dispute as to the particular meaning in a given case. When using this interpretation technique, a court will read the unclear portion of the statute together with, and with reference to, the rest of the statute. In that way, the word or phrase is interpreted as it relates to the legislative enactment as a whole. The word is read within the statutory context in which it is being used.

The Spirit or Purpose of the Statute

Someone may observe the letter of a certain law but violate its spirit. What that generally means is that the behavior of the person in question is consistent with a literal reading of the words of a statute. However, a statute or a rule is not merely a set of words. It exists for a reason and was enacted to further a goal of the legislature. The expression means that the behavior is contrary to legislative purpose, even though it is technically correct given the meaning of the words of the statute. In such a case, a court may interpret the statute consistent with its purpose rather than with the plain meaning of its words.

Return to the garden trespassing statute, discussed earlier in this section, for an example. The statute prohibited individuals from walking across a public flower garden. If a person ran across the garden, would the statute apply? Clearly, the aim of the statute was to prevent people from trampling flowers in the public park. Yet the plain meaning of the word *walk* does not include the act of running. In this sense, the behavior of the runner was within the letter of the law but not within the spirit. However, a court may well hold that running too is prohibited by the statute. The court would be applying the statute to specific incidents as they arise consistent with the purpose and aim of the statute.

As previously noted, sometimes events occur after the passage of an act that could not have been anticipated by the legislators as they were drafting the statute. Perhaps mores have changed. Perhaps new technology has been developed. Either of those instances might give rise to a situation not specifically covered by the terms of the statute but clearly covered by its spirit. In the example of the flower garden statute, the act as passed in 1876 prohibited vehicles from crushing the flowers. Suppose that in 1994 an automobile is driven across the flower garden. Clearly, under a legislative history test, the statute could not be applied to automobiles, since they did not exist at the time of the enactment and perhaps were not even considered except in the imaginations of inventors. Yet given the act's purpose, it should include the prohibition of automobile use. A court may well apply the purpose of the statute to the facts of the case and extend its applicability to automobiles.

Statutes, through such interpretation, can remain vital and useful in the everchanging world. A legislator could not hope to consider all the factors a statute should cover. Courts, working with the legislature and writing opinions consistent with the aim of the statute, expand or contract its coverage to meet the needs and demands of modern society.

The following case is an example of the purpose of a statute being used to interpret it in a certain situation.

Lennon v. Immigration and Naturalization Service
United States Court of Appeals, Second Circuit
527 F.2d 187 (1975)

On October 18, 1968, detectives from the Scotland Yard drug squad conducted a warrantless search of John Lennon's apartment at 34 Montague Square, London. There, the officers found one-half ounce of hashish inside a binocular case and thereupon placed Lennon under arrest. Lennon pleaded guilty to possession of cannabis resin in Marylebone Magistrate's Court on November 28, 1968; he was fined £150.

On August 13, 1971, Lennon and his wife, Yoko Ono, arrived in New York. They had come to this country to seek custody of Mrs. Lennon's daughter by a former marriage to an American citizen.

The Immigration and Nationality Act § 212(a) lists thirty-one classes of "excludable aliens" who are ineligible for permanent residence. Among those excludable is "any alien who has been convicted of a violation of any law or regulation relating to the illicit possession of marihuana." Since John Lennon's conviction appeared to render him excludable, the Immigration and Naturalization Service (INS) specifically waived excludability. The Lennons were then given temporary visas valid until September 24, 1971; the INS later extended the expiration date to February 29, 1972.

The day after Lennon's visa expired, March 1, Sol Marks, the New York District Director of the INS, notified the Lennons by letter that, if they did not leave the country by March 15, deportation proceedings would be instituted. On March 3, Lennon and his wife filed third preference petitions. In response to these applications, the INS instituted deportation proceedings three days later.

In March, April, and May, 1972, deportation hearings were held before Immigration Judge Fieldsteel. The immigration judge filed his decision on March 23, 1973. Since Yoko Ono had obtained permanent resident status in 1964, he granted her application. But, because he believed that John Lennon was an excludable alien, the immigration judge denied his application and ordered him deported.

Kaufman, Chief Judge

We have come a long way from the days when fear and prejudice toward alien races were the guiding forces behind our immigration laws. The Chinese exclusion acts of the 1880's and the "barred zone" created by the 1917 Immigration Act have, thankfully, been removed from the statute books and relegated to the historical treatises. Nevertheless, the power of Congress to exclude or deport natives of other countries remains virtually unfettered. In the vast majority of deportation cases, the fate of the client must therefore hinge upon narrow issues of statutory construction. To this rule, the appeal of John Lennon, an internationally known "rock" musician, presents no exception. We are, in this case, called upon to decide whether Lennon's 1968 British conviction for possession of cannabis resin renders him, as the Board of Immigration Appeals believed, an excludable alien under § 212(a)(23) of the Immigration and Nationality Act (INA), which applies to those convicted of illicit possession of marihuana. We hold that Lennon's conviction does not fall within the ambit of this section.

We base this result upon our conclusion that Lennon was convicted under a law which in effect makes guilty knowledge irrelevant and such a law does not render the convicted alien excludable.

The language of the British statute under which Lennon was convicted is deceptively simple: "A person shall not be in possession of a drug unless . . . authorized. . . ." But around this concise provision, judicial interpretation has created a scholastic maze as complex and baffling as the Labyrinth at Knossos in ancient Crete. However, we conclude, from analyzing British law as it existed in 1968, that Lennon was convicted under a

statute which made guilty knowledge irrelevant. Under British law a person found with tablets which he reasonably believed were aspirin would be convicted if the tablets proved to contain heroin. And a man given a sealed package filled with heroin would, if he had had any opportunity to open the parcel, suffer the same fate—even if he firmly believed the package contained perfume.

The general purpose of § 212(a)(23) is, of course, to bar undesirable aliens from our shores. There is also, we note, some indication that Congress, in enacting § 212(a)(23), was far more concerned with the trafficker of drugs than with the possessor. We do not believe that our holding will subvert these Congressional ends. Virtually every undesirable alien covered by the drug conviction provision would also be barred by other sections of the statute. Moreover, addicts are barred. Finally, our holding will not, of course, give any comfort to those convicted in the United States of drug violations.

Given, in sum, the minimal gain in effective enforcement, we cannot imagine that Congress would impose the harsh consequences of an excludable alien classification upon a person convicted under a foreign law that made guilty knowledge irrelevant.

Before closing with the traditional words of disposition, we feel it appropriate to express our faith that the result we have reached in this case not only is consistent with the language and purpose of the narrow statutory provision we construe, but also furthers the intent of the immigration laws in a far broader sense. The excludable aliens statute is but an exception, albeit necessary, to the traditional tolerance of a nation founded and built by immigrants. If, in our two hundred years of independence, we have in some measure realized our ideals, it is in large part because we have always found a place for those committed to the spirit of liberty and willing to help implement it. Lennon's four-year battle to remain in our country is testimony to his faith in this American dream.

Accordingly, the denial of Lennon's application for adjustment of status and the order of deportation are vacated and the case remanded for reconsideration in accordance with the views expressed in this opinion.

Mulligan, Circuit Judge (dissenting)

That statute would exclude any alien who has been convicted of a violation of any law or regulation relating to the illicit possession of narcotic drugs or marihuana. Since the statute applies to any alien it makes no difference whether he be John Lennon, John Doe or Johann Sebastian Bach.

The undisputed fact however is that Lennon did plead guilty to the possession of cannabis resin, and while this may have been convenient or expedient because of his wife's pregnancy and his disinclination to have her testify in court, it is elementary that we cannot go behind the plea.

The majority here concludes that the Congress was more concerned with trafficking in drugs than in possession and their opinion does not cover the trafficker who obviously is fully aware of the nature of the business he is pursuing. The statute however bars the possessor as well as the trafficker. If there were no users there would be no trafficking. It must also be emphasized that the vast majority of those who are arrested with illicit drugs in their homes or on their persons are users who are fully aware of their presence and their properties. It is the unusual case where contraband such as this is surreptitiously planted in one's reticule or blue jeans pocket. Yet by disregarding convictions under the British statute or any other foreign counterpart, the majority would admit to the United States those who knowingly possessed any illicit drugs. This holding seems to me to conflict with INS § 212(a)(23), which plainly bars those who have been convicted of a violation. Lennon's guilty plea here puts him within the statute.

THE EXECUTIVE BRANCH

Although throughout this section the executive branch of government will be referred to as the presidency, that branch includes many officials besides the president (see Figure 5.1). The executive branch also contains a number of agencies, called executive agencies; examples include the Department of Agriculture, the Department of Commerce, the State Department on the federal level, and the office of the prosecutor and the police department on the state or local level. Note that the discussions in Chapter 7 concerning administrative agencies are applicable to executive agencies as well.

Normally, one thinks of the executive branch as being primarily responsible for carrying out statutes enacted by the legislature and orders issued by courts. In classic separation of powers theory the legislature makes the law, the courts interpret the law, and the executive branch enforces the law. But, as noted in earlier chapters, clear delineation between the branches, particularly when it involves lawmaking, is not appropriate. Each branch, within its government role, makes law that can affect business. The following discussion will focus on this activity of the executive branch.

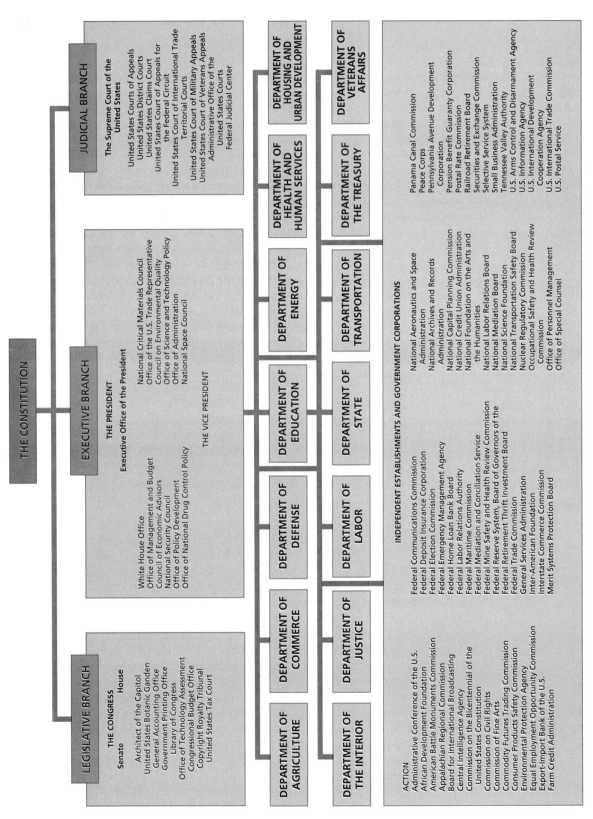

Figure 5.1 The Government of the United States

Source: Office of the Federal Register. *The United States Government Manual 1988/89*, Washington DC: U.S. Government Printing Office, 1988, p. 21.

Relationship of the Executive with Other Branches of Government

The three branches of government act to check and balance one another's power, so that no one branch or individual acquires too much power. Both the Congress and the courts act as checks on the president and are at the same time dependent on the president in the carrying out of their government functions. The Congress is largely dependent on the executive branch for the implementation of the laws it enacts. A president who supports certain legislation will most likely vigorously enforce the congressional policy. However, a president who does not agree with a statute may well frustrate the purposes of the enacted law by having a weak enforcement program. An example from the 1980s was the Reagan administration's enforcement policies in a number of regulatory areas—for example, antitrust and environmental protection. By not enforcing the legislation as did prior administrations, the Reagan administration in fact was changing the "law," even though no formal legislative or regulatory modifications occurred. Thus, the antitrust law factor, for example, was less significant in corporate merger decisions under Reagan than under Carter, Ford, or Nixon. The risk of government interference in such activities, being less, lowered the "cost" of executives' acquisition decisions. Note that the Bush administration increased somewhat the enforcement effort in both antitrust and environmental protection. Thus, the legal environment changed again.

The Congress, however, does have leverage over the executive branch, and can certainly frustrate the plans and policies of a president. The ultimate control by Congress is the power to impeach and remove the president from office. However, other congressional powers act more regularly as checks on the executive branch. Congress has control over the appropriation of federal funds, and may either underfund or refuse to fund an executive's key programs. Congress also has the power to refuse to consent to certain presidential appointments. The Senate's rejection of Robert Bork, one of President Reagan's nominees to the Supreme Court, was an example. Bork, unquestionably, had superb credentials; however, his positions on key issues that could come before the Court led to the Senate refusing to consent to the appointment. Lastly, the Congress has the ability to shape legislative programs. Although most program initiatives come from the executive, the final form is the province of the Congress.

The judicial branch may also act to check the power of the executive. Judges do not seize property, keep people in jail, or make sure a school is integrated on a day-to-day basis. A judge may order that any of those things occur, but the judge does not execute those orders. Their implementation is left to the executive branch of government. However, at the same time that the court relies on the executive, the court also has the power to set the limits of the executive's power. This function of the judiciary will be noted later.

Lawmaking Powers of the Executive

The lawmaking powers of the president may be divided into three groups: first, the general power to draft rules called executive orders; second, the ability to make law through the carrying out of the general executive duties; and third, the ability to make law by virtue of policy initiation.

Executive Orders

The president has the power to issue **executive orders**, which can have the same force and effect as statutes enacted by the Congress or regulations promulgated by an administrative agency. Often these orders are merely housekeeping rules—setting government job categories at certain salary levels, authorizing the creation of boards or committees to coordinate compliance with a statute. However, executive orders may have a much greater effect. Executive orders have controlled wages and prices, set curfews, and made energy policy.

One of the most noteworthy executive orders was President Lyndon Johnson's 1965 executive order requiring affirmative action in hiring by contractors who did business with the federal government. This was an important and far-reaching rule in that it, in effect, regulated business practices of a large number of firms throughout the United States. Johnson's executive order went far beyond any existing policy or law of the goverment at that time to remedy racial discrimination. This executive order was the source of an employment discrimination claim brought by women and minority group members against Harris Trust & Savings Bank. The bank was considered a federal contractor because it held federally insured deposits; thus, its activities were governed by the executive order. Harris Bank settled the claim for fourteen million dollars. It also agreed to modify its hiring policies as well as enhance its training programs to provide advancement opportunities for women and minority group employees.

The president, however, does not have unlimited power and authority to create law through executive order. That power is limited by the Constitution and by congressional legislation. For example, the president would not have the authority to make an executive order prohibiting federal courts from applying the antitrust laws. Although a president may support such a limitation, the Constitution confers that power solely on the Congress. Additionally, executive orders must be drafted within the confines of the express or implied powers set by the Congress for the president to make such an order. A president does not have the ability to draft executive orders to fit any situation that may come to mind. The order must not conflict with limits set by the Congress or the Constitution.

Therefore, the executive's lawmaking power is far more limited than that of the legislature or even that of the courts. The law may be made only pursuant to authority granted by the Constitution or by Congress to draft executive orders covering certain topics. When a dispute arises, it is the duty of the courts to determine whether the executive order was properly made and therefore effective.

To illustrate, President Harry Truman ordered the steel mills seized during the Korean War because of a labor dispute. Truman argued that he had this power both under constitutional authority and as implied by a number of war-related congressional statutes. Article 2, Section 3 of the Constitution requires that the president "take care that the laws be faithfully executed." Truman contended that his executive order calling for seizure of the mills was necessary to execute wartime legislation concerning material procurement and wage and price stability. Truman lost. The United States Supreme Court found neither congressional nor constitutional support for Truman's action. Justice Black, writing for the Court, noted:

The President's order does not direct that a congressional policy be executed in a manner prescribed by Congress—it directs that a presidential policy be executed in a manner prescribed by the President. . . . The Constitution does not subject this lawmaking power of Congress to presidential or military supervision or control.

Figure 5.2 is an example of an executive order concerning drugs in the federal workforce. How would such an order affect the legal environment of business?

Lawmaking through Action

The president also makes law by virtue of various actions taken in the role of executive. This type of lawmaking does not involve the drafting of any rules or regulations. Instead, through judgment and policy choices, the executive makes law in determining how to enforce it. This type of lawmaking may arise directly from the exercise of powers granted the executive by the Constitution, or it may arise from the exercise of judgment by the executive in carrying out the duty to faithfully execute the laws of Congress.

Under the Constitution, the president has certain powers with respect to law made by the legislature and by the judiciary. The president has the right to veto any bill passed by the Congress. The possibility of a veto will often move the Congress to draft legislation compatible with the goals of the president. In this way, through this constitutional power, the president is closely involved with the creation of legislation.

The president has similar constitutional power over decision making by the federal courts. Federal judges are appointed by the president (with the advice and consent of the Senate). As a practical matter, the overwhelming majority of judges appointed by the president are confirmed by the Senate. Therefore, over time, a president has the ability to appoint judges with certain political and social philosophies. (Remember the discussion of the factor of the judge's personality in Chapter 4.) A president may be able to influence the law for years after leaving office by appointing certain individuals to the federal bench.

The decision-making function of a court may also be affected by constitutional powers given to the president to pardon a person from criminal acts that may have been committed or to commute a sentence imposed by a court. By pardoning an individual from alleged crimes, the president removes the judiciary from adjudicating the guilt of that individual. By commuting a sentence imposed by a court, the president overrides a judgment of the court that is designed to render such decisions. The executive may also make law through the exercise of judgment while carrying out the law. Note the effect of the Reagan administration's enforcement policies on both antitrust and environmental law, mentioned earlier.

Therefore, the personality of the executive, like the personality of the judge, is important in the law. The law at any given time is a function of the actions and decisions of the legislative, judicial, and executive branches of government as well as the working of relevant administrative agencies. To understand the legal environment, a general appreciation of the interaction of these various government units is needed.

Executive Order 12564 of September 15, 1986

DRUG-FREE FEDERAL WORKPLACE

Section 1. *Drug-Free Workplace.*

(a) Federal employees are required to refrain from the use of illegal drugs.
(b) The use of illegal drugs by Federal employees, whether on duty or off duty, is contrary to the efficiency of the service.
(c) Persons who use illegal drugs are not suitable for Federal employment.

Sec. 2. *Agency Responsibilities.*

(a) The head of each Executive agency shall develop a plan for achieving the objective of a drug-free workplace with due consideration of the rights of the government, the employee, and the general public.
(b) Each agency plan shall include:
(1) A statement of policy setting forth the agency's expectations regarding drug use and the action to be anticipated in response to identified drug use;
(2) Employee Assistance Programs emphasizing high level direction, education, counseling, referral to rehabilitation, and coordination with available community resources;
(3) Supervisory training to assist in identifying and addressing illegal drug use by agency employees;
(4) Provision for self-referrals as well as supervisory referrals to treatment with maximum respect for individual confidentiality consistent with safety and security issues; and
(5) Provision for identifying illegal drug users, including testing on a controlled and carefully monitored basis in accordance with this Order.

Sec. 3. *Drug Testing Programs.*

(a) The head of each Executive agency shall establish a program to test for the use of illegal drugs by employees in sensitive positions.
(b) The head of each Executive agency shall establish a program for voluntary employee drug testing.
(c) Each Executive agency is authorized to test an employee for illegal drug use under the following circumstances:
(1) When there is a reasonable suspicion that any employee uses illegal drugs;
(2) In an examination authorized by the agency regarding an accident or unsafe practice; or
(3) As part of or as a follow-up to counseling or rehabilitation for illegal drug use through an Employee Assistance Program.
(d) The head of each Executive agency is authorized to test any applicant for illegal drug use.

RONALD REAGAN

THE WHITE HOUSE
September 15, 1986.

Figure 5.2   Executive Order 12564 of September 15, 1986: Drug-Free Federal Workplace

Lawmaking through Policy

The president also has another effect on the law, by virtue of the policy-making function of the office. Legislation is generally initiated by the executive branch. The president presents the Congress with a legislative package, often with drafts of bills included in the package. Congress works through that package in its task of enacting legislation. This is a powerful lawmaking tool for the executive, who sets the lawmaking priority for the Congress and then has the ability to lobby and pressure various lawmakers to get that package enacted. This key aspect of the power of the president did not always exist. In the latter part of the nineteenth century, the president was more of an administrator, and the power for initiating legislation, as well as enacting it, rested with the Congress. The shift of the legislation-initiating power began in this century and was fully developed during the Roosevelt administration with the flurry of legislative proposals sent to Congress to combat the Great Depression.

Limits on Executive Lawmaking Power

The limits on the lawmaking power of the president are generally based upon unwritten rules, past practice, and basic political accommodation among the various branches of government. Limits are not explicitly set until the president goes beyond what could generally be considered to be proper boundaries of executive power. The national experiences with the Vietnamese war and with the revelations of Watergate served to move Congress to legislate limits on certain lawmaking powers of the president where in the past only unwritten rules existed. In the end, however, the people will act or demand that action be taken to curb executive abuses. An example demonstrates this point.

Although the Constitution gives Congress the power to declare war, the president, as commander-in-chief of the armed forces, committed troops to a number of areas (the Caribbean, North Africa to fight the Barbary pirates) throughout American history without a formal congressional declaration of war. However, none of those actions was on as large a scale as the conflict in Vietnam, nor did these actions last as long. During the Vietnamese war, Congress never acted to formally declare war. As a result, after the war, Congress sought to limit the unwritten power of the president alone to make war through the War Powers Act.

Recall that Congress did vote to grant President Bush the right to implement United Nations' resolutions concerning Iraq's invasion of Kuwait. However, hundreds of thousands of American troops were in the war zone before any Congressional action was taken. This area of power sharing between the Executive and Legislative branches remains controversial.

General Issues Involving the Executive Branch

The limits of the power of the executive branch are only rarely adjudicated by the courts. Such issues necessarily involve a test of our form of government. Although a court may well limit the power of the executive, who is to enforce that limitation? Courts may use public opinion and the prestige of their position, but in the end the executive must voluntarily accept the limits imposed by the courts. Any other decision by the executive may well lead to the loss of our system of government.

As a result, courts do not generally confront the executive branch on the limitation of its powers. Frequently courts will simply refuse to decide a challenge to executive action, holding it to be a political, not a judicial, issue. In the end, most questions of executive authority are solved through the give-and-take of the political arena.

WILL HAVE HARD QUESTION 000

Political and Foreign Policy Questions

COURT WON'T TOUCH!! b

As suggested earlier, courts will at times refuse to review the extent of the power exercised by a president. After all, both the president and the courts are sworn to uphold the Constitution. Furthermore, as suggested in Chapter 6, on the Constitution, the meaning of the various terms of the Constitution is certainly subject to diverse good-faith interpretations.

A court, therefore, may refuse to even hear a challenge to an action taken by the president, claiming that such an action is a political question or that the issue is not **justiciable.** This means that the issue presented to the court is not one that is in its power to decide. Other forums in the government or the ballot box may be more appropriate for resolving the conflict.

Courts will similarly usually refuse to review the decision of the president in the area of international relations. This is a recognition of the power of the president and a recognition of the expertise of the executive branch to conduct foreign affairs.

An example of this judicial deference was the issue of the constitutionality of the Vietnamese war. Cases were brought while the war was being fought. Congress had never declared war. Instead, the conflict was fought pursuant to executive order and a resolution passed by the Congress called the Tonkin Gulf Resolution. However, Congress continually funded the war effort. The following case is from a lower court where the issue was raised.

Orlando and Berk v. Laird
United States Court of Appeals, Second Circuit
443 F.2d 1039 (1971)

This case consolidates two actions by servicemen to challenge the constitutional sufficiency of the authority of the executive branch to wage war in Vietnam. The servicemen, in separate actions in June 1970, sought to enjoin the secretary of defense, the secretary of the army, and the commanding officers, who signed their deployment orders, from enforcing them. The plaintiffs contended that these executive officers exceeded their constitutional authority by ordering them to participate in a war not properly authorized by Congress.

Anderson, Circuit Judge

The Government takes the position that the suits concern a nonjusticiable political question; that the military action in South Vietnam was authorized by Congress in the "Joint Resolution to Promote the Maintenance of Internal Peace and Security in Southeast Asia" (the Tonkin Gulf Resolution) considered in connection with the Seato Treaty; and that the military action was authorized and ratified by congressional appropriations expressly designated for use in support of the military operations in Vietnam.

Although appellant-servicemen do not contend that Congress can exercise its war-declaring power only through a formal declaration, they argue that congressional authorization cannot, as a matter of law, be inferred from military appropriations that does not contain an express and explicit authorization for the making of war by the President. Putting aside for a moment the explicit authorization of the Tonkin Gulf Resolution, we disagree with appellants' interpretation of the declaration clause for neither the language nor the purpose underlying that provision prohibits an inference of the fact of authorization from such legislative action as we have in this instance. The framers' intent to vest the war power in Congress is in no way defeated by permitting an inference of authorization from legislative action furnishing the manpower and materials of war for the protracted military operation in southeast Asia.

The choice, for example, between an explicit declaration on the one hand and a resolution and war-implementing legislation, on the other, as the medium for expression of congressional consent involves "the exercise of a discretion demonstrably committed to the . . . legislature," and therefore, invokes the political question doctrine.

Such a choice involves an important area of decision making in which, through mutual influence and reciprocal action between the President and the Congress, policies governing the relationship between this country and other parts of the world are formulated in the best interests of the United States. If there can be nothing more than minor military operations conducted under any circumstances, short of an express and explicit declaration of war by Congress, then extended military operations could not be conducted even though both the Congress and the President were agreed that they were necessary and were also agreed that a formal declaration of war would place the nation in a posture in its international relations which would be against its best interests. For the judicial branch to enunciate and enforce such a standard would be not only extremely unwise but also would constitute a deep invasion of the political question domain. What has been said and done by both the President and the Congress in their collaborative conduct of the military operations in Vietnam implies a consensus on the advisability of not making a formal declaration of war because it would be contrary to the interests of the United States to do so. The making of a policy decision of that kind is clearly within the constitutional domain of those two branches and is just as clearly not within the competency or power of the judiciary.

SUMMARY

The legislative and executive branches of government have a major effect on the legal environment of business. Although the legislature is usually considered to be the lawmaking branch of government, the executive branch is also involved in crafting legal rules that affect business. Thus, business organizations must work with the political branches in order to protect their interests. Dealing with the legal environment not only means considering how given legal rules affect business decisions, it also means learning how to influence the activities of the political branches. Lobbying and campaign contributions are used to ensure access to both legislative and executive branch members before their positions on an issue are developed fully.

This chapter also illustrated doctrines of statutory interpretation. Referring to the legislative history, the words of the statute, and its purpose are all techniques courts use to apply a statute in a case. Note, therefore, how the statutory legal environment consists of both judiciary and legislative activity.

REVIEW QUESTIONS

1. Define the following terms:
   a. Ejusdem generis
   b. Executive order
   c. Plain meaning doctrine

2. Use statutory interpretation techniques to discuss how the statute involved in the following problem should be interpreted. Make sure you can identify the technique urged on the court by each party in the dispute.

   Glen filed a lawsuit against the United States government. He represents a class of plaintiffs who are terminally ill with cancer and would like to use the drug Laetrile as part of their treatment. The United States government would not permit the interstate shipment and sale of Laetrile, since it was not approved by the secretary of the Department of Health, Education, and Welfare pursuant to the Food, Drug, and Cosmetic Act. The act will not permit the distribution of any new drug without such approval. The act defines a "new drug" as "any drug not generally recognized, among experts qualified by scientific training and experience to evaluate the safety and effectiveness of drugs, as safe and effective for use under the conditions prescribed, recommended or suggested in the labeling."

   Scientific experts have determined that Laetrile is not generally recognized as safe and effective as a treatment for cancer, since no adequate studies exist that demonstrate the drug's safety or effectiveness. Remarks made in Congress at the time of the act's passage show that the lawmakers were concerned about drugs being placed on the market before adequate testing was done, the danger being the harm that their use could cause to the people. Furthermore, the Congress was concerned about fraudulent cures being offered as drugs to people who were ill. However, terminally ill patients might be distinguished from the general population because there is no cure leading to recovery from their disease.

3. Use statutory interpretation techniques to discuss how the statute involved in the following problem should be interpreted. Make sure you can identify the technique urged on the court by each party in the dispute.

   A jury returned a verdict for Baker against Jacobs. Immediately thereafter, Baker treated the jury to cigars at a local hotel as a gesture of appreciation. Upon learning of this, Jacobs sought to have a court set aside the verdict rendered by the jury. He relied on the following statute: "If a party obtaining a verdict in his favor shall, during the term of the court in which such a verdict is obtained, give to any of the jurors in the case, knowing him to be such, any victuals or drink, or procure the same to be done, by way of treat, either before or after such verdict, on proof thereof being made the verdict shall be set aside and a new trial granted."

4. Congress enacted general statutes concerning the importance of wage and price stability in this country. They specifically prohibited the president from ordering wage and price controls. However, the president has the power to enter into contracts on behalf of the government to carry out the appropriation-of-funds decisions made by Congress. Assume that the president drafts an executive order requiring all companies

that do business with the government to freeze their prices and wages on pain of losing future government contracts if they do not comply. Is that executive order within the power of the president to make?

5. Compare lawmaking by the legislature with lawmaking by judicial decision.

6. Discuss the techniques of statutory construction.

7. Discuss the lawmaking powers existing in the executive branch of government.

8. What is the purpose of judicial use of legislative history when construing a statute? Discuss its advantages and disadvantages.

9. You are an executive with the XYZ Corporation. The corporation is involved in the landscaping business. A major part of its business is supplying plants and seeds. A statute reads as follows: "No flower, vegetable, bush or other plant may be imported into the United States without approval from the USDA." You learn that a unique variety of tree, found only in Japan, is available for your corporation to import into the United States. However, the delay and cost in obtaining approval for importing the special trees would make them too expensive to import. Must the corporation obtain approval before importing the trees? Give reasons.

10. Why do courts often defer political questions and foreign policy issues to the discretion of the executive branch?

11. A statute reads as follows: "No business may keep a large, vicious dog on its premises." The statute was enacted after several children were attacked by guard dogs that broke loose from the businesses they were protecting. During consideration of the bill, several representatives filed reports showing similar incidents throughout the country. Many argued that innocent citizens, especially children, should not have to fear attack from beasts. A few noted that alarm systems, if properly installed, would adequately protect any business.

You own a small business that has been robbed several times. After reading the statute just referred to, you buy a mountain lion to keep at your business to deter burglars. Are you in violation of the statute? Give reasons.

12. Does business have more influence in lawmaking by the legislature or in lawmaking by the courts? Explain.

13. Compare the process of enacting a statute by the legislature with the techniques used by courts to interpret that statute. Do those techniques reflect the reality of the legislative process?

CHAPTER 6

Constitutional Law and Business

- The United States Constitution
- Federal Power to Regulate Business
- State Power to Regulate Business
- Limitations on Governmental Power
- The First Amendment and Business

A study of the Constitution of the United States, its amendments, and its judicial interpretations embodies the history of this country. This chapter presents a discussion of the Constitution as a means of providing an appreciation for that document and its place in the American legal environment.

The major focus of this chapter concerns the power of the government to regulate business. We first address the question: To what extent may the federal government regulate business? As will be evident from the material in the chapter, the federal government has enormous power to control the activities of business. The primary source of federal power, the commerce clause, has been interpreted as a very broad grant of power to Congress. We then move to the power of state governments to regulate business. Their power comes from what is known as the police power. It permits the states to place extensive controls over business.

In this chapter, we address various limits on the powers of both the federal and state governments to regulate business. The drafters of the United States Constitution placed certain constitutional limits on the power of federal and state governments to keep them from dealing unfairly with people.

THE UNITED STATES CONSTITUTION

Carefully read the Constitution (see Appendix B of this text). Note its two major functions. First, the articles of the Constitution set forth the basic structure of the government. Many of the amendments also pertain to government organization (for example, the Twenty-second Amendment, limitation on the number of terms a president may serve, and the Twenty-fifth Amendment, presidential succession). The second major function of the Constitution is to provide for individual rights. Most often the provisions in the Bill of Rights (the first ten amendments) are cited as performing this function. However, individual freedoms, such as the right to trial by jury in a criminal case (Article III, Section 2), are also provided in the articles of the Constitution and in other amendments—for example, the Civil War Amendments (the Thirteenth, Fourteenth, and Fifteenth Amendments), which were the constitutional basis for the legal battle for civil rights.

FEDERAL POWER TO REGULATE BUSINESS

The commerce clause is of great significance with respect to the power of the federal government to regulate business. This clause appears in the United States Constitution in Article I, Section 8, Subsection 3. It reads as follows: Congress shall have the power "To regulate Commerce with foreign Nations, and among the several States, and with the Indian Tribes." The commerce clause serves not only as a source of congressional power to regulate commerce, but also as a limitation on the power of the states to enact legislation that regulates commerce.

This clause gives Congress three areas over which it can regulate commerce—that involving the Indian tribes, commerce with foreign nations, and commerce among the states. We will leave the matter of trade with the Indian tribes to another course. The latter two areas are very important to business.

Foreign Commerce

Throughout the history of the United States, there has never been any question that the federal government has the exclusive right to regulate foreign commerce and that this power extends to all aspects of foreign trade. Chief Justice Marshall in 1824 so held in *Gibbons* v. *Ogden*. The states and local governments therefore may not interfere in any way with foreign trade. Suppose that a city wished to bar the importation of goods from Russia. If it passed an ordinance to this effect, such an ordinance would be struck down by a court as beyond the power of the city. The commerce clause reserves the power to pass such legislation exclusively to the federal government.

Commerce among the States

Most legislation passed by Congress related to business must be within Congress's power under the commerce clause in order for a court to uphold the legislation. This clause is a major source of congressional power, although by no means the only source of power. For example, some legislation has been held to be within the power of Congress to pass because of its taxing power. The commerce clause, however, is the most significant source of congressional power. As interpreted today, this clause grants enormous power to the federal government.

The United States Supreme Court, in examining this grant of power to Congress, initially adhered to one interpretation of the clause. In the classic case *Gibbons* v. *Ogden* (1824), the Court took a very broad view of the meaning of this phrase. The Court regarded "commerce" as activity that concerns or affects more than one state. This was the "commerce" that constitutionally could be regulated by Congress.

A New York statute gave Ogden a monopoly to run a steamboat on a New York river. The federal government enacted a statute awarding Gibbons the right to operate a steamboat on the same waterway. Ogden initially obtained an injunction prohibiting Gibbons from operating his steamboat on the waterway. The Supreme Court decided, in light of the federal statute, that the grant given to Ogden by New York must fall. The commerce clause gave Congress the power to regulate this activity. Article VI of the Constitution (the supremacy clause) provides that the Constitution, laws, and treaties of the United States "shall be the supreme law of the land." As the New York statute conflicted with a statute lawfully enacted by Congress pursuant to the commerce clause, the United States law prevailed because of the supremacy clause.

As time passed, the Court moved away from the interpretation expressed in *Gibbons* v. *Ogden*. The Court chose to interpret the clause more restrictively, essentially saying that the commerce clause dealt with physical, interstate movement. This made it more difficult for Congress to lawfully pass regulations involving purely local acts.

During this period, state legislatures passed innumerable statutes dealing with commercial activities. In the absence of federal legislation, the Court interpreted the clause in such a way as to uphold this legislation. Such an interpretation worked well until Congress began to regulate business activity. Sustaining federal legislation while adhering to a narrow interpretation of the commerce clause posed significant problems for the Court. The Court adopted various interpretations of the clause in order to sustain some federal business regulatory legislation.

In the early 1900s, the Court decided that various federal statutes were enacted beyond the power of Congress to regulate commerce. For example, in 1918, in *Hammer* v. *Dagenhart,* the Court refused to sustain an act dealing with goods manufactured by firms employing children. The Court held that manufacturing was not commerce and was therefore beyond the power of Congress to regulate.

In the 1930s, the United States found itself in the midst of the Great Depression. Franklin D. Roosevelt assumed the office of the presidency in 1933. He immediately proposed statutes, which were enacted by Congress as part of the New Deal, that were aimed at pulling the United States out of the Depression. The Supreme Court held that much of the New Deal legislation was outside Congress's commercial clause power. For example, in *Schechter Poultry* (1935), the Court ruled that Congress lacked the power to regulate the chicken-processing industry under the commerce clause. The Court also refused to uphold federal legislation dealing with prices, working hours, and wages.

These cases caused a major confrontation between President Roosevelt and the Court. In the wake of the controversy over Roosevelt's proposal to change the composition of the United States Supreme Court by increasing its membership, the Supreme Court reversed its long-held interpretation of the commerce clause. In *N.L.R.B.* v. *Jones & Laughlin Steel Corp.* (1937), it laid to rest the idea that Congress cannot reach intrastate activities.

Although activities may be intrastate in character when considered separately, if they have such a close and substantial relation to interstate commerce that their control is essential or appropriate to protect that commerce from burdens and obstructions, Congress cannot be denied the power to exercise that control.

In a later case, *Wickard* v. *Filburn* (1942), the Court examined a federal marketing quota concerning the amount of wheat a farmer could grow. The farmer planted 23 acres of wheat in violation of the order to plant only 11.9 acres. The farmer argued that his activity was purely local and therefore could not be regulated by Congress. Nonetheless, the Court upheld the federal legislation. Furthermore, it held the government may regulate something that is *not* commerce, if that activity could have a substantial effect on commerce in a cumulative sense. That is, if the action of all farmers, taken as a group, will affect commerce, Congress may regulate the activity in question.

Today, the power of Congress to regulate both intrastate and interstate commerce of private enterprises remains inviolable. Congress possesses the power to pass a wide array of legislation regulating private businesses through the power granted to it by the commerce clause of the United States Constitution as interpreted by the Supreme Court.

The following is a famous case in which the Supreme Court upheld the provisions of the Civil Rights Act of 1964. It illustrates the approach of today's Supreme Court with respect to the scope of the federal government's power to regulate business activities.

Katzenbach v. McClung
United States Supreme Court
379 U.S. 294 (1964)

Ollie McClung had operated Ollie's Barbeque in Birmingham, Alabama, since 1927. Ollie's was located eleven blocks from the nearest interstate highway, somewhat farther from the nearest railroad or bus terminal, and six miles from the airport. Two-thirds of Ollie's thirty-six employees were blacks, but the restaurant had from its beginning refused to serve blacks in its dining room. Approximately forty-six percent of the food served by Ollie's was shipped from outside Alabama.

Title II of the Civil Rights Act of 1964 prohibits racial discrimination by a restaurant if it serves or offers to serve interstate travelers or if a substantial portion of the food it serves has moved in interstate commerce. Ollie's continued to refuse service to blacks after the passage of the act. When the Justice Department sought to enforce the act against similar restaurants, McClung sought a declaratory judgment in the federal district court that the act would interfere with his business and property rights. He demonstrated that the restaurant would lose a substantial portion of its business if forced to serve blacks.

The district court held that (1) the food shipped to Ollie's from out of state ceased to be in commerce when it reached its destination, and the serving of it became a wholly intrastate activity; (2) Congress may not make a presumptive finding that any particular restaurant activities affect interstate commerce; and (3) Ollie's would be deprived of its property rights without due process of law in violation of the Fifth Amendment.

The government appealed the decision to the United States Supreme Court.

COURT RASHIONEL ?
BLACKS TO TRAVEL INTERSTATE

Justice Clark

The record is replete with testimony of the burdens placed on interstate commerce by racial discrimination in restaurants. A comparison of per capita spending by Blacks in restaurants, theaters, and like establishments indicated less spending, after discounting income differences, in areas where discrimination is widely practiced. This condition, which was especially aggravated in the South, was attributed in the testimony of the Under Secretary of Commerce to racial segregation. In addition, the Attorney General testified that this type of discrimination imposed "an artificial restriction on the market" and interfered with the flow of merchandise.

Moreover there was an impressive array of testimony that discrimination in restaurants had a direct and highly restrictive effect upon interstate travel by Blacks. This resulted, it was said, because discriminatory practices prevent Blacks from buying prepared food served on the premises while on a trip, except in isolated and unkempt restaurants and under most unsatisfactory and often unpleasant conditions. This obviously discourages travel and obstructs interstate commerce, for one can hardly travel without eating. Likewise, it was said, that discrimination deterred professional, as well as skilled, people from moving into areas where such practices occurred and thereby caused industry to be reluctant to establish there.

We believe that this testimony afforded ample basis for the conclusion that established restaurants in such areas sold less interstate goods because of the discrimination, that interstate travel was obstructed directly by it, that business in general suffered and that many new businesses refrained from establishing there as a result of it. Hence the District Court was in error in concluding that there was no connection between discrimination and the movement of interstate commerce. The court's conclusion that such a connection is outside "common experience" flies in the face of stubborn fact.

It goes without saying that, viewed in isolation, the volume of food purchased by Ollie's Barbecue from sources supplied from out of state was insignificant when compared with the total foodstuffs moving in commerce. But, as our late Brother Jackson said for the Court in *Wickard v. Filburn*:

> That appellee's own contribution to the demand for wheat may be trivial by itself is not enough to remove him from the scope of federal regulation where, as here, his contribution, taken together with that of many others similarly situated, is far from trivial.

Congress has determined for itself that refusals of services to Blacks have imposed burdens both upon the interstate flow of food and upon the movement of products generally. Of course, the mere fact that Congress has said when particular activity shall be deemed to affect commerce does not preclude further examination by this Court. But where we find that the legislators, in light of the facts and testimony before them, have a rational basis for finding a chosen regulatory scheme necessary to the protection of commerce, our investigation is at an end.

Confronted as we are with the facts laid before Congress, we must conclude that it has a rational basis for finding that racial discrimination in restaurants had a direct and adverse effect on the free flow of interstate commerce. Insofar as the sections of the Act here relevant are concerned Congress prohibited discrimination only in those establishments having a close tie to interstate commerce, i.e., those, like the McClungs', serving food that has come from out of the State. We think in so doing that Congress acted well within its power to protect and foster commerce in extending the coverage of Title II only to those restaurants offering to serve interstate travelers or serving food, a substantial portion of which has moved in interstate commerce.

The power of Congress in this field is broad and sweeping; where it keeps within its sphere and violates no express constitutional limitation it has been the rule of this Court, going back almost to the founding days of the Republic, not to interfere. The Civil Rights Act of 1964, as here applied, we find to be plainly appropriate in the resolution of what the Congress found to be a national commercial problem of the first magnitude. We find it in no violation of any express limitations of the Constitution and we therefore declare it valid.

To determine if an exercise of congressional power under the commerce clause is valid, the courts go through the following analysis. First, if there is any rational basis for a congressional finding that an activity affects interstate commerce, a court must defer to this finding. In the *Katzenbach* case, the Court noted the extensive information in the record that supported the conclusion that racial discrimination in restaurants affects interstate commerce. Consequently, it deferred to the congressional finding that discrimination affects interstate commerce. Second, the courts examine whether the means chosen by Congress are reasonably adapted to the end permitted by the Constitution. If a court finds Congress acted rationally in adopting a particular regulatory scheme, it must uphold the legislation.

Congress may regulate even an activity that is purely intrastate in character when the activity, combined with like conduct by others similarly situated, affects commerce among the states or with foreign nations. Thus, even if a particular restaurant engaged in purely intrastate sales, Congress still may regulate its activities if, when combined with conduct by other restaurants, such activity affects commerce among the states or with foreign nations.

In light of this test, it would appear that, as a practical matter, there is no real limit today on the power of the federal government to regulate business.

It is not only the federal government that may regulate business; state governments may do so also. In the next section we address this power of state governments.

STATE POWER TO REGULATE BUSINESS

POLICE POWER

The power of the states to regulate is referred to as the police power of the states. The states reserved this power when they banded together to form the United States. The states in turn have delegated some of their power to regulate to local governments.

The power of the states to regulate is not without limitation. As noted earlier, the commerce clause is not only a source of congressional power to regulate commerce, it also is a limitation on the power of the states to enact legislation that regulates commerce.

National Uniformity

STATE LIMITATION

If a state passes legislation that is local in character, that legislation may still be held to be unconstitutional under certain circumstances. Some areas of regulation are deemed to be areas in which only the federal government can regulate. These are areas where uniformity on a nationwide basis is essential. A famous example of this involved an attempt by the state of Arizona to limit the length of passenger trains to fourteen cars and the length of freight trains to seventy cars. The United States Supreme Court in *Southern Pacific R.R.* v. *Arizona* ruled that even though Congress had not passed any legislation pertaining to the length of trains, Arizona could not limit the length of trains passing through the state of Arizona. The Court reasoned that if train length were to be regulated at all, then national uniformity would be necessary and could be prescribed only by Congress.

Statutory Preemption

A second area in which states may not regulate commerce is those situations where Congress has preempted an area. By **preemption** the courts mean that Congress has completely occupied a field. Sometimes Congress will expressly state in an act that it intends to preempt the field.

In the following case, the United States Supreme Court considered a federal statute that expressly preempted the states from passing legislation. In light of the fact that Congress included an express preemption provision in the statute, the Court decided that it needed only to identify exactly what Congress intended to preempt.

Cipollone v. Liggett Group, Inc.
United States Supreme Court
112 S. Ct. 2608 (1993)

Rose Cipollone began smoking in 1942. In a suit initially filed by her and then continued by her son following her death from lung cancer in 1984, she claimed that the cigarette manufacturers were liable for her illness and subsequent death. Rose Cipollone wished to recover damages from the cigarette manufacturers according to several theories of recovery. These theories of recovery were created by case law, also called the common law, as opposed to theories of recovery created by statutes passed by a legislature (referred to as positive enactments by the Court in the following opinion).

In 1965, Congress adopted a statute which, in section 4, made it unlawful to sell or distribute a cigarette package unless it bore the following label: "CAUTION: CIGARETTE SMOKING MAY BE HAZARDOUS TO YOUR HEALTH." The statute in section 5, captioned "Preemption," provided that no other statement shall be required on any cigarette package and that no statement shall be required in any advertising of any cigarettes. In 1969, Congress strengthened this warning.

The narrow question addressed by the Court in this case is whether this statute preempted Rose Cipollone's common law claims against the cigarette manufac turers. The United States Supreme Court decided, with respect to the 1965 statute, that this statute only prevented state rule-making bodies from requiring any statement other than that specified in the federal statute. The statute did not preempt damage actions under state law.

Justice Stevens

Article VI of the Constitution provides that the laws of the United States "shall be the supreme Law of the Land; . . . any Thing in the Constitution or Laws of any state to the Contrary notwithstanding." Art. VI, cl. 2. Thus, since our decision in *McCulloch v. Maryland* (1819), it has been settled that state law that conflicts with federal law is "without effect." Consideration of issues arising under the Supremacy Clause starts with the assumption that the historic police powers of the States are not to be superseded by . . . Federal Act unless that is the clear and manifest purpose of Congress. Accordingly, the purpose of Congress is the ultimate touchstone of preemption analysis.

Congress' intent may be explicitly stated in the statute's language or implicitly contained in its structure and purpose. In the absence of an express congressional command, state law is pre-empted if that law actually conflicts with federal law, or if federal law so thoroughly occupies a legislative field as to make reasonable the inference that Congress left no room for the States to supplement it.

In our opinion, the pre-emptive scope of the 1965 Act and the 1969 Act is governed entirely by the express language in §5 of each Act. When Congress has considered the issue of pre-emption and has included in the enacted legislation a provision explicitly addressing that issue, and when that provision provides a reliable indicium of congressional intent with respect to state authority, there is no need to infer congressional intent to pre-empt state laws from the substantive provisions of the legislation. Such reasoning is a variant of the familiar principle of *expressio unius est exclusio alterius:* Congress' enactment of a provision defining the pre-emptive reach of a statute implies that matters beyond that reach are not pre-empted. In this case, the other provisions of the 1965 and 1969 Acts offer no cause to look beyond

§5 of each Act. Therefore, we need only identify the domain expressly pre-empted by each of those sections.

In the 1965 pre-emption provision regarding advertising (§5(b)), Congress spoke precisely and narrowly: "No *statement* relating to smoking and health shall be required *in the advertising of* [properly labeled] cigarettes." Section 5(a) used the same phrase ("No *statement* relating to smoking and health") with regard to cigarette labeling. As §5(a) made clear, that phrase referred to the sort of warning provided for in §4, which set forth verbatim the warning Congress determined to be appropriate. Thus, on their face, these provisions merely prohibited state and federal rule-making bodies from mandating particular cautionary statements on cigarette labels (§5(a)) or in cigarette advertisements (§5(b)).

Beyond the precise words of these provisions, this reading is appropriate for several reasons. First, as discussed above, we must construe these provisions in light of the presumption against the pre-emption of state police power regulations. This presumption reinforces the appropriateness of a narrow reading of §5. Second, the warning required in §4 does not by its own effect foreclose additional obligations imposed under state law. That Congress requires a particular warning label does not automatically pre-empt a regulatory field. Third, there is no general, inherent conflict between federal pre-emption of state warning requirements and the continued vitality of state common law damages actions. . . . All of these considerations indicate that §5 is best read as having superseded only positive enactments by legislatures or administrative agencies that mandate particular warning labels.

For these reasons, we conclude that §5 of the 1965 Act only pre-empted state and federal rule-making bodies from mandating particular cautionary statements and did not pre-empt state law damages actions.

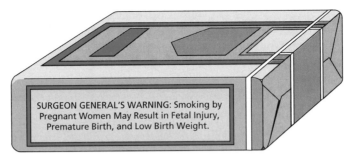

Figure 6.1   The Use of Rotating Warnings Is Required on Cigarette Packages

---

Postmortem

In July of 1992, Wayne McLaren, who portrayed the rugged "Marlboro Man" in cigarette advertisements died of lung cancer at age 51. McLaren smoked for about 25 years. After developing lung cancer McLaren became an antismoking crusader. Some of his last words were: "Take care of the children. Tobacco will kill you, and I am living proof of it."

Preemption by Implication

If congressional legislation is extensive in a particular area, the courts may find that Congress has preempted the area by implication. A good example of this can be found in *City of Burbank* v. *Lockheed Air Terminal, Inc.* That case dealt with an ordinance passed by the city of Burbank, California, which attempted to prohibit aircraft from taking off between the hours of 11:00 P.M. and 7:00 A.M. After examining the extensive federal regulation of aircraft takeoffs, the Court concluded that even though Congress never expressly preempted this area, it had preempted the area by implication. Such a decision makes sense in light of the chaos that would be created if every town could create its own rules relating to aircraft takeoffs and landings.

Businesses are subject to a great deal of regulation by the states. In particular, the insurance, banking, and savings-and-loan industries are heavily regulated by the states. Likewise, most regulations relating to professional conduct have been passed by the state governments.

The following case involves the issue of whether the federal government's extensive regulation of the field of nuclear energy precludes a state court from rendering a punitive damage award.

Silkwood v. Kerr-McGee Corporation
United States Supreme Court
104 S.Ct. 615 (1984)

Karen Silkwood was a laboratory analyst for Kerr-McGee at a plant engaged in fabricating plutonium fuel pins for use as reactor fuel in nuclear power plants. She was contaminated by plutonium from the Kerr-McGee plant. Thereafter she was killed in an unrelated automobile accident. Her father brought suit based on common law tort principles under Oklahoma law to recover for the contamination injuries to Karen's person and property. The jury awarded Silkwood actual damages of $505,000 and punitive damages of $10 million. Kerr-McGee argued that federal law precluded an award of punitive damages. The Tenth Circuit agreed, but the United States Supreme Court reversed, holding federal law did not preclude an award of punitive damages.

Justice White

This case requires us to determine whether a state-authorized award of punitive damages arising out of the escape of plutonium from a federally-licensed nuclear facility is preempted either because it falls within that forbidden field or because it conflicts with some other aspect of the Atomic Energy Act.

As we recently observed in *Pacific Gas & Electric Co. v. State Energy Resources Conservation & Development Comm'n*, state law can be preempted in either of two general ways. If Congress evidences an intent to occupy a given field, any state law falling within that field is preempted. If Congress has not entirely displaced state regulation over the matter in question, state law is still preempted to the extent it actually conflicts with federal law, that is, when it is impossible to comply with both state and federal law, or where the state law stands as an obstacle to the accomplishment of the full purposes and objectives of Congress.

Although the Price-Anderson Act does not apply to the present situation, the discussion preceding its enactment and subsequent amendment indicates that Congress assumed that persons injured by nuclear accidents were free to utilize existing state tort law remedies.

No doubt there is a tension between the conclusion that safety regulation is the exclusive concern of the federal law and the conclusion that a state may nevertheless award damages based on its own law of liability. But as we understand what was done over the years in the legislation concerning nuclear energy, Congress intended to stand by both concepts and to tolerate whatever tension there was between them. We can do no less. It may be that the award of damages based on the state law of negligence or strict liability is regulatory in the sense that a nuclear plant will be threatened with damages liability if it does not conform to state standards, but that regulatory consequence was something that Congress was quite willing to accept.

We do not suggest that there could never be an instance in which the federal law would preempt the recovery of damages based on state law. But insofar as damages for radiation injuries are concerned, preemption should not be judged on the basis that the federal government has so completely occupied the field of safety that state remedies are foreclosed but on whether there is an irreconcilable conflict between the federal and state standards or whether the imposition of a state standard in a damages action would frustrate the objectives of the federal law. We perceive no such conflict or frustration in the circumstances of this case.

We conclude that the award of punitive damages in this case is not preempted by federal law.

Other Limitations

Assuming Congress has not preempted a field and it is not one deemed to be an area in which only Congress can pass regulations, then a state, pursuant to its police power, may pass legislation that regulates business. However, there still are some limitations on state power. For example, a state law may not be in irreconcilable conflict with a federal law. In the event of such an irreconcilable conflict, the supremacy clause of the United States Constitution requires that the state law be struck down. Furthermore, a state law must not discriminate in favor of intrastate commerce. States cannot pass legislation that favors local businesspersons at the expense of out-of-state businesses. It should also be noted that a state law must not place an undue burden on interstate commerce.

The following case discusses the issue of discrimination against interstate commerce by a state government.

Maine v. Taylor
United States Supreme Court
106 S.Ct. 2440 (1986)

The state of Maine by statute prohibited the importation of live baitfish into Maine. The golden shiner, a species of minnow, is commonly used as live bait in sport fishing. Robert Taylor, who operated a bait business in Maine, arranged to have 158,000 live golden shiners delivered to him outside the state. He was arrested for violating the Lacey Act, which makes it a federal crime to import fish in violation of any state law. Taylor argued that the indictment should be dismissed because Maine's import ban unconstitutionally burdens interstate commerce and therefore could not form the basis for a federal prosecution under the Lacey Act. The district court found Maine's statute to be constitutional and convicted Taylor. The court of appeals reversed his conviction. The Supreme Court reversed the court of appeals. It held Maine's statute to be constitutional.

Justice Blackmun

The Commerce Clause of the Constitution grants Congress the power "[t]o regulate Commerce with foreign Nations, and among the several States, and with the Indian Tribes." Although the Clause thus speaks in terms of powers bestowed upon Congress, the Court long has recognized that it also limits the power of the States to erect barriers against interstate trade. Maine's statute restricts interstate trade in the most direct manner possible, blocking all inward shipments of live baitfish at the State's border. Still, as both the District Court and the Court of Appeals recognized, this fact alone does not render the law unconstitutional. The limitation imposed by the Commerce Clause on state regulatory power is by no means absolute, and the States retain authority under their general police powers to regulate matters of "legitimate local concern," even though interstate commerce may be affected.

In determining whether a State has overstepped its role in regulating interstate commerce, this Court has distinguished between state statutes that burden interstate transactions only incidentally, and those that affirmatively discriminate against such transactions. While statutes in the first group violate the Commerce Clause only if the burdens they impose on interstate trade are clearly excessive in relation to the putative local benefits, statutes in the second group are subject to more demanding scrutiny. The Court explained in *Hughes* v. *Oklahoma* that once a state law is shown to discriminate against interstate commerce "either on its face or in practical effect," the burden falls on the State to demonstrate both that the statute "serves a legitimate local purpose" and that this purpose could not be served as well by available nondiscriminatory means.

Maine's ban on the importation of live baitfish is constitutional only if it satisfies the requirements ordinarily applied under *Hughes* v. *Oklahoma* to local regulation that discriminates against interstate trade: the statute must serve a legitimate local purpose, and the purpose must be one that cannot be served as well by available nondiscriminatory means.

The District Court found after an evidentiary hearing that both parts of the *Hughes* test were satisfied.

After reviewing the expert testimony presented to the magistrate we cannot say that the District Court clearly erred in finding that substantial scientific uncertainty surrounds the effect that baitfish parasites and nonnative species could have on Maine's fisheries. Moreover, we agree with the District Court that Maine has a legitimate interest in guarding against imperfectly understood environmental risks, despite the possibility that they may ultimately prove to be negligible.

Nor do we think that much doubt is cast on the legitimacy of Maine's purposes by what the Court of Appeals took to be signs of protectionist intent. Shielding in-state industries from out-of-state competition is almost never a legitimate local purpose, and state laws that amount to "simple economic protectionism" consequently have been subject to a virtually *per se* rule of invalidity. But there is little reason in this case to believe that the legitimate justifications the State has put forward for its statute are merely a sham or a "*post hoc* rationalization."

The Commerce Clause significantly limits the ability of States and localities to regulate or otherwise burden the flow of interstate commerce, but it does not elevate free trade above all other values. As long as a State does not needlessly obstruct interstate trade or attempt to place itself in a position of economic isolation, it retains broad regulatory authority to protect the health and safety of its citizens and the integrity of its natural resources. The evidence in this case amply supports the District Court's findings that Maine's ban on the importation of live baitfish serves legitimate local purposes that could not adequately be served by available nondiscriminatory alternatives. This is not a case of arbitrary discrimination against interstate commerce; the record suggests that Maine has legitimate reasons, apart from their origin, to treat [out-of-state baitfish] differently. The judgment of the Court of Appeals setting aside appellee's conviction is therefore reversed.

LIMITATIONS ON GOVERNMENTAL POWER

The drafters of the United States Constitution realized that government power could be abused. Consequently, they placed some limits on the exercise of government power in the Constitution. In particular, they were concerned about the intrusion of the government on the rights supposedly retained by the people at the time the United States government was formed.

State Action Requirement
ONLY GOVT

The Constitution of the United States provides protection for individual rights. As originally drafted, the Constitution did not contain many protections of individual freedoms. Some of our most cherished rights were added by amendment (for example, freedom of speech, freedom from unreasonable search). The articles in the original document did contain a few basic provisions protecting individual

ONLY   FROM   GOV'T

State Action

After a lengthy investigation, the National Collegiate Athletic Association's (NCAA's) Committee on Infractions determined that Jerry Tarkanian, the head basketball coach at the University of Nevada, Las Vegas (UNLV), had violated NCAA rules. The Committee on Infractions imposed a number of sanctions on UNLV and suggested other penalties should be imposed on the school should it fail to suspend Tarkanian from its program during a probation period. Tarkanian brought suit, alleging that the NCAA had deprived him of his due process rights.

The United States Supreme Court ruled that the NCAA's actions did not constitute state action. The NCAA is a private association, not a state agency. The NCAA's actions were private conduct—not state action. That being the case, the protections afforded by the due process clause of the Fourteenth Amendment did not apply. The NCAA was not obligated to assure Tarkanian the same due process rights that government agencies must extend to persons with whom they deal.

National Collegiate Athletic Association v. *Tarkanian*, 109 S.Ct. 454 (1988).

rights, but during the ratification process many of the states were concerned that protections of additional rights were not explicitly contained in the document.

The concern for individual rights was genuine, and arose from recent experiences. When the country was under British rule, troops were placed in homes without permission, and searches were made without warrants. However, the British government was not the only source of rights violations. Some of the states under the Articles of Confederation also abused individual rights. Certain state legislatures passed bills of attainder, sentencing certain individuals to death without the benefit of a jury trial. At least one state levied a tax that was so burdensome to newspapers as to severely limit freedom of the press.

The drafters of the constitutional rights guarantees were concerned with abuse by government, not abuse by various individuals. The actions of the British colonial government and the governments of the states under the Articles of Confederation gave rise to practical concern by many leaders in the late eighteenth century that individual rights had to be expressly protected from abuse by the government. This is the foundation of an important idea behind the protection of constitutional rights: the concept of ''state action.'' Purely private and individual activity is not covered by the Bill of Rights. It is against the government and the power of the government, with its attendant danger to the freedom of all, that the individual is protected by the Bill of Rights. For example, it is not constitutionally prohibited for an individual to refuse to invite a classmate to a party solely because that person wrote poetry. It may not be a decision one would approve, but it does not violate the Constitution. However, the government may not pass a statute prohibiting poets from attending parties. The statute would be stricken as having a ''chilling effect'' on First Amendment freedoms.

There are constitutional protections for individual rights other than those contained in the first ten amendments. These protections can be found, for the most part, in the Civil War Amendments (the Thirteenth, Fourteenth, and Fifteenth Amendments), which were enacted between 1865 and 1870. These amendments provided the constitutional foundations for the revolution in civil rights law and criminal procedure that has occurred in this country in the last thirty-five years. Of those amendments, the most influential is the Fourteenth Amendment, with its "due process" and "equal protection" clauses.

Due Process Clause

Section 1 of the Fourteenth Amendment provides that no state shall "deprive any person of life, liberty, or property, without due process of law." A similar provision applicable to the federal government is contained in the Fifth Amendment. Although this phrase has a nice ring to it, what does it mean? What is the liberty and property of an individual that the state may not take away without due process? Furthermore, what exactly is "due process"—that is, what procedures must a state provide before it can deprive a person of life, liberty, or property? These questions have been raised and litigated in countless cases. Quite frankly, there is no clear answer.

What has occurred in this area of constitutional law is a large amount of judicial lawmaking concerning the applicability of the amendment language. For example, note the precise choice of words in the Bill of Rights. It is worded in such a way as to limit the power of *Congress* as that power applies to individuals. It does not mention state governments. Years ago, the Bill of Rights did not apply to the states. Many states had bills of rights in their own constitutions, but they were not necessarily construed in the same manner as the Bill of Rights in the United States Constitution. However, by use of the Fourteenth Amendment's due process clause, most of the rights guaranteed to the individual by the Bill of Rights have been held by the courts to be applicable to the states.

At one time the United States Supreme Court not only required the federal and state governments to adopt and follow fair procedures, it also required the provisions of any rule enforced by the governments to be fair and reasonable. This latter method of analysis under the due process clause is called substantive (as opposed to procedural) due process. Substantive due process requires that the provisions of a government rule be fair and reasonable.

To illustrate how the Supreme Court applied the doctrine of substantive due process at one time, consider the concept of freedom of contract. In the 1800s, the Supreme Court regarded freedom of contract as a liberty protected by the term *due process*. The Supreme Court reviewed any legislation that was alleged to be an interference with the freedom of the parties to a contract to voluntarily enter an agreement. The Supreme Court decided whether the law in question interfered with the parties' freedom to contract in an unreasonable manner. The *Lochner* case, which appears in Chapter 9, is an example of a case in which the United States Supreme Court struck down a piece of state legislation because the Court viewed the state legislation as an unconstitutional deprivation of the parties' right to freely contract. The substantive due process doctrine made it very difficult for the federal or state governments to pass any legislation that regulated the economy. During the 1930s, the Supreme Court finally rejected the substantive due process doctrine once and for all, at least as it applied to economic legislation. This enabled the federal and state governments to pass much of the legislation now on the books that regulates how business is conducted. Today, the Court no longer reviews the wisdom of economic regulations passed by the government.

Today, due process analysis is for the most part a guarantee of procedural protection against unfair or intrusive government behavior. It does not refer to what the government may *do* to people; it concerns itself with *how* the government may do it. Due process is a general term that stipulates that government owes duties of fairness in its treatment of individuals.

A few general principles of due process must be observed before people are deprived of life, liberty, or property. One principle is that the affected individuals must have notice of the government activity being taken against them. Notice allows the individuals to prepare a defense or challenge to the government's activity. It eliminates the horror of being subjected to government processes without knowing the basis for the action.

A second principle involves various components of a fair hearing. Merely knowing the basis of the government's action would be valueless if the individual could not effectively challenge that action. A fair hearing involves a neutral, unbiased decision maker who renders a judgment on the evidence presented at the hearing. This is an important factor in that it requires the government to justify its activities to the decision maker. It also provides a forum in which the individual may raise a defense. Additional factors include the rights to present evidence and to test the evidence of the government at the hearing.

In the following case, the state of Connecticut failed to provide for either notice of a pending government activity concerning the defendant or a hearing. This case deals with a matter previously considered by the Supreme Court in a number of other cases: the circumstances under which a plaintiff may seize the assets of a defendant prior to a decision of the trial court in favor of the plaintiff.

Connecticut v. Doehr
United States Supreme Court
111 S.Ct. 2105 (1991)

John DiGiovanni submitted an application for an attachment in the amount of seventy-five thousand dollars on Brian Doehr's home in Connecticut. DiGiovanni sought the prejudgment attachment of Doehr's home in conjunction with a civil action he had filed against Doehr for assault and battery. Connecticut law allowed prejudgment attachment of real estate without first giving the person whose property is subject to attachment notice or the opportunity for a prior hearing (referred to as **ex parte** attachment). The statute did not require DiGiovanni to post a bond. A judge could order the attachment after making a finding, based on the plaintiff's oath, that there was probable cause to sustain the validity of the plaintiff's claims. After the sheriff attached Doehr's home, Doehr received notice of the attachment. At this point, the statute gave Doehr a right to a hearing.

Doehr challenged the constitutionality of this statute under the due process clause of the Fourteenth Amendment. The United States Supreme Court ruled that the Connecticut statute violated the due process clause.

DUE PROCESS
• HEARING
• CHANCE TO OPPOSE

Justice White

With this case we return to the question of what process must be afforded by a state statute enabling an individual to enlist the aid of the State to deprive another of his or her property by means of the prejudgment attachment or similar procedure. Our cases reflect the numerous variations this type of remedy can entail.

These cases underscore the truism that due process, unlike some legal rules, is not a technical conception with a fixed content unrelated to time, place and circumstances.

Prejudgment remedy statutes ordinarily apply to disputes between private parties rather than between an individual and the government. Such enactments are designed to enable one of the parties to make use of state procedures with the overt, significant assistance of state officials, and they undoubtedly involve state action substantial enough to implicate the Due Process Clause. Nonetheless, any burden that increasing procedural safeguards entails primarily affects not the government, but the party seeking control of the other's property. For this type of case, therefore, the relevant inquiry requires, first, consideration of the private interest that will be affected by the prejudgment measure; second, an examination of the risk of erroneous deprivation through the procedures under attack and the probable value of additional or alternative safeguards; and third, principal attention to the interest of the party seeking the prejudgment remedy, with, nonetheless, due regard for any ancillary interest the government may have in providing the procedure of forgoing the added burden of providing greater protections.

We agree with the Court of Appeals that the property interests that attachment affects are significant. For a property owner like Doehr, attachment ordinarily clouds title; impairs the ability to sell or otherwise alienate the property; taints any credit rating; reduces the chance of obtaining a home equity loan or additional mortgage; and can even place an existing mortgage in technical default where there is an insecurity clause. Nor does Connecticut deny that any of these consequences occurs.

Our cases show that even the temporary or partial impairments to property rights that attachments, liens, and similar encumbrances entail are sufficient to merit due process protection.

We also agree with the Court of Appeals that the risk of erroneous deprivation that the State permits here is substantial.

Permitting a court to authorize attachment merely because the plaintiff believes the defendant is liable, or because the plaintiff can make out a facially valid complaint, would permit the deprivation of the defendant's property when the claim would fail to convince a jury. . . . The potential for unwarranted attachment is self-evident and too great to satisfy the requirements of due process absent any countervailing consideration.

Finally, we conclude that the interests in favor of an *ex parte* attachment, particularly the interests of the plaintiff, are too minimal to supply such a consideration here. Plaintiff had no existing interest in Doehr's real estate when he sought the attachment. His only interest in attaching the property was to ensure the availability of assets to satisfy his judgment if he prevailed on the merits of his action. Yet there was no allegation that Doehr was about to transfer or encumber his real estate or take any other action during the pendency of the action that would render his real estate unavailable to satisfy a judgment. Our cases have recognized such a properly supported claim would be an exigent circumstance permitting postponing any notice or hearing until after the attachment is effected. Absent such allegations, however, the plaintiff's interest in attaching the property does not justify the burdening of Doehr's ownership rights without a hearing to determine the likelihood of recovery.

We believe that the procedures of almost all the States confirm our view that the Connecticut provision before us, by failing to provide a preattachment hearing without at least requiring a showing of some exigent circumstances, clearly falls short of the demands of due process.

Equal Protection Clause

Section 1 of the Fourteenth Amendment also provides that no state shall "deny to any person within its jurisdiction the equal protection of the laws." As with due process, it is not quite clear what this section of the amendment means. Its meaning has changed during the one-hundred-plus years since its adoption. As noted in Chapter 1, the language did not always prohibit legislated segregation of the races. Such an interpretation is a recent phenomenon. In fact, the use of the equal protection clause to attack government-imposed discrimination based on a host of individual characteristics (such as race, sex, wealth, alienage) is also a rather recent development.

The **equal protection clause** does not prohibit the law from treating different groups of people differently. What it does is to require that the state show that such differential treatment serves an interest of the state. The Supreme Court, in interpreting the clause, employs a sliding scale of interests that the government must demonstrate are furthered by the classification. Certain government classifications are examined by the Court under a *strict scrutiny test*. This test requires government classifications to be closely related to the furtherance of a government purpose and that no less discriminatory alternative means of achieving the government's aims be available. For example, racial classifications are considered by the Court to be "suspect," and to require the strictest standard of judicial review. Any legislation that treats people differently on the basis of race does not meet the equal protection standard, unless the government can show that it had a compelling interest in making that classification, which could not be served in any other way. This is a very difficult standard to meet.

The minimum review standard, generally applicable to regulation of business, is whether the legislature had some reasonable basis for the classification. This is referred to as the *rational basis test*. Government classifications must have a rational relationship to the achievement of a valid government objective. In general, the courts tend to defer to the legislature's judgment, as is illustrated by the following case.

State by Humphrey v. Ri-Mel, Inc.
Court of Appeals of Minnesota
417 N.W.2d 102 (1987)

Minnesota required that for-profit health clubs post a bond. The bond was required to protect members from losses arising if the club were to go out of business. Such a bond was *not* required for nonprofit health clubs. Ri-Mel argued that the bond requirement violated the equal protection clause. The court of appeals found that the bonding requirement was rationally related to a legitimate state goal of reducing losses experienced by persons who belonged to for-profit clubs.

Forsberg, Judge

Appellants claim the standard of review to be applied in analyzing the constitutionality of the Act is the strict scrutiny standard or an intermediate standard because the Act limits the fundamental right to enter into contracts, and impermissibly restricts the contractual relationship between health clubs and its members. However, in *Essling v. Markman* the supreme court explained that freedom of contract has not been recognized as a fundamental right sufficient to invoke strict judicial scrutiny, and thus minimum judicial scrutiny is appropriate. Under the "rational basis" test an Act should be upheld as constitutional if the record shows the Act is rationally related to achievement of a legitimate government purpose. There is a presumption in favor of the constitutionality of legislation and a party challenging constitutionality has the burden of demonstrating beyond a reasonable doubt a statute violates a provision of the constitution.

Appellants assert the legislative distinction between for profit and nonprofit health clubs is not rationally related to the purpose of the Act and bears no relation to the question whether prepayments by club members require the security of a bond.

The purpose of the Club Contracts Act is to protect consumers by preventing the collection by corporations of large "prepayments" to capitalize the venture and then closing their business without providing services or making refunds. The Act achieves this purpose by requiring for profit clubs to post surety bonds to protect members from loss of money if the club should cease doing business unexpectedly without adequate funds to make refunds to consumers.

The Minnesota Attorney General's Office argues it is unaware of any nonprofit health club in Minnesota ever going out of business after taking consumer prepayments. There has been no showing that the harms sought to be protected against by the Act have occurred in nonprofit organizations or clubs offering health or fitness facilities. Nonprofit health clubs do not have the same incentive to use high pressure sales tactics or to take large prepayments to maximize profits.

The Club Contracts Act distinction between profit and nonprofit organizations is a permissible one, rationally related to the legitimate purpose of minimizing potential harms which have occurred in for profit clubs. Therefore, the Act is not unconstitutional on its face as a violation of equal protection guarantees.

In between the strict scrutiny test as it is applied to race and the rational basis test as it is applied to business, there are a number of different standards of review, depending upon the type of classification. For example, discrimination based upon sex, the right to travel, and the right of access to justice have different standards of equal protection review.

The following case is an example of the Court's analyzing a piece of legislation that classified people on the basis of sex.

Craig v. Boren
United States Supreme Court
429 U.S. 190 (1976)

The interaction of two sections of an Oklahoma statute prohibits the sale of "nonintoxicating" 3.2 percent beer to males under the age of twenty-one and to females under the age of eighteen. The question to be decided is whether such a gender-based differential constitutes a denial to males eighteen to twenty years of age of the equal protection of the laws in violation of the Fourteenth Amendment.

Justice Brennan

After the Court of Appeals for the Tenth Circuit held in 1972, on the authority of *Reed v. Reed,* that the age distinction was unconstitutional for purposes of establishing criminal responsibility as adults, the Oklahoma Legislature fixed age 18 as applicable to both males and females. In 1972, 18 also was established as the age of majority for males and females in civil matters except that sections 241 and 245 of the 3.2% beer statute were simultaneously codified to create an exception to the gender-free rule.

Analysis may appropriately begin with the reminder that *Reed* emphasized that statutory classifications that distinguish between males and females are "subject to scrutiny under the Equal Protection Clause." To withstand constitutional challenge, previous cases establish that classifications by gender must serve important governmental objectives and must be substantially related to achievement of those objectives.

Clearly, the protection of public health and safety represents an important function of state and local governments. However, appellees' statistics in our view cannot support the conclusion that the gender-based distinction closely serves to achieve that objective and therefore the distinction cannot under *Reed* withstand equal protection challenge.

The appellees introduced a variety of statistical surveys showing differences between young male and female drinking problems.

Even were this statistical evidence accepted as accurate, it nevertheless offers only a weak answer to the equal protection question presented here. The most focused and relevant of the statistical surveys, arrests of 18–20-year-olds for alcohol-related driving offenses, exemplifies the ultimate unpersuasiveness of this evidentiary record. Viewed in terms of the correlation between sex and the actual activity that Oklahoma seeks to regulate—driving while under the influence of alcohol—the statistics broadly establish that .18% of females and 2% of males in that age group were arrested for that offense. While such a disparity is not trivial in a statistical sense, it hardly can form the basis for employment of a gender line as a classifying device. Certainly if maleness is to serve as a proxy for drinking and driving, a correlation of 2% must be considered an unduly tenuous "fit." Indeed, prior cases have consistently rejected the use of sex as a decision-making factor even though the statutes in question certainly rested on far more predictive empirical relationships than this.

Moreover, the statistics exhibit a variety of other shortcomings that seriously impugn their value to equal protection analysis. Setting aside the obvious methodological problems, the surveys do not adequately justify the salient features of Oklahoma's gender-based traffic-safety law. None purports to measure the use and dangerousness of 3.2% beer as opposed to alcohol generally, a detail that is of particular importance since, in light of its low alcohol level, Oklahoma apparently considers the 3.2% beverage to be "nonintoxicating." Moreover, many of the studies, while graphically documenting the unfortunate increase in driving while under the influence of alcohol, make no effort to relate their findings to age-sex differentials as involved here. Indeed, the only survey that explicitly centered its attention upon young drivers and their use of beer—albeit apparently not of the diluted 3.2% variety—reached results that hardly can be viewed as impressive in justifying either a gender or age classification.

There is no reason to belabor this line of analysis. It is unrealistic to expect either members of the judiciary or state officials to be well versed in the rigors of experi-mental or statistical technique. But this merely illustrates that proving broad sociological propositions by statistics is a dubious business, and one that inevitably is in tension with the normative philosophy that underlies the Equal Protection Clause. Suffice to say that the showing offered by the appellees does not satisfy us that sex represents a legitimate, accurate proxy for the regulation of drinking and driving. In fact, when it is further recognized that Oklahoma's statute prohibits only the selling of 3.2% beer to young males and not their drinking the beverage once acquired (even after purchase by their 18–20-year-old female companions), the relationship between gender and traffic safety becomes far too tenuous to satisfy *Reed's* requirement that the gender-based difference be substantially related to achievement of the statutory objective.

We hold, therefore, that under *Reed*, Oklahoma's 3.2% beer statute invidiously discriminates against males 18–20 years of age.

The government is also limited in its power to restrict the freedom of speech by people, as is discussed in the following material.

THE FIRST AMENDMENT AND BUSINESS

The first amendment to the United States Constitution reads as follows: "Congress shall make no law respecting an establishment of religion, or prohibiting the free exercise thereof; or abridging the freedom of speech, or of the press, or the right of the people peaceably to assemble, and to petition the government for a redress of grievances."

This section of the chapter concerns that portion of the First Amendment which governs freedom of speech, with an emphasis on business. Freedom of speech is one of the most important guarantees in the Constitution. The free exchange of information helps ensure the preservation of democracy. The drafters of the Constitution believed that through the free and open exchange of ideas the truth, sooner or later, would be exposed. Once the citizens know the truth, they are able to make more intelligent decisions.

What Is "Freedom of Speech"?

Many rules have been found in the First Amendment that a person could not find by looking at the literal language of the amendment. What is speech? Is slander speech? Is threatening another person speech? Are pornographic statements speech? Are agreements to fix prices speech? If so, how can Congress regulate or prohibit such speech? The Constitution, after all, says Congress may pass *no* law. It does not say Congress may restrict pornography, or threats to other people, or slander.

To obtain a *workable* reading of the First Amendment, the justices read certain things into the language of the Constitution that a literal reading would not permit. This is true not only of the First Amendment but of the rest of the Constitution, treaties, statutes, contracts, and so on. The ability to "interpret" the law gives judges considerable discretion to determine what the law is. By the same token, the more imprecise and vague the language used in a document, the more open to varying interpretations it is.

Instead of using extremely precise terms, the drafters of the United States Constitution elected in many places to use phrases that left the courts considerable discretion in interpreting the Constitution. The drafters hoped to create a document that would last this country for many generations. By drafting the Constitution in imprecise terms in certain places, they created a flexible Constitution that could be reinterpreted according to the needs of the times.

Nowhere is this flexible approach more obvious than in the area of freedom of speech. One could interpret this language, by reading it literally, as prohibiting any form of restriction on pure speech whatsoever. Former Supreme Court Justices Black and Douglas probably came closest to adopting such an interpretation. Other justices sitting on the Supreme Court have been more inclined to

---

Freedom of Speech at Penn State

Penn State adopted a regulation for its residence halls that permitted canvassing in its living areas only if a majority of the residents of the hall voted in favor of "open" canvassing at the beginning of the school term. A vote to ban canvassing precludes canvassers from entering the living areas of the dorms. A canvasser still may contact residents in the dining hall buildings and in the main lobbies of each residence hall. Canvassers also post notices in the halls and place material in the residents' mailboxes. Steven Brush sought to canvass the living area of the "closed" residence halls. When permission was refused, he filed a class action suit seeking an injunction against Penn State's enforcement of the canvassing regulations.

The Supreme Court of Pennsylvania determined that this university regulation did not abridge Brush's freedom of expression. The regulation in question furthers a legitimate government interest (the need of the university to provide students a quiet place to study). The regulation placed reasonable restrictions on the place and manner of expression, but at the same time afforded canvassers reasonable alternatives for communication of their messages. The court thus denied injunctive relief.

Brush v. *Pennsylvania State University,* 414 A.2d 48 (1980).

Begging

Young wished to beg for money in the New York City subway system. He was prevented from doing so by a New York City law that prohibits begging on trains, near subway stairways, escalators, and elevators, and within 25 feet of token booths. Young argued that this law violated his right of free speech. The United States Court of Appeals for the Second Circuit ruled that begging falls outside the scope of the First Amendment because beggars do not convey a social or political message. They just want money. Thus, the Court upheld this prohibition on begging.

Young v. *New York City Transit*, 903 F.2d 1461 (2nd cir., 1990).

---

permit restrictions on speech. For example, Justice Holmes once wrote that a person does not have the right to yell ''fire'' in a crowded theater. In other cases, the justices characterized the activity discussed in the case as more than speech, and therefore beyond the scope of the First Amendment.

In spite of the Constitution's provisions protecting free speech, a person may not exercise his or her right to speak in every circumstance. Reasonable time, place, and manner restrictions may be placed by the government on the exercise of free speech, as the Penn State box illustrates.

The homeless create special problems for major metropolitan cities. Some of these people engage in behavior that a large segment of people find offensive. For this reason, the cities have attempted to place restrictions on their right to engage in free speech, as the box on begging illustrates.

The core of the First Amendment clearly is the protection of freedom of political expression. To the extent that speech involves something other than political expression, the Court has been more willing to permit state regulation of such peripheral areas. One example is the area of commercial speech, or speech by business. Do corporations have the same First Amendment rights as human beings? Are corporate advertisements ''speech'' as protected by the First Amendment?

Business and Free Speech

The Supreme Court, in *First National Bank of Boston* v. *Bellotti* (1978), clarified the issue of whether corporations, as well as private citizens, may exercise the right of free speech.

First National Bank of Boston v. Bellotti
United States Supreme Court
435 U.S. 765 (1978)

A Massachusetts statute prohibited corporations from making contributions or expenditures "for the purpose of . . . influencing or affecting the vote on any question submitted to the voters, other than one materially affecting any of the property, business or assets of the corporation." It specifically prohibited such contributions or expenditures on votes relating to taxation. The statute provided for penalties of fines and imprisonment. Appellants, the bank, wanted to spend money to publicize their views on a proposed constitutional amendment relating to a graduated income tax. They sought to have the law declared unconstitutional. The Supreme Court of Massachusetts upheld this act. The United States Supreme Court ruled the statute violated the Constitution.

Justice Powell

The referendum issue that appellants wish to address falls squarely within the First Amendment. In appellants' view, the enactment of a graduated personal income tax, as proposed to be authorized by constitutional amendment, would have a seriously adverse effect on the economy of the State. The importance of the referendum issue to the people and government of Massachusetts is not disputed. Its merits, however, are the subject of sharp disagreement.

The question in this case, simply put, is whether the corporate identity of the speaker deprives this proposed speech of what otherwise would be its clear entitlement to protection. We turn now to that question.

We find no support in the First or Fourteenth Amendment, or in the decisions of this Court, for the proposition that speech that otherwise would be within the protection of the First Amendment loses that protection simply because its source is a corporation that cannot prove, to the satisfaction of a court, a material effect on its business or property. The "materially affecting" requirement is not an identification of the boundaries of corporate speech etched by the Constitution itself. Rather, it amounts to an impermissible legislative prohibition of speech based on the identity of the interests that spokesmen may represent in public debate over controversial issues and a requirement that the speaker have a sufficiently great interest in the subject to justify communication.

The Act permits a corporation to communicate to the public its views on certain referendum subjects—those materially affecting its business—but not others. It also singles out one kind of ballot question—individual taxation—as a subject about which corporations may never make their ideas public. The legislature has drawn the line between permissible and impermissible speech according to whether there is a sufficient nexus, as defined by the legislature, between the issue presented to the voters and the business interests of the speaker.

In the realm of protected speech, the legislature is constitutionally disqualified from dictating the subjects about which persons may speak and the speakers who may address a public issue. Especially where, as here, the legislature's suppression of speech suggests an attempt to give one side of a debatable public question an advantage in expressing its views to the people, the First Amendment is plainly offended.

Conflict of Cultures

In the late 1980s, the author Salman Rushdie wrote *The Satanic Verses,* published by the Macmillan Company. The Ayatollah Khomeini and other religious leaders in Iran interpreted this book as blasphemous. The Ayatollah Khomeini stated that Rushdie should be murdered. Calls for Rushdie's death for his attack on the Muslim religion conflict with the generally held Western belief in the freedom of religion, speech, and press. In particular, the United States Constitution in the First Amendment protects the right of persons to write and speak their minds.

Disputes of this nature arise because, as the world community gets smaller, people in one area of the world often feel compelled to challenge the established social order in other countries. Challenges to existing customs and religious beliefs sometimes deeply upset persons in other parts of the world.

Businesses need to recognize not only the laws of other countries, but their religious and social customs. Businesses need to be sensitized to such beliefs in light of the growing interconnectedness of the world.

Commercial Speech and the Right to Receive Information

The public benefits from hearing all sides to a story. The more information presented to the public, the more likely members of the public are to make intelligent decisions. This concept is important to a business that advertises.

The seminal case in the commercial speech area is *Valentine* v. *Chrestensen* (1942). In this case, a submarine owner protested an ordinance that prohibited him from distributing handbills to advertise the exhibition of his submarine. The Supreme Court upheld the ordinance because of the commercial nature of his message. In a unanimous opinion the Court stated: "This Court has unequivocally held that the streets are proper places for the exercise of communicating information and disseminating opinion. . . . We are equally clear that the Constitution imposes no such restraint on government as respects purely commercial advertising." The courts interpreted this opinion as meaning that commercial speech was not entitled to the protections afforded by the Constitution to noncommercial speech. The Supreme Court continued to adhere to the decision in *Valentine* for many years.

In the mid-1970s the Supreme Court discarded the **commercial speech doctrine.** In *Virginia State Board of Pharmacy* v. *Virginia Citizens Consumer Council, Inc.,* it decided that speech which does no more than propose a commercial transaction is also protected by the First Amendment. The court based its decision on the need of the public for commercial information.

As noted on the following page, the Court in 1980 in *Central Hudson Gas* v. *Public Service Commission of New York* announced a four-part test to be applied in deciding First Amendment cases involving commercial speech.

In commercial speech cases a four-part analysis has developed. At the outset, we must determine whether the expression is protected by the First Amendment. For commercial speech to come within that provision, it at least must concern lawful activity and not be misleading. Next, we ask whether the asserted governmental interest is substantial. If both inquiries yield positive answers, we must determine whether the regulation directly advances the government interest asserted, and whether it is not more extensive than is necessary to serve that interest.

In later cases the Court indicated that a governmental body need not necessarily adopt a manner of restriction that is absolutely the least burdensome restriction on commercial speech that will achieve the government's desired ends. All that is required is that the government demonstrate a reasonable fit between the government's ends and the means chosen to achieve those ends; in other words, the government must choose a means narrowly tailored to achieve the desired objective.

The following case deals with the increasingly common problem of newsracks on city sidewalks. Many cities, in the interests of keeping their towns attractive, want to limit the use of these devices. This case is an example of a governmental regulation that ran afoul of the test requiring a reasonable fit between the government's interests and the means the government chose to serve those interests.

Cincinnati v. Discovery Network, Inc.
United States Supreme Court
113 S. Ct. 1505 (1993)

The city of Cincinnati initially allowed the Discovery Network to place 38 free-standing newsracks on public property. The material in their newsracks primarily consisted of promotional material pertaining to Discovery's adult education courses. The city also permitted about 1,500 to 2,000 other newsracks on public property which were used by local newspapers. Cincinnati withdrew Discovery's permit for its 38 newsracks in the interests of safety and esthetics while at the same time permitting the newspapers to continue to distribute their papers in newsracks.

Under the *Central Hudson* test, the city had the burden of showing a "reasonable fit" between its legitimate interests of safety and esthetics and its decision to prohibit Discovery's newsracks in order to promote these interests. The lower courts as well as the United States Supreme Court ruled that the city had failed to establish the requisite reasonable fit and ruled on behalf of Discovery Network that Cincinnati's categorical ban on Discovery's newsracks conflicts with the requirements of the First Amendment.

Stevens, Justice

The city argues that there is a close fit between its ban on Discovery's newsracks and its interest in safety and esthetics because every decrease in the number of such dispensing devices necessarily effects an increase in safety and an improvement in the attractiveness of the cityscape. In the city's view, the prohibition is thus entirely related to its legitimate interests in safety and esthetics.

We consider the city's position an insufficient justification for the discrimination against Discovery's use of newsracks that are no more harmful than the permitted newsracks, and have only a minimal impact on the overall number of newsracks on the city's sidewalks. The major premise supporting the city's argument is the proposition that commercial speech has only a low value. Based on that premise, the city contends that the fact that assertedly more valuable publications are allowed to use newsracks does not undermine its judgment that its esthetic and safety interests are stronger than the interest in allowing commercial speakers to have similar access to the reading public.

We cannot agree. In our view, the city's argument attaches more importance to the distinction between commercial and noncommercial speech than our cases warrant and seriously underestimates the value of commercial speech.

We agree with the Court of Appeals that Cincinnati's actions in this case run afoul of the First Amendment. Not only does Cincinnati's categorical ban on commercial newsracks place too much importance on the distinction between commercial and noncommercial speech, but in this case, the distinction bears no relationship whatsoever to the particular interests that the city has asserted. It is therefore an impermissible means of responding to the city's admittedly legitimate interests.

The city has asserted an interest in esthetics, but respondent publishers' newsracks are no greater an eyesore than the newsracks permitted to remain on Cincinnati's sidewalks. Each newsrack is equally unattractive. As we have explained, the city's primary concern, as argued to us, is with the aggregate number of newsracks on its streets. On that score, however, all newsracks, regardless of whether they contain commercial or noncommercial publications, are equally at fault.

We are unwilling to recognize Cincinnati's bare assertion that the "low value" of commercial speech is a sufficient justification for its selective and categorical ban on Discovery's newsracks. Our holding, however, is narrow. We do not reach the question whether, given certain facts and under certain circumstances, a community might be able to justify differential treatment of commercial and noncommercial newsracks. We simply hold that on this record Cincinnati has failed to make such a showing. Because the distinction Cincinnati has drawn has absolutely no bearing on the interests it has asserted, we have no difficulty concluding, as did the courts below, that the city has not established the required "fit" between its goals and its chosen means.

Commercial Speech by Professionals

Starting with the case *Goldfarb* v. *Virginia State Bar* (1975), the Supreme Court showed a growing interest in the activities of professionals such as lawyers and doctors. In this case, the Supreme Court struck down the power of attorneys to jointly agree upon the minimum prices they would charge for certain professional services. The Court characterized the activities of attorneys in drafting minimum fee schedules as a clear example of illegal price fixing in violation of the Sherman Antitrust Act. *Goldfarb* represents the first step by the Court to inject some competition in the field of professional services.

The Court in 1977 considered the question of advertising by two attorneys for the purpose of increasing their business—clearly commercially motivated speech. In *Bates* v. *State Bar of Arizona*, two Arizona attorneys, John Bates and Van O'Steen, had decided to advertise in order to attract the volume of business necessary to sustain their legal clinic. They reasoned that it would be necessary to advertise to attract a large number of clients.

The clinic performed only routine services, such as uncontested bankruptcies, uncontested divorces, uncontested adoptions, and changes of names. To attract more business, the clinic placed an advertisement in the *Arizona Republic*, a daily newspaper of general circulation in the Phoenix metropolitan area. The advertisement stated that the clinic offered ''legal services at very reasonable fees,'' and the fees for certain services were listed. This advertisement violated

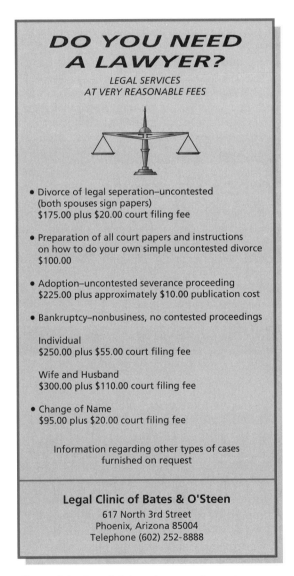

Figure 6.2 Legal Advertisement from *Bates* v. *State Bar of Arizona*

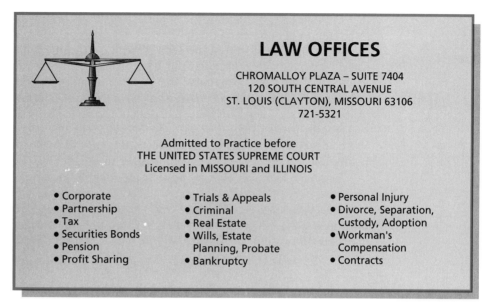

Figure 6.3 Legal Advertisement from *In. Re R.M.J.*

Figure 6.4 Legal Advertisement from *Zauderer* v. *Office of Disciplinary Counsel of the Supreme Court of Ohio*

the Arizona rules governing the practice of law, under which attorneys were forbidden to advertise.

The Court decided that the First Amendment of the United States Constitution invalidated the prohibition on advertising by attorneys. A majority of the members of the Court concluded that a state may not prevent the publication in a newspaper of a truthful advertisement concerning the terms and availability of routine legal services. The state may regulate advertising by attorneys, but it may not prohibit advertising outright. The Court listed some permissible limitations: False, deceptive, or misleading advertising may be restrained, and reasonable restrictions on the time, place, and manner of advertising may be required.

Famous examples of legal advertising include the advertisements from the *Bates* case, the *In re R.M.J.* case, and the *Zauderer v. Office of Disciplinary Counsel of the Supreme Court of Ohio,* case (see Figures 6.3, 6.4, and 6.5). In all three cases, the United States Supreme Court upheld the right of the attorneys to use their advertisements. Today, we see a wide range of legal advertisements not only in newspapers but on television as well.

SUMMARY

In addition to providing individuals with basic rights, the Constitution of the United States created the general structure of our government. The government structure is one of relationships between sources of power. The Constitution provided that the executive, judicial, and legislative powers be confined to separate units of the federal government.

The Constitution grants extensive power in the commerce clause to the federal government. This power has been used to pass innumerable rules that control the conduct of business in America. The states get their power from the police power. They also extensively regulate the activities of businesspeople. Both the power of the states and the power of the federal government are limited by various provisions in the United States Constitution.

Provisions for protecting individual rights from government infringement may be found in a number of places in the Constitution. The Bill of Rights and the Civil Rights Amendments are prime sources of those protected individual freedoms. One of the most important areas of constitutional protection for business is the First Amendment's freedom-of-speech guarantee. Corporations are protected by that provision, and recently the concept of speech has been interpreted by the Supreme Court to include business advertising, or commercial speech.

REVIEW QUESTIONS

1. Define the following terms:
   a. Commerce clause
   b. Commercial speech doctrine
   c. Due process
   d. Equal protection clause

2. Why are most of the protections for individual rights in the Constitution procedural protections?

3. Explain the concept of "state action" in constitutional law.

4. Should business speech be protected by the First Amendment?

5. The city of Columbus, Ohio, wishes to require that any product from a communist country be labeled with the country of origin. Is is within the power of the city to pass such a regulation?

6. Dirks wishes to plant one hundred acres of corn. The federal government orders him to plant only twenty acres of corn. Dirks argues that because he intends to use the corn only to feed the cattle on his farm, his activities are purely intrastate and thus cannot be regulated by Congress. Is he correct?

7. The state of Oklahoma wants to pass a law that requires local utility companies to use oil produced in the state of Oklahoma. The state wants to pass this statute to help support local oil producers. Would such a statute be within the state's power under the United States Constitution?

8. Warren, a man, wishes to join a local garden club that restricts its membership to women. The club refuses to take him as a member. Warren asserts that the club's action violates the equal protection clause of the Constitution. What could the club argue in its defense?

9. Wisconsin passed a statute that permitted creditors to seize debtors' wages without first giving the debtors a hearing. If the debtors wish to challenge this statute, what could they argue?

10. A state legislature wishes to pass a statute that treats one race of persons differently from another race. Is such a statute ever lawful under the equal protection clause?

11. Acme College, a state-run institution, experienced a problem with students of one race making racist remarks about other students in class, at sports events, and at other places on campus. In an attempt to protect all students, the college adopted a hate code speech that prohibited students from making racist remarks. Does such a college rule violate the United States Constitution?

12. The Lakes Mall, a major shopping center, adopted a policy to ask teenagers who assembled in large groups and used the mall as a social gathering place to either limit the size of the group of leave. The teenagers argued that this policy violates their right, guaranteed to them in the United States Constitution, to assemble. Are they correct?

13. An association of coal producers challenged the constitutionality of the Surface Mining Control and Reclamation Act of 1977. The act was passed by Congress to protect the environment from the adverse effects of surface coal mining operations. Congress held extended hearings in both houses concerning the effects of surface mining on the environment. The House committee documented the adverse effects of surface coal mining on interstate commerce as the source of damage to eleven thousand miles of streams, the loss of forests, the destruction of wildlife habitat, and the sedimentation of river systems. Is the application of this act to the coal companies a lawful exercise of congressional power under the commerce clause? Would it be useful for the coal producers to argue that they were engaged in local activities only?

14. The federal government passed a statute that prohibited the mailing of unsolicited advertisements for contraceptives. Youngs Drug Product Company wished to mail to the public unsolicited advertisements including informational pamphlets promoting the use of contraceptives. Youngs Drug Product brought an action for declaratory and injunctive relief that alleged, as applied to the proposed mailings, the statute violated the First Amendment. Is Youngs Drug Product correct?

15. Minnesota banned the retail sale of milk in plastic, nonreturnable, nonrefillable containers. Minnesota permitted the sale of milk in other nonreturnable, nonrefillable contain-

ers, such as paperboard. The state was concerned about solid waste management problems posed by plastic containers. Clover Leaf Creamery alleged that the act violated the equal protection clause of the Constitution. Is Clover Leaf correct?

16. The Virginia Board of Pharmacy adopted a rule that prohibited pharmacists within the state from advertising the prices of prescription drugs. The plaintiff, in this case, wished to receive drug price information. It challenged the rule, asserting that it violated the First Amendment. Did this rule violate the First Amendment?

17. Rock Against Racism sponsored a yearly program of rock music at the Naumberg Acoustic Bandshell in New York City's Central Park. The city received numerous complaints about excessive noise at these concerts. The city also experienced problems at bandshell events put on by other sponsors because of problems with the quality of the sound of the performances. The city adopted a rule whereby it furnished high-quality sound equipment and an independent sound technician for all performances. Rock Against Racism argued that this rule violated the First Amendment. Is it correct?

18. The State University of New York permitted only certain businesses to operate in University facilities. American Future Systems, Inc. sells housewares through a party plan. Products are offered for sale to groups of prospective buyers. An AFS representative was arrested for refusing to leave a university dormitory after she was advised she was violating this regulation. Must the state of New York prove that its rule was absolutely the least severe that would achieve its desired goal of keeping students' privacy from being violated unnecessarily?

CHAPTER 7

The Administrative Agency

- Administrative Agencies and Administrative Law
- Functions of Administrative Agencies

An administrative agency is a government body other than a court or a legislature. Agencies exist at all levels of government and affect individuals and businesses through rule making, adjudicating, and enforcing laws and policies that have been delegated to them. In the past thirty years, administrative agencies have become increasingly involved in various aspects of American life. Their power and law-making ability have affected the ways in which the largest corporations conduct day-to-day business. Their ability to dispense government funds has affected even the poorest individuals' daily lives.

Administrative agencies control various substantive areas of the law. Such diverse legal topics as air and water pollution, safety in the workplace, product safety, and equal employment opportunities are covered by different administrative agencies. Volumes might be written on the workings of just one agency and the areas of substantive law that it covers. Therefore, rather than review new substantive legal rules that happened to be produced by the administrative law system, this chapter will focus on several general issues concerning the administrative agency in our legal system.

This chapter is divided into two sections. First, a general discussion of administrative agencies and administrative law will be presented, which will identify some general characteristics of agencies. Second, three main functions of administrative agencies will be explored: the investigative or enforcement function, the adjudicative function, and the rule-making function. Various issues and limits imposed on the agency in the carrying out of those functions will also be discussed.

ADMINISTRATIVE AGENCIES AND ADMINISTRATIVE LAW

Importance of Agencies

Although the great influence of administrative agencies in the legal environment is a relatively recent development, administrative agencies are not new to our form of government. The first agencies were established by Congress in 1789. They were created to affix duties on foreign imports (the forerunner of today's customs office) and to provide pensions for the soldiers who were disabled in the Revolutionary War (the forerunner of today's Veterans Administration).

The First Congress created those agencies for practical reasons. Processing applications for disability benefits and administering duties on imported products would take an enormous amount of congressional time. Furthermore, use of the judicial branch for these matters would similarly overload it so that the cases and disputes normally associated with the judicial process would be left waiting. The decision-making bodies established by the Constitution were not appropriate for handling such matters, and specialized bodies were necessary to carry out congressional policy. The rationale of practicality that led the First Congress to establish those agencies is still the driving force behind new ones being created today.

Administrative agencies exist at all levels of government. Federal agencies regulate such areas as the environment, workplace safety, and civil rights, as well as distribute welfare and social security payments. States are also filled with various administrative agencies. Such state offices as the division of motor vehicles, workers' compensation department, and the fish and game control board are examples. Local government also contains a number of administrative agencies—police and fire departments, zoning commissions, and park boards.

Virtually no business decision can be made without complying with a rule or regulation concerning the type of decision, the outcome of the decision, or the decision-making process itself. For example, personnel questions in business often involve rules and regulations of the Equal Employment Opportunities Commission (EEOC). Business decisions involving finance or capital accumulation may bring into play rules and regulations of the Securities and Exchange Commission (SEC). The workplace and its design often involve the Environmental Protection Agency (EPA) or the Occupational Safety and Health Administration (OSHA). Selling and marketing the product that has been produced may involve the Federal Trade Commission (FTC) or the Federal Reserve Board. State or local regulation may also affect these business decisions. Administrative regulation of business is a pervasive force in the legal system and in the business world. Some writers call agencies the fourth branch of government, even though they are not mentioned in the Constitution.

Agencies Created by the Legislature

Administrative agencies are creations of the legislature. Their lives are begun through the enactment of a statute, called an **enabling act,** which briefly outlines the desired policy goals. Often, however, the specific implementation provisions for those goals are not included in the statute. Instead, the agency is charged with the responsibility of carrying out the intention of the legislature. Note that the legislature need not create a new agency to administer the areas it chooses to regulate. Frequently, an existing agency is given the authority.

Two of the most important features of an administrative agency are its expertise and its ability to constantly monitor and review regulatory programs. Agencies are staffed with experts in the area over which the agency has jurisdiction. They can provide the technical skill needed to properly carry out the legislative policies that led to the agency's creation.

General Functions of an Agency

The doctrine of separation of powers places the legislative, the judicial, and the executive powers in separate branches. This doctrine was an important element in the Constitution's plan to minimize the risk of too much power being concentrated in one government body. However, administrative agencies have all these functions.

The agency is able to legislate—that is, to make rules and draft regulations that serve as statutory guidelines for the type of conduct necessary to follow the regulatory scheme. Agencies may also exert the power of the executive; that is, an agency may investigate whether the rules it enacted have been properly followed by businesses and individuals. Some agencies are empowered to assess fines against those who violate their rules as well as to file complaints in court against them. Finally, an administrative agency is able to perform the same tasks as the judiciary; that is, to decide cases in the area of its expertise and, like the courts, to make law by virtue of its decisions in those cases.

The National Labor Relations Board (NLRB), for example, is very active in its role as an agency that adjudicates. Its decisions are published in bound volumes, much the same as court decisions, and the NLRB uses its past decisions as precedent in current cases. Most interestingly, the NLRB rarely makes rules or drafts regulations in its capacity as an agency. Instead, it relies on its case decisions to make the law and create rules of conduct in interpreting congressional policy under the National Labor Relations Act (NLRA) governing labor-management relations in the private sector.

Criticism of Administrative Agencies

The increased influence of administrative agencies and the effect of their regulations on business have caused dissatisfaction. Certain agency decisions restrict formerly allowable business activity. For example, the EPA has set emission standards for certain types of pollutants emitted by factories. Companies constrained by this standard must modify their production practices. Laws that compel certain activities seem antithetical to our system, and those encumbered by them can be expected to harbor distaste for the body that applies them.

In addition, administrative agencies are insulated from voter control. Although the heads of agencies are often political appointees, the general functionaries remain in their jobs regardless of a change in political climate. In the federal government, those jobs are protected by the civil service system. Thus, voters have no input into the activities of administrative agencies, another source of dissatisfaction.

Karl Llewellyn, a renowned American legal scholar, once wrote: ''A man's rights must be accessible, but to be right rights, they must call also for some share on his part in initiating or working out their procurement, their fulfillment. Else law remains remote, the government becomes an enemy or a dairy cow, and the morale of official, citizen, and group alike bogs in morass, and pressure-groups become a byword.''[1]

Writers frequently describe a typical evolution of an agency. At the outset, the agency, usually with public and political support, will work with enthusiasm and flexibility in carrying out the goals set in its enabling act. After a few years of operation, complaints begin to arise that the agency has lost its sense of purpose and that complacency has set in. Public and political support wanes, perhaps because early agency successes have solved the most pressing problems, perhaps because more urgent problems gain public attention. In its third state, the agency falls into a routine, and the focus of its attention is making sure others abide by the norms of the bureaucracy rather than initiating innovative approaches to the problems that may still exist. There is no final stage in the life of a typical administrative agency. The legislature rarely phases one out of existence.

Thus, as administrative agencies become more important in the legal environment, concern over their role seems to increase. Politicians, quick to detect these feelings, frequently campaign for office against the bureaucracy. Ronald Reagan, for example, made reducing the burdens of government on business a major theme of his administration.

Checks on Agency Power

Checks do exist on the activities of administrative agencies. The agencies are not simply loose guns going off in whatever directions they see fit. Courts exercise review over the decisions of agencies. The legislature also has tools available to check the agency. Since the legislature created the agency, the legislature can abolish or change the agency in virtually any way it sees fit. Furthermore, since the legislature controls the funding of the various agencies, subtle pressures may be exerted during the time that funding decisions are being made for the next fiscal year.

Congress has enacted general statutes that affect the processes and procedures of administrative agencies. The Administrative Procedure Act sets forth standards and procedures that an agency must follow in its rule-making and adjudication functions. These standards are due process protections for those who may be affected by agency activity. Hearing procedures must contain the general processes similarly available to parties in a judicial hearing. The procedural requirements for rule making call for public notice of the proposed rule making and the opportunity for interested or affected parties to comment. In short, the Administrative Procedure Act legislatively commands the federal agencies to follow minimum standards of procedural fairness.

Sunset legislation exists that requires that an agency cease to exist after a set period of years, unless the legislature re-creates it. In effect, this control plan envisions legislative study of the work of the agency to determine if a further extension of its existence is warranted.

However, legislative oversight of agency activities primarily occurs indirectly. Use of the budgetary process to forbid the expenditure of funds for certain programs or to designate that funds be used in a certain way can channel agency activity. Furthermore, agency commissioners generally owe their appointments (and reappointments) to Congress. Unless the president makes those decisions a major part of his policies, that leverage remains with Congress. Finally, hearings and investigations of agency activities are used by legislators to influence agency activities and to thwart unwanted agency policy initiatives. Thus, agencies generally consult with Congress informally before undertaking policy initiatives.

FUNCTIONS OF ADMINISTRATIVE AGENCIES

Function of the Executive

Inspection and Data Gathering

An administrative agency could not function without the ability to gather and analyze information. Information is vital to the agency in its tasks of rule making and adjudication. One of the reasons that agencies are created is to have experts available to study and respond to a problem that the legislature seeks to regulate. Without the ability to acquire information, agencies would be unable to fulfill their assigned tasks.

Most of the information received by agencies is voluntarily transmitted to them. Private parties respond to requests by the agency to produce documents and other data. Some agencies also inspect public records and reports in order to gather the information needed for their work.

However, agencies are not dependent upon voluntary cooperation. Agencies generally have the power to legally require the necessary cooperation. In fact, the first administrative agencies created by Congress in 1789 had the power to require that records and reports be kept. The record-keeping power is necessary so that an agency can monitor a business in order to effectively regulate pursuant to commands from the legislature. Business managers often complain about this function of administrative regulation. Record keeping and reporting are both costly and time-consuming, especially when a business is required to do so by several agencies. Some critics question whether the need for this information outweighs the burden placed on businesses.

Administrative agencies can also subpoena witnesses and documents. This power is important in any hearing process that may be undertaken by an agency, either as a means of gathering information as a part of the rule-making process, or as a part of a hearing before an administrative law judge or hearing examiner.

The third information-gathering power of an agency is the power to investigate by inspection of the business's books and records or to visit the premises of parties subject to the agency's regulation. Inspection is a very important tool for enforcement of administrative rules and regulations. For example, local health and safety regulation for housing would be difficult to enforce without the agency's having the ability to inspect premises where such regulations may be violated. Spot inspections by OSHA investigators of various workplaces determine if any safety rules have been violated. Although inspections are an important form of law enforcement, they need to be balanced against the general rights provided to the people by the Constitution.

Marshall v. Barlow's, Inc.
United States Supreme Court
436 U.S. 30 (1978)

Petitioner, Barlow's, Inc., brought this action to obtain an injunction against a warrantless search of his business premises in accordance with the Occupational Safety and Health Act of 1970 (OSHA), which allows agents of the secretary of labor to search the work area of any employment facility under OSHA's jurisdiction for safety hazards and violations of OSHA regulations. The three-judge district court rules in petitioner's favor, holding that a warrantless search violated the Fourth Amendment. The United States Supreme Court affirmed.

Justice White

The Warrant Clause of the Fourth Amendment protects commercial buildings as well as private homes. To hold otherwise would belie the origin of that Amendment, and the American colonial experience. An important forerunner of the first 10 Amendments to the United States Constitution, the Virginia Bill of Rights, specifically opposed general warrants, whereby an officer or messenger may be commanded to search suspected places without evidence of a fact committed. The general warrant was a recurring point of contention in the Colonies immediately preceding the Revolution. The particular offensiveness it engendered was acutely felt by the merchants and businessmen whose premises and products were inspected for compliance with the several parliamentary revenue measures that most irritated the colonists.

Against this background, it is untenable that the ban on warrantless searches was not intended to shield places of business as well as of residence.

The businessman, like the occupant of a residence, has a constitutional right to go about his business free from unreasonable official entries upon his private commercial property. The businessman, too, has that right placed in jeopardy if the decision to enter and inspect for violation of regulatory laws can be made and enforced by the inspector in the field without official authority evidenced by a warrant.

Certain industries have such a history of government oversight that no reasonable expectation of privacy could exist for a proprietor over the stock of such an enterprise. Liquor and firearms are industries of this type; when an entrepreneur embarks upon such a business, he has voluntarily chosen to subject himself to a full arsenal of governmental regulation.

The element that distinguishes these enterprises from ordinary businesses is a long tradition of close government supervision, of which any person who chooses to enter such a business must already be aware. The clear import of our cases is that the closely regulated industry is the exception.

We are unconvinced, however, that requiring warrants to inspect will impose serious burdens on the inspection system or the courts will prevent inspections necessary to enforce the statute, or will make them less effective. In the first place, the great majority of businessmen can be expected in normal course to consent to inspection without warrant; the Secretary has not brought to this Court's attention any widespread pattern of refusal.

Whether the Secretary proceeds to secure a warrant or other process, with or without prior notice, his entitlement to inspect will not depend on his demonstrating probable cause to believe that conditions in violation of OSHA exist on the premises. Probable cause in the criminal law sense is not required. For purposes of an administrative search such as this, probable cause justifying the issuance of a warrant may be based not only on specific evidence of an existing violation but also on a showing that reasonable legislative or administrative standards for conducting an inspection are satisfied with respect to a particular establishment.

Nor do we agree that the incremental protections

afforded the employer's privacy by a warrant are so marginal that they fail to justify the administrative burdens that may be entailed.

The authority to make warrantless searches devolves almost unbridled discretion upon executive and administrative officers, particularly those in the field, as to when to search and whom to search. A warrant, by contrast, would provide assurances from a neutral officer that the inspection is reasonable under the Constitution, is authorized by statute, and is pursuant to an administrative plan containing specific neutral criteria. Also, a warrant would then and there advise the owner of the scope and objects of the search, beyond which limits the inspector is not expected to proceed. These are important functions for a warrant to perform, functions which underlie the Court's prior decisions that the Warrant Clause applies to inspections for compliance with regulatory statutes. We conclude that the concerns expressed by the Secretary do not suffice to justify warrantless inspections under OSHA or vitiate the general constitutional requirements that for a search to be reasonable a warrant must be obtained.

Giving Advice

One of the most common activities of an administrative agency is giving advice to businesses that have questions concerning their duties under the law. Inquirers are often seeking information concerning how to comply with the various rules and rulings of the agency. As a practical matter, in the vast majority of the cases, the information received from the agency is reliable. The business can follow that advice with the virtual assurance of compliance with the rules of the agency.

However, the agency is not bound to follow the advice given by one of its employees. Of course, when that happens the result may be devastating to the person who has relied on that advice. Yet there is an important reason in the public interest why an agency may not be considered legally bound by advice given by an employee. If such advice could bind the agency, there would be a danger that the agency could begin to assume powers that the legislature did not wish it to have solely because of its inability to disavow any acts by its employees. In a sense, this doctrine, although sometimes unfair to the inquiring individual who erroneously relies on agency advice, is a protective device to control the powers and activities of an administrative agency. The following case is an example.

Federal Crop Insurance Corp. v. Merrill
United States Supreme Court
332 U.S. 380 (1947)

The Federal Crop Insurance Corporation is a government-owned corporation created for the purpose of insuring wheat producers against crop losses due to unavoidable causes, including drought. The corporation promulgated and published in the *Federal Register* regulations specifying the conditions on which it would insure wheat crops, including a provision making "spring wheat which has been reseeded on winter wheat acreage" ineligible for insurance. The corporation accepted an application for insurance from a wheat grower, who, without knowledge of the provision, informed the local Federal Crop Insurance Corporation agent that most of the wheat to be insured was being reseeded on winter wheat acreage. Later, most of the wheat on the reseeded acreage was destroyed by drought. The corporation, after discovering that the destroyed acreage had been reseeded, refused to pay the loss, and this litigation was begun in one of the lower courts of Idaho. The supreme court of Idaho affirmed the judgment of the lower court, in effect adopting the theory of the trial judge: Since the knowledge of the agent of a private insurance company, under the circumstances of this case, would be attributed to, and thereby bind, a private insurance company, the corporation is equally bound. The United States Supreme Court reversed.

Justice Frankfurter

We assume that recovery could be had against a private insurance company. But the Corporation is not a private insurance company. It is too late in the day to urge that the Government is just another private litigant, for purposes of charging it with liability, whenever it takes over a business theretofore conducted by private enterprise or engages in competition with private ventures. Government is not partly public or partly private, depending upon the governmental pedigree of the type of a particular activity or the manner in which the Government conducts it. The Government may carry on its operations through conventional executive agencies or through corporate forms especially created for defined ends. Whatever the form in which the Government functions, anyone entering into an arrangement with the government takes the risk of having accurately ascertained that he who purports to act for the Government stays within the bounds of his authority. The scope of this authority may be explicitly defined by Congress or be limited by delegated legislation, properly exercised through the rule-making power. And this is so even though, as here, the agent himself may have been unaware of the limitations upon his authority.

Congress has legislated in this instance, as in modern regulatory enactments it so often does, by conferring the rule-making power upon the agency created for carrying out its policy. Just as everyone is charged with knowledge of the United States Statutes at Large, Congress has provided that the appearance of rules and regulations in the Federal Register gives legal notice of their contents.

Accordingly, the Wheat Crop Insurance Regulations were binding on all who sought to come within the Federal Crop Insurance Act, regardless of actual knowledge of what is in the Regulations or of the hardship resulting from innocent ignorance. The oft-quoted observation in that "Men must turn square corners when they deal with the Government," does not reflect a callous outlook. It merely expresses the duty of all courts to observe the conditions defined by Congress for charging the public treasury. The "terms and conditions" defined by the Corporation, under authority of Congress, for creating liability on the part of the Government preclude recovery for the loss of the reseeded wheat no matter with what good reason the respondents thought they had obtained insurance from the Government. Indeed, not only do the Wheat Regulations limit the liability of the Government as if they had been enacted by Congress directly, but they were in fact incorporated by reference in the application as specifically required by the Regulations.

| **Function of the Judiciary** | An administrative agency not only investigates rule violations but also hears complaints brought concerning those violations either by the agency or by private parties. **Agency adjudication** of a dispute is very similar to the adjudicative |

function of a court. Witnesses are heard, evidence is submitted, the law and policy are applied to the facts at hand, and a decision is reached. The materials on judicial decision making would be applicable also to decision making by an administrative law judge or hearing examiner.

Basic adjudication practices and procedures followed by federal administrative agencies are contained in the Administrative Procedure Act. The act codifies traditional court practices as a means of providing fair procedures in administrative hearings. For example, the act provides that notice or appraisal of an agency complaint be provided to the affected party or parties. These parties are given the opportunity to respond to the complaint and to have counsel available to assist them at the hearing. The conduct of a hearing is similar to a court proceeding. Witnesses are called and examined. The opposing party has the opportunity to confront and cross examine the witnesses as well as provide evidence. The proceeding is conducted by a hearing examiner who performs much the same function as a judge in a courtroom hearing.

In addition to these procedures provided by the Administrative Procedure Act, various administrative agencies have adopted rules of practice for the hearings that they hold. This is similar to the judicial practice in which various jurisdictions create rules governing cases to be heard. Administrative agency rules of practice are published in the **Federal Register,** which is the official public notice organ of the federal administrative agencies.

Comparison: Court and Agency Hearings

A few general observations may be made in comparing the administrative agency adjudication process and a trial before a court. Both are usually open to the public and conducted formally, although agency hearings are often not as formal as those in a court. The hearing process, from its initiation to its rendered decision, is also similar. Initiation of the proceeding by a complaint, response by answer, prehearing discovery, and pretrial conferences are common to both forums. Additionally, evidence is presented in a question-answer format with the opportunity for the parties to call witnesses and cross-examine the opposing party's witnesses.

An agency hearing is presided over by a hearing examiner who performs functions similar to those of a judge. The hearing examiner conducts the hearing and rules on motions raised by the parties. The examiner also renders a decision based on the evidence presented. Usually this decision is written and accompanied by findings of fact.

However, some major differences exist between hearings conducted by the judicial system and by administrative agencies. Agency hearings are never heard by a jury. The decisions are made solely by a hearings examiner. As a result, the evidentiary rules designed to insulate juries from unreliable evidence are not applied with the same degree of strictness in an administrative hearing. Furthermore, since some agencies use the adjudicative process more as a rule-making than a dispute-settling mechanism, they are more willing to accept general evidence about the problem surrounding the hearing than information solely relating to the parties to the action. The National Labor Relations Board (NLRB) is an example of such an agency.

Decisions by administrative agencies under their adjudication function have precedential effect, much like judicial decisions. These decisions are often published, as are judicial decisions, and cited as authority by the agency (and by courts) to justify a decision in a similar case.

Doctrines of Judicial Review of Agency Adjudications

Courts will exercise review of agency adjudicative decisions on four levels. In general, courts will review them for questions of law and constitutional procedure. A court will determine whether the agency (1) had exceeded its authority as provided in its enabling statute or (2) had properly interpreted and applied the law in the case. Courts will also (3) review the hearing conducted by the agency to determine whether it was fair; that is, whether it was in keeping with constitutional due process requirements. Courts will also (4) review whether the agency has acted reasonably and not arbitrarily in its decision making.

This type of review is generally not a trial de novo. It is more of an appellate review of the agency decision. Courts will usually not substitute their own view of the facts for that of the agency. Instead, the facts will be reviewed to determine if the agency decision was rationally based upon the evidence presented at the hearing.

The following cases are examples of judicial review of the adjudicatory function of administrative agencies.

Federal Trade Commission v. Colgate-Palmolive Co.
United States Supreme Court
380 U.S. 374 (1964)

The Federal Trade Commission charged Colgate-Palmolive with deceptive advertising under Section 5 of the Federal Trade Commission Act. Commercials purported to give viewers visual proof that Colgate-Palmolive's shaving cream could soften sandpaper. Unknown to the viewers, the "sandpaper" test was actually done with simulated sandpaper made of plexiglass to which sand had been applied. This became "moisturized" by the shaving cream differently from actual sandpaper. The prop was shaved of sand immediately after the application of Rapid-Shave shaving cream. Actual sandpaper would require an approximately eighty-minute soaking before it could be shaved. The commission ordered respondent to cease and desist. On appeal, the court of appeals reversed, holding that the order could be broadly interpreted to forbid the use of all undisclosed simulations. This appeal to the United States Supreme Court followed.

Chief Justice Warren

In reviewing the substantive issues in the case, it is well to remember the respective roles of the Commission and the courts in the administration of the Federal Trade Commission Act. When the Commission was created by Congress in 1914, it was directed by Section 5 to prevent "[u]nfair methods of competition in commerce." Congress amended the Act in 1938 to extend the Commission's jurisdiction to include "unfair or deceptive acts or practices in commerce"—a significant amendment showing Congress' concern for consumers as well as for competitors. It is important to note the generality of these standards of illegality; the proscriptions in Section 5 are flexible, "to be defined with particularity by the myriad of cases from the field of business."

This statutory scheme necessarily gives the Commission an influential role in interpreting Section 5 and in applying it to the facts of particular cases arising out of unprecedented situations. Moreover, as an administrative agency which deals continually with cases in the area, the Commission is often in a better position than are courts to determine when a practice is "deceptive" within the meaning of the Act. This Court has frequently stated that the Commission's judgment is to be given great weight by reviewing courts. This admonition is especially true with respect to allegedly deceptive advertising since the finding of a Section 5 violation in this field rests so heavily on inference and pragmatic judgment. Nevertheless, while informed judicial determination is dependent upon enlightenment gained from administrative experience, in the last analysis the words "deceptive practices" set forth a legal standard and they must get their final meaning from judicial construction.

We agree with the Commission, therefore, that the undisclosed use of plexiglass in the present commercials was a material deceptive practice. We find unpersuasive respondents' objections to this conclusion. Respondents claim that it will be impractical to inform the viewing public that it is not seeing an actual test, experiment or demonstration, but we think it inconceivable that the ingenious advertising world will be unable, if it so desires, to conform to the Commission's insistence that the public be not misinformed. If, however, it becomes impossible or impractical to show simulated demonstrations on television in a truthful manner, this indicates that television is not a medium that lends itself to this type of commercial, not that the commerical must survive at all costs.

We turn our attention to the order issued by the Commission. It had been repeatedly held that the Commission has wide discretion in determining the type of order that is necessary to cope with the unfair practices found, and that Congress has placed the primary responsibility for fashioning orders upon the Commission. For these reasons the courts should not "lightly modify" the Commission's orders. However, this Court has also warned that an order's prohibitions "should be clear and precise in order that they may be understood by those against whom they are directed," and that "[t]he severity of possible penalties prescribed for violations of orders which have become final underlines the necessity for fashioning orders which are, at the outset, sufficiently clear and precise to avoid raising serious questions as to their meaning and application."

The Court of Appeals has criticized the reference in the Commission's order to "test, experiment or demonstration" as not capable of practical interpretation.

The crucial terms of the present order—test, experiment or demonstration represented as actual proof of a claim—are as specific as the circumstances will permit. If respondents in their subsequent commercials attempt to come as close to the line of misrepresentation as the Commission's order permits, they may without specifically intending to do so cross into the area proscribed by this order. However, it does not seem unfair to require that one who deliberately goes perilously close to an area of proscribed conduct shall take the risk that he may cross the line. In commercials where the emphasis is on the seller's word, and not on the viewer's own perception, the respondents need not fear that an undisclosed use of props is prohibited by the present order. On the other hand, when the commercial not only makes a claim, but also invites the viewer to rely on his own perception for demonstrative proof of the claim, the respondents will be aware that the use of undisclosed props in strategic places might be a material deception. We believe that respondents will have no difficulty applying the Commission's order to the vast majority of their contemplated future commercials. If, however, a situation arises in which respondents are sincerely unable to determine whether a proposed course of action would violate the present order, they can, by complying with the Commission's rules, oblige the Commission to give them definitive advice as to whether their proposed action, if pursued, would constitute compliance with the order.

Citizens to Preserve Overton Park v. Volpe
United States Supreme Court
401 U.S. 402 (1971)

Overton Park is a 342-acre city park located near the center of Memphis, Tennessee. The park contains a zoo, a nine-hole municipal golf course, an outdoor theater, nature trails, a bridle path, an art academy, picnic areas, and one hundred seventy acres of forest. The proposed highway, which is to be a six-lane, high-speed expressway, will sever the zoo from the rest of the park. Although the roadway will be depressed below ground level except where it crosses a small creek, twenty-six acres of the park will be destroyed. The highway is to be a segment of Interstate Highway I-40, part of the National System of Interstate and Defense Highways. I-40 will provide Memphis with a major east-west expressway that will allow easier access to downtown Memphis from the residential areas on the eastern edge of the city.

Justice Marshall

Section 4(f) of the Department of Transportation Act and section 138 of the Federal-Aid Highway Act are clear and specific directives. Both the Department of Transportation Act and the Federal-Aid to Highway Act provide that the Secretary shall not approve any program or project that requires the use of any public parkland unless (1) there is no feasible and prudent alternative to the use of such land, and (2) such program includes all possible planning to minimize harm to such park. This language is a plain and explicit bar to the use of federal funds for construction of highways through parks—only the most unusual situations are exempted.

In most cases considerations of cost, directness of route, and community disruption will indicate that parkland should be used for highway construction whenever possible. Although it may be necessary to transfer funds from one jurisdiction to another, there will always be a smaller outlay required from the public purse when parkland is used since the public already owns the land and there will be no need to pay for right-of-way. And since people do not live or work in parks, if a highway is built on parkland no one will have to leave his home or give up his business. Such factors are common to substantially all highway construction. Thus, if Congress intended these factors to be on an equal footing with

preservation of parkland there would have been no need for the statutes.

Congress clearly did not intend that cost and disruption of the community were to be ignored by the Secretary. But the very existence of the statutes indicates that protection of parkland was to be given paramount importance. The few green havens that are public parks were not to be lost unless there were truly unusual factors present in a particular case or the cost of community disruption resulting from alternative routes reached extraordinary magnitudes. If the statutes are to have any meaning, the Secretary cannot approve the destruction of parkland unless he finds that alternative routes present unique problems.

But the existence of judicial review is only the start: the standard for review must also be determined. For that we must look at section 706 of the Administrative Procedure Act, which provides that a reviewing court shall hold unlawful and set aside agency action, findings, and conclusions found not to meet six separate standards. In all cases agency action must be set aside if the action was arbitrary, capricious, an abuse of discretion, or otherwise not in accordance with law or if the action failed to meet statutory, procedural, or constitutional requirements. In certain narrow, specifically limited situations, the agency action is to be set aside if the action was not supported by substantial evidence. And in other equally narrow circumstances the reviewing court is to engage in a de novo review of the action and set it aside if it was unwarranted by the facts.

The court is first required to decide whether the Secretary acted within the scope of his authority. This determination naturally begins with a delineation of the scope of the Secretary's authority and discretion. As has been shown, Congress has specified only a small range of choices that the Secretary can make. Also involved in this initial inquiry is a determination of whether on the facts the Secretary's decision can reasonably be said to be within that range. The reviewing court must consider whether the Secretary properly construed his authority to approve the use of parkland as limited to situations where there are no feasible alternative routes or where feasible alternative routes involve uniquely difficult problems. And the reviewing court must be able to find that the Secretary could have reasonably believed that in this case there are no feasible alternatives or that alternatives do involve unique problems.

Scrutiny of the facts does not end, however, with the determination that the Secretary has acted within the scope of his statutory authority. Section 706(2)(A) re-quires a finding that the actual choice made was not arbitrary, capricious, an abuse of discretion, or otherwise not in accordance with law. To make this finding the court must consider whether the decision was based on a consideration of the relevant factors and whether there has been a clear error of judgment. Although this inquiry into the facts is to be searching and careful, the ultimate standard of review is a narrow one. The court is not empowered to substitute its judgment for that of the agency.

The final inquiry is whether the Secretary's action followed the necessary procedural requirements. Here the only procedural error alleged is the failure of the Secretary to make formal findings and state his reason for allowing the highway to be built through the park.

The administrative record is not before us. The lower courts based their review on the litigation affidavits that were presented. And they clearly do not constitute the "whole record" compiled by the agency: the basis for review required by section 706 of the Administrative Procedure Act.

Thus, it is necessary to remand this case to the District Court for review of the Secretary's decision. That review is to be based on the full administrative record that was before the Secretary at the time he made his decision.

Function of the Legislature

A third function of an administrative agency is promulgating rules and regulations, much as a legislature enacts a statute. These rules are agency statements of policy or interpretation that will be applied in the future. Administrative rules and regulations have the same force and effect as a statute enacted by a legislature. Agencies, ideally, work together with the legislature in carrying out the representatives' desires for regulating a certain area.

An administrative agency's **rule-making** process resembles that of a legislature. Its rules and regulations set forth guidelines to govern the conduct of those individuals and businesses that are subject to its jurisdiction. Since the commands of the legislature in the agency's enabling act are rather general in nature, the rules and regulations crafted by the administrative agency will often be of greater practical importance to businesses than the actual legislation. Frequently, the administrative agency will make rulings interpreting the statute, giving guidance to those who must abide by its terms. In some commercial law areas, the agency may draft a business form that, if used, will virtually ensure compliance with the regulatory requirements.

[margin handwritten notes: • GIVE NOTICE • FOLLOW PROCEDURES • BE FAIR]

The Administrative Procedure Act provides basic practices to be followed by a federal agency involved in formal rule making. These practices, like those pertaining to administrative agency judicial functions, are guidelines to ensure fairness in the agency activity. In general, three steps are required. First, the administrative agency must give notice to the public of its proposed rule-making activity. This notice is made through publication in the *Federal Register*. Thereafter, interested persons are given the opportunity to participate in the process. Such participation may be limited to filing written comments, arguments, or facts with the agency. Second, the agency may provide for oral testimony by having formal presentations made at a rule-making hearing. However, the agency is not limited in the construction of the rule to information presented during the public participation phase of the procedure. The purpose of the participation procedures is to give interested parties some voice in the rule-making process. Finally, once the rule has been promulgated, it must be made public, through publication in the *Federal Register*, at least thirty days before it becomes effective. This gives those who are affected by the rule the opportunity to learn of it and conform to its provisions.

Administrative rules, like statutes, are uniform in treatment. However, this uniformity exists at the cost of a loss of flexibility on the part of the agency. Case-by-case adjudication of issues over which the agency has jurisdiction provides more tailored justice. A uniform rule does not necessarily do this. Rather than rendering a decision on each case based on its merits, the existence of rules and regulations allows disposal of cases based on preexisting rules. The efficiency that rules bring also helps the agency plan its work. Businesses that are required to conform to the commands of the agency are better able to do so if there is an existing body of rules to follow. However, in practice some of the rules are so complex that many have great difficulty in understanding what their conduct requirements are. As a result, new rules and official explanations of the rules are given by the agency, increasing the amount of material that must be digested by those who are subject to the regulations.

The advantages and disadvantages of administrative agency rule making raise questions that have already been considered in studying the American legal environment. These questions revolve around the struggle in the law between certainty and stability on the one hand and fairness and flexibility on the other.

Did the Agency Have the Authority to Make the Rule?

Although an agency action need not pass muster with the other branches of government before it is effective, there are standards of review that the courts apply to agency rules and regulations that serve to keep the agency rule-making process in line. First, an agency rule may be reviewed to determine whether it was within the power of the agency to enact. Agencies are creatures of their enabling acts, limited in scope and power by the act's terms. For example, the EPA, which was created to respond to pollution problems, would not have the ability to promulgate rules concerning discrimination in employment. Discrimination may be an important issue deserving legal control, but the powers of the EPA do not include the power to act on employment discrimination matters. This limitation on agency power is called an **ultra vires** limitation, which means that no act outside the power granted to the agency may be performed.

Forging Industry Association v. Secretary of Labor
United States Court of Appeals, Fourth Circuit
748 F.2d 210 (1984)

An occupational noise exposure standard has existed the enactment in 1970 of the Occupational Safety and Health Act. The current standard was promulgated for the purpose of protecting employees from workplace exposure to damaging levels of noise. The standard establishes a permissible workplace limit of ninety decibels calculated using an eight-hour time-weighted average. If the ninety-decibel exposure limit is exceeded, the employer must reduce noise to or below this level by using feasible engineering or administrative controls. If such controls are infeasible, employers may use hearing protectors, such as earmuffs or plugs, to reduce employee noise exposure to permissible limits. The standard also contained a generally phrased requirement that employers administer a continuing effective hearing conservation program in workplaces where sound levels exceeded the permissible exposure level.

When studies revealed that many employees suffered significant hearing impairment at noise levels below the ninety-decibel threshold, OSHA began the process of collecting and evaluating the information necessary to issue a comprehensive new regulation with a reduced permissible exposure level of eighty-five decibels. As an interim measure, OSHA adopted a hearing conservation amendment to replace the general conservation program requirement.

Despite its interim nature, the requirements of the amendment are substantial. The amendment requires employers to determine which employees are exposed to or above an "action level" of eighty-five decibels measured as an eight-hour time-weighted average. Such employees must be notified of the amount of sound they are exposed to and provided with an audiometric test to determine their hearing level.

Chapman, Circuit Judge

An initial inquiry that must be made in determining the validity of any regulation adopted by a federal agency is whether the regulation is within the scope of the agency's statutory authority. Examining the language of the Occupational Safety and Health Act and the Supreme Court decisions interpreting it, we find it clear that Congress only authorized the Secretary to adopt those standards which relate to health and safety at the workplace.

A standard is invalid if it requires an employer to take actions in regard to hazards existing outside the workplace. It is clear from the language of the hearing conservation amendment that employers may be subjected to requirements and penalties that may be imposed as a result of non-workplace hazards. The amendment's requirements are triggered whenever an employee suffers a standard threshold shift loss in hearing. It is obvious that such a hearing loss can result from non-occupational noise exposure just as easily as it can from occupational exposure. Airplanes, hunting rifles, loud music and a myriad of other sources produce noise potentially as damaging as any at the workplace. Yet the Amendment makes no distinction between hearing loss caused by workplace sources and loss caused by non-workplace sources. The rule-making record clearly provides that once a hearing loss is found, the amendment requires the same actions by the employer whether or not the loss is work-related, and that the subject rule contains no requirement that there be a determination of work relatedness.

Thus the hearing conservation amendment clearly imposes responsibilities on employers based on non-work-related hazards. Under the amendment, an employer whose workers are unaffected by workplace noise may be subject to numerous requirements simply because its workers choose to hunt, listen to loud music or ride motorcycles during their non-working hours. Hearing loss caused by such activities is regrettable but it is not a problem that Congress delegated to OSHA to remedy. The amendment is therefore vacated and remanded to OSHA for the creation of a valid standard.

Was the Rule-Making Procedure Fair?

A second type of judicial review over agency regulations is review of the agency rule-making procedures to determine if the agency followed the proper course outlined in its enabling act, the Administrative Procedure Act, or other relevant statutes. If the agency failed to follow the required procedures, then its regulations may be attacked through judicial review.

Is the Rule Reasonably and Not Arbitrarily Made?

Courts will also review the regulation itself. However, they will not simply impose their judgment for that of the agency. Relevant judicial opinions often state that, although the court disagrees with the wisdom of a certain rule, it will not substitute its own judgment concerning the rule for the expertise of the agency. (In understanding this limitation on the scope of judicial review, refer to Chapter 4 on judicial reasoning.) However, in practice, predicting when the court will defer to the agency's expertise and when it will attack a regulation is problematic. Nonetheless, deferring to agency expertise is the most frequent action.

Administrative regulations that are found to be unreasonable or arbitrary will be stricken. The court will review the agency rule-making record to determine whether there is a rational relationship between the rule and the enabling act passed by the legislature, or with the information used by the agency to study the problem before drafting the rule. The following cases illustrate the reasonable-and-not-arbitrarily-made review standard being applied.

Federal Security Administration v. Quaker Oats Co.
United States Supreme Court
318 U.S. 218 (1943)

The federal security administrator promulgated regulations under the Federal Food, Drug, and Cosmetic Act establishing standards of identity for certain milled wheat products. Under the new regulations, the respondent's product could not be marketed as "farina" because it contained vitamin D, which was permitted only in "enriched farina." On the other hand, the product could not be marketed as "enriched farina" because it did not contain the minimum quantities of vitamin B_1, riboflavin, nicotinic acid, and iron required by the regulations. The respondent, Quaker Oats Co., argued that the regulations are not valid as applied to it.

Chief Justice Stone

In recent years millers of wheat have placed on the market flours and farinas which have been enriched by the addition of various vitamins and minerals. The composition of these enriched products varies widely. There was testimony of weight before the Administrator, principally by expert nutritionists, that such products, because of the variety and combination of added ingredients, are widely variable in nutritional value; and that consumers generally lack knowledge of the relative value of such ingredients and combinations of them.

These witnesses also testified, as did representatives of consumer organizations which had made special studies of the problems of food standardization, that the number, variety and varying combinations of the added ingredients tend to confuse the large number of consumers who desire to purchase vitamin-enriched wheat food products but who lack the knowledge essential to discriminating purchase of them; that because of this lack of knowledge and discrimination they are subject to exploitation by the sale of foods described as "enriched" wheat products which would ensure fairly complete satisfaction of dietary needs, and a somewhat lesser number recommended the disallowance, as optional ingredients in the standards for unenriched wheat products, of individual vitamins and minerals whose addition would suggest to consumers an adequacy for dietary needs not in fact supplied.

The court below characterized this evidence as speculative and conjectural, and held that because there was no evidence that respondent's product had in fact confused or misled anyone, the Administrator's finding as to consumer confusion was without substantial support in the evidence.

None of the testimony which we have detailed can be said to be speculative or conjectural unless it be the conclusion of numerous witnesses, adopted by the Administrator, that the labeling and marketing of vitamin-enriched foods, not conforming to any standards of identity, tend to confuse and mislead consumers. The exercise of the administrative rule-making power necessarily looks to the future. The statute requires the Administrator to adopt standards of identity which in his judgment will promote honesty and fair dealing in the interest of consumers. Acting within his statutory authority he is required to establish standards which will guard against the probable future effects of present trends.

We cannot say that the Administrator made an unreasonable choice of standards when he adopted one which defined the familiar "farina" of commerce without permitting addition of vitamin enrichment, and at the same time prescribed for "enriched farina" the restoration of those vitamins which had been removed from the whole wheat by milling, and allowed the optional addition of vitamin D, commonly found in milk but not present in wheat. Consumers who buy farina will have no reason to believe that it is enriched. Those who buy enriched farina are assured of receiving a wheat product containing those vitamins naturally present in wheat, and, if so stated on the label, an additional vitamin D, not found in wheat.

We conclude that the Administrator did not depart from statutory requirements in choosing these standards of identity for the purpose of promoting fair dealing in the interest of consumers, that the standards which he selected are adapted to that end, and that they are adequately supported by findings and evidence.

Home Box Office, Inc. v. Federal Communications Commission

United States Court of Appeals, District of Columbia Circuit

567 F.2d 9 (1977)

Fifteen consolidated cases challenged four orders of the Federal Communications Commission that regulate and limit the programming that can be offered by cablecasters and subscription broadcast television stations to the public for a fee set on a per-program or per-channel basis. The four 1975 orders prohibited pay exhibitions of (1) feature films between three and ten years old; (2) specific sports events shown on broadcast television within the previous five years; (3) more than the minimum number of regular-season sports events that had not been broadcast in any of the five preceding years, and in some cases only half that number; and (4) all series programs. The FCC also prohibited commercial advertising with pay programming and limited the overall number of hours of pay operation that could be devoted to sports and feature films to ninety percent of total pay operations.

The FCC's stated purpose for these orders was to prevent competitive bidding away (also known as "siphoning") of popular program material from the free television service to a service for which the audience would have to pay a fee to see the same material. The appeals court issued a *per curiam opinion*, with all members of the court concurring.

Per Curiam

We have recently had occasion to review at length our obligation to set aside agency action which is arbitrary, capricious, an abuse of discretion, or otherwise not in accordance with law. It is axiomatic that we may not substitute our judgment for that of the agency. Yet our review must be searching and careful, and we must ensure both that the Commission has adequately considered all relevant factors, and that it has demonstrated a rational connection between the facts found and the choice made.

Equally important, an agency must comply with the procedures set out in Section 4 of the Administrative Procedure Act. The APA sets out three procedural requirements: notice of the proposed rulemaking, an opportunity for interested persons to comment, and a concise general statement of the basis and purpose of the rule ultimately adopted. As interpreted by recent decisions of this court, these procedural requirements are intended to assist judicial review as well as to provide fair treatment for persons affected by a rule.

At the outset, we must consider whether the Commission has made out a case for undertaking rulemaking at all since a regulation perfectly reasonable and appropriate in the face of a given problem may be highly capricious if that problem does not exist. Here the Commission has framed the problem it is addressing as: "...how cablecasting can best be regulated to provide a beneficial supplement to over-the-air broadcasting without at the same time undermining the continued operation of that 'free' television service." To state the problem this way, however, is to gloss over the fact that the Commission has in no way justified its position that cable television must be a supplement to, rather than an equal of, broadcast television. Such an artificial narrowing of the scope of the regulatory problem is itself arbitrary and capricious and is ground for reversal. Moreover, by narrowing its discussion in this way the Commission has failed to crystalize what is in fact harmful about "siphoning."

Setting aside the question whether siphoning is

harmful to the public interest, we must next ask whether the record shows that siphoning will occur. The Commission assures us that siphoning is real, not imagined. We find little comfort in this assurance, however, because the Commission has not directed our attention to any comments in a voluminous record which would support its statement. As to the potential financial power of cable television we are left to draw the inference from two facts—that championship boxing matches often appear only on closed-circuit television in theaters and that Evil Knievel chose to televise his jet-cycled dive into the Snake River in the same fashion—and a series of mathematical demonstrations. While the former may be directly relevant to siphoning of what the Commission has characterized as "specific" sports events, it is not at all clear the light they shed on the question of who is going to pay how much to see feature films and nonspecific sports events on pay cable.

We find the Commission's argument that "siphoning" could lead to loss of programming for those too poor to purchase cable television plausible. Here again, however, we find that the Commission has not documented its case that the poor would be deprived of adequate television service and, worse, that the Commission, by prohibiting advertising in connection with subscription operations, has virtually ensured that the price of pay cable will never be within reach of the poor. There is little disagreement at the theoretical level about the mechanism through which the poor would be deprived of broadcast service in markets served by cable television. Cable operators, to be able to sell a show, would require exclusive exhibition rights in the markets they served, with the result that events purchased by cable operators

for subscription presentation would be unavailable to broadcasters, or would be available only after a delay. What follows from this scenario, even assuming that cable operators would have the financial strength to outbid broadcasters, is by no means clear. There is uncontradicted evidence in the record, for example, that the popularity of film material does not decline with an increase in the interval between first theater exhibition and first television broadcast. At least as to movies, therefore, "siphoning" may not harm the poor very much.

Equally important, the pay cable rules taken as a whole scarcely demonstrate a consistent solicitude for the poor. Thus, although "free" home viewing relies upon advertisement-supported programming, the Commission has in this proceeding barred cable firms from offering advertising in connection with subscription operations. As a result, the Commission forecloses the possibility that some combination of user fees and advertising might make subscription cable television available to the poor, giving them access to the diverse programming cable may potentially bring. The advertising ban section of the regulations was developed to meet wholly different regulatory problems and it has been retained here, not because of its intrinsic merit, but only because no one objected too much. We are thus left with the conclusion that, if the Commission is serious about helping the poor, its regulations are arbitrary; but if it is serious about its rules, it cannot really be relying on harm to the poor. Whatever may be the ultimate validity of this argument, its principal defect in this review is that there is no record evidence to support it.

Rescission of Agency Rule

A similar standard of review is used by the court when an agency wants to rescind a certain regulation. Not all regulations are disliked by those affected. The automobile industry may dislike regulations requiring airbags on cars and welcome agency action that rescinds the rule. However, insurance companies and consumer groups may argue that the regulation is a good idea, since it was made to encourage safety in auto design. Remember, even though a deregulation climate may exist, all regulations benefit some group. No administrative agency creates rules and regulations that bedevil everyone. One can expect that if an agency moves to rescind a particular rule, groups that have benefited from it or that agree with it will seek judicial review.

This is not to suggest that all regulations that are enacted by administrative agencies become permanent legal fixtures. Regulations can certainly be amended or abolished. However, in doing so the agency may not abuse its discretion or act arbitrarily. The following case is an example of an arbitrary change of an existing agency rule. Note how the court reviewed this rescinding action.

State Farm Mutual Automobile Insurance Company v. Department of Transportation

United States Court of Appeals, District of Columbia Circuit

608 F.2d 206 (1982)

Mivka, Circuit Judge

Petitioners in this action seek review of a final order by the National Highway Traffic Safety Administration (NHTSA) rescinding the automatic crash protection requirements of Federal Motor Vehicle Safety Standard 208 ten months before the standard's effective date. The standard would have required that large and mid-size automobiles manufactured after September 1, 1982, and all automobiles manufactured after September 1, 1983, carry passive restraints such as airbags or "passive" seatbelts. Airbags are cushions stored under the dashboard that, when triggered by a frontal collision, fill with stored or rapidly generated gas to protect the rider from collision with the car's interior. Passive seatbelts, also called "automatic" seatbelts, move into place automatically when a passenger enters a vehicle and closes the door. Petitioners challenge NHTSA's rescission of the standard as arbitrary, capricious, an abuse of discretion, and a violation of law as defined by the Administrative Procedure Act.

We agree. This case is complicated because it has far-reaching implications and involves a politically controversial safety standard, but the determining principle is simple. An administrative agency, possessing power delegated by the legislative branch of government, must comply with the legislative requirement that its decisions be reasoned and in accordance with the purposes for which power has been delegated. NHTSA's rescission of the safety standard presents a paradigm of arbitrary and capricious agency action because NHTSA drew conclusions that are unsupported by evidence in the record and then artificially narrowed the range of alternatives avail-

able to it under its legislative mandate. NHTSA thus failed to demonstrate the reasoned decisionmaking that is the essence of lawful administrative action.

In February 1981, approximately one month after taking office, Secretary of Transportation Andrew Lewis opened rulemaking. He based his decision at least in part on "the fact that economic circumstances have changed since the standard was adopted in 1977: and the "difficulties of the automobile industry," citing high unemployment, sales "at a very depressed level," and losses "by even the largest of the domestic manufacturers." Two months later, the agency ordered a one-year delay in the application of the standard to large cars, extending the deadline to September 1982. This notice also observed that the "economic situation of the industry and consumers and the economy as a whole have drastically changed since the standard was adopted in 1977." On the same day, NHTSA proposed the possible rescission of the entire standard. Both decisions were announced by the White House Press Office on April 6, 1981, as part of economic recovery measures. After receiving written comments and holding public hearings, NHTSA issued a final rule (Notice 25) that rescinded the passive restraint requirement, and amended Standard 208.

Even when there is no claim that the agency has exceeded its jurisdiction, as there is not in this case, sudden and profound alterations in an agency's policy constitute "danger signals" that the will of Congress is being ignored.

Our review of the legislative history of the 1974 Amendments to the Safety Act and the subsequent congressional reaction to Modified Standard 208 suggests that the standard has come as close as an agency-made regulation can come to being affirmatively endorsed by Congress, without Congress actually having done so. Although Congress has always considered the standard politically controversial, the regulation has received sufficient congressional approval to raise doubts that NHTSA's rescission necessarily demonstrates an effort to fulfill its statutory mandate.

Reading the legislative history as a whole suggests a congressional commitment to the concept of automatic crash protection devices for vehicle occupants that we may not take lightly.

Based on the legislative reaction to the passive restraint standard discussed above, we conclude that rescission of the standard must be subject to "thorough probing, in-depth review" lest the congressional will be ignored.

Although there may be situations in which an agency may repeal a regulation on no basis at all, such is not the case here. NHTSA has the burden of explaining why it has changed course, and of showing that rescission of Modified Standard 208 was reasonable.

This does not mean that NHTSA may not revoke the standard. If the agency clearly articulates a reasonable basis for that action, we must defer to the policy judgments and expertise of the agency.

The rescission of Modified Standard 208 on the grounds stated by NHTSA was arbitrary and illogical for two general reasons. The agency has offered no evidence that seatbelt usage will fail to increase as was expected when the standard was first promulgated, and has therefore made no showing that the standard is unjustified as written. More important, NHTSA has failed to consider and analyze obvious alternatives to rescission, and has thus artificially foreclosed attempts to further the purpose of the Safety Act. When the agency so narrows its options that it fails to heed the goals that Congress has asked it to meet, the agency violates its basic legislative mandate. Simply put, NHTSA's discussion was wholly inadequate, and rescission was therefore arbitrary and unlawful.

On balance, it is difficult to find anything positive to say about NHTSA's decisionmaking in this case. Based on the record and the statements in Notice 25, we must conclude that NHTSA has acted capriciously, wearing blinders that prevented it from reasoned evaluation of methods to fulfill the purposes of the Safety Act. The rescission of Modified Standard 208 is reversed.

SUMMARY

The administrative agency plays an important role in the American legal environment. It is a government body that has a profound effect on the law and day-to-day business conduct.

Problems needing expertise and efficiency that fall outside the institutional limits of other branches of government led to the creation of administrative agencies. Within the limits specified by their enabling acts, they were deliberately granted all the powers that the Constitution had carefully divided among the three branches of government. The agency may make rules and regulations—that is, act like a legislature. The agency may also hold hearings to determine whether its rules have been violated or to resolve disputes concerning them. This function is like that generally associated with the judiciary. Finally, the agency is empowered to enforce the rules and laws in the area of its jurisdiction—in effect, to act like the executive branch of government.

However, administrative agency activities are not without limitation or review. The legislature, which created the agency, has powerful tools available to control agency activity. Courts also play a major role in reviewing the work of administrative agencies. Agency hearing decisions and regulations must comply with the relevant enabling act, statutes concerning administrative procedures, and fundamental notions of due process. Although administrative agencies are powerful government bodies, their activities may be restrained by other branches of government.

REVIEW QUESTIONS

1. Define the following words and terms:
   a. Agency adjudication
   b. Agency rule making
   c. Enabling act
   d. Ultra vires

2. What are the reasons that a legislature creates an administrative agency?

3. What are the ways in which agency activity may be reviewed by the courts?

4. The Securities and Exchange Commission (SEC) is a federal administrative agency created and authorized by Congress to regulate securities (e.g., stocks, bonds) and securities markets. In July, the SEC filed suit claiming that XYZ, Inc., had discriminated against its female employees by not paying them at the same rate as male employees holding comparable jobs. The SEC based its suit on a regulation it recently made forbidding discrimination in employment. What argument may be raised by XYZ in response to that suit?

5. Assume the SEC rule in question 4 was drafted without any public opportunity for comment and was promulgated without providing any notice. Furthermore, the rule was never published before it was applied to the XYZ matter. What additional arguments can XYZ make based upon these facts?

6. An administrative agency properly promulgated the following regulation: ''All applications for variances and exceptions to the rules of this agency must be filed by March 15 of the year for which such variance or exception is sought.'' On March 10, Mary Smith called the local office of the agency and asked an employee when an application for a variance must be filed. Smith was told that all applications must be on file no later than April 4 to qualify for a variance that year. If Mary Smith files her variance on April 3, will she be able to rely on the information given to her by the agency employee if the agency cites the regulation as grounds for denying her variance application?

7. What are the three main functions of an administrative agency? Discuss each function.

8. What are the advantages and disadvantages of the functions in question 7 being concentrated in one government body?

9. Jones owns a small manufacturing business. The by-products of the manufacturing process include some toxic chemicals. The Environmental Protection Agency (EPA) regulates the disposal of those chemicals. One afternoon an investigator from the EPA appears at the factory to inspect its chemical disposal process. No one from the EPA had received a court warrant to search the business. Must Jones permit the investigator to inspect the factory? Give reasons.

10. A new administration takes office in the federal government. One of the major issues on which it was elected was to eliminate government red tape and regulation. On the day after the inauguration, three federal agencies act to rescind over one hundred regulations. No studies were done by the agencies before taking this action, nor was there any evidence that the regulations were not working. They were rescinded in order to satisfy the election's antiregulation mandate. Discuss how a court might review this rescinding action.

11. In numerous agency adjudications and other actions, the SEC has interpreted the Securities Exchange Act of 1934 to prohibit trading securities on the basis of information that is not public. Is a court bound to follow that agency interpretation?

12. Compare and contrast hearings before an agency and hearings before a court.

13. Your company manufactures fine wooden furniture. Precision-cut pieces of wood are joined together with dowels that require exactly measured holes be drilled in the pieces to be joined. A $\frac{3}{4}$-inch metal drill bit is used to make the holes. Assume that the Occupational Safety and Health Administration (OSHA) has promulgated a regulation that prohibits the use of $\frac{1}{2}$-inch or larger drill bits in woodworking businesses because they create a great risk of harm should human tissue come in contact with them. In promulgating the regulation, OSHA did not study alternatives to banning the bits. In fact, properly installed safety shields can cut injuries dramatically. Further, human tissue can also be injured by drill bits under the $\frac{1}{2}$-inch size. OSHA did not consider banning all drill bits, nor were these studies consulted. Would a court be likely to uphold this regulation? Give reasons.

14. Assume that all administrative agencies were abolished. How do you think the following would operate in the legal environment? For each, create an operational plan:

a. Title VII of the Civil Rights Act of 1964, prohibiting discrimination in employment

b. A new statute passed by Congress that extends the time period when unemployed workers can qualify for unemployment payments

c. A state statute that requires all automobile drivers to have a valid license

15. Your firm has a factory on the outskirts of town. It operates only one eight-hour shift and is shut down from 5:00 P.M. to 8:00 A.M. daily. Assume that the EPA promulgated a regulation that requires each factory to limit the amount of pollutants emitted into the air on an average, measured twenty-four hour basis. Thus, measurements are taken of air quality near each factory at various times throughout the day. Your firm is cited for a violation. However, you learn that often in the evenings the farms that surround your factory burn their waste products, emitting pollution into the air. Furthermore, three other factories (that operate three shifts) are located downwind. Does your company have any valid arguments?

NOTE

[1] Karl N. Llewellyn, *Jurisprudence: Realism in Theory and Practice* (University of Chicago Press, 1962), p. 211.

Part 3

The Ethical Elements of the Legal Environment

CHAPTER 8

Ethics: Its Relationship with the Legal Environment and Business Decision Making

- What Is Business Ethics or Socially Responsible Decision Making?
- Critiques of Common Misconceptions
- Why Should a Business Seek to Act Ethically?
- The Role of Ethics in the Legal Environment
- An Analytical Model for Making Ethically Based Decisions

The study of ethics is the study of what is right or good. It is a branch of philosophy useful in determining conduct in any given instance. Philosophers study problems of ethics that arise in many professional fields—medicine, law, engineering, and business. But ethics is no longer the sole province of philosophers and theologians who at their leisure can contemplate questions of "right." The business manager, at all levels of the organization, may be confronted with complex ethical problems about which even philosophers and theologians disagree. The executive cannot merely join this intellectual battle; a decision must be made that can be of major importance to the business.

Consider the current debate over "abortion pills" that is undoubtedly occurring in American pharmaceuticals companies. Questions like those involving RU-486 are extremely complex. Theologians and philosophers disagree about the morality of abortion; so do individuals from diverse political and social backgrounds. But business executives are faced with a practical problem concerning the product. Ironically, even refusing to decide will, in effect, be choosing one side in that debate.

How should you evaluate this problem? Focus only on your firm's self-interest? Perhaps look to the legal environment for guidance or consult public opinion polls? Maybe there is a third way, based on ethical reasoning. It is this "third way" that is the topic of this chapter.

Ethics is a major force that affects the legal environment of business as well as the "self-interest" of a business. No longer is ethical conduct considered a

Whether to Market an Abortion Pill

In 1988, a French company, Roussel-Uclaf, began to market a new drug, RU-486, more commonly known as an "abortion pill." The drug is an alternative to surgical abortions. It is estimated that one hundred twenty-five thousand women die each year, worldwide, as a result of current abortion methods. Health care and pro-choice advocates praised the drug as a means to lessen injuries and deaths to women who have abortions. One estimate puts the market for the drug to be currently one billion dollars per year. But the drug is available only in France and in China. No American company has sought the right to distribute RU-486 in this country. Antiabortion activists have condemned the drug as being a poison designed to kill fetuses. American companies are concerned about product boycotts led by those activists. But with the rejuvenation of the pro-choice movement and the election of Bill Clinton, American drug companies may face pressure from advocates of safe abortion procedures, too. Furthermore, demand for the drug could create a black market in which smugglers, rather than doctors, will be prescribing RU-486.

Currently, American business is watching the storm brew. What would you recommend that your company do?

management ideal. For the modern firm, it is a necessity. Unethical conduct can affect the application of basic legal principles or can influence an award of damages. As noted in later chapters, legal doctrines are filled with trapdoors and trip wires that can ensnare those whose decision making falls short. Often, this "falling short" is the result of decision making that is not based on a solid ethical foundation.

Thus, not only must business managers develop an appreciation for the legal environment and design corporate activities to stay within its bounds, they must also look to ethical norms for guidance. Many of the changes that have occurred in the legal environment of business reflect a concern that these norms have been ignored. Managing within the legal environment of business will therefore require an outlook broader than simply understanding legal rules.

Two questions then arise. First, *why* is it imperative that ethics play a key role in operating a business within the legal environment? Shouldn't following the rules of law be enough? The first portion of this chapter provides what we believe to be the answer from a legal environment perspective: Making ethically based decisions is a means by which business managers can lessen the risk of adverse legal consequences.

The second question takes a more practical stance: *How* do executives ethically manage their businesses? As a response, the latter part of this chapter will construct an ethically based decision-making model. However, note that this (or any other) model will not yield *the* ethical answer. For many complex problems, there will be no ethical "answer." Instead, the business manager should expect that ethically based decision making will provide an opportunity for creativity in devising the action that the company ultimately adopts.

But as an interlude, consider the following material. It distinguishes what this chapter means by business ethics (or corporate social responsibility) from common alternative characterizations. Furthermore, it sketches some responses to often held misconceptions about ethics as a practical tool. Review this section carefully.

WHAT IS BUSINESS ETHICS OR SOCIALLY RESPONSIBLE DECISION MAKING?

Definitions of the Term

Corporate social responsibility, or business ethics, is an elusive term that has been defined in many ways. However, none of the definitions provides guidance to business managers as they attempt to make socially responsible decisions. Consider a first definition of corporate social responsibility: earning a profit in one's business while inflicting the least possible harm to society. This definition is very broad, raising more questions than it answers. From a corporate viewpoint, how would a manager determine "social" injuries?

For example, do social injuries occur to employees who are furloughed in recessionary times? Or would social injuries occur to shareholders if the firm refused to reduce its workforce in a recession, thereby jeopardizing its financial position? Should noncorporate members of the community who are affected by corporate decisions be included in its sphere of responsibility? (For example, worker layoffs may hurt the business of a local movie theater.) Should there be an ordering of the groups that may be injured by a corporate decision? Even though such social injuries may occur, apparently a value must be attached to them to balance against corporate dollars otherwise lost. This seems simple, but how are social injuries to be so weighted? Placing a numerical value on the social injury to an unemployed worker is a vague approximation at best. As H. L. Mencken wrote: "Explanations exist; they have existed for all time; There is always a well-known solution to every human problem—neat, plausible, and wrong."[1]

In summary, the first definition is too vague and therefore, not useful. In trying to describe what the firm should do—balance profits against social injury—the definition fails to tell us how to strike that balance or how to measure social injury.

By contrast, a second definition is a very narrow characterization: Corporate social responsibility involves voluntary activity undertaken for nonbusiness reasons, the marginal return of the expenditures for socially responsible activity being less than an alternative business-related expenditure of the same funds. This definition ignores any ethical decisions except one based solely on altruistic reasons, which results in economic loss to the corporation. But suppose that ABC, Inc., gave one thousand dollars to the community ballet company. If the contribution garners a great deal of "free" publicity for the corporation and contributes to the quality of life in the community, thereby making it more attractive to employees, the return from that contribution may be much greater than any alternative business use of the funds (such as purchasing advertising or offering bonuses to key employees). This contribution could not be considered socially responsible, given a definition based on pure altruism, because market mechanisms would have yielded such a decision anyway. In this case, good citizenship was good business. However, if ABC had given the money anonymously, thereby gaining no publicity for its act, then it may be assumed that any return to the corporation would be less than the marginal return of alternative uses of the money. Thus, the contribution would be considered socially responsible according to the second definition. However, it is not clear why, when a corporation benefits, the activity should *not* be labeled socially responsible.

In any event, this characterization of the term also provides little guidance to the business manager. The definition suggests that such conduct must be in addition to obeying the laws and using corporate resources in an economically efficient manner. It requires that socially responsible conduct "harm" the corporation by imposing a negative effect on its total return. There seems little practical reason for this narrow definition of corporate social responsibility, since the business manager can make decisions that benefit not only the corporation, but also the community.

A third definition of corporate social responsibility maintains: Should the corporation function in a manner that raises criticism, then the company has not acted in accordance with community values and, therefore, is not a responsible firm. This version is frequently used by those who seek to make a political issue of certain corporate behavior. For example, if ABC, Inc. sells cigarettes or supports Planned Parenthood or manufactures electronic components for nuclear weapons, then some persons and communities might hold that ABC is not acting in a socially responsible manner. This concept of corporate social responsibility is the one most often encountered. Newspaper articles and television commentaries focus on such issues as being "tests" of the responsible nature of corporate behavior. The only value of such a characterization is that it clearly labels the speaker's position on social or political issues. It provides no guidance to the manager, nor is it a useful way to understand the concept.

The existence of broad, narrow, and sometimes cynical definitions of the term *corporate social responsibility* highlights the confusion this idea causes. Corporate social responsibility has a nice ring to it—like patriotism or justice—but it may seem that the term has no real meaning. If one cannot state a clear definition of social responsibility or business ethics, how is it possible to use it as a decision-making tool?

The three common descriptions of the ethical business or the socially responsible corporation provide neither guidance nor a practical framework for the business manager. The first definition is driven by the belief that everything can be quantified and plugged into a formula, and an answer generated. Its error can best be illustrated by Oscar Wilde's definition: "A cynic is a man who knows the price of everything, and the value of nothing."[2] The second definition disconnects "ethics" from practical business activity, as if wearing a hair shirt is a prerequisite for doing good. Its error is that it ignores the fact that ethical conduct can be in the best interests of business. Finally, the third definition confuses ethics with "answers" or "tests." Its error is that it connects responsible business behavior to the opinion polls.

As an alternative, we offer the following definition: Ethical business decision making (or corporate social responsibility) is a search for the good. The key in this definition is the word *search*. Using the model constructed later in this chapter will constitute the search. Decisions arising from it will be as close to "the good" as we can expect to be. The good is an ethereal concept, undefinable, perhaps untouchable. To focus on good as an end is to forget that ethics is a means to make decisions; it is the intellectual journey, not the destination.

CRITIQUES OF COMMON MISCONCEPTIONS

Perhaps, believing that ethics can provide "answers" is a source of common misconceptions about its study. In fact, by focusing on "the good," from the above definition, one might easily become so bogged in the depths of its meaning as to throw up one's hands in surrender. This surrender is often preceded by the adherence to confused ideas about ethical decision making. This section will consider some of them.

A first misconception is that ethics is merely a question of personal values. That is, what is right or wrong in any business situation depends upon who is asked for an opinion. Of course, since everyone has an opinion, in the final analysis, ethics boils down to my opinion versus your opinion. In a business setting (the cynic argues), the opinion that will prevail is the one held by the person of highest rank.

What is mixed up here are two distinct ideas: preference and process. Indeed, everyone has an opinion (preference). Thus, one person may prefer Mozart and another, Garth Brooks. That's fine and in fact, on the level of preference, there is no way to choose between them. The concept reflects purely subjective taste. Ethics, however, is something different. It is the process of reaching a decision. Much like musicologists can evaluate composition techniques to rank quality of compositions (Mozart will win without question), the ethicist uses a model to reach a decision. The incidental fact that some prefer Garth Brooks or would prefer a different outcome to a business problem has no bearing on the issue at all. Consequently, the first misconception is about the nature of ethics itself. To reiterate: Ethics does not provide *the* answer; instead it is the means to reach *an* answer.

A related misconception about ethics is that given disagreements of opinion, there is no way to choose which is best. Consider the following: Assume that XYZ, Inc., has devised the perfect crime, one that can never be detected or proved so that no legal liability will arise. XYZ has decided to have the sales forces of all its competitors murdered. In this way, XYZ can quickly become the dominant firm in its market. Now, also assume that two persons' opinions differ: One argues that XYZ's plan is unethical, the other that it is ethical. Under this misconception, there would be no way to choose, ethically, between the opinions. Thus, murdering competitors would be the ethical equivalent to not murdering them.

Absurd, isn't it? But this misconception does have some power. Not all

Tylenol Poisonings and Socially Responsible Business Decision Making

In 1982, seven people in the Chicago area died after taking cyanide-laced Tylenol capsules. Investigators found that someone unknown (and never found) had tampered with the capsules. Tylenol is made by Johnson & Johnson, and accounted for approximately fifteen percent of the corporation's $468 million in net earnings the previous year. It held an approximately thirty-five percent share of the $1.2 billion painkiller market.

Immediately, consumers throughout the country stopped using Tylenol in both capsule and tablet form. The price of Johnson & Johnson stock dropped eighteen percent in one week. Tylenol users stated that they would never again use the product. Should the product continue to be sold?

A variety of responses to this crisis was considered. Food and Drug Administration officials urged that no mass recall be undertaken, fearing that such an action would increase the national panic over the Chicago deaths. The FBI argued that a recall, which would be very expensive, would encourage terrorist groups to use similar tactics as means to attack major corporations.

Nonetheless, corporate officials decided to recall the thirty-one million boxes of Tylenol capsules in stores throughout the country at a cost of fifty million dollars. The corporation cooperated fully with the investigation, and its CEO appeared on television programs to discuss the incident. Within ten weeks, the product was again on the market, this time in triple-seal tamper-resistant packaging. Eighty million Tylenol coupons, each worth $2.50, were provided to consumers. Within a year, Tylenol had regained most of its lost market share and customer confidence.

problems that arise provide such a clear-cut scenario as the XYZ plan. What if, instead, XYZ's decision involved the production of inexpensive handguns or popular music with violent lyrics? Finding an easy "right" answer suddenly becomes elusive. One might be tempted to shift back to the first misconception, or, if seeking the answer, look only to what is legal (both gun production and violent lyrics are) or what the opinion polls suggest.

Thus, one might consider methods of choice as another misconception about ethics. A decision that concludes that XYZ should make the guns or sell the music because either one is legal is an error of choice. If confuses an ethical analysis with other ways in which decisions are made. One of these other ways is whether the decision is "legal." Of course, legal analysis is valid. Most of this text involves legal analysis of various business problems. But legal analysis is not the same thing as ethical analysis. Suggesting that what is legal is also ethical confuses the two analytical methods. Obviously, the concepts are related, but such an equation makes about as much sense as arguing that a chocolate bar is a steak. Both are food, but their differences are vast.

A similar response can be given to the method of following public opinion polls. It can also be a means that a business uses to make decisions. However, accommodating public opinion does not make one's actions ethical; it just makes them popular. It is the path of the cynic, and can cause as much harm to the business organization as ignoring ethical questions altogether. Furthermore, assuming that public opinion can be known, this method considers that there are no subsidiary ethical questions. Problems facing the business manager (and those arising in life) are simply not so easy.

Although the application of ethical principles may produce disagreement, it is not impossible for business managers to determine socially responsible corporate conduct. By way of analogy, corporations often operate in areas where the application of legal rules is uncertain. Executives are not thereby absolved of decision-making responsibility because disagreements may arise about the "correct" application of the laws. Similarly, when differences occur about the proper ethical mode of conduct, a consensus can be found in order to devise the socially responsible business decision.

Arriving at a consensus requires an informed analysis of the proposed activity, the surrounding circumstances, and the applicable ethical principles. In a business context, one must look to the effect of the decision on various groups in society and then determine to which groups a duty is owed. This model for ethical decision making will be outlined in the last section of the chapter.

WHY SHOULD A BUSINESS SEEK TO ACT ETHICALLY?

Before embarking on a discussion of the ethical decision-making process, a preliminary problem must be addressed. Namely, why should a business seek to act in an ethical manner? A common naive belief is that such inquiries are "soft" or otherworldly. Perhaps ethical thinking is appropriate for the clergy or professors, the argument goes, but in the "real world" such decision-making techniques are fruitless and perhaps harmful to the organization. In this real world, the race is won by the strong, the swift, and the cunning. Nice guys finish last.

Ethical Expectations of Today's Businesses

Although there are complexities when a firm adopts socially responsible decision making, there is little doubt that the role of American business has been reevaluated, and that its behavior is affected by these nonlegally mandated goals. In the early history of American corporations, the organizations were chartered with a business purpose as well as a public purpose in mind. These early corporations were akin to public utilities in that their businesses included such public interest activities as the operation of canals and turnpikes. In such organizations, public benefits and profits to the membership mixed naturally.

As the Industrial Revolution became firmly established, the corporate form was used more for traditional, purely private business purposes. The attitude regarding the corporation's responsibility to the public changed too. Duties were owed to maximize the return of the shareholders. Responsibility to the public was deemed to accrue from the overall operation of the market, which would work best if all firms were operated solely for the benefit of their shareholders. For example, in the mid-1930s Du Pont Corporation tried to convince General Motors to use its newly developed safety glass in its cars. Alfred P. Sloan, the president of GM, responded: "It is not my responsibility to sell safety glass. . . . You can say, perhaps, that I am selfish. We are not a charitable institution—we are trying to make a profit for our shareholders."[3]

Today, of course, a corporation deciding to act ethically or in a socially responsible manner is acting for a valid purpose. The attitude that a corporation's decisions should take into account the interests of the community is firmly established. However, except for certain statutory regulations (for example, the antipollution laws), there is no legal requirement for such behavior. The corporation, except for following its legal duties, is under no compulsion to consider the effect of alternative courses of action on its surrounding environment. Doing so is a part of ethical decision making.

The ethical expectations of modern business firms can be justified in two ways. First, remember that corporations are merely groups of people that the law categorizes in a certain way. Corporate behavior is therefore the decisions and actions of certain individuals in that group. The more cultivated and civilized individuals recognize that responsible behavior goes beyond what is mandated by law. They do not change somehow by making decisions on behalf of a corporation instead of individually.

Second, a market requires an overall acceptance of ethical conduct by its participants. As noted later in this text, a market consists of contracts that transfer property rights. A contract is merely a formal legal recognition of a type of promise. The parties are free, with minimal legal requirements, to negotiate whatever terms of the contract are deemed necessary. The legal environment's role is to act as "promises enforcer" of last resort. That is, upon breach of contract the aggrieved party may use the courts to seek damages.

Corporate decisions, therefore, are governed by the same standards of civilized behavior that govern individual decisions. Society expects respect for others and that promises be kept, even in absence of law. The corporate fictitious personality does not remove this expectation from its activities. Thus, a nebulous, unwritten compact exists to make life in an organized society tolerable. For example, no legal rule prohibits a person from laughing at the handicapped. However, the compact condemns such behavior as boorish and crude. Such a person may not have legal sanctions imposed, but will lose respect and credibility. The person may be shunned by others. Similarly, corporations that violate the compact risk losing the intangible image of respectability they seek to create.

Assume a world without ethics—one in which parties to contracts acted only out of self-interest and would consider breaching the contracts if the expected benefit would exceed the risk that the legal environment would impose damages. In such a world, what would happen to the market? First of all, contracts would probably become more elaborate documents, since all participants would need to look solely to legal sanction to discourage breaches. Promises would be kept only if convenient, otherwise. The more elaborate the document, the higher the transaction cost. Or the participants would try to "game" the process, which would also be an added cost. Resources that a company could use for productive purposes would be spent instead on creatively designed self-protective contract terms or gamelike strategic devices. In addition, if the law was the only factor discouraging breach, one would expect more use of the judicial process. Litigation is quite expensive. Once again, resources would be used for nonproductive purposes. Consequently, participation in such a market would be discouraged because reliance on others' promises (ethics) was not a value that was uniformly held.

Consider this example. List the steps you take when buying a new sweatshirt from the university bookstore. What do you expect will happen if, when you take it home, you discover a rip on an inside seam? But what if no sellers of sweatshirts considered ethics a part of their business activities? They would only replace the sweatshirt if the benefit from doing so outweighed the cost. Now list the steps you would take when making a purchase. Further, if the sweatshirt was defective, under what circumstances would you take legal action against the seller? Finally, what if an enterprising sweatshirt seller in this "world without ethics" decided to make socially responsible decisions? Where would buyers most likely shop?

Thus, one might even characterize ethics as good business practice. Society expects companies to be good citizens and supportive members of the communities in which they operate. By recognizing this expectation, a business is responding to the market. Long-term profitability is influenced not merely by economic forces but also by social and political forces.

THE ROLE OF ETHICS IN THE LEGAL ENVIRONMENT

Justifications for ethical decision making that rely on long-term business interests or a general duty owed to civilized society are not the sole (or even most vital) reason a business executive should implement a socially responsible decision-making process. Civilization will not crumble if a manager concludes that a short-term capture of market share is an acceptable rationale for a business decision, even though to do so means using unethical tactics. Furthermore, the market system will survive that executive's rejection of ethical values. In fact, in the short term, the manager's firm might prosper. Thus, one needs more than a long-term business self-interest rationale to justify ethically based decision making.

Two legal environment justifications should also be considered. One, a longer-term reason, is that government regulation of business arises from circumstances in which overall business behavior falls below ethical expectations. As a result, broadly considered, what were once decisions that businesses could freely make are now dictated by government agencies. Consider the Truth-in-Lending Act, discussed in Chapter 17. It requires certain disclosures be formally made to individuals who are seeking credit. Prior to the act, it was not unusual for creditors to fail to divulge the annual interest rate or the total amount of interest to be paid on a loan. What was "sold" to the debtor was simply the "affordable" monthly payment. Since the legitimate interests of debtors were ignored by this practice, the political climate acted and consumer credit is now regulated. (Note how the "interests analysis" in this example and the ones that follow fit within the ethical model outlined later in this chapter.)

As another example, consider *Boomer* v. *Atlantic Cement Co.* in Chapter 12. In that case, the court refused to prohibit a factory's pollution on the basis of common law doctrines of nuisance and trespass. One might suggest that the factory ignored the legitimate interests of adjoining landowners to use their property unhindered by someone else's waste. What followed a few years after that case were the environmental laws that changed how all such factories did business (see Chapter 21).

Further, government regulation of business leads to costly compliance procedures. Companies, by necessity, spend money in order to report on how they acted within the rules. Sometimes compliance reports are legally required. Government regulation also imposes investment costs. Environmental standards required companies to spend billions of dollars simply to meet the goals. Imagine the increased profitability of a Fortune 500 company if none of the regulations discussed in Chapters 17 to 24 of this text existed.

Of course, making ethically based decisions may also be costly. Forty years ago an executive who concluded that polluting a river with factory waste was unethical would have had a most difficult time convincing the board of directors to spend millions of dollars on an alternative waste disposal system. No immediate incentive would have been thought to exist for the firm to act responsibly (in absence of regulatory mandate) if none of its competitors were. Note that this is a commonly made argument about why environmental regulation is necessary. However, consider that decision making in business should not lead to either-or propositions: Pollute the river or spend millions not to.

An ethically based decision-making process should generate other alternatives. All that occurs with the process is that the analysis will point out the ethical problem with the decision to continue polluting the river. But consider an ethically based alternative: What if the company, forty years ago, decided to invest some funds in research and development for less polluting technology? Since regulation later arose, might not that firm have been in an enhanced competitive position or even have been able to supply technology to others? If no regulation arose, would not the company have benefited anyway by generating less waste and thus becoming a more cost-efficient producer?

Nonetheless, one need not solely consider the long-term legal implications. There are also short-term reasons for using ethically based decision making. First, the legal rules themselves often have ethics components. As an example, consider the promissory estoppel material in Chapter 10. Pay particular note to the case of *Hoffman* v. *Red Owl Stores*. Promissory estoppel is an ethics rule of contract law. In *Hoffman,* the formal elements of a legal contract (e.g., offer, acceptance, consideration) did not exist. Formalistically, there should not be any contractual liability. However, the contract doctrine of promissory estoppel treats the parties as if they had a contract, for ethical reasons. Business managers who consider only the formal characteristics of a body of law when making a decision will risk that an ethics component of that law will capture their behavior as it did for Red Owl.

As another illustration, consider the following. Corona Extra beer, imported from Mexico, had sudden and enormous success at cracking the American beer market. For a while, it was considered a "Yuppie" beer, as upscale young people made a point of ordering it (with its customary wedge of lime). In 1987, Corona Extra faced declining sales that some people attributed to a rumor that the beer was contaminated with human urine. Barton Beers, Inc., Corona's importer, filed suit against a beer wholesaler who it contended had defamed Corona Extra. The wholesaler sold only Heineken beer, Corona's main competitor in the imported beer market. The suit was settled a month and a half later after the wholesaler agreed to state publicly that Corona Extra was not contaminated.

Whether or not the false statements about Corona beer threatened the civilized world or would risk large-scale government regulation of corporate speech are not the practical reasons why other business managers should refrain from spreading lies as a means of winning in the marketplace. The reason is that honesty (as a fundamental moral value) is compromised by such behavior, and the legal system will react to rectify the unethical conduct. (Consider the discussion of the tort of defamation in Chapter 11.) Thus, the workings of the legal environment have short-term, immediate implications for unethical behavior.

A second short-term justification was suggested by the material in Chapter 1 concerning the predictability and flexibility of the law. Also note the materials on judicial reasoning in Chapter 4, in which doing "what is right" is a factor in judicial decisions. This material suggests that a particular legal rule may apply differently to very similar sets of facts. That is, the underlying ethical (or unethical) conduct of a party may influence a decision maker's application of the law. Consequently, assessing the legal implications of any business decision also requires an ethical evaluation. This "ethics flexibility" feature of the legal environment illustrates that managers who ignore the ethical underpinnings of their decisions increase the risk of adverse legal consequences.

As an example, consider the *Blankenship* v. *Cincinnati Milacron Chemicals* case in Chapter 11. Management refused to consider that factory employees had a legitimate interest in learning about their exposure to hazardous chemicals. The company's position raised ethical questions. *Blankenship* carved an exception to the employer's tort immunity under a workers' compensation statute. The *Midler* case and the *Wagenseller* case in the same chapter can be similarly analyzed. After studying the ethical decision-making model in the next section, try to assess the defendant companies' behavior according to that model. What legitimate interests were ignored? Can you suggest an alternative decision?

As an additional illustration, examine the materials on contracts in Chapters 9 and 10. Under the basic principles discussed, a bargain must fit the requirements of a contract before the law will enforce it. But the application of those requirements to any situation may be affected by ethical considerations. To illustrate: Pennzoil won over $10.5 billion in a suit against Texaco. This was the largest amount ever awarded by a court. Pennzoil had complained that Texaco had tortiously interfered with a contract it had with Getty Oil to purchase that company.

In January 1984, Pennzoil and Getty Oil announced that they had entered into an "agreement in principle" under which Pennzoil would purchase Getty stock for $115 per share. After the Getty board approved the transaction, the president of Pennzoil, J. Hugh Liedtke, and Gordon Getty shook hands and toasted the future with a glass of champagne. But was that a *contract?* The "agreement in principle'' was made subject to the development of a fully crafted merger agreement. Additionally, the prevailing view among investment bankers and takeover counsel was that an ''agreement in principle'' was not a binding contract. Texaco, soon after the announcement, secretly bid $128 per share and snared the deal from Pennzoil. Thus arose Pennzoil's contract interference claim against Texaco. The fundamental issue for the jury was whether Pennzoil and Getty Oil had a contract.

From the facts of the case, it was not obvious that the requirement for a legal contract existed. Thus, the jury's finding that there was a contract may be described as a judgment about the ethics of honoring promises. That Texaco had acted without concern for this principle, by clandestinely pushing its way into the deal at the last minute, may be considered the primary motivation for the finding that an enforceable contract did exist and, thus, that Texaco should be liable for wrongfully interfering with it. The law of contracts provided the jury with enough flexibility to make that decision. Note that the legal rules pertaining to creation of contracts do not include an ethics element. But that element can act to mold the legal rules so as to affect the legal environment for business activity.

A final short-term justification for making ethically based decisions is that unethical business conduct may affect any monetary award entered by the court. An excellent example is the awarding of punitive damages in civil litigation. (Note that three billion dollars of the award to Pennzoil was for punitive damages). Most often the damage measure in a civil suit will be to recompense the injured party for what was lost. Thus, when the van owned by ABC, Inc., hits a pedestrian, the corporation can be expected to be liable for medical bills, lost earnings, and pain and suffering. In addition to these damages, the awarding of punitive damages recognizes something else. It reflects the jury's finding that the corporate conduct was far removed from social expectations. In effect, unethical behavior becomes a measure of damages.

In addition, Federal Sentencing Guidelines for business crimes provide a strong incentive for companies to institute ethical programs. The guidelines, which became effective in November 1991, substantially increased the penalties that can be assessed against those convicted of certain crimes (fraud is one example). However, companies that have strong, well-managed, in-house ethics programs could receive more lenient treatment. In fact, a company that might otherwise be fined one million dollars could have that amount reduced by over ninety percent by cooperating with the prosecutor and by having an ethics program that meets the guideline standards.

Consequently, the penalty phase of the legal environment may be managed by the use of ethics. Not only are civil damage awards affected by unethical conduct of a defendant, but federal criminal penalties may be reduced for companies that show a commitment to ethical behavior.

Business managers will be best able to consider the legal implications of their decisions by plotting those decisions along an imaginary risk continuum, rather than on a yes-or-no chart. The risk continuum will not only take into account the anticipated application of relevant legal rules, but will also consider ethical issues. Consider an example in which the management of ABC, Inc. is evaluating the legality of rejecting a hostile tender offer by XYZ, Inc. The analysis of this question on a risk continuum may provide a definite yes, something close to a yes (a ''perhaps''), the gray area in between (a ''toss-up''), something close to a no (a ''perhaps not''), or a definite no. The decision's placement along the risk continuum will depend on a variety of factors that legal counsel will consider. One of these factors should be the ethical implications, if any, involved in the decision to reject the tender offer.

The following cases provide practical examples of companies that acted with questionable ethics and courts responding to their decisions. The first case, *Tennant*, concerns the liability of a company for the acts of its employees. Something is amiss when those employees comb through the trash of a competitor trying to secure shreds of secret information. Note the court's comment about a lack of ethical concern by management. Note also the large jury award, including punitive damages, which was upheld. The second case, *Du Pont*, involves a circumstance in which employee health and safety interests were ignored in the firm's quest for profit. Note again the subsequent jury award.

Tennant Company v. Advance Machine Company
Minnesota Court of Appeals
355 N.W.2d 720 (1984)

Tennant and Advance are competitors in manufacturing and marketing floor cleaning equipment. From fall 1978 through spring 1979, certain Advance employees rummaged through the trash in a dumpster behind Tennant's Western regional sales offices in California. The raids uncovered some confidential sales information that George McIntosh, an Advance employee, forwarded to other Advance sales representatives and to company officers. McIntosh, who reported directly to Jerry Rau, Advance's vice-president for industrial sales, sent Rau memos summarizing information stolen from the Tennant documents.

Rau testified that when he learned of the clandestine activity, he handled it very lightly because he did not consider it a terrible thing. He considered it a joke. Jerry Pond, president of Advance, learned about this activity from Rau early in 1979. Pond also handled it in a very light fashion until this lawsuit was commenced in early 1980. Then he discharged McIntosh. When asked whether he thought raiding the dumpster and rifling through a competitor's trash was unethical, Pond equivocated by saying that he did not have enough information to make a judgment on those practices.

The jury determined that Advance engaged in unlawful business practices, and that Tennant was entitled to one hundred thousand dollars compensatory damages and four hundred thousand dollars punitive damages.

Parker, Judge

California law imposes punitive damages to deter employment of unfit persons for important positions. It reflects certain policy judgments about corporations, primarily that top management sets the company's ethical tone. Accountability of the principal is necessary to enforce corporate responsibility: If we allow the master to be careless of his servants' torts we lose hold upon the most valuable check in the conduct of social life. In this case the president of Advance, who personally hired the individuals responsible for illegal activity, was indifferent to the ethics of their behavior.

Anything which convincingly shows the intention of the principle to adopt or approve the act in question is sufficient to establish ratification and therefore liability. It may also be shown by implication. Where an agent is authorized to do an act, and he transcends his authority, it is the duty of the principal to repudiate the act as soon as he is fully informed of what has been thus done in his name, else he will be bound by the act as having ratified it by implication. Both the president and vice president of Advance, Pond and Rau, were aware of McIntosh's activities early in 1979. Rau had discussed the matter directly with McIntosh. He also received memos containing the illegal information. The obviously sensitive nature of the material would have caused suspicions about their source. Pond had been informed by Rau and received the same memos when Rau was recovering from his heart attack.

Advance officers took no action against McIntosh until nearly one year after the fact. The failure to discharge or even reprimand an agent for illegal activity is evidence of the principal's approval. Pond never repudiated the act by informing Tennant of its occurrence. In fact, he was equivocal about the ethics of the activity.

While there was no direct evidence of ratification, the jury nonetheless had ample circumstantial evidence to sift through.

Millison v. E. I. du Pont de Nemours & Company
Supreme Court of New Jersey
501 A.2d 505 (1985)

Plaintiffs-employees are all past or present workers at defendant Du Pont's Chamber Works or Repauno plants. Both plants are involved in the manufacture of chemicals; each contains an extensive amount of piping through its facilities. As asbestos was often used for insulation purposes, the pipes in these plants were at one time surrounded by asbestos. It is therefore reasonably inferable that certain employees at the Chamber Works and Repauno plants were exposed to the asbestos insulation and inhaled asbestos fibers.

Plaintiffs allege that Du Pont and the company physicians fraudulently concealed from plaintiffs the fact that company medical examinations had revealed that certain plaintiffs-employees had contracted asbestos-related diseases. They assert that each year the Du Pont doctors would give employees complete physical examinations, including chest X rays, pulmonary function tests, electrocardiograms, urine analyses, and blood tests. Plaintiffs contend that the results of these physical exams indicated that plaintiffs-employees had contracted serious pulmonary and respiratory abnormalities associated with exposure to asbestos. They further maintain that rather than provide medical treatment for these ailing employees, defendants fraudulently concealed plaintiffs' asbestos-related diseases and sent them back into the workplace, where their initial infirmities were aggravated by additional exposure to asbestos. Plaintiffs claim that the time from defendants' first knowledge of an employee's condition to the time when the employee was told of the danger was as long as eight years.

It is undisputed that plaintiffs' injuries, if proven, are compensable under the Workers' Compensation Act. The controversy presented, however, calls for a determination of whether the legislature intended that the Compensation Act should serve as a worker's sole and exclusive remedy under circumstances such as those alleged.

Clifford, Justice

We acknowledge a certain anomaly in the notion that employees who are severely ill as a result of their exposure to asbestos in their place of employment are forced to accept the limited benefits available to them through the Workers' Compensation Act. Despite the fact that the current system sometimes provides what seems to be, and at times doubtless is, a less-than-adequate remedy to those who have been disabled on the job, all policy arguments regarding any ineffectiveness in the current compensation system as a way to address the problems of industrial diseases and accidents are within the exclusive province of the legislature.

Plaintiffs have, however, pleaded a valid cause of action for aggravation of their initial occupational diseases under the second count of their complaints. Count two alleges that in order to prevent employees from leaving the workforce, defendants fraudulently concealed from plaintiffs the fact that they were suffering from asbestos-related diseases, thereby delaying their treatment and aggravating their existing illnesses. Du Pont's medical staff provides company employees with physical examinations as part of its package of medical services. Plaintiffs contend that although plaintiff's physical examinations revealed changes in chest X rays indicating asbestos-related injuries, Du Pont's doctors did not inform plaintiffs of their sicknesses, but instead told them that their health was fine and sent them back to work under the same hazardous conditions that had caused the initial injuries.

These allegations go well beyond failing to warn of potentially dangerous conditions or intentionally exposing workers to the risks of disease. There is a difference between, on the one hand, tolerating in the workplace conditions that will result in a certain number of injuries or illnesses, and, on the other, actively misleading the employees who have already fallen victim to those risks of the workplace. An employer's fraudulent concealment of diseases already developed is not one of the risks an employee should have to assume. Such intentionally deceitful action goes beyond the bargain struck by the Compensation Act. But for defendants' corporate strategy of concealing diseases discovered in company physical examinations, plaintiffs would have minimized the dangers to their health. Instead, plaintiffs were deceived—or so they charge—by corporate doctors who held themselves out as acting in plaintiffs' best interests. The legislature, in passing the Compensation Act, could not have intended to insulate such conduct from tort liability. We therefore conclude that plaintiffs' allegations that defendants fraudulently concealed knowledge of already contracted diseases are sufficient to state a cause of action for aggravation of plaintiffs' illnesses, as distinct from any claim for the existence of the initial disease, which is cognizable only under the Compensation Act.

Under our holding, all degrees of negligence continue to be subject to the "exclusive remedy" bar of compensation. Thus, these plaintiffs now face the unenviable burden of proving a deliberate corporate strategy to conceal plaintiffs' asbestos-related diseases that were discovered by defendants-doctors in corporate physical examinations. Proof that the doctors negligently misdiagnosed plaintiffs' X rays or estimated poorly concerning the seriousness of plaintiffs' maladies will be insufficient to establish a cause of action outside the

Compensation Act. If, however, plaintiffs can in fact prove their allegations of fraudulent concealment of known diseases by defendants-doctors, we think it wholly proper that defendants be held to answer for their misconduct. Those corporations that would use their medical departments as a tool to prevent employees from learning of known injuries that are substantially certain to be aggravated by lack of disclosure must be deterred from embarking on such a course of conduct.

Following the court's ruling, a trial was held, and in the spring of 1989 a jury awarded six of the workers $1.4 million.

AN ANALYTICAL MODEL FOR MAKING ETHICALLY BASED DECISIONS

The balance of this chapter will construct a model that business managers can use to make ethically based decisions. As noted above, such decisions will lessen the legal risk for any course of action when compared with alternative means of reaching a decision. Consequently, by reducing legal risk, a manager acts in the firm's best interest.

But at the outset, note a couple of conditions about the model. First, it is not the only model that can be used to make ethical decisions. Numerous philosophers have suggested systems through which one might make ethical choices. Of course, other philosophers have pointed out the flaws, drawbacks, and ways each of the systems can be manipulated. So be it. This is not a philosophy text. The purpose of our model is to illustrate the value of ethical decision making and to provide a means by which a manager can accomplish it. If you have taken an ethics course (if not, we urge you to do so) and prefer another model, we have no qualms in encouraging you to use it in your professional career. We would also make the same arguments, as above, about its value as a means to limit legal risk.

Second, we do not intend to provide a survey of the great ethical philosophers or sketch a summary of their models for ethical decision making. That is the subject of a separate course of study. In our view, a manager can derive more benefit from considering one model in a legal environment course than from a summary of many in a few paragraphs. In any event, consider the following as a means to make ethically based (or socially responsible) business decisions.

Emphasis on Obeying Rules

Making ethical decisions first involves an emphasis on following the law and rules of society. The initial inquiry in any social responsibility analysis should, therefore, be whether the corporation has obeyed the law. For example, a corporation that intentionally files false financial information with the SEC in connection with a bond offering violates federal securities law and is also not acting ethically (as honesty is a fundamental moral value). One might hesitate to say that obeying the securities laws automatically makes a corporation responsible. However, it is clear that a decision to violate them shows irresponsibility.

Rules of law reflect the values of a society. Although they cannot require a corporation to be "good," they can limit behavior that society considers to be wrong. However, merely obeying the commands of the legal system will not alone yield corporate social responsibility. Often, important behavioral controls exist outside the commands of the legal system. As in following the legal rules, a corporation that violates "unwritten rules" may be considered irresponsible.

Unwritten rules are general norms of civilized human conduct. They permit society to function without an overburdensome legal system. However, if groups begin to act outside these general norms, the law will be used to regulate their behavior. For example, before the enactment of environmental laws, some corporations dumped their waste products into rivers adjoining their factories. There were no legal rules forbidding that type of waste disposal. However, as rivers grew polluted and fish began to die, communities became alarmed. General norms of civilized behavior required that those who produced waste refrain from leaving it for others. Polluting rivers, though not illegal, violated unwritten rules.

However, following laws and unwritten social rules will not alone provide socially responsible conduct. In fact, just the opposite might occur. Obeying rules and customs may instead yield irresponsible conduct. In the case of *State of Israel* v. *Adolph Eichmann* (in Chapter 4), Adolph Eichmann was being tried for millions of deaths in the concentration camps and gas chambers of Nazi Germany. Eichmann was in charge of the human extermination programs of the Nazis during World War II. Eichmann and many others followed the rules of their government. Yet they did not act responsibly—in fact, had they *disobeyed* the rules they would have been acting responsibly. In another example, many businesses throughout the United States (before the enactment of antidiscrimination legislation) openly discriminated against black people and women. Certain jobs were not available to them. Rates of pay were less than for white male workers. In many communities, such discrimination was an accepted social practice. However, conforming to such rules was not responsible behavior. Therefore, some other element must enter the picture in defining ethically based decisions.

Emphasis on a Thinking Process

Making ethical decisions also involves a thinking process, beyond mere obedience of laws or social rules. But in order to be effective, this process must be supported by top management, and the goal of ethical corporate actions must be reflected in the reward structure of the organization. Social scientists have found that an organization's culture may determine whether its employee's behavior will be ethical. Thus, if a person is hired by a corporation having corrupt conduct as a norm, it is likely that the person will accept that behavior. Amitai Etzioni, an eminent social scientist, related that "[a] study of price fixing in the electrical equipment industry found that the defendants almost invariably testified that they came new to a job, found price fixing an established way of life, and simply entered into it as they did into other aspects of their job."[4] Thus, without an organizational commitment, corporate social responsibility becomes just empty rhetoric.

But assume that the justifications for ethical decision making mentioned in the first part of this chapter have convinced top management to implement an ethical decision-making process. The key to successful implementation is a method of analysis for business issues that incorporates factors in addition to a review of the legal rules and social customs. Two factors compose this thinking process: first, thorough reflection or examination of the problem as opposed to an immediate, instinctive reaction to it; second, consideration of various alternatives available and how they might affect the corporate environment (this factor requires a familiarity with the external corporate environment and the groups within a corporation's sphere of responsibility).

Reflection

A thorough examination of a business problem requires not only reflection on the actions that might be taken, but also consideration of the available alternatives and an awareness of their implications. These alternatives need to be carefully considered in relation to the goals of the corporation and with respect to the way each might affect the firm, the recipients, and the community.

Simple reflection, however, will not necessarily yield an ethical decision. A methodology, or thinking process, needs to be followed. For any problem, no multiple choice will be apparent, with one "right" choice waiting to be selected. Instead, creative thinking about the types of alternatives available to solve the problem will be required.

The reflection process really takes place in two steps. First, the manager needs to devise alternatives on the basis of the areas of responsibility, to be discussed. Then, one alternative needs to be selected. The selection should be based on the alternative that is best for the most people within the corporation's sphere of responsibility. Of course, quantitative comparison will not be possible. Estimates, rules of thumb, and the like will provide the standards for comparison. The key is to identify the possible effects of various solutions and then to make the decision that provides the most benefit. Admittedly, this will be an imprecise task; but the active interest in searching for the good should, overall, yield ethical corporate conduct.

Effect on Surrounding Environment: Identifying Areas of Responsibility

In weighing alternatives, the manager must understand that all corporate activities affect the surrounding environment, since corporations do not exist in a vacuum. They are organizations of people and capital. Corporate decisions can have unlimited effects. However, no corporation is responsible for *all* the implications of its decisions. No manager could possibly act in a socially responsible manner if the corporation's responsibilities extended far beyond its sphere of control. To determine whether a particular corporate decision is socially responsible, the definition of *external environment* must be limited.

The key to this inquiry is to understand not only the environment in which the corporation exists, but also to whom the corporation is responsible for the consequences of its actions. This process is aided by dividing the relevant environment into four areas: first, the corporation as an institution; second, the people who make up the organization, such as employees and the firm's shareholders; third, the customers, or the ultimate consumers of the firm's products or services;

and fourth, the community or area where the company operates or where its business has an economic influence.

The Corporation As an Entity

Probably the core of a corporation's responsibility environment is the entity itself. Unethical decisions can have a devastating effect on an institution. For example, Johns-Manville (currently Manville) was a corporation that mined and sold asbestos. Asbestos was a major ingredient in insulation, but it caused lung disease in people who inhaled its fibers. Corporate management had long known of the health hazards of the product, perhaps since the 1930s. Nonetheless, Johns-Manville continued to manufacture and sell asbestos products without giving warnings of the health hazards. Product liability suits were filed against the company, and by the early 1980s new cases accrued at the rate of over four hundred per month.

In 1982, the liability exposure became so great that Johns-Manville filed for reorganization under Chapter 11 of the Bankruptcy Act. However, until that time the corporation continued to market asbestos. The year before, it earned over $38 million on $138 million in sales.

Under the Chapter 11 proceedings, an agreement was reached to provide compensation for those injured by the asbestos. But the company that emerged from the bankruptcy proceeding was a far different entity from the pre-products liability Johns-Manville. In 1977, its stock sold for three hundred dollars per share. In June 1989, the stock could be purchased for eight dollars. Most of the stock (eighty percent) was transferred to a special trust created to compensate injured parties. The original shareholders hold only about two and a half percent of the shares. Further, Manville was ordered to pay seventy-five million dollars annually to the trust, with an additional twenty percent of its profits going to the trust beginning in 1992.

Clearly, a corporation must be concerned that its decisions do not threaten its existence. But with socially responsible decision making comes the recognition of the profit-making reason for the existence of the business. Shareholders, employees, and the surrounding community rely on the profitability of the institution. Thus, decisions that yield higher profits are not necessarily wrong or insensitive. The corporation as an institution can justifiably make such decisions to ensure its continued existence. But such a concern is only one aspect of the socially responsible decision-making process.

Furthermore, ignoring the profitability of the entity may be deemed irresponsible when it threatens the existence of the firm. For example, Control Data is a computer corporation. Its former president was deeply concerned about various social ills, and he used corporate resources in an attempt to remedy some of them. An auto leasing subsidiary provided used cars to ex-convicts at low interest rates. No prescreening was done, and large-scale payment defaults led to an end to the program. Further, beginning in 1979 a committee within Control Data was budgeted three million dollars annually to spend on social problems. However, business operations slumped. In 1981, the corporation earned over $170 million on sales of $4.1 billion. The 1985 figures showed a loss of over $567 million on sales of $4.8 billion. The social problems still exist.

Members of Organization

The corporation's environment also consists of its members, primarily employees and shareholders. Corporate decision making should take into account the effect of various alternatives on these internal groups. As members of the corporate organization, they may be greatly affected by various decisions and, therefore, are within the sphere of the corporation's responsibility. One can simply note the effect of the Johns-Manville asbestos problem (discussed previously) on its shareholders to illustrate the effect of unethical decision making on an organization's members. Furthermore, legions of investment firm employees have lost their jobs in the wake of the October 1987 market crash and the insider trading scandals on Wall Street. Thus, jobs and shareholder wealth can be sacrificed by unethical business behavior. But note that management has responsibilities beyond the institution's members.

The following case is a shareholder challenge to certain corporate spending decisions. The shareholders are arguing that the corporation wrongfully spent funds that would have been better used for a direct business purpose—perhaps as dividends. The shareholders were affected by the decisions, but was the effect negative? The expenditures did enhance the community, through college scholarships. Could these be characterized as long-term "investments" creating intangible benefits for the corporation and, therefore, for its members?

A. P. Smith Mfg. Co. v. Barlow
Superior Court of New Jersey
97 A.2d 186 (1953)

Stein, Judge

The question calling for decision is whether a New Jersey corporation may lawfully in 1951 donate from its funds for the general maintenance of an educational institution like Princeton University. The plaintiff-stockholders claim that this is a wrongful use of corporate funds.

It is from the millions of young men and women who are the products of higher American education that industry has picked, and will have need to pick, its scientists and its business executives. It is the youth of today which also furnishes tomorrow's leaders in economics and in government, thereby erecting a strong breastwork against any onslaught from hostile forces which would change our way of life either in respect of private enterprise or democratic self-government. The proofs before me are abundant that Princeton emphasizes by precept and indoctrination the principles which are very vital to the preservation of our own democratic system of business and government. I cannot conceive of any greater benefit to corporations in this country than to build, and continue to build, respect for and adherence to a system of free enterprise and democratic government, the serious impairment of either of which may well spell the destruction of all corporate enterprise. It is no answer to say that a company is not so benefited unless such need is immediate. A long-range view must be taken of the matter. A small company today might be under no imperative requirement to engage the services of a research chemist or other scientist, but its growth in a few years may be such that it must have available an ample pool from which it may obtain the needed service.

It must also be remembered that industry cannot function efficiently or enjoy development and expansion unless it has at all times the advantage of enlightened leadership and direction. The value of that kind of service depends in great measure upon the training, ideologies and character of the personnel available. All of these considerations must lead the reflecting mind to the conclusion that nothing conducive to public welfare, other than perhaps public safety, is more important than the preservation of the privately supported institutions of learning which embrace in their enrollment about half the college-attending youth of the country.

I am strongly persuaded by the evidence that the only hope for the survival of the privately supported American college and university lies in the willingness of corporate wealth to furnish in moderation some support to institutions which are so essential to public welfare and therefore, of necessity, to corporate welfare. What promotes the general good inescapably advances the corporate weal. I hold that corporate contributions to Princeton and institutions rendering the like public service are, if held within reasonable limitations, a matter of direct benefit to the giving corporations, and this without regard to the extent or sweep of the donors' business.

Customers or Consumers of Corporate Products and Services

A third group in a corporation's environment is the customers or the ultimate consumers of its products or services. This element involves not only the typical business-related decision of, for example, making a quality product, but also concern for the health and safety of the users of the corporation's output. In the mid-1970s, three major corporations were competing in the baby food market: Gerber Products, Beech-Nut Nutrition, and H. J. Heinz. To gain an edge, in 1977 Beech-Nut began to market a product it labeled as apple juice that contained no apple juice. During the next five years it sold sixty million dollars worth of its falsely labeled juice. Beech-Nut also saved substantial money because the raw materials for its mixture were cheaper to purchase than apple juice. As investigators began to uncover this fraud, Beech-Nut refused to cooperate and shipped its phony apple juice inventory to a location where the investigators had no jurisdiction. Finally, the corporation was charged with violating the Food, Drug, and Cosmetics Act. It pled guilty and was fined two million dollars. Its president and vice-president of operations were convicted of similar charges. One reporter noted: "Two executives of a company with an excellent reputation breached a trust and did their company harm. Since 1987, when the case was brought to a close, Beech-Nut's share of the overall baby food market has fallen from 19.1% to 15.8%."[5]

Clearly, unethical corporate practices involving customers can destroy the most difficult asset to acquire—credibility. As with Beech-Nut, that loss can translate into a loss of market share. Furthermore, the legal system, through its consumer legislation and through product liability and warranty litigation, enforces the need for corporations to perceive their actions as they affect their customers. Socially responsible decision making requires that their interests be considered as a part of the corporate environment. The following case is an example of corporate decision making which resulted in the placing of an unsafe product on the market. Examine the implications of that unfortunate decision, especially the legal system's concern with it.

Toole v. Richardson-Merrell, Inc.
California Court of Appeal
60 Cal. Rptr. 398 (1967)

Salsman, Justice

Appellant Richardson-Merrell, Inc., appeals from a judgment on a jury's verdict awarding respondent Toole $175,000 general damages and $500,000 punitive damages for injuries suffered as a result of the use of a drug manufactured and marketed by appellant and prescribed for respondent's use by his physician.

Respondent, 43 years of age, developed cataracts in both eyes as a result of taking the drug triparanol, manufactured and sold by appellant under the trade name of "MER/29." He developed a condition known as ichthyosis, characterized by dry, flaky, red and inflamed skin. He also suffered hair loss over his entire body. His sight is now distorted, peripheral vision is reduced, his eyes have lost their ability to adjust for distances, are painfully sensitive to light and he is required to wear corrective glasses. There was also evidence that he is now more apt to suffer detached retinas, which could lead to blindness. He has an emotional overlay of fear that the drug may have some other long-term ill effect that may manifest itself later in life.

Appellant's Toxicology Department began animal testing of MER/29 in 1957. In the first six-week test, all female rats on a high dosage died. All were found to have suffered abnormal blood changes.

A second rat study was begun, using a reduced dosage of MER/29. This test also produced abnormal blood changes in the rats.

In March 1959 a test of MER/29 in monkeys was completed. Again, abnormal blood changes were found. But Dr. Van Maanen ordered Mrs. Beulah Jordan, the laboratory technician, to falsify a chart of this test by recording false body weights for the monkeys, by extending their records beyond dates after which the monkeys had been killed, and by adding data for an imaginary monkey that had never been in the test group at all. Mrs. Jordan protested but was told: "He (Van Maanen) is higher up. You do as he tells you and be quiet."

Knox Smith had prepared a brochure reflecting Merrell's test results of MER/29 on rats. This literature was intended for use of medical doctors clinically testing the drug on human beings. This brochure was revised and the revision eliminated all reference in it to the abnormal blood findings previously recited. Dr. McMaster, of the Medical Science Division, who was in charge of medical research on MER/29, had knowledge of the deletions, and consented to them.

On July 21, 1959 appellant filed a drug application with the FDA seeking permission to place MER/29 on the market. The application contained many false statements, among them these:

1. It was reported that only four out of eight rats had died during a certain study, whereas in truth all had died.

2. Wholly fictitious body and organ weights and also blood tests were reported for dead rats as if they had continued to live and to take MER/29.

3. None of the abnormal blood changes encountered in experiments was disclosed.

4. False data was related for a monkey being tested with the drug, and also data was stated for a monkey that was never part of the test group.

5. The falsified chart, prepared by Mrs. Jordan under protest, was included in the application.

The FDA informed appellant that its new drug application was incomplete. Dr. Murray, appellant's liaison officer, replied to the FDA and specifically informed it that there had been no blood changes in appellant's test of MER/29 on rats or monkeys, and that a 16-month study in monkeys had adequately demonstrated the safety of MER/29. These statements concerning absence of blood changes in animals were of course untrue.

In January 1960 appellant completed another study on the effect of MER/29 in rats. Nine out of ten rats in this study developed eye opacities. Appellant's report to the FDA of the results of this study was false or misleading because it reported that eight out of twenty rats had developed mild inflammation of the eye, but did not disclose the eye opacities seen in the test animals.

In February 1960 appellant reported to the FDA the results of its further tests of MER/29 in dogs. One dog in the test group developed eye opacities and blindness, but again this information was eliminated from the report to the FDA. In the same month, appellant completed a long-term test of the drug used in rats. Of 36 test rats in this group, 25 developed eye opacities. The results of this test were also withheld from the FDA.

In April 1960 the FDA granted appellant's application to market MER/29.

MER/29 was introduced to the market by the greatest promotional and advertising effort ever made by appellant in support of a product. There was testimony that doctors had never before seen so much promotion of a single drug. Doctors were bombarded with sales promotion, and subjected to brainwashing sessions with detailmen (salesmen). One advertising brochure stated that MER/29 was ". . . virtually nontoxic and remarkably free from side effects even in prolonged clinical use."

Appellant's drug salesmen were told that MER/29 was a "proven drug. There is no longer any valid question as to its safety or lack of significant side effects."

In April 1961 appellant began a long-term study of MER/29 in rats and dogs. By June opacities had begun to develop in the eyes of the rats, and by August, 35 out of 46 rats in the experiment had developed eye opacities. Despite these findings, and a field report that a doctor using MER/29 had suffered a change of eyesight, promotion of the drug continued unabated. Appellant gave no report to the FDA or warning to the medical profession in general concerning these developments.

In April 1962 FDA officials made an unannounced visit to appellant's laboratories and took all of appellant's records relating to its animal experiments. After the records were seized, President Getman drafted a letter to the FDA requesting withdrawal of MER/29 from the market.

MER/29 was administered to approximately 400,000 persons during its relatively short market life. In its first year at large it contributed $7,000,000 to appellant's gross sales. 490 cases of cataracts caused by use of the drug were reported. The majority of those on the drug maintained its use for less than three months. There was evidence that a very high percentage of those taking the drug would have developed cataracts if the drug had remained on the market and they had continued its use.

The judgment is affirmed.

The Community

The final group that should be considered as part of the corporate decision-making environment is the community in which the corporation does business. Of all the corporate environmental factors, this one is least closely tied to the traditional operations of a business. Concerns about how management decisions affect the vitality of the corporate organization, its employees, shareholders, and the marketplace arise in most business decision making. As already noted, these elements are also a part of a socially responsible corporation's thinking process. This final element involves consideration of the effect of the corporation's decisions upon those who are not connected with the organization. However, this community does not include the entire world. The community factor is limited to those areas in which the corporation does business, has offices or operations, or has other significant economic influences. In so characterizing this factor, business managers will be able to recognize and consider the direct community consequences of their decisions. They should be able to more readily recognize (through community and social pressure) the concerns of those outside the traditional corporate spheres of responsibility.

One instance in which the interests of the surrounding community were considered carefully by management was the decision not to install lights in the Chicago Cubs home baseball park, Wrigley Field, discussed in Chapter 14 (see *Shlensky* v. *Wrigley et al.*). Note that traditional corporate interests (the long-term effect of night baseball on the team's attendance) and the interests of the community were important factors in the decision. Although lights have now been erected at Wrigley Field, compromise with the neighborhood was essential to bringing night baseball to Chicago Cub fans. The team promised to limit the number of night games it plays and to start the games at an earlier time than is typical for the rest of the major leagues.

Finally, focusing on the community interest may also provide business opportunities. Investment houses market "social interest" stock portfolios that claim to be free of shares in unethical corporations. Other firms evaluate individual companies for clients seeking to make socially responsible investments. Billions of dollars are invested in this manner. Thus, recognizing the social interests of certain investors can be a benefit not only to brokerage houses, but also to individual corporations which might see their shares shunned by what appears to be a growing number of investors.

SUMMARY

Corporate social responsibility is an important factor in assessing the legal environment of business. It is the result of a deliberate decision-making process. As long as difficult decisions must be made, as long as resources are limited, the effects of corporate decisions (both positive and negative) will be felt. However, there is no neat definition with which to characterize corporate decisions as responsible or not. Instead, an inquiry should focus on the corporate decision-making process and the effects of that decision on various components of the corporation's environment.

In a sense, corporate social responsibility requires an analysis of the traditional constituents of the business firm as well as the outside community. However, to determine the extent of the corporation's community responsibility, two inquiries must be made. First, the effect of the exercise of corporate power must be noted. Second, groups that are within the corporate sphere of influence must be identified. It is to these groups that the corporation owes its responsibility. Once a group of possible alternatives to a problem has been identified, the solution that benefits the most people within the corporation's spheres of responsibility should be selected.

The discussion of corporate social responsibility is illustrative of a major influence on corporate behavior. It is, therefore, an important component of the legal environment of business.

REVIEW QUESTIONS

1. Analyze the following case using the suggested corporate social responsibility decision-making model discussed in this chapter.

   XYZ, Inc. operates a hospital. The hospital is a profit-making business. The relevant legal rule, in this case, concerns the duty to rescue. Under the common law, which is applicable here, a person has no obligation to rescue another person in distress. For example, if A notices that B is drowning, A has no legal duty to rescue B even if what would be required of A (tossing B a life preserver) would not endanger or inconvenience A. Additionally, assume that for-profit hospitals have no legal duty to treat anyone who seeks assistance.

   Margaret O'Neill awoke at 5:00 A.M. and saw her husband standing at the window, rubbing his arms and chest. His mouth was open and he was trying to get as much air as he possibly could. He was perspiring, his face was white, as contrasted with his normally ruddy complexion, and he complained of severe pains in his chest and arms. With Mrs. O'Neill's assistance, John O'Neill dressed and walked to XYZ's hospital, which was three blocks away. The O'Neills did not own an automobile, and no taxis were available at that time.

   The hospital maintained an emergency room. When the O'Neills arrived, they were directed to the nurse in charge. Mrs. O'Neill told the nurse that her husband was very ill. She explained the symptoms she observed and stated that she thought he was having a heart attack. She requested the services of a doctor. At that point, John O'Neill mentioned that they were members of the Health Insurance Plan (HIP). Thereupon, the nurse, following corporate policy, stated that the XYZ Hospital had no connection with that insurance plan and did not, therefore, care for HIP patients. She did allow Mr. O'Neill to telephone an HIP doctor, who informed Mr. O'Neill that HIP services would be available at 8:00 A.M.

   Mrs. O'Neill asked the nurse to have a doctor examine her husband anyway, since it was an emergency. The nurse refused. Thereafter, the O'Neills left the hospital and returned home. They walked, pausing occasionally to permit John O'Neill to catch his breath. After they arrived at their apartment, and as Mrs. O'Neill was helping her husband to undress, he fell to the floor and died before any medical attention could be obtained.

2. General Motors Corporation (GM) has its headquarters in Detroit, Michigan. GM, like other major American automobile concerns, has a number of factories in the Detroit area that produce a large number of cars. In the spring of 1980, General Motors notified the city of Detroit that it would close one of its major Detroit plants within three years. Detroit, like many other old Northern industrial communities, had for some time experienced deteriorating economic conditions.

   General Motors' decision to close the plant would inevitably worsen the economic problems: over six thousand jobs would be lost directly, as well as millions of dollars in tax revenue, and the effect on other businesses would make the loss even more costly to the city. GM, therefore, offered to build the replacement facility in Detroit if a suitable site could be found. Otherwise, the plant would be built in another part of the country.

   A number of sites were considered by the city, but none was suitable, except a 465-acre tract that included an area known as Poletown. Poletown was an ethnic neighborhood consisting primarily of Polish-American families. The city of Detroit condemned the 465-acre tract, including the Poletown area, so that it could be cleared, converted into an industrial park, and then conveyed to General

Motors. The condemnation action affected approximately three thousand people, sixteen churches, and one hundred businesses. The area was not a slum.

Was General Motors' decision to build in the Detroit area on the Poletown site a socially responsible one, given the loss of Poletown?

3. Dunes Park is an ecologically sensitive area. It consists of fifty acres of lakefront property. The land is sandy, and large sand hills dot the area. A few shrubs and trees grow in the sandy soil and tend to provide a uniquely landscaped area. It is a very popular area. Dunes Park is not protected under any federal environmental legislation. However, it is a state park, having been dedicated in 1920. During the past ten years, various environmental groups have attempted to have the federal government take over the park and bring it under its control. However, there is no interest on behalf of the federal government to do so. The standard response given to the groups was that "there are a number of other dune areas under federal environmental protection and there is no reason to add another."

Last year the state's budgetary problems became virtually insurmountable. While searching for new sources of revenue, the state received a report from a university geologist that predicted that Dunes Park contained large quantities of natural gas. However, the report also noted that current natural gas-drilling technology, if used, would severely strain the environmental capacity of the park. In fact, there was a great danger that the ecological makeup of the park would be destroyed. On the basis of this information, the state decided to offer natural gas-drilling permits to various corporations with the expectation that a discovery would lead to improved financial conditions for the state.

You are an executive with XYZ, Inc., an energy development firm. You are contacted by the state concerning a possible bid for drilling rights in Dunes Park. You are aware of the university geologist's report, which confirms a number of internal exploration reports. In fact, internal reports project that huge reserves of natural gas may be found beneath the park. During the past five years, the natural gas reserves of XYZ have been greatly depleted. New discoveries have not kept pace with the removal of gas from existing fields. As a result, the stock price of XYZ has been decreasing. Industry analysis paints a grim picture for energy firms that fail to replace the resources they use. One of the firms so pictured is XYZ. Environmental groups are expected to vigorously protest any move to explore for gas in Dunes Park. This may well result in unfavorable publicity for the firm that does the exploring.

On the basis of the socially responsible decision-making model discussed in the chapter, should XYZ seek to drill for gas in the park? Justify whatever decision you make.

4. XYZ, Inc. manufactures automobiles. The industry is very competitive, and the corporation has lost twenty percent of its market share over the last ten years. Furthermore, its current share is being threatened by lower-priced cars being produced overseas and imported to the American market. Therefore, XYZ has become very cost conscious. Labor, materials, and design features for the cars must be proved to be cost effective.

You are the senior project manager for the production of the new low-priced car being produced by XYZ. Sales of the car are scheduled to begin in about eighteen months. Currently, the goal is to be able to produce a high-quality small car to effectively compete with the imports. Already the corporation is advertising its determination to "drive the imports from the highways." Your responsibility is to make absolutely sure that the car will be profitable when sold in the intended five-thousand-dollar range. Additionally, the car must be a high-quality product.

Company engineers recommend that the gasoline tank system be redesigned for the car. The current design made the tank somewhat vulnerable to puncture (and explosion) during rear-end collision tests that were conducted. In order to meet their suggested specifications, an additional fifteen million dollars would need to be invested in the car. Doing so would make the five-thousand-dollar price impossible to meet. Furthermore, company actuaries estimate that the current design would produce ten million dollars in damage awards that the corporation would have to pay as a result of exploding gasoline tanks. This figure is already factored into overall costs that go toward computing the five-thousand-dollar sales price.

What decision should you make? Justify your decision. Would it be different if the design change would not affect the five-thousand-dollar price? Would your decision be different if you and members of your family would be driving the car?

5. You are the vice-president of marketing for a major corporation. Every regional sales manager reports directly to you. One of your jobs is to determine which, if any, of the sales representatives should be promoted to regional manager. These positions open only occasionally and selecting a top person for that job is of vital concern to the company. The industry is very competitive and the regional manager is key in keeping current customers satisfied and in working with the representative in garnering new customers.

Last week one of the regional managers retired and you have been studying the pool of sales representatives, seeking a replacement. The most qualified person, by far, is Mary Smith. In fact, her performance to date has been among the strongest ever recorded for the corporation. However, you know that three of your major customers in that region have serious misgivings about dealing with women in business settings. You heard one mention that women are unsuited for responsible sales management positions.

Should you promote Mary Smith? Base your evaluation on the materials in this chapter.

6. You are an executive with ABC, Inc. The corporation manufactures a very popular jet ski. Although the market for this recreational product is quite competitive, your firm's design has proved to be the winner. This morning ABC's engineers deliver a report to you that states that certain uses of the jet ski, given its design, can be very dangerous. These uses are not atypical for jet skiers. You also have a report that states that recreational products users are quite concerned about safety and will quickly turn on a once-popular product that they discover risks injuries.

What, if anything, should you do? Base your evaluation on the materials in this chapter.

7. You are an executive with a very large company. Six years ago you began to deal with a small supplier of rubber fittings that are used in the production of your firm's products. Your firm has become virtually the sole customer of this supplier. Because of your demands for quickly delivered inventory, the small supplier has borrowed heavily to redesign its operations. In fact, one might consider the survival of the supplier to be tied to its contract with your firm.

Last year your firm signed a ten-year contract with the supplier. The price per unit was designated. However, the economic climate has become uncertain. You would like to cut costs here and there. One of your assistants suggests that you simply withhold payment from the small supplier. When the supplier is sufficiently squeezed financially, the assistant assures you, it will readily accept a renegotiation of the contract.

What do you think? Should you use this strategy? Base your evaluation on the materials in this chapter.

NOTES

[1] H. L. Mencken, *Selected Prejudices* (New York: Octagon, 1926), p. 67.

[2] Oscar Wilde, *Lady Windemere's Fan,* in *The Portable Oscar Wilde,* Richard Aldington, ed. (New York: Viking Press, 1965), p. 686.

[3] Dan Cordtz, "Detroit's Catch-22," in *Financial World,* 36 (June 27, 1989).

[4] A. Etzioni, "The Moral Dilemma," in *The New York Times* (February 12, 1989).

[5] S. Kindel, "Bad Apple for Baby," in *Financial World,* 48 (June 27, 1989).

Part 4

The Legal Foundations of American Business: Common Law and Its Development

CHAPTER 9

The Legal Basis of Enforceable Bargains: Contracts—The Essential Elements

- Meaning of the Word *Contract*
- Sources of the Rules of Contracts
- Historical Look at Contract Law Development
- Nonlegal Considerations
- Contract Requirements—The Essential Elements

The American law, while at one time largely judge-made law, is increasingly becoming codified—that is, the rules appear in statutes. Even so, many rules still are determined by examining cases. This is especially true of the law of contracts. Though statutes have been passed, particularly in the area of consumer protection, that alter traditional contract rules, most of the law of contracts may still be found in cases.

This chapter first discusses what a contract is and covers some of the forces that created contract law as we now know it. The law of contracts evolved over many years, and the body of contract law is a reflection of the political and social forces of the past. Social forces continue today to affect the law of contracts.

The focus of most of this chapter is on the development of the law of contracts and the essential elements necessary to create a valid contract: offer, acceptance, consideration, capacity, and legality.

MEANING OF THE WORD *CONTRACT*

Each day people throughout the United States enter into contracts. Quite often, the persons involved fail to recognize a contract ever came into existence. The average person probably enters into hundreds of contracts a year without realizing it. Buying clothing, purchasing groceries, and subscribing to a magazine are just a few examples of the many contracts we all enter into every year.

A person not trained in the law often assumes that a contract must be drawn up in a formal written document drafted by an attorney. In fact, contracts may result, without either party's signing a formal written agreement, from the exchange of letters between persons, from conversations, or even from the actions of persons who have neither written nor said anything.

Suppose that today you decide to purchase a candy bar. You go to a vending machine on campus, deposit some change, and out comes your selection. Even though you never signed anything or spoke to anyone, your actions created a contract between the seller and yourself. If the machine fails to give you a candy bar after you deposited your money, the contract created by the deposit of money has been breached.

To understand how these actions created a contract, we first need to know what a contract is.

What Is a Contract?   In the law, contract refers to a transaction in which two or more persons have entered into an agreement that is legally enforceable. Quite often the parties first engaged in some discussion of their differences before arriving at an adjustment.

In arriving at a technical definition of the term *contract*, the courts sometimes rely upon the **Restatement of Contracts**. The *Restatement of Contracts* is *not* the law in any state. It is an effort of legal scholars, sponsored by the American Law Institute, to analyze existing judicial decisions and to distill from them some sound principles of contract law. The *Restatement* has often been relied on by the courts as a guide in resolving cases involving contracts.

The drafters of the *Restatement of Contracts* suggest the following definition of a contract: "A contract is a promise or set of promises for breach of which the law gives a remedy, or the performance of which the law in some way recognizes as a duty." The next question, then, is: What is a promise? A **promise** is a voluntary commitment by a person to another person to perform in some manner or refrain from some action in the future.

Often it is helpful to approach the contract law by focusing on the promises of the parties. Consider the following example. Acme Drugstore enters into an employment contract with Janice Hartman. Hartman agrees (or promises) to work for Acme and Acme agrees (or promises) to pay Hartman. According to this agreement, Hartman is obligated to work for Acme and has the right to receive payment for her work. Acme has the right to receive Hartman's services and is obligated to pay her for these services. Thus, a contract may be thought of as an agreement which consists of a promise or set of promises that creates legal rights and obligations.

SOURCES OF THE RULES OF CONTRACTS

The Common Law   Contract law, unlike other areas of law, primarily is found in legal cases rather than in statutes. Case law consists of the rules of law announced in court decisions. Each decision in a case dealing with contracts becomes part of law in this area and serves as a precedent that binds courts in the future. Certain types of contracts, however, are governed by statutory provisions, as noted in the next section.

The Uniform Commercial Code

The Uniform Commercial Code in General   *GOVNS COMMERCIAL TRANSATION*

The **Uniform Commercial Code** (UCC) covers many areas of commercial law. Before the twentieth century, the law came primarily from cases, and the laws dealing with commercial transactions varied greatly from state to state. In order to simplify the law, model statutes (codes) were drafted covering several areas of commercial law. These codes were enacted by the legislatures in a number of states. Based on the experience gained in these early attempts at simplifying the law, the National Conference of Commissioners on Uniform State Laws and the American Law Institute set about drafting new codes that would eliminate some of the problems associated with the earlier codes.

This effort culminated in what we now call the Uniform Commercial Code. This model code, consisting of ten articles, deals with the sale of goods, commercial paper, secured transactions, and other commercial activities.

Though the UCC is merely a model code, all the states have enacted it (except Louisiana, which adopted parts of it, but not Article Two, dealing with the sale of goods). States have generally followed the language that appears in the model version. Some states have altered the language of the model code in certain places. We will confine our discussion of the UCC to that part of it dealing with the sale of goods.

Article Two of the UCC   *ESPECIALLY GOODS*

Unlike the law of contracts covering items other than the sale of goods, in which the primary source of law is cases, the law dealing with the sale of goods is embodied in Article Two of the UCC. It is still necessary, of course, for the courts to decide cases to elaborate the meaning of the UCC, but the code itself is the primary source of law. Judges and attorneys turn first to the UCC to resolve legal disputes dealing with contracts for the sale of goods.

Section 2-105(1) of the UCC defines goods as all things that are movable at the time of identification to the contract for sale. A contract for the sale of a house is *not* a contract for the sale of goods because the house is permanently attached to ground. It is not movable. Contracts for the sale of services, such as the services of a house painter or a typist in a business office, are not goods either. Such services are covered by the common law of contracts and not by the UCC. On the other hand, an automobile qualifies as a good, and the sale of an automobile is covered by the UCC.

The law of contracts basically comes from prior court cases in the area of real estate contracts, employment contracts, service contracts, and other non-sale-of-goods transactions. When goods are involved in a contract, the principles in the UCC control.

Contract As Defined by the UCC

The Uniform Commercial Code gives a broader definition to the term *contract* than a mere group of promises that the law will enforce, or the performance of which is recognized as a duty. The UCC does not use the term *promise* but refers to an *agreement* between the parties. An agreement is defined in Section 1-201(3) of the UCC as "the bargain of the parties in fact as found in their language or by implication from other circumstances including course of dealing or usage of trade or course of performance." This definition recognizes that not only words but also acts, prior understandings between the parties, customs in the industry, and the manner in which the parties perform the contract are all relevant in determining what the bargain between the parties is.

It should be noted that while the UCC creates certain special rules dealing with contracts for the sale of goods, in many places the UCC is silent as to the rule of law that should be applied. In this situation, the common law of contracts governs. In certain situations, special statutes passed by the states also have a bearing on sales contracts.

The law of contracts pertaining to the sale of goods is therefore found in two places: case law and Article Two of the Uniform Commercial Code.

The principles of the law of contracts as we know them today developed to a great extent in the nineteenth century, and the rules are a product of the economic, social, and political thought of that era. In examining the basic requirements of a contract, bear in mind the forces that produced these rules. The law of contracts is still evolving. The next section describes the forces at work in society today that are contributing to a change in the attitude of the courts and legislatures as to the nature and enforceability of contracts.

HISTORICAL LOOK AT CONTRACT LAW DEVELOPMENT

Enforcement of Promises

If the courts failed to enforce contractual promises, the system of business would collapse. Buyers and sellers count on the delivery of goods and services from the other parties to a contract. Because the courts enforce contractual promises, businesses are assured of the delivery of goods and services.

Yet this was not always the case in contract law. In the very early development of the law of contracts in England, the courts recognized liability only for a faulty performance of a promise, and declined to penalize a failure or refusal to perform a promise. By the sixteenth century, the courts had begun to enforce promises made by parties to a contract.

Later, such British writers as Adam Smith (1723–1790) and John Stuart Mill (1806–1873) pleaded for the courts to enforce contractual promises. They believed once a buyer and seller signed a contract, each person needed to be able to count on the other person's promise to deliver or accept these goods and services in the future.

John Stuart Mill, a major writer of the nineteenth century, advocated the freedom of the individual to guide his own destiny unimpeded by government. Only through individual freedom, he believed, could the greatest human development occur. Mill believed in the school of *laissez-faire* economics. To Mill and his followers, laissez-faire economics permitted the full development of the individual and permitted production and trade to follow their natural courses unimpeded by government. Followers of this theory believed that the government should interfere with free trade only to the minimum extent necessary to preserve order.

Advocates of laissez-faire economic theory, who believed that a contract represented the free choice of individuals, influenced the nature of contract law. This stress on individualism and free choice was manifested in the widespread belief that freedom to contract was essential to the development of the economic system. They encouraged government, by and large, to let the economy operate free of government intrusion.

Freedom of Contract

Complete Freedom?

There really never has been *complete* freedom of contract. No court has ever been willing to enforce a contract that contemplated a crime. Today, we refer to such contracts as *illegal*.

Suppose a criminal entered into a contract to kill someone for five thousand dollars. If he or she committed the act called for by the contract, could the murderer go to court to force the other party to live up to the promise to pay five thousand dollars? No. If a court were to enforce such a contract, it would encourage unacceptable behavior in society. This is true today and has always been true.

Contract Law in the United States

Laissez-faire economic thinking, with its great emphasis on the freedom of individuals to contract, greatly influenced the development of the law in the United States during the nineteenth century.

For example, American courts generally followed the doctrine of *caveat emptor*—let the buyer beware—at that time. The courts expected buyers to look out for themselves. They assumed people would exercise a high degree of caution before entering into any transaction. If a person entered into a contract and then became unhappy with the bargain, the courts rarely permitted the party to escape from the contract.

American society began to change radically after the Civil War and many large industrial enterprises flourished. Some of the industrialists became fabulously wealthy. Protest movements took root in response to this concentration of economic power. Doubt began to arise among persons in the country about the wisdom of freedom of contract.

Legislators pushed through legislation dealing with needed reforms in the workplace, but the judges were reluctant to change with the times. In the late nineteenth century, Congress and the state legislatures tried to adopt restrictions on the concept of freedom of contract, but the courts routinely struck down such statutes on a variety of grounds, one ground being the right to freely contract. The following case illustrates this view.

Lochner v. New York
United States Supreme Court
198 U.S. 45 (1905)

Lochner, owner of a bakery, was convicted of violating a New York labor law because he required his employees to work more than ten hours a day and more than sixty hours in one week. His appeals in state court were all denied, so he appealed to the Supreme Court, which reversed the lower court decision.

Justice Peckham

The New York statute necessarily interferes with the right of contract between the employer and employees, concerning the number of hours in which the latter may labor in the bakery of the employer. The general right to make a contract in relation to his business is part of the liberty of the individual protected by the Fourteenth Amendment of the Federal Constitution. Under that provision no State can deprive any person of life, liberty or property without due process of law. The right to purchase or to sell labor is part of the liberty protected by this amendment, unless there are circumstances which exclude the right. There are, however, certain powers, existing in the sovereignty of each State of the Union, somewhat vaguely termed police powers, the exact description and limitation of which have not been attempted by the courts. Those powers, broadly stated, relate to the safety, health, morals and general welfare of the public. Both property and liberty are held on such reasonable conditions as may be imposed by the governing power of the State in the exercise in those powers, and with such conditions the Fourteenth Amendment was not designed to interfere.

The question whether this act is valid as a labor law, pure and simple, may be dismissed in a few words. There is no reasonable ground for interfering with the liberty of person or the right of free contract, by determining the hours of labor, in the occupation of a baker. There is no

contention that bakers as a class are not equal in intelligence and capacity to men in other trades or manual occupations, or that they are not able to assert their rights and care for themselves without the protecting arm of the State, interfering with their independence of judgment and of action. Viewed in the light of a purely labor law, with no reference whatever to the question of health, we think that a law like the one before us involves neither the safety, the morals nor the welfare of the public, and that the interest of the public is not in the slightest degree affected by such an act. The law must be upheld, if at all, as a law pertaining to the health of the individual engaged in the occupation of a baker. The limitation of the hours of labor does not come within the police power on that ground.

We think the limit of the police power has been reached and passed in this case. There is, in our judgment, no reasonable foundation for holding this to be necessary or appropriate as a health law to safeguard the public health or the health of the individuals who are following the trade of a baker.

The act is not, within any fair meaning of the term, a health law, but is an illegal interference with the rights of individuals, both employers and employees, to make contracts regarding labor upon such terms as they may think best, or which they may agree upon with the other parties to such contracts. Statutes of the nature of that under review, limiting the hours in which grown and intelligent men may labor to earn their living, are mere meddlesome interferences with the rights of the individual.

The Twentieth Century

Inequality of Bargaining Power

What the courts were overlooking was the *inequality of bargaining power* between the parties. They wrote about freedom of contract between two knowledgeable, intelligent, and equally positioned persons. But large companies, perhaps the only employment in town, frequently drafted one-sided contracts that required persons to work long hours in unsafe working conditions for unreasonably low wages. Workers accepted the terms offered by the industrialists. But the resulting contracts were hardly freely and voluntarily negotiated agreements.

The courts gradually began to recognize the gross inequality of bargaining power that is present in many bargaining situations, particularly in contracts between consumers and businesses. The more powerful party, often the seller, presents the other party with a choice: Either sign the printed contract presented or go elsewhere. The agent of the seller negotiating the deal often lacks the power to alter the terms of the printed form. The seller deprives the buyer of the opportunity to read the contract. In some cases, the buyer needs additional background to understand the terms of the contract. And even if he or she does have the time and understanding, the buyer lacks the bargaining power to force the other party to alter the terms of a written contract. As a practical matter, the buyer cannot go elsewhere, because other businesses use the same terms. Gradually, as the belief in unrestrained individualism and liberty declined, the legislatures, Congress, and the courts began to erode the doctrine of freedom of contract.

By the beginning of the twentieth century, the courts had become more receptive to social legislation. The courts started to sustain social legislation that restricted the number of hours women and children could work. They upheld minimum wage laws and many other restrictions on the ability of an employer to dictate the terms of employment.

With the election of Franklin D. Roosevelt as president and his implementation of the New Deal, Congress made further inroads on the right to freely contract. Congress passed legislation regulating many facets of the economy. Eventually the United States Supreme Court upheld most of this legislation.

NONLEGAL CONSIDERATIONS

Before we launch into a technical discussion of the law of contracts, let us look at some nonlegal considerations that influence the parties' behavior during the bargaining process. These nonlegal considerations often shape the relationship between the parties far more than simple legal rules.

Repeat Players

Some people engage in businesses that require them to repeatedly enter into one contract after another. To stay in business, they must continually enter into a lot of contracts of the same nature—for example, with an apartment complex, a life insurance company, a bank, or a real estate broker. Think about the opportunity the law affords to such people—and the dangers associated with the power to freely contract unsupervised by government rules. Once these repeat players grasp the legal system, they start to attempt to structure their future relationships in a manner that favors them.

The uninformed often assume that legal rules alone govern a transaction. This overlooks the critical role of *strategy*—a master game plan—in business transactions.

Consider for a moment the enormous advantage enjoyed by a *repeat player*—a party who engages in the same type of transaction over and over. First of all, repeat players have the opportunity to structure the law to their advantage by making donations to legislators, congresspeople, senators, governors, and presidents in order to influence legislation. Repeat players also can elect to litigate those cases that most likely will generate precedents useful to them in the future. Repeat players can hire top legal talent with specialized knowledge in every area of the law. Finally, repeat players understand the rules of the law before legal problems even arise. Their "opponents" quite often tend to learn the rules of law as the case unfolds. This can be very dangerous, as a naive opponent can fall into a trap constructed by the repeat player.

Experienced, But Not Repeat, Players

Even people who infrequently engage in contracts of a particular nature learn through their limited experience. They have "been around the block before" so they tend to be more alert. Experience increases their ability to know what to look for in a contract. A person who purchases a first home knows very little about home buying. The second time around, such a person knows a lot more about how to successfully negotiate a contract for the purchase of the right home in the right area. We all learn, to some extent, through experience. However, learning by doing can result in some costly errors.

Negotiation

To get a good deal, we need to think about the entire process of bargaining.

Bargaining position

A person in a strong bargaining position is more likely to get whatever he or she wants in a contract than a person in a weak bargaining position. In contemplating what sort of strategy to adopt during the bargaining process, we first need to assess the strength of our bargaining position. We should recognize *prior* to the commencement of the bargaining process just how many concessions we have the power to extract from the opposing party.

Labor unions and employers engage in just such an assessment of their respective strengths and weaknesses prior to sitting down at the bargaining table to thrash out the terms of the next labor contract. If a union perceives itself to be in a strong bargaining position, it will aggressively bargain even to the point of ordering its members to go out on strike in order to force the employer to meet the union's demands. On the other hand, if the union's position is weak, it probably will be more amenable to management's proposals. If either party miscalculates the strength of its bargaining position, it can do serious damage to itself and sometimes to the other party as well.

Suppose that the union thinks that management can be forced to agree to the union's demands. If the union miscalculates the strength of management's resolve, and orders its members out on strike, the strike will eventually fail. In this situation the union loses face, the workers lose needed income, and everyone must unnecessarily endure a great deal of stress.

Sometimes parties recognize their lack of bargaining power, but they want to contract anyway. In such a case, the party must take whatever the other side is willing to offer. Suppose that Mogul Records asked a band, the Blues, to sign a record contract. The Blues consulted with a lawyer, who suggested various changes in the contract. Will Mogul Records modify this contract for an unknown group like the Blues? Suppose, instead, that in 1968 the Beatles had asked for a similar change in their contract. Would they have gotten it?

Hollywood contracts tend to be very one-sided agreements. Consider the following passage from the book *Indecent Exposure*:

> In analyzing Hollywood's abuses, the truly sophisticated experts tend to focus not so much on the occasional instances of flagrant illegality as on the more prosaic standard terms and conditions of the average Hollywood contract— perfectly legal terms and conditions—that give the studio or the network enormous advantages over the actor, director, writer, or small production company. The powerful and arrogant few tend to take full advantage of every situation, and the lure of working in the industry is so strong that the fearful mass of prospective employees will sign just about anything to do so—often to their later regret. Hollywood is full of people who argue, *after* a film or TV series becomes a hit, that they deserve more money and are being cheated, when in fact they signed a legal contract—onerous perhaps, but legal nonetheless—that entitles them to no more than they are getting.[1]

A good example of such an unpleasant predicament involved the dispute between humorist Art Buchwald and Paramount Pictures. In 1983, Buchwald wrote a screen treatment called "It's a Crude, Crude World," which he pitched to Jeff Katzenberg, head of motion picture production at Paramount Pictures. Buchwald developed the treatment with the intention that Paramount expand it into a movie starring Eddie Murphy. Buchwald received a fee for his work. Subsequently, Paramount dropped work on his treatment. Thereafter, it produced a film starring Eddie Murphy—the hit movie *Coming to America*. The contract Buchwald signed gave him 1.5 percent of the net profits of any film produced by Paramount based on his treatment. In spite of the fact that *Coming to America* grossed hundreds of millions of dollars, Paramount refused to pay Buchwald any more money because it argued that the film had not earned any profits. This made Buchwald's contract essentially worthless. In 1990 California Superior Court Judge Schneider found the entire contracting system to be grossly unfair because only a few people in the industry possessed enough bargaining power to share in the gross profits. Judge Schneider found the standard movie contract to be excessively one-sided, and he set aside the net profit formula as written in the contract. In 1992 Buchwald settled the case for around $750,000, after spending over $2 million to sue.

The point to bear in mind is that you must assess your position prior to the commencement of the bargaining process. If your bargaining position appears weak, you probably will have to enter into a contract that tends to favor the other side. You may nonetheless want to contract, even on unfavorable terms, with the hope of being able to extract better terms from the other party in the future. (As an illustration of the fact that this does not always happen, review the *Flood* v. *Kuhn* case in Chapter 4.)

Using a Third Party to Bargain on Your Behalf

Sometimes it helps to employ a third party to bargain for you. If nothing else, he or she can remain emotionally detached from the situation, even one that is highly stressful. Lawyers spend a lot of time representing clients in just this fashion. In baseball, for example, few if any players negotiate their own deals, because they recognize the value associated with employing a detached, knowledgeable third party to act on their behalf. The negotiator can drive a hard bargain—and even engage in insults and name calling if the bargaining process falls to that. The player could not do the same without jeopardizing his place on the team.

#3 Psychology

Many writers have pointed out the importance of psychology in bargaining. A host of psychological factors influence the outcome in any bargaining situation. The most important information a person can acquire about an "adversary" is that person's *needs*. In the negotiating process, by asking pointed questions, making statements, listening to the other's responses, and watching for physical reactions, a person can rather rapidly acquire some information about the other person's desires. Body language reveals a lot as well. Don't just look at a person's face—it is, in fact, the most controlled portion of the body. Instead, watch a person's arms, legs, and feet. All provide clues about a person's psychological state. During the process of negotiating, people have a tendency to reveal, directly or indirectly, what they really want.

#4 Lying

It is a regrettable fact, but a negotiator needs to recognize that sometimes people adopt the *strategy of lying*. As the famous circus impresario P. T. Barnum declared, "There's a sucker born every minute." It is naive to think that the people you deal with will not lie every now and then.

Lying is not uncommon in business. In this respect, consider the following comment in the *Harvard Business Review*:

Most executives from time to time are almost compelled, in the interests of their companies or themselves, to practice some form of deception when negotiating with customers, dealers, labor unions, governments or even other departments in their companies. By conscious misstatements, concealments of pertinent facts or exaggerations—in short, by bluffing—they seek to persuade others to agree with them. I think it is fair to say that if the individual executive refuses to bluff from time to time, if he feels obligated to tell the truth—he is ignoring opportunities permitted under the rules and is at a heavy disadvantage in his business dealings.[2]

The question of the ethics of lying, bluffing, and other behavior is taken up later in this text. Even so, at this juncture you might ask yourself: "Would I lie to myself? If not, is it ethical to treat other people in a way that I would not treat myself?" German philosopher Immanual Kant (1724–1804) held that there was an absolute moral law that could never be compromised by expediency. His "categorical imperative," in contrast to the above quotation, maintains that it is unethical to lie.

The Win-Win Strategy

People employ a host of other negotiating styles and techniques. When you bargain with other people, keep in mind the *win-win style* of negotiating. A person employing this strategy hopes to conclude the deal with all parties feeling pleased with the outcome of the negotiating process. Each side must come out of the deal with a sense of gaining something valuable.

For example, suppose that a professor's tenants broke a house lease in September, just three months after signing for a year's rental. The tenants found the home of their dreams, bought it, and moved out. In an academic town, most people secure their rentals by August for the coming school year, so the professor was afraid he would be unable to locate suitable new tenants. In such a situation, anger could easily dominate the professor's reactions. But a "take no hostages" posture of winning at all costs is emotionally wearing and often self-defeating. Moreover, it overlooks the tenants' perspective. Is it unreasonable that the tenants want to move into a home of their own?

A better strategy would be for the professor to resist the temptation to release his anger on the tenants. Instead, he should use the win-win approach. The professor occupies a powerful negotiating position—after all, the tenants agreed to pay rent until the following August. He should call the tenants and firmly, but politely, point out to them that he intends to hold them to their contract. However, at the same time, he should suggest that if they locate someone else to take over their lease, he will release them from their obligations. This gives the tenants some incentive to find a substitute party. Through pointing out to the tenants not the landlord's needs, but rather the tenants' own need to resolve the matter to avoid a suit, and by adopting a flexible attitude, the professor ensures that both parties are likely to come out of the transaction as winners.

Making the Offer   The prudent negotiator always tries to get an "opponent" to make the initial offer. As a general proposition, the person who makes the initial offer occupies the weaker bargaining position. Thus, the local car dealer tries to get the shopper to make the initial offer. The dealer in effect says to a prospect: "What will it take to put you in this car?'' The dealer hopes the buyer will state a very large figure, a figure much higher than the price the dealership intends to sell the car for. If the buyer states too low a figure, the dealer simply rejects the buyer's offer on the spot.

The job interview poses a similar situation. Employers want to get their employees at the lowest possible salary. The interviewer might say to the prospective employee: ''How much are you currently making?'' This gives the person conducting the interview some idea of how much the applicant wants. A person looking for work should strive to avoid divulging information that indicates the lowest salary he or she would work for. Instead, let the employer make the initial offer and force that offer up.

Knowing when to stop talking and when to get down to ironing out the final terms of a deal is an art. At some point, making additional statements or demands will crush the other person's spirit and kill any chance of striking a deal. The artful negotiator stops just short of this point. Presumably, practice helps hone one's natural intuition.

Explicitly Covering All Aspects of the Agreement in Writing

After negotiations are completed and a bargain has been struck, the time comes to present the agreement to a lawyer for the formal drafting of a contract. A client typically has a general idea for an agreement, one that the client wants fleshed out into a formal contract. At this point, the client's attorney will have various provisions to suggest that the client has not considered. More often than not, the final document drafted by the attorney will strike the client as a needlessly complex and detailed agreement filled with arcane language. Why do lawyers draft such complex documents?

One reason is that lawyers prefer to use terms in their agreements that have been judicially interpreted. The use of such terms or phrases adds certainty to the agreement. Many of these phrases are clear to lawyers but not necessarily to the general public.

U.S. lawyers also know from experience that problems arise in business transactions. They tend to believe that the best way to address this fact is to draft a document that at the outset spells out the relationship between the parties so they know exactly what the deal between them is. Spelling out the agreement in crystal-clear language will reduce the possibility of misunderstandings in the future. It also tends to make the agreement more complex.

In the course of drafting such a very explicit agreement, a lawyer may raise issues that the parties to the contract never thought of—issues that, in fact, may never come up during the life of the agreement. Then the question arises: Should a contract include provisions that might be totally academic? A lot of people view lawyers as *deal killers* because they bring such issues up. The negotiations must then be reopened and may become bogged down in haggling over seemingly insignificant or irrelevant terms. Of course, lawyers want to reduce risk. Complex terms may seldom make a difference, but if things go wrong, these provisions can be critical. The real question in a business transaction is: How much risk are you willing to undertake? A businessperson might view the whole transaction on a *risk continuum*. If a person insists upon a document that reduces his or her legal risk to zero, the other side may refuse to sign.

Having given some thought to the nonlegal considerations that influence the negotiating of a contract and the steps leading up to the final agreement, we now turn to the rules that must be observed in order to create a valid contract.

CONTRACT REQUIREMENTS—THE ESSENTIAL ELEMENTS

In General   In considering the following material, bear in mind that the law of contracts varies from state to state to some degree, particularly in the area of consumer contracts. The following remarks are generalizations about the state of the law across the United States.

As suggested at the beginning of the chapter, a contract essentially is an agreement the court will recognize and enforce. The following are the elements necessary to fulfill the legal requirements for a *valid* contract:

1. Offer
2. Acceptance
3. Consideration
4. Capacity
5. Legality

Each of these requirements is discussed in turn in this chapter. In addition, the parties must have truly assented to the agreement. Finally, certain types of contracts must be in writing to be enforceable. The last two topics are covered in Chapter 10.

The following material is a very general, simplified discussion of the basic provisions necessary to create a contract. The law of contracts is complex, but this material is presented to give you a broad overview.

Offer   An **offer** is a manifestation by the person making the offer of a desire to enter into a contract. The person making the offer is called the **offeror** and the person to whom the offer is made is referred to as the **offeree**.

Preliminary Negotiations — NOT AN OFFER

Some contracts are very simple, such as the purchase of candy from a vending machine. Others are more complex, such as the purchase of a home. The more complex the transaction, the more likely there will be some bargaining before the making of an offer.

Suppose a major corporation wishes to dispose of some but not all of its properties located in Los Angeles. An officer of the corporation then decides to write a letter to other corporations the president feels might be interested in the properties. The president's letter merely states: "We are considering selling some of our commercial properties located in Los Angeles. Please write us if you are interested in acquiring property in the Los Angeles market." A recipient of this letter could not write back and state: "I accept your offer." The recipient cannot accept because no offer has yet been made. The parties are in the preliminary negotiations stage. The negotiations between the parties may give rise to a specific offer at a later date.

There was no offer in this example because the letter was too indefinite. The recipient of the letter would not know which properties were being offered, or the terms of the offer, or the price. Until these and perhaps some other matters are specified by the seller, no offer to sell has been made. The seller in this instance has merely invited other businesses to indicate their interest in acquiring these properties.

To constitute a valid offer, the statement in question must (1) indicate the intention to enter into a contract, (2) be certain and definite, and (3) be communicated to the offeree.

INTENTION TO CONTRACT

In the preceding example, no intention to contract could be implied. The corporation merely wanted to learn of the interest of other parties in purchasing Los Angeles property. In order to determine if a statement or writing indicates an intent to contract, the conduct or words used by the offeror must suggest to the offeree that the offeror genuinely desires to enter into a contract. A court bases its decision as to whether the words in question manifest an intent to contract by employing an objective test: Would a hypothetical reasonable person have thought that the offeror intended to make an offer? Courts consider such factors as the language of the statement or writing, the surrounding circumstances, and the relationship of the parties in applying this test. Offers made in anger, jest, or undue excitement may or may not constitute a serious offer on the part of the offeror. Courts try to determine the response such words would evoke in a reasonable person hearing these words under the given circumstances. Suppose that the queen of the United Kingdom said to a British subject, "I will trade my throne for a new car." Would a reasonable person think the queen of England actually intended to trade her title for an automobile? On the other hand, consider Richard III's famous plea: "A horse! A horse! My kingdom for a horse!" With an army closing in on the king, and the prospect of imminent death growing quite near, the exchange of even an old nag for the British crown probably seemed to King Richard, under those circumstances, a fair trade.

CERTAIN AND DEFINITE

To constitute an offer, the statement or writing must cover enough terms so that a contract could be enforced. At the minimum, the following terms must be included in the offer for a common law contract to be certain and definite: who the offeree is, the subject matter of the contract, the price, the terms of payment, delivery, or performance.

Offers involving the *sale of goods*, which are covered under Article Two of the Uniform Commercial Code, need not be this precise. This is because many

Figure 9.1   An Advertisement That Is Too Indefinite to Constitute an Offer

terms, such as price, time of performance, and time of delivery, will be supplied by reference to specific provisions in the UCC. These provisions enable a court to fill in the blanks in a contract. All that is necessary for a valid offer of the sale of goods is a manifestation of an intent to contract by the offeror, expressed to the offeree, which states some quantity of goods is being offered for sale. Thus, the UCC provides that the absence of some terms will not invalidate an offer.

Most advertisements are not certain and definite with respect to the terms on which an item is being offered for sale. Courts generally treat the typical advertisement not as an offer but as an invitation to negotiate and make an offer (see Figure 9.1 on p. 247).

In the following case, the Changs argued that the advertisement placed by the First Colonial Savings Bank created an offer when the bank placed the advertisement in the newspaper.

Chang v. First Colonial Savings Bank
Supreme Court of Virginia
410 S.E.2d 928 (1991)

RATIONAL

First Colonial Savings Bank placed the following advertisement in a Richmond, Virginia newspaper. It stated in part:

You Win 2 Ways With First Colonial's Savings Certificates.

1. Great Gifts

2. High Interest

Saving at First Colonial is a very rewarding experience. In appreciation for your business we have Great Gifts for you to enjoy NOW—and when your investment matures you get your entire principal back PLUS GREAT INTEREST. . . . Plan B: $3\frac{1}{2}$ Year Investment. Deposit $14,000 and receive two gifts—a Remington Shotgun and GE CB Radio OR an RCA 20″ Color-Trac TV—and $20,136.12 upon maturity in $3\frac{1}{2}$ years. Substantial penalty for early withdrawal. Allow 4–6 weeks for delivery. Wholesale cost of gifts must be reported on IRS Form 1099. Rates shown are $8\frac{3}{4}$% for Plan B. All gifts are fully warranted by manufacturer. DEPOSITS INSURED TO $100,000 by FSLIC. Interest can be received by monthly check.

The Changs saw the advertisement in question. Relying on the advertisement, they deposited $14,000 at Colonial. They received the gifts. When they returned three and a half years later to cash in the CD, Colonial informed them of an error in the advertisement. They should have deposited $15,000 to receive $20,136.12. They were never informed of the error in the advertisement until this point in time. First Colonial did display in its lobby pamphlets which contained the correct figures when the Changs made their deposit. The Changs argued that under these circumstances the advertisement constituted an offer which when accepted was binding. The trial court ruled for Colonial. The Supreme Court of Virginia reversed and ruled for the Changs.

Hassell, Justice

The general rule followed in most states, and which we adopt, is that newspaper advertisements are not offers, but merely invitations to bargain. However, there is a very narrow and limited exception to this rule. "Where the offer is clear, definite, and explicit, and leaves nothing open for negotiation, it constitutes an offer, acceptance of which will complete the contract."

In any event, there can be no doubt that a positive offer may be made even by an advertisement or general notice. . . . The only general test which can be submitted as a guide is an inquiry whether the facts show that some performance was promised in positive terms in return for something requested.

Applying these principles to the facts before us, we hold that the advertisement constituted an offer which was accepted when the Changs deposited their $14,000 with the Bank for a period of three and one-half years. A plain reading of the advertisement demonstrates that First Colonial's offer of the television and $20,136.12 upon maturity in three and one-half years was clear, definite, and explicit and left nothing open for negotiation.

Even though the Bank's advertisement upon which the Changs relied may have contained a mistake caused by a typographical error, under the unique facts and circumstances of this case, the error does not invalidate the offer. First Colonial did not inform the Changs of this typographical error until after it had the use of the Changs' $14,000 for three and one-half years. Additionally, applying the general rule to which there are certain exceptions not applicable here, a unilateral mistake does not void an otherwise legally binding contract.

Accordingly, we will reverse the judgment here in favor of the Changs.

Reversed and final judgment.

COMMUNICATED TO OFFEREE

An offer must also be communicated to the offeree. One cannot accept an offer one does not know about. For example, suppose Mrs. Rich offers a one-hundred dollar reward for the return of her dog, FuFu. This is an offer made to the general public. Nancy never saw or heard about the reward. While walking down the street, she finds FuFu. Noting the address on the dog tag, she realizes the dog is lost. Nancy returns the dog to Mrs. Rich. Nancy's actions are not an acceptance of the offer because the offer was not communicated to her. Had Nancy known of the offer, her actions would have created an acceptance of the offer and created a contract.

Termination of the Offer

An offer may be terminated in a number of ways—by the offeror or the offeree, and by operation of law. In this limited discussion, we will cover only a few of the ways in which a termination may occur.

TERMINATION BY OFFEROR

The person who makes an offer, the offeror, may terminate the offer by communicating the withdrawal of the offer to the offeree. In general, an offer may be terminated—*revoked*—at any time before the offer has been accepted. A revocation is therefore not effective until it is received by the offeree.

There are several exceptions to the rule that an offer may be withdrawn any time until it has been accepted. One exception is when the parties have signed an **option contract.** If the offeree gives something of value to the offeror to keep the offer open for a certain period of time, the offer may not be revoked during the time period agreed upon by the parties. The offeror and offeree here have created an option contract.

A second situation, which applies only to contracts for the sale of goods, is dealt with in Section 2-205 of the UCC. This rule applies if the person making the offer is a merchant. Generally speaking, a merchant is a person who regularly deals in goods. The UCC states that if a merchant in a signed writing agrees to hold an offer open, the offer may not be revoked during the time stated. If no time is stated, it may not be revoked for a reasonable time. A reasonable time, in this situation, may not exceed three months.

Another exception is when the party trying to enforce the bargain relies on the doctrine of promissory estoppel, which is dealt with in Chapter 10.

TERMINATION BY OFFEREE

An offer may be terminated by an express rejection by the offeree. Suppose that Sharon offers a job to Marc. Marc replies, "No thanks." This constitutes an express rejection by the offeree. Marc's actions terminate the offer. Unless Sharon renews the offer to Marc, Marc no longer possesses the power to accept. Therefore, the next day when Marc says to Sharon, "I will take the job you offered me yesterday," no contract is created because Marc no longer has the power to accept the offer.

Suppose, instead of expressly rejecting the job, Marc stated: "I will take the job if you agree to pay me $10 per day more than you offered." Such a statement is a **counteroffer.** A counteroffer is an attempted acceptance that varies the terms of the original offer. It operates in effect as a rejection of the original offer. The person making the counteroffer is treated as having made a new offer. An acceptance generally must be in exactly the same language as the offer. The courts refer to this as a **mirror-image rule.** A counteroffer terminates the power of acceptance by the offeree. After making such a statement, Marc may no longer accept the original offer unless Sharon renews it.

The UCC, which controls contracts for the sale of goods, permits an acceptance that varies the terms of the offer under certain circumstances. This is covered in Section 2-207 of the UCC. Because it is a rather complex provision, we will not discuss it; merely note that the UCC permits acceptances that alter the terms of an offer under certain specified conditions.

In several situations, an offer terminates automatically, although the parties fail to take any action. One such situation is when the offer states it will terminate at a particular time. An offer that states that it must be accepted on January 1, automatically terminates at that time.

TERMINATION BY OPERATION OF LAW

Sometimes an offer does not state a definite time at which it will terminate. In that case, the offer terminates after a reasonable period of time. What constitutes a *reasonable period of time* depends on the circumstances.

Acceptance

MIRROR IMAGE [handwritten annotation]

An acceptance is a manifestation of assent to the terms of an offer in the manner required or authorized by the offer. Only the offeree, the person to whom the offer has been made, has the power of acceptance.

The person making an offer may specify the manner of acceptance. He or she may indicate a desire for acceptance in a particular manner (by mail, for example), within a specified time period (by June 1, say), and at a particular place (perhaps at his or her place of business).

If the offer does not place any restrictions on the acceptance, then any kind of acceptance that takes place within a reasonable period of time will create a contract. However, in any nongoods transaction, acceptances must not change the terms of the offer. If they do, the acceptance is treated as a counteroffer, and will automatically terminate the offer.

If the offer does not state that the acceptance will not be effective until it is received, the moment an acceptance is sent by an authorized means a contract is effective. Courts call this the **implied agency rule** (or mailbox rule). In general, the same means or a faster means of communication than that by which the offer was made will be authorized. For example, if the offer was made by mail, an acceptance by mail is effective when the letter of acceptance is deposited in the mailbox—assuming the letter is properly addressed and stamped.

Consider the following case. Morris offers by mail to sell his home to Anne. The offer is clear and definite in every respect. On June 1, Anne deposits a properly stamped and addressed letter of acceptance in the mailbox. Louise, on June 1, after Anne mails her letter of acceptance, meets with Morris personally. She offers to purchase the home, and Morris accepts because he does not know of Anne's acceptance of his offer. On June 2, Morris receives Anne's letter. In this case, a contract between Morris and Anne came into existence on June 1—the date the letter of acceptance was deposited in the mail. Unfortunately for Morris, he also created a contract on June 1 with Louise. Thus, he has sold his home twice! Clearly, Morris cannot deliver the home to both women. Therefore, the person to whom he fails to deliver the home may sue him for breach of contract.

This example illustrates the pitfalls associated with the mailbox rule. Morris could have protected himself in this example by stating in the original offer to Anne that the acceptance would not be effective until it was received. In that case, when he sold the home to Louise, he could have called Anne on June 1 and withdrawn the offer—even after she had deposited her acceptance in the mailbox on June 1. This is true because under these circumstances, her acceptance would not be effective until it was received.

If the offeree accepts by an unauthorized means, the acceptance is not effective until received. Suppose that on June 1 Acme Paints sends a telegram to a chemist in which it offers to employ the chemist. On June 3, the chemist sends Acme a letter of acceptance. Acme receives the letter on June 6. Since the chemist

---

Breach of Oral Promise

After numerous visits and phone calls, Linda called a salesman at a Chevrolet dealer, Mike. She convinced him to ask the sales manager if he would accept an offer of $24,000 for a specific car if she agreed to come in that day at 1:00 P.M. to purchase the car. The dealer agreed to sell her the Chevrolet for $24,000. Such an agreement for the purchase of goods must be in writing to be enforceable under the UCC. Bob, her close friend, knocked on her door five minutes after she finished talking to the salesman. Bob convinced her to visit Acme Motors. While there, she agreed to purchase the same car for $22,500. When Mike learned she purchased the Chevrolet elsewhere, he became very irate. Mike told her it is hard to raise a family as a salesman. Was it ethical for Linda, after making a promise—albeit oral—to buy the car elsewhere?

---

used a slower means of communication than a telegram, his choice of communication was unauthorized. No contract would come into existence until the date on which Acme received the acceptance, June 6. In this situation, Acme could have revoked its offer any time prior to receiving the chemist's letter on June 6.

Bargain and Exchange

[handwritten margin note: Consideration]

[handwritten note: PROMISE A GIFT IS NOT CONSIDERATION]

The parties to a contract must have bargained with each other and exchanged something for something else. The courts will not enforce a mere gift promise. Suppose that Vanessa promises to give her diamond bracelet to Virginia, but Virginia has not promised anything in return. In this case, the courts will not enforce Vanessa's promise because Virginia has not exchanged anything in return.

In addition to a bargain and an exchange, the agreement must impose a **legal detriment** on the **promisee** (the person to whom a promise is made) or the **promisor** (the person making the promise) must receive a **legal benefit.**

A promisee can incur a legal detriment by doing something that she or he was under no prior obligation to do. For example, suppose that Paul, a free-lance journalist, agreed to write an article for a magazine. As Paul was not previously obligated to write an article for anyone, he agreed to do something that he had no prior obligation to do. Alternatively, a promisee can incur a legal detriment by refraining from doing something the person was not previously obligated to refrain from doing. Suppose that Paul agreed not to submit his article in handwritten form as opposed to typewritten. In this case, Paul has agreed to refrain from doing something that he was not previously obligated to refrain from doing.

A promisor can obtain a legal benefit by obtaining something which he or she had no prior legal right to obtain. Suppose that the magazine in the prior example agreed to pay Paul four hundred dollars for his article. The magazine, the prom-isor, thus will receive something that it was not otherwise entitled to receive—Paul's article. A promisor can also benefit when the promisee refrains from doing something that he or she otherwise had a legal right to do. The magazine, the promisor, by promising to pay Paul for the article only if he agreed not to submit it in handwriting, obtained a benefit because Paul must refrain from doing something he had a legal right to do—submit the article in his own handwriting.

A promisee who merely agrees to perform a preexisting duty is not doing anything that he or she was not previously obligated to do anyway. Thus, the promisee has not incurred a legal detriment. Suppose that Bill and Frances Fuller enter into a contract with a home builder. The builder agrees to build them a home according to specifications drawn up by their architect in return for three hundred thousand dollars. During the construction of the home the builder threatens to stop work on the project unless the Fullers agree to pay an additional thirty-five thousand dollars. Bill and Frances agree to pay thirty-five thousand dollars more and the builder completes the home. If Bill and Frances refused to pay any more than three hundred thousand dollars, the builder will be unable to collect the additional thirty-five thousand dollars. There was no legal benefit to the Fullers because they got only what they were contractually entitled to receive. Likewise, there was no legal detriment to the builder because the builder did not do anything that he was not already contractually obligated to perform. The builder should have agreed to do something other than what he was obligated to do under the contract with the Fullers in return for the extra thirty-five thousand dollars.

In the following case the court found both a legal detriment to the promisee and a legal benefit to the promisor.

Jennings v. Radio Station KSCS
Court of Appeals of Texas, Fort Worth
708 S.W.2d 60 (1986)

Steve Jennings, a prisoner in Texas, filed suit against Radio Station KSCS. He alleged that his only contact with the outside world was through the radio. Jennings claimed that the radio station had a policy to play "at least three in a row, or we pay you $25,000. No bull, more music on KSCS." He contacted the station on several occasions after the station failed to play at least three consecutive songs, but the station refused to pay him $25,000. The station moved for a summary judgment. It argued that there can be no enforceable contract because there was no consideration flowing to the station as offeror. The trial court granted the station's motion for summary judgment denying Jennings' right of recovery. The court of appeals reversed.

Ashworth, Justice (retired, sitting by assignment)

It is elementary contract law that a valuable and sufficient consideration for a contract may consist of either a benefit to the promisor or a loss or detriment to the promisee. Thus when a promisee acts to his detriment in reliance upon a promise, there is sufficient consideration to bind the promisor to his promise. In the instant case, appellant's petition alleged that he stopped listening to KSCS when appellee refused to pay him $25,000.00. Implicit in this statement is an allegation by appellant that he listened to KSCS *because* appellee promised to pay him $25,000.00 if he could catch the radio station playing fewer than three songs in a row. Appellant thus relied to his detriment. He could have listened to *any* station, but he listened to KSCS because of the promise. Appellee also benefitted by the promise. KSCS gained new listeners, like appellant, who listened in the hope of winning $25,000.00. We hold that appellant's petition sufficiently alleges a cause of action sounding in breach of contract to necessitate a trial on the merits.

We reverse the summary judgment and remand the cause to the trial court.

Adequacy

The items in a bargained-for exchange need not be of equal value. Courts refer to this as the *adequacy of the consideration*. If A in the earlier example agrees to take fifty thousand dollars for a home worth fifty-five thousand dollars, A cannot ask the court at a later date to ''set aside'' the contract because the consideration was not adequate. In general, the courts will not examine the adequacy of the consideration exchanged.

Example Where There Is No Consideration to Support Agreement

Suppose Stacy sells her home to Gertrude. After signing all the papers, Gertrude asks Stacy to give her the refrigerator and stove in the home. Stacy had planned on taking these with her, and the contract specified that they could be removed by Stacy. If Stacy agrees, is there any consideration to support this new agreement? No. Even if she made such an agreement, no contract would be created. Stacy did not receive anything in exchange for her promise to give the refrigerator and stove to Gertrude. Likewise, Gertrude did not give anything to Stacy in exchange for the new bargain. In light of this fact, there is no consideration to support Stacy's promise; therefore, no contract was created.

In order to make a binding deal, Gertrude should have done something that she was not legally already obligated to do. For example, she could have said, ''Will you sell me the stove and refrigerator for five dollars?'' If Stacy accepted this offer, a contract for the sale of these appliances, supported by consideration, would have been created. That the appliances were worth more than five dollars is irrelevant. The courts do not examine the adequacy of consideration exchanged.

A related topic, promissory estoppel, is dealt with in Chapter 10.

Capacity   The parties to a contract must have the capacity to contract. Some persons are legally regarded as lacking the capacity to contract. One such group of persons is

Contracts of Minors

Famed filmmaker Charlie Chaplin spent well over a year shooting the film *City Lights*. At that point, he decided to fire the star of the film. Chaplin substituted another performer, but he thereafter realized the high costs associated with reshooting the entire film. This forced him to return to the first actress to get her to complete the movie. In the meantime, the first actress had consulted with actress Marion Davies, who suggested she use her minority status as a bargaining tool. When Chaplin called, the actress informed Chaplin that no contract existed between them because she had signed the contract as a minor and she told him to call his lawyers. Chaplin called his lawyers. He thereafter agreed to the actress's demand that he double her salary for the rest of the film in order to induce her to finish *City Lights*.

the insane. A second important group is minors. The term *minor* is defined by state law. Most states consider a person a minor until he or she reaches the age of eighteen, although a few states require the person to reach twenty-one before he or she has the capacity to contract.

Insanity

People who have been declared insane in a court of law have no capacity to contract whatsoever. Contracts involving such people are *void*; that is, the agreement never has any legal effect because one of the requirements of a valid contract (capacity) is missing. Contracts involving people who are insane, but have not yet been legally declared so, are treated slightly differently. Such contracts are said to be *voidable*; that is, the agreement is said to be binding against the competent party, but may be voided by the incompetent party.

Minors

Contracts entered into by minors also are treated as voidable. A minor may disaffirm (avoid) his or her contract any time up to the time he or she reaches the age of *majority* (the age specified by the state when a person has the capacity to contract), or a reasonable time thereafter.

Necessaries

It should be noted that contracts by minors for necessaries are generally enforceable. Necessaries are such things as food, clothing, and medical services, if they are not already being provided for the minor.

One method to protect a person dealing with a minor is for that person to require an adult, as well as the minor, to sign the contract. In the event the minor disaffirms, the adult would still be bound by the provisions of the contract.

Legality   A contract must have a lawful purpose or object to be valid. The general rule is that if the parties enter into an illegal bargain, the courts "leave the parties where they find them." That means the courts will do nothing to assist either party to an illegal agreement. There are some exceptions to this rule, but in most cases a party that enters into an illegal bargain may not petition a court for relief.

Suppose Tony entered into a gambling contract, which in his state was illegal. He paid Susan one hundred dollars to bet on a horse. He now wants to receive his hundred dollars back, claiming the contract is illegal. In general, the courts will not require Susan to return the hundred dollars because the contract is illegal. Contracts are also illegal, of course, if it is necessary to do something illegal, such as a crime, to perform the contract.

Courts typically refuse to enforce gambling contracts on the grounds of illegality. For centuries, courts have refused to enforce such bargains. In 1710, Queen Anne of England signed the Statute of Anne. Parliament passed this statute, designed to invalidate notes given in payment of gambling debts, in order to protect the landed gentry in England. It made all gambling debts unenforceable. The puritanical settlers in the United States passed similar antigambling statutes which made gambling debts uncollectible. In most cases, because such contracts are illegal, the courts "leave the parties where it finds them." Interestingly, although gambling has been legal for years in Nevada, until 1983 gambling debts were not enforceable by the courts in Nevada. In 1983, the Nevada legislature finally permitted the enforcement of gambling debts.

The following case deals with the enforceability of a gambling debt. The debtor lost the money in one place; then the casino attempted to enforce the debt in another state.

Dorado Beach Hotel Corporation v. Jernigan
District Court of Appeals, First District
202 So.2d 831 (1967)

W. A. Jernigan, a Florida resident, gave a check for six thousand dollars to pay for his gambling debts in Puerto Rico. Gambling is legal there. The Dorado Beach Hotel Corporation is a licensed casino. Jernigan stopped payment on his check. The hotel brought this action in Florida. The Florida court ruled that this debt is uncollectible because it is contrary to the public policy of Florida.

Rawls, Judge

We are in accord with the pronouncement in *Young v. Sands, Inc.*, to the effect that a gambling obligation although valid in the state where created cannot be enforced in Florida because it is contrary to public policy, and therefore affirm.

The public policy of this State is that the forms of gambling made legal are contests staged for those seeking pleasure in the State—primarily tourists. These contests are staged between men, horses or dogs, and part of the entertainment afforded to the spectators is the

State's permission to wager on the outcome of these restricted events provided the State receives its "cut of the take." In essence the public policy of the State of Florida is established to permit a restricted type of gambling which is incidental to spectator sports. This State has consistently refused to permit gambling on non-spectator sports such as bookie parlors, football parlors, et cetera. Thus, the public policy of the State of Florida is well established that the State will condone certain selected forms of gambling, but it has likewise been established that the State will not lend its judicial arm to the collection of monies wagered in such enterprises not authorized by the law of the State of Florida. Although many efforts have been made to obtain legal sanction for wagering at gaming tables, such authorization has never been given and should a citizen of the State of Florida lose at a gaming table in the State, clearly the operator could not collect through the judicial processes. It is our conclusion that this forum will not extend its judicial arm to aid in the collection of this type gambling debt whether the transaction giving rise to the loss arose in Nevada, Puerto Rico or Monte Carlo.

Affirmed.

Contract of Adhesion

Just as courts generally refuse to enforce gambling debts on the grounds of illegality, they also will refuse to enforce a contract of adhesion. A contract of adhesion is an extremely one-sided contract with provisions that favor only the drafter, which is presented on a take-it-or-leave-it basis to a party in a very weak bargaining position. The courts refuse to enforce such agreements on the basis of illegality.

We will next consider two other theories on which courts refuse to enforce contracts: public policy and unconscionability.

Public Policy

A court may refuse to enforce a contract that has been found to be contrary to public policy. Alternatively, a clause within a contract may be ruled contrary to public policy, and the court may elect to enforce all of the contract except the offensive clause.

What Courts Mean by Public Policy

In general, conduct that conflicts with generally accepted standards of conduct in the community violates public policy. By examining the applicable statutes and judicial precedents, a judge determines what these community standards are. There is no precise rule or formula for a judge to determine what is and what is not contrary to public policy. As social, economic, moral, and ethical vaues change, the concept of public policy also changes.

Public policy has recently evolved into another concept. Today, the courts will refuse to enforce contracts not only if they are illegal or contrary to public policy, but also if they are unconscionable. The concept of unconscionability is an evolution of judicial thinking, building on the ideas of illegality, contracts of adhesion, and contracts that are contrary to public policy.

(+) NOT FOR BUISINESSES

Unconscionability

The doctrine of unconscionability is as murky a concept as the concept of public policy. The courts recognize it as a ground for invalidating contracts under both the common law and the Uniform Commercial Code.

The Uniform Commercial Code

The drafters of the Uniform Commercial Code adopted the concept of unconscionability in Section 2-302.

The UCC gives a court that finds a contract or a clause in a contract to be unconscionable *at the time it was made* several options. It may: (1) refuse to enforce the contract, (2) enforce the remainder of the contract without the unconscionable clause, or (3) limit the application of any unconscionable clause so as to avoid any unconscionable result.

The UCC fails to clearly define the term *unconscionability*. The drafters of the UCC offer this test:

> The basic test is whether, in the light of the general commercial background and the commercial needs of the particular trade or case, the clauses involved are so one-sided as to be unconscionable under the circumstances existing at the time of the making of the contract. . . . The principle is one of the prevention of oppression and unfair surprise . . . and not of disturbance of allocation of risks because of superior bargaining power.

The UCC seems to be directed at contracts with provisions that heavily favor one party over the other. Such a contract must be unconscionable *at the time the contract was entered into* by the parties—as opposed to a contract that, at a later date, becomes unfair because of some event the parties had not anticipated.

The failure to adequately define the term *unconscionability* or at least to set some standards for guiding the courts has met with criticism, as has the broad authority given to the courts to remake a contract. This provision clearly gives judges vast power and discretion to tamper with the provisions of a contract negotiated between private parties.

Typical Case

Generally, it would seem that the party in the best position to assert the doctrine of unconscionability as a defense is a person who was not engaged in business (for example, a consumer), who did not regularly enter into contracts, and who had a limited education, especially in business affairs. This party probably dealt with a businessperson who presented a form contract drafted by an attorney in such a manner that it unfairly favored the businessperson over the consumer. The contract probably was presented on a take-it-or-leave-it basis, and the consumer had few other places to go to obtain the goods or services. Generally, the purchaser had little time to examine the terms of the contracts. Very possibly he or she had been pressured into signing "at once" without being given the opportunity to reflect on the terms.

In many cases, the courts have struck down a contract because the sale price was unconscionable, as the following case illustrates.

Frostifresh Corp. v. Reynoso
District Court, Nassau County, New York, Second District
274 N.Y.S.2d 757 (1966)

A contract for a refrigerator-freezer was negotiated orally in Spanish between the Reynosos and a Spanish-speaking salesman representing Frostifresh. In that conversation, Mr. Reynoso told the salesman that he had but one week left on his job and he could not afford to buy the appliance. The salesman distracted and deluded the Reynosos by advising them that the appliance would cost them nothing because they would be paid bonuses or commissions of $25 each on the numerous sales that would be made to their neighbors and friends. Thereafter the Reynosos signed a retail installment contract entirely in English. The retail contract was neither translated for nor explained to the defendants. In that contract, there was a cash sales price set forth of $900. To this was added a credit charge of $245.88, making a total of $1,145.88 to be paid for the appliance. The cost to Frostifresh for the freezer was $348.00.

Frostifresh brings action for $1,364.10, alleging that this amount is owed by the Reynosos on account of the purchase of the refrigerator-freezer, for which they agreed to pay $1,145.88. The balance of the amount consists of a claim for attorney fees of $227.35 and a late charge of $22.87. The only payment made by the Reynosos is the sum of $32.

Donavan, Judge

The court finds that the sale of the appliance at the price and terms indicated in this contract is shocking to the conscience. The service charge, which almost equals the price of the appliance, is in and of itself indicative of the oppression which was practiced on these defendants. Defendants were handicapped by a lack of knowledge, both as to the commercial situation and the nature and terms of the contract, which was submitted in a language foreign to them.

The question presented in this case is simply this: Does the court have the power under section 2-302 of the Uniform Commercial Code to refuse to enforce the price and credit provisions of the contract in order to prevent an unconscionable result?

It is normally stated that the parties are free to make whatever contracts they please so long as there is no fraud or illegality.

However, it is the apparent intent of the Uniform Commercial Code to modify this general rule by giving the courts power "to police explicitly against the contracts or clauses which they find to be unconscionable. . . . The principle is one of the prevention of oppression and unfair surprise."

In the instant case the court finds that here it was "too hard a bargain" and the conscience of the court will not permit the enforcement of the contract as written. Therefore the plaintiff will not be permitted to recover on the basis of the price set forth in the retail installment contract, namely $900.00 plus $245.88 as a service charge.

However, since the defendants have not returned the refrigerator-freezer, they will be required to reimburse the plaintiff for the cost to the plaintiff, namely $348.00. No allowance is made on account of any commissions the plaintiff may have paid to salesmen or for legal fees, service charges or any other matters of overhead.

Accordingly the plaintiff may have judgment against both defendants in the amount of $348.00 with interest, less the $32.00 paid on account, leaving a net balance of $316.00 with interest from December 26, 1964.

Unconscion-ability—Business-persons

While unconscionability enables consumers on occasion to avoid their contractual obligations, businesspersons fare poorly under this doctrine. By and large, the courts tend to reject unconscionability as a ground for escaping contracts when persons in business assert it.

The reasons for declining to apply this doctrine to business contracts essentially are: (1) the parties generally are knowledgeable, sophisticated corporations; (2) the negotiations leading up to the consummation of the contract are deliberate and detailed; (3) the contracts are not presented on a take-it-or-leave-it basis but are generally negotiated transactions; and (4) usually the parties have the assistance of legal counsel or are aware they could use legal counsel. Such contracts rarely involve a person who is unaware of his or her legal rights and has very little bargaining power. The parties rarely have been oppressed or surprised by the terms.

Typically, the businessperson asserting unconscionability as a defense simply made a bad deal and is looking to the courts for relief from the consequences of his or her bad judgment. The courts, in light of the unusual negotiations and awareness of the terms of the contract, are quite unlikely to be receptive to the argument of unconscionability in the business context. The following case is typical of the treatment of businesspersons who assert unconscionability as grounds for not enforcing the contract.

Potomac Electric Power Co. v. Westinghouse Electric Corp.
United States District Court, District of Columbia
385 F. Supp. 572 (1974)

After several years of contract negotiations, in the summer of 1970, a turbine-generator was placed in commercial operation in Maryland. A few months later, a malfunction developed, causing substantial damage to the turbine. As a consequence, the unit was out of service for six months.

Potomac Electric Power Company (PEPCO) seeks compensatory and punitive damages from Westinghouse arising from an alleged contract breach for the manufacture and sale of the steam turbine-generator. The complaint alleges negligence, gross negligence, misrepresentation, breach of contract to repair or replace, breach of warranties, breach of express guarantees, and unconscionability. In response to the complaint, Westinghouse relies upon various defenses and contends that PEPCO is estopped from asserting any claim and has waived any right to consequential damages by virtue of the express provisions of the contract.

Parker, Judge

The rights and obligations of the parties are contained in a fully detailed and integrated written contract. Under the first subsection the defendants expressly warranted that the equipment would be of the kind and quality described in the contract and would be free of defects in workmanship or material for one year. In the event of a breach of this warranty, upon notification of the defect and substantiation of proper maintenance and operation, the defendant was only required to repair or replace the nonconforming part at its expense. The parties further agreed that there were no other warranties, express or implied, or merchantability, fitness for purpose, or other warranties. This last provision of the warranty was conspicuously underlined. The liability limitation subsection of the contract also specifically provided that the defendant would in no event be liable ''. . . for special, or consequential damages, such as, but not limited to, damage or loss of other property or equipment, loss of profits or revenue, loss of use of power system, cost of capital, cost of purchased or replacement power, or claims of customers of Purchaser for service interruption. . . .''

Within the framework of this commercial transaction the Court perceives no valid legal reason why PEPCO should not be held to the clear and express provisions of the written agreement between the parties. Warranty and limitation of liability clauses such as found in the present contract, which restrict PEPCO's remedies to the repair and replacement of nonconforming parts and limit Westinghouse's liability, regardless of its negligence in causing such nonconformities, are valid and enforceable and have been consistently upheld by the courts. They are also consistent with Sections 2-316(4) and 2-719(1)(a) and (3), Uniform Commercial Code. Provisions such as those precluding PEPCO from recovering consequential damages have likewise been upheld as valid and enforceable.

Finally, plaintiff raises the issue of the unconscionability of the exculpatory clauses. The negotiated agreement between these parties was not a contract between two small unknowledgeable shop keepers but between two sophisticated corporations each with comparable bargaining power and fully aware of what they were doing. The negotiations leading to the consummation of the contract were deliberate, detailed and consumed more than two years. PEPCO's representatives were experienced and the final agreement was reviewed by their corporate legal staff. While the evidence shows that other than Westinghouse, there was only one other domestic manufacturer with the capability of marketing the turbine-generator, there is nothing to indicate that PEPCO was precluded from contracting with that manufacturer or even foreign manufacturers. Nor is there any evidence in the record showing that PEPCO was a reluctant and unwilling purchaser, overreached and forced to yield to onerous terms imposed by Westinghouse.

In short, the facts have been sufficiently developed and the Court finds that there is no genuine issue as to any material fact and concludes that the law clearly supports the defendant.

Illegal Contracts: Cohabitation

Courts refuse to enforce contracts for the sale of sexual services. Such contracts amount to nothing more than a contract to engage in prostitution—an agreement that violates the law in most states.

A famous case, *Marvin v. Marvin*, dealt with an agreement allegedly entered into between actor Lee Marvin and Michelle Triola (who subsequently changed her last name to ''Marvin''). The couple agreed to live together. As part of that agreement, they agreed to combine their incomes and share equally in the property they accumulated. Michelle agreed to render services as a companion, homemaker, housekeeper, and cook. After living together for seven years, they separated, but Lee refused to share his assets with Michelle. She subsequently brought suit to enforce this agreement. While such an arrangement obviously involves sex, the California Supreme Court ruled that because it involved more than a mere contract to provide sexual services, it was not a contract for prostitution. The court ruled that if Michelle could prove that such an agreement between she and Lee existed, it could be enforced between the parties. [*Marvin v. Marvin*, 134 Cal. Rptr. 815 (1986).] After the decision in this case, some courts around the United States followed the *Marvin* decision and others rejected it.

This case suggests that at least some courts will enforce agreements between parties living together, even if the arrangement involves a sexual relationship.

Covenants Not to Compete

One type of anticompetitive restraint that is sometimes justified as a *reasonable* restraint of trade is the covenant not to compete. This is an agreement restricting the right of a person to practice a trade or profession or to operate a particular kind of business, but this agreement or promise not to compete is just one part of a larger, lawful agreement. Courts often enforce these ancillary agreements even though they do restrain trade.

Enforceable covenants not to compete are common in employment contracts and contracts involving the sale and purchase of a business. In these and similar contexts the covenant not to compete can serve a very useful function.

In order for a covenant not to compete to be enforceable, the restriction must be necessary to protect the legitimate interests of one of the parties to the contract and the restriction must not be excessive given this legitimate need. Courts often focus on whether the agreement is reasonable in scope. Specifically, they focus on the dimensions of the restriction in terms of time and territory.

There are many cases holding that restrictions for a year or two are reasonable. In some employment cases, however, courts have refused to enforce restrictions for shorter durations, expressing concern for the employee's inability to earn a livelihood and the imbalance between the restrictive burden on the employee and the employer's need for protection. Some restrictions for periods considerably longer than two years have been upheld, especially in connection with the sale of a business.

Covenant Not to Compete

H & R Block, Inc., is a corporation that franchises individuals and other concerns to operate a business solely for the preparation of income tax returns under the name of H & R Block.

Earl Lovelace, of Yates Center, Kansas, entered into such a franchise agreement with H & R Block. As part of that agreement, he agreed to not enter into competition with H & R Block for five years should he cease operating an H & R Block franchise. Several years after entering into the agreement, Lovelace terminated the agreement and opened a tax preparation business under his own name at the same location in Yates Center where he had operated under the Block name.

Block felt that it should be entitled to prevent Lovelace from engaging in the tax preparation business for five years. While restrictive covenants of this nature are frequently enforceable, they must be reasonable in the area and the time restrained. The court ruled that an agreement preventing a person from competing with H & R Block anywhere for a five-year period was an unreasonable restraint on competition and was not enforceable.

Had Block limited the restrictive covenant to cover only Yates Center for a period such as two years, the agreement would probably have been enforceable. However, a restrictive covenant that prevents a person from engaging in a business for an unreasonable period of time or in an unreasonable area will not be enforceable.

When combined with reasonable time periods, territorial restrictions that cover small areas, such as "within a one-mile radius" or "within the city of Beverly Hills, California," have nearly always been upheld; though there are some exceptional cases to the contrary. Under appropriate circumstances restrictions involving considerable territories can be enforced.

There are no hard-and-fas rules regarding what is reasonable. Reasonableness depends on the totality of circumstances in a given situation.

SUMMARY

The law of contracts has evolved over hundreds of years into the court-enforced laws of today. Over a period of centuries, the courts gradually accepted the notion that they should enforce a contract freely entered into by the parties. Nineteenth-century philosophers, many of whom espoused the doctrine of freedom of contract, argued that the free enterprise system depended upon the willingness of the courts to enforce every contract. The courts, persuaded by this thinking, developed the doctrine of caveat emptor—let the buyer beware. For many years few persons succeeded in escaping their contractual obligations.

More recently, the courts have moved away from this doctrine because of the harsh consequences associated with enforcing certain contracts. The courts have come to recognize that many contracts are not the product of the free will of individuals, as John Stuart Mill believed, but rather are the product of an inequal-ity of bargaining power between the parties. This inequality of bargaining power often gives the stronger party the opportunity to insert unfair clauses into a contract. Today, the courts are inclined to set aside unfair contracts.

Before any contract comes into existence, certain requirements must have been fulfilled. The person seeking the transaction must manifest a desire to enter into a contract, referred to as an offer. The person to whom this offer is made must manifest an assent to the terms of the offer in a manner required or authorized by the offer, referred to as an acceptance. The entire transaction must be supported by consideration; that is, the contract must have been the product of a bargain and exchange between the parties to the contract. Finally, no contract will be enforced if the parties to the contract lack the capacity to contract or if the bargain in question is illegal.

REVIEW QUESTIONS

1. Define the following terms:
   a. Caveat emptor
   b. Contract
   c. Contract of adhesion
   d. Promise
   e. Public policy
   f. *Restatement of Contracts*
   g. Unconscionability
   h. Uniform Commercial Code

2. Why did the concept of freedom of contract develop as part of contract law?

3. Why did John Stuart Mill feel that it was important for the courts to enforce a contrac-tual promise?

4. Can Sheila enforce a contract if she accepts an offer that was not made to her?

5. Is the meaning of the term *unconscionability* understood by everyone?

6. Acme Corporation decides to divest itself of one of its subsidiary corporations, a soft drink bottling company. While at the country club, the president of Acme mentions to an-other member, Peter West, that Acme in-tends to sell its bottling plant. On hearing this information, West responds "sold." Does this statement create a contract between Acme and West?

7. K-Mart places an advertisement in the *Chicago Tribune* showing an RCA color TV and a price of seven hundred dollars. Janice Bradwell appears at the K-Mart store the next day. Can she create a contract merely by saying "I accept your offer to sell the RCA color TV for seven hundred dollars"?

8. On June 1, Franklin offered to sell an office building to Miller. Miller wanted some more time to make up her mind. She paid a thou-sand dollars to Franklin for an option con-tract that expired August 1. On July 1, another buyer agreed to buy the building. Can Franklin sell the building to the new buyer?

9. Rawls offers to sell her house to Jackson for one hundred and fifty thousand dollars. Jackson responds, "I will take your house for one hundred and fifty thousand dollars if you agree to first repaint all the walls inside the house." Does Jackson's statement cre-ate a contract? Suppose that Rawls refuses to repaint the walls in his house, and Jackson thereafter says: "I will take your house for one hundred fifty thousand dollars." Does his second statement create a contract?

10. On March 1, 1974, Padgett offers to sell her home to Blackburn. The offer does not state

a definite time at which it will terminate. On March 1, 1994, Blackburn accepts the offer. Does this create a contract?

11. Wong offers to sell his hundred-acre farm to Walters. Wong sends an offer by telegram to Walters on September 1. Walters receives the telegram on September 1. On September 2 he mails Wong a letter of acceptance. Wong receives Walter's letter of acceptance on September 5. On what date is a contract formed? Would it make a difference if Walters telegraphed back an acceptance on September 2?

    Suppose instead that on September 2 Walters mails a letter of acceptance. On September 3 Wong telegraphs a revocation to Walters, which Walters receives that day. Wong thereafter receives Walter's letter of acceptance on September 5. What would be the outcome in this situation?

12. Pareja thinks very highly of her neighbor Cohen. One day Pareja offers to give Cohen her brand new refrigerator for free. Cohen says "Thank you. I accept." When Cohen comes to pick up the refrigerator, Pareja informs her that she no longer wants to give the refrigerator to Cohen. Is there an enforceable bargain between Pareja and Cohen?

13. Acme Corporation entered into a contract with Giant Construction. Giant contractually agreed to erect a new plant for Acme at a cost of eight million dollars. Midway into the project the builder threatened to stop work on the plant unless Acme agreed to pay an extra three hundred thousand dollars. Acme agreed to pay the extra money. Is there any consideration to support Acme's promise to pay the extra money?

14. Tina goes into the Alaskan Fur store. She selects a twenty-five-thousand dollar mink coat. Tina signs an agreement to pay twenty-five thousand dollars for the coat. Tina is seventeen years old. Is this contract enforceable? Is it ethical to purchase a mink coat?

15. Quick Lubrication Corporation sells a store to Bill Drews. The store is located in Los Angeles, California. The agreement between Quick and Drews forbids Drews, should he ever terminate his relationship with Quick, from ever opening up a competing lubrication shop anywhere in the world for the rest of his life. What is such an agreement called? Is it enforceable?

16. In 1898, Congress passed a law prohibiting employers from requiring employees, as a condition of employment, to agree not to join labor unions. Adair required his employee, Coppage, to sign such an agreement and fired him when he joined a union. In the absence of a valid contract between the parties, can Congress make it a crime for Adair to fire Coppage without just cause?

17. McConnell entered into a contract with Commonwealth Pictures. The contract obligated Commonwealth to pay McConnell for obtaining the distribution rights for certain pictures. McConnell negotiated these rights, but Commonwealth refused to pay for his services because McConnell procured the rights by bribing a representative of the company. Is this contract legal and thus enforceable?

18. Capitol sued Mary for the $406 balance due under a contract for household goods. The merchandise was valued at $595 plus $18 sales tax. The credit charge for purchase over a two-year period equaled $219. The cost of the goods to Capitol was $234. Mary claimed that the goods were grossly overpriced, that she had already paid their fair market value, and that the contract terms were unconscionable. Are the contract terms unconscionable?

19. After three years of talks, Westinghouse and a public service utilities company entered into a contract for the purchase of a turbine generator manufactured by Westinghouse. Both parties are very large industrial organizations. Westinghouse is one of only two

companies that can manufacture the required generator. The contract involved over ten million dollars and limited Westinghouse's liability to corrections of defects in workmanship and material appearing within one year of installation. Is this liability limitation unconscionable?

NOTES

[1] David McClintock, *Indecent Exposure* (New York: William Morrow, 1982), p. 514.

[2] Albert Carr, "Is Business Bluffing Ethical?" in *Harvard Business Review* (January–February 1968), p. 144.

CHAPTER 10

The Legal Basis of Enforceable Bargains: Contracts—Other Important Considerations

- Genuine Assent
- The Statute of Frauds
- Interpretation of Contractual Provisions
- Rights of Third Parties
- Termination of a Contract
- Damages
- Remedies
- Enforcing a Contract When None Exists

In Chapter 9 we discussed the elements that must be present to have a valid contract: offer, acceptance, consideration, capacity, and legality.

In this chapter we note that the courts will not enforce a contract unless the parties entered into it freely and voluntarily. The courts also refuse to enforce *some* contracts because of the failure of the parties to reduce their agreement to writing. We then make some observations concerning the interpretation of contractual provisions. Next we examine the ways in which a person's contractual obligations may be terminated and what damages the injured party may receive. We conclude by noting that, in some instances, the courts will impose contractual liabilities on the parties even though the contractual requirements discussed in Chapter 9 have not been met.

GENUINE ASSENT

Sometimes parties will agree to a contract, but the agreement will not be freely and voluntarily arrived at by one of the parties to the contract. Assent has not been freely and voluntarily given if it was the result of mistake, duress, fraud, undue influence, or misrepresentation. When any of these are present, the courts may refuse to enforce an agreement.

267

Mistake

MUTUAL MISTAKE

NO CONTRACT

+

JUST ONE = TOUGH LUCK

Sometimes a person or persons enter into a contract because of a mistake. If the mistake was material—that is, if it involved a fact that induced the party trying to avoid the contract to enter into the bargain—it may be possible to set aside the contract.

The courts examine whether only one person to the contract was in error, or whether all parties to the contract were operating under a mistaken belief. A mistake is *unilateral* if only one party held a mistaken belief; it is *bilateral* if both the parties were mistaken.

If the mistake is a unilateral mistake of fact, the courts generally will enforce the contract. On the other hand, if one party knew or should have known of the unilateral mistake by the other, that party will not be able to take advantage of the mistake by enforcing the contract. For example, suppose that Acme Construction solicited bids from several companies. One bid that Acme received was much lower than all the other bids for no apparent reason. In such a case, a court would not permit Acme to take advantage of the obvious mistake.

If both parties make a mistake concerning an important fact on which the contract is based, the contract is voidable. Suppose that Wilson and Petry enter into a contract for the sale of a rare book. At the time they enter into the contract, neither Wilson nor Petry is aware that the book has been destroyed in a fire. Such a contract will not be enforced by a court, on the grounds of mutual mistake.

Fraud

Fraud is a deliberate misrepresentation or nondisclosure of a material fact made with the intent that the other party will rely upon it. A fact is material if the person trying to avoid the contract would not have entered into the contract had he or she known of the misrepresentation. If the other party does in fact rely upon such a statement, and if this causes an injury, the person may bring an action to rescind

---

Baseball Card

Twelve-year-old Bryan Wrzesinski purchased a 1968 Nolan Ryan rookie card at Joe Irmen's Ball-Mart store in Chicago, Illinois for twelve dollars. Bryan did not know the true value of the card—over one thousand dollars, but he realized he was getting a good deal. Bryan owned over fifty thousand baseball cards. When Joe Irmen asked him to return the card because his clerk misread the "1200" price tag as $12.00 in selling the card to Bryan, Bryan refused. Joe then sued Bryan in small claims court. Does the mistake by Joe's clerk entitle him to rescind the contract of sale? Before the judge ruled in the case, the parties settled the dispute. In this case, Bryan could have argued that the store made a unilateral mistake and therefore was not entitled to make him return the card. On the other hand, the store could have argued that Bryan knew of the store's mistake; thus, the contract was voidable.

The law aside, one might ask whether it is *ethical* to snap up the baseball card knowing the store had made a pricing mistake.

(set aside) the contract. The misrepresentation must be of a present or past fact. False statements as to events in the future are not actionable.

Statements of opinion usually may not be used as the basis of a fraud or misrepresentation case. If the seller says, "These dishes are the best buy in town," such a statement is treated as a statement of opinion—not fact. However, if the person making the misrepresentation has superior knowledge, such as the statement of an expert, a person may rely on this statement of opinion.

In general, silence is not fraudulent, although in some instances the law does impose a duty to speak. If a person chooses to speak, he or she must tell the whole truth. Deceptive partial disclosures probably will be treated as fraudulent.

In the following case Geraldine Blane argued that Riley Business College perpetrated a fraud upon her. The court thought otherwise.

Blane v. Alabama Commercial College, Inc.
Supreme Court of Alabama
585 So. 2d 886 (1991)

RATIONAL

In 1988, Blane was a thirty-four-year-old housewife and part-time cook with a ninth-grade education. While watching television, she heard about Riley Business College (operated by Alabama Commercial College, Inc.). Blane spoke with a representative, Linda Brown, and expressed concern about her inability to type. Brown assured Blane of her ability to learn, explaining that the course was twenty-six weeks long and that thirteen weeks were devoted solely to typing instruction. Brown told Blane that the policy of Riley Business College was to require each student to pass a typing proficiency test at thirty-five words per minute before the student could receive a diploma. According to Brown, the test was designed to qualify students to compete in the job market. Blane enrolled and attended every class. At the completion of the course, Blane passed the final proficiency examination with a score of forty-six words per minute and nine errors. Blane graduated from the course in May 1989. Blane applied for approximately fifteen clerical positions to no avail. She then sued Riley Business College for breach of contract, fraud, and educational malpractice. The Supreme Court of Alabama ruled that Riley Business College was not guilty of fraud.

Steagall, Justice

Blane contends that Riley Business College represented to her that it would provide her with the necessary training to compete in the job market and that before she graduated she would have the minimum skills necessary to do so. Blane claims that these representations were fraudulent and that she relied on them prior to entering into a contract with the college. Riley Business College argues that its representations to Blane were in no way fraudulent, because Brown had explained to Blane prior to entering into the contract that the college's view of minimum skills for clerical positions is the ability to type 35 words per minute.

The essential elements of a fraud claim have been stated many times by this Court: "The essential elements of a fraud claim are (1) misrepresentation of a material fact; (2) made willfully to deceive, or recklessly without knowledge; (3) which was justifiably relied upon by the plaintiff under the circumstances; and (4) which caused damage as a proximate consequence."

We have also stated that evidence that a defendant made mere statements of opinion will not suffice as evidence of fraud inducing the signing of a contract. There must be a false assertion of fact that is relied on by the other party. The standard by which reliance is assessed in fraud cases is "justifiable reliance."

The record before us does not contain sufficient evidence to support an action for fraud. At the time Blane and Riley Business College entered into their agreement, the college promised to provide Blane with minimum clerical skills for her to compete in jobs in the clerical field. Prior to Blane's entering into a contract with Riley Business College, the college disclosed that its view of minimum skills was a typing proficiency of 35 words per minute. Blane agreed to pay Riley Business College $3,625 for a 26-week course that would enable her to obtain the minimum skills. At the end of the 26-week course, Blane was able to type at least 35 words per minute, as promised. Blane clearly received what she bargained for with Riley Business College.

The essence of Blane's claim is that she was unable to find employment in the computer/clerical field despite the training she received from Riley Business College. However, we find no cause of action for breach of contract or fraud stemming from such a claim, because there is no evidence that anyone from Riley Business College guaranteed Blane a job or gave her the assurance that she would find a job upon completing the 26-week course. Thus, the summary judgment was proper [in dismissing] the breach of contract and fraud claims.

Fraud in the sale of real estate is a very common occurrence. For example, suppose that Meyer knows her home has a leaky roof. She refuses to show her home when it is raining and fails to disclose the condition of the roof to the buyer prior to the sale. This situation and countless others have resulted in a tidal wave of suits by disgruntled buyers who felt the seller failed to make material disclosures about the property being offered. In response, many real estate agents have begun to require sellers to disclose all known defects in the property in question. Figure 10.1 illustrates the type of questions that might appear on a seller's disclosure form. These forms vary widely around the country. In places such as California, the form might include questions about mud slides and earthquakes, whereas in Florida such a form might ask for information about termites. When sellers make such disclosures, there is a much lower likelihood of a subsequent suit by a buyer, since the buyer knows in advance all the defects in the home.

Misrepresentation

A misrepresentation occurs when a person, by words or acts, creates in the mind of another person an impression not in accordance with the facts. If the seller of an automobile states, "The engine of this car has been rebuilt," when it has not been, and the buyer relies upon this statement in deciding to purchase the automobile, the buyer's assent is not freely and voluntarily given. The buyer may ask a court to free him or her of the contractual obligations under the automobile purchase contract.

Unlike fraud, in this cause of action it is not necessary to establish that the person making the misrepresentation did so intentionally. An unintentionally false statement will be sufficient to establish a case.

SELLER'S DISCLOSURE STATEMENT

SELLER: _____

BUYER: _____

PROPERTY: _____

THIS FORM IS AN INTEGRAL PART OF THE CONTRACT BETWEEN SELLER AND BUYER RESPECTING THE ABOVE PROPERTY. THIS FORM IS NOT A WARRANTY OR GUARANTEE OF ANY KIND BY SELLER, OR ANY REALTOR INVOLVED IN THE TRANSACTION, AND IS NO SUBSTITUTE FOR BUYER HAVING THE PROPERTY CAREFULLY EXAMINED FOR POTENTIAL PROBLEMS OR DEFECTS BY QUALIFIED PROFESSIONALS.

In this section , SELLER discloses in SELLER'S own words any material defects in the property of which SELLER is aware. A defect may be considered material if it is one which a buyer might reasonably regard as important in making the decision to purchase. SELLER should clearly describe any current problems and indicate any past history of problems even if they have been fully corrected. In paragraph No. 7, any significant repairs or alterations should be disclosed. Copies of repair invoices and inspection reports should be attached, if possible.

1. Do you know whether there has ever been any water leakage in the house or basement? If yes, explain and describe the frequency, location and extent:

   ☐ Yes ☐ No _____

2. Do you know whether the property has ever had termites or other wood destroying insects? If yes, state when it was treated and describe any damage:

   ☐ Yes ☐ No _____

3. Do you know whether there has ever been a problem with the foundation, roof, framing, or structure of the house? If yes, explain and describe any damage:

   ☐ Yes ☐ No _____

   Approximate Age of House _____ Approximate Age of Roof _____ Well or City Water? _____

4. Do you know whether the property has ever had radon gas, UFFI insulation, asbestos or other potential environmental hazards? Explain:

   ☐ Yes ☐ No _____

5. This house has: ☐ Sewer ☐ Septic. Do you know whether there has ever been a problem? If yes, explain:

   ☐ Yes ☐ No _____

6. Check if you are aware of serious defects in any of the following or if not in operating condition (strike it if it is not being sold to BUYER):

_____ Utility Lines or Hook-Ups	_____ Air Cleaning System	_____ Plumbing	_____ Fences or Gates
_____ Water Service	_____ Central Vacuum	_____ Plumbing Fixtures	_____ Lawn Sprinkler System
_____ Electrical System	_____ Microwave	_____ Washer/Dryer Hook-Up	_____ Wood Framing or Siding
_____ Heating or Ventilation	_____ Trash Compactor	_____ Water Softener	_____ Gas Heater/Propane Tank
_____ Central Air Conditioner	_____ Disposal	_____ Hot Water Heater	_____ Garage Door Opener
_____ Window Air Conditioner	_____ Dishwasher	_____ Sauna or Hot Tub	_____ Antenna/TV Dish
_____ Attic Fan	_____ Range	_____ Fireplace or Chimney	_____ Intercom
_____ Ceiling Fan	_____ Oven	_____ Fire/Smoke Detector	_____ Humidifier
_____ Exhaust Fan	_____ Refrigerator	_____ Burglar Alarm	_____ Pool/Pool Equipment

Check if you are aware of any of the following with respect to the property:

_____ Additions/Improvements	_____ Zoning/Set-Back Violations	_____ Encroachments/Easements
_____ Flooding/Sump Pumps	_____ Existing/Threatened Legal Action	_____ Fire Damage at Any Time
_____ Party Walls or Common Areas	_____ Code Violations/Liens/Assessments	_____ Landfill or Subterranean Problems
_____ Reappraisal/Reclassification	_____ Homes Association	_____ Problems with Water Supply

If you have checked any of the above, please explain what you know: _____

7. Disclose any material defects in the property not fully described above. Describe any significant repairs or alterations to the property and who did the work:

   _____

8. SELLER agrees to update this form when the property is sold and whenever conditions change at the property between now and the closing.

SELLER: _____ Date: _____   SELLER: _____ Date: _____

BUYER'S ACKNOWLEDGEMENT AND AGREEMENT

1. I HAVE CAREFULLY INSPECTED THE PROPERTY. SUBJECT TO ANY INSPECTIONS ALLOWED UNDER MY CONTRACT WITH SELLER, I AGREE TO PURCHASE THE PROPERTY IN ITS PRESENT CONDITION ONLY, WITHOUT WARRANTIES OR GUARANTEES OF ANY KIND BY SELLER OR ANY REALTOR CONCERNING THE CONDITION OR VALUE OF THE PROPERTY.

2. I AGREE TO VERIFY ANY OF THE ABOVE INFORMATION THAT IS IMPORTANT TO ME BY AN INDEPENDENT INVESTIGATION OF MY OWN. I HAVE BEEN ADVISED TO HAVE THE PROPERTY EXAMINED BY PROFESSIONAL INSPECTORS.

3. I ACKNOWLEDGE THAT NEITHER SELLER NOR ANY REALTOR INVOLVED IN THIS TRANSACTION IS AN EXPERT AT DETECTING OR REPAIRING PHYSICAL DEFECTS IN THE PROPERTY. I STATE THAT NO IMPORTANT REPRESENTATIONS CONCERNING THE CONDITION OF THE PROPERTY ARE BEING RELIED UPON BY ME EXCEPT AS DISCLOSED ABOVE OR AS FULLY SET FORTH AS FOLLOWS: ___

_____

BUYER: _____ Date: _____   BUYER: _____ Date: _____

THIS IS A LEGALLY BINDING AGREEMENT. IF NOT UNDERSTOOD, CONSULT AN ATTORNEY.

LISTING COMPANY

Figure 10.1 Seller's Disclosure Statement

The concepts of fraud and undue misrepresentation come into play in the following case.

Vokes v. Arthur Murray, Inc.
District Court of Appeal of Florida
212 So. 2d 906 (1968)

Audrey E. Vokes filed an action to rescind (set aside) her contracts entered into with Arthur Murray, Inc., alleging fraud and undue influence on the part of agents of this business. Vokes entered into over thirty-one thousand dollars in contracts with the defendant. The trial court dismissed her complaint for failure to state a cause of action. The court of appeals disagreed, stating that Vokes had stated enough facts to merit a trial, and reversed the trial court's finding.

Pierce, Judge

Defendant Arthur Murray, Inc., a corporation, authorizes the operation throughout the nation of dancing schools under the name of "Arthur Murray School of Dancing" through local franchised operators, one of whom was defendant J. P. Davenport, whose dancing establishment was in Clearwater.

Plaintiff Mrs. Audrey E. Vokes, a widow of 51 years and without family, had a yen to be "an accomplished dancer" with the hopes of finding "new interest in life." So, on February 10, 1961, she attended a "dance party" at Davenport's "School of Dancing," where she whiled away the pleasant hours, sometimes in a private room during which her grace and poise were elaborated upon and her rosy future as "an excellent dancer" was painted for her in vivid and glowing colors. She was sold eight one-half-hour dance lessons to be utilized within one calendar month therefrom, for the sum of $14.50 cash in hand paid, obviously a baited "come-on."

Thus, she embarked upon an almost endless pursuit of the terpsichorean art during which, over a period of less than sixteen months, she was sold fourteen "dance courses" totalling in the aggregate 2,302 hours of dancing lessons for a total cash outlay of $31,090.45, all at Davenport's dance emporium. All of these fourteen courses were evidenced by execution of a written "Enrollment Agreement—Arthur Murray's School of Dancing" with the addendum in heavy black print. "No

one will be informed that you are taking dancing lessons. Your relations with us are held in strict confidence," setting forth the number of "dancing lessons" and the "lessons in rhythm sessions" currently sold to her from time to time, and always of course accompanied by payment of cash of the realm.

At one point she was sold 545 additional hours of dancing to be entitled to award of the "Bronze Medal" signifying that she had reached "the Bronze Standard," a supposedly designation of dance achievement by students of Arthur Murray, Inc.

Later she was sold an additional 926 hours in order to gain the "Silver Medal," indicating she had reached "the Silver Standard," at a cost of $12,501.35.

At one point, while she still had to her credit about 900 unused hours of instructions, she was induced to purchase an additional 24 hours of lessons to participate in a trip to Miami at her own expense, where she would be "given the opportunity to dance with members of the Miami Studio."

She was induced at another point to purchase an additional 126 hours of lessons in order to be not only eligible for the Miami trip but also to become "a life member of the Arthur Murray Studio," carrying with it certain dubious emoluments, at a further cost of $1,752.30.

At another point, while she still had over 1,000 unused hours of instruction she was induced to buy 151 additional hours at a cost of $2,049.00 to be eligible for a "Student Trip to Trinidad," at her own expense as she later learned.

Also, when she still had 1,100 unused hours to her credit she was prevailed upon to purchase an additional 347 hours at a cost of $4,235.74, to qualify her to receive a "Gold Medal" for achievement, indicating she had advanced to "the Gold Standard."

On another occasion, while she still had over 1,200 unused hours, she was induced to buy an additional 175 hours of instruction at a cost of $2,472.75 to be eligible "to take a trip to Mexico."

Finally, sandwiched in between other lesser sales promotions, she was influenced to buy an additional 481 hours of instruction at a cost of $6,523.81 in order to "be classified as a Gold Bar Member, the ultimate achievement of the dancing studio."

All the foregoing sales promotions, illustrative of the entire fourteen separate contracts, were procured by defendant Davenport and Arthur Murray, Inc., by false representations to her that she was improving in her dancing ability, that she had excellent potential, that she was responding to instructions in dancing grace, and that they were developing her into a beautiful dancer, whereas in truth and in fact she did not develop in her dancing ability, she had no "dance aptitude," and in fact had difficulty in "hearing the musical beat." The complaint alleged that such representations to her "were in fact false and known by the defendant to be false and contrary to the plantiff's true ability, the truth of plaintiff's ability being fully known to the defendants, but withheld from the plaintiff for the sole and specific intent to deceive and defraud the plaintiff and to induce her in the purchasing of additional hours of dance lessons." It was averred that the lessons were sold to her "in total disregard to the true physical, rhythm, and mental ability of the plaintiff." In other words, while she first exulted that she was entering the "spring of her life," she finally was awakened to the fact there was "spring" neither in her life nor in her feet.

The complaint prayed that the Court decree the dance contracts to be null and void and to be canceled, that an accounting be had, and judgment entered against the defendants "for that portion of the $31,090.45 not charged against specific hours of instruction given to the plaintiff." The Court held the complaint not to state a cause of action and dismissed it with prejudice. We disagree and reverse.

Defendants contend that contracts can only be rescinded for fraud or misrepresentation when the alleged misrepresentation is as to a material fact, rather than an opinion, prediction or expectation, and that the statements and representations set forth at length in the complaint were in the category of "trade puffing," within its legal orbit.

It is true that "generally a misrepresentation, to be actionable, must be one of fact rather than opinion." But this rule has significant qualifications, applicable here. It does not apply where there is a fiduciary relationship between the parties, or where there has been some artifice or trick employed by the representor, or where the parties do not in general deal at "arm's length" as we understand the phrase, or where the representee does not have equal opportunity to become apprised of the truth or falsity of the fact represented. As stated by Judge Allen of this Court: " . . . A statement of a party having . . . superior knowledge may be regarded as a statement of fact although it would be considered as opinion if the parties were dealing on equal terms."

It would be reasonably supposed here that defendants had "superior knowledge" as to whether plaintiff had "dance potential" and as to whether she was noticeably improving in the art of terpsichore. And it would be a reasonable inference from the undenied averments of the complaint that the flowery eulogiums heaped upon her by defendants as a prelude to her contracting for 1,944 additional hours of instruction in order to attain the rank of the Bronze Standard, thence to the bracket of the Silver Standard, thence to the class of the Gold Bar Standard, and finally to the crowning plateau of a Life Member of the Studio, proceeded as much or more from the urge to "ring the cash register" as from any honest or realistic appraisal of her dancing prowess or a factual representation of her progress.

Even in contractual situations where a party to a transaction owes no duty to disclose facts within his knowledge or to answer inquiries respecting such facts, the law is if he undertakes to do so he must disclose the whole truth. From the face of the complaint, it should have been reasonably apparent to defendants that her vast outlay of cash for the many hundreds of additional hours of instruction was not justified by her slow and awkward progress, which she would have been made well aware of if they had spoken the "whole truth."

In *Hirschman v. Hodges* it was said that " . . . what is plainly injurious to good faith ought to be considered as a fraud sufficient to impeach a contract," and that an agreement may be avoided " . . . because of surprise, or mistake, *want of freedom, undue influence, the suggestion of falsehood, or the suppression of truth.*" (Emphasis supplied.)

We repeat that where parties are dealing on a contractual basis at arm's length with no inequities or inherently unfair practices employed, the Courts will in general "leave the parties where they find themselves."

But in the case sub judice, from the allegations of the unanswered complaint, we cannot say that enough of the accompanying ingredients as mentioned in the foregoing authorities, were not present which otherwise would have barred the equitable arm of the Court to her. In our view, from the showing made in her complaint, plaintiff is entitled to her day in Court.

Undue Influence

Undue influence is present if a person agrees to a contract because of the stronger personality or will of the other party. Undue influence differs from duress in that, in the case of duress, a person yields his or her assent because of fear, whereas in the case of undue influence, the person assents to the contract because he or she is unable to hold out against the will of the other party. A person under stress for example, might assent to a contract because of the other person's pressure.

Duress

Suppose that a person coerces another person to enter into a contract through the use of a wrongful act or a wrongful threat. This constitutes duress. The person subjected to the coercion assents to the contract because of an extreme fear that precludes the exercise of free will and judgment. An obvious example is holding a gun to someone's head to force that person to consent to the contract. Under such circumstances, the person would be unable to exercise free will and judgment, fearful of the consequences associated with *not* entering into the contract. The law would refuse to recognize such an agreement.

THE STATUTE OF FRAUDS + PURGURIES

It is not necessary for a contract to be in writing to be valid. Many oral contracts are perfectly enforceable. When a person purchases candy, the purchase constitutes a sale of goods which the law treats as a contract. A contract for the sale of goods need not be in writing if the price of the goods is less than five hundred dollars.

Certain types of contracts, however, must be in writing to be enforceable. The requirement of a writing has its origins in the British statute of frauds enacted by Parliament in 1677. The British statute was designed to prevent perjury—false testimony under oath. The British thought that certain types of contracts were likely to give rise to perjured testimony in the absence of a writing. To remedy this problem, the British Parliament required proof of certain types of contracts in writing. If the person claiming a contract could not produce a writing reflecting the agreement between the parties, the agreement would not be enforced.

Every state has passed a statute of frauds. The terms of these statutes vary from state to state, but in general they prevent the following types of contracts from being enforced in the absence of writing:

1. Contracts to be liable for another person's debts

2. Contracts involving real property

3. Contracts that cannot by their terms be performed within one year from the date the contract was entered into by the parties *12 MONTHS COUNTS AS IN ONE YEAR*

For example, if Peters says to Swanson, "I will pay Harvey's debt if Harvey fails to pay you," such a statement must be in writing to be enforceable. If Peters agrees to purchase a home from Anderson, because such a contract involves real estate, it must be in writing to be enforceable. If Peters asks his bank to extend the time during which he can pay his note to the bank by two years, a contract to extend the note for two years cannot be performed within one year therefore it must be in writing to be enforceable.

States may require other types of contracts to be in writing, but these contracts generally must be in writing everywhere to be enforceable. Certain exceptions exist. For example, in some cases partial performance of a contract will take it out of the statute of frauds.

A contract that has been fully performed by both parties in the contract is not subject to the statute of frauds. Suppose A orally offers to sell his home to B for fifty thousand dollars, and B accepts. B pays the fifty thousand dollars and takes title to and possession of the home. Neither party may ask to get out of this contract on the basis of the statute of frauds, because both parties have fully performed.

Contracts involving the sale of goods are subject to a separate statute of frauds found in Article Two of the Uniform Commercial Code. The UCC states that contracts for the sale of goods for a price of five hundred dollars or more are not enforceable unless they are evidenced by some writing sufficient to indicate a contract of sale has been made. As with the statute of frauds that applies to common law contracts, the code statute of frauds is subject to exceptions. For example, a person who admits in court that a contract for sale was made is bound by his or her admission.

Type of Writing Required

A formal writing drafted by an attorney is not required to make a contract enforceable. Generally all that is required is a writing that covers the basic terms of the agreement and that is signed by the party against whom enforcement is sought.

The Parol Evidence Rule

The parol evidence rule states that oral testimony that adds to, alters, or varies the terms of the written agreement cannot ordinarily be used as evidence in court. This rule establishes that where parties reduce their agreement to a detailed, complete writing, only the writing should serve as evidence of their agreement.

The following example shows how the parol evidence rule operates in practice. Four students rent an apartment for four hundred dollars per month. One of the students moves out and the remaining three students locate another person, Chuck, who agrees to move in the apartment. He visits with the manager of the apartment complex. Chuck asks the manager if he will be responsible for only one-fourth of the rent, or one hundred dollars. The manager confirms this. No one else hears the conversation, Chuck signs a contract, which includes a clause that he does not understand: ''In the event the premises are rented to one or more individuals, each of the individuals shall be jointly and severally liable for the rental due under this agreement and the performance of the terms and conditions of this agreement.'' Soon thereafter, the other three students decide they dislike Chuck, and they vacate the apartment. The manager then informs Chuck that he must pay the entire rent of four hundred dollars. The parol evidence rule creates a serious problem for Chuck. The clause in question makes him individually responsible for the entire rent of $400. The parol evidence rule prohibits the introduction at trial of what the manager told him.

The parol evidence rule focuses on promises that were made prior to the making of the writing or at the same time as the making of the writing. The parol evidence rule does not affect an agreement entered into subsequent to the writing. Such a modification of an existing agreement, of course, might in its own right require a writing under the provisions of the statute of frauds, and might also require its own separate consideration.

Rationale for Rule

The underlying rationale is that if a writing is produced to establish or memorialize an agreement, the writing should be considered to be an embodiment of all the terms that were agreed upon at the time. The practical significance of this rule is clear—if you have a written agreement, make sure that it includes all the important terms.

Exceptions to Rule

Under certain circumstances courts will admit testimonial evidence of terms that are not part of the writing. Clearly this makes sense if the written contract is obviously incomplete. Testimony is permitted to fill in gaps. Similarly, testimony may be used to clear up ambiguity in the written agreement or to correct an obvious clerical error. Oral evidence is also admissible to show that a contract is void or voidable. Thus, if a party was induced—through misrepresentation, fraud, mistake, undue influence, or duress—to enter into a contract, testimony can be used to prove the absence of genuine assent.

It is true that the courts generally will not permit a party to introduce evidence of an oral understanding to alter the terms of a detailed, complete writing. It is also true that certain contracts must be in writing to be enforceable. It is not true that one must read such a written contract before signing it. On the other hand, as noted in the next section, it can be risky to fail to read an agreement before signing it.

Duty to Read

General Rule

The general rule regarding the duty to read before signing a contract is that a person is bound by what he or she signs. The *Restatement of Contracts*, Section

70 (1932), states: "One who makes a written offer which is accepted, or who manifests acceptance of the terms of a writing which he should reasonably understand to be an offer or proposed contract, is bound by the contract though ignorant of the terms of a writing or of its proper interpretation."

This rule suggests that before signing a written contract, a person needs to read the contract provisions. If a person signs without reading, he or she runs the risk of being bound by the contract even though failing to read or comprehend its terms.

This general rule is subject to some exceptions. Certainly people are not bound by an illegal contract. Other exceptions also exist.

Rationale for Rule

By enforcing a contract against someone who failed to read a document or failed to comprehend it, the courts lend certainty to the law of contracts. No one could rely on a signed document if the other party could avoid the transaction by saying he or she had not read or did not understand the writing. If the courts let a person out of a contract under these circumstances, all predictability and certainty of business contractual relationships would be destroyed. Parties to a contract would never be certain whether the contract would be enforced or not. The way to avoid the harsh results that might flow from the doctrine of the duty to read is to read contracts before signing them.

Modern Trend

The more modern cases search for a true assent to the terms of a contractual agreement. Simply having presented a complex contract to the other party for an immediate signature quite frequently will not be sufficient to convince a court that the person signing really agreed to all the terms in the contract. To adopt a contrary rule would reward the unethical seller who cleverly drafts a contract with many inconspicuous, harsh provisions and then pressures the other person into signing the contract without reading it.

Thus, in determining whether a person actually assented to the terms of a contract, a court should determine whether that person had the opportunity to read the contract, understood the provisions in question, and had a real opportunity to accept or reject the provisions.

This view is not necessarily followed by all courts: The law in this area is changing, and unformity of results does not exist.

Suppose that Andrews, the owner of an apartment complex, proposed that Wilson sign a one-year lease on an apartment. A provision in the lease stated that Wilson would be liable for any injury to any person coming into her apartment— even if Andrews caused the injury in question. Andrews stated that he needed to go somewhere immediately, therefore he did not have time to wait for Wilson to read the contract. Furthermore, Andrews stated that if Wilson failed to sign right then, he would not rent the apartment to her. Wilson needed to find an apartment right away because she had come from out of town for the day to locate a place to live and she needed to return home that evening. Under these circumstances, a court quite likely would find that Andrews was not bound by the liability provision in the contract.

You should bear in mind, however, that many courts still rigidly follow the rule stated in the *Restatement of Contracts*, Section 70. It is possible that a court might rule that Wilson would be bound by even the liability provision in the contract if she signed it.

The best course of action is to assume that you will be bound by whatever is in a contract. One should always read a contract before signing it. If anything about the contract is unclear, one should consider getting legal advice before signing the agreement.

INTERPRETATION OF CONTRACTUAL PROVISIONS

Once the parties have entered into a valid contract, problems still can arise over the meaning of the contract language itself. The English language, even when the words are carefully chosen by competent attorneys representing all the parties, is subject to varying interpretations.

Who Interprets the Words in a Contract?

A contract is a privately negotiated agreement. Lawyers or judges are called upon to *interpret* a contract only when the parties choose to avail themselves of these sources of interpretation.

In most situations, the parties never utilize the services of a lawyer or a judge to interpret a contract. Even when a law firm or in-house legal staff drafts an agreement, in the final analysis the parties to the contract end up interpreting the agreement. Quite often, for various reasons, they bypass the legal staff and simply give their own interpretation to a document—perhaps a meaning the lawyers who drafted it never intended. The parties may actually guess what they think the document means, especially if they find themselves pressed for time and the words or phrases in question deal with a relatively trivial matter.

Thus, the parties may entirely distort the "true" meaning of an agreement. Consider this example. Bill Moore of Wet Pools, Inc., using a standard industry contract, fills in the blanks on the form. On the date set for completion, he writes "May 1". Frances and Curtis Heck, the buyers, sign the agreement. Bill finishes digging the hole and pouring the cement walls by May 1. However, the concrete deck around the pool remains unfinished and he still must install the pool equipment. Has Bill complied with the agreement? What can the Hecks do about his failure to finish the deck by May 1?

As a practical matter, there is no way to force the pool company to complete the job by May 1 (even if a court would disagree with the contractor's interpretation) without going to court. If the Hecks sued the contractor, he might stop working on the job. The Hecks might find it difficult, if not impossible, to locate another contractor at the last minute. Furthermore, it costs a lot of money and takes time to litigate a case. To avoid such a situation, it is best to draft a contract in the first place that penalizes the builder in some way for failure to complete the pool by the stated date.

The parties also may distort the meaning of a contract because of misunderstandings between them. Consider the following situation. The tenant says to the landlord, "Do you mind if I put a fence around the yard?" The landlord gives the tenant permission to erect a fence. The landlord envisions a standard, three-foot-high hurricane fence. The tenant thereafter puts up an eight-foot-high chicken wire fence and uses stakes that look like telephone poles, anchored in cement. Obviously, the parties failed to communicate. The landlord simply assumed the tenant intended to erect a standard fence. Yet the landlord gave the tenant a blanket right to construct any sort of fence whatsoever. A more thorough discussion might have resulted in a better understanding on the part of the parties.

It is, of course, possible for a party to intentionally misinterpret the language of a contract. Suppose that a real estate broker hires a real estate agent to make sales by merely filling in the blanks on forms that the broker supplies to the agent. In other words, the broker hires the agent to collect information, not to act as a legal advisor for the parties. When the agent sits down at a table and fills out the purchase agreement, a few buyers may actually insist upon *reading* the contract first. In the course of reviewing it, such buyers sometimes discover phrases they fail to comprehend. In such a situation, the agent fears that the buyers may ask to discuss the terms of the contract with an attorney. Consultation merely slows the whole process down and gives either the buyers or the sellers time to change their minds. The agent, on the other hand, wants his or her commission. Under such circumstances, an unethical agent might succumb to the temptation to give a personal explanation of the phrase in question—an explanation that satisfies the buyers sufficiently to convince them to sign the contract at that time.

Personality is an added factor here. Imagine a meek purchaser in the hands of a self-confident, strong-willed, aggressive agent. The agent states her or his interpretation of the contract very forcefully and very authoritatively, all the while secretly knowing she or he really has no idea what the particular contractual provision means. The buyers, hearing that tone of confidence, accept the agent's interpretation as definitive. Of course, it is not. The agent is not a legal advisor. When in doubt, a party should first consult an attorney to obtain a legal interpretation before signing a contract.

The moral is to draft more precise contracts. The greater the need for interpretation, the more discretion the attorney places in the hands of the interpreter. The more explicit the agreement, the less room exists for an incorrect interpretation of the document—assuming that the parties, in fact, read the contract and know its contents.

When parties disagree about the meaning of contract language, they may be forced to turn to a court for interpretation of the agreement, as is illustrated by the following case.

Burroughs v. Metro-Goldwyn-Mayer, Inc.
United States District Court, Southern District New York
519 F. Supp. 388 (1981)   *RATIONALE*

Edgar Rice Burroughs wrote the book *Tarzan of the Apes* in 1912. He later transferred his interest in this book to Edgar Rice Burroughs, Inc. In 1931, MGM acquired the right to use the Tarzan character and other characters appearing in Burroughs's works in an original story to be created by MGM as a screenplay for a motion picture. MGM also acquired the right to produce remakes of the first film. Any remake had to be based <u>substantially</u> on the first MGM film, without material changes or material departures from the original MGM story line. MGM released the first film in 1932. It issued a remake of the film in 1959. By 1980, MGM had begun work on yet another Tarzan film. The heirs of Burroughs brought suit to enjoin release of the new MGM film. They contended this new film, starring Bo Derek, was a material departure from the original film. After viewing all three films in question, the court concluded MGM had not breached the contract.

Werker, District Judge

The 1931 agreement provides as follows:

. . . Metro agrees . . . that all "remakes" of the first photoplay produced by it hereunder, as well as all other photoplays produced by it hereunder subsequent to the making of said first photoplay, shall be based substantially upon the same story as that used by Metro in connection with said first photoplay and that in such subsequent remakes and/or additional photoplays there will be no material changes or material departures from the story used in connection with said first photoplay . . . .

After viewing the films in question, I must conclude for the reasons that follow that MGM's 1981 remake of the film "Tarzan, The Ape Man" is based substantially on the 1931 photoplay and that there are no material changes or material departures from the story used in that photoplay. My analysis will focus on the storyline as well as the portrayal of the characters and their relationships.

The 1931 photoplay is based on the story of an explorer James Parker, whose daughter Jane joins him in Africa. The movie opens with Jane's arrival and her father's decision shortly thereafter to set off on a safari in search of the fabled "elephants' graveyard" for ivory. In this film, Parker is portrayed as a strong man and Jane as his admiring daughter. There is a suggestion of sexuality in their relationship. The expedition consists of Parker, Jane, Parker's partner Harry Holt, and several natives. On the journey, the party is faced with nearly insurmountable struggles with nature. For example, Jane almost falls off a cliff in the scene of the party crossing the escarpment and Holt is nearly devoured by crocodiles as the

party crosses a river on rafts. It is the scene where the party crosses the escarpment that Tarzan's cry is heard for the first time.

After the party crosses the river, Jane is terrorized by an attacking animal and Tarzan appears from the jungle to rescue her. He carries her off and at this point, Jane discovers that Tarzan is human. She gradually begins to trust him and they appear to fall in love. After a brief stay with Tarzan in which Jane seems quite content, she is found by her father and Holt. They are exceedingly distrustful of the ape-man. She rejoins the safari and the group sets out again for the elephants' graveyard. While enroute, the party falls prey to a tribe of pygmies and they are threatened with death when they are thrown into a pit with a huge gorilla. Tarzan, of course, comes to their rescue. Holt, Parker, Jane and Tarzan then follow a wounded elephant to the elephant's graveyard, where Parker dies. Jane decides to stay with Tarzan and Holt returns to civilization.

In the 1981 film, the story similarly opens with Jane's arrival at her father's camp in Africa. This time, however, Parker is a professional adventurer rather than an explorer. He is a strong man and a bit more eccentric than in the first film. Jane, though admiring, is more hostile toward her father. There again is an element of sexuality in their relationship. As in the 1931 photoplay, shortly after Jane's arrival, Parker, Holt, Jane and some natives set out on an expedition to find the elephants' graveyard. While on the journey, the group hears Tarzan's cry and in contrast to the 1931 film, this time Parker speculates that this is the famed 100 foot ape-man. Jane again is imperilled by wild animals enroute and rescued by Tarzan. Holt and Parker are highly distrustful of Tarzan as they were in the original film, but Jane again perceives that he is human. Although his initial encounter with Jane is brief, Tarzan clearly is fascinated by her. He later captures her while she is swimming in a river. She gets away from him, but is then attacked by a snake. As in the original photoplay, Tarzan comes to her rescue. It is at this point that Jane becomes enamored of Tarzan. After what seems to be a couple of days, Parker finally finds his daughter and she rejoins the safari. The group is soon attacked by an African tribe, however, and Tarzan comes to their rescue. Parker nevertheless dies at the hands of the ivory king and Jane and Tarzan leave Holt to live together in the wild.

While there are some differences between the films in the jeopardies and dramatic sequences employed, as well as in the emphasis accorded different elements of the story, they are insufficient to warrant the conclusion that this Tarzan movie is not based substantially upon the 1931 story. The use of the phrase ''based substantially'' contemplates some deviation from the original story. In addition, the fact that the contract prohibits only material departures and material changes demonstrates that changes and departures were in fact contemplated by the parties.

Plaintiffs argue that the changes and departures in the 1981 photoplay are material. Their principal contention is that the film is no longer suitable for young children. Considering the shift in social mores over the half century from 1931 to 1981, I simply cannot agree that a change of the nature complained of constitutes a material change from the 1931 photoplay. Indeed, the 1931 film itself contained scenes which for its time were rather suggestive.

Since the overall theme of the 1981 film, development of the plot, order of sequence and locus of the 1981 photoplay as edited conform to the 1931 photoplay, I can only conclude that the storyline in the 1981 film is based substantially on the 1931 film and does not contain material departures or changes from that photoplay.

Since I have concluded that the 1981 film as edited is based substantially on the 1931 film and does not contain material changes or material departures from the 1931 film, an injunction permanently restraining release and distribution of the film will not be issued.

Burroughs v. *Metro-Goldwyn-Mayer* demonstrates the fact that two persons, looking at the *same* language within a contract, may arrive at differing interpretations of the meaning of the contract. Even words carefully selected by a skilled attorney may lead to differences of opinion.

The heirs of Burroughs regarded the book *Tarzan of the Apes* and the original photoplay based on that book as wholesome, family entertainment. When they saw the 1980 film staring Bo Derek, the heirs thought that the new film lacked the wholesome quality of the original photoplay. In the absence of this attribute, they alleged that MGM had breached its obligation to base the new film ''substantially upon the same story'' as the 1932 film. MGM took the position that the contract permitted it to deviate, in minor respects, from the original story.

The inability of the parties to come to an agreement on the meaning of the terminology ''based substantially on the same story'' forced the parties to resort to a court for a definitive interpretation of the agreement. In interpreting the meaning of a contractual phrase, a court might attempt to inquire what the parties to the contract intended to accomplish through the use of the particular language that appears in the contract. In this case, the death of Edgar Rice Burroughs made it impossible to ask for his opinion of the contract. Quite likely the other parties involved in the drafting of the agreement either also had died or had forgotten what they intended to accomplish.

Refer back to Chapter 4, ''Judicial Reasoning and Decision Making.'' In that chapter we discuss a number of factors that judges acknowledge in making decisions. One of those factors was "doing what is right." The judge in this case probably in effect was attempting to "do what is right." In this task, the judge needed to rely on his subjective judgment of the proper resolution of this dispute as there was very little else to guide him in resolving this case. A more explicit contract might have not only assisted the judge in his role as interpreter of this contract, it might have eliminated the need to go to court in the first place as the contract might have been clear on its face as to what type of remake was permitted.

While it is often difficult to determine the "true" meaning of a contract, a more difficult question in some cases is whether to enter into a contract at all. The box below addresses this issue in the context of the sale of military weapons.

RIGHTS OF THIRD PARTIES

In most situations, only the parties to a contract have any rights in the contract. However, there are two situations in which someone who was not a party to a contract may have an interest in a contract: (1) by assignment or (2) as a third-party beneficiary.

Assignments
An **assignment** is a transfer by one party to a contract of his or her rights under the contract to someone who was not a party to the original contract. The party who transfers the rights is called the **assignor**. The party to whom rights are transferred is called the **assignee**. As a general rule, a party may assign all of his or her rights under a contract.

Suppose that Lawrence Heating and Cooling sells an air-conditioning unit to Janice Brooks for seventeen hundred dollars. Lawrence needs money immediately in order to keep its business running so it assigns its right to payment from Brooks to the First National Bank. First National pays Lawrence fifteen hundred

---

The Military/Industrial Complex: International Sales/Ethics

A government accounts for a great deal of the consumption and spending in the United States. Between the federal, state, and local governments, governmental entities account for at least 30 percent of the gross domestic product in America. This means that much of business entails not selling to private businesses or persons but selling to a governmental entity.

The federal government is responsible for entire industries that supply services and equipment to the military:

McDonnell Douglas, Boeing, Allied Signal, and Ratheon, to name but a few, are all huge suppliers of products to the U. S. military.

During World War II, the fortunes of military contractors blossomed. Following World War II, the cold war encouraged the United States to keep its military spending at historically high peace time levels. This kept a lot of people employed in the military and in the defense industry.

As the military began to shrink in size in the mid 1990's, both the military and military contractors began to face new questions. One of the most difficult ethical questions is: Should the defense industry move from producing weapons for the U. S. military to producing weapons for foreign governments?

On the plus side of this issue is the fact that these companies need business in order to survive. If the U.S. government no longer provides them with an adequate amount of work to keep the companies in business, these companies could replace the work lost to the U.S. government with sales abroad. Such sales would enhance the number of exports from the United States which would improve our balance of trade with other nations. We can also take the position that if we do not make these sales, some other company elsewhere in the world will do so.

American companies cannot simply enter into a contract to sell weaponry to a foreign government—especially in the case of weapons involving our national security. In many cases, a company must first obtain the permission of the U.S. government to make a sale of weapons abroad. Even assuming the federal government gives its blessing to the sale of weapons, ethical questions arise in such sales.

Some governments intend to use their weapons not only defensively but offensively as well. The Gulf War in 1990 between Kuwait and Iraq is one recent instance of the aggressive use of weapons. A war, even a short war, can kill and maim many people, result in massive property losses, disrupt the free enterprise system, destroy irreplaceable natural resources, and change the very course of history.

The dilemma of whether to sell weapons becomes all the more frightening when one considers the question of the sale of rocket and nuclear technology to potentially aggressive countries. For many years the U.S. government tried to discourage the proliferation of nuclear weapons in the world. Taking into consideration the massive potential for destruction posed by even a 20-megaton bomb, it is difficult to question the wisdom of this policy. While it is unlikely that U.S. contractors would ever be permitted to sell such knowledge to foreign countries, that does not mean they will not acquire this information elsewhere.

As conventional weapons and nuclear technology proliferate, we are setting the stage for a war that no one can control.

dollars for the contract. Lawrence is the assignor of the right to receive money from Brooks. First National is the assignee. The bank now has a right to receive seventeen hundred dollars from Brooks.

When an assignment is made, the assignee takes whatever rights the assignor possessed. The assignee also takes the contract subject to any defenses that exist against the assignor. The assignee in effect "steps into the shoes of the assignor." In the prior example, suppose that Lawrence defrauded Brooks. When First National attempts to collect from Brooks, Brooks could assert the defense of fraud against First National.

While it is generally true that an assignor may assign all of his or her rights under a contract, there are exceptions. Sometimes it is not possible to assign rights under a contract without the consent of the other party to the contract to such an assignment. For example, if a contract is highly personal in nature, such that it involves a relationship of special confidence or trust, the contract cannot be assigned. Suppose that Mildred Smith hires Jack Lansky to paint her portrait. Smith may not assign her rights under this personal service contract to Hoffman.

Further, a contractual right cannot be assigned when the assignment would place an additional burden or risk on the original party obligated to perform under the contract. Suppose that a corporation in St. Louis agrees to deliver goods to a buyer in Chicago. The buyer in Chicago could not assign its rights to another business in Honolulu and expect that St. Louis seller to deliver the goods to Honolulu instead.

In certain instances, a contract may contain a clause that expressly prohibits assignment. Courts today tend to disfavor such provisions with respect to the assignment of rights, particularly in the case of the assignment of the right to receive money.

When a contract is assigned, the assignee needs to notify the party originally obligated under the contract. Notification protects the assignee in case the party originally obligated to perform pays the original assignor or the assignor attempts to assign this right to other persons. For example, suppose that debtor owes creditor five hundred dollars. Creditor assigns the right to five hundred dollars to First National Bank. The bank needs to notify debtor to pay it, rather than the original creditor. If the bank fails to provide such a notice and debtor pays the original creditor, the bank will be unable to collect from debtor. It would, of course, have rights against creditor in this situation.

Delegation of Duties

In general, if a person's duties under a contract do not involve personal skill or a relation of trust and confidence, and the contract does not expressly prohibit the delegation of duties, a person may delegate his or her duties under a contract. Delegation of a contractual duty does not relieve the original party of responsibility for the competent performance of that duty. Suppose that Smith agrees to paint Jones's home. Smith delegates his duty under this contract to Akins. Akins does a very poor job of painting Jones's house. In this situation, Jones could recover damages from Smith.

Third-Party Beneficiaries

A contract may confer benefits upon a person who was not a party to the original contract. The person who receives such benefits is called a **third-party beneficiary**. There are two broad categories: intended beneficiaries and incidental beneficiaries.

Intentional Benefit

A third party who benefits from a contract is an **intended beneficiary** if a major purpose of one of the contracting parties was to benefit the third party. The courts recognize two such persons: donee beneficiaries and creditor beneficiaries.

If a person entered into a contract in order to make a gift upon a third party, the third party is called a *donee beneficiary*. For example, suppose that John Johnson purchases a life insurance policy from Acme Insurance. John names his daughter, Christina, as the beneficiary of the life insurance policy. Even though Christina was not a party to the contract between Acme and her father, she can require the company to pay her the benefits due under the policy in the event her father dies.

If the major purpose of the contract is to discharge debts or duties that one of the parties to the contract owes to someone else, then the third party is a *creditor beneficiary*. Suppose that Mark Russell agrees to sell his home to Cheryl Sanders for one hundred thousand dollars. Cheryl pays Mark seventy-five thousand dollars in cash and also gives Mark a twenty-five-thousand-dollar note. At a later date Cheryl sells the home to Beth Salvani. Beth, as part of the purchase price, agrees to assume the twenty-five-thousand-dollar note payable to Mark Russell. Mark is a third-party creditor beneficiary of the contract between Cheryl and Beth. Mark can enforce Beth's contractual promise to pay the twenty-five-thousand-dollar note.

Incidental Benefit

Sometimes parties enter into a contract which, if the contract is performed, will also benefit a person who is not a party to the contract. The parties did not intend to discharge a debt owed to this third party, nor did they intend to confer a gift upon this person. The parties did not intend to benefit this person at all. Such a person, called *an incidental beneficiary*, does not have any rights under the contract and is not permitted to sue for the nonperformance of the contract. Suppose that Acme Construction contracts to build a thousand-unit apartment complex in which it agrees to install Whirlpool appliances. Acme instead installs GE appliances. Although this contract would have benefited Whirlpool, Whirlpool has no right to sue the builder for not using its products in the apartment complex.

■■■ TERMINATION OF A CONTRACT

Methods of Discharge

A contract may come to an end in one of three ways: by performance, agreement, or operation of law.

Performance

The vast bulk of contracts are terminated by the parties to the contract performing their obligations under the contract. When the law requires no further performance from the parties, their obligations are said to be discharged.

Agreement

Sometimes a contract is discharged through an agreement of the parties to terminate the original contract. The agreement to terminate a contract by mutual consent must be supported by consideration. Suppose that Jackson Transportation entered into a contract to employ Mike Walters as a manager. Walters thereafter learns of a better employment opportunity and Jackson locates a person who appears better qualified than Walters. In such a situation, the parties might mutually agree to terminate the original employment contract.

Operation of Law

A contract may be discharged by operation of law. Various legal rules exist which will cause contractual obligations to be discharged under certain circumstances. For example, courts will discharge the parties from a contract if a change in the law makes performance of the contract illegal. Suppose that a person enters into a contract to sell alcohol and then the state legislature outlaws such sales. The courts will discharge the parties from their contractual obligations.

Conditions of Performance

As noted above, at some point in time the parties to a contract no longer have any obligations under the contract. In most cases, the parties are discharged when they perform the acts specified in the contract. For example, Acme Construction agrees to dig a trench for Southwestern Bell for twenty-five thousand dollars. The contract will be discharged after Acme digs the trench and Southwestern Bell pays Acme twenty-five thousand dollars.

The performance obligation may also be discharged by the occurrence or failure of a *condition* upon which the contract is based. A condition is an expressly stated or implied event upon which the performance of a contract is dependent. If the condition is not satisfied, the parties are excused from fulfilling what would otherwise have been their obligations. Thus, the parties may "condition" their performance upon the occurrence or nonoccurrence of some facts or events.

There are three types of conditions: conditions precedent, conditions subsequent, and concurrent conditions.

Conditions Precedent

A provision which requires that an event must occur before a party's duty of performance arises is known as a condition precedent. For example, a fire policy might require the insured to notify the insurance company within a certain specified time—say, ten days—that a fire has occurred. Notification permits the insurance company to make an investigation of the fire soon after it took place. Suppose that Richard Brownley, who lived in New York, owned a rental house in Kansas City. On April 1, a hailstorm struck his house. His tenants said nothing, but the hailstorm seriously damaged the roof. Six months passed, then water started to leak into the house. At that point the tenants informed Brownley of the problem. After a few more weeks, a roofing expert informed him that hail had damaged the building. The condition precedent clause in the insurance policy is likely to create a problem for Brownley because so much time has passed.

Conditions Subsequent

A provision that will terminate a party's duty of performance *if* an event occurs is known as a condition subsequent. Thus if the event in question occurs, the condition subsequent terminates a party's duty to perform any further. For example, the University of Kansas enters into a contract with Joan Potter to work as head resident at a dormitory for two years. The contract provides that this employment will terminate if she ceases to be enrolled as a full-time student at the university. If after one year Joan drops out of school, the contract is terminated.

Concurrent Conditions

When a concurrent condition is imposed, each party's duty to perform is contingent on the other's performance. Thus, neither is required to perform unless the other party also performs. Such a provision necessitates a simultaneous performance by both parties. Suppose that Janice Smith agrees to deliver the deed to her home on June 1 to Lois Schubert in exchange for one hundred twenty-five thousand dollars. If either Janice or Lois is unwilling or unable to perform, then the other party need not perform. Lois cannot recover from Janice for a breach of contract unless Lois first tenders her own performance. Likewise, Janice cannot recover from Lois for a breach of contract unless Janice first tenders her own performance.

Degrees of Performance

As noted earlier, most contracts are terminated by the parties to a contract performing their obligations under the contract. Sometimes, however, a party fails to live up to its contractual obligations—that is, the party breaches the contract. Courts recognize three degrees of contract performance: complete performance, substantial performance, and material breach.

Complete Performance

A complete performance occurs when parties have fully and perfectly performed their contract duties. Obviously, if this occurs, the performing parties' obligations are discharged and they are entitled to enforce their rights under the contract.

Substantial Performance   — *DEAL GOES THROUGH*

Substantial performance occurs when parties essentially perform their contractual obligations, but with minor deviations. Because there are minor deviations, a breach of contract exists.

Some contract obligations are of such a nature that it is not unusual for actual performance to fall short of complete performance. Often this is the case with construction contracts that involve performance according to a detailed set of plans and specifications. No matter how conscientious the builder may be, it is understandable that the finished work may deviate from the plans and specifications in minor respects. In a contract of this kind, when a party renders substantial performance (i.e., involving a relatively minor breach), the other party's obligation ordinarily will not be discharged as a result of the breach.

Consider the following example. Rush Builders entered into a contract with Amy and Frank Jam for the construction of a three-hundred-thousand-dollar home. The contract specified that the builder would use a particular grade of Du Pont Stainmaster carpet. Because of circumstances beyond the builder's control, he was unable to purchase this brand of carpet, so he substituted a carpet of similar price and quality. Since the builder's failure to comply with the contract was minor and done in good faith, Rush will be held to have substantially complied with its obligations under the contract. The buyers are not permitted to refuse to take the home because Rush breached the contract. Rush is entitled to

Cost/Benefit Analysis: To Breach or Not to Breach

When a party begins to question a deal, he or she might ask: "Should I *intentionally* breach the contract even though I freely and voluntarily entered into it in the first place?" Instances may arise in which the law imposes small penalties for breaching a contract, but great benefits might be realized by breaching it. In such a case, society in general might obtain more economic benefit if the party breached the agreement than if he or she complied with the provisions of the agreement.

It could be argued that the law ought to be structured in such a way that encourages businesses to engage in *value-maximizing behavior*—even if that includes occasionally breaching a contract. For example, suppose that Acme Steel agrees to sell a thousand tons of steel to Superior Motors. In the meantime, Zenith Motors, which needs steel desperately because of a great surge in demand for its cars, offers to pay more for this same thousand tons of steel. In such a case, if Zenith offers enough for the steel, it might actually pay Acme to breach the agreement with Superior. The damages a court forces Acme to pay for breaching the agreement with Superior may be smaller than the increased income it derives from the sale to Zenith. Of course, in practice, Acme must take into consideration the effect of the breach on its business relationship with Superior and other matters.

Looking at the typical contract from a practical standpoint, one should ask: Even if one of the parties to the contract willfully breaches the contract, will the other party file suit? If the parties contemplate a continuing contractual relationship, the aggrieved party probably will not file suit. If they do not contemplate a continuing contractual relationship and one of the parties inflicts a serious injury on the other, the aggrieved party quite likely will file suit. Suppose that Acme Mowers supplies mowers to a major retailer. This contract represents a major portion of Acme's business. The retailer has flagrantly violated the contract in the past, and now and then it refuses, without excuse, to take mowers that Acme delivers. In light of the uncertainty caused by this arrangement, Acme may attempt to charge more for its products if it is able to do so. However, because Acme wants the business of the retailer very much, it probably will overlook even flagrant violations of the contract—assuming of course that the cost/benefit analysis works out.

For a more thorough discussion of this line of thinking, see Richard Posner, *Economic Analysis of Law*, 2nd ed. (Boston: Little Brown & Co. 1977), and other law and economics books and articles

the contract price of three hundred thousand dollars minus any damages that the buyers are able to establish were caused by the breach of contract.

Material Breach — DOES NOT GO THROUGH

A material breach occurs when a party fails to substantially perform contract duties. When a material breach occurs, the nonbreaching party is discharged, is excused from further performance, and has a right to damages caused by the breach. Suppose in the prior example that Rush Builders promised to include a kitchen in the home. Owing to an oversight, it failed to build the kitchen. In such a case, Rush could not force the Jams to accept the home. Furthermore, the Jams would be entitled to damages because Rush did not deliver the home it contractually promised to them.

Another way a contract may be terminated is if one of the parties is unable to perform the contract prior to the date set for performance. If an unforeseeable event occurs that makes it impossible for one of the parties to perform, the parties will be released from their obligations under the contract. Generally, what is required is that the promisor cannot legally or physically perform the contract, such as when one of the parties becomes seriously ill and his or her personal performance is required. For example, if Dr. Kelly is scheduled to perform an operation and has a heart attack, she would be excused from her obligation to operate.

DAMAGES

When one of the parties to a contract fails to perform properly under the contract, this is a breach of the agreement. In such a case, the injured party may sue for any damages he or she sustained as a result of the breach of contract.

Types of Damages

There are four types of damages a plaintiff might request in a breach-of-contracts action.

Compensatory damages

Certain damages compensate the injured party only for the injury suffered and caused by the breach of contract. For example, Kroeger hires Shin to work for the month of June. Shin is to perform certain services in return for the sum of one thousand dollars. Kroeger wrongfully cancels the contract. Shin is unable to find work during June. Shin can sue Kroeger for breach of contract and collect one thousand dollars as compensatory damages.

Consequential Damages

Damages that do not flow directly from the acts of a party but arise only indirectly are said to be consequential damages. They are caused by special circumstances beyond the contract itself. The nonbreaching party may not recover for such damages unless a reasonable person could have foreseen those damages at the time of contracting.

A famous illustration of this rule is found in *Hadley* v. *Baxendale*, a case arising in England in 1854. The crankshaft in the Hadleys' flour mill in Gloucester broke, causing the mill to close. The Hadleys delivered the crankshaft to Baxendale, who operated a transportation company. Baxendale promised to take the crankshaft to the foundry in the following day. The delivery of the crankshaft was delayed by some neglect. The Hadleys did not receive the new shaft until several days after they could have reasonably expected to receive it. The Hadleys sued Baxendale for the profits lost during the additional days the flour mill was closed. The court refused to permit the Hadleys to recover for their lost profits because it was not reasonable to anticipate that a broken shaft would cause the mill to close. Most mills at that time kept more than one crankshaft on hand to deal with just such an emergency. Thus, a loss would not have occurred under ordinary circumstances. The special circumstances—the fact that the Hadleys had only one crankshaft—were never communicated to Baxendale; therefore, the loss of profits as a consequence of a breach of contract could not have been reasonably contemplated by the parties when they entered into the contract.

Nominal Damages

A very small sum of money may be awarded if a plaintiff is unable to prove substantial loss. For example, a court might rule that the defendant technically violated the contract, but in light of the plaintiff's inability to establish a loss, the court awards the plaintiff one dollar. **Nominal damages** are a classic example of a Pyrrhic victory.

Punitive Damages

Sometimes damages are awarded to the plaintiff in order to punish the defendant so as to deter conduct of this nature in the future. It is extremely rare for a party to collect **punitive damages** in a breach of contract case unless there is fraud or some other kind of willful or tortious conduct.

Duty to Mitigate Damages   While it is true that a party that is injured by a breach of contract has a right to collect damages, the injured party has a duty to limit the losses that result from the breach. The obligation to keep the losses as low as possible is known as **mitigation of damages**. Suppose that a person rents an apartment for one year. After living in the apartment only a month, the tenant moves out. While it is true that the landlord is entitled to damages resulting from the wrongful breach of the contract by the tenant, the landlord nonetheless must try to rent the apartment. If the landlord succeeds in finding another tenant, the damages owed by the first tenant are reduced by whatever rent the landlord receives from the substitute tenant.

This does not mean that the landlord must rent to anyone who comes along simply to reduce the first tenant's losses. The landlord certainly could refuse to rent to someone with a poor credit history, for example, even if this person was willing to take over the apartment in question. Similar problems arise in the employment context. If an employee who is working under a contract is wrongfully fired, he or she has an obligation to find employment elsewhere. This does not mean, however, that the worker must take just any job. Courts generally require the employee only to take comparable work. This point is discussed in the following case.

Parker v. Twentieth Century–Fox Film Corp.
California Supreme Court
474 P.2d 689 (1970)

Shirley MacLaine Parker, a film star, entered into a contract with Twentieth Century-Fox to act in a picture entitled *Bloomer Girl*. It was to be filmed starting May 23, 1966, and she was to be paid for fourteen weeks. In April 1966, Fox decided not to make the film. It requested MacLaine to act instead in a film tentatively entitled *Big Country, Big Man*. Although it agreed to pay her the same compensation, the films were different. *Bloomer Girl* was to have been a musical, but *Big Country* was a western. *Bloomer Girl* was to have been filmed in California. *Big Country* was scheduled to be filmed in Australia. MacLaine was given one week to accept. She brought this suit seeking compensation for breach of contract. Fox defended by arguing that MacLaine had failed to mitigate damages. The court ruled for MacLaine.

Burke, Justice

The general rule is that the measure of recovery by a wrongfully discharged employee is the amount of salary agreed upon for the period of service, less the amount which the employer affirmatively proves the employee has earned or with reasonable effort might have earned from other employment.

However, before projected earnings from other employment opportunities not sought or accepted by the discharged employee can be applied in mitigation, the employer must show that the other employment was comparable, or substantially similar, to that of which the employee has been deprived; the employee's rejection of or failure to seek other available employment of a different or inferior kind may not be resorted to in order to mitigate damages.

The sole issue is whether plaintiff's refusal of defendant's substitute offer of "Big Country" may be used in mitigation. Nor, if the "Big Country" offer was of employment different or inferior when compared with the original "Bloomer Girl" employment, is there an issue as to whether or not plaintiff acted reasonably in refusing the substitute offer. Despite defendant's arguments to the contrary, no case cited or which our research has

discovered holds or suggests that reasonableness is an element of wrongfully discharged employee's option to reject, or fail to seek, different or inferior employment lest the possible earnings therefrom be charged against him in mitigation of damages.

Applying the foregoing rules to the record in the present case, with all intendments in favor of the party opposing the summary judgment motion—here, defendant—it is clear that the trial court correctly ruled that plaintiff's failure to accept defendant's tendered substitute employment could not be applied in mitigation of damages because the offer of the "Big Country" lead was of employment both different and inferior, and that no factual dispute was presented on that issue.

In view of the determination that defendant failed to present any facts showing the existence of a factual issue with respect to its sole defense—plaintiff's rejection of its substitute employment offer in mitigation of damages—we need not consider plaintiff's further contention that for various reasons, plaintiff was excused for attempting to mitigate damages.

The judgment is affirmed.

People entering into contracts quite often wonder what will happen if the other party to the agreement fails to comply with his or her obligations under the contract. The option always remains open to file suit. However, because of the time, energy, and money involved, this option is far from attractive. An alternative that may reduce the likelihood of needing to file suit is to specify in the contract that if a party fails to comply with the provisions, that party will pay the nonbreaching party a sum specified in the contract as damages.

The courts will not enforce a provision added to the contract as a penalty. Courts often look to two criteria in deciding whether a liquidated damages clause should be enforced. First, at the time the parties make their contract, the loss expected to result from a potential breach should be such that it would be difficult to estimate. Second, the sum or formula set forth in the contract as liquidated damages must be a reasonable forecast of what would seem to be just compensation. If these standards are not met, a court may refuse to enforce a liquidated damages clause, classifying it instead as an unreasonable penalty.

Suppose that Mark and Judy Timmons want to build a tennis court in their backyard for their children. They want the court done in the early spring so their children can have spring and summer to practice. To make certain that the contractor finishes the job in time, Mark and Judy should probably include a liquidated damages clause in the contract. For example, they might penalize the builder by twenty-five dollars per day, the amount it costs their children to practice at a local club, if the builder fails to complete the job by April 1. Such a clause encourages the builder to perform in a timely manner.

REMEDIES

The general goal of the courts when handling a breach of contract is not to punish the wrongdoing party but rather to attempt to restore the injured party to the same position that he or she would have occupied had the contract not been breached in the first place. This is generally accomplished by awarding the aggrieved party a certain sum of money.

In addition, *equitable remedies* are available when the remedy at law—that is, monetary damages—is not adequate to fully compensate the aggrieved party. Two frequently used equitable remedies are the decree of specific performance and the injunction.

Sometimes the plaintiff wants the defendant to perform the acts called for in the contract but the defendant refuses to perform its obligations under the contract. In such a case, the aggrieved party may ask a court for a decree of **specific performance**. A decree of specific performance is a court order requiring a party who is guilty of a breach of contract to perform its obligations under the contract. A person who fails to obey such a court order may be imprisoned for contempt of court.

As a general rule, the courts will not require the defendant to perform the acts specified in the contract if the payment of damages would adequately compensate the injured party. Courts generally permit a party to request specific performance of a contract if the subject matter of the contract is unique or if the contract involves the sale of real estate. For example, suppose that an art collector purchases a famous painting by Renoir. The seller thereafter refuses to deliver the picture to the collector. In such a case, as the Renoir painting is unique, a court will order the seller to deliver the painting to the buyer.

Injunction

A court issues an **injunction** for the purpose of requiring a party to refrain from engaging in a particular act or activity. Suppose that Mike Waters signs a three-year contract to play baseball for the Kansas City Royals at two million dollars per year. In the contract he agrees that if he does not play baseball for the Royals, he will not play for any other baseball team during the contract period. Soon after signing the contract, he realizes that the Chicago Cubs are willing to pay him three million dollars per year. If Waters even attempted to start playing for the Cubs, the Royals could go to court and obtain an injunction ordering Waters to stop playing for the Cubs or any other ball team.

ENFORCING A CONTRACT WHEN NONE EXISTS

In this section we examine two situations in which no contract exists but the courts impose contractual obligations on the parties anyway. The doctrines of quasi contract and promissory estoppel are discussed in turn.

Quasi Contract

Before signing the typical contract, the parties often discuss the subject matter and major contractual terms. After they come to an agreement on the major terms, one of the parties makes an offer and the other person accepts the offer. In such a case, whether the contract is oral or written, there is a clear express intention to contract. But in some situations the parties never indicate, nor do they in fact have, an intent to contract.

Suppose that today a student decides to drive his car to the record store. On the way to the store, another vehicle collides with his automobile. Because of the serious injuries he sustains, he is in a comatose state. An ambulance driver rushes him to a hospital. While the student is unconscious, the hospital attendants rush him to the operating room for emergency surgery to save his life. The physician in charge operates on him to stop the bleeding. The next day the student awakens in a hospital bed. After several days in the hospital attempting to recover, he finally decides to go home. When he leaves the hospital, the cashier presents him with a bill for the use of the emergency room, the hospital room, and various services and supplies. When he arrives home, he discovers the physician's bill in his mailbox.

Although the student *never had an intent to contract*, the law requires him to pay the reasonable value of the services rendered. Suit may be brought against him on the basis of a quasi-contractual theory of recovery.

Quasi contracts (also called *contracts implied in law*) are not technically contracts, because one of the parties never intended to contract. Even so, the law recognizes an implied contract in order to do justice. If the student received hospital and medical services but was not required to pay for them, he would be unjustly enriched. Thus, the duty to pay is imposed to prevent the unjust enrichment of one person at the expense of another.

Another situation in which recovery may be had under a quasi contract is one in which a minor purchases necessities such as food, clothing, and medical services, assuming the minor does not have a parent or guardian who is able and willing to supply those necessities. In such a situation, the minor must pay for the items purchased, even though one of the elements for a valid contract is missing—capacity. No contract technically ever comes into existence. Nonetheless, to let the minor purchase these things without an obligation to pay for them would unjustly enrich the minor at the expense of the adult or business. Consequently, the courts will permit such a person or business to contract under a quasi-contractual theory of recovery.

Clearly, the doctrine of quasi contract may be used in many situations where it appears that one party has been unjustly enriched at the expense of another. The courts have used it in instances in which a contract was too indefinite to be enforced, in cases where a person who partially performed personal services had died, and in innumerable other situations to ensure that one party was not unjustly enriched at the expense of another.

The case that follows presents a contract implied by the law.

County of Champaign v. Hanks
Court of Appeals of Illinois
353 N.E.2d 405 (1976)

Gary Hanks was accused of a crime. Hanks claimed at the time of his arrest that he had no money to hire an attorney to defend himself. This statement was in fact false, because he owned real estate worth over fifty thousand dollars. Relying on these false statements, the state provided a free attorney to Hanks. When it discovered that the statements were false, the state sued to recover the cost of providing an attorney. Hanks argued that there was no contract on his part to pay for the legal services. The court ruled Hanks had to pay for the services rendered by the state.

Stengel, Justice

A quasi contract, or contract implied in law, is one which reason and justice dictate and is founded on the equitable doctrine of unjust enrichment. A contract implied in law does not depend on the intention of the parties, but exists where there is a plain duty and a consideration. The essential element is the receipt of a benefit by one party under circumstances where it would be inequitable to retain that benefit without compensation.

The county does not officiously confer the benefits of free legal representation, but furnishes legal services to those criminal defendants who qualify by virtue of their indigency. The undisputed facts reveal that defendant received free legal representation when he clearly was not entitled to such representation and that defendant failed to disclose his assets. Under these circumstances the law will imply a promise by defendants to compensate the county and, accordingly, we find that summary judgment was properly granted.

The measure of damages for an implied in law contract is the amount by which defendant has been unjustly enriched or the value of the actual benefit received by defendant, and recovery is usually measured by the reasonable value of the services performed by plaintiff.

Defendant, by his misrepresentations, received legal services which were found by the trial court to have a reasonable value of $2000. The services rendered by three different attorneys from the Public Defender's Office were not only competent but lengthy and most thorough. The records reveals that between March 28, 1972, and July 17, 1972, they appeared in court at least nine days on various matters from preliminary hearing and arraignment to motions to suppress the in-court identification. The jury trial consumed four days from July 17 to July 20, 1972. Motions for mistrial, post-trial motions, probation hearing and finally sentencing hearing were not completed until October 6, 1972. Thus the damage award does not exceed the extent of defendant's unjust enrichment as it is no more than defendant would have paid for such services had he not misrepresented his assets. This damage award more nearly reflects the value of the benefit received by defendant, and a lesser measure of damages would be tantamount to allowing defendant to profit from his wrongful conduct.

Promissory Estoppel

Section 90 of the *Restatement of Contracts Second* states the doctrine of **promissory estoppel**:

> A promise which the promisor should reasonably expect to induce action or forbearance on the part of the promisee or a third person and which does induce such action or forbearance is binding if injustice can be avoided only by enforcement of the promise. The remedy for breach may be limited as justice requires.

A person may, by making a promise to another person, cause the person to whom the statement is made to take some sort of action or to abstain from taking action of some sort. In this situation the person making the statement should not be able to avoid his or her promise by asserting that the promise in question was not supported by consideration. A court in this situation may treat the promise as enforceable even though it is not supported by consideration.

As promissory estoppel is currently being applied, however, it serves as much more than a simple substitute for the doctrine of consideration. *Hoffman* v.

Red Owl Stores, the case that follows, is a good illustration of the broad application some courts make of the promissory estoppel doctrine. Even when many of the terms have never been agreed upon, as in *Hoffman*, courts have been willing to recognize a contract where no contract ever existed.

The *Restatement of Contracts Second* requires a court to find:

1. that the promise was one that the promisor should have reasonably expected would induce action or forbearance of a definite and substantial character on the part of the person to whom the promise was made; and
2. the promise induced such action of forbearance; and
3. injustice can be avoided only by enforcement of the promise.

The trend of the cases is to apply the doctrine of promissory estoppel to any promise that meets these requirements. Many cases have applied this doctrine.

For example, promissory estoppel has come up frequently in construction cases. Suppose a general contractor is building a ten-story building. The contractor asks for bids from various subcontractors. An electrical subcontractor, XYZ, makes the low bid for the electrical work on the building, which the general contractor uses in making his bid for the job. On August 1, the general contractor is awarded the contract. He then goes to XYZ, which informs him its bid has been withdrawn. Some courts have taken the position that once a subcontractor makes a bid, because of the doctrine of promissory estoppel, the subcontractor may not withdraw the bid. The rationale is that the subcontractor, at the time it made its bid, knew the general contractor might rely upon the bid to its detriment, because it would use the subcontractor's bid in making a bid for the entire building. In effect, the courts have altered the general rule that an offeror may withdraw an offer any time before it is accepted in the construction contract situation.

The following case is a well-known illustration of the rule of promissory estoppel.

Hoffman v. Red Owl Stores
Supreme Court of Wisconsin
133 N.W. 2d 267 (1965)

In this case, the Hoffmans claimed that Red Owl's representatives made a number of representations to them upon which they relied to their detriment. They urged the court to apply the doctrine of promissory estoppel to create an enforceable bargain. The Wisconsin Supreme Court ruled that it was properly applied in this case.

Currie, Chief Justice

Many courts of other jurisdictions have seen fit over the years to adopt the principle of promissory estoppel, and the tendency in that direction continues. As Mr. Justice McFaddin, speaking in behalf of the Arkansas court, well stated, that the development of the law of promissory estoppel "is an attempt by the courts to keep remedies abreast of increased moral consciousness of honesty and fair representations in all business dealings."

Because we deem the doctrine of promissory estoppel, as stated in sec. 90 of Restatement, 1 Contracts, is one which supplies a needed tool which courts may employ in a proper case to prevent injustice, we endorse and adopt it.

The record here discloses a number of promises and assurances given to Hoffman by Lukovitz on behalf of Red Owl upon which plaintiffs relied and acted upon to their detriment.

Foremost were the promises that for the sum of $18,000 Red Owl would establish Hoffman in a store. After Hoffman had sold his grocery store and paid the $1,000 on the Chilton lot, the $18,000 figure was changed to $24,000. Then in November, 1961, Hoffman was assured that if the $24,000 figure were increased by $2,000 the deal would go through. Hoffman was induced to sell his grocery store fixtures and inventory in June, 1961, on the promise that he would be in his new store by fall. In November, plaintiffs sold their bakery building on the urging of defendants and on the assurance that this was the last step necessary to have the deal with Red Owl go through.

There remains for consideration the question of law raised by defendants that an agreement was never reached on essential factors necessary to establish a contract between Hoffman and Red Owl. Among these were the size, cost, design, and layout of the store building; and the terms of the lease with respect to rent, maintenance, renewal, and purchase options. This poses the question of whether the promise necessary to sustain a cause of action for promissory estoppel must embrace all essential details of a proposed transaction between promisor and promisee so as to be the equivalent of an offer that would result in a binding contract between the parties if the promisee were to accept the same.

Originally the doctrine of promissory estoppel was invoked as a substitute for consideration rendering a gratuitous promise enforceable as a contract. In other words, the acts of reliance by the promisee to his detriment provided a substitute for consideration. If promissory estoppel were to be limited to only these situations where the promise giving rise to the cause of action must be so definite with respect to all details that a contract would result were the promise supported by consideration, then the defendants' instant promises to Hoffman would not meet this test. However, sec. 90 of Restatement, 1 Contracts, does not impose the requirement that the promise giving rise to the cause of action must be so comprehensive in scope as to meet the requirements of an offer that would ripen into a contract if accepted by the promisee. Rather the conditions imposed are:

1. Was the promise one which the promisor should reasonably expect to induce action or forbearance of a definite and substantial character on the part of the promisee?

2. Did the promise induce such action or forbearance?

3. Can injustice be avoided only by enforcement of the promise?

We conclude the injustice would result here if plaintiffs were not granted some relief because of the failure of defendants to keep their promises which induced plaintiffs to act to their detriment.

SUMMARY

Even if all the requirements for a valid contract have been met—offer, acceptance, consideration, capacity, and legality—the contract will still not be enforceable if the parties did not freely and voluntarily enter into the agreement.

Furthermore, the courts will not enforce certain contracts if they are not evidenced by a writing. Before signing a contract, a person should take care to make certain that the written contract actually reflects the oral agreement entered into between the parties. The parol evidence rule may create serious problems for a party if the final written contract does not reflect the oral agreement between the parties.

Even a contract that seems clear at the outset must be interpreted. First the parties to the contract give their own interpretation to the contract terms. If they cannot come to an agreement as to what these terms mean, they may be forced to go to court to get an official interpretation of the language used in the contract.

A contract may be terminated in a variety of ways, but most commonly it is terminated by the parties to the contract performing their contractual obligations. If one of the parties to the contract does not comply with his or her obligations, the law provides various remedies to the nonbreaching party.

Finally, under certain circumstances, the courts will impose contractual obligations on the parties even when no contract technically exists between the parties.

REVIEW QUESTIONS

1. Define the following terms:
   a. Assignee
   b. Assignor
   c. Creditor beneficiary
   d. Donee beneficiary
   e. Incidental beneficiary
   f. Liquidated damages
   g. Material breach
   h. Mitigation of damages
   i. Parol evidence rule
   j. Promissory estoppel
   k. Quasi contract
   l. Statute of frauds
   m. Substantial performance

2. Does a person have a duty to read a contract before signing it? Is that person bound by the contract if she or he fails to read it before signing?

3. Can a contract be imposed upon a person who never intended to contract?

4. Under what circumstances will a court enforce a contract even when it is *not* supported by consideration?

5. Darla Paxton operates an antiques store. She hires Neil Clark to fill in for her at times. Daphne Martin, a collector with over two hundred rare dolls, asks the price of a particular doll. Neil misreads the price tag and informs her it costs $15 rather than the $1500 Darla marked on the tag. Daphne purchases the doll. Thereafter Darla asks for it back because of Neil's mistake. Must Daphne return the doll? If she knew of the mistake, is it ethical to take advantage of Neil's error?

6. Verlyn Fuller spoke with a representative of the Acme Trucking School. The representative told him that he would learn to drive a truck and the training he would receive was designed to qualify a student to compete in the job market. After Verlyn graduated from the school, he was unable to locate a job. Is Acme guilty of fraud?

7. On June 1, Donna Mello spoke with Phyllis Miles. Donna orally agreed to sell her home to Phyllis. They agreed upon all the terms necessary to create a binding contract. The

next day, Neil Delacruz offered Donna five thousand dollars more for her home. Can Donna sell her home to Neil? Why or why not?

8. Chen Wang recently moved to the United States. Wang spoke with an agent for a shopping center about leasing a restaurant in the center. The restaurant occupied two buildings in the center. Wang inquired whether he could cancel the lease on one of the buildings if business in the restaurant turned out to be poor. The agent said yes. The contract Wang signed was for ten years for both buildings. It said nothing about a right to cancel the lease. Business turned out to be very poor. Can Wang cancel the contract?

9. Kilroy owes Acme Corporation five thousand dollars. Acme needs money to continue operating so it assigns its right to the five thousand dollars to First National Bank. It later develops that Kilroy has a claim of breach of warranty against Acme. In this example, which party is the assignor and the assignee? Is it possible to assign such an obligation? Can Kilroy assert his defense against First National Bank?

10. Simpson sells her home to Atwood. Atwood pays Simpson one hundred thousand dollars and also gives Simpson a twenty-thousand-dollar note in payment for the home. Atwood thereafter sells the home to Hogan. Hogan agrees to assume the twenty-thousand-dollar note payable to Simpson. Can Simpson enforce this note against Hogan? What sort of a beneficiary of the Atwood–Hogan contract is Simpson?

11. On June 1, Richard's home caught fire, causing substantial damage. The insurance contract required him to notify the company of a loss within ten days. Richard did not call the company for three months. What is the clause in the contract called? Does it make any difference that Richard waited three months to call the company?

12. Carolyn Kenyon hired a contractor to build a home for her at a cost of four hundred-twenty-five thousand dollars. The contract required the builder to use Kohler plumbing fixtures. Because of a strike, the builder was unable to purchase Kohler fixtures. The builder substituted plumbing fixtures of equal quality and value. When Carolyn saw the completed house, she refused to pay the builder because he failed to comply with the contract. She viewed his actions as a material breach of contract, thus discharging her from any obligations under the contract. Is she correct?

13. Book Company's printing press stopped working because of a defective part. The company contacted the manufacturer of the press, which agreed to repair the part in two days. The manufacturer assumed that Book Company had a spare part it could use in the meantime. The actual repair took three weeks. Book Company wants to recover from the manufacturer the lost profits it would have made during this time period. What types of damages are these? Can Book Company recover these damages?

14. Marc Stanfield was president of a medium-size computer company working under a three-year contract. The company wrongfully fired him after two years. As a condition of collecting the last year of salary under his contract, does he have an obligation to look for work elsewhere? If he learns of a job as a cashier at the local McDonald's, must he take this job?

15. Sharon Blair entered into a contract with a builder for the construction of a home for one hundred seventy-five thousand dollars. The home was to be completed by June 1. The contract provided that the builder would pay her ten thousand dollars per day for each day after June 1 until the contractor completed the home. What is such a provision called? Is it enforceable?

16. Acme Painters contracted to paint a house at 1212 Main Street. Because the manager made an error in writing down the address, the work crew went out to Edward Goddard's home at 121 Main Street. When they arrived, Goddard was home. He said nothing to them while they painted his house. When they finished, Goddard informed them he would not pay them because he did not enter into a contract with Acme. Is there any way he can be forced to pay?

17. Janell McNearney's college contacted her about making a donation to the school. Janell offered to give the school one hundred thousand dollars. Relying on her statement, the school entered into a contract to build a four-million-dollar building. Janell now refused to give the school the hundred thousand dollars. She contends it was a mere gift promise, unsupported by consideration. Is there any way the school can compel her to pay the hundred thousand?

18. Marie Bredemann worked for the Vaughan Manufacturing Company for a number of years. The president of Vaughan orally promised to pay her three hundred seventy-five dollars per month for life when she retired. In reliance on his statement, she retired. Several years later, the company, which had been paying her three hundred seventy-five dollars per month, stopped making payments. It argued that there was no consideration to support the alleged contract between Vaughan and Bredemann. What could Bredemann argue?

19. Parker, a thirty-seven-year-old bachelor, entered into a series of contracts with Arthur Murray for dancing lessons. During the lessons, he was told he had "exceptional potential to be a fine and accomplished dancer." The contracts he signed stated in bold type at the bottom, "Noncancellable Contract," and also stated, "I understand that no refunds will be made under the terms of this contract." He was thereafter severely injured in an automobile accident and was incapable of continuing his dancing lessons. At that time, he had contracted for a total 2,734 hours of lessons. He contends he should be released from these contracts on the basis of impossibility. Should he win?

20. Vargas is an artist, and a native of Peru. He has lived in the United States for over thirty years. He entered an employment contract with the publishers of *Esquire* magazine, after having looked at and signed it. The contract was written in plain English. Vargas now wishes to cancel the contract on the ground that he failed to know and understand its contents when it was signed. Is this a good defense to a breach of contract claim?

21. Colburn contracted for the construction of a home on his property and executed a mortgage to secure his purchase. He signed a mortgage in the presence of a notary public, but had some questions about the instrument. Colburn paid the installments as they became due for four years. Then he sought to void the mortgage on the ground that he failed to read and understand it when he signed it. Will the court accept this argument?

22. Smith signed a contract with Standard Oil to sell a piece of property. In a suit to enforce the contract against Smith, Smith argued that she was unable to read the contract when it was presented for signature because of her faulty eyesight. She did not have eyeglasses with her, so she signed the contract only upon the assurances given to her by Standard Oil. As soon as she arrived home, she put on her glasses and discovered that the contract did not contain a provision that she was led to believe was in it. Can she have the contract set aside?

23. Christopher Kitsos claimed that he was offered an oral contract for lifetime employment by the Mobile Gas Service Corporation. The company fired him. When sued by Kitsos, it argued that this contract had to be in writing in order to be enforceable. Is the company correct?

CHAPTER 11

Assessing External Costs of Doing Business: Tort Liability

- What Is Tort Liability?
- Tort Law Classifications: Focusing on the Nature of the Conduct
- Examples of Intentional Torts
- Tort Law and History
- Developments in Tort Law

WHAT IS TORT LIABILITY?

The common law legal environment regulates business organizations by imposing a general duty to act reasonably in all their activities. Thus, management decision making in such areas as employer-employee relations, marketing, capital formation, and manufacturing must be made in accordance with this standard of conduct. If not, the potential for tort liability looms if an injury to a person or property arises. In a sense, the common law doctrine of tort liability creates an incentive for careful decision making. In its absence, firms may be required to pay damages arising from harms caused by their faulty management activities.

Thus, the tort system seeks to shift the cost of injury from those actually harmed to those that caused the harm. For example, management for Gourmet Stores, Inc. would have both a business and a tort law concern about the quality of the food items it sells. Offering salads with wilted lettuce and shriveled vegetables is a sure way of inviting customers to shop elsewhere. One might therefore consider a lack of attention to quality as a potential cost to the business. Careful management seeks to eliminate that cost. Similarly, assume that some perishable food was not stored properly and that a customer became violently ill after eating it. Not only will that customer be likely thereafter to shop elsewhere, but a tort claim may arise. Gourmet Stores' faulty management procedures led to the food spoiling, which caused the injury to its customer. Thousands of dollars in tort liability ''cost'' may be assessed against the firm.

This chapter will focus on the tort law system and try to show how that system affects the behavior of business managers. Note, from the discussion of the basic legal doctrines, that it is only at the decision stage that tort liability comes into play. How management decisions affect others is what raises the potential of tort liability. The scope of liability, however, is not fixed. This chapter contains both historical and trends discussions to illustrate this changing scope.

General Factors That Make Up the Law of Torts

Many writers have attempted to draft a good working definition of the term **tort.** They have failed, mainly because of the nature of the legal concept of the term. Tort law is a certain body of civil (noncriminal) law covering civil wrongs other than breaches of contract. Recall the material in Chapters 9 and 10 on contracts. The "wrongs" (breaches of contract) in that area involve parties that have a relationship arising from their exchanged promises. Those parties are known, and liability is generally limited, under contract law, to them. Thus, a business can avoid (or limit) exposure to contract "wrongs" by either not entering into a contract with a certain party or by carefully drafting the contract to protect its interests in the event of a breach. By way of contrast, torts arise without any prerequisite of an initial relationship being formed between the parties. Any person is a potential victim; any action has a risk of leading to a tort. Thus, tortious wrongs or injuries can be tied to a business's actions irrespective of the fact that the injured person was not somehow identified beforehand. Clearly, the scope of liability risk is both greater and less precisely definable for tort theory than for contract theory.

Torts may arise from a wide range of conduct. A few examples include theft of a competitor's trade secret, faulty design of a product, drunk driving, punching someone in the nose, and improper supervision of employees. The common element of these examples is that they reflect a lack of reasonably prudent care. In cases involving torts, a court will usually provide money damages to parties injured by the acts of others.

The system of tort law is based on three major factors or aims: first, to provide a means for those injured by another's unreasonable conduct to be compensated; second, to allocate the risk of loss between those who cause harm and those who are injured; finally, and closely related to the second factor, to encourage (or discourage) certain types of behavior.

The goal of the compensation award or damages in tort is to restore, through the award of money, the injured parties to their condition before the injury. This means that the elements of a damage award are made up of a number of possible factors, depending on the nature of the case. The more tangible elements in the computation of a damage award are out-of-pocket costs and expenses incurred by the injured party (doctor bills and medical expenses, for example) and income lost because of the injury. However, the injured party may have suffered in less clearly measurable ways. Pain and suffering or embarrassment may certainly be consequences of an injury. These intangible factors, too, may be included in the total compensation awarded to the plaintiff in order to make the injured party whole (that is, by awarding money damages, to put the injured party in the same position as before the accident occurred).

However, tort law is not a general social insurance system by which people who somehow receive an injury automatically are compensated for it. Some are not awarded damages because it could not be established that their injuries were caused by the actions of another. Similarly, compensation will not follow if the parties' own misbehavior caused their injuries. Further, a judicial award of tort damages must thereafter be collected. If the tortfeasor has no money or property, no compensation will be received.

The second aim of the tort law system is to assign fault or risks. This assignment may also be described as an allocation of costs. For example, corporations recently began to face tort liability arising from the actions of their employees who become intoxicated at company picnics. Thus, the "cost" to corporations of serving liquor at those functions (or doing so without close monitoring) increased. Furthermore, the "cost" to those injured by intoxicated picnickers decreased, since the system provided an additional party (the corporation) from whom compensation could be assessed.

As will be seen in this chapter, the assignment of fault or risk often shifts. Courts that decide cases and develop doctrine in tort law are aware that their decisions do not operate in a vacuum. Holding that certain conduct may be an actionable tort may have the effect of inhibiting that conduct, because compensation will be awarded to those injured. If the effect is to make manufacturers take greater care in their production procedures, society benefits. However, if the effect is to inhibit the development of new and useful tools, one might question the overall benefit to society. Yet limiting the types of conduct that lead to tort liability might result in the inevitable misfortunes of a complex and highly industrialized society being borne by the unlucky few who are injured. This conflict within the system of torts is a primary source for the change in its doctrines.

The final aim of the tort law system is to encourage certain types of behavior. With the imposition of "costs" on the consequences of certain activities, one can expect that those activities will be changed to minimize the effects of tort law. For economic reasons, a more reasonable mode of behavior will be chosen. This factor may also be considered to have a regulatory effect. Instead of an administrative agency or a legislature creating precise rules of conduct for a business activity, the business is given an option: Either reevaluate that activity so that fewer injuries are caused or face a greater risk of damage awards.

Tort Law, Business Behavior, and Insurance

As noted above, when activities of a business cause injury, tort law is available to impose damages on that business. As a result, an additional "cost" must be computed for all business activities—the cost of potential tort liability arising from that activity. However, an exact figure for these costs may be difficult to compute for any individual company. For example, the Acme Grocery Store would be able to compute labor costs by reviewing the contract with its employees' union and making reasonable assumptions about industry labor costs over the long term. However, the store would have no way to predict how many people will slip on cottage cheese spilled in an aisle or the severity of any of their injuries. Nonetheless, Acme Grocery Store may become liable for a damage award and thus needs to determine how to factor those awards, over time, into its pricing.

The usual way to approach the problem would be for Acme to purchase liability insurance. In fact, most businesses (and individuals) hedge against the risk of major damage awards depleting their assets by purchasing insurance. The insurance company will, consistent with the terms and coverage purchased, defend Acme and, if necessary, ultimately pay any customers injured in the store. The cost of the insurance policy, like labor costs, will be used to make grocery pricing decisions.

Thus, tort law and insurance together operate to further the major goals of tort doctrine. Through insurance, a compensation pool is readily available to satisfy tort damage awards. Otherwise, a **defendant** without either insurance or sufficient assets will be unable to pay the award, thereby causing the injured party to forgo compensation for injuries even though a court provided an award. Furthermore, an ongoing business, like Acme Grocery Store, can plan its liability costs and need not realistically fear a loss of its assets. Finally, the insurance company, in order to minimize tort claims, may cause Acme Grocery Store to modify some of its business procedures. For example, employees may be assigned to police aisles for spilled food. Lower rates or perhaps the availability of insurance itself may be conditioned on such actions. A safer shopping environment and ultimately fewer accidents will result.

Thus, day-to-day activities of business are tied to tort law and insurance. However, the relationship between tort law and insurance today is a tenuous one. Beginning in the 1980s business insurance premiums skyrocketed or the coverage itself became very difficult to obtain. Why this problem arose was subject to great dispute.

One analysis suggested that jury damage awards and the tort law system had run amok. As will be seen by the developments section of this chapter, the compensation of victims policy of tort doctrine has become dominant. Legal doctrines once available as defenses to tort claims have been eliminated or weakened. The *Flagiello* v. *Pennsylvania Hospital* case in Chapter 4 illustrates the abandonment of the charitable immunity doctrine, a tort rule that prevented charitable institutions from being held liable for torts. Furthermore, the scope of tort liability has been expanded to provide remedies for once uncompensated injuries. However, tort law changes are merely reflecting a social belief that injured individuals should not have to absorb certain losses on their own.

Others suggested that the liability insurance crisis was a ruse under which insurance companies have been able to shift the loss of their investment miscalculations. Tort law doctrine has been slowly evolving for the past thirty years, while the insurance crisis is of very recent vintage. No sudden change occurred to precipitate the problem. The only sudden change that did occur was economic: Inflation and interest rates fell very rapidly. Insurance companies were writing insurance at bargain rates, counting on continued inflation and a large return from their investments. When interest rates fell, the companies were responsible for far greater tort liability losses than premium income and their investments could cover. (Some people, however, contended that skillful accounting had as much to do with the claimed "loss" as did the change in the economy.) As a result, insurance companies began to demand huge premium increases for business insurance.

Some businesses were unable to cope with the large insurance rate increases. Their price structures could not support passing the increase along to their consumers. Thus, in some instances businesses found their insurance protection diminished, risking a loss of assets if a major damage award were assessed. Furthermore, some businesses decided to forgo all insurance. A few quit doing business in the areas in which rate increases were the highest.

Predictably, legislative solutions were proposed. Tort law "reforms" that limited damage awards or modified tort law doctrine were enacted. Tighter regulation of insurance companies also occurred. However, basic to these concerns are general tort law principles that are embodied in the close relationship between tort law doctrine and insurance. Two questions should be considered: First, how does (or should) society provide for compensation to be paid to those persons injured as a result of someone else's activity; and second, how can business best hedge against potential tort liability? These are issues seeking a solution.

A Three-Hundred-Billion-Dollar Tax?

The American tort system has recently been the recipient of a barrage of criticism. It has been accused of imposing a three-hundred-billion-dollar "tax" on American business through its damage awards, attorney's costs, and the efforts undertaken by business solely to avoid tort liability. Furthermore, American business is allegedly reluctant to innovate because of fears that unexpected tort liability arising from new products or processes could be devastating. The conclusion: The tort law system seriously hampers the ability of American business to compete internationally because foreign firms do not face similar liability risks at home. These arguments have been used to justify calls for narrowing the scope of tort doctrines, capping damage awards, or making it more difficult for injured parties to sue.

A number of studies, however, have raised substantial questions about these criticisms and suggest that the "remedies" urged by the critics may be misguided. One of the studies compared the American liability system with those of six Western Euro

pean nations. As expected, in Europe the damage awards are smaller and more predictable than in the United States. Further, litigation costs more in the United States, primarily because of the amount spent on attorney's fees. However, the study also noted major legal and social differences between the United States and Western Europe. The European nations have a vast network of government entitlements (e.g., national health care, expansive income security programs) that do not have counterparts in the United States. Consequently, injured Europeans need not resort to tort law litigation for monetary relief. Note, however, that the study found that European accident victims, like their American counterparts, expect compensation for their injuries. The difference is the source: Americans seek a party to "blame" via tort litigation; Europeans have a social program safety net. Thus, the study concluded that no tort law "crisis" has arisen in Europe because the countries provide benefits that injured Americans must seek through the tort law system.

TORT LAW CLASSIFICATIONS: FOCUSING ON THE NATURE OF THE CONDUCT

One might envision the tort system as assessing increased costs according to the intent behind the action that caused an injury. The more despicable the intent, the greater the assessed costs. If there was no wrongful intent, just mere carelessness, a tort would arise, but the assessed costs would be less. But what if there was not even carelessness? For example, assume that because of economic woes, ABC, Inc. lays off fifty employees. These employees clearly have been "injured." They lost their jobs. The "cause" of this injury can be directly attributed to the corporation's action. But no tort arises.

The question is why.

ABC, Inc.'s action is evaluated by the tort law system on the basis of where it would fit on an imaginary conduct scale. On one end are decisions, like the layoff, that do not violate a duty that the firm is deemed to owe. The layoff was an economic necessity, tied to a slumping economy and the need to control costs for the future benefit of the firm. Thus, the firm has no duty to refrain from layoff decisions even though harm to its employees is clearly foreseeable. No purposeful harm to employees or careless actions by management led to the workers' loss of employment.

Consequently, only when some duty is violated will tort liability be said to arise. This section of the chapter will focus on two types of torts, distinguished by the nature of the duty breach: intentional torts and torts of negligence.

Regulating Purposeful Conduct: Intentional Torts

Consider the following example of a corporate decision that injured its workers. It summarizes the Du Pont case from Chapter 8. Compare it with the layoff illustration above. Workers at two Du Pont Corporation plants were required to have annual physical examinations. A number of them were exposed to asbestos, and in 1965 the first harmful effects was discovered during their physicals. By 1976, indications were that all had developed an asbestos-related disease. However, corporate management concealed this information from the workers until 1978 and 1979, when the government cited the plants for asbestos-related safety violations. Thus, the workers continued to be exposed to the asbestos without knowing of their health problems for over thirteen years after Du Pont had learned of them. This management action was deemed an intentional tort, and in the spring of 1989 a jury awarded six of the workers $1.4 million in damages. Note, as discussed later in this chapter, under the workers' compensation system no damage award would have been rendered if management had not purposefully concealed the workers' medical records.

An **intentional tort** focuses on whether the aim of a certain act was to result in an injury. The conduct involved may be malicious or may actually be designed to cause harm (punching someone in the nose). A defendant who commits an intentional tort may be liable to the injured party for damages caused by the tort and may be assessed punitive damages, an award not linked to the injury, but instead designed to penalize the defendant. Furthermore, some intentional torts may also cause criminal charges to be filed against the wrongdoer. For example, assume that Mary was fired from her job with an investment firm. In a rage, she hit her supervisor with an umbrella, causing serious injuries. Mary committed an intentional tort. The purpose of her action was to harm her supervisor. Furthermore, criminal charges of assault and battery may be filed against Mary.

However, the scope of what is considered an intentional tort is considerably broader than might first appear. Determining the precise intent of a person who has committed a tort is an impossible undertaking. The best that can be done is to establish a standard based on all the facts surrounding the act in order to determine whether that act would be considered intentional. The legal standard is: Would a reasonable person in the position of one who committed the act in question believe that the injury that did occur was certain to follow from that act? For example, assume that a practical joker pulls a chair from under another person about to sit. The person then falls to the ground and is injured. It is unlikely that the practical joker acted maliciously or actually intended to harm the other person. At most the joker hoped to get a few laughs from the pratfall. Yet such an act has been held to be an intentional tort. A reasonable person pulling a chair out from another would expect that person to fall on the floor and could reasonably expect injury to occur. It may be considered that the wrongdoer knew or was certain that the other person would fall on the floor even though injury was not meant to occur. Further, it is this standard for an intentional tort that would apply to the Du Pont example above. Undoubtedly, the managers did not conceal the asbestos problems from their workers for the purpose of encouraging disease. But a reasonable person would expect that result to almost certainly arise from their actions.

Even though the legal standard for "intentional" may not be precisely fulfilled, similar tort liability can still arise, as the following case illustrates.

Hackbart v. Cincinnati Bengals, Inc.
United States Court of Appeals, Tenth Circuit
601 F.2d 516 (1979)

The question in this case is whether in a regular-season professional football game an injury inflicted by one professional football player on an opposing player can give rise to liability in tort where the injury was inflicted by the intentional striking of a blow during the game.

The injury occurred in 1973, in Denver, during a game between the Denver Broncos and the Cincinnati Bengals. A Broncos defensive back, Dale Hackbart, was the recipient of the injury, and a Bengals offensive back, Charles "Booby" Clark, inflicted the blow that produced it.

Just before the injury, Clark had run a pass pattern to the right side of the Denver Broncos' end zone. The pass was intercepted by Billy Thompson, a Denver free safety, who returned it to midfield. The subject injury occurred as an aftermath of the pass play.

As a consequence of the interception, the roles of Hackbart and Clark suddenly changed. Hackbart, who had been defending, instantaneously became an offensive player. Clark, on the other hand, became a defensive player. Acting as an offensive player, Hackbart attempted to block Clark by throwing his body in front of him. He thereafter remained on the ground. He turned, and with one knee on the ground, watched the play following the interception.

The trial court's finding was that Charles Clark, "acting out of anger and frustration, but without a specific intent to injure stepped forward and struck a blow with his right forearm to the back of the kneeling plaintiff's head and neck with sufficient force to cause both players to fall forward to the ground." Both players, without complaining to the officials or to one another, returned to their respective sidelines, since the ball had changed hands and the offensive and defensive teams of each had been substituted. Clark testified at trial that his frustration was brought about by the fact that his team was losing the game.

The officials did not notice the incident, and no foul was called. However, the game film showed very clearly what had occurred. The plaintiff did not report the happening to his coaches or to anyone else during the game. However, because of the pain he experienced, he was unable to play golf the next day. He did not seek medical attention, but the continued pain caused him to report this fact and the incident to the Broncos' trainer, who gave him treatment. Apparently, he played on the specialty teams for two successive Sundays, but after that the Broncos released him on waivers. (He was in his thirteenth year as a player.) Hackbart sought medical help, and it was then that the physician discovered that he had a serious neck fracture injury.

Doyle, Circuit Judge

The evidence at the trial uniformly supported the proposition that the intentional striking of a player in the head from the rear is not an accepted part of either the playing rules or the general customs of the game of professional football. The trial court, however, believed that the unusual nature of the case called for the consideration of underlying policy which it defined as common law principles which have evolved as a result of the case to case process and which necessarily affect behavior in various contexts. From these considerations the belief was expressed that even intentional injuries incurred in football games should be outside the framework of the law.

We are forced to conclude the result reached is not supported by evidence.

Contrary to the position of the trial court then, there are no principles of law which allow a court to rule out certain tortious conduct by reason of general roughness of the game or difficulty of administering it.

The general customs of football do not approve the intentional punching or striking of others. That this is prohibited was supported by the testimony of all of the witnesses. They testified that the intentional striking of a player in the face or from the rear is prohibited by the playing rules as well as the general customs of the game. Punching or hitting with the arms is prohibited. Undoubtedly these restraints are intended to establish reasonable boundaries so that one football player cannot intentionally inflict a serious injury on another. Therefore, the notion is not correct that all reason has been abandoned, whereby the only possible remedy for the person who has been the victim of an unlawful blow is retaliation.

The Restatement of Torts Second, section 500, distinguishes between reckless misconduct and intentional wrongdoing. To be reckless the act must have been intended by the actor. At the same time, the actor does not intend to cause the harm which results from it. It is enough that he realized, or from the facts should have realized, that there was a strong probability that harm would result even though he may hope or expect that his conduct will prove harmless. Nevertheless, existence of probability is different from substantial certainty which is an ingredient of intent to cause the harm which results from the act.

Therefore, recklessness exists where a person knows that the act is harmful but fails to realize that it will produce the extreme harm which it did produce. It is in this respect that recklessness and intentional conduct differ in degree.

In the case at bar the defendant Clark admittedly acted impulsively and in the heat of anger, and even though it could be said from the admitted facts that he intended the act, it could also be said that he did not intend to inflict serious injury which resulted from the blow which he struck.

In ruling that recklessness is the appropriate standard and that assault and battery is not the exclusive one, we are saying that these two liability concepts are not necessarily opposed one to the other. Rather, recklessness under section 500 of the Restatement might be regarded, for the purpose of analysis at least, a lesser included act.

EXAMPLES OF INTENTIONAL TORTS

The theoretical discussion of civil wrongs can be given a practical context by reviewing three specific types of intentional torts that have developed their own bodies of law: battery, defamation, and intentional interference with a contract. The first involves wrongful injury to a person. The latter two illustrate intentional torts by business, although both may also occur in nonbusiness settings. In all three cases, a diverse range of conduct can lead to tort liability risk. All are well suited for consideration by business managers.

Battery

Battery may be defined as purposeful touching of a person without consent. Although batteries are commonly thought of as violent assaults—knifings, punchings, kickings, and the like—the tort of battery is not so limited. *Any* unpermitted contact with another person may suffice, even if no physical injury arises. Thus, spitting in someone's face can be considered a battery.

The broad scope of this tort may be traced to its common law origins. Battery was deemed a means to keep the peace. It was a substitute, provided by the legal system, for retribution. Thus, a nineteenth-century gentleman who was slapped with a glove would have a legal claim of battery against the wrongdoer, as opposed to resorting to the traditional private remedy—a duel at dawn. Consequently, today, when damages are computed for a battery, the element of indignity is given great weight. One need not have sustained physical injuries in order to be compensated.

In addition to causation and injury (discussed in more depth in the next section), battery has three elements. First, the defendant's act must be voluntary. Second, the defendant must have intended either to harm the plaintiff or to otherwise impart an offensive touch. Third, the touching must have produced a physical injury or an offense to a reasonable person's sense of dignity.

Assume that George is trying to walk across a crowded room. He taps Sam lightly on the shoulder so he can get by. Battery? Although George did voluntarily touch Sam, without permission, no intentional tort would arise. There was no intent to injure or offend George. Social convention permits such touching as a means to request that someone move aside. Furthermore, even if Sam was greatly offended by the touch, a reasonable person (given social convention again) would not be. Consequently, neither the second nor third element of a battery could be established.

However, if George had tackled Sam in order to clear a path through the crowded room, a battery would have occurred. Tackling is not an accepted convention for moving through crowds, and a reasonable person would be offended by it. Then again, if George and Sam were playing football and Sam was racing for the goal line, George's tackle would not be tortious.

Thus, one needs to consider battery (and its concept of lack of consent to being touched) to be affected by circumstances, time, and place. Recall the *Hackbart* case. Although the physical contact occurred during a football game, the surrounding circumstances were such as to remove it from the acceptable touching that football games permit.

Defamation

Defamation is an intentional tort that injures with words. No physical damage occurs. Instead, the injured party sustains a loss of reputation or esteem, adverse public opinion, or a sense of disgrace. Thus, a business may be defamed by words that attack its honesty, creditworthiness, product quality, and the like. (Recall the Corona Extra example in Chapter 8).

In England, where the legal concept of defamation developed, cases were originally heard in the ecclesiastical courts. Defamation was considered a sin and it was punished (or remedied) by penance. When the common law courts began to hear defamation claims in the early eighteenth century, those cases that could not be shown to have caused some specific injury were considered spiritual wrongs and thus left to the church for remedy.

In addition to causation and injury, a tort of defamation has two elements. First, the defendant's words concerning the plaintiff must be communicated to a third party—orally, in writing, or through the media—with the specific intent that the communication occurs. Thus, if a third person eavesdrops or accidentally picks up a cellular phone conversation between the plaintiff and defendant, the intent-to-communicate criterion would not be met. Second, the defendant's statements must be understood by the third party as being derogatory about the plaintiff. Note that the plaintiff need not prove that the comments were false in order to prevail. The burden of establishing the truth of the statements rests with the defendant. If the defendant does so, it is an absolute defense.

A recent case provides a business illustration of the tort of defamation. On November 17, 1992, during its *Dateline* program, NBC aired a segment about General Motors pickup trucks manufactured between 1973 and 1987. Automobile safety groups had asserted that three hundred people had been killed in crashes in which the gasoline tanks of these trucks caught fire. Numerous suits were filed against General Motors as a result. To illustrate the fire risk for those pickup trucks, the *Dateline* program presented film footage of a staged crash in which the gasoline tank in a GM pickup burst into flames.

General Motors, which denied that its pickup trucks were inherently unsafe, received a tip that the NBC crash simulation had been rigged. Investigation proved that NBC had attached incendiary devices to the fuel tank of the pickup truck used in the crash. This fact was not revealed to the *Dateline* audience. GM sued NBC for defamation. The case was soon settled. NBC apologized, admitting the misleading nature of the staged crash. It also agreed to reimburse General Motors for costs the automaker incurred in investigating the matter.

Interference with a Contractual Relationship

Wrongful interference with another person's business activity can take many forms. Intentional interference with a contract is one of the most important for the business manager to consider. Establishing this tort can be quite complex in a market economy in which competition for relative advantage is considered a virtue.

The claim of interference with a contractual (or economic) relationship has a long history. In ancient Rome, the male head of household had a personal claim against those who had injured one of his servants. The claim was that the legal relationship between master and servant had been harmed. In fourteenth-century Britain, the Ordinance of Labourers created a system of compulsory labor and penalized workers who fled their jobs. In addition, it provided that employers could institute a legal claim against those who had enticed their workers to flee. Although the ordinance may seem to be a puzzling and rather harsh piece of legislation, it grew out of a labor shortage crisis caused by the Black Death. As discussed in Chapter 1, historical and social forces shape the development of law.

In addition to causation and injury, two elements are needed to establish a claim of intentional interference with a contract. First, a valid contract must exist that was the subject of the interference. Otherwise, the actions of the defendant would be legitimate market-oriented "bidding" for some good or service. Second, the defendant must have interfered with the knowledge that the contract existed and with intent to disrupt the relationship.

A recent case involving Texaco, Pennzoil, and Getty Oil illustrates this type of tort. Getty Oil and Pennzoil had entered into a merger agreement. The final terms of the complex legal transaction were still being worked out. During this time, Texaco began to negotiate with Getty officials and proposed a better merger deal than had been offered by Pennzoil. Getty accepted the Texaco bid. Pennzoil sued Texaco, claiming tortious interference with its contract with Getty.

Pennzoil argued that the initial agreement with Getty was a binding contract to work in good faith toward a final merger agreement. Texaco's bid was described as tortiously preventing this development. For its part, Texaco argued that Pennzoil and Getty did not have a valid contract. At most it was a promise to negotiate a merger agreement, if possible. With so little definiteness, no legal contract could arise. Additionally, Texaco asserted that Pennzoil could not establish that it knew about the existence of the "contract" when it began to negotiate with Getty officials.

Nonetheless, a Texas jury found for Pennzoil. It was awarded $7.53 billion in compensatory damages and another $3 billion in punitive damages.

Regulating Careless Conduct: The Tort of Negligence

Unlike intentional torts, torts of **negligence** are not based on a wrongful purpose behind the act that caused an injury. Torts of negligence merely involve an injury being caused by heedless or careless actions. Being the wrongdoer in a tort of negligence does not require an evil mental state or purposeful act. The focus of the doctrine is not the intent of the action that caused the injury, but the conduct itself. Negligence involves a lapse in an acceptable pattern of conduct that creates an unreasonable risk of injury. When injury occurs, a tort of negligence exists.

A common example of a tort of negligence is professional malpractice. Accountants, for example, have a duty of reasonable care when conducting an audit on behalf of a client. Auditors who do not follow generally accepted procedures create a risk that their work will be faulty and that their client, relying on the audit, may suffer some financial loss. Assume that Mary's accounting firm was hired by ABC, Inc. to audit its subsidiary. ABC's management intends to use the audit to help it decide whether to sell the subsidiary or try to revitalize its fortunes. Unfortunately, during the audit, Mary's mind wandered. She rushed through the work, anticipating an upcoming vacation. Consequently, she overlooked numerous contingent liabilities and counted a number of accounts receivable as accounts payable. On the basis of the audit, management undervalues the subsidiary, sells it, and soon learns that it made a disastrous deal.

Mary committed a tort of negligence. She did not intend to perform a subpar audit, since she knew it was so important to ABC, Inc. Nor was she reckless in her work. She was careless, and as a result, ABC's reliance on her work was misplaced and the company was injured. Thus, Mary (and her accounting firm) would be liable for damages to ABC, Inc.

Consequently, business managers (and accounting firms) need to plan to minimize the risk of negligent conduct arising. Of course, the simplest decision is not to do the activity at all. Mary's accounting firm, in the above example, could refuse to perform audits. But, more realistically, the accounting firm will need to evaluate its auditing procedures and determine how best to confront the possibility of a tort occurring. Using Mary as an example again, there are at least three things that can be done to change her faulty auditing habits. First, another accountant could spot-check Mary's auditing work, looking for signs of carelessness. Second, a written procedure could be developed that Mary must follow in any audit she conducts. Third, the firm could simply not assign Mary to an audit too near an upcoming vacation.

Consider these three choices. Each has a different risk potential for repeating the type of faulty audit that led to ABC's financial loss. The less "cost" involved in implementing the choice, the greater the risk of negligence arising. For example, it would be easier (and cheaper) for the accounting firm to bar Mary from client audits within one week of her vacation than it would be to pay a second accountant to check her work or to develop a written procedure. The question, of course, is which method to choose. This is the heart of the management dilemma that the tort law system poses. One can only know the "answer" at a time well after the choice has been made.

Basic Legal Principles: General

Both intentional torts and torts of negligence have four elements that the injured party (the plaintiff) must establish: duty, breach of duty, causation, and injury. The discussion that follows will focus on the tort of negligence. Note that the key distinction between intentional torts and torts of negligence arises in the "breach of duty" element.

Apply the four elements to a tort of negligence: First, a legal duty must exist that establishes a standard of care that a person must follow. This standard of care is based upon reasonableness. For example, the driver of a company automobile is required to act as a reasonable and prudent person would act in the operation of an automobile. That is the driver's legal duty of care. Second, there must be a breach of the duty of care. For example, if the driver looks from the road in order to change a tape, this conduct breaches the duty of care. Reasonable and prudent drivers do not take their eyes from the road. Third, the breach of legal duty must cause an injury to another: The driver's car crashes into Tom, who is crossing the street. Fourth, actual loss or damage must occur. In our example, Tom's leg is broken.

Standard of Care

The law of negligence imposes liability on all persons who deviate from a certain standard of care. This standard of care is not derived from a list of approved rules of behavior for all types of human activity. There is no book to consult. Instead, the law creates a general standard, which it imposes on all types of behavior. This standard is called the **reasonable person** standard of care.

The reasonable person is a fictitious individual in the law whose behavior sets the standard that all other persons must meet. The issue in a tort of negligence is whether the wrongdoer acted as a reasonable person would have acted under similar circumstances. In the previous example, a reasonable person would not have looked from the road in order to change a tape in a cassette player. Therefore, by not meeting the reasonable person standard, the driver was negligent. Furthermore, in the auditing example, since Mary did not follow careful procedures in her work, she too would be considered negligent. An old English case defined the tort of negligence as follows: "Negligence is the omission to do something which a reasonable man, guided upon those considerations which ordinarily regulate the conduct of human affairs, would do, or doing something which a prudent and reasonable man would not do."[1] The following case provides a further illustration.

Weirum v. RKO General, Inc.
Supreme Court of California
539 P.2d 36 (1975)

Radio station KHJ is a successful Los Angeles broadcaster with a large teenage following. In order to attract an even larger portion of the available audience and thus increase advertising revenue, KHJ inaugurated in July of 1970 a promotion entitled "The Super Summer Spectacular." Among the programs included in the "spectacular" was a contest broadcast on July 16, 1970, the date of the accident.

On that day, "The Real Don Steele," a KHJ disc jockey, traveled in a conspicuous red automobile to a number of locations in the Los Angeles metropolitan area. Periodically, he apprised KHJ of his whereabouts and his intended destination, and the station broadcast the information to its listeners. The first person to physically locate Steele and fulfill a specified condition would receive a cash prize.

In Van Nuys, seventeen-year-old Robert Sentner was listening to KHJ in his car while searching for The Real Don Steele. Upon hearing that The Real Don Steele was proceeding to Canoga Park, he immediately drove to that vicinity. Meanwhile in Northridge, nineteen-year-old Marsha Baime heard and responded to the same information. Both of them arrived at the Holiday Theater in Canoga Park to find that someone had already claimed the prize. Without knowledge of the other, each decided to follow the Steele vehicle to its next stop and thus be the first to arrive when the next contest question or condition was announced.

For the next few miles the Sentner and Baime cars jockeyed for position closest to the Steele vehicle, reaching speeds up to eighty miles an hour. About a mile and a half from the Westlake offramp the two teenagers heard the following broadcast: "11:13—The Real Don Steele with bread is heading for Thousand Oaks to give it away." The Steele vehicle left the freeway at the Westlake offramp. Either Baime or Sentner, in attempting to follow, forced Ronald Weirum's car onto the center divider, where it overturned, killing Weirum. Baime stopped to report the accident. Sentner, after pausing momentarily to relate the tragedy to a passing peace officer, continued to pursue Steele, successfully located him, and collected a cash prize.

Weirum's wife and children brought an action for wrongful death against Sentner, Baime, and RKO General, Inc. as owner of KHJ. Sentner settled prior to trial. The jury returned a verdict against Baime and KHJ in the amount of $300,000. Baime did not appeal.

Mosk, Justice

The primary question for our determination is whether defendant owed a duty to Ronald Weirum, the decedent, arising out of its broadcast of the giveaway contest. Any number of considerations may justify the imposition of duty in particular circumstances, including the guidance of history, our continually refined concepts of morals and justice, the convenience of the rule, and social judgment as to where the loss should fall. While the question whether one owes a duty to another must be decided on a case-by-case basis, every case is governed by the rule of general application that all persons are required to use ordinary care to prevent others from being injured as the result of their conduct. However, foreseeability of risk is a primary consideration in establishing the element of duty.

We conclude that the record amply supports the finding of foreseeability. These tragic events unfolded in the middle of a Los Angeles summer, a time when young people were free from the constraints of school and responsive to relief from vacation tedium. Seeking to attract new listeners, KHJ devised an "exciting" promotion. Money and a small measure of momentary notoriety awaited the swiftest response. It was foreseeable that defendant's youthful listeners, finding the prize had eluded then at one location, would race to arrive first at the next site and in their haste would disregard the demands of highway safety. It is of no consequence that the harm to decedent was inflicted by third parties acting negligently. Here reckless conduct by youthful contestants, stimulated by defendant's broadcast, constituted the hazard to which decedent was exposed.

It is true, of course, that virtually every act involves some conceivable danger. Liability is imposed only if the risk of harm resulting from the act is deemed unreasonable. We need not belabor the grave danger inherent in the contest broadcast by defendant. The risk of a high-speed automobile chase is the risk of death or serious injury. Obviously, neither the entertainment afforded by the contest nor its commercial rewards can justify the creation of such a grave risk. Defendant could have accomplished its objectives of entertaining its listeners and increasing advertising revenues by adopting a contest format which would have avoided danger to the motoring public.

The judgment and the orders appealed from are affirmed.

Causation

Not every negligent act will create a tort of negligence. The negligent act must cause the injury. If the driver, in our example discussed before the case, had simply changed the tape and had not hit Tom, no tort would have occurred. The conduct still fell below the reasonable person standard, but no injury arose from it.

However, a more difficult problem of causation occurs when injuries are less closely related to the negligent conduct. In the example, the driver's negligence was clearly the cause of Tom's injury. However, what if Tom had been carrying a package, which fell from his arms when he was struck? A passer-by tripped over the package, falling into a ladder. A painter on the ladder slipped and fell onto a second passer-by. The second passer-by was injured. Did the driver's negligence cause the injury to the second passer-by?

This issue of causation is called **proximate cause.** Proximate cause is a term of art in the law. It essentially means that the injury in question must be within the scope of foreseeability of the defendant's conduct. Or to put it another way, the injury must be a "natural and probable" consequence of the conduct of the defendant. Proximate cause responds to a need in tort law to limit the liability exposure of a negligent person to injuries reasonably related to the negligent conduct. In the example, it is unlikely that the driver's negligence would be found to be the proximate cause of the injury to the second passer-by. That injury was not foreseeable, nor was it a natural consequence of the driver's inattentiveness.

The following case involves a tort of negligence. See if you can identify the duty, the breach of duty, the breach being the cause of an injury, and an actual damage or loss to the plaintiff. What element was found to be missing by the court?

Palsgraf v. Long Island R. Co.
Court of Appeals of New York
162 N.E.99 (1928)

Palsgraf was standing on a platform of defendant's railroad after buying a ticket to go to Rockaway Beach. A train stopped at the station, bound for another place. Two men ran forward to catch it. One of the men reached the platform of the car without mishap, though the train was already moving. The other man, carrying a package, jumped aboard the car but seemed unsteady, as if about to fall. A guard on the car, who had held the door open, reached forward to help him in, and another guard on the platform pushed him from behind. In this act, the package was dislodged, and fell upon the rails. It was a small package, about fifteen inches long, and was covered by a newspaper. In fact it contained fireworks, but there was nothing in its appearance to give notice of its contents. The fireworks exploded when they fell. The shock of the explosion threw down some scales used for weighing at the other end of the platform many feet away. The scales struck the plaintiff, Palsgraf, causing injuries for which she sued.

Cardozo, Chief Justice

The conduct of the defendant's guard, if a wrong in its relation to the holder of the package, was not a wrong in its relation to the plaintiff, standing far away. Nothing in the situation gave notice that the falling package had in it the potency of peril to persons thus removed. Negligence is not actionable unless it involves the invasion of a legally protected interest, the violation of a right. "Proof of negligence in the air, so to speak, will not do." If no hazard was apparent to the eye of ordinary vigilance, an act innocent and harmless, at least to outward seeming, with reference to her, did not take to itself the quality of a tort because it happened to be a wrong, though apparently not one involving the risk of bodily insecurity, with reference to some one else. "In every instance, before negligence can be predicated of a given act, back of the act must be sought and found a duty to the individual complaining, the observance of which would have averted or avoided the injury." "The ideas of negligence and duty are strictly correlative."

One who jostles one's neighbor in a crowd does not invade the rights of others standing at the outer fringe when the unintended contact casts a bomb upon the ground. The wrongdoer as to them is the man who carries the bomb, not the one who explodes it without suspicion of the danger. Life will have to be made over, and human nature transformed, before prevision so extravagant can be accepted as the norm of conduct, the customary standard to which behavior must conform.

The risk reasonably to be perceived defines the duty to be obeyed, and risk imports relation; it is risk to another or to others within the range of apprehension. Here, by concession, there was nothing in the situation to suggest to the most cautious mind that the parcel wrapped in newspaper would spread wreckage through the station. If the guard had thrown it down knowingly and willfully, he would not have threatened the plaintiff's safety, so far as appearances could warn him. His conduct would not have involved, even then, an unreasonable probability of invasion of her bodily security. Liability can be no greater where the act is inadvertent.

Negligence is not a tort unless it results in the commission of a wrong, and the commission of a wrong imports the violation of a right.

Andrews, Justice (dissenting)

Negligence may be defined roughly as an act or omission which unreasonably does or may affect the rights of others, or which unreasonably fails to protect one's self from the dangers resulting from such acts.

There must be both the act or the omission, and the right. It is the act itself, not the intent of the actor, that is important.

Where there is the unreasonable act, and some right that may be affected there is negligence whether damage does or does not result. That is immaterial. Should we drive down Broadway at a reckless speed, we are negligent whether we strike an approaching car or miss it by an inch. The act itself is wrongful. It is a wrong not only to those who happen to be within the radius of danger, but to all who might have been there—a wrong to the public at large.

Due care is a duty imposed on each one of us to protect society from unnecessary danger, not to protect A, B, or C alone.

Negligence does involve a relationship between man and his fellows, but not merely a relationship between man and those whom he might reasonably expect his act would injure; rather, a relationship between him and those whom he does in fact injure. If his act has a tendency to harm some one, it harms him a mile away as surely as it does those on the scene.

The proposition is this: Every one owes to the world at large the duty of refraining from those acts that may unreasonably threaten the safety of others. Such an act occurs. Not only is he wronged to whom harm might reasonably be expected to result, but he also who is in fact injured, even if he be outside what would generally be thought the danger zone.

As we have said, we cannot trace the effect of an act to the end, if end there is. Again, however, we may trace it part of the way. An overturned lantern may burn all Chicago. We may follow the fire from the shed to the last building. We rightly say the fire started by the lantern caused its destruction.

A cause, but not the proximate cause. What we do mean by the word "proximate" is that, because of con-venience, of public policy, of a rough sense of justice, the law arbitrarily declines to trace a series of events beyond a certain point. This not logic. It is practical politics.

We look back to the catastrophe, the fire kindled by the spark, or the explosion. We trace the consequences, not indefinitely, but to a certain point. And to aid us in fixing that point we ask what might ordinarily be expected to follow the fire or the explosion.

This last suggestion is the factor which must determine the case before us. The act upon which defendant's liability rests is knocking an apparently harmless package onto the platform The act was negligent. For its proximate consequences the defendant is liable. If its contents were broken, to the owner; if it fell upon and crushed a passenger's foot, then to him; if it exploded and injured one in the immediate vicinity, to him also as to A in the illustration. Mrs. Palsgraf was standing some distance away. How far cannot be told from the record—apparently 25 to 30 feet, perhaps less. Except for the explosion, she would not have been injured. We are told by the appellant in his brief, "It cannot be denied that the explosion was the direct cause of the plaintiff's injuries." So it was a substantial factor in producing the result—there was here a natural and continuous sequence—direct connection. The only intervening cause was that, instead of blowing her to the ground, the concussion smashed the weighing machine which in turn fell upon her. There was no remoteness in time, little in space. And surely, given such an explosion as here, it needed no great foresight to predict that the natural result would be to injure one on the platform at no greater distance from its scene than was the plaintiff. Just how no one might be able to predict. Whether by flying fragments, by broken glass, by wreckage of machines or structures no one could say. But injury in some form was most probable.

Under these circumstances I cannot say as a matter of law that the plaintiff's injuries were not the proximate result of the negligence.

The following case also raises the issues of negligence and proximate cause.

Crankshaw v. Piedmont Driving Club, Inc.
Court of Appeals of Georgia
156 S.E.2d 208 (1967)

On January 15, 1966, Elizabeth Crankshaw, R. M. Harris, and Arlene Harris patronized the dining room of the Piedmont Driving Club. Arlene Harris ordered shrimp and began eating, at which time she noticed a peculiar odor emanating from the shrimp dish that caused her to feel nauseated. Arlene excused herself and proceeded toward the rest room. Shortly thereafter Elizabeth Crankshaw proceeded toward the rest room to give aid and comfort to Arlene. As Elizabeth entered the rest room, she saw Arlene leaning over one of the bowls. Unbeknownst to Crankshaw, Arlene Harris had vomited just inside the entrance to the rest room. As she hurried toward Arlene, Elizabeth stepped into the vomit, and her feet flew out from under her, causing her to fall and break her hip.

Elizabeth Crankshaw contends that the heart of the legal question presented is whether or not the negligent serving of unwholesome food to Arlene Harris was the proximate cause of Crankshaw's injury.

You write the opinion. Does Elizabeth Crankshaw have a tort claim against the Piedmont Driving Club?

TORT LAW AND HISTORY

Developments in the tort of negligence in the United States reflect changes in lifestyle and technology. Much of the increased capacity of negligent acts to cause injuries is an outgrowth of the availability of machines and new technology. For example, if a person walking along a pathway bumps into another walker it is unlikely that an injury would occur. However, if that same person was daydreaming while driving an automobile, thereby causing a collision, the probability of injury would be very great.

Tort law, especially the law of negligence, was a child of the Industrial Revolution, before which the law of negligence was not well developed. Most actions for tort concerned intentional torts, usually arising out of the use of physical force. In fact, the first major work on negligence law was not written until 1850. The leading commentators on the law before that time mentioned it only briefly. But as the machine age began, and especially as railroads spread throughout the country, a great number of machine-related injuries began to occur. Not only did the Industrial Revolution change the way people lived, where people lived, and how people worked, but it also had a profound effect on the law of torts. As Lawrence Friedman wrote: ''The modern law of torts must be laid at the door of the industrial revolution, whose machines had a marvelous capacity for smashing the human body.''[2]

However, the same machines that smashed human bodies also created wealth, provided jobs, and were the key to growth and development of the country. Railroads served to open the West by linking wilderness and farm areas to cities and markets. An inherent problem, one that continues to surface in tort law, became apparent. Courts, in creating tort law doctrines, must continually be aware that too narrow a reading of the tort doctrines may impose harsh consequences on injured victims, while a very broad concept of tort could cripple a new industry by draining its resources. Compare the following descriptions of the legal environment of workplace injuries in the nineteenth century and today. Note how the law reflected contemporary social and economic forces.

Nineteenth-Century Limitations on Tort Law Recovery

In the latter part of the nineteenth century, courts were sympathetic to the interests of developing industry and created a number of doctrines that limited the ability of the injured individual to collect damages. Three major doctrines arose that were defenses to be used by a defendant in an action for negligence. The effects of these defenses were particularly severe to the worker who happened to be injured on the job. These legal rules favored the developing industrial base of the country by limiting its exposure to liability claims. Thus, a ''cost'' of doing business was subsidized by the tort law system. As a result, the legal environment fostered the values of economic growth by placing the risk of loss on those who were injured.

Contributory Negligence

One of these doctrines was called the doctrine of **contributory negligence.** It provided that if the plaintiff (the injured party) and the defendant were both negligent, resulting in the plaintiff's injury, then the plaintiff would be unable to recover damages in tort from the defendant. The injured party would in a sense have to establish that the defendant alone was at fault. Some writers have suggested that even the slightest degree of negligence by the injured party was enough to deny recovery from the defendant.

Note the facts in the following nineteenth-century contributory negligence case and consider its effect on the railroad business. The court's ruling lowered the railroad's costs in two ways. First, the railroad did not have to pay tort law damages to Haring's family. Second, executives for the railroad did not need to consider modifying crossings so that oncoming trains could more easily be seen from the road.

Haring v. New York and Erie Railroad
Supreme Court of New York
13 Barb. 2 (N.Y. 1851)

The complaint alleged that Haring was thrown out of his sleigh with great force and violence and was so severely and seriously injured as to cause his death in a few hours, and that the injury was caused by the gross carelessness, negligence, or willful mismanagement of the defendants. The defendants denied that the death of Haring was caused by their carelessness, or negligence, or willful misconduct, but alleged that it was caused by the gross carelessness and negligence of Haring and of the person who was with him in the sleigh at the time.

Barculo, Justice

The undisputed evidence introduced by the plaintiff, established the fact that her deceased husband, whose death is the subject of the action, was riding in a sleigh with another person, who was driving at the rapid rate of a mile in four or five minutes, across the track of the railroad when the collision occurred. It also appeared that near the point of intersection, high embankments between the railroad, and highway, render it impossible for a person on the highway to see the cars coming until he gets on the track. Upon this state of facts, the simple question was presented to the circuit judge, whether such fast driving at such a place constituted a degree of negligence that defeated the plaintiff's right of recovery.

That the deceased was guilty of negligence, cannot for a moment be doubted. A man who rushes headlong against a locomotive engine, without using the ordinary means of discovering his danger, cannot be said to exercise ordinary care. And the rule is well settled that where the carelessness and imprudence of the person injured contributed to the injury, an action for damages cannot be sustained.

It is contended by the counsel for the plaintiff, that the question of negligence should have been submitted to the jury. But when, upon the plaintiff's own showing, he has defeated his claim by his own misconduct, there can be no propriety in requiring the jury to pass upon the evidence. We cannot shut our eyes to the fact that in certain controversies between the weak and the strong —between a humble individual and a gigantic corporation, the sympathies of the human mind naturally, honestly and generously, run to the assistance and support of the feeble, and apparently oppressed; and that compassion will sometimes exercise over the deliberations of a jury, an influence which, however honorable to them as philanthropists, is wholly inconsistent with the principles of law and the ends of justice. There is, therefore, a manifest propriety in withdrawing from the consideration of the jury, those cases in which the plaintiff fails to show a right of recovery.

The facts here are plain, simple and undisputed; and upon them the law is clear that the plaintiff cannot recover.

Assumption of the Risk and the Fellow Servant Rule

Two other doctrines were very effective in limiting the ability of workers who were injured on the job to bring successfully a tort claim against an employer. One doctrine, assumption of the risk, provided that if a person was voluntarily in a position where risk of injury existed, and that injury occurred, then no tort would be found. For example, if you knowingly and voluntarily enter the cage of a hungry and ferocious lion, which then uses your leg for lunch, you have no tort claim against its owner, since you will have assumed the risk of being attacked by the beast upon entering the cage. Although this seems to be a fair doctrine, in the nineteenth century workers were frequently held to have assumed the risks involved in their jobs merely upon accepting the job.

A second rule that further limited the ability of workers to collect damages was called the fellow servant rule. This rule provided that workers could not sue employers for job-related injuries caused by another employee. Since very few employers were actually on the shop floor or in the mine or in the railroad yard, this doctrine too limited the ability of the worker to recover for injuries. The only tort claim would be against the negligent fellow employee. A damage claim is worthless unless the party who is liable has the funds to pay it. Few ordinary laborers would have such money.

The following case illustrates the application of the doctrines of assumption of the risk and fellow servant rule to workplace injuries. How does the legal environment, as described in *Farwell*, affect the cost of doing business?

Farwell v. Boston and Worcester Railroad
Supreme Court of Massachusetts
45 Mass. 49 (1842)

The plaintiff was employed by the defendant as an engineer. His duties included the management and care of the engines and cars running on the railroad between Boston and Worcester. He alleged that on October 30, 1837, another employee, Whitecomb, negligently operated the switching apparatus, causing the engine and cars upon which the plaintiff was working to be thrown from the tracks. In the process, the plaintiff was thrown to the ground, and his hand was crushed and destroyed when one of the wheels of one of the cars passed over it.

Shaw, Chief Justice

The question is, whether, for damages sustained by Farwell by means of the carelessness and negligence of Whitecomb, the party injured has a remedy against their common employer.

The general rule, resulting from considerations of justice as well as of policy, is, that he who engages in the employment of another for the performance of specified duties and services, for compensation, takes upon himself the natural and ordinary risks and perils incident to the performance of such services, and in legal presumption, the compensation is adjusted accordingly. And we are not aware of any principle which should except the perils arising from the carelessness and negligence of those who are in the same employment. These are perils which the servant is as likely to know, and against which he can as effectually guard, as the master. They are perils incident to the service, and which can be as distinctly foreseen and provided for in the rate of compensation as any others.

We are of opinion that where several persons are employed in the conduct of one common enterprise or undertaking, and the safety of each depends much on the care and skill with which each other shall perform his appropriate duty, each is an observer of the conduct of the others, can give notice of any misconduct, incapacity or neglect of duty, and leave the service, if the common employer will not take such precautions, and employ such agents as the safety of the whole party may require. By these means, the safety of each will be much more effectually secured, than could be done by a resort to the common employer for indemnity in case of loss by the negligence of each other. Regarding it in this light, it is the ordinary case of one sustaining an injury in the course of his own employment, in which he must bear

the loss himself, or seek his remedy, if he have any, against the actual wrong-doer.

In applying these principles to the present case, it appears that the plaintiff was employed by the defendants as an engineer, at the rate of wages usually paid in that employment, being a higher rate than the plaintiff had before received as a machinist. It was a voluntary undertaking on his part, with a full knowledge of the risks incident to the employment; and the loss was sustained by means of an ordinary casualty, caused by the negligence of another servant of the company. Under these circumstances, the loss must be deemed to be the result of a pure accident, like those to which all men, in all employments, and at all times, are more or less exposed; and like similar losses from accidental causes, it must rest where it first fell, unless the plaintiff has a remedy against the person actually in default; of which we give no opinion.

Of course not all courts and cases exactly paralleled these situations. Juries were often very sympathetic to the injured party. But the legal doctrines of contributory negligence and assumption of the risk, and the fellow servant rule, often provided the means to remove the case from the sympathy of the jury. Note that in both *Haring* and *Farwell* the issues were considered questions of law, thus properly decided by judges who may be described as reflecting the mores of their era. Nonetheless, these and other similar doctrines were criticized even at the time for their harsh treatment of the injured. Attorneys began attacking those doctrines, and a number of exceptions were developed by the courts. As the nineteenth century moved toward its end, political pressure arose from labor unions and other groups for reforms in this area of law.

DEVELOPMENTS IN TORT LAW

Tort law is an ever-changing, ever-expanding field. The United States in the 1990s is vastly different from the United States in the latter half of the nineteenth century, when many of the basic doctrines of tort law developed. The railroad, which some writers suggest was central in the development of many of the doctrines, today has been replaced by the automobile and consumer products as generators of tort law claims. No longer a new, undeveloped nation, the United States is now heavily industrialized, and a new service- and information-based economy is emerging. Furthermore, insurance has arisen to cushion the effects of tort liability for individuals and industry. Many of the rules designed to protect the capital of new industry have been questioned and seriously challenged. In fact, the tort law system itself is being scrutinized to discover whether it is a viable system for providing compensation to the victims in modern society. The following discussion examines the movement and growth of some tort law doctrines today.

GUARANTEE OF PAYMENT / NO LAWSUITS

Compensation of Injured Workers

In response to the effect of the nineteenth-century application of contributory negligence, assumption of the risk, and the fellow servant rule to the workplace, states in 1910 began to enact **workers' compensation** statutes. By the early 1920s, virtually every state legislature, and the Congress in the case of government employees, had enacted a plan. The statutes removed accidents and injuries to a worker on the job from the tort law system. Workers' compensation was a system of no-fault social insurance. The injured workers would collect a sum of damages, prescribed by statute, from the workers' compensation fund. The employer would be assessed premiums to pay into the fund, and the employee would be barred from bringing a negligence suit against the employer. The system provided a number of advantages. The employer was no longer subject to lawsuit by an employee negligently injured on the job. The employer knew what payments would be made and it would be able to plan for them, as for any other regular cost of doing business. The employee would be assured of reasonably prompt payment for work-related injuries. The doctrines that made it extremely difficult to collect for injuries from an employer no longer would have an effect. Furthermore, the new system eliminated much litigation, which had formerly caused a great deal of delay in the injured worker's receiving any money. The costs and attorney's fees associated with the lawsuit had often substantially decreased the money actually paid to the worker.

By the late 1960s, the workers' compensation system began to be criticized for its low payments to injured workers. States had not raised the statutory amounts to keep pace with rising costs. As a result, in 1972, a commission created by President Nixon recommended steep increases in benefits. (For example, one of the recommendations was to provide eighty percent of net income to those whose injuries prevented them from working.) Over time, many states raised payments to injured workers, as well as expanded the scope of eligibility. However, such actions caused increased assessments against employers to support the compensation fund. Thus, some have argued that, other things being equal, a new employer would decide not to locate in a benefit-generous state in order to save on a cost of doing business. In the long run, the argument suggested, generosity in workers' compensation would cost a state jobs.

Other changes can also be noted since the enactment of the first workers' compensation statutes. With government assistance plans available today, as well as private insurance and disability coverage, an injured worker is often no longer without a source of funds and can better afford to await the outcome of litigation than a nineteenth-century counterpart. In addition, although the workplace today is certainly not injury-free, it in no way resembles the conditions in factories and industries prior to the enactment of the compensation acts. The government now regulates safety in the workplace and inspects factories, mines, and other areas to determine if the employer is complying with safety regulations. Lack of compliance could well mean government action being taken against the employer. Further, the relationship between the employer and employee is much different today from what it was in the nineteenth century, and the attitude of the courts is certainly less protective of industry than it was in the nineteenth century.

Nonetheless, the benefits received by an injured worker under workers' compensation (and other programs) is far less than could be gained in litigation with the employer. Consequently, pressures arose to provide a means by which some injured workers could seek damages from their employers for on-the-job injuries. Attorneys sought to skirt the prohibition against employee suits by convincing the courts that tort law suits other than those based on negligence are not barred by the statute. One such attempt was to show that the injury was caused by an intentional tort. As previously discussed, an intentional tort is different from one based on negligence and is not limited to situations in which the action was hostile or was meant to cause harm, like a punch in the nose. A practical joke that results in an injury may be considered an intentional tort. The key is the concept of intent, which has been interpreted by courts to mean whether a reasonable person would expect that the result was almost certain to follow from an act. Plaintiffs' attorneys have filed cases arguing that clients' injuries on the job, caused by exposure to dangerous chemicals, were suffered as a result of an intentional tort of the employer. The employer would not actually have intended that an employee be injured by exposure to the chemicals, but by failing to correct the unsafe working conditions, the employer created a situation in which a reasonable person would expect injuries to occur. Thus, it is argued, the conduct would be considered an intentional tort.

The following case is illustrative. Note the argument made by the dissent. Which of the statutory interpretation techniques (see Chapter 5) did Justice Krupansky use?

Blankenship v. Cincinnati Milacron Chemicals
Supreme Court of Ohio
433 N.E.2d 572 (1982)

On February 22, 1979, eight current or former employees of Cincinnati Milacron instituted an action seeking compensatory and punitive damages against their employer. They alleged in their complaints that while they were stationed at Milacron's chemical manufacturing facility in Reading, Ohio, they were exposed to the fumes and otherwise noxious characteristics of certain chemicals within the scope of their employment. They further alleged that notwithstanding the knowledge of Milacron that such conditions existed, Milacron failed to correct the conditions, failed to warn the employees of the dangers and conditions that existed, and failed to report conditions to the various state and federal agencies to which the company was required to report by law. They alleged that the failure was intentional, malicious, and in willful and wanton disregard of the health of employees, and that as a direct and proximate result of this failure they have been injured.

The trial court issued an order on October 5, 1980, that dismissed the action on the ground that the action was barred by relevant sections of the Ohio Workers' Compensation Act, which afforded an employer and its employees total immunity from civil suit.

This holding was appealed and subsequently affirmed by the court of appeals on January 14, 1980. The Ohio supreme court reviewed the case.

Brown, Justice

The sole issue raised in this appeal is whether the trial court properly granted appellees' motion to dismiss appellants' complaint.

The primary focus of the dispute between the parties centers upon the question of whether the Workers' Compensation Act is intended to cover an intentional tort committed by employers against their employees.

The pertinent statutory language does not expressly extend the grant of immunity to actions alleging intentional tortious conduct by employers against their employees. The statutory language clearly limits the categories of injuries for which the employer is exempt from civil liability. By designating as compensable only those injuries received or contracted in the course of or arising out of employment the General Assembly has expressly limited the scope of compensability. By its use of this phrase, the General Assembly has seemingly allowed the judiciary the freedom to determine what risks are incidental to employment in light of the humanitarian purposes which underlie the Act.

Where an employee asserts in his complaint a claim for damages based on an intentional tort, the substance of the claim is not an "injury . . . received or contracted by any employee in the course of or arising out of his employment." No reasonable individual would equate intentional and unintentional conduct in terms of the degree of risk which faces an employee nor would such individual contemplate the risk of an intentional tort as a natural risk of employment. Since an employer's intentional conduct does not arise out of employment, the Act does not bestow upon employers immunity from civil liability for their intentional torts and an employee may resort to a civil suit for damages.

The worker's compensation system is based on the premise that an employer is protected from a suit for negligence in exchange for compliance with the Workers' Compensation Act. The Act operates as a balance of mutual compromise between the interests of the employer and the employee whereby employees relinquish their common law remedy and accept lower benefit levels coupled with the great assurance of recovery and employers give up their common law defenses and are protected from unlimited liability. But the protection afforded by the Act has always been for negligent acts and not for intentional tortious conduct. Indeed, workers' compensation Acts were designed to improve the plight of the injured worker, and to hold that intentional torts are covered under the Act would be tantamount to encouraging such conduct, and this clearly cannot be reconciled with the motivating spirit and purpose of the Act.

In addition, one of the avowed purposes of the Act is to promote a safe and injury-free work environment. Affording an employer immunity for his intentional behavior certainly would not promote such an environment, for an employer could commit intentional acts with impunity with the knowledge that, at the very most his workers' compensation premiums may rise slightly. The judgment of the Court of Appeals is reversed.

Krupansky, Justice (dissenting)

The majority opinion, while appearing on the surface to be a humanitarian gesture, in effect undermines the beneficent purposes for which the Ohio Workers' Compensation Act was created.

Nowhere in the language of the statute is there support for the conclusion that the workers' compensation system was designed to compensate employees solely for employer negligence. The majority claims, if intentional torts are covered under the Act then intentional torts are encouraged. If this is true, then are not negligence and industrial accidents similarly encouraged, since they are covered under the Act?

Such reasoning leads ultimately to releasing the floodgates to a whole vista of lawsuits, each claiming exceptions to the all-inclusive language of the Act. The majority opinion represents a foot in the door policy to encourage workers to sue their employers for damages in addition to compensation provided under the Act.

The intent of the General Assembly, was to eliminate all damage suits outside the Act for injury or disease arising out of employment, including suits based on intentional tort. If the General Assembly desired to create an exception for intentional misconduct it surely could have done so.

The majority's myopic approach disrupts the delicate balance struck by the Act between the interests of labor, management and the public and signals the erosion of a valuable system which has served its purpose of providing a common fund for the benefit of all workers.

While that Act provides for a liberal construction, it must not be used as a panacea to justify reasoning which suffers from logical malnutrition. One of the long-range effects of permitting recovery in these types of cases is the additional costs that will ultimately have to be borne by the consumer through increased product prices. Goods manufactured in this state will thereby suffer a competitive disadvantage, and a less hospitable climate is created to attract and maintain industry in this state. Since industry provides jobs, the labor force has an interest in encouraging industry. Thus, while some workers may benefit from recovery against the employer for intentional torts in addition to collecting workers' compensation benefits, we would be ill-advised to engage in such irresponsibility for the benefit of a few at the detriment of so many.

The workers' compensation system is now approximately eighty years old. As noted, changes occurred within the last twenty years to make the system more responsive to the needs of workers: Benefits payments were raised and the definition of job-related injuries that would be covered was broadened. At the same time, countervailing forces created pressures within the system. Health care expenses skyrocketed and competitive forces required employers to cut costs. Furthermore, some states, in setting employer premiums, did not reflect the costs that insurers argued they faced. Instead, premiums reflected what the regulators thought employers could pay.

An additional countervailing force was the reappearance of an age-old vice: greed. Recent reports indicate that rampant fraud exists within the workers' compensation system. In some cases, lawyers and doctors have induced workers to lie about their health or sources of injuries in order to file false claims. Such workers, of course, had no qualms when "free" money was at stake. It has also been found that some employers lied about the number of people they employ or created scams in order to evade premium assessment. Some reports suggest that up to twenty percent of the current workers' compensation claims are tainted with fraud. As an illustration, Pittsburgh had a fifteen percent decrease in workers' compensation costs after the city began a program of secretly taping activities of some of its "injured" workers. Tapes showed that some who were collecting benefits for workplace injuries were healthy enough to play basketball or fix roofs.

Consequently, in 1991 workers' compensation cost three times what it did in 1980. In that year too, insurance companies reported losses for workers' compensation coverage of over seven billion dollars. Recently, a number of states, including Maine, New York, and California, have seen their workers' compensation system in financial jeopardy.

Query: How should the legal environment deal with workplace injuries? Tort law negligence litigation has its costs, inefficiencies, and delays. In the nineteenth century, workers who were injured were left without remedy. Litigation was deemed to be an ineffective tool. So workers' compensation was hailed as a new no-fault alternative. But, as noted above, it currently has substantial drawbacks. This is a problem awaiting all who are about to begin business careers.

The Demise of Contributory Negligence— and the Rise of Something to Replace It?

Earlier, in the section on tort law during the nineteenth century, the doctrine of contributory negligence was briefly discussed. Judges used this doctrine to remove a case from consideration by a jury if an injured person's own negligence contributed to the injuries, even if the defendant was also negligent. At its harshest, contributory negligence was an all-or-nothing proposition. If the defendant was found to have been even the slightest bit negligent, then no recovery was allowed. Contributory negligence was one of the common law doctrines that reflected the business-subsidizing values favoring economic development in the late nineteenth century.

Today, the doctrine is disfavored. In its place, all but seven of the states have substituted comparative negligence. Comparative negligence provides a proportional recovery to the injured party, based upon a comparison of the plaintiff's negligence with that of the defendant. Thus, in the *Haring* case if the plaintiff was forty percent negligent for fast sleigh driving and the railroad was sixty percent negligent for failing to remove sight obstructions, an award of one hundred thousand dollars would be reduced forty percent. The railroad would be responsible only for its portion of the negligence that led to the injury: sixty thousand dollars.

The rise of comparative negligence reflected a modern trend in tort law that favored compensation of injured parties, weighing this factor more heavily than the factor of assigning fault for the injury. However, there are indications that the victim compensation policy driving tort law development may be slowing down. Consider the following, using comparative negligence. That is, can you roughly determine some negligence on both sides? If so, what percentage?

1. A high school football player, exhausted from play, was nonetheless left in the game even though his team was greatly overmatched. He sustained injuries that left him a quadriplegic. A negligence action was filed against his school.

2. An experienced water skier was skiing backward and barefoot in a narrow channel that was popular with water skiers. His boat driver angled very close to the shore, where untrimmed tree branches hung over the water. The skier crashed into a branch. Would a negligence action be successful against either the boat driver or the property owners?

Both scenarios above are taken from actual cases in which all recovery was denied to the injured persons. Courts used the doctrine of assumption of the risk, since the football player and water skier were both engaged in risky activities that they should have known could cause an injury. Yet others too may have been at fault, given the particular circumstances of each injury.

Consider, then, whether contributory negligence is being "reborn" within comparative negligence doctrine under the guise of assumption of the risk? If so, the pendulum of liability exposure may be beginning to shift toward lesser tort law "cost" for business. Note the precarious current economic climate, the demise of certain industries, the rise of strong foreign competition. Could the legal environment be beginning to respond by narrowing the risk of tort liability exposure? Watch for developments.

New Torts— Wrongful Discharge

NOT IN GA

The employer-employee relationship is sometimes a precarious affair. Most people are employees and earn their living working for someone else. Yet frequently these employees do not have job security. Their employment may be terminated at any time, for any reason. This notion is called the at-will employment doctrine.

The at-will employment doctrine holds that in the absence of an express contract to the contrary, an employee may be fired for no cause or for any cause whatsoever without a legal wrong being committed by the employer. However, the doctrine gives like rights to the employee, who may quit for any reason, in absence of express contract terms to the contrary, without committing a compensable legal wrong against the employer. Practically, the doctrine works most often against the interests of the employee. The doctrine recognizes the great degree of control the employer has over an employee.

The doctrine arose in the late nineteenth century and became the general rule throughout the country. The Wagner Act in the 1930s limited the scope of the discharge right by making it unlawful for employers to fire employees who engaged in union activities. But for that exception, and the employment discrimination laws, employees without contractual protection remained at the mercy of their employers. Examples of past judicially approved at-will discharges involve an employee fired because of refusal to commit perjury on behalf of the employer and an employee fired for refusing to participate in illegal price fixing.

Recently, a trend in the law has been to limit the absolute right of an employer to fire an at-will employee. Employees who have been unjustly fired from their jobs have instituted lawsuits alleging damages for tortious discharge by an employer. For example, in May 1992 a jury in Texas found that an executive was wrongly discharged for refusing to file a false financial report. The executive was awarded $124 million.

Consider that "wrongful discharge" developed through litigation in the United States. Fired workers brought suit, and cases established that the at-will employment doctrine does have limits. No other industrialized country has had a similar rise in wrongful discharge litigation. At the same time, the United States is the only major industrialized country without a "just cause" statute that limits an employer's discretion in firing workers.

Nonetheless, how should a business manager respond to the rise of wrongful discharge litigation? An article in *The Wall Street Journal* noted that companies are seeking more legal advice in their hiring and firing decisions. Furthermore, some firms are offering discharged executives generous severance payments, provided that each executive agrees to refrain from taking legal action against the company. Other firms have created alternative dispute resolution systems (see the materials in Chapter 3 for a general discussion of ADR) by which a discharged employee can seek redress for any grievance.

However, as with any trend, a lack of uniformity exists in the law. Some states continue to recognize the at-will employment doctrine. Others provide limited exceptions only if the employer's actions violate a statutory or constitutional public policy. Still other states take a broader view of emloyee discharges that contravene public policy. The following case is an example.

Wagenseller v. Scottsdale Memorial Hospital
Supreme Court of Arizona
710 P.2d 1025 (1985)

Catherine Wagenseller began her employment at Scottsdale Memorial Hospital as a staff nurse in March 1975, having been personally recruited by the manager of the emergency department, Kay Smith. Wagenseller was an at-will employee—one hired without a specific contractual term.

Most of the events surrounding Wagenseller's work at the hospital and her subsequent termination are not disputed. For more than four years, Smith and Wagenseller maintained a friendly, professional working relationship. In May 1979, they joined a group consisting largely of personnel from other hospitals for an eight-day camping and rafting trip down the Colorado River. According to Wagenseller, "an uncomfortable feeling" developed between her and Smith as the trip progressed—a feeling that Wagenseller ascribed to "the behavior that Kay Smith was displaying." Wagenseller states that this included public urination, defecation, and bathing; heavy drinking; and "grouping up" with other rafters. Wagenseller did not participate in any of these activities. She also refused to join in the group's staging of a parody of the song "Moon River," which allegedly concluded with members of the group "mooning" the audience. Smith and others allegedly performed the "Moon River" skit twice at the hospital following the group's return from the river, but Wagenseller declined to participate there as well.

Wagenseller contends that her refusal to engage in these activities caused her relationship with Smith to deteriorate and was the proximate cause of her termination. She claims that following the river trip Smith began harassing her, using abusive language, and embarrassing her in the company of other staff. Other emergency department staff reported a similar marked change in Smith's behavior toward Wagenseller after the trip, although Smith denied it. On November 1, 1979, Wagenseller was terminated.

Up to the time of the river trip, Wagenseller had received consistently favorable job performance evaluations. Two months before the trip, Smith completed an annual evaluation report in which she rated Wagenseller's performance as "exceed[ing] results expected," the second highest of five possible ratings.

Feldman, Justice

As early as 1562, the English common law presumed that an employment contract containing an annual salary provision or computation was for a one-year term. In the early nineteenth century, American courts borrowed the English rule. The legal rationale embodied in the rule was consistent with the nature of the predominant master-servant employment relationship at the time because it reflected the master's duty to make provision for the general well-being of his servants. The late nineteenth century, however, brought the Industrial Revolution; with it came the decline of the master-servant relationship and the rise of the more impersonal employer-employee relationship. In apparent response to the economic changes sweeping the country, American courts abandoned the English rule and adopted the employment-at-will doctrine. This new doctrine gave the employer freedom to terminate an at-will employee for any reason, good or bad. Thus, an employer was free to fire an employee hired for an indefinite term "for good cause, for no cause, or even for cause morally wrong, without being thereby guilty of legal wrong."

In recent years there has been apparent dissatisfaction with the absolutist formulation of the common law at-will rule. With the rise of large corporations conducting specialized operations and employing relatively immobile workers who often have no other place to market their skills, recognition that the employer and employee do not stand on equal footing is realistic. In addition, unchecked employer power, like unchecked employee power, has been seen to present a distinct threat to the public policy carefully considered and adopted by society as a whole. As a result, it is now recognized that a proper balance must be maintained among the employer's interest in operating a business efficiently and profitably, the employee's interest in earning a livelihood, and society's interest in seeing its public policies carried out. Today, courts in three-fifths of the states have recognized some form of a cause of action for wrongful discharge.

The most widely accepted approach is the "public policy" exception, which permits recovery upon a finding that the employer's conduct undermined some important public policy. There is no precise definition of the term, "public policy." In general, it can be said that public policy concerns what is right and just and what affects the citizens of the state collectively. It is to be found in the state's constitution and statutes and, when they are silent, in its judicial decisions. Although there is

no precise line of demarcation dividing matters that are the subject of public policies from matters purely personal, a survey of cases in other states involving retaliatory discharges shows that a matter must strike at the heart of a citizen's social rights, duties, and responsibilities before the tort will be allowed.

It may be argued, of course, that our economic system functions best if employers are given wide latitude in dealing with employees. We assume that it is in the public interest that employers continue to have that freedom. We also believe, however, that the interests of the economic system will be fully served if employers may fire for good cause or without cause. However, the interests of society as a whole will be promoted if employers are forbidden to fire for cause which is "morally wrong." We hold that an employer may fire for good cause or for no cause. He may not fire for bad cause—that which violates public policy.

In the case before us, Wagenseller refused to participate in activities which arguably would have violated our indecent exposure statute. While this statute may not embody a policy which "strikes at the heart of a citizen's social rights, duties and responsibilities," we believe that it was enacted to preserve and protect the commonly recognized sense of public privacy and decency. The statute does, therefore, recognize bodily privacy as a "citizen's social right." The nature of the act, and not its magnitude, is the issue. The legislature has already concluded that acts fitting the statutory description contravene the public policy of this state. The relevant inquiry here is not whether the alleged "mooning" incidents were either felonies or misdemeanors or constituted purely technical violations of the statute, but whether they contravened the important public policy interests embodied in the law. The law enacted by the legislature establishes a clear policy that public exposure of one's anus is contrary to public standards of morality. We are compelled to conclude that termination of employment for refusal to participate in public exposure of one's buttocks is a termination contrary to the policy of this state, even if, for instance, the employer might have grounds to believe that all of the onlookers were voyeurs and would not be offended. In this situation, there might be no crime, but there would be a violation of public policy to compel the employee to do an act ordinarily proscribed by the law.

We have little expertise in the techniques of mooning. We cannot say as a matter of law, therefore, whether mooning would always violate the statute. We deem such an inquiry unseemly and unnecessary in a civil case. Compelled exposure of the bare buttocks, on pain of termination of employment, is a sufficient violation of the policy embodied in the statute to support the action, even if there would have been no technical violation of the statute.

A Tort Arising from Newly Recognized Property

The doctrines of tort law are as readily applicable to injuries to property rights as they are to personal injuries. Recall the earlier discussion of the elements of a tort. The hypothetical example involved an automobile colliding with Tom, who received a broken leg. If the facts are changed so that the automobile instead collided with a parked delivery van, a tort would still arise. The analysis of the matter would be the same. The only difference is that the injury element that needs to be established in order for a tort to exist would focus on the delivery van instead of Tom's leg.

Glance at the property rights materials in Chapter 12. Technological developments may give rise to complex questions of who is the owner of something newly created. The case of the removed spleen in that chapter is an illustration. Once property questions have been answered, the tort system provides a means through which the owner can seek damages from those who wrongfully use or harm that property. An issue recently raised is whether a popular performer's style is "property" that belongs to that performer. If so, mimicking it, without the performer's consent, may be considered similar, for tort liability purposes, to using a person's car without permission.

The practice of hiring "sound-alikes" to make commercials has long been common in advertising. Copyright law, which protects property interest in musical compositions, generally prohibits the use of any song without its owner's permission. A particular musician's interpretation of the song, however, falls outside copyright law's protection. As a result, advertisers would acquire rights to a song and then seek an unknown performer to mimic the style of a famous rendition. Until recently, such a practice was permitted by the courts. For example, in 1970 a court rejected a claim by Nancy Sinatra against the use of a sound-alike version of "These Boots Are Made for Walking" in a tire commercial. Sinatra's recording of that song had been very popular.

The following case, however, changed direction. A property right in a certain singing style was recognized and Bette Midler was awarded $400,000 against the advertising agency that used a "sound-alike" recording of one of her most popular songs.

Midler v. Ford Motor Company
United States Court of Appeals, Ninth Circuit
849 F.2d 460 (1988)

Ford Motor Company and its advertising agency, Young & Rubicam, Inc., in 1985 advertised the Ford Lincoln Mercury with a series of nineteen 30- or 60-second television commercials in what the agency called the "Yuppie Campaign." The aim was to make an emotional connection with yuppies, bringing back memories of when they were in college. Different popular songs of the 1970s were sung on each commercial.

When Young & Rubicam was preparing the Yuppie Campaign, it presented the commercial to its client by playing an edited version of Bette Midler singing "Do You Want to Dance?" taken from the 1973 album *The Divine Miss M.* Thereafter, the agency contacted Midler's manager, Jerry Edelstein. The conversation went as follows: "Hello, I am Craig Hazen from Young & Rubicam. I am calling you to find out if Bette Midler would be interested in doing . . . ?" Edelstein: "Is it a commercial?" "Yes." "We are not interested."

Undeterred, Young & Rubicam sought out Ula Hedwig, whom it knew to have been one of "The Harlettes," backup singers for Midler for ten years. Hedwig was told by Young & Rubicam that "they wanted someone who could sound like Bette Midler's recording of ['Do You Want to Dance?']." She made an a capella demo and got the job.

After the commercial was aired, Midler was told by "a number of people" that it "sounded exactly" like her record of "Do You Want to Dance?" Hedwig was told by "many personal friends" that they thought it was Midler singing the commercial. Neither the name nor the picture of Midler was used in the commercial; Young & Rubicam had a license from the copyright holder to use the song. At issue in this case is only the protection of Midler's voice.

Noonan, Circuit Judge

If Midler were seeking to prevent the defendants from using that song she would fail. But that is not the case. Midler does not seek damages for Ford's use of "Do You Want To Dance." Copyright protects "original works of authorship fixed in any tangible medium of expression." A voice is not copyrightable. The sounds are not "fixed." What is put forward as protectable here is more personal than any work of authorship. Further, we do not find unfair competition here. One-minute commercials of the sort the defendants put on would not have saturated Midler's audience and curtailed her market. Midler did not do television commercials. The defendants were not in competition with her.

However, a voice is as distinctive and personal as a face. The human voice is one of the most palpable ways identity is manifested. We are all aware that a friend is at once known by a few words on the phone. A fortiori, these observations hold true of singing, especially singing by a singer of renown. The singer manifests herself in the song. To impersonate her voice is to pirate her identity.

Why did the defendants ask Midler to sing if her voice was not of value to them? Why did they studiously acquire the services of a sound-alike and instruct her to imitate Midler if Midler's voice was not of value to them? What they sought was an attribute of Midler's identity.

Its value was what the market would have paid for Midler to have sung the commercial in person. We need not and do not go so far as to hold that every imitation of a voice to advertise merchandise is actionable. We hold only that when a distinctive voice of a professional singer is widely known and is deliberately imitated in order to sell a product, the sellers have appropriated what is not theirs and have committed a tort.

Finding that Bette Midler had a property right in her singing style and that it was tortiously taken by use of a sound-alike is a new "cost" imposed on advertisers seeking to tie popular songs to a certain product. However, application of this principle has not been uniform. A Michigan court refused Mitch Ryder's claim arising from a beer commercial imitation of his version of "Devil With a Blue Dress On." By way of contrast, a $2.5 million award was upheld on behalf of singer Tom Waits in his suit against an advertising agency that used a sound-alike of his distinctive voice in radio commercials.

However, the development of tort law is not static. Lawsuits relying on the *Midler* principle have been filed alleging other performance misappropriations. For example, the rap group Fat Boys filed suit against comedian Joe Piscopo's imitation of their stage presence during a beer commercial. Vanna White sued Samsung Electronics for an advertisement in which a mannequin, wearing a gown and wig, was place in a setting similar to her role on *Wheel of Fortune*.

How would you as an advertising executive deal with the implications of *Midler* when you want to create consumer interest in a client's product? Will this legal development hinder advertising creativity? Will it protect entertainers?

SUMMARY

Various doctrines of tort law (such as negligence, contributory negligence, comparative negligence, and wrongful discharge) are judicial creations. These creations are based on a number of policies in the law. These policies include compensating injured parties, deterring socially unreasonable conduct, adjusting the competing claims of litigating parties, weighing the interests of society that are affected by the legal rule, and assigning fault for the mishap among the conflicting parties.

Since these policies often conflict, there is continued tension within a given tort law doctrine. As shown by the historical material, judicial weight placed on any one of these policies may change over time, resulting in a change in the law. You should understand that the law is not static. It, like society as a whole, is constantly changing to meet the needs of today.

REVIEW QUESTIONS

1. Define the following terms:
   a. Comparative negligence
   b. Intentional tort
   c. Negligence

d. Tort

e. Workers' compensation

2. What are the major differences between a tort of negligence and an intentional tort? Give an example of each.

3. What are the functions of tort law?

4. Discuss the defenses to tort claims that arose during the nineteenth century and that limited an injured person's right to recover damages.

5. Sandra brought suit against a grocery store, alleging that the manager of the store included a dead rat with the groceries that were delivered to her home. She alleged that, as a practical joke, the manager caused the package to be prepared for delivery with the dead rat inside. When the package was delivered, the person who delivered it stated, "The store manager said you had better open the package while I am here." When Sandra opened the package, she saw the dead rat, whereupon she fainted, fell to the floor, and was injured.

 What type of tort should Sandra allege took place? Would your answer change if a rat from a grocery store's storage area had simply crawled into the package without the knowledge of anyone in the store? Could a tort still be said to exist?

6. Computer and recording technology is rapidly changing the world of music. Digital sampling techniques may soon be able to create computer programs that can replicate a musician's unique style. Thus, perhaps recordings could be made of new songs "performed" via a computer program mimicking the special "sound" of long-dead musicians. Assume that you are an executive with the XYZ Entertainment Corporation. Your research and development department has created a new Beatles record through the use of cutting-edge computer technology. Actual Beatles records made over twenty-five years ago are still brisk sellers today. But with the death of John Lennon, any reunion recor-

ding is impossible. Your company, however, has developed a seemingly excellent alternative. What legal environment questions need to be considered in evaluating whether to market that recording? Note, your corporation owns the copyrights to all Lennon-McCartney (Beatles) songs.

7. Discuss at-will employment. How is that doctrine affected by the tort of wrongful discharge?

8. Tom owned a fast-food restaurant business. The restaurant sold sandwiches. It stocked a table with ketchup, mustard, and relish for customers to use. One afternoon while filling the mustard container, Tom accidentally spilled some mustard on the floor. Before he had a chance to clean it up, a customer entered the restaurant. Tom promptly waited on the customer and soon forgot about the mustard on the floor. A few hours later, another customer entered the restaurant, slipped on the mustard, fell, and broke a leg. Does the injured customer have a tort claim against Tom? Explain.

9. Discuss the relationship between tort law and insurance as they affect the behavior of a business.

10. Jack was walking in the city. As he strolled past a high-rise construction site, a board fell and struck him, causing injury. Jack was walking in a safety area, and no one could tell exactly how that board happened to fall. Discuss how Jack might proceed with his claim against the construction company.

11. The ABC Corporation owned a delivery business. One evening one of its trucks was parked negligently, in neutral with its parking brake only partly engaged. Furthermore, the truck was parked on a steep incline. That evening the truck rolled downhill and struck a car, causing the car to hit a telephone pole. The pole fell to the ground and demolished a fire hydrant. Water began to spray. Before the hydrant could be turned off, Smith's

basement was flooded. Does Smith have a tort claim against the ABC Corporation?

12. Mary Jones was jogging. She was wearing a Walkman with the volume nearly on maximum. She was concentrating on the music instead of watching where she was running. As a result, she entered a busy intersection against the light and a clearly noted "Do Not Walk" sign. She was struck by a car that was exceeding the speed limit by fifteen miles per hour. If Mary brings a tort action against the driver of the car, what defenses could be raised? First, assume the case arose in a state that retained its nineteenth-century tort law doctrines and note the arguments. Thereafter, assume the state has adopted doctrines in line with a majority of other states today and note the arguments anew.

13. Jenkins worked for the ABC Chemical Corporation. The factory where he worked produced a certain chemical that emitted dangerous fumes during the production process. Exposure to those fumes over a period of time could cause permanent injury. ABC Corporation knew about the dangers in the production process and also knew that its safety procedures were below standard. The only time the corporation met required safety procedures was when a government inspector toured the factory. At other times, the procedures were such that fumes were likely to be emitted. One day Jenkins was exposed to a dangerous level of fumes and was injured. What contentions and claims could Jenkins and ABC Chemical Corporation make?

14. Smith was an executive with the XYZ Corporation, which sells gasoline products. The corporation is governed by the antitrust laws and is prohibited from agreeing with its competitors to fix prices charged for the products sold. Smith worked for the company without any written contract. One day she was asked by the vice-president of marketing to meet with executives from competing companies in order to set prices on the firms' kerosene, which sold in various regions throughout the country. Smith refused and was therefore fired. Does Smith have a claim against the XYZ Corporation?

15. What would you recommend that business executives for the defendant companies in questions 5, 8, and 13 do in order to minimize similar suits arising in the future?

16. Assess current developments in the American economy. Assume that they presage long-term changes. Then review some of the tort law doctrines in the chapter and suggest possible modifications that may arise. Note the materials in Chapter 1: One theme in the legal environment is that it reflects social and historical movements.

NOTES

[1] *Blyth* v. *Birmingham Waterworks Co.,* 156 Eng. Rep. 1047 (1856).

[2] Lawrence Friedman, *A History of American Law* (New York: Simon & Schuster, 1974), p. 409.

CHAPTER 12

Property Rights

- The Nature of Property
- Where Does a Rule of Property Come From?
- Predictability of Property Rights and Business
- The Use of Property: Scope and Conflicts

Business may be described as the acquisition, use, and transfer of property. Whether a firm is a sole proprietorship or a multinational corporation, those three activities describe the core of their operations. A business school education, therefore, involves the study of the most effective means to accomplish those ends.

Consider the following scenarios:

1. ABC, Inc. has been manufacturing industrial equipment in the United States for fifty years. The company intends to seek additional opportunities for its equipment in foreign markets.

2. Aero, Inc., is a newly created corporation that intends to begin leasing sunlight to farmers who now use it rent-free throughout the country.

3. Jones and Fleener are partners. They have a terrific idea, which they intend to share with others for a price.

Before one can create plans for these businesses using such concepts as marketing, economics, and finance, a preliminary question must be considered: How does the system of property define the scope of the acquisitions, uses, and transfers that those businesses propose? For ABC, Inc., one must consider whether there are relevant differences in property concepts among the countries where the company intends to do business. If so, how might those differences affect, for example, advertising or financing decisions concerning ABC's industrial equipment? With Aero, Inc., and the Jones and Fleener partnership, a more basic question is whether sunlight or ideas are even recognized as property. If not, business principles, such as marketing and economics, simply cannot be applied.

Thus, the foundation for all business activity is the idea of property. This chapter focuses on that concept and describes how the legal system defines property rights. Pay particular attention to how changes in the legal environment affect the scope of property rights. Additionally, note how the law classifies types of property: real or personal, tangible or intangible. Finally, keep in mind that property issues are not static. Questions continue to arise about what should be afforded property rights status and what that status actually means. The materials on intellectual property and the discussion of conflicts between property rights illustrate ongoing areas of development in the legal environment.

THE NATURE OF PROPERTY

Property As a Relationship

IS A BUNDLE OF RIGHTS

Property may be defined as a relationship between its owner and all other people. Thus, to own an acre of land means that the person designated by the legal environment as "owner" has certain powers with respect to that acre that others do not have. Common owner activities such as selling the acre, leasing it to a neighbor, and using it as collateral for a loan are examples of such powers. They provide the owner with choices that may freely be made and that all others are obliged to honor. It is these powers that are the key to the concept of property— what they are, how they can be used, and whether they are subject to change. More commonly they are called property rights.

The term *property rights*, in the legal environment, refers to the adjustment and balance of relationships between individuals, government, and business, or any combination of them. Property, itself, is most accurately considered to be a bundle of rights. Often people speak of property as it relates to a thing: "This is my car, my book, my land." Although it is a convenient way of describing property, what is really meant is that the person has rights in that car, book, or land, and those rights describe certain legally recognized and protected relationships.

In the novel *Robinson Crusoe* by Daniel Defoe, Crusoe was shipwrecked on a deserted island and lived alone for many years. During that time he captured and raised a herd of goats. Could it be said that Robinson Crusoe had property rights in those goats? Think about this question and compare Robinson Crusoe's "rights" with those of Mary, who purchased this textbook from the bookstore. One might say she owns the book—or more accurately, she has all the rights in the book. Those rights include the right to sell the book, perhaps to a friend taking the course next semester. If she needs to borrow ten dollars from her roommate, Mary can use the book as collateral for the loan; that is, in the event Mary does not repay the loan, her roommate may sell the book to get back her ten dollars. Mary has the right to use the book or let someone else use it. If a thief takes the book, Mary may call upon the police to arrest the thief and return the book to her. These are just a a few of the property rights Mary acquired when she purchased the book from the bookstore.

Now compare Mary with Robinson Crusoe. Can Robinson Crusoe sell the goats or use any of them as collateral for a loan? Is there any difference between what Crusoe and Mary can do with their "property"? Anything that Crusoe can do with the goats he is able to do simply because he is in control of them and is alone. One cannot say that Crusoe has property rights in the goats. Against whom would such rights exist? Mary's rights regulate her relationship with others concerning the textbook. Property rights have meaning only as they regulate certain relationships.

Property and Government

Property also requires a system under which relationships with others are both regulated and enforced. However, this system (or laws) in a capitalist economy does not generally act to grant certain defined rights. For example, Mary did not receive a government-approved list of "rights" when she purchased the book. Instead, as the choices she makes concerning her book yield disputes with others, the limits of her property rights will be defined by government's settling the disputes. The outcomes will either recognize rights that Mary possesses or limit her choices, thereby creating boundaries for her property rights in the book. Consequently, property might be seen as arising from the relationships among people, not from government fiat. Nonetheless, government plays a major role in the capitalist concept of property.

Return to Defoe's novel for further elaboration. Later in the novel, another person appears on the island—Friday. Since there is now more than one person, there can be relationships that property rights concepts can regulate. For example, Crusoe may sell a goat to Friday or permit Friday to borrow a number of goats to begin his own herd. But there is still something very important missing to establish that Robinson Crusoe has property rights in the goats, as Mary has property rights in her book. Who says that Crusoe, who captured the goats, should own them rather than Friday? If Robinson Crusoe is stronger or better-armed than Friday, that would settle the matter. But Mary need not be a weight lifter in order to have her rights enforced against the thief who stole her textbook. The government is there to recognize and enforce her property rights. On Robinson Crusoe's island, there is no government or system of laws to adjust claims that Robinson Crusoe might want to make with respect to the goats. Therefore, it is not accurate to say that he has any property rights with respect to the goats. A system of law must exist which acts to define the scope of the property relationship. Thus, clarifying Mary's relationship with all others concerning the textbook is a function of the legal environment. Clarifying Robinson Crusoe's powers with respect to the goats is a personal matter between Crusoe and any other individual who may have a competing claim in the goats.

In summary, property has two elements. First, there must be others against whom property rights claims may be asserted because property rights describe certain relationships among people. Second, there must be a system of government or laws that can recognize, adjust, and enforce claims of property rights.

The following case illustrates this basic concept of property. It involves a college professor and claims of property rights in the professor's lectures. The professor has a property right in his lectures, called a **common law copyright**. Under this right, the profesor has exclusive control of the use and publication of his lectures. The relationship between the professor and others with respect to those notes is regulated by the government.

Williams v. Weisser
California Court of Appeals
78 Cal. Rptr. 542 (1962)

Plaintiff is assistant professor at UCLA in the Anthropology Department. Defendant's business, Class Notes, in Westwood, California, sold outlines for various courses given at UCLA. The defendant paid Karen Allen, a UCLA student, to attend plaintiff's class in Anthropology 1, to take notes from the lectures, and to type up the notes. Allen delivered the typed notes to defendant, and defendant placed a copyright notice thereon in defendant's name, reproduced the typed notes, and offered them for sale. Plaintiff objected. Defendant did not cease these activities until served with summons, complaint, and temporary restraining order. Plaintiff seeks a permanent injunction, general damages, and punitive damages.

One of the grounds on which the judgment was based was that the defendant infringed on the plaintiff's common law copyright (property right) in his lectures.

Kaus, Presiding Judge

The oral delivery of the lectures did not divest plaintiff of his common law copyright to his lectures. Nothing tangible was delivered to the students. The principle which pervades the whole of that reasoning is, that where the persons present at a lecture are not the general public, but a limited class of the public, selected and admitted for the sole and special purpose of receiving individual instruction, they may make any use they can of the lecture, to the extent of taking it down in shorthand, for their own information and improvement, but cannot publish it. It is defendant's position that, copyright aside, he was privileged to publish the notes and to use plaintiff's name in connection with such publication because "[p]laintiff intentionally placed himself in the public eye when he undertook his employment as an instructor."

An author who owns the common law copyright to his work can determine whether he wants to publish it and, if so, under what circumstances. Plaintiff had prepared his notes for a specific purpose—as an outline to lectures to be delivered to a class of students. Though he apparently considered them adequate for that purpose, he did not desire a commercial distribution with which his name was associated. Right or wrong, he felt that his professional standing could be jeopardized. There is evidence that other teachers at UCLA did not object to representatives of Class Notes being in the classroom; indeed some cooperated with defendants in revising the product of the note takers. Plaintiff considered the Anthropology 1 notes sold by defendant as defective in several respects, chiefly because of certain omissions. Any person aware of the cooperation given by other faculty members could reasonably believe that plaintiff had assisted in the final product. We think that these considerations easily bring the case within the ambit of *Fairfield* v. *American Photocopy*. There the defendant used the plaintiff's name in advertising a certain product. He was said to be one of the many satisfied users of the product. He had been a user, but had returned the product to the defendant. The court held that defendant's conduct was "an unauthorized and unwarranted appropriation of plaintiff's personality as a lawyer for pecuniary gain and profit." We think that the *Fairfield* case is indistinguishable from the one at bar.

Pretty Woman, Roy or Rap?

Acuff-Rose Music, Inc. owns the copyright to the song "Oh, Pretty Woman," which was written by Roy Orbison and William Dees in 1964. The Orbison-Dees song has become a popular music standard and Acuff-Rose, as copyright owner, has earned substantial income by licensing it to other musicians who then record the song.

In 1989, Luther Campbell of the rap group 2 Live Crew wrote a rap version of "Oh, Pretty Woman" that he called "Pretty Woman." This version was recorded and released by 2 Live Crew on an album entitled *As Clean As They Want to Be*. Following the release of 2 Live Crew's album, a letter was sent to Acuff-Rose informing it of the rap group's version of "Oh, Pretty Woman." Acuff-Rose refused to grant a license for that use of the song. Nonetheless, *As Clean As They Want to Be* continued to be sold. In 1990 Acuff-Rose sued 2 Live Crew and its recording company for violating its copyright. 2 Live Crew contends that its version of "Oh, Pretty Woman" is a parody, and thus would not violate Acuff-Rose's copyright. Note that under copyright law, parodies are considered a "fair use" to which the copyright owner has no claim. In August 1992 the Sixth Circuit Court of Appeals held that 2 Live Crew's use of "Oh, Pretty Woman" violated Acuff-Rose's copyright. 2 Live Crew appealed this decision and the matter is now pending with the U.S. Supreme Court.

WHERE DOES A RULE OF PROPERTY COME FROM?

One might wonder whether the distinction between property rights arising from the people, being recognized by the law, and property rights being conferred by the law is merely a chicken-and-egg phenomenon. Does a property right really exist before the government recognizes it? If so, then presumably a property owner has a variety of rights that no one, as yet, knows about or can identify. Although this distinction may seem to be esoteric, it is quite important for business, particularly in the era of new property arising from biotechnology and digital computer networks. The key to the distinction, perhaps, may be seen from competing property system concepts. In the capitalist sense, individuals are deemed to have freedom of choice until inconsistent choices arise. Thereafter, the legal system will settle or adjust that dispute. From that activity of the legal system, a clearer definition of acceptable property rights choices can be determined. Under a government-origin theory, by contrast, individuals have no free choice. They are merely authorized to use property in a certain way. The government is the body that makes the "choices."

For example, assume that Billy Bob intends to build a fence in his yard. As a result, a portion of his neighbor Betty Sue's view of a meadow will be obstructed. Under a capitalist system, both parties should have the "right" to choose how to use their land: Billy Bob, as a place on which to erect a fence; Betty Sue, as a place from which to view a meadow. The law, however, in adjusting their inconsistent claims, helps define, or recognize, the scope of each owner's right of use. In this case, Billy Bob will prevail.

The question, of course, is why.

Property rights and rules that define property rights do not exist in a vacuum. They are the results of a careful consideration of a variety of factors that society values. Some of those factors may conflict. But the end result is a rule of property or the recognition of a property right that reflects a number of important things. The best way to understand this notion is to take a long-established rule for the creation of property rights and seek to determine why that rule is as it is.

In an article published in the 1950s, Felix Cohen, a prominent legal scholar, discusses the values and balances inherent in a timeless rule of property.[1] He begins with a discussion of who owns a newborn mule, and through the discussion the reader is led to understand the reasons for the legal rule, in existence for thousands of years in numerous places, that the newborn mule belongs to the owner of its mother. One reason is that the rule seems to be in accordance with the laws of nature. Cohen asks whether it would be just as consistent with the laws of nature if the owner of the father owned the newborn mule. An additional factor then becomes apparent, based upon the difficulty in determining a newborn mule's paternity: the basic need for certainty in the establishment of property law rules. Cohen then asks whether an alternative simple and definite rule for newborn mule ownership should be that the first person to rope or capture it would be its owner. Two final factors are raised from this inquiry: a concept of fairness and the contribution the rule makes to economic productivity. The owner of the mother had cared for it during pregnancy, and thereafter the newborn depends on its mother for its survival. Furthermore, without ownership vesting in the mother's owner, one could expect problems in the livestock business because of the disincentive to breed one's herd.

The interesting thing about Cohen's dialogue is that the values and considerations that make up the rule seem to flow so effortlessly to the result. Yet it is not difficult to imagine major disputes arising thousands of years ago over this issue. Property rights disputes today reflect a similar weighing of considerations. Four considerations should be noted: productivity, or contribution to the economy; certainty and ease of application; enforceability; and fairness. Apply these factors to the dispute between Billy Bob and Betty Sue that was discussed previously. How do these factors support the fact that Billy Bob has the right to build the fence?

The following case is an illustration of the legal environment being asked to find ''new'' property. The question posed by the plaintiff, John Moore, is as vexing as that proposed by the ancient mule owners in Felix Cohen's example noted above. Given the rapid developments in biotechnology, one might suggest that similar questions will be occurring in the future. Nonetheless, note the considerations that were important to the court in holding that Moore did not have any property right in the discovery that was made from his removed spleen.

Moore v. Regents of the University of California
Supreme Court of California
271 Cal. Rptr. 146 (1990)

John Moore first visited UCLA Medical Center on October 5, 1976, shortly after he learned that he had hairy-cell leukemia. On October 8, 1976, his physician, David Golde, recommended that Moore's spleen be removed. Golde informed Moore that he had reason to fear for Moore's life, and that the proposed operation was necessary to slow down the progress of the disease. On the basis of Golde's representations, Moore signed a written consent form authorizing the splenectomy. Before the operation, Golde and Shirley Quan, a researcher employed by the medical center, made arrangements to study portions of Moore's removed spleen. These research activities were not intended to have any relation to Moore's medical care. However, neither Golde nor Quan informed Moore of the plans to conduct this research or requested his permission.

Moore returned to the UCLA Medical Center several times between November 1976 and September 1983. He did so at Golde's direction and on the advice that such visits were necessary and required for his health and well-being. In fact, defendants were conducting research on Moore's cells and planned to benefit financially and competitively by exploiting the cells and their exclusive access to the cells by virtue of Golde's ongoing physician-patient relationship. Sometime before August 1979, Golde established a cell line from Moore's T-lymphocytes. On January 30, 1981, the regents of the University of California applied for a patent on the cell line, listing Golde and Quan as inventors. By virtue of an established policy, the regents, Golde, and Quan would share in any royalties or profits arising out of the patent.

Moore theorizes that he continued to own his cells following their removal from his body, at least for the purpose of directing their use, and that he never consented to their use in potentially lucrative medical research. Thus, to complete Moore's argument, defendants' unauthorized use of his cells constitutes a **conversion** or wrongful taking of his property. As a result of the alleged conversion, Moore claims a proprietary interest in each of the products that any of the defendants might ever create from his cells or the patented cell line.

WOULD STIFLE REASERCH

Panelli, Justice

To establish a conversion a plaintiff must establish an actual interference with his *ownership* or *right of possession*. Where the plaintiff neither has title to the property alleged to have been converted, nor possession thereof, he cannot maintain an action for conversion. Since Moore clearly did not expect to retain possession of his cells following their removal, to sue for their conversion he must have retained an ownership interest in them.

Moore's novel claim to own the biological materials at issue in this case is problematic, at best. Accordingly, his attempt to apply the theory of conversion within this context must frankly be recognized as a request to extend that theory. While we do not purport to hold that excised cells can never be property for any purpose whatsoever, the novelty of Moore's claim demands express consideration of the policies to be served by extending liability.

Of the relevant policy considerations, two are of overriding importance. The first is protection of a competent patient's right to make autonomous medical decisions. That right is grounded in well-recognized and long-standing principles of fiduciary duty and informed consent. This policy weighs in favor of providing a remedy to patients when physicians act with undisclosed motives that may affect their professional judgment. The second important policy consideration is that we not threaten with disabling civil liability innocent parties who are engaged in socially useful activities, such as researchers who have no reason to believe that their use of a particular cell sample is, or may be, against a donor's wishes.

Research on human cells plays a critical role in medical research. This is so because researchers are increasingly able to isolate naturally occurring, medically useful biological substances and to produce useful quantities of such substances through genetic engineering. These efforts are beginning to bear fruit. The extension of conversion law into this area will hinder research by restricting access to the necessary raw materials. Thousands of human cell lines already exist in tissue repositories. These repositories respond to tens of thousands of requests for samples annually. At present, human cell lines are routinely copied and distributed to other researchers for experimental purposes, usually free of charge. This exchange of scientific materials, which still is relatively free and efficient, will surely be compromised if each cell sample becomes the potential subject matter of a lawsuit.

The theory of liability that Moore urges us to endorse threatens to destroy the economic incentive to conduct important medical research. If the use of cells in research is a conversion, then with every cell sample a researcher purchases a ticket in a litigation lottery. Because liability for conversion is predicated on a continuing ownership interest, companies are unlikely to invest heavily in developing, manufacturing, or marketing a product when uncertainty about clear title exists.

In this case, limiting the expansion of liability under a conversion theory will only make it more difficult for Moore to recover a highly theoretical windfall. Any injury to his right to make an informed decision remains actionable through the fiduciary-duty and informed-consent

theories. For these reasons, we hold that the allegations of Moore's complaint state a cause of action for breach of fiduciary duty or lack of informed consent, but not conversion.

Mosk, Justice (dissenting)

The majority claims that a conversion cause of action threatens to "destroy the economic incentive" to conduct the type of research here in issue. In my view whatever merit the majority's single policy consideration may have is outweighed by two contrary considerations. First, our society acknowledges a profound ethical imperative to respect the human body as the physical and temporal expression of the unique human persona. One manifestation of that respect is our prohibition against direct abuse of the body by torture or other forms of cruel or unusual punishment. Another is our prohibition against indirect abuse of the body by its economic exploitation for the sole benefit of another person. Yet the specter of abuse and exploitation haunts the laboratories and boardrooms of today's biotechnological research-industrial complex. It arises wherever scientists or industrialists claim, as defendants claim here, the right to appropriate and exploit a patient's tissue for their sole economic benefit—the right, in other words, to freely mine or harvest valuable physical properties of the patient's body. Such research tends to treat the human body as a commodity—a means to a profitable end. The dignity and sanctity with which we regard the human whole, body as well as mind and soul, are absent when we allow researchers to further their own interests without the patient's participation by using a patient's cells as the basis for a marketable product.

A second policy consideration adds notions of equity to those of ethics. Our society values fundamental fairness in dealings between its members, and condemns the unjust enrichment of any member at the expense of another. This is particularly true when, as here, the parties are not in equal bargaining positions. We are repeatedly told that the commercial products of the biotechnological revolution "hold the promise of tremendous profit." These profits are currently shared exclusively between the biotechnology industry and the universities that support that industry. There is, however, a third party to the biotechnology enterprise—the patient who is the source of the blood or tissue from which all of these profits are derived. While he may be a silent partner, his contribution to the venture is absolutely crucial. But for the cells of Moore's body taken by defendants, there would have been no Mo-cell line at all. Yet defendants deny that Moore is entitled to any share whatever in the proceeds of this cell line. This is both inequitable and immoral.

Biotechnology depends upon the contributions of both patients and researchers. If not for the patient's contribution of cells with unique attributes, the medical value of the bioengineered cells would be negligible. But for the physician's contribution of knowledge and skill in developing the cell product, the commercial value of the patient's cells would also be negligible. Failing to compensate the patient unjustly enriches the researcher because only the researcher's contribution is recognized. In short, if this science has become science for profit, then I fail to see any justification for excluding the patient from participation in those profits.

PREDICTABILITY OF PROPERTY RIGHTS AND BUSINESS

In Chapter 1, predictability was described as one of the required characteristics of law: One must be able to judge the future legal implications of one's decisions. Otherwise the risk in proceeding would be intolerable. In a market economy, predictability of property rights is fundamental. For example, a business executive must be certain that owning a machine means that the machine can be used, sold, leased, used as collateral for a loan, and the like. In absence of that certainty, the legal risk arising from doing anything with the machine (or even buying it) may make any decision making impossible.

Consider the following: What if the court in the *Moore* case had decided that John Moore did have property rights in the medical discovery? Suddenly, any similar discovery based on research that used human tissues would be subject to conficting property claims: the researchers', the person from whom the tissue was taken. But then, what about those persons whose tissues led to preliminary discoveries? Shouldn't they too have some claim? Because without their tissues, the current discovery could not have arisen. Would there be any others with justifiable claims? How about the researchers' professors who taught the techniques that led to the discovery?

These are not idle questions for the business manager in, say, a medical products company that is interested in marketing new biotechnology discoveries. Who owns the discovery and who should this manager deal with are *the* fundamental questions upon which marketing and financial analyses of the new discovery's profitability will be based. In absence of predictability of the property rights questions, the business manager's task becomes a high-risk adventure.

Of course, unlike the discussions above, most questions concerning property rights in business are very predictable. The owner of land can sell it. The owner of a pen can write with it. But it is important to remember that with new property (and at the margins of established property) questions of rights suddenly become central to business decision making. It is from these defined property rights, their sale and use by business, that a market is derived.

**Classifi-
cation of
Types of
Property**

The law divides property into a number of classifications. Once property is found to fit within one of the classifications, various legal rules and procedures, which differ from one classification to another, apply to determine the extent of the rights held by the owner of that property. For example, the legal rules associated with the transfer of land require more formalities than those concerning the transfer of a compact disc player. Procedures for establishing ownership in a song or an invention are more heavily regulated than those for establishing ownership in a jacket. But the same thing is happening in either example. In the first example, property rights are being transferred; and in the second, an owner's claim is being recognized. The legal environment thus refines property rights concepts based on the practical grounds of the nature of the property.

**Real and
Personal
Property**

The law provides two major categories of property. Property may be either real property (land and anything firmly attached to it) or personal property (everything else). Personal property may be either tangible (it can be seen, felt, touched—it has a physical existence) or intangible (ideas, accounts receivable, other items with economic value but without a physical existence). When a person buys a new home, that purchase is considered a purchase of real property. The land and the house, firmly attached to the land, are transferred to the buyer. This textbook is personal property, as are shoes, as are the songs heard on the radio, as is a new short story. Such types of personal property may be tangible (the shoes or the textbook) or intangible (the song or the short story). If someone steals a textbook, the owner has a claim against that person. Similarly, if another band records a songwriter's work without permission or a company publishes a story without the author's consent, the songwriter or author would have claims for property rights infringement even though the song and the short story by themselves do not have a physical existence. They have a physical existence only when placed upon a record or printed on paper.

Note the definitions of real and personal property in the preceding paragraph. Which of the following can always be placed in one category or the other?

1. A house   2. A painting   3. Fertile topsoil   4. A rug

The answer: none of them. Normally, of course, the items can be readily classified. But the law of property at times requires a more focused review of the definitions. The legal environment makes each item of property subject to factual evaluation, rather than relying on general notions of what is normal. Thus, consider the painting above. Typically, it would be a framed canvas and would be personal property. But "typically" does not include the mural painted on the side of a three-story building. That painting is an indivisible part of the building and thus would be considered a part of the real property.

The classification of atypical types of property has its own set of guidelines and is known as the law of fixtures. Note the practical nature of these guidelines, as they seek to assist in the classification. They illustrate the flexible nature of the definitions of real and personal property.

A **fixture** may be defined as personal property that is so attached to or used with real property that it is considered to be part of that real property (see Figure

12.1). For example, a doorknob at the hardware store is personal property. It is stacked on a shelf and is in no way connected with the land or the building. But as soon as a home owner purchases the doorknob and affixes it to the front door, that item of personal property has been transformed into a part of the house, part of the real property.

The legal standard generally applied to fixtures questions is a reasonable person standard. That is, would a reasonable person familiar with the community and with the facts and circumstances of the case be justified in assuming that the person attaching or using the personal property with the real property intended the item of personal property to become a fixture and therefore part of the real property? Courts have developed four guidelines to determine what this mythical reasonable person would do. One is whether there is a written agreement labeling an item as a fixture. The written agreement shows intent and is a strong but not conclusive factor in determining whether something is a fixture. Courts will also analyze the facts concerning the relationship of the item of personal property to the real property. These facts revolve around three general concepts. The first is the degree of attachment or annexation of the item of personal property to the real property. The greater the attachment, the more a part of the real property the item appears to be. Certainly a brick that becomes part of the wall of a building is more solidly affixed to the real property than a throw rug lying on one of the room's floors. Second, courts analyze the ease or difficulty of removing the item of personal property, and whether such removal would damage the real property or the item of personal property. Ease of removal suggests that the item is not a part of the real property. Removing the brick from a wall in the building would without question result in damage to the wall and probably also result in damage to the brick. Since the throw rug could easily be rolled up and carried out of the room there would be no damage occasioned by its removal. Third, the appropriateness of the use of the personal property item with the real property; that is, by its use alone, should the item of personal property be considered part of the real property? For example, the throw rug in the above examples may fit into this category if it was custom designed to fit wall to wall in an unusually shaped room—perhaps a room shaped as a star—as well as being a necessary part of the particular decor of that room. In such a case, the easy-to-remove, unaffixed throw rug begins to appear to have been intended to be a part of the real property.

These factors help when determining whether the item in question should be considered a part of the real property or an independent item of personal property. The following case illustrates the importance of analyzing property classifications by the definition rather than by what would be a usual finding.

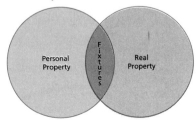

Figure 12.1   Fixtures

Sigrol Realty Corp. v. Valcich
Supreme Court Appellate Division, New York
212 N.Y.S.2d 224 (1961)

In 1891, six members of the Wilmore family acquired the tract of waterfront land in Richmond County known as Robinson's Beach. During the Wilmore ownership, seven frame bungalows were placed on the land by various tenants who rented the land space from the landowners for that purpose. The tenants paid rent for the use of the land; they paid for the maintenance and insurance of the bungalows; and from time to time they repaired, altered, and sold the bungalows without hindrance from the landowners. The tenants occupied the bungalows during the summer months only.

The bungalows rested on cinder blocks that were not sunk into the ground. The bungalows were not bolted to the ground, and they had no basements. It is not disputed that the bungalows were so constructed that, upon severance of the water and electrical connections, they could be removed without injury either to them or to the land.

On April 9, 1959, the Wilmores, for the sum of $12,250, contracted to sell to the plaintiff the land with the buildings and improvements thereon, subject to the rights of tenants, if any. The contract contained the printed provision that fixtures and articles of personal property attached or appurtenant to the premises "which are owned by the seller, are free from all liens and encumbrances."

When defendants, the sellers of the land, attempted to remove the bungalows, plaintiff, on October 6, 1959, instituted this action to declare that it had title to the bungalows and to restrain defendants from removing them.

Beldock, Justice

For the purpose of determining whether chattels annexed to realty remain personalty or become realty, chattels are divided into three classes: (1) some chattels, such as gas ranges, because of their character as movables, remain personalty even after their annexation, regardless of any agreement between the chattel owner and the landowner; (2) other chattels, such as brick, stone and plaster placed in the walls of a building, become realty after annexation, regardless of any agreement to the contrary between the chattel owner and the landowner; such personal property does not retain its character as such if it be annexed to the realty in such a manner as to become an integral part of the realty and be immovable without practically destroying the personal property, or if all or a part of it be essential to the support of the structure to which it is attached; and (3) still other chattels, after attachment, continue to be personalty or become realty, in accordance with the agreement between the chattel owner and the landowner.

In my opinion, these bungalows were movables which continued to be personalty. The bungalows were erected by defendants or by their predecessors in title without any intention of making them permanent accessions to the realty. The manner of their annexation was such as to make them easily removable without injury either to them or to the land. Defendants repaired, maintained, insured, altered, and sold the bungalows without the consent or interference by the Wilmores.

Only the fixtures and articles of personalty owned by the Wilmores were sold. Under the contract the Wilmores sold and the plaintiff purchased the land subject to the rights of the defendants in the bungalows.

Intangible Personal Property: Intellectual Property and Its Growing Importance to Business

As noted above, personal property may be further classified as tangible or intangible. The distinguishing characteristic is whether an item of property has a physical existence. If it does, it is considered tangible personal property. Basic industries that produce goods—steel, automobiles, and textiles, for example—create wealth through the production of tangible personal property. These industries were the heart of the growth of the American economy in the late nineteenth century and throughout the twentieth. Not only did these industries have products protected by laws of property but, as foreign competition arose, various protectionist devices were instituted to salvage their market share. Although this development is beyond the scope of the text, it illustrates the importance of tangible personal property to the economy.

Of perhaps even greater importance in today's post-industrial economy is intangible personal property. It has no physical existence, but that does not mean that it is not real or that it cannot have extraordinary value. As was noted in *The Ramayana*: "There are three things which are real: God, human folly and laughter. Since the first two pass our comprehension, we must do what we can with the third."[2] Perhaps then, one can consider intangible personal property as having a heightened or more sophisticated reality than tangible personal property.

Accounts receivable and business goodwill are common forms of intangible personal property that have long been important to business. But of growing importance to the economy is a type of intangible personal property called *intellectual property*. Intellectual property includes patents, trademarks, copyrights, and trade secrets. Each are doctrines of law designed to protect original ideas ranging from computer programs, to production processes, to corporate logos, to the persona of a celebrity. (Note the discussion of the "new tort" that arose from the recognition of new property rights in Chapter 11.)

In absence of property rights status, original ideas would be available for any company to use. Further, originating firms would have little incentive to develop any ideas, since the products they produced could easily be pirated by competitors. Thus, in the last decade the legal environment protecting intellectual property has been strengthened. Computer software is subject to patent protection. Congress, in 1982, created a new federal circuit court of appeals designed to hear intellectual property disputes. This new court has upheld eighty percent of the asserted patents, while previously only thirty percent were upheld when challenged by competitors. Royalty payments from intellectual property have grown as a source of corporate revenue. For example, routinely, licenses granted by patent holders so others could use their ideas provided a one percent royalty on sales. In 1987, Texas Instruments raised its charge to five percent, and its licensing revenues increased by $281 million over the next two years. Lawsuits over intellectual property have also proliferated, increasing sixty percent over the last decade.

Note how this development reflects one of the themes discussed in Chapter 1. The computer revolution was not ignored by the legal environment.

Midway Mfg. Co. v. Artic International, Inc.
United States Court of Appeals, Seventh Circuit
704 F.2d 1009 (1983)

Midway Manufacturing Co., the plaintiff, makes video game machines. Inside these machines are printed circuit boards capable of causing images to appear on a television picture screen and sounds to emanate from a speaker when an electric current is passed through them. Each machine can produce a large number of related images and sounds. These sounds and images are stored on the machine's circuit boards. How the circuits are arranged and connected determines the set of sounds and images the machine is capable of making. Playing a video game involves manipulating the controls on the machine so that some of the images stored in the machine's circuitry appear on its picture screen and some of its sounds emanate from its speaker.

Artic International, Inc., the defendant, sells printed circuit boards for use inside video game machines. One of the circuit boards the defendant sells speeds up the rate of play—how fast the sounds and images change—of "Galaxian," one of the plaintiff's video games, when inserted in place of one of the "Galaxian" machine's circuit boards. Another of the defendant's circuit boards stores a set of images and sounds almost identical to that stored in the circuit boards of the plaintiff's "Pac-Man" video game machine; thus, the video game that people play on machines containing the defendant's circuit board looks and sounds virtually the same as the plaintiff's "Pac-Man" game.

Midway Manufactuing Co. sued Artic International, Inc., alleging that Artic's sale of these two circuit boards infringes its copyrights in its "Galaxian" and "Pac-Man" video games.

Cummings, Chief Judge

Midway Manufacturing claims that its "Pac-Man" and "Galaxian" video games are "audiovisual works" protected under the 1976 Copyright Act. However, there is a difficulty that must be overcome if video games are to be classified as audiovisual works. Strictly speaking, the particular sequence of images that appears on the screen of a video game machine when the game is played is not the same work as the set of images stored in the machine's circuit boards. The person playing the game can vary the order in which the stored images appear on the screen by moving the machine's control lever. That makes playing a video game a little like arranging words in a dictionary into sentences or paints on a palette into a painting. The question is whether the creative effort in playing a video game is enough like writing or painting to make each performance of a video game the work of the player and not the game's inventor. If so, then the games are not "audiovisual works" as protected by the Act.

We think it is not. Television viewers may vary the order of images transmitted on the same signal but broadcast on different channels by pressing a button that changes the channel on their television. The creative effort required to do that did not make the sequence of images appearing on a viewer's television screen the work of the viewer and not of the television station that transmitted the images. Playing a video game is more like changing channels on a television than it is like writing a novel or painting a picture. The player of a video game does not have control over the sequence of images that appears on the video game screen. He cannot create any sequence he wants out of the images stored on the game's circuit boards. The most he can do is choose one of the limited number of sequences the game allows him to choose. He is unlike a writer or a painter because the video game in effect writes the sentences and paints the painting for him; he merely chooses one of the sentences stored in its memory, one of the paintings stored in its collection.

Thus we affirm the district court's order that enjoins the defendant from manufacturing or distributing circuit boards that can be used to play video games substantially similar to those protected by the plaintiff's copyrights.

Currently, the legal environment is struggling to define property rights for various developments in high-technology industries. For example, as noted in *Diamond* v. *Chakrabarty* in Chapter 5, patent protection is now available for genetically engineered life forms. Although that case dealt with bacteria, a more familiar form, a mouse that was engineered to have a defective immunity system similar to AIDS, has also received patent protection.

Another illustration concerns the computer industry. Digital technology promises mindboggling developments. Information as diverse as books, music, and movies can become instantaneously available once it has been put into digital form. Thereafter, rather than being "accessed" the traditional way—by purchasing a textbook or CD or renting a film—the information will be available on computer networks. Thus, anyone with access to the network may be able to view any movie on demand or mix together vast amounts of information to create customized reports. Of course, that person may also become a mini publishing house by making copies of the movies or books that are available on the network. This is not an idle fear. A telecommunications company recently provided high-speed digital telephone lines to its business customers. One of the first uses the customers made of this technology was to make perfect copies of CDs onto digital audiotape.

Although such actions may violate the property rights of the owners of the music, movies, and books, the enforcement of those rights may be impossible. Consequently, the lack of a practical means for the property law system to protect the information may inhibit its translation into digital form. In absence of a means to protect the data, the digital revolution may not arrive. Thus, the fundamental concept of property rights has moved to the forefront in developing technologies in this country.

THE USE OF PROPERTY: SCOPE AND CONFLICTS

One of the benefits of property ownership is the right to use that property. But as a practical matter, merely listing a "use right" does not provide the business that owns the property with information about what that right actually means. For example, does it mean that a corporation can use the property in a way that is inconsistent with another firm's use of its property? Perhaps it means that the corporation can enforce its property rights in a manner that harms the liberty interests of those who come in contact with that property.

Defining the scope and use of property rights is essential for the business manager who must construct corporate plans on the basis of specific things the firm can do with its property. Although a complete and detailed list of those things does not exist, some general principles can be noted from which the legal environment of a property use right can be constructed.

Conflict between Property Rights and Individual Rights

Property rights and individual rights have the same legal foundation. Each is a system of protection of the rights of the minority against the wishes of the majority. The minority in this case is the rights holder; the majority is the rest of society or the government. Thus, the rights holder, within limits, may exercise power in certain relationships with others. For example, if Jack owned a tract of land, he would be considered to have property rights in that land. Jack could cultivate corn on the land, thus making productive and reasonable use of it. Or Jack could let the land lie fallow and use it for picnics—even if the corn he could have grown would be needed by the community for food. Jack could prohibit anyone else from picnicking on his land or charge a fee for the privilege. The government would, through its laws, enforce such personal choices made by Jack. Under classic property rights theory, Jack, the owner, is generally not answerable to the community, his neighbors, or the government for his use of his land. The majority yields to the dictates of the minority when the minority has property rights.

Individual rights (or liberty) work much the same way. The major distinction is the focus of those rights. Property rights focus on the creation and protection of items of economic value, whether that value is great (a gold mine) or negligible (a mangy old dog or a swamp). Individual rights are the other rights the law recognizes. Examples of individual rights are the right to travel, the right to vote, the right not to be discriminated against on the basis of sex, the right to a jury in a criminal case, and the right to stay out of jail except upon the state's following a rigorous procedure to prove guilt. These rights, too, involve relationships. In fact, historically, liberty and property concepts were treated much the same. Each allowed the individual who possessed any of those rights to make personal (and perhaps illogical, unreasonable, or stupid) choices. The rights insulated the individual from the necessity to conform to the norms of the community through the force of the government.

A problem arises when the rights of a property owner and those of an individual clash. Whose choices should prevail? A brief discussion of *Plessy* v. *Ferguson* from Chapter 1 is illustrative. A law was enacted that protected the choices of property owners in that it forbade the racial integration of railway passengers. In that case, the interests of the individual, to be free of racial discrimination, clashed with the interest of the property owner in enforcing segregation. Although *Plessy* upheld the statute, note that changing historical forces have led to a number of laws that now recognize the individual's interests. Fair housing laws are one example.

Furthermore, beginning in the late nineteenth century the choices provided by the law to property owners began to have detrimental effects on individual interests. The population movement from the farms to urban factories made an individual's living dependent on the property choices of the industrialist. Great concentrations of wealth and power arose in the form of private corporations and trusts. The labor union movement, the populist movement, the grange movement, and the enactment of antitrust laws were attempts to regulate the private decision-making power of property owners by those individuals whose interests were in conflict.

During the Great Depression the clash between property rights and individual rights was at a peak. New Deal legislation, which attempted to deal creatively with an economic crisis, was attacked in court as unconstitutionally infringing on property rights. After a few widely unpopular decisions that upheld the concept of property rights, the Supreme Court changed its mind, indicating that it would use a less stringent standard for reviewing claims of property rights infringement than would apply to individual rights.

As a result, over a half century of precedent and regulation of property has followed. Clearly, the choice between individual rights and property rights, when they clash, now favors individual rights. However, this change of view of the relative importance of property and individual rights did not result in a shift of power from the few to the many.

No property redistribution or corporate breakup occurred to return control to the individual. Instead, the change in the legal environment resulted in the power and control being transferred to the government, another large and powerful body. As a result, individuals remained subject to decisions made by those who control large amounts of property, but at the same time any individual's property has become subject to the control of the government. The material in Chapter 21 focuses on government regulation of property rights.

In the following two cases, property rights and individual rights seem to be in conflict. Each case seems to favor individual rights, thereby relegating property rights to a lower status. Can the cases be characterized another way?

State of New Jersey v. Shack and Tejeras
Supreme Court of New Jersey
277 A.2d 369 (1971)

Tedesco, a farmer, employed migrant workers for his seasonal needs. As part of their compensation, these workers were housed at a camp on his property.

Defendant Tejeras was a field worker for the Farm Workers Division of the Southwest Citizens Organization for Poverty Elimination, known by the acronym SCOPE, a nonprofit corporation funded by the Office of Economic Opportunity pursuant to an act of Congress. The role of SCOPE included providing for the health services of the migrant farm worker.

Defendant Shack was a staff attorney with the Farm Workers Division of Camden Regional Legal Services, Inc., known as CRLS, also a nonprofit corporation funded by the Office of Economic Opportunity pursuant to an act of Congress. The mission of CRLS included legal advice and representation for these workers.

Differences had developed between Tedesco and these defendants before the events that led to the tresspass charges in this case. Hence, when defendant Tejeras wanted to go upon Tedesco's farm to find a migrant worker who needed medical aid for the removal of twenty-eight sutures, he called upon defendant Shack for his help with respect to the legalities involved. Shack, too, had a mission to perform on Tedesco's farm; he wanted to discuss a legal problem with another migrant worker. Defendants arranged to go to the farm together.

Defendants entered upon Tedesco's property, and as they neared the campsite where the farmworkers were housed, they were confronted by Tedesco, who inquired as to their purpose. Tejeras and Shack stated their missions. In response, Tedesco offered to find the injured worker. Tedesco also offered to locate the worker who needed legal advice but insisted that the consultation take place in Tedesco's office and in his presence. Defendants declined, saying they had the right to see the workers in the privacy of their living quarters and without Tedesco's supervision. Tedesco thereupon summoned a state trooper, who, however, refused to remove defendants except upon Tedesco's written complaint. Tedesco then executed the formal complaints, charging violations of the trespass statute.

Weintraub, Chief Justice

Property rights serve human values. They are recognized to that end, and are limited by it. Title to real property cannot include dominion over the destiny of persons the owner permits to come upon the premises. Their well-being must remain the paramount concern of a system of law. Indeed the needs of the occupants may be so imperative and their strength so weak, that the law will deny the occupants the power to contract away what is deemed essential to their health, welfare, or dignity.

Here we are concerned with a highly disadvantaged segment of our society. The migrant farmworkers come to New Jersey in substantial numbers. The migrant farmworkers are a community within but apart from the local scene. They are rootless and isolated. Although the need for their labors is evident, they are unorganized and without economic or political power. It is their plight alone that summoned government to their aid. In response, Congress provided under the Economic Opportunity Act of 1964 for "assistance for migrant and other seasonally employed farmworkers and their families."

These ends would not be gained if the intended beneficiaries could be insulated from efforts to reach them. It is in this framework that we must decide whether the camp operator's rights in his lands may stand between the migrant workers and those who would aid them. The key to that aid is communication. Since the migrant workers are outside the mainstream of the communities in which they are housed and are unaware of their rights and opportunities and of the services available to them, they can be reached only by positive efforts tailored to that end.

A man's right in his real property is not absolute. It was a maxim of the common law that one should so use his property as not to injure the rights of others. Although hardly a precise solvent of actual controversies, the maxim does express the inevitable proposition that rights are relative and there must be an accommodation when they meet. Hence, it has long been true that necessity, private or public, may justify entry upon the lands of another.

The process involves not only the accommodation between the right of the owner and the interests of the general public in his use of this property, but involves also an accommodation between the right of the owner and the right of individuals who are parties with him in consensual transactions relating to the use of the property.

We see no profit in trying to decide this case upon a conventional category and then forcing the present subject into it. That approach would be artificial and distorting. The quest is for a fair adjustment of the competing needs of the parties, in the light of the realities of the relationship between the migrant worker and the operator of the housing facility.

Thus, approaching the case, we find it unthinkable that the farmer-employer can assert a right to isolate the migrant worker in any respect significant for the worker's well-being. The farmer, of course, is entitled to pursue his farming activities without interference, and this defendants readily concede. But we see no legitimate need for a right in the farmer to deny the worker the opportunity for aid available from federal, State, or local services, or from recognized charitable groups seeking to assist him. Hence, representatives of these agencies and organizations may enter upon the premises to seek out the worker at his living quarters. So, too, the migrant worker must be allowed to receive visitors there of his own choice, so long as there is no behavior hurtful to others, and members of the press may not be denied reasonable access to workers who do not object to seeing them.

It is not our purpose to open the employer's premises to the general public if in fact the employer himself has not done so. We do not say, for example, that solicitors or peddlers of all kinds may enter on their own; we may assume for the present that the employer may regulate their entry or bar them, at least if the employer's purpose is not to gain a commercial advantage for himself or if the regulation does not deprive the migrant worker of practical access to things he needs.

And we are mindful of the employer's interest in his own and in his employees' security. Hence, he may reasonably require a visitor to identify himself, and also to state his general purpose if the migrant worker has not already informed him that the visitor is expected. But the employer may not deny the worker his privacy or interfere with his opportunity to live with dignity and to enjoy associations customary among our citizens. These rights are too fundamental to be denied on the basis of an interest in real property and too fragile to be left to the unequal bargaining strength of the parties.

It follows that defendants here invaded no possessory right of the farmer-employer. Their conduct was therefore beyond the reach of the trespass statute.

Katko v. Briney
Supreme Court of Iowa
183 N.W.2d 657 (1971)

In 1957, defendant Bertha L. Briney inherited her parents' farmland. Included was an eighty-acre tract where her grandparents and parents had lived. No one occupied the farmhouse. Her husband, Edward, attempted to care for the land. He kept no farm machinery thereon. The outbuildings became dilapidated.

From 1957 to 1967, there was a series of trespassings and housebreakings with loss of some household items, the breaking of windows, and "messing up of the property in general." The latest occurred on June 8, 1967.

Defendants through the years boarded up the windows and doors in an attempt to stop the intrusions. They had posted "no trespass" signs on the land several years before 1967. The nearest one was thirty-five feet from the house. On June 11, 1967, defendants set "a shotgun trap" in the north bedroom. After Mr. Briney cleaned and oiled his twenty-gauge shotgun, the power of which he knew well, defendants took it to the old house where they secured it to an iron bed with the barrel pointed at the bedroom door. It was rigged with wire from the doorknob to the gun's trigger so it would fire when the door was opened. Mr. Briney admitted he set the trap "because I was mad and tired of being tormented," but he did not intend to injure anyone. He gave no explanation of why he used a loaded shell and set it to hit a person already in the house. Tin was nailed over the bedroom window. The spring gun could not be seen from the outside. No warning of its presence was posted.

Plaintiff lived with his wife and worked regularly as a gasoline station attendant in Eddyville, seven miles from the old house. He had observed it for several years while hunting in the area and considered it as being abandoned. He knew it had long been uninhabited. In 1967, the area around the house was covered with high weeds. Before July 16, 1967, plaintiff and his friend, McDonough, had been to the premises and found several old bottles and fruit jars, which they took and added to their collection of antiques. An old organ fascinated the plaintiff. Arriving at the house a second time, they found that the window by which they had entered before was now a "solid mass of boards" and walked around the house until they found the porch window, which offered less resistance. They crawled through this window. While searching the house, the plaintiff came to the bedroom door and pulled it open, thus triggering the gun, which delivered a charge that struck him in the leg.

Much of his leg, including part of the tibia, was blown away. Only by McDonough's assistance was plaintiff able to get out of the house. After crawling some distance, he was put in his vehicle and rushed to a doctor and then to a hospital. He remained in the hospital for forty days.

Plaintiff's doctor testified he seriously considered amputation, but eventually the healing process was successful. Some weeks after his release from the hospital, plaintiff returned to work on crutches. He was required to keep the injured leg in a cast for approximately a year and wear a special brace for another year. He continued to suffer pain during this period.

There was undenied medical testimony that plaintiff had a permanent deformity, a loss of tissue, and a shortening of the leg.

Plaintiff knew he had no right to break into and enter the house with intent to steal bottles and fruit jars therefrom. He entered a plea of guilty, was fined fifty dollars and costs, and paroled during good behavior from a sixty-day jail sentence. Other than minor traffic charges, this was plaintiff's first brush with the law.

Plaintiff sued the defendant for damages for his injuries, which is the subject of this case.

[You write the opinion. How should these rights be balanced?]

Conflicting Uses of Property

Even though the legal environment upholds individual rights over property rights, there is no similar doctrine of favoritism that applies when property rights conflict. Consider ABC, Inc.'s decision to construct a tannery on land adjacent to XYZ, Inc.'s scented flower garden. The uses are mutually exclusive. The value of XYZ's garden would be ruined by the foul odors emanating from ABC's factory. Conversely, the factory cannot be built if preserving the garden is of importance.

The legal environment attempts to resolve such conflicts in two ways: through the common law and through land use planning. The common law seeks to control the effects of one property owner's use decisions on surrounding land. In general, an owner is free to make even eccentric land use choices until those choices infringe on the enjoyment of adjoining land by its owner. Common law doctrines of trespass and nuisance were designed to accomplish this end.

Trespass is an unauthorized, intentional entry upon the land of another. It may occur if someone walks across another's land or if one causes particles to enter the airspace above another person's land. Thus, the odors wafting from ABC's factory may be a trespass when they enter XYZ's garden area. Furthermore, **nuisance** has been defined as an act that annoys or disturbs the enjoyment of a landowner's property. Acts that make the use of adjoining property physically uncomfortable, endanger the user's health, or revolt the senses are considered a nuisance. Clearly, the tannery seems to fit this definition, too.

But the application of the common law is not that mechanical. Courts balance the relative importance of the uses of the property as part of the trespass or nuisance analysis. Trespass and nuisance proved ineffective in controlling air and water pollution when the alternative was closing the offending factory as the following case illustrates. The environmental law materials in Chapter 21 provide the regulatory response.

Boomer v. Atlantic Cement Co.
Court of Appeals of New York
257 N.E.2d 870 (1970)

Bergan, Judge

Defendant operates a large cement plant near Albany. These are actions for injunction and damages by neighboring landowners alleging injury to property from dirt, smoke and vibration emanating from the plant. A nuisance has been found after trial, temporary damages have been allowed; but an injunction has been denied.

The public concern with air pollution arising from many sources in industry and in transportation is currently accorded ever wider recognition accompanied by a growing sense of responsibility in State and Federal Governments to control it. Cement plants are obvious sources of air pollution in the neighborhoods where they operate.

But there is now before the court private litigation in which individual property owners have sought specific relief from a single plant operation. The threshold question raised by the division of view on this appeal is whether the court should resolve the litigation between the parties now before it as equitably as seems possible; or whether, seeking promotion of the general public welfare, it should channel private litigation into broad public objectives.

It seems apparent that the amelioration of air pollution will depend on technical research in great depth; on a carefully balanced consideration of the economic impact of close regulation; and of the actual effect on public health. It is likely to require massive public expenditure and to demand more than any local community can accomplish and to depend on regional and interstate controls.

A court should not try to do this on its own as a by-product of private litigation and it seems manifest that the judicial establishment is neither equipped in the limited nature of any judgment it can pronounce nor prepared to lay down and implement an effective policy for the elimination of air pollution. This is an area beyond the circumference of one private lawsuit. It is a direct responsibility for government and should not thus be undertaken as an incident to solving a dispute between property owners and a single cement plant—one of many—in the Hudson River valley.

The rule in New York has been that a nuisance will be enjoined although marked disparity be shown in economic consequence between the effect of the injunction and the effect of the nuisance.

But to follow the rule literally would be to close down the plant at once. This court is fully agreed to avoid that immediately drastic remedy; the difference in view is how best to avoid it.

To grant the injunction unless defendant pays plaintiffs permanent damages as may be fixed by the court seems to do justice between the contending parties. All of the attributions of economic loss to the properties on which plaintiffs' complaints are based will have been redressed.

The nuisance complained of by these plaintiffs may have other public or private consequences, but these particular parties are the only ones who have sought remedies and the judgment proposed will fully redress them.

It seems fair to both sides to grant permanent damages to plaintiffs which will terminate this private litigation. The theory of damage is the "servitude on land" of plaintiffs imposed by defendant's nuisance.

The judgment, by allowance of permanent damages imposing a servitude on land, which is the basis of the actions, would preclude future recovery by plaintiffs or their grantees.

Jasen, Judge (dissenting)

It has long been the rule in this State that a nuisance which results in substantial continuing damages to neighbors must be enjoined. To now change the rule to permit the cement company to continue polluting the air indefinitely upon the payment of permanent damages is, in my opinion, compounding the magnitude of a very serious problem in our State and Nation today.

I see grave dangers in overruling our long-established

rule of granting an injunction where a nuisance results in substantial continuing damage. In permitting the injunction to become inoperative upon payment of permanent damages, the majority is, in effect, licensing a continuing wrong. It is the same as saying to the cement company, you may continue to do harm to your neighbors so long as you pay a fee for it. Furthermore, once such permanent damages are assessed and paid, the incentive to alleviate the wrong would be eliminated, thereby continuing air pollution of an area without abatement.

In a day when there is a growing concern for clean air, highly developed industry should not expect acquiescence by the courts, but should, instead, plan its operations to eliminate contamination of our air and damage to its neighbors.

A second problem with conflicting uses of land illustrates a further limitation of the property rights system. Not every important value that is associated with the ownership of property is considered a property right. Fresh breezes, afternoon sunlight, and picturesque views may be important aspects of a certain piece of land, but they are not among the property rights that comprise that land. Consequently, they may be lost when a neighbor uses adjoining land.

For example, assume that the owner of a home most values the view of a mountain range that can be seen from the front porch. Even though the price of that home reflected the picturesque view, the owner does not "own" it. Thus, if a neighbor plants a fast-growing line of trees that obstructs the view, the homeowner has no legal right to assert to reclaim the view. This is so even though the value of that home may diminish because the mountain range is now obstructed. In absence of a right to the view, the neighbor's right to plant trees may proceed unhindered.

The following case illustrates this limitation in the common law. Note the materials on land use planning in Chapter 21. The regulatory environment often acts to balance these conflicting uses. Consider the comment in the last paragraph of the decision in the *Fontainebleau* case.

Fontainebleau Hotel Corp. v. Forty-Five Twenty-Five, Inc.
Florida District Court of Appeal
114 So.2d 357 (1959)

Appellee, plaintiff below, owns the Eden Roc Hotel, which was constructed in 1955, about a year after the Fontainebleau Hotel, owned by the defendant, and adjoins the Fontainebleau on the north. Both are luxury hotels facing the Atlantic Ocean. The Fontainebleau is constructing an addition. During the winter months, from around two o'clock in the afternoon for the remainder of the day, the shadow of the addition will extend over the cabana, swimming pool, and sunbathing areas of the Eden Roc, which are located in the southern portion of its property.

In this action, plaintiff-appellee sought to enjoin the defendants-appellants from proceeding with the construction of the addition to the Fontainebleau (it appears to have been roughly eight stories high at the time suit was filed), alleging that the construction would interfere with the light and air on the beach in front of the Eden Roc and cast a shadow of such size as to render the beach wholly unfit for the use and enjoyment of its guests, to the irreparable injury of the plaintiff. It was alleged that the construction would interfere with the sunlight and air enjoyed by plaintiff and the previous owners of that property for more than twenty years.

Per Curiam

It is well settled that a property owner may put his own property to any reasonable and lawful use, so long as he does not thereby deprive the adjoining landowner of any right of enjoyment of his property which is recognized and protected by law, and so long as his use is not such a one as the law will pronounce a nuisance.

No American decision has been cited, and independent research has revealed none, in which it has been held that—in the absence of some contractual or statutory obligation—a landowner has a legal right to the free flow of light and air across the adjoining land of his neighbor. Even in English common law, the landowner had no legal right, in the absence of an easement or uninterrupted use and enjoyment for a period of 20 years, to unobstructed light and air from the adjoining land. And that doctrine has been unanimously rejected in this country.

There being, then, no legal right to the free flow of light and air from the adjoining land, it is universally held that where a structure serves a useful and beneficial purpose, it does not give rise to a cause of action, either for damages or for an injunction.

If, as contended, public policy demands that a landowner in the Miami Beach area refrain from constructing buildings on his premises that will cast a shadow on the adjoining premises, an amendment of the city's comprehensive planning and zoning ordinance, applicable to the public as a whole, is the means by which such purpose should be achieved.

SUMMARY

Property is the fundamental concept in a market economy. It identifies and defines various rights concerning the ownership and use of ideas and things that have an economic value. These rights are what are bought and sold in the marketplace. The extent of their legitimate use in the legal environment affects the price that is paid for them. Consequently, the business executive needs to appreciate how the legal environment provides a system of property rights.

The study of property in the American legal environment involves more than focusing of a variety of legally protected ownership rights. Property is a relationship among people that is recognized and enforced by the government. Since property consists of a bundle of rights, it is subject to change as the relationships among people in society change. Today, with the developments in computers and biotechnology, basic questions of what should be protected as property often arise. These questions are important, since the legal environment regulates conflicts that arise when property is being used. This chapter examined those conflicts and discussed how the property rights system alleviates them. The limitations of that system were also noted. Chapter 21 focuses on the regulatory response to those limitations.

REVIEW QUESTIONS

1. Define the following terms:
   a. Fixtures
   b. Intangible personal property
   c. Intellectual property
   d. Nuisance
   e. Real property

2. List and discuss the factors and values that make up a rule of property or a property right.

3. List the factors a court may consider in determining whether something is a fixture.

4. Determine from the following facts whether rain should be considered a property right associated with ownership of land. What factors or values make up the arguments of each side in the dispute?

   Weather Research, Inc. began a program of cloud seeding for the purpose of suppressing hail. A number of farmers had hired Weather Research because their lands were frequently ravaged by damaging hailstorms. However, a group of ranchers brought suit against Weather Research, contending that the cloud seeding destroyed potential rain clouds over their property. Seeding was done on clouds directly over the ranchers' property. Ten to twenty minutes thereafter a potential rain cloud or thunderhead would be destroyed, leaving only a fuzzy or wispy mist. The ranchers claim that they have a property right in the precipitation that nature deigns to bestow and that Weather Research, Inc. is interfering with that right.

5. Jones is an archaeologist. He has traveled the world seeking archaeological treasures.

Some of his finds have been placed in his home. For example, in the family room there is a huge stone slab that he pried from the tomb of an Egyptian pharaoh. Jones brought the slab to his house while it was being constructed. He had the family room specially designed so that the slab would stretch from wall to wall. It is used as a table or shelf. The room also has a triple-size door through which the slab was transported into the room. The slab weighs two thousand pounds. The balance of the room is designed and painted to look like the inside of an Egyptian tomb. The slab adds authenticity to the decor.

In July 1991, Jones sold his "house and real property" to Smith. When Smith moved into the house, he noticed that the slab in the family room was missing. He demanded that Jones return it. Jones refused. Discuss in full.

6. Prah constructed a home with a solar heating system. The properties to the north and south of Prah's home were vacant. Therefore, sunlight could, without obstruction, strike the solar collectors that were installed on Prah's roof. Subsequently, Maretti began to construct a home on vacant land adjacent to Prah's residence. Completion of the home would result in a shading of Prah's solar collectors during the cold Wisconsin winters. The shading would reduce the system's efficiency. In addition, there was a possibility of damage through freezing to the solar energy system and to Prah's home itself. The parties attempted, unsuccessfully, to negotiate a settlement concerning the location of Maretti's home.

Should Prah have a property right to the sunlight needed for his solar energy collector? Discuss in light of *Fontainebleau*.

7. How does the law distinguish real property from personal property?

8. Would the law classify a brick in the same way if that brick was one of a stack of fifty at a construction site or if it was part of a wall of a three-story building? If so, why? If not, why not?

9. Why does the law provide property rights status to ideas?

10. How would nuisance or trespass theory apply to the following?

    Jim lives next door to Bill. In the autumn, he builds a fire in his yard to burn the leaves. The smoke drifts onto Bill's land and into his house, causing great discomfort.

11. How would nuisance or trespass theory apply to the following?

    ABC, Inc. is the largest employer in the city. Its factory chimneys belch smoke that drifts onto Bill's land and into his house, causing great discomfort.

12. George owns an herb business. Each summer his garden is filled with aromatic herbs. In the fall he picks what has not been sold and dries the herbs in the sunlight that fills his yard each afternoon. Mary owns the adjacent land. She expands her business by adding a second story to the building. This addition obstructs the sunlight that had been flowing into George's yard. How does the property rights system handle the conflict?

13. How does the law distinguish between tangible and intangible personal property?

14. ABC, Inc. purchased a ten-story building from XYZ, Inc. This building had been XYZ's corporate headquarters. A new headquarters complex was built outside the city. ABC intends to use the old XYZ building for its offices. However, upon moving in, ABC discovered that all the doors had been removed and taken by XYZ to its new complex. Does ABC have a claim against XYZ?

NOTES

[1] F. Cohen, "Dialogue on Private Property," 9 *Rutgers L. Rev.* 357 (1954).

[2] A. Menen, *Rama Retold* (London: Chatto and Windus, 1954), p. 231. Menen's book is a prose version of Valmiki's epic poem from the Indian Enlightenment, *The Ramayana*.

Part 5

Legal Aspects of the Firm and the Regulation of Its Power

CHAPTER 13

Legal Aspects of Business Organizational Forms

- A Focus on Business Organizational Forms: General Ideas
- The Sole Proprietorship
- The Partnership
- The Limited Partnership
- The Corporation
- The Limited Liability Company: An Emerging Organizational Form

A business organization is a type of human relationship, one among workers, managers, owners, and investors. These individuals and their interactions are the focus of the next two chapters. In this chapter, we examine the forms of organization: the sole proprietorship, the partnership, the limited partnership, the corporation, and the limited liability company.

Chapter 14 examines the relationship among organization members. Note how the law facilitates one person's acting on behalf of another (the law of agency) as well as how it controls that person's actions (the law of fiduciary relationships). Recall that these two important features of law, control and facilitate, were discussed in Chapter 1 as ways in which the legal environment affects business activities.

A FOCUS ON BUSINESS ORGANIZATIONAL FORMS: GENERAL IDEAS

Which Form to Choose?

Each legal organizational form facilitates certain combinations of labor, capital, and management that will serve varied business or economic goals. Although the same type of business may be operated using any of the forms, certain ones may not be appropriate given the specific goals of the business executives involved. In fact, as will be noted throughout this chapter, depending upon their goals or interests, one group of business executives may prefer to operate a business as, say, a partnership instead of a corporation. Another group may prefer to use a limited partnership. In either event, the key factor in their decision making is the legal attributes of each form.

As an illustration, consider the following:

1. Mozart and Salieri intend to pool their resources to begin a computer software company. Each wants to have the legal right to share in the profits and to exercise direct management and control of the software company's operations.

2. Hemingway and Fitzgerald intend to invest in a cattle ranch. Neither knows anything about ranching, but they believe, in the long run, the venture will provide a healthy return on their money. Thus, they plan to hire an expert to manage the ranch. Furthermore, since ranching is a rather volatile business, neither Hemingway nor Fitzgerald wants to risk more than his initial investment.

Note the differences between the goals of the two groups: The first pair of investors want to manage their investment, with a legal right to share in profits. The second pair of investors seek protection of their assets beyond what was invested and intend to disassociate themselves from day-to-day concerns of the business. The law of business organizational forms seeks to aid each pair of investors in meeting their goals by providing a number of choices as to how to structure their business. This chapter outlines the basic features of each choice. When you have finished reading the materials, decide on the form that best serves the needs of the investor groups.

Legal Aspects of Business Functions May Differ

Common features or functions can be found among most business organizations. For example, capital will be needed, and those who provide it generally will be investors in the business. In addition, to operate the business, individuals will be placed in charge of day-to-day management. Furthermore, the person considered the "owner" will have the power to make final decisions.

However, each of these functions may have different *legal* consequences, depending upon the form of organization that has been chosen. The legal status of an "investor," for example, will be different depending on whether a person invests in a corporation (investor as shareholder), a partnership (investor as partner), or a limited partnership (investor as limited partner). All other things being equal, investing as a partner will have a greater risk of personal liability for business debts than investing as a limited partner or as a corporate shareholder. Understanding the legal aspects of organizational forms, therefore, plays a vital role in business decision making.

Evaluating Organizational Forms on the Basis of Business Interests

The sole proprietorship, partnership, limited partnership, corporation, and limited liability company can be distinguished in numerous ways. This chapter focuses on four of the most fundamental from the perspective of the business manager.

Limited Liability Principle

Do the members of the organization face any risk of personal liability for claims that are made against the organization? Assume that Mary Smith wants to ensure

TABLE 13.1	Organizational Forms and Business Interests			
	Business Interest			
Business Form	Limited Liability	Profit Share	Management Rights	Control
Sole proprietorship	No	Yes	Yes	Yes
Partnership	No	Yes	Yes	Yes
Limited Partnership	Only for limited partners	Yes	Only for general partner	Only for general partner
Corporation	Yes	No	No	No
Limited liability company	Yes	Yes	Yes	Yes

that her inheritance is safe from creditor claims against her environmental protection company. Are there any legal organizational forms that she should avoid? As we will see, some forms of business protect the owner through **limited liability.**

Profit Share Principle

Do any of the members of the business organization have a legal right to a share of its profits? Thus, if at the end of the current fiscal year an environmental protection company has five hundred thousand dollars in profit, which of its members, if any, have a right to share it?

Management Rights Principle

Which members of the business organization have a legal right to participate in its management? Thus, if Jack Jones intends to assume an active role in decision making at the environmental protection company, are there any organizational forms that will facilitate this choice?

Control Principle

How does the law determine "control" for each of the business organizations? If Mary Smith invests more in an environmental protection business than Jack Jones, which of the forms will give her the power to control the business?

Each of the organizational forms that follows provides a different answer to these four questions. Table 13.1 presents a summary.

THE SOLE PROPRIETORSHIP

The **sole proprietorship,** the least complex form of business organization, consists of one owner, the proprietor. No legal formalities precede its creation. A sole proprietorship may be any size, although most are small businesses. In fact, the sole proprietorship need not have employees; it can proceed on a Garboesque formulation: "I want to be alone." Consequently, the sole proprietor could be the

only one involved in the business. (Of course, most sole proprietors take on employees. Once this occurs, the principles discussed in Chapter 14 regulate the sole proprietor–employee relationship.)

As an illustration, assume that Mary Smith's environmental protection company starts out as a sole proprietorship. As owner, Mary will have control of the business and will make all the management decisions. In order to start the company, she secures a loan from a local bank, using her home as collateral. She selects the firm's equipment and works at its offices throughout the day. Although her conduct is regulated by certain bodies of law (contract law in her dealings with clients; licensing requirements of the state and local governments; and so forth), she is not required to follow any legal procedure to become a sole proprietor. If the environmental protection company is successful, Mary Smith will reap the benefits. If it is a failure, then she will be responsible for its losses. There is no legal distinction between Smith and her business.

As a result, no separate body of "sole proprietorship law" exists. Since there is only one owner, no special legal rules are needed to regulate co-owner relations. Furthermore, since the sole proprietor (without employees) is also the manager of the business, no legal rules are necessary to govern the separation between the control and management functions of the business. The sole proprietor and the business have a single identity. Therefore, the "law of sole proprietorship" encompasses the laws of contracts, torts, property, and agency, as well as government regulations applicable to any business.

But what if more than one person owns the same business? Note, for example, the intentions of Mozart and Salieri or Hemingway and Fitzgerald outlined earlier. A number of questions suddenly arise that were of no concern to Mary Smith. For example: Which of the co-owners will make management decisions? Who will exercise control? How is profit sharing to be determined (if it is to be at all)? Will either be liable for any unpaid claims against the business? The law of business organizations provides a framework under which such questions can be analyzed.

THE PARTNERSHIP

Consider two sole proprietors who decide, informally, to merge their businesses. Each would retain three legal attributes of a sole proprietor: management rights, profit share, and personal liability for business losses. But suddenly problems appear. No longer would either sole proprietor have unfettered control of the business. Furthermore, the management rights, profits, and liability risks will need to be shared. The legal aspects of this "sharing" can be called the law of **partnership**. It is a business organizational form with its own body of law.

As noted in Chapter 1, one of the themes in the legal environment is how historical and social movements influence the creation of today's law. The law of business organizations is an illustration. The use of a partnership as a profit-seeking business organization can be traced to arrangements between ancient Babylonian sharecroppers. The arrangement was also used in ancient Greece and

Rome, where it was called a *societas*. A more direct ancestor of current American partnership law is the Law Merchant, a body of informal rules that derived from business practices during the Middle Ages. The Law Merchant was international in scope and was initially developed apart from the formal legal rules created by any country's government. In the sixteenth and seventeen centuries, England merged the Law Merchant into its common law. Thereafter, it (and the law of partnership) grew with the common law.

In both England and the United States, the nineteenth century was a time of significant use of the partnership form. This reflected heightened business activity in both countries as well as the difficulty in securing corporate charters. By the end of that century, confusion among common law principles (judicial opinions would disagree) led to a movement to codify the law of partnership. The English Parliament enacted the Partnership Act of 1890. In the United States, statutes were passed by individual states following a model called the Uniform Partnership Act, which was drafted in 1914. This act and its successor, the Revised Uniform Partnership Act, are the current sources of American partnership law.

Creation of a Partnership

The Uniform Partnership Act defines a partnership as "an association of two or more persons to carry on as co-owners of a business for profit." If a business organization fits within this definition, it will be considered a partnership. No formal action is needed to create the form. Let us consider Mary Smith and her environmental protection business from the perspective of this definition.

First, according to the definition, another person will need to be involved in the business. That person, Jack Jones, is a product designer and thus Smith and Jones will pool their talents in environmental protection and product design. Of course, this arrangement alone will not make them partners. A number of other legal arrangements (employer-employee, for example) could yield the same result. Consequently, something more will be needed for there to be a Smith and Jones partnership.

A second part of the definition requires that Smith and Jones be co-owners of the business. Attributes of co-ownership can be gleaned from the operation of the firm. They include investment of capital, sharing of management, sharing of profits, and responsibility for any business losses. If Smith and Jones's business exhibits these attributes, Mary and Jack will be considered co-owners and thus partners in the eyes of the law.

And that is all they will need to do. No formal legal procedures are required to form a partnership. Nothing needs to be filed with a state office. No documents or contracts need to be signed by the partners. Having one's business fit within the definition is sufficient. In fact, the law of partnership acts as a stopgap when people operate a business as co-owners without having considered the law of organizational forms. The *Zajac* v. *Harris* case at the end of this section illustrates such a situation.

Of course, partnership contracts that regulate certain aspects of partner relations are not prohibited. In fact, the astute partner may seek to customize the partnership arrangement. As noted in Chapters 9 and 10, contracts are means by which parties can legally enforce their expectations. Although contracts are often thought to concern buying or selling things, they are an important component of business organizations. For example, Mary Smith may want a larger share of the profits than Jack Jones. Or perhaps Jones would like to have a greater say in their firm's management. In absence of a partnership agreement, the Uniform Partnership Act provides that each will have equal legal rights to profits, management, and control. Consequently, Smith and Jones may want to draft a partnership agreement at the time they begin doing business that meets their particular needs.

The following case illustrates a number of points discussed above. First, it is an example of how courts determine whether a certain business arrangement is a partnership. Note how messy and confusing the facts of the case are. Real-life business arrangements do not always follow textbook-perfect models. Second, reflect on the importance of an agreement being negotiated at the outset of a business relationship. If Harris and Zajac intended to be partners, a written partnership agreement could have clarified their relationship. Similarly, an employer-employee relationship could also have been formalized.

Zajac v. Harris
Supreme Court of Arkansas
410 S.W.2d 593 (1967)

The appellee, George Harris, brought this suit to compel the appellant, Carl A. Zajac, to account for the profits and assets of a partnership that assertedly existed between the parties for two years. Zajac denied that a partnership existed, insisting that Harris was merely an employee in a business owned by Zajac.

Smith, Justice

At first blush the testimony appears to be in such hopeless conflict that the controlling issue at the trial must have been one of credibility. Upon reflection, however, we arrive at a somewhat different view of the case. The business association that is known in the law as a partnership is not one that can be defined with precision. To the contrary, a partnership is a contractual relationship that may vary, in form and substance, in an almost infinite variety of ways.

These two laymen went into business together without consulting a lawyer or attempting to put their agreement into writing. It is apparent from the testimony that neither man had any conscious or deliberate intention of entering into a particular legal relationship. When the testimony is viewed in this light the conflicts are not so

sharp as they might otherwise appear to be. Our problem is that of determining from the record as a whole whether the association they agreed upon was a partnership or an employer-employee relationship.

Before the two men became business associates Zajac had conducted a combination garage-and-salvage company, filling station, and grocery store. In the salvage operation now in controversy the parties bought wrecked automobiles from insurance companies and either rebuilt them for resale or cannibalized them by reusing or reselling the parts. Harris, the plaintiff, testified that he and Zajac agreed to go into business together, splitting the profits equally—except that Harris was to receive one fourth of the proceeds from any parts sold by him. Harris borrowed $9,000 from a bank, upon the security of property that he owned, and placed the money in a bank account that he used in buying cars for the firm. The profits were divided from time to time as the cars were resold, so that Harris's capital was used and reused. He identified checks totaling more than $73,000 that he signed in making purchases for the business.

Zajac, by contrast, took the position that Harris was merely an employee working for a commission of one half the profits realized from cars that Harris himself had bought. Zajac denied that he had ever agreed that Harris would spend his own money in buying cars. "I told him, when you go out there, when you bid on a car, make a note that I will pay for it." We have no doubt, however, that Harris did use his own money in the venture and Zajac knew that such expenditures were being made.

Zajac and his wife and their accountant had charge of the books and records. No partnership income tax return was ever filed. Harris was ostensibly treated as an employee, in that federal withholding and Social Security taxes were paid upon his share of the profits. The firm also carried workmen's compensation insurance for Har-

ris's protection. In our opinion, however, any inference that might ordinarily be drawn from these bookkeeping entries are effectively rebutted by the undisputed fact that Harris, apart from being able to sign his name, was unable to read or write. There is no reason to believe that he appreciated the significance of the accounting practices now relied upon by Zajac. They were unilateral.

Zajac paid Harris one half of the profits derived from cars that Zajac bought with his own money and sold by his efforts. Zajac has insisted from the outset that Harris was working upon a commission basis, but that view cannot be reconciled with Harris's admitted right to receive his share of the profits derived from business conducted by Zajac alone.

Harris invested, as we have seen, substantial sums of his own money in the acquisition of cars for the firm. Zajac concedes that Harris was entitled to a share of the profits from transactions that Harris certainly did not handle on a commission basis. When the testimony is reconciled, as we have attempted to do, it does not appear that the chancellor was wrong in deciding that a partnership existed.

**Business
Interests
and the
Partnership**

At the beginning of this chapter, it was noted that four business interests can be used to compare various organizational forms. A brief discussion of their application to a partnership follows.

Limited Liability Principle

Partners are liable for the losses suffered by a partnership business. Thus, if unpaid claims remain after all business assets have been spent and the firm's insurance coverage has been exhausted, the partners will be required to use their own property to satisfy the claims. Personal liability has recently become a substantial problem for large accounting and law partnerships

During 1991 over one billion dollars in damages were assessed against law and accounting partnerships. Approximately three thousand lawsuits are currently pending against accounting partnerships that seek about ten billion dollars in damages. This is twice the number of lawsuits and about five times the damages that were sought in claims filed just five years earlier. If an award is made that cannot be covered by partnership insurance (or assets), then the individual partners will be responsible to make up the difference.

Because of large damage awards and increased risk to personal assets, large professional partnerships are lobbying state legislatures for changes in the law so that a partner's personal assets will be protected. An impetus for this activity was

Almost Liable at Price Waterhouse

Price Waterhouse, a Big Six public accounting firm, is one of the largest accounting partnerships in the world. It has about nine hundred and fifty partners as well as hundreds of accountant-employees and support staff. In May 1992 an Arizona jury awarded a claimant $338 million against Price Waterhouse. The suit involved an audit that the accounting firm performed on behalf of an Arizona bank. This bank was purchased by a London bank and when problems arose with the sale, the London bank sued Price Waterhouse, claiming that its negligent audit was a cause of the London bank's loss that arose from the purchase.

Price Waterhouse's malpractice insurance would have covered only about a third of the judgment. Therefore, if the award had been upheld on appeal, firm assets could have been tapped or partners in Price Waterhouse may have faced personal assessments to make up the difference of about $200 million. Partners who may never have been to Arizona or may not even know anyone in the office that performed the audit could have been as liable as those who supervised the work.

In late December, 1992 the trial judge threw out the jury verdict and granted Price, Waterhouse's motion for a new trial. The judge found that the jury's award of damages was irreconcilably inconsistent in its attribution of the amounts to the plaintiff's claims.

Nonetheless, consider the personal liability risk that partnership status imparts.

the demise of a former Big Eight accounting firm, Laventhol & Horwath. Some former partners in the bankrupt accounting partnership have been assessed $400,000 each to pay firm creditors. About a dozen former partners have filed bankruptcy, hoping to shelter some of their personal assets from creditor claims. In addition, the Big Six accounting firms are studying ways to restructure to lessen partner liability risk. One suggestion is to spin off their consulting businesses into separate corporations in each state where they do business.

Consequently, as illustrated above, the business executive needs to consider the liability disadvantage when evaluating the partnership organizational form. Although insurance and firm assets can act as a buffer, the ultimate sources for unpaid business claims are the partners. However, there are compensating advantages that, for some executives, make the partnership an attractive organizational form.

Profit Share Principle

Partners have a legal right to a share of business profits. Becoming a partner in a large professional partnership has been synonymous with earning a large income. It is not uncommon for such partners to earn well into six figures annually. Thus, although personal liability is a risk with this form of business, a successful arrangement can produce huge gains for a partner. Note in *Zajac* v. *Harris* that George Harris sought to have the business declared a partnership. Most likely it was profitable enough that his partnership share would far exceed what he was paid in "wages."

Management Rights Principle

Partners have a legal right to manage the partnership business. Consequently, another advantage of this form is that the partners have input into the operation of the business. In theory, then, one can assume that by careful management, partners can limit the risk of personal liability that is a part of the organizational form. Today's litigation climate, however, somewhat belies that theory. (See the discussion of the changes and trends in the scope of tort liability in Chapter 11.) Further, not all individuals want to have an active role in the operation of a business.

Control Principle

Partners are co-owners of the business. As such, their work for the partnership is not compensated by wages or a salary. Instead, they work for a share in the profits. Furthermore, as co-owners, each partner has the same right to vote on issues affecting the firm. Unless specified otherwise in the partnership agreement, this equal right to control is unaffected by the amount a partner has invested in the business or the skills and experience a partner may possess. Control is a fundamental attribute of the partnership form. The determination of control is quite different in a corporation, as discussed later in the chapter.

Although a partner's right to control, manage, and share profits in the business make the partnership an attractive form, the risk of personal liability always must be considered. Of course, a firm with ample assets and impressive insurance coverage will insulate a partner from that risk. But, as noted above, the risk can never fully be alleviated. Thus, there is a need for an organization in which a person can invest money, share in the profits, but have no risk of personal liability. This form is called the limited partnership.

THE LIMITED PARTNERSHIP

The **limited partnership** can be traced to the *commenda* in the Middle Ages. In principle, the commenda was much like today's limited partnership, in which the investor (the commendator) provided funds for a business that was managed by another person (the commendatarius). Most of the profits would go to the commendator, but no liability for losses would attach.

Limited partnership law in the United States arose in the early nineteenth century as a response to concerns about partners' personal liability risk, as well as to the difficulty of obtaining a corporate charter. In 1822, New York became the first state to enact a limited partnership statute. It was based on the French

Commercial Code of 1807. Chancellor Kent, in *Commentaries on American Law*, described it as the first instance in which non-British law was adopted in the United States. Today, limited partnership law in the states is based primarily on one of two model statutes: the Uniform Limited Partnership Act or the Revised Uniform Limited Partnership Act.

One might consider (if reading ahead a few pages) that the limited partnership contains elements of both the partnership and corporate forms. Like a corporation, a limited partnership must be formed pursuant to a statute. Formalities prescribed by the statute and required filings must take place before the limited partnership is created. Once the limited partnership exists, the investors (limited partners) have limited liability. Furthermore, the limited partners do not take part in the management of the business. A limited partnership is also similar in some ways to a partnership. The persons who manage the business are called general partners and are governed by the terms of partnership law. Also, limited partners share in the profits of the business.

Limited partnerships are used primarily for investments in rather risky business. Broadway shows, professional sports franchises, and oil exploration are examples. Limited partnerships and tax shelters are virtually synonymous. Investors in limited partnerships generally can be assured that their loss will be no more than what they invested, since they have a limited liability. Furthermore, since the limited partnership is not a legal entity like a corporation, income and losses for taxes purposes are apportioned among the investors. Thus, the limited partnership is an attractive business organization for investment purposes. Note, however, that if limited partners are found to be taking part in managing the business, they lose their limited liability protection. The following case is an example.

Holzman v. De Escamilla
California District Court of Appeal
195 P.2d 833 (1948)

Early in 1943, Hacienda Farms, Limited, was organized as a limited partnership with Ricardo de Escamilla as the general partner and James L. Russell and H. W. Andrews as limited partners.

The partnership went into bankruptcy in December 1943, and Lawrence Holzman was appointed and qualified as trustee of the estate of the bankrupt. On November 13, 1944, he brought this action for the purpose of determining that Russell and Andrews, by taking part in the control of the partnership business, had become liable as general partners to the creditors of the partnership. The trial court found in favor of the plaintiff on this issue and rendered judgment to the effect that the three defendants were liable as general partners.

Marks, Justice

The record shows the following testimony of de Escamilla:

"Q. Did you have a conversation or conversations with Mr. Andrews or Mr. Russell before planting the tomatoes? A. We always conferred and agreed as to what crops we would put in.

"Q. Who determined that it was advisable to plant watermelons? A. Mr. Andrews.

"Q. Who determined that string beans should be planted? A. All of us. There was never any crop that was planted or contemplated in planting that wasn't thoroughly discussed and agreed upon by the three of us; particularly Andrews and myself."

De Escamilla further testified that Russell and Andrews came to the farms about twice a week and consulted about the crops to be planted. He did not want to plant peppers or egg plant because, as he said, "I don't like that country for peppers or egg plant; no, sir," but he was overruled and those crops were planted. The same is true of the watermelons.

Hacienda Farms, Limited, maintained two bank accounts. It was provided that checks could be drawn on the signatures of any two of the three partners. The general partner had no power to withdraw money without the signature of one of the limited partners.

The Civil Code provides as follows:

"A limited partner shall not become liable as a general partner, unless, in addition to the exercise of his rights and powers as a limited partner, he takes part in the control of the business."

The foregoing illustrations sufficiently show that Russell and Andrews both took "part in the control of the business." The two men had absolute power to withdraw all the partnership funds in the banks without the knowledge or consent of the general partner. Either Russell or Andrews could take control of the business from de Escamilla by refusing to sign checks for bills contracted by him and thus limit his activities in the management of the business. They were active in dictating the crops to be planted, some of them against the wish of Escamilla. This clearly shows they took part in the control of the business of the partnership and thus became liable as general partners.

Business Interests and the Limited Partnership

Consider, then, how the limited partnership organizational form will facilitate the four business interests outlined at the beginning of this chapter.

Limited Liability Principle

Limited partners, those who invest in the business but refrain from managing it, have no personal liability for unpaid claims of the business. The most the limited partner can lose is the amount that was invested. Thus, the limited partner knows the extent of the worst-case scenario at the time of the investment. However, limited partners who are found to be managing the business, as in *Holzman* v. *De Escamilla*, forgo this limited liability protection.

Profit Share Principle

Both limited and general partners have a legal right to share in the profits from the business.

Management Rights and Control Principles

A limited partnership is managed and controlled by the general partner. If a limited partner is deemed to be exercising these rights, as noted above, then no limited liability will protect personal assets. The general partner, of course, is fully liable for business losses in any event.

One might thus consider the general partner here to be like the partner in a partnership. Both have rights to manage, control, and share in the profits of the business. The limited partner, by contrast, can be characterized as a passive investor. The reward for the passivity is a share in the profits and limited liability. (Note that under the limited partnership statutes, limited partners need not be inert. Approval of new general and limited partners joining the firm and occasional consulting with the general partner are examples of activities that will not threaten their limited liability.)

THE CORPORATION

The **corporation** is a legal entity, separate from any of its members. The law considers that type of business organization to be a person, having its own rights, duties, and responsibilities. The concept of an organization of individuals having a single personality has deep historical roots. Some writers date this idea to primitive societies; others contend that the seeds of the modern business corporation can be found in ancient Greece. Still others submit that it was first developed in Rome. Under Roman law, a corporation was empowered to do many things that an actual person could do: hold and convey property, inherit land and goods, and acquire assets or incur liabilities. Early Christian societies continued to use a corporate concept of organization. These early forms of incorporation greatly influenced the development of English law, which became the basis for American corporate law.

The direct antecedents of American corporations, however, were the joint stock companies that were begun in sixteenth-century England. At first, these were temporary arrangements, organized for single overseas trading expeditions. Later, a more permanent structure was developed. One of the most well-known was the Governor and Companies of Merchants Trading in the East Indies (the British East India Company). Organized by charter granted by Elizabeth I in 1600, the British East India Company thrived for over two hundred years.

Many other joint stock companies were chartered in England; some of them played an important role in colonizing North America. In 1607, for example, the Virginia Company of London settled Jamestown, Virginia. The Massachusetts Bay Company, chartered in 1629, settled New England. This joint stock company was unique in that the colonists were its controlling members instead of merely its employees. Note that these companies were more than simple commercial enterprises. They also governed the settlements that they established.

The first corporation in the American colonies was chartered in 1768, in what would become the state of Pennsylvania. The company was called the Philadelphia Contributionship for Insuring Houses from Loss by Fire. As the name implies, it was an insurance company, and was the only corporation organized in this country before the Revolution. Thereafter, a number of American businesses received corporate charters. Most of these companies were involved in banking or insurance or in establishing the country's system of overland turnpikes, toll bridges, and canals.

Early American corporations were granted their charters by state legislatures, a time-consuming and quite expensive process. Of course, before the Industrial Revolution, the United States had primarily an agrarian economy. Thus, little need or demand arose for a simplified incorporation process. New York, in 1811, was the first state to enact an enabling act for manufacturing companies. An enabling act provides an administrative procedure that relieves the legislature of the task of acting on each corporate charter application. However, the New York statute was quite restrictive. Not until New Jersey's General Corporation Act of 1875 did enabling acts reject strict state control over corporate formation and activities. The New Jersey act can be seen as the prototype of today's corporate organization statutes.

These statutes outline a procedure that must be followed in order for a corporation to come into existence. Generally, this includes filing articles of incorporation with the secretary of state. If the filed documents meet the requirements of the enabling statute, the secretary will issue a certificate of incorporation signifying the formal beginning of a corporation's legal existence. Thereafter, bylaws must be adopted, directors and officers elected, and shares of stock issued. Additionally, regular meetings of directors and shareholders must occur. Compare these formalities with the simple and uncomplicated way in which a partnership organization can be created.

Characteristics of the Corporate Form

The corporation is a unique form of business organization. Legally, it is a separate entity—a person in the eyes of the law, distinguishable and apart from any of its members. The separate entity concept of the corporation was described by Chief Justice John Marshall of the United States Supreme Court in the famous case of *Dartmouth College* v. *Woodward* in 1819:

> A corporation is an artificial being, invisible, intangible, and existing only in contemplation of law. Being the mere creature of law, it possesses only those properties which the charter of its creation confers upon it, either expressly or as incidental to its very existence. These are such as are supposed best calculated to effect the object for which it was created. Among the most important are immortality, and if the expression may be allowed, individuality.

Individuality

A corporate individual cannot be seen or touched. It is an intangible organizational idea that is given life, personality, and an existence by the law. It is solely a creature of the law, being formed pursuant to statute. Corporations have many of the legal characteristics of any natural person. For example, the corporation can sue and be sued. It can own property and invest it. A corporation can make money, lose money, and go bankrupt. Corporations can enter into contracts.

Since a corporation has no physical form, its individuality is obviously limited. A corporation can only act through agents (see the materials in Chapter 14.) Agents are people (workers, managers, vice-presidents, and so on) who are empowered to do certain tasks on behalf of the corporation. For example, when General Motors produces a new type of sports car, legally the corporation used its capital and resources to design a new car for the market. However, practically speaking, people, acting on behalf of General Motors, actually produced the car. Corporate agents made decisions concerning all aspects of design and production. Other agents built the car, tested it, and developed its unique features. Nonetheless, the corporation is bound by the contracts those agents enter on its behalf and may be liable for torts committed by them. Thus, a contract negotiated by a General Motors executive to buy steel from Inland Steel Corporation for use in constructing the sports car will bind GM. Further, if the braking system was negligently developed by people in the company's design department, the corporation, General Motors, may be liable for injuries caused by the defect.

Shareholders

The shareholders in a corporation are considered to be its owners. They invest money in the enterprise through the purchase of stock. However, shareholders do not participate in the management or operation of the corporation unless they occupy some position other than shareholder—for example, shareholder-director or shareholder-division manager. The only control that shareholders exercise is through the election of the board of directors.

Generally, each share of common stock is entitled to one vote. Thus, the shareholders who control sufficient shares can indirectly control the corporation through the election of a board of directors who will carry out those shareholders' aims. The other shareholders, although able to vote, will have no effective voice in corporate affairs. In large, publicly held corporations, shareholders who are dissatisfied with management may simply sell their shares on the market. But in small, privately held corporations in which there is no market for the shares, this is not an alternative.

Directors

The board of directors of a corporation is vested with the duty to manage the corporation. This does not mean that they are involved in the day-to-day decision making of the business. These decisions are made by the officers of the corporation, who are elected by the directors. However, the board of directors is legally responsible for the management of the corporation. In fulfilling this responsibility, the directors must operate as a board. One or two directors may not act independently. Also, the board only has authority to act as a group.

In a sense, the directors act as the representatives of the shareholders. They have control over the shareholders' investments and the assets of the corporation. Their decisions affect the future of the business. Consequently, the law imposes specific duties of care and loyalty upon them. These are called the directors' fiduciary duties. This concept is discussed in Chapter 14.

One might thus characterize the corporation as a series of legally defined roles: shareholder, director, the corporate entity itself. Each has certain attributes that together constitute the business enterprise. Compare this defined-role structure of a corporate organization to the loose construction of a partnership, for example. In a partnership, the investor is the owner, has management power, and is legally identified with the business. By contrast, a corporate investor (the shareholder) has no management role and is distinct from the corporate entity. Keep this difference in mind as the four business interests are discussed for the corporate form.

Business Interests and the Corporate Form

Limited Liability Principle

The members of the corporation are not liable for claims made against the business. Corporate debts belong to the corporation, and creditors may not seek contribution from individuals within the organization to pay them, even if the corporation is insolvent. Directors, officers, shareholders, or employees of the corporation may not be charged with corporate liabilities.

Furthermore, corporate shareholders can lose only the amount of their investment in the business. For instance, if a shareholder buys one hundred dollars' worth of stock, the most a shareholder could lose is the one-hundred-dollar investment. Limited liability is a protective device that encourages people to contribute capital to business enterprises. The investor need not fear calamitous personal financial exposure should the business fail.

Although the concept of limited liability is virtually synonymous with the corporate form, it should be considered in its historical and economic contexts. Doing so illustrates that limited liability arose later than the use of the corporate form for business organizations. Further, modern multinational enterprises' use of the corporate form has led to changes in the protection that "limited liability" will provide. In fact, one might consider that there are two standards of limited liability: one for corporations with individual shareholders, and one for corporations whose shareholders are other corporations (parent-subsidiary relationships).

Corporate charters granted in the early nineteenth century rarely provided for limited liability for members of the organization. Not until New Hampshire's actions in 1816 were manufacturing companies provided with such protection for their investors. But that change in the law was not uniformly adopted. For example, in a ten-year period between 1820 and 1830 Massachusetts and Rhode Island did not provide limited liability, while nearby states (Maine, New Hampshire, and Connecticut) did. Phillip I. Blumberg, in his four-volume treatise *Corporate Groups and Enterprise Liability,* noted that there was little evidence of different economic activity in those states.

Rhode Island, in 1847, was the last state to adopt limited liability. But uniformity among the states still did not exist. Until 1931, California provided that shareholders were liable, pro rata, for debt incurred by the corporation. Today, both New York and Wisconsin refuse to extend shareholder limited liability to wage claims by corporate employees. Thus, the evidence is far from clear that the concept of limited liability is a natural consequence of corporate individuality. More likely, it is a political response to investor interests. Nonetheless, limited liability is a central feature of the corporate form and distinguishes it from the partnership and sole proprietorship.

PIERCING THE CORPORATE VEIL

Although a corporation confers limited liability protection upon its members, there are times when the shield is ignored and a court will hold the members liable for debts of the business. This doctrine, known as **piercing the corporate veil**, is an equitable approach to handling abuses of the law. Such abuse may occur when the corporation becomes the "alter ego" of its members or when recognition of the corporation as a separate entity would perpetrate a fraud.

A corporate entity becomes the alter ego of its members when those members fail to treat it as a separate legal being. This is a management problem in which the formalities of the law are ignored. One might consider these formalities a "cost" that management must bear in order to capture the benefit that limited liability provides. One major area of concern arises if management fails to follow the basic legal organizational requirements once the corporate charter has been obtained. Examples include neglecting to elect directors or officers, never issuing shares of stock, and not holding annual director and shareholder meetings, as corporate enabling statutes generally require.

A second area of concern arises if management mingles personal and corporate property to such an extent that the financial individuality of the corporation is lost. For example, management may use its own funds for the business or take corporate funds for personal use without documentation. However, such "intermingling" will not always prompt the courts to pierce the corporate veil. For example, management legitimately may use its funds to lend money to the business or to purchase additional shares of stock. Further, business funds can be paid to management in salary (or dividends for shareholders).

The key to the alter ego problem is that the corporate individual recognized at law is ignored in business practice. Doing so risks that a court will hold members of the corporate organization liable for debts of the business.

Courts will also pierce the corporate veil, for reasons of equity and justice, when upholding limited liability would perpetrate a fraud. A classic example of fraud committed by a corporation's members is an arson case from the early part of this century. X was the principal behind a small corporation whose sole asset was a warehouse of tailor clippings worth approximately thirty thousand dollars. X was president and a director; he owned nearly all the shares of stock in the corporation. He was also a creditor of the corporation for over twenty-nine thousand dollars. X arranged to have the warehouse burned by an arsonist. Later, X was tried and convicted of the crime. However, the corporation filed a claim with its insurance company to collect approximately thirty thousand dollars on its policy for the loss. The insurance company refused to pay, and the court upheld this decision. The court pierced the corporate veil and refused to allow X to gain through the corporate personality what he would not have gained individually. A person may not collect insurance on property that the person willfully destroyed. In this case, recognizing the legal entity would have allowed just that result to occur, although circuitously.

Regardless of piercing theory, courts are wary of too readily ignoring the corporate entity to seek contribution from individual shareholders. The reliance interests of investors in limited liability is a strong factor in retaining the protection the corporate shield provides. Thus, individual shareholders generally can be confident that the most they can lose from their investment is the amount of that investment. But this policy of limited liability to protect individual shareholders becomes strained in a parent-subsidiary relationship, in which the investor is not an individual but merely another corporation.

Corporations in the early nineteenth century rarely had the power to own shares in other corporations. Thus, a business's organizational structure was reasonably simple: individual shareholders owned the corporation, which owned the business. Beginning with New Jersey in 1888, corporations were permitted to own shares in other corporations. Thus, the business enterprise itself could be divided into a group of corporations with interlocking interests and ownership, but with central control.

The railroad corporations were the first to use this ''enterprise organization.'' A single railroad company would be transformed into an amalgam of parent and subsidiary corporations. Today, enterprise organization is a common form by which large ''corporations'' do business. Mobil, for example, operates its business through over five hundred corporate subsidiaries. British Petroleum Corporation operates through more than one thousand corporate subsidiaries.

The law, however, did not create new doctrines for these multicorporate business organizations. It simply extended the limited liability concept to them, even though they are quite different from the simple corporate organization model from which limited liability arose. As a result, multiple layers of liability protection were recognized that were not necessary to protect the assets of individual shareholders. What was being protected were assets of a corporate shareholder. Individual investors in the parent corporation were thus protected twice: first, by the limited liability for their investment; and second, by the corporation's limited liability in holding shares of stock in a subsidiary. The courts, however, have begun to treat individual corporate shareholder cases differently from those involving parent-subsidiary relationships. In parent-subsidiary cases, piercing the corporate veil and other doctrines are interpreted broadly so as to provide a compensation source for claimants.

The following case involves a parent-subsidiary corporate enterprise that is a small business.

Walkovszky v. Carlton
New York Court of Appeals
233 N.E.2d 6 (1966)

The plaintiff, Walkovszky, was severely injured four years ago in New York City when he was run down by a taxicab owned by Seon Cab Corporation. Carlton is a stockholder in ten corporations, including Seon, each of which has but two cabs registered in its name. Only the minimum automobile liability insurance required by law (in the amount of ten thousand dollars) is carried on any one cab. These corporations are alleged to be operated as a single entity with regard to financing, supplies, repairs, employees, and garaging, and all are named as defendants. Walkovszky asserts that he is also entitled to hold their stockholders personally liable for the damages sought because the multiple corporate structure constitutes an

unlawful attempt to defraud members of the general public who might be injured by the cabs.

Fuld, Judge

The law permits the incorporation of a business for the very purpose of enabling its proprietors to escape personal liability but, manifestly, the privilege is not without its limits. Broadly speaking, the courts will disregard the corporate form, or, to use accepted terminology, "pierce the corporate veil," whenever necessary to prevent fraud or to achieve equity.

In the case before us, the plaintiff alleged that none of the corporations had a separate existence of their own. However, it is one thing to assert that a corporation is a fragment of a larger corporate combine which actually conducts the business. It is quite another to claim that the corporation is a "dummy" for its individual stockholders who are in reality carrying on the business in their personal capacities for purely personal rather than corporate ends. Either circumstance would justify piercing the corporate veil, but a different result would follow in each case. In the first, only a larger corporate entity would be held financially responsible while, in the other, the stockholder would be personally liable. Either the stockholder is conducting the business in his individual capacity or he is not. If he is, he will be liable; if he is not, then, it does not matter—insofar as his personal liability is concerned—that the enterprise is actually being carried on by a larger "enterprise entity."

Carlton is alleged to have organized, managed, dominated and controlled a fragmented corporate entity. But there are no allegations that he was conducting business in his individual capacity. Had the taxicab fleet been owned by a single corporation, it would be readily apparent that the plaintiff would face formidable barriers in attempting to establish personal liability on the part of the corporation's stockholders. The fact that the fleet ownership has been deliberately split up among many corporations does not ease the plaintiff's burden in that respect. The corporate form may not be disregarded merely because the assets of the corporation, together with the mandatory insurance coverage of the vehicle which struck the plaintiff, are insufficient to assure him the recovery sought. If Carlton were to be held individually liable on those facts alone, the decisions would apply equally to the thousands of cabs which are owned by their individual drivers who conduct their businesses through corporations.

The principle relied upon in the complaint to sustain the imposition of personal liability on Carlton is fraud. Such a cause of action cannot withstand analysis. If it is not fraudulent for the owner-operator of a single cab corporation to take out only the minimum required liability insurance, the enterprise does not become either illicit or fraudulent merely because it consists of many such corporations. The plaintiff's injuries are the same regardless of whether the cab which strikes him is owned by a single corporation or part of a fleet with ownership fragmented among many corporations. Whatever rights he may be able to assert against parties other than the registered owner of the vehicle come into being not because he has been defrauded but because he is entitled to hold the whole enterprise responsible.

In sum, then, the complaint falls short of adequately stating a cause of action against the defendant Carlton in his individual capacity.

Keating, Judge (dissenting)

The issue presented by this action is whether the policy of this State, which affords those desiring to engage in a business enterprise the privilege of limited liability through the use of the corporate device, is so strong that it will permit that privilege to continue no matter how much it is abused, no matter how irresponsibly the corporation is operated, no matter what the cost to the public. I do not believe that it is.

The defendant Carlton claims that, because the minimum amount of insurance required by the statute was obtained, the corporate veil cannot and should not be pierced despite the fact that the assets of the corporation which owned the cab were trifling compared with the business to be done and the risks of loss which were certain to be encountered. I do not agree.

The Legislature in requiring minimum liability insurance of $10,000, no doubt, intended to provide at least some small fund for recovery against those individuals and corporations who just did not have and were not able to raise or accumulate assets sufficient to satisfy the claims of those who were injured as a result of their negligence. It certainly could not have intended to shield those individuals who organized corporations, with the specific intent of avoiding responsibility to the public, where the operation of the corporate enterprise yielded profits sufficient to purchase additional insurance. Moreover, it is reasonable to assume that the Legislature believed that those individuals and corporations having substantial assets would take out insurance far in excess of the minimum in order to protect those assets from depletion. Given the costs of hospital care and treatment and the nature of injuries sustained in auto collisions, it would be unreasonable to assume that the Legislature believed that the minimum provided to the statute would in and of itself be sufficient.

The defendant, however, argues that the failure of the Legislature to increase the minimum insurance requirements indicates legislative acquiescence in this scheme to avoid liability and responsibility to the public.

In the absence of a clear Legislature statement, approval of a scheme having such serious consequences is not to be so lightly inferred.

What I would merely hold is that a participating shareholder of a corporation vested with a public interest, organized with capital insufficient to meet liabilities which are certain to arise in the ordinary course of the corporation's business, may be held personally responsible for such liabilities. Where corporate income is not sufficient to cover the cost of insurance premiums above the statutory minimum or where initially adequate finances dwindle under the pressure of competition, bad times or extraordinary and unexpected liability, obviously the shareholder will not be held liable.

The only types of corporate enterprises that will be discouraged as a result of a decision allowing the individual shareholder to be sued will be those such as the one in question, designed solely to abuse the corporate privilege at the expense of the public interest.

Profit Share, Management Rights, and Control Principles

In a corporate organization, management rights and profit share concepts are inextricably intertwined. Both are driven by the issue of control or, more directly, by the actions of the person who has the legal power to make decisions for the corporation.

The concept of a profit share is different in a corporation than it is in the other organizational forms reviewed thus far. No member of a corporate organization has a right to its profits. How those profits are used is a decision that is vested in the board of directors. Consequently, a highly profitable corporation may choose to invest all its profits in new factories or equipment. Conversely, it may distribute the money to the shareholders in the form of dividends. Of course, comparable decisions can also be made in partnership and limited partnership organizations. The distinguishing feature, however, is that unlike the partners in a partnership or the general and limited partners in a limited partnership, corporate shareholders have no legal right to any of the profit. In those other organizations, the profit right would need to be relinquished. This is not the case with the corporation. Thus, the key "profit share" decisions in a corporate form involves control of the board of directors.

Similarly, only certain formally designated members of the corporation have the legal rights to manage it. As noted above, this group is the board of directors. Consequently, an investor's ability to influence the direction of corporate management is directly tied to the question of control of the board of directors.

Thus, it is important for the business manager to focus on the unique control issue that arises with the corporate form. In general, the investor (or group) who owns the majority of a corporation's shares of stock controls the corporation. (In large corporations in which ownership is diffuse, this control can be obtained by a much smaller percentage.) Since a simple majority is sufficient to elect the directors, the majority shareholder, in effect, elects the board. Since the board of directors makes dividend payment decisions, one can expect that those decisions will be consistent with the goals of the majority shareholder. Compare this for a moment with the partnership form. There, each investor, irrespective of the amount contributed, retains a right to share in the profits as well as management rights.

A concern therefore becomes apparent for the minority shareholders: Their investment in the organization may leave them disenfranchised. But how this affects a particular investor will depend on whether the corporation is a close corporation or a publicly traded one. The following discussion will sketch out this distinction.

A **close corporation** has few shareholders and its shares of stock are not traded on any organized market. Often a close corporation is a small, family-owned business. The local bakery, dry-cleaner, and auto shop are examples. But "small-ness" is not a requirement. Hallmark, a greeting card company based in Kansas City, is a close corporation that has worldwide operations.

However, let us examine a more typical close corporation. Assume that Mozart and Salieri, in the example that opened the chapter, formed a corporation that issued one hundred shares, none of which are traded on a public market. Mozart invested $51,000, thereby receiving fifty-one of the company's issued shares. Salieri invested $49,000, receiving forty-nine shares of stock. Mozart and Salieri are also members of the board of directors, by unanimous vote of the shareholders. Each also holds an officer position, by unanimous vote of the board. Additionally, both work every day in the business. Since Mozart and Salieri are friends, they jointly decide all issues involving the business.

Note the similarities between this typical close corporation, as an operating business and a partnership. In both, the investors manage the company as a partner or by serving on the board. Their friendship fosters joint control, which would include a determination about the distribution of company earnings. In practice, then, the operation of Mozart and Salieri's business would differ little, whether it is a partnership or a corporation.

But consider the following development. Mozart and Salieri soon begin feuding. The disagreement escalates. At the next shareholders' meeting Mozart refuses to vote to renew Salieri's membership on the board of directors. Instead, he uses his majority of fifty-one votes to elect Cosima to the board. The new board consists of Mozart and Cosima. Their first duty is to cut corporate costs. As a result, Salieri also loses his job with the company. Mozart and Cosima share his tasks and also substantially raise their salaries. Further, they refuse to pay any more dividends. Salieri's investment has been rendered worthless to him.

However, one might ask: Why can't Salieri simply sell his stock to someone else, since shares of stock are freely transferable property? Two reasons come to mind. First, there is no organized market for close corporate shares. Salieri would need to find a buyer for his particular investment. Second, it is unlikely that anyone would buy his minority shareholder interests, which provide neither income nor the likelihood of market appreciation (since there is no market).

What happened to Salieri is called a *corporate squeeze-out*. It is a source of bitter litigation in close corporations. However, a recent trend in the law has seen some courts reviewing close corporation squeeze-outs on the basis of certain "duties" that the majority shareholders would owe the minority shareholders. These duties arise from a concern about the majority's position of control and its potential for abuse. In addition, since a close corporation, like Mozart and Salieri's is operated in ways similar to a partnership, a similar duty (the fiduciary duty) that exists in a partnership would be deemed applicable. (See Chapter 14 for a discussion of fiduciary duties.) Consequently, in the example above, a court following the trend would find that Mozart abused his majority position by squeezing out Salieri. The next case illustrates this new approach.

Hagshenas v. Gaylord
Illinois Court of Appeals
557 N.E.2d 316 (1990)

This case was initiated on April 29, 1982, when Bruce Hagshenas (Bruce) sued for dissolution of Imperial Travel Ltd. because of the dissension and corporate deadlock between himself, a fifty percent shareholder, and Robert Gaylord (Robert) and Virginia Gaylord (Virginia), the other fifty percent shareholders. The Gaylords filed a counterclaim alleging breach of fiduciary duties and sought damages.

On October 2, 1982, Bruce and his wife, Barbara, resigned from Imperial as officers and directors. The following day they purchased a new travel agency and began competing with Imperial. On November 1, 1982, the Gaylords moved for a preliminary injunction to stop Bruce from competing with Imperial.

On October 1, 1987, the trial court found in favor of the Gaylords on their complaint for breach of fiduciary duty.

In the present case, Bruce argues that the court erred in finding he owed a fiduciary duty to the Gaylords after he resigned as a director and officer of Imperial. He contends that he was free to compete with Imperial once he resigned. Ordinarily, after a director or officer resigns from a corporation, he or she owes no fiduciary duty to that corporation. The Gaylords contend, however, that Bruce continued to owe a fiduciary duty similar to that of a partner, since he continued to own half the stock of Imperial, a company that was essentially a close corporation.

Dunn, Justice

In general, a mere owner of stock in a company does not owe a fiduciary duty to that company. We believe that Imperial acted as a close corporation. A close corporation is defined as "one in which the stock is held in a few hands, or in a few families, and wherein it is not at all, or only rarely, dealt in by buying or selling." Imperial meets this test. Its stock was equally split between Bruce and the Gaylords, and there was no buying or selling of this stock. We also find it significant that the shareholders elected themselves directors and officers and participated in the day-to-day operations.

Though Imperial was a corporation, it clearly was an enterprise closely resembling a partnership. Hagshenas and the Gaylords were not only equal 50% shareholders; they were the directors and officers of the company; they oversaw the day-to-day operations. A partner owes a duty to exercise the highest degree of honesty and good faith in the dealings and in handling of business assets, thereby prohibiting enhancement of personal interests at the expense of the interests of the enterprise.

We find Bruce, as a 50% shareholder in this closely held corporation, owed a fiduciary duty similar to a partner to Imperial and its shareholders. He violated his fiduciary duty when he opened a competing business and hired away all of Imperial's employees. The sales employees were of great significance to Imperial's success. It was obvious Imperial would lose the majority of its customers if the sales people left. This action clearly benefited Bruce at the expense of Imperial.

In finding Bruce owed a fiduciary duty as a 50% shareholder in this closely held corporation, we recognize a significant difference between a shareholder of a closely held corporation and a shareholder of public stock. Unlike the holders of public stock, who can sell their stock when disagreements over management arise, shareholders in a small corporation do not usually have an available market to sell their shares. We find it implicit that people who enter into a small business enterprise, as in this case, place their trust and confidence in each other.

A fiduciary relation exists in all cases in which a confidential relationship has been acquired. Bruce argues there can be no finding of trust and confidence in this case because the parties were openly hostile to each other by the time he resigned. The important point in time is not the time at which the parties' differences became irreconcilable but, rather, the time in which they entered into the business relationship. We find no evidence of hostility or mistrust between the parties when they entered this business.

The fact that the parties were in disagreement when Bruce began competing with Imperial does not excuse his conduct. The parties, being equal shareholders, were at each other's mercy. If there were problems that could not be resolved, then the proper course of action would have been to negotiate a sale or buy-out of the shares or file for dissolution. We are aware that Bruce made an attempt to sell his shares and filed for dissolution. Until a final sale or order for dissolution, however, Bruce owed a fiduciary duty to Imperial.

We find that Bruce is liable for breaching a fiduciary duty as a shareholder.

The issue of corporate control, then, has a particular meaning for the close corporation form of business organization. However, in large, publicly traded corporations, there are additional factors to be considered in a definition of control.

A **publicly traded corporation** is one whose shares are bought and sold in an organized marketplace, such as the New York Stock Exchange. Often publicly traded corporations have thousands of employees, scattered operations, and shareholders that change almost by the minute. Frequently such corporations are international in scope. Although the basic principles of corporate law apply (shareholders elect the directors, who elect the officers), there are some practical differences.

First, a relatively small percentage of the shares will control the corporation, since few shareholders actually vote in director elections. Second, **management generally will be in control of those shares' votes (either through ownership or** through an alliance with the owners). Third, the directors will be selected by management and will then be offered to the shareholders to approve, disapprove, or abstain. Given management control, invariably these director candidates will prevail. Only in the rare event of a contest for control will shareholders have a choice in the slate of directors.

The realities of corporate control raise complex issues. Corporate legal theory suggests that management is selected by the board, which is chosen by the shareholders. Yet, for the most part, in publicly traded corporations management is the key and the directors are beholden to management for their positions. Although directors owe fiduciary duties to the shareholders, corporate critics frequently point to this lack of shareholder democracy as a source of corporate ills. One well-known criticism is leveled at the enormous income levels of top management at publicly traded American corporations—levels far exceeding what is earned by often better performing Japanese and European counterparts. The board of directors, of course, sets the top executive salary level.

What is a noncontrolling shareholder in such a corporation to do? The typical response is to sell the shares. Since an organized public market exists, this dissatisfied investor is not stuck to the company, as was Salieri in the example above. Another response is to pressure management. Of course, this will not work for Joe Smith, owner of only one hundred shares. But a trend in share ownership suggests that pressure may become a powerful device. Many individuals who invest in public companies do so through institutions such as mutual funds and pension plans. These large institutions are beginning to use their clout to pressure certain corporate managements to be more responsive to shareholder interests. The question of stratospheric executive salaries is one of those interests. The implicit threat, of course, is that the mutual fund or pension plan will sell its shares or support an insurgent who seeks to oust current management.

In any event, the concept of corporate control for the business executive is tied more to the nature of the corporation than to legal theory. As with the issue of piercing the corporate veil, the nature of the corporation affects the application of the legal theory.

The complex issues of corporate control go far beyond the brief survey in this chapter and merit an additional course of their own.

THE LIMITED LIABILITY COMPANY: AN EMERGING ORGANIZATIONAL FORM

As noted from the discussions above, each of the traditional legal business organizational forms (partnership, limited partnership, corporation) has unattractive features. The partnership imposes a risk of personal liability on its partners. In a limited partnership, limited partners cannot manage the firm. In a corporation, management and profit share are tied to control. Those investors without a controlling interest have neither a management right nor a right to have corporate earnings distributed to them.

In recent years, a few states (eighteen by the middle of 1993) have enacted legislation that created a new business organizational form, the limited liability company. The first state to enact a limited liability company statute was Wyoming, in 1977, reportedly at the behest of an oil company. More states are actively considering similar legislation, and the American Bar Association has charged a committee with drafting a uniform statute that can be used as a model for legislatures that are considering limited liability company statutes. A similar business form exists in some foreign countries, including Brazil, Germany, Portugal, and Saudi Arabia.

The limited liability company combines the "best" features of the other business organizational forms. Its owners (called members) have limited liability. In addition, they share the profits from the business. Finally, the members may directly manage the business. As an added attraction, in 1988 the IRS issued a revenue ruling that indicated it would treat limited liability companies as partnerships for income tax purposes. That is, the business organization itself would not be a taxable entity.

Business Interests and the Limited Liability Company

Note how the limited liability company facilitates the four business interests outlined at the beginning of the chapter.

Limited Liability Principle

Members (including investors) have limited liability.

Profit Share Principle

Members have a right to a share of the profits from the business.

Management Rights and Control Principles

Members have a right to both manage and exercise control in the business without affecting their profit share right or their limited liability. However, members need not be active in the business. They are free to select an outsider as manager or to have some members opt out of any such responsibilities.

Consider the following illustration. Barbara is a Kansas entrepreneur who developed a new way to send radio signals that enhances their clarity as well as the number that can be sent without overlap or distortion. She jerry-built a prototype and has impressed a couple of very wealthy investors. These investors are willing to risk a million dollars in the business because they anticipate a huge profit potential. However, they refuse to put their other assets at risk and intend to work together with Barbara to develop her idea.

In Kansas, a limited liability company is an organizational alternative that can be selected. Barbara and her investors formally elect that form by filing a document with the requisite state office. Thereafter, as members of a limited liability company, all will have a right to a share in the profit. Each will have management rights and none of them will risk personal liability for business debts.

Compare this scenario with a similar business group working in another state that does not offer the limited liability company form. The partnership, corporation and limited partnership forms have limitations that might discourage potential investors from risking their funds.

Although to date there have been few legal developments with limited liability companies, one might suggest that if they become widely available they could replace the partnership for most businesses and, in some instances, be preferable to the corporation. Limited liability companies might be particularly attractive for start-up, risky, entrepreneurial ventures. Investors can provide funding, lend their expertise in management, and share in the wealth that is generated without exposing noninvested assets to loss. The limited liability company clearly illustrates how the law can be used to facilitate business conduct.

SUMMARY

Five legal forms under which a business can be operated were discussed in this chapter: the sole proprietorship, the partnership, the limited partnership, the corporation, and an emerging form, the limited liability company. For the business executive, these are more than mere legal technicalities. Each can have profound implications for any business that chooses to operate under one of the forms. In fact, failing to choose can lead to one being presumed by the law—partnership. Consequently, it is important that the executive select the form that best meets certain business interests.

Legal organizational forms can be distinguished in many ways. This chapter focused on four of the most basic: the limited liability principle, the profit share principle, the management right principle, and the control principle. The business executive should evaluate the relative importance of these interests before deciding which organizational form to use. Each legal form tends to favor certain interests over the others.

All business organizational forms are governed by state law. Thus, one can expect some differences among them. Nonetheless, since the partnership, limited partnership, and corporation have had a long history of use, their contours should be relatively easy to predict. Not so with the limited liability company, a new and untested organizational form that is available in eighteen states. Numerous other states are considering it and undoubtedly more will adopt it. The business executive should therefore pay careful attention to developments in the state legislature.

REVIEW QUESTIONS

1. Define the following terms:
   a. Limited liability
   b. Limited partnership
   c. Parent-subsidiary corporation
   d. Partnership
   e. Piercing the corporate veil

2. Mary and Sam would like to become co-owners of a bike shop. Discuss whether they can do so under the sole proprietorship form of doing business.

3. Tom and Bill are involved in a bakery business. Bill invested all the money. They share gross income, by agreement: twenty percent to Tom and the balance to Bill, who pays all the expenses of the business from his share. Since Tom is a master baker, he makes all decisions concerning breads, cookies, and cakes. Do Tom and Bill have a partnership?

4. Under what circumstances would you suggest that a partnership form would be least attractive to a business executive?

5. George and Susan own an oil well under the limited partnership form of business organization. George is the limited partner and Susan is the general partner. If the business cannot pay one million dollars in creditor claims, how much can the creditors seek from George? How much from Susan?

6. Would your answer to the above question change if George were closely involved in making management decisions for the oil well business?

7. How does the doctrine of piercing the corporate veil operate to remove the corporate limited liability shield?

8. Jack and Molly decide to operate their restaurant as a corporation. They begin to call each other "shareholder" and put a sign out in front that says "Eats, Inc." However, they do not file any documents with the state. Have they created a corporate organizational form?

9. For a birthday gift, Jim's uncle gives him two shares of stock in XYZ, Inc., a publicly traded corporation that does business throughout the world. In yesterday's newspaper, Jim reads that XYZ, Inc. is insolvent and has millions of dollars of unpaid bills. Should Jim be concerned that the creditors will seek contribution from him?

10. Betty is an investor in small, risky businesses. She has been very successful because many of those businesses have become quite successful. She learns that a number of state legislatures are considering adopting the limited liability company form as a way in which business can be conducted. Should Betty lobby in favor or against that proposed statute?

11. Bill and Jane would like to jointly own a bookstore. Neither has any interest in managing the business, but each would like to have a share in the profits. Which of the business organizational forms fit their needs?

12. June and Sam intend to begin a deep-sea diving and salvage company. Since both are expert divers, they intend to be active in the business and jointly make all management decisions. However, neither wants to risk any of their personal assets, beyond what they invest in the business. Which of the business organizational forms fit their needs?

13. Tom and Mary would like to open a custom-made automobile shop. Since both are experts in auto design and construction, they intend to have a personal involvement in all aspects of production and jointly make all management decisions for the business. Further, they believe that this business can produce huge profits and each would like the legal right to a share. Which of the business organizational forms fit their needs?

14. May and June each have net worth in the hundreds of millions of dollars. Their friend George, though penniless, is a computer design genius. He has shown them his new ideas, which are revolutionary. May and June would like to invest in George's new design ventures. However, they know nothing about computers and are too busy to bother with managing the business. They want to share in its profits, but are emphatic that their personal fortunes should not be

placed at risk. Which of the business organizational forms fit their needs?

15. Compare the concept of control in a partnership with control in a corporation.

16. Tom and Jane operate a business together. Jane invested ten thousand dollars in the business; Tom invested eight thousand. What added risk would Tom have if the business was a corporation instead of a partnership?

17. Lilly and Yolanda want to open a fitness center where people can work out and get in condition. They decide that the best organizational form for them is the partnership. They begin to call each other "partner" and consider themselves to be co-owners. Do Lilly and Yolanda have a partnership? If so, why? If not, why not?

18. Assume that your answer to question 17 was that there was no partnership formed. What facts might you add to show that Lilly and Yolanda did create a partnership?

19. Bill decided to invest ten thousand dollars in a Broadway show. The show was being operated as a limited partnership. The investors were the limited partners, and the producers of the show were general partners. Unfortunately, the show was a flop, and after all the assets were liquidated, two hundred thousand dollars was still owed to various creditors. Is Bill liable for all or any portion of that debt? Note that there are twenty limited partners in this organization.

20. Maude invested five thousand dollars in a limited partnership. There were three other limited partners and one general partner. The limited partnership was engaged in growing and marketing avocados. After two years, with no return on her investment, Maude became rather concerned. She visited Jack, the general partner, and demanded his resignation. Instead, he agreed, at her urging, to allow her to co-sign all checks the firm issued. Thereafter, she had input into all expenditures of the limited partnership. Within six months the firm was bankrupt, and forty thousand dollars remained in unpaid debts. Do the creditors have claims against the limited partners?

21. Smith took care of the formalities necessary for his computer programming business to be incorporated. Upon issuance of the certificate of incorporation, the business was known as ABC, Inc. Although Smith was to own all the shares of stock in the business, no shares were ever issued. Furthermore, the corporation kept no formal records, as required by law. Frequently, Smith used money produced by the business to meet his personal expenses. He also used his home and car in the business. Neither of these events was accounted for. If a disgruntled customer sues ABC, will Smith be successful in interposing the corporation's limited liability to protect his personal assets? Explain.

22. What are the roles of a shareholder and a director in a corporation?

CHAPTER 14

Members of Business Organizations: Regulation of Their Activities Through Agency and Fiduciary Duty Principles

- Business Concerns Arising From an Organization Member's Actions
- The Law of Agency
- Agency Relationships within Business Organizational Forms
- Business Consequences of the Agency Relationship
- Principles of Fiduciary Duties
- The Fiduciary Duty and Director-Shareholder Relationships

Irrespective of the legal form under which a business operates (see Chapter 13 for a discussion of the forms), the business is actually run by its members. Individuals design the products, acquire financing, and keep the books and records. The legal implications of their work and their relationship to the business organization are the subject of this chapter. Emphasis is placed on the rules under which an individual's actions are deemed to be those of the business organization. These rules are called the law of agency. The chapter also reviews the rules that control and limit those individuals' actions. This regulation occurs under the principles of fiduciary relationships.

BUSINESS CONCERNS ARISING FROM AN ORGANIZATION MEMBER'S ACTIONS

The legal environment responds to a number of problems that may arise when people work on behalf of business organizations. Some of the most basic involve the legal roles of those individuals and the duties that the law imposes upon them. Consider the following questions: Do individuals within a business organization owe one another any special duties that will regulate their conduct? Why can a sales representative working for a large corporation make a sale on behalf of the corporation since, as noted in Chapter 13, the corporation itself has a legal identity apart from its members? Finally, do members of business organizations have any risk of personal liability arising from torts committed by their fellow members?

To more fully develop these questions, consider the following scenarios:

1. Lazy Larry and Busy Betty formed a partnership. After about two months, Lazy Larry begins to neglect his work. He spends most of his time at the beach, charging his leisure expenses to the business. Consequently, Busy Betty is required to work ever harder to pick up the slack. Would she have any legal claim against him? Stated another way, does Lazy Larry owe Busy Betty any special legal duties because he is her partner? These questions can be answered by the legal principles of fiduciary relationships.

2. ABC, Inc. is a multinational corporation that manufactures automobiles. Jack Smith is an employee of ABC, Inc. His job is to buy high-quality loudspeakers to be installed in the cars. Yesterday he signed a contract to purchase ten thousand pairs of speakers. Who are the parties to the contract: ABC, Inc.? Jack Smith? the speaker manufacturer? These questions are addressed by the authority principles of the law of agency.

3. Jane Jones is employed by an oil exploration company organized as a limited partnership. She is neither a general nor a limited partner in this business organization. Her role is to drive a truck. One afternoon, while delivering some equipment to a drilling site, she falls asleep and the truck collides with a parked car. Assuming that Jones committed a tort, will the limited partnership face any liability because she was its employee? (See Chapter 11 for a discussion of tort liability principles.) This question is addressed by an agency law doctrine: vicarious liability.

After finishing this chapter, you should be able to evaluate the above scenarios and answer the questions posed. However, at the outset, a fundamental question must be raised: Under what circumstances will relationships between individuals be regulated by agency law and fiduciary duty principles?

THE LAW OF AGENCY

Understanding the three scenarios above requires identification of the legal relationship that exists between the individuals. For example, what is the relationship between Lazy Larry and Busy Barbara, or between Jack Smith and Jane Jones and their employers? If they can be considered agency relationships, then a number of legal doctrines arise that will provide answers to their dilemmas.

The law of agency may be traced to ancient Rome, where ''agents'' were actually slaves, who had no legal status under Roman law. Their legal identities were absorbed into the Roman families they served. Since the master (male head of the household) represented the family in the eyes of the law, he also became liable for the actions of his slaves. Today, the law of agency carries forward the legal consequences of the Roman relationship, even though the relationship no longer exists in its original form.

An agency relationship is created by consent of two persons, **agent** and **principal.** The agent has the power to act on behalf of the principal. Consequently, the agent also owes legal duties to the principal. On the other hand, the principal has the legal right to control the activities of the agent. In the example of Mary Smith's environmental protection business (see Chapter 13), if she hires an employee, Jack Jones, an agency relationship is created. Mary is the principal. She has control over the actions of Jack and is the one on whose behalf Jack will be acting. Jack, the agent, has the power to act in place of Mary and owes her a fiduciary duty throughout this employment. This duty attaches to the agent, because by having the power to act in Mary's place, Jack can cause certain legal liabilities to attach to Mary. Thus, in order to regulate this power, the law imposes the fiduciary duty on Jack.

However, not every consensual relationship between two persons creates an agency relationship. Buyer–seller relations are consensual, but the parties are not each other's agents and principals. A debtor–creditor relationship is another example. Although the creditor may have control over certain aspects of the debtor's business, the debtor is not given the power to act on behalf of the creditor. Therefore, no agency relationship arises.

In order for an agency relationship to be formed, two factors must exist. First, the principal must have the right to control the activities of the agent. In a typical employer-employee agency relationship, the employer (principal) has the right to control work activities of the employee (agent). Second, the agent must have the power to act on behalf of the principal.

The following case concerns the issue of identifying a principal-agent relationship. Before the legal doctrines that bind the principal to the consequences of certain actions by the agent can arise, the relationship must be established.

Hurla v. Capper Publications, Inc.
Supreme Court of Kansas
87 P.2d 552 (1939)

The defendant Arthur Capper and Capper Publications, Inc. operated several routes of the Topeka *Daily Capital* in the neighborhood of Delia, Kansas. The defendant John Lane collected subscriptions and delivered the Sunday edition of that paper. On September 26, 1937, the Hurla family was driving east on a county highway in a Chevrolet coach. At a point two miles east of Delia, the county highway is intersected by a township road running north and south. At the intersection, the Hurla car collided with a Ford V–8 car traveling north on the township road. The Ford car was owned and driven by the defendant John Lane.

As a result of the collision, the plaintiff Michael Hurla suffered severe injuries for which he asks damages.

The defendant Arthur Capper denied that he at any time, either in his personal capacity or as owner of the Topeka *Daily Capital*, operated any newspaper route or routes in the neighborhood of Delia. He also denied that John Lane was his agent, or employee. Capper further alleged that the defendant John Lane was the owner of and was operating a newspaper route on his own responsibility for the purpose of delivering the Sunday edition of the Topeka *Daily Capital*.

Allen, Justice

A principal employing another to achieve a result but not controlling nor having the right to control the details of his physical movement is not responsible for incidental negligence while such person is conducting the authorized transaction. Thus, the principal is not liable for the negligent physical conduct of an attorney, a broker, a factor, or a rental agent, as such. In their movements and their control of physical forces, they are in the relation of independent contractors to the principal. It is only when to the relationship of principal and agent there is added that right to control physical details as to the manner of performance that the person in whose service the act is done becomes subject to liability for the physical conduct of the actor.

The general rule is that when a person lets out work to another, the contractee reserving no control over the work or workmen, the relation of contractor and contractee exists, and the contractee is not liable for the negligence or improper execution of the work by the contractor.

Under the established rule in this state it is necessary to show by competent testimony that the relation of principal and agent existed between John Lane and Arthur Capper. It is not sufficient to show that John Lane had a paper route, and that he solicited and collected subscriptions and delivered papers to the subscribers. These acts are consistent with the conduct of an independent contractor. On the subscription card delivered by Lane to the subscriber appeared the title "Topeka Daily Capital," "Topeka Sunday Capital" and was endorsed "Carrier, J. A. Lane." It is argued that this establishes the relation of principal and agent between the parties. We think however this is consistent with the view that Lane was an independent contractor. Giving the plaintiff the benefit of every reasonable inference arising from the evidence adduced it fails to show that Arthur Capper controlled or had the right to control the physical conduct of John Lane in the performance of his duties as a paper carrier over the route.

Agency Relationships within Business Organizational Forms

Doctrines of agency law occur in every organizational form in which one person (the agent) works on behalf of another (the principal). Consequently, the legal doctrines that follow apply to any employee working in any business, irrespective of its form. Once an employer–employee relationship is created, agency law will apply.

However, additional, unique agency relationships exist within each particular

TABLE 14.1	The Agency Relationship and Business Organizational Forms	
	Agency Relationship	
Business Form	Who Are Agents?	Who Is the Principal?
Sole proprietorship	Employees*	Sole proprietor
Partnership	Partners	Partners
Corporation	Corporate officers†	Corporate entity
Limited partnership	General partner	Other general partners and the limited partners
Limited liability company	Members	Company

* Employees of any organizational form are considered agents.
† Only officers elected by directors, as required by enabling acts, since they are distinct from being mere corporate employees.

business organization. They arise because of the legal structure of the organizational form (see table 14.1). In a partnership, the partners are considered both agents and principals of one another. A partner may contract on behalf of the organization. Torts of a partner are binding on the firm. Thus, one need not look further than the existence of a partner–partner relationship for the agency principles to apply.

In a limited partnership, the general partner has agency powers. (Note that the limited partners are not agents. Their role in the organization does not include a management and control right.) The principal here is the limited partners (and any other general partners). Since a limited partnership, like the partnership, is not a legal entity, unsatisfied claims arising because of agent (or general partner) actions may be collected from the general partner.

A corporation provides a contrast. Its agents are officers (president, vice-president, secretary) elected by the board, with powers as described in the corporate bylaws. The principal is the corporation. Since the corporation is a legal entity, it is the party for whom the agents work. Note that the members of the board of directors are not agents (unless they serve the corporation in some other capacity). Board members have no power to act individually. Their power exists solely from their decisions as a collective group.

Finally, in the limited liability company, any members who are managing the firm are acting as agents. The principal is the company.

BUSINESS CONSEQUENCES OF THE AGENCY RELATIONSHIP

Torts and Vicarious Liability

A tort committed by an agent within the course and scope of the agency relationship (or the principal's business) binds the principal. This is known as the doctrine of respondeat superior, or **vicarious liability**. (The agent who committed the tort, of course, would also be liable.) The principal did not commit a tort but is liable simply because of the relationship with the agent.

Vicarious liability may, at first, seem at odds with notions of fairness or justice; liability is imposed on someone who has committed no wrong. However, the doctrine serves some major purposes. It provides that those who have others act in their stead may not thereby escape liability. If the principal had committed the tort, liability would exist; thus, by hiring an agent as a substitute, liability should also follow. Today, probably the strongest rationale for vicarious liability is the "deep pocket." The injured party will be more likely to receive damages from the principal (a business with assets or insurance) than from the individual who committed a tort.

The doctrine of vicarious liability has been a part of the common law for nearly three hundred years. It was first created by Justice Holt, in England, in the case of *Jones* v. *Hart* in 1698. However, vicarious liability is not unique to American and English common law. Legal systems influenced by the French Napoleonic Code also use the principle. In fact, the French legal writer Domat was urging such a rule for France at about the same time Justice Holt decided *Jones* v. *Hart*. The Code Napoléon of 1804, with some modifications, adopted Domat's ideas. As an aside, in the 1804 Code Napoléon, teachers were held to be vicariously liable for damages caused by their students during the time they were under the teachers' supervision. Fortunately for today's professors, this was never a principle of the common law. It has also been changed in France, by amendment to the code in 1937.

Determining whether a tort was committed within the course and scope of the business is often not an easy task. The basic question is whether the tort was committed by the agent while conducting the business of the principal. However, some agent torts may involve both business and nonbusiness (personal) elements. For instance, while on route, a delivery driver stops at home to check the mail and has an accident. Or a delivery driver has an order to deliver a special package to an important customer by 3:00 P.M., but cannot because the road is blocked by a person protesting high taxes. The driver, unable to convince the protester to move and concerned because the deadline is near, throws the protester to the side of the road, causing injury. Neither example involves solely business or personal activities by the agent.

Generally, the courts analyze these and other situations case by case. Courts use a number of factors in deciding whether or not an agent has acted in the course and scope of the business. Some pertinent questions are:

1. Were the agent's actions common among other employees? Consider again the case of the delivery driver making a convenient stop at home. If delivery drivers often stopped at home on personal errands while delivering goods for the employer, then the tort may be considered in the course of the business.

2. Was the agent's action unexpected by the employer? For example, if personal errands by delivery persons were tolerated and therefore not unexpected by the employer, then the tort may be considered normal business conduct.

3. When and how did the act occur? (Did it occur during normal business hours, on the premises of the business, or with property owned by the business?)

4. If physical violence by the agent was involved, was it fully unexpected by the employer? In the example of the delivery driver with a deadline, it might be expected that an employee would take whatever actions were necessary in order to make an important delivery. At least, the reaction in the example would seem less unexpected than if the employee had punched an innocent passerby.

In studying these considerations, note that there is no single answer to the ultimate question posed by the courts: Was an activity within the course and scope of the business? Since the trend in tort law is toward victim compensation, the scope of principal liability under vicarious liability is broadly interpreted. The following cases are illustrative.

Williams v. Community Drive-In Theater, Inc.
Kansas Supreme Court
520 P.2d 1296 (1974)

Jerry Williams was a patron at the theater operated by defendant Community Drive-In Theater, Inc. Donna McKenna, a theater employee, testified that at the time of the incident she was sixteen years of age and had been working at the Community Drive-In Theater for about three weeks. She worked at the concession stand; sometimes she helped close the theater. On April 7, 1970, at about 10:30 P.M., while she was still working at the cash register, the assistant manager, Mr. Robertson, asked her if she would help him close the theater. She agreed. Robertson parked his car close to the entrance so they could view the movie and also see if anyone tried to get in without paying. While sitting there, Donna McKenna saw the plaintiff's car come into the drive–in and go to the concession stand. Robertson drove his car to the concession stand and spoke with one of the three men who was in the plaintiff's car. Donna McKenna accompanied Robertson and then went to her car nearby to get her husband's .410–gauge shotgun. Since there were three men against Robertson, she thought the shotgun would give him a little more authority. After retrieving the gun, she walked behind the plaintiff as they moved toward the manager's office. The men stopped. She then put the gun against the plaintiff's shoulder and told him, "Let's go to the other side of the building." The plaintiff turned as if to walk in front of her. The shotgun dropped so she grasped it tighter, which probably released the trigger. The plaintiff was shot.

The manager, Mr. Barnhardt, testified as to the duties of various drive-in employees. The assistant manager, Robertson, was in charge that night after Barnhardt had left; Robertson was expected to investigate any disturbance, maintain discipline among patrons, watch and protect property, and take appropriate action. Robertson had obtained a deputy sheriff's commission and a deputy sheriff's shirt to use on occasions when deemed necessary. Robertson also obtained a permit to carry a gun and carried one at times while on duty. Security was needed on weekends and when the drive-in had large crowds. Fights occurred; people threw beer cans. It was a pretty rough place and on those occasions the manager would try to break up disturbances with the use of force. On several occasions the police were called. Leon Barker, a doorman, carried a gun and once "put a gun to a guy's head for throwing gravel." The incidents mentioned occurred prior to the night in question: The manager was sure Robertson knew Donna McKenna had the shotgun in her car because everyone knew that her husband owned a shotgun. The manager had never told Donna McKenna to leave the gun at home.

Harmon, Commissioner

If an assault by an employee is motivated entirely by personal reasons such as malice or spite or by a desire to accomplish some unlawful purpose and does not have for its purpose the furtherance of the employer's business, it will be considered personal to the employee and not such as will make the employer answerable. If the assault is committed by the employee while furthering the employer's interest in some way, the employer is liable. Thus, we see the relation of the act to the employer's business becomes an important criterion in determining the employer's liability.

In the case at bar the trial court in reaching its decision apparently regarded the employee in question as merely a concession stand employee. We think the record indicates she was more than that. She was specifically requested to remain after the concession stand closed and assist in closing the theater. Part of those duties consisted of preventing unauthorized entry after the ticket office had closed. Despite the fact she may not later have been paid by her employer for her services that night, she was the drive-in's employee at the crucial time. Although she may have used poor judgment in her actions, her own testimony indicates she was motivated by a desire to further theater interests rather than personal reasons such as malice or spite. She was shepherding two apparent intruders to the assistant manager for investigation when the shotgun discharged. There was evidence that the fact she had the gun on the premises was known to that individual, who himself carried a gun. The facts presented indicate certain employment at the drive-in was of a nature where the display and use of guns was contemplated in the furtherance of the employer's business in preserving order. We think the facts bearing upon whether she acted within the scope of her employment were such as to raise an issue requiring jury determination. Accordingly it must be held the trial court erred in granting summary judgment. The judgment is reversed and the cause remanded with directions to proceed with trial of the action.

Harris v. Trojan Fireworks Company
California Court of Appeals
174 Cal. Rptr. 452 (1981)

Anthony Barajas was an employee of defendant Trojan Fireworks Company. On Friday, December 21, 1979, at the Trojan manufacturing plant in Rialto, commencing at noon and continuing until 4:00 P.M., Trojan held a Christmas party at which all employees were required to attend. Some imbibed large quantities of alcoholic beverages. Barajas attended the party and became intoxicated to the extent that his ability to drive an automobile was substantially impaired. Nevertheless, he attempted to drive home. In this attempt he was involved in the accident which resulted in the death of James Harris and injury to Dawn and Steven Griffin.

[You write the opinion. Should Trojan Fireworks Company be vicariously liable for its employee's tort? If so, how would you manage future Christmas parties?]

Since an employee's torts may be binding on the business organization, the doctrine of vicarious liability can have an effect on management decision making. Management, through supervision and control of the organization's employees, can limit the risk that certain types of torts will be committed. The lower the risk, the lower the "costs" imposed on the firm through the doctrine of vicarious liability. However, managing too has its costs. For example, as noted in Chapter 11, insurance can be purchased to act as a buffer against tort claims.

Contracts and Agent Authority

The agency relationship does not merely create tort liability risks for a business; it also facilitates the operation of the business itself. Imagine a business organization in which the principal was required to sign every contract on behalf of the firm. This might be feasible for a small company, but would be impossible for a corporate organization. Since a corporation is merely a legal idea, there is no person who occupies the role of principal. Furthermore, even in a small firm operated as a partnership, where the partners could sign such contracts, the cost in terms of time and lost opportunities would create enormous inefficiencies.

Under agency law, a number of doctrines that can be grouped together under the heading "agent's authority" solve these hypothetical problems. An agent who possesses the requisite authority binds the principal to contracts that the agent enters into. For these contracts, generally, only the principal will be bound; the agent will not become a legal party to them.

Three doctrines regulate an agent's power to bind a principal to a contract: actual authority, apparent authority, and ratification. The doctrine of **actual authority** requires that the principal has given expressly or by implication some specific contracting powers to the agent. Determining whether an agent has actual authority requires a review of the directions given by the principal to that agent. If the agent's power is definite and precise, the agent is considered to have express authority. For example, if the principal directs the agent to purchase a certain brand of computer software for the business, the agent, when purchasing the software, is using the express authority given by the principal.

However, not all instructions given to the agent will be so unequivocal. Sometimes the agent will be assigned a job with a general description—computer supplies manager—or the agent will be given somewhat vague directions—"Buy some computer software for the business.'' Although the principal has empowered the agent to do some act, the exact contours of the act have not been stated. Nonetheless, the agent still has actual authority. However, to determine the scope of that authority will require that assumptions be made about the nature of the business and the intent of the principal. In short, the inquiry is to determine what can be implied from the general grant of authority. This doctrine is called implied authority.

Implied authority is practical. No principal could be expected to precisely convey every action for the agent to take. Furthermore, some contracting activities may require choices to be made that can readily be delegated to the agent. Thus, the doctrine of implied authority works together with express authority to describe the contracting rights given by the principal to the agent.

Consider the following example. Warren was recently hired by ABC, Inc. as a warehouse manager and is therefore its agent. His job description grants him the power to ''hire employees and generally manage the warehouse.'' If Warren hires a forklift operator, he will be acting with express authority. That is, Warren has expressly been given the right to hire warehouse workers on behalf of ABC. Therefore, his principal (the corporation) is bound by the employment contract. However, assume Warren hired a local pest control firm to rid the warehouse of vermin. Nothing in his job description expressly states that he is empowered to hire pest control firms. However, his position as warehouse manager and the general language of his grant of authority, to ''generally manage the warehouse,'' clearly suggest that authority was granted to him by ABC.

A second doctrine concerning agents and contracts with third parties is known as **apparent authority**. Apparent authority arises in the absence of actual authority. The agent does not have the right to enter into the contract on behalf of the principal. However, owing to certain circumstances, the agent has the power to do so. In this event, the principal would be bound to the contract even though no such authority was granted to the agent.

Apparent authority has two elements. First, the principal must have created the impression that the agent had the authority to enter into the contract. Second, the third party must have reasonably relied upon an agent's having the authority. For example, assume that Jill has the actual authority to negotiate spare automobile parts contracts worth no more than ten thousand dollars; that is, she has been given an express limit on her actual authority. Jill, however, enters into a contract on behalf of her principal to purchase eleven thousand dollars in spare automobile parts. Under the doctrine of apparent authority, she would have the power to bind her principal to that contract.

By granting Jill the actual authority to enter into automobile parts contracts, her employer created the impression that she was empowered to enter into the contract at issue. The employer would have had to give notice of Jill's authority limitation for the contract to be voidable. Failing to do so established the appearance that Jill's actual authority did not have an express dollar ceiling. Furthermore, the party with whom Jill contracted had no way of knowing about the ten-thousand-dollar limitation. The mere thousand dollars more in parts would hardly seem unusual or out of line.

Apparent authority may thus be seen as a fairness device designed to protect the interests of third parties contracting with agents. Principals cannot escape liability for the misimpressions of agent authority they allow to reasonably exist.

A final doctrine concerning agents and contracts is **ratification**. Ratification binds the principal to an agent's contract in the absence of either actual or apparent authority. If the principal accepts the benefits of an unauthorized contract or in some other way affirms that contract, then the principal is bound. For example, assume in the previous example that Jill signed a promissory note borrowing five thousand dollars from a bank. She had no actual authority, since she was limited to purchasing spare automobile parts. Furthermore, she had no apparent authority because the principal created no impression that she was empowered to borrow money for the firm. However, if the principal were to take the five thousand dollars and use it for business, then the contract would be ratified and the principal would be bound by it. The doctrine of ratification is based on common sense. If the principal accepts the benefits of the contract, then the obligations of that contract should also apply.

The most important aspect of an agent's contracting authority is that the law provides a mechanism for one person to legally act on behalf of another. No business could function if concepts of agency were not in existence. However, as suggested by the discussion above, business managers are advised to pay close attention to the authority that their firms' agents possess. Limiting an agent's actual authority—or more precisely, defining that agent's role in the business—can limit the exposure of the company to unwanted contracts. As an exercise, assume that you were promoted to regional sales manager for ABC, Inc. You have been asked to create a policy manual that deals with issues involving the sales representatives. Describe problems of agent authority that might be of concern to ABC, Inc., and propose standards that will help alleviate them.

The case that follows shows the operation of the authority doctrines. Note that often multiple doctrines of authority can be raised simultaneously. Upon any one of them being established, the principal will be bound to the terms of the contract.

Lind v. Schenley Industries, Inc.
United States Court of Appeals, Third Circuit
278 F.2d 79 (1960)

Lind, the plaintiff–appellant, sued Park & Tilford Distillers Corporation for a compensation that he assserts is due him by virtue of a contract expressed by a written memorandum supplemented by oral conversations. Lind also sued for certain expenses he incurred when moving from New Jersey to New York when his position as New Jersey state manager of Park & Tilford terminated.

Lind had been employed for some years by Park & Tilford. In July 1950, Lind was informed by Herrfeldt, then Park & Tilford's vice-president and general sales manager, that he would be appointed assistant to Kaufman, Park & Tilford's sales manager for metropolitan New York. Subsequently, Lind received a communication, dated April 19, 1951, signed by Kaufman, informing Lind that he would assume the title of "district manager." The letter went on to state: "I wish to inform you of the fact that you have as much responsibility as a State Manager and that you should consider yourself to be of the same status." The letter concluded with the statement: "An incentive plan is being worked out so that you will not only be responsible for increased sales in your district, but will benefit substantially in a monetary way."

Lind assumed his duties as district sales manager for metropolitan New York. During the weeks following Lind's new appointment, Lind inquired of Kaufman frequently what his remuneration would be under the incentive plan and was informed that details were being worked out. In July 1951, Kaufman informed Lind that he was to receive one percent commission on the gross sales of the men under him. This was an oral communication and was completely corroborated by Kaufman's former secretary. On subsequent occasions, Lind was assured by Kaufman that he would get his money. Lind was also informed by Herrfeldt, in the autumn of 1952, that he would get a one percent commission on the sales of the men under him. Early in 1955, Lind negotiated with Brown, then president of Park & Tilford, for the sale of Park & Tilford's New Jersey Wholesale House, and Brown agreed to apply the money owed to Lind by reason of the one percent commission against the value of the goodwill of the Wholesale House.

Biggs, Chief Judge

The problems of "authority" are probably the most difficult in that segment of law loosely termed "Agency." Two main classifications of authority are generally recognized, "actual authority," and "apparent authority."

"Actual authority" means, as the words connote, authority that the principal, expressly or implicitly, gave the agent. "Apparent authority" arises when a principal acts in such a manner as to convey the impression to a third party that an agent has certain powers which he may or may not actually possess. "Implied authority" has been variously defined. It has been held to be actual authority given implicitly by a principal to his agent. Another definition of "implied authority" is that it is a kind of authority arising solely from the designation by the principal of a kind of agent who ordinarily possesses certain powers. It is this concept that is called "inherent authority." Usually it is not necessary for a third party attempting to hold a principal to specify which type of authority he relies upon.

From the evidence it is clear that Park & Tilford can be held accountable for Kaufman's actions on the principle of "inherent authority." Kaufman was Lind's direct superior, and was the man to transfer communications from the upper executives to the lower. Moreover, there was testimony tending to prove that Herrfeldt, the vice-president in charge of sales, had told Lind to see Kaufman for information about his salary and that Herrfeldt himself had confirmed the 1 percent commission arrangement. Thus Kaufman, so far as Lind was concerned, was the spokesman for the company.

There is no doubt that New York accepts the "apparent authority" doctrine if change of position is shown. "[T]he principal is often bound by the act of his agent in excess or abuse of his actual authority, but this is only true between the principal and third person, who believing and having a right to believe that the agent was acting within and not exceeding his authority, would sustain loss if the act was not considered that of the principal."

Testimony was adduced by Schenley tending to prove that Kaufman had no authority to set salaries, that power being exercisable solely by the president of the corporation, and that the president had not authorized Kaufman to offer Lind a commission of the kind under consideration here. However, this testimony, even if fully accepted, would only prove lack of actual or implied authority in Kaufman but is irrelevant to the issue of apparent authority.

The opinion below seems to agree with the conception of the New York agency law as set out above but the court reversed the jury's verdict and the judgment based on it on the conclusion, as a matter of law, that Lind could not reasonably have believed that Kaufman was authorized to offer him a commission that would, in the trial judge's words "have almost quadrupled Lind's then salary." But Lind testified that before he had become Kaufman's assistant in September 1950, he had earned $9,000 for the period from January 1, 1950 to August 31, 1950, that figure allegedly representing half of his expected earnings for the year. Lind testified that a liquor salesman can expect to make 50 percent of his salary in the last four months of the year owing to holiday sales. Thus Lind's salary two years before his appointment as district manager could have been estimated by the jury at $18,000 per year, and his alleged earnings, as district manager, a position of greater responsiblity, do not appear disproportionate. On the basis of the foregoing it appears that there was sufficient evidence to authorize a jury finding that Park & Tilford had given Kaufman apparent authority to offer Lind 1 percent commission of gross sales of the salesmen under him and that Lind reasonably had relied upon Kaufman's offer.

It must be remembered that when dealing with internal corporate management matters an employee must be able to rely on the word of his superiors, or their apparent spokesmen, lest operation of such organizations becomes impossible. A salesman cannot check every promise made to him by a superior with the president and the board of directors of the corporation.

PRINCIPLES OF FIDUCIARY DUTIES

After reading the preceding material, you should be aware of one substantial problem: The agent is granted extraordinary power to affect the property owned by the principal. Consequently, an agent's carelessness could make the principal vicariously liable to an injured third party. Unwanted agent contracts, through apparent authority, would nonetheless bind the principal. Thus, the law imposes on the agent higher standards of behavior than apply in nonagency relationships. These standards are called **fiduciary duties.**

But first, one needs to determine when someone becomes a fiduciary.

What is a Fiduciary?

A fiduciary is vested with power and authority over another person's property and is charged with managing that property for the other person's benefit. This other person, therefore, places trust and confidence in the work of the fiduciary, hoping to benefit from that work. A fiduciary relationship, then, is one of power and dependence. Let us consider this definition in light of the agent–principal materials discussed above.

The agent is granted power over the principal's property, as may be illustrated by the above discussion of the vicarious liability and authority doctrines. Through these doctrines the agent can either benefit or harm the finances of the principal. Furthermore, when entering into the relationship, the principal necessarily must place trust and confidence in the abilities of the agent who will be performing various tasks on the principal's behalf. Thus, the agent owes fiduciary duties to the principal.

In general, this fiduciary duty may be divided into two categories: The first is the fiduciary duty of care, which imposes a burden of diligence, attention, and concern in all aspects of the agent's work on behalf of the principal. For example, an employee negotiating a contract must do so with concern and skill, keeping the best interests of the employer in mind. This duty balances against the employer's risk that the employee may, through careless action, bind it to an unwanted or unfavorable contract.

The second aspect of the fiduciary relationship is the duty of loyalty. Once the principal–agent relationship has been created, the agent must make the interests of the principal paramount. Given the power that is vested in the agent, a temptation may arise to use it for the personal benefit of the agent, rather than on the principal's behalf. To combat this temptation, the law imposes the fiduciary duty of loyalty on the agent.

As an illustration: Jack is employed by ABC, Inc. His job is to order parts for compact disc players that ABC, Inc. manufactures. A supplier offers Jack a percentage of the purchase price to commit ABC to a long-term contract. By accepting this bribe, Jack would violate the trust that ABC placed in him by making him its agent. Furthermore, the percentage that was offered to Jack should belong to ABC, because the supplier was willing to accept less than its usual price for the compact disc player parts. Accepting the bribe would place Jack's interests ahead of ABC's and, thus, be a breach of Jack's duty of loyalty.

Fiduciary Relationships within Business Organizations

As suggested by the discussion above, all employees owe fiduciary duties to their employers. Thus, for all organizational forms that have employees (sole proprietorship, partnership, limited partnership, corporation, and limited liability company), the fiduciary duty principles apply. However, as with the discussion of the agency materials, other fiduciary relationships arise from the particular nature of the organizational form (see Table 14.2). The following material notes these relationships.

Partners owe fiduciary duties to one another. Recall the nature of their

TABLE 14.2	The Fiduciary Relationship and Business Organizational Forms	
	Fiduciary Relationship	
Business Form	**Who Owes a Fiduciary Duty?**	**To Whom Is the Fiduciary Duty Owed?**
Sole proprietorship	Employees*	Sole proprietor
Partnership	Partners	Partners
Corporation	Directors and officers	Shareholders
Limited partnership	General partner	Other general partners and the limited partners
Limited liability company	Members who manage	Members

* Employees of any organizational form owe fiduciary duties.

relationship: each partner, as an agent, can enter into contracts on behalf of the firm; torts committed by the partner may be binding on the firm. Further, note that the partners have a risk of personal liability for unpaid claims against their business. Consequently, each partner has a great deal of power in relation to the property of the others. As a result, the partners are dependent and, by necessity, have placed trust in one another when they entered into the relationship.

Similarly, in a limited partnership and limited liability company, those who manage the firm owe fiduciary duties. In a limited partnership, the general partner owes the duties to the limited partners. Since the limited partners are precluded from management and control of the firm, they must rely on the skills of the general partner for the operation of the business. Thus, the legal restrictions on the limited partner create the need for such a duty to arise.

In a limited liability company, those members who manage the firm owe fiduciary duties to the other members, since as managers they are empowered to make business decisions that affect the others' investment.

Within a corporation, the board of directors and officers owe a fiduciary duty to the shareholders. Note that under corporate law the shareholders do not have a role in managing the firm. Their influence is "indirect"; they elect the board of directors, which in turn elects officers. Therefore, the shareholders rely on others to manage the firm. Under corporate law, the board of directors is vested with this power. Consequently, the classic relationship arises between power and dependence. As a result, the directors owe fiduciary duties to the shareholders.

THE FIDUCIARY DUTY AND DIRECTOR—SHAREHOLDER RELATIONSHIPS

As noted above, the fiduciary duty compels a standard of behavior that exceeds what normally would be acceptable in the legal environment. It is distinguished from the reasonable person standard (see Chapter 11). Rather than being evaluated as "reasonable persons," according to how people really act, fiduciaries are held to standards consistent with how people ought to act. A fiduciary duty imposes a higher level of care and loyalty than the law ordinarily requires.

This section will explore the requirements that the law imposes on a fiduciary, focusing on the director–shareholder relationship. (Note that fiduciary relationships exist in numerous other areas of business law, including trustee–beneficiary, attorney–client, accountant–client, and mutual fund manager–investor.) This fiduciary relationship has been the source of much litigation and development in the law. Consequently, it provides a good source of information about the fiduciary duty. Note, however, that the precise contours of any fiduciary's obligations are driven by the specific nature of the relationship.

The fiduciary duty of corporate directors obligates them to use the utmost good faith and loyalty and to exercise care and prudence in all matters concerning the management of the corporation. Normally acceptable standards of business practice are not sufficient to satisfy their duty. The duty of care involves diligent decision making by the board; the duty of loyalty requires that corporate interests be placed ahead of any personal interests of the directors.

Fiduciary Duty of Care

Directors have a fiduciary duty to be thorough and viligant in their decision making. The law requires them to use the amount of care an ordinarily prudent person in a like position would use under similar circumstances. This is not an easy standard to apply. In effect, it is a standard of hindsight. Shareholders will argue breach of the fiduciary duty of care or will review the directors' decision making when a particular decision turns out to be wrong or costs the shareholders potential profits. Although the standard requires the directors to exercise prudent procedures, it is no guarantee that all decisions will be correct.

The following case is an example of the fiduciary duty of care. It involves a bank fraud and claims that the fiduciaries violated their duty of care by not detecting the fraud before it became a disaster. Note that the duty of care was applied differently to the board of directors than it was to the president (who also owed a fiduciary duty). Although each owed the shareholders a fiduciary duty of care, their positions in the day–to–day operation of the bank were different. Thus, the diligence each needed to exercise on behalf of the corporation was found to be factually different.

Bates v. Dresser
United States Supreme Court
251 U.S. 524 (1920)

The bank was a little bank in Cambridge, Massachusetts, with a capital of $100,000 and average deposits of about $300,000. Coleman, who made the trouble, entered the service of the bank as messenger in September 1903. In January 1904, he was promoted to bookkeeper.

In November 1906, he began the thefts that come into question here. Having a small account at the bank, he would draw checks for the amount he wanted, exchange checks with a Boston broker, get cash for the broker's check, and, when the checks came to the bank through the clearinghouse, abstract his own from the envelope, enter the others on his book, and conceal the difference by a charge to some other account or a false addition in the column of drafts or deposits in the depositors' ledger. He handed to the cashier only the slip from the clearinghouse that showed the totals. The cashier paid whatever appeared to be due, and thus Coleman's checks were honored. So far as Coleman thought it necessary, in view of the absolute trust in him on the part of all concerned, he took care that his balances should agree with those in the cashier's book.

By May 2, 1907, Coleman had abstracted $17,000, concealing the fact by false addition in the column of total checks and false balances in the deposit ledger. Then for the moment a safer concealment was effected by charging the whole to the inactive account of Dresser, then the bank's president. Coleman adopted this method when a bank examiner was expected. Of course, when the fraud was disguised by overcharging a depositor, it could not be discovered except by calling in the passbooks, or taking all the deposit slips and comparing them with the depositors' ledger in detail. By February 21, 1910, when the bank closed, the amount taken by Coleman was $310,143.02.

The directors considered the matter in September 1909, but concluded that the falling off in deposits was due in part to the springing up of rivals, whose deposits were increasing, but was parallel to a similar decrease in New York. An examination by a bank examiner in December 1909 disclosed nothing wrong.

In this connection it should be mentioned that in the previous semiannual examinations by national bank examiners, nothing was discovered pointing to malfeasance. The cashier was honest, and everybody believed that they could rely upon him, although in fact he relied too much upon Coleman, who also was unsuspected by all. If the cashier had opened the envelopes from the clearinghouse and had seen the checks, or had examined the deposit ledger with any care, he would have found out what was going on. The scrutiny of anyone accustomed to such details would have discovered the false addition and other indicia of fraud that were on the face of the book. But it may be doubted whether anything less than a continuous pursuit of the figures through pages would have done so except by a lucky chance.

Justice Holmes

The question of the liability of the directors in this case is the question whether they neglected their duty by accepting the cashier's statement of liabilities and failing to inspect the depositors' ledger. The statements of assets always were correct. Of course liabilities as well as assets must be known to know the condition and, as this case shows, speculations may be concealed as well by a false understatement of liabilities, as by a false show of assets. But the former is not the direction in which fraud would have been looked for, especially on the part of one who at the time of his principal abstractions was not in contact with the funds. A debtor hardly expects to have his liability understated. Some animals must have given at least one exhibition of dangerous propensities before the owner can be held. This fraud was a novelty in the way of swindling a bank so far as the knowledge of any experience had reached Cambridge before 1910.

We are not prepared to reverse the finding of the master and the Circuit Court of Appeals that the directors should not be held answerable for taking the cashier's statement of liabilities to be as correct as the statement of assets always was. If he had not been negligent without their knowledge it would have been. Their confidence seemed warranted by the semi-annual examinations by the government examiner and they were encouraged in their belief that all was well by the president, whose responsibility, as executive officer; interest, as large stockholder and depositor; and knowledge, from long daily presence in the bank, were greater than theirs. They were not bound by virtue of the office gratuitously assumed by them to call in the pass–books and compare them with the ledger, and until the event showed the possibility they hardly could have seen that their failure to look at the ledger opened a way to fraud. We are not laying down general principles, however, but confine our decision to the circumstances of the particular case.

The position of Dresser, the president, is different. Practically he was the master of the situation. He was daily at the bank for hours, he had the deposit ledger in his hands at times and might have had it at any time. He had had hints and warnings in addition to those that we have mentioned, warnings that should not be magnified unduly, but still would have induced scrutiny but for an invincible repose upon the status quo. In 1908 one Fillmore learned that a package containing $150 left with the bank for safe keeping was not to be found, told Dresser of the loss, wrote to him that he could but conclude that the package had been destroyed or removed by someone connected with the bank, and in later conversation said that it was evident that there was a thief in the bank. He added that he would advise the president to look after Coleman, that he believed he was living at a pretty fast pace, and that he had pretty good authority for thinking that he was supporting a woman. In the same year or the year before, Coleman, whose pay was never more than twelve dollars a week, set up an automobile, as was known to Dresser and commented on unfavorably, to him. There was also some evidence of notice to Dresser that Coleman was dealing in copper stocks. In 1909 came the great and inadequately explained seeming shrinkage in deposits. No doubt plausible explanations of his conduct came from Coleman and the notice as to speculations may have been slight, but taking the whole story of the relations of the parties, we are not ready to say that the two courts below erred in finding that Dresser had been put upon his guard.

In accepting the presidency Dresser must be taken to have contemplated responsibility for losses to the bank, whatever they were, if chargeable to his fault. Those that happened were chargeable to his fault, after he had warnings that should have led to steps that would have made fraud impossible, even though the precise form that the fraud would take hardly could have been foreseen.

Business Judgment Rule

The directors' defense to any shareholder claim of breach of fiduciary duty of care is called the business judgment rule. The business judgment rule provides that when an act or omission involves a question of policy or business judgment, the directors will not be liable for an erroneous decision, in absence of a showing of fraud or bad faith. This defense recognizes that mistakes may be made and that people may disagree about the proper business policies in a given situation. If the directors make their business decisions honestly and use sound business judgment, then they have not breached their fiduciary duty of care.

However, the directors may not ignore what is happening around them in the business. They must be inquisitive. Furthermore, the standard of honest judgment reflects the notion that the directors have used careful decision-making procedures. Generally, this requires the directors to make reasonable efforts to gather information concerning the decisions to be made.

The following case illustrates the business judgment rule defense. Note that the court was not concerned with whether the business decision was correct or whether the court itself would have made a similar one. Instead, the court held that the decision was proper because it found that the directors had exercised sound decision-making practices.

Shlensky v. Wrigley et al.
Appellate Court of Illinois
237 N.E.2d 776 (1968)

Plaintiff is a minority stockholder of defendant corporation, Chicago National League Ball Club (Inc.), a Delaware corporation with its principal place of business in Chicago, Illinois. Defendant corporation owns and operates the major league professional baseball team known as the Chicago Cubs. The individual defendants are directors of the Cubs and have served for varying periods of years. Defendant Philip K. Wrigley is also president of the corporation and owner of approximately eighty percent of the stock therein.

Plaintiff alleges that since night baseball was first played in 1935, nineteen of the twenty major league teams have scheduled night games. In 1966, out of a total of 1,620 games in the major leagues, 932 were played at night. Plaintiff alleges that every member of the major leagues, other than the Cubs, scheduled substantially all its home games in 1966 at night, exclusive of opening days, Saturdays, Sundays, holidays, and days prohibited by league rules. This has been done for the specific purpose of maximizing attendance and thereby maximizing revenue and income.

The Cubs, in the years from 1961 to 1965, sustained operating losses from its direct baseball operations. Plaintiff attributes those losses to inadequate attendance at Cubs' home games. He concludes that if the directors continue to refuse to install lights at Wrigley Field and schedule night baseball games, the Cubs will continue to sustain comparable losses, and its financial condition will continue to deteriorate.

Plaintiff alleges that defendant Wrigley has refused to install lights, not because of interest in the welfare of the corporation but because of his personal opinions "that baseball is a 'daytime sport' and that the installation of lights and night baseball games will have a deteriorating effect upon the surrounding neighborhood." It is alleged that he has admitted that he is not interested in whether the Cubs would benefit financially from such action because of his concern for the neighborhood, and that he would be willing for the team to play night games if a new stadium were built in Chicago.

Sullivan, Justice

Plaintiff in the instant case argues that the directors are acting for reasons unrelated to the financial interest and welfare of the Cubs. However, we are not satisfied that the motives assigned to Philip K. Wrigley, and through him to the other directors, are contrary to the best interests of the corporation and the stockholders. For example, it appears to us that the effect on the surrounding neighborhood might well be considered by a director who was considering the patrons who would or would not attend the games if the park were in a poor neighborhood. Furthermore, the long run interest of the corporation in its property value at Wrigley Field might demand all efforts to keep the neighborhood from deteriorating. By these thoughts we do not mean to say that we have decided that the decision of the directors was a correct one. That is beyond our jurisdiction and ability. We are merely saying that the decision is one properly before directors and the motives alleged in the amended complaint showed no fraud, illegality or conflict of interest in their making of that decision.

There is no allegation that the night games played by the other nineteen teams enhanced their financial position or that the profits, if any, of those teams were directly related to the number of night games scheduled. There is an allegation that the installation of lights and scheduling of night games in Wrigley Field would have resulted in large amounts of additional revenues and incomes from increased attendance and related sources of income. Further, the cost of installation of lights, funds for which are allegedly readily available by financing, would be more than offset and recaptured by increased revenues. However, no allegation is made that there will be a net benefit to the corporation from such action, considering all increased costs. No mention was made of operation and maintenance of the lights or other possible increases in operating costs of night games and we cannot speculate as to what other factors might influence the increase or decrease of profits if the Cubs were to play night home games.

Finally, we do not agree with plaintiff's contention that failure to follow the example of the other major league clubs in scheduling night games constituted negligence. Plaintiff made no allegation that these teams' night schedules were profitable or that the purpose for which night baseball had been undertaken was fulfilled. Furthermore, it cannot be said that directors, even those

of corporations that are losing money, must follow the lead of the other corporations in the field. Directors are elected for their business capabilities and judgment and the courts cannot require them to forego their judgment because of the decisions of directors of other companies. Courts may not decide these questions in the absence of a clear showing of dereliction of duty on the part of specific directors and mere failure to "follow the crowd" is not such a dereliction.

Fiduciary Duty of Loyalty

The directors' fiduciary duty of loyalty does not regulate their decision–making process. Instead, it regulates the relationship between an individual director and the corporation. Board members are privy to secret corporate plans and information. By virtue of their powerful position they have the ability to influence management policy for their own benefit. They have the ability to make investments and personal business decisions that could garner large profits at the expense of the corporation.

The danger the fiduciary duty of loyalty seeks to avoid is that of individual directors' taking advantage of their positions for personal gain. Directors, therefore, are held to a duty to promote the interests of the corporation without regard for individual profit.

Dealings with the Corporation

The law does not prohibit a director from engaging in business deals with the corporation. However, there exists the danger of a conflict of interest in such transactions. The director owes a duty to the corporation, yet stands to gain financially from the terms of the contract. Furthermore, by virtue of a position on the board, a director may have an undue advantage in securing or negotiating the contract.

The directors' fiduciary duty requires a standard different from that which exists in the marketplace. For example, the director must make a full disclosure concerning all aspects of the contract affecting the value of the property or services involved, as well as the amount of profit to be made. This full disclosure must be made to an independent board of directors. Essentially, this means that the other directors of the corporation must not be influenced by the contracting director. Alternatively, the contract must, in all respects, be fair and reasonable to the corporation. If one or the other of these standards is not met, then the contract is considered legally voidable.

Under either of these standards, fairness is the key. Not only is this standard based on a review of the contractual terms, but one can expect that a board that is not unduly influenced by a particular director will exercise its fiduciary duty of care in reviewing the contract proposal. Consequently, a board-approved contract will also be "fair." In any event, the duty of loyalty standard responds to a concern that directors may take advantage of their position in dealing with the corporation.

The following case is an example of a breach of the fiduciary duty of loyalty. Note that the director who negotiated the startlingly one-sided contract was on the boards of both corporations. Yet he owned stock only in one of them—the corporation for whose benefit the contract was drafted.

Globe Woolen Co. v. Utica Gas & Electric Co.
Court of Appeals of New York
121 N.E.378 (1918)

The plaintiff is the owner of two mills in the city of Utica. One is for the manufacture of worsteds and the other for the manufacture of woolens. The defendant generates and sells electricity for light and power. For many years, John F. Maynard has been the plaintiff's chief stockholder, its president, and a member of its board of directors. He has also been a director of the defendant and chairman of its executive committee. He received a single share of the defendant's stock to qualify him for office. He returned the share at once, and he has never held another. His property interest in the plaintiff is large. In the defendant he has none.

At the beginning, the mills were run by steam, and the plant was antiquated and inadequate. Greenidge, the general manager of the defendant's electrical department, suggested to Mr. Maynard the substitution of electric power. Mr. Maynard was fearful that the cost of equipment would be too great unless the defendant would guarantee a saving in the cost of operation. Nonetheless, a change was felt to be important. The plaintiff's books were thrown open to Greenidge, who calculated for himself the cost of operation with steam and the probable cost with electricity.

When the investigation was over, a contract was closed. The defendant proposed to supply the plaintiff's mills with electricity at a maximum rate of $.0104 per kilowatt–hour, and to guarantee that the cost for heat and light and power would show a saving each month of $300 each as compared with the cost for the corresponding month in the year previous to the change. In addition, the contract would apply to "current used for any purposes in any extensions or additions to the mills." There was to be a trial period ending July 1, 1907. Then, at the plaintiff's option, the contract was to run for five years, with a privilege of renewal for a like term. Six weeks later, on December 1, 1906, Mr. Maynard laid the contract before the defendant's executive committee. He went to the meeting with Mr. Greenidge. The contract was read. Mr. Lewis, the vice–president, asked Mr. Greenidge what the rate would be, and was told about $.0104 per kilowatt–hour. Mr. Beardsley, another director, asked whether the contract was a profitable one for the company, and was told by Mr. Greenidge that it was. Mr. Maynard kept silent. A resolution was moved and carried that the contract be ratified. Mr. Maynard presided at the meeting, and put the resolution, but was excused from voting.

It quickly appeared that the defendant had made a losing contract, but only gradually did the extent of the loss, its permanence, and its causes unfold themselves. Greenidge had miscalculated. The plaintiff dyed more yarn and less slubbing than before. But the dyeing of yarn takes twice as much heat as that of slubbing, and thus doubles the cost of fuel. These and like changes in the output of the mills had not been foreseen by Greenidge, and Maynard had not warned of them. In 1909, the defendant became alarmed at the mounting loss. Finally, in February 1911, the defendant gave notice of rescission. At that time, it had supplied the plaintiff with electricity worth $69,500.75 if paid for at the maximum rate fixed by the contract, and $60,000 if paid for at the lowest rate charged to any customer in Utica. Yet not only had it received nothing, but it owed the plaintiff under its guaranty $11,721.41. The finding is that a like loss prolonged to the end of the term would amount to $300,000.

Cardozo, Justice

We think the evidence supports the conclusion that the contracts are voidable at the election of the defendant. The plaintiff does not deny that this would be true if the dual director had voted for their adoption. But the argument is that by refusing to vote he shifted the responsibility to his associates, and may reap a profit from their errors. One does not divest oneself so readily of one's duties as director. A dominating influence may be exerted in other ways than by a vote. A beneficiary, about to plunge into a ruinous course of dealing, may be betrayed by silence as well as by the spoken word.

The director is free to stand aloof, while others act, if all is equitable and fair. He cannot rid himself of the duty to warn and to denounce, if there is improvidence or impression, either apparent on the surface, or lurking beneath the surface, but visible to his practiced eye.

There was an influence here, dominating, perhaps, and surely potent and persuasive, which was exerted by Mr. Maynard from the beginning to the end. In all the stages of preliminary treaty he dealt with a subordinate, who looked up to him as to a superior, and was alert to serve his pleasure. There was no clean–cut cleavage in those stages between his conflicting offices and agencies. No label identified the request of Mr. Maynard, the plaintiff's president, as something separate from the advice of Mr. Maynard, the defendant's chairman. The members of the committee, hearing the contract for the first time, knew that it had been framed by the chairman of the meeting. They were assured in his presence that it

was just and equitable. Faith in his loyalty disarmed suspicion.

There was, then, a relation of trust reposed, of influence exerted, of superior knowledge on the one side and legitimate dependence on the other. At least, a finding that there was this relation was evidence to sustain it. A director may not cling to contracts thus won, unless their terms are fair and just.

The contracts before us do not survive these tests. The unfairness is startling, and the consequences have been disastrous. The mischief consists in this: no matter how large the business, no matter how great the increase in the price of labor or of fuel, no matter what the changes in the nature or the proportion of the products, no matter even though there be extensions of the plant, the defendant has pledged its word that for ten years there will be a saving of $600 a month, $300 for each mill, $7,200 a year. As a result of that pledge it has suppplied the plaintiff with electric current for nothing, and owes, if the contract stands, about $11,000 for the privilege. These elements of unfairness Mr. Maynard must have known, if indeed his knowledge be material. He may not have known how great the loss would be. But he cannot have failed to know that he held a one-sided contract which left the defendant at his mercy. He was not blind to the likelihood that in a term of ten years there would be changes in the business.

We hold that the constant duty rests on a director to seek no harsh advantage to the detriment of his corporation, but rather to protest and renounce it through the blindness of those who treat with him he gains what is unfair. And, because there is evidence that in the making of these contracts that duty was ignored, the power of equity was fittingly exercised to bring them to an end.

Corporate Opportunity Doctrine

The corporate opportunity doctrine imposes two more loyalty standards. First, a director may not compete with the corporation. Consider that a director has access to corporate strategy and plans that would make a competitive enterprise particularly harmful to the corporation. In effect, the director would be using the position for personal gain rather than for the benefit of the corporation.

The second standard prohibits a director from taking advantage of a business opportunity that may be of interest to or could be used by the corporation. The director owes the corporation a right of first refusal, that being the right to acquire a particular opportunity at the same terms and conditions as were first offered to the individual director. If the opportunity is presented and the corporation refuses it, the director is generally able to legally take advantage of it. For example, assume that a director knows that the corporation has building plans. A real estate agent offers the director land that is in a prime location for the corporation to expand. The director may not purchase this land, even though it may be an outstanding investment, without first giving the corporation the opportunity to do so.

An example further illustrates the operation of the corporate opportunity doctrine. Assume that Jane Jones is a member of the board of directors of XYZ, Inc., which owns a large chain of fast-food restaurants. The restaurants specialize in a wide variety of soft drinks, its most popular being an orange-flavored beverage. The corporation has attempted to negotiate bulk rates with the small firm that supplies the popular orange drink, but to no avail. On February 15, Jones learns that this supplier is in financial trouble. She purchases a controlling interest in the company and thereafter decides to expand its operations to include quick-stop restaurants that sell the orange drink and sandwiches.

Jane Jones has violated the corporate opportunity doctrine. First, Jones, through her controlling interest in the firm, is in direct competition with XYZ. The Jones-controlled firm will be selling products similar to XYZ's, including the most popular item at XYZ's restaurants. Furthermore, since both businesses will be selling fast food, their clientele will be similar. Thus, the danger to XYZ shareholders is that Jones's personal success conflicts with the success of the corporation, and her access to corporate plans and strategies can be used to harm it. A director's duty of loyalty requires that corporate interests supersede individual ones.

Furthermore, Jones took for herself an opportunity that rightfully belonged to XYZ. Since XYZ sold the very popular orange drink, the opportunity to acquire the firm that produces it would be a business opportunity that would most likely interest the corporation. A director's duty of loyalty requires that such business opportunities be made available to the corporation before the individual director can consider them. Since Jones did not provide the corporation with the right of first refusal, she breached her duty of loyalty.

SUMMARY

Business organizations are operated by individuals. In Chapter 13, the forms of those organizations were explored. Here, the powers and duties that the law provides to people within the organizations were discussed. Note, at the outset, how basic legal environment concepts, as discussed in Chapter 1, are illustrated by these materials: first, the legal environment facilitates the operation of the business organizations (the law of agency); second, the legal environment controls the power that it grants to agents (the law of fiduciary relationships).

An agent-principal relationship is not limited to that of an employee and employer. Although that is its most common identity, it also has other identities within each of the organizational forms. For example, partners are agents and principals of one another. Corporate officers are agents, the corporate entity is the principal. In any event, agents are empowered to act on behalf of the principal. Two major aspects of this power were explored: the ability of agents to create contracts on behalf of the principal, and the liability risk to the principal arising from torts committed by the agent.

In addition, while granting agents these powers, the law also imposes a fiduciary duty on them. Fiduciaries owe their beneficiaries duties of care and loyalty that exceed standards normally imposed by the legal environment. Note that the fiduciary duty extends not only to agents and their principals but to other organizational relationships as well—corporate director-shareholder is an example. In fact, any relationship with an imbalance of power and dependence is a candidate for fiduciary duty regulation.

REVIEW QUESTIONS

1. Define the following terms:
   a. Agent
   b. Apparent authority
   c. Business judgment rule
   d. Corporate opportunity doctrine
   e. Vicarious liability

2. Under what circumstances could a person who owns shares in ABC, Inc. be considered an agent of ABC, Inc.?

3. While on vacation, Jack is approached by an artist who has a booth where he sketches portraits. Jack agrees to have a drawing made but insists that it be of his left side and that only a blue pencil be used. Do Jack and the artist have a principal and agent relationship?

4. Mary and Jane are partners in a bookstore. Jane's role is limited to buying used books from wholesalers. One afternoon, Jane purchases a big-screen television set, charging it to the bookstore. When the set is delivered, the partners install it against a wall and show advertising videos to their customers. Would the partnership be bound to Jane's contract? Why?

5. Jack is a shareholder in ABC, Inc., a publicly traded company that manufactures mobile homes. It is his only role in the firm. One

day while visiting a furniture store, Jack orders custom-made items to be used in ABC-manufactured mobile homes. He negotiated an excellent price. However, ABC does not want that furniture. Is ABC bound to the contract?

6. Bill works for a sole proprietor. He has a written job description that lists as one of his responsibilities ''to purchase computers as needed by the business.'' Would Bill have the authority to purchase a printer (assuming the business needed one)?

7. Mary is an auditor with the Smith & Jones partnership. She was assigned to audit the books of a major client, but thought a few days on the beach would be more exciting. So instead of following office audit procedures, she fabricated the numbers. If the client suffers a financial loss because of this audit, does the Smith & Jones partnership face any risk of liability?

8. Jim is a shareholder in XYZ, Inc., a publicly traded company with headquarters in Lawrence, Kansas. It is his only role in the corporation. The firm intends to expand its office space, but has been unable to secure the needed land. If the opportunity is presented to Jim to purchase a site that would be perfect for XYZ's needs, must he offer it first to the corporation?

9. Do partners owe the same duties toward one another that limited partners owe to general partners?

10. George is on the board of directors of ABC, Inc. He attends meetings only occasionally. When he does, he often dozes through most of them. He also doesn't bother to read reports prepared for the directors, instead relying on management to keep him informed. In fact, he supports anything that management proposes. Does this behavior increase George's risk of legal liability?

11. Smith, Inc. received an offer to purchase its assets in September for five hundred million dollars. The offer was made after months of negotiations and evaluation of the assets of the corporation. However, the deal was never consummated. On December 18, another offer of five hundred million dollars was received. The offer must be accepted or rejected by December 21. A special meeting of the board of directors was called to consider the offer. The directors met for one hour and heard a report roughly outlining the offer. They neither asked questions nor requested that corporate experts be called to advise them concerning its soundness. Furthermore, general inflation had increased by ten percent in the last quarter of the year. The directors accepted the offer. Have the directors fulfilled their duty to the shareholders?

12. Mary is a member of the board of directors of XYZ, Inc., which operates a popular restaurant in the city. In February, the directors met to discuss the possibility of expanding the restaurant onto the vacant lot next to it. However, because interest rates were high, the board deferred action on the proposal. In April, Mary was approached by the owner of the lot, who offered Mary an excellent deal, including low-interest financing, to purchase the lot. Mary immediately agreed. Discuss this problem with relation to Mary's duty to the shareholders of XYZ.

13. Tom was the sole proprietor of a grocery store. He hired Jane to stock the shelves in his store. One afternoon, Jane was putting bars of soap in a large basket located in an aisle of the store. She was bored with the task so to make it more enjoyable, she invented a game in which, for each bar of soap placed in the basket, the next one would have to be tossed in from one step farther away. A bar of soap missed the basket and skidded down the aisle. A customer stepped on the soap, fell, and was injured. Would Tom be liable for that tort?

14. Jim began working at Harry's Book Shop. His job was to sell books to customers. One Thursday afternoon a bedraggled old professor was browsing through the shelves and noticed an early edition of Walt Whitman's poetry. The price marked on the book was $150. Jim approached the professor and they began to speak and haggle about the price. They agreed, finally, that the professor could purchase the book for $128. When the professor attempted to pay for the book, Harry refused to accept the agreed-upon $128 and insisted on the full $150. Must Harry sell the book for the price negotiated by Jim? (Note that negotiating over the price of books is standard practice in many used-book stores.)

15. Jane Jones is the sole owner of a small business that manufactures pencils. She is also a member of the board of directors of XYZ Corporation. May Jones legally enter into a contract to sell pencils manufactured by her business to XYZ Corporation? If so, may she negotiate with XYZ to the same extent she is able to do so with all other pencil manufacturers?

CHAPTER 15

White-Collar and Business Crime: Regulation of Business Through the Criminal Process

- Classes of Crimes
- Prosecution of Cases
- Constitutional Protection
- White–Collar Crime

Many people read about, and in some cases are the victims of, crimes. Businesses suffer billions of dollars in losses each year from crime. In spite of the enormous impact of crime on society, many people have no idea how the criminal system operates. This chapter is designed to briefly explain what activities are classified as criminal and how criminal cases are handled within the American judicial system. The chapter also covers some of the limitations in the United States Constitution on the operation of the criminal system. The Constitution protects the rights of all people accused of a crime to make certain that every person receives a fair trial. The final section discusses the topic of white-collar crime, which is increasingly recognized as a major problem in society. Every year, more effort is devoted by the government to prosecuting such crimes.

CLASSES OF CRIMES

Crimes   A *crime* is an act or omission for which a sentence or a fine may be imposed by the presiding judge. Crimes are thought of as wrongs not only against the injured parties but also against society. The federal government, state governments, and city and county governments make certain types of behavior criminal.

Felonies   The most serious crime is called a **felony**. A felony generally is punishable by imprisonment in a penitentiary for more than a year. A fine may also be imposed in some cases. Theft of property worth more than a specified sum of money (for example, over one hundred dollars) usually constitutes a felony. Other examples of felonies are murder, rape, and possession of such drugs as heroin. Persons in business who violate the antitrust laws in certain cases may be guilty of a felony, as discussed in Chapters 23 and 24.

Mis-demeanors

All crimes that are not felonies normally are classified as **misdemeanors**. Misdemeanors are punishable by up to one year in jail. A fine also may be imposed. Theft of property of small value and assaulting another person are examples of misdemeanors. Violations of county and city laws sometimes may be punished by a jail sentence. Driving while intoxicated is a good example of an offense in violation of a local law. People refer to crimes that violate city and county laws as *petty crimes*. It should be noted that violations of local ordinances are frequently civil violations rather than criminal violations. In the case of felonies, misdemeanors, or petty crimes, the judge may impose a jail sentence.

PROSECUTION OF CASES

Criminal As Opposed to Civil Litigation

The American legal system handles cases in two separate ways: *civil litigation* and *criminal litigation*. The same action may result in both a civil case and a criminal case, but usually a set of facts gives rise to either one or the other.

Civil Cases

In a **civil case**, the plaintiff institutes suit against the defendant for some civil wrong allegedly committed by the defendant. Civil suits may be instituted by private citizens, businesses, or the government. The law creates the right and duties of persons. The term *civil law* refers to suits dealing with the rights and duties of persons other than those created in the criminal law. The plaintiff quite often seeks monetary damages in these cases. The goal of the civil system, in general, is to restore the injured party to the position he or she occupied prior to the defendant's wrongful actions. For example, if a person drives a vehicle at an excessive speed and as a result, an accident occurs, that individual probably has committed a civil wrong—a tort. If the injured party broke a leg, the courts would require the defendant to compensate the plaintiff for the damages caused to the plaintiff. By the payment of a certain sum of money, the plaintiff in theory is restored to his or her position before the accident.

Criminal Cases

In a **criminal case**, a prosecutor representing either the state or the federal government brings suit against the defendant for an alleged violation of the state or federal criminal laws. The prosecutor in effect represents the public at large. The law penalizes a violation of the criminal law with a fine or imprisonment. The victim is not, as a general rule, compensated for the damages done.

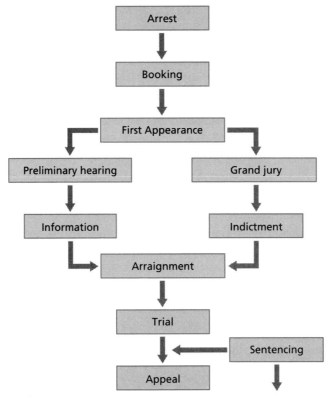

Figure 15.1   Steps in a Criminal Proceeding

**Steps in a
Criminal
Prosecution**

The following are the typical stages of a felony case after the arrest of a person (see Figure 15.1). Practices vary from state to state. The federal procedure is somewhat different from the states' procedure. This material is presented to give readers a general idea of the steps in a criminal case.

The Arraignment, or Appearance

The first appearance before a judge of a person accused of a crime is generally called the *arraignment*, or appearance. At this stage, the charges are read to the accused, and the judge inquires how that person pleads—guilty or not guilty. The judge also determines whether the person is assisted by an attorney. If not, the judge inquires whether the person has the funds to hire an attorney. A person who lacks the money to hire an attorney will be provided one. The question of a person's release on bond or on his or her own recognizance (without a bond) is also discussed. A person may also at this point waive presentment of the case to a grand jury or waive presentment of the preliminary hearing.

The prosecutor is required to take a person before a judge without an unreasonable delay following his or her arrest.

The Preliminary Hearing

In place of a grand jury (when one is not required), most states use a preliminary hearing. At this stage the prosecution must prove that some evidence exists to establish that a crime was committed and that evidence exists that indicates the accused committed the crime. A formal hearing is conducted in front of the judge. If the judge agrees that the case merits further prosecution, the judge "binds" the defendant over" for trial—that is, the judge holds the person for trial.

The Grand Jury

The function of a **grand jury** is to determine whether there exists probable cause to initiate a criminal prosecution. Grand juries are used only in *criminal* cases.

The United States Constitution in the Fifth Amendment guarantees a right to a grand jury in certain instances: "No person shall be held to answer for a capital, or otherwise infamous crime, unless on a presentment or indictment of a Grand Jury."

Murder is one of the types of crimes for which the Fifth Amendment guarantees an accused person the right to a grand jury. It should be noted that the Supreme Court has decided that states are not required to use grand juries. However, some state constitutions require that a grand jury be provided in certain types of cases.

What is the purpose of the grand jury? To prevent the unjustified criminal prosecution of a person accused of a crime. Unless the grand jury hands down an **indictment**, the prosecutor may not pursue the case further. The prosecutor representing the state or federal government must convince the members of the grand jury (typically twenty-three in number) that a crime has been committed and, if the prosecutor claims a particular person committed a crime, that some evidence exists that suggests that the accused committed the crime. If the grand jury agrees with the prosecutor, it signs the indictment, referred to as a **true bill**.

The Arraignment

At this point, the defendant appears before the trial judge and the charges are read to the accused. The judge inquires how the defendant pleads. If the defendant pleads not guilty, the judge sets the case for trial. Some persons plead guilty at this stage. Others plead not guilty, but enter a guilty plea at a later date before the date set for trial.

A common practice in the United States is for the prosecution to agree to drop or reduce the charges against the defendant if the defendant will agree to plead guilty to certain charges. This is called a *plea bargain*.

The Trial

If the case is not settled before this time, the case will be tried. Most criminal cases are settled by a plea of guilty by the accused to reduced charges. The prosecution might prove at trial, beyond a reasonable doubt, (1) that a crime was committed, and (2) that the accused committed the crime in question. If the prosecution fails to establish its case, the person will go free.

Several provisions in the United States Constitution relate to criminal trials. Article III, Section 2 requires, excepting the case of the impeachment of the president, that the trial of the crime must be held in the state in which the crime was committed. The Sixth Amendment to the Constitution adds to this the right, in criminal cases, to be tried in the district where the crime was committed. It also requires a speedy and public trial by an impartial jury. In addition, as noted earlier, the Fifth Amendment guarantees the right to a grand jury for murder and other capital crimes.

Sentencing

Following either a plea or a conviction, court personnel generally study a person's past history and talk with the convicted person to decide whether the person should go to prison or not. The findings or recommendations are made to the judge. The judge takes this information into consideration in deciding whether to send the convicted person to prison. If a judge decides on prison, the statute governing the crime typically specifies the length of time the person must be confined.

Appeal

If a person is convicted, he or she may appeal the conviction to a higher court. In general, the state may not appeal when the defendant is found to be not guilty as charged. The appeals court, if it disagrees with the decision of the trial court, may dismiss the case against the defendant. In most cases, if a prejudicial error took place at trial, the appeals court orders a new trial. This new trial does not violate the **double jeopardy clause** of the Constitution.

A person in prison who feels that his or her conviction ought to be set aside may also file a **writ of habeas corpus**. The sole function of such a suit is to obtain the release of a person from unlawful imprisonment.

CONSTITUTIONAL PROTECTION

Bill of Rights

Many of the issues litigated in a criminal case involve constitutional principles. The Constitution guarantees each person in the United States a fair trial. The framers of the Constitution feared abuse of the rights of innocent persons. For this reason, they adopted ten amendments to the United States Constitution that collectively are referred to as the **Bill of Rights**. These first ten amendments ensure that every person is treated in a fair and just manner. Several of them protect persons appearing in a court in a criminal case.

The Fourteenth Amendment

For many years, the provisions in the first ten amendments were applied only to actions of the federal government. In the 1950s, the mood on the Supreme Court shifted, and the Court began to extend some of the provisions of the Bill of Rights to state actions as well as federal. The device used to extend some of the provisions in the Bill of Rights to state action was the due process clause of the Fourteenth Amendment. The Court essentially was saying that the failure of the states to abide by certain provisions in the Bill of Rights was a denial of due process. Today, most of the provisions in the Bill of Rights apply to both federal and state proceedings.

We next turn to the three constitutional amendments most frequently dealt with in criminal cases—the Fourth, Fifth, and Sixth Amendments to the Constitution.

The Fourth Amendment

The Fourth Amendment protects the public from "unreasonable" searches and seizures. It does not prohibit all searches and seizures. It also requires that no warrants be issued "but upon probable cause, supported by oath or affirmation, and particularly describing the place to be searched, and the persons or things to be seized." A cursory examination reveals a certain degree of vagueness in the language adopted. What is an *unreasonable* search and seizure? What is *probable cause*? The Constitution leaves a number of points unresolved, and the courts must examine and interpret the material in the Constitution. Because the members of the courts change over time, *the meaning attributed to various phrases in the Constitution also changes over time.* Different factual situations give rise to different applications of these rules. For this reason, people charged with a crime quite often challenge the introduction of evidence against them. They assert that somehow the Constitution was violated when certain evidence was obtained. A matter frequently contested is the failure of the police to obtain a search warrant prior to conducting a search.

Search Warrants

A **search warrant** is a written order by a court that gives the police the right to search certain premises or property for certain items, which if found may be seized and used as evidence in a criminal trial. A warrant also may be issued by a court to the police directing them to arrest someone.

Once an officer is in possession of sufficient information to warrant a search, the Constitution requires a review of this information by a judge to determine if probable cause for a search exists. After discussing the matter, if the judge thinks probable cause for a search exists, he or she will issue a warrant. Probable cause is more than a mere suspicion that certain facts are true—there should be sufficient evidence that a reasonable person would believe the facts alleged to be true. The warrant must be precisely worded—it must particularly describe the place to be searched and the item or items to be seized.

Justice Jackson, a former member of the Supreme Court, made the following statement in *Johnson* v. *United States*, 333 U.S. 10, 13 (1948), concerning the purpose of the warrant requirement:

> The point of the Fourth Amendment, which often is not grasped by zealous officers, is not that it denies law enforcement the support of the usual inference which reasonable men draw from evidence. Its protection consists in requiring that those inferences be drawn by a neutral and detached magistrate instead of being judged by the officer engaged in the often competitive enterprise of ferret-

ing out crime. Any assumption that evidence sufficient to support a magistrate's disinterested determination to issue a search warrant will justify the officers in making a search without a warrant would reduce the amendment to a nullity and leave the people's homes secure only in the discretion of police officers.

The drafters of the Constitution struck a balance between the need to apprehend criminals and the right to privacy. If the police have a reason to search a place, they must first convince a third party (a judge) of the merits of the search. If the judge agrees, a warrant is issued.

While the Fourth Amendment refers to the right of people "to be secure in their persons, houses, papers, and effects, against unreasonable searches and seizures," this right has been interpreted by the Supreme Court to extend to businesses as well as people. The government must comply with the Fourth Amendment when dealing with businesses as well as people, as is illustrated by the following case.

G. M. Leasing Corp. v. United States
United States Supreme Court
429 U.S. 338 (1977)

The Internal Revenue Service (IRS) determined that a taxpayer owed it money. The IRS, after determining that the corporation was the alter ego of the taxpaper, made a warrantless seizure of several automobiles in the company's possession and made a warrantless forced entry into a building owned by the corporation. Two days later, the IRS again returned without a warrant and seized certain books, records, and other property. The corporation, claiming it was not the taxpayer's alter ego, brought a suit for damages based on the warrantless search conducted by the IRS. The district court ruled for the plaintiff. The court of appeals reversed. The Supreme Court ruled for the plaintiff. It held that the IRS had violated the Fourth Amendment rights of the corporation by conducting a warrantless search. The portion of the Court's opinion dealing with the search of the business premises follows.

Justice Blackmun

The seizure of books and records involved intrusion into the privacy of petitioner's offices. Significantly, the Court has said:

"[O]ne governing principle, justified by history and by current experience, has consistently been followed: except in certain carefully defined classes of cases, a

search of private property without proper consent is "unreasonable" unless it has been authorized by a valid search warrant.

The respondents do not contend that business premises are not protected by the Fourth Amendment. Such a proposition could not be defended in light of this Court's clear holdings to the contrary nor can it be claimed that corporations are without some Fourth Amendment rights.

The Court, of course, has recognized that a business, by its special nature and voluntary existence, may open itself to intrusions that would not be permissible in a purely private context.

In the present case, however, the intrusion into petitioner's privacy was not based on the nature of its business, its license, or any regulation of its activities. Rather, the intrusion is claimed to be justified on the ground that petitioner's assets were seizable to satisfy tax assessments. This involves nothing more than the normal enforcement of the tax laws, and we find no justification for treating petitioner differently in these circumstances simply because it is a corporation.

One of the primary evils intended to be eliminated by the Fourth Amendment was the massive intrusion on privacy undertaken in the collection of taxes pursuant to general warrants and writs of assistance.

The intrusion into petitioner's office is governed by the normal Fourth Amendment rule that "except in certain carefully defined classes of cases, a search of private property without proper consent is 'unreasonable' unless it has been authorized by a valid search warrant."

We therefore conclude that the warrantless entry into petitioner's office was in violation of the commands of the Fourth Amendment.

The Fifth Amendment

The Fifth Amendment creates a number of safeguards to protect persons accused of crimes from being prosecuted unfairly. In certain federal cases, it requires a grand jury to first issue an indictment before a person is tried for a crime. After an indictment by a grand jury, if one is used, the defendant is arraigned in trial court. The Fifth Amendment prevents people from being tried twice for the same offense.

Self-Incrimination

The Fifth Amendment prohibits the government from compelling a person to be a witness against himself or herself. The drafters of the Bill of Rights feared the police might abuse a suspect in order to extract a confession. At one point in history, prosecutors placed people accused of crimes on the rack. They tortured suspects until they admitted a violation of the law. Naturally, the rack proved to be an effective device in obtaining confessions. People either admitted their guilt or died.

The courts have held that a confession may be used against a defendant—but only when the confession was *knowingly*, *freely*, and *voluntarily* given. The United States Supreme Court has decided that before confessions may be used against defendants, the accused must first be informed of certain rights guaranteed to all persons under the Constitution.

Business Records

The Fifth Amendment is also relevant to the question of attempts by the government to obtain business records from companies. The argument has been made that requiring a person to turn over certain records violates the Fifth Amendment privilege that prevents a person from being compelled in a criminal case to be a witness against himself or herself.

Over the years, the Court has interpreted the Fifth Amendment in such a manner that it applies only when the accused is compelled to make some testimonial communication that is incriminating. The Court has refused to extend the Fifth Amendment privilege to the giving of blood samples, voice samples, and other nontestimonial evidence.

Some laws require people in business to maintain certain records. If the government wishes to examine these records, the law requires that the business turn these papers over to the government agents. The act of relinquishing control over such business papers does not require anyone to make a testimonial communication. For this reason, the Fifth Amendment does not permit a businessperson to refuse to surrender such documents to the government.

Because the law permits the government to seize such papers as long as the businessperson holds them in his or her possession, the government also may seize such business records even if the business transferred them to an attorney or accountant. Suppose that Jack prepared certain records in the course of operating his business. Jack used these records to prepare his income taxes. He thereafter turned the material over to his attorney. The IRS may force Jack's attorney to turn this information over to it.

The Sixth Amendment

The Sixth Amendment guarantees anyone tried in either federal or state court the following rights: (1) the right to a speedy and public trial, (2) the right to trial by an impartial jury of the state and district where the crime was committed, (3) the right to be informed of the charges against him or her, (4) the right to confront witnesses against him or her, (5) the right to an attorney, and (6) the right to subpoena witnesses in his or her favor. The right to a trial would mean very little if the government conducted the trial unfairly. These safeguards merely help ensure that a person receives a trial likely to achieve a just result.

The Right to Counsel

The Sixth Amendment specifically states: "In all criminal prosecutions, the accused shall . . . have the assistance of counsel for his defense." The Constitution guarantees everyone the right to an attorney.

The Constitution is silent on the question of providing attorneys for poor persons accused of crimes. Before 1963 many people were tried by the government without the assistance of an attorney because they lacked the funds to hire one. The state or federal government, of course, was represented by an attorney.

The Court, in *Gideon* v. *Wainright* (1963), decided that the Constitution requires the government to provide an attorney for a person who is accused of a felony but who lacks the funds to hire an attorney. Since the *Gideon* decision, the Court has expanded this doctrine to cover any situation in which a conviction on the charges brought by the government would result in a jail sentence. This means that even for less serious offenses, the state or federal government must provide an attorney to indigent persons if there is a chance a jail sentence could be imposed.

Having examined the major constitutional provisions related to criminal trials, we will now focus on a problem of great concern to business—white-collar crime.

WHITE-COLLAR CRIME

The most widely talked about form of crime often involves violence (as in murder or rape) or a loss of property (as in theft or arson). These crimes may be distinguished from some less frequently discussed crimes, which are often referred to under the general heading of ''white-collar crime.'' The term *white-collar crime* was first popularized by Edwin H. Sutherland in 1939. He defined it as ''crime committed by a person of respectability and high social status in the course of his occupation.'' Since that time, the term has taken on a much broader significance. A possible definition, although there is widespread disagreement on the meaning of this term, is *an illegal act or series of illegal acts committed by nonphysical means and by concealment or guile, to obtain money or property, or to obtain business or personal advantage.* While definitions of white–collar crime vary, most people in using this phrase are referring to criminal activity by persons who use neither force nor violence. The people who commit white–collar crimes tend to bilk the public through fraud, not strong-arm tactics.

White–collar crimes often are committed against businesses or by businesses.

Mail and Wire Fraud

Businesspeople frequently use the mail, the telephone, and other devices to communicate with the public. People who transmit messages to others may be opening themselves up for prosecution under the federal statutes relating to mail and wire fraud.

With respect to mail fraud, merely using the mail as an incident to an essential part of a fraudulent scheme is sufficient to make the person subject to possible prosecution under the mail fraud act. For example, a real estate promoter might try to induce people to purchase worthless land from her by mailing letters to prospective buyers concerning the land she is offering for sale. Sending the letter may make the sender subject to prosecution under the mail fraud act. Alternatively, using a telephone, telegraph, television, radio, or other device to transmit the same message may result in the sender being subject to prosecution under the federal wire fraud act.

The mail and wire fraud statutes outlaw the same type of behavior—that is, using the mails (or wire) for the purpose of executing a scheme or artifice to defraud the public in order to obtain money or property. The acts do not define the term *defraud*. However, the courts have given this term a very broad interpretation. A ''scheme or artifice'' to defraud refers to using some plan or devising some trick to perpetrate a fraud upon another.

In order to prosecute a person, the government must establish that the scheme or artifice was reasonably calculated to deceive persons of ordinary prudence and intelligence in order to bring about some harm or to obtain some undeserved advantage. In other words, the defendant must have intended to defraud an average person.

Suppose Mort plans to try to encourage people to invest in a business he is organizing. Mort intends to abscond with the funds once he tricks investors out of their money. Use of the mail or wire by the promoter to further his fraudulent scheme will make it possible to prosecute him under these acts.

These statutes can be used in a wide variety of situations. Each violation is subject to a fine of not more than one thousand dollars and/or imprisonment of not more than five years. Needless to say, because of the broad scope of these acts, a businessperson should be exceedingly careful when using the mail or wire transmission devices. It should also be noted that these acts are quite often used with other federal statutes. For example, a person might be charged by federal prosecutors with both securities fraud and mail fraud.

The following case illustrates the point that, in order to establish a case of mail fraud, the mailings in question need not be an essential element of a scheme to defraud, but are sufficient so long as they are incident to an essential part of the scheme. Thus, it is quite easy to establish a case of mail fraud, even when the letters themselves do not have fraudulent statements in them.

Schmuck v. United States
United States Supreme Court
109 S. Ct. 1443 (1989)

Wayne Schmuck sold used cars after he rolled back their odometer readings. He turned the odometers back on about one hundred and fifty automobiles. He then sold these vehicles to retail dealers at inflated prices. Schmuck contended that the government could not convict him of mail fraud because he never mailed anything to anyone. The items mailed in this case were title application forms. However, the retail dealers, not Schmuck, mailed these to the Wisconsin Department of Transportation of behalf of their customers. The government contended that the mailing of the title applications by the dealers could serve as the basis for a mail fraud conviction. The United States Supreme Court agreed.

Justice Blackmun

"The federal mail fraud statute does not purport to reach all frauds, but only those limited instances in which the use of the mails is a part of the execution of the fraud, leaving all other cases to be dealt with by appropriate state law." *Kann* v. *United States*. To be part of the execution of the fraud, however, the use of the mails need not be an essential element of the scheme. It is sufficient for the mailing to be incident to an essential part of the scheme, or a step in the plot.

Schmuck argues that mail fraud can be predicated only on a mailing that affirmatively assists the perpetrator in carrying out his fraudulent scheme. The mailing element of the offense, he contends, cannot be satisfied by a mailing, such as those at issue here, that is routine and innocent in and of itself, and that, far from furthering the execution of the fraud, occurs after the fraud has come to fruition, is merely tangentially related to the fraud, and is counterproductive in that it creates a "paper trail'' from which the fraud may be discovered. We disagree both with this characterization of the mailings in the present case and with this description of the applicable law.

Schmuck's was not a ''one–shot'' operation in which he sold a single car to an isolated dealer. His was an ongoing fraudulent venture. A rational jury could have concluded that the success of Schmuck's venture depended upon his continued harmonious relations with and good reputation among retail dealers, which in turn required the smooth flow of cars from the dealers to their Wisconsin customers.

Under these circumstances, we believe that a rational jury could have found that the title–registration mailings were part of the execution of the fraudulent scheme, a scheme which did not reach fruition until the retail dealers resold the cars and effected transfers of title. Schmuck's scheme would have come to an abrupt halt if the dealers either had lost faith in Schmuck or had not been able to resell the cars obtained from him. These resales and Schmuck's relationships with the retail dealers naturally depended on the successful passage of title among the various parties. Thus, although the registration-form mailings may not have contributed directly to the duping of either the retail dealers or the customers, they were necessary to the passage of title, which in turn

was essential to the perpetuation of Schmuck's scheme. As noted earlier, a mailing that is incident to an essential part of the scheme, satisfies the mailing element of the mail fraud offense. The mailings here fit this description.

In *Parr* the Court specifically acknowledged that ''innocent'' mailings—ones that contain no false information—may supply the mailing element. In other cases, the Court has found the elements of mail fraud to be satisfied where the mailings have been routine.

We also reject Schmuck's contention that mailings that someday may contribute to the uncovering of a fraudulent scheme cannot supply the mailing element of the mail fraud offense. The relevant question at all times is whether the mailing is part of the execution of the scheme as conceived by the perpetrator at the time, regardless of whether the mailing later, through hindsight, may prove to have been counterproductive and return to haunt the perpetrator of the fraud. The mail fraud statute includes no guarantee that the use of the mails for the purpose of executing a fraudulent scheme will be risk free. Those who use the mails to defraud proceed at their peril.

For these reasons, we agree with the Court of Appeals that the mailings in this case satisfy the mailing element of the mail fraud offenses.

Obviously, mail fraud may be very easily established. Businesspeople need to be careful with respect to every mailing or wire transmission to avoid making statements that could be used against them at a later date.

The mail and wire fraud acts are especially important because violations of these acts can give rise to liability under the Racketeer Influenced Corrupt Organizations Act, which is discussed in the next section.

Racketeer Influenced Corrupt Organizations Act (RICO)

When persons violate the law by engaging in illegal activities, their actions sometimes generate great sums of money. Suppose a group of college students decides to deal in cocaine. Even if they sell the drugs to a limited number of people, the drug dealers very likely will take in more money than the cocaine cost them. Just as in legitimate businesses, the object in many criminal enterprises is to make a profit. The people from whom the college students purchase the cocaine hope to make a profit, as do other individuals in the chain of distribution.

Criminal behavior can generate immense sums of money for everybody concerned. The college students may cease dealing in drugs after graduating from school, but many dealers belong to a more complex organization that operates for years. Such enterprises often resemble the organizational structure of a corporation. When a member dies or retires, another person moves up in the enterprise to take his or her place.

The traditional approach to dealing with crime has emphasized the detection of crime and imprisonment of those responsible for the crimes in question. The police often find it difficult to establish any evidence against mobsters high up in such organizations. Even when prosecutors succeed in obtaining convictions, crime never halts for a moment. That is because a criminal enterprise, much like a corporation, fills the vacant slot with another person. Just like a legitimate corporation, a criminal enterprise has a life of its own.

In the course of engaging in criminal conduct, such enterprises generate considerable sums—quite often, in cash. The money obtained through an activity such as drug peddling then needs to be ''cleaned'' so that the source of such money will be hidden. One device frequently used to cleanse money is to acquire control of a seemingly legitimate business—such as a bank, restaurant, motel, or auto dealership. Alternatively, a legitimate business may be operated in a perfectly legal manner and not used to cleanse money, but may have been acquired with funds generated by criminal activities. Thus, sooner or later, some or all of the illicit profits produced by an unlawful venture winds up in ''legitimate'' businesses. Competitors of these businesses, who acquired their companies by investing money they accumulated through lawful means, find themselves in competition with criminals.

To effectively deter crime, Congress deemed it necessary to seize the funds generated by enterprises that break the law. Without such a law, criminal enterprises would continue to flourish even after one or more of their members had been placed behind bars. Congress wished to halt the infiltration of legitimate businesses by organized crime.

To accomplish this goal, Congress passed the Racketeer Influenced Corrupt Organizations Act (RICO), which was enacted as part of the Organized Crime Control Act of 1970. This act is designed to economically cripple organized crime by attacking its economic base. Congress hoped that if the underworld lost the money it generated through its illicit activities, eventually its members would find it unprofitable to continue to break the law.

RICO makes it unlawful to conduct or acquire an interest in an ''enterprise'' through a ''pattern of racketeering activity'' or through the collection of an ''unlawful debt.''

Collecting an illegal gambling debt is an example of a violation of the latter provision. It is largely addressed to loan sharking. Most RICO defendants, however, are alleged to be engaged in a ''pattern of racketeering.''

Suppose that the college students mentioned earlier eventually acquire a substantial sum of money as a result of selling cocaine. They then invest their profits by purchasing a college pizza parlor. The students violated RICO because the income in this instance was produced by a pattern of racketeering activity.

RICO prohibits using money generated by a pattern of racketeering activity (1) to gain or maintain control over an enterprise, (2) to invest in an enterprise, or (3) to participate in the conduct or the affairs of an enterprise. The term *enterprise* includes all legal entities and any union or group of individuals associated in fact even though they are not a legal entity.

In *United States* v. *Turkette*, 452 U.S. 576 (1981), the United States Supreme Court ruled that RICO applies to the activities of illegitimate enterprises. In that case, the enterprise in question dealt with the trafficking of narcotics. The Supreme Court decided that a group of persons dealing in drugs was an ''enterprise'' because of the use of the language in the statute that defines an enterprise as ''a group of persons associated together for a common purpose of engaging in a course of conduct.'' The government established an enterprise at trial by introducing evidence that the defendants participated in an ongoing organization, formal or informal, and by introducing evidence that the various associates functioned as a continuing unit. Thus, a wholly criminal organization can be a RICO enterprise. In addition to establishing that the defendants are engaged in an enterprise, the government must prove that they conducted or acquired this enterprise through a ''pattern of racketeering activity.''

A ''pattern of racketeering activity'' is defined in the act as ''at least two acts of racketeering activity . . . committed within ten years of each other. . . .'' There are four basic types of racketeering activities. First, certain activities that are felonies under state law, (for example, arson) are categorized as racketeering under RICO. Second, acts indictable under Title 18 of the United States Code, such as mail fraud, are racketeering activities. Third, violations of Title 29 of the United States Code, which prohibits such activities as loans to labor organizations, also constitute racketeering. Finally, bankruptcy fraud and fraud in the sale of securities and drug-related offenses also are regarded as racketeering activities.

Because the act defines drug-related offenses as racketeering activities, if the college students mentioned earlier engaged in two sales of cocaine within a ten-year period, a court could find they had been engaged in a ''pattern of racketeering activity'' for purposes of establishing a violation of the RICO Act. RICO is very important to individuals engaged in legitimate businesses as well as to persons involved in a criminal organization.

RICO is a significant statute in the field of white-collar crime because of the types of offenses that the statute defines as racketeering activities (predicate acts). Within a ten-year period, if a person engages in two acts such as mail (or wire) fraud, securities fraud, arson, bribery, bankruptcy fraud, embezzlement from pension funds, or a host of other criminal activities, he or she has engaged in a ''pattern of racketeering activity'' insofar as RICO is concerned.

Obviously, since many transactions in business utilize the mail or wire, if these transactions are subsequently established to be fraudulent, they may give rise to a RICO suit. This creates an enormous likelihood that any white-collar crime perpetrated by a businessperson may subsequently be attacked as a violation of the RICO Act.

Congress included significant penalties in RICO. The act authorizes the government to bring actions to enjoin RICO violations. Each violation may be punished by a maximum fine of twenty-five thousand dollars and/or a maximum sentence of twenty years. Furthermore, RICO permits a judge to order a forfeiture of any interest in property that was acquired or maintained in violation of the act, or a forfeiture of any interest in property that gives the defendant influence over

Banks and Forfeiture

Suppose a bank lends money to a person to purchase a home. The individual makes a substantial down payment—for example, twenty-five percent of the total purchase price. The bank summarily approves the loan without carefully examining the source of the funds. It later develops that the purchaser acquired the funds to buy the home through the sale of illegal drugs. After the arrest of the homeowner, the local police then seize the home because the homeowner purchased it with drug money. Federal law requires the lender, before it can recover the money it loaned on the home, to establish that it had no actual knowledge of drug activities. If the lender made the loan knowing of the source of the down payment, the law prevents it from recovering its money. Lenders need to very carefully establish the source of a person's money before making loans. If a lender acts improperly, the government may seize the property and refuse to permit the lender to recover its funds used to purchase the property.

an enterprise that the defendant has "established, operated, controlled, conducted or participated in the conduct of" in violation of the act.

Forfeiture of Property Under Federal and State Laws

The purpose of the forfeiture penalty is to take the property in question from the racketeer, thus depriving him or her of the ability to continue to control the property.

Russello v. *U.S.* (1983) decided by the Supreme Court dealt with the forfeiture provision. Russello had been convicted of violating the RICO Act because of his involvement in an arson ring. He received compensation from an insurance company for a fire he caused to a building he owned. A person convicted under the RICO Act shall forfeit to the United States "any interest he has acquired or maintained in violation" of the act. Russello argued that this language permitted the United States to seize only interests in an enterprise. The Supreme Court rejected his interpretation of this provision. It ruled that the insurance proceeds he received as a result of a violation of the RICO Act were subject to forfeiture to the U.S. government.

The seizure of private property has become a multibillion-dollar operation for federal and state law-enforcement personnel. A number of acts, in addition to the RICO Act, provide for the forfeiture of private property to the government.

In order to strengthen law enforcement throughout the United States, many states passed their own versions of the federal Racketeer Influenced and Corrupt Organizations Act. The states modeled their acts after the federal law. As with RICO, the state statutes include criminal as well as civil provisions. Business managers need to realize that these state laws also contain forfeiture provisions. These forfeiture provisions permit the pretrial seizure of property. This is true even if no one has been convicted of a crime, or even if criminal charges have not

Forfeiture

In *Alexander* v. *U.S.*, 1993, a unanimous decision of the United States Supreme Court held that a criminal forfeiture under RICO could be challenged as an excessive fine under the Eighth Amendment's ban on excessive fines. In *Austin* v. *U.S.*, 1993, a unanimous court also ruled that the Eighth Amendment's ban on excessive fines applies to civil forfeiture of property. These two cases signal a very clear desire of the Supreme Court to eliminate the abusive use of forfeiture powers by the government.

been filed against a person, because the laws treat the forfeiture of property as a civil, as opposed to a criminal, offense.

Under the 1984 Comprehensive Crime Control Act, the federal government granted the police sweeping power to seize private property held by persons engaged in criminal activities. Many states also adopted similar legislation. These laws permit the police to seize property used in an illegal transaction (for example, a car used to transport heroin) and property purchased as a result of engaging in illegal activities. For example, if John sells narcotics to Lance for one hundred thousand dollars, and then invests this money in a restaurant, the government may seize the restaurant.

Forfeiture of Private Property

The government possessed the right to seize property long before the drafting of the Declaration of Independence or the United States Constitution. Many of the important legal principles that protect us today were derived from the experience of the colonists while living under the oppressive rule of the British government.

Colonial courts permitted the British to seize ships and their cargoes for violation of the customs and revenue laws. High on the colonists' list of abuses of power by the British government were the general warrants known as writs of assistance. These court orders gave customs officials blanket authority to search in any place for goods imported in violation of the British tax laws. These laws enabled low level governmental employees to interfere with the liberty of every person. Abuse of power by the British lead to rebellion by the colonists in 1761 at the Boston Tea Party and eventually to revolution and war.

As the Spanish philosopher George Santayana once observed, those who forget history are doomed to relive it. The colonists learned that unchecked power can and will be abused. In the hundreds of years since the Revolutionary War apparently Congress and the state legislatures in their quest for more effective law enforcement overlooked the fact that even a well-intentioned law sometimes leads to unfortunate results.

While drugs have been with us always, we did not always prohibit their sale. In the late 1800s, the general public came to recognize the danger posed by certain types of widely available medicines such as cocaine. Congress passed the Food and Drug Administration Act to try to curtail the use of medicines perceived to be harmful to the general public. Even so, drug use continued—albeit in a more clandestine manner than before the passage of this act. By the 1960s, the hippie movement brought the issue of drug abuse to the forefront of the American conscience. The middle class began to see their own sons and daughters abusing drugs, and this heightened the awareness of the general public with respect to the illegal drug traffic in America. The public began to demand more antidrug laws and more vigorous enforcement of the existing drug laws. Congress responded with such laws as the Comprehensive Drug Abuse Prevention and Control Act of 1970. We also began to see a steady increase in the amount of law enforcement time and effort devoted to fighting illegal drug sales. Lots of drug traders started going to prison.

But law enforcement officials slowly began to expand their efforts beyond the narrow confines of putting drug traders in jail. They started to vigorously enforce the laws that allowed them to seize private property as well. By the late 1980s, numerous property owners began to complain of abuses of power by the government in its zealous quest to eradicate crime in America. They found themselves thrust into the battle between the police and drug sellers. These property owners alleged they had lost their property even though they had never committed any crime. The government had seized their property even though they had never been convicted of, or even charged with, a criminal offense.

The burden fell on them to challenge the government's action in court following the seizure of their property.

One such case involved the purchase of a $240,000 home by a woman who lived with Joseph Brenna. Although there was probable cause to believe that Joseph Brenna generated the $240,000 in question by engaging in illegal drug trafficking, the woman swore that she had no knowledge of the origins of the money. These two persons separated in 1987. In 1989, the government seized the house in question. The Comprehensive Drug Abuse Prevention and Control Act of 1970 permitted the forfeiture of any property acquired with money traceable to the unlawful sale of a controlled substance. (Prior to the *Warden* v. *Hayden* case in 1967, although the government could seize property, it was only permitted to seize property that a private citizen was not permitted to possess. For example, if a person possessed heroin, the government could seize the heroin. It was not at that time possible for the government to seize the proceeds of illegal drug transactions.)

In her defense, the homeowner argued the innocent owner defense— that she acquired the property without knowing that the funds provided to her by Joseph Brenna were derived from the sale of illegal drugs. The Comprehensive Drug Abuse Prevention Act specifically prohibits the seizure of proceeds owned by a person who is unaware of the criminal source of the money used to purchase the property. The government took the position that the money given by Joseph Brenna to her belonged to the government because it was traceable to illegal drug transactions. Anything purchased with this money became the property of the government. As the United States Supreme Court noted, the flaw in this argument is that it could result in the forfeiture of property innocently acquired by persons who had been paid with illegal proceeds for providing goods or services to drug traffickers. The United States Supreme Court ruled that the property could not be seized if, in fact, she acquired the property without knowing the funds in question resulted from the sale of illegal drugs. *United States* v. *A Parcel of Land*, 1993 U. S. Lexis 1782 (1993).

This case perhaps suggests a shift in the orientation of the Supreme Court with respect to the seizure of private property. The Court seems more willing to entertain arguments that favor the private property owner even if such decisions might hamper law enforcement. The pendulum thus may be beginning to swing away from the position that vigorous law enforcement is more important than any other rights recognized by society, to a rec-

ognition that the government ought not to infringe on private property rights. This position may make law enforcement more difficult. It may also reduce the likelihood that the government may seize private property from totally innocent persons.

To a very great extent, criminal law in America involves a political struggle between those who believe that effective law enforcement is paramount to all other possible rights in society—such as private property rights and individual rights—and those who believe that other rights in America deserve equal recognition along with the need to effectively enforce our criminal laws. The pendulum in the 1970's and 1980's swung very far in the direction of law enforcement and it now appears to be swinging away from this political position.

The Right to Hire a Private Attorney

In recent years, persons accused of violating the RICO Act, as well as some other federal laws, have found they could not use their assets to defend themselves. This happens when the government freezes the assets of a person accused of violating a federal law that provides for a pretrial seizure of the defendant's assets. If the court convicts the defendants, it may order a forfeiture of the assets in question. Congress gave the courts this power to keep a person accused of a crime from disposing of his or her assets.

The question then arises: If the government seizes all of a defendant's assets, how can such a person afford to hire an attorney to defend himself or herself? Attorneys prefer to receive their fee prior to trial. A person without funds must then use the services of an attorney provided by the government. In numerous cases, defendants have argued that a pretrial freeze on their assets deprives them of their constitutional right to an attorney. The Supreme Court resolved this issue in the following case.

Caplin & Drysdale v. United States
United States Supreme Court
109 S.Ct. 2646 (1989)

The government charged Christopher Reckmeyer with running a drug importation and distribution scheme—an alleged continuing criminal enterprise. Reckmeyer retained Caplin & Drysdale to defend him. The law permitted the court to order a forfeiture of any of Reckmeyer's assets derived from drug law violations. The trial court issued a restraining order forbidding the transfer of all of his assets that were potentially forfeitable. Thereafter, Reckmeyer paid twenty-five thousand dollars to Caplin & Drysdale for pretrial services. The firm placed this money in a special account. Reckmeyer requested the court to permit him to use some of his restrained assets to pay the law firm. Prior to a resolution of this question, Reckmeyer on his own motion pled guilty to a drug-related offense and agreed to forfeit the assets in question.

Caplin & Drysdale then filed an action on behalf of the firm that asserted an interest of one hundred and seventy thousand dollars in Reckmeyer's forfeited assets. The firm argued that the forfeiture law violated the Constitution because it failed to provide an exemption that would permit Reckmeyer to use his assets to hire an attorney. The Court of Appeals for the Fourth Circuit found this statutory scheme constitutional. The United States Supreme Court affirmed the judgment of the Fourth Circuit.

Justice White

We address petitioner's constitutional challenges to the forfeiture law. Petitioner contends that the statute infringes on criminal defendants' Sixth Amendment right to counsel of choice.

Petitioner's first claim is that the forfeiture law makes impossible, or at least impermissibly burdens, a defendant's right "to select and be represented by one's preferred attorney." *Wheat v. United States.* Petitioner does not, nor could it defensibly do so, assert that impecunious defendants have a Sixth Amendment right to choose their counsel. The amendment guarantees defendants in criminal cases the right to adequate representation, but those who do not have the means to hire their own lawyers have no cognizable complaint so long as they are adequately represented by attorneys appointed by the courts. "[A] defendant may not insist on representation by an attorney he cannot afford." *Wheat.*

Petitioner urges that a violation of the Sixth Amendment arises here because of the forfeiture, at the instance of the Government, of assets that defendants intend to use to pay their attorneys.

Even in this sense, of course, the burden the forfeiture law imposes on a criminal defendant is limited. The forfeiture statute does not prevent a defendant who has nonforfeitable assets from retaining any attorney of his choosing.

Nonetheless, there will be cases where a defendant will be unable to retain the attorney of his choice, when that defendant would have been able to hire that lawyer if he had access to forfeitable assets, and if there was no risk that fees paid by the defendant to his counsel would later be recouped under § 853(c). It is in these cases, petitioner argues, that the Sixth Amendment puts limits on the forfeiture statute.

This submission is untenable. Whatever the full extent of the Sixth Amendment's protection of one's right to retain counsel of his choosing, that protection does not go beyond "the individual's right to spend his own money to obtain the advice and assistance of . . . counsel." *Walters v. National Assn. of Radiation Survivors*. A defendant has no Sixth Amendment right to spend another person's money for services rendered by an attorney, even if those funds are the only way that that defendant will be able to retain the attorney of his choice. A robbery suspect, for example, has no Sixth Amendment right to use funds he has stolen from a bank to retain an attorney to defend him if he is apprehended. The money, though in his possession, is not rightfully his; the government does not violate the Sixth Amendment if it seizes the robbery proceeds, and refuses to permit the defendant to use them to pay for his defense.

Petitioner seeks to distinguish such cases for Sixth Amendment purposes by arguing that the bank's claim to robbery proceeds rests on "pre-existing property rights," while the Government's claim to forfeitable assets rests on a "penal statute" which embodies the "fictive property-law concept of . . . relation-back" and is merely "a mechanism for preventing fraudulent conveyances of the defendant's assets, not . . . a device for determining true title to property." Brief for Petitioner 40-41. In light of this, petitioner contends, the burden placed on defendant's Sixth Amendment rights by the statute outweighs the Government's interest in forfeiture.

The premises of petitioner's constitutional analysis are unsound. A major purpose motivating congressional adoption and continued refinement of the RICO forfeiture provision has been the desire to lessen the economic power of organized crime and drug enterprises. This includes the use of such economic power to retain private counsel. When a defendant claims that he has suffered some substantial impairment of his Sixth Amendment rights by virtue of the seizure or forfeiture of assets in his possession, such a complaint is no more than the reflection of "the harsh reality that the quality of a criminal defendant's representation frequently may turn on his ability to retain the best counsel money can buy." *Morris v. Slappy*.

We therefore reject petitioner's claim of Sixth Amendment right of criminal defendants to use assets that are the government's—assets adjudged forfeitable, as Reckmeyer's were—to pay attorney's fees, merely because those assets are in their possession. See also *Monsanto*, which rejects a similar claim with respect to pretrial orders and assets not yet judged forfeitable.

Justice Blackmun, with whom Justice Brennan, Justice Marshall, and Justice Stevens join (dissenting)

Those jurists who have held forth against the result the majority reaches in these cases have been guided by one core insight: that it is unseemly and unjust for Government to beggar those it prosecutes in order to disable their defense at trial. The majority trivializes "the burden the forfeiture law imposes on a criminal defendant." *Caplin & Drysdale v. United States*. Instead, it should heed the warnings of our district court judges, whose day-to-day exposure to the criminal-trial process enables them to understand, perhaps far better than we, the devastating consequences of attorney's fee forfeiture for the integrity of our adversarial system of justice.

The right to retain private counsel serves to foster the trust between attorney and client that is necessary for the attorney to be truly effective advocate. Not only are decisions crucial to the defendant's liberty placed in counsel's hands, but the defendant's perception of the fairness of the process, and his willingness to acquiesce in its results, depend upon his confidence in his counsel's dedication, loyalty, and ability. When the Government insists upon the right to choose the defendant's counsel for him, that relationship of trust is undermined: counsel is too readily perceived as the Government's agent rather than his own.

The right to retain private counsel also serves to assure some modicum of equality between the Government and those it chooses to prosecute. The Government can be expected to "spend vast sums of money . . . to try defendants accused of crime," *Gideon v. Wainwright*, and of course will devote greater resources to complex cases in which the punitive stakes are high. Precisely for this reason, there are few defendants charged with crime, few indeed, who fail to hire the best lawyers they can get to prepare and present their defenses. But when the Government provides for appointed counsel, there is no guarantee that levels of compensation and staffing will be even average. Where cases are complex, trials long, and stakes high, that problem is exacerbated.

In sum, our chosen system of criminal justice is built

upon a truly equal and adversarial presentation of the case, and upon the trust that can exist only when counsel is independent of the Government. Without the right, reasonably exercised, to counsel of choice, the effectiveness of that system is imperilled.

Civil RICO

RICO creates a very significant right for *private parties*—the right to sue for any damages a person sustains as a result of a violation of RICO. These damages, if established, will be *trebled* by the court. Attorney fees also may be recovered.

Civil RICO claims have been asserted in a wide variety of cases, such as securities, commodities, and contract disputes.

A person who engages in mail fraud can be sued under RICO. Because the federal mail fraud statute is so broad, it is relatively easy for private litigants to establish a case under the RICO Act. Each mailing is generally treated as a separate violation of the mail fraud act. Thus, two such mailings can be treated as a "pattern of racketeering activity." Every transaction involving the wrongful use of the mails, telephone, or interstate wire facilities creates the potential for a civil lawsuit under RICO.

Although Congress was concerned with the takeover of legitimate businesses by organized crime when it passed RICO, the primary focus of the act is now civil lawsuits. As the categories of racketeering activities are so broad, it is relatively easy for a plaintiff to state a case. Therefore, it is highly likely that RICO suits will become even more common as time passes. Businesspeople should be aware of the possibility that any unlawful actions they engage in could result in a civil suit under RICO.

In *Sedima, S.P.R.I.* v. *Imrex Co., Inc.*, the United States Supreme Court ruled that a civil RICO suit may proceed even if the defendant has not been convicted of a crime. It also ruled that it is not necessary to establish an injury other than the defendant's commission of the predicate acts. All that is necessary to establish a case under RICO is (1) conduct (2) of an enterprise (3) through a pattern (4) of racketeering activity.

In *Holmes* v. *Securities Investor Protection Corporation*, the United States Supreme Court added an additional element to civil RICO suits: The plaintiff must prove he or she was directly harmed by the alleged wrongdoing.

Scope of Civil RICO

In the 1980s, once attorneys began to recognize that RICO could be used in civil suits, a tremendous upsurge in the number of civil RICO suits began to swamp the courts. Many civil suits routinely included a RICO claim. Some of these suits resulted in enormous judgments against people and businesses who had only the most distant relationship to the operation of the alleged criminal enterprise.

The following case represents an attempt by the United States Supreme Court to curtail the use of RICO in suits against persons who were not actively engaged in managing or operating a business. This case limits abusive cases by limiting the potential defendants to those actually running the enterprise. Even so, it should be noted that an outsider associated with the operation and management of an enterprise still can be subject to damages under civil RICO.

Reves v. Ernst & Young
United States Supreme Court
1993 U.S. Lexis 1940 (1993)

Jack White, the general manager of the Farmer's Cooperative of Arkansas and Oklahoma, Inc. (the Co-Op) began taking loans from the Co-Op to finance the construction of a gasohol plant by his company, White Flame Fuels, Inc. In 1980, White proposed that the Co-Op purchase White Flame. Thereafter, White and the Co-Op entered into a consent decree relieving White of his debts and providing that the Co-Op had owned White Flame since February 15, 1980.

The Co-Op retained Joe Drozal of Russell Brown to perform its 1981 financial audit. In 1982, Russell Brown was merged with Arthur Young and Company, which later became Ernst & Young. In the course of the audit, Drozal concluded that White Flame's 1981 fixed-asset value was approximately $4.5 million. Drozal had to determine how that value should be treated for accounting purposes. Suffice it to say that he chose to value it at $4.5 million, rather than a lower figure which would have indicated the Co-Op was insolvent.

On April 22, 1982, Arthur Young presented its 1981 audit report to the Co-Op's board. In that audit's note 9, Arthur Young expressed doubt whether the investment in White Flame could ever be recovered. Arthur Young did not tell the board of its conclusion that the Co-Op had always owned White Flame or that without that conclusion the Co-Op was insolvent. At the Co-Op's 1982 annual meeting, Arthur Young distributed to the Co-Op's members condensed financial statements. These included White Flame's $4.5 million asset value among its total assets but omitted the information contained in the audit's Note 9.

In February 1984, the Co-Op filed for bankruptcy. The trustee in bankruptcy filed suit against 40 individuals and entities including Arthur Young on behalf of the Co-Op and certain noteholders. The Court of Appeals applied a "manage or operate" test in arriving at its conclusion that Arthur Young was not liable under RICO. The United States Supreme Court affirmed the decision of the Court of Appeals on behalf of Arthur Young.

Blackmun, Justice

In determining the scope of a statute, we look first to its language. If the statutory language is unambiguous, in the absence of a clearly expressed legislative intent to the contrary, that language must ordinarily be regarded as conclusive. Section 1962(c) makes it unlawful "for any person employed by or associated with any enter-

prise . . . to conduct or participate, directly or indirectly, in the conduct of such enterprise's affairs through a pattern of racketeering activity . . . ."

The narrow question in this case is the meaning of the phrase "to conduct or participate, directly or indirectly, in the conduct of such enterprise's affairs." As a verb, "conduct" means to lead, run, manage, or direct. Congress could easily have written "participate, directly or indirectly, in an enterprise's affairs," but it chose to repeat the word "conduct." We conclude therefore that "conduct" requires an element of direction.

The more difficult question is what to make of the word "participate." Petitioners argue that Congress used "participate" as a synonym for "aid and abet." Within the meaning of 1962(c) "participate" appears to have a narrower meaning. It seems that Congress chose a middle ground, consistent with a common understanding of the word "participate"—to take part in.

Once we understand the word "conduct" to require some degree of direction and the word "participate" to require some part in that direction, the meaning of section 1962(c) comes into focus. In order to "participate, directly or indirectly, in the conduct of such enterprise's affairs," one must have some part in directing those affairs. The "operation or management" test expresses this requirement in a formulation that is easy to apply.

Of course, "outsiders" may be liable under section 1962(c) if they are "associated with" an enterprise and participate in the conduct of its affairs—that is, partici-

pate in the operation or management of the enterprise itself.

In sum, we hold that "to conduct or participate, directly or indirectly, in the conduct of such enterprise's affairs," one must participate in the operation or management of the enterprise itself.

In the existing case, it is undisputed that Arthur Young relied upon existing Co-Op records in preparing the 1981 and 1982 audit reports. The AICPA's professional standards state that an auditor may draft financial statements in whole or in part based on information from management's accounting system. It is also undisputed that Arthur Young's audit reports revealed to the Co-Op's board that the value of the gasohol plant had been calculated based on the Co-Op's investment in the plant. Thus, we only could conclude that Arthur Young participated in the operation or management of the Co-Op itself if Arthur Young's failure to tell the Co-Op's board that the plant should have been given its fair market value constituted such participation. We think that Arthur Young's failure in this respect is not sufficient to give rise to liability under section 1962(c).

The judgment of the Court of Appeals is affirmed.

Criminal Liability of Officers of Corporations

While it is true that businesses often are the victim of crimes, sometimes, acting through their employees, businesses commit crimes. Many major companies have been convicted of major violations of the law. Companies have been found guilty of violating the antitrust laws, giving kickbacks, and evading their tax liabilities, to name just a few of the crimes. (For a discussion of antitrust legislation, see Chapters 23 and 24.)

Some scholars attribute business crimes to excessive competitive pressure in certain industries. As managers are evaluated only in the short run and quite often only on the basis of financial returns, the temptation to violate the law sometimes proves irrestible. Another possible explanation for criminal activities is industry custom and structure. The problems associated with certain industries encourage criminal activities. For example, in the construction industry, the need to meet deadlines may contribute to bribery. The fact that crime frequently pays also contributes to criminal activity. If it is profitable to violate the law, many people will do so—hoping, of course, they will be able to escape detection.

In the following case, the United States Supreme Court found the chief executive of a corporation criminally liable even though there was no direct proof of wrongful action by the president. The issue in the *Park* case essentially deals with the issue of accountability. Park held a responsible position within the corporation, and by virtue of this position, he had authority and responsibility to deal with the problems for which he was subsequently held accountable. This case perhaps reflects a trend among courts and lawmakers toward forcing chief executive officers to assume more direct responsibility for their actions. It should be noted, however, that the case was brought pursuant to the Food, Drug, and Cosmetic Act, which creates special standards of behavior for covered businesses.

United States v. Park
United States Supreme Court
421 U.S. 658 (1974)

Acme Markets, Inc., a large national food chain, and its president were charged with violating Section 301(k) of the Federal Food, Drug, and Cosmetic Act, which prohibits the adulteration of food held for sale after shipment in interstate commerce. The government alleged that Acme had caused food shipments to be exposed to rodent contamination. Acme pleaded guilty but its president did not. Evidence was admitted that tended to show that the president was "responsible for . . . the entire operation of the company" and that he knew of the unsanitary conditions at Acme's warehouse. The president was advised by the Food and Drug Administration (FDA) of unsanitary conditions at Acme's Philadelphia warehouse in April 1970, and of similar conditions in 1971, at the Baltimore warehouse. In January 1972, after receiving an FDA letter, the president conferred with the vice-president of legal affairs, who informed him the Baltimore division vice-president was taking corrective action. The president contended he assigned the issue of sanitation to dependable subordinates. The president was convicted at the trial level. He was required to pay a fine of fifty dollars on each violation for which he was found guilty. The court of appeals reversed, arguing that the president could not be found guilty without evidence of "wrongful action" on his part. The government appealed to the Supreme Court. The Supreme Court ruled against Park.

Chief Justice Burger

The question presented by the Government's petition for certiorari in *United States v. Dotterweich*, and the focus of this Court's opinion, was whether the manager of a corporation, as well as the corporation itself, may be prosecuted under the Federal Food, Drug, and Cosmetic Act of 1938 for the introduction of misbranded and adulterated articles into interstate commerce.

In reversing the judgment of the Court of Appeals and reinstating Dotterweich's conviction, this Court looked to the purposes of the Act and noted that they "touch phases of the lives and health of people which, in

the circumstances of modern industrialism, are largely beyond self-protection." It observed that the Act is of "a now familiar type" which "dispenses with the conventional requirement for criminal conduct—awareness of some wrongdoing. In the interest of the larger good it puts the burden of acting at hazard upon a person otherwise innocent but standing in responsible relation to a public danger."

Central to the Court's conclusion that individuals other than proprietors are subject to the criminal provisions of the Act was the reality that "the only way in which a corporation can act is through the individuals who act on its behalf."

The Court concluded, settled doctrines of criminal law dictated that the offense was committed "by all who . . . have . . . a responsible share in the furtherance of the transaction which the statute outlaws."

The rule that corporate employees who have "a responsible share in the furtherance of the transaction which the statute outlaws" are subject to the criminal provisions of the Act was not formulated in a vacuum. Cases under the Federal Food and Drugs Act of 1906 reflected the view both that knowledge or intent were not required to be proved in prosecutions under its criminal provisions, and that responsible corporate agents could be subjected to the liability thereby imposed. Moreover, the principle had been recognized that a corporate agent, through whose act, default, or omission the corporation committed a crime, was himself guilty individually of that crime. The principle had been applied whether or not the crime required "consciousness of wrongdoing," and it had been applied not only to those corporate agents who themselves committed the criminal act, but also to those who by virtue of their managerial positions or other similar relation to the actor could be deemed responsible for its commission.

In the latter class of cases, the liability of managerial officers did not depend on their knowledge of, or personal participation in, the act made criminal by the statute. Rather, where the statute under which they were prosecuted dispensed with "consciousness of wrongdoing," an omission or failure to act was deemed a sufficient basis for a responsible corporate agent's liability. It was enough in such cases that, by virtue of the relationship he bore to the corporation, the agent had the power to prevent the act complained of.

Thus *Dotterweich* and the cases which have followed reveal that in providing sanctions which reach and touch the individuals who execute the corporate mission—and this is by no means necessarily confined to a single corporate agent or employee—the Act imposes not only a positive duty to seek out and remedy violations when they occur but also, and primarily, a duty to implement measures that will insure that violations will not occur. The requirements of foresight and vigilance imposed on responsible corporate agents are beyond question demanding, and perhaps onerous, but they are no more stringent than the public has a right to expect of those who voluntarily assume positions of authority in business enterprises whose services and products affect the health and well-being of the public that supports them.

The Act does not, as we observed in *Dotterweich*, make criminal liability turn on "awareness of some wrongdoing" or "conscious fraud." The duty imposed by Congress on responsible corporate agents is, we emphasize, one that requires the highest standard of foresight and vigilance, but the Act, in its criminal aspect, does not require that which is objectively impossible. The theory upon which responsible corporate agents are held criminally accountable for "causing" violations of the Act permits a claim that a defendant was "powerless" to prevent or correct the violation to "be raised defensively at a trial on the merits." If such a claim is made, the defendant has the burden of coming forward with evidence, but this does not alter the Government's ultimate burden of proving beyond a reasonable doubt the defendant's guilt, including his power, in light of the duty imposed by the Act, to prevent or correct the prohibited condition. Congress has seen fit to enforce the accountability of responsible corporate agents dealing with products which may affect the health of consumers by penal sanctions cast in rigorous terms, and the obligation of the courts is to give them effect so long as they do not violate the Constitution.

The *Park* case establishes the rule that an executive who possesses the authority and responsibility to prevent a violation of the Food, Drug, and Cosmetic Act may be held criminally liable for a failure to comply with the law. Park had the power and authority to take action to bring the corporation in compliance with the law. His failure to take measures to ensure that a violation of the law did not occur resulted in his criminal liability. The absence of personal knowledge of the wrongdoing by Park and the delegation of the task to a dependable subordinate did not prevent him from being found guilty.

Merely having the power and authority to correct a violation of the law does not, however, always result in criminal liability on the part of the officers of a company. In fact, the *Park* case is somewhat unusual. Many criminal statutes require proof that a manager, to be guilty of a crime, have a culpable state of mind—which Park argued he did not have.

SUMMARY

Society imposes prison sentences and fines on persons engaging in illegal activities or crimes. More serious crimes are called felonies, while less serious crimes generally are referred to as misdemeanors.

In the typical felony case, the government must, after informing the defendant of the crime he or she is accused of having committed, convince a judge, or a grand jury in some cases, that a crime was committed and that evidence indicates the accused committed the crime. The defendant is then bound over for trial.

The United States Constitution protects persons accused of a violation of the law. The Constitution, in the Bill of Rights, places important restraints on the manner in which the legal system may operate. The Fourth Amendment protects the public, including businesses, from unreasonable searches and seizures. A judge must generally issue a search warrant before a lawful search can be made. The Fifth Amendment prohibits the government from compelling a person to be a witness against himself or herself. Business records, while possibly harmful if released to the government, must be turned over to the prosecutor if the government requests them. The Sixth Amendment guarantees everyone a right to the assistance of a defense attorney. This is true even if a person cannot afford a lawyer.

One of the most significant statutes dealing with white–collar crime is the Racketeer Influenced Corrupt Organizations Act (RICO). This act makes it unlawful to conduct or acquire an interest in an enterprise through a pattern of racketeering activity or through the collection of an unlawful debt. Through a series of Supreme Court interpretations of RICO it became evident that a wide range of organizations could be subject to the provisions of RICO.

Among other penalties, RICO provides for the forfeiture of any interest in property that gives the defendant influence over an organization that the defendant has established or operated in violation of the act. In recent years, the Supreme Court has indicated some willingness to restrict the ability of the government to seize certain property without first having a trial to determine if a seizure of property is lawful.

It is possible for a defendant to obtain treble damages from a defendant if it can be established that the defendant violated the provisions of RICO. All that is necessary to establish a case for treble damages is proof of conduct of an enterprise through a pattern of racketeering activity. The plaintiff must also establish that he or she was directly harmed by the alleged wrongdoing. In the *Reeves* case the Supreme Court adopted the operation or management test which limits potential defendants under civil RICO to those persons who actually run an enterprise.

It should be noted that certain laws dispense with the requirement that a manager of a business have a culpable state of mind in order to be found in violation of a criminal statute.

REVIEW QUESTIONS

1. Define the following terms:
   a. Bill of Rights
   b. Civil case
   c. Criminal case
   d. Felony
   e. Grand jury
   f. Misdemeanor
   g. Search warrant

2. What is the significant point of the *Park* case?

3. What process do the police follow before conducting a search of a business or home?

4. Why does the Supreme Court require the government to provide a person accused of a crime an attorney if he or she cannot afford one?

5. Discuss the stages in the criminal prosecution of a felony.

6. If the police violate the Fifth Amendment in obtaining a confession, why do the courts refuse to admit such a confession?

7. Couch turned her financial records over to her accountant for the purpose of preparing her income tax records. The Internal Revenue Service now wishes to obtain those records. Couch asserts that requiring these records to be turned over to the IRS would violate her Fifth Amendment privilege against compulsory self-incrimination. Must Couch's accountant turn the records over to the IRS?

8. The Food and Drug Administration inspected the warehouse of Chaney Brothers Food Corporation. Its secretary-treasurer, Starr, was charged with violating the Food, Drug, and Cosmetic Act by allowing contamination of food stored in the warehouse. Starr was convicted at trial. The warehouse in question had been infected by mice. Mr. Starr, following an investigation by the FDA, knew of the condition and took some corrective measures, but on the next inspection, the FDA again found mice. May Starr lawfully be convicted of a crime?

9. Scalon Corporation sold products to Greenmass Corporation. In the course of the transactions, Scalon sent a number of letters to Greenmass with fraudulent representations. Greenmass brought a civil suit against Scalon for treble damages caused by Scalon's acts. Scalon made two arguments: Suit may not be commenced against him because he had never been convicted of mail fraud, and suit may not be brought against him under the RICO Act because he is a respectable businessman. Is Scalon right?

10. Sedima entered into a joint venture with Imrex. A dispute arose between the parties, and Sedima charged that Imrex and its officers had engaged in the predicate acts of mail and wire fraud. First, Imrex argued that Sedima could not bring a civil suit against it under RICO unless Imrex had first been convicted of a crime. Second, Imrex argued that Sedima must be able to establish an injury separate and apart from any injury caused by Imrex's commission of the predicate acts. Is Imrex correct in arguing that Sedima must establish these two points before it can bring a civil suit under RICO?

11. Anne Meyer operated a retail motorcycle store. In order to increase her income, she

started buying used motorcycles. She thereafter began to roll the odometers back on the used cycles, which she sold at inflated prices to her customers. The customers mailed title applications for their cycles to the state. The government attempted to prosecute Anne for mail fraud. She responded that, as she had never mailed anything to anyone, she could not be prosecuted for mail fraud. Is she correct?

12. Can the government seize all the assets of a person that are potentially forfeitable prior to trial, even if this means that the person will not have the funds to hire a private attorney to defend himself or herself?

Part 6

Regulation of Business Activity: Customers and Employees

CHAPTER 16

Products Liability

- Products Liability and History
- Negligence
- Warranty
- Misrepresentation
- Strict Liability

In the torts chapter, we discussed the theories of recovery injured parties have relied upon when they have sustained an injury as a result of the actions of another party. This chapter is devoted to the very serious problem of products that cause injuries to people. Very often, even when the seller exercises the very highest level of care with respect to its products, those products sometimes injure people.

As a society we have several options. One is to take no action whatsoever when products injure people. A second possibility is to allow people who have been injured to sue the person or company responsible for their injuries. A third approach is for the government to pass laws that are designed to make certain that unsafe products are kept off the market. In this chapter, we discuss the second approach to the problem.

As you will note, the law in this area actually comes in part from tort law and in part from contract law. The law evolved over a period of years and slowly permitted more and more people to recover from an ever larger pool of defendants. This tendency to increase the pool of defendants liable to injured parties seems to still be taking place, causing grave concerns to people in business.

PRODUCTS LIABILITY AND HISTORY

Historically, the law permitted only the person who purchased a product to sue, and it permitted that person to sue only his or her immediate seller. Before the Industrial Revolution, this policy probably created very few problems, because of the small number of rather simple products purchased by the average person. The farmer who purchased a plow to pull behind his ox probably bought it directly from a village blacksmith. Any disputes could be resolved directly between the blacksmith and the farmer.

Because people purchased just a few simple products in the course of their lives, the courts tended to believe that purchasers could easily determine for themselves the quality of products. For centuries, the courts followed the doctrine of caveat emptor. In other words, the courts placed the risk of loss for dangerous products on the injured party. Such courts assumed that the injury occurred because of the failure of the injured party to carefully examine a product before purchasing and using it. Such decisions mirrored the prevailing American desire for everyone to look out for himself or herself—that is, to be self-reliant. The public and the courts believed that the injured parties, not society, should take care of themselves.

The doctrine of caveat emptor furthered the development of American industry by making the production of products less expensive. Injured parties, rather than manufacturers, absorbed the losses associated with product injuries. During the Industrial Revolution, however, the courts slowly began to alter their approach to this problem. The public began to question whether an individual, as opposed to business, should bear the costs of being injured by a product. As products and the manufacturing process became more complex, avoiding injuries became more difficult—even for highly self-reliant persons. The thinking in America shifted from an acceptance of the proposition that self-reliant individuals should protect themselves to a belief that society and business should bear the cost of the inevitable injuries some people sustained.

Privity of Contract

During most of the nineteenth century, the courts permitted injured parties to recover solely on the basis of a contractual theory of recovery. However, in 1852 the New York Court of Appeals accepted the argument that a seller could be held liable in tort. Even so, many injured people found it difficult, if not impossible, to recover any compensation for their injuries. The major doctrine that prevented people from recovering was the requirement that the plaintiff in a personal injury suit be in **privity of contract** with the defendant—that is, there must have been a direct contractual relationship between the injured party and the defendant. In many cases, the injured person had purchased the goods from a retailer. Thus, the buyer was in privity of contract only with the retailer and not with anyone else in the distributive chain. As a practical matter, plaintiffs generally prefer to institute suit against well-heeled defendants, especially if the plaintiffs have sustained very serious injuries. It is pointless to receive a large judgment against a defendant who has very little money. For this reason, the average plaintiff would prefer filing suit against a manufacturer as opposed to a retailer or, worse yet, against a private individual. Now that is possible.

Suppose that Tom purchased a new automobile manufactured by Acme Corporation. Acme, in turn, purchased component parts from various suppliers. One of Acme's suppliers delivered a defective wheel, which Acme used on the vehicle sold to Tom. Tom, of course, purchased the vehicle from an automobile dealer in his hometown, not directly from Acme. While Tom was driving the car, the wheel collapsed. At one time, the only person Tom could bring suit against was the retail dealer from whom he purchased the automobile. A major departure occurred in 1916 in *MacPherson* v. *Buick Motor Co.*, when the New York Court of Appeals abandoned the requirement of privity of contract in negligence suits. The case is presented below. As time passed, other courts followed the lead set by

New York. More recently, the courts have abandoned the requirement of privity of contract in most products liability suits. Thus, today, in most states, Tom could bring suit against the manufacturer, the distributor, or the retailer.

MacPherson v. Buick Motor Co.
Court of Appeals of New York
111 N.E. 1050 (1916)

Defendant, Buick Motor Co., a manufacturer of automobiles, sold an automobile to a retail dealer who in turn resold the car to the plaintiff, MacPherson. While MacPherson was operating the car, the wheel suddenly collapsed, throwing him out and injuring him. One of the wheels had been made out of defective wood, and its spokes had crumbled into fragments. Defendant had not made the wheels, but had bought them from another manufacturer. There was evidence, however, that its defects could have been discovered by reasonable inspection, and inspection had been omitted. The charge in this case was one, not of fraud, but of negligence. The question to be determined was whether Buick owed a duty of care and vigilance to anyone but its immediate purchaser—the retail automobile dealer. The court ruled for the plaintiff.

Cardozo, Justice

The foundations of this branch of the law, at least in this state, were laid in *Thomas v. Winchester*. A poison was falsely labeled. The sale was made to a druggist, who in turn sold to a customer. The customer recovered damages from the seller who affixed the label. "The defendant's negligence," it was said, "put human life in imminent danger." A poison, falsely labeled, is likely to injure anyone who gets it. Because the danger is to be foreseen, there is a duty to avoid the injury.

We hold, then, that the principle of *Thomas v. Winchester* is not limited to poisons, explosives, and things of like nature, to things which in their normal operation are implements of destruction. If the nature of a thing is such that it is reasonably certain to place life and limb in peril when negligently made, it is then a thing of danger. Its nature gives warning of the consequences to be expected. If to the element of danger there is added knowledge that the thing will be used by persons other than the purchaser, and used without new tests, then, irrespective of contract, the manufacturer of this thing is under a duty to make it carefully. That is as far as we are required to go for the decision in this case.

From a survey of the decisions, there emerges a definition of the duty of a manufacturer which enables us to measure this defendant's liability. Beyond all question, the nature of an automobile gives warning of probable danger if its construction is defective. This automobile was designed to go 50 miles an hour. Unless its wheels were sound and strong, injury was almost certain. The defendant knew the danger. It knew also that the car would be used by persons other than the buyer.

There is nothing anomalous in a rule which imposes upon A., who has contracted with B., a duty to C. and D. and others according as he knows or does not know that the subject-matter of the contract is intended for their use. Subtle distinctions are drawn by the defendant between things inherently dangerous and things imminently dangerous, but the case does not turn upon these verbal niceties. If danger was to be expected as reasonably certain, there was a duty of vigilance, and this is true whether you call the danger inherent or imminent.

We think the defendant was not absolved from a duty of inspection because it bought the wheels from a reputable manufacturer. It was not merely a dealer in automobiles. It was a manufacturer of automobiles. It was responsible for the finished product. It was not at liberty to put the finished product on the market without subjecting the component parts to ordinary and simple tests. Under the charge of the trial judge nothing more was required of it. The obligation to inspect must vary with the nature of the thing to be inspected. The more probable the danger the greater the need of caution.

Courts across the United States followed the decision of Judge Cardozo. Today, plaintiffs who wish to bring suit on the basis of negligence need not prove a direct contractual relationship with the defendant. As time passed, courts across the United States eventually abandoned this requirement in warranty cases as well.

Thus, until rather recently, most cases in the products liability field used either breach of warranty or negligence as a theory of recovery. Since the mid- to late 1970s, strict liability in tort has become the most favored theory of recovery. The following material therefore briefly discusses negligence and warranty.

NEGLIGENCE

Manufacturers

The law relating to torts varies from state to state. Efforts have been made to encourage uniformity in the law. One such effort, the work of scholars examining the state of the law in the field of torts, resulted in a number of recommendations as to rules states should adopt in this area. It is called the ***Restatement (Second) of Torts***. Many judges have followed the provisions in the *Restatement* in deciding the proper rule of law to adopt for their states.

In Section 395, the *Restatement (Second) of Torts sets forth a standard by which the courts may judge the actions of a manufacturer of a product. It states:*

A manufacturer who fails to exercise reasonable care in the manufacture of a chattel which, unless carefully made, he should recognize as involving an unreasonable risk of causing physical harm to those who use it for a purpose for which the manufacturer should expect it to be used and to those whom he should expect to be endangered by its probable use, is subject to liability for physical harm caused to them by its lawful use in a manner and for a purpose for which it is supplied.

A manufacturer can be held liable for physical injuries to a person caused by a defective product because of poor design, improper construction, or assembly of the product. In Section 398, the *Restatement (Second) of Torts* announces a standard for design of products.

A manufacturer of a chattel made under a plan or design which makes it dangerous for the uses for which it is manufactured is subject to liability to others whom he should expect to use the chattel or to be endangered by its probable use for physical harm caused by his failure to exercise reasonable care in the adoption of a safe plan or design.

This means that a manufacturer must exercise due care in the design of all products. Putting a product on the market that later is determined to be unsafe for normal use may result in liability for physical injuries caused to people by the product.

DUTY OF DUE CARE

The manufacturer generally must exercise due care to make certain the product he or she places on the market is safe. This means the manufacturer must conduct reasonable tests and exercise reasonable care in inspecting a product to discover latent defects before putting it on the market.

It is not sufficient for a manufacturer merely to inspect and test a product. The manufacturer also sometimes has a duty to warn the public of the dangerous propensities of a product. In Section 388, the *Restatement (Second) of Torts* suggests the following standard with respect to a duty to warn:

> One who supplies directly or through a third person a chattel for another to use is subject to liability to those whom the supplier should expect to use the chattel with the consent of the other or to be endangered by its probable use, for physical harm caused by the use of the chattel in the manner for which and by a person for whose use it is supplied, if the supplier
>
> a. knows or has reason to know that the chattel is or is likely to be dangerous for the use for which it is supplied, and
> b. has no reason to believe that those for whose use the chattel is supplied will realize its dangerous condition, and
> c. fails to exercise reasonable care to inform them of its dangerous condition or of the facts which make it likely to be dangerous.

Numerous cases have arisen with respect to the issue of duty to warn. All too often people coming into contact with cerain products do not realize the dangers associated with using them.

Not only must sellers warn people of the dangers associated with proper uses of a product, sellers must also warn the public of foreseeable dangers associated with the misuse of their products. For example, the manufacturer of a lawn mower should warn users of the mower not to put their hands inside the mower housing while the blade is still spinning. Although this seems highly improbable, a person may mow a lawn while it is wet. The wet grass may clog the exhaust chute. A person in a rush to finish mowing the lawn may be tempted to try to dislodge the grass without shutting off the mower. For this reason, mowers sold today have a warning label next to the exhaust chute cautioning users against such behavior.

Even if a manufacturer places a warning on its products, other questions concerning the warning can arise. For example, was the warning adequate? Was the warning clear and intelligible? Was it written in a language people coming into contact with the product could read? Another problem concerns who should receive the warning. Is it sufficient to warn physicians of the dangers of a drug and not the consuming public?

The *Restatement* requires a manufacturer to use reasonable care in every step of the manufacturing process—design, construction, testing, labeling, and packaging—if it realizes that the product poses an unreasonable risk of causing physical harm to users of the product. The manufacturer owes this duty to exercise reasonable care to any person who uses or is endangered by the use of its product. This provision dispenses with the defense of the lack of privity of contract—that is, the necessity of establishing a direct contractual relationship between buyer and seller. If a manufacturer fails to exercise such care, it will be liable for physical harm caused by the product.

Retailers   Retailers also owe a duty of due care to the public. Some states require the retailer to inform purchasers of any defect that could be discovered by an inspection of the product. Other states do not require the retailer to take such steps to warn purchasers. In general, recovery from a retailer under negligence theory is difficult. Retailers quite often deal in packaged containers that they know very little about. Courts take this into consideration when evaluating the obligations of retailers.

The chief problem with negligence is the difficulty for the plaintiff in establishing that the defendant failed to exercise due care. This creates a very substantial burden of proof for the plaintiff in many cases. Furthermore, the defendant may be able to establish to the satisfaction of a court that it did in fact exercise a reasonable amount of care in manufacturing, assembling, testing, and packaging the product. In this situation, because the defendant acted reasonably, the plaintiff receives nothing. Certain theories of recovery discussed later in this chapter permit the plaintiff to recover even if the manufacturer exercised all care possible. That being the case, pursuing a case under negligence in many instances makes very little sense.

Warranty

Because of the problems with respect to negligence, injured parties began to attempt to bring suit under other theories of recovery. The next theory of recovery to gain popular acceptance by the courts was warranty. Unlike negligence, which is a tort theory of recovery, warranty theory is contractual in nature.

Today, courts across the United States permit a person injured by a product to recover if the injured party is able to show that there was a breach of warranty by the defendant and that the injury was sustained as a result of the breach of warranty.

Sellers may create warranties by express agreement. Other warranties arise automatically by operation of law whenever a seller enters into a contract.

Express Warranty   An **express warranty** may be created in one of three ways: (1) by a promise made by the seller to the buyer that relates to the goods, (2) by a specific description of the goods made by the seller, or (3) by the seller's sample of model.

For example, a tire manufacturer's statement that its tires will not blow out during the life of the tread creates an express warranty. Suppose the manufacturer made such a statement and the tire on a driver's car exploded. If the explosion caused her car to run off the road into a tree, would she have a cause of action against the tire manufacturer for her injuries? Yes. The manufacturer breached its warranty when the tire exploded. It would be liable for the resulting injuries to the driver.

The following case deals with an express warranty created by an advertisement.

Drayton v. Jiffee Chemical Corp.
United States District Court
395 F. Supp. 1081 (1975)

RATIONALE

This suit arose out of a severe facial disfigurement incurred by a child. Terri Drayton. On December 21, 1968, Terri and her parents were living in a boarding house in Cleveland, Ohio. Terri's father was attempting to clear a clogged sink in the bathroom. He was using a bottle of "liquid-plumr' that he had borrowed from the landlady, Mrs. Sorrell. At the trial, Terri's father testified that he had entered the bathroom alone and poured half a bottle of liquid-plumr into the drain. He then placed a towel over the open drain and stepped back from the sink. At that moment, Terri grabbed his leg and screamed. When he looked down at the child it appeared that she had been doused with the drain cleaner. He testified that he was unaware of the child's presence in the bathroom until he heard her scream.

Battisti, Chief Judge

Plaintiffs contend that defendant's use of such a highly caustic concentration of sodium hydroxide in liquid-plumr rendered such product unsafe, unmerchantable, and unfit for the use intended—that of a common, household drain cleaner. Besides breaching such implied warranties of merchantability and fitness for the use intended, plaintiffs also argue that the defendant breached its express warranty, contained in its advertising, that liquid-plumr was "safe" for ordinary household use.

At trial there was introduced into evidence a copy of a letter from The Code Authority, National Association of Broadcasters to Mr. Harold F. Bull, president of the Bull Advertising Agency, which had as one of its accounts the Jiffee Chemical Corporation. The letter requested documentation in support of Jiffee's claim that liquid-plumr is "safe." Also introduced into evidence was Mr. Bull's letter in response wherein he stated that as of March 28, 1967 all references to the word "safe" were being deleted from Jiffee's advertisements for liquid-plumr. Such

advertising, however, continued beyond the point in time when Mrs. Sorrell purchased the bottle of liquid-plumr that was used on the night of the accident. Mrs. Sorrell testified that she bought the drain cleaner before Terri was born (1966) and that she had seen the product advertised on television and that it was represented to be "safe" and capable of "fast action." It is clear that Mrs. Sorrell relied, at least in part, on such representations in making her choice of which product to purchase. Under those circumstances Mrs. Sorrell would have a viable cause of action against Jiffee for breach of express warranty:

> Under modern merchandising practices, where the manufacturer of a product in his advertising makes representations as to the quality and merit of his product aimed directly at the ultimate consumer and urges the latter to purchase the product from a retailer, and such ultimate consumer does so in reliance on and pursuant to the inducements of the manufac-

turer and suffers harm in the use of such product by reason of deleterious ingredients therein, such ultimate consumer may maintain an action for damages immediately against the manufacturer on the basis of express warranty, notwithstanding that there is no direct contractual relationship between them. *Rogers v. Toni Home Permanent Co.*, 167 Ohio St 244, 147 N.E.2d 612 (1958).

Such cause of action would also be vested in Terri Drayton as "one whose presence at the [scene of the accident] was foreseeable and whose safety it was the duty of the manufacturer to protect by producing a chattel that when used as intended would not endanger the safety of those lawfully at the place of its use."

Defendant is therefore liable to plaintiff for breach of warranty.

Implied Warranty of Merchantability

Warranties may be created by operation of law. Here the seller neither says nor writes down any warranties, but the law creates a warranty anyway. One such type of warranty is the implied warranty of merchantability. Only a merchant seller creates such a warranty. The foremost question in deciding whether goods are merchantable or not is whether the goods are fit for the ordinary purposes for which such goods are used. If the buyer orders a furnace for his or her home, the buyer expects a certain level of performance from the heater even though the seller said nothing regarding its performance. Suppose the buyer turned the heater on after its installation and the heater exploded. Obviously, a heater that explodes on its first use fails to comply with the implied warranty of merchantability. The buyer may bring suit for any injuries caused by the defective heater.

Implied Warranty of Fitness for a Particular Purpose

This warranty also is created by operation of law. If at the time of contracting, the seller has reason to know any particular purpose for which the goods are required and that the buyer is relying on the seller's skill or judgment to select or furnish suitable goods, there is an implied warranty that the goods shall be fit for such purpose. Suppose a consumer purchased a gas range installed by the seller. If the seller used a defective brass tube to connect the range to the gas pipe, and if the defective pipe caused an explosion, the seller is liable to the purchaser. The seller knew the buyer was relying upon it to furnish a suitable tube. Its failure to do so breaches the implied warranty of fitness for a particular purpose.

Breach of Warranty As a Basis for a Products Liability Suit

If a seller creates an express warranty or if an implied warranty exists and the seller breaches this warranty, a person injured as a result of the breach of warranty may bring suit to recover for his or her injuries if the plaintiff also establishes that the express or implied warranty was part of the basis of the bargain between the parties.

Even today, in some states a plaintiff will be unable to recover if he or she is unable to establish a direct contractual relationship with the defendant.

Proceeding on a personal injury suit based on a warranty theory of recovery creates a number of other hurdles for plaintiffs to overcome. In some cases, the defendant may be able to successfully demonstrate that it disclaimed all warranties. A defendant who makes no warranties obviously cannot be liable for breach of an express warranty. Even though the implied warranties arise by operation of law, and not by express warranty, sellers may exclude the operation of these warranties. The power to disclaim warranties gives sellers the opportunity to limit their liability under this theory of recovery. Furthermore, in the case of the implied warranty of merchantability, the plaintiff must establish that the defendant is a merchant. If the defendant is not a merchant, the implied warranty of merchantability does not arise. Finally, if a plaintiff wishes to institute suit on the basis of breach of warranty, it must notify the defendant of breach. If requisite notice of breach of warranty is not given at the appropriate time, the plaintiff may not use breach of warranty as a basis for recovery.

Warranties and Computer Software

James A. Cummings, Inc., was a construction firm. It purchased Lotus Development Corporation's business program "Symphony" and used it to prepare a bid for constructing an office building complex. As the bid was being prepared, an employee noticed that it did not include $254,000 in general costs. The preparer then inserted this figure at the top of the column of figures used to calculate the bid. The number appeared on the preparer's computer screen but was never added to the bid amount by the computer program. Cummings did not know this until after the miscalculated bid was accepted.

Cummings filed suit against Lotus seeking $254,000 in consequential damages, contending that its Symphony software did not perform properly, thereby causing the loss. However, Lotus's software package provides a written limited warranty under which the company will replace only a defective disc. Furthermore, these limited warranties are a part of licensing agreement common to software purchases under which the buyer does not own the product. Instead, the buyer simply purchases a license to use the software maker's product.

This issue of software maker liability may be viewed from two perspectives. The companies contend that no maker represents that its software is flawless, since there are too many ways a computer program can go wrong. The problems that arise, they contend, are with users who blindly rely on computer output for their major decisions without adequate controls. Furthermore, some small software companies are concerned that potential liability for consequential damages arising from flawed software might stifle innovation and cause some to go out of business because of a costly lawsuit or increased liability insurance premiums. On the other hand, software companies are selling a very sophisticated product that they intend their customers to rely on. Software is sold to business as a major time-saving device that can be used for complex operations. Thus, should not the maker be liable if the software does not perform according to specifications?

MISREPRESENTATION

Another theory of recovery in the products liability field developed even more recently than negligence or warranty. This theory of recovery, referred to generally as *misrepresentation,* permits the injured party to recover in certain instances when the defendant has misrepresented the product and the misrepresentation causes the injury. Untrue statements in radio or television broadcasts, newspapers, magazines, billboards, posters, or pamphlets may lead to liability for personal injuries if the statements mislead the public.

During the last decade, an increasing number of plaintiffs have chosen to establish their case on the basis of **innocent misrepresentation**. Liability arises under innocent misrepresentation even though the seller never intended to mislead the public. The *Restatement (Second) of Torts* suggests that a plaintiff be permitted to collect for any physical injuries she or he sustained, if the harm in question resulted from a misrepresentation of the character or quality of the product sold, even though the misrepresentation was an innocent one, and not made fraudulently or negligently, and the plaintiff demonstrates that she or he relied upon the misrepresentation in purchasing or using the product. The absence of privity of contract is not a defense.

In the following case, the court adopts innocent misrepresentation as a theory of recovery. Note that the facts in this case clearly indicate that Klages had been misled by General Ordnance's statements. As a result of his reliance on the statements in question, he sustained an injury for which the court permitted him to recover.

Klages v. General Ordnance Equipment Corporation
Superior Court of Pennsylvania
367 A.2d 304 (1976)

Plaintiff, John R. Klages, was employed as a night auditor at Conley's Motel. After once being held up by armed robbers, plaintiff purchased the defendant's mace weapon for protection. He sued for injuries sustained while using the mace weapon. The lower court ruled in his favor and the superior court affirmed the lower court decision.

Hoffman, Judge

The instant case presents a question of first impression in Pennsylvania: Is the *Restatement (Second) of Torts* Section 402B the law of this Commonwealth?

The facts are not in dispute. The appellee, John R.

Klages, was employed as a night auditor at Conley's Motel on Route 8, Hampton Township. He worked from eleven o'clock at night until seven o'clock in the morning, five days a week. On March 30, 1968, at approximately one-thirty in the morning, two individuals entered the motel and announced "This is a stickup. Open the safe."

The next day Klages and a fellow employee, Bob McVay, decided that they needed something to protect themselves against the possibility of future holdups. After reading an article concerning the effects of mace, McVay suggested that they investigate the possibility of using mace for their protection. McVay secured four leaflets describing certain mace weapons from the Markl Supply Company. The leaflets were distributed to retail outlets by the appellant manufacturer, General Ordnance Equipment Corporation. The literature indicated that three different types of mace weapons were available. Two of the weapons were too large for Klages' and McVay's purposes, but the third, the MK-II, was easily concealable and otherwise appeared to meet their requirements. The literature contained, in pertinent part, the following description of the mace's effectiveness:

> Rapidly vaporizes on face of assailant effecting instantaneous incapacitation. . . . It will instantly stop and subdue entire groups . . . instantly stop assailants in their tracks . . . an attacker is subdued—instantly, for a period of 15 to 20 minutes. . . . Time Magazine stated the Chemical Mace is "for police the first, if not the final answer to a nationwide need—a weapon that disables as effectively as a gun and yet does no permanent injury." . . . The effectiveness is the result of a unique incapacitating formulation (patent pending), projected in a shotgun-like pattern of heavy liquid droplets that, upon contact with the face, cause extreme tearing, and a stunned, winded condition, often accompanied by dizziness and apathy.

After reading and discussing the literature with their employer, McVay purchased an MK-II mace weapon from Markl Supply Company.

At approximately 1:40 A.M., on the morning of September 22, 1968, while the appellee was on duty, two unknown individuals entered the motel office and requested a room. After the appellee had placed a registration form in front of one of the men and had turned to secure a room key, the individuals announced a stickup. One of the intruders took out a gun and directed the appellee to open the safe. Klages, planning to use the mace before the intruder used the gun, moved from the counter to the cash register where the mace was kept. Using the cash register as a shield, Klages squirted the

mace, hitting the intruder "right beside the nose." Klages immediately ducked below the register, but the intruder followed him down and shot him in the head. The intruders immediately departed and Klages called the police. The bullet wound caused complete loss of sight in the appellee's right eye.

The appellee, Klages, commenced separate actions against the Markl Supply company and the General Ordnance Equipment Corporation. The Markl Supply company also joined the General Ordnance Corporation as an additional defendant in each of its cases. On October 26, 1973, the cases were consolidated for trial. A jury trial commenced on March 4, 1974, and the jury returned a a verdict in the amount of $42,000.00, in favor of Klages against the appellant, General Ordnance Equipment Corporation, and a verdict in favor of the Markl Supply Company. This appeal followed.

The appellant raises as grounds for reversal the argument the lower court erred in charging the jury on misrepresentation of a material fact under section 402B of the *Restatement (Second) of Torts.*

Section 402B of the *Restatement (Second) of Torts* provides as follows:

> One engaged in the business of selling chattel who, by advertising, labels, or otherwise, makes to the public a misrepresentation of a material fact concerning the character or quality of a chattel sold by him is subject to liability for physical harm to a consumer of the chattel caused by justifiable reliance upon the misrepresentation, even though (a) it is not made fraudulently or negligently, and (b) the consumer has not bought the chattel from or entered into any contractual relation with the seller.

Having adopted Section 402B of the *Restatement (Second) of Torts* as the law of this Commonwealth, we must determine whether the appellant misrepresented "a material fact concerning the character or quality of a chattel sold by him. . . ."

The comments to Section 402B are helpful in this regard. First, Comment f states that "[t]he fact misrepresented must be a material one, upon which the consumer may be expected to rely in making his purchase. . . ." Comment g states that section 402B

does not apply to statements of opinion, and in particular it does not apply to the kind of loose general praise of wares sold which, on the part of the seller, is considered to be "sales talk," and is commonly called "puffing"—as, for example, a statement that an automobile is the best on the market for the price. . . . In addition, the fact misrepresented must be a material one, of importance to the normal purchaser by which the ultimate buyer may justifiably be expected to be influenced in buying the chattel.

The facts and circumstances surrounding the purchase of a product are helpful in determining whether the representation is of a material fact. In this case, the appellant sold a product designed as a tool to deter violence. Its sole anticipated use was to protect the purchaser from harm under extremely dangerous circumstances and the appellee specifically purchased the product with these explicit purposes in mind. Specific representations about the effectiveness of the weapon under such dangerous circumstances are clearly material. The mace weapons were described as effecting an instantaneous, immediate, complete incapacitation of an assailant. This is not "loose, general praise"; rather it is specific data on the capability of a product.

STRICT LIABILITY

As the years passed, plaintiffs became weary of the difficult problems of proof associated with negligence and the various defenses to warranty cases. In many cases, people who sustained injuries as a result of a defective product found themselves unable to recover, not because they were not injured, but because of some technical rule of law. As more and more people sustained injuries, the mood in the courts and the legislatures gradually began to shift from protecting business to protecting consumers. People began to argue that the manufacturer is in the best position to shoulder any loss caused by its products. A manufacturer has the power to produce better and safer products. The public is powerless to control the quality of products on the marketplace. Lawyers argued that by placing more responsibility on corporations to produce safe products, corporations would be encouraged to take more care in the design, manufacture, testing, and inspection of products.

In some instances, neither the manufacturer nor the consumer really is at fault. Sometimes a bad product reaches the marketplace even though the manufacturer takes every step possible to keep this from occurring. When this happens, who ought to bear the loss—the injured party or the manufacturer? Lawyers increasingly began to accept the idea that a manufacturer is in the best position to insure against any possible loss caused by its products. If one of two innocent persons must bear the loss caused by a defective product, let the manufacturer purchase insurance and bear the loss.

This idea of **strict liability** gained popularity following Judge Traynor's famous comments in *Escola v. Coca Cola Bottling Co. of Fresno*. A waitress in a restaurant was injured when a bottle of Coca Cola exploded in her hand. Neither she nor anyone else was able to explain why this accident occurred. In ruling in her favor, Judge Traynor wrote:

I believe the manufacturer's negligence should no longer be singled out as the basis of a plaintiff's right to recover in cases like the present one. In my opinion it should now be recognized that a manufacturer incurs an absolute liability when an article he has placed on the market, knowing that it is to be used without inspection, proves to have a defect that causes injury to human beings. . . . Even if there is no negligence, however, public policy demands that responsibility be fixed wherever it will most effectively reduce the hazards to life and health inherent in defective products that reach the market.

From Fault to No Fault

HARM MUST RESULT

A breakthrough came in 1963 when the California Supreme Court in *Greenman* v. *Yuba Power Products* accepted the concept of strict liability in tort. After the acceptance of this theory of recovery by the California Supreme Court, other courts and legislatures throughout the country slowly began to adopt this rule. By the late 1970s, most states across the United States permitted parties to sue under strict liability in tort.

Prior to the adoption of strict liability in tort, the law permitted a person to recover under negligence only if he or she could prove that the seller failed to act reasonably and prudently. The law therefore limited recovery to cases in which the injured party was able to demonstrate that the defendant acted in some manner that the law regarded as improper.

A seller who acted with reasonable care would prevail in a negligence suit. However, if the plaintiff sued on the basis of strict liability in tort, the plaintiff might prevail even if "the seller has exercised all possible care in the preparation and sale of his product"—in other words, even though the seller acted with reasonable care. Thus, strict liability in tort shifts some of the risk associated with products from the buyer to the seller. The courts assume that sellers may protect themselves from the costs of suits by purchasing insurance.

Section 402A

The *Restatement (Second) of Torts* adopted the concept of strict liability in tort, which now appears in Section 402A. It reads as follows:

1. One who sells any products in a defective condition unreasonably dangerous to the user or consumer or to his property, is subject to liability for physical harm thereby caused to the ultimate user or consumer, or to his property, if

   (a) the seller is engaged in the business of selling such a product, and
   (b) it is expected to and does reach the consumer or user without substantial change in the condition in which it is sold.

2. The rule stated in subsection (1) applies although

   (a) the seller has exercised all possible care in the preparation and sale of his product, and
   (b) the user or consumer has not bought the product from or entered into any contractual relation with the seller.

The *Restatement* adopts a rule that is almost one of absolute liability on the part of the seller. It makes the seller liable even if it exercised "all possible care in the preparation and sale" of the product. In a negligence case, evidence of this type would absolve the defendant of any liability. Under strict liability in tort, it is irrelevant whether the seller acted negligently. As long as the plaintiff is able to establish the other elements, he or she recovers even if there is no evidence of negligence on the part of the defendant.

The *Restatement* also eliminates the need to establish a direct contractual relationship between the plaintiff and the defendant; that is, it eliminates the absence of privity of contract as a defense in a strict liability case. This permits an injured party to sue anyone in the distributive chain: manufacturers, distributors, or retail sellers. Any user or consumer is permitted to bring suit. Further, many states permit bystanders to bring suit. Suppose a person on a skateboard lost control because a roller came off the skateboard. If the person on the skateboard crashed into John, John would be an innocent bystander injured by the failure of the skateboard. Many states permit a person in John's position to bring suit against the manufacturer of the skateboard, the distributor, or the retail seller.

Plaintiffs must establish that the product in question was expected to and in fact did reach the consumer without substantial change in the condition in which it was sold. In the case of packaged goods, such a requirement creates few difficulties for the plaintiff. Suppose Mrs. Jones purchases some hair dye to change the color of her hair. If the formula of the dye causes users to lose their hair, and Mrs. Jones's hair falls out, she may sue the seller for damages. As the dye comes in a package, she will have no problems proving the product was in the same condition as when it was sold. But suppose Mrs. Jones was injured instead in her two-year-old car when the brakes failed. If she brings suit against the manufacturer, will she be able to prove the brakes were in the same condition as when the vehicle was sold to her? Obviously, this creates a substantial burden of proof. Many people may have touched the brakes. These people might have somehow tampered with the brakes and caused them to fail; in that case, the manufacturer would not be liable.

Section 402A applies only to persons regularly engaged in selling a particular product. If a person purchases an automobile from a local automobile dealer, clearly the dealer is in the business of selling automobiles. The dealer could be liable. But suppose the buyer purchased the automobile from a next-door neighbor. The neighbor, as he or she is not regularly engaged in selling automobiles, would have no liability.

A company must provide adequate instructions and warnings with its products. Suppose a company sold paint with the following warning: "Keep away from heat and open flame. Use with adequate ventilation." Does this fully inform users of the product of all dangers inherent in using the product? What if flammable vapors could accumulate in a closed area? Does this warning adequately alert potential users to this danger? A product that is otherwise safe may be rendered unreasonably dangerous by the failure of the seller to provide adequate warnings of the dangerous characteristics of its products. Such a warning might be inadequate if it failed to clearly warn users of all dangers in using the product.

On the other hand, when a seller adopts adequate warnings on its products, courts rule for the defendant. Today, in response to the pressure of potential liability, most sellers take great care in creating instructions and warnings for their products. These warnings often result in verdicts for the manufacturer.

The following case deals with a mother who desired to cure her acne problem. The drug she took, Accutane, caused birth defects in her child.

Failure to Warn
Outlaw v. *Firestone Tire and Rubber*, 770 F.2d 1012 (1985)

Jay Outlaw pumped air into his tire. The gauge registered between thirty-five and forty-five pounds per square inch. When he began to release air from the tire, the tire exploded, injuring his right eye and ear. The exposion was caused when heat, produced by continuous contact of the deflated tire with the surface of the highway, created a temperature hot enough to melt the sidewall. Firestone, the manufacturer of the tire, knew of this risk. Out-law contended that Firestone failed to give an adequate warning that a tire operated at low pressure for an extended period of time would melt down and explode. The Eleventh Circuit Court of Appeals ruled that a seller must warn of any nonobvious risk of serious injury when the product is used in its intended manner. The jury could therefore have concluded that Firestone should have warned Outlaw of this risk.

Accutane presents very real risks to its users. Consumption of the antiacne drug Accutane resulted in over one thousand babies born with birth defects by the year 1988. The desperation of many people with acne causes them to reach out for cures. If these people receive *complete* disclosure of the risks associated with the product, they possess the information to evaluate the risks and to exercise their free choice. Of course, a person in dire straits may discount very real long-term risks in order to resolve her or his short-term problem. Can a person in such a situation be expected to really objectively evaluate the risks involved?

In any case, if the seller fails to disclose the problems associated with its products, no one may exercise free choice and make an informed consent to treatment. In the *Felix* case, the court ruled in favor of Hoffman-LaRoche.

Felix v. Hoffman-LaRoche, Inc.
District Court of Appeal of Florida
513 So.2d 1319 (1987)

Yolanda Felix consulted with a physician concerning treatments for acne. The physician prescribed a drug called Accutane. As a result of taking this drug, Yolanda gave birth to a deformed child. She sued Hoffman-LaRoche for failure to warn her of the danger of taking Accutane. The court ruled for Hoffman-LaRoche because the company provided an adequate warning to her physician.

Per Curiam

We affirm the trial court's final summary judgment, entered in favor of Hoffmann-LaRoche, Inc., Roche Biomedical Laboratories, Lester M. Wachman, Bindley Western Industries, Inc., Gray Drug Stores, Inc. of Miami, Gray Drug Stores, Inc., and Sherwin Williams Company. A drug manufacturer owes a duty to warn prescribing physicians of the dangerous side effects of its prescription drugs.

If the warning given to the medical community is sufficient, then the drug manufacturer is not liable for injuries sustained by the physician's patients as a result of the side effects of the drugs. The warning given was adequate as a matter of law. It is inconceivable that reasonable persons could disagree as to the adequacy of the warnings in conveying to physicians that the prescription drug, Accutane, is dangerous to pregnant women and should not have been prescribed.

Besides using the term "teratogenicity," the package insert accompanying the drug also warned:

Women of child-bearing potential should not be given Accutane unless an effective form of contraception is used, and they should be fully counseled on the potential risk to the fetus should they become pregnant while undergoing treatment. Should pregnancy occur during treatment, the physician and patient should discuss the desirability of continuing the pregnancy period.

It is also uncontested that the Physician's Desk Reference gave a similar warning.

While we recognize that whether a warning is adequate is usually a jury question, summary judgment is proper where, as here, the warning is clear and unambiguous, the injuries arising as a result of the failure to heed the warning are identical to those the warning described, and the undisputed evidence demonstrates that at the time the prescribing physician prescribed the drug, he was completely aware of the dangers it posed. Accordingly, the trial court's final summary judgment is affirmed.

Courts treat a product as defective if it lacks a warning necessary to alert persons to dangers associated with its use. Manufacturers need not warn users of obvious dangers—only those dangers not apparent to an ordinary person using the product. If a person picks up a knife, most people realize the dangers associated with carelessly handling the knife. For that reason, knife manufacturers need not place a warning on the blade of each knife. The *Outlaw* case, discussed in a box in this chapter, deals with the potential of a hot tire to explode. Few people appreciate this risk; thus, they need a warning of such a potential danger.

Some products pose obvious risks. Anyone who ever drank a six-pack of beer in a couple of hours realizes that the consumption of excessive quantities of alcohol in a short duration of time makes certain activities risky—such as coming home in dad's car after drinking the six-pack, climbing up the stairs of the bar, or trying to walk a straight line. Anyone who consumes a few drinks can experience the effects of alcohol for himself or herself.

Excessive consumption of alcohol creates a host of problems in the United States and throughout the world. It touches the lives of virtually everyone. In America, as in the rest of the world, excessive drinking causes many tragedies. For example, in 1989, the actions of the allegedly intoxicated captain of the *Exxon Valdez* may have caused the tragic eleven-million-gallon oil spill in Alaska's Prince William Sound. Every year drunk drivers kill over twenty thousand persons and permanently injure thousands of others. The influence of alcohol plays a

Sports and Steroids

Following the sports axiom "if you don't take it, you won't make it," track star Ben Johnson took anabolic steroids for five years before the Seoul Olympics. At the games, Johnson won a gold medal for the one-hundred-meter race. He tested positive for steroids at the games.

It is a known fact that steroids may lead to serious medical problems. In spite of this fact, the urge to place first in sports leads a number of athletes to engage in the unlawful use of prescription drugs. This urge to win a short-term victory may lead to disastrous long-term consequences for the people using steroids.

"Johnson Took Steroids 50 Times, Doctor Says," *The Kansas City Times*, May 25, 1989, p. F-3.

part in many criminal acts. Excessive consumption of alcohol contributes to innumerable cases of spouse and child abuse. Businesses lose billions of dollars because of loss of work, on-the-job injuries, and medical problems caused by the long-term abuse of alcohol. Obviously, most people realize the typical dangers associated with the abuse of alcohol. The law requires no warning for these dangers.

At the same time, alcohol poses certain risks that may not be obvious even to a regular drinker. These dangers are not necessarily obvious merely because a person drank a lot of alcohol one evening. The following case discusses the question of the duty to warn in this situation.

Brune v. Brown Forman Corp.
Court of Appeals of Texas, Corpus Christi
758 S.W.2d 827 (1988)

RATIONALE

Marie Brinkmeyer was eighteen years old and in her first semester at Texas A&I University. On November 14, 1983, Marie went to the University Liquor Store and purchased a bottle of Pepe Lopez Tequila. She drank straight shots of tequila with her friends that evening. Around 10:00 P.M. her friends escorted her to her room. They found her dead the following morning, allegedly as a direct result of acute alcohol intoxication. Brown Forman manufactured the tequila in question. The plaintiff alleged that the tequila was defective because it was an unreasonably dangerous product in the absence of a warning that it could cause an overdose resulting in death. The court ruled that a genuine issue of material fact exists concerning whether tequila is safe for its intended purposes without a warning. Therefore, the trial court erred in granting a motion for a summary judgment.

Utter, Justice

Appellee contends that the comments to Section 402A indicate that good alcoholic beverages properly made without contamination or deleterious material are not defective. However, we do not read these provisions so narrowly. Comment h states that:

A product is not in a defective condition when it is safe for normal handling and consumption. If the injury results from . . . abnormal consumption, as where a child eats too much candy and is made ill, the seller is not liable. *Where, however, he has reason to anticipate that danger may result from a particular use, as where a drug is sold which is safe only in limited doses, he may be required to give adequate warning of the danger (See comment j), and a product sold without such warning is in a defective condition* (emphasis added).

A close look at comment h, reveals that in a situation where the manufacturer can anticipate a danger from a particular use, such as death resulting from acute alcohol poisoning, he may be required to give an adequate warning of that danger. Nowhere does comment h state that there is no duty to warn under any circumstances involved. In fact, appellee may have had reason to anticipate that danger may result from this particular use.

Likewise, comments i and j do not preclude a cause of action based on a duty to warn. In pertinent part, comment i states:

Many products cannot possibly be made entirely safe for all consumption, and any food or drug necessarily involves some risk of harm, if only from overconsumption. . . . *The article sold must be dangerous to an extent beyond that which would be contemplated by the ordinary consumer who purchases it, with the ordinary knowledge common to the community as to its characteristics.* Good whiskey is not unreasonably dangerous merely because it will make some people drunk and is especially dangerous to alcoholics . . . (emphasis added).

It is readily apparent that comment i only speaks of those characteristics that result from general intoxication and dangers peculiar to alcoholics. Comment i neither speaks of the fatal propensities of alcohol, nor does it state that those fatal propensities are ordinary knowledge common to the community.

Lastly, comment j states in relevant part:

Directions or warning. In order to prevent the product from being [in a defective condition] unreasonably dangerous [to the user or consumer], the seller may be required to give directions or warning, on the container, as to its use. . . . *In the case of poisonous drugs, or those unduly dangerous for other reasons, warning as to use may be required.*

But a seller is not required to warn with respect to products, or ingredients in them, which are only dangerous, or potentially so, when consumed in excessive quantity, or over a long period of time, *when the danger, or potentiality of danger, is generally known and recognized.* Again the dangers of alcoholic beverages are an example, as are those of foods containing such substances as saturated fats, which may over a period of time have a deleterious effect upon the human heart (emphasis added).

Appellee interprets comment j to mean that the dangers of excessive alcohol consumption are well known to the public. Comment j, however, does not say that the dangers of acute ethyl ingestion resulting in death are necessarily generally known. Rather, it says that when the danger is generally known, no warning is required. As noted in *Hon* , when read in context, comment j does nothing more than extend to the duty to warn the *Restatement's* general exception for cases in which the consumer knows or should know of the product's dangerous propensities. In other words, it does not say that the danger of acute alcohol intoxication resulting in death is generally known and that no warning is required. We conclude, therefore, that comments h, i and j do not preclude liability where death results from acute alcohol intoxication. Likewise, there is no basis for concluding that alcohol should be treated any differently than any other drug or poison on the market.

In its response to appellee's motion for summary judgment, appellant offered evidence which showed that, prior to the time of her death, Brinkmeyer had little exposure to the use of alcohol. Brinkmeyer's mother stated that she had warned Brinkmeyer of the dangers of impaired physical capacity which can result from the consumption of alcohol, but that she had not warned her daughter that alcohol was lethal because she had no knowledge of that fact. The liquor store owner that sold Brinkmeyer the tequila stated that he knew you could die from an alcohol overdose, but admitted that he had acquired his knowledge through college chemistry courses. In addition, appellant submitted documents showing that the United States Congress has been considering legislation on whether to require warning labels on bottles of alcohol and that the government of Mexico has already instituted such legislation. Appellant further showed that warning labels are presently used in the United States on "Everclear" grain alcohol bottles. These warnings state that the overconsumption may endanger your health and instruct the user not to consume the product in excessive quantities or to drink it without mixing it with non-alcoholic beverages.

The appellant alleged that tequila, taken in the quantity and manner Brinkmeyer consumed it, can have fatal consequences. There is nothing in the record which sug-gests that Brinkmeyer was aware of this fact. Moreover, the record reveals that the general public may be unaware that consumption of tequila in this quantity and manner can be potentially fatal. The fatal propensities of acute alcohol poisoning cannot be readily categorized as ordinary common knowledge. Although there is no question that drinking alcoholic beverages will cause intoxication and possibly even cause illness is a matter of common knowledge, we are not prepared to hold, as a matter of law, that the general public is aware that the consumption of an excessive amount of alcohol can result in death.

It should be noted that as of November 1989, the Alcoholic Beverage Labeling Act requires beverage containers to bear the following warning:

> GOVERNMENT WARNING: (1) According to the Surgeon General women should not drink alcoholic beverages during pregnancy because of the risk of birth defects. (2) Consumption of alcoholic beverages impairs your ability to drive a car or operate machinery, and may cause health problems.

The act specifically states that no other statement relating to health may be required by any state.

Unreasonably Dangerous

The requirement that gives the courts the greatest problem is the requirement that the product be in a "defective condition unreasonably dangerous to the user or consumer or to his property." The states have adopted various positions regarding the terminology "defective condition unreasonably dangerous." Some states have greatly modified these concepts.

Duty to Warn
Pemberton v. *American Distilled Spirits Company*, 644 S.W.2d 690 (1988)

Pemberton consumed a bottle of grain alcohol and thereafter died. His father brought suit against American Distilled Spirits Company. He alleged that the company failed to warn his son of the risk of death from consuming too much alcohol. The Supreme Court of Tennessee ruled that the average person understands the dangers associated with the use of alcohol. Therefore, no warning need be provided of such dangers to the general public because the alcohol could not be unreasonably dangerous.

For example, some courts have found that the marketing of handguns is an unreasonably dangerous activity. Courts that are willing to hold sellers of handguns liable are attempting to stretch strict liability law to its limits. The following case also represents a willingness by a court to give a very broad interpretation to the term **unreasonably dangerous**.

Fraust v. Swift and Company
United States District Court, W.D. Pennsylvania
610 F. Supp. 711 (1985)

A products liability action was brought against Swift and Company, a peanut butter manufacturer, by Judith Fraust, the mother of Isaac Fraust, a sixteen-month-old child who choked while eating peanut butter spread on bread. The child subsequently died of severe brain damage. Swift claimed that as a matter of law its product should be declared to be not unreasonably dangerous.

The plaintiff's theory is that the peanut butter supplied by the defendant was unsafe for its intended use because it lacked a warning that it should not be fed to children under four years of age. Fraust contends that peanut butter is dangerous to children under four years of age because of its texture and consistency and the immature eating and swallowing abilities of children of that age.

Teitelbaum, Chief Judge

Liability cannot be imposed on the seller for failure to warn of a danger associated with its product if the danger was or should have been known to the user. The issue of necessity of warnings must also be considered in light of any contradictory promotional activities on the part of the seller. The Court cannot say as a matter of law that Isaac's mother knew or should have known of the danger associated with feeding a peanut butter sandwich to him.

As its second argument, defendant contends that because plaintiffs do not allege that the peanut butter was not in the condition expected by the ordinary consumer it was not unreasonably dangerous as a matter of law. Although at first this argument appears different from defendant's first argument, it is really a variant of the same argument.

Comment (i) to section 402A of the *Restatement (2nd) of Torts* differentiates those products which are by

their very nature unsafe but not defective from those which can truly be called defective. Comment (i) states:

> Good whiskey is not unreasonably dangerous merely because it will make some people drunk, and is especially dangerous to alcoholics; but bad whiskey, containing a dangerous amount of fuel oil, is unreasonably dangerous. Good tobacco is not unreasonably dangerous merely because the effects of smoking may be harmful; but tobacco containing something like marijuana may be unreasonably dangerous. Good butter is not unreasonably dangerous merely because, if such be the case, it deposits cholesterol in the arteries and leads to heart attacks; but bad butter, contaminated with poisonous fish oil, is unreasonably dangerous.

Defendant argues that similarly good peanut butter is not unreasonably dangerous because a young child may choke on it. Defendant then prematurely ends its analysis. However, comment (j) goes on to explain why good whiskey and good butter; and by inference, good tobacco; although "unsafe" are not defective, even without a warning of their dangers.

> . . . a seller is not required to warn with respect to products, or ingredients in them, which are only dangerous, or potentially so, when consumed in excessive quantity, or over a long period of time, when the danger, or potentiality of danger, is generally known and recognized. Again the dangers of alcoholic beverages are an example, as are also those of foods containing such substances as saturated fats, which may over a period of time have a deleterious effect upon the human heart.

That is, because these "unsafe" products present known dangers no warning is required. Therefore, although "unsafe," they are not defective.

Again the Court cannot say as a matter of law that the danger of a sixteen month old choking on a peanut butter sandwich is generally known and recognized so that admittedly good peanut butter, without warning of such a danger, is not unreasonably dangerous.

Emotional Injuries

Generally, the courts have not been willing to permit people to recover mere mental injuries. There is a trend, however, for more and more courts to permit recovery for their emotional injuries—a point discussed in the following case.

Sease v. Taylor's Pets, Inc.
Court of Appeals of Oregon
700 P.2d 1054 (1985)

The defendants appeal judgments of twenty thousand dollars for plaintiffs Nora Thayer, Paula Hill, and Bradford Hill in a products liability action. On June 21, 1979, Janice Sease bought a pet skunk from defendant, Perfected Pets, Inc., a pet shop in Portland, Oregon. It had purchased the skunk from defendant Taylor's Pets, Inc. Nine or ten days after Janice bought the skunk, it began to attack and bite people, lose fur, and develop sores on its body. It bit Paula Hill. Although it did not bite Nora Thayer, she handled it, fed it, and came in contact with its saliva. The skunk did not bite Brad Hill either, but he came in contact with its saliva when he had open cuts and scratches on his arms. The skunk also bit Janice Sease.

The skunk died, and Janice took it to a veterinarian for an autopsy. The veterinarian told her the skunk was rabid. A doctor from the Oregon State Health Division ordered rabies treatments for Nora and Paula and others whom the skunk had bitten or who had been exposed to its saliva. Brad's physician concluded that because of his history and allergies, the rabies injections could cause anaphylactic shock of death and advised against them. Brad did not take the injections. Both Paula and Nora were aware that their lives were in danger even after taking the treatments. None of the plaintiffs contracted rabies.

Newman, Judge

As to the right to recover for emotional distress in a strict products liability action, ORS 30.920 provides:

> One who sells or leases any product in a defective condition unreasonably dangerous to the user or consumer or to his property is subject to liability for *physical harm* or damage to property caused by that condition. . . . ORS 30.920(1). (Emphasis supplied.)

Defendants concede that Nora, whom the rabid skunk bit, and Paula, who was also in contact with the skunk's saliva, did suffer "physical harm," because they received the rabies injections. Defendants argue, however, that Brad did not suffer physical harm, because he did not take the injections and did not suffer illness or death from contact with the skunk's saliva. They argue that the evidence shows only that he suffered anxiety because he knew that he might develop rabies. They assert that the court should have directed a verdict against Brad and should have granted judgment notwithstanding the verdict, because he suffered no "physical harm." We agree.

Although we reject the Illinois rule that a live animal is not a product, we find helpful two cases from Illinois bearing on the recovery of damages for emotional distress in an action for strict products liability. In *Woodill v. Parke Davis & Co.*, the plaintiffs sought damages based on strict products liability for injuries to their son, and for their emotional distress because of his injuries, which they alleged resulted from the administration of a prescription drug to the mother while she was pregnant. The Appellate Court affirmed the dismissal of the count for plaintiffs' emotional distress, stating:

> [W]e do not believe that strict liability should be extended to include recovery for emotional distress and mental anguish to the parents of a minor who had suffered injury. First, because section 402A of the *Restatement* expressly limits recovery to physical harm. That section is entitled "Special Liability of Seller of Product for *Physical Harm* to User or Consumer" (emphasis added), and it provides that "[o]ne who sells any product in a defective condition unreasonably dangerous to user or consumer or to his property is subject to liability for physical harm thereby caused to the ultimate user or consumer. . . ." (emphasis added). Given the limitation underlined above in section 402A, we conclude that the *Restatement* did not intend a strict liability action for mental anguish or emotional distress. Furthermore, at present, Illinois recognizes no such action. Case law here allows a cause of action only for severe emotional distress caused by intentional conduct.

In *Mink v. University of Chicago*, the court relied on section 402A as stating the law of Illinois. It held that women who had been subjected to an increased risk of cancer by administration of DES without their knowledge had failed to state a claim for strict products liability:

> [O]ne of the essential elements in a claim for strict liability is physical injury to the plaintiff. The closest the complaint comes to alleging physical injury is the allegation of a "risk" of cancer. The mere fact of a risk without any accompanying physical injury is insufficient to state a claim for strict products liability. Likewise, the plaintiffs may not rely on injury to their children to state a claim for relief for themselves, even though they allege mental anxiety and emotional distress as a consequence of the injury to their children.

Here, Brad's exposure to and contact with the rabid skunk increased the risk that he would suffer physical harm. He did not, however, suffer physical harm. Accordingly, we reverse the judgment for Brad Hill.

In other cases, the courts have permitted plaintiffs to recover even though they did not sustain a physical injury. The *Sease* case represents the traditional view followed by courts with respect to this issue.

Developments in Products Liability Law

As indicated earlier, the courts assumed when they adopted strict liability in tort as a theory of recovery that businesses would be able to protect themselves from suits by purchasing liability insurance. However, because the insurance industry lacked information on its risk exposure under this theory of recovery, insurance companies responded to the adoption of strict liability in tort in the late 1970s by drastically raising their insurance rates, limiting coverage, and in some cases refusing to sell insurance to certain businesses. The response created a products liability crisis as many manufacturers found themselves paying astronomical increases in premiums. This trend continued as courts awarded large judgments to people in America on the basis of strict liability in tort. Throughout the 1970s and 1980s many courts expanded the ability of people to sue by accepting new arguments posed by injured parties. The Market Share Liability box illustrates one such innovative argument.

Some companies, particularly small ones, found themselves unable to purchase an adequate amount of insurance to protect themselves from potential suits. Many of these businesses closed their doors.

Other companies closed their doors because the large number of strict-liability-in-tort suits filed against them overwhelmed the businesses. Many companies that sold highly dangerous products, such as asbestos, found refuge in the federal bankruptcy laws. The Johns Manville Corporation, a seller of asbestos, in 1982 filed a bankruptcy petition to reorganize the company. So many people filed

Market Share Liability

Abbott Laboratories, as well as a number of other drug companies, many years ago manufactured the synthetic drug, DES. DES was administered to mothers who were pregnant for the purposes of preventing miscarriages. At the time of the administration of the drug it was unknown, but it was later discovered, that the drug might cause cancerous vaginal and cervical growths in the daughters exposed to it before birth. In recent years, a number of women have in fact developed cancer. They want to recover but are unable to prove which company manufactured the drug that injured them.

In the seminal case, *Sindell* v. *Abbott Laboratories*, 607 P.2d 924 (California Supreme Court, 1980), the court decided that each manufacturer's liability would approximate its responsibility for the injuries caused by its own products. This has since been referred to as market share liability. A number of courts, but not all courts, have adopted this as a theory of recovery when the plaintiff is unable to identify which company manufactured the product that injured him or her. In the states that have adopted this theory of recovery, it is much easier for an injured party to establish a case, and thus the possibility of recovering for injuries is much higher than in states that have not adopted this theory of recovery.

personal injury suits against Johns Manville that it needed to resort to the protection of the bankruptcy laws to stay in business. When a company produces a product that injures a large number of persons, it may be faced with a situation in which the claims of all of the plaintiffs exceed the total assets of the company. In such a case, the courts need a system to divide up the available assets of the company in an orderly manner. Bankruptcy laws allow a company to set aside a pool of money to be divided up among all those injured by a company's products.

The vast number of suits filed by plaintiffs generated a lot of activity by business. For years, manufacturers lobbied Congress to adopt a federal law of products liability that would preempt all state laws—thus making products liability law uniform throughout the United States. Such lobbying efforts failed because the bills proposed by industry sought to eliminate strict liability in tort as a theory of recovery. Manufacturers tried to get Congress to return the law in the United States to a negligence theory of recovery. The effort generated widespread opposition by consumer groups and plaintiff's lawyers.

Business groups also attempted to attack the contingency fee system of paying plaintiff's lawyers. Plaintiffs' attorneys share in the award or settlement obtained by the injured parties. Sometimes the attorneys receive as much as the injured party receives—or more! Industry argues that the contingency fee system encourages litigation. Businesses argue that allowing only billing on an hourly basis for services might reduce the number of suits that attorneys file. Needless to say, the bar rejects the abolition of the contingency fee system.

On other fronts, industry prevailed over the bar. Some states adopted legislation that makes it more difficult for injured persons to recover. For example, some states prohibited suits arising from the failure of products over ten years old. Other states placed limits on the amount of punitive damages a plaintiff may recover.

Industry also responded to the flood of suits by ceasing production of certain products—or by reducing the number of changes in existing products. Does a decline in innovations in products serve the best interests of the country? At one time, many sellers manufactured football helmets. Because of the number and size of the verdicts, the law whittled down the number of football helmet manufacturers to just a handful, while at the same time the price of helmets soared. At one time, many drug companies manufactured whooping cough vaccine. Today, only one firm manufactures this product.

Many firms follow a better and more successful approach to dealing with the onslaught of suits. Suits arise because sellers fail to properly design, manufacture, assemble, test, or inspect their products. Astute companies today work to correct these problems by getting everyone involved in producing high-quality products. This involves eliminating design errors, selecting better raw materials, reducing assembly line errors, increasing the testing of products, and improving warnings. When bad products reach the market, their manufacturers act faster to correct the defects in the products. They try to get everyone involved who can reduce the risk of producing bad products. To some extent, therefore, products liability law has forced industry in a very positive direction. It has forced companies to produce better products.

Unavoidably Unsafe Products
Johnson v. *American Cyanamid Company*, 718 P.2d 1318 (1986)

Emil Johnson brought suit against American Cyanimid Company. His physician vaccinated his infant daughter with Orimune, an oral polio vaccine manufactured by Lederle Laboratories, a division of American Cyanamid. She thereafter contracted poliomyelitis. This type of injury will occur on an extremely infrequent, but predictable, ratio known to the manufacturer. This risk cannot be eliminated. The court found that Orimune is an unavoidably unsafe product which is socially useful in spite of the dangers associated with its use. Public policy requires that the manufacturer not be held responsible on the ground of design defect. The court also found the warning given in this case to be adequate.

By the late 1980s, the courts began to respond to the widespread outcry over higher insurance rates, failures of companies, withdrawals of products from the market, and a slowdown in product innovations. Some courts have become more receptive to defenses asserted by the seller. The Unavoidably Unsafe Products box presents an example.

When a manufacturer does a good job designing and assembling products and warning users, many courts and legislatures are willing to accept the manufacturer's argument that it should not be liable to the plaintiff for his or her injuries. Even so, in light of the tremendous number of settlements and verdicts against companies, the best long-term strategy for a company is to continue to make very possible effort to ensure that it produces the highest quality, best designed products. These products need to be accompanied by clearly written, easily understood instructions that warn persons coming into contact with the products how to use them.

SUMMARY

Over the last hundred years or so, the courts and the legislatures have expanded the theories of liability in the products liability field. They have gradually made it easier and easier for an injured person to recover for any injuries he or she has sustained as a result of coming into contact with a product. At one time, it was virtually impossible for a person injured by a product to sue at all unless he or she actually purchased the product in question. Furthermore, the injured person could sue only the business that actually sold the product. As a result, it was extremely difficult to sue anyone other than retail sellers. Today, it is possible to sue virtually anyone in the distributive chain. Furthermore, a person does not have to be the purchaser of a product in order to sue.

For many years, plaintiffs had to establish their cases by relying upon negligence as a theory of recovery. This was not a totally satisfactory theory of recovery from the plaintiff's standpoint because he or she needed to establish that the defendant was in fact negligent. As time passed, some people began to bring suit on the basis of breach of warranty as a theory of recovery. More recently, the courts and state legislatures have permitted injured parties to sue according to the concept of strict liability in tort or misrepresentation. If a plaintiff can prove that he or she was personally injured as a result of a misrepresentation by the defendant of the character or quality of its product, the plaintiff may recover damages on the basis of misrepresentation. A business that sells a product in a defective condition unreasonably dangerous to people can be sued for any personal injuries caused by the defective product. This is true even if the seller exercised all possible care in the preparation and sale of the product.

Suits by consumers have encouraged sellers to take more care in making certain that their products are safe.

REVIEW QUESTIONS

1. Define the following terms:
   a. Innocent misrepresentation
   b. Privity of contract
   c. Strict liability

2. List the theories under which a manufacturer or seller of personal property may have liability to one injured by a product and explain each theory.

3. Plaintiff was riding as a passenger in the front seat of a 1956 model Ford automobile owned and operated by Clarence Dailey. Plaintiff had dropped a lighted cigarette, and as he was attempting to retrieve it from the floor of the vehicle, with his head down, the brakes of the automobile were applied suddenly and with great force, throwing the plaintiff forward and causing his face to come into contact with the dashboard. (Dailey, the driver, had applied the brakes to avoid a collision with another automobile that had pulled out in front of his car.) Immediately following the plaintiff's contact with the dashboard, he realized that his right eye had been seriously injured.

   The Ford automobile was equipped with an ashtray, which was located in the center of the dashboard. This tray was found on the floor of the vehicle after plaintiff was in-

jured. After taking plaintiff to the hospital, Dailey examined the ashtray and for the first time discovered a "jagged" edge on the top right-hand front corner. This sharp edge is the defect upon which plaintiff predicates his case. Is the defendant, Ford Motor Company, which designed and manufactured the automobile containing the allegedly defective ashtray, liable?

4. Defendants manufacture and sell the Golfing Gizmo, a training device designed to aid unskilled golfers in improving their games. In 1966, Louise Hauter purchased a Gizmo and gave it to Fred Hauter, her thirteen-and-a-half-year-old son, as a Christmas present. On July 14, 1967, Fred was seriously injured while using defendant's product when the ball flew back and struck him sharply on the forehead.

   The label on the shipping carton and the cover of the instruction booklet urged players to "drive ball with full power" and further stated: "Completely Safe Ball Will Not Hit Player." This is the statement that plaintiffs sued upon, alleging false representation. Should plaintiffs recover on the basis of a misrepresentation theory of recovery?

5. A suit by decedent's (that is, the deceased's)

family alleged that the manufacturer of a bulldozer was liable in negligence and strict liability in tort for the defective design of the machine. When decedent was struck, the bulldozer was in the process of reversing to position itself to move forward to spread and tamp down fill; decedent was behind the bulldozer directing dump trucks in depositing fill that was to be spread and tamped by the bulldozer at the later time. Before backing up, the operator of the bulldozer, who had not observed decedent for about five minutes, looked to the rear to ascertain if it was clear, but he did not see decedent, who was standing thirty to forty feet behind the vehicle. The operator testified that there was a substantial blind spot to the rear of the bulldozer because of its design. The bulldozer had no rearview mirrors and no audible or visible backup warning signal. Is the manufacturer liable for its failure to include these design features?

6. Martin applied Ben-Gay to his chest because he was suffering from a cold. When he attempted to light a cigarette, the match head fell off and struck his chest. This caused the Ben-Gay to catch on fire. Martin was severely burned. Nowhere on the package did the company warn Ben-Gay was flammable. Is the company liable to Martin for his injuries?

7. When Ford produced the 1966 Ford Fairlane, it used a flange-mounted gasoline tank rather than a strap-mounted tank. The top of the flange-mounted tank served as the floor of the trunk. The only shield separating the trunk compartment from the passenger compartment was a fiberboard panel and the rear seat padding. Neither of these materials significantly limits the passage of fire. The cost of placing a shield between the passenger compartment and the fuel-containing system would only be one dollar plus one-half hour of labor time. Buehler was involved in a rear-end collision in which he was seriously injured. Had such a shield been in place, it would have substantially reduced the risk of injury to Buehler by having provided him additional time to escape from the accident. Should Ford be held liable to Buehler under the strict liability in tort theory of recovery?

8. Selectone is the manufacturer of mobile pagers, which it had promoted as being suitable for use by police agencies. Hollenbeck, a police officer, used his Selectone mobile pager to obtain assistance during an arrest. The pager failed to activate, and Hollenbeck was severely injured by the family of the person he was attempting to arrest. Hollenbeck brought suit on the basis of misrepresentation as a theory of recovery. Selectone argued that the assault by the family members was an intervening criminal act that broke the causal connection between the product and the injury. Is Selectone correct?

9. Lamb was eating an oven-roasted chicken that her daughter had prepared. She accidentally swallowed the pop-up thermometer inserted in the chicken by the supplier which indicated when the chicken was properly cooked. Lamb brought suit on the theory that the thermometer was dangerous because it could be inadvertently ingested, that the arrowlike points at its ends made it prone to being caught in the intestine if swallowed, and that the defendant had neither tested the thermometer for safety nor issued warnings concerning the danger of ingestion. Will the plaintiff prevail?

10. Woodworth was copiloting a Learjet. He was killed when a loon flew through the jet's windshield. Woodworth's family alleged that the windshield should have been designed to resist bird impact. Learjet argued that windshields should not have to withstand the impact of the 11.5-pound loon. Who should win?

11. Maybelline is the manufacturer of cosmetic products. Walker was applying Maybelline mascara and accidentally scratched the cornea of her left eye with the applicator brush.

Walker eventually became blind in her eye as a result of an infection from the defendant's mascara.

Maybelline knew that scratching of the eye surface with a mascara brush posed a danger of infection by the bacteria present in the mascara. Maybelline placed the following warning on the back side of the card that went with the mascara: "Note: In case of eye irritations or infections or scratches, do not use this or any eye cosmetic. Consult a physician at once." Does this constitute an adequate warning by Maybelline?

12. Cox brought a products liability suit. He alleged that he developed asbestosis as a result of exposure to Eagle-Picher's asbestos products. At trial, Cox was permitted to show that having asbestosis increased his risk of contracting lung cancer. He sought damages for present emotional distress caused by his fear of developing cancer and damages for the risk of developing cancer in the future. Will he be able to recover on either of these theories?

13. Hurley injured his right leg during a skiing lesson. The ski school program was designed to teach beginners to ski. While he was attempting to get up on the skis, the wooden tow handle that he was holding snapped and struck his leg. Hurley sued Larry's Water Ski School for breach of the implied warranty of fitness for a particular purpose. Is Larry's liable?

14. Winter purchased the book *The Encyclopedia of Mushrooms*. The book contained erroneous and misleading information. After consuming several mushrooms, Winter became seriously ill and subsequently required a liver transplant. Winter argued that under the innocent misrepresentation theory of recovery the publisher should be held liable for his injuries. Is Winter correct?

15. The Boy Scouts of America—now called Scouting, U.S.A.—published a sixteen page supplement to the September 1988 edition of *Boy's Life* magazine. This material dealt with shooting and firearms. The National Shooting Foundation and Remington Arms Company, Inc., among others, sponsored the supplement in *Boy's Life*.

Rocky Miller, a twelve-year-old boy, and several other youthful companions read the supplemental edition, and in particular, the Remington Arms Company advertisement. Thereafter, the boys located an old gun and a .22 cartridge. On November 19, 1988, while examining the rifle, Rocky accidentally shot himself. He died from the gunshot. Should either Scouting, U.S.A. or Remington be held liable based on innocent misrepresentation?

CHAPTER 17

Consumer Law

- Consumer Law and Business Behavior
- The Consumer As Buyer
- The Consumer As Borrower

Freedom of contract is a basic principle of American business and the common law. Parties are said to bargain over various terms for the purchase of a product or the borrowing of funds. The resulting agreement reflects their individual needs and choices. The courts would enforce that contract, on the basis of freedom-of-contract theory, with few exceptions.

Recent trends in society have emphasized concerns over contract fairness. The freedom to bargain may be illusory if one of the parties to the contract had little power to bargain or was confronted with a transaction of such complexity that it could not be understood. As a result, numerous legislative and regulatory changes in basic contract law occurred that were aimed at alleviating this problem.

CONSUMER LAW AND BUSINESS BEHAVIOR

Most businesses deal with **consumers**; thus, businesspeople need to be alert to the restrictions placed on them by law when dealing with consumers. The law generally holds businesspeople to a higher standard of behavior when dealing with consumers. The courts and legislatures assume that people in business know the law and know how to protect themselves. In order to protect consumers from abusive practices, the law places many restrictions on businesses when they deal with consumers.

President Kennedy ushered in the most recent wave of consumer legislation when in 1962 his consumer bill of rights stated that consumers had the right to better protection. Ralph Nader, a consumer activist, also encouraged the growth of the consumer movement. His book on the Chevrolet Corvair, entitled *Unsafe at Any Speed*, sharply criticized General Motors for its indifference to consumer safety. From these two seeds grew an enormous movement that spanned the 1960s and 1970s. Throughout this period many persons worked for the passage of legislation to protect consumers, civil rights, the environment, and workers. A great deal of the material discussed in this book resulted from the activities of these people. The consumer movement resulted in a host of federal and state laws that greatly increased the complexity of doing business in America.

As an illustration of the changes that took place in the lending industry, consider a typical lender. Suppose that International Lenders wants to loan out money to customers at the highest possible rate of interest. International also wishes to make certain its borrowers repay their loans in a timely fashion; thus, it wants to lend to reliable borrowers. To further protect itself, International wants to secure repayment of its loans with property owned by the borrowers. To the extent market conditions force it to lend to less creditworthy borrowers, the firm probably will attempt to charge more for its loans. Prior to the enactment of the laws discussed in this chapter, a company such as International exercised considerable discretion in structuring its actions.

Some lenders abused this discretion by making it difficult for creditworthy people to obtain credit. These lenders denied credit to certain persons who they believed posed a higher risk to them. However, widely held views in society influenced the perceptions of lenders concerning risk. This illustrates the interrelationship of widely held beliefs in society and business behavior.

For example, lenders tended to stereotype women. Most lenders assumed that typical women wanted to stay at home rather than to continue to work throughout their lives. Thus, lenders viewed women as only temporarily in the workforce until they got married or had babies. Because many lenders operated on this assumption, they refused to consider the income of working women in deciding whether or not to make loans.

Industry beliefs failed to track the pervasive changes taking place in American society during the early 1970s. Many women entered the workforce in the early 1970s with the intention of remaining permanently employed. Such stereotypical beliefs on the part of lenders probably never coincided with the actual behavior of the majority of women. Throughout the history of this nation, millions of women have worked their entire lives. Even so, lenders continued to refuse to recognize this fact. They treated women stereotypically and refused to recognize their incomes in deciding whether to grant loans or not.

Congress responded with the Equal Credit Opportunity Act, discussed below. This act, along with much of the other legislation dealt with in this chapter, was passed because industry failed to adopt practices consistent with the needs and wants of the general public.

This suggests an important rule for business: It behooves businesspeople to act in a socially responsible manner, if for no other reason than to prevent the courts and legislatures from taking actions adverse to the interests of business in America. If businesses act irresponsibility, Congress and the state legislatures may feel compelled to pass additional laws to protect the public from its own lack of knowledge.

Businesses also need to recognize the fact that a judge who witnesses a constant procession of consumers complaining about unfair treatment by business very likely may attempt to interpret the law strictly—against business. This has happened with respect to the courts' interpretation of the Truth-In-Lending Act, discussed later in this chapter. Very minor technical violations of the act sometimes result in judgments against lenders.

Such government restraints on action imposed costs on doing business. Valuable worker time must be devoted to complying with government rules; thus, businesses become less efficient and less productive. This increase in legislation left many managers complaining of the frustration associated with their jobs. They suddenly had to devote an inordinate amount of their time, not to manufacturing and selling goods and services, but to answering to federal, state, and local government officials. Furthermore, the very cost of operating the government increased. More laws and regulations take more employees to administer.

Because of the adverse effect of government regulations on business, businesses tended to resist the consumer movement in the 1960s and 1970s. As businesspeople witnessed Congress passing more and more consumer legislation throughout this period, industry gradually mobilized itself to try to stop the tide of consumer legislation and to reduce the complexity of these regulations. Industry worked to get people elected to government who had a more favorable attitude with respect to business. It put pressure on Congress to reign in the activities of such agencies as the Federal Trade Commission.

At the same time, because the states and the federal government enacted so much legislation, by the early 1980s the law finally addressed the most pressing needs of the public. Support for consumer protection probably peaked in the early 1980s. Throughout the 1980s Congress passed very few laws and regulations, and consumer attention shifted to other pressing problems.

THE CONSUMER AS BUYER

Deceptive and Unfair Trade Practices

The marketing and sales efforts of a large company often generate considerable public comment. These facets of a company's operations are the most visible to the general public—few persons escape hearing or seeing advertising every day. Other operations within a company, such as accounting, never come to the attention of the average American consumer. For this reason, unfair and deceptive sales practices of any company very likely will not escape the attention of the general public or government regulators.

As is noted in Chapters 23 and 24 on antitrust law, the Federal Trade Commission was created to help strengthen the enforcement of the antitrust laws and to help further fair competition. The FTC interpreted its mission to also encompass the protection of consumers. In 1938, with the passage of the Wheeler-Lea amendment to the Federal Trade Commission Act, Congress expanded the language of the original act from "unfair methods of competition" to include "unfair and deceptive acts." Congress wanted the FTC to protect not only competition, but consumers as well, by prohibiting unfair and deceptive practices by business.

Over the years, the FTC has vigorously enforced this rather vague language prohibiting unfair and deceptive acts. The FTC prohibits the use of deceptive price advertising. For example, advertisers must exercise great caution when advertising a free product. Suppose Burger Company used the following promotion: "Buy one burger, get the second burger free." The day before, Burger

Company had doubled the price of its burgers. Such a course of action clearly is deceptive. Likewise, the FTC has found television advertising that fails to disclose the use of mock-ups in place of the real object to be deceptive. In a case involving a television commercial that stated a given brand of shaving cream could shave sandpaper, the FTC found the advertising to be deceptive. The advertiser failed to discose to viewers that what appeared on television to be sandpaper covered with shaving cream was in fact merely sand on glass covered with shaving cream.

In order to correct the false impression left by deceptive advertising, the FTC developed the corrective advertising remedy. This remedy requires a company to place advertisements that attempt to correct the false impression created by earlier deceptive advertising.

Not only does the Federal Trade Commission Act prohibit unfair and deceptive acts, but many states also prohibit such practices by statute. In addition, competitors may seek to have deceptive advertising curtailed.

Figure 17.1 shows the structure of the Federal Trade Commission.

Federal Warranty Act

Studies in the late 1960s concluded that written warranties on consumer products were often unfair. They were difficult to understand, and consumers were confused concerning the amount of protection the warranties provided. Sometimes the warranties were so limited in scope that they provided less protection than if no warranty had been given at all. Nonetheless, these written warranties were advertised as providing protection or guarantees for buyers. The Magnuson-Moss Warranty–Federal Trade Commission Improvement Act created special rules relating to written warranties on consumer products. The act defines a consumer product as "any tangible personal property which is distributed in commerce and which is normally used for personal, family or household purposes." For example, if John Doe purchases a stereo for his home, any written warranty relating to this purchase must comply with the Magnuson-Moss Act.

The purpose of the act was to provide purchasers of consumer products with knowledge of the terms of a written warranty before purchase in language comprehensible to the average consumer. Oral warranties are not covered by the act. The act does not require sellers to provide a written warranty, and a seller who wishes to avoid the provisions of this act may simply not provide one with its products. The act also does not prevent a seller from limiting the duration of an express warranty.

When a written warranty is given on a consumer product that costs more than ten dollars, the warranty must be clearly and conspicuously designated a **full warranty** or a **limited warranty**. Congress wished to make it easy for purchasers to differentiate between the types of warranties offered by companies. If a product has a written full warranty, it must provide at least the following:

1. Any defects, malfunctions, or inability to conform to the terms of a written warranty must be corrected by the warrantor without charge and within a reasonable length of time.

A Defective Transmission and the Magnuson-Moss Warranty Act

In 1977, Arlie Skelton purchased a new Oldsmobile Delta 88. When the transmission did not seem to work properly, he returned to the dealer who told him the transmission was fine and to keep driving the car. When the transmission broke, after the warranty expired, Skelton went to a mechanic, who charged him five hundred dollars but could not assure Skelton that the transmission would last for another six months. The mechanic explained that the transmission in Skelton's car was too small. It was designed for small General Motors' cars, such as the Chevrolet Chevette, rather than the full-size models, such as Skelton's Delta 88.

Skelton attempted to resolve this problem, without success, through the dealer, where he had purchased eight or nine other cars, and through representatives of General Motors. Finally, in 1979, he filed a lawsuit against GM under the Magnuson-Moss Warranty Act. This suit evolved into a class action with thousands of plaintiffs having the same complaint against GM and is considered one of the largest suits ever filed under the Magnuson-Moss consumer protection statute.

In February 1987, the suit was settled, with General Motors agreeing to place $19.5 million in an escrow account to be used to reimburse car owners for transmission repairs. The lawsuit contended that as many as 4.7 million cars could be involved. General Motors also agreed to contact present or former car owners about the defective transmissions and the settlement.

2. The warrantor cannot limit the period within which implied warranties will be effective with respect to the consumer product.

3. The warrantor cannot limit or exclude consequential damages in a consumer product unless noted conspicuously on the face of the warranty.

4. The warrantor must allow the consumer to choose between a refund of the purchase price or replacement of the defective product or part whenever a reasonable number of attempts to remedy the defect or malfunction have occurred.

A limited warranty is any warranty that does not give the consumer these guarantees. Such a product warranty must be conspicuously labeled as limited. Figure 17.2 is an example.

The act excuses a seller if it demonstrates that the defect, malfunction, or failure of the product resulted from consumer misuse.

Door-to-Door Sales

Buyers seem most vulnerable to sales pitches at home because they do not expect to be purchasing products in this setting. Some sellers exert enormous pressure on consumers at home in order to convince them to buy. Frequently, the consumer regrets the purchase.

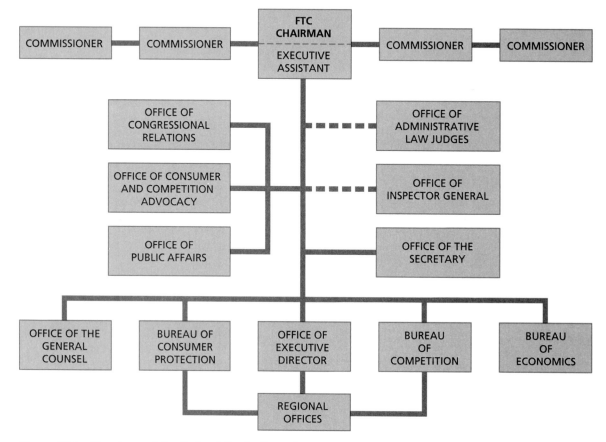

Figure 17.1   Structure of the Federal Trade Commission
Source: The United States Government Manual 1991/92, Washington, DC: U.S. Government Printing Office, 1991.

A Federal Trade Commission rule regulates door-to-door sales. It states that contracts used by such companies must conspicuously disclose that the buyer has a right to cancel the contract any time before midnight of the third business day after the contract date. The product purchased must cost twenty-five dollars or more for the rule to apply. The rule does not cover sales of real estate, insurance, or securities, or sales for emergency home repairs.

If a person elects to cancel a contract within the three-day period, the merchant must within ten days cancel the order and return any papers signed by the buyer, refund any money paid, inform the buyer whether any product left will be picked up, and return any trade-in. Within twenty days, the merchant must either pick up the items left with the buyer or pay any shipping expenses necessary for the buyer to ship the goods back if the buyer agrees to ship them back.

While the rule applies to door-to-door sales, the scope of the rule is broader than one might think. It applies not only to sales made at a person's home but to any sale made at some place other than the seller's normal place of business. In other words, the rule is also designed to cover sales made by companies using party plans. Suppose Melinda's neighbor, Alice, invites Melinda to her home for a

LIMITED WARRANTY

Touch Control by Moen products have been manufactured under the highest standards of quality and workmanship. We warrant to the **consumer** all parts of your Touch Control by Moen products against defects in material and workmanship for TEN (10) YEARS from date of purchase. Any defective part will be replaced FREE OF CHARGE, excluding labor or service charges. We will not be responsible for any product damage due to installation error, product abuse, or product misuse whether performed by a contractor, service company, or yourself. Use of other than genuine Moen factory parts may void this warranty.

This warranty applies **only to the consumer use** of the product and any inquiries regarding warranty claims are to be directed to:

Stanadyne/Moen Division
377 Woodland Avenue
Elyria, Ohio 44036.

This warranty gives you specific legal rights and you may also have other rights which vary from state to state.

Figure 17.2   Sample Limited Warranty

party with some other neighbors. At the party, Alice demonstrates and sells some dishware to the women. This transaction is a door-to-door sale even though it took place at Alice's home rather than Melinda's.

THE CONSUMER AS BORROWER

In today's economic environment, borrowing money has become common for both consumers and businesses. The average consumer finances the purchase of a home, a car, clothing, and many other items.

People desiring to finance the purchase of products have a variety of sources from which to acquire credit. A borrower may go to a bank or credit union to finance the purchase of an automobile. A person who lacks an established credit record may choose to borrow money from a finance company. Many stores provide financing for the purchase of products. For higher-priced purchases, the retailer may sell the instrument signed by the debtor to a finance company or bank. Alternatively, the buyer may use a credit card.

A credit card purchase is an example of **open-end credit**. Under an open-end credit plan, the consumer is permitted to make periodic charges up to a certain credit limit, and may pay the balance owed either in full or in installments. The finance charge is computed on the basis of the outstanding balance on the account at the time of billing.

On the other hand, if a person borrows one thousand dollars from the bank and agrees to repay it in twelve months, this type of financing is called **closed-end credit**. In such a situation, a specific sum is borrowed, which will be repaid over a particular period of time, with a certain number of payments to be made at certain designated times.

Truth in Lending

In 1969, Congress passed the Consumer Credit Protection Act, one section of which is commonly referred to as the **Truth-in-Lending Act**. The purpose of the act was to enable consumers to make meaningful comparisons among the rates charged by different lenders. Before this time, lenders expressed the amount charged for the use of money in different manners, which made a comparison of rates difficult. The Truth-in-Lending Act acts as a full disclosure mechanism for consumer borrowers. The theory of the act was that if the borrower had information about various loan offers, comparisons could be made and lenders would have to compete on terms and conditions of the consumer loans. However, in practice, accomplishing that goal proved elusive.

Creditors had difficulty complying with the act. In 1980, one study noted that eighty percent of the banks were in violation. The problem was in the act's complexity and numerous judicial and administrative interpretations. Between 1969 and 1980, over fifteen hundred administrative regulations and interpretations were issued. Furthermore, most litigation involved very technical violations of the act. Note that the act provided for attorney's fees and statutory damages irrespective of actual damages that were incurred by the debtor. Often these technical violations were raised as defenses by debtors sued for nonpayment. For example, in one case, a bank creditor sued a debtor for nonpayment of a seven-hundred-and-fifty-dollar loan. The debtor counterclaimed with both federal and state truth-in-lending contentions. Both were based on the same disclosure error. The court found that the error did occur and awarded statutory damages to the debtor under both acts, totaling approximately four thousand dollars.

By the late 1970s, it was clear that the act needed revision. Congress, in 1980, passed the Truth-in-Lending Simplification and Reform Act. Its purpose was to reduce the number of required disclosures and make compliance easier. Model forms were provided that, if used, would guarantee compliance. Figure 17.3 is a typical Truth in Lending Disclosure Statement.

Finance Charge and Annual Percentage Rate

Two very important figures must be provided to borrowers—the finance charge and the annual percentage rate (APR). These figures make the comparison of borrowing costs relatively simple. The finance charge is the total dollar amount the borrower pays to use credit. It includes interest costs and such other costs as service charges and appraisal fees. The annual percentage rate is the percentage cost of the credit on a yearly basis.

FEDERAL TRUTH-IN-LENDING DISCLOSURE STATEMENTS

APPLICATION#:
LOAN#:

Borrowers

John Doe
1500 Main Street
Anywhere, U.S.A.

Property

1500 Main Street
Anywhere, U.S.A.

Itemization of Amount Financed

$	Total amount financed	$
$	TAX SERVICE FEE	
$	Interim Interest	
$	MI Premium	
$	MI Renewal Reserves	
$	Total Prepaid finance charges	$
$	1992 COUNTY TAXES	
$	Appraisal fee	
$	Credit report	
$	Hazard insurance reserves	
$	County tax reserves	
$	Settlement or closing fee	
$	Document preparation	
$	Title insurance	
$	Recording fees	
$	State tax/stamps	
$	SEPTIC INSPECTION	
$	Proc/Underwriting Fee	
$	Total amount paid to others	
	LOAN AMOUNT	$

THE FIRST PAYMENT
FOR YOUR ADVANCE 7/23

FOR: $200,000
AT: 7.65%

WHICH WILL PAY OFF IN 84 PAYMENTS

IS BROKEN DOWN AS FOLLOWS:

PRINCIPAL &/OR INTEREST $

Mortgage Insurance

Taxes

Insurance

Other

TOTAL OF PAYMENT $

ANNUAL PERCENTAGE RATE	FINANCE CHARGE	Amount Financed	Total of Payments
The cost of your credit as a yearly rate.	The dollar amount the credit will cost you. $	The amount of credit provided to you or on your behalf.	The amount you will have paid after you have made all payments as scheduled.

Your Payment Schedule Will Be:

THIS LOAN MUST EITHER BE PAID IN FULL AT MATURITY OF MODIFIED TO A MARKET LEVEL FIXED RATE OVER THE REMAINING 30 YEAR TERM. YOU MUST REPAY THE ENTIRE PRINCIPAL BALANCE OF THE LOAN AND UNPAID INTEREST THEN DUE IF YOU DO NOT QUALIFY FOR THE CONDITIONAL MODIFICATION AND EXTENSION FEATURE AS SPECIFIED IN THE NOTE ADDENDUM AND MORTGAGE RIDER. THE LENDER IS UNDER NO OBLIGATION TO REFINANCE THE LOAN IF QUALIFICATION CONDITIONS ARE NOT MET. YOU WILL, THEREFORE, BE REQUIRED TO MAKE PAYMENT OUT OF OTHER ASSETS YOU MAY OWN, OR YOU WILL HAVE TO FIND A LENDER, WHICH MAY BE THE LENDER YOU HAVE THIS LOAN WITH, WILLING TO LEND YOU THE MONEY. IF YOU REFINANCE THIS LOAN AT MATURITY YOU MAY HAVE TO PAY SOME OR ALL OF THE CLOSING COSTS NORMALLY ASSOCIATED WITH A NEW LENDER EVEN IF YOU OBTAIN REFINANCING FROM THE LENDER.

Security Interest: You are giving a security interest in the property located at

Late Charge: If payment is 15 days late, you will be charged 5.0000% of the payment.
Prepayment: If you pay off early, you will not have to pay a penalty.
    If you pay off early, you will not be entitled to a refund of part of the finance charge.
Assumption: Someone buying your home cannot assume the remainder of the mortgage on the original terms.
This Obligation: WILL have a demand feature.

Insurance: You may obtain property insurance from anyone you want that is acceptable to
Lender. See your contract documents for any additional information about nonpayment, default,
any required repayment in full before the scheduled date, prepayment refunds and penalties.

I (We) hereby acknowledge receiving a completed copy of this disclosure.   Date: __/__/__

DOUGLAS F. WHITMAN

Figure 17.3 Federal Truth-in-Lending Disclosure Statement

Notice to customer required by Federal law:

You have entered into a transaction on _____ which may result in a lien,
(date)
mortgage, or other security interest on your home. You have a legal right under Federal law to cancel this transaction, if you desire to do so, without any penalty or obligation within three business days from the above date or any later date on which all material disclosures required under the Truth in Lending Act have been given to you. If you so cancel the transaction, any lien, mortgage, or other security interest on your home arising from this transaction is automatcally void. You are also entitled to receive a refund of any downpayment or other consideration if you cancel. If you decide to cancel this transaction, you may do so by notifying

by mail or telegram sent not later than midnight of _____. You may also use
(date)
any other form of written notice identifying the transaction if it is delivered to the above address not later than that time. This notice may be used for that purpose by dating and signing below.

I hereby cancel this transaction.

_____   _____
(date)   (customer's signature)

See reverse side for important information about your right of rescission.

Receipt is herewith acknowledged of the foregoing NOTICE, the undersigned CUSTOMERS having received copies thereof, this the ___ day of _____, 19___.

_____   _____
Customer   Customer

Effect of rescission. When a customer exercises his right to rescind under paragraph (a) of this section, he is not liable for any finance or other charge, and any security interest becomes void upon such rescission. Within 10 days after a receipt of a notice of rescission, the creditor shall return to the customer any money or property given as earnest money, downpayment, or otherwise, and shall take any action necessary or appropriate to reflect the termination of any security interest created under the transaction. If the creditor has delivered any property to the customer, the customer may retain possession of it. Upon the performance of the creditor's obligations under this section, the customer shall tender this property to the creditor, except that if return of the property in kind would be impracticable or inequitable, the customer shall tender its reasonable value. Tender shall be made at the location of the property or at the residence of the customer, at the option of the customer. If the creditor does not take posession of the property within 10 days after tender by the customer, ownership of the property vests in the customer without obligation on his part to pay for it.

Figure 17.4 Typical Rescission Form

If a person goes to a bank for a loan, the bank must tell the customer the finance charge and the APR. One lender may agree to loan one thousand dollars for one year for a finance charge of one hundred and fifty dollars at an APR of 15 percent. If another lender agrees to loan the same one thousand dollars for one year for a finance charge of one hundred and twenty-five dollars at an APR of 12.5 percent, obviously the borrower would save money by patronizing the second lender.

Right to Cancel Contract

3 DAYS → HOME LOAN CANCLE (FROM STATEMENT) DATE

A very important right given to consumers under truth in lending is the right to cancel contracts involving loans on their homes. Section 1635 permits a consumer to rescind a transaction for three business days after entering into a contract, if the consumer uses his or her home as security for the loan. If a person elects to rescind the loan, the security interest is voided and the consumer is not liable for any finance charge. Figure 17.4 is a typical rescission form.

It should be noted that the three-day period during which a person has the right to cancel a contract does not start to run until the proper truth-in-lending disclosures are provided to the consumer. This means that even several years after a person enters into a transaction the loan still may be canceled, as the three-day period has not yet run. Suppose on January 1, 1989, Mary hires Acme Home Improvement Company to remodel her bathroom. She agrees to pay Acme five thousand dollars to perform this work. One of the papers she signs gives Acme a mortgage on her home. If the proper disclosures have been provided to Mary, she has three business days from January 1 to cancel the transaction. Suppose instead that Acme carelessly fails to provide her with certain information required by the Truth-in-Lending Act. The contractor performs the work. Mary starts paying on her note on February 1, 1989. Later in that year, she falls behind on the note and Acme starts a legal action to foreclose its mortgage. At this point, Mary may exercise her right to cancel the transaction because the three-day period has not yet begun to run. Acme, therefore, may not take her home in payment of this debt. Mary is not liable for any finance charges on this loan. Of course, she still must pay the contractor for the work it performed on her home.

FDIC v. Hughes Development Co., Inc.
United States District Court, District of Minnesota
684 F. Supp. 616 (1988)

Mr. and Mrs. Hughes took out a loan from the Guaranty State Bank of St. Paul. The Hughes gave the bank a mortgage on their home. The proceeds of the mortgage were to be used to remodel the family residence. In 1984, the Federal Deposit Insurance Corporation (FDIC) was appointed receiver of the bank's business after the bank was adjudged insolvent. Prior to the takeover of the bank by the FDIC, the Hughes sent a letter to the bank. They stated that the bank had failed to make some disclosures required by the Truth-in-Lending Act (TILA). The Hughes exercised their right to rescind and cancel the loan on their home.

The FDIC thereafter brought a foreclosure action on the mortgage executed by Mr. and Mrs. Hughes. It contended that they could not rescind the transaction because the FDIC, rather than the Guaranty State Bank, now held the mortgage. The court disagreed and ruled for the Hughes.

Doty, District Judge

The FDIC requests summary judgment on its claim for foreclosure on the Lombard loan. In response, the defendants request summary judgment dismissing FDIC's foreclosure action on the Lombard residence because Mr. Hughes effectively rescinded the Lombard Mortgage as allowed under the Truth-in-Lending Act and thereby voided FDIC's security interest in the residence.

The defendants request this Court to enforce their right to rescind a consumer loan under 15 U.S.C. § 1635. The FDIC asserts that the entire TILA is inapplicable to the FDIC because 15 U.S.C. § 1612(b) creates a statutory exemption for governmental agencies.

Because § 1612(b) clearly constitutes a statutory exemption, this Court cannot impose civil or criminal sanctions against the FDIC. The question then becomes whether rescission pursuant to § 1635 . . . constitute[s] a civil penalty.

The Fifth Circuit held that the purpose of the TILA is to enable the individual consumer to credit shop and avoid the uninformed use of credit, that the recovery under § 1635 runs to the individual and that the purpose of the rescission remedy is to restore the parties, as much as possible, to the *status quo ante*.

Under this analysis, the right to rescission under § 1635 is not a civil penalty and, therefore, is a remedy outside of the scope of § 1612(b). This conclusion is consistent with the general policy of the Act "to assure a meaningful disclosure of credit terms." There is no public policy reason for disallowing a valid rescission merely because the creditor has become insolvent and has sold the underlying note and mortgage to a governmental agency.

Lost or Stolen Credit Cards

People have only a limited liability in the event unauthorized charges appear on their credit cards. The most one can be liable for as a result of unauthorized credit card use is fifty dollars on each card. This applies only to charges made before the loss or theft of the card is reported to the credit card company. The following case illustrates the issue of determining when the use of a credit card is unauthorized.

Oclander v. First National Bank of Louisville
Court of Appeals of Kentucky
700 S.W.2d 804 (1985)

Monica Oclander and Bonifacio Aparicio opened a MasterCard account on October 20, 1981. In July 1982, Monica notified the bank that she was separated from

Bonifacio. The bank "blocked" the account from additional charges. It informed Monica how to restore her credit. She returned the forms sent to her by the bank. Monica informed the bank that she had destroyed the credit card issued to Bonifacio and she had retained the other card. On the basis of this representation, the bank unblocked her account. Bonifacio, who in fact still held a credit card, thereafter charged $11,319.43 to the account while traveling in Spain. Monica argued that she was not responsible for the charges because they were unauthorized. The court disagreed and ruled for the bank.

Dunn, Judge

Congress recognized some time ago that the area of credit card liability needed to be dealt with in a uniform manner. Accordingly, 15 U.S.C.A. § 643 provides protection for a card holder against "unauthorized" charges made on an account. Obviously, this was to protect the card holder in cases where the card had been stolen or lost and was being used to make "unauthorized charges. § 1643 limits the liability of a card holder where there has been "unauthorized use." Title 15 U.S.C.A. § 1602(o) defines the term "unauthorized use" to mean "a use of a credit card by a person other than the card holder who does not have actual, implied, or apparent authority for such use and from which the card holder receives no benefit." If the person using the card has either actual, implied, or apparent authority then the charges are authorized and the limitations imposed by § 1643 do not apply and Ms. Oclander would be liable for all charges made on the account as set out under the "Terms of Agreement." Thus, the issue of liability turns on whether the charges made by Bonifacio Aparicio were authorized.

Apparent authority exists where a person has created such an appearance of things that it causes a third person to reasonably and prudently believe that a second party has the power to act on behalf of the first person. *Walker Bank & Trust Company v. Jones.*

Bonifacio Aparicio did in fact have a card in his possession with his name on it as a joint card holder and presented the card to merchants who had no reason to question his authority to use it. Mr. Aparicio was in possession of a card which was a representation to merchants (third parties) to whom they were presented that he (second-parties/card bearers) was authorized to make the charges. This is not a case where charges were made on an expired card, or the card was obtained through fraud or other wrongdoing. Mr. Aparicio was actually in possession of one of the cards and at all times was ostensibly authorized to make charges on the account. If Ms. Oclander had accurately explained the situation to the Bank and told them that Mr. Aparicio was in possession of one of the cards, or at the very least, that she did not have possession of both cards, then the Bank would have maintained the "block" it had originally placed on the account in July, and none of the charges made during Mr. Aparicio's buying spree would have been chargeable to the Bank.

The Bank did not even require that the cards be surrendered but only that they be accounted for by Ms. Oclander. Ms. Oclander failed to do so, and as a result the Bank has suffered damages for which she should be held accountable.

| Fair Credit Reporting Act | Lenders, insurance companies, and the like may subscribe to consumer reporting services that provide information on applicants they are evaluating. For example, a person seeking a loan to purchase a sailboat will most likely have a credit report forwarded by a credit bureau to the bank. The report will provide a record of the credit activity of the consumer and will assist the bank in determining whether that person is a good credit risk. |

STATEMENT OF CREDIT DENIAL, TERMINATION, OR CHANGE

After giving your application every possible consideration, we regret that we are unable to extend credit for the Reason(s) indicated below.

Description of Account, Transaction, or Requested Credit: <u>Home equity line-of-credit</u>

Applicant's name and address

Description of Adverse Action Taken: <u>denial</u>

PRINCIPAL REASON(S) FOR ADVERSE ACTION CONCERNING CREDIT

☐ Credit application incomplete
☐ Insufficient credit references
☐ Unable to verify credit references
☐ Temporary or irregular employment
☐ Unable to verify employment
☐ Length of employment
☐ Insufficient income
☐ Excessive obligations
☐ Unable to verify income
☒ Inadequate collateral
☐ Too short a period of residence

☐ Temporary residence
☐ Unable to verify residence
☐ No credit file
☐ Insufficient credit file
☐ Delinquent credit obligations
☐ Garnishment, attachment, foreclosure, repossession, or suit
☐ Bankruptcy
☐ We do not grant credit to any applicant on the terms and conditions you request.

Other, specify: _____

DISCLOSURE OF USE OF INFORMATION OBTAINED FROM AN OUTSIDE SOURCE

☐ Disclosure inapplicable

☒ Information obtained in a report from a consumer reporting agency

Name: <u>Credit Bureau</u>

Street Address: _____ Phone: _____

☐ Information obtained from an outside source other than a consumer reporting agency. Under the Fair Credit Reporting Act, you have the right to make a written request, within 60 days of receipt of this notice, for disclosure of the nature of the adverse information.

EQUAL CREDIT OPPORTUNITY ACT NOTICE

The Federal Equal Credit Opportunity Act prohibits creditors from discriminating against credit applicants on the basis of race, color, religion, national origin, sex, marital status, age, (provided that the applicant has the capacity to enter into a binding contract); because all or part of the applicant's income derives from any public assistance program; or because the applicant has in good faith exercised any right under the Consumer Credit Protection Act. The Federal agency that administers compliance with this law concerning this creditor is **Comptroller of the Currency, Consumer Affairs Division, Washington, D.C., 20219.**

Figure 17.5 Typical Credit Denial Form

RECENTLY ?

BAD INFO

FINED

+

INFO SOURCE

However, errors may arise in consumer credit reports. Assume that the person seeking the loan is turned down because the report noted that bills were never paid to Smith's Department Store and Jones's Used Cars. The person, however, had never dealt with either business, but was being denied credit because of misinformation on the credit report. Congress passed the Fair Credit Reporting Act to protect consumers from unfair and inaccurate credit reports.

A consumer who has been denied credit because of an adverse credit rating has the following rights: (1) the right to receive the name and address of the agency that keeps the consumer's report; (2) the right to review at least a summary of the information held by the credit bureau; (3) the right to demand that any important error be investigated and corrected if the bureau finds an error in the report; and (4) if the person disagrees with the findings of the bureau, the right to prepare a short statement, which must be included in the record in the future. Figure 17.5 is a typical credit denial form.

When a credit reporting agency is requested to investigate an error in its report, it must act reasonably—a point illustrated by the following case.

Pinner v. Schmidt
United States Court of Appeals, Fifth Court
805 F.2d 1258 (1986)

Thomas K. Pinner was employed as a sales representative for Sherwin-Williams at a paint store managed by James E. Schmidt. Pinner had a personal charge account at the store.

As the district judge noted, considerable tension developed between Pinner and Schmidt. A relationship began to develop between Pinner and one of the female employees. Unfortunately, Schmidt also was obsessed with this same employee. This rivalry led to a dispute over Pinner's personal charge account bill. Pinner believed that Schmidt had entered several fictitious charges to his account.

Pinner left Sherwin-Williams in 1980. His account balance was $171.11. At trial, it was established that the correct balance was only $121.71. Sherwin-Williams reported his account as delinquent to C.B.M. of Louisiana (Chilton), a credit reporting agency. Sherwin-Williams never reported Pinner's objections to the amount due.

In October 1981, Pinner tried to buy some tires on credit. This purchase was refused after the tire company checked with Chilton. Pinner thereafter obtained his credit report from Chilton. He sent a letter to Chilton on January 11, 1982, notifying Chilton that he disputed the charges and asked Chilton to investigate the matter. Chilton then contacted *Schmidt*, who verified the account as delinquent. In February 1982, Pinner was again denied credit on the basis of a report furnished by Chilton. Pinner once again requested his credit report. The report indicated the amount owed to Sherwin-Williams was an undisputed delinquent account. Chilton had not amended to Pinner's credit file the fact that the amount was in dispute. After Pinner filed suit, Chilton amended his file "Litigation Pending," without specifying whether Pinner was the plaintiff or defendant in the litigation.

The court ruled that Pinner could recover for a violation of the Fair Credit Reporting Act (FCRA).

Hunter, Jr., District Judge

Congress, in enacting the FCRA, sought to require consumer reporting agencies to adopt reasonable procedures for meeting the needs of commerce for consumer credit in a manner both fair and equitable to the consumer. 15 U.S.C.A. § 1681(b). The legislative history of the FCRA indicates that its purpose is to protect an individual from inaccurate or arbitrary information about himself in a consumer report that is being used as a factor in determining the individual's eligibility for credit, insurance, or employment.

The facts of this case present two possible bases of liability under the FCRA. First, the FCRA provides that in preparing a consumer report a credit reporting agency must follow reasonable procedures to assure maximum possible accuracy of the information concerning the individual about whom the report relates. This section imposes a duty of reasonable care in the preparation of a consumer report. Second, the FCRA imposes a duty upon reporting agencies to reinvestigate and to delete information found to be inaccurate or no longer verifiable once the consumer has protested the inclusion of the material. A negligent violation of either of these sections subjects the credit reporting agency to liability for any actual damages sustained as a result of the violation, together with the costs of the action and a reasonable attorney's fee. A willful violation of either section subjects the agency to punitive damages as well.

The record reveals evidence from which a jury could find a negligent violation of § 1681i. Once Chilton received notice of the dispute over the Sherwin-Williams account from Pinner's attorney it was obligated to re-verify the accuracy of the delinquent entry. The letter informed Chilton of the Pinner-Schmidt dispute. It was unreasonable for Chilton to contact only Schmidt in its reinvestigation. Here, Chilton not only called the creditor to re-verify the report but consulted the man they knew to have had disagreements with Pinner in the past. Because of Schmidt's involvement, contacting only him was insufficient to re-verify the entry as Chilton was required to do under § 1681i(a). If, as Chilton argues, there was no other authority to turn to to verify Pinner's account, Chilton should have deleted the information altogether, as is required by § 1681i(a).

Turning to liability under § 1681e(b), any person could easily have construed the notation "Litigation Pending" as an indication that the plaintiff was being sued by Sherwin-Williams, while the actual situation was the reverse. It would have been a simple matter to prevent this ambiguity, particularly in light of Chilton's knowledge of Pinner's dispute with Sherwin-Williams.

We find that the district court was eminently correct in denying Chilton's motions for directed verdict, judgment notwithstanding the verdict, or a new trial in regard to negligent violations of the FCRA.

Equal Credit Opportunity Act

The Equal Credit Opportunity Act (ECOA) makes it illegal for creditors to discourage applicants from applying for a loan, refuse a loan to a qualified person, or lend money on terms different from those granted to similar persons because of the applicant's sex, race, marital status, national origin, religion, or age, or because the applicant receives public assistance income. The act initially was aimed at sex and marital status discrimination. Studies in the early 1970s indicated that women had a far more difficult time securing credit than did men. For example, single women were less likely to obtain credit than single men. Those who did receive credit, upon marriage would need to reapply for credit in the husband's name. Newly married men were not required to reapply. Furthermore, creditors were often unwilling to count a wife's income when a married couple sought credit.

Thus, the Equal Credit Opportunity Act attempted to remove barriers to the credit markets that existed for certain people for reasons unrelated to financial status. Since credit is an important aspect of society, Congress acted to make it available on a nondiscriminatory basis to anyone who is creditworthy.

Although the act addressed a widespread problem, only a relatively few cases have arisen under it. Some reasons have been advanced for the lack of development under the act. First, most overt types of credit discrimination have been eliminated. Credit institutions, for example, as a matter of policy stopped discounting the wife's income in a marital loan application. In addition, compliance with the act has been furthered by industry educational efforts and forms provided by the Federal Reserve Board (the agency responsible for ECOA matters). Finally, the more complex forms of discrimination are more difficult to find and far more difficult to prove.

Nonetheless, some cases do illustrate the types of discriminatory treatment that violate the act. Note that discrimination is prohibited in any aspect of the credit transaction.

United States v. American Future Systems, Inc.
United States Court of Appeals, Third Circuit
743 F.2d 169 (1984)

American Future Systems, Inc. sells china, cookware, crystal, and tableware and extends credit to its customers. Since its incorporation, AFS's sales on a credit basis have amounted to over ninety-five percent of its total sales.

AFS alleges that it has two separate marketing programs. One program comprises only single white females who are upperclasspersons (sophomores, juniors, and seniors) in a four-year college or nursing schoool. The district court found this to be the preferred program. The other program comprises minorities, males, and married people attending college or vocational school. The district court found this to be the nonpreferred program.

The applicants for the preferred credit program for single white females are treated as preferred sales targets, regardless of age, prior credit histories, or any other normal indicia of creditworthiness. They receive immediate credit. Sales to this group are always made on an immediate-shipment basis unless there is a specific request for a delay in shipment.

Unlike the preferred credit program, the nonpreferred credit program withholds the shipment of goods to its credit applicants until the applicant makes three successive monthly payments. If nonpreferred applicants fail to make three consecutive monthly payments, AFS retains the payments made and retains the goods earmarked for shipment.

Both programs are designed to meet the "special social need" for credit shared by eighteen- to twenty-one-year-olds. The distinction between the two programs—based on race, sex, and marital status—is not, however, a matter of differential "social need." Rather, it stems from a marketing judgment made by AFS. AFS does not inform potential credit applicants that they are participants in an alleged special-purpose credit program. As the district court noted, "All applicants between 18 and 21 are carefully led to believe that they are being treated the same as all other applicants."

Potential credit applicants who fall into the nonpreferred category because of their race, sex, or marital status are therefore unable to decline credit offered through an alleged special-purpose credit program. Moreover, these same nonpreferred credit applicants are not told that they are being rejected for the credit terms extended to other persons identically situated, except for the characteristics of race, sex, marital status, or year in school.

Higginbotham, Jr., Circuit Judge

The Equal Credit Opportunity Act (ECOA) proscribes discrimination in the extension of credit. The ECOA does provide, however, for special purpose credit programs responsive to special social needs of a class of persons.

AFS readily admits that its treats participants in its two credit programs, members of the class of persons between the ages of 18 and 21, differently on the basis of race, sex and marital status. Thus the specific issue before us is whether the ECOA permits such differential treatment where the district court expressly found that each person in the group of individuals between the ages of 18 and 21 shares the same credit disability. That is, once the social need is defined only as extending credit to a particular age group, can a creditor use factors such as race, sex and marital status in setting up special purpose credit programs designed to address that social need when such factors are not related to the need? Although special program participants may be required to share one or more of those characteristics ordinarily considered prohibited bases, we believe they may be required to share only those factors inextricably tied to the need being addressed.

In this case, AFS identified one broad class of persons excluded from the customary credit market: the 18 to 21 year old age group. The district court found that each

person in this age group irrespective of race, sex, or marital status shared the same credit disability. In our view, where each person in the class shares the same special need but does not receive the same credit terms solely because of the individual's sex, race or marital status the program in question violates the ECOA. . . .

There is a particular irony in AFS's approach where it singles out white women as a "disadvantaged" group and gives them a special advantage that it unhesitatingly denies to black and other minority women. Certainly we recognize that this country has a tragic history in gender discrimination in that women have not been and still today are often not, treated as equals.

Despite all of the disadvantages that women have had, historically and at present, the significant disadvantages suffered by white women have been far less than those disadvantages black women, Native American women (Indians), Hispanic and other minority American women have had to endure for centuries. Yet, the paradox of AFS's plan is that it perpetuates the past disparities between white and minority women and rather than helping all women it aids only white women and slams the door of equal credit opportunity in the faces of minority women.

Fair Debt Collection Practices Act

CAUSES ?

Br

Since litigation is often a time-consuming and uneconomic way to proceed against delinquent debtors, some creditors become rather aggressive in trying to collect the unpaid account. If the loan was secured by collateral—for example, an automobile loan—the creditor may simply repossess the property. However, if the loan was not backed by collateral, the only nonlitigation remedy for the creditor is to convince the debtor to continue repaying the debt.

Aggressive creditor collection practices may at times cross the line and be considered harassment. When that occurs, the debtor may have a claim for damages against the creditor.

Unscrupulous debt collection practices led to the passage of the Fair Debt Collection Practices Act. When Congress held hearings before the passage of this act, it determined that debt collection practices contributed to a number of personal bankruptcies, to marital instability, to the loss of jobs, and to the invasion of individual privacy.

The act is designed to protect consumers from unfair and abusive collection practices. Thus, the term **debt**, in the act, is restricted to obligations arising out of a transaction in which the property, services, insurance, or money received is used primarily for personal, family, or household purposes.

Whether a person or entity is protected by this act is for the most part determined by the definition of the term **debt collector**. The act defines the term to cover the activities of all third-party debt collectors—that is, anyone other than the creditor who regularly collects debts for others.

Debt collectors may not use unfair or unconscionable means to collect a debt. The following case illustrates this point.

Juras v. Amon Collection Service, Inc.
United States Court of Appeals, Ninth Circuit
829 F.2d 739 (1987)

Juras attended Montana State University. He took out several loans under the National Defense (later "Direct") Student Loan Program to finance his education. Juras defaulted on the loans. Montana State assigned the notes to Amon Collection Services for purposes of collection. Amon informed Juras that his grade transcripts would not be released until he paid his debt, even if his debt was discharged in bankruptcy. Juras filed suit in federal court, alleging several violations of the Fair Debt Collections Practices Act, including the refusal of Montana State to provide his transcript to him. The court held that Montana State did not violate the act by refusing to provide the transcript to Juras.

Per Curiam

Under federal law, "[a] debt collector may not use unfair or unconscionable means to collect or attempt to collect any debt." 15 U.S.C. § 1629f. Juras claims that withholding his transcript is an unfair means of debt collection because it violates a provision of the NDSL statutes requiring institutions to make loans "without security." We disagree.

The loan statutes do not define the term "security"; the legislative history is equally silent. We therefore turn to more general sources for aid in construing the term.

Standard definitions indicate that the term "security," in the loan context, refers to property belonging to a debtor that provides some assurance of repayment.

Even if the transcript is property, it is unlikely that it belongs to Juras. A property interest is a creation of state law, rule, or policy. In determining whether such an interest exists, Montana looks to its definition of property. That definition is as follows:

Property defined—ownership. The ownership of a thing is the right of one or more persons to possess and use it to the exclusion of others. In this code, the thing of which there may be ownership is called property. *Mont. Code Ann.* § 70-1-101 (1985).

As between Juras and the university, it appears the latter is the owner of the official transcript. It creates, maintains, and possesses the grade record and excludes all others, except the student, from using it.

If Congress' desire for diligent enforcement is to be fulfilled, reasonable enforcement mechanisms, including withholding of transcripts, must be permitted. Dismissal of the claim challenging the withholding of the transcript was proper.

False misleading representations used to collect a debt have also been prohibited. For example, a debt collector cannot imply that nonpayment of a debt will result in property or wages being seized, unless the action threatened is lawful and the debt collector intends to take such action. A person may not be imprisoned for failing to pay a debt. Thus, threatening to file criminal charges because a person fails to pay a debt would be unlawful. On the other hand, a civil action may be instituted if a person refused to pay a debt. If the creditor prevails in such a suit, it may be possible to seize and sell certain assets of the debtor. However, merely threatening to file such a civil suit is unlawful unless the person making such a threat actually intends to take such action.

Communicating with the debtor may in certain instances violate the act. Communicating with the consumer at any unusual time or place or at a time or place that should be known to be inconvenient to the consumer is unlawful. The act specifies that the convenient time for communicating with a consumer is after 8:00 A.M. and before 9:00 P.M.. Normally, if the debt collector knows a consumer is represented by an attorney, all communications should be solely with the attorney and not with the debtor. The debt collector also may not communicate with the consumer at work if the debt collector knows or has reason to know the employer prohibits such communication.

Holder-in-Due-Course Doctrine as Modified by the FTC

During the 1970s, the legislation we have been discussing paved the way for easier-to-understand credit terms, fairer treatment of persons desiring credit, and easier resolution of disputes dealing with credit payments. One more related development of the 1970s deserves attention here.

The holder-in-due-course doctrine is a very old doctrine in the field of negotiable instruments. The courts developed this doctrine hundreds of years ago to encourage the free transferability of commercial paper—instruments such as checks and notes. A person who takes such an instrument in good faith, for value, and without notice that it is overdue or has been dishonored or of any defense against it or claims to it on the part of any person is a holder in due course and is given special treatment by the courts. The holder in due course takes an instrument free of most defenses that exist between the original parties to an instrument.

As an illustration, consider the following situation. A person purchases a new eighteen-foot boat from Stanley's Marine. He signs a promissory note for fourteen thousand dollars, which Stanley negotiates to a local bank for fourteen thousand dollars cash. Thereafter, the boat fails to perform properly. Neither Stanley nor the manufacturer is willing to remedy the defect in the boat. The buyer, infuriated over the problems with the boat, refuses to pay the bank. Can he do this?

The answer to this question, historically, was no—if the bank qualified as a holder in due course.

The courts reasoned that if the signer of an instrument could assert defenses against the person to whom the note was negotiated, such a rule would discourage financial institutions from accepting instruments. It was thought that, in order to keep commerce functioning, the transferability of such instruments as notes was very important.

In many instances, the holder-in-due-course rule resulted in a very unfair deal for consumers. Purchasers of products often were forced to pay for goods that did not function, or even for goods that they did not receive!

This rule has been modified by a trade regulation rule promulgated by the Federal Trade Commission. The rule largely eliminates the problems associated with the holder-in-due-course doctrine—at least for consumer transactions.

Federal Trade Commission Action

The Federal Trade Commission has outlawed the use of the holder-in-due-course rule in the case of consumer purchases. When a person signs a note today to finance the purchase of a product for personal or household use, any person or business that takes the note from the seller takes it subject to any defenses that exist between the seller and the buyer. The rule requires the seller to include a provision, in any note or contract for the sale or lease of goods or services to consumers, that in bold type states that any person taking the note or contract takes it subject to any defenses or claims that the debtor could assert against the seller. It is an unfair trade practice to fail to comply with this FTC rule.

The FTC rule has virtually eliminated this doctrine as a problem in consumer transactions. However, persons in business should realize that the holder-in-due-course doctrine still applies to nonconsumer transactions, such as a note signed by a business buyer and given to a business seller in payment for goods purchased for a business.

Mahaffey v. Investor's National Security Co.
Supreme Court of Nevada
747 P.2d 890 (1987)

Warren & Kristina Mahaffey entered into a home insulation contract in March 1980. They signed a note which was secured by their home. The insulation company, Five Star Solar Screens, sold the note to Mortgage Finance Corporation, a subsidiary of Investor's National Security Company; Five Star never performed the work it agreed to do. The Mahaffeys refused to pay the note. Mortgage Finance Corporation filed this suit to collect on the note. The court refused to permit the company to collect.

Per Curiam

Although the Mahaffeys rightfully had at least three days to rescind the contract, Five Star employees arrived at their home the next day and completed most of the work ever done. The workmen left the job half completed, with large holes in the interior walls and improperly installed "solar screens" on the windows and doors. One of the workmen falsely assured Mr. Mahaffey that insulation had been poured into the walls from the attic. This was physically impossible, since a solid block of wood was built into the top of each wall. This block of wood is called a "firebreak" and is a normal part of home construction, a fact which should have been well known to these professional insulation contractors. Additionally, the heater blanket and roof turbines promised by the salesman were never delivered.

Despite this state of affairs, another Five Star salesman coerced the Mahaffeys into signing a completion certificate, note, and deed of trust two weeks after they signed the initial bid order. When the Mahaffeys resisted signing the documents, the salesman told them the original contract was worthless, and threatened them with "trouble" and "skyrocketing interest rates" unless they signed immediately. Under the pressure thus applied, they signed. The next day, Five Star sold the contract to Mortgage Finance Corp. Five Star never finished the job

at the Mahaffey residence, and none of the promises made by the salesmen were ever kept. In fact, it was later discovered that the insulation which had been installed was completely inadequate. The net result was that the Mahaffeys received no benefit from the agreement, which nevertheless obligated them to pay a total of $8,832.96.

Upon these facts, we conclude that the district court was correct in finding that the contract was fraudulently induced. We further agree with the district court's finding that the Mahaffeys were entitled to assert any defenses against Mortgage Finance Corp. which they could have asserted against Five Star. First, we note the contract plainly states on its face that any buyer of the note takes it subject to all claims and defenses available against the seller. Mortgage Finance Corp. thereby had notice of possible claims and defenses, and was not a holder in due course. Since it was not a holder in due course, the Mahaffeys could assert any of their defenses, including fraudulent inducement and failure of consideration, against payment of the note.

We conclude that, by virtue of fraudulent inducement and failure of consideration, the contract is null and void.

Bankruptcy   Bankruptcy is a safety valve. It provides an orderly mechanism for salvaging the financial affairs of those who have acquired overly burdensome debts. Although a system of credit depends on enforceable legal obligations to repay money, at times debtors through misfortune or poor planning may acquire more obligations than they can bear. In those circumstances, bankruptcy law is available to mitigate the otherwise harsh effects.

Purposes

The bankruptcy laws can be seen as having two major purposes. They provide debtors with a fresh start so that they may seek new opportunities without being burdened by the pressure and hardship of preexisting debts. Risk taking and entrepreneurship are thereby enhanced, since bankruptcy does limit the ultimate risk of failure. Those who do fail are given a new start. Without bankruptcy protection for debtors, productive risk-taking behavior would be more costly and perhaps, as a result, not taken.

Implicit in this discussion is the fact that the bankruptcy laws are also designed to protect creditors. They provide for a fair distribution of debtor property among similarly situated creditors. Thus, a creditor need not fear that another creditor will strip a nearly insolvent debtor of most assets and thereby gain a windfall. The law contains provisions whereby those assets will be returned and divided equitably among all creditors.

History

Providing a system of relief for debtors as a part of a credit system is not a recent phenomenon nor is it uniquely American. Bankruptcy originated under Roman law and has been available in England for over three hundred years. In fact, the Bible refers to periodic relief from debts: "At the end of every seven years thou shalt make a release. And this is the manner of the release: every creditor shall release that which he has lent unto his neighbor and his brother; because the Lord's release hath been proclaimed." Deut. 15:1-2.

The United States Constitution, Article 1, Section 8, which appears in the Appendix, states: "The Congress shall have the power . . . to establish . . . uniform laws on the subject of bankruptcies throughout the United States." Bankruptcy is a federal law, and it is applicable throughout the United States. The states thus delegated the power to establish bankruptcy laws to Congress and for the most part relinquished any role in bankruptcy proceedings. States do, however, regulate other debtor-creditor relationships.

Congress passed the first bankruptcy act in 1800, but it soon repealed the act in 1803. During the nineteenth century, Congress enacted various bankruptcy acts only to repeal them at a later date. Thus, no bankruptcy law was in effect at various intervals during the nineteenth century. By the conclusion of the nineteenth century, Congress enacted the National Bankruptcy Act of 1898. Ever since, there has been a federal bankruptcy law. In 1938, Congress amended the bankruptcy law when it passed the Chandler Act which involved a major overhaul of the law. It again extensively revised the bankruptcy law when it passed the

Ethics

Suppose that Joe and Mary Doaks never saved any money. They just lived from paycheck to paycheck like a lot of people. If they had adopted a more frugal lifestyle, the Doaks might have been able to save up some money to protect themselves in the event of an emergency. Instead, they spent a lot of money on prepepared gourmet foods, dinners out at nice restaurants on the weekends, and tickets to all the professional athletic games and concerts. The Doaks always managed to scrape by and they always paid their debts on time. One day Joe's employer notified him that due to a sharp decline in orders, it was necessary to lay him off. Joe looked feveriously for work. In the meantime, they lived off their credit cards. After just a few months, the Doaks started receiving hostile calls from creditors and stern letters in the mail demanding immediate payment of their ever increasing debts. They hated picking up the telephone.

One day while looking at the classified advertisements for employment opportunities Joe noticed an advertisement placed by a local attorney. It read: "Can't pay your debts? Creditors hounding you? Looking for a solution? Call Carl White." Joe called the number listed in the advertisement. White's secretary made the Doaks an appointment the next day. At the conference with the attorney the following day, after evaluating the Doaks' situation, White concluded the only option left open to them was to file for bankruptcy. The Doaks took his advice. Much to their surprise, immediately after filing the bankruptcy petition, they stopped receiving any hostile phone calls or demanding letters.

The Doaks did a perfectly lawful act. Carl White, as noted in the Constitutional law chapter, had a constitutional right to advertise. Even so, many people feel that the actions of both White and the Doaks are unethical. Some people argue that an attorney who advises the fact that people can eliminate their debts by filing for bankruptcy relief is encouraging people not to pay their lawful debts. Such people ought to instead be encouraged to make a greater effort pay off their obligations. Other people find it unethical to file for bankruptcy relief at all. At one time in history, if a debtor failed to pay his lawful obligations, he or she could land in jail. Obviously, the law takes a less stringent attitude with respect to the issue of debt repayment than was the case centuries ago. The question nonetheless remains: In light of the fact that lenders extended credit on the expectation that the Doaks would repay the debts in question, are the Doaks really acting in an ethical manner by not paying off their debts?

The attitude of the general public in the United States with respect to this question has changed over the years. Fifty years ago, there was a *great* stigma attached to bankruptcy. For this reason, not a lot of people filed for bankruptcy relief even though the law permitted them to do so. In the last few decades, in light of the high number of bankruptcy filings today, it appears that the general public no longer attaches as much of a stigma to bankruptcy as was previously the case. In light of this fact, creditors must exercise a high degree of care in deciding whether to make a loan or not.

Bankruptcy Reform Act of 1978. Other less significant amendments have been passed since that time.

Bankruptcy provisions can provide relief for vastly different types of debtors, from large corporations (W. T. Grant, Johns Manville) to small business owners to consumers. Once a bankruptcy proceeding has begun, all other creditor actions against the debtor must stop (for example, repossessing property or filing a lawsuit for nonpayment for a loan). Thereafter, any creditor actions must take place pursuant to bankruptcy law.

Chapter 7 Liquidations

If a debtor elects to file under Chapter 7 of the Bankruptcy Act, the debtor's assets will be liquidated and the proceeds distributed to the debtors' creditors. At the time of the filing of the bankruptcy petition, the trustee in bankruptcy takes control of certain assets owned by the debtor. The trustee then sells these assets and uses the proceeds to pay off the debtor's creditors.

VOLUNTARY BANKRUPTCY

If a debtor on his or her own motion decides to file for bankruptcy relief, the debtor begins the case by filing a bankruptcy petition. Any person, firm or corporation may file for such relief (with some exceptions). It is not necessary to be insolvent in order to file a voluntary bankruptcy petition; that is, it is not necessary that one's debts exceed one's assets. Most persons and businesses probably are insolvent when they file.

The voluntary petition contains the following information:

1. A list of the creditors which indicates the amount owed to each creditor.

2. A list of the property owned by the debtor which the debtor wishes to claim as exempt.

3. A list of all of the property owned by the debtor.

4. A statement of the financial affairs of the debtor.

5. A list of current income and expenses.

When a debtor files this petition with the Bankruptcy court, the actual filing of the petition, assuming it is not challenged, constitutes an order of relief. The purpose in filing this information with the court is to give the court the information necessary to proceed with the case. The court will notify the creditors listed in the bankruptcy petition of the filing and inform them of the need to file a formal claim within six months of the filing of the bankruptcy petition. A trustee will be appointed by the court.

The bankruptcy estate consists of all property owned by the debtor at the time of filing the bankruptcy petition except for exempt property. Certain property that the debtor acquires within six months of the filing of the bankruptcy petition such as inheritances and property settlements also become part of the bankruptcy estate. All other property acquired by the debtor after the filing of the bankruptcy petition cannot be reached by the trustee in bankruptcy. A very typical example might involve a couple who both file bankruptcy petitions. Both the husband and the wife have jobs. Every dollar of income they earn after the filing of the bankruptcy petition is their property to keep.

The debtor need not part with all of the assets he or she owns at the time of the filing of the bankruptcy petition. The law permits the debtor to keep certain property. The law refers to this property as **exempt property**. What property is exempt can be determined by either federal or state law. The debtor decides whether to elect the federal exemptions or the state exemptions. Among other things, the federal exemptions include $7,500 equity in one's principal residence and $1,200 equity in a motor vehicle. State laws can be more or less generous than federal law. If a person lives in a state that permits the debtor to keep more property than federal law does, the debtor probably will elect the state exemptions. States like Kansas, Texas, and Florida are very liberal in the amount of property a debtor may keep. In other states, the states permit a debtor to keep less property than the federal law does. If a debtor lives in such a state, the debtor probably will elect to claim his or her exemptions under the federal statute.

At the first meeting of the creditors, the trustee, the creditors and the debtor meet. At this time the trustee has the opportunity to question the debtor about the information in the bankruptcy petition. Among other things, the trustee generally will inquire if the debtor has wrongfully transferred any assets to other people. Everything the debtor testifies as to is under oath and penalties can be assessed if the debtor lies.

Sometime soon after the first meeting of the creditors, in most cases the case comes to an end. The debtor will receive a formal notice from the court discharging him or her from all the debts listed on the bankruptcy petition. If a debtor did not act honestly, the court may refuse to grant the debtor a discharge on his or her debts. Certain types of debts cannot be discharged by filing a bankruptcy petition, for example, debts that arise as a result of the failure to make one's child support payments and taxes due within three years of filing a bankruptcy petition.

INVOLUNTARY BANKRUPTCY

In rare cases, a creditor may file a petition with the bankruptcy court asking that a debtor be forced into bankruptcy. This generally does not occur because in most cases the creditors of a debtor will be better off if a debtor does not go bankrupt and keeps trying to pay off his or her debts.

An involuntary bankruptcy case can be started by a single creditor if the debtor owes that creditor $5,000 or more and the debtor has fewer than twelve creditors. If the debtor has more than twelve creditors, then any three creditors with aggregate claims of $5,000 or more can file such a petition. A debtor may be forced into bankruptcy if one of the two following things can be established:

1. The debtor was not paying his or her debts as they came due; or

2. A custodian was appointed or took possession of substantially all of the property of the debtor during the 120 days preceding the filing of the petition.

If the court finds either of these things to be true, it will grant an order of relief. At this point, an involuntary case becomes exactly like a voluntary bankruptcy case.

Chapter 11   Reorganizations

The second general type of relief provided by the bankruptcy law is to restructure the debtor's financial affairs. A corporation that wishes to continue to operate (as opposed to liquidating the business) may elect to reorganize pursuant to Chapter 11. Individuals (although it would be very unusual for an individual to do so) and partnerships also may file under Chapter 11. Either a debtor or the debtor's creditors may initiate reorganization.

After the court accepts the bankruptcy petition and grants an order of relief, a creditors' committee is selected from the unsecured creditors of the debtor. The creditors' committee investigates the debtors' financial affairs and may propose a plan for reorganization. It may recommend that the debtor not be permitted to continue to operate the business. In the absence of a court order, the debtor may continue to operate the business during the reorganization.

The debtor has 120 days following the court order of relief to submit a plan to the Bankruptcy court. The plan must be in the best interests of the creditors. If the plan has not been accepted and confirmed within 120 days, anyone may file a reorganization plan. A plan must be submitted to each class of the debtors' creditors for acceptance. Thereafter, it must be confirmed by the court. It is possible for a court to confirm a plan that has been accepted by only one class of creditors. Once a plan has been confirmed by the court, it will govern the operation of the business in the future and the relationship of the debtor to its creditors.

Chapter 13   *Adjustment of Debts of Individuals With Regular Income*

Rather than liquidating the debtor's assets to pay creditor's claims, this process provides that the debtor formulate a plan under which a certain portion of creditor obligations will be paid. Chapter 13 permits a person with regular income, including debtors engaged in business (other than partnerships and corporations), to file a plan. Only those persons or businesses with regular income and unsecured debts of less than $100,000 and secured debts of less than $350,000 may file for relief under Chapter 13. Creditors may not force a debtor into such a plan. Unlike Chapter 11 cases, only the debtor may file a plan.

The plan filed by the debtor must provide that the debtor will submit his or her income in the future to the trustee. A court will confirm the plan if it was proposed in good faith and was accepted by all of the debtor's secured creditors covered by the plan. There is no requirement that unsecured creditors approve the plan. If a court approves the debtors' plan, the plan will bind all creditors covered by the plan.

If the debtor complies with his or her obligations as stated in the plan, at the conclusion of the plan, the debtor will receive a discharge on all debts listed in the plan (with the exception of certain debts on which the law does not permit a debtor to receive a discharge.)

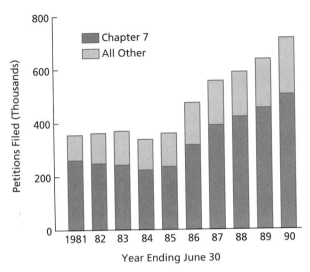

Figure 17.6   Filings in U.S. Bankruptcy Courts, 1981–1990
Source: Annual Report of the Director of the Administrative Office of the United States Courts, 1990.

As Figure 17.6 indicates, there has been a steady increase in the number of persons filing for bankruptcy relief.

SUMMARY

Consumer law illustrates a recent trend in the law of contracts. Principles of contract freedom have been modified by concerns over contract fairness. Consumers, those who enter transactions for personal, family, or household purposes, are given certain statutory protections to remedy their lack of bargaining power or marketplace sophistication.

Innumerable statutes and regulations protect consumers from unfair business practices. Deceptive and unfair practices have been violations of the Federal Trade Commission Act for many years. The FTC has attempted to cut down on the use of deceptive advertising by sellers.

In the 1960s and 1970s, Congress and the state legislatures passed statutes and regulations outlawing particular types of business practices. Written warranties on consumer products costing more than ten dollars must be labeled full or limited, and must be disclosed prior to purchase. Credit has been extensively regulated. The law today requires that credit terms be presented in a simple, comparable manner. It provides an easier resolution of disputes dealing with credit payments. Debt collectors must act with caution to avoid harassing or abusing debtors.

In virtually every area in which business deals with consumers, business must apprise itself of federal and state statutes and regulations. Consumer law limits the ability of business to set its own contract terms when dealing with certain persons.

American law permits persons and businesses to discharge their debts by filing a petition for relief with the Bankruptcy court. Two general types of relief are available: liquidation and reorganization. If a person or business files for reorganization, the trustee acquires title to the debtor's nonexempt assets. The trustee disposes of these assets and uses the proceeds to pay off the creditors listed in the debtor's petition. A debtor does not forfeit all property he or she owns. Most property acquired by the debtor after the filing of the bankruptcy petition is not part of the bankruptcy estate. The debtor may also claim certain property as exempt.

A business that wishes to avail itself of the bankruptcy laws may either file under Chapter 7 for a liquidation or under Chapter 11 in order to reorganize. If a court accepts a plan to reorganize a business, the plan will govern the operation of the business in the future.

Individuals, including individuals engaged in businesses (but not partnerships and corporations) may formulate a plan under which a certain portion of the debtor's obligation to his or her creditors will be paid pursuant to the plan proposed by the debtor. Only a debtor may file such a plan. Creditors may not force a debtor into a Chapter 13 proceeding. If a debtor complies with its obligations under the plan, the debtor will receive a discharge on the debts listed in the plan.

REVIEW QUESTIONS

1. Define the following terms:
   a. Bankruptcy
   b. Consumer
   c. Truth-in-Lending Act

2. ABC, Inc. manufactures and sells turbine engines that are used for power-generating plants. The engines cost five hundred thousand dollars each and are fifteen feet high. All customers of ABC are major corporations or public utilities. Should ABC be concerned with consumer regulation? If not, develop a scenario that would give rise to such a concern.

3. XYZ, Inc. sells small television sets that are used primarily in households. Carl Smith purchases such a television so he can watch the early morning news while getting ready for work. The corporation gave Smith a written warranty when he purchased the television. The warranty was five pages long, written in very fine print in technical legal language. The warranty is labeled a "full warranty." It provided that implied warran-ties will be recognized for three months after the date of purchase. Furthermore, it provided that the buyer will be liable for any defects except problems with the picture tube. Can XYZ expect to have problems with this written warranty? Explain.

4. Sally Jenkins purchased an automobile for her private use from Joe's Used Cars. She agreed to pay Joe in equal installments for the car over the next two years. Although Joe told Jenkins that the installment payments included an interest charge, the amount of interest to be paid was never disclosed. Furthermore, the interest rate was also not disclosed. Can Joe's Used Cars expect to have problems with this loan transaction? Explain.

5. Discuss the relationship of consumer regulation with the principle of freedom of contract.

6. Continental Baking Company advertised Profile bread as being effective for weight

reduction. The FTC charged Continental with false, misleading, and deceptive advertising. It alleged the bread was not low-calorie, but simply sliced very thinly. If the FTC proves its case, may the FTC compel any special form of advertising by Continental in the future?

7. The Firestone Tire and Rubber Company was charged with unfair and deceptive advertising practices in violation of the Federal Trade Commission Act. The charge was in relation to two particular ads, one called the "Safe Tire" ad, and the other the "Stop 25% Quicker" ad. The "Safe Tire" ad naturally had safety as its dominant theme and contained the following statement: "Every new Firestone design goes through rugged tests of safety far exceeding any driving condition you'll ever encounter." The other ad made claims that a specific tire stopped "25% quicker" than "regular" tires. Do you see any problems with the ads?

8. When Jill Student enrolled in the university, her parents gave her a credit card. They arranged with the Charge-it Credit Card Company for a card to be issued in her name on their account. After Jill began to receive low grades, her parents decided to take away her credit card. She refused to relinquish it. They telephoned Charge-it to cancel their credit account. Charge-it informed them to send in all the outstanding cards on their account. This procedure for cancellation was provided in the credit card contract. No cards were submitted to the company for three months. In the meantime, Jill charged two thousand dollars' worth of merchandise. Her parents have been sued for that amount by Charge-it. They contend that they should, at most, be liable for fifty dollars. Discuss.

9. Mary Jones and Tom Smith were accountants, employed by the same firm. Their positions and salaries were identical. Both were unmarried, with approximately the same monthly expenses. They also had a similar credit history. On July 5, each visits

Loan Company to borrow five thousand dollars. Smith is given a one-page information sheet to fill out. Jones must prepare a ten-page questionnaire as well as provide three personal references. Upon completion of the documents, Smith is immediately granted the loan. Jones must meet with officers of Loan Company for a personal interview. Note that the financial information on both Smith and Jones's information sheets was virtually the same. Jones was granted the loan, but was to pay interest at three percent higher than market rates. When Jones learned about Smith's different experience with the same company, she became angry. Does Jones have a claim against Loan Company? Discuss.

10. Discuss the functions of bankruptcy law in the legal environment of business.

11. Bristol-Myers Company employed Christina Ferrare to star in a television commercial for its shampoo, Body on Tap. In the commercial, Ferrare claimed, "In shampoo tests with over nine hundred women like me, Body on Tap got higher ratings than Prell . . . higher than Flex . . . higher than Sassoon." During the shampoo tests, no woman tried more than one shampoo, and in reality one-third of the women were ages thirteen to eighteen. Is Bristol-Myers guilty of false advertising?

12. Gloria Harlan was a VISA cardholder who requested the Walker Bank and Trust to issue a card to her husband. The Harlans separated, and Mrs. Harlan notified the bank by letter that she wanted the account closed or wanted the bank to deny further extensions of credit to her husband. The account agreement contained an explicit provision requiring the return of all outstanding credit cards to close the account. Mr. Walker continued to make purchases on the account. Are the charges made by Mr. Walker "unauthorized" charges such that Mrs. Walker is liable for only fifty dollars?

13. Fire Fighter's Fund hired O'Hanlon Reports to conduct a personal investigation of James Millstone. When he was denied credit, he asked to see his credit report. The agency failed to provide the entire report to him until he had gone to great effort to obtain it. The report contained a number of false statements, such as the allegation that Millstone used drugs and gave wild parties. The agent who filed the report talked to only one person in obtaining this information. Did O'Hanlon violate the Fair Credit Reporting Act?

14. Carla and Steve Melton entered into a contract to have work performed by Acme Improvement Company on their personal residence. The work performed by Acme failed to meet up to their expectations. In the meantime, Acme transferred a note signed by the Meltons to International Finance Company. International now wishes to recover five thousand dollars from them. Can the Meltons assert the defense they have against Acme against International?

15. Wilson owes three creditors a total of $4,000. The creditors call and write him all the time. Wilson is unable to pay these creditors because she lost her job and she has not paid them anything on these bills. Can the creditors force her into bankruptcy? If Wilson files for bankruptcy relief, will she be forced to give up all the property she currently owns?

16. Anderson operated a small business as a sole proprieter. After a year, she owed the bank $25,000 on a secured loan and owed some other parties $15,000. The $15,000 debt was not secured. Can her creditors force her to file for Chapter 13 relief? If Anderson files for Chapter 13 relief, can the creditors file a plan? Can Anderson receive a discharge of these debts by filing a petition for Chapter 13 relief?

CHAPTER 18

Employment Discrimination

- Historical Background
- Title VII: Civil Rights Act of 1964
- What Is Discrimination?
- Permitted Discrimination: The Bona Fide Occupational Qualification
- Developments in Equal Employment Law
- Selected Statutes

The equal employment opportunity laws reflect the influence of historical and social movements. In Chapter 1 of this text, a discussion of race relations and law concluded with a brief mention of the Civil Rights Act of 1964. One of the major provisions of that statute is Title VII, which prohibits discrimination in employment because of race, color, sex, national origin, or religion.

This chapter provides an overview of the major aspects of Title VII of the Civil Rights Act of 1964. Note that this is not the only source of discrimination in employment law. Other federal statutes, such as the Equal Pay Act, also play a role. Additionally, executive orders, administrative regulations, and state law concern employment discrimination. However, none of the other sources of law has had as great an effect on business as has Title VII. Thus, a more focused study of that provision will provide the background for further study in employment law or will provide an appreciation for additional developments that are sure to be proposed in this area. A final section of the chapter examines three important federal statutes, enacted since Title VII, that have had a significant impact on equal opportunity protection.

Consider how the legal environment through its discrimination laws modified all aspects of a firm's employment practices. In doing so, evaluate each section two ways: first, take a model based on common law contract and note how it was changed by the discrimination laws; then, consider what steps a company might take in order to make sure that its personnel practices do not violate Title VII.

HISTORICAL BACKGROUND

The demise of slavery did not mean that black people were accepted into the mainstream of American life. Jim Crow laws created a dual society, one black and one white. Private attitudes reinforced the legal segregation, and many employers refused to hire black workers or placed them in low-level jobs. Women, too, were treated differently, on the basis of certain stereotypes.

Discrimination based on sex reflected society's view of the traditional roles of men and women: Men were strong and aggressive, and they worked to support their families; women were nurturing and cared for their families at home. Some of this attitude was reflected in the progressive movement at the turn of the century. The Industrial Revolution led to the employment of women in factories. Long hours, low pay, and poor working conditions for the women workers led reformers to seek legislation that would outlaw certain practices. The United States Supreme Court in *Muller* v. *Oregon* (1908) upheld an Oregon statute that prohibited women from working in factories longer than ten hours per day. By 1920, most states had enacted similar protective legislation.

The attitudes of society toward women consisted of more than simply a concern that women not be exploited in the workplace. As the following case notes, solely on the basis of their sex, women were commonly thought to be ill-equipped to do certain work.

Bradwell v. The State of Illinois
United States Supreme Court
83 U.S. 130 (1872)

Myra Bradwell made application to the judges of the Supreme Court of Illinois for a license to practice law. The practice of law without a license was forbidden by an Illinois statute. Mrs. Bradwell's application for the license was refused. After the announcement of this decision, Mrs. Bradwell filed an appeal, maintaining that she had a right to admission under the Fourteenth Amendment of the United States Constitution.

The decision of the Supreme Court was to deny her appeal on the now overruled grounds that the Fourteenth Amendment does not apply to the laws of a state. Justice Bradley (joined by two other justices) filed the following concurring opinion.

Justice Bradley

The civil law, as well as nature herself, has always recognized a wide difference in the respective spheres and destinies of man and woman. Man is, or should be, woman's protector and defender. The natural and proper timidity and delicacy which belongs to the female sex evidently unfits it for many of the occupations of civil life. The constitution of the family organization, which is founded in the divine ordinance, as well as in the nature of things, indicates the domestic sphere as that which properly belongs to the domain and functions of womanhood. The harmony, not to say identity, of interests and views which belong, or should belong, to the family institution is repugnant to the idea of a woman adopting a distinct and independent career from that of her husband. So firmly fixed was this sentiment in the founders of the common law that it became a maxim of that system of jurisprudence that a women had no legal existence separate from her husband, who was regarded as her head and representative in the social state; and, notwithstanding some recent modifications of this civil status, many of the special rules of law flowing from and dependent upon this cardinal principle still exist in full force in most States. One of these is, that a married woman is incapable, without her husband's consent, of making contracts which shall be binding on her or him. This very incapacity was one circumstance which the Supreme Court of Illinois deemed important in rendering a married woman incompetent fully to perform the duties and trusts that belong to the office of an attorney or counselor.

It is true that many women are unmarried and not affected by any of the duties, complications, and incapacities arising out of the married state, but these are exceptions to the general rule. The paramount destiny and mission of women are to fulfill the noble and benign offices of wife and mother. This is the law of the Creator. And the rules of civil society must be adapted to the general constitution of things, and cannot be based upon exceptional cases.

It is the prerogative of the legislator to prescribe regulations founded on nature, reason, and experience for the due admission of qualified persons to professions and callings demanding special skill and confidence. This fairly belongs to the police power of the State; and, in my opinion, in view of the peculiar characteristics, destiny, and mission of women, it is within the province of the legislature to ordain what offices, positions, and callings shall be filled and discharged by men, and shall receive the benefit of those energies and responsibilities, and that decision and firmness which are presumed to predominate in the sterner sex.

The civil rights movement and the national concern with racial segregation led to legislation, proposed during the Kennedy administration, that would extend the aspirations of *Brown* v. *Board of Education* (noted in Chapter 1) to the private job market. But, as initially proposed, this legislation did not prohibit sex discrimination. In the early 1960s, the idea that women could be police officers, construction workers, or business executives was considered too foreign. Nonetheless, the statute, when finally enacted, did list "sex" as one of the prohibited categories of job discrimination. Ironically, during the statute's debate in the House of Representatives, the sex discrimination amendment was offered by an opponent as a tactic for defeating the bill. The gambit misfired, and sex discrimination became part of civil rights legislation in 1964.

TITLE VII: CIVIL RIGHTS ACT OF 1964

Title VII of the Civil Rights Act of 1964 prohibits discrimination in any aspect of employment because of race, color, sex, religion, or national origin. Note that other types of discrimination may be prohibited by law, as examined later in this chapter. For example, age (over forty) and disability are other personal characteristics that in some circumstances may not influence employment decisions.

Two major policy goals are contained in Title VII. First, the decision to eliminate race, color, sex, religion, and national origin from being used as employment criteria was designed to limit social conflict by providing the opportunity for all workers to compete without regard to certain personal characteristics. In addition, nondiscriminatory employment practices were considered a means of entry for black people, especially, into the economic mainstream of the country. At the time of the passage of the act, dramatic economic inequality existed between black and white people.

Note, however, that these policy goals have raised conflicts about the extent of equal employment opportunity laws. Should employment practices be designed in a "color-blind" (or sex-neutral, etc.) manner, or should those practices be designed to hasten the economic integration of historically disadvantaged groups? This conflict will be illustrated by some of the materials that follow.

The **Equal Employment Opportunity Commission (EEOC)** is the federal administrative agency charged with enforcing Title VII. The EEOC has the power to investigate allegations of employment discrimination and file charges against businesses, unions, or employment agencies. Additionally, the EEOC, in its fact-finding role, may hear evidence from employee and employer and attempt to reach a resolution of the complaint. Finally, the agency promulgates regulations that provide guidance to businesses concerned with the agency's attitude toward certain employment practices.

The Equal Employment Opportunity Commission was created by the Civil Rights Act of 1964. Its powers were strengthened in 1972 by the Equal Employment Opportunity Act, which gave the commission authority to file suit on behalf of aggrieved parties.

Most of the developments in Title VII of the Civil Rights Act have occurred in case law. The judicial branch has been active in clarifying and applying the act's rather general language. As will be noted in the following materials, these decisions tried to clarify the statutory requirements so that business could more readily plan its personnel practices. In addition, the cases tended to favor protecting workers from discriminatory practices.

The election of Ronald Reagan (1980 and 1984) and George Bush (1988) to the presidency heralded a change in judicial approach. Their appointments to the United States Supreme Court gave it a conservative majority. Consequently, by the late 1980s numerous Title VII precedents were being reevaluated or distinguished. Often these cases created technical legal barriers (e.g., restated standards of proof) that made a successful claim under Title VII less likely. Note the materials in Chapter 4 on judicial reasoning and Chapter 5 on statutory interpretation. The "personality" factor influenced the newly appointed Supreme Court justices' use of statutory interpretation techniques, thus changing the meaning of Title VII.

However, after months of haggling between Congress and President Bush as well as vetoes and threatened vetoes of proposed legislation, a new civil rights bill was enacted, the Civil Rights Act of 1991. This statute did not create any new type of employment right. Nor did it require employers, as did the 1964 Act, to revise their personnel practices. Instead, the Civil Rights Act of 1991 reversed six Supreme Court precedents from 1989 that hindered a worker's ability to raise, successfully, a Title VII claim.

WHAT IS DISCRIMINATION?

Discriminate means to choose or differentiate. A generation or two ago, to indicate that someone was "discriminating" was to compliment that person. The choices referred to by that word usually involved high-quality taste in music, literature, and lifestyle. Today, however, the choices suggested by the word *discriminate* are far from complimentary. However, the idea behind the use of the word remains the same. *Discriminate* now means—instead of, say, differentiating between a fine Bordeaux wine and a wine cooler—distinguishing between people on the basis of innate characteristics.

Thus, the antidiscrimination provisions of Title VII may be considered to prohibit certain bases for choice in employment decisions. Any other factors can be used; whether or not they are wise is a decision left to the employer. For example, assume George and Sam are vying for a special training program offered by ABC, Inc. The employer may select the worker who has the best job record or who, through past performance, has shown the most aptitude for that program. Or, perhaps, ABC will make the choice on the basis of whether or not one of the workers likes tomatoes. None of these criteria for choosing between George or Sam would violate Title VII, since they do not involve any of the prohibited decision-making rationales. Title VII, therefore, does not eliminate employer discretion in distinguishing between employees, even if the means to make the distinction is foolish (enjoying tomatoes). The only concern is that race, color, sex, national origin, and religion do not play a part in the decision.

Thus, the initial inquiry in an employment discrimination problem is whether the basis for the employer's decision was prohibited by Title VII. Otherwise, no violation of the act will arise. The following case illustrates that even though an employer's action may be unfair, it may not violate Title VII. What statutory interpretation technique was used by the court?

Ulane v. Eastern Airlines, Inc.
United States Court of Appeals, Seventh Circuit
742 F.2d 1081 (1984)

Plaintiff, as Kenneth Ulane, was hired in 1968, as a pilot for defendant, Eastern Airlines, Inc., but was fired as Karen Frances Ulane in 1981. Ulane filed a timely charge of sex discrimination with the Equal Employment Opportunity Commission, which subsequentlly issued a right-to-sue letter. This suit followed.

Ulane became a licensed pilot in 1964, serving the United States Army from that time until 1968 with a record of combat missions in Vietnam for which he received the Air Medal with eight clusters. Upon discharge in 1968, Ulane began flying for Eastern. With Eastern, Ulane progressed from second to first officer, and also served as a flight instructor, logging over eight thousand flight hours.

Ulane was diagnosed as a transsexual in 1979. She explains that although embodied as a male, from early childhood she felt like a female. Ulane first sought psychiatric and medical assistance in 1968 while in the military. Later, Ulane began taking female hormones as part of her treatment, and eventually developed breasts from the hormones. In 1980, she underwent "sex reassignment surgery." After the surgery, Illinois issued a revised birth certificate indicating Ulane was female, and the FAA certified her for flight status as a female. Ulane's own physician explained, however, that the operation would not create a biological female in the sense that Ulane would not "have a uterus and ovaries and be able to bear babies." Ulane's chromosomes, all concede, are unaffected by the hormones and surgery. Ulane, however, claims that the lack of change in her chromosomes is irrelevant. Eastern was not aware of Ulane's transsexuality, her hormone treatments, or her psychiatric counseling until she attempted to return to work after her reassignment surgery. Eastern knew Ulane only as one of its male pilots.

The district court judge held that Karen Ulane was protected under Title VII of the Civil Rights Act. The case was appealed.

Wood Jr., Circuit Judge

The district judge first found that Eastern discharged Ulane because she was a transsexual and that Title VII prohibits discrimination on this basis. While we do not condone discrimination in any form, we are constrained to hold that Title VII does not protect transsexuals, and that the district court's order on this count therefore must be reversed.

Even though Title VII is a remedial statute, and even though some may define "sex" in such a way as to mean an individual's "sexual identity," our responsibility is to interpret this congressional legislation and determine what Congress intended when it decided to outlaw discrimination based on sex.

While we recognize distinctions among homosexuals, transvestites, and transsexuals, we believe that the same reasons for holding that the first two groups do not enjoy Title VII coverage apply with equal force to deny protection for transsexuals.

The phrase in Title VII prohibiting discrimination based on sex, in its plain meaning, implies that it is unlawful to discriminate against women because they are women and against men because they are men. The words of Title VII do not outlaw discrimination against a person who has a sexual identity disorder, i.e., a person born with a male body who believes himself to be female, or a person born with a female body who believes herself to be male; a prohibition against discrimination based on an individual's sexual identity disorder or discontent with the sex into which they were born.

When Congress enacted the Civil Rights Act of 1964 it was primarily concerned with race discrimination. This sex amendment was the gambit of a congressman seeking to scuttle adoption of the Civil Rights Act. The ploy failed and sex discrimination was abruptly added to the statute's prohibition against race discrimination.

The total lack of legislative history supporting the sex amendment coupled with the circumstances of the amendment's adoption clearly indicates that Congress never considered nor intended that this 1964 legislation apply to anything other than the traditional concept of sex.

Members of Congress have, moreover, on a number of occasions, attempted to amend Title VII to prohibit discrimination based upon "affectional or sexual orientation." Each of these attempts has failed.

In our view, to include transsexuals within the reach of Title VII far exceeds mere statutory interpretation. Congress had a narrow view of sex in mind when it passed the Civil Rights Act, and it has rejected subsequent attempts to broaden the scope of its original interpretation. For us to now hold that Title VII protects transsexuals would take us out of the realm of interpreting and reviewing and into the realm of legislating. This we must not and will not do.

If Congress believes that transsexuals should enjoy the protection of Title VII, it may so provide. Until that time, however, we decline on behalf of the Congress to judicially expand the definition of sex as used in Title VII beyond its common and traditional interpretation.

Outlawing certain employment practices does not necessarily change attitudes. Nor will the effects of long-time discrimination become irrelevant. Barriers to equal employment opportunities proved far more complex than the enactment of a statute could remedy. The concerns that led to the passage of Title VII remained to create complex questions concerning the application of equal employment opportunity laws. To illustrate, what follows are four theories or categories of employment discrimination that have arisen under Title VII.

Disparate Treatment

The most evident employment practice that violates the act has been labeled *disparate treatment*. The term means that a person is treated differently from others on the basis of the prohibited categories of Title VII. For example, if George, in the example that precedes the *Ulane* case, is rejected for the ABC training program because he is a Methodist (rather than because he doesn't like tomatoes), then the act is violated on the basis of disparate treatment. Religion is one of the categories in Title VII that may not be used to make employment decisions. Similarly, if an employer disciplines Spanish-surnamed workers more harshly than others for the same rule infraction, a violation occurs on the basis of disparate treatment. Discrimination based on national origin is prohibited. Thus, the first step for business executives evaluating personnel policies in light of Title VII was rather straightforward: Any employment-related practice that made use of one of the prohibited criteria must be changed. No longer could there be jobs for males and females, and black workers could not be excluded from corporate training programs that led to higher-paying jobs. These changes in American business practices were easy to accomplish.

However, disparate treatment issues may arise in less obvious ways. An employer that does not recognize that stereotypical attitudes may affect executives' judgments about job applicants or employees creates an environment in which Title VII violations can arise. In the case that follows, there was no question about Hopkins's abrasive personality and lack of interpersonal skills. Such shortcomings may have been sufficient to squelch her hopes of partnership. But the Title VII problem arose from the inference that Hopkins being a female made those characteristics far more negative in the partnership evaluation. Stereotypical attitudes about the proper decorum for women created the potential for disparate treatment in the promotional process. In fact, after Hopkins's partnership candidacy was first rejected, one of her male partner supporters suggested that she act more "female" in the future: walk differently, wear makeup and jewelry, and have her hair styled.

What suggestions would you have made to Price Waterhouse in the partnership evaluation process so that the Hopkins discrimination issue would not have arisen. Note that in 1990 the federal district court, upon rehearing the *Hopkins* case in light of the following opinion, again found that Price Waterhouse had discriminated against Ann Hopkins. For the remedy, the court ordered that she be made a partner.

Price Waterhouse v. Hopkins
United States Supreme Court
109 S. Ct. 1775 (1989)

Ann Hopkins had worked at Price Waterhouse's Office of Government Services in Washington, D.C., for five years when the partners in that office proposed her as a candidate for partnership. Thirteen of the thirty-two partners who had submitted comments on Hopkins supported her. Three partners recommended that her candidacy be placed on hold; eight stated that they did not have an informed opinion about her; and eight recommended that she be denied partnership. Consequently, Hopkins was neither offered nor denied admission to the partnership; instead, her candidacy was held for reconsideration the following year.

During the evaluation, the partners in Hopkins's office praised her character as well as her accomplishments, describing her in their joint statement as "an outstanding professional" who had a "deft touch," a "strong character, independence, and integrity." Clients appear to have agreed with these assessments.

On too many occasions, however, Hopkins's aggressiveness apparently spilled over into abrasiveness. Staff members seem to have borne the brunt of Hopkins's brusqueness. Long before her bid for partnership, partners evaluating her work had counseled her to improve her relations with staff members. Although later evaluations indicated an improvement, Hopkins's perceived shortcomings in this important area eventually doomed her bid for partnership. Virtually all of the partners' negative remarks about Hopkins, even those of partners supporting her, had to do with her "interpersonal skills."

There were clear signs, though, that some of the partners reacted negatively to Hopkins's personality because she was a woman. One partner described her as "macho"; another suggested that she "overcompensated for being a woman"; a third advised her to take "a course at charm school." Several partners criticized her use of profanity; in response, one partner suggested that those partners objected to her swearing only "because it's a lady using foul language."

In previous years, other female candidates for partnership also had been evaluated in sex-based terms. As a general matter, candidates were viewed favorably if partners believed that they maintained their femininity while becoming effective professional managers; in this environment, to be identified as a "women's libber" was regarded as a negative comment. In previous years, one partner repeatedly commented that he could not consider any woman seriously as a partnership candidate and believed that women were not even capable of functioning as senior managers—yet the firm took no action to discourage his comments and recorded his vote in the overall summary of the evaluations.

When the partners in Hopkins's office refused to repropose her for partner-ship, she sued Price Waterhouse under Title VII, charging that the firm had discriminated against her on the basis of sex in its decisions regarding partnership.

Justice Brennan

According to Price Waterhouse, an employer violates Title VII only if it gives decisive consideration to an employee's gender, race, national origin, or religion in making a decision that affects that employee. On Price Waterhouse's theory, even if a plaintiff shows that her gender played a part in an employment decision, it is still her burden to show that the decision would have been different if the employer had not discriminated.

In passing Title VII, Congress made the simple but momentous announcement that sex, race, religion, and national origin are not relevant to the selection, evaluation, or compensation of employees. Congress' intent to forbid employers to take gender into account in making employment decisions appears on the face of the statute. We take these words to mean that gender must be irrelevant to employment decisions. To construe the words "because of" as colloquial shorhand for "but-for causation," as does Price Waterhouse, is to misunderstand them. When, therefore, an employer considers both gender and legitimate factors at the time of making a decision, that decision was "because of" sex and other, legitimate considerations—even if we may say later, in the context of litigation, that the decision would have been the same if gender had not been taken into account.

To say that an employer may not take gender into account is not, however, the end of the matter, for that describes only one aspect of Title VII. The other important aspect of the statute is its preservation of an employer's remaining freedom of choice. We conclude that the preservation of this freedom means that an employer shall not be liable if it can prove that, even if it had not taken gender into account, it would have come to the same decision regarding a particular person.

In saying that gender played a motivating part in an employment decision, we mean that, if we asked the employer at the moment of the decision what its reasons were and if we received a truthful response, one of those reasons would be that the applicant or employee was a woman. In the specific context of sex stereotyping, an employer who acts on the basis of a belief that a woman cannot be aggressive, or that she must not be, had acted on the basis of gender. As for the legal relevance of sex stereotyping, we are beyond the day when an employer could evaluate employees by assuming or insisting that they matched the stereotype associated with their group, for in forbidding employers to discriminate against individuals because of their sex, Congress intended to strike at the entire spectrum of disparate treatment of men and women resulting from sex stereotypes.

An employer who objects to aggressiveness in women but whose positions require this trait places women in an intolerable and impermissible Catch-22: out of a job if they behave aggressively and out of a job if they don't. Title VII lifts women out of this bind.

The stereotyping in this case did not simply consist of stray remarks. On the contrary, Hopkins proved that Price Waterhouse invited partners to submit comments; that some of the comments stemmed from sex stereotypes; that an important part of the Policy Board's decision on Hopkins was an assessment of the submitted comments; and that Price Waterhouse in no way disclaimed reliance on the sex-linked evaluations. This is not, as Price Waterhouse suggests, "discrimination in the air"; rather, it is, as Hopkins put it, "discrimination brought to ground and visited upon" an employee.

Neutral Practices or Policies That Discriminate

Title VII may be violated even though the employer has not used any of the prohibited factors in any employment-related decision. All employment policies or practices are then considered to be neutral on their face, meaning that there has been no disparate treatment. However, the effect of the application of those policies might be as if direct discrimination had been practiced. The next two theories of discrimination apply to such situations.

Policies or Practices That Have a Disparate Impact on a Protected Group

The application of some employment standards may have the effect of discriminating against members of a group protected by Title VII, as if the employer had used one of the prohibited factors. For example, assume that ABC, Inc. is inteviewing applicants for an entry level management trainee position. One of the factors used to distinguish among candidates is height. No job candidate under six feet tall would be considered. At first glance, although the requirement seems silly, it appears that there is no violation of Title VII. The factors of disparate treatment do not include size. However, on further reflection, that "neutral" standard would have a discriminatory effect on women. Far fewer females than males would be able to meet the height standard; thus, the standard has a disparate impact based on sex.

The Supreme Court's initial interpretation of a Title VII "neutral" practices theory occurred in 1971 in *Griggs* v. *Duke Power Co.* In a unanimous opinion, written by Chief Justice Burger, the Court focused on whether job requirements that disproportionately affect groups protected by the act are predictive of success in the job itself.

> The Act proscribes not only overt discrimination but also practices that are fair in form, but discriminatory in operation. The touchstone is business necessity. If an employment practice which operates to exclude Negroes cannot be shown to be related to job performance, the practice is prohibited.
>
> We do not suggest that either the District Court or the Court of Appeals erred in examining the employer's intent; but good intent or absence of discriminatory intent does not redeem employment procedures or testing mechanisms that operate as "built-in headwinds" for minority groups and are unrelated to measuring job capability.
>
> Nothing in the Act precludes the use of testing or measuring procedures; obviously they are useful. What Congress has forbidden is giving these devices and mechanisms controlling force unless they are demonstrably a reasonable measure of job performance. Congress has not commanded that the less qualified be preferred over the better qualified simply because of minority origins. Far from disparaging job qualifications as such, Congress has made such qualifications the controlling factor, so that race, religion, nationality, and sex become irrelevant. What Congress has commanded is that any tests used must measure the person for the job and not the person in the abstract.

Thus, after *Griggs*, the analysis of the example in which height was a job requirement would proceed as follows.

No intent to exclude women from the management trainee jobs would need to be established. The key was that the standard used served as a substitute for direct sex discrimination. However, simply because a neutral job evaluation standard had a disparate impact on one of the Title VII categories did not automatically result in a violation of Title VII. If the employer could show that the standard was related to the job in question, then the standard could be used. However, the courts closely scrutinized any such job requirement. In the management trainee example, height would have nothing to do with the job. Therefore, the use of that standard would be impermissible sex discrimination.

Note the requirement that the employer must show the job-related nature of the neutral category. Such a requirement led managers to evaluate various jobs in their companies to determine what skills were central to those jobs. Thereafter, job requirements would need to relate to the needed skills as well as be predictive of success in performance of the job. One example would be a typing skills test given to all applicants for word processing jobs at ABC, Inc. The typing test, assuming it was properly designed, is directly related to the job. ABC is not required to hire people who cannot type, even if the effect of such a test would be to exclude, for example, most Catholics from the job.

Thus, after *Griggs*, companies planned their job selection criteria keeping this Title VII theory in mind. Chevron Corporation, for example, provided its executives with expertly crafted job selection guidelines by which applicants were to be evaluated. In doing so, the corporation sought to strengthen its argument that ''job relatedness'' was at the heart of its procedures in the event women or minorities were underrepresented in a certain job group and an employment discrimination claim was filed.

In *Ward's Cove Packing* v. *Atonio* (1989) the Supreme Court reinterpreted this issue. Various proof requirements were changed that made challenging ''neutral'' practices far more difficult. However, the Civil Rights Act of 1991 overturned this judicial construction of Title VII, returning things to pre–*Ward's Cove* practices. Consequently, business executives again need to ensure that job-related standards actually measure the job in question. Consider the following case.

Bradley v. Pizzaco of Nebraska, Inc. d/b/a Domino's Pizza
United States Court of Appeals, Eighth Circuit
939 F.2d 610 (1991)

Domino's grooming policy prohibits company employees from wearing beards. Pizzaco, a Domino's franchisee, hired Bradley to deliver pizzas, but fired him within two weeks because he would not remove his beard. Bradley is a black man who suffers from pseudofolliculitis barbae (PFB), a skin disorder affecting almost half of all black males. The symptoms of PFB—skin irritation and scarring—are brought on by shaving, and in severe cases PFB sufferers must abstain from shaving altogether. Domino's policy, however, provides for no exceptions. As Pizzaco's owner explained, "You must be clean-shaven to work for Domino's."

Langston Bradley brought a disparate impact case against Domino's Pizza, Inc. and Pizzaco of Nebraska, Inc. (collectively Domino's), claiming his discharge for failure to comply with Domino's no-beard policy violates Title VII because the policy discriminates against black males.

Fagg, Circuit Judge

This case is about a facially neutral employment policy that discriminates against black males when applied. Title VII forbids employment policies with a disparate impact unless the policy is justified by legitimate employment goals. To make a prima facie case of disparate impact, the EEOC must identify a specific employment practice that has a significantly disparate impact on black males. Through expert medical testimony and studies, the EEOC demonstrated Domino's policy necessarily excludes black males from the company's work force at a substantially higher rate than white males. In so doing, the EEOC has shown Domino's facially neutral grooming requirement operates as a "built-in headwind" for black males.

The record shows PFB almost exclusively affects black males, and white males rarely suffer from PFB or comparable skin disorders that may prevent a man from appearing clean-shaven. Nevertheless, Domino's contends that the EEOC failed to show black males with PFB who could not shave were turned away or were fired for failing to comply with Domino's no-beard policy. We

disagree. There is no requirement that disparate impact claims must always include evidence that actual job applicants were turned down for employment because of the challenged discriminatory policy. The reason is self-evident: a discriminatory work policy might distort the job applicant pool by discouraging otherwise qualified workers from applying.

The EEOC's evidence makes clear that Domino's strictly-enforced no-beard policy has a discriminatory impact on black males. PFB prevents a sizable segment of the black male population from appearing clean-shaven, but does not similarly affect white males. Domino's policy—which makes no exceptions for black males who medically are unable to shave because of a skin disorder peculiar to their race—effectively operates to exclude these black males from employment with Domino's. Thus, having concluded the EEOC has shown Domino's grooming policy falls more harshly on blacks than it does on whites, we must reverse the district court's holding that the EEOC failed to make a prima facie showing of disparate impact.

Policies or Practices That Perpetuate the Effects of Past Discrimination

A second type of "neutral" employment practice will also violate Title VII if it continues the discriminatory conditions that existed prior to passage of the Civil Rights Act of 1964. A couple of examples taken from Title VII cases will illustrate.

A union restricted its membership to white workers until that practice was forbidden by Title VII. Thereafter, the union adopted a rule requiring any new members to be either related to a current member or recommended by a current member. Note that at the time, because of the union's long-time discrimination, few if any black applicants could meet the "neutral" membership rule. Thus, the rule was held to perpetuate the effects of past racial discrimination.

In a second example, an employer assigned white workers to one type of job and black workers to another (paying less) until the practice was forbidden by Title VII. The employer also prohibited workers from transferring between types of jobs. The second practice remained in effect. However, although "neutral," this rule perpetuated the past discrimination that assigned black workers to low-paying jobs, since they would be unable to transfer out of them. It thus violated Title VII.

Today, about thirty years since Title VII became effective, few current practices or rules can be tied to discriminatory conditions prior to 1964. However, two major issues have been litigated under this issue, neither of which was found to violate Title VII.

SENIORITY SYSTEMS

Seniority systems are a means to protect workers from arbitrary and subjective treatment by employers. For example, during a layoff, the application of seniority would require the last-hired workers to be the first laid off. This criterion is viewed as unbiased and is common throughout the unionized workplace. Since seniority is based on the time-in-job, employment discrimination that kept certain workers from being hired is carried forward through seniority. If a factory before 1964 refused to hire black workers, then blacks hired after Title VII was enacted may have less seniority than if a nondiscriminatory hiring policy had always existed. During an economic decline, those black workers would be the first to be laid off because of their relatively low seniority.

The Civil Rights Act of 1964 contained a provision designed to protect bona fide seniority systems from the terms of Title VII. Those systems were deemed by Congress to be an important part of workplace harmony, and thus employment decisions based on a bona fide seniority system were not in violation of Title VII. However, questions arose concerning whether a seniority system that reflected pre-1964 employment discrimination could be considered "bona fide." In *Teamsters* v. *United States* (1977) the United States Supreme Court upheld such seniority systems. A "neutral" seniority system did not become illegal simply because it perpetuated past employment discrimination. Employees with seniority rights could be favored even over those who had less seniority because of past discrimination.

COMPARABLE WORTH

A wage gap exists between certain jobs (e.g., librarian and city planner) in which the credentials (a master's degree) and skills of the workers are similar. The jobs themselves are not the same, but each reflects a common level of worker talent and importance to employers. What if some of these jobs were closed to women and minorities prior to the enactment of Title VII? As a result, those jobs paid more than comparable ones that were open to all. Would continued differences in compensation between those jobs be considered to perpetuate the effects of the past discrimination? This issue is cental to **comparable worth** theory.

The first government use of comparable worth appeared in 1942, when the National War Labor Board issued General Order Number 16 allowing employers to adjust pay to equalize wage rates for men and women. However, when Congress adopted the Equal Pay Act in 1963, the issue of comparable worth was considered and rejected in favor of requiring equal pay for equal work.

The current theory of comparable worth developed in response to the belief that, because of a variety of factors, women are underpaid in comparison with men. Comparable worth is a principle of wage determination involving the evaluation of the worth or value of an employee's job and the relative value of that job compared with all others within the company. Those who espouse the comparable worth doctrine argue that employees who perform work of comparable value to their employer should receive equal pay, even though the jobs being compared are not the same.

Proponents of comparable worth argue that market-based wage rates perpetuate past, pre-1964 discrimination against women, when many high-paying jobs were closed to women. Typical jobs that were available were relatively low paying. The low pay, proponents argue, resulted from the fact that these jobs were considered women's work. Today, those jobs remain relatively low paying.

Opponents of the theory dispute that the value of jobs can be measured independently of the workings of the market. Another layer of bureaucracy would be needed to assess and compare the worth of dissimilar work with their results being highly subjective and questionable. Although women as a group are paid less than men, the comparable worth theory is seen as unfit to address that problem.

The following case refused to extend Title VII to comparable worth theory. Thus comparable worth arguments will not give rise to a finding of sex discrimination. However, simply because the judiciary has so construed Title VII does not mean that business managers may ignore such claims. Unions [such as the American Federation of State, County, and Municipal Employees (AFSCME) and the United Auto Workers (UAW)] have successfully negotiated comparable worth settlements on behalf of the workers they represent. For example, the UAW and the state of Michigan settled a comparable worth suit the union had brought; employees in clerical and other low-paying jobs that are generally filled by women received pay raises of between forty and sixty cents per hour.

As an aside, the judge, Anthony Kennedy, who wrote the following opinion, was President Reagan's last appointee to the United States Supreme Court. His vote was the key to the much-touted conservative majority that emerged on the Court. However, Justice Kennedy has not followed a predictable conservative agenda. He is now considered a part of the moderate "swing vote" faction of the Court.

American Federation of State, County, and Municipal Employees v. State of Washington
United States Court of Appeals, Ninth Court
770 F.2d 1401 (1985)

In 1974, the state commissioned a study to determine whether a wage disparity existed between employees in jobs held predominately by women and jobs held predominately by men. The study examined sixty-two classifications in which at least seventy percent of the employees were men. It found a wage disparity of about twenty percent, to the disadvantage of employees in jobs held mostly by women, for jobs considered of comparable worth. The state of Washington conducted similar studies in 1976 and 1980, and in 1983 the state enacted legislation providing for a compensation scheme based on comparable worth. The scheme was to take effect over a ten-year period.

In 1982, AFSCME brought this action in the district court, seeking immediate implementation of a system of compensation based on comparable worth. The district court found the state discriminated on the basis of sex, in violation of Title VII of the Civil Rights Act of 1964, by compensating employees in jobs where women predominate at lower rates than employees in jobs where men predominate, if these jobs, though dissimilar, were identified by certain studies to be of comparable worth. The state appealed. The court of appeals held that a violation of Title VII was not established.

Kennedy, Circuit Judge

AFSCME alleges sex–based wage discrimination throughout the state system, but its explanation and proof of the violation is, in essence, Washington's failure as early as 1979 to adopt and implement at once a comparable worth compensation program. The comparable worth theory, as developed in a case before us, postulates that sex-based wage discrimination exists if employees in job classifications occupied primarily by women are paid less than employees in job classifications filled primarily by men, if the jobs are of equal value to the employer, though otherwise dissimilar.

AFSCME contends discriminatory motive may be inferred from the study, which finds the State's practice of setting salaries in reliance on market rates creates a sex-biased wage disparity for jobs deemed of comparable worth. AFSCME argues from the study that the market reflects a historical pattern of lower wages to employees in positions staffed predominately by women; and it contends the State of Washington perpetuates that disparity, in violation of Title VII, by using market rates in the compensation system. The inference of discriminatory motive which AFSCME seeks to draw from the State's participation in the market system fails, as the State did not create the market disparity and considerations in setting salaries.

Neither law nor logic deems the free market system a suspect enterprise. Economic reality is that the value of a particular job to an employer is but one factor influencing the rate of compensation for that job. Other considerations may include the availability of workers willing to do the job and the effectiveness of collective bargaining in a particular industry. We recognize that employers may be constrained by market forces to set salaries under prevailing wage rates for different job classifications. We find nothing in the language of Title VII or its legislative history to indicate Congress intended to abrogate fundamental economic principles such as the laws of supply and demand or to prevent employers from competing in the labor market.

While the Washington legislature may have the discretion to enact a comparable worth plan if it chooses to do so, Title VII does not obligate it to eliminate an economic inequality which it did not create.

Reasonable Accommodation

The final theory of discrimination that arises under Title VII involves only discrimination on the basis of religion. In 1972, the Civil Rights Act was amended to impose an additional requirement on employers whose policies have the effect of discriminating against a person because of religion. The employer was placed under a duty to reasonably accommodate an employee's religious beliefs unless doing so would cause undue hardship.

Most of the cases that have arisen under this theory have involved workers whose beliefs forbade Saturday work. Like the case following, those cases have not required the employer to go to extraordinary lengths to accommodate the workers. However, the courts do note any reasonable attempts that have been made in such cases. What does this suggest to business managers who may be asked to change an employee's work schedule because of that employee's religious beliefs?

Trans World Airlines v. Hardison
United States Supreme Court
431 U.S. 324 (1977)

Hardison started to work at the overhaul base of Trans World Airlines on June 5, 1967. In the spring of 1968, he began to study religion under the Worldwide Church of God. One of its tenets is that people must not work from sunset on Friday until sunset on Saturday. Hardison informed the manager of his religious beliefs. TWA found Hardison a job that permitted him to observe his religious beliefs. Hardison then bid for and received another job in another building. The two buildings had separate seniority lists. Hardison lacked enough seniority to qualify for a schedule that permitted work at a time he desired. TWA tried to accommodate his religious beliefs, but was unable to do so because of the seniority list. Hardison refused to report for work on Saturdays. TWA fired him. He then brought charges of religious discrimination against TWA. The trial court ruled for TWA. The Eighth Circuit Court of Appeals ruled for Hardison. The Supreme Court ruled for TWA.

Justice White

It might be inferred from the Court of Appeals' opinion and from the brief of the EEOC in this Court that TWA's efforts to accommodate were no more than negligible. The findings of the District Court, supported by the record, are to the contrary. In summarizing its more detailed findings, the District Court observed:

> TWA established as a matter of fact that it did take appropriate action to accommodate as required by Title VII. It held several meetings with plaintiff at which it attempted to find a solution to plaintiff's problems. It did accommodate plaintiff's observance of his special religious holidays. It authorized the union steward to search for someone who would swap shifts, which apparently was normal procedure.

It is also true that TWA itself attempted without success to find Hardison another job. The District Court's view was that TWA had done all that could reasonably be expected within the bounds of the seniority system.

As will become apparent, the seniority system represents a neutral way of minimizing the number of occasions when an employee must work on a day that he would prefer to have off. Additionally, recognizing that weekend work schedules are the least popular, the company made further accommodation by reducing its work force to a bare minimum on those days.

Hardison and the EEOC insist that the statutory obligation to accommodate religious needs takes precedence over both the collective-bargaining contract and the seniority rights of TWA's other employees. We agree that neither a collective-bargaining contract nor a seniority system may be employed to violate the statute, but we do not believe that the duty to accommodate requires TWA to take steps inconsistent with the otherwise valid agreement. Collective bargaining, aimed at effecting workable and enforceable agreements between management and labor, lies at the core of our national labor policy, and seniority provisions are universally included in the contracts. Without a clear and express indication from Congress, we cannot agree with Hardison and the EEOC that an agreed-upon seniority system must give way when necessary to accommodate religious observances. To require TWA to bear more than a de minimus cost in order to give Hardison Saturdays off is an undue hardship. Like abandonment of the seniority system, to require TWA to bear additional costs when no such costs are incurred to give other employees the days off that they want would involve unequal treatment of employees on the basis of their religion. By suggesting that TWA should incur certain costs in order to give Hardison Saturdays off the Court of Appeals would in effect require TWA to finance an additional Saturday off and then to choose the employee who will enjoy it on the basis of his religious beliefs. While incurring extra costs to secure a replacement for Hardison might remove the necessity of compelling another employee to work involuntarily in Hardison's place, it would not change the fact that the privilege of having Saturdays off would be allocated according to religious beliefs.

PERMITTED DISCRIMINATION: THE BONA FIDE OCCUPATIONAL QUALIFICATION

In certain circumstances, the Civil Rights Act permits disparate treatment in employment; that is, one of the Title VII categories may be used to distinguish among job applicants. The circumstance when the otherwise prohibited category may be used is when the characteristic is a **bona fide occupational qualification (BFOQ)**. Note however, that the BFOQ analysis does not apply to discrimination on the basis of race or color. Its applicability is limited to employment decisions made on the basis of religion, sex, or national origin.

A bona fide occupational qualification arises when religion, sex, or national origin is a requirement that is reasonably necessary to operate the business. For example, a gym could hire only women to work in the women's locker room. Although a person of either sex could adequately perform the job of locker room attendant, the circumstances of the job create a business necessity that gender be used as a means to distinguish between job applicants.

Courts have construed narrowly the BFOQ exception to Title VII's discrimination prohibition. The employer has a heavy burden to establish a business necessity for a job qualification concerning sex, religion, or national origin. Three elements must be established before a BFOQ will be found.

First, there must be a connection between the classification and job performance. Women, for example, were frequently denied certain job opportunities on the basis of stereotypical or romantic notions. Thus, under the assumption that women were not aggressive, sales jobs were assigned to men. However, there is no link between the sex of a sales representative and the job of selling. Personal characteristics other than the sex of the applicant are central to that job.

Second, the classification must be necessary for the successful performance of the job. However, this necessity test is not to be based on customer or fellow employee preferences. For example, even if customers prefer female sales representatives, requiring that sales representative applicants be women will not generally be found to be necessary for the successful performance of the job. Instead, the classification itself must be somehow intertwined with the job. Hiring women for wet nurse positions or actors and actresses for certain roles needed to ensure authenticity in a play are examples.

Finally, the job performance affected by the classification must be the "essence" of the employer's business. For example, in the case that follows, the "essence" of the airline's business is safe air transport. The tasks that women attendants may perform better than men (comforting or reassuring passengers) are

Applying the BFOQ Exception

On August 17, 1978, Wade Kern entered into a written contract of employment with Dynalectron Corporation to perform duties as a helicopter pilot in Saudi Arabia. The work to be performed in Saudi Arabia consisted of flying helicopters over crowds of Muslims making their pilgrimage along Muhammad's path to Mecca. The purpose of these flights was twofold: to protect against any violent outbreaks and to help fight fires.

Those pilots who were stationed at Jeddah would be required to fly into the holy area, Mecca. Saudi Arabian law, based upon the tenets of the Islamic religion, prohibits the entry of non-Muslims into Mecca under penalty of death. Thus, Dynalectron required all pilots stationed at Jeddah to be (or become) Muslim. Wade Kern went through such a course, chose his new Islamic name, signed his certificate of conversion, and then changed his mind about his conversion.

Dynalectron offered Kern a job as a member of the air crew, a position not requiring his conversion. However, Kern declined to take that job. Kern filed suit, alleging discrimination under Title VII. His employer sought to apply the BFOQ exception. The court held that Dynalectron proved a factual basis for believing that *all* non-Muslims would be unable to perform this job safely. Specifically, non-Muslims flying into Mecca are, if caught, beheaded. Thus, the court found that non-Muslims pilots stationed in Jeddah were not safe as compared with Muslim pilots. Therefore, Dynalectron's discrimination against non-Muslims in general, and Wade Kern specifically, was not unlawful since to hire Muslims exclusively for this job was a bona fide occupational qualification reasonably necessary to the normal operation of Dynalectron's business.

Kern v. *Dynalectron Corp.*, 577 F.Supp. 1196 (N.D. Tex. 1983).

tangential to the safety aspect of the business. Thus, refusing to hire men as flight attendants cannot be justified because those features of the job are an insignificant part of the airline's business.

As suggested by this discussion, very few bona fide occupational qualifications will be found. Title VII was designed to remove stereotyping and replace it with measuring the individual for the job. Below is an example of a claimed BFOQ that was not allowed.

Diaz v. Pan American World Airways, Inc.
United States Court of Appeals, Fifth Circuit
442 F.2d 385 (1971)

Celio Diaz applied for a job as flight cabin attendant with Pan American Airlines in 1967. He was rejected because Pan Am had an admitted policy of restricting its hiring for that position to females. Thus, both parties stipulated that the primary issue for the district court was whether, for the job of flight cabin attendant, being a female is a "bona fide occupational qualification reasonably necessary to the normal operation" of Pan American's business.

Having reviewed the evidence submitted by Pan American regarding its own experience with both female and male cabin attendants it had hired over the years, the trial court found that Pan Am's current hiring policy was the result of a pragmatic process "representing a judgment made upon adequate evidence acquired through Pan Am's considerable experience, and designed to yield under Pan Am's current operating conditions better average performance for its passengers than would a policy of mixed male and female hiring." The performance of female attendants was better in the sense that they were superior in such nonmechanical aspects of the job as "providing reassurance to anxious passengers, giving courteous personalized service and, in general, making flights as pleasurable as possible within the limitations imposed by aircraft operations."

The trial court also found that Pan Am's passengers overwhelmingly preferred to be served by female stewardesses. Moreover, on the basis of the expert testimony of a psychiatrist, the court found that an airplane cabin represents a unique environment in which an air carrier is required to take account of the special psychological needs of its passengers. These psychological needs are better attended to by females. This is not to say that there are no males who would not have the necessary qualities to perform these nonmechanical functions, but the trial court found that the actualities of the hiring process would make it more difficult to find these few males.

In what appears to be a summation of the difficulties, which the trial court found would follow from admitting males to this job, the court said "that to eliminate the female sex qualification would simply eliminate the best available tool for screening out applicants likely to be unsatisfactory and thus reduce the average level of performance."

Tuttle, Circuit Judge

This appeal presents the important question of whether Pan American Airlines' refusal to hire appellant and his class of males solely on the basis of their sex violates Title VII of the 1964 Civil Rights Act. Because we feel that being a female is not a "bona fide occupational qualification" for the job of flight cabin attendant, appellee's refusal to hire appellant's class solely because of their sex, does constitute a violation of the Act.

We begin with the proposition that the use of the word "necessary" in section 703(e) requires that we apply a business necessity test, not a business convenience test. That is to say, discrimination based on sex is valid only when the essence of the business operation would be undermined by not hiring members of one sex exclusively.

The primary function of an airline is to transport passengers safely from one point to another. While a pleasant environment, enhanced by the obvious cosmet-

ic effect that female stewardesses provide as well as, according to the finding of the trial court, their apparent ability to perform the non-mechanical functions of the job in a more effective manner than most men, may all be important, they are tangential to the essence of the business involved. No one has suggested that having male stewards will so seriously affect the operation of an airline as to jeopardize or even minimize its ability to provide safe transportation from one place to another.

We do not mean to imply, of course, that Pan Am cannot take into consideration the ability of individuals to perform the non-mechanical functions of the job. What we hold is that because the non-mechanical aspects of the job of flight cabin attendant are not "reasonably necessary to the normal operation" of Pan Am's business, Pan Am cannot exclude all males simply because most males may not perform adequately.

Before sex discrimination can be practiced, it must

not only be shown that it is impracticable to find the men that possess the abilities that most women possess, but that the abilities are necessary to the business, not merely tangential.

Similarly, we do not feel that the fact that Pan Am's passengers prefer female stewardesses should alter our judgment. A BFOQ ought not be based on "the refusal to hire an individual because of the preferences of co-workers, the employer, clients or customers."

While we recognize that the public's expectation of

finding one sex in a particular role may cause some initial difficulty, it would be totally anomalous if we were to allow the preferences and prejudices of the customers to determine whether the sex discrimination was valid. Indeed, it was, to a large extent, these very prejudices the Act was meant to overcome. Thus, we feel that customer preference may be taken into account only when it is based on the company's inability to perform the primary function or service it offers. The judgment is reversed."

DEVELOPMENTS IN EQUAL EMPLOYMENT LAW

Affirmative Action Plans

The issue of **affirmative action plans** illustrates a conflict between goals of Title VII. On the one hand, employees are to be free of job-related decisions based on their race, color, sex, religion, or national origin. Those decisions are to be made according to neutral standards. However, victims of historical discriminatory practices are to be moved into the mainstream of economic life in America. Elimination of the gap in earnings between black and white workers as an effect of discrimination was also an aim of the Civil Rights Act.

Minority workers have argued that simply removing the barriers to equal opportunity in employment is not enough. The lasting economic effects of long-term discrimination can be overcome only if minority workers are given a fair share of the available positions. Affirmative action is needed to provide employment advantages to certain people to remedy the ingrained inequalities of long-term discrimination. Some beneficiaries of affirmative action plans, however, cite a stigma of being considered "preferred" and thus not really qualified for their jobs. They fear that their talents and accomplishments will be overlooked once they are labeled as affirmative action hires.

Critics of affirmative focus on the color-blind or neutral standard goal of Title VII. By allowing preferences to be given to certain groups, the discrimination that the act meant to eliminate remains. Primarily white, male workers are made the new victims of discrimination. The real culprits, the decision makers, were doing the same thing under affirmative action that they did before the Civil Rights Act—using a person's race or sex as a means of assigning the benefits or burdens of society.

In 1979, the United States Supreme Court upheld a union-management voluntary affirmative action plan that was aimed at ending racial imbalance in Kaiser Aluminum Corporation's craft workforce. However, affirmative action as a legal issue was not settled by that case, *United Steelworkers* v. *Weber*. Cases and disputes continue to arise. The difficulty is in reconciling the dual goals of Title VII.

After *Weber*, business managers were able to reduce the risk of employment discrimination liability by adopting an affirmative action plan. Consequently, minority workers would be less likely to make a successful Title VII case. Further, as in *Weber*, white male workers adversely affected by the plan would have a difficult task of establishing ''reverse discrimination.'' *Weber* and the case that follows may thus be described as creating a ''safe harbor'' for business. Adopting affirmative action plans provided business a means to comply with the requirements of Title VII without creating the inordinate uncertainty that would otherwise arise. Recall the materials in Chapter 1 concerning predictability as an important characteristic of an effective law.

The following case is an example of the operation of an affirmative action plan that provided a job promotion to a woman, Diane Joyce. Interestingly, a few years after this case, Joyce sought another promotion, this time to road foreman. She scored first on both the oral and written tests required of applicants, but she did not get the job. A man, who ranked fifth, was promoted to road foreman instead.

Johnson v. Transportation Agency, Santa Clara County
United States Supreme Court
55 U.S.L.W. 4379 (1987)

In December 1978, the Santa Clara County Transit District Board of Supervisors, adopted an Affirmative Action Plan for the County Transportation Agency. In reviewing the composition of its workforce, the agency noted in its plan that women were represented in numbers far less than their proportion of the county labor force in both the agency as a whole and in five of seven job categories. The agency stated that its plan was intended to achieve a statistically measurable yearly improvement in hiring, training, and promoting women throughout the agency in all major job classifications where they are underrepresented. Its long-term goal was to attain a workforce whose composition reflected the proportion of women in the area labor force. The agency's plan set aside no specific number of positions for women, but authorized the consideration of sex as a factor when evaluating qualified candidates for jobs in which members of such groups were poorly represented.

On December 12, 1979, the agency announced a vacancy for the promotional position of road dispatcher. Nine of the applicants, including Diane Joyce and Paul Johnson, were deemed qualified for the job and were interviewed by a two-person board. Seven of the applicants scored above 70 on this interview, which meant that they were certified as eligible for selection. Johnson was tied for second with a score of 75, while Joyce ranked next with a score of 73. A second interview was conducted by three agency supervisors, who ultimately recommended that Paul Johnson be promoted. Prior to the second interview, Joyce had contacted the county's Affirmative Action Office because she feared that her application might not receive disinterested review. Joyce testified that she had disagreements with two of the three members of the second interview panel. The office in turn contacted the agency's Affirmative Action Coordinator, whom the agency's plan makes responsible for keeping the agency director informed. At the time, the agency employed no women in any skilled craft position and had never employed a woman as a road dispatcher. The coordinator recommended to the director of the agency, James Graebner, that Diane Joyce be promoted. After deliberation, Graebner concluded that the promotion should be given to Joyce. Paul Johnson filed a complaint with the EECO, alleging that he had been denied promotion on the basis of sex in violation of Title VII.

Justice Brennan

Paul Johnson, the plaintiff, bears the burden of proving that the Agency's Plan violates Title VII. Once a plaintiff establishes a prima facie case that race or sex has been taken into account in an employer's employment decision, the burden shifts to the employer to articulate a nondiscriminatory rationale for its decision, such as the existence of an affirmative-action plan. The burden then shifts to the plaintiff to prove that the plan is invalid and that the employer's justification is pretextual.

In reviewing the employment decision at issue in this case we must first examine whether that decision was made pursuant to a plan prompted by concerns similar to those of the employer in *Weber*. Thus, an employer seeking to justify the adoption of an affirmative-action plan need not point to its own prior discriminatory practice, but need point only to a conspicuous imbalance in traditionally segregated job categories. Voluntary employer action can play a crucial role in furthering Title VII's purpose of eliminating the effects of discrimination in the workplace, and Title VII should not be read to thwart such efforts. Next, we must determine whether the effect of the plan on males and non-minorities is comparable to the effect of the plan in the *Weber* case.

The first issue is whether consideration of the sex of applicants for skilled craft jobs was justified by the existence of a "manifest imbalance" that reflected underrepresentation of women in "traditionally segregated job categories." The requirement that the "manifest imbalance" relate to a "traditionally segregated job category" provides assurance both that sex will be taken into account in a manner consistent with Title VII's purpose of eliminating the effects of employment discrimination and that the interests of those employees not benefitting from the plan will not be unduly infringed.

It is clear that the decision to hire Joyce was made pursuant to an Agency plan that acknowledged the limited opportunities that have existed in the past for women to find employment in certain job classifications where women have not been traditionally employed in significant numbers. The Plan sought to remedy these imbalances through hiring, training, and promoting women throughout the Agency in all major job classifications where they are underrepresented.

As an initial matter, the Agency adopted as a bench mark for measuring progress in eliminating underrepresentation the long-term goal of a work force that mirrored in its major job classifications the percentage of women in the area labor market. Even as it did so, however, the Agency acknowledged that such a figure could not by itself necessarily justify taking into account the sex of applicants for positions in all job categories. The Plan stressed that such goals should not be construed as "quotas" that must be met, but as reasonable aspirations in correcting the imbalance in the Agency's work force. These goals were to take into account factors such as turnover, layoffs, lateral transfers, new job openings, retirements and availability of women in the area work force who possess the desired qualifications or potential for placement. The Plan specifically directed that, in establishing such goals, the Agency work with the County Planning Department and other sources in attempting to compile data on the percentage of women in the local labor force that were actually working in the job classifications comprising the Agency work force.

Had the Plan simply calculated imbalances in all categories according to the proportion of women in the area labor pool, and then directed that hiring be governed solely by those figures, its validity fairly could be called into question. This is because analysis of a more specialized labor pool normally is necessary in determining underrepresentation in some positions. If a plan failed to take distinctions in qualifications into account in providing guidance for actual employment decisions, it would dictate mere blind hiring by the numbers. The Agency's

Plan emphatically did not authorize such blind hiring. It expressly directed that numerous factors be taken into account in making hiring decisions, including specifically the qualifications of female applicants for particular jobs. Thus, the Agency's management nevertheless had been clearly instructed that they were not to hire solely by reference to statistics.

Given the obvious imbalance in the Skilled Craft category, and given the Agency's commitment to eliminating such imbalances, it was plainly not unreasonable for the Agency to determine that it was appropriate to consider as one factor the sex of Ms. Joyce in making its decision. The promotion of Joyce thus satisfies the first requirement since it was undertaken to further an affirmative-action plan designed to eliminate Agency work force imbalances in traditionally segregated job categories.

We next consider whether the Agency Plan unnecessarily trammeled the rights of male employees or created an absolute bar to their advancement. The Plan sets aside no positions for women. Rather, the Plan merely authorizes that consideration be given to affirmative action concerns when evaluating qualified applicants. As the Agency Director testified, the sex of Joyce was but one of numerous factors he took into account in arriving at his decision. The Agency Plan requires women to compete with all other qualified applicants. No persons are automatically excluded from consideration; all are able to have their qualifications weighed against those of other applicants.

Seven of the applicants were classified as qualified and eligible, and the Agency Director was authorized to promote any of the seven. Thus, denial of the promotion unsettled no legitimate firmly rooted expectation on the part of the petitioner Paul Johnson. Furthermore, while the petitioner in this case was denied a promotion, he retained his employment with the Agency, at the same salary and with the same seniority, and remained eligible for other promotions.

In this case, substantial evidence shows that the Agency has sought to take a moderate, gradual approach to eliminating the imbalance in its work force, one which establishes realistic guidance for employment decisions, and which visits minimal intrusion on the legitimate expectations of other employees. Given this fact, as well as the Agency's express commitment to "attain" a balanced work force, there is ample assurance that the Agency does not seek to use its Plan to maintain a permanent sexual balance.

We therefore hold that the Agency appropriately took into account as one factor the sex of Diane Joyce in determining that she should be promoted to the road dispatcher position. The decision to do so was made pursuant to an affirmative action plan that represents a moderate, flexible, case-by-case approach to effecting a gradual improvement in the representation of women in the Agency's work force. Such a plan is fully consistent with Title VII, for it embodies the contribution that voluntary employer action can make in eliminating the vestiges of discrimination in the workplace.

Sexual Harassment

The issue of **sexual harassment** is one of today's major Title VII issues. As more women have entered the workplace, concern has arisen about unwanted advances or demands for sexual favors as a condition of employment. Such conduct is considered sex discrimination and thus, violates Title VII of the Civil Rights Act of 1964. Sexual harassment is an abuse of power. Often the cases involve a male supervisor exploiting his authority by preying on female employees. The victim must choose between tolerating or submitting to the supervisor's demands or risking unfavorable consequences concerning her job.

Note that although most sexual harrassment cases have a woman victim, the principles also apply to men. In Wisconsin, a jury awarded damages to a male employee who was demoted because he rejected a female superivsor's sexual advances. In another case, sexual harassment was found to exist when two male employees had to choose between having sex with their boss's secretary or losing their jobs.

A business organization's interest in preventing sexual harassment was heightened after the following case, *Meritor Savings Bank* v. *Vinson*. It is not merely the transgressive supervisor who may face Title VII sanctions, but also his or her employer. Cases involving sexual harassment often name the company as a defendant. This takes on added significance because the Civil Rights Act of 1991 permits the award of compensatory and punitive damages in sexual discrimination cases.

Consequently, business executives face the risk of higher "costs" being assessed against their firms if they do not confront the issue of sexual harrassment in the workplace. In fact, major corporations have been doing just that. For example, Honeywell had a detailed handbook prepared that clearly indicates prohibited conduct in the workplace (e. g., wolf whistles, leers). In 1988, Du Pont instituted a sexual harassment prevention program that has been attended by nearly seventy-five percent of its employees. As a result, sexual harassment complaints have decreased.

The *Meritor Savings Bank* case makes note of EEOC guidelines defining sexual harassment. The guidelines state:

> Harrassment on the basis of sex is a violation of Sec. 703 of Title VII. Unwelcome sexual advances, requests for sexual favors, and other verbal or physical conduct of a sexual nature constitute sexual harassment when (1) submission to such conduct is made either explicitly or implicitly a term or condition of an individual's employment, (2) submission to or rejection of such conduct by an individual is used as the basis for employment decisions affecting such individual, or (3) such conduct has the purpose or effect of unreasonably interfering with an individual's work performance or creating an intimidating, hostile or offensive working environment.

In *Meritor Savings Bank* the issue was under what circumstances an employer would be held liable for sexual harassment committed by one of its employees. Some courts had held that an employer's liability exposure extended beyond traditional agency principles. (See Chapter 14 for a discussion of agency.) In order to encourage the employer to ensure that those practices were eliminated, the courts adopted a standard of absolute liability. The Supreme Court rejected that approach.

Meritor Savings Bank v. Vinson
United States Supreme Court
54 U.S.L.W. 4703 (1986)

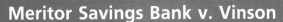

In 1974, respondent Mechelle Vinson met Sidney Taylor, a vice-president of what is now petitioner Meritor Savings Bank and manager of one of its branch offices. When respondent asked whether she might obtain employment at bank, Taylor gave her an application, which she completed and returned the next day; later that same day, Taylor called her to say that she had been hired. With Taylor as her supervisor, respondent started as a teller-trainee, and thereafter was promoted to teller, head teller, and assistant branch manager. She worked at the same branch for four years, and it is undisputed that her advancement there was based on merit alone. In September 1978, respondent notified Taylor that she was taking sick leave for an indefinite period. On November 1, 1978, the bank discharged her for excessive use of that leave.

Respondent brought this action against Taylor and the bank, claiming that during her four years at the bank she had "constantly been subjected to sexual harassment" by Taylor in violation of Title VII. Respondent testified that during her probationary period as a teller-trainee, Taylor treated her in a fatherly way and made no sexual advances. Shortly thereafter, however, he invited her out to dinner and, during the course of the meal, suggested that they go to a motel to have sexual relations. At first she refused, but out of what she described as fear of losing her job, she eventually agreed. According to respondent, Taylor thereafter made repeated demands upon her for sexual favors, usually at the branch, both during and after business hours. She estimated that over the next several years she had intercourse with him some forty or fifty times. In addition, respondent testified that Taylor fondled her in front of other employees, followed her into the women's rest room when she went there alone, exposed himself to her, and even forcibly raped her on several occasions. These activities ceased after 1977, respondent stated, when she started going with a steady boyfriend. Finally, respondent testified that because she was afraid of Taylor she never reported his harrassment to any of his supervisors and never attempted to use the bank's complaint procedure.

Taylor denied respondent's allegations of sexual activity, testifying that he never fondled her, never made suggestive remarks to her, never engaged in sexual intercourse with her, and never asked her to do so. He contended instead that respondent made her accusations in response to a business-related dispute. The bank also denied respondent's allegations and asserted that any sexual harassment by Taylor was unknown to the bank and engaged in without its consent or approval.

Although it concluded that respondent had not proved a violation of Title VII, the district court nevertheless went on to address the bank's liability. After noting the bank's express policy against discrimination and finding that neither respondent nor any other employee had ever lodged a complaint about sexual harassment by Taylor, the court ultimately concluded that "the bank was without notice and cannot be held liable for the alleged actions of Taylor."

The court of appeals for the District of Columbia Circuit reversed.

STRICT LIABILITY

Justice Rehnquist

This case presents important questions concerning claims of workplace "sexual harassment" brought under Title VII of the Civil Rights Act of 1964.

Title VII of the Civil Rights Act of 1964 makes it "an unlawful employment practice for an employer . . . to discriminate against any individual with respect to his compensation, terms, conditions, or privileges of employment, because of such individual's race, color, religion, sex, or national origin." Without question, when a supervisor sexually harasses a subordinate because of the subordinate's sex, that supervisor "discriminate[s]" on the basis of sex. Petitioner apparently does not challenge this proposition. It contends instead that in prohibiting discrimination with respect to "compensation, terms, conditions, or privileges" of employment, Congress was concerned with what petitioner describes as "tangible loss" of "an economic character," not "purely psychological aspects of the workplace environment."

We reject petitioner's view. First, the language of Title VII is not limited to "economic" or "tangible" discrimination. The phrase "terms, conditions, or privileges of employment" evinces a congressional intent "to strike at the entire spectrum of disparate treatment of men and women" in employment. Second, the EEOC guidelines fully support the view that harassment leading to noneconomic injury can violate Title VII. The EEOC drew upon a substantial body of judicial decisions and EEOC precedent holding that Title VII affords employees the right to work in an environment free from discriminatory intimidation, ridicule, and insult.

Since the guidelines were issued, courts have uniformly held, and we agree, that a plaintiff may establish a violation of Title VII by proving that discrimination based on sex has created a hostile or abusive work environment.

For sexual harassment to be actionable, it must be sufficiently severe or pervasive "to alter the conditions of [the victim's] employment and create an abusive working environment." Respondent's allegations in this case— which include not only pervasive harassment but also criminal conduct of the most serious nature— are plainly sufficient to state a claim for "hostile environment" sexual harassment.

The District Court's conclusion that no actionable harassment occurred might have rested on its earlier "finding" that "[i]f [respondent] and Taylor did engage in an intimate or sexual relationship . . . that relationship was a voluntary one." But the fact that sex-related conduct was "voluntary," in the sense that the complainant was not forced to participate against her will, is not a defense to sexual harassment suit brought under Title VII. The gravamen of any sexual harassment claim is that the alleged sexual advances were "unwelcome." The correct inquiry is whether respondent by her conduct indicated that the alleged sexual advances were unwelcome, not whether her actual participation in sexual intercourse was voluntary.

Although the District Court concluded that respondent had not proved a violation of Title VII, it nevertheless went on to consider the question of the bank's liability. Finding that "the bank was without notice" of Taylor's alleged conduct, and that notice to Taylor was not the equivalent of notice to the bank, the court concluded that the bank therefore could not be held liable for Taylor's alleged actions. The Court of Appeals took the opposite view, holding that an employer is strictly liable for a hostile environment created by a supervisor's sexual advances, even though the employer neither knew nor reasonably could have known of the alleged misconduct. The court held that a supervisor, whether or not he possesses the authority to hire, fire, or promote, is necessarily an "agent" of his employer for all Title VII purposes, since "even the appearance" of such authority may enable him to impose himself on his subordinates.

The EEOC, in its brief as amicus curiae, contends that courts formulating employer liability rules should draw from traditional agency principles. Examination of those principles has led the EEOC to the view that where a supervisor exercises the authority actually delegated to him by his employer, by making or threatening to make decisions affecting the employment status of his subordinates, such actions are properly imputed to the employer whose delegation of authority empowered the supervisor to undertake them. Thus, the courts have consistently held employers liable for the discriminatory discharges of employees by supervisory personnel, whether or not the employer knew, should have known, or approved of the supervisor's actions.

This debate over the appropriate standard for employer liability has a rather abstract quality about it given the state of the record in this case. We do not know at this stage, whether Taylor made any sexual advances toward respondent at all, let alone whether those advances were unwelcome, whether they were sufficiently pervasive to constitute a condition of employment, or whether they were "so pervasive and so long continuing . . . that the employer must have become conscious of [them]."

We therefore decline the parties' invitation to issue a definitive rule on employer liability, but we do agree with the EEOC that Congress wanted courts to look to agency principles for guidance in this area. While such common-law principles may not be transferable in all their particulars to Title VII, Congress' decision to define "employer" to include any "agent" of an employer, surely evinces an intent to place some limits on the acts of employees for which employers under Title VII are to be held responsible. For this reason, we hold that the Court of Appeals erred in concluding that employers are always automatically liable for sexual harassment by their supervisors. For the same reason, absence of notice to an employer does not necessarily insulate that employer from liability.

Finally, we reject petitioner's view that the mere existence of a grievance procedure and a policy against discrimination, coupled with respondent's failure to invoke that procedure, must insulate petitioner from liability. While those facts are plainly relevant, the situation before us demonstrates why they are not necessarily dispositive. Petitioner's general nondiscrimination policy did not address sexual harassment in particular, and thus did not alert employees to their employer's interest in correcting that form of discrimination. Moreover, the bank's grievance procedure apparently required an em-ployee to complain first to her supervisor, in this case Taylor. Since Taylor was the alleged perpetrator, it is not altogether surprising that respondent failed to invoke the procedure and report her grievance to him. Petitioner's contention that respondent's failure should insulate it from liability might be substantially stronger if its procedures were better calculated to encourage victims of harassment to come forward.

Accordingly, the judgment of the Court of Appeals reversing the judgment of the District Court is affirmed.

Note the facts in the case above. It involves a classic sexual predator type of harassment claim. However, the definition of sexual harassment is far broader. A violation of Title VII might also occur if the workplace environment becomes intolerable because of activities of fellow employees. Jokes, slurs, comments, leers, and the like may be so burdensome that continuing in the job becomes intolerable. These types of violations may be classified as "hostile workplace environment" sexual harassment. If certain actions unreasonably interfere with an employee's job performance or create an intimidating work environment, then Title VII will be violated.

Examples of such behavior that have led to findings of sexual harassment include repeated unwanted propositions for sexual favors or dates. In addition, crude gestures, graffiti, and explicit drawings or photographs festooning the workplace may also lead to a finding of a hostile environment. The problem for the law is determining from what perspective such activities should be evaluated.

The common method is to measure such conduct by the reasonable person standard. Thus, if a reasonable person's job performance would be impaired or if the reasonable person would be intimidated by the actions, then sexual harassment would arise. But, as noted in Chapter 11, this reasonable person is a fictitious individual. Since "person" is sexless, one presumes that both men's and women's perceptions will be treated the same.

The problem, of course, is that harassment is a subjective judgment of the victim. An all-male workplace in which lewd comments, crude jokes, and the like are tolerated may not seem harassing to the employees. However, add a few women to the workforce and one might expect that their perceptions of the nature of the workplace would be different. Consequently, a trend seems to be developing that focuses on the perception of the reasonable victim. This has come to be known as the "reasonable woman" standard. If a reasonable woman would feel intimidated or her job performance impaired, then a hostile work environment would be found. The following case provides an illustration of the trend. Note that a similar victim-specific standard, "a reasonable black person," was applied in a racial harassment case.

Ellison v. Brady
United States Court of Appeals, Ninth Circuit
924 F.2d 872 (1991)

Kerry Ellison worked as a revenue agent for the Internal Revenue Service in San Mateo, California. During her initial training in 1984 she met Sterling Gray, another trainee. The two co-workers never became friends, and they did not work closely together. In June 1986 when no one else was in the office, Gray asked Ellison to lunch. She accepted. Ellison alleges that after the June lunch Gray started to pester her with unnecessary questions and hang around her desk. On October 9, 1986, Gray asked Ellison out for a drink after work. She declined. One day during the following week, Gray, uncharacteristically dressed in a three-piece suit, asked Ellison out for lunch. Again, she did not accept.

On October 22, 1986, Gray handed Ellison a note he wrote on a telephone message slip which read:

> I cried over you last night and I'm totally drained today. I have never been in such constant term oil [sic]. Thank you for talking with me. I could not stand to feel your hatred for another day.

When Ellison realized that Gray wrote the note, she became shocked and frightened and left the room. Gray followed her into the hallway and demanded that she talk to him, but she left the building. The next month Ellison started four weeks of training in St. Louis, Missouri. Gray mailed her a card and a typed single-spaced, three-page letter. She describes this letter as "twenty times, a hundred times weirder" than the prior note. Explaining her reaction, Ellison stated: "I just thought he was crazy. I thought he was nuts. I didn't know what he would do next. I was frightened."

She immediately telephoned her supervisor, telling her that she was frightened and really upset. Ellison requested that either she or Gray be transferred because she would not be comfortable working in the same office with him. That same day the supervisor had a counseling session with Gray. She informed him that he was entitled to union representation. During this meeting, she also told Gray to leave Ellison alone and reminded Gray many times over the next few weeks that he must not contact Ellison in any way. Gray subsequently transferred to the San Francisco office. Ellison returned from St. Louis in late November and did not discuss the matter further with her supervisor.

After three weeks in San Francisco, Gray filed union grievances requesting a return to the San Mateo office. The IRS and the union settled the grievances in Gray's favor, agreeing to allow him to transfer back to the San Mateo office provided that he promise not to bother Ellison. On January 28, 1987, Ellison first learned of Gray's request in a letter from her supervisor explaining that Gray would return to the San Mateo office. After receiving the letter, Ellison was "frantic." She filed a formal complaint alleging sexual harassment on January 30, 1987, with the IRS. She also obtained permission to transfer to San Francisco temporarily when Gray returned. The IRS employee investigating the allegation agreed with Ellison's supervisor that Gray's conduct constituted sexual harassment. In its final decision, however, the Treasury Department rejected Ellison's complaint because it believed that the complaint did not describe a pattern or practice of sexual harassment covered by the EEOC regulations. After an appeal, the EEOC affirmed the Treasury Department's decision on a different ground. It concluded that the agency took adequate action to prevent the repetition of Gray's conduct.

Ellison filed a complaint in September 1987 in federal district court. The court granted the government's motion for summary judgment on the ground that Ellison had failed to state a prima facie case of sexual harassment owing to a hostile working environment. Ellison appealed.

Beezer, Circuit Judge

We have closely examined *Meritor* and we believe that Gray's conduct was sufficiently severe and pervasive to alter the conditions of Ellison's employment and create an abusive working environment. We first note that the required showing of severity or seriousness of the harassing conduct varies inversely with the pervasiveness or frequency of the conduct. Although a single act can be enough, repeated incidents create a stronger claim of hostile environment, with the strength of the claim depending on the number of incidents and the intensity of each incident. Next, we believe that in evaluating the severity and pervasiveness of sexual harassment, we should focus on the perspective of the victim. If we only examined whether a reasonable person would engage in allegedly harassing conduct, we would run the risk of reinforcing the prevailing level of discrimination. Harassers could continue to harass merely because a particular discriminatory practice was common, and victims of harassment would have no remedy.

We therefore prefer to analyze harassment from the victim's perspective. A complete understanding of the victim's view requires, among other things, an analysis of the different perspectives of men and women. Conduct that many men consider unobjectionable may offend many women. We realize that there is a broad range of viewpoints among women as a group, but we believe that many women share common concerns which men do not necessarily share. For example, because women are disproportionately victims of rape and sexual assault, women have a stronger incentive to be concerned with sexual behavior. Women who are victims of mild forms of sexual harassment may understandably worry whether a harasser's conduct is merely a prelude to violent sexual assault. Men, who are rarely victims of sexual assault, may view sexual conduct in a vacuum without a full appreciation of the social setting or the underlying threat of violence that a woman may perceive.

In order to shield employers from having to accommodate the idiosyncratic concerns of the rare hypersensitive employee, we hold that a female plaintiff states a prima facie case of hostile environment sexual harassment when she alleges conduct which a reasonable woman would consider sufficiently severe or pervasive to alter the conditions of employment and create an abusive working environment.

We adopt the perspective of a reasonable woman primarily because we believe that a sex-blind reasonable person standard tends to be male-biased and tends to systematically ignore the experiences of women. The reasonable woman standard does not establish a higher level of protection for women than men. By acknowledging and not trivializing the effects of sexual harassment on reasonable women, courts can work toward ensuring that neither men nor women will have to run a gauntlet of sexual abuse in return for the privilege of being allowed to work and make a living.

We note that the standard we adopt today classifies conduct as unlawful sexual harassment even when harassers do not realize that their conduct creates a hostile working environment. Well-intentioned compliments by co-workers or supervisors can form the basis of a sexual harassment cause of action if a reasonable victim of the same sex as the plaintiff would consider the comments sufficiently severe or pervasive to alter a condition of employment and create an abusive working environment. That is because Title VII is not a fault-based tort scheme. Title VII is aimed at the consequences or effects of an employment practice and not at the motivation of co-workers or employers.

We hope that over time both men and women will learn what conduct offends reasonable members of the other sex. When employers and employees internalize the standard of workplace conduct we establish today, the current gap in perception between the sexes will be bridged.

Stephens, District Judge (dissenting)

Title VII presupposes the use of a legal term that can apply to all persons and the impossibility of a more individually tailored standard. It is clear that the authors of the majority opinion intend a difference between the "reasonable woman" and the "reasonable man" in Title VII cases on the assumption that men do not have the same sensibilities as women. This is not necessarily true. A man's response to circumstances faced by women and their effect upon women can be and in given circumstances may be expected to be understood by men.

It takes no stretch of the imagination to envision two complaints emanating from the same workplace regarding the same conditions, one brought by a woman and the other by a man. Application of the "new standard" presents a puzzlement which is born of the assumption that men's eyes do not see what a woman sees through her eyes. I find it surprising that the majority finds no need for evidence on any of these subjects. I am not sure whether the majority also concludes that the woman and the man in question are also reasonable without evidence on this subject. I am irresistibly drawn to the view that the conditions of the workplace itself should be examined as affected, among other things, by the con-

duct of the people working there as to whether the workplace as existing is conducive to fulfilling the goals of Title VII.

The circumstances existing in the workplace where only men are employed are different than they are where there are both male and female employees. The existence of the differences is readily recognizable and the conduct of employees can be changed appropriately. This is what Title VII requires. Whether a man or a woman has sensibilities peculiar to the person and what they are is not necessarily known. Until they become known by manifesting themselves in an obvious way, they do not become part of the circumstances of the workplace. Consequently, the governing element in the equation is the workplace itself, not concepts or viewpoints of individual employees. This does not conflict with existing legal concepts.

The creation of the proposed "new standard" which applies only to women will not necessarily come to the aid of all potential victims of the type of misconduct that is at issue in this case. I believe that a gender-neutral standard would greatly contribute to the clarity of this and future cases in the same area.

Sexual Orientation and AIDS

Some state and local governments prohibit discrimination in employment on the basis of sexual orientation. Title VII does not cover this issue. As noted in the *Ulane* case early in this chapter, the definition of sex discrimination under federal law is tied to gender rather than orientation. Nonetheless, other levels of government may regulate that type of discriminatory activity. Massachusetts, for example, merely lists sexual orientation as one of several bases upon which employment decisions cannot be made. California, on the other hand, provides a more extensive statute. Thus, a business manager must consider "local" or "regional" expansion of the discrimination rules. A company with offices in areas with relevant statutes could not base employment decisions on the sexual orientation of its workers.

Sexual orientation is a controversial addition to the list of prohibited discrimi-

The Sexual Orientation Bias
California Labor Code, C. 915, L. 1992

Sec. 1102.1. Sexual Orientation Prohibited; Definitions

(a) Sections 1101 and 1102 prohibit discrimination or different treatment in any aspect of employment or opportunity for employment based on actual or perceived sexual orientation.

(b) For purposes of this section: (1) "Employer" as used in this chapter includes any person regularly employing five or more persons, or any person acting as an agent of an employer, directly or indirectly, including the state or any political subdivision of the state.

(2) "Employer" as used in this chapter does not include a religious association or corporation not organized for private profit, whether incorporated as a religious or public benefit corporation.

(c) Nothing in this section shall invalidate any marital status classification that is otherwise valid.

(d) Nothing in this section shall require or permit the use of quotas or other such affirmative action.

(e) Nothing in this section shall interfere with whatever existing rights an employer has to base employment actions on the commission of conduct illegal in California.

(f) Section 1103 on criminal penalties shall not apply to a violation of this section.

natory factors. Proponents of the addition argue that sexual orientation has nothing to do with one's ability to do a job and that homosexuals are frequent targets of discrimination. Opponents contend that sexual orientation is a lifestyle preference that the full force of the employment laws should not countenance. Note the recent Colorado citizen initiative, Amendment 2, which banned state or local extensions of antidiscrimination laws to include sexual orientation. The amendment, currently being challenged in the courts, acted to overturn some city-enacted ordinances that had done just that.

As a manager, how will you deal with this issue? What if one of your offices is in a jurisdiction that prohibits discrimination on the basis of sexual orientation and another office is in a jurisdiction that has no rule? Should your firm have a uniform policy? Or will it suffice to contour employment decision making to the specific rules of each jurisdiction? Is the material on ethics in Chapter 8 of value in helping you make the decision? These are questions awaiting you when you begin your business career.

As a further illustration of the expansive effect that local statutes can have on equal opportunity laws, consider San Francisco Ordinance No. 49985, which prohibits discriminatory treatment of victims of AIDS (see box). As we will see later in this chapter, the AIDS crisis has raised issues of discrimination in a number of employment areas, including health insurance coverage. As noted in Chapter 1, the law changes with social and historical forces, whether good or ill. How might these developments affect employment decisions in your business?

San Francisco Ordinance No. 49985
Municipal Code Part II, Ch. VIII, Art. 38 (1985)

Sec. 3801. Policy. It is the policy of the City and County of San Francisco to eliminate discrimination based on the fact that a person has AIDS or any medical signs or symptoms related thereto. In adopting this ordinance, the Board of Supervisors does not intend to proscribe any activity the proscription of which would constitute an infringement of the free exercise of religion as guaranteed by the United States and California constitutions.

• • •

Sec. 3803. Employment.—(a) *Prohibited Activity.* It shall be unlawful for any person to do any of the following acts as a result of the fact, in whole or in part, that another person has AIDS or any of the associated conditions covered by this article.

(1) *By an employer*: To fail or refuse to hire, or to discharge any individual; to discriminate against any individual with respect to compensation, terms, conditions or privileges of employment, including promotion; or to limit, segregate or classify employees in any way which would deprive or tend to deprive any individual of employment opportunities, or otherwise adversely affect his/her status as an employee;

• • •

(4) *By an employer, employment agency or labor organization*;
(i) to discriminate against any individual in admission to, or employment in, any program established to provide apprenticeship or other training or retraining, including any on-the-job training program;
(ii) to print, publish, advertise or disseminate in any way, or cause to be printed, published, advertised or disseminated in any way, any notice or advertisement with respect to employment, membership in, or any classification or referral for employment or training by any such organization, which indicates an unlawful discriminatory act or preference.

SELECTED STATUTES

Although Title VII of the Civil Rights Act of 1964 is at the heart of the employment discrimination laws, a number of other important federal statutes should also be considered. This section reviews three of them: Americans with Disabilities Act, Age Discrimination in Employment Act, and Pregnancy Discrimination Act.

Americans with Disabilities Act

Title VII of the Civil Rights Act of 1964 did not apply to discrimination based on a physical or mental disability. Consequently, denying jobs to qualified wheelchair users, for example, *because* of that fact was not illegal. The first attempt to remedy this situation occurred in 1973 with the passage of the Rehabilitation Act. The Rehabilitation Act prohibited discrimination based on a disability, but was limited to employers having ties to the federal government (e.g., government contractors or recipients of federal funds). Thus, most private employment practices were not affected. Furthermore, the Rehabilitation Act did not explicitly authorize federal administrative agencies to create enforcing regulations. Not until 1980, after an executive order, was the regulatory rule-making process begun and not until 1985 did some administrative rules become final.

Consequently, the disabled had few remedies when faced with discriminatory treatment. Hearings before Congress provided evidence that confirmed this supposition: The disabled were denied jobs, prevented from eating in restaurants, required to sit in the back of theaters, and unable to use public transportation. In one shameful incident, children with Down's syndrome were prohibited entry to a zoo because the keeper thought they would upset the chimpanzees.

Scope and Basic Provisions of ADA

In 1990 the Americans with Disabilities Act was enacted. It is a broad–ranging statute that seeks to integrate the disabled into the economic and social mainstream of the country. Not only does it cover employment situations (the focus of this section); it also addresses other areas of American life where the disabled have faced barriers: public services, private transportation, accommodations and services provided by private companies, and telecommunications. Thus, virtually no business is untouched by ADA: Restaurants may need to print menus in braille or provide a reader for customers with visual impairments. Professional offices (e.g., legal and accounting firms) may need to remove or modify architectual barriers that impede access of the wheelchair-bound. Telecommunications companies may need to provide equipment so that the hearing-impaired can use their services.

Under ADA, a person is considered disabled if a physical or mental impairment substantially limits one or more of that person's major life activities. Businesses may not discriminate against such individuals and, furthermore, are required to reasonably accommodate them. Consequently, the Americans with Disabilities Act does not merely forbid the making of arbitrary distinctions. It also mandates that affirmative steps be taken by business to facilitate full participation by the disabled, provided that doing so would not be an undue hardship.

But what *exactly* does this mean? When does accommodation stop being ''reasonable'' and begin to become undue hardship? What steps must a business take to minimize the risk of liability exposure under ADA? These questions have no precise answers. The act is vague here, anticipating communications between businesses and the affected disabled. As a business manager, you might consult the ethics material in Chapter 8 for some ideas.

Through the end of 1992, few cases have arisen that can provide guidance. Although over 1800 complaints were filed with the Department of Justice (under the nonemployment provisions of ADA), the department pursued only one to litigation. Additionally, over 3300 complaints were filed with the Equal Employment Opportunity Commission (under the employment provision of ADA). Yet the EEOC too brought only one suit. The prevailing enforcement activities seem to be based on education and negotiation.

Nonetheless, some of the private suits filed under ADA illustrate its broad scope and the effect its provisions may have on all aspects of operating a business.[1] In one case, a superior court judge who was paraplegic was denied the opportunity to coach at third base for his son's Little League team. The national Little League office had a policy that prohibited wheelchairs from the playing field because of concern over player injuries. The judge sued under ADA and a federal district court overturned the Little League policy on two grounds. First, the policy did not provide that the condition of the disabled wheelchair user be individually assessed in relation to the safety concern. Second, the policy failed to provide for any means of **reasonable accommodation**.

Another example concerned the Becker CPA Review Course. The Department of Justice sued on behalf of a hearing-impaired individual who was not provided a sign language interpreter when taking the review course. A movie theater complex was sued because it failed to provide wheelchair-accessible seating throughout the theater. The issue in both of these cases is the meaning of the reasonable accommodation provision of the act.

However, business need not merely consider the Americans with Disabilities Act as an additional government-imposed burden or cost. It can also be seen as a means by which energetic companies can create market opportunities. One example is Meridian Bancorp, a banking firm based in Reading, Pennsylvania. In 1992 Meridian received an award for its commitment to providing accessibility to the disabled. For example, the year before, the bank promised to make all its automatic bankteller machines wheelchair-accessible. By the end of 1992, sixty percent met that goal. The company asserts that all will be accessible by 1997. In addition, Meridian has created "audio brochures" for the visually impaired describing the full range of bank services—from checking accounts and mortgages to discount brokerage. Furthermore, the bank intends to introduce account statements in large type and braille.

Consider, as a manager, that such activities should expand your customer base. Obviously, a disabled bank customer would be encouraged to switch to the institution that made banking activities easier. Consider also: Are there other target customer groups to whom such innovations would appeal *in addition* to those with disabilities? Audio brochures, for example, might appeal to commuters, who could learn about banking (or other) services while driving to work.

Employment and ADA

The Americans with Disabilities Act prohibits discrimination in any aspect of employment if a disabled person with (or without) reasonable accommodation by the employer can perform the essential functions of the job. This standard contains two quite complex ideas. First, one must be able to separate the essential features of a particular job from those that are merely tangential, convenient, or customary. It is only the essential features that are germane to determining whether a disabled person is qualified for the job.

For example, assume that ABC, Inc. requires that its retail salesclerks stand near the merchandise when dealing with customers. On its face, it would seem that a wheelchair-bound applicant could readily be rejected because of an inability to meet the "standing" requirement. However, under ADA one must inquire about the essential features of the salesclerk position. Such a job, at its core,

Health Insurance and ADA

In July 1991 a New York-based construction union changed its workers' health insurance coverage to exclude HIV infections and AIDS or AIDs–related illnesses. A construction worker who had been a member of the union since 1988 had tested positive for HIV. Because of the coverage change, the worker was unable to obtain needed medical treatment.

The worker filed a complaint with the EEOC contending that the union's unilateral change of coverage violated the Americans with Disabilities Act. In February 1993 after evidence was heard, the New York district director for the EEOC found that the union's sudden refusal to provide full insurance coverage under its benefits plan was discriminatory under ADA and

that the union had no viable defense. The director instructed the parties to meet in order to create a plan to comply with the decision. If compliance does not occur, then either the EEOC or the worker's attorneys can file suit.

Technically, such a localized, low-level ruling carries little precedential weight. However, such an important construction of an employment discrimination statute will not generally be rendered by a district director without prior approval at the highest levels of the EEOC. Consequently, employment law experts contend that the decision may signal the EEOC's intent to pursue employers that change health insurance coverage in order to deny benefits to employees who have AIDS.

involves marketing goods on a one-to-one basis with the customer. Whether this occurs while standing or sitting seems incidental. Consequently, ABC, Inc.'s rejection of a wheelchair-bound applicant because of an inability to meet its "standing" requirement would most likely raise a liability risk under ADA.

"A second complex idea arising from the ADA employment standard concerns reasonable accommodation. Once the essential functions of the job are identified, an individual may not be rejected for that job because of a disability if through reasonable accommodation that individual could successfully perform those functions. In short, the employer must make an effort to modify normal business practices that impede the disabled. The statute, however, does not provide the business executive with a comprehensive list cross-referencing disabilities with required accommodations. Instead, the act is open-ended in this regard, contemplating that the employer and the individual can jointly determine what steps would be necessary to minimize the effects of the disability. Some typical responses would include making the workplace accessible and usable, restructuring the job requirements; and acquiring special equipment.

For example, assume that XYZ, Inc. needed to hire a typist to transcribe audiotapes. Since an essential function of the job is the ability to hear the tapes, a hearing-impaired applicant would be at a decided disadvantage. However, that alone would not be a sufficient reason to reject the applicant. Special amplification equipment can be acquired that would enable the disabled applicant to do the job. Consequently, typing skills of the applicant should be the key factor, independent of the hearing impairment. If the disabled applicant was the better typist, XYZ would be required to acquire the equipment in order to meet the reasonable accommodation standard.

Note, however, that the employer is not required to undergo unreasonable hardship in making such an accommodation. Cost, resources of the business, and the effect on the operation of the business are all factors that can transform an accommodation into a hardship. Thus, if the amplification equipment in the example above was extraordinarily expensive, XYZ would not be required to acquire it in order to accommodate the applicant. However, if other, less expensive means exist to ameliorate the effects of the applicant's hearing impairment, XYZ will need to consider them.

As noted earlier, the Americans with Disabilities Act is not limited to the job application. All aspects of employment are covered: job testing, selection procedures, promotions, and more. The Health Insurance box illustrates the wideranging impact of ADA.

AGE DISCRIMINATION IN EMPLOYMENT ACT

Age is an additional category that raises employment discrimination questions. The primary focus is the older worker. In 1967, when the Age Discrimination in Employment Act was passed, the concern of Congress was unemployment among older workers and the difficulty they often encountered in finding new jobs after being laid off. As a rule, older workers earn a higher wage and consume more benefits than their younger counterparts. Consequently, for economic reasons, a firm might be tempted to arbitrarily discharge or refuse to hire older workers. The purpose of the statute was to refocus workplace decisions on ability rather than age of employees.

The 1967 Act protected employees between ages forty and sixty-five. The upper limit was extended to age seventy in 1978, and in the 1986 amendments the upper limit was removed altogether—with, one exception (until the end of 1993): University professors were protected only to age seventy.

Common remedies assessed for violating the act are back pay and reinstatement. However, the reinstatement remedy is often infeasible because of the acrimony that develops during litigation. In fact, a survey covering the years 1973 to 1980 found that over fifty percent of the workers who had been awarded reinstatement refused to return to their former jobs because, at least in part, they were concerned about possible ill-treatment by the company. A more startling finding was that eighty-seven percent of those who accepted reinstatement left the job within a year, often citing the company's way of dealing with them as a reason. Consequently, a trend in the courts has been to award lost future income and benefits as a remedy in age discrimination cases. In this way, a dollar approximation of reinstatement is made available.

However, not all age-based job classifications are prohibited. A couple of exceptions in the statute can be noted. First, if age can be shown to be a bona fide occupational qualification, then no violation of the act will arise. Recall the discussion of airline flight attendants earlier in the chapter. The same BFOQ concept that applies to using a sex-based job qualification also applies to age. For example, a Federal Bureau of Prisons policy that excluded applicants over age thirty-four from consideration for certain prison jobs was found to be a BFOQ, given the conditions of the job.

A second exception, known as the *high policy maker exception*, provides that top executives who have held their positions for at least two years can be made to retire at age sixty-five. The purpose of this exception is to open opportunities for advancement within organizations. (Studies have shown that one high-level retirement results in five to eight promotions within the hierarchy.) Furthermore, objective performance evaluations of such executives are quite difficult to devise; finally, the company is deemed to benefit by turnover in such positions.

PREGNANCY DISCRIMINATION ACT

The Pregnancy Discrimination Act of 1978 was actually an amendment to Title VII. It expanded the definition of sex discrimination to include discrimination based on pregnancy, thereby overturning the Supreme Court's decision in *General Electric* v. *Gilbert* (1976).

In that case, General Electric had excluded from its employee health benefits package any disabilities arising from pregnancy. The move precipitated a Title VII challenge claiming that such an exclusion was sexually discriminatory, since only women could become pregnant. The Supreme Court rejected the argument, basing its construction of Title VII on the assertion that "sex discrimination" in Title VII was limited to gender distinctions. The GE policy was found not to be a gender-based discrimination. It merely distinguished between pregnant women and nonpregnant persons. This, the Court held, was not prohibited under Title VII.

Public outcry led Congress to amend Title VII to include distinctions based on pregnancy as a form of sex discrimination. The *Ulane* case (on transsexuality) described early in this chapter raises a similar issue concerning the scope of the sex discrimination prohibition under Title VII. In that case too, the court adopted a narrow reading of the term.

SUMMARY

For many years, a large segment of society struggled to overcome unfair treatment. Although the Supreme Court outlawed government-caused racial segregation in *Brown* v. *Board of Education*, the decision failed to address the problem of discrimination in the private workplace. While the civil rights movement took a giant stride forward as a result of *Brown*, many people still dealt with discrimination on a day-to-day basis—particularly in getting and keeping a good job.

Title VII of the Civil Rights Act of 1964 prohibited employment discrimination on the basis of race, color, religion, sex, or national origin. Four theories of Title VII discrimination have been advanced. They involve both direct and indirect forms of discrimination. Note that even benign employment practices may have the effect of discriminating and therefore violate the act.

Business managers, in response to employment discrimination laws, modified their personnel policies. Job qualifications were carefully assessed to ensure that they reflected the skills necessary for the work to be done. Further, affirmative action plans were often adopted as a means of integrating the workforce. These business policies were designed to limit company exposure to employment discrimination claims.

However, complex Title VII issues remain. Note the *Hopkins* case and how a procedure for selecting partners from employee candidates could lead to discrimination problems. In addition, affirmative action continues to raise complex questions about the twin goals of the Civil Rights Act: equal opportunity and integrating members of one-time disfavored groups into the economic mainstream. Finally, given the increasing presence of women in the workplace, the issues of sex discrimination and sexual harassment have taken on added importance. Business managers should note that a Title VII violation will occur if the workplace is deemed to create a hostile environment.

Since the enactment of Title VII, three important federal statutes have affected the scope of equal employment opportunity protection. The first two statutes extended protection to include disability (Americans with Disabilities Act) and age (Age Discrimination in Employment Act). The third statute, by contrast, overturned a narrow judicial construction of sex discrimination under Title VII (Pregnancy Discrimination Act).

State law, too, prohibits discrimination in employment, and local governments have enacted ordinances concerning this issue. At times, these regional legal rules provide greater protection than what is offered through federal legislation. Consequently, a business manager must be aware of the equal opportunity laws from all three levels of government. For large businesses, with operations in numerous states, this may well mean that the legal environment for employment decisions may differ from one factory to another.

REVIEW QUESTIONS

1. Define the following terms:
   a. Affirmative action plans
   b. Bona fide occupational qualification
   c. Comparable worth
   d. Equal Employment Opportunity Commission
   e. Sexual Harrassment

2. Why should employers be held liable for sexually harassing actions of their employees?

3. The Southern Pacific Co. refused to hire Ann Rosenfeld as an agent telegrapher. It argued that because of the arduous nature of the work, women were physically unsuited for the job. At times, the job requires work in excess of ten hours a day and eighty hours a week. It requires heavy physical effort, such as lifting objects weighing more than twenty-five pounds. May the company refuse to hire Ann Rosenfeld for this position?

4. Fernandez was a female employee of Wynn Oil Company. When she was denied a promotion that went to a male employee, she alleged sex discrimination in violation of Title VII of the Civil Rights Act of 1964. Wynn alleged that Fernandez lacked the qualifications necessary for the job. She lacked proficiency in the English language, had difficulty with articulation, had no secondary educa-

tion, and suffered from a drinking problem and erratic work habits. Alternatively, Wynn argued that the male sex was a bona fide occupational qualification for a job performed in foreign countries where women are barred from business. Who should prevail?

5. Donnell, a black employee of General Motors, sought entrance into two skilled trades training programs established by GM. GM required a high school degree. Donnell asserted that such a requirement violated Title VII because it operated to disqualify more blacks than whites and was not justified as a business necessity. Only 0.3 percent of black employees were in skilled trades, while 3.2 percent of white employees were in skilled trade positions. Did the educational requirement violate Title VII?

6. Rawlinson was a twenty-two-year-old female applying as a prison guard trainee at an Alabama penitentiary. She was rejected because she failed to meet the one-hundred-twenty-pound minumum weight requirement of an Alabama statute, which also established a height minimum of five feet two inches. Rawlinson asserted this practice violated Title VII. The Alabama statute would exclude 33.2 percent of the women in the United States between the ages of eighteen and seventy-nine while excluding only 1.28 percent of the men in the same age group. Does this statute violate Title VII?

7. Female matrons who worked at the Washington County jail in Oregon brought suit against the county, maintaining that although their jobs were comparable (not equal) in skill, effort, responsibility, and working conditions to the male-held guard jobs, the women were paid less money. The matrons argued that part of the pay disparity could be explained only by sex discrimination. Do the matrons have a case?

8. Discuss the historical background of Title VII of the Civil Rights Act of 1964.

9. XYZ Corporation had a policy not to hire any black workers until it was sued in 1971 under Title VII of the Civil Rights Act. Thereafter, the corporation eliminated the policy. However, it instituted a new policy that required all new employees to be recommended by at least two current employees with at least twenty years' seniority or by retired XYZ employees. Would this rule raise problems for the corporation under Title VII?

10. Mary Jones is an athletic trainer. She has studied, taught, and worked for a number of years in the specialty of athletic injuries. She has one of the finest backgrounds for this type of work in the country. Jones applies to be an assistant trainer with a National Football League team. Each NFL team has four assistant trainers. Usually only one assistant trainer is present at each game; the assistant trainers work out a game rotation schedule.

   Because of her religion, Jones informs the team that she will not be able to work on Sundays. As a result, the team refuses to consider her application. Does Jones have a claim under Title VII?

11. For each of the above questions that relate a story and ask whether a Title VII problem might arise, creatively assess the same facts and devise a corporate policy for each that seeks to limit such incidents from arising.

12. Bill Jones, a recent college graduate, was hired for an entry level management position at ABC, Inc., a large corporation. His immediate supervisor is Mary Smith, two years older than Jones. They knew each other in college and dated occasionally when Jones was a sophomore. Smith believes that Jones has matured quite a bit in the last three years. She would like to date him. Would she

risk a claim of sexual harassment if she asks Jones out? What if she compliments Jones on his tie? What if they had never dated in the past?

13. You are the manager of a department in ABC, Inc., a major corporation. Six employees, all in their late twenties, of the same sex, race, religion, and national origin, and having no disabilities, work under your supervision. The atmosphere of your department is festive in an odd sort of way. Any person in the news who is different (in the areas noted above) is the subject of jokes, wall posters, lunchtime skits, and the like. You believe that, although crude, this behavior creates workplace cohesion that is necessary for the department's success. If a candidate for a new position in your department is different (as noted above) from the current six employees, would you decide not to hire that person? If so, are there any risks? If not, and the person is hired, are there any risks?

14. You have been appointed vice president of sales for ABC, Inc. Thirty top sales representative report to you. They are divided into five team according to the areas of the world where they work. Three of the teams are fully integrated: men and women representing a number of races. The other two teams are homogeneous: white men only. ABC's policy of not sending sales representatives to locations in which they may face hardship on the basis of race or sex is the reason for two nonintegrated teams. Do you detect any problems with this policy? What if the last three promotions from the groups of sales representatives went to people who had been assigned, at one time, to each of the five teams?

15. You are the director of nursing services in a major private hospital. Virtually every nurse in the hospital is a woman. A new hospital policy provides that in each department, all hires, promotions, and transfers should aim for a goal of creating an employee profile to match that of the surrounding community. Note that fifty-one percent of the members of your community are women. Should you follow the directive? If so, explain the program you might establish to do so. If not, why not?

NOTE

[1] The ADA illustrations are described in R. Samborn, "A Quiet Birthday," *National Law Journal*, March 1, 1993, pp. 1, 42.

CHAPTER 19

Labor–Management Relations: The Regulation of Management

- Historical Background
- General Explanation of Collective Bargaining
- Unfair Labor Practices by Employers

For many years, unions struggled to obtain recognition by employers. The unions often met with frustration and hostility. On some occasions, this hostility erupted into virtual open warfare between the companies and the employees. A major piece of legislation drafted in the 1930s, the Wagner Act, sought to cool the fires between labor and management. Congress hoped to institute a period of labor peace.

The first part of this chapter will present an overview of the conditions that led to the unionization of many industries in America. The text will then address the specific laws passed by Congress to promote collective bargaining and explain the nature and function of the chief federal agency in this area, the National Labor Relations Board (NLRB). One of the board's important functions is the conduct of representation elections in which the employees are permitted to vote for or against unionization. The text next discusses the way the government handles these representation elections.

Managers need to be aware of the types of activities they must avoid when dealing with unions. Certain types of activities will result in the filing of unfair labor practice charges against their corporations. The activities that were outlawed by the Wagner Act will be given considerable attention in the latter part of this chapter.

In the next chapter we will discuss improper activities by unions under the federal labor laws.

HISTORICAL BACKGROUND

Before the 1930s, the courts strove for but failed to formulate a workable labor relations policy. In a typical case early in the nineteenth century, *Commonwealth v. Pullis*, a Pennsylvania court ruled that any joint employee action violated the criminal laws of Pennsylvania. The court imprisoned workers because they joined together for purposes of gaining better working conditions. In the mid-nineteenth century, the courts began to reject the application of the criminal laws to union activities.

In the early nineteenth century, many employees tried to form unions on a city-by-city basis. Union activities tended to be localized, rather than statewide or nationwide. These unions sought a number of goals, such as a ten-hour working day, an end to child labor, and improved working conditions. When the Civil War broke out in 1861, it stimulated industrial activity. During the war, a railroad system was built stretching out to the Midwest. By the end of the Civil War, a huge number of local unions operated in the Northern states, and a few national unions had begun to take root. Several unions attempted to consolidate their organizing efforts on a nationwide basis.

Early Union Goals

Early union leaders often advocated a major restructuring of the United States economic system. The leaders in these movements argued that manufacturers in the United States ought to be required to treat their employees in a more decent, humane manner. One such union, the National Labor Union of Baltimore, worked for many years to encourage workers to form cooperatives in which the workers would own the company for which they worked. The National Labor Union envisioned happy workers producing goods in worker-owned plants.

Very little came of these efforts to restructure the economic system. Over time, the unions in America turned from grandoise plans to alter the conduct of business to more immediately attainable goals, such as higher wages.

Injunctions

In spite of a groundswell in favor of unions throughout the United States, the courts failed to reflect their increasing acceptance by the general public. Initially, the courts stifled the growth of union membership by sentencing union members to prison. The courts eventually turned to the use of civil sanctions, and in particular favored the injunction, a court order requiring the person or group against which it is issued to refrain from a particular activity. A judge quite often issued a temporary ex parte injunction restraining a union from engaging in certain activities. In other words, on the basis of a motion by the employer and without hearing evidence presented by the union, the judge temporarily restrained certain types of union activity pending a formal trial on the merits of the case. Injunctions were vaguely worded. The only safe way to avoid violating the injunction was to cease acting collectively. Quite often, such temporary relief broke the union. The injunction became very unpopular with unions, and the unions in turn became disenchanted with the courts.

Violence   The use of injunctions exacerbated the unfriendly relationship between unions and management. Companies in the 1890s opposed unions with force. The unions met force with force, and violence erupted throughout the United States. Workers of the Amalgamated Association of Iron and Steel Workers and the management of the Carnegie Steel Company fought a heated battle in 1892. Carnegie brought in Pinkerton detectives to fight the strikers. The strike culminated in the deaths of ten people and the injury of numerous others. In 1894, the American Railway Union led a strike against the Pullman Palace Parlor Car Company. Twenty-five people died and sixty were injured in this strike. All of this violence merely increased the hostility of the company owners to the union movement.

Legislative Successes and Union Growth   The unions fought companies in the streets and in the halls of Congress and the state legislatures in the early twentieth century. At the state level, they succeeded in enacting legislation regulating the employment of women and children. Most states passed workers' compensation laws. In 1913, the Congress created a separate Department of Labor. In 1914, Congress passed the Clayton Antitrust Act, which attempted to limit the issuance of injunctions by federal courts in labor disputes. The act failed to stop the courts from enjoining strikes and picketing because the courts failed to interpret and apply the act in such a manner as to limit the use of injunctions.

Railway Labor Act

In the 1920s, the unions intensified their efforts to unionize industry. In 1926, Congress passed the Railway Labor Act, which regulated labor relations in the railroad industry. The act heralded the beginning of public acceptance of unions. The Railway Labor Act gave railroad employees the right to organize and join unions without employer interference and the right to bargain collectively. The act was based on the premise that peaceful labor-management relations are best promoted through collective bargaining between employers and unions.

Norris-LaGuardia Act

In 1932, Congress passed the Norris-LaGuardia Act, which drastically limited the power of the federal courts to issue injunctions against strikes, picketing and boycotts. It outlawed the "yellow dog" contract which prohibited workers, as a condition of employment, from joining a union. It also limited the liability of unions and union members for unlawful acts committed by union officers, agents, or members.

Wagner Act

Congress tried in 1933 to guarantee the right of employees to organize and to bargain collectively through the passage of the National Industrial Recovery Act. The Supreme Court ruled the act unconstitutional in 1935 in *Schechter Poultry*

Co. v. *United States.* Congress responded by enacting the Wagner Act that same year. The Wagner Act guaranteed employees ''the right to self-organization, to form, join, or assist labor organizations to bargain collectively through representatives of their own choosing, and to engage in concerted activities for the purpose of collective bargaining or other mutual aid or protection.'' The act created the National Labor Relations Board (NLRB) and outlawed a number of practices by employers, which we will examine in depth later in this chapter. In *NLRB* v. *Jones and Laughlin Steel Corp.*, the Supreme Court upheld the constitutionality of the Wagner Act.

Congress continued to pass legislation favorable to labor throughout the 1930s. In order to ensure workers a minimum wage and to set maximum hours of work, it passed the Fair Labor Standards Act in 1938. Earlier, in 1935, it had attempted to secure some income for the elderly through the adoption of the Social Security Act.

The Norris-LaGuardia Act and the Wagner Act served as the impetus for the growth of the labor movement. In 1937, 7.25 million workers belonged to unions. The unions succeeded in organizing much of the heavy industry in the United States, such as automobile, rubber, and steel plants. Union membership continued to grow for many decades, aided by this favorable regulatory environment.

Shift in the Law in Favor of Management

Taft-Hartley Act

The mood in Congress turned against the unions in the 1940s, and the tide turned in favor of management. Many people thought organized labor had become too strong in relation to the power of the companies. To offset this imbalance in bargaining power, Congress passed the Labor Management Relations Act (Taft-Hartley) in 1947. The act outlawed a number of practices by unions. (We will examine this act in the next chapter.)

Landrum-Griffin Act

Congress continued to strengthen the rules regulating the behavior of unions with the passage of the Landrum-Griffin Act in 1959. The act outlawed certain activities by labor and management. Landrum-Griffin requires a large amount of information to be disclosed by unions. It closes loopholes in the protection against secondary boycotts and limits organizational and jurisdictional picketing. Congress hoped the Landrum-Griffin Act would serve as a bill of rights for union members. (This act is also dealt with in the next chapter.)

Over the years, the mood of Congress shifted back and forth on the issue of labor relations. The goal of Congress in the 1940s and 1950s was to equalize the bargaining power between management and labor in order to promote peaceful collective bargaining.

We will now examine the manner in which the labor laws are structured at the federal level to enable management and labor to achieve their goals through the collective bargaining process.

GENERAL EXPLANATION OF COLLECTIVE BARGAINING

Organization of the National Labor Relations Board

The national Labor Relations Board (**NLRB**) has two structural divisions: the office of the general counsel, and the board.

The general counsel's office has the responsibility for the day-to-day operations of the agency, both in Washington and in the regional offices. All regional offices work under the auspices of the general counsel, which administers the operations of the field offices. Much of the work of the agencies is done by the regional offices, which look into complaints brought within their respective regions, file charges, and prosecute complaints. The regional offices also conduct representation elections. The general counsel's office is responsible for filing petitions to enforce board orders, if necessary, and for prosecuting any appeals.

The board is composed of five members, each of whom serves for five years. Each board member has a staff of attorneys. Cases are initially taken before an administrative law judge. These judges are controlled by the board.

The agency has two major functions: the conduct of representation elections, and the resolution of unfair labor practices charges.

The Conduct of Representation Elections

A regional office of the NLRB determines the composition of the bargaining units and conducts representation elections. The goal of the board is to provide conditions in which the workers may exercise a free, uncoerced choice in any election.

Support for Election

Before a union files a petition with the board calling for an election, the board must first obtain some evidence of support from the workers. A union often starts with an employee in the plant to spearhead the organizing effort—when possible an intelligent, respected worker with a good record.

The unions prefer to line up the support of a *majority* of the employees in the bargaining unit for tactical reasons. However, in order to call for an election, the union needs to demonstrate the *support of thirty percent* or more of the workers. The union requests employees to sign a card and date it. These cards constitute proof of support by the employees for an election.

Pre-Election Activities

In the event an unfair labor practice occurs during the election campaign, the NLRB can set aside the election. It also may put aside an election if acts by either management or labor prevent the workers from exercising a free, uncoerced choice. The board considers only conduct after the date of the filing of a petition for an election. After an election, the complaining party must immediately file an objection to any improper conduct during the election campaign if it wishes to protect the outcome of the election.

During the period after the filing of a petition for an election but before the election, an employer must exercise great caution in talking to employees. While Section 8(c) of the Taft-Hartley Act guarantees employers the right of free speech, an employer still must not threaten or coerce its employees. An employer also

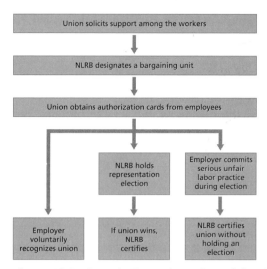

Figure 19.1 Steps in Becoming a Bargaining Representative for Employees

must refrain from talking to the employees in a group within twenty-four hours of the election. Unions too must exercise restraint in their pre-election activities. In order to prevail if an election takes place, the union must receive the vote of a majority of the employees who *actually* vote—not a majority of the employees qualified to vote.

The Bargaining Unit

One complex issue is that of defining the appropriate unit in which to conduct an election. The NLRB tries to find a cohesive unit of employees whose interests are basically the same. Section 9(a) of the National Labor Relations Act makes the union designated by a majority of the employees in an appropriate unit the exclusive representative of all employees in that unit "for purposes of collective bargaining in respect to rates of pay, wages, hours of employment, or other conditions of employment." But which unit of employees is appropriate? The *board* makes this determination. Needless to say, the makeup of a unit may be critical to the outcome of an election.

A court has very limited powers in examining the designation of a bargaining unit.

Establishing Representative Status Through Unfair Labor Practice Proceedings

A union becomes the representative of the employees in the designated bargaining unit in one of three ways: (1) by a voluntary agreement entered into with the company after the union demonstrates majority support by the employees, (2) by winning an election conducted by the NLRB, or (3) through an unfair labor practice proceeding. Figure 19.1 summarizes the steps in becoming a bargaining representative for employees.

Voluntary Recognition

The easiest way for a union to obtain recognition is to demonstrate union support by presenting the employer with authorization cards. The employer may voluntarily recognize the union when it presents cards signed by a majority of the employees.

An Election *For if 50 % want*

Alternatively, the union might seek an election conducted by the NLRB. This normally is quicker than bringing an unfair labor practice charge.

Unfair Labor Practice Charges

The circumstances may be such that a free election appears impossible because the employer has tainted the atmosphere by violating some rights of the employees. In this case, a union may choose to bring a Section 8(a)(5) charge rather than calling for an election. Section 8(a)(5) of the Wagner Act makes it an unfair labor practice for an employer to refuse to bargain collectively with the representatives of its employees.

When an employer commits an unfair labor practice, many employees feel coerced or frightened. They may feel unable to exercise their own free will and judgment. In this situation, an election would be of minimal value. The union would surely lose, not because the employees opposed the union, but because they feared reprisals if they voted in favor of the union. In this case, the board—assuming the union can demonstrate that a majority of the employees signed authorization cards—may certify the union as the bargaining representative for the employees without calling for an election.

In *Linden Lumber* v. *NLRB* (1974), the Supreme Court ruled that ''unless an employer has engaged in an unfair labor practice that impairs the electoral process, a union with authorization cards purporting to represent a majority of the employees, which is refused recognition, has the burden of taking the next step in invoking the Board's election procedures.'' In other words, if the employer did *not* commit an unfair labor practice before the union's request for recognition, the union *must call for an election*.

UNFAIR LABOR PRACTICES BY EMPLOYERS

Employer Interference with Employee Rights

Section 8(a) of the Wagner Act declared it an unfair labor practice for an employer ''to interfere with, restrain, or coerce employees in the exercise of the rights guaranteed in section 7.'' Section 7 reads as follows:

> Employees shall have the right to self-organization, to form, join or assist labor organizations, to bargain collectively through representatives of their own choosing, and to engage in other concerted activities for the purpose of collective bargaining or other mutual aid or protection, and shall also have the right to refrain from any or all of such activities except to the extent such right may be affected by an agreement requiring membership in a labor organization as a condition of employment.

Termination of Contract

In September of 1983, Continental Air Lines, a major air carrier, filed a petition to reorganize. In a very innovative move, Continental rejected the contracts it had with the various unions with whom Continental had previously entered into collective bargaining agreements.

It was in fact possible for Continental to reject all executory contracts, including labor relations contracts, at the time it took this action. In 1984, Congress modestly reformed the law pertaining to this issue. Prior to filing an application for rejection of a collective bargaining agreement, the company must propose to the authorized representative of the union any modifications of the contract that are necessary to permit a reorganization of the company. It must also supply any relevant information required to evaluate the proposal. Thereafter, a court should permit a rejection of a collective bargaining agreement only if it finds that the union has refused to accept the proposal without good cause, and the balance of the equities clearly favors rejection of the agreement.

A collective bargaining agreement may not, therefore, be unilaterally terminated or altered without first complying with these procedures.

Organizing Efforts on Employer's Property

To what extent may an employer limit the ability of unions to speak and distribute literature on company property? Is such an attempt an unfair labor practice under Section 8(a)? Once again, the law must resolve a conflict between the property rights of an employer and the rights of other persons—in this case, unions. A union obviously wishes to come into the plant to speak with the workers in order to get its message across to them. An employer often wishes to limit this contact in the hope the employees will not gain an interest in unionizing.

An employer might go further than merely trying to keep the union and the workers apart. For example, the company could threaten to fire anyone engaged in union activities. Such threats stifle discussion and promote fear. Remarks of this character are calculated to intimidate the employees and violate Section 8(a).

With respect to organizational activities on an employer's premises, the property rights of the company must be weighed against the union's need for access to convey its message to the employees.

As indicated in Section 8(a), the employer must not interfere with rights guaranteed to the employees in Section 7. To prove a violation, the board need not demonstrate that any particular person was coerced, but merely that an employer's actions had a natural tendency to restrain or coerce employees in the exercise of their rights.

Nonemployee Distribution of Literature

In *NLRB* v. *Babcock & Wilcox Co.*, the Court examined Babcock's nondistribution-of-literature rule. The rule prohibited nonemployees from distributing literature in the company parking lot. The union argued that contact with employees was practically impossible except on company property. Ninety percent of the workers drove to the plant. This argument failed to persuade the Court, which ruled that Babcock & Wilcox had no obligation to permit distribution of union literature by nonemployees. It did suggest that if no other means of communication with the employees exists, then the board might be justified in ordering a company to permit contacts on company property. In the *Babcock* case, the Court found it was possible to reach the employees without entering company property.

What if the employees worked at a lumber camp and lived on the premises? Or suppose they lived and worked at a resort. In these situations, perhaps no reasonable alternatives for contact exists. The Court probably would require the company to let the union distribute literature on the company property. The following case expands on the question of whether an employer may prohibit nonemployees from distributing literature in a company parking lot.

Lechmere, Inc. v. NLRB
United States Supreme Court
112 S.Ct. 841 (1992)

The United Food and Commercial Workers Union wanted to organize the employees at a retail store owned by Lechmere, Inc. The store is located in the Lechmere Shopping Plaza. A parking lot, partly owned by Lechmere, adjoins the shopping plaza. Nonemployee union organizers entered Lechmere's parking lot and placed handbills on cars in an area used mainly by employees. Lechmere's manager informed them that Lechmere prohibited solicitation or handbilling of any kind on its property.

The union alleged that Lechmere had violated the National Labor Relations Act by barring nonemployee organizers from its parking lot. The United States Supreme Court disagreed and ruled for Lechmere.

Justice Thomas

This case requires us to clarify the relationship between the rights of employees under § 7 of the National Labor Relations Act, 49 Stat. 452, as amended, 29 U.S.C. § 157, and the property rights of their employers.

Section 7 of the NLRA provides in relevant part that "[e]mployees shall have the right to self-organization, to form, join, or assist labor organizations." Section 8(a)(1) of the Act, in turn, makes it an unfair labor practice for an employer "to interfere with, restrain, or coerce employees in the exercise of rights guaranteed in [§ 7]." By its plain terms, thus, the NLRA confers rights only on *employees*, not on unions or their nonemployee organizers. In *NLRB v. Babcock & Wilcox Co.*, however, we recognized that insofar as the employees' "right of self-organization depends in some measure on [their] abili-

ty . . . to learn the advantages of self-organization from others," § 7 of the NLRA may, in certain limited circumstances, restrict an employer's right to exclude nonemployee union organizers from his property. It is the nature of those circumstances that we explore today.

While no restriction may be placed on the employees' right to discuss self-organization *among themselves*, unless the employer can demonstrate that a restriction is necessary to maintain production or discipline, no such obligation is owed nonemployee organizers. As a rule, then, an employer cannot be compelled to allow distribution of union literature by nonemployee organizers on this property. As with many other rules, however, we recognized an exception. Where the location of a plant and the living quarters of the employees place the employees beyond the reach of reasonable union efforts to communicate with them, employers' property rights may be required to yield to the extent needed to permit communication of information on the right to organize.

The threshold inquiry in this case, then, is whether the facts here justify application of *Babcock*'s inaccessibility exception.

As we have explained, the exception to *Babcock*'s rule is a narrow one. It does not apply wherever nontrespassory access to employees may be cumbersome or less-than-ideally effective, but only where the *location of a plant and the living quarters of the employees* place the employees *beyond the reach* of reasonable union efforts to communicate with them. Classic examples include logging camps and mountain resort hotels.

Babcock's exception was crafted precisely to protect the § 7 rights of those employees who, by virtue of their employment, are isolated from the ordinary flow of information that characterizes our society. The union's burden of establishing such isolation is, as we have explained, "a heavy one," and one not satisfied by mere conjecture or the expression of doubts concerning the effectiveness of nontrespassory means of communication.

Because the union in this case failed to establish the existence of any "unique obstacles" that frustrated access to Lechmere's employees, the Board erred in concluding that Lechmere committed an unfair labor practice by barring the nonemployee organizers from its property.

The judgment of the First Circuit is therefore reversed, and enforcement of the Board's order denied.

It is so ordered.

Employee Conversations

Bear in mind that the *Lechmere* case involved *nonemployee* distribution of literature, as opposed to distribution of literature by an employee. An employee has a legitimate reason for being on company property, but a nonemployee does not. This suggests that an employee may be able to distribute literature or talk to workers at times and places not accessible to nonemployees.

Normally, an employee may speak with other employees during nonworking hours in *working or nonworking areas* unless a nonsolicitation rule is necessary to maintain discipline. Companies may prohibit such solicitation during working hours. The rationale for such a rule is fairly clear. In many cases, speaking with employees distracts them from their jobs.

Employee Distribution of Literature

What about the distribution of literature by employees? In general, employers may prohibit the distribution of literature in a working area but not in a nonworking area unless the company demonstrates special circumstances. Any such rule against distribution of literature must be nondiscriminatory; that is, the rule must apply to everyone who wishes to distribute literature. A company that prohibits the distribution of literature in working areas must apply the rule to the Red Cross, the Salvation Army, or any other organization that wishes to distribute literature as well as to unions. The basic problem with any literature is the litter it creates. When employees receive handbills, they often throw the material on the floor and create a hazard to others working in that area.

In some instances, determining whether a union activity is solicitation or distribution is difficult. For example, what if an employee handed out union cards while he spoke with other employees? The board found this activity to be solicitation, although it possesses the characteristics of distribution. In other cases, the facts suggest that an activity possibly amounts to solicitation. What if an employee wears a union button while on the job? The cases vary, but *generally* an employee is permitted to wear a union button at all times. A case decided against an employee involved a button reading "Ma Bell is a cheap mother." The employee lost because the button created a disturbance.

In Summation

The following rules apply to solicitation and distribution of literature by employees:

1. An employee may be restricted from distributing literature in working areas, in working or nonworking times.

2. A rule forbidding the distribution of literature in nonworking areas during nonworking times is presumptively invalid.

3. A rule against solicitation during nonworking times is presumptively invalid, even if confined to working areas.

Threats and Benefits

Because the NLRB wishes to conduct an election in an atmosphere conducive to the free exercise of an employee's beliefs, coercive tactics by an employer violate that act.

But threats of reprisal are not the only form of coercion. An employee's right to exercise free will may be influenced by promises of benefits. In these cases, the board examines (1) the timing and impact of the benefits, (2) whether the employer places conditions on the granting of benefits, and (3) whether any valid reasons exist for the conferring of benefits other than the election. The employer is placed in an awkward position when benefits are conferred before an election. Custom is crucial in these cases. An employer that regularly grants increases each year around October 1 probably may grant one at that time even if an election is scheduled. The following case discusses the issue of granting benefits.

NLRB v. Exchange Parts Co.
United States Supreme Court
375 U.S. 405 (1964)

A representation election to unionize Exchange Parts employees was to be held. Shortly before the election, respondent, Exchange Parts, sent its employees a letter denouncing the union and listing all previous benefits granted by the company to the employees. The list also announced new benefits for the employees, including a birthday holiday, longer vacations, and increased wages for holiday work. The union lost the election. The NLRB held that the letter violated Section 8(a)(1) of the National Labor Relations Act. The court of appeals would not enforce the

NLRB's order and the NLRB appealed. The Supreme Court ruled in favor of the NLRB.

Justice Harlan

This case presents a question concerning the limitations which section 8(a)(1) of the National Labor Relations Act places on the right of an employer to confer economic benefits on his employees shortly before a representation election. The precise issue is whether that section prohibits the conferral of such benefits, without more, where the employer's purpose is to affect the outcome of the election. For reasons given in this opinion, we conclude that the judgment below must be reversed.

Section 8(a)(1) makes it an unfair labor practice for an employer "to interfere with, restrain, or coerce employees in the exercise of the rights guaranteed in section 7." We think the Court of Appeals was mistaken in concluding that the conferral of employee benefits while a representation election is pending, for the purpose of inducing employees to vote against the union, does not "interfere with" the protected right to organize.

The broad purpose of section 8(a)(1) is to establish "the right of employees to organize for mutual aid without employer interference." We have no doubt that it prohibits not only intrusive threats and promises but also conduct immediately favorable to employees which is undertaken with the express purpose of impinging upon their freedom of choice for or against unionization and is reasonably calculated to have that effect. The danger inherent in well-timed increases in benefits is the suggestion of a fist inside the velvet glove. Employees are not likely to miss the inference that the source of benefits now conferred is also the source from which future benefits must flow and which may dry up if it is not obliged. The danger may be diminished if, as in this case, the benefits are conferred permanently and unconditionally. But the absence of conditions or threats pertaining to the particular benefits conferred would be of controlling significance only if it could be presumed that no question of additional benefits or renegotiation of existing benefits would arise in the future; and, of course, no such presumption is tenable.

Domination or Support of a Union

Another prohibited activity, employer domination or support of a union, is covered in Section 8(a)(2) of the Wagner Act. At one time, employers who foresaw unionizataion as inevitable often attempted to subvert the employees' effort to organize by forming their own unions—without informing the employees of the company's support for the union. In this manner, companies assured themselves of weak unions, favorably disposed to their goals and easier to deal with than powerful independent unions. Ostensibly, the company union represented the employees. In fact, the union operated as an arm of the company.

While the law today forbids company domination of a union, the factual situations may make it difficult to distinguish employer domination from employer cooperation with a union. The Wagner Act requires cooperation but forbids domination.

The courts view as improper any assistance or support of a union to such an extent that the union must be regarded as the employer's own creation and subject to its control. What if a company permitted a union to use the company printing equipment—does this constitute cooperation or support of a union? Too much activity of this nature looks like company support. An employer must remain neutral in order to avoid running afoul of Section 8(a)(2).

Recognition of Union

The prohibition of employer domination or support of a union appears in the act to allow unions to organize without any hindrance by companies. What if a company agrees to bargain with a union that in fact represents less than a majority of the employees? Does this recognition of the union violate Section 8(a)(2)? The Supreme Court has ruled that the recognition of a union in this situation provides encouragement to join a union, and thus deprives the employees of their freedom of choice. A company must not recognize a union that represents less than a majority of the employees.

The wise course of action for an employer confronted by a union that demands recognition is to carefully review the cards signed by the employees calling for an election or to insist upon an election conducted by the NLRB. Before an employer bargains with a union, the union must represent a *majority* of the employees.

Discrimination to Encourage or Discourage Union Membership

It is also unfair labor practice for an employer "by discrimination in regard to hiring or tenure of employment or any term or condition of employment to encourage or discourage membership in any labor organization" (Wagner Act, Section 8[a][3]). Generally, the *motive* of an employer is critical.

Discharging Employees

For the government to establish an unfair labor practice when a company discharges an employee, it must demonstrate that (1) the company has a deep-seated hostility toward unions, (2) the person involved in the charges was active in the union, (3) the employer knew that the employee was active in the union, (4) prior treatment by the company of other employees was not as harsh, and (5) the employer did not have just cause for the discharge. In the event an employer wrongfully discharged an employee in violation of Section 8(a)(3), the board has the power to order reinstatement of the employee with pay if it determines the employee was fired in order to discourage union activity. On the other hand, an employee discharged for a legitimate reason, such as missing work, may not be reinstated.

What if an employee violates a rule in the plant? May the employer safely fire him or her? As indicated, an employer must not discriminate in the employment of workers on the basis of union membership. If it treats a person active in the union more harshly for an offense than other employees, the company runs the risk of violating this part of the act. When the board examines the case, it looks at the past practices in the plant, the severity of the violation, the type of disciplinary actions imposed in the past, and other factors.

The following case involves an attempt by an employer to punish its employees for engaging in union activities.

Sure-Tan, Inc. v. NLRB
United States Supreme Court
104 S.Ct. (1984)

A small employer, Sure-Tan, was organized by a union. The union won an election conducted by the NLRB in 1976. After receiving notice that the union would be certified as the bargaining representative of the employees, the president of Sure-Tan, Surak, sent a letter to the Immigration and Naturalization Service (INS) asking that it check the status of a number of his employees as soon as possible. The president knew these employees were Mexican nationals present illegally in the United States without visas or immigration papers authorizing them to work. The INS agents discovered five illegal aliens. These people soon left the country. The NLRB brought unfair labor charges against Sure-Tan. It alleged Sure-Tan had violated Section 8(a)(3) by requesting the INS to investigate these employees solely because they had supported the union and with full knowledge that the employees in question had no papers or work permits. The Supreme Court ruled that Sure-Tan had violated Section 8(a)(3).

NOW ILLEGAL TO HIRE ILLEGAL ALIENS

Justice O'Connor

We first consider the predicate question whether the NLRA should apply to unfair practices committed against undocumented aliens. The Board has consistently held that undocumented aliens are "employees" within the meaning of § 2(3) of the Act. That provision broadly provides that "[t]he term 'employee' shall include any employee," subject only to certain specifically enumerated exceptions. Since undocumented aliens are not among the few groups of workers expressly exempted by Congress, they plainly come within the broad statutory definition of "employee."

Counterintuitive though it may be, we do not find any conflict between application of the NLRA to undocumented aliens and the mandate of the Immigration and Nationality Act (INA). Since the employment relationship between an employer and an undocumented alien is not illegal under the INA, there is no reason to conclude that application of the NLRA to employment practices affecting such aliens would necessarily conflict with the terms of the INA.

Accepting the premise that the provisions of the NLRA are applicable to undocumented alien employees, we must now address the more difficult issue whether, under the circumstances of this case, petitioners commit-

ted an unfair labor practice by reporting their undocumented alien employees to the INS in retaliation for participating in union activities. Section 8(a)(3) makes it an unfair labor practice for an employer "by discrimination in regard to hire or tenure of employment or any term or condition of employment to encourage or discourage membership in any labor organization."

The Board, with the approval of lower courts, has long held that an employer violates this provision not only when, for the purpose of discouraging union activity, it directly dismisses an employee, but also when it purposefully creates working conditions so intolerable that the employee has no option but to resign—a so-called "constructive discharge."

Petitioners do not dispute that the antiunion animus element of this test was, as expressed by the lower court, "flagrantly met." Petitioners contend, however, that their conduct in reporting the undocumented alien workers did not force the workers' departure from the country; instead, they argue, it was the employees' status as illegal aliens that was the actual "proximate cause" of their departure.

This argument is unavailing. According to testimony by an INS agent, petitioners' letter was the sole cause of the investigation during which the employees were taken into custody. And there can be little doubt that Surak foresaw precisely this result when, having known about the employees' illegal status for some months, he notified the INS only after the Union's electoral victory was assured.

It is only when the evidence establishes that the reporting of the presence of an illegal alien employee is in retaliation for the employee's protected union activity that the board finds a violation of § 8(a)(3). Absent this specific finding of anti-union animus, it would not be an unfair labor practice to report or discharge an undocumented alien employee.

Encouraging Union Membership

While an employer violates the Wagner Act by discouraging union membership, it also violates the act by discrimination that encourages union membership. A company must strive to remain neutral in order to let the employees freely and voluntarily decide in favor of or against union affiliation.

Lockouts

A **lockout** can also result in legal problems for the company. (In a lockout, the employer refuses to permit the employees to work.) A lockout is unlawful if it is used to oppose unionization or to force the employees to choose the union the employer prefers.

Sometimes a lockout is legal. A single-employer economic lockout is legal when used to avoid unusual economic losses or operational difficulties that would result from a threatened strike.

A union may negotiate with a multiemployer group (more than one company in the bargaining unit) but choose to strike only one member of the association. United Auto Workers usually operates in this fashion. It bargains with all the automobile companies at once, but if a strike occurs, only one company gets closed down. Rather than continuing to operate, the other automobile companies might stage a lockout. The Supreme Court has ruled that a lockout is legal under these circumstances.

Worker Adjustment and Retraining Notification Act

The subject of plant closings and relocations has caused workers a great deal of anxiety and has resulted in various suits. Many employers have closed plants or relocated plants in order to discourage union membership.

To combat this practice, in 1988 Congress passed the Worker Adjustment and Retraining Notification Act. This law forces an employer to provide a written notice to its employees before ordering a mass layoff or a plant closing. An employer may not order a plant closing or a mass layoff (subject to certain exceptions) until sixty days after it has given a written notice to the union or to the employees, to the appropriate state agency which deals with worker dislocation, and to the chief elected official of the appropriate government unit. Separate provisions in the law deal with plant relocations and the sale of businesses.

Discrimination against Employees Who File Charges

In order to increase the cooperative spirit among the employees, Section 8(a)(4) makes it an unfair labor practice for an employer to "discharge or otherwise discriminate against an employee because he has filed charges or given testimony under this Act." Many employees might refuse to cooperate with the NLRB field agent if they believed their employers could fire them. This provision restricts the employer from taking any vindictive actions against the employees for either filing charges with the NLRB or giving testimony. The phrase "giving testimony" has been construed by the Supreme Court to also cover the process of collecting information before the filing of formal charges. Any employee who cooperates with the board field agents or participates in a trial is protected by this provision.

Collective Bargaining

The Wagner Act, Section 8(a)(5), makes it an unfair labor practice for an employer "to refuse to bargain collectively with the representatives of his employees." This provision escorts the parties to the door of the bargaining room. It prohibits fictitious negotiation and a de facto refusal to recognize and bargain with the union.

The Taft-Hartley Act added some additional guidance on this point in Section 8(d):

> For the purposes of this section, to bargain collectively is the performance of the mutual obligation of the employer and the representative of the employees to meet at reasonable times and confer in good faith with respect to wages, hours, and other terms and conditions of employment, or the negotiation of an agreement, or any question arising thereunder, and the execution of a written contract incorporating any agreement reached if requested by either party, but such obligation does not compel either party to agree to a proposal or require the making of a concession.

The Taft-Hartley Act thus specifies that the parties must *meet and confer*, but it does not compel the parties to arrive at an agreement or to make concessions. Congress added this language to the National Labor Relations Act because it felt the board was going too far in requiring the parties to agree to specific terms. Section 8(d) was a response to the zealous enforcement of this provision by the board. Even so, in examining Section 8(a)(5) claims, the board still examines the substance of the parties' discussion. It is not blinded by empty talk.

A tension exists between the right to not agree to any specific points, as set forth in Taft-Hartley, and the obligation to make a serious effort to resolve the differences between the parties, but some fairly clear rules exist as to one's obligation to bargain.

Mandatory Subjects of Bargaining

TOPIC

In general, the parties may insist to the point of impasse on *mandatory* subjects of bargaining. They may not insist to the point of impasse on nonmandatory (voluntary) subjects; that is, if a union goes on strike over a nonmandatory issue, the workers are not protected. The employer may fire the employees in this situation. Examples of mandatory subjects on which the parties must bargain are wages, merit increases, pensions, disciplinary rules, seniority, nonstrike provisions, and contracting work out. An example of a nonmandatory issue is a request by the union that the employer change its negotiator.

A unilateral change by an employer on a mandatory subject of bargaining is a violation of the act. For example, if an employer changed its sick leave policy during the negotiation sessions, without first offering this to the union, the company has violated Section 8(a)(5). However, an employer may give its employees something it offered the union at the bargaining table, if the union rejected the offer and the parties *reached an impasse* in their negotiations. In this situation, an employer could unilaterally grant the employees the benefit the union rejected. This is true even though negotiations continue after the expiration of the old contract. Either party may decline to negotiate after a true impasse is reached. Determining when the parties have reached an impasse poses problems for the negotiators. Both the union and the company must make certain an impasse has been reached before a refusal to negotiate further, or they run the risk of being guilty of a failure to bargain in good faith.

The following case deals with the question of whether an employer violates the law if it offers the employees something different from the offers it proposed to the union representative.

Southwest Forest Industries, Inc. v. National Labor Relations Board
United States Court of Appeals, Ninth Circuit
841 F.2d 270 (1988)

A collective bargaining agreement existed between the Graphic Communications Union District Council #1, Local 388, and Southwest Forest Industries. After it expired, the employees went out on strike. The parties continued to bargain but as of November 23, they reached an impasse. Southwest thereafter sent a letter to its employees. The employment conditions differed significantly from those discussed with the union. The union filed an unfair labor practice charge. The court agreed that by sending such a letter, Southwest violated the law.

Fletcher, Circuit Judge

An employer must maintain the *status quo* after the expiration of the collective bargaining agreement until a new agreement is reached or until the parties bargain in good faith to impasse. Where, as in this case, an impasse is reached, "the employer may unilaterally impose changes in the terms of employment *if* the changes were reasonably comprehended in the terms of its contract offers to the union." *Cuyamaca Meats, Inc. v. San Diego*

& Imperial Counties Butchers' & Food Employers' Pension Trust Fund. Unilateral changes not comprehended in pre-impasse proposals constitute a refusal to bargain in violation of sections 8(a)(5) and (1) of the Act.

It is undisputed that the changes made by Southwest were not on the bargaining table prior to impasse.

. . .Substantial evidence in the record before the Board supports the Board's finding that Southwest did not afford the Union a meaningful opportunity to bargain about the changes before instituting them.

Accordingly, we affirm the Board's finding that Southwest's implementation of unilateral changes in the terms of employment violated sections 8(a)(5) and (1) of the Act.

Bargaining in Good Faith

Much of the negotiation process between the company and the union takes place on a give-and-take basis. Presumably, the company devises a range of wages and benefits it will offer, and the union sets up a scale of wages and benefits it hopes to receive. If the parties fail to agree, a strike may occur. What if, rather than secretly holding back the best offer, a company puts the best offer on the table at the beginning of the bargaining session and then communicates the information to the employees? The following case discusses this strategy.

NLRB v. General Electric Co.
United States Court of Appeals, Second Circuit
418 F.2d 736 2nd Cir. (1969), Cert. Den. 397 U.S. 965 (1970)

After a crippling strike in 1946, GE changed its bargaining tactics. It made its best offer to the union at the very beginning of negotiations, and then it heavily publicized the offer to employees. The NLRB found three specific unfair labor practices and an overall failure to bargain in good faith, a violation of Section 8(a) of the National Labor Relations Act. The court of appeals was petitioned to enforce the NLRB's order against GE.

Kaufman, Judge

In addition to the three specific unfair labor practices, G. E. is also charged with an overall failure to bargain in good faith.

The Board chose to find an overall failure of good faith bargaining in G. E.'s conduct. Specifically, the Board found that G. E.'s bargaining stance and conduct, considered as a whole, were designed to derogate the Union in the eyes of its members and the public at large. This plan had two major facets: first, a take-it-or-leave-it approach ("firm, fair offer") to negotiations in general which emphasized both the powerlessness and uselessness of the Union to its members, and second, a communications program that pictured the Company as the true defender of the employees' interests, further denigrating the Union, and sharply curbing the Company's ability to change its own position.

Given the effects of take-it-or-leave-it proposals on the Union, the Board could appropriately infer the presence of anti-Union animus, and in conjunction with other similar conduct could reasonably discern a pattern of illegal activity designed primarily to subvert the Union.

G. E. argues forcefully that it made so many concessions in the course of negotiations—concessions which, under section 8(d), it was not obliged to make—that its good faith and the absence of a take-it-or-leave-it attitude were conclusively proven, despite any contrary indicia on which the Trial Examiner and the Board rely.

The company's stand, however, would be utterly inexplicable without the background of its publicity program. Only when viewed in that context does it become meaningful. We have already indicated that one of the central tenets of "the Boulware approach" is that the "product" or "firm, fair offer" must be marketed vigorously to the "consumers" or employees, to convince them that the Company, and not the Union, is their true representative. G. E., the Trial Examiner found, chose to rely "entirely" on its communications program to the virtual exclusion of genuine negotiations, which it sought to evade by any means possible. Bypassing the national negotiators in favor of direct settlement dealings with employees and local officials forms another consistent thread in this pattern. The aim, in a word, was to deal with the Union through the employees, rather than with the employees through the Union.

The Company's refusal to withhold publicizing its offer until the Union had had an opportunity to propose suggested modifications is indicative of this attitude. The ees and the general public must be barraged with communications that emphasized the generosity of the offer, and restated the firmness of G. E's position.

In order to avoid any misunderstanding of our holding, some additional discussion is in order. We do not today hold that an employer may not communicate with his employees during negotiations. Nor are we deciding that the "best offer first" bargaining technique is forbidden. Moreover, we do not require an employer to engage in "auction bargaining," or compel him to make concessions, "minor" or otherwise.

We hold that an employer may not so combine "take-it-or-leave-it bargaining methods with a widely publicized stance of unbending firmness that he is himself unable to alter a position once taken. Such conduct, we find, constitutes a refusal to bargain "in fact." It also constitutes, as the facts of this action demonstrate, an absence of subjective good faith, for it implies that the Company can deliberately bargain and communicate as though the Union did not exist, in clear derogation of the Union's status as exclusive representative of its members under section 9(a).

The petition for review is denied, and the petition for enforcement of the Board's order is granted.

Employer's Free Speech

The First Amendment of the Constitution prohibits Congress from passing laws that restrict the right of free speech. Although the Constitution guarantees the right of free speech, employers for many years ran into trouble when they exercised it. Quite often, the NLRB construed a statement by an employer before an election as an unfair labor practice. In response to the decisions of the NLRB, Congress passed Section 8(c) of the Taft-Hartley Act. This provision reads as follows: "The expressing of any views, argument or opinion, or the dissemination thereof, whether in written, printed, graphic or visual form, shall not constitute and be evidence of an unfair labor practice under any of the provisions of this act, if such expression contains no threat of reprisal or force or promise of benefit."

Section 8(c) permits employers to communicate their general views as to unionization so long as they do not make any threats or promises. Employers are free only to state what they feel will be the economic consequences of unionization, which are outside of their control and do not constitute reprisals.

The NLRB has taken the position that conduct that creates an atmosphere that renders free choice improbable sometimes may warrant invalidating an election, even though the conduct does not rise to the level of an unfair labor practice. Some employer statements, which may not constitute a threat of reprisal under

Section 8(c), may so cloud the atmosphere as to warrant the board's setting aside an election.

In the following case, the court considered a statement by management prior to a representation election that unionization might result in the closing of the plant. The court ruled in favor of management and approved such a statement under these circumstances.

United Automobile, Aerospace and Agricultural Implement Workers of America v. National Labor Relations Board
United States Court of Appeals, Ninth Circuit
834 F.2d 816 (1987)

Kawasaki manufactures motorcyles at a plant in Lincoln, Nebraska. Prior to a union election, Kawasaki management made certain statements to the employees that the union alleged violated the labor law. The court ruled that the statements in question came within Kawasaki's freedom of speech.

Wiggins, Circuit Judge

Before the NLRB's order was enforced, the UAW requested a new election, which was scheduled for October 21, 1982. On October 18 and 19, Kawasaki held a series of one hour meetings on company time with small groups of employees. Each meeting began with plant manager Hanson describing the plant's poor financial health. He reminded the employees about recent layoffs, work hour reductions, overstocked inventory, and losses. He explained that the plant had not shown a profit since it opened in 1975, and had its greatest loss, $9,000,000 in the prior year.

The company president Saeki said he was sent to the plant the year before to correct "some big problems," a $36,000,000 loss in seven years," and that at that time "we had to make a decision either to change the plant to make it profitable or to close the plant." The company's parent he explained, refused to subsidize it any further and so more losses would lead to plant closure. He noted the plant's productivity was lower than that of plants in developing countries, but had improved recently. His goal for the year was to break even. He cited slack motorcycle demand as the cause of the plant's recent financial woes, and concluded: "I do not like more new problems. Please understand our serious situation. I think

at first we must survive. Survival is the most important thing."

Hanson predicted Kawasaki would find it difficult to operate under a UAW contract with restrictive job classifications because the company needed versatility in moving employees among jobs. He said the plant had until the year's end to break even or close. When employees asked him if Kawasaki would close the plant if the UAW won the election, he replied the question was a "trap" which he could not legally answer.

An employer may express opinions or predictions, reasonably based in fact, about the possible effects of unionization on its company. But such a prediction must be carefully phrased on the basis of objective fact to convey an employer's belief as to demonstrably probable consequences beyond his control or to convey a management decision already arrived at. A prediction is a coercive threat of retaliation if it implies that the employer may take an action solely on his own initiative for reasons unrelated to economic necessity and known only to him.

Kawasaki intimated that due to the company's mounting losses and the union's inefficient work rules, a union victory might push the plant over the brink. Our inquiry is whether these statements were predictions based on economic fact or coercive threats of actions the company might take if it so chose.

A prediction of plant closure is unlawful unless the employer can show that it is the probable consequence of unionization for reasons beyond its control.

The Board found Kawasaki's prediction of plant closure to be based on economic necessity. Kawasaki documented its economic concerns with detailed financial information showing heavy losses. An employer is privileged to warn its employees truthfully of its precarious financial condition, even if its purpose for the disclosure is to discourage unionization. But an employer that pre-dicts unionization will cause plant closure cannot rely exclusively on its financial condition, but must further show that plant closure is the demonstrably probable consequence of unionization.

The board found that Kawasaki lawfully predicted that the union's restrictive work rules would reduce the company's flexibility, threaten its profitability, and—in light of its precarious financial condition likely push it over the edge.

We AFFIRM the Board's order finding Kawasaki's statements to be protected speech under section 8(c) of the NLRA and DENY the UAW's petition for review.

SUMMARY

In the late 1800s and early 1900s, relations between management and labor were very poor. Workers tried to improve working conditions through collective action, while most companies tried to thwart the workers' organizing efforts. This led to a period of social unrest and violence. The workers finally turned to Congress to obtain just treatment in the workplace. Congress responded by passing a series of acts, the most important of which, the Wagner Act, gave employees the right to organize and bargain collectively.

The Wagner Act created the National Labor Relations Board, whose function is to conduct representation elections and process labor disputes. (Much of this work is done by the board's local offices.) Persons who disagree with the decisions of the regional offices may appeal their cases to the board itself, and from there, to the courts.

Much of the board's time is devoted to conducting representation elections. An employer may voluntarily recognize a union that represents a majority of the employees, but elections are customarily held to determine if a majority of the employees favor unionization. An employer must act carefully after a representation petition has been filed. Employers may not threaten workers or promise them benefits in order to influence the outcome of a representation election. A company that commits a serious unfair labor practice after the filing of a petition runs the risk that the board will certify the union as the bargaining representative of the employees solely on the basis of authorization cards signed by the employees.

Prior to asking the board for a representation election, the union will attempt to organize the workers. The circumstances under which union representatives may speak with workers and distribute union literature in the workplace are governed by the labor law. Generally, employee-representatives have greater right to speak with workers and distribute literature than nonemployees would have.

The labor laws place a number of obligations on management. Certain types of activities are treated as unfair labor practices. An employer may not discriminate against workers to encourage or discourage union membership. An employer may not discriminate against workers who file charges under the Wagner Act. Once the board recognizes a union as the bargaining representative of a designated group of employees, it is an unfair labor practice for the employer to refuse to bargain in good faith with the union. The union and the employer must meet and confer with each other. They are not required to arrive at an agreement or to make concessions; however, certain subjects must be considered at the bargaining table.

It should finally be noted that the labor law guarantees employers a right of free speech.

REVIEW QUESTIONS

1. Define the following terms:
   a. Injunction
   b. Lockout

2. Why did Congress pass the Norris-LaGuardia Act?

3. Steel Corporation learns from the NLRB that a union has filed a petition to conduct a representation election. One week before the election, Steel Corporation grants the employees two extra paid vacation days and agrees to increase everyone's salary by twenty-five cents per hour if the employees vote against the union. Does this violate the labor law?

4. Darling Toys produced most of its toys during the spring and summer because the bulk of its toys were sold at Christmas. The company engaged in collective bargaining and reached an impasse with the with the union. The company feared the employees intended to strike during the spring, so it locked them out starting on December 25. Is this legal?

5. Is it legal for a company to make its best offer immediately to the union, then inform the employees of its actions?

6. A union obtained thirteen signed authorization cards from a plant with thirty employees and demanded recognition as the bargaining agent for the company's production and maintenance employees. The employer refused to recognize the union, and the union filed unfair labor practice charges with the NLRB. How should the NLRB rule on the charge? Has the union done enough to obtain recognition?

7. During contract negotiations, an employer unilaterally implemented a new system of automatic wage increases, changes in sick-leave benefits, and merit increases, even though these matters were subjects of pending contract negotiation. Was this a violation of the duty to bargain collectively?

8. A nonprofit general hospital had a rule prohibiting solicitation by its employees in any area of the hospital that was accessible to the public—including lobbies, gift shops, cafeterias, main floor entrances, corridors, sitting rooms, and public restrooms. Is this rule valid? What part(s) may be enforceable?

9. Metropolitan Edison Company had a collective bargaining agreement with the International Brotherhood of Electrical Workers. The agreement had a no-strike clause that prohibited strikes during the term of the agreement. Despite the no-strike clause, union members participated in an unlawful work stoppage. Another union set up an informational picket line in front of the construction site. The Electrical Workers refused to cross the picket line. Metropolitan Edison asked the union president to cross the picket line, but he refused to do so. The company suspended the workers for ten

days, but suspended the president for twenty-five days. Did the company violate the labor laws?

10. Employees of Eastex sought to distribute a union newsletter in nonworking areas of Eastex's property during nonworking times. The company refused to permit the newsletter to be distributed. The newsletter urged support for the union. It also discussed a right-to-work statute and the federal minimum wage. Did Eastex commit an unfair labor practice?

11. What restrictions does the law place on plant closings?

12. A union waged an organizational campaign against Gissel Packing. The union obtained authorization cards signed by a majority of the employees. During this time, Gissel Packing engaged in unfair labor practices which made the holding of a fair election unlikely. Under these circumstances, must the union win a representation election to become the bargaining agent for the employees?

13. Pizza Crust prohibited off-duty employees from using its parking lot to distribute union literature. Is the refusal of the employer to let the employees use the parking lot an unfair labor practice?

14. Ford Motor Company increased the price of the food in its plant cafeteria. The union requested bargaining over the prices. Ford refused the union's request. Is this an unfair labor practice?

15. The NLRB scheduled a representation election. Prior to the election, the employer told the employees that if they voted in favor of a union, the plant would be closed. Is it lawful to make such a statement with a representation election pending?

CHAPTER 20

Labor-Management Relations: The Regulation of Unions

- Bargaining
- Duty of Fair Representation
- Unfair Labor Practices
- Protected Concerted Activities
- The Right to Strike
- Picketing
- Secondary Pressure

In the preceding chapter, we dealt with the historical forces that resulted in the creation of the present extensive body of federal regulatory law in the area of labor relations. In particular, we covered the manner in which the National Labor Relations Board regulates employers and employees, and certain types of activities by employers that are unfair labor practices.

In this chapter, we will focus on some of the major types of union activities. In the first section, we will deal with some issues unions and management bargain over. We will then discuss the duty of a union to fairly represent *all* persons in the bargaining unit. After examining very briefly a few unfair labor practices, we will focus in depth on three important concerted activities permitted to unions—strikes, picketing, and secondary activities.

BARGAINING

Must Meet and Confer

As with employers, the National Labor Relations Act creates certain obligations for unions with respect to bargaining with an employer. It is an unfair labor practice for a union certified by the board as the representative of the employees to refuse to bargain collectively with the employer [Section 8(b)(3)].

Both the company and the union must bargain collectively if the union has been certified by the board. The obligation to bargain collectively means that the union and the company must "meet at reasonable times and confer in good faith with respect to wages, hours, and other terms and conditions of employment . . . but such obligation does not compel either party to agree to a proposal or require the making of a concession" [Section 8(d)].

One of the issues unions typically are quite concerned over and may wish to discuss with employers when they bargain is whether employees will be required to join a union as a condition of employment.

Union Security

Closed Shop

If a union signs a contract to bargain collectively, it may wish to include in the collective bargaining agreement provisions that help it survive. At one time, unions sought **closed shop** agreements from employers. A clause such as "The employer hereby agrees to employ only members in good standing of the union" is a closed shop clause. Such a clause in contracts today is illegal. With such a clause, before a person could be eligible to work, he or she would first have to be a member of a union. Such a clause gave unions great power over the pool of available workers because the union had power to control its own membership. The closed shop is illegal because it discriminates in the hiring or tenure of employees so as to encourage union membership.

Union Shop

The act recognizes the **union shop** as a valid agreement. With a union shop clause, employees must join a union within a certain period after they begin to work for the employer. Section 8(a)(3) permits a company and a union to agree that employees must join after thirty days of employment. [Section 8(f) lowers the number of days to seven in the case of construction industry jobs.]

Section 8(b)(2) makes it clear that a union may not request the company to discharge an employee for any reason other than failure to pay the initiation fee or dues. This means that union employees could not be discharged from the company because, for example, they failed to attend a union meeting.

While the union shop agreement forces employees to join a union after so many days, new employees still are in a stronger position than they would be if the company signed a closed shop agreement. With the closed shop, the union determines which employees are eligible for hiring. Furthermore, a union possesses more power to control which employees continue to work under a closed shop, because the union could force the discharge of employees if they failed to comply with a union rule or regulation. The Taft-Hartley Act protects workers from losing their jobs because of a failure to comply with the union's rules. Only the failure to pay the dues and initiation fees exposes employees to the possible loss of their jobs.

Agency Shop

An **agency shop** agreement requires employees to pay union dues and initiation fees, but does not require an employee to join a union as a condition to gaining employment. Some religious groups refuse to join unions. The agency shop permits these people to work without joining a union. At the same time, it forces them to pay for the services rendered to them by the union. The Taft-Hartley Act permits the agency shop as well as the union shop.

Right to Work

Both the union shop and the agency shop may be outlawed by state law. Section 14(b) of the Taft-Hartley Act permits each state to adopt a law giving workers in the state the "right to work." These state laws are designed to outlaw the use of agreements that require membership in a labor organization as a condition of employment. A number of states have adopted right-to-work legislation.

In addition to meeting and conferring with employers over such issues as whether employees must join a union, unions must negotiate wages, terms, and conditions of employment for the workers in the unit the union represents. They must try to fairly represent everyone in the bargaining unit—both in negotiating and in enforcing the bargain eventually struck with the employer.

DUTY OF FAIR REPRESENTATION

The union must represent all the members in the unit that it was certified by the board to represent—not just the people who voted in favor of unionization. It is the representative of all the people in the bargaining unit. This is true even in right-to-work states that prohibit the use of the union or agency shop.

The duty of fair representation began as a court doctrine. The courts ruled that the union must fairly represent *all* people in the bargaining unit. Even so, a union violates its obligation of fair representation only if it acts in an arbitrary, discriminatory, or bad-faith manner. A union needs wide discretion in how it handles various matters brought to its attention. Over time, the board came to the conclusion that a union violates Section 8(b)(1) when it fails to fairly represent all the people in the bargaining unit. If a company permits a union to unfairly represent the employees, the company violates Section 8(a)(1).

A union must investigate cases in a fair and impartial manner. It must represent an employee even if she or he is not a member of the union.

UNFAIR LABOR PRACTICES

While it is certainly improper for a union to fail to represent a worker in the bargaining unit, this is not the only activity that may run a union afoul of the National Labor Relations Act. A number of practices by unions were made unfair by the Taft-Hartley Act. A few of them will be briefly noted here.

A union must not restrain or coerce the employees in the exercise of their right to engage in concerted activities [Section 8(b)(1)]. Forcing employees to vote for a union in a representation election is an example of a violation of this provision.

A union coerces an employee if it offers the employee a bribe to vote for a union—a point discussed in the following case.

Revco D.S. Inc. (D.C.) v. NLRB
United States Court of Appeals, Sixth Circuit
830 F.2d 70 (1987)

The National Labor Relations Board conducted a representation election, the results of which the NLRB subsequently set aside. The board ordered a second election which a regional office of the NLRB conducted. The union won the second election by a single vote. Following the election, Revco refused to bargain with the union. The NLRB applied to the court of appeals for an order of enforcement to compel Revco to bargain with the union. Owing to the wrongful acts of the union's agent, the court refused to order Revco to bargain with the union.

Lively, Chief Judge

Wayne Hanna, a member of the organizing committee offered to pay Sandy Crosby, an anti-union employee, $100 to vote for the union. These two employees worked in the same department. After the first election Crosby told Hanna that she was against the union, and Hanna tried several times to talk her into supporting the union. The hearing officer found that Hanna made the offer to Crosby immediately before the polls opened for the second election, though Hanna denied the incident. Another employee who was present corroborated Crosby's testimony.

The hearing officer found that Hanna was joking when he made the offer. This conclusion was based on Crosby's reply: "[Give] me the $100 and you won't know which way I vote," and the fact that none of the three employees discussed the matter further. The hearing officer characterized this conversation as a "witty exchange rather than a serious offer and acceptance." This determination was made in spite of Crosby's testimony that Hanna was "straight-faced, said it serious as can be," and that she believed him. Crosby testified that she and Hanna never joked about the question of union representation. In fact, Hanna had been persistent in his efforts to persuade Crosby over a period of several months to support the union. Most important, perhaps, is the fact that Hanna himself did not claim that he had jokingly offered Crosby $100; he denied that the incident had occurred. On the entire record we conclude that the finding of the hearing officer, adopted by the Board, that Hanna was only joking when he offered Crosby money to vote for the union is not supported by substantial evidence.

As is so often the case, neither the hearing officer nor the Board cited any case from this court dealing with objections similar to those made by Revco in the present case. Instead, they relied on cases in which the Board reached a different result. Revco's petition for review is granted and the Board's order finding the employer in violation of sections 8(a)(5) and (1) of the Act is set aside; the Board's cross-application for enforcement is dismissed, and enforcement is denied. Revco will recover its cost on appeal.

While unions may charge their members initiation fees or dues, and the failure to pay such fees may result in an employee's expulsion from the union and dismissal from his or her job, a union may not charge excessive or discriminatory fees [Section 8(b)(5)].

The Taft-Hartley Act made it an unfair labor practice for a union to require an employer to pay for work not performed, otherwise known as **featherbedding**. There has been very little activity recently concerning featherbedding.

PROTECTED CONCERTED ACTIVITIES

The Wagner Act guarantees workers

> the right to self-organization, to form, join, or assist labor organizations, to bargain collectively through representatives of their own choosing, and to engage in other concerted activities for the purpose of collective bargaining or other mutual aid or protection, and . . . the right to refrain from any and all of such activities except to the extent that such right may be affected by an agreement requiring membership in a labor organization as a condition of employment.

Not only does the act give employees the right to engage in concerted activities, it also gives them the right to refrain from such activities. The following case deals with this provision.

Pattern Makers' League of North America v. NLRB
United States Supreme Court
105 S.Ct. 3064 (1985)

The Pattern Makers' League of North American AFL-CIO (the league), a labor union, fined ten of its members who, in violation of the league's constitution, resigned during a strike and returned to work. The National Labor Relations Board ruled that the league had committed an unfair labor practice by fining the employees. The Supreme Court upheld the board's decision in this case.

Justice Powell

Section 7 of the Act grants employees the right to "refrain from any or all [concerted] . . . activities. . . ." This general right is implemented by § 8(b)(1)(A). The latter section provides that a union commits an unfair labor practice if it "restrain[s] or coerce[s] employees in the exercise" of their § 7 rights. When employee members of a union refuse to support a strike (whether or not a rule prohibits returning to work during a strike), they are refraining from "concerted activity." Therefore, impos-

ing fines on these employees for returning to work "restrain[s]" the exercise of their § 7 rights. Indeed, if the terms "refrain" and "restrain or coerce" are interpreted literally, fining employees to enforce compliance with any union rule or policy would violate the Act.

Despite this language from the Act, the Court in *NLRB v. Allis-Chalmers* held that § 8(b)(1)(A) does not prohibit labor organizations from fining current members. In *NLRB v. Textile Workers* and *Machinists & Aero-*

space *Workers v. NLRB*, the Court found as a corollary that unions may not fine former members who have resigned lawfully. Neither *Textile Workers* nor *Machinists*, however, involved a provision like League Law 13, restricting the members' right to resign. We decide today whether a union is precluded from fining employees who have attempted to resign when resignations are prohibited by the union's constitution.

The Court's reasoning in *Allis-Chalmers* supports the Board's conclusion that petitioners in this case violated § 8(b)(1)(A). In *Allis-Chalmers*, the Court held that imposing court-enforceable fines against current union members does not ''restrain or coerce'' the workers in the exercise of their § 7 rights. In so concluding, the Court relied on the legislative history of the Taft-Hartley Act. It noted that the sponsor of § 8(b)(1)(A) never intended for that provision ''to interfere with the internal affairs or organization of unions'' (statement of Sen. Ball), and that other proponents of the measure likewise disclaimed an intent to interfere with unions' ''internal affairs.'' From the legislative history, the Court reasoned that Congress did not intend to prohibit unions from fining present members, as this was an internal matter.

The Congressional purpose to preserve unions' control over their own ''internal affairs'' does not suggest an intent to authorize restrictions on the right to resign. Traditionally, union members were free to resign and escape union discipline. The Board has found union restrictions on the rights to resign to be inconsistent with the policy of voluntary unionism implicit in § 8(a)(3). We believe that the inconsistency between union restrictions on the right to resign and the policy of voluntary unionism supports the Board's conclusion that League Law 13 is invalid.

Therefore, the Board was justified in concluding that by restricting the right of employees to resign, League Law 13 impairs the policy of voluntary unionism.

To what extent may employees engage in concerted activities? They may act together without the assistance of a union. Washington Aluminum asked its employees to work on a bitterly cold day, and the employees, finally unable to tolerate the cold, left the job without first receiving the permission of their foreman. Washington Aluminum fired them for walking off the job. Such joint action by the employees constitutes a concerted activity protected by the Wagner Act. The company violated the employees' rights to engage in concerted activity by firing them.

While the act protects collective actions by employees, the employees lose the protection afforded by the Wagner Act if they use unprotected means (such as violence and destruction of property) or if the objective of the employees violates the labor law (as would a strike to compel an employer to commit an unfair labor practice).

Are the actions of a single employee, acting *pursuant to* rights guaranteed to employees in a collective bargaining agreement, concerted activity protected by Section 7?

In *NLRB* v. *City Disposal Systems* (1984) the Supreme Court ruled that even if only a single employee protests a violation of the collective bargaining agreement, his or her actions amount to concerted activity protected by Section 7.

THE RIGHT TO STRIKE

A concerted activity of great importance to workers is the right to strike. Employees utilize the right to strike as a means of protecting their rights and of obtaining benefits. When employees strike, they act together to obtain what the workers believe will serve their collective interests. Clearly, when employees exercise the right to strike they are engaging in a concerted activity for the purpose of mutual aid or protection.

There are two important types of strikes. If employees go out on strike to obtain better wages or working conditions, they are engaging in an **economic strike**. A strike in protest over an unfair labor practice allegedly committed by an employer is called an **unfair labor practice strike**.

Situations When Employees May Not Strike

Injunctions

While Section 7 and Section 13 of the National Labor Relations Act reflect the view that employees have a right to strike, this right is a qualified one. A court, because the right is protected, generally may not enjoin a strike. (The Norris-LaGuardia Act generally prohibits federal courts from enjoining such strikes. This area of law has been preempted by federal law.) In some circumstances, when the means and ends of a strike are unlawful, an employer may obtain an injunction. For example, if a company's employees engage in violence, a state court, in spite of Norris-LaGuardia, may enjoin violence by strikers. Furthermore, strikers who block access to a plant may be enjoined. If workers engage in a strike, and the collective bargaining agreement contains a no-strike clause, both federal and state courts may enjoin the strike. If a union gives notice of an intent to terminate or modify a collective bargaining agreement, it may not strike for sixty days after the union serves written notice upon the company. If employees strike during this period, they may be fired. Finally, in the event of a national emergency, the Taft-Hartley Act gives the federal courts the right to enjoin a strike for eighty days if the strike threatens the national health and safety. After the eighty-day elapses, the strike may resume. Not only may employees be prevented from striking in these cases, but they also may be enjoined for engaging in a jurisdictional dispute.

Jurisdictional Disputes

Section 8(b)(4) deals with the problem of **jurisdictional disputes**. The act makes it an unfair labor practice to engage in or encourage a strike or refusal to handle goods, or to threaten or coerce any person, where the object is

> forcing or requiring an employer to assign particular work to employees in a particular labor organization or in a particular trade, craft or class rather than to employees in another labor organization or in another trade, craft or class, unless such employer is failing to conform to an order or certification of the board determining the bargaining representative for employees performing such work.

Congress included this provision in the labor laws in 1947 to counteract the many work stoppages in industry arising out of controversies between unions as to which union was entitled to perform certain work. The Wagner Act failed to set up any machinery to deal with such disputes between unions. Essentially, the Taft-Hartley Act prohibits a union from striking to force an employer to assign work to a certain group of workers unless the employer is failing to comply with a board order. It is the board's duty to consider the merits of a dispute when requested to do so, and to make an award of work to one union or the other. The courts require the board to make such an assignment of work because the board possesses experience with such problems.

National Emergency Disputes

While the National Labor Relations Act goes to great lengths to protect the right to strike, in some cases employees may not strike. One such instance is when a strike threatens to cripple the economy of the entire nation. Some strikes not only cripple an individual company, but also threaten the safety and well-being of the entire nation. The Taft-Hartley Act set up a system for dealing with severe strikes without impairing the system of collective bargaining created by the Wagner Act.

Process Followed

The president of the United States may order an eight-day postponement of a strike, a threatened strike, or a lockout affecting an entire industry when the president determines such a strike or lockout would impair the national health or safety. The president may appoint a board of inquiry to examine the issues involved in the dispute and to make a written report to him. This board is for fact finding only; Congress did not want the government setting the terms for wages and working conditions. On receipt of the report from the board, the president may direct the attorney general to file a petition to enjoin the strike or lockout. If the court finds that the threatened or actual strike or lockout (1) affects an entire industry or a substantial part thereof, and (2) if permitted to occur or to continue, will imperil the national health or safety, the court may issue an injunction.

Federal Mediation and Conciliation Service

Whenever a court issues such an injunction, it is the duty of the parties to make every effort to adjust and settle their differences with the assistance of the **Federal Mediation and Conciliation Service**.

Created by the Taft-Hartley Act, this service assists parties to labor disputes in industries affecting commerce in settling such disputes through conciliation and mediation. The service may offer its assistance whenever a dispute threatens to cause a substantial interruption of commerce. The service does not mediate disputes that have only a minor effect on interstate commerce.

Neither party, in a national emergency dispute, is under any duty to accept any proposal of settlement made by the Federal Mediation and Conciliation Service. However, if the service fails to convince the parties to settle the dispute at the end of sixty days, the board of inquiry will issue another report to the president. The president makes this report available to the public. Fifteen days after the publication of the report, the National Labor Relations Board takes a secret ballot of the employees of each employer involved in the dispute on the question of whether they wish to accept the final offer of settlement made by their employer. This vote permits the employees, rather than the union leaders, to determine whether the offer should be accepted. The NLRB has five days to report the result of the vote to the attorney general. The attorney general, if the workers reject the company's final offer, must discharge the injunction. The president then makes a report to Congress of the proceeding. At this point, the strike or lockout could resume.

Reinstate-ment of Employees Following a Strike

Not only may strikes in certain instances be enjoined, but the employer may replace the workers who go out on strike. Whether the employees who strike may be reinstated depends upon the nature of the strike.

In examining this question, strikes for *economic* benefits are distinguished from *unfair labor practice* strikes. A worker has an absolute right to strike if the strike is in protest over an unfair labor practice by an employer. If an employer fires an unfair labor practice striker, the employer may be compelled to reinstate the employee. But if an employee engages in an economic strike, the employer may hire a *permanent* replacement.

In the following case, the Court discusses the question of rehiring workers following an economic strike.

NLRB v. Mackay Radio & Telegraph Co.
United States Supreme Court
304 U.S. 333 (1938)

Negotiations between Mackay and the union regarding wages and employment terms failed, so employees in one of Mackay's offices went on strike. After the strike ended, Mackay required strikers who were prominent in organizing the strike to fill out applications for reinstatement and did not allow them to return to work, although it did reinstate the rest of the striking employees. The NLRB held that Mackay committed an unfair labor practice by violating its employees' rights guaranteed by Section 7 of the National Labor Relations Act. The court of appeals refused to uphold the NLRB's ruling, and the board appealed. The Supreme Court ruled for the NLRB.

Justice Roberts

It is contended that the Board lacked jurisdiction because respondent was at no time guilty of any unfair labor practice. Section 8 of the Act denominates as such practice action by an employer to interfere with, restrain, or coerce employees in the exercise of their rights to organize, to form, join or assist labor organizations, and to engage in concerted activities for the purpose of collective bargaining or other mutual aid or protection, or "by discrimination in regard to . . . tenure of employment or any term or condition of employment to encourage or

discourage membership in any labor organization. . . .'' The claim put forward is that the unfair labor practice indulged by the respondent was discrimination in reinstating striking employees by keeping out certain of them for the sole reason that they had been active in the union. As we have said the strikers retained under the Act, the status of employees. Any such discrimination in putting them back to work is therefore, prohibited by Section 8.

The Board's findings as to discrimination are supported by evidence. There was evidence, which the Board credited, that several of the five men in question were told that their union activities made them undesirable to their employer. The Board found, and we cannot say that its finding is unsupported, that, in excluding five who were active union men, the respondent's officials discriminated against them on account of their union activities and that the excuse given was an afterthought and not the true reason for the discrimination against them.

As we have said, the respondent was not bound to displace men hired to take the strikers' places in order to provide positions for them. It might have refused reinstatement on the ground of skill or ability, but the Board found that it did not do so. It might have resorted to any one of a number of methods of determining which of its striking employees would have to wait because five men had taken permanent positions during the strike, but it found that the action taken by the respondent was with the purpose to discriminate against those most active in the union. There is evidence to support these findings.

Economic Strikes

An employer may not punish his or her employees for engaging in a protected activity. A company may not discharge employees as a reprisal. However, an employer may hire other people in order to keep the business running. If employers hire replacements following an economic strike, they still must rehire the strikers on a nondiscriminatory basis as vacancies appear. The former employees are entitled to reinstatement unless in the meantime they have acquired regular and substantially similar employment.

Until recently, most employers rejected the option of hiring replacements in an economic strike, although the *Mackay Radio* case has permitted them to do so since 1938, because of the problem of ending up with less skilled workers and creating tension between the replacements and the returning strikers. However,

---

Economic Strikes

On August 17, 1985, the meat packers began a strike at the main plant of George A. Hormel & Company. During the course of this strike, there were more than two hundred arrests as well as assorted acts of violence. Union members were upset when Hormel hired replacements for the fourteen hundred workers out on strike.

The strike finally ended on September 12, 1986, with the signing of a new contract. The new contract restored wage cuts instituted in 1984.

The contract signed by the union did not guarantee the strikers their jobs back. There was no immediate rehiring of the eight hundred workers who stayed out on strike for the whole year. However, the company agreed to let the strikers return on the basis of seniority as openings arose.

The Hormel incident illustrates the great risk to workers who go out on an economic strike. The fact that these employees did not immediately get their jobs back undoubtedly was a severe economic hardship for the employees and their families.

increasing worldwide competition has resulted in more employers hiring permanent replacements than in the past. This arguably dampens the enthusiasm of union members to willingly strike for fear of losing their jobs.

In *National Labor Relations Board* v. *Curtin Matheson Scientific, Inc.*, the Court announced a rule that makes it more difficult for a company to oust a union by hiring permanent replacements following an economic strike.

National Labor Relations Board v. Curtin Matheson Scientific, Inc.
United States Supreme Court
100 S.Ct. 1542 (1990)

Curtin Matheson Scientific, Inc. buys and sells laboratory instruments and supplies. In 1970, the board certified Teamsters Local 868, General Drivers, Warehousemen and Helpers as the collective bargaining agent for Curtin's production and maintenance employees. After the collective bargaining agreement expired in 1979, Curtin made its final offer for a new agreement. The union rejected that offer. Curtin then locked out the twenty-seven bargaining-unit employees. The union then commenced an economic strike. The company thereafter hired permanent replacement employees to replace the strikers. The union ended its strike on July 16, and offered to accept the last contract offer. Curtin informed the union that the offer was no longer available. In addition, it withdrew recognition from the union and refused to bargain further, stating that it doubted that the union was supported by a majority of the employees in the unit.

On July 30, the union filed an unfair labor practice with the board. Following an investigation, the general counsel issued a complaint, alleging that Curtin's withdrawal of recognition, and the refusal to execute a contract embodying the terms of the May 25 offer, violated Sections 8(a)(1) and 8(a)(5) of the National Labor Relations Act. The board held that Curtin lacked an objective basis to doubt the union's majority status and the evidence was insufficient to rebut the presumption of the union's continuing majority status. The court of appeals rejected the board's decision not to apply any presumption in evaluating striker replacements' union sentiments and decided to adopt a rule that striker replacements oppose the union. The Supreme Court reversed the decision of the court of appeals.

Justice Marshall

This case presents the question whether the National Labor Relations Board, in evaluating an employer's claim that it had a reasonable basis for doubting a union's majority support, must presume that striker replacements oppose the union. We hold that that the Board acted within its discretion in refusing to adopt a presumption of replacement opposition to the union and therefore reverse the judgment of the Court of Appeals.

Upon certification by the NLRB as the exclusive bargaining agent for a unit of employees, a union enjoys an irrebuttable presumption of majority support for one year. During that time, an employer's refusal to bargain with the union is *per se* an unfair labor practice under sections 8(a)(1) and 8(a)(5) of the National Labor Relations Act. After the first year, the presumption continues but is rebuttable. Under the Board's long-standing approach, an employer may rebut that presumption by showing that, at the time of the refusal to bargain, either (1) the union did not *in fact* enjoy majority support, or (2) the employer had a good-faith doubt, founded on a sufficient objective basis of the union's majority support. The question presented in this case is whether the Board must, in determining whether an employer has presented sufficient objective evidence of a good-faith doubt, presume that striker replacements oppose the union.

The Board has long presumed that new employees hired in nonstrike circumstances support the incumbent union in the same proportion as the employees they replace. The Board's approach to evaluating the union sentiments of employees hired to replace strikers, however, has not been so consistent.

In 1987 the Board determined that no universal generalization could be made about replacements' union sentiments that would justify a presumption either of support for or of opposition to the union. Accordingly, the Board held that it would not apply any presumption regarding striker replacements' union sentiments, but would determine their views on a case-by-case basis.

The starting point for the Board's analysis is the basic presumption that the union is supported by a majority of bargaining-unit employees. The employer bears the burden of rebutting that presumption, after the certification year, either by showing that the union in fact lacks majority support or by demonstrating a sufficient objective basis for doubting the union's majority status. Curtin urges that in evaluating an employer's claim of a good-faith doubt, the Board must adopt a second, subsidiary presumption—that replacement employees oppose the union. Under this approach, if a majority of employees in the bargaining unit were striker replacements, the employer would not need to offer *any* objective evidence of the employees' union sentiments to rebut the presumption of the union's continuing majority status. The presumption of the replacements' opposition to the union would, in effect, override the presumption of continuing majority status. In contrast, under its no-presumption approach, the Board takes into account the particular circumstances surrounding each strike and the hiring of

replacements, while retaining the longstanding requirement that the employer must come forth with some objective evidence to substantiate his doubt of continuing majority status.

Curtin insists that the interest of strikers and replacements are diametrically opposed and that unions inevitably side with the strikers. Unions often negotiate with employers for strike settlements that would return strikers to their jobs, thereby displacing some or all of the replacements.

The extent to which a union demands displacement of permanent replacement workers logically will depend on the union's bargaining power. Under this Court's decision in *NLRB v. Mackay Radio & Telegraph Co.*, an employer is not required to discharge permanent replacements at the conclusion of an economic strike to make room for returning strikers; rather, the employer must only reinstate strikers as vacancies arise. The strikers only chance for immediate reinstatement, then, lies in the union's ability to force the employer to discharge the replacements as a condition for the union's ending the strike. Unions' leverage to compel such a strike settlement will vary greatly from strike to strike. A union with little bargaining leverage is unlikely to press the employer—at least not very forcefully or for very long—to discharge the replacements and reinstate all the strikers. Cognizant of the union's weak position, many if not all of the replacements justifiably may fear that they will lose their jobs at the end of the strike. They may still want that union's representation after the strike, though, despite the union's lack of bargaining strength during the strike, because of the union's role in processing grievances, monitoring the employer's actions, and performing other non-strike roles. Because the circumstances of each strike and the leverage of each union will vary greatly, it was not irrational for the Board to reject the antiunion presumption and adopt a case-by-case approach in determining replacements' union sentiments.

The Board's refusal to adopt an antiunion presumption is also consistent with the Act's overriding policy of achieving industrial peace.

It was reasonable for the Board to conclude that the antiunion presumption could allow an employer to eliminate the union merely by hiring a sufficient number of replacement employees. That rule thus might encourage the employer to avoid good-faith bargaining over a strike settlement, and instead to use the strike as a means of removing the union altogether. Restricting an employer's ability to use a strike as a means of terminating the bargaining relationship serves the policies of promoting industrial stability and negotiated settlements.

If an employer could remove a union merely by hiring a sufficient number of replacements, employees considering a strike would face not only the prospect of being permanently replaced, but also a greater risk that they would lose their bargaining representative, thereby diminishing their chance of obtaining reinstatement through a strike settlement. It was rational for the Board to conclude, then, that adoption of the antiunion presumption could chill employees' exercise of their right to strike.

We hold that the Board's refusal to adopt a presumption that striker replacements oppose the union is rational and consistent with the Act. We therefore reverse the judgment of the Court of Appeals.

NLRB v. *Curtin Matheson Scientific, Inc.* thus curtails the ability of a company to hire replacements as a tactic to assist it in ousting a union engaged in an *economic* strike.

Unfair Labor Practice Strikes

On the other hand, if employees strike because the employer committed an unfair labor practice, when the strike ends, they have an *absolute* right to return even if this means replacing the workers the employer hired during the strike. An economic strike may be converted to an unfair labor practice strike if the employer commits an unfair labor practice during the strike. Those replacements hired before the unfair labor practice may not be bumped, but those hired after the violation will be replaced by the strikers.

In *Mastro Plastic Corp.* v. *NLRB*, an employer was faced with a struggle between two unions. The union holding a collective bargaining agreement with Mastro served notice it intended to renegotiate its contract. This started the sixty-day period running. The employer, which supported another union, precipitated a strike by committing an unfair labor practice. The employer fired the strikers, contending they violated Section 8(d) by striking during the sixty-day period. Furthermore, the collective bargaining agreement contained a no-strike clause. The Supreme Court construed the no-strike clause in this case as covering only economic strikes, not unfair labor practice strikes. The contract did not say the employees gave up the right to *any* strike. The Court also construed Section 8(d) as applying only to economic strikes. The Court stated the sixty-day cooling-off period is to encourage peaceful, reflective discussion of economic questions and not to render the union defenseless in the event of unfair labor practices by an employer that might destroy the union.

Employees place a high value on the right to strike It gives them some leverage to attempt to force the employer to meet their demands. Of course, in some instances, a strike is of little value—for example, when a plant has not yet been organized by a union. In this situation, the employees must resort to some other form of concerted activity.

PICKETING

A very important type of concerted activity that the law permits employees to engage in for mutual aid or protection is picketing. The United States Constitution protects picketing—it is a form of free speech which was guaranteed to everyone in the First Amendment.

Constitutional Protections

In *Hudgens* v. *NLRB* (1976), the Supreme Court considered the question of whether the owner of a privately owned shopping center could obtain an injunction against a union picketing at his center. The Court noted that the First Amendment prohibits the *government*, not private persons, from passing laws restricting freedom of speech. For example, if a union attempted to picket on the lawn of Tracy's home, Tracy could call the police and request that the police remove the picketers from her lawn. Although her actions restrict the speech of the picketers, the law permits Tracy to limit the speech of persons on her property. Contrast this to a law passed by the government that prohibits anyone from advocating unionization of America's industrial plants. The First Amendment prohibits the *government* from enacting such legislation.

Speech at privately owned shopping centers creates a dilemma for the courts. Such centers include places such as sidewalks. In most cases, the government owns the sidewalks, so the law generally permits people to exercise a right of free speech on them. Do people suddenly lose the right of free speech simply because a private party constructs a sidewalk rather than the government?

The United States Supreme Court first considered this question in *Food Employees Local 590* v. *Logan Valley Plaza* (1968). It characterized the actions of the owners of the shopping center, in trying to stop a union from picketing on the sidewalks of the center, as state action. Streets and sidewalks are places where First Amendment rights traditionally have been exercised. The justices reasoned that a shopping center has the same characteristics as public property if the owners open the center to the public.

In the *Hudgens* case, the Supreme Court overruled the *Logan Valley* case. It decided that because private parties, not the government, restricted the speech of the union members, the union could not argue that the First Amendment protected its speech. Even so, in light of the fact that the case dealt with speech by union members, the Court decided the National Labor Relations Act, not the First Amendment, governed the resolution of the case. It recognized that under the NLRA, there must be an accommodation between the employees' Section 7 rights and the employer's property rights.

Violence As a Ground for an Injunction

Both the United States Constitution and the National Labor Relations Act protect picketing. Picketing may not be banned outright. The basic approach of most state courts to picketing is that peaceful, noncoercive picketing for lawful purposes is legal. What if the picketing becomes violent? Should a state court enjoin all forms of picketing in the future? Once pickets become violent, a court might consider a prohibition of peaceful picketing as appropriate in order to punish the pickets, or because it suspects violence will recur, or because the previous violence gives any future peaceful picketing a coercive effect.

Today, the state courts, because of the preemption doctrine, may enjoin future acts of violence by the pickets but may *not* enjoin future *peaceful picketing*.

In the event picketing is not violent, it is generally lawful. There have been some restrictions, however, placed on the right to picket. These are discussed in the next section.

SECONDARY PRESSURE

The law in the area of **secondary pressure** is complex. Section 8(b)(4) of the Taft-Hartley Act as amended by the Landrum-Griffin Act states the law relating to secondary activity. What does a court mean by secondary pressure?

The courts, in using this phrase, are speaking of a boycott of an employer other than the employer with whom the employees have a dispute. The **boycott** is named after Captain Charles Boycott, a British estate manager in Ireland. Captain Boycott evicted his tenants. The tenants banded together to urge people in the community not to deal with the captain. The term *boycott* now describes a concerted effort to stop people from doing business with someone.

Suppose that the employees of a meat packer wished to put pressure on the packer. The employees could stage a strike at the meat packer's plant, or they might urge *customers* shopping at a retail grocery store not to buy the products of the meat packer. The **primary pressure** in this situation would be against the packer. Primary pressure is pressure put on an employer by the employees of that company. If the employees exert pressure on the grocery store, urging consumers not to buy the products of the meat packer, they are exerting secondary pressure.

There are three parties to any case involving a secondary boycott: employer A, the union of employer A, and employer B. The union working for employer A puts pressure on employer B by striking, picketing, and so on. Quite frequently, employer B is a customer or supplier of employer A. In this fashion, the union exerts pressure indirectly against the ultimate target—employer A.

Why would a union attempt to exert pressure on an employer in this round-about fashion? Perhaps employer A is not unionized, thus making actions such as picketing against it ineffective, or perhaps, though the union represents the employees of employer A, a strike against employer A would be futile. The ultimate objective of such secondary pressure is to force employer B to stop doing business with employer A. This puts pressure on employer A to settle the dispute with the union.

At one time, the courts regarded such secondary pressure as a violation of the antitrust laws—a conspiracy in restraint of trade. The Norris-LaGuardia Act prohibited the classification of such secondary activity as a violation of the antitrust laws.

The Taft-Hartley Act

Over time, the pro-labor mood in Congress shifted, and in 1947 Congress passed the Taft-Hartley Act. Congress concluded that secondary pressure should not be permitted, because it is unfair to subject employer B to this type of economic pressure. In such a situation, there is no manner in which employer B may settle the dispute. It is an innocent neutral. Congress also wanted to confine disputes to employer A to keep commerce from being disrupted. Section 8(b)(4) now covers secondary activity.

Primary Activity

In the statute, Congress used complicated language. It did not use the terms *boycott* or *secondary*. Even so, it is clear that when a union's activity is primary, it does not fall under the ban of the act.

Suppose agents of a union picketed a mill even though they were not certified or recognized as representatives of the employees. The union hoped to secure recognition of the union as the collective bargaining representative of the mill employees. A driver from another company arrived at the mill to pick up supplies. The union members asked the driver to turn away. The conduct of the union was lawful primary activity.

Generally, when pickets are at a plant gate and employees of other companies refuse to cross the picket line, the effect is secondary but **legal**. Section 8(b)(4)(B) states that primary strikes and primary picketing are legal in this situation.

Consumer Boycotts

Publicity

Merely handing out leaflets to encourage people not to purchase a product usually poses no problems under Section 8(b)(4). The act contains a proviso permitting *publicity, other than picketing,* for the purpose of truthfully advising the public that a product or products produced by an employer with whom the labor organization has a primary dispute are being distributed by another employer. (See Figures 20.1 and 20.2.) This right to advise is subject to several limitations. It must not have the effect of inducing any employee of secondary employers to refuse to pick up, deliver, or transport any goods, or not to perform any services at the establishment of the employer engaged in such distribution. The proviso ensures the right to free speech guaranteed to every person under the Constitu-

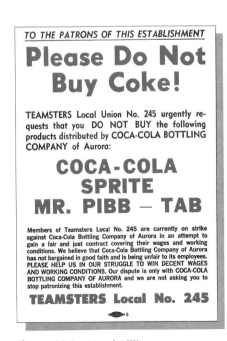

Figure 20.1   Hand Billing   **Figure 20.2**   Boycott Announcement

tion. The union's aim here must not be to induce the employees of the secondary employer not to work. The union must solely intend to exercise its *right to inform* the public of its dispute with the primary employer.

The following case deals with the right of the employees to use handbills.

DeBartolo Corporation v. Florida Gulf Coast Building and Construction Trades Council
United States Supreme Court
108 S.Ct. 1392 (1988)

A dispute arose between the Florida Gulf Coast Building and Construction Trades Council (the union) and the H. J. High Construction Company over the allegedly substandard wages and fringe benefits paid by High to its employees. DeBartolo hired H. J. Wilson to build a department store. H. J. Wilson, the general contractor, hired High, a subcontractor, to construct a department store in a mall owned by the Edward J. DeBartolo Corporation. DeBartolo and the mall tenants lacked the contractual right to influence the selection of contractors. The union sought to influence Wilson and High by distributing handbills asking mall customers not to shop at any of the stores in the mall until DeBartolo promised that all construction would be performed by contractors who paid fair wages. The handbills clearly stated that the union was seeking only a consumer boycott of the mall tenants, not a secondary strike by their employees. The union peacefully distributed handbills at all the entrances to the mall. DeBartolo filed a complaint with the NLRB, charging the union with unfair labor practices under Section 8(b)(4). The court of appeals found in favor of the union. The Supreme court affirmed.

Justice White

The handbills involved here truthfully revealed the existence of a labor dispute and urged potential customers of the mall to follow a wholly legal course of action, namely, not to patronize the retailers doing business in the mall. The handbilling was peaceful. No picketing or patrolling was involved. On its face, this was expressive activity arguing that substandard wages should be opposed by abstaining from shopping in a mall where such wages were paid. Had the union simply been leafletting the public generally, including those entering every shopping mall in town, pursuant to an annual educational effort against substandard pay, there is little doubt that legislative proscription of such leaflets would pose a substantial issue of validity under the First Amendment. The same may well be true in this case, although here the handbills called attention to a specific situation in the mall allegedly involving the payment of unacceptably low wages by a construction contractor.

The case turns on whether handbilling such as involved here must be held to "threaten, coerce, or restrain any person" to cease doing business with another, within the meaning of § 8(b)(4)(ii)(B). There is no suggestion that the leaflets had any coercive effect on customers of the mall. There was no violence, picketing, or patrolling and only an attempt to persuade customers not to shop in the mall.

Neither do we find any clear indication in the relevant legislative history that Congress intended § 8(b)(4)(ii) to proscribe peaceful handbilling, unaccompanied by picketing, urging a consumer boycott of a neutral employer.

In our view, interpreting § 8(b)(4) as not reaching the handbilling involved in this case is not foreclosed either by the language of the section or its legislative history . . . . Accordingly, the judgment of the Court of Appeals is affirmed.

Picketing

Suppose a union places members outside the plant of a candy manufacturer with which it has a dispute. If the union members hand out leaflets concerning their dispute with the candy company, this is clearly lawful primary activity. Secondary activity becomes a problem if a union places people around an establishment with which the union has no dispute but which carries goods manufactured by a company with which the union has a dispute. If a union that worked for a candy company places pickets outside retail stores carrying the candy, the union is engaging in secondary activity.

A union may try to enlist public support for its strike against an employer. In *NLRB* v. *Fruit and Vegetable Packers & Warehousemen* (the *Tree Fruits* case), the Court dealt with the problem of picketing. The packers commenced a strike in Washington State over apples. The union organized a consumer boycott of Washington State apples. It placed pickets in front of retail stores urging customers not to purchase these apples. The union tried to make clear its desire merely to discourage people from buying apples and not to discourage customers from patronizing the retail stores. No deliveries or pickups were stopped. Customers were not interfered with. The Supreme Court held the union may picket and urge people not to buy the apples. However, had the union requested the customers to not trade at all with the secondary employer (the retail grocery store), this would have violated Section 8(b)(4). Whether the grocery store experienced a drop in business or not, the Court sanctioned picketing to urge customers not to purchase the apples. The union's activities in this case were closely confined to the primary dispute—the strike against the apple producer. Note in this case that the product was clearly identifiable—apples. Retail grocery stores sell many products in addition to apples. When the pickets asked people not to purchase apples, little chance of a misunderstanding existed. What if the union decided to picket a company with only a single product, such as gasoline? The Court implied that a union may not boycott a store that sells only one product. (See the *Retail Store Employees Union, Local 1001* case, which follows, on this point.)

Generally, if the union asks consumers not to buy a particular product, no unfair labor practice has been committed. Asking customers not to patronize the secondary employer is unlawful.

In the following case, on secondary picketing, the Supreme Court ruled that the attempted consumer boycott violated the Taft-Hartley Act.

NLRB v. Retail Store Employees Union, Local 1001
United States Supreme Court
447 U.S. 607 (1980)

Safeco Title Insurance Co. does business with several title companies that derive over ninety percent of their gross incomes from the sale of Safeco insurance policies. When contract negotiations between Safeco and respondent union, the bargaining representative for certain Safeco employees, reached an impasse, the employees went on strike. The union picketed each of the title companies, urging customers to support the strike by canceling their Safeco policies. Safeco and one of the title companies filed complaints with the NLRB, charging that the union had engaged in an unfair labor practice by picketing in order to promote a secondary boycott against the title companies. The board agreed and ordered the union to cease picketing. The board held that the union's secondary picketing violated Section 8(b)(4)(ii)(B) of the National Labor Relations Act. The court of appeals reversed, holding that the union's activity was lawful product picketing. The NLRB appealed. The Supreme Court reversed.

Justice Powell

Section 8(b)(4)(ii)(B) of the National Labor Relations Act makes it "an unfair labor practice for a labor organization . . . to threaten, coerce, or restrain" a person not party to a labor dispute "where . . . an object thereof is . . . forcing or requiring [him] to cease using, selling, handling, transporting, or otherwise dealing in the products of any other producer . . . or to cease doing business with any other person. . . ."

In *Tree Fruits*, the Court held that Section 8(b)(4)(ii)(B) does not prohibit all peaceful picketing at secondary sites. There, a union striking certain Washington fruit packers picketed large supermarkets in order to persuade consumers not to buy Washington apples. Concerned that a broad ban against such picketing might run afoul of the First Amendment, the Court found the statute directed to an isolated evil. The evil was the use of secondary picketing to persuade the customers of the secondary employer to cease trading with him in order to force him to cease dealing with, or to put pressure upon the primary employer. Congress intended to protect secondary parties from pressures that might embroil them in the labor disputes of others, but not to shield them from business losses caused by a campaign that successfully persuades consumers to boycott the primary employer's

goods. Thus, the Court drew a distinction between picketing "to shut off all trade with the secondary employer unless he aids the union in its dispute with the primary employer" and picketing that "only persuades his customers not to buy the struck product." The picketing in that case, which "merely follow[ed] the struck product," did not, "'threaten, coerce, or restrain'" the secondary party within the meaning of Section 8(b)(4)(ii)(B).

Although *Tree Fruits* suggested that secondary picketing against a struck product and secondary picketing against a neutral party were "poles apart," the courts soon discovered that product picketing could have the same effect as an illegal secondary boycott.

There is a critical difference between the picketing in this case and the picketing at issue in *Tree Fruits*. The product picketed in *Tree Fruits* was but one item among the many that made up the retailer's trade. If the appeal against such a product succeeds, the Court observed, it simply induces the neutral retailer to reduce his orders for the product or "to drop the item as a poor seller." The decline in sales attributable to consumer rejection of the struck product puts pressure upon the primary employer, and the marginal injury to the neutral retailer is purely incidental to the product boycott. The neutral therefore has little reason to become involved in the labor dispute. In this case, on the other hand, the title companies sell only the primary employer's product and perform the services associated with it. Secondary picketing against consumption of the primary product leaves responsive consumers no realistic option other than to boycott the title companies altogether. If the appeal succeeds, each company stops buying the struck product, not because of a falling demand, but in response to pressure designed to inflict injury on its business generally. Thus, the union does more than merely follow the struck product; it creates a separate dispute with the secondary employer.

As long as secondary picketing only discourages consumption of a struck product, incidental injury to the neutral is a natural consequence of an effective primary boycott. But the Union's secondary appeal against the central product sold by the title companies in this case is reasonably calculated to induce customers not to patronize the neutral parties at all. Product picketing that reasonably can be expected to threaten neutral parties with ruin or substantial loss simply does not square with the language or the purpose of Section 8(b)(4)(ii)(B). Since successful secondary picketing would put the title companies to a choice between their survival and the severance of their ties with Safeco, the picketing plainly violates the statutory ban on the coercion of neutrals with the object of forcing or requiring them to cease dealing in the primary product or to cease doing business with the primary employer.

Accordingly, the judgment of the Court of Appeals is reversed, and the case is remanded with directions to enforce the National Labor Relations Board's order.

What if, rather than objecting to the product handled by the other employer, the employees of the primary employer wish to influence the political affairs of the country? Such activities would be an illegal secondary boycott because the Court has ruled that there is no exemption in the act for political boycotts.

Damages

In the event a union violates the rights of a company by engaging in unlawful secondary activity, the union may be liable to the company for damages caused by the illegal activity. Punitive damages are not available. In the event a union engages in such illegal secondary activity, an employer may file an unfair labor practice charge with the NLRB. It also may file a separate damages suit in federal court.

We have now examined the extent to which unions may engage in certain types of activities. Employees have considerable leeway in engaging in such collective activities as strikes and picketing, but they must be careful not to place pressure on an employer with which they do not have a dispute.

As Figure 20.3 indicates, the percentage of workers who are members of unions has been steadily declining. It is difficult to say whether this trend will continue as the character of American industry changes.

SUMMARY

A union may not enter into a contract with an employer that requires people to become union members before they are eligible to work. However, an employee

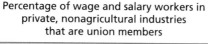

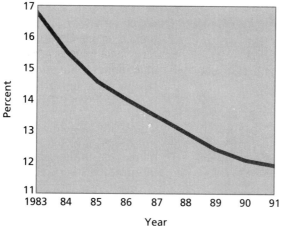

Figure 20.3   Decline in Union Membership, 1983–1991
Source: U.S. Bureau of Labor Statistics.

may be required to join a union after thirty days of employment unless a state has outlawed such a contractual agreement.

The Taft-Hartley Act made a number of union practices a violation of the labor laws. A union must fairly represent all the members in the unit that it was certified by the board to represent. It may not coerce employees in the exercise of their right to engage in concerted activities or charge its members excessive or discriminatory fees.

One of the most important rights guaranteed to unions by the labor laws is the right to strike. Only under very limited circumstances can an injunction be issued against a strike, such as when a strike threatens to cripple the economy of the entire nation. If employees do engage in an economic strike, they may be permanently replaced. However, when workers go out on an unfair labor practice strike, they have an absolute right to reinstatement.

Another important right guaranteed to labor by the labor laws is the right to picket. The law places some restrictions, however, on the exercise of this right. For example, a union may not picket an employer to obtain recognition if the board has certified another union as the bargaining representative of the employees.

The law also places restrictions on the right of unions to exert secondary pressure in order to obtain concessions for the workers of the primary employer. Secondary pressure is a significant problem in the construction and manufacturing businesses.

Generally, a union may picket to inform the public of its dispute with the primary employer. In most cases, a union may urge the public not to purchase products produced by the primary employer.

REVIEW QUESTIONS

1. Define the following terms:

    a. Agency shop
    b. Closed shop
    c. Featherbedding
    d. Federal Mediation and Conciliation Service
    e. Jurisdictional disputes
    f. Secondary pressure
    g. Union shop

2. Under what circumstances must an employer rehire strikers—if ever?

3. May the employees of Company X form a picket line in front of the plant if it has the effect of discouraging other persons from doing business with X?

4. Under what circumstances may an employee who is discharged from the union be fired at the union's request?

5. E Company changed its method of computation to pay to employees from a piece-rate basis to an hourly rate. As a result, the wages of the employees were significantly reduced. Five employees responded to the changes with a work slowdown and were subsequently fired for unsatisfactory production. Is the employees' action protected by Section 7 of the National Labor Relations Act as a concerted activity? Was their discharge an unfair labor practice?

6. The union, while on strike against Dow Chemical Co., picketed six gas stations that sold gasoline refined by Dow. The union asked consumers to boycott only Dow-refined gasoline. The sales of this gas represented most of each gas station's gross revenues. The gas stations were neutral parties to the dispute and the picketing was peaceful. Was the picketing lawful?

7. A typographical union insisted that newspaper publishers pay printers for reproducing advertisements that had been already furnished by the advertiser. The publisher charged the union with an unfair labor practice in violation of Section 8(b)(6) regarding featherbedding. How should the NLRB rule?

8. Several employees were discharged by their employer for alleged dishonesty. Their union did not investigate the employees' claims of wrongful discharge, and the employees sued the union and the employer, alleging that the falsity of the charges could easily have been discovered. Did the union breach its duty of fair representation?

9. A union wishes to distribute handbills to the general public. It intends to ask the public not to buy products produced by the company with which it has a dispute: Petco. Petco is a wholly owned subsidiary of International Products. In its handbills, the union also intends to ask the public not to purchase any products produced by International Products. Is it legal for the union to distribute such handbills?

10. The employees of East Corporation went out on an economic strike. The company hired permanent employees to replace the strikers. The union ended the strike and offered to accept the last contract offer. East refused to bargain with the union because, in light of the large number of replacement employees it had hired, it now doubted the union was supported by a majority of the employees. Is this an unfair labor practice by East?

Part 7

Regulation of Business Activity: Property and the Market

CHAPTER 21

Regulation of Property Rights: Eminent Domain, Zoning, and Environmental Law

- Land Use Regulation: Eminent Domain
- Land Use Regulation: Zoning
- Environmental Law

This chapter will focus on government regulations that affect property rights. Recall the material in Chapter 12: The concept of property rights provides an owner with decision-making power that is recognized and enforced by the government. However, conflicts may arise which are not readily handled by the property rights system. Note the *Fontainebleau* and *Atlantic Cement* cases in that chapter.

Local government influences the use of property primarily in two ways: through eminent domain and zoning. Consider how a new regulation could affect business decision making. In your community, most likely, there is an ordinance that prohibits the construction of apartment buildings in certain neighborhoods. A person owning vacant land in one of those neighborhoods would have limited choice about its development: Either build single-family homes or keep the land vacant. Of course, those who live in the neighborhood will be assured of less traffic, congestion, and noise. Review the materials in Chapters 5 and 6 and consider how neighborhood residents and developers might respond to proposed changes in the ordinance.

A third area of regulation, environmental law, has been dominated by activities of the federal government, although local and state regulations do play a role. The chapter materials focus on recent developments at the federal level. Note, however, that the environmental movement is not a U.S. phenomenon. International efforts have focused on controlling pollution both through laws of individual countries and through treaties among countries.

LAND USE REGULATION: EMINENT DOMAIN

What Is Eminent Domain?

As discussed in Chapter 12, property in the legal environment is a bundle of rights. One of the rights associated with ownership controls the power of government to seize privately held property. This does not mean that government is prohibited from taking private property, only that its power to do so is limited. Consequently, all property is held subject to the **eminent domain** power of government.

The provision for eminent domain is contained in the Fifth Amendment to the United States Constitution as well as in the constitutions of the states. Although eminent domain may seem harsh, it is in fact a protective device. The government must pay the landowner just compensation (generally fair market value) for any property that it takes. (This ''taking'' is accomplished by a process called *condemnation.*) Furthermore, the government can take the property only for a public use. Consequently, unbridled exercise of government power is limited. A glance at a newspaper will show that uncontrolled government expropriation of private property is not uncommon in other parts of the world.

However, eminent domain is not merely a protective provision for landowners. It also recognizes the claim that a community may have upon a certain parcel of land. Without the right to condemn property, the government could be stymied by one landowner who refused to convey needed property or demanded a very high price. As a result, vital public works projects could be severely curtailed.

The requirement for public use of the condemned property is a far broader concept than one may first think. It covers not only property taken by the government for projects to benefit the general public (such as roads, schools, or hospitals), but also property that is used to produce a public advantage, convenience, or benefit, even if the general public makes no use of the property. For example, local governments have condemned slum areas, taking the property from its owners upon paying them just compensation. The local government then clears the land and sells it to a developer, who constructs new housing, commercial, or industrial buildings. The general public will certainly not have the use of that property. The use will be limited to the new developer and those who purchase or rent from the developer. However, such use has been considered by the courts as a permissible public use of the property.

In *Berman* v. *Parker,* for example, the United States Supreme Court held that condemnation of land on which a department store was located as a part of an areawide redevelopment plan was consistent with the public use requirement of the Constitution. Even though the store itself was not blighted and the land was to be transferred to a private developer, the Court upheld the decision to remove a slum in total instead of on a piecemeal basis. The elimination of a slum was considered well within the public use limitation, since it was found to further the public welfare. As Justice Douglas, writing for the Court, noted:

> Miserable and disreputable housing conditions may do more than spread disease and crime and immorality. They may also suffocate the spirit by reducing the people who live there to the status of cattle. They may indeed make living an almost insufferable burden. They may also be an ugly sore, a blight on the

community which robs it of charm, which makes it a place from which men turn. The misery of housing may despoil a community as an open sewer may ruin a river.[1]

As a practical matter, it is not often that a use to which the local government wants to put condemned property will be successfully challenged as a nonpublic use. The definition of the term is very broad. Most of the fights in the eminent domain area of law are over the amount of compensation paid to the property owner.

Although the power of the government to condemn property for public use is generally exercised to acquire land, it is not so limited. Personal property may also be acquired by the government for public purposes. The following case is an example. Note the virtual lack of practical restrictions on local government's taking an individual's property.

City of Oakland v. Oakland Raiders
Supreme Court of California
183 Cal. Rptr. 673 (1982)

In 1966, the Oakland Raiders football team signed a five-year licensing agreement for use of the Oakland Coliseum. The Raiders subsequently exercised three of its three-year renewal options but failed to do so for the 1980 football season. The City of Oakland brought this action in eminent domain to prevent the football team from moving to Los Angeles, when plans were announced to do so.

The city argues that it is seeking to condemn "property," which is the subject of eminent domain law. The Raiders contend that the law of eminent domain does not apply to "intangible property not connected with reality," like a football franchise. Thus, the case presents two issues, one dealing with the intangible nature of the property the city proposes to take, and the second focusing on the scope of the condemning power as limited by the doctrine of public use.

Richardson, Justice

We conclude that the trial court erred in granting the summary judgment and we reverse and remand the case for trial of the issues on the merits.

Because the power to condemn is an inherent attribute of general government, we have observed that "constitutional provisions merely place limitations upon its exercise." The two constitutional restraints are that the taking be for a "public use" and that "just compensation" be paid therefor. No constitutional restriction, federal or state, purports to limit the nature of the property

that may be taken by eminent domain. In contrast to the broad powers of general government, "a municipal corporation has no inherent power of eminent domain and can exercise it only when expressly authorized by law." We examine briefly the source of that statutory power.

The statutory power appears to impose no greater restrictions on the exercise of the condemnation power than those which are inherent in the federal and state Constitutions. Further, the power which is statutorily extended to cities is not limited to certain types of property, nor was it intended to be. In discussing the broad scope of property rights which are subject to a public taking under the new law, the Law Revision Commission comment significantly notes that "Section 1235.170 is intended to provide the broadest possible definition of property and to include any type of right, title or interest in property that may be required for public use." To that end the commission eliminated the "duplicative listing of property types and interests subject to condemnation" which had appeared in the earlier eminent domain statutes.

We are aware of nothing peculiar to a franchise which can class it higher, or render it more sacred, than other property. A franchise is property, and nothing more; it is incorporeal property.

For eminent domain purposes, neither the federal nor the state Constitution distinguishes between property which is real or personal, tangible or intangible. Nor did the 1975 statutory revision. Bearing in mind that the Law Revision Commission, after an extensive national study, made its legislative recommendations, including a definition of condemnable property which is characterized as "the broadest possible," we conclude that our eminent domain law authorizes the taking of intangible property. To the extent that the trial court based its summary judgment on a contrary conclusion it erred.

In fairness it must be said that the trial court fully acknowledged "the intent of the Legislature to allow the taking of any type of property, real or personal, if it was in fact necessary for a public use." But the court concluded as a matter of law that (1) no statutory or charter provision specifically authorized the taking of a professional football franchise, and (2) the operation of such a franchise is not a recognized public use which would permit its taking under general condemnation law. Assuming, for purposes of discussion, the propriety of the first premise, this fact alone is insufficient to support summary judgment, and we cannot agree with the second premise which we now explore.

Is City's attempt to take and operate the Raider's football franchise a valid public use? We have defined "public use" as "a use which concerns the whole com-

munity or promotes the general interest in its relation to any legitimate object of government." Further, "Public uses are not limited, in the modern view, to matters of mere business necessity and ordinary convenience, but may extend to matter of public health, recreation and enjoyment."

The examples of Candlestick Park in San Francisco and Anaheim Stadium in Anaheim, both owned and operated by municipalities, suggest the acceptance of the general principle that providing access to recreation to its residents in the form of spectator sports is an appropriate function of city government. In connection with the latter stadium, the appellate court upheld the power of the City of Anaheim to condemn land for parking facilities at the stadium on the ground that "the acquisition, construction, and operation of a stadium by a county or city represents a legitimate public purpose."

The obvious difference between managing and owning the facility in which the game is played, and managing and owning the team which plays in the facility, seems legally insubstantial. If acquiring, erecting, owning and/or operating a sports stadium is a permissible municipal function, we discern no valid reason why owning and operating a sports franchise which fields a team to play in the stadium is not equally permissible.

We caution that we are not concerned with the economic or governmental wisdom of City's acquisition or management of the Raider's franchise, but only with the legal propriety of the condemnation action. In this period of fiscal constraints, if the city fathers of Oakland in their collective wisdom elect to seek the ownership of a professional football franchise are we to say to them nay? And, if so, on what legal ground? Constitutional? Both federal and state Constitutions permit condemnation requiring only compensation and public use. Statutory? The applicable statutes authorize a city to take any property, real or personal. Decisional? Courts have consistently expanded the eminent domain remedy permitting property to be taken for recreational purposes with the public either as playing participants or observing spectators.

Bird, Chief Justice (concurring and dissenting)

The power of eminent domain claimed by the City in this case is not only novel but virtually without limit. This is troubling because the potential for abuse of such a great power is boundless. Although I am forced by the current state of the law to agree with the result reached by the

majority, I have not signed their opinion because it endorses this unprecedented application of eminent domain law without even pausing to consider the ultimate consequences of their expansive decision. It should be noted that research both by the parties and by this court has failed to disclose a single case in which the legal propositions relied on here have been combined to reach a result such as that adopted by the majority.

There are two particularly disturbing questions in this case. First, does a city have the power to condemn a viable, ongoing business and sell it to another private party merely because the original owner has announced his intention to move his business to another city? For example, if a rock concert impresario, after some years of producing concerts in a municipal stadium, decides to move his productions to another city, may the city condemn his business, including his contracts with the rock stars, in order to keep the concerts at the stadium? If a small business that rents a storefront on land originally taken by the city for a redevelopment project decides to move to another city in order to expand, may the city take the business and force it to stay at its original location? May a city condemn any business that decides to seek greener pastures elsewhere under the unlimited interpretation of eminent domain law that the majority appear to approve?

Second, even if a city were legally able to do so, is it proper for a municipality to drastically invade personal property rights to further the policy interests asserted here?

At what point in the varied and complex business relationships involved herein would this power to condemn end? In my view, this court should proceed most cautiously before placing a constitutional imprimatur upon this aspect of creeping statism. These difficult questions are deserving of more thorough attention than they have yet received in this litigation.

It strikes me as dangerous and heavy-handed for the government to take over a business, including all of its intangible assets, for the sole purpose of preventing its relocation. The decisional law appears to be silent as to this particular question. It appears that the courts have not yet been confronted with a situation such as that presented by this case. However, a review of the pertinent case law demonstrates that decisions as to the proper scope of the power of eminent domain generally have been considered legislative, rather than judicial, in nature. Therefore, in the absence of a legislative bar to the use of eminent domain in this manner, there appears to be no ground for judicial intervention.

Some writers have argued that the expanded notion of eminent domain illustrated by the *Oakland Raiders* case may create an impediment to the free flow of capital investment thought necessary for the efficient use of corporate resources. Some major Northern industrial cities (for example, Boston, Pittsburgh, and Chicago) have threatened local industries with eminent domain rather than endure additional job migration. Although no such actions have occurred, the Massachusetts city of New Bedford found that such a threat persuaded Gulf & Western to decide not to relocate one of its subsidiaries.

Typically, if such an action were taken, the city would hope to quickly sell the factory (or the Raiders) to a group of local owners. These owners would then keep the jobs and tax revenue within the community. But what would happen to the original owner? The law provides that market value be paid, not replacement cost. Further, in some industries, the original owner would be unable to participate at the same level as before. New start-up costs and new market participant problems would arise. Remember, the original business would now be its former owner's competitor. Further, with the Raiders, a new professional sports franchise might simply be unavailable.

Thus, the expansive doctrine of eminent domain has a major potential effect on business activity and some decision making. Can you now suggest one reason why the Baltimore Colts professional football team secretly moved to Indianapolis in the middle of the night? Materials in Chapter 2 might also be useful.

LAND USE REGULATION: ZONING

Zoning and Property Rights

Not all property use decisions made by local governments involve the condemning of and payment for private property. Government could not afford it. The most common decisions made about property involve regulations concerning its use. These regulations are commonly referred to as zoning ordinances or land use planning rules. Note the *Fontainebleau* case at the end of Chapter 12. Local regulations concerning building height, for example, could have protected the Eden Roc's sunbathing area from being shaded by the Fontainebleau's construction. From one perspective, the regulation limits land use decisions: The Fontainebleau could not build the addition it might have needed. On the other hand, the regulation assures the Eden Roc that investment in a sunbathing area will not be rendered worthless by an adjoining landowner's building plans. Thus, zoning may be seen as a means of planning to minimize future disputes over land use.

Although zoning and land use regulations affect property rights (and may limit them, as in the Fontainebleau Hotel example), the landowner has no right to receive compensation. Thus, if the building height limitation made the Fontainebleau's property worth fifty thousand dollars less, the hotel must absorb the loss. The government is empowered to enact such regulations under its police power as long as they protect the health, safety, morals, or welfare of the general public.

Zoning regulation is a means for a local government to plan the growth and development of the community. It is a way to balance the needs and rights of the community against the rights of the individual landowner. It recognizes, as society advances, that what some people do with their property may well affect how others enjoy their property. Zoning provides orderly regulation of the varied uses of property. In that way, an individual who purchases a home need not fear that a tannery or pig farm will be put on the land next door or that an all-night bistro will open across the street. As Samuel Johnson said, "A cow is a very good animal in the field; but we turn her out of a garden."[2] Thus, zones for residential, commercial, and industrial uses have been created in communities throughout the country.

Of course, there is a limit to the extent to which local government may regulate land use. Regulation may so affect the use and value of a property as to make it seem that the government has almost taken the property away from the landowner. This problem—how much regulation before compensation must be paid—is one of the thorniest issues in land use law.

If the regulation goes too far, it will be considered a "taking," similar to condemnation of the land under eminent domain. The local government will then be required to pay just compensation to the affected landowner, and the regulation will be declared unconstitutional. In *Lucas* v. *South Carolina Coastal Commission* (1992), the United States Supreme Court held that land use regulations that destroy a property's value are a taking and, thus, the government must compensate the landowner. In 1986 David Lucas paid $975 thousand for two undeveloped beachfront lots in South Carolina. In 1988 the state barred new building on coastal land, rendering Lucas's land worthless. This action led to the above-noted case. Note that surrounding parcels had already been developed.

However, except for destruction of value, no set standard or predictable test exists to determine when a certain amount of regulation of land use by a local government will lead a court to hold that the landowner must be compensated. Oliver Wendell Holmes, Jr., writing in the *Pennsylvania Coal Co.* v. *Mahon* case, stated: "Government hardly could go on if to some extent values incident to property could not be diminished without paying for every such change in the general law. As long recognized, some values are enjoyed under an implied limitation and must yield to the police power."[3]

Zoning controls basically involve a redistribution of property rights from a landowner to other community residents. These residents, through local government, are able to determine the uses of property within the community. In essence, the means of control over property use is removed from those who own the property and transferred to those who have political control in the community. The goal, no matter who exercises control, is for the land to be efficiently and wisely used. However, it is not clear that government control, as opposed to control by the owner, will necessarily lead to wise choices.

One of the problems with land use control is that it sometimes places an inequitable burden on the affected landowner. It is one thing to prohibit the keeping of a piggery in the city limits, but it is another thing to prohibit the construction of homes or businesses in an area that already has similar homes or businesses. Benefits may flow to the community, but is it fair for the burdens of no or little additional similar development to be borne by an individual landowner? Nonetheless, business managers need to appreciate the importance of the political branches of government in determining basic questions concerning property use.

Zoning and Conflicts of Property Use

The traditional application of zoning is to prevent use conflicts among property owners. Thus, most regulations concern such issues as the location of factories and fast-food restaurants, the height of office towers in a large city, and the number of parking spaces a new retail establishment must provide. Since the regulation of property rights has greater acceptance in the legal environment than the regulation of individual liberty, the scope of that regulation has increased.

As a result, businesses may find themselves "zoned out" of a particular community. For example, the town of Lawrence, Kansas, is located about forty miles from Kansas City and twenty-five miles from Topeka. Lawrence has a pleasant, traditional downtown shopping district. The closest shopping malls are in the nearby cities. For the past dozen years, at least three major nationwide shopping center developers have tried to receive zoning approval to construct a regional, enclosed shopping mall in Lawrence. All attempts have failed. The city has refused to modify a development plan that centers retail activity in the downtown area. In the meantime, however, numerous strip centers have been developed, with zoning approval, along the major roads on the south and northwest sides of the city. One study indicated that, as a result, the retail center of the city is no longer the downtown.

The example illustrates the power that zoning and land use planning practices may exert over business decision making. Since the courts generally refuse to intervene, the disputes become a part of the political process. "Downtown or mall" has become an issue is Lawrence's local elections, and property rights become defined by who is elected. Ponder whether the political and legal environment is being used properly by a local government when its land use regulations act to restrict some new business entry while approving others that have the same effect on the community.

The following case is another illustration of the expanded use of zoning to protect what some consider "quality of life" issues.

Village of Belle Terre v. Boraas
United States Supreme Court
416 U.S. 1 (1974)

The village of Belle Terre near the State University of New York at Stony Brook, located on the north shore of Long Island, has an area of less than one square mile. In 1973, it had two hundred homes with a total population of about seven hundred people. The village passed a zoning ordinance requiring that only single-family homes be built and that households of more than two unrelated persons be prohibited. The owners of a house who rented to six college students were ordered to remedy their violation. The district court held the ordinance constitutional. The court of appeals reversed. The United States Supreme Court reversed, holding that such an ordinance was constitutional.

Justice Douglas

The present ordinance is challenged on several grounds: that it interferes with a person's right to travel; that it interferes with the right to migrate to and settle within a State; that it bars people who are uncongenial to the present residents; that it expresses the social preferences of the residents for groups that will be congenial to them; that social homogeneity is not a legitimate interest of government; that the restriction of those whom the neighbors do not like trenches on the newcomers' rights of privacy; that it is of no rightful concern to villagers whether the residents are married or unmarried; that the ordinance is antithetical to the Nation's experience, ideology, and self-perception as an open, egalitarian, and integrated society

We find none of these reasons in the record before us. It is not aimed at transients. It involves no procedural disparity inflicted on some but not on others. It involves no "fundamental" right guaranteed by the Constitution, or any rights of privacy. We deal with economic and social legislation where legislatures have historically drawn lines which we respect against the charge of violation of the Equal Protection Clause if the law be "reasonable, not arbitrary" and bears a rational relationship to a permissible state objective.

It is said, however, that if two unmarried people can constitute a "family," there is no reason why three or four may not. But every line drawn by a legislature leaves some out that might well have been included. That exercise of discretion, however, is a legislative, not a judicial, function.

The ordinance places no ban on other forms of association, for a "family" may, so far as the ordinance is concerned, entertain whomever it likes.

The regimes of boarding houses, fraternity houses, and the like present urban problems. More people occupy a given space; more cars rather continuously pass by; more cars are parked; noise travels with crowds.

A quiet place where yards are wide, people few, and motor vehicles restricted are legitimate guidelines in a land-use project addressed to family needs. This goal is a permissible one. The police power is not confined to elimination of filth, stench, and unhealthy places. It is ample to lay out zones where family values, youth values,

and the blessings of quiet seclusion and clean air make the area a sanctuary for people.

Zoning and Its Effect on Individual Rights

As noted in Chapter 12, property rights and individual rights are conceptually the same. They are distinguished by what they concern, and by the broad acceptance of property rights regulation by the judiciary. But at some point, the regulation of property may have the effect of infringing on individual rights. At that point, the resolution is far less certain than if only property interests were involved. The following cases are illustrative of this dilemma. In the first, the property regulation is upheld (and such regulations generally are). The regulation is aimed at indirectly limiting perceived "adult" entertainment and is an attempt to circumvent First Amendment objections. The second case seeks to control the location of a certain type of business, abortion clinics. It arose at a time when courts were regularly rejecting more direct regulation of abortion.

City of Renton v. Playtime Theatres, Inc.
United States Supreme Court
106 S.Ct 925 (1986)

This case involves a constitutional challenge to a zoning ordinance, enacted by the city of Renton, Washington, that prohibits adult motion picture theaters from locating within one thousand feet of any residential zone, single- or multiple-family dwelling, church, park, or school. In early 1982, the respondents, Playtime Theatres, acquired two existing theaters in downtown Renton, with the intention of using them to exhibit feature-length adult films. The theaters were located within the area proscribed by the ordinance. At about the same time, the respondents filed a lawsuit challenging the ordinance on First and Fourteenth Amendment grounds.

Justice Rehnquist

This Court has long held that regulations enacted for the purpose of restraining speech on the basis of its content presumptively violate the First Amendment. On the other hand, so-called "content-neutral" time, place, and manner regulations are acceptable so long as they are designed to serve a substantial governmental interest and do not unreasonably limit alternative avenues of communication.

To be sure, the Renton ordinance treats theaters that specialize in adult films differently from other kinds of theaters. Nevertheless the ordinance is aimed not at the content of the films shown at "adult motion picture theaters," but rather at the secondary effects of such theaters on the surrounding community.

The ordinance by its terms is designed to prevent crime, protect the city's retail trade, maintain property values, and generally protect and preserve the quality of the city's neighborhoods, commercial districts, and the quality of urban life, not to suppress the expression of unpopular views.

The Renton ordinance is completely consistent with our definition of "content-neutral" speech regulations as those that are justified without reference to the content of the regulated speech. Cities may regulate adult thea-

ters by dispersing them or by effectively concentrating them, as in Renton. It is not our function to appraise the wisdom of the city's decision to require adult theaters to be separated rather than concentrated in the same areas. The city must be allowed a reasonable opportunity to experiment with solutions to admittedly serious problems.

Justice Marshall (dissenting)

The fact that adult movie theaters may cause harmful "secondary" land use effects may arguably give Renton a compelling reason to regulate such establishments; it does not mean, however, that such regulations are content-neutral. Because the ordinance imposes special restrictions on certain kinds of speech on the basis of content, I cannot simply accept, as the Court does, Renton's claim that the ordinance was not designed to suppress the content of adult movies. Other motion picture theaters, and other forms of "adult entertainment," such as bars, massage parlors, and adult bookstores, are not subject to the same restrictions as adult theaters. This selective treatment strongly suggests that Renton was interested not in controlling the "secondary effects" associated with adult businesses, but in discriminating

against adult theaters based on the content of the films they exhibit.

Additionally, shortly after this lawsuit commenced, the Renton City Council amended the ordinance, adding a provision explaining that its intention in adopting the ordinance had been to promote the City of Renton's great interest in protecting and preserving the quality of its neighborhoods, commercial districts, and the quality of urban life through effective land use planning. Prior to the amendment, there was no indication that the ordinance was designed to address any "secondary effects" a single adult theater might create. The ordinance greatly restricts access to lawful speech, and is plainly unconstitutional.

Framingham Clinic, Inc. v. Board of Selectmen
Supreme Court of Massachusetts
367 N.E.2d 367 (1977)

The town of Southborough, Massachusetts, passed a zoning bylaw that prohibited the operation of abortion clinics within the town. Framingham Clinic, Inc., a corporation that had been attempting to establish a gynecological clinic in the town, wished to provide first-trimester abortions in that clinic. The corporation sued the town.

Kaplan, Justice

We hold for the corporation. The by-law amendment is invalid. The conclusion becomes clear when attention is

paid to the constitutionally protected rights of a woman in respect to termination of her pregnancy (and the correlative rights of an attending physician or a health facility), as expounded by the Supreme Court of the United States in the line of cases beginning with *Roe v. Wade.*

The by-law amendment would have the effect of banishing from the town any clinic in which first-trimester abortions, themselves admittedly lawful, were performed. But clinics offering other lawful medical procedures could locate themselves and carry on in this or any other industrial park district that might appear on the town map. This indicates strongly that discrimination was at work against the constitutional right.

The desires of members of the community to disfavor an "abortion clinic"—desires which, reflexively, may cause these persons to see an economic detriment to themselves in the existence of the clinic—cannot extenuate such a violation. The report of the Southborough planning board about public sentiment was thus an irrelevancy, and a dangerous one, for that way would lie the extinction of many liberties which are, indeed, constitutionally guaranteed against invasion by a majority.

Neither could Southborough justify its own exclusionary rule by saying that a woman might overcome it by going elsewhere in the Commonwealth. May a "fundamental" right be denied in Worcester County because it remains available in Suffolk or Barnstable? Such a proposition cannot be seriously maintained. The picture of one community attempting thus to throw off on others would not be a happy one.

ENVIRONMENTAL LAW

Few areas of government activity have had as great an effect on all aspects of business as environmental regulation. Nonetheless, environmental regulation is rather new and still evolving as more pollution problems are discovered. Although the federal environmental statutes and the activities of the Environmental Protection Agency (EPA) are more widely known, state and local governments also act to protect the environment.

Environmental regulation aims to control pollution. Thus, business decisions such as factory construction and operation, disposal of waste from a manufacturing process, and even whether to purchase land, since owners are responsible for any remaining toxic contamination, are tied to various provisions of environmental law.

As a result, environmental regulation is most often seen as imposing a cost on business activity: Automobile manufacturers are required to equip their cars with emission controls; coal-burning plants must install scrubber devices in their smokestacks; and chemical products companies are regulated in their disposal of hazardous wastes. But the "cost" effect of environmental regulation also provides business opportunities for the creative manager.

For example, in 1985, California promulgated regulations designed to curb leakage of underground storage tanks. Some instances of water pollution had been traced to gasoline and chemicals seeping from underground tanks. J. W. DeWitt, Inc., a gasoline marketer, was concerned that some of its customers would be unable, financially, to comply with the new regulations and would therefore be forced out of business. Consequently, DeWitt organized seminars for its customers to explain the new regulations and suggest low-cost compliance methods. Thereafter, a number of DeWitt's gasoline customers requested assistance in remedying their storage tank problems. Seizing the opportunity, DeWitt devel-

Antipollution Technology in Japan

Japan, unlike the United States, has few natural energy resources. It depends heavily on imported oil. Over twenty years ago, Japan adopted tough air and water pollution control standards as well as antipollution incentives for its industry. Since pollution is waste, these actions had a number of effects. Not only did Japanese industries pollute less; they also became more efficient energy users. Japanese industries thus have a cost advantage in international trade. By way of comparison, the United States has a far higher energy cost per item produced than do competing firms in Japan.

An additional effect of the antipollution activity in Japan was the development of highly efficient, nonpolluting technology. This technology is at least ten years ahead of what is available in other countries. The Japanese Ministry of International Trade and Industry (MITI) foresees a large international market for this technology. As worldwide interest in the environment rises, Japanese firms are positioned to supply the basic equipment to meet the need. In fact, Japanese international diplomatic policy promotes such an end. In 1990, MITI proposed a plan for international consideration, called New Earth 21, that would restore the environment to its pre–Industrial Revolution condition over the next hundred years. Note which country has the technology to begin meeting this goal. As one writer commented: "[A] world community that decides to save itself by saving the global environment will be promoting many large Japanese interests."

The comment is from J. Newhouse, "The Diplomatic Round: Earth Summit," *The New Yorker*, June 1, 1992, pp. 64, 69.

oped a new line of business: testing, monitoring, and renovating storage tanks to comply with the California environmental regulations. By late 1988, DeWitt employed fifteen people in this area and anticipated revenues of three million dollars per year. Note that in 1988 the Environmental Protection Agency (EPA) adopted similar nationwide regulations. About one million small businesses are affected.

What Is the Environment?

The environment consists of all the physical elements of the world except human beings. A study of environmental law, therefore, is a study of the regulation of human conduct in relation to air, water, land, plant and animal life, and natural resources. Environmental law protects the environment in order to preserve it for people to use and enjoy.

Three major benefits or functions of the environment may be noted. First, the environment provides a place for life. Clean air and pure water are essentials to human life and health. The land is also essential in that it provides minerals and animal and plant life for food and shelter. Environmental regulation, therefore, reflects a concern of the legal system for the survival of human life.

A second important function of the environment is to provide resources needed for the production of goods. Clothing, houses, office buildings, books, televisions, automobiles, and countless other products are derived from the environment. Environmental law seeks to preserve and manage our resources. Waste management regulation and controls on the use of pesticides are examples of such laws.

A final function of the environment is to symbolize or personify certain intangible qualities that are important to people. These qualities include the majesty of a range of snow-capped mountains, the tranquility of a pine forest, and the timelessness of the sea crashing into a rocky coastline. Environmental law seeks to preserve these qualities of nature. National parks and wildlife refuges are examples of the law protecting the intangible qualities of the environment.

The environment, therefore, provides a broad range of benefits. Not surprisingly, the environmental statutes that encompass those benefits and the various policies of those statutes may at times create conflict. One commentator identified four goals promoted by the environmental statutes: first, to protect the environment; second, to provide recreational opportunities (for example, national parks); third, to avoid social dislocation that would result from excessive environmental controls; and fourth, to promote economic growth.

Thus, understanding the nature of the environment is the first step in the study of environmental law. Although providing a clean environment is a major facet of the laws, the importance of economic growth and development is not to be ignored. The first task of the business manager, therefore, is to appreciate the breadth and complexity of the topic.

Pollution

What Is Pollution?

Pollution is more extensive than emitting particles into the air or dumping waste into a river. **Pollution** may be defined as the human-caused diminished capacity of the environment to perform its functions. This may involve dumping noxious chemicals into a groundwater supply, thereby making the water unsafe to drink. It may involve harvesting trees or planting crops in such a manner as to deplete the soil or encourage erosion. It may involve a mine that leaves a scar on the earth where rolling hills once existed. All these activities adversely affect one of the primary functions of the environment. All may be considered polluting and all are monitored by environmental laws.

Concern over damage to the environment emerged during the 1960s. Some writers trace its origins to Rachel Carson's book *Silent Spring,* which chronicled the harmful effect pesticides had on the environment. In addition, studies were published that predicted the death of all life in certain lakes and rivers. One river in Ohio, the Cuyahoga, was so polluted that it caught fire. Weather forecasts began to include reports on air quality as well as temperature and precipitation.

However, pollution is not a modern phenomena. In the late thirteenth century, smog was already a problem in London because soft coal was used for fuel. With the development of cannons in the fourteenth century came deforestation in some areas of Europe caused by the newly created demand for potash, sulfur, iron ore, and charcoal.

Causes of Pollution

Although pollution is not new, its extent and its consequences became very serious in the 1960s because of the convergence of four factors. One was high population densities. An old saying has it that a river cleans itself every ten miles. This aphorism may have been true decades ago. A community of five thousand may have been able to dispose of its untreated sewage in a passing river without environmental harm. But as the community grew to thirty-five thousand, the dumping of the untreated sewage began to pollute. The river could no longer handle the increased waste. Large numbers of people concentrated in smaller areas strained the capacity of the environment.

Not only did the community increase in population, but its members used more resources than their predecessors, a second factor in the ecology crisis. Modern appliances created a greater demand for electricity. Families that may have had one automobile began to acquire two or more. As personal income increased, people were able to afford more products and luxuries. Pollution occurs at each stage of the production cycle. It occurs in the making of the product, during its distribution, and in its consumption. As demand for products increased, so did the demands on the environment to supply the resources.

Business practices made up another major factor of the pollution problem. Factories that were built to meet increased demand spewed added particles into the air and dumped more waste into the water. New types of products and manufacturing processes created more deadly forms of pollutants. Disposable products (for example, beverage containers, cigarette lighters, and pens) replaced reusable or returnable products. Nonbiodegradable plastic containers began to replace paper products.

A final factor in the ecology crisis was that the legal and economic systems did not discourage the use of the environment as a dumping ground. The firm that refused to use a river as a sewer would need to make additional expenditures in order to purify its wastes. Competitors who continued to pollute would have those funds available for alternative productive uses. Since the legal system did not prevent such dumping, the economic system, in a sense, rewarded those who chose the "free" method of waste disposal.

None of these factors was alone the culprit, but coming together they caused a crisis in the ability of the environment to fulfill its important functions. During the late 1960s and early 1970s, concern for the environment led the different levels of government to seek legal solutions to the problems of pollution.

Of course, a concern with environmental quality is not uniquely American. Environmental movements have arisen throughout the world. In Germany, for example, the "Greens" have become a political party, with members elected to offices throughout the country. But an interesting contrast in approaches might be seen by comparing Japan with the United States. As noted above, the impetus for an environmental movement in the United States was an increasing number of polluted rivers, seemingly ubiquitous foul-smelling air, and endangerment to wildlife. In Japan, an environmental movement arose out of national outrage over pollution-caused diseases.

In Japan, during the mid-1950s, new maladies began to be encountered:

Minamata disease (caused by mercury poisoning), Itai-Itai disease (caused by cadmium poisoning), and severe pulmonary problems. These diseases were traced to industrial pollution. The plight of the victims were graphically depicted: "the splintering of bone tissue, disfigurement, excruciating pain, paralysis, and death."[4] A national protest movement developed. The traditional mediation approach to solving Japanese disputes did not work, and litigation became a force in the antipollution movement. During the 1960s, four major cases were decided by Japanese courts that made it far easier for victims of pollution-caused disease to pursue claims against industry. (It is interesting that no comparable American body of case law relying on statistical correlations for causation developed in the environmental injury area.) Consequently, in Japan in 1973, a law was passed, with the support of industry, that created an administrative system for making compensation payments to victims of certain pollution-caused diseases. (The funding is provided by Japanese companies.) Although the victims retained their right to sue in court, no major cases have been brought since the act has been in effect.

A business executive should appreciate that the environmental policy goals in the United States are not necessarily identical with those of other countries. Thus, the regulations that affect business activity in each country may differ. Compensation for victims of pollution in the United States is generally handled through litigation (asbestos-caused diseases, for example). In Japan, no statute comparable to NEPA, discussed later, has been able to overcome opposition from growth-oriented businesses and MITI. The focus of the environmental regulation discussion that follows, however, will be the United States.

Local and State Environmental Regulation

Local Regulation

Local regulation of pollution occurs in a variety of ways. Zoning and land use planning are frequently used to control property development—one of the goals being to reduce the risk of further pollution. For example, a few years ago, Tiburon, California, a small and wealthy suburban community, enacted an open-space zoning ordinance. The purpose of the ordinance was to limit the density of new housing. The community believed that overbuilding would lead to traffic congestion, environmental hazards, and destruction of scenic beauty. The ordinance was therefore a preventive measure. Instead of limiting its concern to the removal of environmental problems, the community sought to limit the occurrence of those problems. Thus, although federal environmental law did not affect density of housing, developers in Tiburon had their building decisions influenced by the local environmental open-space ordinance.

Local government can also play a role in the identification and cleaning of toxic land sites. An ordinance passed in 1986 in San Francisco requires applicants for building permits to conduct soil tests to determine if any hazardous substances are present on the land. Thereafter, if cleanup is required, the applicant must certify that the work was done and will remain liable for carrying out the cleanup plan.

Local governments have a variety of other tools to regulate the environment.

Ordinances designed to limit the size of outdoor advertising signs and billboards work to preserve the aesthetic features of the local area. Antilitter ordinances and city offices, such as the parks and recreation department, work to eliminate wastes being dumped in the city. Some local governments require that public projects be preceded by an analysis of the effect on the local environment.

However, the power of local government is not unlimited. Zoning and other ordinances apply only to the local community that enacts them. Pollution problems may exist outside its boundaries or enter the community by air or water. Furthermore, there are both federal and state constitutional controls on a local community's power. For example, one community in California was concerned about noise pollution caused by the taking off and landing of airplanes at night. Therefore, the community enacted an ordinance restricting the nighttime use of its airport. However, the federal government has exclusive control of air traffic. Upon legal challenge, the ordinance fell, since community residents were found to be unable to regulate an area from which the federal government excluded them.

State Regulation

State governments regulate pollution through legislation, administrative agency actions, and their judicial systems. A number of states have adopted a process in which written analyses must be prepared when any major state activity has an effect on the environment. This is a process similar to that adopted by some cities. Both city and state environmental analyses were patterned after the environmental impact statement requirements placed on the federal government by the National Environmental Policy Act of 1969 (see below). Some states have extended this requirement to private projects. In addition, laws have been enacted that protect ecologically sensitive areas (for example, shore and coastal regions). State agencies oversee parklands, wildlife, and soil and water conservation programs. These activities, too, regulate the use of the environment and may affect business decisions.

Sometimes local and state regulation work together. In Michigan, for example, restrictions have been placed on construction on lakefront dunes. Lakes Michigan, Superior, Huron, and Erie border the state, providing unique recreational and tourist-oriented business opportunities. One of the most arresting ecological features is the sand dunes that are located primarily along the shores of Lakes Michigan and Superior. Here is the largest concentration of freshwater dunes in the world. Increasingly, dune acreage has become prime real estate development property. Consequently, some dunes have been demolished, and others are threatened with erosion as their natural state is disturbed. In response, the Michigan legislature enacted a model zoning ordinance for local government to adopt in order to restrict development on the dunes. The ordinance will be enforced either locally or, if sufficient resources are lacking, by the State Department of Natural Resources.

The goal of the ordinance, of course, is to preserve the unique dunes resource. But it also will have an effect on business. Can you suggest at least three effects?

Federal Regulation of the Environment

Federal environmental law may be divided into two categories. One is a full disclosure of the environmental effects of major federal government activity. The second category consists of a number of statutes (and accompanying administrative regulations) aimed at limiting pollution. Together these approaches have resulted in over hundreds of billions of dollars being spent on compliance by business since the laws' enactment. It has also resulted in tremendous strides being made in reducing the amount of environmental damage.

NEPA

The National Environmental Policy Act of 1969 (**NEPA**) was enacted as a full-disclosure statute. It recognized that federal activity had major environmental consequences. The purposes of the act were stated by Congress in Section 2:

> To declare a national policy which will encourage productive and enjoyable harmony between man and his environment; to promote efforts which will prevent or eliminate damage to the environment and biosphere and stimulate the health and welfare of man; to enrich the understanding of the ecological systems and national resources important to the Nation; and to establish a Council on Environmental Quality.

NEPA requires an environmentally related decision-making technique. If federal activity has a major effect on the environment, then a detailed report, called an **environmental impact statement,** must be prepared. This report analyzes the effect of the project on the human environment. If the activity *might* have an effect on the environment, then the environment is to be considered along with the other factors involved in the planning.

The act is significant in that it clearly recognizes federal government responsibility for the quality of the environment. However, it is not a means for eliminating causes or sources of pollution. Nor does it provide a legal right to a clean and unpolluted environment. The following case is an example of the application of NEPA. Note that if the federal activity is challenged in court because no environmental impact statement (or an inadequate statement) has been prepared, a court may order the project stopped until a statement has been properly prepared. NEPA does not require an analysis of all effects on federal activities. It is aimed at the protection of the environment.

Breckinridge v. Rumsfeld
United States Court of Appeals, Sixth Circuit
537 F.2d 864 (1976)

On November 22, 1974, the secretary of defense announced 111 actions involving realignment of units and the closing of particular military bases. One of the actions affected the Lexington-Bluegrass Army Depot (LBAD) to the extent that 18 military and 2,630 civilian jobs would be eliminated in the Lexington area. The army prepared an environmental assessment, which concluded that because there was to be no significant effect on the human environment, a formal environmental impact statement was not required. Additionally, a nongovernment research institution, Batelle Columbus Laboratories, studied the possible socioeconomic impact of the action and concluded that the Lexington area would suffer only minimal short-term unemployment as a result of the partial closing.

The question presented on this appeal involves the breadth to be given to the term *human environment* as used in the National Environmental Policy Act (NEPA). Specifically, does action by the United States Army that reduces jobs and transfers personnel from the Lexington-Bluegrass Army Depot to depots in California and Pennsylvania constitute "a major Federal action significantly affecting the quality of the human environment"?

Phillips, Chief Judge

In the present case there is no long term impact, no permanent commitment of a national resource and no degradation of a traditional environmental asset, but rather short term personal inconveniences and short term economic disruptions. We conclude that such a situation does not fall within the purview of the act.

The contention that NEPA goes beyond what might be stated to be the "physical environment" is not in dispute. Environmental impact statements have been mandated in such diverse instances as construction of a federal jail in the back of the United States Court House in Manhattan.

Although factors other than the physical environment have been considered, this has been done only when there existed a primary impact on the physical environment.

In discussion of NEPA on the floor of the Senate, Senator Jackson provided insight into the breadth of the statute:

What is involved is a congressional declaration that we do not intend, as a government or as a people, to initiate actions which endanger the continued existence or the health of mankind: That we will not intentionally initiate actions which will do irreparable damage to the air, land, and water which support life on earth.

An environmental policy is a policy for people. Its primary concern is with man and his future. The basic principle of the policy is that we must strive in all that we do, to achieve a standard of excellence in man's relationships to his physical surroundings.

To extend the meaning of NEPA to apply to the factual situation involved in this case would distort the congressional intent.

NEPA is not a national employment act. Environmental goals and policies were never intended to reach social problems such as those presented here.

Direct Statutory Control of Pollution

In addition to NEPA, there is another type of federal environmental law. This is a series of statutes that address certain environmental problems such as air pollution, water pollution, toxic waste disposal, use of insecticides and pesticides, and strip mining.

These direct controls of pollution involve efforts by Congress, which enacts the statutes, and an administrative agency (usually the Environmental Protection

WATER ACT
→ + *OTHER (2)*

Agency), which promulgates regulations to carry out the policies of the statutes. For example, the policy behind the Clean Air Act and its amendments was to limit the emission of certain pollutants into the air. The Environmental Protection Agency (EPA) was given the authority to set and enforce these limits. As a result, automobiles were redesigned in order to meet pollution standards for exhaust emissions. Factories and power plants installed devices to cleanse the smoke they emitted of pollutants.

Typically, violations of environmental regulations will result in a fine being assessed. However, recently criminal sanctions have been applied against officers of polluting corporations.

During 1991 there were 125 indictments and 72 convictions for environmental crimes. Fines assessed totaled $14.1 million and prison terms increased dramatically. However, none of those sentenced to jail were members of the large companies that violated the law. For seemingly similar environmental crimes, managers of small companies had a greater likelihood of serving time. In fact, a study over a six-year period (1984–1990) showed a similar reluctance to jail convicted managers of large companies as compared with small ones.

Furthermore, civil fines paid to the EPA have increased substantially. In 1990 the $61.3 million in fines was a seventy-four percent increase over the previous year. In addition, in May 1991 the largest fine ($6 million) in a water pollution case was assessed against Wheeling Pittsburgh Steel Company.

However, direct controls of pollution through statute and administrative activity raise problems, which may be divided into two categories: first, the ability of the EPA (or another government agency) to determine the "correct" level of pollution; second, the effect such an approach has on a business.

Some contend that it is extremely difficult for the EPA to determine the correct level of pollution. Any controls imposed on business to reduce the level of pollutants use resources that could have been used for the production of additional goods and services. Therefore, there is a trade-off between the tolerable levels of pollution and the costs of compliance. What is "tolerable" for various pollutants has caused great controversy. Furthermore, some argue that if a desirable level of pollution is determined, the allocation of permissible polluting would not be done efficiently. That is, assuming that there are numerous sources of a certain pollutant being emitted into the air, how should permissible levels of pollution be allocated among polluters? For example, it may be more efficient to allow plant X to emit a higher proportion of pollutants than plant Y, with the total amount of particles being within the level set by the government. Efficiency suggests that plant X should be governed by a different emission standard than plant Y.

Although this distinction has not been made, an EPA definition of pollution source has been extended to cover plantwide pollution. The definition has been called the *bubble concept* and provides that so long as the entire plant does not increase its pollution, the replacement or modification of any individual piece of equipment is exempt from meeting emissions requirements.

Chevron v. Natural Resources Defense Council, Inc.
United States Supreme Court
81 L.Ed.2d 694 (1984)

In the Clean Air Act Amendments of 1977, Congress enacted certain requirements applicable to states that had not achieved the national air quality standards established by the Environmental Protection Agency (EPA) pursuant to earlier legislation. The amended Clean Air Act required these "nonattainment" states to establish a permit program regulating "new or modified major stationary sources" of air pollution. Generally, a permit may not be issued for a new or modified major stationary source unless several stringent conditions are met. The EPA regulation promulgated to implement this permit requirement allows a state to adopt a plantwide definition of the term "stationary source." Under this definition, an existing plant that contains several pollution-emitting devices may install or modify one piece of equipment without meeting the permit conditions if the alteration will not increase the total emissions from the plant. The question presented by this case is whether the EPA's decision to allow states to treat all the pollution-emitting devices within the same industrial grouping as though they were encased within a single "bubble" is based on a reasonable construction of the statutory term *stationary source.*

Justice Stevens

When a court reviews an agency's construction of the statute which it administers, it is confronted with two questions. First, always, is the question whether Congress has directly spoken to the precise question at issue. If the intent of Congress is clear, that is the end of the matter; for the court, as well as the agency must give effect to the unambiguously expressed intent of Congress. If, however, the court determines Congress has not directly addressed the precise question at issue, the court does not simply impose its own construction on the statute, as would be necessary in the absence of an administrative interpretation. Rather, if the statute is silent or ambiguous with respect to the specific issue, the question for the court is whether the agency's answer is based on a permissible construction of the statute.

In light of these well-settled principles it is clear that the Court of Appeals misconceived the nature of its role in reviewing the regulations at issue. Once it determined, after its own examination of the legislation, that Congress did not actually have an intent regarding the applicability of the bubble concept to the permit program, the question before it was not whether in its view the concept is "inappropriate" in the general context of a program designed to improve air quality, but whether the Administrator's view that it is appropriate in the context of this particular program is a reasonable one. Based on the examination of the legislation and its history we agree with the Court of Appeals that Congress did not have a specific intention on the applicability of the bubble concept in these cases, and conclude that the EPA's use of that concept here is a reasonable policy choice for the agency to make.

The 1977 Amendments contain no specific reference to the "bubble concept." Nor do they contain a specific definition of the term "stationary source." The legislative history of the portion of the 1977 Amendments dealing with nonattainment areas does not contain any specific comment on the "bubble concept" or the question whether a plantwide definition of a stationary source is permissible under the permit program. It does, however, plainly disclose that in the permit program Congress sought to accommodate the conflict between the economic interest in permitting capital improvements to continue and the environmental interest in improving air quality.

Our review of the EPA's varying interpretations of the word "source"—both before and after the 1977 Amendments—convinces us that the agency primarily responsible for administering this important legislation has consistently interpreted it flexibly—not in a sterile textual vacuum, but in the context of implementing policy decisions in a technical and complex arena. The fact that the agency has from time to time changed its interpretation of the term "source" does not, as respondents argue, lead us to conclude that no deference should be accorded the agency's interpretation of the statute. An initial agency interpretation is not instantly carved in stone. On the contrary, the agency, to engage in informed rulemaking, must consider varying interpretations and the wisdom of its policy on a continuing basis. Moreover, the fact that the agency has adopted different

definitions in different contexts adds force to the argument that the definition itself is flexible, particularly since Congress has never indicated any disapproval of a flexible reading of the statute.

In this case, the Administrator's interpretation represents a reasonable accommodation of manifestly competing interests and is entitled to deference: the regulatory scheme is technical and complex, the agency considered the matter in a detailed and reasoned fashion, and the decision involves reconciling conflicting policies. When a challenge to an agency construction of a statutory provision, fairly conceptualized, really centers on the wisdom of the agency's policy, rather than whether it is a reasonable choice within a gap left open by Congress, the challenge must fail.

We hold that the EPA's definition of the term "source" is a permissible construction of the statute which seeks to accommodate progress in reducing air pollution with economic growth.

A second group of problems raised by federal efforts to control environmental pollution directly involves business. The first problem is the imposition of unrealistic pollution standards. This raises an issue of cost/benefit analysis. A second problem is the inflexible nature of set standards. Extensive regulation potentially strains a firm's ability to meet the standards—some standards may even require that new technology be developed to meet them.

Cost/Benefit Analysis and Pollution Standards

An environmental regulation often sets a precise numerical limit on the amount of permissible pollution. It may establish the number of particles a factory can emit from its smokestack or the amount of waste that may be dumped into a nearby river. It may also reflect a concern over the exposure of workers to certain chemicals.

Often questions are raised concerning the relationship of the standard to the benefit it affords society, as well as the cost it imposes on business. For example, assume a regulation limits the amount of pollution in the air to one hundred parts per million. A factory currently emits five hundred particles. A two-million-dollar expenditure will lower the emission to one hundred and twenty-five particles. However, in order to reach the one-hundred-particle standard, an additional two million dollars will have to be spent. To remove twenty-five additional particles, twice the sum of money will be needed. The question posed by business is whether the cost of removing the "last" twenty-five particles is worth the benefits it will produce.

Cost/benefit analysis is an economic tool used to determine the efficient allocation of funds. The business decision to allocate money to a certain project will be made if the expected benefits from that expenditure exceed the costs. Therefore, businesses argue that the administrative agency that sets a pollution standard should employ a similar technique. The agency should determine industry cost of compliance with a proposed standard and the amount of benefit the standard is expected to produce. The costs and benefits should be weighed and the standard issued only if it is determined that its benefits outweigh its costs.

The use of cost/benefit analysis in environmental regulation raises questions because of the difficulty of measuring quality-of-life cost and benefits. Antipollution standards are not always limited to what could be achieved given present technology. Standards may require industry to create new technology in order to be in compliance. The costs of such a standard are highly speculative, since it may be an estimate of technology development.

Assigning a dollar value to the benefits to be gained from the standard is even more difficult. Often the benefits associated with cleaner air or water have no dollar value. Longer life expectancy, less disease, and fewer foul smells are quality-of-life benefits that are not readily measured in terms of dollars.

However, cost/benefit analyses based on similar intangibles are made every day. Automobiles are not banned or made impregnable even though it is predictable that thousands of people will be injured or die in accidents each year. The highway speed limit is between fifty-five and sixty-five miles per hour even though lives would be saved if it was set and enforced at thirty miles per hour. Trade-offs are accepted, even though a precise measure of the costs and benefits of automobiles, accidents, and speed limits is impossible. Instead, an approximation is made. Similarly, businesses contend, the costs and benefits of environmental regulation must be considered before their implementation.

The *Cotton Dust* case (1981) is an example of this argument by business. It involved an issue of particle pollution in the workplace and a regulation setting forth a precise standard limiting those particles. The agency that created the regulation was the Occupational Safety and Health Administration (OSHA). By the time the case reached the United States Supreme Court, it appeared that OSHA was ready to agree with business criticism concerning that regulation. The reason for this apparent change of position was that the Reagan administration took office at about the same time. In fact, President Reagan was inaugurated the day before oral arguments were held. The new administration filed a motion with the Supreme Court requesting a return of the case to OSHA for further consideration. Reagan campaigned on an antiregulation platform, and it was expected that if the Court approved the request, OSHA would decide that it had the discretion to use cost/benefit analysis in promulgating this type of regulation.

The Supreme Court denied OSHA's motion. It rejected the claim that the agency could use cost/benefit analysis at its discretion. As a further note, in February 1981, President Reagan issued an executive order that required agency regulations to be issued only if the costs of compliance were less than the potential benefits to society.

Economic and Technological Infeasibility

Federal environmental regulation is a creation of Congress. As in the *Cotton Dust* case, important balances of various interests are made by Congress during the course of the enactment of the applicable environmental law. An important issue for businesses is that some environmental regulation is set beyond the limits of current technology or the financial ability of a firm to comply. Two acts that raise this issue are the Clean Air Act and the Water Pollution Control Act. These acts have had a great effect on business. One writer estimated that two-thirds of the funds business has spent in complying with environmental regulations have been required by these acts. At times the standards were set beyond the technological or economic limits of an industry. One commentator noted that Congress may have viewed a corporation's survival instinct as the strongest motivator in encouraging compliance with the antipollution standards. Therefore, infeasibility claims have caused much concern in the business world.

The following case is an example of a corporation seeking judicial relief from air pollution regulations on the basis of claims of **technological infeasibility** or economic infeasibility. Note that the request for relief on those grounds was denied by the Supreme Court. However, the Court did not foreclose all consideration of the issue.

Union Electric Co. v. Environmental Protection Agency
United States Supreme Court
427 U.S. 246 (1976)

Petitioner is an electric utility supplying power in the St. Louis metropolitan area, a large part of Missouri, and parts of Illinois and Iowa. It alleges that it cannot continue to operate if forced to comply with the sulfur dioxide restrictions contained in the Missouri implementation plan of the Clean Air Act which was approved by the administrator. Specifically, petitioner alleges that since the administrator's approval of the plan, low-sulfur coal has become too scarce and expensive to obtain; reliable and satisfactory sulfur dioxide removal equipment that would enable it to comply with the plan's requirements simply has not been devised; the installation of the unsatisfactory equipment that is available would cost over five hundred million dollars, a sum impossible to obtain by bonds that are contingent on approval by regulatory bodies and public acceptance; and, even if the financing could be obtained, the carrying, operating, and maintenance costs of over one hundred and twenty million dollars a year would be prohibitive. Petitioner further alleges that recent evidence has disclosed that sulfur dioxide in the ambient air is not the hazard to public health that it was once thought to be, and that compliance with the sulfur regulation in the Missouri plan is not necessary to the attainment of national primary and secondary ambient air standards in the St. Louis area.

Justice Marshall

After the Administrator of the Environmental Protection Agency (EPA) approves a state implementation plan under the Clean Air Act, the plan may be challenged in a court of appeals within 30 days, or after 30 days have run if newly discovered or available information justifies subsequent review. We must decide whether the operator of a regulated emission source, in a petition for review of an EPA-approved state plan filed after the original 30-day appeal period, can raise the claim that it is economically or technologically infeasible to comply with the plan.

The Clean Air Amendments reflect congressional dissatisfaction with the progress of existing air pollution programs and a determination to take a stick to the States, in order to guarantee the prompt attainment and maintenance of specified air quality standards. The heart of the Amendments is the requirement that each State formulate, subject to EPA approval, an implementation plan designed to achieve national primary ambient air quality standards—those necessary to protect the public health—as expeditiously as practicable but in no case later than three years from the date of approval of such plan. Each State is given wide discretion in formulating its plan.

After the promulgation of the national standards, the State of Missouri formulated its implementation plan and submitted it for approval.

We reject at the outset petitioner's suggestion that a claim of economic or technological infeasibility may be considered upon a petition for review based on new information and filed more than 30 days after approval of an implementation plan even if such a claim could not be considered by the Administrator in approving a plan or by a court in reviewing a plan challenged within the original 30-day appeal period.

Since a reviewing court—regardless of when the petition for review is filed—may consider claims of economic and technological infeasibility only if the Administrator may consider such claims in approving or rejecting a state implementation plan, we must address ourselves to the scope of the Administrator's responsibility. After surveying the relevant provisions of the Clean Air Amendments of 1970 and their legislative history, we agree that Congress intended claims of economic and technological infeasibility to be wholly foreign to the Administrator's consideration of a state implementation plan.

As we have previously recognized, the 1970 Amendments to the Clean Air Act were a drastic remedy to what was perceived as a serious and otherwise uncheckable problem of air pollution. The Amendments place the primary responsibility for formulating pollution control strategies on the States, but nonetheless subject the States to strict minimum compliance requirements. These requirements are of a "technology-forcing character," and are expressly designed to force regulated sources to develop pollution control devices that might at the time appear to be economically or technologically infeasible.

This approach is apparent on the face of the Act. The provision sets out eight criteria that an implementation plan must satisfy, and provides that if these criteria are met and if the plan was adopted after reasonable notice and hearing, the Administrator shall approve the proposed state plan. The mandatory "shall" makes it quite clear that the Administrator is not to be concerned with factors other than those specified and none of the eight factors appears to permit consideration of technological or economic infeasibility.

If a State makes the legislative determination that it desires a particular air quality by a certain date and that it is willing to force technology to attain it—or lose a certain industry if attainment is not possible—such a determination is fully consistent with the structure and purpose of the Amendments, and they provide no basis for the EPA Administrator to object to the determination on the ground of infeasibility.

In sum, we have concluded that claims of economic or technological infeasibility may not be considered by the Administrator in evaluating a state requirement that a primary ambient air quality standard be met in the mandatory three years.

Our conclusion is bolstered by recognition that the Amendments do allow claims of technological and economic infeasibility to be raised in situations where consideration of such claims will not substantially interfere with the primary congressional purpose of prompt attainment of the national air quality standards. Thus, we do not hold that claims of infeasibility are never of relevance in the formulation of an implementation plan or that sources unable to comply with emission limitations must inevitably be shut down.

Perhaps the most important forum for consideration of claims of economic and technological infeasibility is before the state agency formulating the implementation plan. So long as the national standards are met, the State may select whatever mix of control devices it desires and industries with particular economic or technological problems may seek special treatment in the plan itself.

An Experimental Market-Oriented Approach

Not every important value associated with property has the status of a property right. Recall the material in Chapter 12. Property, there, was defined as a bundle of rights that represent certain human relationships that are recognized and enforced by the government. The right to buy or sell an acre of land, the right to plant crops on it, and the right to prohibit another person from walking across it are illustrations of property rights of a landowner. These rights recognize the economic values associated with a tract of land, its productivity potential, and the need to encourage the owner to make the "best" use of it.

Note too the case of *Boomer* v. *Atlantic Cement* (1970), also in Chapter 12. The court refused to prohibit a factory from trespassing on others' land by virtue of emitting pollution from its smokestacks. Consequently, the rights of industrial polluters took precedence over the rights of adjoining landowners to be free of trespassers and nuisances. One implication was that rather than the landowners selling "trespass permits" to polluters through the marketplace, the government stepped in and directly regulated the emissions from the factory.

As noted earlier, these direct environmental regulations have been quite costly. Not only have companies faced stringent pollution controls, but an enforcement bureaucracy has been created to investigate and enforce the regulations. The Clean Air Act of 1990 suggested an alternative.

Under the act, emissions of sulphur dioxide are to be reduced by fifty percent from current levels. (Note that sulphur dioxide is a major component of acid rain.) However, this reduction will occur through a market system rather than through government fiat, as has been past practice. The pollution reduction market will operate as follows.

Each plant emitting sulphur dioxide will be given an allowance for each ton of acceptable emissions. Those factories that pollute more will need to buy additional "allowances." Those that can operate with less, can sell excess allowances. These allowances will be transferable, and thus a market for them is envisioned.

Consequently, factories that expand will need to either pollute less (within their current allowance) or buy surplus allowances on the market. Firms will have an incentive to create pollution reduction systems because salable allowances will result. In fact, ownership and trade in the allowances is not limited to companies. Investors are free to add them to their portfolios, speculating that their price will rise.

The sulphur dioxide market experiment is touted as providing a number of advantages over the current command system. First, fewer government employees will be needed to oversee compliance. Second, industry will have flexibility (and incentives) to adopt cost-effective pollution control systems. Third, innovation in nonpolluting technology may arise as the price of allowances rises. It may be cheaper to innovate than to buy more allowances. The key to this system is whether an operating market for the allowances can be created and maintained.

Thus, note the creativity in the legal environment as it seeks to control pollution. Business executives need to appreciate the ever changing forces that affect the law.

SUMMARY

Major areas in which property rights are regulated involve land use questions and the environment. Land use questions are often raised locally through use of the eminent domain power and through the enactment of zoning ordinances. Local governments have the power under eminent domain to condemn and pay for private property that is to be used for a public purpose. Additionally, an owner's property use choices may be limited without compensation through zoning regulations. Consider how this activity of the political branches of government affects property rights. The more limitations that are placed on the use of property, the less flexibility a landowner has in deciding how to use that property. On the other hand, these regulations also provide a degree of certainty for surrounding landowners. They can enjoy their land without risking inconsistent uses of an adjoining landowner.

Environmental regulation seeks to control pollution. All levels of government are active in this effort; thus, the business manager must appreciate the multiple sources from which this regulation can arise. Federal regulation, however, is the dominant source of environmental laws.

Two aspects of federal environmental regulation should be emphasized: first, the full disclosure policy of NEPA through the environmental impact statement. This law requires that harmful environmental effects of public projects be revealed and considered before work on the projects begins. The second important aspect of federal environmental regulation is its direct control of certain pollution problems. Federal statutes regulate such areas as water pollution, air pollution, and toxic substances. The main issues that have arisen under environmental regulation should be noted: first, cost/benefit analysis as a tool for imposing specific regulations; and second, the effect of burdensome regulations, economically or technologically, on business.

REVIEW QUESTIONS

1. Define the following terms:
   a. Eminent domain
   b. Environmental impact statement
   c. NEPA
   d. Pollution
   e. Zoning
2. Jones is a rock concert impresario. He brings the most popular groups to the city for concerts. All concerts are held in Municipal Auditorium, which was built with tax revenues. The city built the auditorium primarily as a place where concerts could be held to encourage people to visit the community and to enhance its urban renewal goals. In addition, when Jones began to use the auditorium fifteen years ago, the city agreed to abate his taxes by fifty percent. Jones's business, which is made up of contracts with various rock musicians, has grown, and he intends to move his concerts from Municipal Auditorium to a privately owned facility in a community thirty miles away. What action might

the city take, based on the Oakland Raiders' case? (See *City of Oakland* v. *Oakland Raiders* at the beginning of this chapter.)

3. Hut is a very exclusive suburb with many wealthy residents. Twenty years ago, Hut was a small rural community. Today it has a very large, urban population. Most of its growth is attributable to white upper-middle-class residents who have left the city, which Hut adjoins. Although areas surrounding Hut are economically and racially integrated, Hut's population is almost all white. It ranks as one of the wealthiest, per capita, communities in the nation. One reason for Hut's particular development is a series of land use regulations. These regulations are such as to virtually foreclose any low or moderately priced housing from being built. Furthermore, the acknowledged purpose of those regulations is to keep low-income people from moving to Hut and to keep the town homogeneous. Construct an argument that questions the validity of those regulations.

4. What are the advantages and disadvantages of zoning and land use controls?

5. You are an executive with XYZ Corporation, a manufacturing firm. The corporation recently purchased a large tract of land, zoned for industrial development, on which it plans to build a new factory. The land cost ten million dollars. Last week the county commission rezoned the land for "open space" in order to protect a mountain range view that can be seen from the downtown business district. As a result, no factory can be built on that land by XYZ and it is, for all practical purposes, now worthless. Does XYZ Corporation have a claim against the commission for its loss? Explain.

6. Recall the *City of Renton* case on zoning. How does the decision affect the "adult entertainment" business? What if there were only two parcels of land that qualified under the ordinance, but demand in the community was for many more theaters?

7. Discuss the functions of the environment and give an example of each function.

8. What is pollution and why did it become a major problem in the 1960s?

9. Discuss the two general methods by which the federal government regulates the environment.

10. Discuss business problems arising from federal efforts to control environmental pollution through regulation.

11. You are project manager for ABC Corporation. Your job involves coordinating all aspects of new factory construction that the corporation undertakes. One of the major concerns you have is satisfying the EPA concerning possible pollution that may be emitted once the factory is operating. Currently, ABC is constructing a factory in California. You have worked closely with the EPA and anticipate no problems with it. Is your concern about environmental regulation at an end?

12. Discuss the "bubble concept," noting particularly its effect on corporate decision making.

13. The Army Corps of Engineers is planning to dam a river in order to create a large reservoir. The reservoir will replace farmland and woodland that currently surrounds the dam site. Discuss how this project is regulated by the federal environmental laws. Limit your discussion to materials contained in the chapter.

NOTES

[1] *Berman* v. *Parker*, 348 U.S. 26 (1954).

[2] James Boswell, *The Life of Samuel Johnson* (1791), p. 421.

[3] 260 U.S. 393 (1922).

[4] A. Marcus, "Compensating Victims for Harms Caused by Pollution and Other Hazardous Substances: A Comparison of American and Japanese Policies," *Law and Policy*, (April 1986), pp. 189, 195. The discussion of the Japanese approach to environmental regulation relies on this article.

CHAPTER 22

Federal Securities Regulation

- Historical Background of the Federal Securities Laws
- Objectives of the 1933 and 1934 Acts
- Federal Securities Law

Capital formation is a business activity with great national importance. In a private, free-market economy the availability of capital from nongovernment sources is vital. If business could not rely on a ready source of investment funds, then either the economy would wither or it would become state-directed. Neither development would preserve the current American business system.

One major source of private capital is the securities markets. Corporations seeking new funds will sell securities, the most common being shares of stock, to investors who risk their private funds for a share of the business. Most major corporations are publicly traded; their stock is available for purchase or sale through a national exchange. Many individuals are investors, at least indirectly, through pension or retirement plans that purchase corporate shares. Thus, the workings of the private securities markets has a major influence on capital formation as well as a great effect on the wealth of corporations and the financial security of individuals.

As a result, the issuance, purchase, and sale of securities are subject to strict government regulation. Most of the regulatory activity is by the federal government through the federal securities laws. However, individual states also regulate securities through what have become known as "blue sky laws."

The law of securities regulation is very broad and complex. This chapter will provide only a brief introduction and overview of some of the major provisions. The focus will be on federal securities regulation, since most major issues occur under its provisions. Throughout the chapter, consider whether the regulatory approach taken by the securities laws is the best way to implement their goals.

HISTORICAL BACKGROUND OF THE FEDERAL SECURITIES LAWS

A common misconception about the major federal securities statutes, the Securities Act of 1933 and the Securities Exchange Act of 1934, is that they grew directly from the stock market crash of 1929. Although the crash and various practices that led to the crash provided the political impetus, the issue of securities regulation had long preceded it.

In Great Britain, concern about controlling the private capital markets can be seen as early as 1285. Edward I authorized the Court of Aldermen to license London brokers as a means of controlling the developing capital markets. The early part of the eighteenth century saw vast speculative investments fueled by the success of a few trading companies in the New World. Many of the investments were dubious schemes. During one morning, a thousand investors paid two guineas each as a first installment for the purchase of a share in a company whose business was advanced to be of major importance, but no one knew what it was. Available speculative investments at one point exceeded the value of all the land in Britain. As a result, in 1720, Parliament passed the "Bubble Act," which was designed to eliminate abuses. Thereafter, many of the schemes collapsed, causing major investor losses. During the nineteenth century, various securities regulation statutes were enacted in Britain, reflecting its maturing industrial economy.

Interest in securities regulation arose later in the United States. In 1903, roughly one-third of the transactions on the New York Stock Exchange were estimated to be a result of attempted manipulation of the market. Federal legislation was proposed in the late nineteenth century, but the first regulations began to appear in the states. Kansas, in 1911, enacted the first major securities regulation statute, which reflected the strong Populist current of the times; the moneyed Eastern interests were exploiting the honest tillers of the soil. By 1913, twenty-two states had followed suit.

However, these state **blue sky laws** were not particularly effective. The laws were limited to the states of their enactment, while the scope of the capital markets was national in character. Furthermore, not all states had such laws, and often no proper enforcement mechanism was available where regulations existed. Nonetheless, at the time, federal intervention was not considered a proper course.

Political philosophies changed by the early 1930s. The Great Depression had begun, heralded by the stock market crash in 1929. In the autumn of that year, the value of the securities traded on the New York Stock Exchange was eighty-nine billion dollars. By 1932, the value had fallen to fifteen billion dollars. The Roosevelt administration had taken office, and federal intervention into economic activity was the byword. Furthermore, revelations about market abuses during the 1920s combined with the other factors to create the political climate for the enactment of federal securities laws. For example, a report of the House of Representatives noted that approximately one-half of the securities issued during the 1920s were worthless.

The Securities Act of 1933 and the Securities Exchange Act of 1934 were enacted to regulate the securities markets. However, Congress did not intend to create a system of insurance to protect bad investments or to cushion the shock of market fluctuations. Instead, the acts were designed to limit market abuses. The acts protected investors from potentially unfair and manipulative practices in the securities markets. They also provided that investors not have less information than corporate insiders when analyzing potential securities transactions.

However, these laudable regulatory goals have come at a price. Today companies that issue securities have an information disclosure cost imposed by the law. Yet it is unclear whether offsetting benefits flow to the individual investor as a consequence. As noted in Chapter 1, many desirable goals cannot be readily achieved by law. Is securities regulation one of them?

Furthermore, policing a market for "fairness" is a complex undertaking that can create uncertainty for securities traders whose access to information is their stock-in-trade. Again, in Chapter 1, note that an effective law is defined as one that is predictable in its application. Are the insider trading laws (discussed below) thus impaired? These regulatory dilemmas surround issues of securities regulation.

OBJECTIVES OF THE 1933 AND 1934 ACTS

Full Disclosure

The federal securities acts of 1933 and 1934 have two major objectives. First, the acts are designed to provide the investing public with adequate information about securities so that investors may make informed decisions. No attempt is made to approve or recommend various types of investments. Instead, the law permits the individual investor to make ill-founded, unwise, or foolish investments as long as the information for a more rational approach is available. One of the major problems with the securities markets in the 1920s was a general unavailability of reliable information on which investors could base their decisions. Furthermore, people with information would withhold it until they had purchased or sold securities. Congress was concerned that such practices inhibited the proper functioning of the securities markets, which requires an informed buying and selling public.

The informational objective of the securities law not only provides the facts to individual investors, but, more importantly, permits professional financial advisors, brokers, and money managers to devise sophisticated tools of investment analysis. Their efforts and advice, which require access to reliable information, can filter down to the investor. The investor may take advantage of the advice by subscribing to a newsletter, using a stockbroker to recommend securities, or purchasing shares in a mutual fund. The informational objective of the federal securities laws may be described as encouraging the markets to work properly.

Fair Securities Markets

A second major objective of the federal securities laws is to provide a fair market for the investor. Note that this objective is not the same as encouraging an efficient market or one that most readily reacts to market-related information. Although a fairness policy may also foster such goals, its aim is to retain investor confidence in the honest workings of the marketplace. The concern is that if a perception develops that the market is rigged or that certain well-placed individuals can exploit their positions relative to other investors, then less money will be placed in the market. If this occurs, a vital source of private capital will diminish.

Thus, the securities laws may also be described as working to deter market abuses by elevating ethical standards of buying and selling securities. (Note the materials in Chapter 8 on ethics in the legal environment.) The tie between ethical conduct and investor confidence in the market is a source of the securities regulation. Note particularly the materials on insider trading later in this chapter for an illustration of federal policy.

FEDERAL SECURITIES LAW

Definition of Securities

The initial regulatory inquiry is whether the items involved in a disputed transaction are considered securities. The legal definition of **securities** is very broad. The 1933 and 1934 acts define them in list fashion, including stocks, bonds, and other common types of investment vehicles. The listing of items also specifies investment contracts. The term **investment contracts** has been construed by courts to include a large number of unusual schemes. The United States Supreme Court devised a three-part test to determine if a particular one is covered by the securities laws: First, there must be money paid from one person to another; second, the money must be an investment in a common enterprise in which the investor is led to expect profits; and third, the profits must arise primarily from the efforts of persons other than the investor. Schemes to sell self-improvement lessons, beauty products, and orange groves have all been held, under this test, to be securities. Review the materials in Chapter 5 on statutory interpretation. Can you suggest a reason why the general term *investment contract* was used by Congress in its definition of a security?

The following case is one of the more unusual examples of an investment contract. Note the application of the three-part test to the facts of the case.

Miller v. Central Chinchilla Group, Inc.
United States Court of Appeals, Eighth Circuit
494 F.2d 414 (1974)

The sole issue on this appeal is whether the district court erred in holding that certain contracts for the sale of chinchillas were not investment contracts subject to the Securities Act of 1933 and the Securities Exchange Act of 1934.

The plaintiffs initiated a class action in the Southern District of Iowa against Central Chinchilla Group, Inc. and individual defendants in March of 1971. The plaintiffs complained that because of material misrepresentations and omissions, they were persuaded to enter into contracts with the chinchilla corporations under which those firms sold chinchillas to the plaintiffs at prices many times in excess of their true market value. The plaintiffs agreed to raise and breed these chinchillas in accordance with the corporations' directions. The chinchilla corporations agreed to repurchase the offspring for one hundred dollars per pair. The plaintiffs maintain, in part, that they were misinformed by the defendants that it was a simple task to raise chinchillas and that the venture would be highly profitable. They assert that in reality, chinchillas are difficult to raise and have a high mortality rate. More important, they contend that the market for chinchillas is such that the venture could return the promised profits only if the defendants repurchased the offspring at the hundred-dollar price and, in turn, resold them to other prospective chinchilla raisers at an inflated price. Thus, they assert, in essence, that the defendants were operating a pyramiding scheme under which profits could be made by the plaintiffs only if the defendants were successful in encouraging new victims to buy into the scheme.

Heaney, Circuit Judge

We consider the fundamental question before us— whether the contracts were investment contracts and hence securities subject to the federal securities laws. The starting point in this determination is the Supreme Court's definition.

The record shows that the plaintiffs invested money in a common enterprise with the expectation that they would profit if the defendants secured additional investors. It also shows that the plaintiffs would not profit from the venture unless they exerted efforts in raising the chinchillas. But this fact does not preclude the conclusion that they had entered into investment contracts because the plaintiffs have alleged: (1) that the defendants persuaded them to invest by representing that the efforts required of them would be very minimal; and (2) that if they did diligently exert themselves, they still would not gain the promised profits because those profits could be achieved under the scheme only if the defendants secured additional investors at the inflated prices. The defendants by their own actions have admitted that the plaintiffs' contribution to the scheme were nominal, and what the plaintiffs really purchased was the defendants'

skill at persuading others to become chinchilla raisers.

In determining whether the plaintiffs' contributions were nominal or significant, the issue is not what efforts, in fact, were required of them. Rather, it is what efforts the plaintiffs were reasonably led to believe were required of them at the time they entered into the contracts.

Viewed in this context, it becomes apparent that the plaintiffs' efforts in raising the chinchillas are really of no significance to the venture's ultimate success. The investor had to contribute two things: his money and his efforts in raising the chinchillas. The latter contribution is alleged to have been represented as being minimal. In both cases, the investor's profit was dependent upon the defendants' efforts to persuade additional persons to invest in the enterprise.

We are convinced on the record before us that the effort to persuade others to invest was the significant effort here. Thus the chinchilla contracts are "investment contracts" and are therefore subject to the 1933 and 1934 Acts. The decision of the District Court is reversed.

Initial Issuance of Securities: The 1933 Act and the Full Disclosure Policy

An illustration of the full disclosure policy of the federal securities laws may be derived from the 1933 Act's registration statement provisions. Although investor confidence in the marketplace is also a factor in these materials, their primary focus is requiring that important information about the securities be made available to the investor. Thus, in theory, the market can operate "properly." Those investors contemplating the purchase of a new securities offering will have the same information to evaluate as does the issuer. Consequently, the market will accurately reflect the true value of that security with neither buyer nor seller profiting from some hidden important facts.

The registration statement provisions of the 1933 Act are concerned with the initial issuance of securities. For example, if a major corporation decides to offer to the public a new series of shares or if the corporation seeks to raise capital through the sale of debentures, then the 1933 Act must be complied with. However, not all new issuances of securities must comply with the general provisions of the act. Some securities are exempt by their nature (government securities). Other securities that would ordinarily be covered are exempt because of the particular transaction that is the subject of the offering (an offering of securities that is private rather than public).

The 1933 Act is sometimes called the *truth-in-securities act*. This reflects its purpose, which is to ensure full disclosure of all material information about the new security to the investing public. The information is contained in filings that must be made by the issuer of the securities to the **Securities and Exchange Commission (SEC),** the administrative agency created to implement and monitor the federal securities laws. These filings are called a **registration statement.** A summary of its contents is called a **prospectus** and must be provided to the investors. The SEC reviews the filed registration statement for full disclosure purposes. It does not judge the wisdom or the soundness of the investment being proposed. Rather, the 1933 Act imposes that responsibility upon the individual investor. Securities markets operate more efficiently and investors are able to make rational investment decisions if they have the necessary information.

However, some economists suggest that the registration statement process of the 1933 Act is not effective in reaching its goals. They contend that the cost of preparing and filing the documents to comply with the regulations exceeds the informational benefit they were designed to provide.

A number of arguments have been advanced supporting this proposition. First, the registration statement and prospectus are written in legal and accounting jargon. Thus, the unsophisticated investor must rely on professional advisors rather than on the information filed by the corporation issuing the securities. These professional advisors have access to similar information without the filing as they seek to serve their clients. Therefore, requiring filing under the 1933 Act is redundant. Second, the issuer does not actively market the new securities. This task is performed by sophisticated middlemen, called underwriters, who would risk professional credibility by misleading investors. Thus, the underwriters will ensure that their clients are fully informed about the issued securities. Again, requiring the corporation to file a registration statement is argued to be redundant. Finally, most investors in initially issued securities are large institutions, such as brokerage houses, pension and mutual funds, and trust companies. These investors can protect their own interests by acquiring the necessary information without the assistance of the 1933 Act's requirements. These factors, some economists contend, illustrate that the capital markets are sufficiently competitive and self-regulating, even without the full disclosure required by the 1933 Act. Nonetheless, the full disclosure requirement remains. Failure to comply with its provisions may be considered a fraud.

The 1933 Act attempts to eliminate fraud by requiring the filing of the registration statement. **Fraud,** under this statute, is a much broader concept than the general legal concept of fraud. This general legal concept requires an intentional distortion of the truth to secure reliance of a person who subsequently parts with money or other legal right. In contrast, the 1933 Act does not question the intentions of the persons involved. Under the act, fraud has occurred if the full disclosure mandate for the initial issuance of the securities has not been complied with. The act provides that when the registration statement contains a misstatement or omission of material fact, the holder of that security may bring a legal action. Material facts are those which would be of interest to the ordinary, prudent investor. For example, assume that ABC, Inc. filed a registration statement concerning its newly issued preferred stock. The financial information in the registration statement failed to indicate that ABC, Inc. was on the verge of insolvency. Instead, the data merely indicated that its fortunes had waned. Furthermore, in the registration statement's listing of the board of directors, Joan R. Toast was erroneously listed as Joan Q. Toast.

Note that two misstatements of fact occurred in ABC, Inc.'s registration statement: one, the financial picture that was presented; the other, the error in Toast's name. However, the 1933 Act and its full disclosure policy are not concerned about information that would not be of interest to investors. Thus, the key to liability is whether either misstatement would be so construed. Were the misstatements material? What do you think?

Liability for fraud in a registration statement may be imposed on a number of parties involved in its preparation. They include the issuer of the securities (the corporation that issues the new series of shares), anyone who signs the registration statement, directors at the time the registration statement is filed, and accountants or other experts who have prepared or certified any report or valuation used in connection with the registration statement.

Although the 1933 Act seems to place a very large burden on people associated with the issuance of new securities, the act does provide a defense, called the **due diligence defense,** which is available to all who may be liable under the act except the issuer of the securities. The issuer has no defense and will be held liable if a fraud in the registration statement is established.

The due diligence defense is maintained when the person against whom a claim has been made had reasonable grounds to believe that all statements in the registration statement were true and that no omissions of material fact had been made. The standard required is the amount of reasonable care that would be used by prudent persons in the management of their property. Thus, assume that you are the vice-president of finance for ABC, Inc., in the example above. What directive would you issue to the corporate staff members who are working on the registration statement? Try to be specific and provide rationales.

The following case is the leading judicial opinion on the Securities Act of 1933. The business events that led to the 1933 Act claim are explained in some detail. Note the application of the antifraud provisions of the act by the court. Note also the due diligence defenses argued by the various defendants.

Escott v. BarChris Construction Corp.
United States District Court, Southern District of New York
283 F. Supp. 643 (1968)

On the main issue of Securities Act liability, the questions to be decided are:

1. Did the registration statement contain false statements of fact, or did it omit to state facts that should have been stated in order to prevent it from becoming misleading?

2. If so, were the facts that were falsely stated or omitted "material" within the meaning of the act?

3. If so, have defendants established their affirmative defenses?

BarChris was engaged primarily in the construction of bowling alleys, referred to here as "bowling centers." These were rather elaborate affairs. They contained not only a number of alleys or "lanes," but also, in most cases, bar and restaurant facilities. The introduction of automatic pin-setting machines in 1952 gave a marked stimulus to bowling. It rapidly became a popular sport, with the result that bowling centers began to appear throughout the country in rapidly increasing numbers. BarChris benefited from this increased interest in bowling. Its construction operations expanded rapidly. It is estimated that in 1960 BarChris installed approximately three percent of all lanes built in the United States.

In general, BarChris's method of operation was to enter into a contract with a customer, receive at that time a comparatively small down payment on the purchase price, and proceed to construct and equip the bowling alley. When the work was finished and the building delivered, the customer paid the balance of the contract price in notes, payable in installments over a period of years. BarChris discounted these notes with a factor and received part of their face amount in cash. The factor held back part as a reserve.

In 1960, BarChris began a practice that is referred to throughout this case as the "alternative method of financing." In substance, this was a sale and leaseback arrangement. It involved a distinction between the "interior" of a building and the building itself—that is, the outer shell. In instances in which this method applied, BarChris would build and install what it referred to as the "interior package." Actually, this amounted to constructing and installing the equipment in a building. When it was completed, BarChris would sell the interior to a factor, James Talcott Inc. (Talcott), who would pay BarChris the full contract price therefor. The factor then proceeded to lease the interior either directly to BarChris's customer or back to the subsidiary of BarChris. In the latter case, the subsidiary in turn would lease it to the customer.

Under either financing method, BarChris was compelled to expend considerable sums in defraying the cost of construction before it received reimbursement. As a consequence, BarChris was in constant need of cash to finance its operations, a need that grew more pressing as operations expanded. By early 1961, BarChris needed additional working capital. The proceeds of the sale of the debentures involved in this action were to be devoted, in part at least, to filling that need.

Although BarChris continued to build alleys in 1961 and 1962, it became increasingly apparent that the industry was overbuilt. Operators of alleys, often inadequately financed, began to fail. Precisely when the tide turned is a matter of dispute, but at any rate, its ebbing was painfully apparent in 1962. In October 1962, BarChris came to the end of the road. On October 29, 1962, it filed in this court a petition for an arrangement under Chapter 11 of the Bankruptcy Act. BarChris defaulted in the payment of the interest due on November 1, 1962, on the debentures.

The registration statement, filed before the sale of debentures, contained a prospectus as well as other information. The prospectus contained, among other things, a description of BarChris's business, a description of its real property, some material pertaining to certain of its subsidiaries, and remarks about various other aspects of its affairs. It also contained financial information. It included a consolidated balance sheet as of December 31, 1960, with elaborate explanatory notes. These figures had been audited by Peat, Marwick.

Plaintiffs challenge the accuracy of a number of these figures. They also charge that the text of the prospectus, apart from the figures, was false in a number of respects, and that material information was omitted. Each of these contentions, after eliminating duplications, will be separately considered.

The various falsities and omissions are as follows:

1. 1960 Earnings

   (a) Sales

As per prospectus	$9,165,320
Correct figure	8,511,420
Overstatement	$ 653,900

   (b) Net Operating Income

As per prospectus	$1,742,801
Correct figure	1,496,196
Overstatement	$ 246,605

   (c) Earnings per Share

As per prospectus	$ .75
Correct figure	.65
Overstatement	$ .10

2. 1960 Balance Sheet

   Current Assets

As per prospectus	$4,524,021
Correct figure	3,914,332
Overstatement	$ 609,689

3. Contingent liabilities as of December 31, 1960, on alternative method of financing

As per prospectus	$ 750,000
Correct figure	1,125,795
Understatement	$ 375,795
Capitol Lanes should have been shown as a direct liability	$ 325,000

4. Contingent liabilities as of April 30, 1961

As per prospectus	$ 825,000
Correct figure	1,443,853
Understatement	$ 618,853
Capitol Lanes should have been shown as a direct liability	$ 314,166

5. Earnings figures for quarter ending March 31, 1961

(a) <u>Sales</u>

As per prospectus	$2,138,455
Correct figure	1,618,645
Overstatement	$ 519,810

(b) <u>Gross Profit</u>

As per prospectus	$ 483,121
Correct figure	252,366
Overstatement	$ 230,755

6. Backlog as of March 31, 1961

As per prospectus	$6,905,000
Correct figure	2,415,000
Overstatement	$4,490,000

7. Failure to disclose officers' loans outstanding and unpaid on May 16, 1961 — $ 386,615

8. Failure to disclose use of proceeds in manner not revealed in prospectus

    Approximately — $1,160,000

9. Failure to disclose customers' delinquencies in May 1961 and BarChris's potential liability with respect thereto — Over $1,350,000

10. Failure to disclose the fact that BarChris was already engaged, and was about to be more heavily engaged, in the operation of bowling alleys

McLean, District Judge

It is a prerequisite to liability under Section 11 of the Act that the fact which is falsely stated in a registration statement, or the fact that is omitted when it should have been stated to avoid misleading, be "material."

The average prudent investor is not concerned with minor inaccuracies or with errors as to matters which are of no interest to him. The facts which tend to deter him from purchasing a security are facts which have an important bearing upon the nature or condition of the issuing corporation or its business.

Judged by this test, there is no doubt that many of the misstatements and omissions in this prospectus were material. This is true of all of them which relate to the state of affairs in 1961.

The misstatements and omissions pertaining to BarChris's status as of December 31, 1960, however, present a much closer question. These debentures were rated "B" by the investment rating services. They were thus characterized as speculative, as any prudent investor must have realized. It would seem that anyone interested in buying these convertible debentures would have been attracted primarily by the conversion feature, by the growth potential of the stock. The growth which the company enjoyed in 1960 over prior years was striking, even on the correct figures. It is hard to see how a prospective purchaser of this type of investment would have been deterred from buying if he had been advised of these comparatively minor errors in reporting 1960 sales and earnings.

Since no one knows what moves or does not move the mythical "average prudent investor," it comes down to a question of judgment. It is my best judgment that the average prudent investor would not have cared about these errors in the 1960 sales and earnings figures, regrettable though they may be. I therefore find that they were not material within the meaning of Section 11. The same is true of the understatement of contingent liabilities by approximately $375,000.

This leaves for consideration the errors in the 1960 balance sheet figures. Would it have made any difference if a prospective purchaser of these debentures had been advised of these facts? There must be some point at which errors in disclosing a company's balance sheet position become material, even to a growth-oriented investor. On all the evidence I find that these balance sheet errors were material within the meaning of Section 11.

Since there was an abundance of material misstatements pertaining to 1961 affairs, whether or not the errors in the 1960 figures were material does not affect the outcome of this case except to the extent that it bears upon the liability of Peat, Marwick. That subject will be discussed hereinafter.

The "Due Diligence" Defenses

Every defendant, except BarChris itself, to whom, as the issuer, these defenses are not available, has pleaded this affirmative defense. Each claims that (1) as to the part of the registration statement purporting to be made on the authority of an expert (which, for convenience, I shall refer to as the "expertised portion"), he had no reasonable ground to believe and did not believe that there were any untrue statements or material omissions, and (2) as to the other part of the registration statement, he made a reasonable investigation, as a result of which he had reasonable ground to believe and did believe that the registration statement was true and that no material fact was omitted. As to each defendant, the question is whether he has sustained the burden of proving these defenses.

The only expert, in the statutory sense, was Peat, Marwick, and the only parts of the registration statement which purported to be made upon the authority of an expert were the portions which purported to be made on Peat, Marwick's authority.

The registration statement contains a report of Peat, Marwick as independent public accountants dated February 23, 1961. This relates only to the consolidated balance sheet of BarChris and consolidated subsidiaries as of December 31, 1960, and the related statement of earnings and retained earnings for the five years then ended. This is all that Peat, Marwick purported to certify. It is perfectly clear that it did not purport to certify the 1961 figures, some of which are expressly stated in the prospectus to have been unaudited.

I turn now to the question of whether defendants have proved their due diligence defenses. The position of each defendant will be separately considered.

Trilling

Trilling was BarChris's controller. He signed the registration statement in that capacity, although he was not a director. Trilling entered BarChris's employ in October 1960. He was Kircher's subordinate. When Kircher asked him for information, he furnished it. On at least one occasion he got it wrong. Trilling was not a member of the executive committee. He was a comparatively minor figure in BarChris.

Trilling may well have been unaware of several of the inaccuracies in the prospectus. But he must have known of some of them. As a financial officer, he was familiar with BarChris's finances and with its books of account.

He did not prove that as to the parts of the prospectus expertised by Peat, Marwick he had no reasonable ground to believe that it was untrue. He also failed to prove, as to the parts of the prospectus not expertised by Peat, Marwick, that he made a reasonable investigation which afforded him a reasonable ground to believe that it was true. As far as it appears, he made no investigation. He did what was asked of him and assumed that others would properly take care of supplying accurate data as to the other aspects of the company's business. This would have been well enough but for the fact that he signed the registration statement. As a signer, he could not avoid responsibility by leaving it up to others to make it accurate. Trilling did not sustain the burden of proving his due diligence defenses.

Auslander

Auslander was an "outside" director, i.e., one who was not an officer of BarChris. He was chairman of the board of Valley Stream National Bank in Valley Stream, Long

Island. In February 1961 Vitolo, the president and a founder of BarChris, asked him to become a director. Vitolo gave him an enthusiastic account of BarChris's progress and prospects. As an inducement, Vitolo said that when BarChris received the proceeds of a forthcoming issue of securities, it would deposit $1,000,000 in Auslander's bank.

In February and early March 1961, before accepting Vitolo's invitation, Auslander made some investigations of BarChris. He obtained Dun & Bradstreet reports which contained sales and earnings figures for periods earlier than December 31, 1960. He caused inquiry to be made of certain of BarChris's banks and was advised that they regarded BarChris favorably.

On March 3, 1961, Auslander indicated his willingness to accept a place on the board. Shortly thereafter, on March 14, Kircher sent him a copy of BarChris's annual report for 1960. Auslander observed that BarChris's auditors were Peat, Marwick. They were also the auditors for the Valley Stream National Bank. He thought well of them.

Auslander was elected a director on April 17, 1961. The registration statement in its original form had already been filed, of course without his signature. On May 10, 1961, he signed a signature page for the first amendment to the registration statement, which was filed on May 11, 1961. This was a separate sheet without any document attached. Auslander did not know that it was a signature page for a registration statement. He vaguely understood that it was something "for the SEC."

Auslander attended a meeting of BarChris's directors on May 15, 1961. At that meeting he, along with the other directors, signed the signature sheet for the second amendment, which constituted the registration statement in its final form. Again, this was only a separate sheet without any document attached. Auslander never saw a copy of the registration statement in its final form.

At the May 15 directors' meeting, however, Auslander did realize that what he was signing was a signature sheet to a registration statement. This was the first time that he had appreciated that fact. A copy of the registration statement in its earlier form as amended on May 11, 1961 was passed around at the meeting. Auslander glanced at it briefly. He did not read it thoroughly.

At the May 15 meeting, the officers stated that everything was in order and that the prospectus was correct. Auslander believed this statement.

In considering Auslander's due diligence defenses, a distinction is to be drawn between the expertised and non-expertised portions of the prospectus. As to the former, Auslander knew that Peat, Marwick had audited the 1960 figures. He believed them to be correct because he had confidence in Peat, Marwick. He had no reasonable ground to believe otherwise.

As to the non-expertised portions, however, Auslander is in a different position. He seems to have been under the impression that Peat, Marwick was responsible for all the figures. This impression was not correct, as he would have realized if he had read the prospectus carefully. Auslander made no investigation of the accuracy of the prospectus. He relied on the assurance of the officers, and upon the information he had received in answer to his inquiries back in February and early March. These inquiries were general ones, in the nature of a credit check. The information which he received in answer to them was also general, without specific reference to the statements in the prospectus, which was not prepared until some time thereafter.

It is true that Auslander became a director on the eve of the financing. He had little opportunity to familiarize himself with the company's affairs. The question is whether, under such circumstances, Auslander did enough to establish his due diligence defense with respect to the nonexpertised portions of the prospectus.

Section 11 imposes liability in the first instance upon a director, no matter how new he is. He is presumed to know his responsibility when he becomes a director. He can escape liability only by using the reasonable care to investigate the facts which a prudent man would employ in the management of his own property. In my opinion, a prudent man would not act in an important matter without any knowledge of the relevant facts, in sole reliance upon representations of persons who are comparative strangers and upon general information which does not purport to cover the particular case. To say that such minimal conduct measures up to the statutory standard would, to all intents and purposes, absolve new directors from responsibility merely because they are new. This is not a sensible construction of Section 11, when one bears in mind its fundamental purpose of requiring full and truthful disclosure for the protection of investors.

I find and conclude that Auslander has not established this due diligence defense with respect to the misstatements and omissions in those portions of the prospectus other than the audited 1960 figures.

Peat, Marwick

The part of the registration statement purporting to be made upon the authority of Peat, Marwick as an expert was, as we have seen, the 1960 figures. But because the statute requires the court to determine Peat, Marwick's belief, and the grounds thereof, "at the time such part of the registration statement became effective," for the purposes of this affirmative defense, the matter must be viewed as of May 16, 1961, and the question is whether at that time Peat, Marwick, after reasonable investigation, had reasonable ground to believe and did believe that the 1960 figures were true and that no material fact had been omitted from the registration statement which should have been included in order to make the 1960 figures not misleading. In deciding this issue, the court must consider not only what Peat, Marwick did in its 1960 audit, but also what it did in its subsequent "S-1 review." The proper scope of that review must also be determined.

Most of the actual work was performed by a senior accountant, Berardi, who was then about thirty years old. He was not yet a C.P.A. He had had no previous experience with the bowling industry. This was his first job as a senior accountant. He could hardly have been given a more difficult assignment.

The purpose of reviewing events subsequent to the date of a certified balance sheet (referred to as an S-1 review when made with reference to a registration statement) is to ascertain whether any material change has occurred in the company's financial position which should be disclosed in order to prevent the balance sheet figures from being misleading. The scope of such a review, under generally accepted auditing standards, is limited. It does not amount to a complete audit.

Peat, Marwick prepared a written program for such a review. I find that this program conformed to generally accepted auditing standards. Among other things, it required the following:

Review minutes of stockholders, directors and committee meetings.

Review latest interim financial statements and compare with corresponding statements of preceding year. Inquire regarding significant variations and changes.

Review the more important financial records and inquire regarding material transactions not in the ordinary course of business and any other significant items.

Inquire as to changes in material contracts.

Inquire as to any significant bad debts or accounts in dispute for which provision has not been made.

Inquire as to newly discovered liabilities, direct or contingent.

Berardi made the S-1 review in May 1961. He devoted a little over two days to it, a total of 20½ hours. He did not discover any of the errors or omissions pertaining to the state of affairs in 1961 which I have previously discussed at length, all of which were material. The question is whether, despite his failure to find out anything, his investigation was reasonable within the meaning of the statute.

What Berardi did was to look at a consolidating trial balance as of March 31, 1961 which had been prepared by BarChris, compare it with the audited December 31, 1960 figures, discuss with Trilling certain unfavorable developments which the comparison disclosed, and read certain minutes. He did not examine any "important financial records" other than the trial balance. As to minutes, he read only what minutes he was given, which consisted only of the board of directors' minutes of BarChris.

In substance, what Berardi did was he asked questions, he got answers which he considered satisfactory, and he did nothing to verify them.

Berardi had no conception of how tight the cash position was. Since he never read the prospectus, he was not even aware that there had ever been any problem about loans from officers.

During the 1960 audit Berardi had obtained some information from factors, not sufficiently detailed even them, as to delinquent notes. He made no inquiry of factors about this in his S-1 review. He was content with Trilling's assurance that no liability theretofore contingent had become direct.

There had been a material change for the worse in BarChris's financial position. That change was sufficiently serious so that the failure to disclose it made the 1960 figures misleading. Berardi did not discover it. As far as results were concerned, his S-1 review was useless.

Accountants should not be held to a standard higher than that recognized in their profession. I do not do so here. Berardi's review did not come up to that standard. He did not take some of the steps which Peat, Marwick's written program prescribed. He did not spend an adequate amount of time on a task of this magnitude. Most important of all, he was too easily satisfied with glib answers to his inquiries.

This is not to say that he should have made a complete audit. But there were enough danger signals in the materials which he did examine to require some further investigation on his part. Generally accepted accounting standards required such further investigation under these circumstances. It is not always sufficient merely to ask questions.

Here again, the burden of proof is on Peat, Marwick. I find that that burden had not been satisfied. I conclude that Peat, Marwick has not established its due diligence defense.

Trading in Securities: The 1934 Act and the Fair Markets Policy

The second major objective of the federal securities laws, providing a fair market, may best be illustrated by a discussion of **insider trading.** Insider trading prohibitions seek to inhibit those with confidential information from acting on it by purchasing or selling securities. Consequently, investors' perceptions of the market will not be tarnished by a belief that certain privileged individuals, those in possession of secret information, are gaining unfairly from their trades.

The Securities Exchange Act of 1934 is the key statute concerning insider trading. The primary focus of the 1934 Act is the secondary purchase or sale of securities, covering transactions other than those involved in an initial offering. The act provides a legal mechanism to combat deceptive or manipulative practices in the securities marketplace. These prohibited practices, which include insider trading, impose a higher standard of conduct in the securities industry than in others.

The major provision to combat such problems in the 1934 Act is Section 10(b). That section makes it unlawful to use or employ any manipulative or deceptive device in connection with the purchase or sale of any security. Section 10(b) was implemented by an administrative regulation drafted by the Securities and Exchange Commission. The SEC is the agency charged with the oversight of federal securities laws. This regulation, known as Rule 10b-5, makes it unlawful for any person to:

1. Employ any device, scheme, or artifice to defraud.

2. Make any untrue statement of a material fact or omit a material fact which would be necessary in order that the statements made not be misleading.

3. Engage in any act, practice, or course of business that operates as a fraud or deceit upon any person in connection with the purchase or sale of any security.

Compare the language of Section 10(b) and Rule 10b-5 with the concept of fraud in the registration statement materials in the 1933 Act. Note that the 1934 Act suggests that a purposeful intent or scienter (guilty knowledge in a matter) will be required in order to violate its provisions. In the 1934 Act, such words as *deceptive, manipulative,* and *scheme* connote a purposeful mental state that is not evident or required in the 1933 Act's antifraud provisions. Consequently, the mere use of confidential information will not be considered insider trading. Something more is required.

Insider Trading

Assume that Nick Adams is the president of HW, Inc., a publicly traded corporation. The corporation has been experiencing financial difficulties, and its share price declined from $20^{1}/_{4}$ to $16^{1}/_{2}$ over the past three months. One might consider that the current share price reflects all public information about HW, Inc. and investors' perceptions of its ability to withstand the difficult times. Adams owns five hundred thousand shares of HW, Inc. This morning, during a secret meeting with top corporate executives, Adams decides that HW, Inc. should file for bankruptcy. Announcement of that decision will be made within the hour. But before that time, Adams sells all his shares. Would Adams's sale of his shares in HW, Inc., based on the undisclosed bankruptcy decision, be insider trading in violation of Section 10(b) and Rule 10b-5 of the 1934 Act?

Note that the discussion of insider trading that follows is based on one theory of liability for insider trading. Although it is the major theoretical foundation of insider trading, a number of other theories, such as misappropriation, mail and wire fraud, and RICO, are often raised simultaneously. Their discussion, however, is beyond this one-chapter survey of federal securities law policies.

Basic insider trading liability theory involves someone (not necessarily an officer or employee of the corporation) trading in securities on the basis of material inside information, knowing that information is not available to the investing public. Material information is information that would be of interest to an investor in making an investment decision. Inside information is that which is not disseminated to the general investing public. Persons who possess material inside information and who have a duty not to use it must either refrain from trading in the securities or wait until the information is disseminated. (See the Ivan Boesky and Insider Trading box.)

Apply the above factors to Nick Adams's trade: As president of HW, Inc., he knew of the bankruptcy decision before it was publicly disclosed. Such a decision by corporate management removes hope that some investors harbored that HW, Inc. could avoid financial disaster. This "hope" was reflected in the $16^{1}/_{2}$ price of the stock. Remove it, and one could be assured that the price would fall. Adams took advantage of this bit of information at a time when other investors could only speculate about the possibility of bankruptcy. Furthermore, the information did not belong to Adams; it was *corporate* information. As president, Nick Adams owed a fiduciary duty not to use corporate property for personal gain. Consequently, by so using the inside information, Adams breached his duty to HW, Inc.

Thus, one can identify two elements that are at the heart of illegal insider trading: first, that the trader (Nick Adams, in the example) knowingly used secret, material corporation information; and, second, that in doing so the trader (Nick Adams) breached a fiduciary duty to the company.

Insider trading activity was one of the major financial news stories of the 1980s. Aggressive investigations by the SEC led to the arrests and convictions of major Wall Street figures. Some were sentenced to prison. A popular movie, *Wall*

Street, chronicled a young stockbroker's experiences with insider trading. Congress in 1984, 1988, and 1990 enacted statutes that greatly enhanced penalties for those involved in insider trading. Clearly, such trading can be highly lucrative. These statutes sought to make the costs of being caught so great as to inhibit such activity.

The potential for enormous profits from insider trading may be shown by an example using call options. A call option is the right to purchase shares of a certain corporation's stock at a fixed price at some future date. Consider, for example, call options for Santa Fe International stock that were selling for less than one dollar each before a takeover bid by Kuwait Petroleum. As soon as the bid was announced (usually such bids involve the offering of a large premium over market price for the shares of the company being taken over), the call option price for Santa Fe rose to over fourteen dollars. Someone with inside information concerning the takeover bid could have made a great deal of money if call options were purchased before the news of the takeover was made public.

Ivan Boesky and Insider Trading

Ivan Boesky was one of the top arbitrage traders on Wall Street. Arbitrage is the near simultaneous purchase and then sale of the same securities in an effort to profit from a small increase in the price. He started his own investment firm in 1975, using $700,000 of family money. By 1980, the firm's capital had reached $90 million. In 1986, his personal fortune had been estimated in the $200 million range.

Beginning in early 1985 and lasting for about one year, Boesky entered into a business relationship with Dennis Levine. Levine, managing director of Drexel Burnham Lambert, Inc., arranged to give Boesky secret information concerning pending corporate mergers, acquisitions, and restructurings. These corporate activities, when announced, would likely lead to higher stock prices for the firms involved. Boesky agreed to pay Levine five percent on profits made on information that caused Boesky to invest in a certain corporation's stock and one percent on profits earned on stock that Boesky already held.

This illegal arrangement produced a $4 million profit for Boesky in the R. J. Reynolds takeover of Nabisco Brands, whose stock was purchased after a Levine tip. He made an additional $4.1 million when he purchased Houston Natural Gas Corporation stock prior to its acquisition by InterNorth, Inc. By spring of 1986, Boesky had agreed to pay Levine $2.4 million pursuant to their arrangement. However, Levine was never paid because soon thereafter he was charged by the SEC with a variety of illegal insider trades that resulted in $12.6 million in profit.

Levine, cooperating with the SEC, implicated Boesky, and in November 1986 Boesky signed a consent decree settling insider trading claims against him. He agreed to put $50 million in an escrow account to benefit investors harmed by his insider trades. He also agreed to pay a $50 million fine and will be barred from the securities business for life. Finally, Boesky pled guilty to one criminal charge and was sentenced to three years in jail.

Breach of Confidentiality

Another example of management breaching its fiduciary duty when trading on the basis of confidential corporate information is illustrated by the classic 1934 Act case, *SEC* v. *Texas Gulf Sulphur*. In November 1963, during some geological surveys and exploratory drilling, a potentially vast and very rich area of ore was discovered. No further drilling or exploration was performed at the site until the end of March 1964. The corporation kept the information secret as it sought to acquire the balance of the section of land surrounding the rich exploratory core. During this five-month period of drilling inactivity, a number of corporate personnel who knew of the discovery, as well as some others who had been told, invested in Texas Gulf Sulphur stock. Before these come-lately investments, the persons owned 1,135 shares and no calls. After the investments, they owned 8,235 shares and 12,300 calls.

By early April, rumors abounded that a rich strike had been made. On April 12, the corporation issued a press release aimed at quelling them. On April 16, the corporation released the information about the ore strike through an article in a Canadian mining journal and via a news conference held that morning. Some corporate officials purchased Texas Gulf Sulphur stock between April 12 and April 16. One official left the press conference early to place an order with his broker.

These purchases were later attacked as being illegal insider trades in violation of the 1934 Act. The information was found to be material, since news of a major ore strike would affect the decisions of the investing public whether to buy or sell the stock. The information was secret. The individuals who purchased stock or calls had therefore traded on the basis of material inside information. The officials who purchased between April 12 and April 16 clearly knew of the materiality of the information. They should not have traded until the information was disseminated to the general investing public, yet they chose to do so.

It is interesting to note that at the time of the initial find, in November 1963, Texas Gulf Sulphur stock was selling at $17^3/8$. On April 16, after the information was disseminated, the stock closed at $36^3/8$. By May 15, shares in Texas Gulf Sulphur were selling for $58^1/4$.

Texas Gulf Sulphur also illustrates the point that the standard of business conduct imposed by the securities regulations is different from that which is acceptable in other types of business transactions. Purchasing land surrounding the ore strike without releasing the information was an acceptable (and probably prudent) business practice. If landowners had known that valuable ore was beneath their property, Texas Gulf Sulphur would have had to pay much higher prices. However, purchasing Texas Gulf Sulphur securities on the basis of the same secret information was considered illegal insider trading under the 1934 Act.

Although corporate insiders are the most obvious targets of insider trading enforcement, they are not the only ones who have been found liable. The following two cases, *In the Matter of Cady, Roberts & Co.* and *Dirks* v. *Securities and Exchange Commission*, illustrate the application of insider trading prohibitions to those outside the ambit of the corporation. Note that in each case, confidential information was used. The distinction between the two cases is whether a fiduciary duty was breached by doing so. In *Cady, Roberts*, Gintel's duty not to use the information arose from his business relationship with a director of Curtiss-Wright, J. Cheever Cowdin. Thus, Gintel was held to have violated the 1934 Act. However, in *Dirks* no duty was breached by the use of confidential information concerning the Equity Funding scandal. Consequently, Dirks did not violate the act.

In the Matter of Cady, Roberts & Co.
Securities and Exchange Commission
40 S.E.C. 907 (1961)

Early in November 1959, Roy T. Hurley, then president and chairman of the board of Curtiss-Wright Corporation, invited two thousand representatives of the press, the military, and the financial and business communities to a public unveiling, on November 23, of a new type of internal combustion engine being developed by the company. On November 24, 1959, press announcements concerning the new engine appeared in certain newspapers. On that day, Curtiss-Wright stock was one of the most active issues on the New York Stock Exchange, closing at 35¼, up 3¼ on a volume of 88,700 shares. From November 6 through November 23, Gintel had purchased approximately 11,000 shares of Curtiss-Wright stock for some thirty discretionary accounts of customers of Cady, Roberts & Co. With the rise in the price on November 24, he began selling Curtiss-Wright shares for these accounts and sold on that day a total of 2,200 shares on the Exchange.

The activity in Curtiss-Wright stock on the Exchange continued the next morning, November 25, and the price rose to 40¾, a new high for the year. Gintel continued sales for the discretionary accounts and, between the opening of the market and about 11:00 A.M., he sold 4,300 shares.

On the morning of November 25, the Curtiss-Wright directors, including J. Cheever Cowdin (Cowdin), then a registered representative of Cady, Roberts & Co., met to consider, among other things, the declaration of a quarterly dividend. The company had paid a dividend of $.625 per share for each of the first three quarters of 1959. The Curtiss-Wright Board, over the objections of Hurley, who favored declaration of a dividend at the same rate as in the previous quarters, approved a dividend for the fourth quarter at the reduced rate of $.375 per share. At approximately 11:00 A.M., the board authorized transmission of information of this action by telegram to the New York Stock Exchange. The secretary of Curtiss-Wright immediately left the meeting room to arrange for this communication. There was a short delay in the transmission of the telegram because of a typing problem, and the telegram, although transmitted to Western Union at 11:12 A.M., was not delivered to the Exchange until 12:29 P.M. It had been customary for the company also to advise the Dow Jones News Ticker Service of any dividend action. However, apparently through some mistake or inadvertence, the *Wall Street Journal* was not given the news until approximately 11:45 A.M., and the announcement did not appear on the Dow Jones ticker tape until 11:48 A.M.

Sometime after the dividend decision, there was a recess of the Curtiss-Wright directors' meeting, during which Cowdin telephoned Cady, Roberts & Co. and left a message for Gintel that the dividend had been cut. Upon receiving this information, Gintel entered two sell orders for execution on the Exchange: one to sell two thousand shares of Curtiss-Wright stock for ten accounts, and the other to sell short (for later repurchase) five thousand shares for eleven accounts. Of the five thousand shares, four hundred were sold for three of Cowdin's customers. According to Cowdin, pursuant to directions from his clients, he had given instructions to Gintel to take profits on these four hundred shares if the stock took a "run up." These orders were executed at 11:15 and 11:18 A.M., at $40\frac{1}{4}$ and $40\frac{3}{8}$, respectively.

When the dividend announcement appeared on the Dow Jones tape at 11:48 A.M., the Exchange was compelled to suspend trading in Curtiss-Wright because of the large number of sell orders. Trading in Curtiss-Wright stock was resumed at 1:59 P.M. at $36\frac{1}{2}$, ranged during the balance of the day between $34\frac{1}{8}$ and 37, and closed at $34\frac{7}{8}$.

Cary, Chairman

The ingredients are here and we accordingly find that Gintel willfully violated Section 10(b) and Rule 10b-5. We also find a similar violation by the registrant, Cady, Roberts & Co., since the actions of Gintel, a member of registrant, in the course of his employment are to be regarded as actions of registrant itself. It was obvious that a reduction in the quarterly dividend by the Board of Directors was a material fact which could be expected to have an adverse impact on the market price of the company's stock. The rapidity with which Gintel acted upon receipt of the information confirms his own recognition of that conclusion.

The anti-fraud provisions are phrased in terms of "any person" and that a special obligation has been traditionally required of corporate insiders, e.g., officers, directors, and controlling stockholders. These three groups, however, do not exhaust the classes of persons upon whom there is such an obligation. Analytically, the obligation rests on two principal elements; first, the existence of a relationship giving access, directly or indirectly, to information intended to be available only for a corporate purpose and not for the personal benefit of anyone, and second, the inherent unfairness involved where a party takes advantage of such information knowing it is unavailable to those with whom he is dealing. In considering these elements under the broad language of the anti-fraud provisions we are not to be circumscribed by fine distinctions and rigid classifications. Thus, our task here is to identify those persons who are in a special relationship with a company and privy to its internal affairs, and thereby suffer correlative duties in trading in its securities. Intimacy demands restraint lest the uninformed be exploited.

The facts here impose on Gintel the responsibilities of those commonly referred to as "insiders." He received the information prior to its public release from a director of Curtiss-Wright, Cowdin, who was associated with the registrant. Cowdin's relationship to the company clearly prohibited him from selling the securities affected by the information without disclosure. By logical sequence, it should prohibit Gintel, a partner of registrant. This prohibition extends not only over his own account, but to selling for discretionary accounts and soliciting and executing other orders.

We do not accept respondents' contention that Gintel was merely carrying out a program of liquidating the holdings in his discretionary accounts—determined and embarked upon prior to this receipt of the dividend information. In this connection, it is further alleged that he had a fiduciary duty to these accounts to continue the sales, which overrode any obligations to unsolicited purchasers on the Exchange.

The record does not support the contention that Gintel's sales were merely a continuance of his prior schedule of liquidation. Upon receipt of the news of the dividend reduction, which Gintel knew was not public, he hastened to sell before the expected public announcement all of the Curtiss-Wright shares remaining in his discretionary accounts, contrary to his previous moderate rate of sales. In so doing, he also made short sales of securities which he then allocated to his wife's account and to the account of a customer whom he had never seen and with whom he had had no prior dealings. Moreover, while Gintel undoubtedly occupied a fiduciary relationship to his customers, this relationship could not justify any actions by him contrary to law. Even if we assume the existence of conflicting fiduciary obligations, there can be no doubt which is primary here. On these facts, clients may not expect of a broker the benefits of his inside information at the expense of the public generally.

Under all the circumstances we conclude that the public interest and the protection of investors will be adequately and appropriately served if Gintel is suspended from the New York Stock Exchange for 20 days and if no sanction is imposed against the registrant.

Dirks v. Securities and Exchange Commission
United States Supreme Court
103 S.Ct. 3255 (1983)

Dirks was an officer of a New York broker-dealer firm who specialized in providing investment analysis of insurance company securities to institutional investors. On March 6, Dirks received information from Ronald Secrist, a former officer of Equity Funding of America. Secrist alleged that the assets of Equity Funding were vastly overstated as the result of fraudulent corporate practices. He urged Dirks to verify the fraud and disclose it publicly.

Dirks decided to investigate the allegations. He visited Equity Funding's headquarters in Los Angeles and interviewed several officers and employees of the corporation. The senior management denied any wrongdoing, but certain corporation employees corroborated the charges of fraud. Neither Dirks nor his firm owned or traded any Equity Funding stock, but throughout his investigation, he openly discussed the information he had obtained with a number of clients and investors. These persons included five investment advisors who liquidated holdings of more than sixteen million dollars of Equity Funding securities.

During the two-week period in which Dirks pursued his investigation and spread word of Secrist's charges, the price of Equity Funding stock fell from twenty-six dollars per share to less than fifteen dollars per share. This led the New York Stock Exchange to halt trading on March 27. Shortly thereafter, California insurance authorities impounded Equity Funding's records and uncovered evidence of the fraud.

The SEC began an investigation into Dirk's role in the exposure of the fraud. After a hearing, the SEC found that Dirks had aided and abetted violations of the Securities Exchange Act of 1934 by repeating the allegations of fraud to members of the investment community who later sold their Equity Funding stock. The SEC concluded: "Where 'tippees'—regardless of their motivation or occupation—come into possession of material 'information that they know is confidential and know or should know came from a corporate insider,' they must either publicly disclose that information or refrain from trading." Recognizing, however, that Dirks "played an important role in bringing Equity Funding's massive fraud to light," the SEC censured only him.

Dirks sought review in the Court of Appeals for the District of Columbia Circuit. The court entered judgment against Dirks "for the reasons stated by the Commission in its opinion." The Supreme Court reviewed the case.

Justice Powell

The SEC's theory of liability appears rooted in the idea that the antifraud provisions require equal information among all traders. We reaffirm today that a duty to disclose arises from the relationship between parties and not merely from one's ability to acquire information because of his position in the market.

Imposing a duty to disclose or abstain solely because a person knowingly receives material nonpublic information from an insider and trades on it could have an inhibiting influence on the role of market analysts, which the SEC itself recognizes is necessary to the preservation of a healthy market. It is commonplace for analysts to ferret out and analyze information and this often is done by meeting with and questioning corporate officers and others who are insiders. And information that the analysts obtain normally may be the basis for judgments as to the market worth of a corporation's securities. The analyst's judgment in this respect is made available in market letters or otherwise to clients of the firm. It is the nature of this type of information, and indeed of the markets themselves, that such information cannot be made simultaneously available to all of the corporation's stockholders or the public generally.

The conclusion that the recipients of inside information do not invariably acquire a duty to disclose or abstain does not mean that such tippees always are free to trade on the information. Not only are insiders forbidden by their fiduciary relationship from personally using undisclosed corporate information to their advantage, but they may not give such information to outsiders for the same improper purpose of exploiting the information for their personal use.

Thus, some outsiders must assume an insider's duty to the shareholders not because they receive inside information, but rather because it has been made available to them improperly.

In determining whether an outsider is under an obligation to disclose or abstain, it thus is necessary to determine whether the insider's "tip" constituted a breach of the insider's fiduciary duty. All disclosures of confidential corporate information are not inconsistent with the duty insiders owe to shareholders. In contrast to the extraordinary facts of this case, the more typical situation in which there will be a question whether disclosure violates the insider's *Cady, Roberts* duty is when insiders disclose information to analysts. In some situations, the insider will act consistently with his fiduciary duty to shareholders, and yet release of the information may affect the market. For example, it may not be clear —either to the corporate insider or to the recipient analyst—whether the information will be viewed as material nonpublic information. Corporate officials may mistakenly think the information already has been disclosed or that it is not material enough to affect the market. Whether disclosure is a breach of duty therefore depends in large part on the purpose of the disclosure. This standard was identified by the SEC itself in *Cady, Roberts*: a purpose of the securities laws was to eliminate "use of inside information for personal advantage." The test is whether the insider personally will benefit, directly or indirectly, from his disclosure. Absent some personal gain, there has been no breach of duty to stockholders. And absent a breach by the insider, there is no derivative breach.

For example, there may be a relationship between the insider and the recipient that suggests a quid pro quo from the latter, or an intention to benefit the particular recipient. The elements of fiduciary duty and exploitation of nonpublic information also exist when an insider makes a gift of confidential information to a trading relative or friend. The tip and trade resemble trading by the insider himself followed by a gift of the profits to the recipient. Determining whether an insider personally benefits from a particular disclosure is a question of fact.

Under the inside-trading and tipping rules set forth above, we find that there was no actionable violation by Dirks. It is undisputed that Dirks himself was a stranger to Equity Funding, with no preexisting fiduciary duty to its shareholders. He took no action, directly or indirectly, that induced the shareholders or officers of Equity Funding to repose trust or confidence in him. There was no expectation by Dirks's sources that he would keep their information in confidence. Nor did Dirks misappropriate or illegally obtain the information about Equity Funding. Unless the insiders breached their *Cady, Roberts* duty to shareholders in disclosing the nonpublic information to Dirks, he breached no duty when he passed it on to investors.

It is clear that neither Secrist nor the other Equity Funding employees violated their *Cady, Roberts* duty to the corporation's shareholders by providing information to Dirks. The tippers received no monetary or personal benefit for revealing Equity Funding's secrets, nor was their purpose to make a gift of valuable information to Dirks. As the facts of this case clearly indicate, the tippers were motivated by a desire to expose the fraud. In the absence of a breach of duty to shareholders by the insiders, there was no derivative breach by Dirks. Dirks therefore could not have been a participant after the fact in an insider's breach of a fiduciary duty.

We conclude that Dirks, in the circumstances of this case, had no duty to abstain from use of the insider information that he obtained. The judgment of the Court of Appeals therefore is reversed.

Clearly, both the 1933 Act's registration statement provisions and the 1934 Act's insider trading prohibitions impose costs on businesses that use American securities markets to raise capital. They also impose costs on those companies that actively trade securities. But securities markets are no longer an American phenomenon. The markets in Tokyo and London are now major players in international finance. Too great a cost burden arising from American securities regulations can make foreign operations more attractive to business. A primary question for the 1990s will be how to balance these costs with the potential loss to the United States of its role in the capital markets. Furthermore, as securities markets become more international in character, the effectiveness of American regulations becomes doubtful. Much like the limited power of blue sky laws to regulate a national capital market, U.S. securities laws have limited power to affect an international market.

What might you propose as a securities market policy for the 1990s? If your proposals are not adopted, how might you, on the basis of securities regulations, evaluate your company's decision to seek additional capital by selling a new series of bonds?

SUMMARY

The securities markets are regulated by state blue sky laws and by the federal securities laws. Most of the major issues that arise, however, involve two federal statutes: the Securities Act of 1933 and the Securities Exchange Act of 1934. Two major objectives of that regulatory scheme may be discerned. The first objective is that the investor should have full disclosure of important information surrounding the securities transaction at issue. No law requires that an investor actually use the information. However, the requirement is meant to create an informed securities marketplace, thereby increasing its efficiency. A second objective of federal securities regulation is to raise the ethical standards of participants in securities transactions. Acceptable business behavior may well run afoul of those regulations. The confidence of investors in the fairness of the market is an important factor in their continued participation. A vigorous private capital market is necessary for the economy, and investor participation is to be encouraged.

Although federal securities regulation is complex and wide-ranging, a few issues recur and also clearly illustrate the objectives of the law. When securities are being newly offered, the first-time buyers need to have full information in order to be able to make an informed purchase decision. The 1933 Act requires public filing of this information. Once the securities are in the marketplace, concerns arise about certain investors taking advantage of others. One such problem is the trading of securities on the basis of information that has not been made public. Those who possess such information are able to make a more complete investment decision. The 1934 Act prohibits certain insider trading, thereby placing a higher ethical standard on securities traders than exists in other businesses.

REVIEW QUESTIONS

1. Define the following terms:
   a. Blue sky laws
   b. Insider trading
   c. Investment contract
   d. Securities and Exchange Commission

2. Discuss the historical background that led to the enactment of the Securities Act of 1933 and the Securities Exchange Act of 1934.

3. What are the purposes of the federal securities laws?

4. ABC Corporation plans to issue a new series of bonds, to be offered to the general public throughout the United States. The bonds are valued at fifty million dollars. What must the corporation do to avoid problems with the SEC? Limit your discussion to materials contained in the chapter.

5. Your spouse is the administrative assistant to the president of Oil Co., Inc., a major petroleum concern. On August 1, your spouse comes home and tells you that the board of directors was told at that day's meeting of a major corporate petroleum discovery. This discovery, it is believed, will be the largest ever recorded. It was decided at the board meeting to withhold announcement of the find until the corporation can purchase the land rights to cover all the drilling sites. The next day you and your spouse use all joint savings to purchase Oil Co. stock. In October, the find is announced and the stock price jumps. Are there any potential problems for you and your spouse under the 1934 Act? Discuss.

6. You are a member of the board of directors of XYZ Corporation. At the annual meeting of the board held in January, you are given a lengthy document that you are told is to be filed with the SEC in the morning. Since the document was distributed about fifteen minutes before the meeting was to adjourn, you do not have an opportunity to read it. What concerns should you have about signing this document?

7. Horace operates a large number of swimming pools throughout the country. He plans to sell memberships in the pools. Current members will get a share of the fee paid by each prospect they recommend who joins

the pools. However, no member actually sells memberships. Instead, members bring prospects to a meeting, which Horace leads. The meeting is carefully orchestrated by Horace, and no pool member has any part in the meeting other than bringing the new prospects. Horace then attempts to convince the prospects to become one of three types of pool members. The types of membership vary in price. But the more one pays to become a member, the higher percentage of new member fees is received from prospects who later join the pool. Is this plan a sale of securities?

8. You are having dinner in a nice restaurant in the financial district of a city you are visiting. At the next table is a group that is discussing a decision to decrease the dividend being paid on ABC Corporation stock. The corporation has never before cut its dividends. You suddenly realize that the group is the board of directors of that company. Furthermore, you enjoy investing in stock and have studied the fortunes of ABC. You are very surprised to hear about the dividend decision. If you sell your ABC stock before the corporation announces its dividend cut, can you expect problems to arise with the SEC? Explain.

9. XYZ Corporation filed a registration statement with the SEC concerning a new issuance of securities. The statement fails to note that most of the proceeds from the sale of those securities will be paid to executives as a year-end bonus. The language of the document states: "The funds will be used to enhance corporate productivity." In addition, the document significantly understates corporate liabilities and overvalues corporate assets. Finally, the document fails to indicate that most of the accounts receivable are actually bad debts. Would a purchaser of those new securities have a claim under federal securities law? Explain.

10. Referring to question 9, discuss defenses that XYZ Corporation may raise to that claim.

11. Jenkins is a close friend of Smith, the president of XYZ Mining Corporation. One afternoon while playing golf, Smith tells Jenkins that XYZ has discovered a very large deposit of diamonds in Montana and that the corporation is quietly purchasing land surrounding the initial find in order to fully exploit the discovery. Smith also tells Jenkins that the information is highly confidential. If Jenkins thereafter begins to purchase land in Montana near the discovery site, will she have problems with the SEC? Explain. If not, change the facts to raise a potential securities law problem.

12. Accounting Firm audits the books and records of Joe's House of Investments, a small brokerage firm. Through negligence, Accounting Firm did not discover that the brokerage firm was engaged in numerous fraudulent investment practices in which client funds were not invested as promised. Instead, the funds were stolen. After the discovery of the fraud and the bankruptcy of Joe's House of Investments, the investors bring an action under the 1934 Act against Accounting Firm. They claim that the negligence of Accounting Firm aided and abetted the 1934 Act violations committed by Joe's House of Investments. Should Accounting Firm be liable as claimed?

13. Research the general scope of securities regulations in the London and Tokyo markets and compare them with the discussion of U.S. securities law in this chapter.

CHAPTER 23

Introduction to Antitrust

- What Is the Meaning of Antitrust?
- Forces That Produced the Antitrust Laws
- Objectives of the Antitrust Laws
- Overview of the Major Federal Antitrust Laws
- Enforcement of the Antitrust Laws
- Remedies
- Exemptions from the Antitrust Laws
- Political Action
- Price Discrimination

Antitrust laws have had and continue to have a profound effect on the manner in which business is conducted in the United States. Business executives for many years have been greatly concerned with this area of the law, owing to the rather large judgments in antitrust cases. It is not uncommon for judgments against major corporations to run into the hundreds of millions of dollars.

The goal of the antitrust laws is to promote competition and the efficient allocation of resources. The federal government, to a lesser extent the state governments, and private parties have the power to enforce the antitrust laws—subject to some of the exemptions noted in this chapter.

This chapter presents a basic introduction to the federal antitrust laws. Specific activities that have been outlawed by these acts are covered in Chapter 24.

WHAT IS THE MEANING OF ANTITRUST?

Trusts Many people are familiar with trusts. As commonly used, the term **trust** refers to a property right held by one person (the trustee) for the benefit of another (the beneficiary). The trustee controls and manages property for the benefit of the beneficiary of the trust. Many people today utilize trusts to lower their estate taxes, designate that their funds be used in a particular manner, or protect their spouses and children. The trustee invests the money and distributes the interest to the beneficiaries. Trusts of this nature are perfectly legal and quite common.

Antitrust   The antitrust laws are directed not at this type of trust, but at unlawful restraints of trade and monopolies. The term *antitrust* in this sense applies to the trusts created by men like John D. Rockefeller, who founded the Standard Oil Trust, the trustees of which managed the business affairs of a number of independent oil companies. Many industries developed large trusts that in effect constituted single businesses run by a board of trustees.

In 1890, Congress tried to put a stop to the consolidation of businesses by enacting the Sherman Antitrust Act. The act outlaws unreasonable attempts to monopolize or restrain trade. Additional legislation in the antitrust field was passed in 1914, when Congress enacted the Clayton Antitrust Act and the Federal Trade Commission Act. Congress strengthened the Clayton Act in the 1930s, through the passage of the Robinson-Patman Act, and again in the 1950s, with the passage of the Cellar-Kefauver amendment to the Clayton Act.

FORCES THAT PRODUCED THE ANTITRUST LAWS

Equal Opportunity   At the heart of the movement for the passage of the antitrust laws lies the American Dream of equal opportunity for those people willing and able to work—the right of people to advance through their own efforts. Vast amounts of unowned land beckoned the early settlers of this country. Many immigrants from Europe arrived hoping to own a piece of that land. Successive waves of settlers moved farther and farther west seeking free land to homestead, until eventually no more free land was available. Frederick Jackson Turner called this the closing of the American frontier.

What of those immigrants who planned to start small businesses? Many millions arrived over the years and started businesses: drugstores, restaurants, grocery stores, shipping lines, newspapers, feed stores, banks, insurance companies, dressmaking shops, millineries, meat-packing plants, oil companies, and lumberyards—every type of business imaginable. And why not? The opportunity to engage in a wide variety of businesses was available to anyone who wanted to take a chance. Often, there were no competing businesses in a town, and a man or woman could simply move to the town and set up shop.

Many persons believed in laissez-faire economics; that is, they opposed government interference in economic affairs beyond the minimum necessary for the maintenance of peace and property rights. The public opposed government interference with individual freedom of choice and action. People felt they should have the opportunity to better themselves.

Why, then, would Congress pass the antitrust laws?

Concentration of Wealth   One of the many forces behind the antitrust movement arose from the concentration of enormous sums of money in the hands of very few persons. As business enterprises like steel, oil, and railroads became larger, their owners became extremely wealthy. At the same time, the average factory worker often lived in poverty. The concentration of wealth in the hands of a few monopolists (persons or groups of persons who exclusively control a particular field of business) offended the public. Some argued that the industrialists profited at the expense of the average person. While many workers lived in slums and worked twelve hours a day, six days a week, fifty-two weeks a year, the industrialists lived in luxury. Many people immigrated to the United States to escape the aristocratic structure of Europe. Is it surprising that these same people would object to an aristocracy of wealth being created in the United States?

Individualism

The American frontier contributed to the growth of a belief in individualism—the right to live life in the manner a person feels is best. The men and women who settled the West wished to live free of government restraints. These self-reliant individuals believed people could advance through individual enterprise. Once the farmland was all settled, it seemed to many that only small business remained as a means to self-betterment. But in the late nineteenth century, many persons also saw wealth gradually falling into the hands of the elite; indeed, with businesses growing larger and larger, some persons foresaw the day when a few persons would control all businesses.

Mass Production

Mass production contributed heavily to the growth of large national and international enterprises. For example, where formerly a rifle had been created by a craftsperson step by step, industrialists learned to assemble rifles by assigning particular steps to various workers on a line. With each person performing a single repetitive task, a manufacturer could produce many more rifles. Industrialists applied this same process to the manufacture of shoes, the slaughter and dressing of beef, the weaving of materials, and the sewing of clothes. Every manufacturing enterprise produced more products faster by using the techniques of mass production. Over time, the neighborhood tailor or cobbler gave way to large, national manufacturers.

Businesses learned how to produce goods cheaply and in quantity. However, they needed a market for the large quantity of goods being produced. Cobblers who sold shoes only to people in their towns did not have any problems disposing of their goods. But a company that manufactured enough goods for hundreds of towns needed new methods to get the goods into the customers' hands.

This increasingly became a possibility in the 1870s and 1880s, with the rapid expansion of the American railway system, which became one of the finest and most extensive systems in the world. The railway system created a means for the mass producer to get its goods to a larger market. Large companies began to compete in many sections of the country virtually overnight. These big businesses became formidable competitors for local manufacturers. The sudden competition created a sort of "shock of the new," and a consequent distaste, among many persons, for big business.

The growth of mass production and the expansion of the railway system, the indigenous American quest for individualism, the growing inequality of the distribution of wealth, and the desire to maximize opportunity for all willing workers all contributed to the legal environment in the late nineteenth century.

The Populist and Farmers

One interest group that worried over the changing structure of America—the move away from small farms and small businesses—was the Populists. The Populists objected to the growth of large oil, packing, and steel companies. They favored small, local, individually owned businesses, which they claimed were more accountable and less corrupt than the large national enterprises springing up across America.

Another group particularly upset by higher prices was the farmers. While the large meat-packing companies and grain elevators kept prices for farm products low, the farmers paid high prices for farm equipment. The farmers argued that big business kept farm prices artificially low, and at the same time sold them products at artificially inflated prices.

Populists, farmers, and small business owners saw competition as the method by which markets could be kept open. They viewed competition as the means to ensure that individual enterprise would be rewarded. The obstructions to competition created by the industrialists appeared to be unfairly eroding the rewards for hard work by the siphoning off of large profits to big business. These groups favored competition as the means for keeping prices to consumers as low as possible.

The widespread belief in the virtues of free, unfettered competition led ultimately to the election of Congressmen committed to passing antitrust legislation. These elected representatives passed the Sherman Act of 1890.

OBJECTIVES OF THE ANTITRUST LAWS

The Sherman Act reflected the wishes of many diverse groups—farmers, Populists, small business owners, frontierspeople, and others—that wished to stop unfair business practices. Congress complied with their desires in passing the Sherman Act.

Not all people agree that the Sherman Act really satisfied the needs of these groups. Congress chose very vague language, rather than specifically spelling out the acts or practices it wished to prohibit. Neither the legislative history of the Sherman Act nor the language of the act itself gave the courts clear-cut direction as to what the Congress wished to accomplish and how Congress intended the act to be enforced. It was therefore up to the courts to develop a body of law in the antitrust field on a case-by-case basis.

Some commentators view the original act as a lukewarm attempt to appease various groups without clearly adopting their aims. Indeed, in the first antitrust case to reach the Supreme Court, *United States* v. *E. C. Knight Co.* (1895), the Court interpreted the power of the government to act pursuant to the Sherman Act very narrowly. The *Knight* case held that manufacturing was not commerce, and therefore a monopoly of the sugar manufacturing industry was not covered by the Sherman Act. Subsequent decisions avoided this doctrine, but the case illustrates the point that the Supreme Court initially construed the act quite narrowly, thus hampering antitrust enforcement, and certainly the Court did not offer the broad interpretation the people who worked for its passage probably hoped for.

Whether or not Congress intentionally watered down the language of the act so as to make vigorous enforcement impossible, the vague language of the act did give the Court great latitude in deciding which business actions Congress intended to prohibit. But it was clear that Congress chose market competition—not government regulation—as the method best suited for achieving its goals.

Competition

Over the years, the courts have identified the furtherance of competition as one of the foremost goals of the antitrust laws. Almost without exception, the courts have favored the promotion of competition over any other social goal that might be accomplished through the enforcement of the antitrust laws. Many people argue that vigorous competition lowers the price of goods and promotes the efficient allocation of resources. competition also limits business power; in a competitive market, individuals cannot take advantage of the people with whom they deal. If a seller charges too high a price for wares, buyers are able to purchase them from someone else. Many people regard this alternative as producing fairer results than would decisions by private people or the government as to what and how much to produce. Arguably competition also helps to keep businesses small and opportunity open for everyone, and to distribute money throughout society rather than to a few powerful people.

Economic Efficiency

Another aim of the antitrust laws is to improve the economic performance of individual firms and the economy as a whole. Through vigorous enforcement of the antitrust laws, the government hopes to ensure that those companies which need resources the most, and are willing to pay the most for them, will receive a proper allocation of society's funds. By this means, it is hoped, output will be increased, new techniques of production will be utilized, and new and better products will be developed. One might label this "progressiveness."

Picture what might happen if we had no competition—if, for example, the government regulated all production. Suppose the government had ordered the production of buggy whips. This action would have consumed some of our resources. When someone came along who wished to make automobiles, extra resources might not be available to develop this new mode of transportation. The automobile might never have been developed if the government had misallocated the available resources to the buggy whip manufacturer.

In general, the courts apply the antitrust law to encourage efficiency. In this way, the courts help those enterprises which can most efficiently utilize our valuable resources and which are best able to devise cheaper methods of production and improved products. These firms will be permitted to prosper. The less efficient, more poorly run business will fall by the wayside. In the final analysis, society will prosper because it will be getting the biggest return on its investment of resources.

The courts also favor competition so long as competition does not interfere with efficiency. *United States* v. *Grinnell Corp.* (1966) supports this proposition in noting that a monopoly resting on economies of scale or obtained by skill, foresight, and industry does not violate the antitrust laws. To the extent that competition promotes efficiency, the courts favor the maintenance of a competitive economic environment.

Limitation on Size

Another possible goal of the antitrust laws is the limitation on the growth of big business—or the protection of small, independent businesses. Essentially, people who espouse this view wish to limit the size of big business, not so much because of the economic advantage of small businesses as because of the political problems associated with big business. These persons fear the power held by large businesses because of its implications for democracy. Concentration of wealth and power in the hands of a very few people, in their eyes, opens the door to abuse of our political system.

Other Possible Goals

The other goals of fairness and the Populist goals of distribution of wealth, limitation on the size of business, and promotion of business opportunities really have not been given great emphasis by the courts in the enforcement of the antitrust laws. Some commentators assert that these Populist goals should not be given *any* weight in formulating rules in the antitrust field, that the courts should focus on a procompetitive policy that promotes economic deficiencies. They contend that to promote these other Populist goals over economic efficiency would make the antitrust laws costly, futile, and impossible to administer. Not every scholar in the antitrust field shares this view. Some argue that noneconomic goals—such as the distribution of economic power, the increase in opportunity for more people to enter business, and the preference for small businesses—are laudable goals that should be promoted through antitrust enforcement. Nonetheless, the cases over the years and the more recent cases, in particular, do seem to favor the goals of economic efficiency and competition. The Populist goals seem to have been ignored over the decades as the courts have chosen not to emphasize them at the expense of economic efficiency.

OVERVIEW OF THE MAJOR FEDERAL ANTITRUST LAWS

This book covers only the broadest principles in antitrust. It does not attempt to discuss every issue or rule covered by the antitrust laws. The goal here is to provide a general introduction to the area of antitrust. The first piece of antitrust legislation, as indicated earlier, was the Sherman Act, which was enacted in 1890. Two important acts followed in 1914—the Clayton Act and the Federal Trade Commission Act. In 1936, Congress passed the Robinson-Patman Act, which amended the Clayton Act, and in 1950, amended it again through the Cellar-Kefauver Act. In order to strengthen antitrust enforcement in the United States, Congress passed the 1976 Antitrust Improvements Act and the 1980 Antitrust Procedural Improvements Act.

**Sherman
Act**

Exactly what does the Sherman Act cover? Section 1 of the act states: "Every contract, combination in the form of trust or otherwise, or conspiracy, in restraint of trade or commerce among the several States, or with foreign nations, is declared to be illegal." This means that no person or company may enter into any arrangement with another person or company to restrain trade (restraints restrict production, affect prices, or otherwise control the market to the detriment of purchasers or consumers of goods and services). Congress provided no definition of restraint of trade, but left it up to the courts to clarify the term on a case-by-case basis.

Section 2 of the act states: "Every person who shall monopolize, or attempt to monopolize, or combine or conspire with any other person or persons, to monopolize any part of the trade or commerce among the several States, or with foreign nations, shall be deemed guilty of a felony." The act declares that any actions by any person that attempt to create or succeed in creating a monopoly violate Section 2 of the Sherman Act. The act also failed to define these terms.

The first antitrust act thus gave the courts broad discretion in creating a body of antitrust law. As noted earlier, the Supreme Court's initial cases dealing with the antitrust laws construed the act very narrowly. As time passed, the Court chose to interpret the words of the act more broadly to cover more situations. In the 1930s, Congress decided small businesses deserved further protection. The feeling spread that a manufacturer should be able to set the price at which its product sold at the retail level. In 1937, Congress passed the Miller-Tydings Act, which exempted from Section 1 of the Sherman Act agreements of this nature. In 1952, Congress passed the McGuire Act, which also related to this issue. In the 1970s, both acts were repealed.

Clayton Act

The next antitrust act was passed in 1914 in response to a public outcry for more effective restraints on big business. The public lacked confidence in the adequacy of the Sherman Act and the interest of the Department of Justice in enforcing the Sherman Act. The Supreme Court also contributed to a climate favorable to the passage of new legislation by announcing its Rule of Reason principle in *Standard Oil Co.* v. *United States*, 221 U.S. 1 (1911), which is discussed in Chapter 24. People who opposed big business pushed for new legislation, as did business executives who wished for further clarification of permissible business conduct.

All this activity culminated in the adoption of the Clayton Act in 1914. The act prohibited price discrimination, sales on the condition that the buyer cease dealing with the seller's competitors, certain types of mergers, and interlocking corporate directorates. This act was amended in 1936 by the Robinson-Patman Act, which rewrote the price discrimination provisions of the original Clayton Act. In 1950, Congress again amended the act to strengthen its merger provisions when it passed the Cellar-Kefauver Act.

**Federal
Trade
Commission
Act**

Also in 1914, Congress created the Federal Trade Commission (FTC) when it passed the Federal Trade Commission Act. This act, like the Clayton Act, was passed in response to the misuse of economic power by the trusts. All of the candidates for president in the election of 1912 vowed to further strengthen the laws to combat the trusts. President Wilson vowed in his State of the Union message to Congress to seek new legislation in the antitrust field. The act stated: "Unfair methods of competition in commerce are hereby declared unlawful." Once again, Congress chose not to define this terminology, but left it up to the FTC to determine on a case-by-case basis the meaning of this phrase. Congress could have chosen to specify certain acts as "unfair methods of competition," but it elected not to do so. In 1938, Congress decided the Federal Trade Commission Act needed further strengthening. It passed the Wheeler-Lea Amendment to the act, which declared illegal, in addition to unfair methods of competition, "unfair or deceptive acts or practices in commerce." This amendment was an express statement by Congress that consumers needed direct protection.

These acts constitute the substantive law in the antitrust field. Clearly, they attempt to prohibit monopolies, attempts to monopolize, restraints of trade, unfair methods of competition, and unfair or deceptive acts or practices by business. Just what all these acts meant was left up to the courts and the Federal Trade Commission to decide. For this reason, the cases in the antitrust field, as opposed to the statutes, assume great importance. A careful examination of all cases is necessary to understand the meaning given by the courts and the FTC to these acts.

ENFORCEMENT OF THE ANTITRUST LAWS

Department of Justice

The Department of Justice represents the federal government in the courts. The head of the department is the attorney general—a cabinet member. The Department of Justice has many functions—among them, working on civil rights issues, federal crimes, and tax questions, and advising the president and other executive agencies on legal matters. One of the most important functions of the Department of Justice is enforcement of the antitrust laws (see Table 23.1). A special division of the department, the antitrust division, has the power to bring either criminal suits or civil suits pursuant to the Sherman Act, and civil suits under the Clayton Act. Figure 23.1 illustrates the structure of the Department of Justice.

Federal Trade Commission

The Department of Justice has exclusive power over criminal actions under the Sherman Act. It shares the enforcement responsibilities involving the Clayton Act with the Federal Trade Commission, which has the power to enforce Sections 2, 3, 7, and 8 of the Clayton Act. The Department of Justice and the Federal Trade Commission coordinate their enforcement activities to avoid conflicts. The Federal Trade Commission has sole authority to enforce Section 5 of the Federal Trade Commission Act. The Federal Trade Commission Act gives the FTC power to challenge any conduct that would violate the Sherman Act or any conduct that violates the spirit of either the Clayton Act or the Sherman Act though not technically a violation of either act. The power of the FTC to reach improper actions of business is greatest under Section 5 of the Federal Trade Commission Act.

Private Parties

The Department of Justice has the exclusive right to bring criminal actions pursuant to the Sherman Act, but private parties who think themselves injured by a violation of the Sherman Act may bring civil actions for either treble damages or

TABLE 23.1		Parties with Power to Enforce Federal Antitrust Laws	
	Department of Justice	Federal Trade Commission	Private Parties and State Attorneys General
Sherman Act	Enforces criminal and civil litigation	No power to enforce	Enforces civil litigation
Clayton Act	Enforces civil litigation	Enforces civil litigation	Enforces civil litigation
Federal Trade Commission Act	No power to enforce	Enforces Federal Trade Commission Act	No power to enforce

the equitable remedies called injunctions. Likewise, the Department of Justice shares its power to enforce the Clayton Act with the FTC and private parties who may request treble damages or equitable relief for a violation of the Clayton Act. Section 4 of the Clayton Act states that "any person who shall be injured in his business or property by reason of anything forbidden in the antitrust laws may sue therefore . . . and shall recover threefold the damages by him sustained, and the cost of the suit, including a reasonable attorney's fee." Section 16 of the Clayton Act permits private parties to sue for injunctive relief.

In many instances, a private action follows upon successful government prosecution of a case. However, many private actions are brought separate and apart from action by the government. The reason most private litigants wait for the government to establish its case is that a final judgment rendered against the defendant in any civil or criminal proceeding brought by the United States is prima facie evidence against the defendant in any suit brought by a private plaintiff in a civil treble damages suit. This means the private litigant need only establish the extent of its injuries and that the injuries resulted from a violation of the antitrust laws. The private plaintiff need not establish a violation of the antitrust laws, because the government established the violation in the earlier case. The burden of proving an antitrust violation is formidable, and the cases often take many years. Many private parties prefer to let the government establish this part of the case for them.

While a person, firm, corporation, or association may sue for treble damages or injunctive relief for a violation of either the Sherman or the Clayton Act, several other devices may be utilized to enforce the antitrust laws. One is the **class action**—a lawsuit brought by members of a large group of persons on behalf of all members of the group. Another possibility is a **parens patriae** action—a suit brought by the attorney general of a state on behalf of persons living in that state.

REMEDIES

As we have noted, several organizations, as well as persons or corporations, may attempt to enforce the antitrust laws. The primary goal to be achieved through the

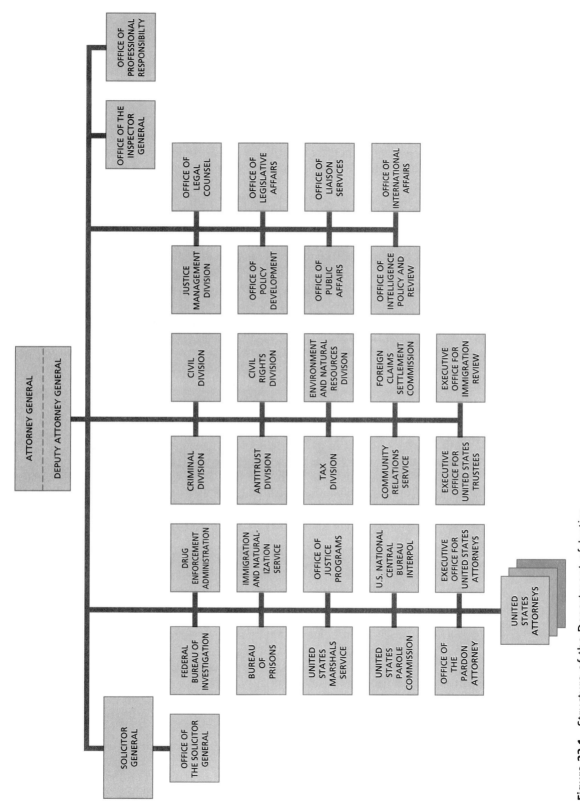

Figure 23.1 Structure of the Department of Justice
Source: The United States Government Manual 1991/92, Washington, DC: U.S. Government Printing Office, 1991.

enforcement of these acts is the furtherance of competition and economic efficiency in the American economy.

In spite of the rather clear preference for competition and economic efficiencies, businesses still run afoul of the antitrust laws. This section discusses how the courts deal with persons who violate the antitrust laws.

The government, if it establishes an antitrust violation, may pursue two remedies: equitable relief, treble damages, and criminal sanctions. Private parties may seek equitable relief and damages.

Equitable Actions

A suit in equity seeks as its objective the control of future behavior rather than punishment for past acts. Section 4 of the Sherman Act and Section 15 of the Clayton Act give the government the power to seek equitable relief from the federal courts. The federal courts have a great deal of discretion in deciding what type of remedy is appropriate in a given situation. The courts may enjoin companies from restraining trade. They may force a company to divest itself of a company it acquired. They may force a company to share its patents with other companies. There are many, many different types of actions a federal court may order a company to take in order to create a remedy for a violation of the antitrust laws.

Section 16 of the Clayton Act also permits private persons to obtain injunctive relief against any threatened loss or damage by a violation of the antitrust laws.

Criminal Sanctions

In certain cases, the activity in question may be of such an unjustifiable nature that the party or parties in question should be punished. In this case, the government will attempt to have fines imposed on the parties or seek prison terms. Only the government may institute a criminal suit. The Department of Justice handles all criminal prosecutions pursuant to the antitrust laws.

A violation of Section 1 or 2 of the Sherman Act is punishable as a crime. Such a violation is a felony. In general, violations of the Clayton Act are not crimes.

In 1976, the Antitrust Procedures and Penalties Act revised the Sherman Act to increase the criminal penalty from a misdemeanor to a felony. Officers and employees of the corporation who are substantially responsible for a criminal offense may be indicted along with the corporation. Changing the penalty from a misdemeanor to a felony has very significant implications for management.

The Antitrust Improvements Act of 1990 provided increased criminal fines—up to three hundred fifty thousand dollars for individuals and ten million dollars for corporations—and gave the federal government the power to get treble damages in actions it brings as an antitrust plaintiff.

Pleas

Prior to the 1976 change, it used to be in the best interest of the company and the executives to dispose of an alleged antitrust violation by entering a plea of **nolo contendere;** that is, the defendants pleaded no contest to the charges brought by the Department of Justice. The advantage of a nolo contendere plea, as opposed to a guilty or not guilty plea, is that a nolo contendere plea may not be used as prima facie evidence of liability in a subsequent suit brought by a private litigant for its damages. On the other hand, a guilty plea or a finding of guilty by a court after a trial is prima facie evidence of liability in any subsequent damages suit. Private persons injured by an antitrust violation still may bring damage suits following a plea of nolo contendere, but they must prove an antitrust violation as well as damages. Many companies forgo suing in light of the substantial problems of proof. A plea of nolo contendere also is advantageous because it avoids a costly trial and possibly more widespread adverse publicity.

Today, more individual defendants are indicted along with the corporation, and there is an increasing tendency to send persons who are convicted to jail. While a plea of nolo contendere might strike the corporation as advantageous, many individuals probably will resist such a plea since the consequences, as far as punishment is concerned, are the same whether the plea is nolo contendere or guilty. A judge can and will sentence an executive to prison whether the defendant pleads guilty or nolo contendere. Since the penalty for such a plea has been increased from a misdemeanor to a felony, many indicted executives probably will desire to take the case to trial rather than pleading guilty.

Treble Damages

As indicated earlier, private persons may enforce the Sherman and Clayton acts. Section 4 of the Clayton Act provides that the plaintiff may recover treble damages if it is able to establish an antitrust violation and damages resulting from that violation. The 1990 Act permits the federal government as well as private parties to get treble damages. That is, if the plaintiff establishes losses of one hundred thousand dollars because of an antitrust violation by the defendant, he or she will actually recover three times this amount, or three hundred thousand dollars plus the cost of the action, including reasonable attorney's fees. As noted earlier, Section 16 of the Clayton Act also permits suits by private parties for injunctive relief.

The reason the law permits treble damages is not only to compensate a private party for its injuries, but also to *punish* the defendant for violating the law. Since the award for an antitrust violation might be very large, treble damage suits encourage private persons to enforce the antitrust laws by bringing these suits. This helps encourage compliance with the antitrust laws and supplements public enforcement.

Even with private treble damage actions and the enforcement powers of the FTC, the Department of Justice, and state attorneys general, the rewards for violating the antitrust laws are very great, and the chances of detection often are slim. One might argue that the remedies are inadequate to deter violations.

Consent Decree

While a plea of guilty or nolo contendere may be utilized to dispose of a criminal case, a different device may be utilized by a corporation should it wish not to go to trial on a civil antitrust case brought by the government. Most cases brought by the Department of Justice terminate with a settlement known as a **consent decree**. A consent decree is a voluntary agreement entered into by a corporation and a government agency in which the business agrees to cease engaging in certain activities. It is not an admission of a violation of the law. A company may enter into a consent decree with the government at any time—even after the case has gone to trial and the government has lost. It might be simpler to enter into a consent decree at this point than to involve the corporation in a costly, time-consuming appeal.

Consent decrees are advantageous to both parties. The government can handle more suits if the parties settle in this fashion instead of going to trial. The defendant saves money and time and avoids adverse publicity. Most important, a consent decree may *not* be used by a private party seeking damages to prove the defendant violated the antitrust laws. Thus, a consent decree minimizes the possibility of subsequent damage suits. If the corporation takes the civil suit to trial and loses, the judgment may be used by persons or companies injured by an antitrust violation in a subsequent suit for damages. A consent decree usually states it is not an adjudication on the merits or an admission of liability on the part of the defendants. Consent decrees must be approved by a court.

Both consent decrees and pleas of nolo contendere are valuable tools for the government. The government is understaffed and inadequately funded. It lacks the workforce to pursue every antitrust violation. If it were forced to try every case it handled, the government would be unable to pursue many antitrust violators.

■■■■■■ EXEMPTIONS FROM THE ANTITRUST LAWS

Labor Certain groups are exempt from the antitrust laws. Labor unions are one such group. Section 6 of the Clayton Act provides:

> The labor of a human being is not a commodity or article of commerce. Nothing contained in the antitrust laws shall be construed to forbid the existence and operation of labor . . . organizations, instituted for the purpose of mutual help . . . or to forbid or restrain individual members of such organizations from lawfully carrying out the legitimate objects thereof.

Section 20 of the Clayton Act prohibits federal courts from issuing injunctions in cases between employers and employees involving or growing out of a dispute concerning the terms or conditions of employment.

While this language indicates an intent by Congress to exempt labor unions from the antitrust laws, the Supreme Court soon made it clear that not all types of union activity were protected from the antitrust laws. Congress responded in 1932 by passing the Norris-LaGuardia Act, which further clarified its wish to prohibit the use of injunctions against labor unions by federal courts.

The activities protected by the Clayton Act and the Norris-LaGuardia Act are activities between employees and unions. The activities between a union and an employer are not expressly exempted. Labor unions generally need not concern themselves with the antitrust laws so long as they do not combine with a nonlabor group in order to restrain trade.

The following case discusses the extent to which the collective bargaining agreement entered into between the Players Association and the National Football League insulates the NFL from the provisions of the antitrust laws.

Powell v. National Football League
United States Court of Appeals, Eighth Circuit
888 F.2d 559, Cert. Den. 111 S.Ct. 711 (1991)

In 1977, the National Football League and the Players Association entered into a collective bargaining agreement. The agreement contained a controversial provision, the first refusal/compensation system, which provided that a team could retain a veteran free agent by matching a competing club's offer. Alternatively, if the old team decided not to match the offer, it would receive compensation from the new team in the form of additional draft choices. This provision also appeared in the 1982 agreement, which expired in August 1987. However, the NFL maintained the status quo on all mandatory subjects of bargaining covered by the agreement.

The Players Association argued that the NFL's continued imposition of the first refusal compensation system after the parties reached an impasse in negotiations was an unlawful restraint of trade in violation of the Sherman Act. The NFL maintained that its actions were protected by the labor exemption to the antitrust laws. The Court of Appeals ruled in favor of the National Football League because the antitrust laws were inapplicable under these circumstances.

Gibson, Circuit Judge

In *Mackey,* we proceeded to analyze the principles which undergird the nonstatutory labor exemption, and the determinative issue of whether relevant federal labor policy was deserving of preeminence over federal antitrust policy under the circumstances of a particular case. In resolving these competing labor and antitrust interests, we found the proper accommodation to be:

First, the labor policy favoring collective bargaining may potentially be given preeminence over the antitrust laws where the restraint on trade primarily affects only the parties to the collective bargaining relationship. . . . Second, federal labor policy is implicated sufficiently to prevail only where the agreement sought to be exempted concerns a mandatory subject of collective bargaining. . . . Finally, the policy favoring collective bargaining is furthered to the degree necessary to override the antitrust laws only where the agreement sought to be exempted is the product of bona fide arm's-length bargaining.

On appeal, the parties do not dispute that the terms of the 1977 and 1982 Agreements establishing the First Refusal/Compensation system: (1) primarily affected only the parties in the collective bargaining relationship; (2) concerned a mandatory subject of collective bargaining;

and (3) were the product of bona fide, arm's-length bargaining. Under *Mackey,* therefore, the nonstatutory exemption precluded an antitrust challenge to those restraints while the Agreements were in effect. Now that the 1982 Agreement is terminated, however, we must decide whether the nonstatutory labor exemption has also expired or, alternatively, whether under the circumstances of this case the exemption continues to protect the League from potential antitrust liability.

The district court adopted "impasse" as the point at which the nonstatutory labor exemption expires, holding that "once the parties reach impasse concerning player restraint provisions those provisions will lose their immunity and further imposition of those conditions may result in antitrust liability." The court reasoned that its impasse standard "respects the labor law obligation to bargain in good faith over mandatory bargaining subjects following expiration of a collective bargaining agreement," and that it "promotes the collective bargaining relationship and enhances prospects that the parties will reach compromise on the issue." The League attacks the district court's standard as providing a union, such as the Players, with undue motivation to generate impasse in order to pursue an antitrust suit for treble damages.

In *Charles D. Bonanno Linen Services, Inc. v. NLRB,*

the Supreme Court defined "impasse" as a temporary deadlock or hiatus in negotiations "which in almost all cases is eventually broken, through either a change of mind or the application of economic force." . . . Furthermore, an impasse may be "brought about intentionally by one or both parties as a device to further, rather than destroy, the bargaining process."

Our reading of the authorities leads us to conclude that the League and the Players have not yet reached the point in negotiations where it would be appropriate to permit an action under the Sherman Act. The district court's impasse standard treats a lawful stage of the collective bargaining process as misconduct by defendants, and in this way conflicts with federal labor laws that establish the collective bargaining process, under the supervision of the National Labor Relations Board, as the method for resolution of labor disputes.

The labor arena is one with well established rules which are intended to foster negotiated settlements rather than intervention by the courts. The League and the Players have accepted this "level playing field" as the basis for their often tempestuous relationship, and we believe that there is substantial justification for requiring the parties to continue to fight on it, so that bargaining and the exertion of economic force may be used to bring about legitimate compromise.

The First Refusal/Compensation system, a mandatory subject of collective bargaining, was twice set forth in collective bargaining agreements negotiated in good faith and at arm's-length. Following the expiration of the 1982 Agreement, the challenged restraints were imposed by the League only after they had been forwarded in negotiations and subsequently rejected by the Players. The Players do not contend that these proposals were put forward by the League in bad faith. We therefore hold that the present lawsuit cannot be maintained under the Sherman Act. Importantly, this does not entail that once a union and management enter into collective bargaining, management is forever exempt from the antitrust laws, and we do not hold that restraints on player services can never offend the Sherman Act. We believe, however, that the nonstatutory labor exemption protects agreements conceived in an ongoing collective bargaining relationship from challenges under the antitrust laws.

National labor policy should sometimes override antitrust policy and we believe that this case presents just such an occasion.

Upon the facts currently presented by this case, we are not compelled to look into the future and pick a termination point for the labor exemption. The parties are now faced with several choices. They may bargain further, which we would strongly urge that they do. They may resort to economic force. And finally, if appropriate issues arise, they may present claims to the National Labor Relations Board. We are satisfied that as long as there is a possibility that proceedings may be commenced before the Board, or until final resolution of Board proceedings and appeals therefrom, the labor relationship continues and the labor exemption applies.

In sum, we hold that the antitrust laws are inapplicable under the circumstances of this case as the nonstatutory labor exemption extends beyond impasse. We reverse the order of the district court and remand the case with instructions to enter judgment in defendants' favor on Counts I, II, and VIII of plaintiffs' amended complaint.

Agricultural Cooperatives

Another group excluded from the antitrust laws is agricultural cooperatives. Congress wanted to reach restraints on competition and monopolization by big trusts when it passed the Sherman Act. It did not intend to reach cooperatives. After all, the farmers pushed hard for the Sherman Act. They felt at a disadvantage in dealing with the large packing companies. They probably did not visualize the antitrust laws being applied against them, yet it was in cases early in the 1900s. Congress, as it has done for labor unions in 1914, attempted to clarify the exemption for agricultural cooperatives when it passed the Clayton Act. In 1922, Congress enacted the Capper-Volstead Act to make it crystal clear it wished to exempt agricultural cooperatives from the antitrust laws. The object of the act was to protect farmers, planters, ranchers, and the like from the antitrust laws to permit them to collectively process, prepare for market, handle, and market their products.

Congress thought farmers needed additional legislation because of the farmer's economic plight. Most farms were relatively small, but the processors with whom farmers dealt were few and very powerful. Furthermore, problems with the weather compounded the farmer's difficulties with the processors. In spite of the rather clear exemption, the act has been construed narrowly so that in some instances the antitrust laws have been applied to the cooperatives. If a cooperative includes among its members any person who or business that is not a farmer, it is not exempt from the provisions of the antitrust laws.

State Action Exemption

Another important exception to the application of the antitrust laws is the *state action exemption* created by the *Parker* v. *Brown* case (1943). In that case, a producer and packer of raisins in California brought suit to enjoin the state director of agriculture from enforcing a program for marketing the raisins produced in the state. The state of California wished to restrict competition among growers to maintain the price of raisins. In an earlier case, the Supreme Court had held states were "persons" within the meaning of the Sherman Act, and therefore entitled to maintain an action for treble damages. Essentially, *Parker* concerned the question of whether the California statute was rendered invalid by the Sherman Act. The Supreme Court held that the Sherman Act did not invalidate the California statute (although the statute quite obviously restricted competition in the raisin-growing market). Instead, the Supreme Court enunciated an exception to the Sherman Act:

> [W]e find nothing in the language of the Sherman Act or in its history which suggests that its purpose was to restrain a state or its officers or agents from activities directed by its legislature. . . . [I]n view of the (Act's) words and history, it must be taken to be a prohibition of individual and not state action. . . . The state . . . imposed the restraints as an act of government which the Sherman Act did not undertake to prohibit.

What the Supreme Court wished to do in deciding *Parker* v. *Brown* was to recognize the fact that states are free to establish their own set of laws absent a conflict with the United States Constitution or preemption of the area by Congress.

Parker reflects the idea of dual federalism. In our system of government, both the federal government and the states are sovereign. The states gave up part of their power in forming the U.S. government. They retained the power not delegated to the United States or reserved to the people. As states are sovereign, states may pass laws in the same areas as the federal government. Only if the state law violates the Constitution, or if Congress preempts the field, must the courts strike down a state law. In the case of the Sherman Act, Congress failed to indicate that it intended to restrain state action in this field. As nothing about the Sherman Act indicated any intent upon the part of Congress to prohibit states from legislating in a manner contrary to the Sherman Act, the Supreme Court upheld the California statute.

Following this decision, the Supreme Court decided a number of cases that further refined the state action exemption. One of them follows.

Southern Motor Carriers Rate Conference, Inc. v. United States
United States Supreme Court
105 S.Ct. 1721 (1985)

The Southern Motor Carriers Rate Conference is a rate bureau composed of common carriers which submits, on behalf of its members, joint rate proposals to the Public Service Commission in North Carolina, Georgia, Tennessee, and Mississippi. The collective rate making is authorized, but not compelled, by these states. The United States brought suit against Southern Motor Carriers. It contended that the collective rate making violated federal antitrust laws. Southern Motor Carriers claimed its actions were immune from the federal antitrust laws by virtue of the state action doctrine of *Parker* v. *Brown*. The Supreme Court ruled for Southern Motor Carriers.

Justice Powell

In *Midcal,* we affirmed a state-court injunction prohibiting officials from enforcing a statute requiring wine producers to establish resale price schedules. We set forth a two-pronged test for determining whether state regulation of private parties is shielded from the federal antitrust laws. First, the challenged restraint must be "one clearly articulated and affirmatively expressed as state policy." Second, the State must supervise actively any private anticompetitive conduct. This supervision requirement prevents the state from frustrating the national policy in favor of competition by casting a "gauzy cloak of state involvement" over what is essentially private anticompetitive conduct.

We hold *Midcal's* two-pronged test applicable to private parties' claims of state action immunity. Moreover, a state policy that expressly *permits,* but does not compel, anticompetitive conduct may be "clearly articulated" within the meaning of *Midcal.* Our holding today does not suggest, however, that compulsion is irrelevant. To the contrary, compulsion often is the best evidence that the State has a clearly articulated and affirmatively expressed policy to displace competition. Nevertheless, when other evidence conclusively shows that a State

intends to adopt a permissive policy, the absence of compulsion should not prove fatal to a claim of *Parker* immunity. A private party may claim state action immunity only if both prongs of the *Midcal* test are satisfied. Here the Court of Appeals found, and the Government concedes, that the State Public Service Commission actively supervises the collective ratemaking activities of the rate bureaus. Therefore, the only issue left to resolve is whether the petitioners' challenged conduct was taken pursuant to a clearly articulated state policy. *Parker* immunity is available only when the challenged activity is undertaken pursuant to a clearly articulated policy of the State itself, such as a policy approved by a state legislature, or a state supreme court.

A private party acting pursuant to an anticompetitive regulatory program need not "point to a specific, detailed legislative authorization" for its challenged conduct. As long as the State as sovereign clearly intends to displace competition in a particular field with a regulatory structure, the first prong of the *Midcal* test is satisfied.

If more detail than a clear intent to displace competition were required of the legislature, States would find it difficult to implement through regulatory agencies their anticompetitive policies. Agencies are created because they are able to deal with problems unforeseeable to, or outside the competence of, the legislature. Requiring express authorization for every action that an agency might find necessary to effectuate state policy would diminish, if not destroy, its usefulness. Therefore, we hold that if the State's intent to establish an anticompetitive regulatory program is clear, as it is in Mississippi, the State's failure to describe the implementation of its policy in detail will not subject the program to the restraints of the federal antitrust laws.

We hold that the petitioners' collective ratemaking activity is immune from Sherman Act liability. This anticompetitive conduct is taken pursuant to a "clearly articulated state policy." The legislatures of North Carolina, Georgia, and Tennessee expressly permit motor common carriers to submit collective rate proposals to public service commissions, which have the authority to accept, reject, or modify any recommendation. Mississippi, the fourth State in which the petitioners operate, has not expressly approved of collective ratemaking, but it has articulated clearly its intent to displace price competition among common carriers with a regulatory structure. Anticompetitive conduct taken pursuant to such a regulatory program satisfies the first prong of the *Midcal* test. The second prong of the *Midcal* test likewise is met, for the government has conceded that the relevant States, through their agencies, actively supervise the conduct of private parties.

We conclude that the petitioners' collective ratemaking activities, although not compelled by the States, are immune from antitrust liability under the doctrine of *Parker v. Brown*. Accordingly, the judgment of the Court of Appeals is reversed.

Regulated Industries

Many businesses operate in industries subject to extensive government regulation. In some cases, government regulation specifies in great detail the manner in which companies must conduct their business. A federal agency or state agency might order a business to conduct itself in a manner contrary to the broad requirements of the antitrust laws. Does this mean that a business that obeys the regulation at the same time violates the antitrust laws? The law in the regulated-industries area cannot be explained in a few general statements. A given action may be subject to the antitrust laws, depending on a number of factors, even when a business operates within a regulated industry.

Such industries as insurance and banking are subject to extensive government regulation. Many professionals in areas like law, medicine, and dentistry must follow rules set down by state regulatory agencies. While precise general rules as to when an industry must comply with the antitrust laws are difficult to state in many instances, if Congress expressly indicated an intent to displace the antitrust laws with agency regulation, the Sherman Act does not apply to matters regulated by the agency. If Congress failed to grant an express immunity, the Courts try to avoid finding an implied immunity unless such a rule is necessary to make the regulation work.

It should be noted that there is a trend to extend the antitrust laws to as many industries as possible, even though they are regulated to some extent by the government.

POLITICAL ACTION

The antitrust laws to a great extent are designed to further competition. What if a businessperson decided that he disliked competition? Could he seek a special rule for his business or industry that exempts it from competition? The answer is yes.

In the discussion of constitutional law, we noted the United States Constitution in the First Amendment provides that "Congress shall make no law . . . abridging the freedom of speech . . . or the right of the people . . . to petition the Government for a redress of grievances."

Because the Constitution permits all persons to freely speak their minds and to petition (that is, request some action from) the government, there is nothing improper about asking government officials for special treatment. To create another rule would be a denial of free speech and the right to petition as guaranteed by the First Amendment. Whether a particular business or industry will succeed in convincing Congress of the need for special protection is another question.

Quite clearly, if a business or industry seeks special legislation from Congress and obtains it, the passage of the legislation constitutes a sort of stamp of approval on its efforts. Congress apparently judged the public interest as being furthered by such a law. This is a legislative judgment. Congress is free to determine how much competition our system needs. Of course, a business might succeed in its lobbying effort even though the public interest was not served by a given piece of legislation. Nonetheless, absent a conflict with the Constitution, the courts must defer to the judgment of Congress.

A business also might elect to lobby a state legislature for favorable treatment. Absent a conflict with federal legislation or with the state constitution or United States Constitution, such efforts may result in special favorable treatment for a business. Once again, the degree of competition in our society is a legislative judgment.

What if a business engaged in a ruthless lobbying effort to obtain favorable anticompetitive legislation? Suppose this legislation was aimed to harm its rivals. Suppose further that the business engaged in unethical and perhaps illegal conduct to induce the Congress or a state legislature to pass this anticompetitive bill. Does all this mean its actions violated the antitrust laws?

In *Eastern Railroad Presidents Conference* v. *Noerr Motor Freight, Inc.* (1961), the United States Supreme Court considered such a case. The Court ruled that the purpose of the Sherman Act is to regulate business practices, not political activities. The First Amendment permits the petitioning of the government for relief. If a business makes a bona fide effort to influence government action, it may not be prosecuted under the Sherman Act, even if the legislation it seeks might injure competition.

Noerr suggests that any attempt to influence any branch of government—legislative, executive, judicial, or administrative—may be exempt from the antitrust laws. As one moves away from the legislative area, however, the courts may be more willing to find the action of a company a mere sham or undertaken in bad faith. Clearly, instituting a suit in bad faith may lead to a countersuit. The standards for when and how a litigant uses the courts are fairly clear. A company might also attempt to seek favorable treatment by the president of the United States or by the governor of a state. These persons possess the power to make law through such devices as the executive order. Furthermore, the executive branch enforces legislation. A company might petition the executive branch to not enforce a piece of legislation against it. Once again, such actions are consistent with the Constitution and do not violate the antitrust law absent a bad faith attempt to injure competition.

Neither bad acts, unethical conduct, nor anticompetitive intent make a company's actions in attempting to influence government illegal under the antitrust laws. Only misuse of the process results in an application of the antitrust laws. While some efforts to influence the administrative branch also fit within this political action exception, the Supreme Court will not permit competitors to abuse the administrative process by instituting proceedings against competitors without probable cause and regardless of the merits.

In *California Motor Transport Co.* v. *Trucking Unlimited* (1972), the Supreme Court discussed the sham exception to the *Noerr* doctrine. In this case, the plaintiffs alleged that the defendants engaged in concerted action to institute state and federal administrative proceedings to defeat plaintiff's applications to conduct trucking business over certain routes. The plaintiffs alleged that the defendant's real purpose in instituting proceedings was to destroy them as competitors. Administrative cases had been instituted sometimes without cause, and regardless of the merits of the case. The Court ruled that a pattern of baseless, repetitive claims constitutes an abuse of process. Such actions barred the plaintiffs from access to the agencies and courts. While all trucking companies legally could use the agencies and the courts, using them with intent to eliminate a competitor by denying it free and meaningful access to the agencies and courts comes within the sham exception to the *Noerr* case.

The defendants' wrongdoing in using the agencies to prevent their competitors from obtaining licenses consisted of contesting every request for a license by the plaintiffs—even when the defendants lacked any grounds for such action. Repeatedly contesting every request for a license constituted an abuse of the administrative process. Consequently, the Court applied the Sherman Act to the defendants in this case.

Business executives should not be deterred by the *California Motor Transport* case from exercising their legitimate rights under the Constitution. Many valid arguments may lawfully be presented to Congress, state legislatures, the president, a governor, or the courts. The Constitution guarantees businesses the right of free speech and the right to petition the government. Business executives need not fear the antitrust laws even if they seek anticompetitive legislation of value only to their business and harmful to their competitors. *Noerr* illustrates the point that even bad acts in seeking favorable legislation will not alone trigger the application of the Sherman Act. However, when a person's actions constitute a mere sham to cover up an attempt to interfere directly with the business relationships of a competitor, such actions result in the application of antitrust laws. If a business crosses this line, and seeks legislative, executive, judicial, or administrative relief solely for this purpose, and without any legitimate political aims, the courts will impose the antitrust sanctions on its activities.

The following case discusses the *Noerr* doctrine in the context of taxicab licenses.

Campbell v. City of Chicago
United States Court of Appeals, Seventh Circuit
823 F.2d 1182 (1987)

In 1963, the city of Chicago enacted an ordinance regulating the manner of acquiring and holding taxicab licenses. The law limited the number of cabs in Chicago, but it provided a system for adding more cabs if needed. If more licenses were added, however, Yellow Cab Company and Checker Taxi Company would be guaranteed at least eighty percent of any newly issued licenses. The plaintiffs sued the city of Chicago, Yellow Cab, and Checker Taxi. The cab companies argued that their actions were immune under the *Noerr* doctrine. The court agreed that their actions were immune.

Flaum, Circuit Judge

In 1963, Mayor Daley and representatives of the cab companies met to discuss how damage claims that the taxicab companies had asserted against the City could be settled. Yellow and Checker had sought damages arising from the City's alleged violation of the 1937 taxi-cab ordinance. The cab companies agreed to drop the damage claims in exchange for a favorable ordinance.

We disagree with the plaintiffs, and conclude that Yellow and Checker's actions are immunized by the *Noerr-Pennington* doctrine. We believe that the settlement effected in 1963, and the ensuing lobbying efforts in the Chicago City Council, were protected efforts to petition the government. Any injury that the plaintiffs may have suffered stems from the result of the plaintiffs' successful lobbying efforts rather than from the lobbying itself.

The plaintiffs argue that the defendant taxi companies are liable under the antitrust laws for conspiring with the City to restrain trade. The cab companies argue that they are immune from liability under the *Noerr-Pennington* doctrine, which provides that "the antitrust laws do not apply to efforts to persuade the government to organize or support a cartel." The plaintiffs assert, however, that the cab companies' lobbying efforts in 1963, which secured the passage of the 1963 ordinance, were not legitimate efforts to petition the government as al-

lowed by the *Noerr-Pennington* doctrine. The plaintiffs argue that the cab companies' actions fall within the so-called "sham exception" to *Noerr-Pennington*. This exception applies in a situation "in which a publicity campaign, ostensibly directed toward influencing governmental action, is a mere sham to cover what is actually nothing more than an attempt to interfere directly with the business relationships of a competitor and the application of the Sherman Act would be justified." *Noerr.* We have recently explained the sham exception:

> [I]t is important to identify the source of the injury to competition. If the injury is caused by persuading the government, then the antitrust laws do not apply to the squelching (*Parker v. Brown*) or the persuasion (*Noerr-Pennington*). If the injury flows directly from the "petitioning"—if the injury occurs no matter how the government responds to the request for aid—then we have an antitrust case. When private parties help themselves to a reduction in competition, the antitrust laws apply. *Premier Electric.*

We agree with the district court that the sham exception does not apply in the case, and that the cab companies are immune from liability under *Noerr-Pennington.*

PRICE DISCRIMINATION

While the antitrust laws are intended to preserve competition and further efficiency, some antitrust legislation may impede competition. Section 2(a) of the Clayton Act, as amended by the Robinson-Patman Act, makes it unlawful to discriminate in price between different purchasers of commodities of like grade and quality where the effect of such discrimination may be to substantially lessen competition or to tend to create a monopoly in any line of commerce, or to injure, destroy, or prevent competition with any person who either grants or knowingly receives the benefit of such discrimination, or with customers of either of them.

In order to establish a violation of the Robinson-Patman Act, the plaintiff must establish the following:

1. A sale of goods. Gifts, leases, and other nonsale transactions are not covered by the act. The sale must be of goods—tangible, movable property. If a business provided services, for example, at discriminatory prices, the act would not apply.

2. A sale in interstate commerce; that is, there must be a physical movement of the relevant product across a state line.

3. Evidence that the seller discriminated in price between a buyer and its competitor at roughly the same time.

4. That the goods in question are of like grade and quality.

5. An injury to competition.

The Robinson-Patman Act is intended to prevent sellers from trying to gain an unfair advantage over their competitors by discriminating as to price among buyers of like commodities. The drafters also hoped to prevent such buyers as chain grocery stores from using their economic power to gain an advantage over competitors.

Congress passed the Robinson-Patman amendment to Section 2 of the Clayton Act in 1936. No doubt, different legislators sought different goals—some wished to protect competition; others wished to protect small businesses. To the extent the act favors small businesses, it may injure competition. If a large retailer operates more efficiently, it may be able to sell goods cheaper to consumers. To the extent that some members of Congress wished to favor small business even at the expense of competition, the Robinson-Patman amendment creates problems in the enforcement of the antitrust laws. It reflects the belief of some congressional representatives and senators that other goals (such as the preservation of small business, the dispersal of economic power, and the preservation of opportunity) rank equally with the goals of competition and efficiency as set forth in the original Sherman Act. In the 1930s, 1940s, and 1950s, Congress saw the demise of small business. It perceived that certain problems arise when too much power falls into the hands of too few persons. To some extent, Congress wished to stop this trend toward concentration of business in the hands of very few companies. This goal conflicts with the goal of reducing prices through the furtherance of competition and efficiency.

As Congress never repealed the earlier acts, the antitrust laws conflict with one another to some extent. Those persons favoring competition and efficiency find the alternative goal of preservation of small, independently owned businesses offensive. Perhaps efficiency and competition ought not to be the sole goal of the law—even if it results in higher prices for consumers. At least some members of Congress though so in the 1930s.

The Robinson-Patman Act has been criticized by the Federal Trade Commission as legislation designed to protect small, independent businesspeople against the growth of chain stores. The FTC stated that this protectionist legislation has cost consumers money.

Although the last Department of Justice suit was in 1963 and the Federal Trade Commission has filed very few suits to enforce the Robinson-Patman Act, suits still can be filed by private parties seeking treble damages and injunctions pursuant to Sections 4 and 16 of the Clayton Act.

SUMMARY

Many forces contributed to the passage of the Sherman Act in 1890: the growth of mass production, the expansion of the railway system, American individualism, a desire to redistribute wealth, and a desire to maximize opportunity for workers. Populists, farmers, and small business owners succeeded in convincing Congress that the best way to achieve these goals was through an act which promoted competition and economic efficiency.

Since the passage of the Sherman Act, Congress has enacted a number of other laws in order to keep our economic system competitive. It vested the Department of Justice and the Federal Trade Commission with the primary responsibility for enforcing these acts. Private businesses and individuals, as well as state attorneys general, also may to some extent enforce the federal antitrust laws. Businesses that violate the antitrust laws may be enjoined from certain types of conduct, may be fined, or may have their employees sentenced to prison. Furthermore, civil suits may be filed for damages wrought by antitrust violations, and treble damages may be assessed against an erring company.

Certain groups and businesses are not subject to the federal antitrust laws. In general, labor unions and agricultural cooperatives are exempt. States also may elect to exempt certain types of business activity from antitrust scrutiny.

The United States Constitution also strongly affects the law in this area. Businesses are free to seek legislation even if it has an anticompetitive effect. The constitution permits businesses and people to petition the government for redress of grievances. The Supreme Court has interpreted this clause in the Constitution as creating a right to seek political action from the government.

Congress passed the Robinson-Patman Act in order to prohibit the discrimination in price between different purchasers of commodities of like grade and quality where the effect is to injure competition. The Robinson-Patman Act is inconsistent with the policy of favoring competition and efficiency. To a great extent, it favors small business even at the expense of efficiency.

REVIEW QUESTIONS

1. Define the following terms:
   a. Class actions
   b. Nolo contendere
   c. Parens patriae

2. What forces produced the antitrust laws?

3. What objectives do the courts regard as furthered by the antitrust laws?

4. What groups, if any, are exempt from the antitrust laws?

5. Why is the state action exemption, as announced in *Parker* v. *Brown,* important?

6. What must be established by the plaintiff in order to prove a violation of the Robinson-Patman Act?

7. Is it a violation of the Sherman Act to seek legislation that destroys some other person or company as a competitor?

8. The National Football League enters into a collective bargaining agreement with the union representing the football players on the teams in the NFL. The contract contains a provision that gives a team the right to retain a free agent by matching any offer from another team the free agent receives. In light of the fact that such a provision restrains trade, does this contractual provision violate the antitrust laws?

9. The state of Kansas requires liquor wholesalers to charge retailers a certain specified price for alcoholic beverages. Why is such a state law not in irreconcilable conflict with the federal antitrust laws? Under what circumstances would such a law be upheld even though it restrains competition?

10. Sunkist Growers, Inc. permitted some people who were not growers or producers to join its organization. Sunkist at the time was organized into local associations, which in turn elected members of the Sunkist board. Is Sunkist an association of persons engaged in the production of agricultural products within the meaning of the Capper-Volstead Act?

11. Noerr Motor Freight alleged that the Eastern Railroad Presidents Conference and a public relations firm hired by it conspired to restrain trade and to monopolize the long-distance freight business. Noerr contended that the railroads had engaged the public relations firm to conduct a "vicious, corrupt and fraudulent" publicity campaign designed to create an atmosphere of distrust for truckers and to influence legislative bodies to adopt and enforce laws to the detriment of the trucking industry. The plaintiff charged that the sole motivation behind these efforts was to injure and ultimately destroy the truckers as competitors in the long-distance freight business. The defendants persuaded the governor of Pennsylvania to veto the Fair Truck Bill. Did the railroads violate the Sherman Act?

12. A manufacturer of plastic conduit, Indian Head, Inc., initiated a proposal before the National Fire Protection Association, a private association, to extend the National Electric Code to permit the use of plastic conduit as well as electrical conduit made of steel. The National Electric Code is routinely adopted into law by most state and local governments. Before the annual meeting of the association, at which a majority of the members could approve this change, members of the steel industry packed the meeting with new members whose only function was to vote against this proposal. The proposal was defeated. Indian Head then brought suit, alleging that the steel manufacturers had unreasonably restrained trade in the electrical conduit market in violation of the Sherman Act. The defendants argued that their actions were entitled to immunity under the *Noerr* doctrine. Are they correct?

CHAPTER 24

Antitrust Law

- Monopolies
- Attempts to Monopolize
- Restraint of Trade
- Resale Price Maintenance
- Group Boycotts
- Tying Contracts
- Section 5 of the Federal Trade Commission Act
- Mergers

In Chapter 23, we discussed the scope and enforcement procedures of the antitrust laws. This chapter briefly examines some major antitrust rules. Antitrust law is very complex. Unlike many other areas of law, the statutes creating the antitrust laws leave it up to the courts to precisely define the limits of corporate activity in the antitrust field. The Sherman and Clayton acts were written in broad, general terms, giving the courts considerable discretion in creating a body of antitrust law. Careful attention to the pronouncements by the courts is essential. We will present in-depth discussion of some cases in this chapter to make it easier to understand the current view of the courts on selected antitrust issues.

The cases should enable you to gain a broad overview of the goals of the antitrust laws as interpreted by the courts. Some important issues have been left out because of the complexity and lack of clear-cut rules. Nonetheless, this chapter presents most of the major issues confronting the courts today. The primary emphasis is on monopolies and restraints of trade. A number of other important areas have been presented briefly to alert readers to potential problem areas in the antitrust field.

MONOPOLIES

As noted in Chapter 23, the Sherman Act outlaws monopolies and attempts to monopolize. Section 2 of the act reads as follows:

> Every person who shall monopolize, or attempt to monopolize, or combine or conspire with any other person or persons, to monopolize any part of the trade or

commerce among the several states, or with foreign nations, shall be deemed guilty of a felony, and, on conviction thereof, shall be punished by fine not exceeding one million dollars if a corporation, or, if any other person, one hundred thousand dollars, or by imprisonment not exceeding three years or by both said punishments, in the discretion of the court.

Most challenges to monopolistic behavior are brought under Section 2 of the Sherman Act.

What Is a Monopoly?

When the courts speak of a **monopoly,** they are referring to a firm that deliberately engages in conduct to obtain or maintain the power to control prices or exclude competition in some part of trade or commerce. The courts do not require a firm to be the sole business operating in a particular market—other firms may be operating in the market but they must lack the power to influence prices or output in the market. Contrast a monopolistic industry with an industry composed of several large firms each possessing a major part of the trade in a given market. The courts refer to these firms as **oligopolies.** In a *competitive system,* there are many firms each producing the same product, with none of the firms possessing the power to control prices or output.

Picture a business that operates the parking lot at the airport in your city. Does not this business, in a sense, have a monopoly? Either you park your automobile at the airport in the airport lot, or you take the bus or a cab or arrange to be driven to the airport. If you want to park your car at the airport, you must park at this lot. Such a parking facility faces competition only from other parking lots, but an airport miles from town really need not concern itself with such lots. The airport parking lot in this situation has a monopoly in the parking business. Contrast this with a person operating a downtown parking lot in a big city. The big city parking lot competes with every other lot downtown, as well as with parking on the street. People also may see the bus or a cab as a substitute for driving and parking if parking downtown becomes too expensive. Which business is in the best position to obtain a premium price for renting its space, the lot downtown or the lot at the airport? Clearly, the airport parking lot ought to earn more money.

In labeling the airport parking lot a monopoly, we must make certain assumptions, assumptions that courts make when they designate a business as a monopoly.

Geographic Market

First of all, we must consider the *geographic market*. Implicit in this analysis is the assumption that we will exclude all other parking lots outside the geographic boundaries of the airport. If we include all parking lots in the city as well as those at the airport, the airport business probably rents only a tiny portion of the parking spaces in the city. However, if the geographic market is the airport, the lot probably rents one hundred percent of the spaces. The latter case looks a lot more like a monopoly. A business that controls one hundred percent of the market probably has the power to control prices. Courts must examine the geographic market in which a business operates.

Product Market

Likewise, courts inspect the nature of the *product sold by a business*. While the airport parking lot sells one hundred percent of the parking spaces at the airport, the parking lot sells only a tiny portion of all goods and services sold at the airport. By first defining the product market as the rental of parking spaces and the geographic market as the airport, we arrive at the conclusion that the parking lot business is a monopolist because it sells one hundred percent of the parking lot spaces (the product market) at the airport (the geographic market). If the court defined the geographic market as the whole city, and the product market as all goods and services sold in the city, would the airport parking lot be a monopolist? Clearly not. Courts go through a very similar analysis in monopoly cases. A court first determines the *geographic market* in which a business operates, then the court decides the *product market,* and then it determines the *anticompetitive effects* of a particular company's activities.

Is Monopolizing Trade Bad?

Not all people share the view that monopolies are bad. Some economists think the most efficient use of resources occurs when market power is concentrated in the hands of one efficient firm—or a few efficient firms—in each industry. They see economic waste and inefficiency resulting from the competitive rivalry of industrial corporations. Many executives at large companies share the view that big business operates more efficiently than a number of small competitors.

Diametrically opposed to those who favor monopoly are those who believe the consumer needs protection through the furtherance of competition. Classic economic theory supports this view. It tells us that competition weeds out inefficiency, results in the most productive use of resources, encourages technological advances, and assures the consumer of an adequate supply of goods at the lowest possible price. Whichever theory is correct, some monopolies violate the Sherman Act.

Are All Monopolies Illegal?

Not every monopoly violates the antitrust laws. Some businesses, such as utilities, are natural monopolies. The states give these businesses the exclusive right to operate in a certain territory. Other businesses fall within an exemption to the antitrust laws. Article I, Section 8, of the United States Constitution gives monopolies to authors in the form of copyrights and gives patents to inventors. The framers of the Constitution reasoned that such protection for authors and inventors encourages work in these areas. One object of marketing certainly is to give a product a unique identification in the minds of consumers. If consumers perceive a company's product as different from any other product on the market, they may pay a higher price for its product. There is nothing illegal about a company trying to project a unique, favorable image of its products in the minds of the public. To the extent such a campaign succeeds, the company has obtained a kind of monopoly.

Absent one of these situations, a company that becomes a monopoly in a given geographic and product market may violate the Sherman Act.

Changing the Law

In determining whether a monopoly violates the antitrust laws, the Supreme Court has altered its position over the years. In an early landmark case in the antitrust area, *Standard Oil Co.* v. *United States* (1911), Justice White stated, ''The dread of enhancement of prices . . . which . . . would flow from the undue limitation on competitive conditions caused by contracts or other acts . . . led . . . to the prohibition . . . of all contracts or other acts which were unreasonably restrictive of competitive conditions.'' Justice White did not interpret Section 2 as condemning all monopolies. On this point he noted that the act ''by the omission of every direct prohibition against monopoly . . . indicates a consciousness that the freedom of the individual to contract when not unduly or improperly exercised was the most efficient means for the prevention of monopoly.''

Justice White viewed the statutory purpose of the act as directed at the ''dread of enhancement of prices.'' What he probably meant by his opinion in *Standard Oil* is that if a company is headed toward a monopoly fairly, the extra profits it earns will attract others into the market. For this reason, there will never be a monopoly unless the company is guilty of bad acts. Essentially his views reflect the early analysis of Section 2 of the Sherman Act—that a court must find that a firm has monopolized its market and engaged in *bad acts* in order to find the company in violation of the Sherman Act.

The view currently applied in the courts no longer follows White's opinion. Today, the focus has shifted from an emphasis on reprehensible behavior to the issue of *monopoly power*. Courts examine the relevant *geographic market* a firm operates in and the *product line* it sells. Once a court defines these markets, it determines the *degree of power* a firm possesses in this market. If a firm reaches the position where it sells forty to sixty percent of the goods in a given geographic and product market, it must act with caution. A firm selling sixty percent or more of such a market probably will be in violation of Section 2.

Rule of Reason

Standard Oil Co. v. *United States* was decided under Section 2 of the Sherman Act. Although Justice White dissolved the Standard Oil Trust, he also announced the famous **Rule of Reason** in this case. In what looks very much like a reversal of earlier cases, he stated that only *unreasonable* restraints of trade and *unreasonable* attempts to monopolize violate the Sherman Act. The courts still follow the Rule of Reason in interpreting the Sherman Act.

Starting with *United States* v. *Aluminum Co. of America,* the courts embarked on a new approach to the handling of monopoly cases. The opinion, written by the distinguished Judge Learned Hand, has served as a model for subsequent judges handling monopoly cases. In this famous decision, Judge Hand analyzed the activities of Alcoa by examining the structure of the aluminum market.

In the *Aluminum Company of America* (Alcoa) case, Judge Learned Hand analyzed the market for aluminum. He considered whether to include recycled and imported ingot in the definition of the aluminum market. Judge Hand decided that the aluminum market consisted of imported ingot plus all of Alcoa's aluminum production but did not include recycled ingot. Alcoa controlled ninety percent of the aluminum market as defined by Judge Hand. He could have defined the market differently, in which case Alcoa's share of the market would have been much smaller—and thus it would have had less power over the price of aluminum ingot. However, Judge Hand's definition gave the appearance that Alcoa possessed virtually total control over aluminum production. The court thus ruled that Alcoa had unlawfully monopolized the aluminum market because it possessed monopoly power in this market.

The *Alcoa* case suggests the following rule: Unless a company can prove a Thrust-Upon Defense, if the government proves that a company possesses monopoly power in a given market, it has violated Section 2 of the Sherman Act.

When courts refer to the thrust-upon defense, they are alluding to the situation in which a business unwittingly finds itself in possession of a monopoly; that is, without having intended to put an end to existing competition, or to prevent competition from arising when none had existed, the business simply ends up as a monopolist. For example, suppose that four companies controlled all the market in the United States for refrigerators. If one company went bankrupt, and two more withdrew from the market, the remaining business would have had the monopoly "thrust upon it." Contrast this situation with the type of activities engaged in by the Aspen Skiing Co. which is discussed in a case later in this chapter. Some people have observed that it may be risky for a company to compete too aggressively. If it ends up with a monopoly, it may be sued by the government for unlawfully monopolizing a market. In such a case, it would be difficult for the company to argue that the monopoly position was thrust upon it.

Since the *Alcoa* case, the courts have focused more attention on *monopoly power* and *market structure*. The courts determine the relevant market— geographic and product—and then examine whether a firm possesses power within that market. Remember, a monopolist is a business that possesses the power to exclude competition or control prices in a given market.

Relevant Market

Determining the relevant product market often is critical to the outcome in a case. In *United States* v. *E. I. du Pont de Nemours & Co.* (1956), the Supreme Court expanded the test for relevant product market. The Court ruled that the relevant product market is composed of products that are reasonably interchangeable for the purposes for which they are produced. It examined the price, use, and quality of all products that might compose a given market. The government, in that case, charged Du Pont with monopolizing interstate commerce in cellophane in violation of Section 2 of the Sherman Act. Du Pont produced seventy percent of all cellophane during the relevant period, but cellophane constituted less than twenty percent of all flexible packaging material sales. The government argued that the proper product market definition was cellophane. The company argued that the market definition should include all flexible packaging materials.

A company has a monopoly in violation of Section 2 only if it has the power to control prices or unreasonably restrict competition. Taking this definition of monopoly into consideration, the Court stated that if it defined the product market as cellophane, Du Pont had monopoly power over that market. The company possessed the power to control the price of cellophane. The Court rejected cellophane as the proper product market definition, however, and adopted flexible packaging materials as the proper market definition. The Court reasoned that control in a market depends upon the availability to buyers of alternative commodities. To determine if buyers will substitute one product for another, a court must examine the price, characteristics, and adaptability of competing commodities. The Court found purchasers were willing to substitute other wrapping papers for cellophane (wax paper, brown wrapping paper, and so on). It therefore ruled for Du Pont.

While a company controlling a product possesses monopoly power if no substitutes are available for that product, it does not follow that merely because a product differs from others, an illegal monopoly exists. Although cellophane differs from other wrapping papers, the Court found these other papers to be reasonably interchangeable with cellophane for the purpose of wrapping articles. In making this determination, the Court examined the price, use, and qualities of the substitute products. It found the proper product market definition, in light of these factors, to be flexible wrapping materials.

The *Du Pont* case suggests that courts will pay more attention to product market definitions and will take into consideration partial substitutes. Du Pont clearly possessed substantial market power over cellophane. It lowered the price and increased its sales over time. But it escaped any sanctions by convincing the Court to adopt flexible wrapping materials as opposed to cellophane as the proper definition of relevant product market. This meant Du Pont controlled only twenty percent of the relevant product market—not enough to constitute a monopoly.

Geographic Market

Not only must a court examine the relevant product market before determining if a firm possesses monopoly power, it must also determine the relevant geographic market. Quite often the geographic market for purposes of the Sherman Act is the nation.

In *United States* v. *Grinell Corp.*, 384 U.S. 563 (1966), the Supreme Court essentially announced a two-part test for monopolization. The defendant must (1) possess monopoly power in the relevant market, and (2) have willfully acquired or maintained that power as distinguished from growth or development as a consequence of a superior product, business acumen, or historical accident.

Football Monopoly Damages

In July 1986, a federal district court ruled, in a suit brought by the United States Football League (USFL) that the National Football League (NFL) was a football monopoly. In spite of victory on this point, the jury awarded the USFL only one dollar in damages, which the trial court trebled to three dollars. The Second Circuit Court of Appeals in 1988 upheld the verdict. Judge Ralph K. Winter ruled that the reason for the decline of the USFL was its decision to move its playing schedule from spring-summer to fall in direct competition with the NFL. Thus, the change in the schedule, not any activities of the NFL, resulted in the demise of the USFL.

In the following case, the court discusses the question of whether a promoter monopolized the market for rock concerts in the Chicago metropolitan area.

Flip Side Productions, Inc. v. JAM Productions, Inc.
United States Court of Appeals, Seventh Circuit
843 F.2d 1024 (1988)

Flip Side Productions alleged that JAM Productions and Tempo International exclusively controlled the Rosemont Horizon, an essential facility for the booking and promotion of pop, rock, and rhythm and blues concerts in the Chicago metropolitan area, in violation of the Sherman Act. Flip Side thus alleged that by entering into exclusive leases for the use of this facility, JAM had monopolized the promotion of concerts in the Chicago metropolitan area. JAM and Tempo argued that the Rosemont Horizon was not an essential facility for the promotion of arena-level concerts in the Chicago metropolitan area, since other suitable facilities were available for staging concerts. The district court found that the relevant market in this case was the promotion of arena-level concerts in the Chicago metropolitan area. The trial judge ruled that Flip Side had failed to produce any evidence that established an antitrust injury, so he granted the defendants' motion for a summary judgment. The court of appeals affirmed the district court's judgment.

Coffey, Circuit Judge

Promoters present concerts for Chicago consumers in facilities in three size categories: the arena-level facility, seating 10,000 or more; the middle-level facility seating 3,000-4,500; and the lower-level facility, which seats approximately 1,000. At least 35 lower-level facilities and 16 middle-level facilities are located in the Chicago metropolitan area.

Prior to 1980, at least two arena-level facilities competed with each other in the Chicago metropolitan area: the Chicago Stadium, which seats approximately 19,000, and the International Amphitheatre, which seats approximately 10,500. The Amphitheatre was constructed during the late 1930s and closed its doors in December of 1982.

Since 1980, at least three additional arena-level facilities have been constructed in the Chicago metropolitan area: namely, the Rosemont Horizon, the Pavilion, and Poplar Creek.

In 1978 the Village of Rosemont, Illinois, decided to construct an 18,000-seat indoor arena, the Horizon, which would compete with the International Amphitheatre and the Chicago Stadium. The Horizon was to stage sporting events, circuses, ice shows, and other entertainment events. The Village of Rosemont financed the project, issuing $19 million worth of revenue bonds. To ensure the marketability of these bonds, the Village contracted with Araserv, Inc. (a concessionaire), the Ringling Brothers Barnum & Bailey Circus, and MFG International, Inc. (the corporate entity now known as Tempo International, Inc.). Pursuant to these agreements, Araserv, Ringling Brothers, and Tempo received long-term contracts for the exclusive use of the Horizon. Under its agreements, Tempo was obligated to pay a *minimum* license fee of $6,000 per event or $300,000 annually, whichever was greater. The exclusive nature of these ten-year contracts protected the guarantors Araserv,

Tempo, and Ringling Brothers, allowing them the opportunity to recoup their substantial fee guarantees and expenditures. THe Horizon opened its doors in May 1980, and concerts, as well as an assortment of other events, have been staged very successfully.

The threat to competition and ultimately to the consumer posed by a monopolist who controls and excludes its competitors from an essential facility ("sometimes called a 'bottleneck'") is that it "can extend monopoly power from one stage of production to another and from one market into another." *MCI Communications.* Under these circumstances, the essential facilities doctrine is used "to preserve horizontal competition at a level other than the bottleneck." *Fishman v. Estate of Wirtz.* Needless to say, the threshold inquiry is whether JAM, Flip Side's competitor, has or had market power in the relevant market. In other words, we determine whether the defendants' (JAM and Tempo's) alleged control of the Horizon created a "bottleneck," i.e., is the Horizon an essential facility?

[A]ssuming Flip Side's best scenario, the defendants would be entitled to summary judgment as a matter of law. Flip Side contended (1) that JAM and Tempo had exclusive control of the Horizon for the promotion of concerts, (2) that neither the Pavilion nor the Amphitheatre (while open) reasonably duplicated the Horizon, and (3) that the Stadium was unavailable because another promoter had the exclusive concert promotion rights in that facility. Under these circumstances, absent collusion between JAM, Tempo, and the promoter of concerts at the Stadium, Flip Side failed to demonstrate an antitrust injury since competition for the concert-going consumer remained as the promoters controlling the Horizon and Stadium necessarily vied for the market. In other words, the Horizon was not a bottleneck (i.e., not an essential facility).

Aggressive Competition Not Based on Efficiency   In the following case, Aspen Skiing Co. was acting aggressively. Aspen Skiing Co. used its monopoly power to exclude a rival on some basis *other than* efficiency. It did not maintain its monopoly power through superior business ability and efficiency.

Aspen Skiing Co. v. Aspen Highlands Skiing Corp.
United States Supreme Court
105 S.Ct. 2847 (1985)

Aspen is a ski resort in Colorado. Private investors in Aspen operated three facilities (Ajax, Highlands, and Buttermilk) for downhill skiing between 1945 and 1960. A fourth mountain (Snowmass) opened in 1967. It is no longer possible to open additional facilities in the area. Starting in 1962, the three independent firms that operated the facilities introduced a six-day, all Aspen ticket that permitted skiers to ski on any of the three mountains then in service. This six-day ticket was offered at a discount from the price of six daily tickets.

Aspen Skiing Co. (Called Ski Co.), the owner of Ajax, purchased Buttermilk in 1964 and opened Snowmass in 1967. It continued to offer all-Aspen tickets in conjunction with Aspen Highlands, but over the years evinced a hostility to the all-

Aspen ticket. In 1978, owing to a difference of opinion as to the sharing of revenues, the parties were unable to come to an agreement, and Ski Co. discontinued selling the all-Aspen ticket. Ski Co. then began to promote its own three-area, six-day ticket in a national advertising campaign that strongly implied that there were only three mountains in Aspen. Highlands continued to try to market an all-Aspen ticket, but Ski Co. took additional actions to make it difficult for Highlands to market the all-Aspen ticket—such as refusing to sell Highlands any lift tickets for use in its all-Aspen ticket. Without the convenient all-Aspen ticket, Highlands's share of the market for downhill skiing services steadily declined from 20.5 percent in 1976 to 11 percent in 1980 to 1981. Its other revenues declined sharply as well.

Highlands brought suit against Ski Co. in 1979. It alleged that Ski Co. had monopolized the market for downhill skiing services at Aspen in violation of Section 2 of the Sherman Act and asked for treble damages. The jury ruled for Highlands and found that Ski Co. had violated Section 2 of the Sherman Act. It calculated Highlands actual damages at two and a half million dollars. The district court entered a judgment awarding Highlands treble damages of seven and a half million dollars, plus costs and attorney's fees. The Supreme Court affirmed this judgment.

Justice Stevens

In her instructions to the jury, the District Judge explained that the offense of monopolization under § 2 of the Sherman Act has two elements: (1) the possession of monopoly power in a relevant market, and (2) the willful acquisition, maintenance, or use of that power by anticompetitive means or for anticompetitive or exclusionary purposes. Although the first element was vigorously disputed at the trial and in the Court of Appeals, in this Court Ski Co. does not challenge the jury's special verdict finding that it possessed monopoly power.

The central message of the Sherman Act is that a business entity must find new customers and higher profits through internal expansion—that is, by competing successfully rather than by arranging treaties with its competitors. Ski Co., therefore, is surely correct in submitting that even a firm with monopoly power has no general duty to engage in a joint marketing program with a competitor. Ski Co. is quite wrong, however, in suggesting that the judgment in this case rests on any such proposition of law. For the trial court unambiguously instructed the jury that a firm possessing monopoly power has no duty to cooperate with its business rivals.

The absence of an unqualified duty to cooperate does not mean that every time a firm declines to participate in a particular cooperative venture, that decision may not

have evidentiary significance, or that it may not give rise to liability in certain circumstances. The absence of a duty to transact business with another firm is, in some respects, merely the counterpart of the independent businessman's cherished right to select his customers and his associates. The high value that we have placed on the right to refuse to deal with other firms does not mean that the right is unqualified.

In the actual case that we must decide, the monopolist did not merely reject a novel offer to participate in a cooperative venture that had been proposed by a competitor. Rather, the monopolist elected to make an important change in a pattern of distribution that had originated in a competitive market and had persisted for several years.

Ski Co.'s decision to terminate the all-Aspen ticket was a decision by a monopolist to make an important change in the character of the market. Such a decision is not necessarily anticompetitive, and Ski Co. contends that neither its decision, nor the conduct in which it engaged to implement that decision, can fairly be characterized as exclusionary in this case.

We must assume that the jury followed the court's instructions. The jury must, therefore have drawn a distinction between practices which tend to exclude or restrict competition on the one hand, and the success of a business which reflects only a superior product, a well-run business, or luck, on the other. Since the jury was unambiguously instructed that Ski Co.'s refusal to deal with Highlands "does not violate § 2 if valid business reasons exist for that refusal," we must assume that the jury concluded that there were no valid business reasons for the refusal. The question then is whether that conclusion finds support in the record.

The question whether Ski Co.'s conduct may properly be characterized as exclusionary cannot be answered by simply considering its effect on Highlands. In addition, it is relevant to consider its impact on consumers and whether it has impaired competition in an unnecessarily restrictive way. If a firm has been attempting to exclude rivals on some basis other than efficiency, it is fair to characterize its behavior as predatory. It is, accordingly, appropriate to examine the effect of the challenged pattern of conduct on consumers, on Ski Co.'s smaller rival, and on Ski Co. itself.

The evidence supports a conclusion that consumers were adversely affected by the elimination of the 4-area ticket. The actual record of competition between a 3-area ticket and the all-Aspen ticket in the years after 1967 indicated that skiers demonstrably preferred four mountains to three.

The adverse impact of Ski Co.'s pattern of conduct on Highlands is not disputed in this Court.

Perhaps most significant, however, is the evidence relating to Ski Co. itself, for Ski Co. did not persuade the jury that its conduct was justified by any normal business purpose. Ski Co. was apparently willing to forgo daily ticket sales both to skiers who sought to exchange the coupons contained in Highlands' Adventure Pack, and to those who would have purchased Ski Co. daily lift tickets from Highlands if Highlands had been permitted to purchase them in bulk. The jury may well have concluded that Ski Co. elected to forego these short-run benefits because it was more interested in reducing competition in the Aspen market over the long run by harming its smaller competitor.

The record in this case comfortably supports an inference that the monopolist made a deliberate effort to discourage its customers from doing business with its smaller rival.

Thus the evidence supports an inference that Ski Co. was not motivated by efficiency concerns and that it was willing to sacrifice short-run benefits and consumer good will in exchange for a perceived long-run impact on its smaller rival.

ATTEMPTS TO MONOPOLIZE

A firm may violate Section 2 of the Sherman Act not only by achieving a monopoly, but also by *attempting* to monopolize a market. As stated earlier, a monopolist possesses the power to control prices or exclude competition in some part of the trade or commerce. Thus, a firm attempting to monopolize a market is trying to achieve a position in a market whereby the firm may control prices or exclude competition.

Presumably, such a company desires to achieve a monopoly position in the market in order to charge prices higher than those which would prevail in a competitive market. The antitrust laws, by preventing monopolies, helps keep prices low.

The approach taken by courts in the attempt-to-monopolize cases is to require a demonstration that the defendant has a specific intent to monopolize a market, is engaging in conduct likely to lead to a monopoly, and possesses significant market power in the relevant geographic and product market.

With respect to intent, Judge Hand observed in the *Alcoa* case: "Conduct falling short of monopoly is not illegal unless it is part of a plan to monopolize, or to gain such other control of a market as is equally forbidden. To make it so, the plaintiff must prove what in the criminal law is known as a 'specific intent'; an intent which goes beyond the mere intent to do the act.'' In other words, by engaging in certain behavior, the firm intends to achieve a monopoly. Most courts merely require proof of improper conduct to establish a specific intent. The defendant is presumed to intend the likely consequences of its acts.

In an attempt-to-monopolize case, courts require evidence that the defendant possesses a significant market share. A firm that intends to monopolize a market and engages in conduct designed to achieve this goal is not guilty of a violation of Section 2 until it achieves a significant market share. The firm must have enough of the market in question to pose a dangerous probability of succeeding in achieving a monopoly.

In monopoly cases, the defendant is accused of trying to control all or a significant portion of a market. In restraint-of-trade cases, a discussion of which follows, the defendant is accused of interfering with free trade.

RESTRAINT OF TRADE

Section 1 of the Sherman Act outlaws **restraint of trade.** The act reads as follows:

> Every contract, combination in the form of trust or otherwise, or conspiracy, in restraint of trade or commerce among the several States, or with foreign nations, is declared to be illegal. Every person who shall make any contract or engage in any combination or conspiracy . . . shall be deemed guilty of a felony, and, on conviction thereof, shall be punished by fine not exceeding one million dollars if a corporation, or, if any other person, one hundred thousand dollars, or by imprisonment not exceeding three years, or by both said punishments, in the discretion of the court.

Elements of Case

What does the Sherman Act require before a corporation or person may be deemed in violation of Section 1? There must be (1) a contract, combination, or conspiracy, and (2) a restraint of trade. Generally, we need not concern ourselves with a careful definition of geographic and product markets or market power when analyzing restraints of trade. Though a careful definition of markets and market power can be useful in some restraint-of-trade cases, such as exclusive dealing agreements (agreements by a buyer to deal only from a particular seller), we will not discuss this type of case.

Although the act used the phrase ''in restraint of trade or commerce,'' Congress left it to the courts to define this phrase. One possible construction of those words is that any action that restrains trade violates the act. If you read the words literally, they imply that the act outlaws all restraints of trade. If a person enters into an employment contract, does this violate the Sherman Act? Obviously, to some extent trade is restrained by this person's agreeing to work for only a certain employer. A more reasonable interpretation of ''in restraint of trade or commerce'' is that the act intended to outlaw only a subset of all contracts that restrain trade or commerce, namely, those that are bad for various reasons.

Early Interpretation of the Act

In the early cases dealing with the Sherman Act, the Supreme Court read Section 1 literally. When faced with the question whether the act outlawed all restraints of trade and commerce, or merely unreasonable restraints of trade and commerce, the Supreme Court chose the former option. In *United States* v. *Trans-Missouri Freight Association* (1897), the Court stated: "The plain and ordinary meaning of such language is not limited to that kind of contract alone which is in unreasonable restraint of trade, but all contracts are included in such language." As noted, outlawing all contracts that restrain trade makes very little sense. Many contracts that restrain trade are highly beneficial to society.

The Rule of Reason

The Supreme Court eventually changed its position in the landmark case *Standard Oil Co.* v. *United States* (1911). In this case, brought against the Standard Oil Trust, the Supreme Court again reconsidered the question of whether the Sherman Act outlaws all restraints of trade. The defendants in this case had entered into agreements to fix prices, limit production, and control the transportation of oil and its products. They turned over the management of all aspects of their businesses to nine trustees. In return for surrendering the control of their businesses to the Standard Oil trustees, they received trust certificates. The Supreme Court decided this trust agreement violated the Sherman Act. The Court enjoined Standard Oil of New Jersey from voting the stocks or otherwise controlling the thirty-seven subsidiaries and the individuals and corporations from entering into any similar combination to evade the decree. The Court enjoined the defendants from engaging in the petroleum business as long as the illegal combination existed.

Justice White, in his opinion in the *Standard Oil* case, described the Sherman Act as an act designed to promote the free marketplace and competition. Congress was concerned with enhancement of prices caused by undue limitations on the competitive process. However, Congress chose to outlaw only *unreasonable* restraints of trade or *unreasonable* attempts to monopolize. The facts of the *Standard Oil* case presented a situation so clearly in violation of the Sherman Act that the trust device used by Standard was found to be illegal without extensive analysis.

Many people viewed the *Standard Oil* case as an outrage. They argued that the Supreme Court adopted this interpretation of the Sherman Act in order to favor big business. This also probably contributed to a feeling of uneasiness among the general population as to the Court's orientation.

Look back at the language of Section 1 of the Sherman Act, quoted at the beginning of this discussion. Does the act refer to "unreasonable" restraints of trade? No. The Court *read the term* unreasonable *into the statute,* though the word does not actually appear in the statute. The Court felt it necessary to interpret the language of the act in this fashion in order to make it workable.

The Supreme Court found support in the common law dealing with restraints of trade. The common law also followed the reasonableness standard, which arguably was incorporated into the Sherman Act by Congress's deliberate use of the common law term **restraint of trade.** Thus there was legislative intent and precedential support for the Rule of Reason announced in the *Standard Oil* case.

It should be borne in mind that courts have the final say as to the actual meaning of a statute. In the case of the Supreme Court, its interpretation of a statute is final and can be overruled only by the decision of Congress or a constitutional amendment. As Congress has never reversed the Court's interpretation on restraints of trade, we continue to apply what is referred to as the Rule of Reason in analyzing some restraints of trade under Section 1 of the Sherman Act.

Per Se Rule   In following the Rule of Reason, a court must examine whether a contract, combination, or conspiracy hinders or promotes the purposes of the Sherman Act. This analysis enmeshes the court in a complex web of facts. Antitrust cases tend to be long and very involved. Yet some types of restraints of trade clearly contravene the spirit of the Sherman Act. Why not adopt a rule that outlaws certain types of practices without an extended analysis of the impact of certain conduct on the economic system? This is exactly what the courts have done with respect to certain business practices. Rather than examining whether a particular act has a bad effect, the courts sometimes rule that if a given set of facts exist, the defendant's conduct violates the antitrust law. This is referred to as the **Per Se Rule,** as opposed to the Rule of Reason. When a situation presents a clear-cut violation of the Sherman Act, the courts use the Per Se Rule and find a violation without extended consideration of the effects of a defendant's conduct. Conversely, if the situation is one in which a violation is not evident, the courts follow the Rule of Reason and examine the impact of particular behavior to determine if it constitutes an *unreasonable* restraint of trade.

Horizontal Market Divisions   In *United States* v. *Topco Associates, Inc.,* 405 U.S. 596 (1972), the United States Supreme Court examined a case dealing with an association composed of twenty-five different grocery chains. Topco operated as a purchasing agent for the member groceries and provided products to them under the Topco name. Topco divided markets among its members. In that case, the Court noted that a classic example of a per se violation of Section 1 is an agreement between competitors at the same level of the market structure to allocate territories in order to minimize competition, called a horizontal restraint on competition. Such horizontal territorial limitations serve no purpose other than limiting competition. Therefore, the Court found Topco's territorial restrictions to be illegal per se.

We know from this case, therefore, that competitors at the same level of market structure—as opposed to combinations of persons at different levels of the market structure (for example, combinations of manufacturers and distributors, which are termed *vertical* restraints)—may not allocate territories in order to minimize competition. These *horizontal* market divisions are illegal per se.

Palmer v. *BRG of Georgia, Inc.,* deals with two publishing companies that offered bar review courses and agreed not to compete in the other's territory.

Palmer v. BRG of Georgia, Inc.
United States Supreme Court
111 S.Ct. 401 (1990)

Harcourt Brace Jovanovich Legal and Professional Publications (HBJ) is the nation's largest provider of bar review materials and lecture services. Both BRG and HBJ offered Georgia bar review courses in the 1970s. In early 1980, they entered into an agreement that gave BRG an exclusive license to market HBJ's material in Georgia and to use its trade name "Bar/Bri." The parties agreed that HBJ would not compete with BRG in Georgia and that BRG would not compete with HBJ outside of Georgia. Palmer contends that the price of BRG's course was enhanced by reason of this agreement and that the agreement violated Section 1 of the Sherman Act. The United States Court of Appeals for the Eleventh Circuit held that to prove a per se violation under a geographic market allocation theory, plaintiff had to show that the defendants had subdivided some relevant market in which they had previously competed.

Per Curiam

The District Court and the Court of Appeals erred when they assumed that an allocation of markets or submarkets by competitors is not unlawful unless the markets in which the two previously competed is divided between them.

In *United States v. Topco Associates, Inc.* we held that agreements between competitors to allocate territories to minimize competition are illegal. One of the classic examples of a *per se* violation of section 1 is an agreement between competitors at the same level of the market structure to allocate territories in order to minimize competition. This Court has reiterated time and time again that horizontal territorial limitations are naked restraints of trade with no purpose except stifling of competition. Such limitations are *per se* violations of the Sherman Act.

The defendants in *Topco* had never competed in the same market, but had simply agreed to allocate markets. Here, HBJ and BRG had previously competed in the Georgia market; under their allocation agreement, BRG received that market, while HBJ received the remainder of the United States. Each agreed not to compete in the other's territories. Such agreements are anticompetitive regardless of whether the parties split a market within which both do business or whether they merely reserve one market for one and another for the other. Thus, the 1980 agreement between HBJ and BRG was unlawful on its face.

Subsidiaries   In *Copperweld Corporation* v. *Independence Tube Corporation*, 104 S.Ct. 2731 (1984), the United States Supreme Court ruled that a corporation and its *wholly owned* subsidiary are incapable of conspiring with each other for the purposes of violating Section 1 of the Sherman Act because they have a complete unity of interest. It is irrelevant whether the subsidiary is an unincorporated division or a wholly owned subsidiary. Congress *exempted* unilateral conduct from Section 1 of the antitrust law.

Price Fixing

This brings us to the issue of price fixing. Price fixing is one of those areas of conduct treated by the courts as a per se violation of Section 1 of the Sherman Act. No extended analysis of the effect of the defendant's activities is necessary. The proof that a defendant entered into a contract, combination, or conspiracy to fix prices is sufficient to find it in violation of the Sherman Act.

In *United States* v. *Trenton Potteries* (1927), the Supreme Court explained why it regarded price-fixing agreements as so offensive to the purposes of the Sherman Act. Trenton Potteries manufactured vitreous pottery. It fixed prices and limited the sale of its pottery to specific companies. Justice Stone, speaking for the majority, wrote the following concerning price-fixing agreements:

> The aim and result of every price fixing agreement, if effective, is the elimination of one form of competition. . . . The reasonable price fixed today may through economic or business changes become the unreasonable price of tomorrow. Once established, it may be maintained unchanged because of the absence of competition secured by the agreement. . . . Agreements which create such potential power may well be held to be in themselves unreasonable unlawful restraints, without necessity of minute inquiry whether a particular price is reasonable or unreasonable.

Trenton Potteries argued that it fixed only *reasonable* prices. The Court rejected the reasonable price defense in this case. This means that even if a company that sets a price for its product at the same level that competition would have produced violates Section 1, if it enters into a contract, combination, or conspiracy with any other firm or person to fix prices at this level. The contracts in this case were between Trenton Potteries and the people to whom Trenton sold its products.

The question remained, however, whether price fixing was illegal per se if the persons or companies that set the prices *lacked the market power* actually to fix prices. The Supreme Court answered this question definitively in the following case.

United States v. Socony-Vacuum Oil Co.
United States Supreme Court
310 U.S. 150 (1940)

At the time of this suit, the major oil refiners were able to respond to changes in demand by increasing or decreasing their inventories, or production, or price. The major refiners thought they were being hurt by the fact that independent refiners lacked storage capacity for their gasoline. Because of this, the independents were forced to offer their gasoline on the spot market for immediate delivery to dealers. This caused the price of gasoline to vary greatly.

To eliminate the price fluctuations, the major producers entered into a program of bidding for and buying gas on the spot market that they were capable of storing. The major producers entered into the arrangement in order to stabilize the price of gasoline. There was no actual formal contractual commitment to purchase the gasoline, either between the majors or between the majors and the independent refiners. It was more of a gentlemen's agreement, or understanding. The prices did rise and stabilize in the markets in which the parties were operating during 1935 and 1936. The government charged that the major oil companies had violated Section 1 of the Sherman Act. The Supreme Court agreed.

Justice Douglas

There was abundant evidence that the combination had the purpose to raise prices. And likewise, there was ample evidence that the buying programs at least contributed to the price rise and the stability of the spot markets, and to increases in the price of gasoline sold in the Mid-Western area during the indictment period. That other factors also may have contributed to that rise and stability of the markets is immaterial. Proof that there was a conspiracy, that its purpose was to raise prices, and that it caused or contributed to a price rise is proof of the actual consummation or execution of a conspiracy under Section 1 of the Sherman Act.

The fact that sales on the spot markets were still governed by some competition is of no consequence. For it is indisputable that that competition was restricted through the removal by respondents of a part of the supply which but for the buying programs would have been a factor in determining the going prices on those markets.

Any combination which tampers with price structures is engaged in an unlawful activity. Even though the members of the price-fixing group were in no position to control the market, to the extent that they raised, lowered, or stabilized prices they would be directly interfering with the free play of market forces. The Act places all such schemes beyond the pale and protects that vital part of our economy against any degree of interference. Congress has not left with us the determination of whether or not particular price-fixing schemes are wise or unwise, healthy or destructive. It has not permitted the age-old cry of ruinous competition and competitive evils to be a defense to price-fixing conspiracies. It has no more allowed genuine or fancied competitive abuses as a legal justification for such schemes than it has the good intentions of the members of the combination.

Under the Sherman Act a combination formed for the purpose and with the effect of raising, depressing, fixing, pegging, or stabilizing the price of a commodity in interstate or foreign commerce is illegal per se. Where the machinery for price-fixing is an agreement on the prices to be charged or paid for the commodity in the interstate or foreign channels of trade, the power to fix prices exists if the combination has control of a substantial part of the commerce in that commodity. Where the means for price-fixing are purchases or sales of the commodity in a market operation or, as here, purchases of a part of the supply of the commodity for the purpose of keeping it from having a depressive effect on the markets, such power may be found to exist though the combination does not control a substantial part of the commodity. In such a case that power may be established if as a result of market conditions, the resources available to the combinations, the timing and the strategic placement of orders and the like, effective means are at hand to accomplish the desired objective. But there may be effective influence over the market though the group in question does not control it. Price-fixing agreements may have utility to members of the group though the power possessed or exerted falls far short of domination and control. Monopoly power is not the only power which the Act strikes down, as we have said. Proof that a combination was formed for the purpose of fixing prices and that it caused them to be fixed or contributed to that result is proof of the completion of a price-fixing conspiracy under Section 1 of the Act. The indictment in this case charged that this combination had that purpose and effect. And there was abundant evidence to support it. Hence the existence of power on the part of members of the combination to fix prices was but a conclusion from the finding that the buying programs caused or contributed to the rise and stability of prices.

Accordingly we conclude that the Circuit Court of Appeals erred in reversing the judgments on this ground. A fortiori the position taken by respondents in their cross petition that they were untitled to direct verdicts of acquittal is untenable.

Socony-Vacuum Oil Case

The *Socony* case illustrates several points. Whether the price established through a contract, combination, or conspiracy is reasonable is irrelevant. The Court also rejected the argument that the manufacturers needed to set prices in order to avoid the ruinous competition created by sellers on the spot market. Ruinous competition is *not* a defense to a price-setting scheme. The Court stated: ''Under the Sherman Act a combination formed for the purpose and with the effect of raising, depressing, fixing, pegging or stabilizing the price of a commodity in interstate commerce is illegal per se.'' The Court also implied that even if the defendants lacked the power to influence prices—that is, even if they lacked market power to influence the price of oil—they violated the Sherman Act simply by entering into such an agreement to fix prices.

Why was the Court so hard on price fixers? After all, if the price that is fixed is the price that would have prevailed in a fully competitive market, how is the public interest prejudiced? The Court answered this in *Trenton Potteries*. The reasonable price fixed today could become an unreasonable price tomorrow. It would place an unreasonable burden on the courts to recognize the reasonable price defense. The government would be forced to monitor prices and relitigate a case if it appeared the price fixers changed their price from a reasonable price to an unreasonable price. A Per Se Rule minimizes the time the courts must spend on a price-fixing scheme. Furthermore, it provides a clear-cut rule for people in business to follow. Anyone who fixes the price of his or her product does so at the risk of being prosecuted for a violation of the antitrust laws. As we noted in Chapter 23, such a violation may lead to substantial civil penalties and even criminal sanctions.

Maximum Prices

What if, rather than agreeing upon a given price, several manufacturers enter into an arrangement in which they agree to charge buyers no more than a certain price—a maximum price. Setting a maximum price, as well as any other tampering with the price system of the free market, violates the antitrust laws.

Rather than agreeing to require their purchasers to resell a commodity at a maximum price, manufacturers may agree simply to charge their customers a minimum price. Agreements among manufacturers to charge all customers no less than a stated price also violates the Sherman Act.

We now know that setting a minimum or a maximum price, stabilizing prices, and fixing prices in any way all violate the Sherman Act.

Analysis of Section 1 Cases

When faced with a Section 1 case, a given court first asks if the parties entered into an agreement. If so, should the agreement be covered by a Per Se Rule? Activities that clearly violate Section 1, such as price fixing, fall under a per se form of analysis. The government, in a price-fixing case, need only prove an agreement to fix prices between two or more parties. It need not prove any harmful effects.

If a court analyzes a case under the Rule of Reason, it looks for harmful effects. It then examines the legitimate beneficial effects of the agreement—that is, those which are procompetitive. The *purpose* of the defendants are often looked to as a guide to interpreting effects. This is often a very critical move by the court in its application of the Rule of Reason approach. (The court does not examine broader social policy arguments other than the furtherance of competition and efficiency.) Finally, the court examines whether *less restrictive alternatives* exist for achieving the goals the defendants wish to achieve. If they are able to achieve the same results in another way, one which does not injure competition, the court likely will rule against the defendants.

Ruinous Competition

What if a company entered into a price-fixing agreement with its competitors in order to stay in business? Suppose competition within the industry reached such a fever pitch that every company was near bankruptcy. Should the competitors be allowed to fix prices in order to stay in business, in light of the otherwise ruthless competition within the industry?

In *Appalachian Coal, Inc.* v. *United States* (1933), the Court examined the social costs of business failure. The coal industry was in disarray. In order to prevent a collapse of the companies in the coal industry, the coal companies formed a cooperative, Appalachian Coal, Inc., to market their coal. The cooperative charged a single price for its coal. While these companies produced only a small percentage of United States coal, the cooperative did tend to stabilize the price of coal in this geographical area. Not all mines in the area belonged to the cooperative. Was this a violation of the Sherman Act? The Supreme Court ruled it was not! The Court noted that the cooperative was formed to combat evils inherent in the coal industry. The cooperative stabilized prices, but to the Court this was insufficient to make out an antitrust violation.

Does the *Appalachian Coal* case make any sense in light of the subsequent decision in 1940 in *Socony?* The Court in *Socony* found that any contract, combination, or conspiracy to fix prices violated the Sherman Act, whether the conspirators had market power to influence prices or not. This suggests the *Appalachian Coal* decision no longer is valid. However, the case illustrates an important point. The Supreme Court in most cases has been unresponsive to fear of ruinous competition. Normally, courts reject social arguments—such as the argument that if competition is not stopped in a given industry, it will destroy all companies within that industry. The Supreme Court probably accepted this argument in 1933 because the United States was in the Great Depression. This caused the Court to be more responsive to arguments that excessive competition was an evil from which companies had a right to protect themselves.

In examining antitrust or any part of the law, keep in mind the *historical forces at work* at the time a court renders a decision or Congress passes an act. All institutions are influenced to some degree by events in society. So it is in the case of *Appalachian Coal*. The Court reflected the basic distrust of competition evident in the New Deal legislation. After the country passed through the Great Depression, the Court reaffirmed its original position that any tampering with prices violates the Sherman Act. But for a few years, the Court listened to and accepted social arguments that put forth goals other than competition as legitimate goals of the antitrust laws. Today, the Court no longer accepts such social arguments as a legitimate justification for price fixing.

RESALE PRICE MAINTENANCE

Suppose a single manufacturer and a retail seller or a distributor agree to set the price at which a commodity may be resold. An arrangement like this between suppliers and customers is commonly referred to as a **resale price maintenance** scheme. Resale price maintenance schemes often run afoul of Section 1 of the Sherman Act. They are a form of *vertical* price fixing (between a manufacturer and a distributor or a retailer). The problem with such an arrangement is that it prevents competition between retailers. If a television manufacturer required all television sets be sold at no more than a certain price, every retailer would be forced to sell the televisions at a price somewhere between the wholesale price and the maximum price. This would lead, possibly, to very little competition at the retail level. Furthermore, a maximum price might result in a price below that level which would occur in the presence of a competitive retail market. In this situation, the retailer's earnings would be lower than he or she would achieve in the absence of such an agreement. Alternatively, the price set by the manufacturer might be too high.

In an early resale price maintenance case, *Dr. Miles Medical Co.* v. *John D. Park & Sons Co.* (1911), the Supreme Court ruled that when a manufacturer parts with title to his property, he may not require the person or company with whom he dealt to resell the product at a particular price. In that case, a manufacturer of patent medicines entered into an agreement with its dealers on the minimum price at which the patent medicine could be resold. The Court acknowledged that such a price-fixing scheme helped increase the profits of dealers handling this patent medicine and seemed to imply that there may be some advantage to Dr. Miles as well. Without determining what that advantage might be, the Court held that a manufacturer may not enter into an agreement with its dealers that restrains trade in this fashion. A resale price maintenance scheme of this nature is illegal per se.

In two subsequent cases, the Court refused to invalidate restrictions on the price at which dealers could resell goods. In *United States* v. *General Electric Company* (1926), the Court ruled in favor of General Electric. Unlike the *Dr. Miles* case, General Electric held a patent on its products and used agents to resell the products to consumers. The Court held that sales through this type of agency relationship were *not* violations of the antitrust laws. In 1964, the Supreme Court decided a case very similar to *General Electric—Simpson* v. *Union Oil Co.* The plaintiff, Simpson, leased a retail gasoline station owned by Union Oil. Simpson signed a consignment agreement under which Union set the price at which he could resell the gasoline. He sold below this price and Union terminated his lease. Simpson asserted this agreement violated the Sherman Act. Without overruling *General Electric,* the Court ruled against Union Oil. The Court held that a resale price maintenance agreement utilizing a coercive consignment agreement violates the antitrust laws.

These cases seem to create a set of rules whereby certain agreements are per se illegal, as those in the *Dr. Miles* case. Agreements that set resale prices and use agents and patented products arguably are legal under the *General Electric* decision. In the middle, probably analyzed under the Rule of Reason, are such agreements as the one discussed in the *Simpson* case. One might argue, however, that the decision in *Simpson* overrules *General Electric.* As to whether a firm may sell to another company (to a jobber or wholesaler, for example) and control the resale price of its product, it may still be possible to enter into such an arrangement if the other firm is an agent of the manufacturer. The *Simpson* case stressed the comprehensiveness of the arrangement and the fact that the consignment agents appeared to be independent businesspersons. In the absence of these factors, the *Simpson* rule might not apply.

The *Simpson* case has been criticized. Justice Stewart wrote a dissent in that case in which he argued that *Simpson* was virtually indistinguishable from *General Electric.*

In *Monsanto Co.* v. *Spray-Rite Service Co.* 104 S.Ct. 1464 (1984), the United States Supreme Court upheld the *Dr. Miles* case. It ruled that it is illegal per se to engage in *concerted* activities to set prices. Thus, in distributor cases, it is illegal per se to engage in a resale price maintenance scheme with distributors.

Whether a case involves an agreement between two manufacturers and their customers or an agreement between a supplier and a customer, resale price maintenance agreements that fix the price at which the buyer may resell its products are a per se violation of Section 1 of the Sherman Act.

In any event, a firm is still free to integrate forward and undertake its own distribution of its products. In such a case, since the firm would not be forcing independent businesspeople to resell its products at a particular price, the rule in *Simpson* would not apply.

The following case is a 1980 decision of the Supreme Court on retail price maintenance.

California Retail Liquor Dealers Association v. Midcal Aluminum, Inc.
United States Supreme Court
100 S.Ct. 937 (1980)

In this case, Midcal Aluminum, the plaintiff-respondent, a wine distributor, challenged California's wine-pricing scheme. The state required all wine producers and wholesalers to file fair trade contracts or price schedules with the state. Wholesalers that sold below these prices could be fined or have their licenses suspended or revoked. Midcal sold below these prices and the state challenged its prices. Midcal claimed this was an illegal resale price maintenance scheme in violation of Section 1 of the Sherman Act. The California Court of Appeals agreed, and the Supreme Court affirmed the ruling for Midcal.

Portions of its opinion dealing with the Twenty-first Amendment to the Constitution have been deleted. The Court noted that the amendment gives the state substantial discretion to establish liquor regulations. However, the federal government also has the power to regulate in this area, and therefore the Sherman Act applies in spite of the Twenty-first Amendment.

Justice Powell

Under Section 24866(b) of the California Business and Professions Code, all wine producers, wholesalers, and rectifiers must file with the State fair trade contracts or price schedules. If a wine producer has not set prices through a fair trade contract, wholesalers must post a resale price schedule for that producer's brands. No state-licensed wine merchant may sell wine to a retailer at other than the price set "either in an effective price schedule or in an effective fair trade contract. . . ."

The State is divided into three trading areas for administration of the wine-pricing program. A single fair trade contract or schedule for each brand sets the terms for all wholesale transactions in that brand within a given trading area. Similarly, state regulations provide that the wine prices posted by a single wholesaler within a trading area bind all wholesalers in that area. A licensee selling below the established prices faces fines, license suspension, or outright license revocation. The State has no direct control over wine prices, and it does not review the reasonableness of the prices set by wine dealers.

The threshold question is whether California's plan for wine pricing violates the Sherman Act. This Court has ruled consistently that resale price maintenance illegally restrains trade. In *Dr. Miles Medical Co. v. Park & Sons Co.* (1911), the Court observed that such arrangements are "designed to maintain prices . . . and to prevent competition among those who trade in [competing goods]." For many years, however, the Miller-Tydings Act of 1937 permitted the States to authorize resale price maintenance. The goal of that statute was to allow the States to protect small retail establishments that Congress thought might otherwise be driven from the marketplace by large-volume discounters. But in 1975 that congressional permission was rescinded. The Consumer Goods Pricing Act of 1975 repealed the Miller-Tydings Act and related legislations. Consequently, the Sherman Act's ban on resale price maintenance now applies to fair trade contracts unless an industry or program enjoys a special antitrust immunity.

California's system for wine pricing plainly constitutes resale price maintenance in violation of the Sherman Act. The wine producer holds the power to prevent price competition by dictating the prices charged by wholesalers. As Mr. Justice Hughes pointed out in *Dr. Miles,* such vertical control destroys horizontal competition as effectively as if wholesalers "formed a combination and endeavored to establish the same restrictions . . . by agreement with each other."

We must consider whether the State's involvement in the price-setting program is sufficient to establish antitrust immunity under *Parker v. Brown* (1943).

Our decisions establish two standards for antitrust immunity under *Parker v. Brown*. First, the challenged restraint must be "one clearly articulated and affirmatively expressed as state policy"; second, the policy must be "actively supervised" by the State itself. *City of Lafayette v. Louisiana Power & Light Co.* (1978). The California system for wine pricing satisfies the first standard. The legislative policy is forthrightly stated and clear in its purpose to permit resale price maintenance. The program, however, does not meet the second requirement for *Parker* immunity. The State simply authorizes price-setting and enforces the prices established by private parties. The State neither establishes prices nor reviews the reasonableness of the price schedules; nor does it regulate the terms of fair trade contracts. The State does not monitor market conditions or engage in any "pointed reexamination" of the program. The national policy in favor of competition cannot be thwarted by casting such a gauzy cloak of state involvement over what is essentially a private price-fixing arrangement. As *Parker* teaches, "[A] state does not give immunity to those who violate the Sherman Act by authorizing them to violate it, or by declaring that their action is lawful. . . ."

Why would a company wish to engage in a program to fix the price at which its product is resold? Normally, one would assume that a manufacturer would want more competition at the retail level. With more competition at the retail level, the manufacturer would sell more of its product. If the manufacturer requires its dealers to sell at a minimum price, its retail sales may be depressed. There are, however, several reasons a manufacturer might attempt to set retail prices: (1) the manufacturer may wish to protect its dealers from price cutters; (2) the manufacturer may wish to cultivate a prestige image for its product by selling the product at a high price; (3) retailers may wish to have the manufacturer set a high resale price in order to increase their profits (a dealer cartel); (4) price setting may encourage retailers to increase their promotional expenses (dealer services); or (5) resale price maintenance programs may help a manufacturer that has entered into a price-fixing agreement with other manufacturers.

If a price cutter handles a company's products, many consumers will purchase the product from the discounter. Local retailers may then drop the company's product from their shelves, as they need a sufficient volume of sales in order to profitably stock a particular line of products.

Given the right product—that is, one which consumers will pay a premium price for over other, similar products—retailers will earn large profits if the manufacturer sets a minimum price for its product. If all manufacturers set a minimum price for their products, retailers will earn large profits.

Another rationale for minimum prices at the retail level is to enhance a company's image. If a perfume sells for fifty dollars an ounce at a prestige store, few manufacturers wish to see that product sold at a discounter for five dollars an ounce.

A manufacturer might engage in setting the resale price of its products if all the manufacturers in the industry have entered into an illegal price-fixing agreement. If four manufacturers sold all the electric irons in the United States, they could enter into an agreement to sell their irons at a certain price to distributors or retailers. But what if one of the parties to a price-fixing scheme decided not to abide by the scheme? Suppose this firm sells to buyers at a price lower than that at which the other manufacturers agreed to sell to their customers. If there were a number of different prices charged by retailers, then it would be more difficult to determine that one of the manufacturers was failing to comply with the unlawful agreement to fix prices. If retailers cut their prices, it would be unclear whether a manufacturer had cut its price to the retailers, or the retailers had cut prices on their own. A retail price maintenance agreement makes it clear that if Company X's retailers cut their prices, Company X must have cut its prices to its retailers. The members of the group that agreed to fix prices would then know they must take some action to force Company X to stop cutting its price to the retailers.

The dealer cartel is also often cited as a reason for the manufacturer's setting a resale price. The dealers might ask the manufacturer to act as their agent in administering the cartel by fixing a uniform resale price. Of course, dealers could enter into such an agreement on their own, but the agreement can be more easily enforced if the manufacturer agrees to it.

One argument that has been vigorously asserted as a justification for a price-fixing scheme is the dealer service theory. If a price is set at a given level, it may encourage retailers to compete by providing more services to purchasers. Many products require substantial retailer service. For example, an automobile manufacturer may wish for its dealerships to give customers a great deal of presale attention. If the price were fixed, the dealers might compete by giving customers more services (often called point-of-sale services).

As none of these reasons for price maintenance schemes strikes the courts as fair, the courts normally invalidate retail price-fixing agreements.

While today these agreements often violate the Sherman Act, at one point Congress permitted such retail price setting by manufacturers. The McGuire Act and the Miller-Tydings amendment to the Sherman Act allowed states to adopt fair trade acts. These acts granted an exemption to the Sherman Act if a state passed a fair trade law. In a state with such a law, manufacturers could require retailers to resell a product at a certain minimum price. The Consumer Goods Pricing Act of 1975 repealed the states' ability to pass fair trade laws.

Colgate
Doctrine

One last device should be mentioned before leaving the resale price maintenance area. It is possible for a company to attempt to maintain retail prices by announcing it will not deal with customers who resell the product at a price different from that set by the manufacturer. The Supreme Court announced this rule in *United States* v. *Colgate Co.* (1919). The **Colgate doctrine** permits a unilateral announcement by a manufacturer that it will not deal with customers who fail to abide by the price set by the manufacturer. The manufacturer may terminate dealers who sell above the stated price.

The Court in *Colgate* basically recognized the right of a company to exercise its own independent judgment as to whom it would deal with—assuming the company has no purpose to create or maintain a monopoly. *Colgate* has been criticized because the Court really did not offer a sound economic argument for adopting such a rule. The *Colgate* doctrine creates an exception, for no apparent economic reason, to the resale price rule adopted by the Court.

The *Colgate* doctrine has been greatly limited by other decisions, but it remains a valid doctrine today. In *United States* v. *Parke, Davis & Co.* (1960), the court held that a manufacturer may not threaten to cut off wholesalers who distribute to retailers selling below the price specified by the manufacturer. The effect of the *Parke, Davis* case is that a manufacturer may avail itself of the *Colgate* doctrine only when it is selling directly to retailers. Even then, of course, the manufacturer may only announce it will not sell to retailers who sell below a certain price, and terminate retailers who sell below the stated price.

In *Monsanto Co.* v. *Spray-Rite Service Co.,* the Supreme Court reaffirmed the validity of the *Colgate* doctrine. So long as a manufacturer acts independently when it announces its resale prices and its refusal to deal with those who fail to comply, it acts lawfully.

Generally, a company can safely warn retailers in advance of a sale that it will not deal with anyone who undercuts its recommended prices. But any action taken by a company to enforce that warning—threatening retailers, for example—can run afoul of the law. This doctrine is not precisely clear. A company must act with *extreme* caution when making such statements.

GROUP BOYCOTTS

A business that does not intend to create or maintain a monopoly may choose the parties with whom it deals. While a simple unilateral refusal to deal with another business does not violate the antitrust laws, a business must take care not to act in concert with other businesses when it decides not to deal with a given company.

A good example of unlawful concerted activity would be if a group of wholesalers asked retailers not to buy from wholesaler X, and threatened the retailers that if they bought from wholesaler X, the other wholesalers would stop selling to them. Such an action would constitute a classic boycott and is unlawful per se. Another example would be if a group of retailers asked some manufacturers not to sell to a retailer—with the sole desire of limiting competition at the retail level. Such a conspiracy would be illegal per se.

In order to be covered by this Per Se Rule, the activity in question must fit within the definition of a boycott. Concerted activity in which the parties agree not to deal with a company or companies or demand that others not deal with a company or companies will be treated as a classic boycott when the purpose of the conspirators is to deprive a competitor of a needed resource and make it harder for the competitor to compete. Such concerted activity constitutes a per se violation of the Sherman Act. The courts regard such activity as inherently harmful to competition.

Even the United States Supreme Court has acknowledged that there is considerable confusion about the operation of the Per Se Rule against group boycotts. The Court has applied a Per Se Rule when a firm (or firms) either directly denies or persuades or coerces suppliers or customers to deny relationships that the competitors need to survive. The boycott often cuts off access to a supply facility or market necessary to enable the boycotted firm to compete, and frequently the boycotting firm possesses a dominant position in the relevant market. Furthermore, the activities of the boycotting firm or firms do not enhance overall efficiency and make markets more competitive.

Fashion Originators' Guild of America v. *Federal Trade Commission* (1941) is a classic boycott case. Members of the guild agreed, in order to drive certain manufacturers out of business, to refuse to deal with retailers who stocked the boycotted manufacturers' products. The guild agreed to this course of action because the boycotted manufacturers were copying original dress designs and selling them at a lower price. These designs could not be copyrighted or patented. The guild members controlled thirty-eight percent of all women's garment wholesaling and sixty percent of the wholesaling of all high-priced garments. *Fashion Originators' Guild* thus involved a classic boycott where competitors were being driven out of the market. The Supreme Court ruled that this combination violated the Sherman and Clayton Acts.

A variety of other situations may fall within the boycott definition, but these arrangements always involve an agreement not to deal with someone when the purpose of the conspirators is to deprive a competitor of a needed resource and make it harder for the competitor to compete.

Absent a showing that the boycotting firm or firms possessed market power or unique access to a business element necessary for effective competition, the courts should apply a Rule of Reason analysis and not the Per Se Rule. Of course, to be safe, a business would be wise not to engage in any boycott, thus avoiding the possibility of being prosecuted for violating the antitrust laws.

TYING CONTRACTS

A seller must be careful when it refuses to deal with another business, and it must also exercise caution if it asks the buyer to purchase certain goods in addition to those the buyer wants.

The antitrust laws may be violated if the seller of a product the buyer wants (the tying product) requires the buyer, as a condition of purchasing the tying product, to also purchase another product (the tied product). Suppose the lessor of a computer (the tying product) requires persons leasing the seller's computer to use only punch cards (the tied product) made and sold by the seller. The Supreme Court ruled against International Business Machines Corporation in just such a case. The Court stated that such an agreement violated the antitrust laws.

Tying agreements are outlawed by Section 3 of the Clayton Act, which states:

> It shall be unlawful for any person engaged in commerce, in the course of such commerce, to lease or make a sale of contract for sale of goods, wares, merchandise, machinery, supplies, or other commodities, whether patented or unpatented, for use, consumption, or resale within the U.S. . . . on the condition, agreement, or understanding that the lessee or purchaser thereof shall not use or deal in the goods . . . of a competitor or competitors of the . . . seller, where the

effect of such lease, sale, or contract for sale or such condition, agreement, or understanding may be to substantially lessen competition or tend to create a monopoly in any line of commerce.

It should be noted that tying agreements may also violate Section 1 of the Sherman Act. Section 3 of the Clayton Act applies only to the sale or lease of a commodity on the condition that the lessee or purchaser not use or deal in commodities of seller's or lessor's competitors. If a tying arrangement deals with the sale of services, suit must be brought on the basis of Section 1 of the Sherman Act.

In many cases, the Court has indicated that a given tying agreement is per se unlawful under one or both of these acts. However, perhaps tying agreements should be viewed as governed by a complex Per Se Rule.

Certainly not every sale is illegal in which the seller conditions the sale of a product on the purchase of some other product. If a tailor requires the purchaser of a suit to also buy a vest with a suit, the tailor has not violated the antitrust laws.

The following elements would seem necessary for a plaintiff to establish an unlawful tying agreement: (1) that the defendant possess economic power over the tying product; and (2) that a not unsubstantial amount of commerce in the tied product be involved. Even if both these conditions have been met, the defendant probably has a good defense if it can show that the purpose of the tie-in is to protect the goodwill of the tying product.

In some cases, such as when the seller has a patent or copyright, the tying product has been regarded as sufficiently unique to give rise to a presumption of economic power.

Purpose of Tying

Some economists have suggested that one of the purposes of a tie-in is often to facilitate price discrimination. What a seller might do is to tie the sale of a product that the buyer wants (the tying product) to a product the buyer does not necessarily want (the tied product). Why would a seller do this? Probably the seller intends to charge a higher-than-market price for the tied product. If the seller intends to sell a great deal of the tied product to the buyer, this may by a very profitable arrangement for the seller. Furthermore, it may enable the seller to discriminate in price among different buyers.

An excellent example of this is the *International Salt* (1947) case. International Salt leased certain machines on which it held a patent (the tying product) to customers, but required the lessees to purchase only International Salt (the tied product) as a condition of receiving the machines. The Supreme Court held that this arrangement violated Section 3 of the Clayton Act because International Salt controlled a major portion of the market for salt and was attempting to monopolize the market.

Consider the effect of such an arrangement. If International Salt charged the same price to three customers for a machine, it could in effect discriminate in price among them because the buyers would not use the same amount of salt. Suppose A intended to use one thousand pounds of salt, B intended to use two thousand pounds of salt, and C intended to use three thousand pounds of salt. If International Salt charged a higher-than-market price for the salt it sold to A, B, and C, they would in effect be paying different prices for the machine. Suppose the price for salt is ten cents per pound regularly, but International Salt charges its customers fifteen cents per pound. At the end of the year, A will have paid $150 for salt it could have purchased for $100, B will have paid $300 for salt it could have purchased for $200, and C will have paid $450 for salt it could have purchased for $300. In effect, A has paid $50 more for the salt than it could have been purchased for on the open market, B has paid $100 more, and C has paid $150 more.

The following case discusses the question of whether the defendants had enough economic power in the market for the tying product to constitute an unlawful tying conspiracy.

Baxley-DeLamar Monuments v. American Cemetery Association
United States Court of Appeals, Eighth Circuit
843 F.2d 1154 (1988)

Baxley-DeLamar alleged that various cemeteries and the cemetery trade association conspired to tie the sale of grave lots (the tying product) to the sale of grave memorials and memorial installation services (the tied product). They adopted rules that either required cemetery lot customers to buy their memorials and installation services from the cemeteries in question or as a practical matter made it too difficult or expensive to buy the memorials and services from anyone else. Together, the cemeteries controlled fifty-seven percent of the potential memorial sales in Pulaski and Saline counties. As a result, Baxley had much lower sales in these cemeteries than in other cemeteries without such restrictive practices. The district court held that the allegation that the defendants controlled only fifty-seven percent of the relevant cemetery lot market demonstrated that the defendants did not have sufficient market power in the cemetery lot market to constitute an illegal tying arrangement.

The district court rules for the defendants. The court of appeals reversed.

Gibson, Circuit Judge

Baxley-DeLamar challenges the district court's conclusion that it did not allege facts showing appellees had sufficient market power in the cemetery lot market to form the basis for illegal tying. In *Jefferson Parish Hospital District No. 2 v. Hyde,* the Supreme Court characterized economic power in the tying market as the *sine qua non* of illegal tying:

[T]he essential characteristic of an invalid tying arrangement lies in the seller's exploitation of its control over the tying product to force the buyer into the purchase of a tied product that the buyer either did not want at all, or might have preferred to purchase elsewhere on different terms.

Economic power over the tying market can be established by proof either of a large enough share of the relevant market in the tying product to give the seller some power over the market or of such uniqueness or desirability of the tying product as to give the seller of the tying product an advantage other competitors in that market cannot meet. Cemetery lots have been considered unique as all land is unique, and this uniqueness in conjunction with other factors contributing to market power has been held sufficient to make possible illicit tying. In addition, Baxley-DeLamar alleged that once some family members are buried in a certain cemetery, competition is curtailed with respect to the other family members by family members' desire to be buried in the same place. This allegation suggests that cemetery lots may be unique in a way that gives appellee cemeteries special leverage. In this case the alleged collective market share of the appellee cemeteries in the cemetery lot market ("a majority") is higher than that in *Rosebrough II* (22%). The combination of uniqueness of the lots and the appellees' alleged market share convinces us the district court erred in determining Baxley-DeLamar did not allege economic power in the tying market adequately to survive the motion to dismiss.

The next section of the book deals with another important antitrust problem—the power of the FTC to regulate businesses.

SECTION 5 OF THE FEDERAL TRADE COMMISSION ACT

Many actions violate the spirit of the antitrust laws but for some technical reason are beyond the reach of the government under the Sherman Act or Clayton Act. Business practices beyond the reach of the Sherman Act may sometimes be struck down by the FTC acting pursuant to Section 5 of the Federal Trade Commission Act. The FTC possesses power to declare invalid trade practices that conflict with the basic policies of the Sherman and Clayton Acts even though such practices may not actually violate these laws.

The Federal Trade Commission Act and the Clayton Act were passed by Congress in 1914 largely in response to a public outcry for more effective control over big business. One important group that supported the creation of the FTC was those people who feared the effect of big business on competition. They favored more competition. President Wilson put his support behind the strengthening of the law in order to promote competition.

To some extent, the Court's lax enforcement of the Sherman Act served as an impetus for this new legislation. In particular, the Supreme Court's decision in 1911 in the *Standard Oil* case, in which it announced the Rule of Reason, created a great demand for new legislation.

Congress, in Section 5 of the Federal Trade Commission Act, outlawed "unfair methods of competition." Many members of Congress believed that a monopoly could be achieved only through unfair competition and that the nation needed an agency decided to check such unfair practices by business.

Congress thought it would be impossible to define every unfair practice. So, rather than defining "unfair methods of competition," Congress left it up to the FTC to determine what constituted unfairness on a case-by-case basis.

In 1938, Congress passed the Wheeler-Lea amendment to the Federal Trade Commission Act. This added the language "unfair or deceptive acts or practices in commerce." Section 5 of the Federal Trade Commission Act, as amended, asserts that "unfair methods of competition in or affecting commerce, and unfair or deceptive acts or practices in or affecting commerce, are declared unlawful." The goal of Congress in adding this language was to make it clear that it wished to protect not only competition, but also competitors.

As indicated earlier, the FTC may reach conduct that violates the spirit of the Sherman and Clayton acts, and even conduct that is simply unfair. Thus, the reach of Section 5 is much greater than that of the Sherman Act or Clayton Act, and Section 5 may be used by the FTC to reach unfair trade practices in general.

MERGERS

Types of Mergers

A merger refers to the joining together of two companies that previously operated as separate entities, whereby one company absorbs the other and continues to exist, while the absorbed company ceases to exist as a separate entity. The courts have identified several types of mergers: (1) **horizontal mergers** involve a merger between two companies that previously competed with each other; (2) **vertical mergers** join together a customer and a supplier; and (3) all other mergers are classified as **conglomerate mergers.** If General Motors merged with Ford, the action would be referred to as a horizontal merger. These companies compete in the sale of automobiles. On the other hand, if General Motors merged with USX, the courts would call this type of merger a vertical merger. General Motors purchases steel and USX makes steel. Suppose, instead, that American Tobacco merged with Continental Can. Since neither company competes with the other—one produces tobacco, the other produces cans—and neither buys or sells to the other, the courts call such a merger a conglomerate merger.

In the 1960s, the merger law became more restrictive. The Supreme Court invalidated a number of mergers. More recently, the Court has upheld a number of mergers.

As noted in Chapter 23, the public sentiment against the growth of big business led to the adoption of the Sherman Act in 1890. The Sherman Act outlaws monopolies, attempts to monopolize, and restraints of trade.

Congress soon decided the antitrust laws needed further strengthening, so in 1914 it passed the Clayton Act, which outlawed certain types of mergers. Congress amended the Clayton Act in 1950 to make it more difficult for firms to lawfully merge.

Clayton Act

The *primary* source of law in the area of mergers today is Section 7 of the Clayton Act. The act currently reads as follows:

> [N]o corporation engaged in commerce shall acquire, directly or indirectly, the whole or any part of the stock or other share capital and no corporation . . . shall acquire the whole or any part of the assets of another corporation engaged also in

commerce, where in any line of commerce in any section of the country, the effect of such acquisition may be substantially to lessen competition, or to tend to create a monopoly.

The language, as it presently stands, comes in part from the original Clayton Act passed in 1914 and in part from the Cellar-Kefauver amendment to Section 7 in 1950. In 1950, Congress deemed it necessary to clarify the law in this area. At one point, the courts applied Section 7 only to horizontal mergers. The Cellar-Kefauver amendment clarified Congress's wish to extend the act to vertical mergers as well. The amendment also extended the act to cover not only acquisitions of the stock of a company, but also acquisitions of the assets of a business.

As the language indicates, Congress wished to reach certain mergers *before* they had an actual anticompetitive impact on trade. Section 7 is designed to reach any merger that *may* substantially lessen competition or that *tends* to create a monopoly. Exactly when a merger may have an anticompetitive effect is not always clear. Therefore, while the Sherman Act requires proof of an actual and substantial adverse effect on competition, the Clayton Act requires only that the action create a probable substantial lessening of competition or a tendency to create a monopoly. The Supreme Court in the 1960s applied Section 7 to a number of cases. Some commentators argue that the Court acted overzealously. The Court arguably applied Section 7 to any merger with even a *possibility* of an anticompetitive effect, as opposed to a merger with a *probable* anticompetitive effect.

Product and Geographic Markets

When analyzing a case under Section 7 of the Clayton Act, two important determinations must be made. The court must determine the *relevant product market* (line of commerce) and the *relevant geographic market*. If a court very narrowly defines these markets, such a definition may have the effect of making the merger look detrimental to competition. Suppose a court defines the relevant product market in a case as rolled steel, as opposed to all types of steel. If two companies that manufacture rolled steel tried to merge, the categorization of the product market as rolled steel makes the merger look more anticompetitive than it would if the court selected all types of steel as the relevant product market. These firms' percentage of the total steel business would be much smaller than their percentage control over the rolled steel business. Likewise, if a defendant operates in St. Louis and the court defines the geographic market as the St. Louis metropolitan area, the defendant's percentage of the business in the relevant geographic market is much larger than the percentage it would have if the market were defined as the nation.

In the *General Dynamics* (1974) case the government challenged the acquisition of the stock of United Electric Coal Companies by Material Service Corporation and its successor, General Dynamics Corporation. The government argued that the takeover substantially lessened competition in the sale of coal. The government introduced evidence that the coal industry was becoming increasingly concentrated. The court decided that because most coal is sold by way of long-term contracts to utility companies, a company's reserves are the best measure of its ability to compete. United had depleted its reserves, and most of its resources were committed under long-term contracts. Therefore, as United was in no position to compete with other companies for the sale of coal, even though it had a large market share, its acquisition by Material Service Corporation would not substantially lessen competition.

The Supreme Court in the 1960s placed its primary emphasis on *market share*. In the 1970s, the Court began to show a broader concern with other factors.

The *General Dynamics* case marks the beginning of the Supreme Court's willingness to consider factors other than market share in analyzing the legality of a merger. Such factors as the ease of entry, the vigor of the industry, the demand for the products, and the characteristics of each firm are now considered in evaluating a merger under Section 7 of the Clayton Act.

SUMMARY

Section 2 of the Sherman Act outlaws monopolies, as well as attempts to monopolize. When a court is confronted with the charge that a firm allegedly has violated Section 2, it must make two important determinations: It must decide what the relevant geographic and product markets are for the purposes of the suit. How the court characterizes these markets will have a great effect on whether a firm is found guilty of violating the law.

Not every monopoly is unlawful—just unreasonable ones. A firm that has monopoly power in the relevant market which was not thrust upon it probably has violated the Sherman Act. It is possible that a firm which arrives at a monopoly position as a result of aggressive competition has not violated the act; however, there is no definitive Supreme Court decision on this point yet.

It is also unlawful to unreasonably restrain trade. The Court has created two rules in this area. Certain types of activities are illegal per se; other conduct is analyzed under the Rule of Reason. Price fixing is a good example of an activity that is always in violation of the Sherman Act. Any attempt to fix prices with another firm violates the law. Attempts by a firm to control the price at which the product it sells are resold are governed by a more complex rule but are generally held to be unlawful. A manufacturer, however, may unilaterally announce the price at which it wants the products resold and may terminate customers who fail to abide by the price specified by the manufacturer.

Sellers are also restricted from entering into most tying agreements. If a seller requires buyers to purchase one product only if they buy some other product sold by the seller, such agreements typically are treated as unlawful per se. Group boycotts also are generally treated as per se violations of the anti-trust laws.

The Federal Trade Commission Act also places restraints upon the manner of conducting business. Certain practices which do not technically violate the Sherman Act or Clayton Act can be held to be violations of the FTC Act.

When two companies that previously operated as separate entities join together, the transaction is called a *merger*. The courts typically use one of three terms in referring to mergers: *horizontal, vertical,* or *conglomerate.*

Because many persons regarded mergers as threatening to the economy, as well as a possible threat to democratic principles, Congress passed the Clayton Act in 1914. Section 7 of the Clayton Act is the primary source of law in this area. The Clayton Act was amended in 1950 to strengthen its prohibitions on mergers.

In identifying whether a merger violates the Clayton Act, a court must first identify the relevant product and geographic markets for purposes of the merger. Once these markets have been determined, a court decides whether a given merger may substantially lessen competition or tends to create a monopoly. If so, the court will find that the merger violates Section 7. At one point, the courts placed almost exclusive reliance on the market shares of the merging firms. Today the courts look at a number of other factors, such as ease of entry in a market and the vigor of an industry, in deciding whether a merger will have an anticompetitive effect.

REVIEW QUESTIONS

1. Define the following terms:
   a. *Colgate* doctrine
   b. Conglomerate merger
   c. Horizontal merger
   d. Monopoly
   e. Oligopoly
   f. Resale price maintenance
   g. Restraint of trade
   h. Rule of Reason
   i. Vertical merger

2. What does a court look at in determining whether a merger violates Section 7 of the Clayton Act? What must the government demonstrate?

3. In determining whether a company has unlawfully monopolized an industry, do courts today emphasize bad acts?

4. Initially, the Supreme Court ruled that the Sherman Act covered all restraints of trade. What is the practical effect of the *Standard Oil* case on Section 1 of the act?

5. What arguments would you advance in favor of accepting ruinous competition as a defense in a price-fixing case? What counterarguments might be asserted? Why did the Supreme Court accept this defense in the *Appalachian Coal* case?

6. If one of a dozen food stores in a community refuses to sell flour unless purchasers also buy sugar, is this an illegal tying arrangement if other sellers offer to sell flour by itself?

7. What is the *Grinnell* two-part test for monopolization?

8. Explain the difference between the Rule of Reason and the Per Se Rule as they are applied to restraints of trade.

9. Is it possible for the Federal Trade Commission to prohibit activities under Section 5 of the Federal Trade Commission Act that could not be outlawed under the Clayton Act or Sherman Act?

10. Hand Tools Corporation gradually grew larger and larger. It availed itself of every opportunity, and through aggressive competition, gradually acquired ninety percent of the market for plumber's tools in the United States. What type of analysis would a court go through in order to determine if such a business is an unlawful monopoly?

11. International Grocery Stores entered into an agreement with Acme Grocery Stores. International agreed to open stores only in the eastern half of the United States in return for Acme agreeing to open stores only in the western half of the United states. Is such an agreement lawful?

12. National Oil Company entered into an agreement with United States Oil Company. The companies agreed to purchase gasoline on the spot market in order to stabilize the price of gasoline. They did not intend to suppress competition. Is such an agreement lawful?

13. Elite Perfumes entered into a contract with all retailers handling its products that required all purchasers of its perfumes to charge at least one hundred dollars per ounce for its product. Elite Perfume wishes to force all retailers handling its products to charge a high price in order to keep any one from selling its products cheaply. Is such an agreement lawful?

14. Chocolate Candy Company announced a policy that it would not deal with any retailer who charged less than the prices suggested by Chocolate for its product. Discount Corporation charged less than the suggested price. Chocolate thereafter refused to sell its candy to Discount. Is this lawful?

15. International Business Machines leased its computer to lessees on the condition that lessees use only IBM punch cards. IBM controlled eighty-one percent of the industry at the time. IBM claimed it needed this agreement to prevent patent infringement on the machine. Has it violated the antitrust laws?

16. Klor's alleged that a competing retailer, Broadway-Hale, had placed pressure on certain manufacturers to get the manufacturers not to deal with Klor's. Some of the manufacturers refused to sell to Klor's. Broadway-Hale did not deny the charge. Does this action violate the antitrust laws?

17. Between 1933 and 1948, the *Lorain Journal,* a newspaper, was the only local business disseminating news and advertising in a small Ohio town. In 1948, a small radio station was started in a nearby town. In order to destroy the radio station as a competitor and to regain its pre-1948 monopoly over the mass dissemination of all news and advertising, the *Journal* refused to sell advertising to advertisers who bought air time from the radio station. The station argued that this was an unlawful attempt to monopolize in violation of Section 2 of the Sherman Act. The publisher argued that it had a right to select its customers and to refuse to deal with other firms. Who is correct?

18. Regal was a wholly owned subsidiary of Copperweld. It is possible for Regal to be found guilty of having conspired with Copperweld to violate Section 1 of the Sherman Act?

19. Monsanto on several occasions contacted distributors that were selling Monsanto herbicides below the price suggested by Monsanto. Monsanto advised the price cutters that if they did not maintain the suggested price, they would not receive adequate supplies of Monsanto's herbicides. When one distributor refused to agree, Monsanto complained to the distributor's parent company. The parent instructed its subsidiary to comply, and the distributor informed Monsanto it would charge the suggested price. Has Monsanto violated Section 1 of the Sherman Act?

Part 8

International Regulation of Business Activity

CHAPTER 25
The International Legal Environment of Business

CHAPTER 25

The International Legal Environment of Business

- Problems Associated with Selling Goods in an International Environment
- Activities by American Companies Overseas
- Legal Disputes with Foreign States
- Developing a Sales Organization Abroad
- Extraterritorial Application of U.S. Laws

Competition, product markets, and supply sources are now international in scope, and even domestically oriented firms are fundamentally affected by international economic pressures. Thus, an awareness of the basic laws associated with international business transactions has become increasingly important.

In no other area of business are legal considerations so central to the success of an enterprise. American multinational businesses must deal with three sets of laws—international, American, and the domestic law of the foreign country in which the firm operates. We focus here on international commercial law and American law. While the domestic legal codes of countries around the world are important, they are too many and too diverse to be considered in this chapter.

But what is international commercial law? Is it just a consensus on legal norms, or the laws of the United Nations, or both? International commercial law is the product of consensus among trading nations that culminated in various unilateral, bilateral, and multilateral government accords and voluntary non-government agreements. Thus, there are numerous international agreements, a few of which we will review, that regulate international commerce.

PROBLEMS ASSOCIATED WITH SELLING GOODS IN AN INTERNATIONAL ENVIRONMENT

Documentary Credits

One of the most important agreements in international commerce is the International Chamber of Commerce's (ICC) Uniform Customs and Practice for Documentary Credits. Issued in 1933 and revised periodically, it establishes a foundation for standardizing worldwide transactions. It is the product of nongovernment action and is based on business practice. As of 1974, banks in 156 countries adhered to its provisions.

A **documentary credit,** also called a letter of credit, is a conditional bank payment instrument. The buyer requests his or her bank to pay the seller or the seller's bank at sight (upon seeing), or at some future date, a stated amount upon receipt of the required documents, assuming the individual documents list the prescribed information (i.e., are ''correct'' documents) and arrive within the prescribed time. The terms of the documentary credit in regard to the documents, their content, and the time limit must be exact and followed to the letter; otherwise, the buyer can refuse shipment. The documentary credit and the underlying sales contract exist separately. Thus, the buyer's bank reviews the presented documents and not the original sales contract before paying the stated sum. As long as the seller delivers the correct documents within the stipulated time, the buyer's bank must pay the seller or the seller's bank.

All documentary credits must indicate which documents are to be presented in order for the seller to be paid. Typically, a transport document listing the goods, the companies involved, and other details is agreed upon. Figure 25.1 demonstrates the process followed when utilizing a letter of credit.

An example will help us better understand the cycle of documentary credits. Assume an American liquor importer wishes to special-order thirty thousand kegs of Wetzlarer Brau from Sabine AG in Wetzlar, Germany, for a client who is celebrating his graduation. The importer has never dealt with Sabine before and thus desires the security of a documentary credit. Sabine in turn requests that the letter of credit be irrevocable for its own protection. Thus, the buyer, the American importer, requests its bank, Americanbank, to establish an irrevocable documentary letter of credit for the seller, Sabine. Americanbank telexes its partner bank, Germanbank, that the buyer opened a letter of credit. Germanbank, which is also Sabine's local bank, informs Sabine that the buyer has established the letter of credit.

To fulfill the terms of the credit, Sabine must deliver the transportation document, an air waybill, and an insurance certificate that states that the beer is insured against spoilage. In addition, the buyer stipulates a certificate of origin. It must state that the beer comes from Wetzlar, Germany. Further, Sabine must submit a certificate of inspection, which assures the buyer of receipt of the one and only Wetzlarer Brau. The credit requires that the thirty thousand kegs be shipped by air two days before graduation. Upon delivery of correct documents, Germanbank will pay Sabine at sight.

A week before graduation, Sabine delivers the prescribed documents. All are predated two days before graduation. Germanbank, however, refuses payment because the air waybill states that one hundred thousand barrels instead of thirty thousand kegs are being shipped. Sabine then requests the air carrier to change the air waybill, after which Sabine resubmits the documents. Germanbank reviews the documents again and determines that it now has correct documents. Germanbank in turn sends the documents to Americanbank and requests payment. After examining the documents, Americanbank pays Germanbank and informs the American importer that Sabine submitted correct documents. (Note

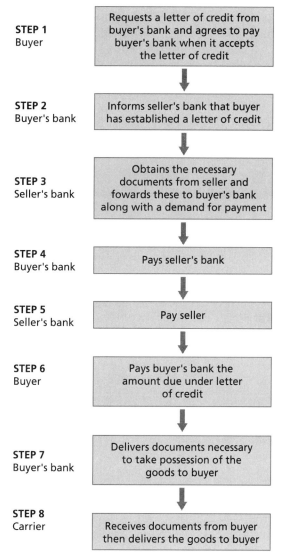

STEP 1
Buyer

Requests a letter of credit from buyer's bank and agrees to pay buyer's bank when it accepts the letter of credit

STEP 2
Buyer's bank

Informs seller's bank that buyer has established a letter of credit

STEP 3
Seller's bank

Obtains the necessary documents from seller and fowards these to buyer's bank along with a demand for payment

STEP 4
Buyer's bank

Pays seller's bank

STEP 5
Seller's bank

Pay seller

STEP 6
Buyer

Pays buyer's bank the amount due under letter of credit

STEP 7
Buyer's bank

Delivers documents necessary to take possession of the goods to buyer

STEP 8
Carrier

Receives documents from buyer then delivers the goods to buyer

Figure 25.1 Method of Payment with a Letter of Credit

that the bank's legal department does not usually review the documents. The review is performed by the bank's staff.) Thus, the American importer owes Americanbank and must pay its debt to obtain the documents so that the shipment can be claimed from the carrier.

Documentary credits offer both the buyer and seller a great deal of convenience and security. They need only deal with their local bank. The banks provide advice and assistance throughout the process. The buyer is assured that no payment will be made until the exact goods arrive, and the seller is certain that the goods will not be delivered to the buyer until payment is received. Thus, in a world in which buyer and seller often do not know each other, documentary credits provide the perfect vehicle for international trade.

The following case deals with a situation in which the court declined to force the bank to pay a letter of credit.

Sztejn v. J. Henry Schroder Banking Corporation
Supreme Court, Special Term, New York County
31 N.Y.S.2d 631 (1941)

Chester Charles Sztejn contracted with Transea Traders, Ltd., a corporation located in Lucknow, India, for the purchase of a quantity of bristles. To pay for the bristles, he contracted with J. Henry Schroder for the issuance of an irrevocable letter of credit to Transea. The letter of credit was delivered to Transea. Transea placed fifty cases of material on board a steamship and received a bill of lading and invoices. The documents described the bristles called for by the letter of credit. Sztejn asserted that in fact the cases were loaded with worthless cow hair. Transea drew a draft under the letter of credit to the order of the Chartered Bank of India and delivered the draft and the fraudulent documents to the bank for collection. The bank presented the draft along with the documents to Schroder for payment.

Sztejn argued that because Schroder had been notified of the seller's fraud before it made payment to the seller, the letter of credit and drafts should be declared null and void. The court ruled for Sztejn.

Shientag, Justice

It is well established that a letter of credit is independent of the primary contract of sale between the buyer and the seller. The issuing bank agrees to pay upon presentation of documents, not goods. This rule is necessary to preserve the efficiency of the letter of credit as an instrument for the financing of trade. One of the chief purposes of the letter of credit is to furnish the seller with a ready means of obtaining prompt payment for his merchandise. It would be a most unfortunate interference with business transactions if a bank before honoring drafts drawn upon it was obliged or even allowed to go behind the documents, at the request of the buyer and enter into controversies between the buyer and the seller regarding the quality of the merchandise shipped. If the buyer and the seller intended the bank to do this they could have so provided in the letter of credit itself, and in the absence of such a provision, the court will not demand or even permit the bank to delay paying drafts which are proper in form. Of course, the application of this doctrine presupposes that the documents accompanying the draft are genuine and conform in terms to the requirements of the letter of credit.

This is not a controversy between the buyer and seller concerning a mere breach of warranty regarding the quality of the merchandise; on the present motion, it must be assumed that the seller has intentionally failed to ship any goods ordered by the buyer. In such a situation, where the seller's fraud has been called to the bank's attention before the drafts and documents have been presented for payment, the principle of the independence of the bank's obligation under the letter of credit should not be extended to protect the unscrupulous seller. It is true that even though the documents are forged or fraudulent, if the issuing bank has already paid the draft before receiving notice of the seller's fraud, it will be protected if it exercised reasonable diligence before making such payment. However, in the instant action Schroder has received notice of Transea's active fraud before it accepted or paid the draft. The Chartered Bank, which under the allegations of the complaint stands in no better position than Transea, should not be heard to complain because Schroder is not forced to pay the draft accompanied by documents covering a transaction which it has reason to believe is fraudulent.

General Agreement on Tariffs and Trade (GATT)

The first real progress toward a global agreement on tariffs and trade came at the end of World War II. In 1947, the United States and twenty-two other nations completed negotiations on the General Agreement on Tariffs and Trade (**GATT**); today some ninety countries are members of the organization. The signators agreed to trade with all other signators on the same terms. The ultimate goal of the GATT is to reduce tariffs and nontariff trade barriers. The GATT has evolved into a complex framework for regulating trade, as it monitors the flow of thousands of products.

Tariffs are taxes placed on imported goods but not on domestic goods. It is frequently very important how an item being imported into the United States is classified. Products may be classified in various ways. Importers are likely to argue the goods in question should be classified in the manner that will result in the lowest possible duty, as is illustrated by the following case.

James S. Baker (Imports) v. United States
United States Customs Court, Second Division
November 19, 1968

In this case, the plaintiffs argued that two importations of lawn rakes manufactured in Japan should not be classified as "rakes, other" under the United States Tariff Schedules. This classification was subject to an assessment of duty at the rate of 15 per centum ad valorem. They argued that the rakes in question should be classified as "agricultural or horticultural tools" instead, and thus subject to a duty at the rate of only 7.5 per centum ad valorem. The question for the court was whether or not a lawn rake should be classified as an "agricultural or horticultural tool" or as "rakes, other." The court ruled on behalf of the importer that the rakes in question were "horticultural tools."

Rao, Chief Judge

The pertinent statutory provisions read as follows:

Tariff Schedules of the United States, schedule 6, part 3, subpart E:

Drainage tools, scoops, shovels, spades, picks, mattocks, hoes, rakes and forks . . . all the foregoing which are hand tools, and metal parts thereof. . .

Hoes and rakes, and parts thereof:

648.55 Agricultural or horticultural tools, and
parts thereof   7.5 % ad val.
648.57 Other   15.0 % ad val.

We deem it appropriate to resort to legislative history and other available data to determine the intent of Congress with respect to this language.

It is defendant's contention that the term "horticultural" does not embrace those tools used on the lawn, as the caring for and growing of a lawn is not a horticultural pursuit. With this we cannot agree.

In reaching our decision we must determine what Congress has intended by including "horticultural" hoes and rakes in item 648.55.

The following definition of the word "horticulture" is pertinent to the resolution of the issue:

The *Random House Dictionary of the English Language,* unabridged edition, 1966:

1. The cultivation of a garden, orchard, or nursery; the cultivation of flowers, fruits, vegetables, or ornamental plants.

2. The science and art of cultivating such plants.

The common meaning of the term as cited above is undisputed. However, defendant argues that under this definition the care and propagation of a lawn is excluded as not being a horticultural pursuit.

We can find no basis for excluding the care of a lawn from being a horticultural activity. In its treatment of horticulture, the *Encyclopaedia Britannica,* volume 11, page 775, 1947 edition, discusses horticulture and the home. It describes the lawn as "one of the first considerations, since it serves as the floor covering of the living room, so to speak, and is the setting for the buildings and ornamental plantings."

Clearly, the treatment of the lawn in this work leaves us with no doubt that the caring of a lawn may properly be considered a horticultural pursuit. Nor do we believe that Congress intended to exclude lawn rakes from the provision for horticultural tools, as it was set forth in item 648.55.

In view of the foregoing considerations, we hold that the lawn rakes here in issue are horticultural tools within the meaning of item 648.55 of the Tariff Schedules of the United States, and are subjected to at the rate of 7.5 per centum ad valorem. The claim in the protest to that effect is sustained.

Judgment will be entered accordingly.

Nontariff Trade Barriers

Nontariff trade barriers (NTBs) are a serious obstacle to free trade. The following are some example of NTBs. A **quota** is probably the most familiar. It stipulates that only a certain amount of a good will be allowed to enter the country during a given period. By paying a special duty, an importer might be able to import an additional amount above the amount specified by the quota.

Domestic content laws, increasingly used by countries, require that a certain percentage of a good's value be produced in the domestic economy. Such laws enable Japan to manufacture certain products in the United States. *Voluntary restraint agreements* are informal, nonbinding constraints on the foreign producer. For example, Japan has agreed to limit its car exports to this country. This also tends to encourage the foreign producer to manufacture or assemble products in the domestic economy.

Direct investment restrictions often require that a certain portion of a business be domestically owned. In the past, Canada required that businesses be at least partially Canadian. Certain industries are closed to foreigners. For example, entry into the airline industry in the United States is restricted to U.S. nationals.

ACTIVITIES BY AMERICAN COMPANIES OVERSEAS

Contractual Problems

Choice of Law Clause

Often in international contracts, the parties insert a **choice of law clause.** By inserting such a clause, the parties determine the governing law of the contract. For example, the agreement may stipulate English law or the law of the state of New York. New York State law rather than American law is specified because the laws of the fifty states differ.

Common law countries, such as the United States and Great Britain, will usually respect the right of the parties to choose the governing law of the contract. (See Chapter 2 for a discussion of common and civil law.) If the clause stipulates English law, American courts will normally apply English law and vice versa. Civil law countries, for example Germany and France, show less respect for the parties' right to contract and may uphold a choice of law clause only if the contract or the parties bear some connection to the chosen law. Certain Latin American nations, also civil law countries, ignore choice of law clauses completely and apply their own laws to contracts that are performed in their countries.

Choice of Forum Clause

A **choice of forum clause** determines the location of the court or arbitration proceeding. An agreement that stipulates arbitration in London or New York implicitly means that English or New York courts will have jurisdiction in proceedings to compel arbitration or enforce arbitral awards. The United States Supreme Court ruled in *The Bremen* v. *Zapata* (1972) that "the forum clause should control absent a strong showing that it should be set aside. . . ." Thus, the more reasonable a choice of forum clause is, the more likely it is that the courts will uphold the clause in the United States.

Arbitration

A clause in a contract may specify that all disputes concerning the contract will be settled by means of arbitration. Usually, arbitration is preferred to litigation because it circumvents several problems associated with litigation—for example, a tremendous backlog of cases may be before the court, causing long delays.

Ideally, an arbitration clause includes exclusive remedies for all issues so that litigation is completely avoided. In addition, all parties should relinquish the right to pursue the matter in the courts. A single arbitrator is generally best. If one party is domiciled in a common law country and the other in a civil law country, the right to engage in discovery should be included, since civil law codes do not always allow for discovery. The location of the proceeding is extremely important, for local law may determine the applicable procedure and substantive law. An arbitral body, such as the American Arbitration Association, United Nations Committee on International Trade Law, or International Chamber of Commerce, should be stipulated. "Ad hoc" arbitration is also a possibility. In this case, the

Documentation in Contracts

Most lawyers in the United States who draft contracts tend to make them as explicit as possible and try to cover every possible future contingency. This approach is favored because when disputes arise at a later date, the contract clearly specifies how the disagreement will be resolved.

This thorough approach leads, in major transactions, to very complex contracts written in technical legal jargon. Consequently, the average person finds it quite difficult to read through a form contract such as an automobile insurance contract or even a rental car agreement.

In sharp contrast to the American practice of careful documentation is the tendency in most Asian countries to keep contracts short and vague. Obviously, when parties from the United States and Asia get together to draft an agreement, they must engage in fierce negotiations to come to an agreement in light of the radical difference in styles of contracting.

arbitration is administered according to the exact specifications of the parties without regard to any institutional framework.

The International Chamber of Commerce is the oldest international arbitral institution and has established rules and procedures for the arbitration process.

Courts worldwide will usually enforce the orders of arbitrators and judgment awards, even though the arbitration agreement prevents the courts from judging the merits. For the parties to obtain the maximum benefit from arbitration, they must construct an arbitration agreement in advance and with great attention to detail, for this will reduce conflicts and expedite the arbitration process.

The following is a United States Supreme Court case dealing with the enforceability of agreements to arbitrate.

Mitsubishi Motors Corporation v. Soler Chrysler-Plymouth, Inc.
United States Supreme Court
105 S.Ct. 3346 (1985)

Mitsubishi entered into a contract with Soler Chrysler-Plymouth. The contract required arbitration by the Japan Commercial Arbitration Association of all disputes arising with respect to the contract. A dispute arose between the parties, and Mitsubishi brought suit in federal court under the federal Arbitration Act and the Convention on the Recognition and Enforcement of Foreign Arbitral Awards seeking an order to compel arbitration. Soler counterclaimed that Mitsubishi had violated the Sherman Act. The court of appeals ruled that Soler could not be forced to arbitrate its antitrust claim. The United States Supreme Court reversed.

Justice Blackmun

As in *Scherk v. Alberto-Culver Co.*, we conclude that concerns of international comity, respect for the capacities of foreign and transnational tribunals, and sensitivity to the need of the international commercial system for predictability in the resolution of disputes require that we enforce the parties' agreement, even assuming that a contrary result would be forthcoming in a domestic context.

Even before *Scherk*, this Court had recognized the utility of forum-selection clauses in international transactions. *Scherk* establishes a strong presumption in favor of enforcement of freely negotiated contractual choice-of-forum provisions. Here, as in *Scherk*, that presumption is reinforced by the emphatic federal policy in favor of arbitral dispute resolution. And at least since this Nation's accession in 1970 to the Convention, and the implementation of the Convention in the same year by amendment of the federal Arbitration Act, that federal policy applies with special force in the field of international commerce.

There is no reason to assume at the outset of the dispute that international arbitration will not provide an adequate mechanism. To be sure, the international arbitral tribunal owes no prior allegiance to the legal norms of particular states; hence, it has no direct obligation to vindicate their statutory dictates. The tribunal, however, is bound to effectuate the intentions of the parties. Where the parties have agreed that the arbitral body is to decide a defined set of claims which includes, as in these cases, those arising from the application of American antitrust law, the tribunal therefore should be bound to decide that dispute in accord with the national law giving rise to the claim.

Having permitted the arbitration to go forward, the national courts of the United States will have the opportunity at the award enforcement stage to ensure that the legitimate interest in the enforcement of the antitrust laws has been addressed. The Convention reserves to each signatory country the right to refuse enforcement of an award where the recognition or enforcement of the award would be contrary to the public policy of that country. While the efficacy of the arbitral process requires that substantive review at the award-enforcement stage remain minimal, it would not require intrusive inquiry to ascertain that the tribunal took cognizance of the antitrust claims and actually decided them.

Accordingly, we require this representative of the American business community to honor its bargain, by holding this agreement to arbitrate enforceable . . . in accord with the explicit provisions of the Arbitration Act.

International Law: Problems of Communication

Attorneys want to help their clients communicate with other people. A well-drafted contract, for example, can help eliminate disagreements arising between the parties at a later date. However, parties often find it difficult to understand even a well-drafted contract because of the complexity of the English language. Two persons may sincerely interpret words, phrases, or entire paragraphs in a totally different manner. In such a case, the parties probably must turn to the courts to resolve such differences of opinion.

Even within English-speaking countries, different words often mean different things. For example, in the United States we use the words *drugstore, truck, line*, and *elevator* to mean the same things as the words *chemist, lorry, queue*, and *lift* in Britain. A man who goes to England needs to learn very quickly to ask for the gents room rather than the bathroom.

If the parties to a transaction speak two or more languages, the usual problems of communication are simply compounded. In such a case, someone must translate all oral and written communications for the parties. In the course of such translations, the translators may create misunderstandings.

Joint Ventures

Joint venture is a descriptive term rather than a legal one. Often joint ventures take the form of a corporation in which each partner has a proportionate interest. They can carry out one-time projects, engage in an ongoing enterprise, or undertake extremely risky, large-scale projects. A master contract between two or more parties determines the rights and responsibilities of the participants.

Joint ventures exist because the partners possess unique characteristics which complement and augment each other. The foreign partner usually brings the necessary technology and human capital (management). The host countries provide inexpensive labor, raw materials, and relief from taxes. Control is usually a major consideration. Mexico, for example, requires fifty-one percent domestic ownership. Having domestic partners offers some protection against expropriation and might allow the enterprise to qualify for participation in local government export programs. Repatriation (return to the home country) of profits is a key consideration for both the investor and the host country. Host countries try to keep profits in the domestic economy. Brazil indirectly requires reinvestment of a portion of profits in Brazil through special taxes and foreign-exchange rationing.

LEGAL DISPUTES WITH FOREIGN STATES

Sovereign Immunity Doctrine

Jurisdiction in cases involving governments and their agents is complicated by the Sovereign Immunity and Act of State doctrines. Originally, the **Sovereign Immunity Doctrine** offered foreign lands complete immunity from lawsuits. The Foreign Sovereign Immunities Act (FSIA) distinguishes between government acts and private or commercial acts, the former being generally immune from lawsuits.

There are several instances in which a foreign land is within the jurisdiction of U.S. courts. If the sovereign grants an explicit or implied waiver of immunity or engages in commercial activities in the United States or in commercial activities that have a direct impact on the United States, U.S. courts have jurisdiction. For example, an arbitration clause that requires arbitration in the United States constitutes a waiver. Examples of commerce are the issuance of debt or purchase of military hardware in the United States.

Where property rights are taken in violation of international law and the property, or property exchanged therefor, is present in the United States in connection with a commercial activity in the United States, or if such property is owned or operated by an agency or instrumentality of the foreign state which is engaged in a commercial activity in the United States, American courts can sit in judgment. For example, a state-owned airline that employs confiscated aircraft for passenger transport to the United States could be sued in U.S. court.

Obtaining a favorable judgment does not mean that the plaintiff can readily satisfy her or his claim. A foreign state is generally immune from attachments and execution (court-ordered payment of the judgment). The FSIA actually affords the foreign state more protection from execution than from suit, which may render litigation useless.

The following case deals with the Foreign Sovereign Immunities Act. In it, the court found that the Republic of South Africa could not be sued in the United States for the actions of its government agencies.

Martin v. Republic of South Africa
United States Court of Appeals, Second Circuit
836 F.2d 91 (1987)

Barry J. Martin is a U.S. citizen. While traveling with a dance group in South Africa, he was a passenger in a car involved in an accident. After the accident, an ambulance from the Transvaal Department of Hospital Services (a service owned and operated by the Republic of South Africa) arrived at the scene of the accident and transported the driver of the car to the Paul Kruger Hospital run by the South African government, where he was treated.

Martin was left at the scene of the accident, allegedly because he was black. Eventually Martin was transported by private automobile to the Paul Kruger Hospital and allegedly was forced to walk into the hospital, where he waited several hours expecting to receive medical care. Martin never received medical treatment at the Paul Kruger Hospital, but instead was transported to the H. F. Verwoerd Hospital (also run by the South African government), sixty-five miles away. Upon arriving at the hospital, he was diagnosed as quadriplegic. After more than twenty-four hours at this hospital, he received medical treatment for the first time, but only after being granted "honorary White status."

Upon his return to the United States, Martin sued the Republic of South Africa and the hospitals in question for his injuries sustained in South Africa. The critical issue was whether South Africa's conduct caused "a direct effect in the United States" with the meaning of the Foreign Sovereign Immunities Act. The district court and the court of appeals ruled for the government of South Africa.

Timbers, Circuit Judge

For there to be original jurisdiction, the claim against the foreign state must fall within an exception to the basic premise, set forth in 28 U.S.C. § 1604 (1982), that foreign states generally are immune from the jurisdiction of federal and state courts.

The specific exception involved on this appeal is 28 U.S.C. § 1605(a)(2) (1982), which provides in relevant part:

(a) A foreign state shall not be immune from the jurisdiction of courts of the United States or of the States in any case—

(2) in which an action is based . . . upon an act outside the territory of the United States in connection with a commercial activity of the foreign state elsewhere and that act causes a direct effect in the United States[.]

The focus of our inquiry is to determine whether the appellees' acts caused a "direct effect in the United States" within the meaning of § 1605(a)(2), i.e., whether the effect was sufficiently "direct" and sufficiently "in the United States" to support the claim of the foreign state to sovereign immunity.

Appellant here asserts that, where South Africa's activities have caused a citizen to return to the United States permanently disabled, the foreign state has caused a "direct effect in the United States." We disagree.

Our holding on the issue raised on this appeal conforms with the holdings of all courts that have considered a claim for *personal injuries* sustained in a foreign state when the plaintiff asserted that the "direct effect in the United States" was the continued physical suffering and consequential damages that persisted once the plaintiff returned.

We hold that South Africa's acts did not have a "direct effect in the United States" within the meaning of § 1605(a)(2) of the FSIA, and that the district court therefore correctly dismissed the complaint for lack of subject matter jurisdiction.

Affirmed.

Act of State Doctrine

The **Act of State Doctrine** was originally based on *Underhill* v. *Hernandez* (1897), in which the Supreme Court stated: "Every sovereign state is bound to respect the independence of every other sovereign state, and the courts of one country will not sit in judgment on the acts of the government of another done within its own territory." The doctrine strikes a balance among the three branches of government. It represents the desire of the Supreme Court to defer to the executive branch in the conduct of foreign policy. The Court recognizes that its actions may interfere with presidential efforts to resolve certain disputes. For example, a foreign state might agree to a negotiated settlement through the State Department, whereas a court order would be counterproductive. The Congress has incorporated these thoughts into legislation.

The Act of State Doctrine no longer grants blanket immunity to foreign governments. A court must analyze the effect of the government action on the foreign investor and determine whether the act was in the public interest as opposed to an act which might be committed by a private person. If a government act was in the public interest, the Act of State Doctrine is a valid defense to suit. For example, if a country nationalizes foreign firms in the oil industry and it was in the public interest, U.S. courts do not have jurisdiction to review the action of the foreign country.

The Court established the commercial exception to the Act of State Doctrine in *Alfred Dunhill of London, Inc.* v. *Republic of Cuba* (1976). Here, the Court held that "in their commercial capacities, foreign governments do not exercise powers peculiar to sovereigns. . . . The concept of an Act of State should not be extended to include the repudiation of a purely commercial obligation owed by a foreign

---

Sovereign Immunity: Mexicana Airlines

An airplane operated by Mexicana Airlines, a business run by the government of Mexico, crashed while operating in Mexico. The flight originated in Mexico and was to terminate in Mexico. Passengers purchased their tickets in Mexico. In response to a suit brought in the United States by heirs of the passengers for damages, the Ninth Circuit Court of Appeals ruled that Mexicana could not be sued in the United States because the government had not waived its sovereign immunity.

Mexicana de Aviacion v. *United States*, 57 USLW 2291 (October 17, 1988).

sovereign or by one of its commercial instrumentalities.'' For example, if the German government sold bonds in the United States and subsequently defaulted on the bonds, it could not avail itself of the Act of State Doctrine to prevent lawsuits.

The following case deals with the actions of the Organization of Petroleum Exporting Countries (OPEC). The court decided that the actions of OPEC were beyond the reach of the U.S. courts because of the Act of State Doctrine.

International Association of Machinists v. OPEC
United States Court of Appeals, Ninth Circuit
649 U.S. 1354 (1981)

The International Association of Machinists (IAM) filed suit against the Organization of Petroleum Exporting Countries (OPEC). IAM argued that the actions of OPEC constituted price fixing in violation of the U.S. antitrust laws. The court ruled that the Act of State Doctrine prohibited it from hearing this dispute.

Choy, Circuit Judge

IAM is a non-profit labor association. Its members work in petroleum-using industries, and like most Americans, they are consumers of gasoline and other petroleum-derived products. They object to the high and rising cost of such products.

OPEC is an organization of the petroleum-producing and exporting nations. . . . The OPEC nations have organized to obtain the greatest possible economic returns for a special resource which they hope will remove them from the ranks of the underdeveloped and the poverty-plagued. OPEC was formed in 1960 by the defendants Iran, Iraq, Kuwait, Saudi Arabia, and Venezuela. The other defendants, Algeria, Ecuador, Gabon, Indonesia, Libya, Nigeria, Qatar, and the United Arab Emirates, joined thereafter.

The OPEC nations produce and export oil either through government-owned companies or through government participation in private companies. Prior to the formation of OPEC, these diverse and sometimes antagonistic countries were plagued with fluctuating oil prices. Without coordination among them, oil was often in oversupply on the world market, resulting in low prices.

After formation of OPEC, it is alleged, the price of crude oil increased tenfold and more. Whether or not a causal relation exists, there is no doubt that the price of oil has risen dramatically in recent years, and that this has become of international concern.

Supporters of OPEC argue that its actions result in fair world prices for oil, and allow OPEC members to achieve a measure of economic and political independence. Without OPEC, they say, in the rush to the marketplace these nations would rapidly deplete their only valuable resource for ridiculously low prices.

Detractors accuse OPEC of price-fixing and worse in its deliberate manipulation of the world market and withholding of a resource which many world citizens have not learned to do without.

In December 1978, IAM brought suit against OPEC and its member nations. IAM's complaint alleged price fixing in violation of the Sherman Act, and requested treble damages and injunctive relief under the Clayton Act.

The act of state doctrine declares that a United States court will not adjudicate a politically sensitive dispute which would require the court to judge the legality of the sovereign act of a foreign state.

The doctrine recognizes the institutional limitations of the courts and the peculiar requirements of successful foreign relations. To participate adeptly in the global community, the United States must speak with one voice and pursue a careful and deliberate foreign policy. The political branches of our government are able to consider the competing economic and political considerations and respond to the public will in order to carry on foreign relations in accordance with the best interests of the country as a whole.

When the courts engage in piecemeal adjudication of the legality of the sovereign acts of states, they risk disruption of our country's international diplomacy.

The act of state doctrine is similar to the political question doctrine in domestic law. It requires that the courts defer to the legislative and executive branches when those branches are better equipped to resolve a politically sensitive question.

The doctrine of sovereign immunity is similar to the act of state doctrine in that it also represents the need to respect the sovereignty of foreign states. The two doctrines differ, however, in significant respects. The law of sovereign immunity goes to the jurisdiction of the court. The act of state doctrine is not jurisdictional. Rather, it is a prudential doctrine designed to avoid judicial action in sensitive areas. Sovereign immunity is a principle of international law, recognized in the United States by statute.

It is the states themselves, as defendants, who may claim sovereign immunity. The act of state doctrine is a domestic legal principle, arising form the peculiar role of American courts. It recognizes not only the sovereignty of foreign states, but also the spheres of power of the co-equal branches of our government. The record in this case contains extensive documentation of the involvement of our executive and legislative branches with the oil question. IAM does not dispute that the United States has a grave interest in the petro-politics of the Middle East, or that the foreign policy aims of the executive and legislative branches are intimately involved in this sensitive area. It is clear that OPEC and its activities are carefully considered in the formulation of American foreign policy.

The remedy IAM seeks is an injunction against the OPEC nations. The possibility of insult to the OPEC states and of interference with the efforts of the political branches to seek favorable relations with them is apparent from the very nature of this action and the remedy sought. The courts should not enter at the will of litigants into a delicate area of foreign policy which the executive and legislative branches have chosen to approach with restraint.

Treaties

In many cases, disputes with foreign nations can be resolved by resort to the wording of a *treaty*. A treaty is an agreement between two or more nations which is binding on the nations and must be performed by them in good faith.

The following case deals with a question of interpretation of a treaty. The Court found that the actions of the agents of the U.S. government did not violate the treaty. In essence, the Court decided that this was a political matter best resolved by the executive branch of government.

United States v. Alvarez-Machain
United States Supreme Court
112 S.Ct. 2188 (1992)

Humberto Alvarez-Machain is a citizen and resident of Mexico. He was indicted for the kidnap and murder of a U.S. Drug Enforcement Administration (DEA) special agent. On April 2, 1990, Alvarez-Machain was forcibly kidnapped from his medical office in Guadalajara, Mexico, and flown by private plane to El Paso, Texas, where he was arrested by DEA officials. The DEA was responsible for his abduction.

Alvarez-Machain moved to dismiss the charges brought against him on the grounds that the U.S. courts lacked jurisdiction to try him because he was abducted in violation of the extradition treaty between the United States and Mexico. The United States Supreme Court ruled in favor of the United States, permitting Alvarez-Machain to be tried in U.S. courts.

Chief Justice Rehnquist

In *Ker v. Illinois,* 119 U.S. 436 (1886), written by Justice Miller, we addressed the issue of a defendant brought before the court by way of a forcible abduction. Frederick Ker had been tried and convicted in an Illinois court for larceny; his presence before the court was procured by means of forcible abduction from Peru. A messenger was sent to Lima with the proper warrant to demand Ker by virtue of the extradition treaty between Peru and the United States. The messenger, however, disdained reliance on the treaty processes, and instead forcibly kidnapped Ker and brought him to the United States. We rejected Ker's argument that he had a right under the extradition treaty to be returned to this country only in accordance with its terms. We rejected Ker's due process argument more broadly, holding in line with "the highest authorities" that such forcible abduction is no sufficient reason why the party should not answer when brought within the jurisdiction of the court which has the right to try him for such an offense, and presents no valid objection to his trial in such court.

The only differences between *Ker* and the present case are that *Ker* was decided on the premise that there was no governmental involvement in the abduction and Peru, from which Ker was abducted, did not object to his prosecution.

Therefore our inquiry must be whether the abduction of respondent from Mexico violated the extradition treaty between the United States and Mexico. If we conclude that the Treaty does not prohibit respondent's abduction, the rule in *Ker* applies, and the court need not inquire as to how respondent came before it. In construing a treaty, as in construing a statute, we first look to its terms to determine its meaning. The Treaty says nothing about the obligations of the United States and Mexico to refrain from forcible abductions of people from the territory of the other nation, or the consequences under the Treaty if such an abduction occurs.

More critical to respondent's argument is Article 9 of the Treaty, which provides:

1. Neither Contracting Party shall be bound to deliver up its own nationals, but the executive authority of the requested Party shall, if not prevented by the laws of that Party, have the power to deliver them up if, in its discretion, it be deemed proper to do so.

2. If extradition is not granted pursuant to paragraph 1 of this Article, the requested Party shall submit the case to its competent authorities for the purpose of prosecution, provided that Party has jurisdiction over the offense.

According to respondent, Article 9 embodies the terms of the bargain which the United States struck: if the United States wishes to prosecute a Mexican national, it may request that individual's extradition. Upon a request from the United States, Mexico may either extradite the individual, or submit the case to the proper authorities for prosecution in Mexico. In this way, respondent reasons, each nation preserved its right to choose whether its nationals would be tried in its own courts or by the courts of the other nation.

This preservation of rights would be frustrated if either nation were free to abduct nationals of the other nation for the purposes of prosecution. More broadly, respondent reasons, as did the Court of Appeals, that all the processes and restrictions on the obligation to extradite established by the Treaty would make no sense if either nation were free to resort to forcible kidnapping to gain the presence of an individual for prosecution in a manner not contemplated by the Treaty.

We do not read the Treaty in such a fashion. Article 9 does not purport to specify the only way in which one country may gain custody of a national of the other country for the purposes of prosecution. The history of negotiation and practice under the Treaty also fails to show that abductions outside of the Treaty constitute a violation of the Treaty. As the Solicitor General notes, the Mexican government was made aware, as early as 1906, of the *Ker* doctrine, and the United States' position that it applied to forcible abductions made outside of the terms of the United States-Mexico extradition treaty. Nonetheless, the current version of the Treaty, signed in 1978, does not attempt to establish a rule that would in any way curtail the effect of *Ker*.

Thus, the language of the Treaty, in the context of its history, does not support the proposition that the Treaty prohibits abductions outside of its terms.

Respondent may be correct that respondent's abduc-

tion was "shocking," and that it may be in violation of general international law principles. Mexico has protested the abduction of respondent through diplomatic notes, and the decision of whether respondent should be returned to Mexico, as a matter outside of the Treaty, is a matter for the Executive Branch. We conclude, however, that respondent's abduction was not in violation of the Extradition Treaty between the United States and Mexico, and therefore the rule of *Ker v. Illinois* is fully applicable to this case. The fact of respondent's forcible abduction does not therefore prohibit his trial in a court in the United States for violations of the criminal laws of the United States.

Settlement of Disputes

Sometimes disputes arise between a nation and a commercial enterprise but there is no treaty to refer to resolve the dispute. The commercial enterprise may file suit in a U.S. court. Such a suit, because it concerns a foreign nation, may involve political as well as financial considerations. Such suits may create tensions with foreign countries. For this reason, the law gives the President the power to settle the claims of U.S. nationals and a foreign government in order to minimize the tensions between the U.S. and the foreign government.

In the next section we consider the options open to a company that wishes to sell its products in foreign countries.

DEVELOPING A SALES ORGANIZATION ABROAD

Foreign Agents and Distributors

American firms that wish to market their products in other countries have several options from which to choose. In terms of direct American involvement, a branch office or production facility ranks at the top of the list. Traveling American sales representatives rank second, followed by foreign distributors, American distributors, and foreign agents in that order. To avoid foreign income and employment taxes, American companies use foreign agents and distributors, thereby circumventing a "permanent establishment" in the foreign country. If the agent is an individual as opposed to a corporation, the firm must exercise caution, for the agent can be viewed as an employee. Thus, the company would have a "permanent establishment" and be liable for income and employment taxes.

International laws tend to give more protection to an agent than to a distributor on the assumption that a company possesses more bargaining power relative to the agent. Companies usually register agents and establish a commission schedule and payment timetable. European laws provide for longer termination notices and more severance pay in the form of lost commissions than does American law. To

Religion and the Law

At one time in the West, clerics exercised enormous influence over governments. Centuries ago, Western nations separated the operation of their governments from the religious beliefs of their people. In the United Kingdom, the kings separated church and state hundreds of years ago. In the United States, from the very outset in 1791, the United States Constitution recognized the concept of separation of church and state as reflected in the First Amendment. However, as recently as the early 1900s, Attaturk in Turkey, a Muslim country, separated the state from religious beliefs.

A close connection remains in other countries worldwide between the government and religion—in some, the two are inseparable. In Saudi Arabia, for example, the Koran *is* the law. As even the Koran must be interpreted, in such countries this gives the religious leader similar powers to that of a judge. Likewise, following the Iranian revolution in 1980 and the overthrow of the Shah, Muslim leaders began to take an active part in the governing of Iran. The mullahs imposed strict standards of dress and behavior.

A corporation that wishes to sell products in a country in which a close relationship is maintained between the religious beliefs of the people and the government must learn about these beliefs and abide by them while in the country—or its employees risk offending the people or, worse yet, going to jail.

protect the company, the agency agreement should include a nonexclusive agency clause, be short term, provide for no automatic extension, and specify causes for termination and the required notice period.

Sale of Data, Patents, and Know-How Abroad— Licensing

Firms that do not want to enter foreign markets, but nonetheless do not want to forgo the additional income from their special technology or know-how, can license the use of their processes. Thus, such firms eliminate the potential risk of establishing a production facility abroad and marketing the output there. The licensee benefits from the arrangement if it thereby has a monopoly or a real competitive advantage in the domestic market.

Licensing becomes more complicated when the export of the technology or know-how involved is restricted by the U.S. government. The rules are very complex and apply to all transactions—not just licensing. Antitrust issues are also involved in licensing arrangements.

EXTRATERRITORIAL APPLICATION OF U.S. LAWS

From time to time, Congress has attempted to extend the reach of U.S. law beyond the borders of the United States. For example, the Civil Rights Act of

The AIDS Crisis

At the present time in America, hundreds of thousands if not millions of persons may develop AIDS—a deadly disease spread through sexual contact. In a very short period of time, some people in virtually every country throughout the world have died from AIDS. The rapid spread of this disease illustrates the close relationship among all the people in the world. Whether we live on a wheat farm in Kansas or in a skyscraper in New York City, we need to realize the close connection between people in distant lands and people in the United States. Modern systems of communication, travel, and world trade make an isolationistic viewpoint, no matter how facially appearing, very myopic. Business and government must keep abreast of significant world developments like AIDS. They need to work in concert with other countries and businesses to address problems that will grow ever larger if we ignore them. The AIDS crisis illustrates the interdependent nature of today's world community.

1991 extended the protection of Title VII of the 1964 Civil Rights Act and the Americans With Disabilities Act to American citizens employed in foreign countries by U.S. employers. When a U.S. company operates in a foreign country, it should be alert to the possibility that it may be required to abide by U.S. law even through it is on foreign soil.

SUMMARY

A number of issues are of interest to executives who are engaged in international trade. Many businesses are engaged in importing and exporting. In such a situation, sellers are concerned about whether they will ever be paid, and buyers are concerned about whether they will receive the goods they ordered. In order to overcome these problems, parties in international transactions frequently use documentary credits.

One of the goals of governments around the world for many years has been the elimination of barriers to free trade. To help achieve this goal, a number of nations have entered into an agreement called the General Agreement on Tariffs and Trade, or GATT.

American companies operating abroad encounter various problems. In order to protect themselves in the event of a suit, they generally use certain clauses in their contracts, such as choice of law and choice of forum clauses. One clause that is frequently utilized is an arbitration clause. Companies often prefer arbitration of disputes to litigation.

When a business tries to sue a foreign government, it generally will have to overcome the Sovereign Immunity Doctrine and the Act of State Doctrine.

Rather than simply exporting or importing goods, a company may choose to develop a sales organization abroad. Companies frequently license foreign businesses to exploit their patents or manufacturing processes.

REVIEW QUESTIONS

1. Define the following terms:
   a. Choice of forum clause
   b. Choice of law clause
   c. Documentary credit

2. Why would a seller use a documentary letter of credit?

3. Why might arbitration be preferred to litigation?

4. If a court determines that a foreign state has engaged in commercial activity, does this mean a plaintiff will always be able to collect damages?

5. What is the difference between the Act of State Doctrine and the Foreign Sovereign Immunities Act?

6. How does the doctrine of separation of powers relate to the Act of State Doctrine?

7. What possible alternatives are open to a business firm that wishes to make money in foreign countries?

8. An American business wishes to sell products to a purchaser in France. Because the French purchaser is located in Europe, the American business knows practically nothing about the creditworthiness of the French company. If the American business decides to sell goods, how should it protect itself to make certain it is paid?

9. Cambridge Sporting Goods Company entered into a contract to purchase boxing gloves from Duke Sports, a Pakistani Corporation. Duke agreed to manufacture twenty-eight thousand pairs of boxing gloves for forty-two thousand dollars. Cambridge opened an irrevocable letter of credit with its bank in New York, Manufacturers Hanover Trust Company. The seller perpetrated a fraud upon Cambridge by shipping worthless fragments of boxing gloves. Can the defense of fraud be asserted against United Bank Limited (Duke's bank) when it requests payment of the letter of credit?

10. Nigeria contracted to purchase huge quantities of Portland cement. It overbought and was unable to accept delivery of the cement because its harbors became clogged with ships waiting to unload. It repudiated its contracts. When sued in the United States, it asserted the Sovereign Immunity Doctrine as defense. Will Nigeria prevail on this defense?

11. Allied Bank made loans to three Costa Rican banks. The Costa Rican banks executed promissory notes for the amounts in question to Allied. Several years later, the Costa Rican government issued a law preventing any institution in Costa Rica from paying any external debt. Allied brought suit in the United States against these Costa Rican banks. The banks raised as defenses the Sovereign Immunity Doctrine and the Act of State Doctrine. Will the Costa Rican banks prevail on any of these arguments?

12. An agency of the Mexican government, Pemex, was conducting mineral exploration in the Bay of Campeche. Zernicek, an employee of an American company hired by Pemex to perform certain work, was exposed to excessive doses of radiation as a result of the negligence of Pemex. After returning to the United States, Zernicek became ill. He filed suit in the United States against Pemex. Pemex alleges that it cannot be sued because of the Foreign Sovereign Immunities Act. Zernicek alleged that his injury constituted a "direct effect in the United States" such that it came within the commercial activities exception to the Foreign Sovereign Immunities Act. Is Zernicek correct?

13. The U.S. government wishes to punish Mendez for activities he engaged in while living in his own country, Spain. An extradition treaty exists between Spain and the United States. Can U.S. officials kidnap Mendez from Spain and try him in the United States?

Where to Find the Law

It takes a considerable period of time to become highly proficient in legal research. The first time you try to locate something generally takes the most time, but the whole process becomes easier with practice.

In order to locate material, one generally needs to know how it is categorized. You can get a very good feel for many of the categories of law by examining the Table of Contents of this text. For example, suppose a person received a serious injury while riding in a defective vehicle. Such a case concerns an issue related to the law of products liability.

In the course of performing their jobs, many nonlawyers find it necessary to keep abreast of some area of law. Jobs often require employees to keep learning about the law even after graduating from school. For example, an engineer may need to know about developments in environmental law in order to make certain the work performed by the engineer complies with the requirements of the law. People in bank trust departments, human resource departments, tax accountants, and a host of other people regularly consult legal publications. Some of these people develop a genuine expertise in an area of law due to their daily contact with certain types of business problems.

Many nonlegal sources provide valuable information about changes in the law. The daily newspaper in your city most likely discusses major United States Supreme Court cases, state supreme court cases, new federal and state laws. *The Wall Street Journal, Business Week, The New York Times, Newsweek,* and *Time* all provide updates on the law. Most companies receive trade publications from their trade associations. These publications contain information on legal developments of interest to people in that line of business. Many business people receive newsletters written expressly for their industry. One might even consult scholarly publications such as *The Harvard Business Review.* All these sources help keep the business community informed about the law.

Attorneys also rely upon other publications such as *The American Bar Association Journal, The National Law Journal* or *U.S. Law Week.* Attorneys receive updates from other sources such as newsletters which keep them posted on changes in the law.

The sources listed below all can be located in the typical university law school law library. One can also often find some of them in the main public library in your city. Large law firms, major corporations and the state legislatures all have extensive legal libraries as do many county bar associations. It may be possible to use these sources simply by asking for permission.

Constitutional Law

All laws in America must conform to the provisions of the United States Constitution (except treaties negotiated by the President and ratified by the Senate). The text of the United States Constitution appears in Appendix B to this book. One could also find the Constitution as well as cases that have interpreted the Constitution by looking at the *United States Code Annotated* or the *United States Code Service*—both of which are discussed in the following material.

All state laws must comply with the provisions of the United States Constitution as well as the state's constitution. For example, a law passed by the California legislature must comply with both the provisions of the U.S. Constitution and the California Constitution. One can locate a state constitution in the same books in which one finds the state statutes.

Federal Statutory Law

One of the most important areas of law today is statutory law—laws enacted by the United States Congress and by state legislatures. Cities and towns also possess the power to pass statutory laws, which we call ordinances. Laws passed by Congress occupy a very important place in American law.

A member of Congress initially proposes a bill. If both houses of Congress adopt this bill and the President of the United States signs the bill (which is generally required), it then becomes law. This law is published in several places. All of the laws passed at the end of a session of Congress are published in chronological order in the *United States Statutes at Law*.

Generally, practicing attorneys try to locate the text of a law in a more user friendly publication, the *United States Code,* published by the U.S. government. The *United States Code* is arranged by title and each title has been given a number. For example, the Sherman Antitrust Act is found in Title 15—''Commerce and Trade.'' Titles in turn are subdivided into sections. Attorneys refer to a federal statute by title and section number. 15 U.S.C. 1 thus refers to a statute that can be found in Title 15 in subsection 1. Lawyers generally do not own the *United States Code* but instead own an unofficial version of it such as the *United States Code Annotated* (published by the West Publishing Company) or the *United States Code Service, Lawyers' Edition* (published by the Lawyers Co-operative Publishing Company). Both of these unofficial sources contain additional useful information such as references to cases that have involved the particular federal statute one is examining and other relevant publications by the same publisher.

Federal Administrative Regulations

Students sometimes confuse the difference between laws passed by Congress, called statutes, and rules passed by federal agencies, called government regulations. Agencies cannot simply create law. All federal agencies must act pursuant to a grant of authority to these agencies contained in a federal statute. Federal agencies only have the power to create regulations governing a certain area of the law designated by Congress.

Federal administrative regulations must first be published in the *Federal Register* to be effective. In order to locate such an administrative regulation, it is easiest to consult the *Code of Federal Regulations.* Just as the *United States Code* is organized by title and section number, the *Code of Federal Regulations* is organized into fifty titles and rules within each title are given section numbers. For example, a reference to the rules relating to the apprehension of aliens can be found in 8 C.F.R.

242.2 *et seq.* The Immigration and Naturalization Service's rule thus can be found in section 242.2 of Title 8. Title 8 deals with aliens and nationality. *Et seq.* refers to all of the sections that relate to the cited section and which follow the section number in sequence. All the regulations issued by an agency may be found in the *Code of Federal Regulations.*

State Statutes

Much of the law in America appears in the form of state statutes. Just as at the federal level of government, a member of a state legislature must propose a bill. If both houses pass the bill and the governor signs the bill (the governor generally must sign a bill), the bill becomes law. State laws passed each session of the legislature generally are published in books called *session laws* which are published in chronological order like the federal *Statutes at Large*.

These statutes have been rearranged in more user friendly publications often referred to as *codes* or *revised statutes* or the like. These are published by the state governments or by private publishers. State codes frequently are annotated; that is, they contain additional information such as references to cases that have involved the respective statutory provisions. One needs to consult the particular publication to see how the material is arranged and supplemented.

Federal Cases

There are three important federal courts—the federal trial courts (district courts), the federal courts of appeals, and the United States Supreme Court.

One can locate the decisions of the federal district courts in the West Publishing Company's *Federal Supplement* (F.Supp.). In referring to (citing) a case lawyers generally state the name of the case, the volume number of the publication in which the case appears, the name of the publication in which it appears, the first page in the volume in which the case appears and the date of the case. You could find the *Powell* case—*Powell v. National Football League,* 678 F. Supp. 777 (1988)—by looking in volume 678 of the *Federal Supplement.* The first page of the case will appear on page 777 of that volume. The case was decided in 1988.

If the parties appeal a case to a federal court of appeals, the citation to the case is very similar. All

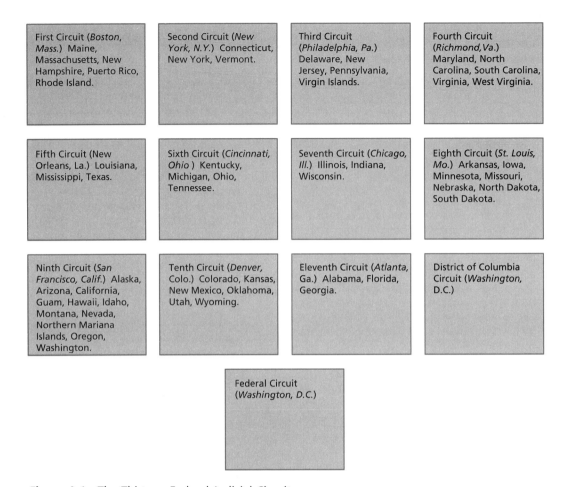

First Circuit (*Boston, Mass.*) Maine, Massachusetts, New Hampshire, Puerto Rico, Rhode Island.

Second Circuit (*New York, N.Y.*) Connecticut, New York, Vermont.

Third Circuit (*Philadelphia, Pa.*) Delaware, New Jersey, Pennsylvania, Virgin Islands.

Fourth Circuit (*Richmond, Va.*) Maryland, North Carolina, South Carolina, Virginia, West Virginia.

Fifth Circuit (New Orleans, La.) Louisiana, Mississippi, Texas.

Sixth Circuit (*Cincinnati, Ohio*) Kentucky, Michigan, Ohio, Tennessee.

Seventh Circuit (*Chicago, Ill.*) Illinois, Indiana, Wisconsin.

Eighth Circuit (*St. Louis, Mo.*) Arkansas, Iowa, Minnesota, Missouri, Nebraska, North Dakota, South Dakota.

Ninth Circuit (*San Francisco, Calif.*) Alaska, Arizona, California, Guam, Hawaii, Idaho, Montana, Nevada, Northern Mariana Islands, Oregon, Washington.

Tenth Circuit (*Denver, Colo.*) Colorado, Kansas, New Mexico, Oklahoma, Utah, Wyoming.

Eleventh Circuit (*Atlanta, Ga.*) Alabama, Florida, Georgia.

District of Columbia Circuit (*Washington, D.C.*)

Federal Circuit (*Washington, D.C.*)

Figure A.1 The Thirteen Federal Judicial Circuits

federal court of appeals cases appear in the West Publishing Company's *Federal Reporter* (F. or F.2d). The appeal of the *Powell* case appears in the Introduction to Antitrust chapter of this text. It is cited as follows: *Powell v. National Football League*, 888 F.2d 559 (1991). You could find the *Powell* case by looking in volume 888 of the *Federal Reporter*. The first page of the case will appear on page 559. The case was decided in 1991.

Note Figure A.1 above. There are thirteen federal judicial circuits, each of which has a court of appeals in it. It is not possible to appeal the decision of a federal trial court to any one of the thirteen courts of appeals listed in this figure that one desires. Decisions of federal trial courts located in a given state *must* be appealed to the court of appeals for the federal circuit indicated in this figure. For

example, appeals relating to matters that arise in the District of Columbia go to the District of Columbia Circuit. The Court of Appeals for the Federal Circuit hears such appeals as those relating to patents and copyrights and other specialized matters. Decisions of the federal trial courts in Illinois must be appealed to the court of appeals for the seventh circuit whereas decisions of the federal trial courts in California must be appealed to the court of appeals for the ninth circuit.

Sometimes the Supreme Court examines a case. Supreme Court cases appear in three different publications: the *United States Reports* (U.S.) published by the federal government, the West Publishing Company's *Supreme Court Reporter* (S.Ct.) and the Lawyers' Co-operative publication *Lawyers' Edition of the Supreme Court Reports* (L.Ed.

or L.Ed.2d). Most lawyers generally use one of the latter two publications. Many of the cases in this text are decisions of the Supreme Court. One cites them in a similar fashion to that discussed earlier. The *Socony-Vacuum Oil* case appears in the Antitrust chapter of this text. Its citation is as follows: *United States v. Socony-Vacuum Oil Co.*, 310 U.S. 150 (1940). You could find this case by looking in volume 310 of the *United States Reports*. The first page of the case will appear on page 150. The case was decided in 1940. Quite often a citation to a Supreme Court decision lists all three of these sources.

State Cases

State cases are an important source of the law. Most state trial court decisions have not been published. It is generally possible to find the decisions of state appellate courts. Many states publish their own cases. Some states do not.

Whether or not a state publishes its own appellate court decisions, a person looking for a state court decision can find that decision in one of the regional units of the *National Reporter System* (West Publishing Company). The *National Reporter System* publishes the state decisions as shown in Table A.1.

For example, if one wanted to locate a decision of the Kansas Supreme Court, one could find that in the *Pacific Reporter*. If one wanted to find a decision of the Missouri Supreme Court, it could be located in the *Southwestern Reporter*.

State court decisions are cited in much the same manner as federal court decisions. Consider the case *Parker v. Twentieth-Century Fox Film Corporation*, which appears in the second contracts chapter. The citation on this case is: 474 P.2d 689 (1970). You can find the original version of this case in volume 474 of the *Pacific Reporter, Second*. (Older cases appear in the *Pacific Report*. More recent cases appear in the *Pacific Reporter, Second* series.)

Finding the Law

A wide variety of approaches may be employed in finding the applicable law. Quite often a person wants more than just the official publication. It is useful to look at some commentary on the law as well. Indeed this may lead to a better understanding of the law.

TABLE A.1   Regional Units of the *National Reporter System.**

Atlantic Reporter

Connecticut	New Jersey
Delaware	Pennsylvania
Maine	Rhode Island
Maryland	Vermont
New Hampshire	

Northeastern Reporter

Illinois	(New York)
Indiana	Ohio
Massachusetts	

Northwestern Reporter

Iowa	North Dakota
Michigan	South Dakota
Minnesota	Wisconsin
Nebraska	

Pacific Reporter

Alaska	Nevada
Arizona	New Mexico
(California)	Oklahoma
Colorado	Oregon
Hawaii	Utah
Idaho	Washington
Kansas	Wyoming
Montana	

Southeastern Reporter

Georgia	Virginia
North Carolina	West Virginia
South Carolina	

Southern Reporter

Alabama	Louisiana
Florida	Mississippi

Southwestern Reporter

Arkansas	Tennessee
Kentucky	Texas
Missouri	

Note: California and New York each have their own Reporter System.

One source that a person with little familiarity with the law might want to examine is a legal encyclopedia. Legal encyclopedias cover all of the law of the United States. Consequently they have many volumes. The Lawyers Co-operative Publishing Company publishes one such encyclopedia—*American Jurisprudence 2d (Am Jur.2d)*. By using the index or table of contents one can find a discussion of the law that governs the topic one wants to research. *Am Jur* also contains references to other useful sources such as the *American Law Reports*. ALR contains in-depth memoranda on the topics it covers.

A very useful source often utilized today by practicing lawyers is the treatise. Treatises are in-depth examinations of a particular area of law by experts in that field of law. In a treatise one will find references to all of the law—constitution, statutory, administrative, or case law—that relates to the topic dealt with by the treatise. For example, one of the authors of this text, John Gergacz, has written a treatise, *Attorney Corporate Client Privilege*, 2nd edition, which is published by Shepard's/McGraw-Hill.

For example, suppose that you wish to research a question relating to the law of the sale of goods. One might turn to the *Uniform Commercial Code Reporting Service*. This multi-volume publication deals with all of the laws concerning the Uniform Commercial Code. The UCC deals with, among other topics, the law relating to the sale of goods. By examining the index or the table of contents it is possible to locate the information desired.

If a person has a particular topic in mind and wants a very high quality discussion of that area of law, he or she might consider reading a law journal article. There are literally hundreds of law journals in America. Journals published by law schools are called "law reviews." The authors of this text have written many law review articles. You can find law journal articles by examining the *Index to Legal Periodicals*. Suppose that you wanted to find an article dealing with whether a misrepresentation in an advertisement can be the basis of a products liability suit. By looking under the term "products liability" in the *Index to Legal Periodicals* one can find all the law review articles relating to products liability. In your search you might come across an article written by one of the authors of this text: Douglas Whitman, *Reliance as an Element in Product Misrepresentation Suits: A Reconsideration*, 35

Southwestern Law Review 741-773 (1981). This citation means that you can find this article in volume 35 of the Southwestern Law Review (published by the Southern Methodist University School of Law). The articles appear on pages 741 to 773. It was published in 1981.

One final note. Because the law changes, it is necessary to keep publications current. Soon after a hard-bound volume comes out, new cases, statutes, and regulations may make the information in the bound volume out of date. Rather than republishing a new hard-bound volume, publisher often issue a "pocket part" (an update on the law) on a quarterly or annual basis. In many of the sources you examine, you will find some material that supplements each hard-bound volume. Sometimes this information is put at the back of a bound book (which is where the phrase "pocket parts" originated). In other cases publishers simply release a paperback supplement to each bound book. When you research the law, look for material that supplements the hardbound book. By examining this additional information your legal search will be more up to date.

Computerized Legal Research

At one time it was necessary to be located near a large law library in order to have access to all of the materials useful to a person who wants to do legal research. While law schools still have certain publications that cannot be found elsewhere, the great bulk of the law today can be located simply by having access to either WESTLAW, operated by the West Publishing Company, or LEXIS, owned by Mead Data Central, Inc. Both of these provide comprehensive, online information service. All of the material discussed in the preceding material can be located in the data bases for these services.

Many persons searching for the law today use a computerized form of legal research because one can find the most current state of the law in these data bases. LEXIS and WESTLAW put statutes, cases, and administrative regulations on their data bases immediately after they are issued.

Both of these legal search systems require users to search only a portion of the entire data base. A user must provide instructions to LEXIS and WESTLAW as to which of the many data bases the user wants the computer to examine. Limiting the search in this manner makes it faster for the computer to find the desired information than if the computer had to search through the entire data base.

Once a person has designated a particular data base to be searched, the next step is to specify a search request. There are many ways to create a search request. A common method is to ask the computer to search for certain designated words. For example, if a person wants to see information on employment discrimination concerning women, one could ask the computer to search for documents in a designated data base that contains the words "employment discrimination" and "women."

Once the computer locates a set of documents, the user can look at the citations retrieved, look at portions of the documents retrieved, or look at the entire text of each document located. If a person finds useful information, he or she can read the material while online or have the information printed for examination at a later date.

We hope this information will be useful to you in your study of the law.

The Constitution of the United States of America

Preamble

We the People of the United States, in Order to form a more perfect Union, establish Justice, insure domestic Tranquility, provide for the common defence, promote the general Welfare, and secure the Blessings of Liberty to ourselves and our Posterity, do ordain and establish this Constitution for the United States of America.

Article I

SECTION 1. All legislative Powers herein granted shall be vested in a Congress of the United States, which shall consist of a Senate and House of Representatives.

SECTION 2. [1] The House of Representatives shall be composed of Members chosen every second Year by the People of the several States, and Electors in each state shall have the qualifications requisite for Electors of the most numerous Branch of the State Legislature.

[2] No Person shall be a Representative who shall not have attained to the Age of twenty five Years, and been seven Years a Citizen of the United States, and who shall not, when elected, be an Inhabitant of that State in which he shall be chosen.

[3] [Representatives and direct Taxes shall be apportioned among the several States which may be included within this Union, according to their respective Numbers, which shall be determined by adding to the whole Number of free Persons, including those bound to Service for a Term of Years, and excluding Indians not taxes, three fifths of all other Persons.] The actual Enumeration shall be made within three Years after the first Meeting of the Congress of the United States, and within every subsequent Term of ten Years, in such Manner as they shall by Law direct. The Number of Representatives shall not exceed one for every thirty Thousand, but each State shall have at Least one Representative; and until such enumeration shall be made, the State of New Hampshire shall be entitled to chuse three, Massachusetts eight, Rhode Island and Providence Plantations one, Connecticut five, New York six, New Jersey four, Pennsylvania eight, Delaware one, Maryland six, Virginia ten, North Caroline five, South Carolina five, and Georgia three.

The clause of this paragraph inclosed in brackets was amended, as to the mode of apportionment of representatives among the several states, by the Fourteenth Amendment, § 2, and as to taxes on incomes without apportionment, by the Sixteenth Amendment.

[4] When vacancies happen in the Representation from any State, the Executive Authority thereof shall issue Writs of Election to fill such Vacancies.

[5] The House of Representatives shall chuse their Speaker and other Officers; and shall have the sole Power of Impeachment.

SECTION 3. [1] The Senate of the United States shall be composed of two Senators from each State, [chosen by the Legislature thereof,] for six Years; and each Senator shall have one Vote.

This paragraph and the clause of following paragraph enclosed in brackets were superseded by the Seventeenth Amendment.

[2] Immediately after they shall be assembled in Consequence of the first Election, they shall be divided as equally as may be into three Classes. The Seats of the Senators of the first Class shall be vacated at the Expiration of the Second Year, of the second Class at the Expiration of the fourth Year, and of the third Class at the Expiration of the sixth

Year, so that one third may be chosen every second Year; [and if Vacancies happen by Resignation, or otherwise, during the Recess of the Legislature of any State, the Executive thereof may make temporary Appointments until the next Meeting of the Legislature, which shall then fill such Vacancies.]

[3] No Person shall be a Senator who shall not have attained to the Age of thirty Years, and been nine Years a Citizen of the United States, and who shall not, when elected, by an Inhabitant of that State for which he shall be chosen.

[4] The Vice President of the United States shall be President of the Senate, but shall have no Vote, unless they be equally divided.

[5] The Senate shall chuse their other Officers, and also a President pro tempore, in the Absence of the Vice President, or when he shall exercise the Office of President of the United States.

[6] The Senate shall have the sole Power to try all Impeachments. When sitting for that Purpose, they shall be an Oath or Affirmation. When the President of the United States is tried, the Chief Justice shall preside: And no Person shall be convicted without the Concurrence of two thirds of the Members present.

[7] Judgment in Cases of Impeachment shall not extend further than to removal from Office, and disqualification to hold and enjoy an Office of honor, Trust, or Profit under the United States: but the Party convicted shall nevertheless be liable and subject to Indictment, Trial, Judgment, and Punishment, according to Law.

Section 4. [1] The Times, Places and Manner of holding Elections for Senators and Representatives, shall be prescribed in each State by the Legislature thereof; but the Congress may at any time by Law make or alter such Regulations, except as to the Places of chusing Senators.

[2] The Congress shall assemble at least once in every Year, and such Meeting shall [be on the first Monday in December,] unless they shall by Law appoint a different Day.

The part included in brackets was changed by Section 2 of the Twentieth Amendment.

Section 5. [1] Each House shall be the Judge of the Elections, Returns, and Qualifications of its own Members, and a Majority of each shall constitute a Quorum to do Business; but a smaller Number may adjourn from day to day, and may be authorized to compel the Attendance of absent Members, in such Manner, and under such Penalties as each House may provide.

[2] Each House may determine the Rules of its Proceedings, punish its Members for disorderly Behavior, and, with the Concurrence of two thirds, expel a Member.

[3] Each House shall keep a Journal of its Proceedings, and from time to time publish the same, excepting such Parts as may in their Judgment require Secrecy; and the Yeas and Nays of the Members of either House on any question shall, at the Desire of one fifth of those Present, be entered on the Journal.

[4] Neither House, during the Session of Congress, shall, without the Consent of the other, adjourn for more than three days, nor to any other Place than that in which the two Houses shall be sitting.

Section 6. [1] The Senators and Representatives shall receive a Compensation for their Services, to be ascertained by Law, and paid out of the Treasury of the United States. They shall in all Cases, except Treason, Felony and Breach of the Peace, be privileged from Arrest during their Attendance at the Session of their respective Houses, and in going to and returning form the same; and for any Speech or Debate in either House, they shall not be questioned in any other Place.

[2] No Senator or Representative shall, during the Time for which he was elected, be appointed to any civil Office under the Authority of the United States, which shall have been created, or the Emoluments whereof shall have been increased during such time; and no Person holding any Office under the United States, shall be a Member of either House during his Continuance in Office.

Section 7. [1] All Bills for raising Revenue shall originate in the House of Representatives; but the Senate may propose or concur with Amendments as on other Bills.

[2] Every Bill which shall have passed the House of Representatives and the Senate, shall, before it become a Law, be presented to the President of the United States; If he approve he shall sign it, but if not he shall return it, with his Objections to the House in which it shall have originated, who shall enter the Objections at large on their Journal, and proceed to reconsider it. If after such Reconsideration two thirds of that House shall agree to pass the Bill, it shall be sent together with the Objections, to the other House, by which it shall likewise be reconsidered, and if approved by

two thirds of that House, it shall become a Law. But in all such Cases the Votes of both Houses shall be determined by Yeas and Nays, and the Names of the Persons voting for and against the Bill shall be entered on the Journal of each House respectively. If any Bill shall not be returned by the President within ten Days (Sundays excepted) after it shall have been presented to him, the Same shall be a Law, in like Manner as if he had signed it, unless the Congress by their Adjournment prevent its Return in which Case it shall not be a Law.

[3] Every Order, Resolution, or Vote, to Which the Concurrence of the Senate and House of Representatives may be necessary (except on a question of Adjournment) shall be presented to the President of the United States; and before the Same shall take Effect, shall be approved by him, or being disapproved by him, shall be repassed by two thirds of the Senate and House of Representatives, according to the Rules and Limitations prescribed in the Case of a Bill.

SECTION 8. [1] The Congress shall have Power To lay and collect Taxes, Duties, Imposts and Excises, to pay the Debts and provide for the common Defence and general Welfare of the United States; but all Duties, Imposts and Excises shall be uniform throughout the United States;

[2] To borrow money on the credit of the United States;

[3] To regulate Commerce with foreign Nations, and among the several States, and with the Indian Tribes;

[4] To establish an uniform Rule of Naturalization, and uniform Laws on the subject of Bankruptcies throughout the United States;

[5] To coin Money, regulate the Value thereof, and of foreign Coin, and fix the Standard of Weights and Measures;

[6] To provide for the Punishment of counterfeiting the Securities and current Coin of the United States;

[7] To Establish Post Offices and Post Roads;

[8] To promote the Progress of Science and useful Arts, by securing for limited Times to Authors and Inventors the exclusive Right to their respective Writings and Discoveries;

[9] To constitute Tribunals inferior to the Supreme Court;

[10] To define and punish Piracies and Felonies committed on the high Seas, and Offenses against the Law of Nations;

[11] To declare War, grant Letters of Marque and Reprisal, and make Rules concerning Captures on Land and Water;

[12] To raise and support Armies, but no Appropriation of Money to that Use shall be for a longer Term than two Years.

[13] To provide and maintain a Navy;

[14] To make Rules for the Government and Regulation of the land and naval Forces;

[15] To provide for calling forth the Militia to execute the Laws of the Union, suppress Insurrections and repel Invasions;

[16] To provide for organizing, arming, and disciplining the Militia, and for governing such Part of them as may be employed in the Service of the United States, reserving to the States respectively, the Appointment of the Officers, and the Authority of training the Militia according to the discipline prescribed by Congress;

[17] To exercise exclusive Legislation in all Cases whatsoever, over such District (not exceeding ten Miles square) as may, by Cession of particular States, and the Acceptance of Congress, become the Seat of the Government of the United States, and to exercise like Authority over all Places purchased by the Consent of the Legislature of the State in which the Same shall be, for the Erection of Forts, Magazines, Arsenals, dock-Yards, and other needful Buildings;—And

[18] To make all Laws which shall be necessary and proper to carrying into Execution the foregoing Powers, and all other Powers vested by this Constitution in the Government of the United States, or in any Department or Officer thereof.

SECTION 9. [1] The Migration or Importation of Such Persons as any of the States now existing shall think proper to admit, shall not be prohibited by the Congress prior to the Year one thousand eight hundred and eight, but a Tax or duty may be imposed on such Importation, not exceeding ten dollars for each Person.

[2] The privilege of the Writ of Habeas corpus shall not be suspended, unless when in Cases of Rebellion or Invasion the public Safety may require it.

[3] No Bill of Attainder or *ex post factor* Law shall be passed.

[4] No Capitation, or other direct, Tax shall be laid, unless in Proportion to the Census or Enumeration herein before directed to be taken.

See also the Sixteenth Amendment.

[5] No Tax or Duty shall be laid on Articles exported from any State.

[6] No Preference shall be given by any Regulation of Commerce or Revenue to the Ports of one State over those of another; nor shall Vessels bound to, or from, one State be obliged to enter, clear, or pay Duties in another.

[7] No money shall be drawn from the Treasury, but in Consequence of Appropriations made by Law; and a regular Statement and Account of the Receipts and Expenditures of all public Money shall be published from time to time.

[8] No Title of Nobility shall be granted by the United States: And no Person holding any Office of Profit or Trust under them, shall, without the Consent of the Congress, accept of any present, Emolument, Office, or Title, of any kind whatever, from any King, Prince, or foreign State.

SECTION 10. [1] No State shall enter into any Treaty, Alliance, or Confederation; grant Letters of Marque and Reprisal; coin Money; emit Bills of Credit; make any Thing but gold and silver Coin a Tender in Payment of Debts; pass any Bill of Attainder, *ex post facto* Law, or law impairing the Obligation of Contracts, or grant any Title of Nobility.

[2] No State shall, without the Consent of the Congress, lay any Imposts or Duties on Imports or Exports, except what may be absolutely necessary for executing it's inspection Laws: and the net Produce of all Duties and Imposts, laid by any State on Imports or Exports, shall be for the Use of the Treasury of the United States; and all such Laws shall be subject to the Revision and controul of the Congress.

[3] No State shall, without the Consent of Congress, lay any Duty of Tonnage, keep Troops, or Ships of War in time of Peace, enter into any Agreement or Compact with another State, or with a foreign Power, or engage in War, unless actually invaded, or in such imminent Danger as will not admit of delay.

Article II

SECTION 1. [1] The executive Power shall be vested in a President of the United States of America. He shall hold his Office during the Term of four Years, and, together with the Vice President, chosen for the same Term, be elected, as follows:

[2] Each State shall appoint, in such Manner as the Legislature thereof may direct, a Number of Electors, equal to the whole Number of Senators and Representatives to which the State may be entitled in the Congress; but no Senator or Representative or Person holding an Office of Trust or Profit under the United States, shall be appointed an Elector.

[3] [The Electors shall meet in their respective States, and vote by Ballot for two Persons, of whom one at least shall not be an Inhabitant of the same State with themselves. And they shall make a List of all the Persons voted for, and of the Number of Votes for each; which List they shall sign and certify, and transmit sealed to the Seat of Government of the United States, directed to the President of the Senate. The president of the Senate shall, in the presence of the Senate and House of Representatives, open all the Certificates, and the Votes shall then be counted. The Person having the greatest Number of Votes shall be the President, if such Number be a Majority of the whole Number of Electors appointed; and if there be more than one who have such Majority, and have an equal Number of Votes, then the House of Representatives shall immediately chuse by Ballot one of them for President; and if no Person have a Majority, then from the five highest on the List the said House shall in like Manner chuse the President. But in chusing the President, the Votes shall be taken by States the Representation from each State having one Vote; A quorum for this Purpose shall consist of a Member or Members from two thirds of the States, and a Majority of all the States shall be necessary to a Choice. In every Case, after the Choice of the President, the Person having the greatest Number of Votes of the Electors shall be the Vice President. But if there should remain two or more who have equal Votes, the Senate shall chuse from them by Ballot the Vice President.]

This paragraph, inclosed in brackets, was superseded by the Twelfth Amendment.

[4] The Congress may determine the Time of chusing the Electors, and the Day on which they shall give their Votes; which Day shall be the same throughout the United States.

[5] No person except a natural born Citizen, or a Citizen of the United States, at the time of the Adoption of this Constitution, shall be eligible to the Office of President; neither shall any Person be eligible to that Office who shall not have attained to

the Age of thirty five Years, and been fourteen Years a Resident within the United States.

[6] In case of the removal of the President from Office, or of his Death, Resignation or Inability to discharge the Powers and Duties of the said office, the Same shall devolve on the Vice President, and the Congress may by law provide for the Case of Removal, Death, Resignation or Inability, both of the President and Vice President, declaring what Officer shall then act as President and such Officer shall act accordingly, until the Disability be removed, or a President shall be elected.

[7] The President shall, at stated Times, receive for his Services, a Compensation, which shall neither be increased nor diminished during the Period for which he shall have been elected, and he shall not receive within that Period any other Emolument from the United States, or any of them.

[8] Before he enter on the Execution of his Office, he shall take the following Oath or Affirmation: "I do solemnly swear (or affirm) that I will faithfully execute the Office of President of the United States, and will to the best of my Ability, preserve, protect and defend the Constitution of the United States."

SECTION 2. [1] The President shall be Commander in Chief of the Army and Navy of the United States, and of the militia of the several States, when called into the actual Service of the United States; he may require the Opinion, in writing, of the principal Officer in each of the Executive Departments, upon any Subject relating to the Duties of their respective Offices, and he shall have Power to grant Reprieves and Pardons for Offenses against the United States, except in Cases of Impeachment.

[2] He shall have Power, by and with the Advice and Consent of the Senate to make Treaties, provided two thirds of the Senators present concur; and he shall nominate, and by and with the Advice and Consent of the Senate, shall appoint Ambassadors, other public Ministers and Consuls, Judges of the supreme Court, and all other Officers of the United States, whose Appointments are not herein otherwise provided for, and which shall be established by Law; but the Congress may by Law vest the Appointment of such inferior Officers, as they think proper, in the President alone, in the Courts of law, or in the Heads of Departments.

[3] The President shall have Power to fill up all Vacancies that may happen during the Recess of the Senate, by granting Commissions which shall expire at the End of their next Session.

SECTION 3. He shall from time to time give to the Congress Information of the State of the Union, and recommend to their Consideration such Measures as he shall judge necessary and expedient; he may, on extraordinary Occasions, convene both Houses, or either of them, and in Case of Disagreement between them, with Respect to the Time of Adjournment, he may adjourn them to such Time as he shall think proper; he shall take Care that the laws be faithfully executed, and shall Commission all the Officers of the United States.

Section 4. The President, Vice President and all civil Officers of the United States, shall be removed from Office on Impeachment for, and Conviction of, Treason, Bribery, or other high Crimes and Misdemeanors.

Article III

SECTION 1. The judicial Power of the United States, shall be vested in one supreme Court, and in such inferior Courts as the Congress may from time to time ordain and establish. The Judges, both of the supreme and inferior Courts, shall hold their Offices during good Behaviour, and shall, at stated Times, receive for their Services a Compensation, which shall not be diminished during their Continuance in Office.

SECTION 2. [1] The judicial Power shall extend to all Cases, in Law and Equity, arising under this Constitution, the laws of the United States, and Treaties made, or which shall be made, under their Authority;—to all Cases affecting Ambassadors, other public Ministers and Consuls;—to all Cases of admiralty and maritime Jurisdiction;—to Controversies to which the United States shall be a Party;—to Controversies between two or more States;—between a State and Citizens of another State;*—between Citizens of different States;—between Citizens of the same State claiming Lands under the Grants of different States, and between a State, or the Citizens thereof, and foreign States, Citizens or Subjects.

[2] In all Cases affecting Ambassadors, other public Ministers and Consuls, and those in which a State shall be a Party, the supreme Court shall have original Jurisdiction. In all the other Cases before mentioned, the supreme Court shall have appellate Jurisdiction, both as to Law and Fact, with such Exceptions, and under such Regulations as the Congress shall make.

* This clause has been affected by the Eleventh Amendment.

[3] The Trial of all Crimes, except in Cases of Impeachment, shall be by Jury; and such Trial shall be held in the State where the said Crimes shall have been committed; but when not committed within any State, the Trial shall be at such Place or Places as the Congress may by Law have directed.

SECTION 3. [1] Treason against the United States, shall consist only in levying War against them, or, in adhering to their Enemies, giving them Aid and Comfort. No Person shall be convicted of Treason unless on the Testimony of two Witnesses to the same overt Act, or on Confession in open Court.

[2] The Congress shall have Power to declare the Punishment of Treason, but no Attainder of Treason shall work Corruption of Blood, or Forefeiture except during the Life of the Person attained.

Article IV

SECTION 1. Full Faith and Credit shall be given in each State to the public Acts, Records, and judicial Proceedings of every other State. And the Congress may by general Laws prescribe the Manner in which such Acts, Records and Proceedings shall be proved, and the Effect thereof.

SECTION 2. [1] The Citizens of each State shall be entitled to all Privileges and Immunities of Citizens in the several States.

[2] A Person charged in any State with Treason, Felony, or other Crime, who shall flee from Justice, and be found in another State, shall on demand of the executive Authority of the State from which he fled, be delivered up, to be removed to the State having Jurisdiction of the Crime.

[3] [No Person held to Service or Labour in one State, under the Laws thereof, escaping into another, shall, in Consequence of any Law or Regulation therein, be discharged from such Service or Labour, but shall be delivered up on Claim of the Party to whom such Service or Labour may be due.]

This paragraph has been superseded by the Thirteenth Amendment.

SECTION 3. [1] New States may be admitted by the Congress into this Union; but no new State shall be formed or erected within the Jurisdiction of any other State; nor any State be formed by the Junction of two or more States, or Parts of States, without the Consent of the Legislatures of the States concerned as well as of the Congress.

[2] The Congress shall have Power to dispose of an make all needful Rules and Regulations respecting the Territory or other Property belonging to the United States; and nothing in this Constitution shall be so construed as to Prejudice any Claims of the United States, or of any particular State.

SECTION 4. The United States shall guarantee to every State in this Union a Republican Form of Government, and shall protect each of them against Invasion; and on Application of the Legislature, or of the Executive (when the Legislature cannot be convened) against domestic Violence.

Article V

The Congress, whenever two thirds of both Houses shall deem it necessary, shall propose Amendments to this Constitution, or, on the Application of the Legislature of two thirds of the several States, shall call a Convention for proposing Amendments, which, in either Case, shall be valid to all Intents and Purposes, as part of this Constitution, when ratified by the Legislatures of three fourths of the several States, or by Conventions in three fourths thereof, as the one or the other Mode of Ratification may be proposed by the Congress; Provided that no Amendment which may be made prior to the Year One thousand eight hundred and eight shall in any Manner affect the first and fourth Clauses in the Ninth Section of the first Article; and that no State, without its Consent, shall be deprived of its equal Suffrage in the Senate.

Article VI

[1] All Debts contracted and Engagements entered into, before the Adoption of this Constitution shall be as valid against the United States under this Constitution, as under the Confederation.

[2] This Constitution, and the Laws of the United States which shall be made in Pursuance thereof; and all Treaties made, or which shall be made, under the Authority of the United States, shall be the supreme Law of the Land; and the Judges in every State shall be bound thereby, any Thing in the Constitution or Laws of any State to the Contrary notwithstanding.

[3] The Senators and Representatives before mentioned, and the Members of the several State

Legislatures, and all executives and judicial Officers, both of the United States and of the several States, shall be bound by Oath or Affirmation, to support this Constitution; but no religious Test shall ever be required as a Qualification to any Office or public Trust under the United States.

Article VII

The Ratification of the Conventions of nine States shall be sufficient for the Establishment of this Constitution between the States so ratifying the Same.

Done in Convention by the Unanimous Consent of the States present the Seventeenth Day of September in the Year of Our Lord one thousand seven hundred and Eighty seven and of the Independence of the United States of America the Twelfth. IN WITNESS whereof We have hereto subscribed our Names,

Go. Washington—Presidt.
and deputy from Virginia

New Hampshire

John Langdon   Nicholas Gilman

Massachusetts

Nathaniel Gorham   Rufus King

Connecticut

Wm. Saml. Johnson   Roger Sherman

New York

Alexander Hamilton

New Jersey

Wil: Livingston   Wm. Paterson
David Brearley   Jona: Dayton

Pennsylvania

B. Franklin   Thos. FitzSimons
Thomas Mifflin   Jared Ingersoll
Robt. Morris   James Wilson
Geo. Clymer   Gouv Morris

Delaware

Geo: Read   Richard Bassett
Gunning Bedford Jun   Jaco: Broom
John Dickinson

Maryland

James McHenry   Danl. Carroll
Dan of St Thos. Jenifer

Virginia

John Blair   James Madison, Jr.

North Carolina

Wm. Blount   Hu Williamson
Richd. Dobbs Spaight

South Carolina

J. Rutledge   Charles Pinckney
Charles Cotesworth   Pierce Butler
 Pinckney

Georgia

William Few   Abr Baldwin
                     Attest William Jackson
                             Secretary

Amendments to the Constitution of the United States

AMENDMENT I [1791]

Congress shall make no law respecting an establishment of religion, or prohibiting the free exercise thereof; or abridging the freedom of speech, or of the press; or the right of the people peaceably to assemble, and to petition the Government for a redress of grievances.

AMENDMENT II [1791]

A well regulated Militia being necessary to the security of a free State, the right of the people to keep and bear Arms, shall not be infringed.

AMENDMENT III [1791]

No Soldier shall, in time of peace be quartered in any house, without the consent of the Owner, nor in time of war, but in a manner to be prescribed by law.

AMENDMENT IV [1791]

The right of the people to be secure in their persons, houses, papers, and effects, against unreasonable searches and seizures, shall not be violated, and no Warrants shall issue, but upon probable cause, supported by Oath or affirmation, and particularly describing the place to be searched, and the persons or things to be seized.

AMENDMENT V [1791]

No person shall be held to answer for a capital, or otherwise infamous crime, unless on a present-ment or indictment of a Grand Jury, except in cases arising in the land or naval forces, or in the Militia, when in actual service in time of War or public danger; nor shall any person be subject for the same offence to be twice put in jeopardy of life or limb, nor shall be compelled in any criminal case to be a witness against himself, nor be deprived of life, liberty, or property, without due process of law; nor shall private property be taken for public use, without just compensation.

AMENDMENT VI [1791]

In all criminal prosecutions, the accused shall enjoy the right to a speedy and public trial, by an impartial jury of the State and district wherein the crime shall have been committed; which district shall have been previously ascertained by law, and to be informed of the nature and cause of the accu-sation; to be confronted with the witnesses against him; to have compulsory process for obtaining Wit-nesses in his favor, and to have the Assistance of Counsel for his defence.

AMENDMENT VII [1791]

In Suits at common law, where the value in controversy shall exceed twenty dollars, the right of trial by jury shall be preserved, and no fact tried by jury shall be otherwise reexamined in any Court of the United States, than according to the rules of the common law.

AMENDMENT VIII [1791]

Excessive bail shall not be required, nor exces-sive fines imposed, nor cruel and unusual punish-ments inflicted.

AMENDMENT IX [1791]

The enumeration in the Constitution, of certain rights, shall not be construed to deny or disparage others retained by the people.

AMENDMENT X [1791]

The powers not delegated to the United States by the Constitution, nor prohibited by it to the States, are reserved to the States respectively, or to the people.

AMENDMENT XI [1798]

The Judicial power of the United States shall not be construed to extend to any suit in law or equity, commenced or prosecuted against one of the United States by Citizens of another State, or by Citizens or Subjects of any Foreign State.

AMENDMENT XII [1804]

The electors shall meet in their respective states and vote by ballot for President and Vice-President, one of whom, at least, shall not be an inhabitant of the same state with themselves; they shall name in their ballots the person voted for as President, and in distinct ballots the person voted for as Vice-President, and they shall make distinct lists of all persons voted for as President, and of all persons voted for as Vice-President, and of the number of votes for each, which lists they shall sign and certify, and transmit sealed to the seat of the government of the United States, directed to the President of the Senate;—The President of the Sen-ate shall, in the presence of the Senate and House of Representatives, open all the certificates and the votes shall then be counted;—The person having the greatest number of votes for President, shall be the President, if such number be a majority of the whole number of Electors appointed; and if no per-son have such majority, then from the persons hav-ing the highest numbers not exceeding three on the list of those voted for as President, the House of Representatives shall choose immediately, by bal-lot, the President. But in choosing the President, the votes shall be taken by states, the representa-tion from each state having one vote; a quorum for this purpose shall consist of a member of members from two-thirds of the states, and a majority of all the states shall be necessary to a choice. [And if the House of Representatives shall not choose a Presi-dent whenever the right of choice shall devolve upon them before the fourth day of March next following, then the Vice-President shall act as Pres-ident, as in the case of the death or other constitu-tional disability of the President.] The person having the greatest number of votes as Vice-Presi-dent, shall be the Vice-President, if such number be a majority of the whole number of electors appoin-ted, and if no person have a majority, then from the two highest numbers on the list, the Senate shall choose the Vice-President; a quorum for the purpose shall consist of two-thirds of the whole number of Senators, and a majority of the whole number shall be necessary to a choice. But no person constitutionally ineligible to the office of President shall be eligible to that of Vice-President of the United States.

The part included in brackets has been superseded by section 3 of the Twentieth Amendment.

AMENDMENT XIII [1865]

SECTION 1. Neither slavery nor involuntary servitude, except as a punishment for crime whereof the party shall have been duly convicted, shall exist within the United States, or any place subject to their jurisdiction.

SECTION 2. Congress shall have power to enforce this article by appropriate legislation.

AMENDMENT XIV [1868]

SECTION 1. All persons born or naturalized in the United States, and subject to the jurisdiction thereof, are citizens of the United States and of the State wherein they reside. No State shall make or enforce any law which shall abridge the privileges or immunities of citizens of the United States; nor shall any State deprive any person of life, liberty, or property, without due process of law; nor deny to any person within its jurisdiction the equal protection of the laws.

SECTION 2. Representatives shall be apportioned among the several States according to their respective numbers, counting the whole number of persons in each State, excluding Indians not taxed. But when the right to vote at any election for the choice of electors for President and Vice President of the United States, Representatives in Congress, the Executive and Judicial officers of a State, or the members of the Legislature thereof, is denied to any of the male inhabitants of such State, being twenty-one years of age, and citizens of the United States, or in any way abridged, except for participation in rebellion, or other crime, the basis of representation therein shall be reduced in the proportion which the number of such male citizens shall bear to the whole number of male citizens twenty-one years of age in such State.

SECTION 3. No person shall be a Senator or Representative in Congress, or elector of President and Vice President, or hold any office, civil or military, under the United States, or under any State, who, having previously taken an oath, as a member of Congress, or as an officer of the United States, or as a member of any State legislature, or as an executive or judicial officer of any State, to support the Constitution of the United States, shall have engaged in insurrection or rebellion against the same, or given aid or comfort to the enemies thereof. But Congress may by a vote of two-thirds of each House, remove such disability.

SECTION 4. The validity of the public debt of the United States, authorized by law, including debts incurred for payment of pensions and bounties for services in suppressing insurrection or rebellion, shall not be questioned. But neither the United States nor any State shall assume or pay any debt or obligation incurred in aid of insurrection or rebellion against the United States, or any claim for the loss or emancipation of any slave; but all such debts, obligations and claims shall be held illegal and void.

SECTION 5. The Congress shall have power to enforce, by appropriate legislation, the provisions of this article.

AMENDMENT XV [1870]

SECTION 1. The right of citizens of the United States to vote shall not be denied or abridged by the United States or by any State on account of race, color, or previous condition of servitude.

SECTION 2. The Congress shall have power to enforce this article by appropriate legislation.

AMENDMENT XVI [1913]

The Congress shall have power to lay and collect taxes on incomes, from whatever source derived, without apportionment among the several States, and without regard to any census or enumeration.

AMENDMENT XVII [1913]

The Senate of the United States shall be composed of two Senators from each State, elected by the people thereof, for six years; and each Senator shall have one vote. The electors in each state shall have the qualification requisite for electors of the most numerous branch of the State legislatures.

When vacancies happen in the representation of any State in the Senate, the executive authority of such State shall issue writs of election to fill such vacancies: *Provided,* That the legislature of any State may empower the executive thereof to make temporary appointments until the people fill the vacancies by election as the legislature may direct.

This amendment shall not be so construed as to affect the election or term of any Senator chosen before it becomes valid as part of the Constitution.

AMENDMENT XVIII [1919]

SECTION 1. [After one year from the ratification of this Article the manufacture, sale, or transportation of intoxicating liquors within, the importation thereof into, or the exportation thereof from the United States and all territory subject to the jurisdiction thereof for beverage purposes is hereby prohibited].

SECTION 2. [The Congress and the several States shall have concurrent power to enforce this article by appropriate legislation].

SECTION 3. [This article shall be inoperative unless it shall have been ratified as an amendment to the Constitution by the legislatures of the several States, as provided in the Constitution, within seven years from the date of the submission hereof to the State by the Congress].

The eighteenth amendment was repealed by the twenty-first amendment to the Constitution of the United States.

AMENDMENT XIX [1920]

The right of citizens of the United States to vote shall not be denied or abridged by the United States or by any State on account of sex.

Congress shall have the power to enforce this Article by appropriate legislation.

AMENDMENT XX [1933]

SECTION 1. The terms of the President and Vice President shall end at noon on the 20th day of January, and the terms of Senators and Representatives at noon on the 3d day of January, of the years in which such terms would have ended if this article had not been ratified; and the terms of their successors shall then begin.

SECTION 2. The Congress shall assemble at least once in every year, and such meeting shall begin at noon on the 3d day of January, unless they shall by law appoint a different day.

SECTION 3. If, at the time fixed for the beginning of the term of the President, the President-elect shall have died, the Vice President-elect shall become President. If the President shall not have been chosen before the time fixed for the beginning of his term, or if the President-elect shall have failed to qualify, then the Vice President-elect shall act as

President until a President shall have qualified; and the Congress may by law provide for the case wherein neither a President-elect nor a Vice President-elect shall have qualified, declaring who shall then act as President, or the manner in which one who is to act shall be selected, and such person shall act accordingly until a President or Vice President shall have qualified.

SECTION 4. The Congress may by law provide for the case of the death of any of the persons from whom the House of Representatives may choose a President whenever the right of choice shall have devolved upon them, and for the case of the death of any of the persons from whom the Senate may choose a Vice President whenever the right of choice shall have devolved upon them.

SECTION 5. Sections 1 and 2 shall take effect on the 15th day of October following the ratification of this article.

SECTION 6. This article shall be inoperative unless it shall have been ratified as an amendment to the Constitution by the legislatures of three-fourths of the several States within seven years from the date of its submission.

AMENDMENT XXI [1933]

SECTION 1. The eighteenth article of amendment to the Constitution of the United States is hereby repealed.

SECTION 2. The transportation or importation into any State, Territory, or possession of the United States for delivery or use therein of intoxicating liquors, in violation of the laws thereof, is hereby prohibited.

SECTION 3. This article shall be inoperative unless it shall have been ratified as an amendment to the Constitution by conventions in the several States, as provided in the Constitution, within seven years from the date of the submission hereof to the States by the Congress.

AMENDMENT XXII [1951]

SECTION 1. No person shall be elected to the office of the President more than twice, and no person who has held the office of President, or acted as President, for more than two years of a term to which some other person was elected President shall be elected to the office of President more than once. But this Article shall not apply to any person holding the office of President when this Article was proposed by the Congress, and shall not prevent any person who may be holding the office of President, or acting as President, during the term within which this Article becomes operative from holding the office of President or acting as President during the remainder of such term.

SECTION 2. This Article shall be inoperative unless it shall have been ratified as an amendment to the Constitution by the legislatures of three-fourths of the several States within seven years from the date of its submission to the States by the Congress.

AMENDMENT XXIII [1961]

SECTION 1. The District constituting the seat of Government of the United States shall appoint in such manner as the Congress may direct:

A number of electors of President and Vice President equal to the whole number of Senators and Representatives in Congress to which the District would be entitled if it were a State, but in no event more than the least populous state; they shall be in addition to those appointed by the States, but they shall be considered, for the purposes of the election of President and Vice President, to be electors appointed by a State; and they shall meet in the District and perform such duties as provided by the twelfth article of amendment.

SECTION 2. The Congress shall have power to enforce this article by appropriate legislation.

AMENDMENT XXIV [1964]

SECTION 1. The right of citizens of the United States to vote in any primary or other election for President or Vice President, for electors for President or Vice President, or for Senator or Representative in Congress, shall not be denied or abridged by the United States or by any State by reason of failure to pay any poll tax or other tax.

SECTION 2. The Congress shall have power to enforce this article by appropriate legislation.

AMENDMENT XXV [1967]

SECTION 1. In case of the removal of the President from office or of his death or resignation, the Vice President shall become President.

SECTION 2. Whenever there is a vacancy in the office of the Vice President, the President shall nominate a Vice President who shall take office upon confirmation by a majority vote of both Houses of Congress.

SECTION 3. Whenever the President transmits to the President pro tempore of the Senate and the Speaker of the House of Representatives his written declaration that he is unable to discharge the powers and duties of his office, and until he transmits to them a written declaration of the contrary, such powers and duties shall be discharged by the Vice President as Acting President.

SECTION 4. Whenever the Vice President and a majority of either the principal officers of the executive departments or of such other body as Congress may by law provide, transmit to the President pro tempore of the Senate and the Speaker of the House of Representatives their written declaration that the President is unable to discharge the powers and duties of his office, the Vice President shall immediately assume the powers and duties of the office as Acting President.

Thereafter, when the President transmits to the President pro tempore of the Senate and the Speaker of the House of Representatives his written declaration that no inability exists, he shall resume the powers and duties of his office unless the Vice President and a majority of either the principle officers of the executive department or of such other body as Congress may by law provide, transmit within four days to the President pro tempore of the Senate and the Speaker of the House of Representatives their written declaration that the President is unable to discharge the powers and duties of his office. Thereupon Congress shall decide the issue, assembling within forty-eight hours for that purpose if not in session. If the Congress, within twenty-one days after receipt of the latter written declaration, or, if Congress is not in session, within twenty-one days after Congress is required to assemble, determines by two-thirds vote of both Houses that the President is unable to discharge the powers and duties of his office, the Vice President shall continue to discharge the same as Acting President; otherwise, the President shall resume the powers and duties of his office.

AMENDMENT XXVI [1971]

SECTION 1. The right of citizens of the United States, who are eighteen years of age or older, to vote shall not be denied or abridged by the United States or by any State on account of age.

SECTION 2. The Congress shall have the power to enforce this article by appropriate legislation.

Warranty Provisions of the Uniform Commercial Code and Unconscionability

Section 2-302. Unconscionable Contract or Clause.

(1) If the court as a matter of law finds the contract or any clause of the contract to have been unconscionable at the time it was made the court may refuse to enforce the contract, or it may enforce the remainder of the contract without the unconscionable clause, or it may so limit the application of any unconscionable clause as to avoid any unconscionable result.

(2) When it is claimed or appears to the court that the contract or any clause thereof may be unconscionable the parties shall be afforded a reasonable opportunity to present evidence as to its commercial setting, purpose and effect to aid the court in making the determination.

Section 2-313. Express Warranties by Affirmation, Promise, Description, Sample.

(1) Express warranties by the seller are created as follows:

(a) Any affirmation of fact or promise made by the seller to the buyer which relates to the goods and becomes part of the basis of the bargain creates an express warranty that the goods shall conform to the affirmation or promise.

(b) Any description of the goods which is made part of the basis of the bargain creates an express warranty that the goods shall conform to the description.

(c) Any sample or model which is made part of the basis of the bargain creates an express warranty

that the whole of the goods shall conform to the sample or model.

(2) It is not necessary to the creation of an express warranty that the seller use formal words such as "warrant" or "guarantee" or that he have a specific intention to make a warranty, but an affirmation merely of the value of the goods or a statement purporting to be merely the seller's opinion or commendation of the goods does not create a warranty.

Section 2-314. Implied Warranty: Merchantability; Usage of Trade.

(1) Unless excluded or modified (Section 2-316), a warranty that the goods shall be merchantable is implied in a contract for their sale if the seller is a merchant with respect to goods of that kind. Under this section the serving for value of food or drink to be consumed either on the premises or elsewhere is a sale.

(2) Goods to be merchantable must be at least such as

(a) pass without objection in the trade under the contract description; and

(b) in the case of fungible goods, are of fair average quality within the description; and

(c) are fit for the ordinary purposes for which such goods are used; and

(d) run, within the variations permitted by the agreement, of even kind, quality and quantity within each unit and among all units involved; and

(e) are adequately contained, packaged, and labeled as the agreement may require; and

(f) conform to the promises or affirmations of fact made on the container or label if any.

(3) Unless excluded or modified (Section 2-316) other implied warranties may arise from course of dealing or usage of trade.

Section 2-315. Implied Warranty: Fitness for Particular Purpose.

Where the seller at the time of contracting has reason to know any particular purpose for which the goods are required and that the buyer is relying on the seller's skill or judgment to select or furnish suitable goods, there is unless excluded or modified under the next section an implied warranty that the goods shall be fit for such purpose.

Section 2-316. Exclusion or Modification of Warranties.

(1) Words or conduct relevant to the creation of an express warranty and words or conduct tending to negate or limit warranty shall be construed wherever reasonable as consistent with each other; but subject to the provisions of this Article on parol or extrinsic evidence (Section 2-202) negation or limitation is inoperative to the extent that such construction is unreasonable.

(2) Subject to subsection (3), to exclude or modify the implied warranty of merchantability or any part of it the language must mention merchantability and in case of a writing must be conspicuous, and to exclude or modify any implied warranty of fitness the exclusion must be by a writing and conspicuous. Language to exclude all implied warranties of fitness is sufficient if it states, for example, that "There are no warranties which extend beyond the description on the face hereof."

(3) Notwithstanding subsection (2)

(a) unless the circumstances indicate otherwise, all implied warranties are excluded by expressions like "as is," "with all faults" or other language which in common understanding calls the buyer's attention to the exclusion of warranties and makes plain that there is no implied warranty; and

(b) when the buyer before entering into the contract has examined the goods or the sample or model as fully as he desired or has refused to examine the goods there is no implied warranty with regard to defects which an examination ought in the circumstances to have revealed to him; and

(c) an implied warranty can also be excluded or modified by course of dealing or course of performance or usage of trade.

(4) Remedies for breach of warranty can be limited in accordance with the provisions of this Article on liquidation or limitation of damages and on contractual modification of remedy (Sections 2-718 and 2-719).

Section 2-317. Cumulation and Conflict of Warranties Express or Implied.

Warranties whether express or implied shall be construed as consistent with each other and as cumulative, but if such construction is unreasonable the intention of the parties shall determine which warranty is dominant. In ascertaining that intention the following rules apply:

(a) Exact or technical specifications displace an inconsistent sample or model or general language of description.

(b) A sample from an existing bulk displaces inconsistent general language of description.

(c) Express warranties displace inconsistent implied warranties other than an implied warranty of fitness for a particular purpose.

Section 2-318. Third Party Beneficiaries of Warranties Express or Implied.

ALTERNATIVE A

A seller's warranty whether express or implied extends to any natural person who is in the family or household of his buyer or who is a guest in his home if it is reasonable to expect that such person may use, consume or be affected by the goods and who is injured in person by breach of the warranty. A seller may not exclude or limit the operation of this section.

Restatement of Torts, Second (excerpts)

Section 402 A. Special Liability of Seller of Product for Physical Harm to User or Consumer.

(1) One who sells any product in a defective condition unreasonably dangerous to the consumer or to his property is subject to liability for physical harm thereby caused to the ultimate user or consumer, or to his property, if

(a) the seller is engaged in the business of selling such a product, and

(b) it is expected to and does reach the user or consumer without substantial change in the condition in which it is sold.

(2) The rule stated in Subsection (1) applies although

(a) the seller has exercised all possible care in the preparation and sale of his product, and

(b) the user or consumer has not bought the product from or entered into any contractual relation with the seller.

Section 402 B. Misrepresentation by Seller of Chattels to Consumer.

One engaged in the business of selling chattels who, by advertising, labels, or otherwise, makes to the public a misrepresentation of a material fact concerning the character or quality of a chattel sold by him is subject to liability for physical harm to a consumer of the chattel caused by justifiable reliance upon the misrepresentation, even though

(a) it is not made fraudulently or negligently, and

(b) the consumer has not bought the chattel from or entered into any contractual relations with the seller.

National Labor Relations Act (excerpts)

Rights of Employees

SECTION 7. Employees shall have the right to self-organization, to form, join or assist labor organizations, to bargain collectively through representatives of their own choosing, and to engage in other concerted activities for the purpose of collective bargaining or other mutual aid or protection, and shall also have the right to refrain from any or all of such activities except to the extent that such right may be affected by an agreement requiring membership in a labor organization as a condition of employment as authorized in section 8(a)(3).

Unfair Labor Practices

SECTION 8. (a) It shall be an unfair labor practice for an employer—

(1) to interfere with, restrain, or coerce employees in the exercise of the rights guaranteed in section 7;

(2) to dominate or interfere with the formation or administration of any labor organization or contribute financial or other support to it: Provided, That subject to rules and regulations made and published by the Board pursuant to section 6, an employer shall not be prohibited from permitting employees to confer with him during working hours without loss of time or pay;

(3) by discrimination in regard to hire or tenure of employment or any term or condition of employment to encourage or discourage membership in any labor organization: Provided, That nothing in this Act, or in any other statute of the United States, shall preclude an employer from making an agreement with a labor organization (not established, maintained, or assisted by any action defined in section 8(a) of this Act as an unfair labor practice) to require as a condition of employment membership therein on or after the thirtieth day following the beginning of such employment or the effective date of such agreement, whichever is the later (i) if such labor organization is the representative of the employees as provided in section 9(a), in the appropriate collective-bargaining unit covered by such agreement when made, and (ii) unless following an election held as provided in section 9(e) within one year preceding the effective date of such agreement, the Board shall have certified that at least a majority of the employees eligible to vote in such election have voted to rescind the authority of such labor organization to make such an agreement: Provided further, That no employer shall justify any discrimination against an employee for nonmembership in a labor organization (A) if he has reasonable grounds for believing that such membership was not available to the employee on the same terms and conditions generally applicable to other members, or (B) if he had reasonable grounds for believing that membership was denied or terminated for reasons other than the failure of the employee to tender the periodic dues and the initiation fees uniformly required as a condition of acquiring or retaining membership;

(4) to discharge or otherwise discriminate against an employee because he has filed charges or given testimony under this Act;

(5) to refuse to bargain collectively with the representatives of his employees, subject to the provisions of section 9(a).

(b) It shall be an unfair labor practice for a labor organization or its agents—

(1) to restrain or coerce (A) employees in the exercise of the rights guaranteed in section 7: Provided, That this paragraph shall not impair the right of a labor organization to prescribe its own rules with respect to the acquisition or retention of membership therein; or (B) an employer in the selection of his representatives for the purposes of collective bargaining or the adjustment of grievances;

(2) to cause or attempt to cause an employer to discriminate against an employee in violation of subsection (a)(3) or to discriminate against an employee with respect to whom membership in such organization has been denied or terminated on some ground other than his failure to tender the periodic dues and the initiation fees uniformly required as a condition of acquiring or retaining membership;

(3) to refuse to bargain collectively with an employer, provided it is the representative of his employees subject to the provisions of section 9(a);

(4) (i) to engage in, or to induce or encourage [the employees of any employer] an individual employed by any person engaged in commerce or in an industry affecting commerce to engage in, a strike or a refusal in the course of his employment to use, manufacture, process, transport, or otherwise handle or work on any goods, articles, materials, or commodities or to perform any services; or (ii) to threaten, coerce, or restrain any person engaged in commerce or in an industry affecting commerce, where in either case an object thereof is—

(A) forcing or requiring any employer or self-employed person to join any labor or employer organization or to enter into any agreement which is prohibited by section 8(e);

(B) forcing or requiring any person to cease using, selling, handling, transporting, or otherwise dealing in the products of any other producer, processor, or manufacturer, or to cease doing business with any other person, or forcing or requiring any other employer to recognize or bargain with a labor organization as the representative of his employees unless such labor organization has been certified as the representative of such employees under the provisions of section 9: Provided, That nothing contained in this clause (B) shall be construed to make unlawful, where not otherwise unlawful, any primary strike or primary picketing;

(C) forcing or requiring any employer to recognize or bargain with a particular labor organization as the representative of his employees if another labor organization has been certified as the representative of such employees under the provisions of section 9;

(D) forcing or requiring any employer to assign particular work to employees in a particular labor organization or in a particular trade, craft, or class rather than to employees in an-

other labor organization or in another trade, craft, or class, unless such employer is failing to conform to an order or certification of the Board determining the bargaining representative for employees performing such work:

Provided, That nothing contained in this subsection (b) shall be construed to make unlawful a refusal by any person to enter upon the premises of any employer (other than his own employer), if the employees of such employer are engaged in a strike ratified or approved by a representative of such employees whom such employer is required to recognize under this Act: Provided further, That for the purposes of this paragraph (4) only, nothing contained in such paragraph shall be construed to prohibit publicity, other than picketing, for the purpose of truthfully advising the public, including consumers and members of a labor organization, that a product or products are produced by an employer with whom the labor organization has a primary dispute and are distributed by another employer, as long as such publicity does not have an effect of inducing any individual employed by any person other than the primary employer in the course of his employment to refuse to pick up, deliver, or transport any goods, or not to perform any services, at the establishment of the employer engaged in such distribution:

(5) to require of employees covered by an agreement authorized under subsection (a)(3) the payment, as a condition precedent to becoming a member of such organization, of a fee in an amount which the Board finds excessive or discriminatory under all the circumstances. In making such a finding, the Board shall consider, among other relevant factors, the practices and customs of labor organizations in the particular industry, and the wages currently paid to the employees affected;

(6) to cause or attempt to cause an employer to pay or deliver or agree to pay or deliver any money or other thing of value, in the nature of an exaction, for services which are not performed or not to be performed; and

(7) to picket or cause to be picketed, or threaten to picket or cause to be picketed, any employer where an object thereof is forcing or requiring an employer to recognize or bargain with a labor organization as the representative of his employees, or forcing or requiring the employees of an employer to accept or select such labor organization as their collective bargaining representative, unless such la-

bor organization is currently certified as the representative of such employees:

(A) where the employer has lawfully recognized in accordance with this Act any other labor organization and a question concerning representation may not appropriately be raised under section 9(c) of this Act;

(B) when within the preceding twelve months a valid election under section 9(c) of this Act has been conducted, or

(C) where such picketing has been conducted within a petition under section 9(c) being filed within a reasonable period of time not to exceed thirty days from the commencement of such picketing: Provided, That when such a petition has been filed the Board shall forthwith, without regard to the provisions of section 9(c)(1) or the absence of a showing of a substantial interest on the part of the labor organization, direct an election in such unit as the Board finds to be appropriate and shall certify the results thereof: Provided further, That nothing in this subparagraph (C) shall be construed to prohibit any picketing or other publicity for the purpose of truthfully advising the public (including consumers) that an employer does not employ members of, or have a contract with, a labor organization, unless an effect of such picketing is to induce any individual employed by any other person in the course of his employment, not to pick up, deliver or transport any goods or not to perform any services.

Nothing in this paragraph (7) shall be construed to permit any act which would otherwise be an unfair labor practice under this section 8(b).

(c) the expressing of any views, argument, or opinion, or the dissemination thereof, whether in written, printed, graphic, or visual form, shall not constitute or be evidence of an unfair labor practice under any of the provisions of this Act, if such expression contains no threat of reprisal or force or promise of benefit.

(d) For the purposes of this section, to bargain collectively is the performance of the mutual obligation of the employer and the representative of the employees to meet at reasonable times and confer in good faith with respect to wages, hours, and other terms and conditions of employment, or the

negotiation of an agreement, or any question arising thereunder, and the execution of a written contract incorporating any agreement reached if requested by either party, but such obligation does not compel either party to agree to a proposal or require the making of a concession: Provided, That where there is in effect a collective-bargaining contract covering employees in an industry affecting commerce, the duty to bargain collectively shall also mean that no party to such contract shall terminate or modify such contract, unless the party desiring such termination or modification—

(1) serves a written notice upon the other party to the contract of the proposed termination or modification sixty days prior to the expiration date thereof, or in the event such contract contains no expiration date, sixty days prior to the time it is proposed to make such termination or modification;

(2) offers to meet and confer with the other party for the purpose of negotiating a new contract containing the proposed modifications;

(3) notifies the Federal Mediation and Conciliation Service within thirty days after such notice of the existence of a dispute, and simultaneously therewith notifies any State or Territorial agency established to mediate and conciliate disputes within the States or Territory where the dispute occurred, provided no agreement has been reached by that time; and

(4) continues in full force and effect, without resorting to strike or lock-out, all the terms and conditions of the existing contract for a period of sixty days after such notice is given or until the expiration date of such contract, whichever occurs later:

The duties imposed upon employers, employees, and labor organizations by paragraphs (2), (3), and (4) shall become inapplicable upon an intervening certification of the Board, under which the labor organization or individual, which is a party to the contract, has been superseded as or ceased to be the representative of the employees subject to the provisions of section 9(a), and the duties so imposed shall not be construed as requiring either party to discuss or agree to any modification of the terms and conditions contained in a contract for a fixed period, if such modification is to become effective before such terms and conditions can be reopened under the provisions of the contract. Any employee who engages in a strike within any notice periods specified in this subsection, or who engages in any strike within the appropriate period specified in subsection (g) of this section, shall lose his status as an employee of the employer engaged in the particular labor dispute, for the purposes of section 8, 9, and 10 of this Act, but such loss of status for such employee shall terminate if and when he is reemployed by such employer. Whenever the collective bargaining involves employees of a health care institution, the provisions of this section 8(d) shall be modified as follows:

(A) The notice of section 8(d)(1) shall be ninety days; the notice of section 8(d)(3) shall be sixty days; and the contract period of section 8(d)(4) shall be ninety days.

(B) Where the bargaining is for an initial agreement following certification or recognition, at least thirty days' notice of the existence of a dispute shall be given by the labor organization to the agencies set forth in section 8(d)(3).

(C) After notice is given to the Federal Mediation and Conciliation Service under either clause (A) or (B) of this sentence, the Service shall promptly communicate with the parties and use its best efforts, by mediation and conciliation, to bring them to agreement. The parties shall participate fully and promptly in such meetings as may be undertaken by the Service for the purpose of aiding in a settlement of the dispute.

(e) It shall be an unfair labor practice for any labor organization and any employer to enter into any contract or agreement, express or implied, whereby such employer ceases or refrains or agrees to cease or refrain from handling, using, selling, transporting, or otherwise dealing in any of the products of any other employer, or to cease doing business with any other person, and any contract or agreement entered into heretofore or hereafter containing such an agreement shall be to such extent unenforceable and void: Provided, That nothing in this subsection (e) shall apply to an agreement between a labor organization and an employer in the construction industry relating to the contracting or subcontracting of work to be done at the site of the construction, alteration, painting, or repair of a building, structure, or other work: Provided further, That for the purposes of this subsection (e) and section 8(b)(4)(B) the terms "any employer,"

"any person engaged in commerce or any industry affecting other producer, processor, or manufacturer," "any other employer," or "any other person" shall not include persons in the relation of a jobber, manufacturer, contractor, or subcontractor working on the goods or premises of the jobber or manufacturer or performing parts of an integrated process of production in the apparel and clothing industry: Provided further, That nothing in this Act shall prohibit the enforcement of any agreement which is within the foregoing exception.

(f) It shall not be an unfair labor practice under subsections (a) and (b) of this section for an employer engaged primarily in the building and construction industry to make an agreement covering employees engaged (or who, upon their employment, will be engaged) in the building and construction industry with a labor organization of which building and construction employees are members (not established, maintained, or assisted by any action defined in section 8(a) of this Act as an unfair labor practice) because (1) the majority status of such labor organizations has not been established under the provisions of section 9 of this Act prior to the making of such agreement, or (2) such agreement requires as a condition of employment, membership in such labor organization after the seventh day following the beginning of such employment or the effective date of the agreement, whichever is later, or (3) such agreement requires the employer to notify such labor organization of opportunities for employment with such employer, or gives such labor organization an opportunity to refer qualified applicants for such employment, or (4) such agreement specifies minimum training or experience qualifications for employment or provides for priority in opportunities for employment based upon length of service with such employer, in the industry or in the particular geographical area: Provided, That nothing in this subsection shall set aside the final proviso to section 8(a)(3) of this Act: Provided further, That any agreement which would be invalid, but for clause (1) of this subsection shall not be a bar to a petition filed pursuant to section 9(c) or 9(e).

(g) A labor organization before engaging in any strike, picketing, or other concerted refusal to work at any health care institution shall, not less than ten days prior to such action, notify the institution in writing and the Federal Mediation and Conciliation Service of that intention, except that in the case of bargaining for an initial agreement following certification or recognition the notice required by this subsection shall not be given until the expiration of the period specified in clause (b) of the last sentence of section 8(d) of this Act. The notice shall state the date and time that such action will commence. The notice, once given, may be extended by the written agreement of both parties.

Representatives and Elections

SECTION 9. (a) Representatives designated or selected for the purposes of collective bargaining by the majority of the employees in a unit appropriate for such purposes, shall be the exclusive representatives of all the employees in such unit for the purposes of collective bargaining in respect to rates of pay, wages, hours of employment, or other conditions of employment: Provided, That any individual employee or a group of employees shall have the right at any time to present grievances to their employer and to have such grievances adjusted, without the intervention of the bargaining representative, as long as the adjustment is not inconsistent with the terms of a collective-bargaining contract or agreement then in effect: Provided further, That the bargaining representative has been given opportunity to be present at such adjustment.

(b) The Board shall decide in each case whether, in order to assure to employees the fullest freedom in exercising the rights guaranteed by this Act, the unit appropriate for the purposes of collective bargaining shall be the employer unit, craft unit, plant unit, or subdivision thereof: Provided, That the Board shall not (1) decide that any unit is appropriate for such purposes if such unit included both professional employees and employees who are not professional employees unless a majority of such professional employees vote for inclusion in such unit; or (2) decide that any craft unit is inappropriate for such purposes on the ground that a different unit has been established by a prior Board determination, unless a majority of the employees in the proposed craft unit vote against separate representation; or (3) decide that any unit is appropriate for such purposes if it includes, together with other employees, any individual employed as a guard to enforce against employees and other persons rules to protect property of the employer or to protect the safety of persons on the employer's premises; but no later organization shall be certified as the representative of employees in a bargaining unit of guards if such organization admits to membership, or is affiliated directly or indirectly with an organization which admits to membership, employees other than guards.

(c)(1) Whenever a petition shall have been filed, in accordance with such regulations as may be prescribed by the Board—

(A) by an employee or group of employees or an individual or labor organization acting in their behalf alleging that a substantial number of employees (i) wish to be represented for collective bargaining and that their employer declines to recognize their representative as the representative defined in section 9(a), or (ii) assert that the individual or labor organization, which has been certified or is being currently recognized by their employer as the bargaining representative, is no longer a representative as defined in section 9(a); or

(B) by an employer, alleging that one or more individuals or labor organizations have presented to him a claim to be recognized as the representative defined in section 9(a);

the Board shall investigate such petition and if it has reasonable cause to believe that a question of representation affecting commerce exists shall provide for an appropriate hearing upon due notice. Such hearing may be conducted by an officer or employee of the regional office, who shall not make any recommendations with respect thereto. If the Board finds upon the record of such hearing that such a question of representation exists, it shall direct an election by secret ballot and shall certify the results thereof.

(2) In determining whether or not a question of representation affecting commerce exists, the same regulations and rules of decision shall apply irrespective of the identity of the persons filing the petition or the kind of relief sought and in no case shall the Board deny a labor organization a place on the ballot by reason of an order with respect to such labor organization or its predecessor not issued in conformity with section 10(c).

(3) No election shall be directed in any bargaining unit or any subdivision within which, in the preceding twelve-month period, a valid election shall have been held. Employees engaged in an economic strike who are not entitled to reinstatement shall be eligible to vote under such regulations

as the Board shall find are consistent with the purposes and provisions of this Act in any election conducted within twelve months after the commencement of the strike. In any election where none of the choices on the ballot receives a majority, a runoff shall be conducted, the ballot providing for a selection between the two choices receiving the largest and second largest number of valid votes cast in the election.

(4) Nothing in this section shall be construed to prohibit the waiving of hearings by stipulation for the purpose of a consent election in conformity with regulations and rules of decision of the Board.

(5) In determining whether a unit is appropriate for the purposes specified in subsection (b) the extent to which the employees have organized shall not be controlling.

(d) Whenever an order of the Board made pursuant to section 10(c) is based in whole or in part upon facts certified following an investigation pursuant to subsection (c) of this section and there is a petition for the enforcement or review of such order, such certification and the record of such investigation shall be included in the transcript of the entire record required to be filed under section 10(e) or 10(f), and thereupon the decree of the court enforcing, modifying, or setting aside in whole or in part the order of the Board shall be made and entered upon the pleadings, testimony, and proceedings set forth in such transcript.

(e)(1) Upon the filing with the Board, by 30 per centum or more of the employees in a bargaining unit covered by an agreement between their employer and a labor organization made pursuant to section 8(a)(3), of a petition alleging they desire that such authority be rescinded, the Board shall take a secret ballot of the employees in such unit, and shall certify the results thereof to such labor organization and to the employer.

(2) No election shall be directed in any bargaining unit or any subdivision within which, in the preceding twelve-month period, a valid election shall have been held.

The Sherman Act
(excerpts)

1. Every contract, combination in the form of trust or otherwise, or conspiracy, in restraint of trade or commerce among the several States, or with foreign nations, is declared to be illegal. Every person who shall make any contract or engage in any combination or conspiracy declared by section 1 to 7 of this title to be illegal shall be deemed guilty of a felony, and, on conviction thereof, shall be punished by fine not exceeding one million dollars if a corporation, or if any other person, one hundred thousand dollars, or by imprisonment not exceeding three years, or both said punishments, in the discretion of the court.

2. Every person who shall monopolize, or attempt to monopolize, or combine or conspire with any other person or persons, to monopolize any part of the trade or commerce among the several States, or with foreign nations, shall be deemed guilty of a felony, and, on conviction thereof, shall be punished by fine not exceeding one million dollars if a corporation, or if any other person, one hundred thousand dollars, or by imprisonment not exceeding three years, or by both said punishments, in the discretion of the court.

Clayton Act (excerpts)

An act to supplement existing laws against unlawful restraints and monopolies, and for other purposes.

SECTION 2. (a) That it shall be unlawful for any person engaged in commerce, in the course of such commerce, either directly or indirectly, to discriminate in price between different purchasers of commodities of like grade and quality, where either or any of the purchases involved in such discrimination are in commerce, where such commodites are sold for use, consumption, or resale within the United States or any Territory thereof or the District of Columbia or any insular possession or other place under the jurisdiction of the United States, and where the effect of such discrimination may be substantially to lessen competition or tend to create a monopoly in any line of commerce, or to injure, destroy, or prevent competition with any person who either grants or knowingly receives the benefit of such discrimination, or with customers of either of them; Provided, That nothing herein contained shall prevent differentials which make only due allowance for differences in the cost of manufacture, sale, or delivery resulting from the differing methods or quantities in which such commodities are to such purchasers sold or delivered: Provided, however, That the Federal Trade Commission may, after due investigation and hearing to all interested parties, fix and establish quantity limits, and revise the same as it finds necessary, as to particular commodities or classes of commodities, where it finds that available purchasers in greater quantities are so few as to render differentials on account thereof unjustly discriminatory or promotive of monopoly in any line of commerce; and the foregoing shall then not be construed to permit differentials based on differences in quantities greater than those so fixed and established: And provided further, That nothing herein contained shall prevent persons engaged in selling goods, wares, or merchandise in commerce from selecting their own customers in bona fide transactions and not in restraint of trade: And provided further, That nothing herein contained shall prevent price changes from time to time where in response to changing conditions affecting the market for or the marketability of the goods concerned, such as but not limited to actual or imminent deterioration of perishable goods, obsolescence of seasonal goods, distress sales under court process, or sales in good faith in discontinuance of business in the goods concerned.

(b) Upon proof being made, at any hearing on a complaint under this section, that there has been discrimination in price or services or facilities furnished, the burden of rebutting the prima facie case thus made by showing justification shall be upon the person charged with a violation of this section, and unless justification shall be affirmatively shown, the Commission is authorized to issue an order terminating the discrimination: Provided, however, That nothing herein contained shall prevent a seller rebutting the prima facie case thus made by showing that his lower price or the furnishing of services or facilities to any purchaser or purchasers was made in good faith to meet an equally low price of a competitor, or the services or facilities by a competitor.

(c) That it shall be unlawful for any person engaged in commerce, in the course of such commerce, to pay or grant, or to receive or accept, anything of value as a commission, brokerage, or other compensation, or any allowance or discount in lieu hereof, except for services rendered in connection with the sale or purchase of goods, wares, or merchandise, either to the other party to such transaction or to an agent, representative, or other intermediary therein where such intermediary is acting in fact for or in behalf, or is subject to the direct or indirect control, of any party to such transaction other than the person by whom such compensation is so granted or paid.

(d) That it shall be unlawful for any person engaged in commerce to pay or contract for the payment of anything of value to or for the benefit of a customer of such person in the course of such commerce as compensation or consideration for any services or facilities furnished by or through such customer in connection with the processing, handling, sale, or offering for sale of any products or commodities manufactured, sold, or offered for sale by such person, unless such payment or consideration is available on proportionally equal terms to all other customers competing in the distribution of such products or commodities.

(e) That it shall be unlawful for any person to discriminate in favor of one purchaser against another purchaser or purchasers of a commodity bought for resale, with or without processing, by contracting to furnish or furnishing, or by contributing to the furnishing of, any services or facilities connected with the processing, handling, sale, or offering for sale of such commodity so purchased upon terms not accorded to all purchasers on proportionally equal terms.

(f) That it shall be unlawful for any person engaged in commerce, in the course of such commerce, knowingly to induce or receive a discrimination in price which is prohibited by this section.

SECTION 4. That any person who shall be injured in his business or property by reason of anything forbidden in the antitrust laws may sue therefor in any district court of the United States in the district in which the defendant resides or is found, or has an agent, without respect to the amount in controversy, and shall recover threefold the damages by him sustained, and the cost of suit, including a reasonable attorney's fee.

SECTION 4A. Whenever the United States is hereafter injured in its business or property by reason of anything forbidden in the antitrust laws it may sue therefor in the United States district court for the district in which the defendant resides or is found or has an agent, without respect to the amount in controversy, and shall recover actual damages by it sustained and the cost of suit.

SECTION 4B. Any action to enforce any cause of action under sections 4 and 4A shall be forever barred unless commenced within four years after the cause of action accrued. No cause of action barred under existing law on the effective date of this act shall be revived by this Act.

SECTION 4C. (a)(1) Any attorney general of a State may bring a civil action in the name of such State, as parens patriae on behalf of natural persons residing in such State, in any district court of the United States having jurisdiction of the defendant, to secure monetary relief as provided in this section for injury sustained by such natural persons to their property by reason of any violation of the Sherman Act. The court shall exclude from the amount of monetary relief awarded in such action any amount of monetary relief (A) which duplicates amounts which have been awarded for the same injury, or (B) which is properly allocable to (i) natural persons who have excluded their claims pursuant to subsection (b)(2) of this section, and (ii) any business entity.

(2) The court shall award the State as monetary relief threefold the total damage sustained as described in paragraph (1) of this subsection, and the cost of suit, including a reasonable attorney's fee.

(b)(1) In any action brought under subsection (a)(1) of this section, the State attorney general shall, at such times, in such manner, and with such content as the court may direct, cause notice thereof to be given by publication. If the court finds that notice given solely by publication would deny due process of law to any person or persons, the court may direct further notice to such person or persons according to the circumstances of the case.

(2) Any person on whose behalf an action is brought under subsection (a)(1) may elect to exclude from adjudication the portion of the State claim for monetary relief attributable to him by filing notice of such election with the court within such time as specified in the notice given pursuant to paragraph (1) of this subsection.

(3) The final judgment in an action under subsection (a)(1) shall be res judicata as to any claim under section 4 of this Act by any person on behalf of whom such action was brought and who fails to give such notice within the period specified in the notice given pursuant to paragraph (1) of this subsection.

(c) An action under subsection (a)(1) shall not be dismissed or compromised without the approval of the court, and notice of any proposed dismissal or compromise shall be given in such manner as the court directs.

(d) In any action under subsection (a)—

(1) the amount of the plaintiffs' attorney's fee, if any, shall be determined by the court; and

(2) the court may, in its discretion, award a reasonable attorney's fee to a prevailing defendant upon a finding that the State attorney general has acted in bad faith, vexatiously, wantonly, or for oppressive reasons.

SECTION 6. That the labor of a human being is not a commodity of article of commerce. Nothing contained in the antitrust laws shall be construed to forbid the existence and operation of labor, agricultural, or horticultural organizations, instituted for the purposes of mutual help, and not having capital stock or conducted for profit, or to forbid or restrain individual members of such organizations from lawfully carrying out the legitimate objects thereof; nor shall such organizations, or the members thereof, be held or construed to be illegal combinations or conspiracies in restraint of trade, under the antitrust laws.

Americans with Disabilities Act of 1990 (excerpts)

Title I—Employment

Sec. 101. Definitions.

Qualified individual with a disability.—The term "qualified individual with a disability" means an individual with a disability who, with or without reasonable accommodation, can perform the essential functions of the employment position that such individual holds or desires. For the purposes of this title, consideration shall be given to the employer's judgment as to what functions of a job are essential, and if an employer has prepared a written description before advertising or interviewing applicants for the job, this description shall be considered evidence of the essential functions of the job.

Reasonable accomodation.—The term "reasonable accommodation" may include—

(A) making existing facilities used by employees readily accessible to and usable by individuals with disabilities; and

(B) job restructuring, part-time or modified work schedules, reassignment to a vacant position, acquisition or modification of equipment or devices, appropriate adjustment or modifications of examinations, training materials or policies, the provision of qualified readers or interpreters, and other similar accommodations for individuals with disabilities.

Undue Hardship.—

(A) **In general.**—The term "undue hardship" means an action requiring significant difficulty or expense, when considered in light of the factors set forth below:

In determining whether an accommodation would impose an undue hardship on a covered entity, factors to be considered include—

(i) the nature and cost of accommodation needed under this Act;

(ii) The overall financial resources of the facility or facilities involved in the provision of the reasonable accommodation; the number of persons employed at such facility; the effect on expenses and resources, or the impact otherwise of such accommodation upon the operation of the facility;

(iii) the overall financial resources of the covered entity; the overall size of the business of a covered entity with respect to the number of its employees; the number, type, and location of its facilities; and

(iv) the type of operation or operations of the covered entity, including the composition, structure, and functions of the workforce of such entity; the geographic separateness, administrative, or fiscal relationship of the facility or facilities in question to the covered entity.

Sec. 102. Discrimination.

(a) **General Rule.**—No covered entity shall discriminate against a qualified individual with a disability because of the disability of such individual in regard to job application procedures, the hiring, advancement, or discharge of employees, employee compensation, job training, and other terms, conditions, and privileges of employment.

(b) **Construction.**—As used in subsection (a), the term "discriminate" includes—

(1) limiting, segregating, or classifying a job appli-

cant or employee in a way that adversely affects the opportunities or status of such applicant or employee because of the disability of such applicant or employee;

(2) participating in a contractual or other arrangement or relationship that has the effect of subjecting a covered entity's qualified applicant or employee with a disability to the discrimination prohibited by this title (such relationship includes a relationship with an employment or referral agency, labor union, an organization providing fringe benefits to an employee of the covered entity, or an organization providing training and apprenticeship programs);

(3) utilizing standards, criteria, or methods of administration—

(A) that have the effect of discrimination on the basis of disability; or

(B) that perpetuate the discrimination of others who are subject to common administrative control;

(4) excluding or otherwise denying equal jobs or benefits to a qualified individual because of the known disability of an individual with whom the qualified individual is known to have a relationship or association;

(5)

(A) not making reasonable accommodations to the known physical or mental limitations of an otherwise qualified individual with a disability who is an applicant or employee, unless such covered entity can demonstrate that the accommodation would impose an undue hardship on the operation of the business of such covered entity; or

(B) denying employment opportunities to a job applicant or employee who is an otherwise qualified individual with a disability, if such denial is based on the need of such covered entity to make reasonable accommodation to the physical or mental impairments of the employee or applicant;

(6) using qualification standards, employment tests or other selection criteria that screen out or tend to screen out an individual with a disability or a class of individuals with disabilities unless the standard, test or other selection criteria, as used by the covered entity, is shown to be job-related for the position in question and is consistent with business necessity; and

(7) failing to select and administer tests concerning employment in the most effective manner to ensure that, when such test is administered to a job applicant or employee who has a disability that impairs sensory, manual, or speaking skills, such test results accurately reflect the skills, aptitude, or whatever other factor of such applicant or employee that such test purports to measure, rather than reflecting the impaired sensory, manual, or speaking skills of such employee or applicant (except where such skills are the factors that the test purports to measure).

GLOSSARY

Act of State Doctrine The doctrine that states that a court in one country will not sit in judgment on the acts of another government done within its own territory.

Actual Authority Authority for an agent to act that is granted either expressly or by implication by the principal.

Administrative Rule Making Administrative agency function to promulgate rules and regulations having the same force and effect as laws passed by a legislature.

Adversary System Theory that all the facts will be uncovered and the truth will come out if each side in a dispute presents its case in the best possible light.

Advisory Opinion Advice given by the courts to other branches of government concerning the law or the constitutionality of a proposed law.

Affirmative Action Plans Plans designed to ensure that all persons have an opportunity to work at a given company.

Agency Adjudication The function of an administrative agency to hear complaints, similar to a judicial function.

Agency Shop A contract with a union that does not require employees to join the union but does require them to pay union dues and initiation fees.

Agent A person who has the power to act on behalf of a principal.

Ally Doctrine The doctrine that permits unions to picket secondary employers doing the work of a primary employer.

Amicus Curiae Brief A brief filed in a case by someone who is not a party to that case. Amicus curiae means "a friend of the court."

Answer The response filed in court by the defendant to the plaintiff's petition. It states the defendant's response to each of the plaintiff's allegations.

Apparent Authority A doctrine covering agents and contracts with third parties by which authority exists in the absence of actual authority.

Appellant Party in a case who petitions a court of appeals to review the decision of a lower court.

Appellate Court A court that reviews the rulings of a trial court when the losing party in a trial case is dissatisfied with the verdict.

Appellee The party in a case against whom an appeal is filed.

Assignee The person to whom an assignment of right is made.

Assignment The process of transferring rights from one person to another.

Assignor A person who makes an assignment of a right.

Attorney-Client Privilege A privilege by which a client's confidential discussions with an attorney remain confidential.

Bankruptcy Estate All of the debtor's legal and equitable interests in property owned as of the date of the filing of the bankruptcy petition, except for exempt property, and interests in certain property that the debtor becomes entitled to within 180 days after the filing of the bankruptcy petition.

Bench Trial A trial that is heard only by a judge and not by a jury.

Bill of Rights The first ten amendments to the Constitution.

Blind Trust A legal and business relationship in which one person holds in trust and invests the property of another. The person whose property is being held is precluded from knowing the assets in the trust or the investments made on his behalf.

Blue Sky Laws State laws attempting to regulate the securities industry.

Bona Fide Occupational Qualification (BFOQ) A job qualification that arises when religion, sex, or national origin is a requirement that is reasonably necessary to operate the business.

Boycott A concerted effort by someone or some

group to encourage people to stop doing business with someone.

Brandeis Brief A brief making use of social science studies to supplement more traditional legal arguments. First used by Louis D. Brandeis.

Brief Written argument to the court concerning points the parties want the court to consider.

Burden of Proof The duty of a party to substantiate an allegation or issue to avoid dismissal of that issue early in the trial or in order to convince the trier of facts as to the truth of the claim and therefore win at trial.

Cause of Action A legal claim or complaint for which a party may seek redress in a court.

Caveat Emptor Literally, let the buyer beware. A doctrine in which the buyer of a product assumed any risk associated with the purchase or use of the product.

Certiorari A procedure of appellate practice whereby a higher court is given the opportunity to review a decision by a lower court.

Challenge for Cause The right of an attorney to ask that a person be disqualified from serving on a jury because of the person's bias or prejudice.

Choice of Forum Clause A contractual provision that specifies where a dispute arising under a contract will be tried.

Choice of Law Clause A contractual provision that specifies the law of the country or state that will be applied in the event of a contract dispute.

Civil Case Case in which the plaintiff institutes suit against the defendant for some civil wrong.

Civil Litigation All the trial work of our judicial system that does not involve the violation of a criminal statute.

Civil War Amendments The Thirteenth, Fourteenth, and Fifteenth Amendments to the Constitution.

Class Action A lawsuit or legal action brought on behalf of a large number of people with similar claims.

Close Corporation A type of corporate organization in which there are few shareholders. Corporate shares are not sold on an organized market. Often, close corporate shareholders are related to one another. Frequently, close corporations are small businesses.

Closed-End Circuit A credit plan in which a person borrows a fixed amount that is to be paid back over a designated period of time.

Closed Shop An agreement, now illegal, by an employer to hire only members of a union.

Closing Argument The point during a trial, after the conclusion of the presentation of evidence, when the attorneys present their final arguments concerning a case to the judge or jury.

***Colgate* Doctrine** A doctrine by which a manufacturer may unilaterally announce that it will not deal with customers who fail to abide by the price it sets for a product.

Commerce Clause A provision in the U.S. Constitution created to protect interstate commerce from discriminatory state action.

Commercial Speech Doctrine The doctrine that states commercial speech is protected by the United States Constitution.

Common Law The body of law formulated and created by judicial decision.

Common Law Copyright The property right in a written item as recognized by common law.

Common Situs A location where employees from several employers work at the same place.

Comparable Worth The concept that employers should pay workers the same wage rate if their jobs are of comparable worth, or equal value, to the employer.

Comparative Negligence A doctrine in the law of torts. The relative negligence of the plaintiff and defendant are considered and the damages ultimately awarded are reduced by the proportion of the plaintiff's negligence.

Compensatory Damages Those damages necessary to place the aggrieved party in the same position he or she would have occupied had the contract not been breached in the first place.

Concurring Opinion An opinion, written by an appellate court justice, that agrees with the appellate court's decision but disagrees with the reasoning of the court.

Conglomerate Merger A business combination or merger in which there are no economic relationships between the acquiring and the acquired firm.

Consent Decree An agreement between parties that they will be bound by a certain stipulated set of facts.

Consequential Damages Special damages that could have been foreseen at the time of the breach of contract but which do not directly flow from the breach of contract.

Consumer A person who buys or borrows for personal, family, or household use.

Contract An agreement, obligation, or legal tie whereby a party binds himself or herself, expressly or impliedly, to pay a sum of money or to perform or omit to do a certain act or thing.

Contract of Adhesion A contract heavily weighted to favor the party that possesses significantly more bargaining power.

Conversion A doctrine in the law of torts. Conversion arises when someone wrongfully uses (or takes) another's property.

Corporation A business organizational form that is considered to be a legal being. It may have perpetual life, and it insulates its owners (shareholders) from personal liability.

Counterclaim A claim presented by a defendant against the plaintiff. Answers often contain counterclaims against the plaintiff.

Counteroffer An offer made by the offeree to the offeror that would materially alter the original offer and thus require acceptance by the offeror.

Countervailing Duties Special duties used to offset a foreign subsidy.

Creditor Beneficiary A person who is not a party to a contract. If the contract is performed, one of the parties to the contract will be discharged from a duty or debt he or she owes to this person.

Criminal Case Case in which a prosecutor representing the state or federal government brings suit against the defendant for an alleged violation of law.

Criminal Law Branch or division of law that defines crimes, treats their nature, and provides for their punishment.

Cross Examination The point when an attorney for the opposing party asks questions of a witness who is testifying.

Custom A nation's present habits and an important aspect of its system of laws.

Debt A financial obligation owed by one person or business to another.

Debt Collector A person or business that tries to collect from persons or businesses who fail to pay a debt.

Defendant The party in a case against whom criminal charges have been filed (in criminal law) or against whom a legal claim has been filed (in a civil suit).

Deposition The process of questioning under oath, prior to trial, the witnesses and parties to a lawsuit.

Dicta Portions of a judge's opinion that are not the ruling in the case.

Dilatory tactics The practice of delaying a case simply for the purpose of delay.

Direct Examination The point when an attorney calls a witness to testify and asks the witness questions.

Discovery A process before a trial begins through which opposing counsel can learn the case to be presented by the other side.

Dissenting Opinion An opinion, written by an appellate court justice, that disagrees with the outcome of the case being decided.

Diversity of Citizenship A situation when all the plaintiffs are from states other than the state of residence of any of the defendants.

Documentary Credit An instrument in which a bank agrees to pay another party if certain conditions in the instrument have been complied with by the presenting party.

Domestic Content Law A law that requires a certain percentage of a good's value be produced in the nation which passed the law.

Donee Beneficiary A person who is not a party to a contract that was made for that person's benefit.

Double Jeopardy Clause The provision in the United States Constitution that prohibits the government from bringing a criminal action against a person twice for the same offense.

Due Diligence Defense A doctrine arising under the 1933 Act in which those liable (other than the issuer) for material omissions or misstatements in the registration statement can be exonerated.

Due Process A constitutional principle which requires that government actions not be arbitrary or capricious. Its concern is with establishing fundamental procedural fairness in our system of government.

Dumping Selling products or services in a foreign market at less than their fair value.

Economic Strike A strike solely to force an employer to grant the employees better wages or working conditions.

Ejusdem Generis Doctrine A method of interpretation in which a general phase is inserted after a series of specific words in a statute. The general phrase shall be interpreted to include words of the same kind as those used in the preceding series.

Eminent domain The right of the government to take property from a private owner for public use. Just compensation must be paid to those private owners.

Enabling Act A congressional statute that calls into existence a federal administrative agency.

Environment Impact Statement An analysis of the effect of major federal activity on the environment as required by the National Environmental Policy Act.

Equal Employment Opportunity Commission (EEOC) Federal administrative agency charged with the enforcement of Title VII of the Civil Rights Act of 1964.

Equal Protection Clause The clause in the United States Constitution that requires equal treatment of people.

Equity justice. Also a separate body of law developed independently from the common law, based upon rules of fairness and justice.

Escape Clause A provision in GATT that permits countries to raise tariffs if there is a serious threat to domestic industry as a consequence of earlier trade reductions.

Executive Order An order issued by the president of the United States or governor of a state.

Executive Privilege Doctrine under which the president is able to keep certain communications from being disclosed in court.

Ex Parte An application by one party to a case made to a judge without first giving notice of the application to the other party.

Express Warranty A statement of fact, description or sample or model that is part of the basis of the bargain between the parties.

Expropriation The seizure of foreign owned property by a government.

Featherbedding A union requirement, now illegal, that an employer pay for work not performed.

Federal Mediation and Conciliation Service An agency created by the Taft-Hartley Act to assist parties to labor disputes in industries affecting commerce to settle such disputes through conciliation and mediation.

Federal Register The official public notice organ of the federal administrative agencies.

Felony Generic term to distinguish certain crimes such as murder, robbery, and larceny from minor offenses known as misdemeanors. The distinction lies in the extent of punishment provided.

Fiduciary Duty The duty of a person who is vested with power over another's property to act with good faith, diligence, and loyalty with regard to that property.

Fixture Personal property that is so attached to or used with real property that it is considered to be a part of real property.

Formal Settlement An agreement to resolve a case entered into after a complaint is filed against a party.

Fraud A deliberate misrepresentation or nondisclosure of a material fact made with the intent that the other party will rely upon it, and in fact the party to whom the statement is made does rely upon it to his or her detriment.

Full Warranty The Magnuson-Moss Act requires certain consumer products to be labeled as having either a full or limited warranty. Products with a full warranty must meet certain requirements specified in the act.

GATT General Agreement on Tariffs and Trade. A trade agreement between many of the world's countries.

General Verdict A decision for one of the parties to a case without any special findings of fact.

Grand Jury A proceeding to determine whether there exists probable cause to initiate a criminal proceeding.

Habeus Corpus (Writ of) A common law writ that brings a prisoner before a court. Prisoners use such writs to obtain a court review as to whether a person was imprisoned in accordance with the requirements of the law.

Hearsay Evidence of a statement which is made other than by a witness while testifying at trial which is offered to prove the truth of the matter stated.

History A nation's past and an important aspect of its system of law.

Holder in Due Course A person who is in possession of a negotiable instrument who has taken it in good faith, for value, and without notice of any claim or defense that exists against the instrument.

Horizontal Merger The acquisition of one company by another company producing the same product or similar product and selling it in the same geographic market.

Hot Cargo A clause, now illegal, stating that

workers are not required to handle nonunion material.

Hung Jury   When a jury is unable to arrive at a verdict.

Illusory Promise   A promise in which the obligation to perform is entirely optional on the part of one of the parties.

Implied Agency Rule   In contract law, if the offer does not state that the acceptance will not be effective until it is received, the moment an acceptance is sent by an authorized means a contract is effective.

Implied Warranty of Merchantability   The guarantee that arises automatically by operation of law that goods sold by a seller will be fit for the purposes for which such goods are normally sold and will pass without objection in the trade.

Incidental Beneficiary   A person who is not a party to a contract who obtains a benefit that was not intended by the parties to the contract.

Indictment   A finding by a grand jury that reasonable grounds exist to believe that a crime has been committed. It is not a final determination or conviction.

Informal Settlement   An agreement to resolve a case entered into before a complaint has been filed against a party.

Informational Picketing   Picketing designed to advise the public that an employer does not have a union contract with its employers.

Injunction   An order by a court that prohibits or restrains a party from doing a particular act.

Innocent Misrepresentation   Unintended misrepresentation of a product that causes injury to a person.

Insider Trading   Trading in securities by someone who has information on those securities not available to the general investing public and who has a duty not to use the information for personal benefit. Under the 1934 Act, certain people who buy or sell securities having secret material information are liable both civilly and criminally.

Intentional Tort   A tort in which the aim of a certain act is to cause injury.

Interrogatories   Written questions submitted to a person concerning a case that must be answered under oath.

Investigative Consumer Report   A report gathered by a company about a person's credit history.

The Fair Credit Reporting Act calls this an investigative consumer report.

Investment Contracts   Type of security that includes a large number of unusual schemes.

Judgment on the Pleadings   A motion at the close of the pleading state made by any party to a suit which alleges the other party is not entitled to prevail at trial.

Judicial Immunity   The inability of a dissatisfied litigant to sue the judge.

Judicial Review   The power of a court to review a statute and declare it void if it violates various constitutional guarantees.

Jurisdiction   The power or authority of a court to hear a particular legal dispute.

Jurisdictional Dispute   A dispute between unions as to which union is entitled to perform certain work.

Justiciable   A dispute that may properly be decided by a court.

Legal   Lawful.

Legal Benefit   Receiving something that one had no prior legal obligation to receive.

Legal Detriment   The requirement that a party does or promises to do something which there was no prior legal duty to do or refraining from doing something that there was no prior legal duty to refrain from doing.

Legislative History   A body of documentation created at the time a statute was drafted. A judge will consult the documents, consisting of reports, studies, speeches, etc., to determine the legislature's purpose in enacting the statute.

Limited Liability   The characteristic of a corporation by which no individual member of the corporation is liable for claims made against it.

Limited Liability Company   A new form of business organization that is rapidly being embraced by the states. It provides limited liability for its owners who can manage the business and who have a right to share in its profits.

Limited Partnership   Business organization with characteristics of both a corporation and a partnership; often used for a tax shelter.

Limited Warranty   The Magnuson-Moss Act requires certain consumer products to be labeled as having either a full or limited warranty. Limited warranties are those that do not comply with the act's requirement for a full warranty.

Liquidated Damages (Clause) A clause in a contract that specifies the amount of damages a party must pay if it breaches the contract.

Lockout An employer's refusal to allow employees to work.

Long-Arm Statutes Statutes that permit a plaintiff to obtain service of a summons and petition beyond the physical borders of a state.

Mediation A proceeding used to try to resolve disputes. The mediator tries to help the parties to a dispute work out their differences.

Minitrial An informal procedure used by parties in which a simplified version of the case is presented to a neutral party for a decision. The decision in the minitrial is not binding on the parties.

Mirror Offer Rule The common law rule of contracts that requires an acceptance to be in exactly the same terms as the original offer.

Misdemeanor Misconduct or offense inferior to a felony.

Missouri Plan A method of appointing judges whereby a panel recommends suitable candidates for the judiciary and voters are periodically questioned in the voting booth whether to retain the judge or not.

Mitigation of Damages The obligation of the injured party in a breach of contract to keep losses or damages as small as possible.

Monopoly The power to fix prices or exclude competition, coupled with policies designed to use or preserve that power.

Motion A request to the court for an order or rule in favor of the party making the motion.

Motion for a Directed Verdict A motion by which the moving party states that the other side has failed to prove all the facts necessary to establish a case.

Motion for a Judgment Notwithstanding the Verdict Motion in which, at the conclusion of a trial, after the verdict is announced, the defeated party asks the judge to set the verdict aside because it was not supported by the evidence or the law.

Motion for Summary Judgment A motion which states that there is no genuine issue of material fact remaining to be decided in the case, therefore the judge should grant the motion and decide who should prevail in the case.

Motion to Dismiss A motion made by the defendant which alleges that even if everything in the plaintiff's petition is assumed to be true, the plaintiff still is not entitled to a remedy, and therefore the plaintiff's petition should be dismissed.

Natural Law An overriding sense of justice or fairness that is fundamental to the law.

Negligence A lapse in an acceptable pattern of conduct that creates an unreasonable risk of injury.

NEPA The National Environmental Policy Act of 1969, the purposes of which are to encourage harmony between man and the environment and to eliminate environmental damage.

NLRB (The National Labor Relations Board) A national public agency created by statute to enforce the provisions of the National Labor Relations Act—not a tribunal for the enforcement of private rights through administrative remedies. An agency of the United States, an entity apart from its members, having legal capacity to sue in the federal courts to carry out its statutory functions.

Nolo Contendere An admission of every essential element of the offense stated in the charge. It is tantamount to an admission of guilt for the purpose of the case, but it is only a confession and does not dispute of the case or constitute a conviction or determination of guilt.

Nominal Damages A token sum awarded to a party in light of a breach of contract that did not produce any financial loss to the aggrieved party.

Nuisance An act that annoys or disturbs the enjoyment of property by its owner.

Offer A manifestation by a person of a desire to enter into a contract.

Offeree The person to whom an offer is made.

Offeror The person who makes an offer.

Oligopoly An industry composed of several large firms, each possessing a major part of trade in a given market.

Open-End Credit A credit plan that permits a person to keep charging on an account until he reaches a certain amount. The account can be paid off in full or in installments.

Opening Statement The statement made by the attorney in a case prior to the actual presentation of evidence. It generally provides an overview of what evidence will be presented and what the attorneys have to prove.

Option Contract   A special contract that provides that a certain offer will remain open to a certain offeree upon the offeree providing some consideration.

Organization Picketing   Picketing designed to convince employees to sign up with the union.

Parens Patriae   Suit brought by the attorney general of a state on behalf of persons living in that state.

Parol Evidence Rule   A rule of evidence that prevents the introduction of oral testimony in a court proceeding which adds to, alters, or varies the terms of a written agreement.

Partnership   A type of business organization. It consists of two or more persons co-owning a business that is a profit-seeking enterprise. These co-owners (called partners) are legally indistinguishable from their partnership business.

Per Curiam Opinion   A latin phrase meaning "by the court." When used in a judicial opinion, it means that the opinion is joined by all the judges of that court.

Per Se   The rule that a court need not inquire into the reasonableness of a case before determining that it is a violation of the antitrust laws, if an anticompetitive business activity is blatant in its intent and pernicious in its effect.

Peremptory Challenge   The right of an attorney to strike certain prospective jurors from the jury panel. This is exercised by the attorneys after the conclusion of the voir dire.

Petition   A document filed with a court by the plaintiff asking the court to grant the plaintiff some type of relief. The petition states paragraph by paragraph the nature of the claims the plaintiff has against the defendant and the relief requested of the court.

Petit Jury   A jury that hears evidence presented by witnesses at trial, and based upon instructions given to them by the judge, renders a decision in a case.

Piercing the Corporate Veil   Doctrine in corporate law under which a court will ignore the limited liability protection of the corporate form and hold those members behind it personally liable.

Plain Meaning Doctrine   A method of statutory interpretation in which the court looks solely at the ordinary and usual meaning of the words of the statute to determine what the statute says.

Plaintiff   The party in a civil suit who commences the action.

Pleadings   The documents filed by the respective parties to a lawsuit that state their contentions. The first pleading is the petition, filed by the plaintiff, to which the defendant is required to file an answer.

Pollution   The human-caused diminished capacity of the environment to perform its function.

Precedent   A previously decided case that serves as authority for a court's decision in a current dispute.

Preemption   The doctrine that deprives a state of the power to pass legislation dealing with the same matters as covered in federal legislation.

Preponderance of the Evidence   The standard of proof required in civil cases. A party has met this burden of proof when its evidence is more convincing to the trier of fact than the opposing evidence.

Prescription   Doctrine that confers a property right on a person who uses another's land without permission and without interruption for twenty years (usually).

Pretrial Conference   A conference held by a judge prior to trial concerning an upcoming trial. The purpose is to try to narrow the issues of the case and to attempt to encourage a settlement of the case.

Preventive Law   A lawyer's advice to a client on a variety of legal matters in order to minimize the possibility of future legal problems for the client.

Primary Employer   The employer for whom employees who are engaged in collective activity work.

Primary Line Competitive Injury   Price discrimination by which a national firm attempts to put a local competitive firm out of business by lowering its prices only in the region where the local firms sell its products.

Primary Pressure   Direct pressure put on an employer by its own employees.

Principal   In agency law, the employer or person for whom an agent acts.

Privity of Contract   A direct relationship between the parties to a contract.

Probate   Process in law by which a will is proven and its terms given effect.

Promise   Voluntary commitment by a person to another person to perform in some manner or refrain from some action in the future.

Promisee   The person to whom a promise is made.

Promisor   The person who makes a promise.

Promissory Estoppel The doctrine that makes certain contracts binding although they are not supported by consideration.

Property A relationship between the holder of rights and all others recognized and enforced by government.

Prospectus A summary of the information contained in a registration statement. It is provided to all offerees of the initial issuance of the securities.

Proximate Cause A term of art in tort law that refers to a policy that limits to scope of a tortfeasor's liability. The act that is the dominant cause or is in a close relation to an injury is said to be the proximate cause of that injury.

Public Use The only reason that entitles government to exercise its right of eminent domain.

Publicly Traded Corporation A type of corporate organization in which the shares of stock are traded on an organized market such as the New York Stock Exchange.

Punitive Damage Damage that is awarded by a court in order to punish a party that has violated the law.

Quota A limit on the importation of a certain type of good imposed by a country.

Ratification The acceptance by the principal of the benefits of a contract entered into by an agent in absence of an authority. The principal is thereafter bound by that contract.

Reasonable Accommodation A term that is used in both Title VII of the Civil Rights Act of 1964 and in the Americans with Disabilities Act. It provides that a business must consider reasonable changes in its operations or procedures to adjust to either the religious practices or disabilities of its employees (or applicants for jobs).

Reasonable Person Used in tort law as a test for actionable conduct. A reasonable person acts with ordinary care and prudence.

Recognition Picketing Picketing used to convince the employer to recognize the union.

Recusal A situation in which a judge declines to hear a case because he fears that a personal bias may affect its outcome.

Registration Statement Under the 1933 Act, a company issuing new nonexempt securities must file a full disclosure statement with the

SEC. This statement is called a registration statement.

Res Ipsa Loquitur A doctrine in the law of torts which presumes that the defendant was the negligent cause of an accident. Rather than requiring the plaintiff to prove that the defendant was negligent, the doctrine shifts the burden to the defendant to prove that he or she was not negligent.

Restatement of Contracts An analysis of contract law based on existing judicial decisions.

Restatement (Second) of Torts A scholarly work that discusses the law of torts as it exists across the United States. It also includes suggestions for changes the scholars think ought to be adopted by the states with respect to the law of torts.

Restraint of Trade In antitrust law, business combinations or practices that seek to stifle competition and obstruct the market from its natural operation.

Restrictive Covenant In a contract, an agreement by one of the parties to the contract not to engage in certain behavior in a designated area for a designated period of time at the conclusion of the contractual relationship.

Retail Price Maintenance Scheme in which a single manufacturer and a retail seller or distributor agree to set the price at which a commodity may be sold.

RICO The Racketeer Influenced Corrupt Organization Act.

Rights Powers of free action that a person has and that are recognized by law.

Rule Making A process by which administrative agencies promulgate regulations.

Rule of Reason Court decision stating that only unreasonable restraints of trade and unreasonable attempts to monopolize violate the Sherman Act.

Search Warrant Written order by a court that gives the police the right to search certain premises or property for items that may be used, if found, as evidence in a criminal trial.

Secondary Line Competitive Injury A price discrimination that causes injury to certain buyers.

Secondary Pressure A boycott of an employer other than the employer with whom the employees have a dispute.

Secondary Pressure Action Action taken against a

customer or supplier of an employer in order to pressure the employer to settle a labor dispute in favor of the employees.

Securities Stocks, bonds, and other investment contracts.

Securities and Exchange Commission (SEC) Federal commission responsible for administering federal securities laws.

Separate but Equal The constitutional doctrine put forth in *Plessy* v. *Ferguson* (1896) that the equal protection clause was not violated if segregated facilities were equivalent.

Separation of Powers The principle by which each of the three branches of government—executive, legislative, and judicial—has different functions so that no one of them becomes too powerful.

Sexual Harassment Unwelcome sexual advances, requests for sexual favors, and other verbal or physical conduct of a sexual nature.

Sole Proprietorship A means by which a business can be owned. It is not a formal type of business organization. Its primary characteristic is that it has one owner and this owner and the sole proprietorship business are legally indistinguishable.

Sovereign Immunity Doctrine The doctrine under which governments are immune from suit when engaging in governmental acts.

Special Verdict A verdict in a case where a jury makes specific findings concerning the facts presented at trial.

Specific Performance (Doctrine of) An order compelling a party to perform his or her obligations under a contract.

Stare Decisis A doctrine of judicial decision making that governs the application of precedent to a current dispute. The doctrine provides for stability in the legal system by having current disputes controlled by decisions in past cases.

Statute of Limitations A statute which specifies that a certain type of case must be filed within a certain designated period of time after the cause of action arises.

Strict Liability The standard of culpability to which a seller will be held for breach of an implied warranty that is imposed as a matter of public policy on a product he sells. Such liability is "strict liability" because it attaches even though the seller has exercised all possible care in the preparation and sale of his or her product.

Summary Judgment A decision by a court in a case without holding a trial. It occurs on motion of a party that since the facts of the case are not in dispute, the court should make a ruling based upon the law.

Summary Trial A trial in which a summary of the case is presented to a judge or jury. Decisions in such cases may not be binding on the parties depending upon the agreement between the parties.

Summons A document issued by a court which is served on the defendant, notifies him that suit has been instituted by the plaintiff, and requires the defendant to answer the plaintiff's petition in a certain designated period of time.

Surface Bargaining A situation in which the employer goes through the outward motions of bargaining but is really not willing to negotiate.

Technological Infeasibility The inability of industry to comply with environmental regulations because existing technology is inadequate.

Third Party Beneficiary A person who is not a party to a contract but who will benefit form the performance of the contract.

Tort A body of law covering civil wrongs other than breaches of contract.

Treaty An agreement between two or more nations which is binding on the nations and must be performed in good faith.

Trespass The unauthorized, intentional entry upon the land of another.

Trial Court The first step in resolving disputes in the judicial system. Evidence is given and a verdict is rendered.

True Bill A grand jury's endorsement of an indictment that it finds supported by the evidence presented to them.

Trust An obligation arising out of confidence reposed in a person, for the benefit of another, to apply property faithfully and according to such confidence.

Trustee in Bankruptcy A person who holds title to the bankrupt's property at the direction of a court. The trustee collects all the property from the bankrupt, liquidates it and distributes the money to the creditors of the bankrupt.

Truth-in-Lending Act Act passed by Congress in 1969 in order to make meaningful comparisons between the rates charged by different lenders.

Ultra Vires Limitation of agency power by which no act outside the power granted may be performed. Such acts would be voidable.

Unconscionablity A lack of meaningful choice in a contractual relationship coupled with a contract term that is so one-sided as to be oppressive.

Unfair Labor Practice Strike A strike in response to an unfair labor practice committed by an employer.

Uniform Commercial Code A model code that deals with sale of goods, commercial paper, secured transactions, and other commercial activities.

Union Shop An agreement that employees must join a union within a certain period after they begin to work for an employer.

Unreasonably Dangerous More dangerous than would be contemplated by an ordinary consumer.

Venue The place in which the suit is tried.

Vertical Merger A merger between or joining of two firms that have a buyer-seller relationship. That is, one produces a product that is then sold to the other.

Vicarious Liability A doctrine in the law of agency. It provides that the principal will be liable to those injured by an agent's tort if that tort occurred within the course and scope of the principal's business. The key is whether the agent's actions that led to the tort can be described as being primarily business-related.

Voir Dire The period in a trial when the attorneys question prospective jurors concerning their qualifications to sit as jurors in the case.

Workmen's Compensation State system of insurance whereby employees injured on the job would receive damages from a fund made up of employers' premiums.

Work Preservation Clause An agreement designed to preserve work for certain employees.

Writ A written court order requiring the party to whom it is addressed to do whatever is required by the writ.

Zoning Local government ordinances regarding use of land.

INDEX